Honoring America

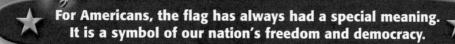

For Americans, the flag has always had a special meaning. It is a symbol of our nation's freedom and democracy.

Flag Etiquette

Over the years, Americans have developed rules and customs concerning the use and display of the flag. One of the most important things every American should remember is to treat the flag with respect.

- The flag should be raised and lowered by hand and displayed only from sunrise to sunset. On special occasions, the flag may be displayed at night, but it should be illuminated.

- The flag may be displayed on all days, weather permitting, particularly on national and state holidays and on historic and special occasions.

- No flag may be flown above the American flag or to the right of it at the same height.

- The flag should never touch the ground or floor beneath it.

- The flag may be flown at half-staff by order of the president, usually to mourn the death of a public official.

- The flag may be flown upside down only to signal distress.

- The flag should never be carried flat or horizontally, but always carried aloft and free.

- When the flag becomes old and tattered, it should be destroyed by burning. According to an approved custom, the Union (stars on blue field) is first cut from the flag; then the two pieces, which no longer form a flag, are burned.

The American's Creed

I believe in the United States of America as a Government of the people, by the people, for the people, whose just powers are derived from the consent of the governed; a democracy in a republic; a sovereign Nation of many sovereign States; a perfect union, one and inseparable; established upon those principles of freedom, equality, justice, and humanity for which American patriots sacrificed their lives and fortunes.

I therefore believe it is my duty to my Country to love it; to support its Constitution; to obey its laws; to respect its flag, and to defend it against all enemies.

The Pledge of Allegiance

I pledge allegiance to the Flag of the United States of America and to the Republic for which it stands, one Nation under God, indivisible, with liberty and justice for all.

The Star-Spangled Banner

O! say, can you see, by the dawn's early light,
What so proudly we hail'd at the twilight's last gleaming?
Whose broad stripes and bright stars, thro' the perilous fight,
O'er the ramparts we watched were so gallantly streaming?
And the rockets' red glare, the bombs bursting in air,
Gave proof thro' the night, that our flag was still there.
O! say, does that Star-Spangled Banner yet wave
O'er the land of the free and the home of the brave?

On the shore, dimly seen thro' the mist of the deep,
Where the foe's haughty host in dread silence reposes,
What is that which the breeze, o'er the towering steep,
As it fitfully blows, half conceals, half discloses?
Now it catches the gleam of the morning's first beam,
In full glory reflected now shines on the stream.
'Tis the Star-Spangled Banner. O long may it wave
O'er the land of the free and the home of the brave.

And where is that band who so vauntingly swore,
That the havoc of war and the battle's confusion
A home and a country should leave us no more?
Their blood has wash'd out their foul footstep's pollution.
No refuge could save the hireling and slave
From the terror of flight or the gloom of the grave,
And the Star-Spangled Banner in triumph doth wave
O'er the land of the free and the home of the brave.

O thus be it e'er when free men shall stand
Between their lov'd home and war's desolation,
Blest with vict'ry and peace, may the Heav'n-rescued land
Praise the pow'r that hath made and preserv'd us a nation.
Then conquer we must, when our cause it is just,
And this be our motto, "In God is our Trust."
And the Star-Spangled Banner in triumph shall wave
O'er the land of the free and the home of the brave.

The American Journey

Joyce Appleby, Ph.D.

Alan Brinkley, Ph.D.

James M. McPherson, Ph.D.

NATIONAL GEOGRAPHIC

Mc Graw Hill **Glencoe McGraw-Hill**

New York, New York   Columbus, Ohio   Chicago, Illinois   Peoria, Illinois   Woodland Hills, California

Joyce Appleby, Ph.D. is Professor of History at UCLA. Dr. Appleby's published works include *Inheriting the Revolution: The First Generation of Americans; Capitalism and a New Social Order: The Jeffersonian Vision of the 1790s;* and *Ideology and Economic Thought in Seventeenth-Century England,* which won the Berkshire Prize. She served as president of both the Organization of American Historians and the American Historical Association, and chaired the Council of the Institute of Early American History and Culture at Williamsburg. Dr. Appleby has been elected to the American Philosophical Society and the American Academy of Arts and Sciences, and is a Corresponding Fellow of the British Academy.

Alan Brinkley, Ph.D. is Allan Nevins Professor of American History at Columbia University. His published works include *Voices of Protest: Huey Long, Father Coughlin, and the Great Depression,* which won the 1983 National Book Award; *The End of Reform: New Deal Liberalism in Recession and War; The Unfinished Nation: A Concise History of the American People;* and *Liberalism and its Discontents.* He received the Levenson Memorial Teaching Prize at Harvard University.

James M. McPherson, Ph.D. is George Henry Davis Professor of American History at Princeton University. Dr. McPherson is the author of 11 books about the Civil War era. These include *Battle Cry of Freedom: The Civil War Era,* for which he won the Pulitzer Prize in 1989, and *For Cause and Comrades: Why Men Fought in the Civil War,* for which he won the 1998 Lincoln Prize. He is a member of many professional historical associations, including the the Civil War Preservation Trust.

The National Geographic Society, founded in 1888 for the increase and diffusion of geographic knowledge, is the world's largest nonprofit scientific and educational organization. Since its earliest days, the Society has used sophisticated communication technologies, from color photography to holography, to convey knowledge to a worldwide membership. The School Publishing Division supports the Society's mission by developing innovative educational programs—ranging from traditional print materials to multimedia programs including CD-ROMs, videodiscs, and software. "National Geographic Geography & History," featured in each unit of this textbook, was designed and developed by the National Geographic Society's School Publishing Division.

About the Cover The images on the cover are: *Apollo* astronaut saluting U.S. flag on the moon, Statue of Liberty, Abraham Lincoln, Rosa Parks, Benjamin Franklin, and Colin Powell.

Glencoe/McGraw-Hill

A Division of The McGraw·Hill Companies

Copyright © 2003 by The McGraw-Hill Companies, Inc. All rights reserved. Except as permitted under the United States Copyright Act of 1976, no part of this publication may be reproduced or distributed in any form or by any means, or stored in a database or retrieval system, without the prior written permission of the publisher.

National Geographic Geography & History © 2003 National Geographic Society. The name "National Geographic Society" and the "Yellow Border Rectangle" are trademarks of the Society and their use, without prior written permission, is strictly prohibited.

TIME Notebook © Time Inc. Prepared by TIME School Publishing in collaboration with Glencoe/McGraw-Hill.

Send all inquiries to:
Glencoe/McGraw-Hill, 8787 Orion Place, Columbus, Ohio 43240-4027

ISBN 0-07-824129-4 (Student Edition) ISBN 0-07-824130-8 (Teacher Wraparound Edition)
Printed in the United States of America.
4   5   6   027/043   06   05   04   03

Academic Consultants

Richard G. Boehm, Ph.D.
Professor of Geography
Southwest Texas State University
San Marcos, Texas

Margo J. Byerly, Ph.D.
Assistant Professor of Social
Studies Methods
Ball State University
Muncie, Indiana

Frank de Varona
Region Superintendent
Dade County Public Schools
Miami, Florida

William E. Nelson, Jr., Ph.D.
Research Professor of Black Studies
and Professor of Political Science
The Ohio State University
Columbus, Ohio

Bernard Reich, Ph.D.
Professor of Political Science and
International Affairs
George Washington University
Washington, D.C.

Donald A. Ritchie, Ph.D.
Associate Historian of the United
States Senate Historical Office
Washington, D.C.

FOLDABLES Dinah Zike
Educational Consultant
Dinah–Might Activities, Inc.
San Antonio, Texas

Teacher Reviewers

John R. Doyle
Director, Division of Social
Sciences
Dade County Public Schools
Miami, Florida

David J. Engstrom
American History Teacher
Discovery Junior High School
Fargo, North Dakota

Harry J. Hancock
Social Studies Teacher
Theodore Roosevelt
Middle School
Kenner, Louisiana

**Elysa E. Toler Robinson,
Ed.D.**
Program Supervisor
Detroit Public Schools
Detroit, Michigan

Kay R. Selah
Social Studies Teacher
Landmark Middle School
Jacksonville, Florida

Deborah N. Smith
Social Studies Teacher
New Albany Middle School
New Albany, Ohio

Larry John Smith
United States History Teacher
Mt. Savage School
Mt. Savage, Maryland

Cheryl Summers
Clinical Supervisor
Albuquerque Public Schools
Albuquerque, New Mexico

Renée Marie Trufant
Social Studies and
Communications Skills
Teacher
Brevard Middle School
Brevard, North Carolina

Sonya Lou Weaver
Social Studies Teacher
Greencastle–Antrim
Middle School
Greencastle, Pennsylvania

Carol Davenport Wood
Social Studies Teacher
Lusher Extension
New Orleans, Louisiana

Contents

Contents

Contents

Features

Features

More About...

What *Life* Was Like...

NATIONAL GEOGRAPHIC — Geography & History

America's Literature

Two Viewpoints

TECHNOLOGY & History

Linking Past & Present

What If...

HANDS-ON HISTORY Lab Activity

TIME NOTEBOOK

Why It Matters

Causes and Effects

Features

SKILLBUILDER

People In History

Fact Fiction Folklore

Primary Source Quotes

A variety of quotations and excerpts throughout the text express the thoughts, feelings, and life experiences of people, past and present.

Primary Source Quotes

Primary Source Quotes

Primary Source Quotes

Charts & Graphs

American Wealth Sent to Spain

NATIONAL GEOGRAPHIC Maps

NATIONAL GEOGRAPHIC Oregon Country

NATIONAL GEOGRAPHIC   D-Day Invasion

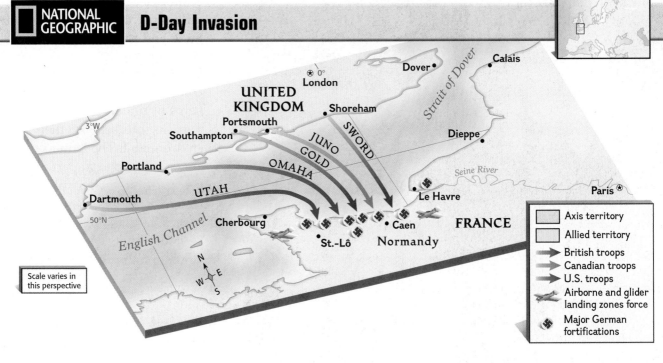

How Do I Study History?

As you read *The American Journey*, you will be given help in sorting out all the information you encounter. This textbook organizes the events of your nation's past and present around 10 themes. A theme is a concept, or main idea that happens again and again throughout history. By recognizing these themes, you will better understand events of the past and how they affect you today.

Themes in *The American Journey*

Culture and Traditions
Being aware of cultural differences helps us understand ourselves and others. People from around the world for generations have sung of the "land of the Pilgrims' pride, land where our fathers died" even though their ancestors arrived on these shores long after these events occurred.

Continuity and Change
Recognizing our historic roots helps us understand why things are the way they are today. This theme includes political, social, religious, and economic changes that have influenced the way Americans think and act.

Geography and History
Understanding geography helps us understand how humans interact with their environment. The United States succeeded in part because of its rich natural resources and its vast open spaces. In many regions, the people changed the natural landscape to fulfill their wants and needs.

Individual Action

Responsible individuals have often stepped forward to help lead the nation. America's strong family values helped create such individuals. These values spring in part from earlier times when the home was the center of many activities, including work, education, and daily worship.

Groups and Institutions

Identifying how political and social groups and institutions work helps us work together. From the beginning, Americans formed groups and institutions to act in support of their economic, political, and religious beliefs.

Government and Democracy

Understanding the workings of government helps us become good citizens. Abraham Lincoln explained the meaning of democracy as "government of the people, by the people, for the people." Democracy, at its best, is "among" the people.

Science and Technology

Americans have always been quick to adopt innovations. The nation was settled and built by people who blended their old ways with new ways. Americans' lives are deeply influenced by technology, the use of science and machines. Perhaps no machine has so shaped modern life as the automobile. Understanding the roles of science and technology helps us see their impact on our society and the roles they will play in the future.

Economic Factors

The free enterprise economy of the United States is consistent with the nation's history of rights and freedoms. Freedom of choice in economic decisions supports other freedoms. Understanding the concept of free enterprise is basic to studying American history.

Global Connections

The world seems smaller than it did only 50 years ago. Modern transportation and communication have brought people around the globe closer together. As a result, countries today are more dependent on one another. As citizens of the United States and members of the global community, we have a responsibility to keep informed about developments in other nations and the world. Being aware of global interdependence helps us make decisions and deal with the difficult issues we will encounter.

Civic Rights and Responsibilities

For a democratic system to survive, its citizens must take an active role in government. The foundation of democracy is the right of every person to take part in government and to voice one's views on issues. An appreciation for the struggle to preserve these freedoms is vital to the understanding of democracy.

Using the Themes

You will find Section Themes at the beginning of every section of your text. You are asked questions that help you put it all together to better understand how ideas and themes are connected across time—and to see why history is important to you today.

REFERENCE ATLAS

NATIONAL GEOGRAPHIC

ATLAS KEY

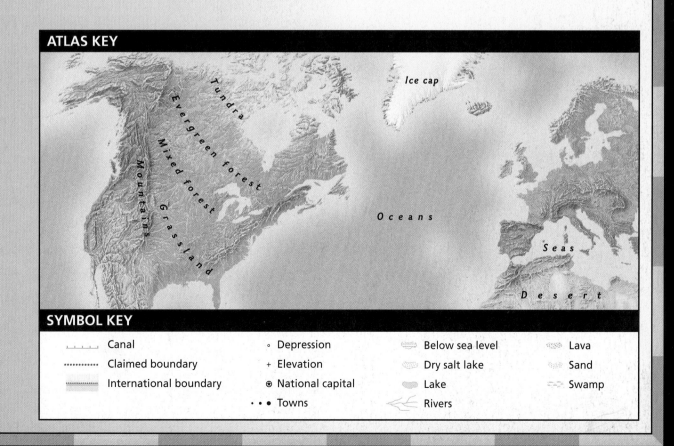

SYMBOL KEY

⌐⌐⌐ Canal	∘ Depression	Below sea level	Lava
·········· Claimed boundary	+ Elevation	Dry salt lake	Sand
International boundary	⊛ National capital	Lake	Swamp
	• • Towns	Rivers	

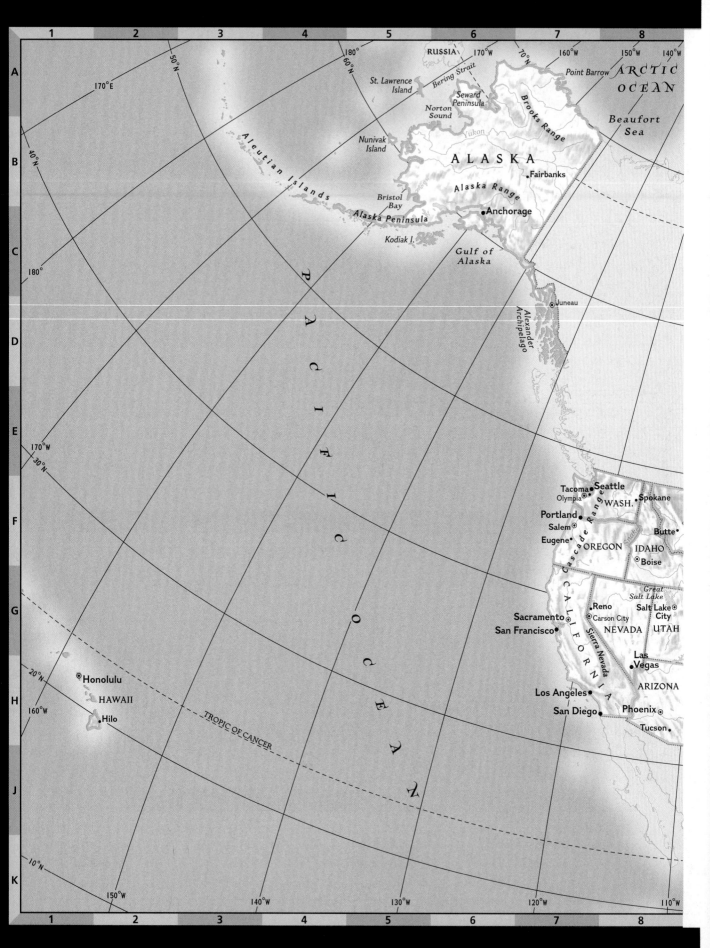

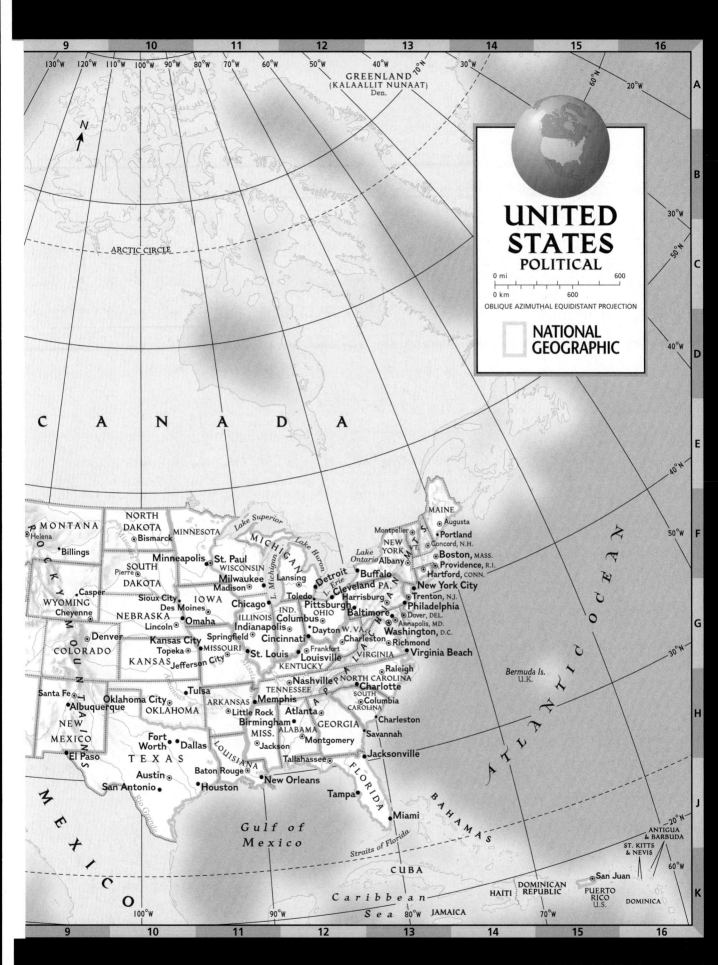

UNITED
STATES
POLITICAL

0 mi   600

0 km   600

OBLIQUE AZIMUTHAL EQUIDISTANT PROJECTION

NATIONAL GEOGRAPHIC

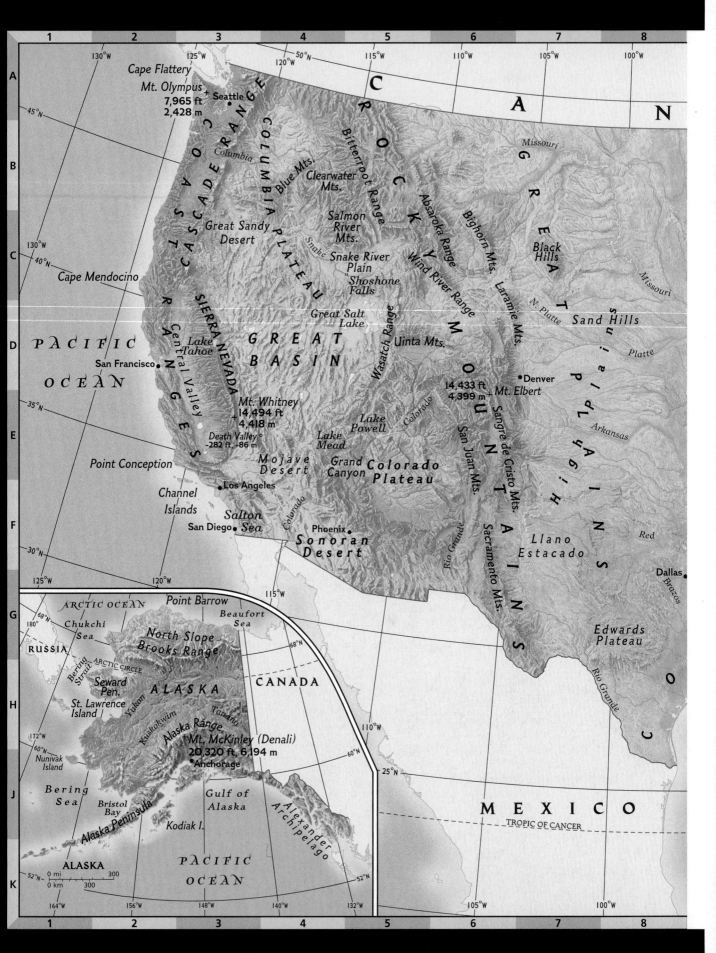

1 | **2** | **3** | **4** | **5** | **6** | **7** | **8**

C A N A N

130°W 125°W 120°W 50°N 115°W 110°W 105°W 100°W

A 45°N

Cape Flattery
Mt. Olympus
7,965 ft
2,428 m · Seattle

Columbia

B 130°W

Missouri

C A S C A D E   R A N G E

COLUMBIA PLATEAU

Blue Mts.
Clearwater Mts.
Bitterroot Range
Salmon River Mts.
Absaroka Range
Bighorn Mts.
Laramie Mts.
Black Hills

Great Sandy Desert

C 40°N

Cape Mendocino

Snake
Snake River Plain
Shoshone Falls
Wind River Range
N. Platte
Sand Hills
Missouri

Great Salt Lake

D 130°W

P A C I F I C

O C E A N

SIERRA NEVADA

Lake Tahoe
San Francisco
Central Valley

G R E A T   B A S I N

Wasatch Range
Uinta Mts.

R O C K Y   M O U N T A I N S

Denver
14,433 ft
4,399 m · Mt. Elbert

H I G H   P L A I N S

Platte

E 35°N

Point Conception

Mt. Whitney
14,494 ft
4,418 m
Death Valley
-282 ft, -86 m

Lake Powell
Lake Mead

Colorado

San Juan Mts.

Arkansas

Mojave Desert
Channel Islands

Grand Canyon
Colorado Plateau

Sangre de Cristo Mts.

F 30°N

Los Angeles

Salton Sea
San Diego

Colorado
Phoenix

Rio Grande
Sacramento Mts.

Llano Estacado

Red

Dallas
Brazos

Sonoran Desert

125°W 120°W 115°W

G 68°N 180°

ARCTIC OCEAN
Point Barrow
Beaufort Sea

Edwards Plateau

RUSSIA
Chukchi Sea
North Slope
Brooks Range

68°N

ARCTIC CIRCLE
CANADA

Bering Strait
Seward Pen.
St. Lawrence Island

A L A S K A

Yukon
Tanana

110°W

H 172°W

Kuskokwim

Alaska Range
Mt. McKinley (Denali)
20,320 ft, 6,194 m
Anchorage

60°N

60°N

Nunivak Island

25°N

J

B e r i n g
S e a

Bristol Bay
Alaska Peninsula

Gulf of Alaska

Alexander Archipelago

Kodiak I.

M E X I C O

Rio Grande
C O

TROPIC OF CANCER

K 52°N

ALASKA
0 mi   300
0 km   300

P A C I F I C
O C E A N

52°N

164°W 156°W 148°W 140°W 132°W

105°W 100°W

1 | **2** | **3** | **4** | **5** | **6** | **7** | **8**

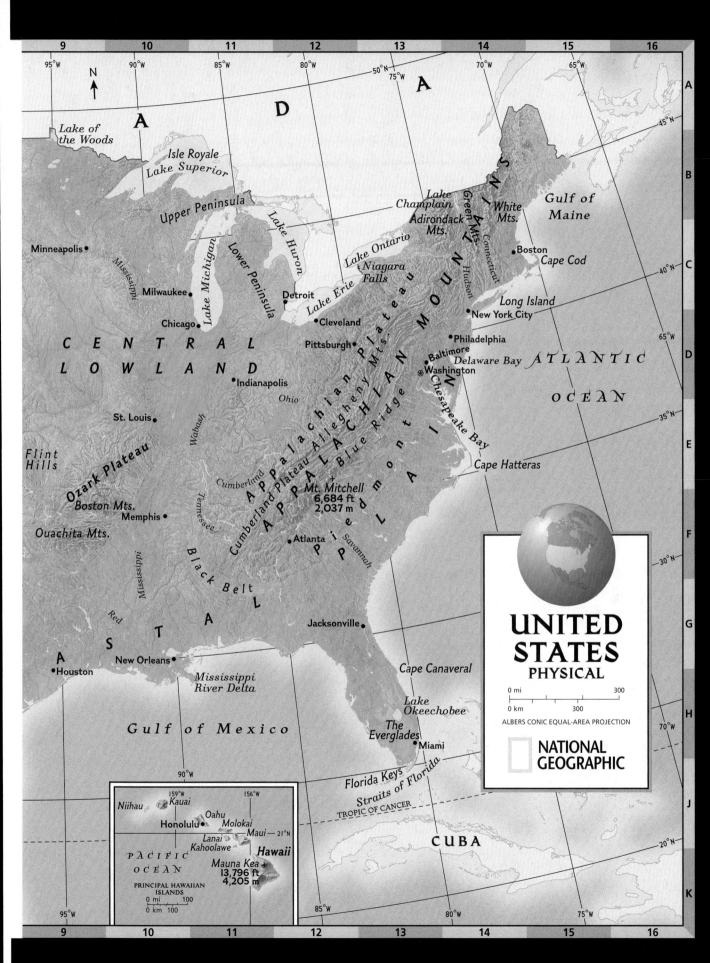

N

9   10   11   12   13   14   15   16

95°W   90°W   85°W   80°W   50°N 75°W

C A N A D A

A

45°N

Lake of the Woods

Isle Royale
Lake Superior

Upper Peninsula

Lake Huron

B

Lake Michigan

Lower Peninsula

Lake Champlain

Adirondack Mts.

Green Mts.

White Mts.

Gulf of Maine

Minneapolis ●

Mississippi

Milwaukee ●

Chicago ●

Detroit ●

Lake Ontario
Niagara Falls

Lake Erie

Cleveland ●

Connecticut

Hudson

● Boston
Cape Cod

40°N

Long Island

New York City ●

C

C E N T R A L

L O W L A N D

Pittsburgh ●

Appalachian Plateau
Allegheny Mts.

Philadelphia ●

Baltimore ●

Delaware Bay

A T L A N T I C

65°W

O C E A N

D

Indianapolis ●

Ohio

A
P
P
A
L
A
C
H
I
A
N

M O U N T A I N S

⊛ Washington

Chesapeake Bay

St. Louis ●

Wabash

Blue Ridge

35°N

Flint Hills

Ozark Plateau

Cumberland

Cumberland Plateau

P
i
e
d
m
o
n
t

Cape Hatteras

E

Boston Mts.

Memphis ●

Tennessee

+ Mt. Mitchell
6,684 ft
2,037 m

Ouachita Mts.

Mississippi

Atlanta ●

Savannah

30°N

F

Black Belt

C
O
A
S
T
A
L

Red

Jacksonville ●

P
L
A
I
N

G

● Houston

New Orleans ●

Mississippi River Delta

Cape Canaveral

Lake Okeechobee

H

G u l f   o f   M e x i c o

90°W

The Everglades

● Miami

70°W

UNITED STATES
PHYSICAL

0 mi ────────── 300
0 km ────────── 300

ALBERS CONIC EQUAL-AREA PROJECTION

NATIONAL GEOGRAPHIC

Florida Keys

Straits of Florida
TROPIC OF CANCER

J

159°W   156°W

Niihau *Kauai*

Oahu
Honolulu ● *Molokai*
Lanai *Maui* — 21°N
Kahoolawe

Hawaii

C U B A

20°N

K

P A C I F I C
O C E A N

Mauna Kea +
13,796 ft
4,205 m

PRINCIPAL HAWAIIAN
ISLANDS
0 mi ──── 100
0 km ──── 100

85°W   80°W   75°W

95°W

9   10   11   12   13   14   15   16

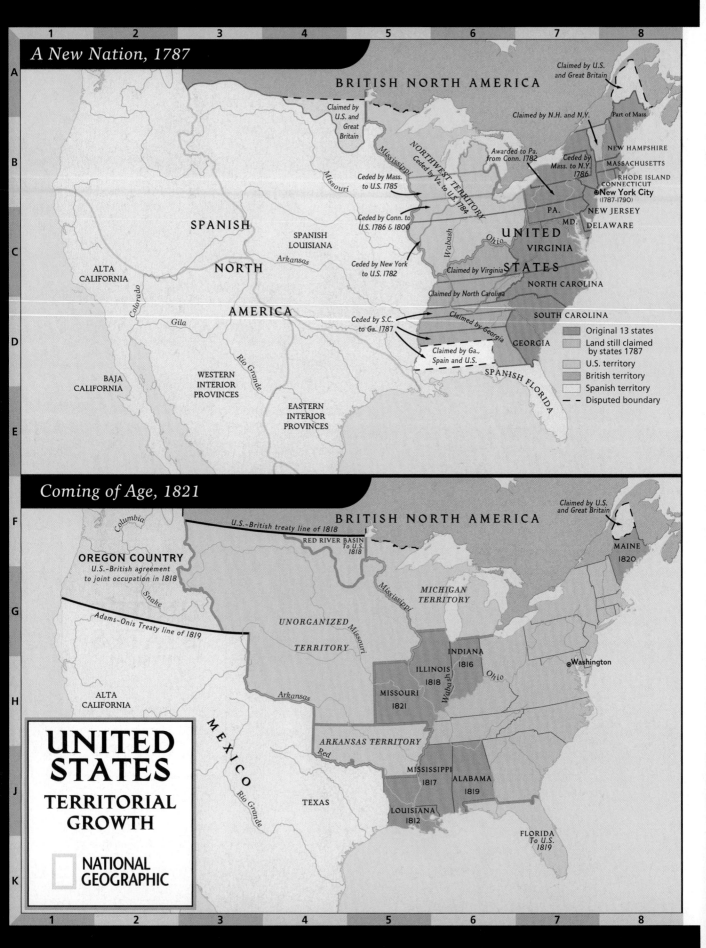

A New Nation, 1787

BRITISH NORTH AMERICA

Claimed by U.S. and Great Britain

Claimed by U.S. and Great Britain

Claimed by N.H. and N.Y.

Part of Mass.

Awarded to Pa. from Conn. 1782

Ceded by Mass. to N.Y. 1786

NEW HAMPSHIRE

MASSACHUSETTS

RHODE ISLAND

CONNECTICUT

Mississippi

NORTHWEST TERRITORY Ceded by Va. to U.S. 1784

Ceded by Mass. to U.S. 1785

Missouri

New York City (1787-1790)

PA.

NEW JERSEY

MD.

DELAWARE

Ceded by Conn. to U.S. 1786 & 1800

SPANISH

SPANISH LOUISIANA

Arkansas

NORTH

Wabash

Ohio

UNITED STATES

VIRGINIA

Ceded by New York to U.S. 1782

Claimed by Virginia

NORTH CAROLINA

ALTA CALIFORNIA

Colorado

AMERICA

Claimed by North Carolina

SOUTH CAROLINA

Gila

Ceded by S.C. to Ga. 1787

Claimed by Georgia

GEORGIA

Original 13 states

Land still claimed by states 1787

U.S. territory

British territory

Spanish territory

Disputed boundary

BAJA CALIFORNIA

WESTERN INTERIOR PROVINCES

Rio Grande

Claimed by Ga., Spain and U.S.

SPANISH FLORIDA

EASTERN INTERIOR PROVINCES

Coming of Age, 1821

Claimed by U.S. and Great Britain

Columbia

U.S.–British treaty line of 1818

BRITISH NORTH AMERICA

RED RIVER BASIN To U.S. 1818

MAINE 1820

OREGON COUNTRY

U.S.–British agreement to joint occupation in 1818

Snake

Mississippi

MICHIGAN TERRITORY

Adams–Onis Treaty line of 1819

UNORGANIZED

Missouri

TERRITORY

INDIANA 1816

Washington

ILLINOIS 1818

Ohio

Wabash

ALTA CALIFORNIA

Arkansas

MISSOURI 1821

M E X I C O

ARKANSAS TERRITORY

Red

MISSISSIPPI 1817

ALABAMA 1819

Rio Grande

TEXAS

LOUISIANA 1812

FLORIDA To U.S. 1819

UNITED STATES

TERRITORIAL GROWTH

NATIONAL GEOGRAPHIC

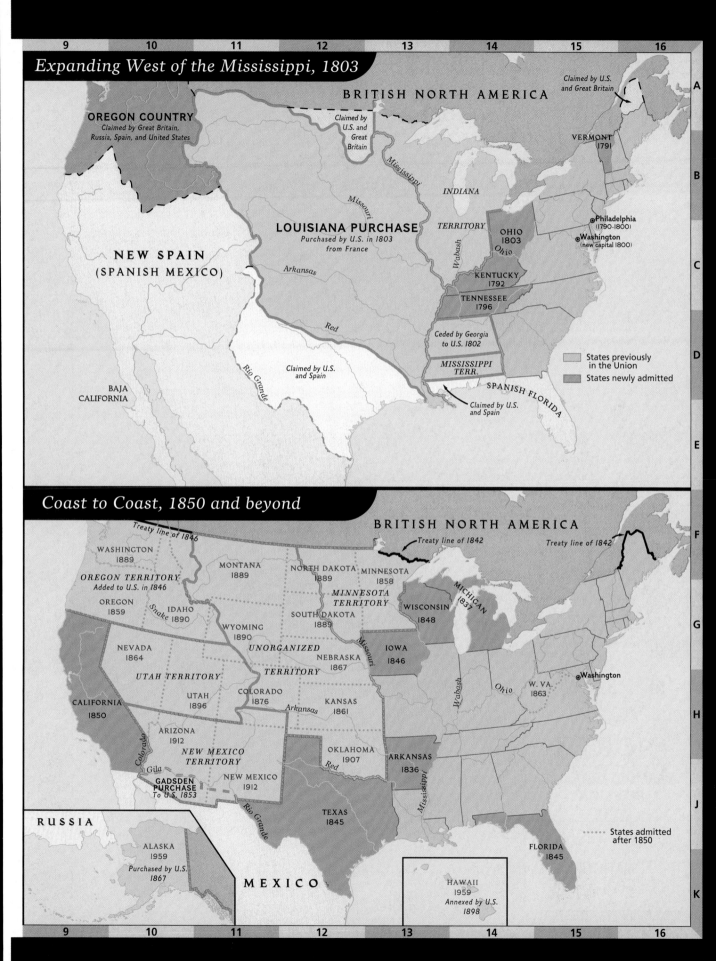

Expanding West of the Mississippi, 1803

9   10   11   12   13   14   15   16

BRITISH NORTH AMERICA

Claimed by U.S. and Great Britain

OREGON COUNTRY
Claimed by Great Britain, Russia, Spain, and United States

Claimed by U.S. and Great Britain

VERMONT 1791

INDIANA

LOUISIANA PURCHASE
Purchased by U.S. in 1803 from France

Mississippi

Missouri

TERRITORY

OHIO 1803
Ohio

Philadelphia (1790-1800)
Washington (new capital 1800)

NEW SPAIN (SPANISH MEXICO)

Arkansas

KENTUCKY 1792

TENNESSEE 1796

Red

Ceded by Georgia to U.S. 1802

Rio Grande

Claimed by U.S. and Spain

MISSISSIPPI TERR.

SPANISH FLORIDA

States previously in the Union

States newly admitted

BAJA CALIFORNIA

Claimed by U.S. and Spain

Coast to Coast, 1850 and beyond

BRITISH NORTH AMERICA

Treaty line of 1846

Treaty line of 1842

Treaty line of 1842

WASHINGTON 1889

MONTANA 1889

NORTH DAKOTA 1889

MINNESOTA 1858

OREGON TERRITORY
Added to U.S. in 1846

Snake

IDAHO 1890

MINNESOTA TERRITORY

MICHIGAN 1837

OREGON 1859

WYOMING 1890

SOUTH DAKOTA 1889

WISCONSIN 1848

NEVADA 1864

UNORGANIZED

Missouri

IOWA 1846

UTAH TERRITORY

NEBRASKA 1867

TERRITORY

CALIFORNIA 1850

UTAH 1896

COLORADO 1876

KANSAS 1861

Arkansas

Wabash

Ohio

W. VA. 1863

Washington

Colorado

ARIZONA 1912

NEW MEXICO TERRITORY

OKLAHOMA 1907

ARKANSAS 1836

Gila

Red

Mississippi

GADSDEN PURCHASE
To U.S. 1853

NEW MEXICO 1912

Rio Grande

RUSSIA

ALASKA 1959
Purchased by U.S. 1867

TEXAS 1845

FLORIDA 1845

States admitted after 1850

MEXICO

HAWAII 1959
Annexed by U.S. 1898

9   10   11   12   13   14   15   16

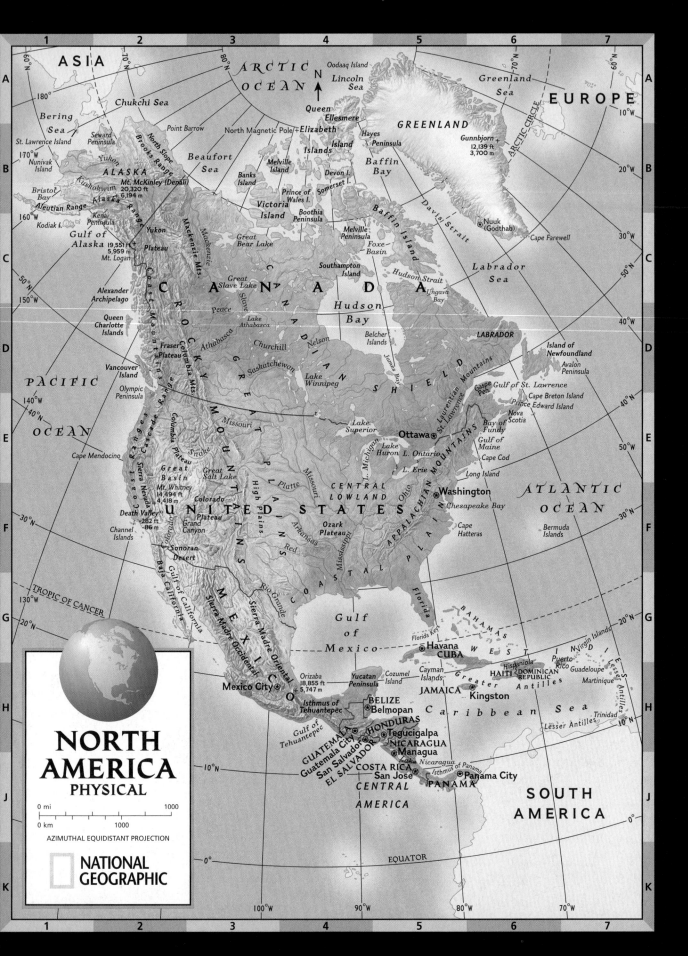

NORTH AMERICA

PHYSICAL

0 mi — 1000

0 km — 1000

AZIMUTHAL EQUIDISTANT PROJECTION

NATIONAL GEOGRAPHIC

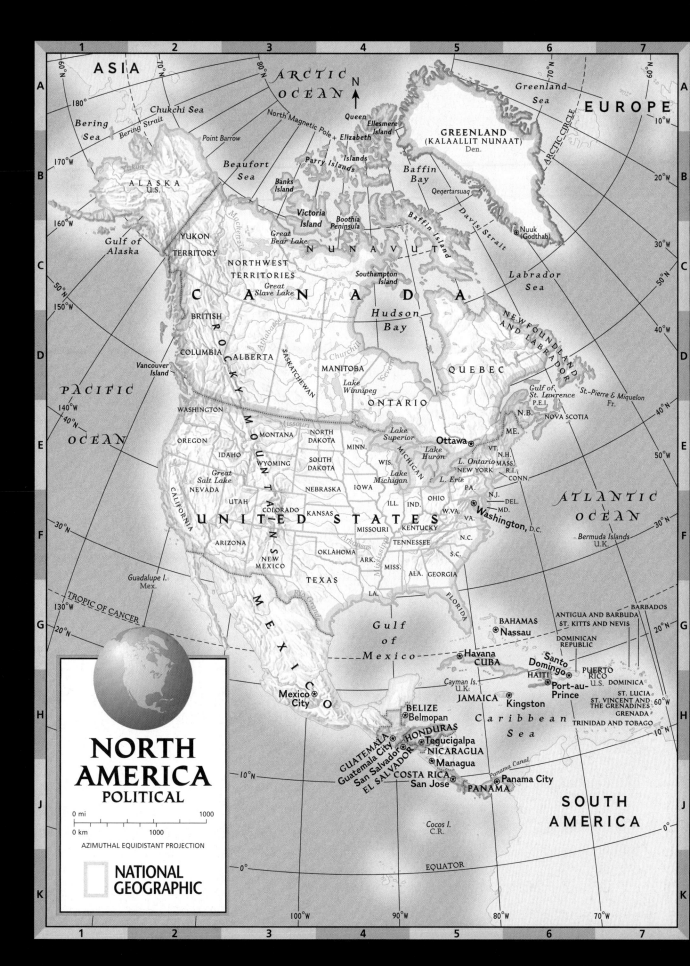

NORTH AMERICA
POLITICAL

0 mi 1000
0 km 1000

AZIMUTHAL EQUIDISTANT PROJECTION

NATIONAL GEOGRAPHIC

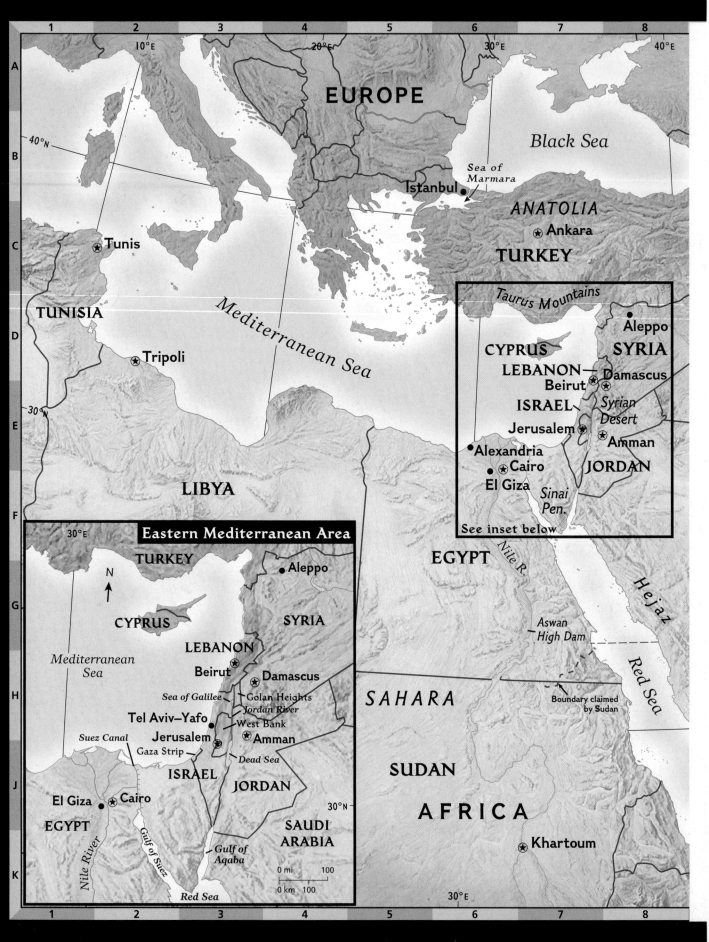

EUROPE

Black Sea

Sea of Marmara

Istanbul

ANATOLIA

Ankara

TURKEY

Tunis

TUNISIA

Tripoli

Mediterranean Sea

Taurus Mountains

Aleppo

CYPRUS

SYRIA

LEBANON — Damascus

Beirut

Syrian
Desert

ISRAEL

Jerusalem

Amman

JORDAN

El Giza

Alexandria

Cairo

Sinai
Pen.

See inset below

LIBYA

EGYPT

Nile R.

Hejaz

Eastern Mediterranean Area

30°E

TURKEY

N

CYPRUS

SYRIA

Aleppo

LEBANON

Mediterranean
Sea

Beirut

Damascus

Sea of Galilee

Golan Heights

Tel Aviv–Yafo

Jordan River

Jerusalem

West Bank

Amman

Suez Canal

Gaza Strip

Dead Sea

ISRAEL

JORDAN

El Giza

Cairo

EGYPT

Nile River

Gulf of Suez

SAUDI
ARABIA

30°N

Gulf of
Aqaba

Red Sea

0 mi   100

0 km   100

Aswan
High Dam

SAHARA

Boundary claimed
by Sudan

Red Sea

SUDAN

AFRICA

Khartoum

30°E

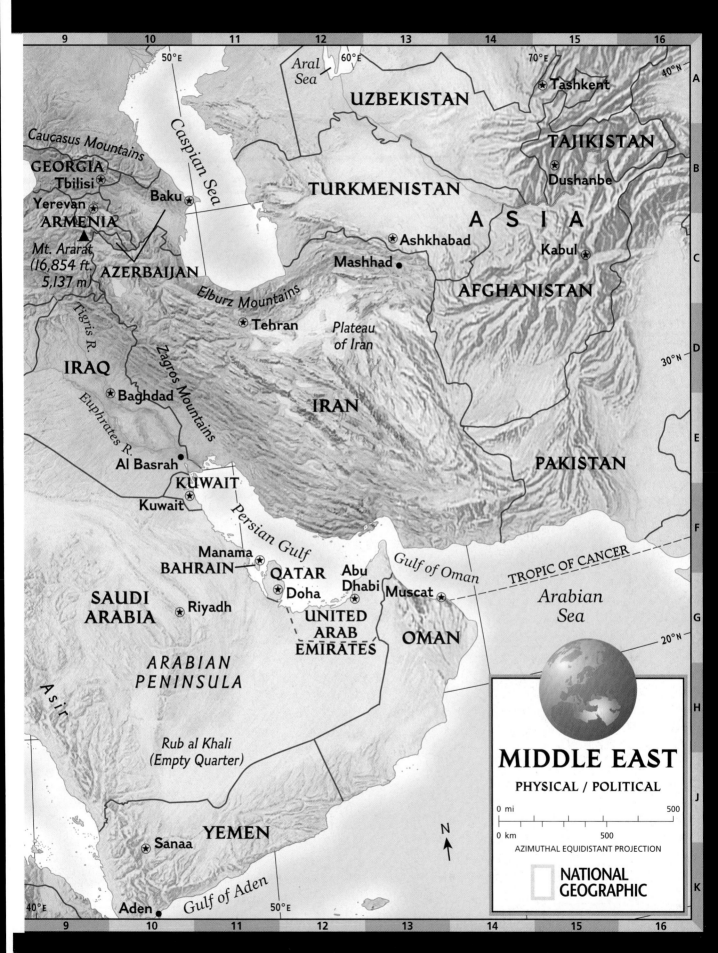

MIDDLE EAST

PHYSICAL / POLITICAL

| 0 mi | | 500 |
| 0 km | 500 | |

AZIMUTHAL EQUIDISTANT PROJECTION

NATIONAL GEOGRAPHIC

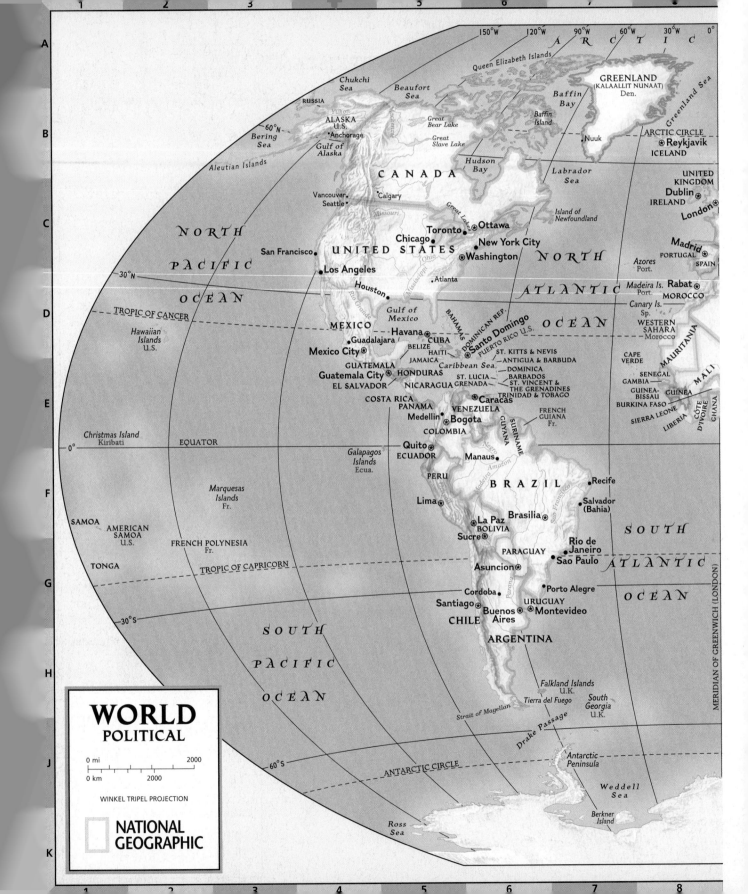

WORLD
POLITICAL

0 mi   2000

0 km   2000

WINKEL TRIPEL PROJECTION

NATIONAL
GEOGRAPHIC

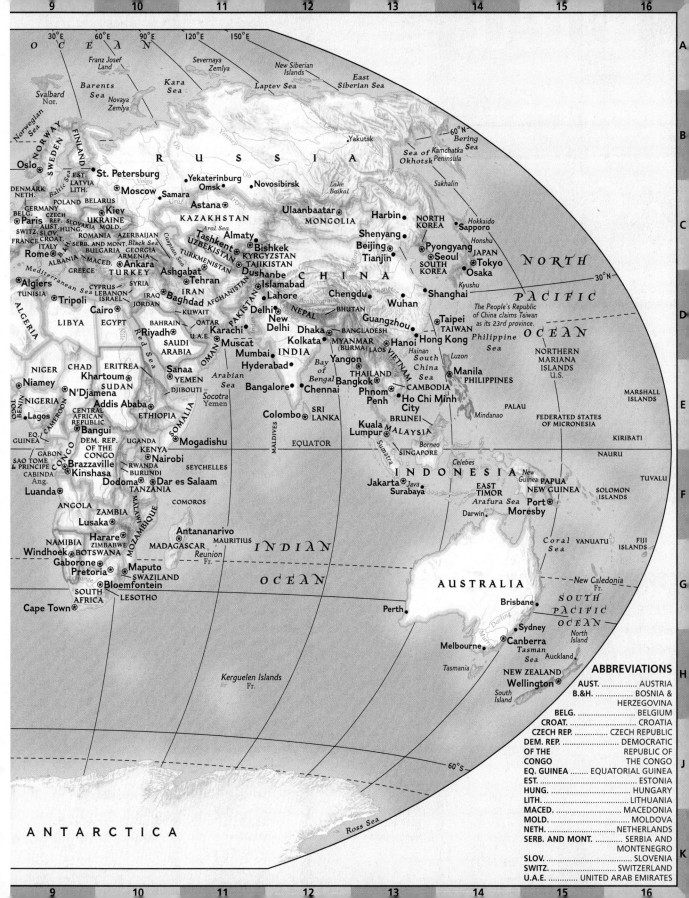

ABBREVIATIONS

AUST.	AUSTRIA
B.&H.	BOSNIA & HERZEGOVINA
BELG.	BELGIUM
CROAT.	CROATIA
CZECH REP.	CZECH REPUBLIC
DEM. REP. OF THE CONGO	DEMOCRATIC REPUBLIC OF THE CONGO
EQ. GUINEA	EQUATORIAL GUINEA
EST.	ESTONIA
HUNG.	HUNGARY
LITH.	LITHUANIA
MACED.	MACEDONIA
MOLD.	MOLDOVA
NETH.	NETHERLANDS
SERB. AND MONT.	SERBIA AND MONTENEGRO
SLOV.	SLOVENIA
SWITZ.	SWITZERLAND
U.A.E.	UNITED ARAB EMIRATES

United States Facts

Washington, D.C.
Population: 572,059
Land area: 61 sq. mi.

U.S. Territories

Puerto Rico
Population: 3,808,610
Land area: 3,425 sq. mi.

Guam
Population: 155,000 (est.)
Land area: 210 sq. mi.

U.S. Virgin Islands
Population: 121,000 (est.)
Land area: 134 sq. mi.

American Samoa
Population: 65,000 (est.)
Land area: 77 sq. mi.

The states are listed in the order they were admitted to the Union.

Population figures are based on U.S. Bureau of the Census for 2000. House of Representatives figures are from the Clerk of the House of Representatives. States are not drawn to scale.

1 Delaware
Year Admitted: 1787
Population: 783,600
Land area: 1,955 sq. mi.
Representatives: 1
Dover

2 Pennsylvania
Year Admitted: 1787
Population: 12,281,054
Land area: 44,820 sq. mi.
Representatives: 19
Harrisburg

3 New Jersey
Year Admitted: 1787
Population: 8,414,350
Land area: 7,419 sq. mi.
Representatives: 13
Trenton

9 New Hampshire
Year Admitted: 1788
Population: 1,235,786
Land area: 8,969 sq. mi.
Representatives: 2
Concord

10 Virginia
Year Admitted: 1788
Population: 7,078,515
Land area: 39,598 sq. mi.
Representatives: 11
Richmond

11 New York
Year Admitted: 1788
Population: 18,976,457
Land area: 47,224 sq. mi.
Representatives: 29
Albany

17 Ohio
Year Admitted: 1803
Population: 11,353,140
Land area: 40,953 sq. mi.
Representatives: 18
Columbus

18 Louisiana
Year Admitted: 1812
Population: 4,468,976
Land area: 43,566 sq. mi.
Representatives: 7
Baton Rouge

19 Indiana
Year Admitted: 1816
Population: 6,080,485
Land area: 35,870 sq. mi.
Representatives: 9
Indianapolis

25 Arkansas
Year Admitted: 1836
Population: 2,673,400
Land area: 52,075 sq. mi.
Representatives: 4
Little Rock

26 Michigan
Year Admitted: 1837
Population: 9,938,444
Land area: 56,809 sq. mi.
Representatives: 15
Lansing

27 Florida
Year Admitted: 1845
Population: 15,982,378
Land area: 53,997 sq. mi.
Representatives: 25
Tallahassee

33 Oregon
Year Admitted: 1859
Population: 3,421,399
Land area: 96,003 sq. mi.
Representatives: 5
Salem

34 Kansas
Year Admitted: 1861
Population: 2,688,418
Land area: 81,823 sq. mi.
Representatives: 4
Topeka

35 West Virginia
Year Admitted: 1863
Population: 1,808,344
Land area: 24,087 sq. mi.
Representatives: 3
Charleston

36 Nevada
Year Admitted: 1864
Population: 1,998,257
Land area: 109,806 sq. mi.
Representatives: 3
Carson City

42 Washington
Year Admitted: 1889
Population: 5,894,121
Land area: 66,582 sq. mi.
Representatives: 9
Olympia

43 Idaho
Year Admitted: 1890
Population: 1,293,953
Land area: 82,751 sq. mi.
Representatives: 2
Boise

44 Wyoming
Year Admitted: 1890
Population: 493,782
Land area: 97,105 sq. mi.
Representatives: 1
Cheyenne

45 Utah
Year Admitted: 1896
Population: 2,233,169
Land area: 82,168 sq. mi.
Representatives: 3
Salt Lake City

What Is Geography?

The story of the United States begins with geography—the study of the earth in all of its variety. Geography describes the earth's land, water, and plant and animal life. It is the study of places and the complex relationships between people and their environments.

Geography of the United States

The United States is a land of startling physical differences. It is also a nation of diverse groups of people. A study of geography can help explain how the United States acquired its diversity.

The United States—with a total land area of 3,537,441 square miles (9,161,930 sq. km)—is the world's fourth-largest country in size.

The 50 States

Most of the United States—48 of the 50 states—spans the entire middle part of North America. This group of states touches three major bodies of water—the Atlantic Ocean, the Gulf of Mexico, and the Pacific Ocean. Two states—Alaska and Hawaii—lie apart from the 48 states.

Our Nation's Growth

Within the borders of the United States stretch a variety of landscapes—dense forests, hot deserts, rolling grasslands, and snow-capped mountains. Because of its large size and diverse regions, the United States throughout its history offered many opportunities. Over the centuries people from Europe, Africa, Asia, and other parts of the Americas have journeyed here. Today more than 281 million people make their homes in the United States.

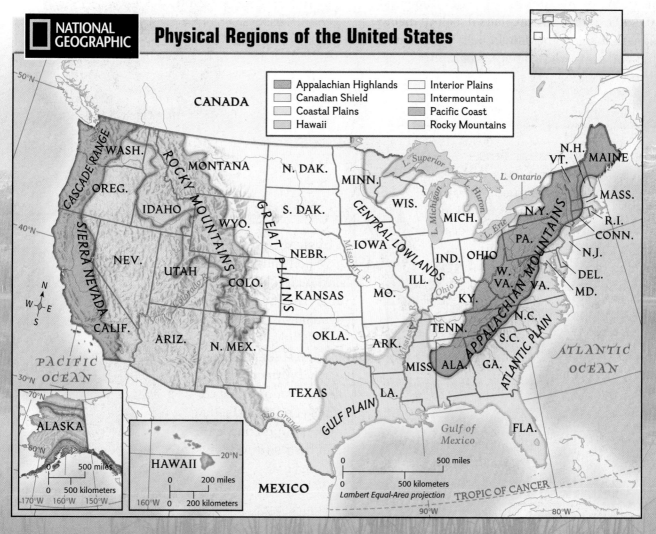

NATIONAL GEOGRAPHIC

Physical Regions of the United States

Legend:
- Appalachian Highlands
- Canadian Shield
- Coastal Plains
- Hawaii
- Interior Plains
- Intermountain
- Pacific Coast
- Rocky Mountains

Lambert Equal-Area projection

I Study Geography?

To understand how our world is connected, some geographers have broken down the study of geography into five themes. The **Five Themes of Geography** are (1) location, (2) place, (3) human/environment interaction, (4) movement, and (5) regions. You will see these themes highlighted in the Geography Skills accompanying the maps of *The American Journey*.

Six Essential Elements

Recently, geographers have begun to look at geography in a different way. They break down the study of geography into **Six Essential Elements,** which are explained below. Being aware of these elements will help you sort out what you are learning about geography.

Element 2

Places and Regions

Place has a special meaning in geography. It means more than where a place is. It also describes what a place is like. These features may be physical characteristics such as landforms, climate, and plant or animal life. They may also be human characteristics, including language and way of life.

To help organize their study, geographers often group places or areas into regions. **Regions** are united by one or more common characteristics.

Element 1

The World in Spatial Terms

Geographers first take a look at where a place is located. **Location** serves as a starting point by asking "Where is it?" Knowing the location of places helps you develop an awareness of the world around you.

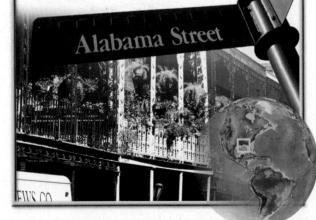

Element 3

Physical Systems

When studying places and regions, geographers analyze how **physical systems**—such as hurricanes, volcanoes, and glaciers—shape the earth's surface. They also look at communities of plants and animals that depend upon one another and their surroundings for survival.

Element 4

Human Systems

Geographers also examine human systems, or how people have shaped our world. They look at how boundary lines are determined and analyze why people settle in certain places and not in others. A key theme in geography is the continual **movement** of people, ideas, and goods.

Element 5

Environment and Society

"How does the relationship between people and their natural surroundings influence the way people live?" This is one of the questions that the theme of **human/ environment interaction** answers. This theme also shows how people use the environment and how their actions affect the environment.

Element 6

The Uses of Geography

Knowledge of geography helps people understand the relationships among people, places, and environments over time. Understanding geography, and knowing how to use the tools and technology available to study it, prepares you for life in our modern society.

I Use Maps?

Maps of many different kinds are used in *The American Journey* to help you see the connection between geography and the history of our nation.

Different Kinds of Maps

Physical Maps

A physical map shows the physical features of an area, such as its mountains and rivers. Physical maps use color and shadings to show **relief**—how flat or rugged the land surface is. Colors also may be used to show **elevation**—the height of an area above sea level.

Political Maps

Political maps generally show political, or human-made, divisions of countries or regions. The political map on pages RA2–RA3, for example, shows boundaries between the states that comprise the United States.

Special-Purpose Maps

Besides showing political or physical features, some maps have a special purpose. Human activities such as exploration routes, territorial expansion, or battle sites appear on special-purpose maps, also called **thematic maps.** The maps on pages RA6–RA7, for example, show territorial growth of the United States.

Latitude and Longitude

Maps have lines of latitude and longitude that form a grid. Lines of latitude circle the earth, either north or south of the Equator (0° latitude). Lines of longitude stretch from the North Pole to the South Pole, either east or west of the Prime Meridian (0° longitude). The distance between the lines is measured in degrees (°). Every place on the earth has a unique position or "address" on this grid.

Knowing this address makes it easier for you to locate cities and other places on a map. For example, the map on page RA5 shows you that the address of New Orleans is 30°N latitude, 90°W longitude.

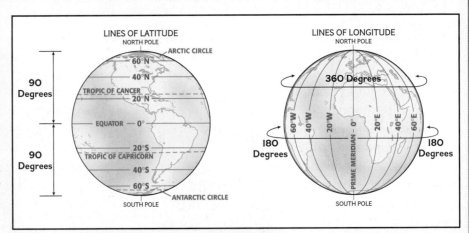

Parts of Maps

Map Key The map key explains the lines, symbols, and colors used on a map. For example, the map on this page shows the various climate regions of the United States. The key shows what climates the different colors represent. Map keys also may show structures created by people. Cities are usually symbolized by a solid circle (•). A star within a circle represents capitals (✪). On this map, you can see the capital of Texas and the cities of New Orleans, Los Angeles, Seattle, and Chicago.

Climate Regions of the United States

Key:
- Desert
- Highland
- Humid continental
- Humid subtropical
- Marine
- Mediterranean
- Steppe
- Subarctic
- Tropical
- Tundra

Lambert Equal-Area projection

Scale A measuring line, often called a **scale bar,** helps you determine distance on the map. The map scale tells you what distance on the earth is represented by the measurement on the scale bar.

Compass Rose An important first step in reading any map is to find the direction marker. A map has a symbol that tells you where the **cardinal directions**—north, south, east, and west—are positioned.

How Does Geography Influence History?

Geographic factors—landforms, waterways, natural resources—have shaped America's history. Here are some examples of geography's influences in history that are highlighted in *The American Journey.*

Unit 1 Different Worlds Meet As settlement spread, Native Americans created distinctive civilizations appropriate to their climates and resources. For example, Native Americans in the Great Plains depended on herds of buffalo for food, clothing, shelter, and tools.

Unit 2 Colonial Settlement Beginning in the 1500s, Europeans came to North America seeking land, riches, and freedom. Groups from Spain, France, Great Britain, and other countries established colonies. The British colonies along the Atlantic coast were hemmed in by the Appalachian Mountains—the first physical barrier to the West.

Unit 3 Creating a Nation The hardships of the land shaped the colonial settlers' cultural identities. The colonists were isolated from much of the world and became more independent. Eventually they broke away from Great Britain and won their independence.

Unit 4 The New Republic When the United States was established, many doubted that the young government could control people over such great distances. New rivers, roads, and canals helped to open up the country. At the same time an Industrial Revolution had begun in New England.

Unit 5 The Growing Nation Through wars, treaties, and purchases, the United States gained control of the lands west of the Mississippi River. Settlers were drawn to Western territories by opportunities. Native Americans were forced onto reservations. Railroads enabled people to overcome geographic barriers.

Unit 6 Civil War and Reconstruction

Demand for cotton by the textile industry increased the demand for labor provided by enslaved African Americans. In 1861 regional differences and a dispute over slavery sparked the Civil War between the North and South.

Unit 7 Reshaping the Nation

After the Civil War, railroads transported goods from the East to the West and carried food products from the West to the East. The workers who advanced this industrial boom were immigrants and people who moved from farms to the cities. Pioneers changed the Great Plains from wilderness to farmland.

Unit 8 Reform, Expansion, and War

As industry grew in the United States, foreign trade became more important. America became more involved with other nations, expanded its empire around the world, and became involved in a world war.

Unit 9 Turbulent Decades

Environmental disasters during the first part of the 1900s affected the national economy. Due to poor farming methods, in the 1930s winds blew away so much of the soil in the Great Plains that the area became known as the Dust Bowl.

Unit 10 Turning Points

After World War II, the world's nations became much more connected and America became more involved in international affairs. Increased technology broke many long-standing geographic barriers. Americans were now able to travel greater distances in less time, leading to increased trade, travel, and opportunities.

Unit 11 Modern America

Americans take a leading role maintaining world peace. Many also are more aware of their impact on the surrounding environment. The government has begun to conserve and protect nature. Americans also face a new century with advanced technology.

Geographic Dictionary

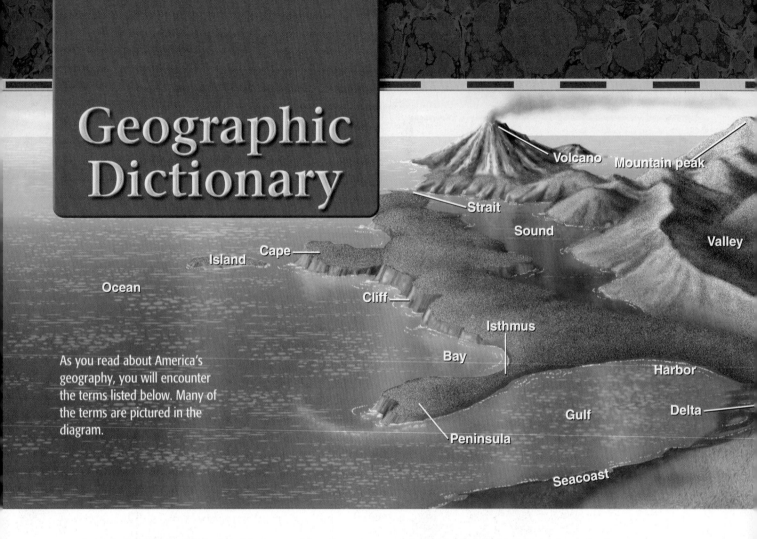

As you read about America's geography, you will encounter the terms listed below. Many of the terms are pictured in the diagram.

Labels on diagram: Volcano, Mountain peak, Strait, Sound, Valley, Cape, Island, Cliff, Ocean, Isthmus, Bay, Harbor, Gulf, Delta, Peninsula, Seacoast

absolute location exact location of a place on the earth described by global coordinates

basin area of land drained by a given river and its branches; area of land surrounded by lands of higher elevations

bay part of a large body of water that extends into a shoreline, generally smaller than a gulf

canyon deep and narrow valley with steep walls

cape point of land that extends into a river, lake, or ocean

channel wide strait or waterway between two land-masses that lie close to each other; deep part of a river or other waterway

cliff steep, high wall of rock, earth, or ice

continent one of the seven large landmasses on the earth

cultural feature characteristic that humans have created in a place, such as language, religion, housing, and settlement pattern

delta flat, low-lying land built up from soil carried downstream by a river and deposited at its mouth

divide stretch of high land that separates river systems

downstream direction in which a river or stream flows from its source to its mouth

elevation height of land above sea level

Equator imaginary line that runs around the earth halfway between the North and South Poles; used as the starting point to measure degrees of north and south latitude

glacier large, thick body of slowly moving ice

gulf part of a large body of water that extends into a shoreline, generally larger and more deeply indented than a bay

harbor a sheltered place along a shoreline where ships can anchor safely

highland elevated land area such as a hill, mountain, or plateau

hill elevated land with sloping sides and rounded summit; generally smaller than a mountain

island land area, smaller than a continent, completely surrounded by water

isthmus narrow stretch of land connecting two larger land areas

lake a sizable inland body of water

latitude distance north or south of the Equator, measured in degrees

longitude distance east or west of the Prime Meridian, measured in degrees

lowland land, usually level, at a low elevation

map drawing of the earth shown on a flat surface

meridian one of many lines on the global grid running from the North Pole to the South Pole; used to measure degrees of longitude

mesa broad, flat-topped landform with steep sides; smaller than a plateau

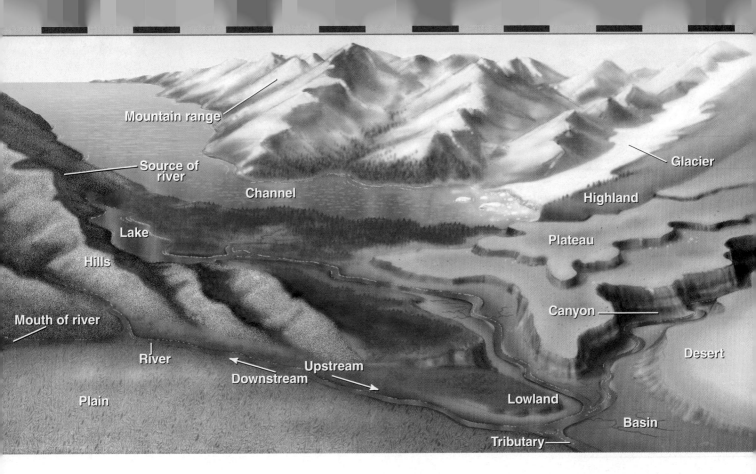

Mountain range

Source of river

Channel

Glacier

Highland

Lake

Plateau

Hills

Mouth of river

Canyon

Desert

River

Upstream

Downstream

Plain

Lowland

Basin

Tributary

mountain land with steep sides that rises sharply (1,000 feet or more) from surrounding land; generally larger and more rugged than a hill

mountain peak pointed top of a mountain

mountain range a series of connected mountains

mouth (of a river) place where a stream or river flows into a larger body of water

ocean one of the four major bodies of salt water that surround the continents

ocean current stream of either cold or warm water that moves in a definite direction through an ocean

parallel one of many lines on the global grid that circle the earth north or south of the Equator; used to measure degrees of latitude

peninsula body of land jutting into a lake or ocean, surrounded on three sides by water

physical feature characteristic of a place occurring naturally, such as a landform, body of water, climate pattern, or resource

plain area of level land, usually a low elevation and often covered with grasses

plateau area of flat or rolling land at a high elevation, about 300–3,000 feet high

Prime Meridian line of the global grid running from the North Pole to the South Pole through Greenwich, England; starting point for measuring degrees of east and west longitude

relief changes in elevation over a given area of land

river large natural stream of water that runs through the land

sea large body of water completely or partly surrounded by land

seacoast land lying next to a sea or ocean

sea level position on land level with surface of nearby ocean or sea

sound body of water between a coastline and one or more islands off the coast

source (of a river) place where a river or stream begins, often in highlands

strait narrow stretch of water joining two larger bodies of water

tributary small river or stream that flows into a large river or stream; a branch of the river

upstream direction opposite the flow of a river; toward the source of a river or stream

valley area of low land between hills or mountains

volcano mountain created as liquid rock or ash erupts from inside the earth

Be an Active Reader

Think about your textbook as a tool that helps you learn more about the world around you. It is an example of nonfiction writing—it describes real-life events, people, ideas, and places. Here is a menu of reading strategies that will help you become a better textbook reader. As you come to passages in your textbook that you don't understand, refer to these reading strategies for help.

✔ Before You Read

Set a purpose
- Why are you reading the textbook?
- How does the subject relate to your life?
- How might you be able to use what you learn in your own life?

Preview
- Read the chapter title to find what the topic will be.
- Read the subtitles to see what you will learn about the topic.
- Skim the photos, charts, graphs, or maps. How do they support the topic?
- Look for vocabulary words that are bold-faced. How are they defined?

Draw From Your Own Background
- What have you read or heard concerning new information on the topic?
- How is the new information different from what you already know?
- How will the information that you already know help you understand the new information?

Question

- What is the main idea?
- How do the photos, charts, graphs, and maps support the main idea?

Connect

- Think about people, places, and events in your own life. Are there any similarities with those in your textbook?
- Can you relate the textbook information to other areas of your life?

Predict

- Predict events or outcomes by using clues and information that you already know.
- Change your predictions as you read and gather new information.

Visualize

- Pay careful attention to details and descriptions.
- Create graphic organizers to show relationships that you find in the information.

Look For Clues As You Read

Comparison and Contrast Sentences

- Look for clue words and phrases that signal comparison, such as *similarly*, *just as*, *both*, *in common*, *also*, and *too*.
- Look for clue words and phrases that signal contrast, such as *on the other hand*, *in contrast to*, *however*, *different*, *instead of*, *rather than*, *but*, and *unlike*.

Cause-and-Effect Sentences

- Look for clue words and phrases such as *because*, *as a result*, *therefore*, *that is why*, *since*, *so*, *for this reason*, and *consequently*.

Chronological Sentences

- Look for clue words and phrases such as *after*, *before*, *first*, *next*, *last*, *during*, *finally*, *earlier*, *later*, *since*, and *then*.

✓ After You Read

Summarize

- Describe the main idea and how the details support it.
- Use your own words to explain what you have read.

Assess

- What was the main idea?
- Did the text clearly support the main idea?
- Did you learn anything new from the material?
- Can you use this new information in other school subjects or at home?
- What other sources could you use to find more information about the topic?

UNIT
1 Different Worlds Meet

Beginnings to 1625

Why It Matters

As you study Unit 1, you will learn that the first immigrants came to the Americas long before written history. From their descendants evolved a rich variety of cultures. The following resources offer more information about this period.

Primary Sources Library

See pages 958–959 for primary source readings to accompany Unit 1.

Use the **American History Primary Source Document Library CD-ROM** to find additional primary sources about Native American life.

Astrolabe, early astronomical instrument

Monument Valley

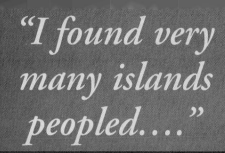

"*I found very many islands peopled....*"

—Christopher Columbus, 1493

The First Americans

Prehistory to 1492

Why It Matters

Thousands of years ago small groups of hunters crossed a bridge of land that connected Siberia and Alaska. Eventually, they spread throughout North and South America.

The Impact Today

These first people, called Native Americans, influenced later cultures. Native Americans are part of the modern world, yet many of them also preserve the ways of life, customs, and traditions developed by their ancestors centuries ago.

The American Journey *Video* *The chapter 1 video, "Before Columbus," examines the diverse cultures of North America before Europeans arrived, focusing on the Anasazi.*

C. 28,000 B.C.
• Asian hunters enter North America

C. 1500 B.C.
• Rise of Olmec in Mexico

C. A.D. 700
• Maya empire reaches peak

C. A.D. 1130
• Drought strikes Anasazi communities

The Americas

Prehistory   *900*   *1100*

World

C. 10,000 B.C.
• Last Ice Age ends

C. A.D. 33
• Jesus Christ is crucified

A.D. 613
• Muhammad preaches Islam in Makkah

A.D. 1095
• The Crusades begin

City in the Sky Inca workers built the city of Machu Picchu high in the Andes mountain ranges.

C. A.D. 1300
• Hohokam civilization begins to decline

A.D. 1325
• Aztec establish Tenochtitlán

C. A.D. 1400
• Inca empire begins to expand

HISTORY
Online

Chapter Overview
Visit taj.glencoe.com and click on **Chapter 1— Chapter Overviews** to preview chapter information.

1300   1500

A.D. 1368
• Ming dynasty begins in China

A.D. 1215
• England's King John signs Magna Carta

A.D. 1295
• Italian traveler Marco Polo returns from China

A.D. 1312
• Mansa Musa begins rule of West African kingdom of Mali

Early Peoples

Guide to Reading

Main Idea
The first Americans spread throughout North, Central, and South America.

Key Terms
archaeology, artifact, Ice Age, nomad, migration, maize, carbon dating, culture

Reading Strategy
Determining Cause and Effect As you read Section 1, re-create the diagram below and explain why the first Americans came to the continent and the consequences of their arrival.

Migration to the Americas	
Causes	Effects

Read to Learn
- how the first people arrived in the Americas.
- which discovery changed the lives of the early Native Americans.

Section Theme
Geography and History The Ice Age made it possible for hunters to migrate to the Americas.

Preview of Events

♦30,000 B.C.	♦10,000 B.C.	♦5000 B.C.	♦1000 B.C.

c. 28,000 B.C.
Asian hunters enter North America

c. 10,000 B.C.
Last Ice Age ends

c. 7000 B.C.
Farming develops in Mexico

c. 3000 B.C.
Early villages established in Mexico

AN
American Story

Arrowhead, hand-chipped stone

No one knows for sure how the first people arrived in America. They may have crossed a land bridge that many scientists think connected Asia and North America thousands of years ago. They may have come by boat from Asia or Europe. Why they came is also a mystery. Possibly they followed mammoths or other game animals or were hunting seals and whales along the coast. Over time, these people settled in America becoming the first "native Americans."

The Journey From Asia

These first Americans arrived thousands of years ago. As food supplies improved, the population of the Americas increased. By A.D. 1500, millions of Native Americans, belonging to more than 2,000 different groups, lived on the two continents of North America and South America.

When Europeans arrived in the Americas in the late 1400s, they found Native Americans living there. The Europeans wondered where these peoples had come from and how they happened to settle in the Americas. Some believed the Native Americans had come from Atlantis, an island that was supposed to have sunk beneath the waves of the Atlantic Ocean.

Modern scientists are still trying to determine how the first people came to North and South America. The story of the first Americans is still being pieced together by experts in archaeology, the study of ancient peoples. Archaeologists learn about the past from artifacts, things left behind by early people, such as stone tools, weapons, baskets, and carvings. Their discoveries show that many early peoples may have come across a land that later sank into the sea. It was not the mythical Atlantis, however, but a strip of land called **Beringia** that once joined Asia and the Americas.

Crossing the Land Bridge

During its long history, the earth has passed through several Ice Ages. These are periods of very cold temperatures when part of the earth was covered with large ice sheets. Much of the water from the oceans was frozen into these sheets, or glaciers. For that reason the sea levels were much lower than they are today.

The most recent Ice Age began 100,000 years ago and ended about 12,000 years ago. During this period many scientists think the lower sea level exposed a wide strip of land between Asia and North America. This land bridge would have run from **Siberia** in northeastern Asia to present-day **Alaska,** the westernmost part of the Americas. The land bridge, Beringia, now lies under the **Bering Strait.**

One popular scientific theory states that the first Americans were people from Asia who crossed over Beringia during the last Ice Age. These early peoples reached the Americas thousands of years ago.

In Search of Hunting Grounds

The early Americans were nomads, people who moved from place to place. They gathered wild grains and fruits but depended on hunting for much of their food. While traveling in search of animals to hunt, they crossed Beringia into what is now Alaska and Canada.

The crossing of the land bridge was a migration, a movement of a large number of people into a new homeland. It did not happen in a single journey. As the centuries passed, many groups of people traveled from Asia either on foot across the land bridge or in boats. From the north, the migrants gradually moved into new territory. They spread out across the Americas, going as far east as the Atlantic Ocean and as far south as the tip of South America.

Hunting for Food

Native American legends tell of giant beasts that roamed the earth in ancient times. When the first Americans arrived from Asia, they did indeed find huge mammals. There was the saber-toothed tiger, the woolly mammoth, and the mastodon. The mammoth and mastodon resembled modern elephants in size and shape but had shaggy fur and long tusks.

The early Americans were skilled at hunting these beasts. The hunters shaped pieces of stone and bone to make tools for chopping and scraping. They chipped rocks into extremely sharp points and fastened them on poles to make spears. Bands of hunters armed with these spears stalked herds of bison, mastodons, or

Causes and Effects of Migration

Causes
- The earth enters a long Ice Age.
- Water from the ocean freezes.
- Sea levels drop, exposing the Beringia land bridge.

Effects
- Hunters from Asia cross into North America.
- People spread into Central America and South America.
- The early Americans create new cultures.

Graphic Organizer → Skills

The settlement of the Americas can be traced to a geographic element—the earth's climate.

Analyzing Information What happened when sea levels dropped?

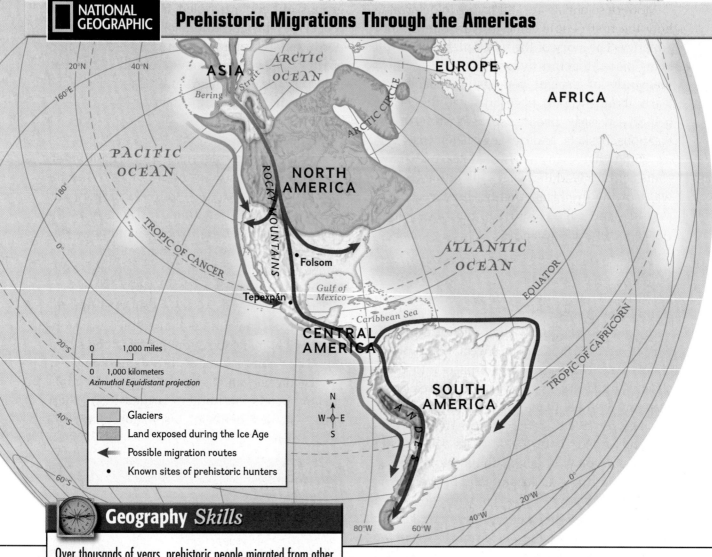

Geography *Skills*

Over thousands of years, prehistoric people migrated from other lands to the Americas.

1. **Movement** Along what major mountain ranges did the migration routes flow?
2. **Interpreting Information** How was it possible for prehistoric people to cross the Bering Strait?

mammoths and then charged at the animals, hurling their weapons.

A single mammoth provided tons of meat, enough to feed a group of people for months. The hunters and their families used every part of the animal. They made the skin into clothing, carved the bones into weapons and tools, and may have used the long ribs to build shelters.

About 15,000 years ago the earth's temperatures began to rise. The Ice Age was drawing to an end. As the great glaciers melted, the oceans rose, and Beringia was submerged again. The

Americas were cut off from Asia. At the same time, the hunters of America faced a new challenge. The mammoths and other large animals began to die out, either from being overhunted or because of changes in the environment. The early Americans had to find other sources of food.

✓ **Reading Check** **Describing** How did early American nomads hunt for food?

Settling Down

As the large animals disappeared, the early Americans found new sources of food. They hunted smaller game, such as deer, birds, and rodents. Those who lived along rivers or near the seacoast learned to catch fish with nets and traps. They continued to gather wild berries and grains.

Planting Seeds

About 9,000 years ago, people living in present-day **Mexico** made a discovery that would shape the lives of Native Americans for thousands of years. They learned to plant and raise an early form of corn called maize. Their harvests of maize provided a steady, reliable source of food. No longer did they have to move from place to place in order to find food.

Early Americans in Mexico also experimented with other kinds of seeds. They planted pumpkins, beans, and squashes. They soon began producing more than enough food to feed themselves. The population grew along with the growing food supply.

Early Communities

With rising numbers of people and a dependable supply of food, early Americans in Mexico started to form stationary communities. Scientists have found traces of early villages that date from about 5,000 years ago. Scientists use a method called carbon dating to find out how old an artifact is. By measuring the amount of radioactive carbon that remains in something that was once alive—such as a bone or a piece of wood—they can tell approximately how long ago it lived. Carbon dating is imprecise and can only give a rough estimate of an artifact's age.

Sometime after the early settlements in Mexico, people began farming in what is now the southwestern United States. Not all the early peoples in the Americas farmed, however. Some remained nomadic hunters, and others relied on fishing or trading instead of agriculture.

The Growth of Cultures

Farming allowed people to spend time on activities other than finding food. Knowing that they would harvest an abundant supply of grains and vegetables, the people of ancient Mexico began to improve their lives in other ways. They built permanent shelters of clay, brick, stone, or wood. They made pottery and cloth and decorated these goods with dyes made from roots and herbs. They also began to develop more complex forms of government.

Agriculture changed the lives of these early people and led to a new culture, or way of life. Rather than move from place to place in search of food, the people who farmed were able to settle down. They formed communities and developed common customs, beliefs, and ways of protecting themselves. Over time, the many different groups of people living in the Americas developed their own cultures.

Reading Check **Summarizing** What did farming mean for nomadic people?

SECTION 1 ASSESSMENT

Checking for Understanding

1. **Key Terms** Use each of the following terms in a complete sentence that will help explain its meaning: archaeology, artifact, Ice Age, migration, culture.
2. **Reviewing Facts** Why did the first people come to the Americas?

Reviewing Themes

3. **Geography and History** How did an Ice Age make it possible for Asian hunters to migrate to the Americas?

Critical Thinking

4. **Determining Cause and Effect** How do you think the first Americans discovered that they could grow their own plants?
5. **Organizing Information** Re-create the diagram below and explain how early Native Americans depended on their environment and natural resources.

Analyzing Visuals

6. **Geography Skills** Study the map on page 18. In which direction did the travelers migrate across the Bering Strait?

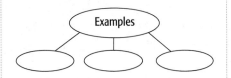

Examples

Interdisciplinary Activity

Geography Create a version of the map on page 18. Your version can be larger, if needed. Label all land masses and bodies of water. Illustrate the map to tell the story of how the first Americans migrated to North America.

New Ways to the New World

An old Virginia sandpit may change our views of the earliest Americans

IT HAS BEEN CALLED THE GREATEST STORY OF IMMIGRATION TO THE Americas. At the end of the last Ice Age, brave women and men from Siberia walked across the Bering Sea land bridge. This is a piece of land that once connected the Asian continent with North America. Within 500 years, their descendants had settled most of the hemisphere, from the Arctic Circle to the tip of South America. But it seems they may not have been first.

Cactus Hill

Well known archaeologist **JOSEPH McAVOY** and his team reported that they have located an ancient campsite that is about 18,000 years old. The place, known as Cactus Hill, is about 45 miles south of Richmond, Virginia (see map).

Scientists now believe the site may actually be thousands of years older than the land-bridge site. If that's true, then people were living in North America much earlier than once believed. "If the dates hold up, and I think they will," says archaeologist Dennis Stanford, "this is probably some of the oldest material in North America, if not the entire New World."

For decades, experts thought that 11,200-year-old stone spear points from a site in Clovis, New Mexico, were the earliest evidence of settlement in the hemisphere. But since the 1970s, older sites have been discovered on both sides of the North American continent. The most important finding has been a 17,000-year-old rock shelter in Meadowcroft, Pennsylvania.

More Proof

Now Cactus Hill presents still more proof that humans settled in North America earlier than anyone had thought. McAvoy's team has unearthed a variety of stone tools, probably used for hunting and butchering animals. The team also found burned bones of mud turtles, white-tailed deer, and other mammals, and bits of charcoal left over from hunters cooking the animals.

High-tech instruments were used to figure out how old the bones and objects are. The Meadowcroft rock shelter's chief archaeologist, James Adovasio, says: "This is another indication that people were running around North America earlier than 13,000 years ago."

McAvoy and wife, Lynn, working on what may be one of the oldest campsites in the Americas

GARRETT—NAT'L GEOGRAPHIC CACTUS HILL

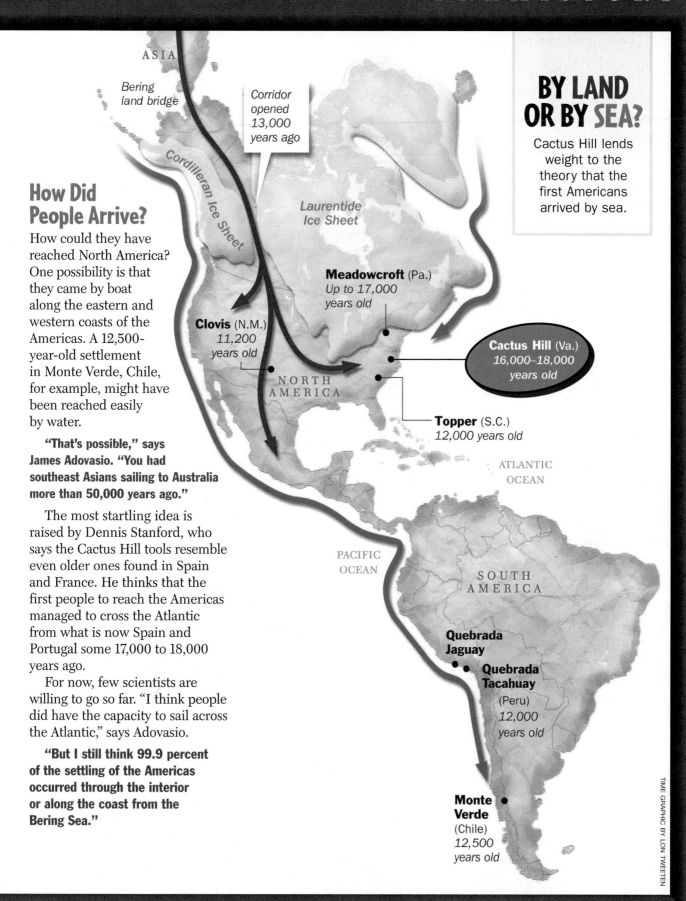

ASIA

Bering
land bridge

Corridor
opened
13,000
years ago

Cordilleran Ice Sheet

Laurentide
Ice Sheet

BY LAND
OR BY SEA?

Cactus Hill lends
weight to the
theory that the
first Americans
arrived by sea.

How Did
People Arrive?

How could they have
reached North America?
One possibility is that
they came by boat
along the eastern and
western coasts of the
Americas. A 12,500-
year-old settlement
in Monte Verde, Chile,
for example, might have
been reached easily
by water.

**"That's possible," says
James Adovasio. "You had
southeast Asians sailing to Australia
more than 50,000 years ago."**

The most startling idea is
raised by Dennis Stanford, who
says the Cactus Hill tools resemble
even older ones found in Spain
and France. He thinks that the
first people to reach the Americas
managed to cross the Atlantic
from what is now Spain and
Portugal some 17,000 to 18,000
years ago.

For now, few scientists are
willing to go so far. "I think people
did have the capacity to sail across
the Atlantic," says Adovasio.

**"But I still think 99.9 percent
of the settling of the Americas
occurred through the interior
or along the coast from the
Bering Sea."**

Meadowcroft (Pa.)
*Up to 17,000
years old*

Clovis (N.M.)
*11,200
years old*

NORTH
AMERICA

Cactus Hill (Va.)
*16,000–18,000
years old*

Topper (S.C.)
12,000 years old

ATLANTIC
OCEAN

PACIFIC
OCEAN

SOUTH
AMERICA

**Quebrada
Jaguay**

**Quebrada
Tacahuay**
(Peru)
*12,000
years old*

**Monte
Verde**
(Chile)
*12,500
years old*

Cities and Empires

Main Idea
Several factors led to the rise and decline of great civilizations and empires in the Americas.

Key Terms
civilization, theocracy, hieroglyphics, terrace

Reading Strategy
Categorizing Information As you read the section, re-create the diagram below and describe the role religion played in each civilization.

Civilization	Religion
Maya	
Aztec	
Inca	

Read to Learn
• why powerful empires arose in the Americas.
• how the people of each empire adapted to their environment.

Section Theme
Culture and Traditions Civilizations such as the Maya, the Aztec, and the Inca arose in present-day Mexico and in Central and South America.

Preview of Events

1500 B.C.	B.C./A.D.	A.D.1200	A.D.1400

c. 1500 B.C.
Rise of the Olmec in Mexico

c. A.D. 700
Maya civilization at its height in Central America

c. A.D. 1325
Aztec establish Tenochtitlán in Mexico

c. A.D. 1400
Inca Empire begins to expand

Artifact, c. A.D. 900

AN
American Story

Rumors of a lost city led American historian Hiram Bingham to the mountains of Peru in 1911. Bingham followed a steep mountain trail, pulling himself along by grabbing vines. After many hours of climbing, he reached a clearing. Suddenly he saw acres of huge, crumbling walls and pillars of white stone covered with vines and moss. "It fairly took my breath away," wrote Bingham. He knew that these temples and monuments were the remains of a very advanced people.

Early American Civilizations

Bingham had discovered the ruins of an early Inca city, Machu Picchu (MAH•choo PEE•choo). It is a small city—Machu Picchu covers only about five square miles (13 sq. km)—but it is an extraordinary place. Its structures, carved from the gray granite of the mountaintop, are wonders of design and craftsmanship and equal the achievements of the civilizations of Europe, Asia, and Africa.

Long before the arrival of Europeans in the early 1500s, several great civilizations, or highly developed societies, arose in present-day Mexico and in

Central and South America. These civilizations built enormous cities in thick jungles and on mountaintops that were hard to reach. They also developed complex systems for writing, counting, and tracking time.

Among the largest and most advanced of these early civilizations were the **Olmec,** the **Maya,** the **Aztec,** and the **Inca.** Each civilization spread out over hundreds of miles, included millions of people, and thrived for centuries.

The Olmec flourished between 1500 B.C. and 300 B.C. along the Gulf Coast of what are now Mexico, Guatemala, and Honduras. Olmec farmers produced enough food to sustain cities containing thousands of people. Olmec workers sculpted large stone monuments and built stone pavements and drainage systems. Their civilization strongly influenced their neighbors.

✓ Reading Check **Identifying** What are civilizations?

The Maya

The Maya built their civilization in the steamy rain forests of present-day **Mexico, Guatemala, Honduras,** and **Belize.** They planted maize, beans, sweet potatoes, and other vegetables. They also pulled enormous stones from the earth to build monuments and pyramids that still stand today. Much of this labor was performed by enslaved people, usually prisoners of war.

Mayan Cities

By A.D. 300 the Maya had built many large cities. Each city had at least one stone pyramid. Some pyramids reached about 200 feet (60 m)—the height of a 20-story building. Steps ran up the pyramid sides to a temple on top. The largest Mayan city, **Tikal,** in present-day Guatemala, was surrounded by five pyramids.

The temples on top of the pyramids were religious and governmental centers. Wearing gold jewelry and detailed headdresses, the priests in the temples performed rituals dedicated to the Mayan gods. On special days, the city's people attended religious festivals.

The Maya believed the gods controlled everything that happened on earth. Because only priests knew the gods' wishes, the priests held great power in Mayan society and made most of the important decisions. The civilization of the Maya was a theocracy, a society ruled by religious leaders.

To keep accurate records for their religious festivals, the Maya became skilled astronomers. The Mayan priests believed that the gods were

America's *Architecture*

In Tikal and other cities, the Maya built huge pyramids where people could gather for ceremonies honoring the deities. A model of a Mayan city is shown (top left). **How were the Maya governed?**

visible in the stars, sun, and moon. They used their knowledge of the sun and stars to predict eclipses and to develop a 365-day calendar. Their desire to measure time increased their knowledge of mathematics. The Maya also developed a form of writing called hieroglyphics. Hieroglyphics use symbols or pictures to represent things, ideas, and sounds.

$ Economics
Transport and Trade

The Maya did not have wheeled vehicles or horses, so everything they transported overland was carried on human backs. Mayan traders traveled on a network of roads that had been carved out of the jungle. Farmers brought maize and vegetables to outdoor markets in the cities. They exchanged their crops for cotton cloth, pottery, deer meat, and salt.

Mayan traders also transported goods by water. Mayan canoes traveled up and down Mexico's east coast. The canoes carried jade statues, turquoise jewelry, cacao beans for making chocolate, and other goods to traders throughout a large area.

Decline of a Civilization

Around A.D. 900 the Maya civilization in the lowlands began to decline. By A.D. 1100 the great cities were almost ghost towns. The jungle crept back across the plazas, roads, and fields. No one knows what caused the decline. Perhaps slaves and farmers revolted against their Mayan masters. Perhaps the soil became too exhausted by erosion and fire to produce enough food for the people. The Maya civilization collapsed, but descendants of the Maya still live in parts of Mexico and Central America.

✓ Reading Check **Explaining** What is a theocracy?

The Aztec

Centuries after the fall of the Maya, a group of hunters called the Aztec wandered through central Mexico, searching for a permanent home. In 1325 they came upon an island in Lake Texcoco, today part of Mexico City. There the

Why It Matters

Farming and the Growth of Civilization

Thousands of years ago, a quiet revolution took place. In scattered pockets of the Middle East, Asia, Africa, and the Americas, people learned to cultivate food-producing plants for the first time. As farming gradually spread, it encouraged the growth of permanent communities.

What, Where, and When

Once they had agriculture, people could settle in permanent communities.

c. 8000 B.C. ➔ **c. 7000 B.C.** ➔
Wheat (Syria)   Barley (Jordan)

Aztec saw a sign: an eagle sitting on a cactus, with a snake in its beak. That meant this island was to be their home.

Tenochtitlán

On this island emerged **Tenochtitlán** (tay•NAWCH•teet•LAHN), one of the greatest cities in the Americas. Its construction was a miracle of engineering and human labor. Directed by priests and nobles, workers toiled day and night. They pulled soil from the bottom of the lake to make causeways, or bridges of earth, linking the island and the shore. They filled parts of the lake with earth so they could grow crops.

In time the Aztec capital expanded to the mainland around the lake. At its height Tenochtitlán was the largest city in the Americas, and one of the largest in the world. Tenochtitlán also served as a center of trade, attracting thousands of merchants to its outdoor marketplaces.

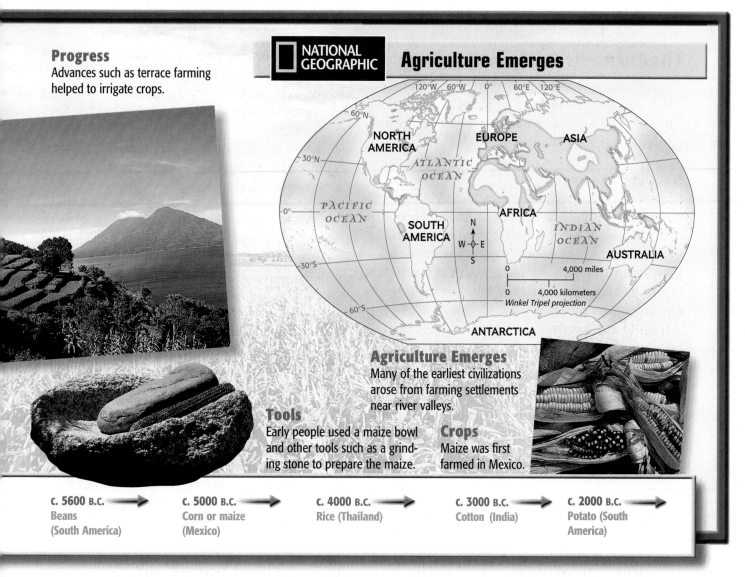

Progress
Advances such as terrace farming helped to irrigate crops.

NATIONAL GEOGRAPHIC — **Agriculture Emerges**

Agriculture Emerges
Many of the earliest civilizations arose from farming settlements near river valleys.

Tools
Early people used a maize bowl and other tools such as a grinding stone to prepare the maize.

Crops
Maize was first farmed in Mexico.

c. 5600 B.C.	c. 5000 B.C.	c. 4000 B.C.	c. 3000 B.C.	c. 2000 B.C.
Beans (South America)	Corn or maize (Mexico)	Rice (Thailand)	Cotton (India)	Potato (South America)

War and Religion

The Aztec civilization grew into a military empire. In the 1400s the Aztec army marched through central and southern Mexico, conquering nearly all rival communities. Aztec warriors took everything they could carry from their victims, including maize, cotton cloth, copper, and weapons. Conquered people were forced to work as slaves in Aztec cities and villages.

Like the Maya, the Aztec organized their society around their religion. The Aztec believed that human sacrifices were necessary to keep the gods pleased and to ensure abundant harvests. Thousands of prisoners of war were sacrificed.

A Great City Remembered

The first Europeans to see the Aztec capital were awed by its splendor. In 1519, 550 Spanish soldiers entered Tenochtitlán, led by Hernán Cortés. He wrote:

❝There are forty towers at least, all of stout construction and very lofty. . . . The workmanship both in wood and stone could not be bettered anywhere.❞

Bernal Díaz del Castillo, one of the soldiers, marveled at the

❝great stone towers and temples and buildings that rose straight up out of the water.❞

Tenochtitlán, he explained, was a city of water, and many of the streets were waterways for canoes. Some of the Spanish soldiers thought that Tenochtitlán was more magnificent than Rome and the other great European capitals of the time.

✓ **Reading Check** **Making Generalizations** Why was the Aztec city of Tenochtitlán a great city?

The Inca

Another great American civilization developed in the western highlands of South America. The empire of the Inca was the largest of the early American civilizations.

The Inca founded their capital city of **Cuzco** (KOOS•koh) around A.D. 1200. In 1438 an emperor named Pachacuti (PAH•chah•KOO•tee) came to the throne and began a campaign of conquest against the neighboring peoples. He and his son, Topa Inca, built an empire that stretched from north to south for more than 3,000 miles (4,800 km), from present-day Colombia to northern Argentina and Chile.

The Incan army was powerful. All men between 25 and 50 years old could be drafted to serve in the army for up to five years. Their weapons included clubs, spears, and spiked copper balls on ropes. Using slings of woven cloth, Incan soldiers could throw stones 30 yards (27 m).

Life in the Empire

At its height, the Inca Empire had a population of more than nine million, including many conquered peoples. To control this large empire, the Inca built at least 10,000 miles (16,000 km) of stone-paved roads that ran over mountains, across deserts, and through jungles. Rope bridges, made from grass, crossed canyons and rivers.

Runners carrying messages to and from the emperor linked remote outposts of the empire to Cuzco. The Inca language, Quechua (KEH•chuh•wuh), became the official language for the entire empire. Although the Inca did not have a system of writing, they developed a system of record keeping with string called *quipus* (KEE•poos). Using various lengths and colors of string, knotted in special patterns, the *quipus* carried information about resources such as grain supplies.

Although mountainous land is not well suited for farming, the Inca devised ways to produce a steady supply of food. They cut terraces, or broad platforms, into steep slopes so they could plant crops. They built stone walls on the terraces to hold the soil and plants in place. Incan farmers grew maize, squash, tomatoes, peanuts, chili peppers, melons, cotton, and potatoes.

All Inca land belonged to the emperor, who was believed to be a descendant of the sun god. Because the Inca thought that the sun god enjoyed displays of gold, they made magnificent gold jewelry and temple ornaments. The Inca also built special cities devoted to religious ceremonies. One of these cities was Machu Picchu, the mountaintop site described in "An American Story" on page 22.

Reading Check **Explaining** How did the Inca farm steep slopes?

SECTION 2 ASSESSMENT

Checking for Understanding

1. **Key Terms** Using standard grammar, write a short paragraph in which you use all of the following terms: civilization, theocracy, hieroglyphics, terrace.

2. **Reviewing Facts** Why did the Aztec choose the location of Tenochtitlán as their permanent home?

Reviewing Themes

3. **Culture and Traditions** Why did priests hold great power in Mayan society?

Critical Thinking

4. **Making Inferences** How does trade help to enrich a civilization? Provide examples in your answer.

5. **Analyzing Information** Re-create the diagram below and give three reasons the Maya, Aztec, and Inca are considered advanced civilizations.

Analyzing Visuals

6. **Picturing History** Study the photograph of the pyramid on page 23. Why do you think the Maya built such large pyramids?

Interdisciplinary Activity

Art Compile illustrations of some of the accomplishments of the Maya, Aztec, and Inca in the areas of communication, science, and math. Use your own drawings or use photographs from newspapers and magazines.

Understanding the Parts of a Map

Why Learn This Skill?

Maps can direct you down the street or around the world. There are as many different kinds of maps as there are uses for them. Being able to read a map begins with learning about its parts.

Learning the Skill

Maps usually include a key, a compass rose, and a scale bar. The map key explains the meaning of special colors, symbols, and lines used on the map.

After reading the map key, look for the compass rose. It is the direction marker that shows the cardinal directions of north, south, east, and west.

A measuring line, often called a scale bar, helps you estimate distance on a map. The map's scale tells you what distance on the earth is represented by the measurement on the scale bar. For example, 1 inch (2.54 cm) on the map may represent 100 miles (160.9 km) on the earth.

NATIONAL GEOGRAPHIC

Empires of the Maya, Aztec, and Inca

- ⊛ Capital City
- • Major City
- Maya
- Inca
- Aztec

Practicing the Skill

The map on this page shows where the ancient Maya, Aztec, and Inca built their empires in North America and South America. Look at the parts of this map, then answer the questions that follow.

1. What information is given in the key?

2. What color shows the Inca Empire?

3. What direction would you travel to go from Tenochtitlán to Chichén Itzá?

4. About how many miles long was the Inca Empire?

5. What was the capital of the Aztec Empire?

Applying the Skill

Drawing a Map Picture a mental image of your house or room. Draw a map showing the location of various areas. Include a map key explaining any symbols or colors you use. Also include a scale bar explaining the size of your map compared to the real area. Finally, add a compass rose and title to your map.

 Glencoe's **Skillbuilder Interactive Workbook CD-ROM, Level 1,** provides instruction and practice in key social studies skills.

North American Peoples

Guide to Reading

Main Idea
Many different cultures lived in North America before the arrival of the Europeans.

Key Terms
pueblo, drought, adobe, federation

Reading Strategy
Taking Notes As you read Section 3, re-create the diagram below and identify locations and ways of living for each culture.

Culture	Where they lived	How they lived
Anasazi		
Mound Builders		
Inuit		

Read to Learn
- what early people lived in North America.
- how different Native American groups adapted to their environments.

Section Theme
Culture and Traditions Early North Americans developed new societies.

Preview of Events

♦ *1000 B.C.*	♦ *B.C./A.D.*	♦ *A.D. 1000*	♦ *A.D. 1300*

C. 1000 B.C.
First ceremonial mounds built

C. A.D. 1000
Anasazi build pueblos in North America

C. A.D. 1100
Cahokia is built

C. A.D. 1300
Hohokam civilization begins to decline

Ancient jar, American Southwest

AN
American Story

In the summer of 1991, a helicopter passenger made an amazing discovery in Arizona's Coconino National Forest. As the helicopter hovered among the sandstone cliffs, the sun shone into a cave 200 feet (61 m) below the rim of one cliff. Standing in the opening of the cave were three large pottery jars. The three jars had been sitting, untouched and unseen, for more than 700 years. The jars and other objects found in the cave were left there by the Sinagua. These people lived hundreds of years ago in what we now call Arizona. The Sinagua are just one of many Native American peoples who are now being studied by archaeologists and historians.

Early Native Americans

Many Native American cultures rose, flourished, and disappeared in North America long before Europeans arrived in the 1500s. Among the most advanced of these early cultures were the Hohokam and Anasazi of the Southwest and the Mound Builders of the Ohio River valley.

The Hohokam

The dry, hot desert of present-day Arizona was home to the **Hohokam** people. They may have come from Mexico about 300 B.C. The Hohokam culture flourished from about A.D. 300 to A.D. 1300 in an area bordered by the Gila and Salt River valleys.

The Hohokam were experts at squeezing every drop of available water from the sun-baked soil. Their way of life depended on the irrigation channels they dug to carry river water into their fields. In addition to hundreds of miles of irrigation channels, the Hohokam left behind pottery, carved stone, and shells etched with acid. The shells came from trade with coastal peoples.

The Anasazi

The **Anasazi** lived around the same time as the Hohokam, roughly A.D. 1 to A.D. 1300, in the area known as the Four Corners (the meeting place of the present-day states of Utah, Colorado, Arizona, and New Mexico). There they built great stone dwellings that the Spanish explorers later called pueblos (PWEH•blohs), or villages. **Pueblo Bonito,** one of the most spectacular of the Anasazi pueblos, can still be seen in New Mexico. The huge semicircular structure of stone and sun-dried earth resembles an apartment building. It is four stories high and has hundreds of rooms. Archaeologists have found traces of a complex road system linking Pueblo Bonito with other villages. This suggests that Pueblo Bonito was an important trade or religious center for the Anasazi.

The Anasazi also built dwellings in the walls of steep cliffs. Cliff dwellings were easy to defend and offered protection from winter weather. **Mesa Verde** in Colorado, one of the largest and most elaborate cliff dwellings, held several thousand inhabitants.

In about 1300 the Anasazi began leaving the pueblos and cliff dwellings to settle in smaller communities. Their large villages may have been abandoned because of droughts, long periods of little rainfall, during which their crops dried up.

Kivas at Pueblo Bonito

Picturing **History**

Pueblo Bonito had more than 800 rooms and 32 kivas, or underground ceremonial chambers. Today, the ruins of Pueblo Bonito are part of Chaco Culture National Historical Park in northwestern New Mexico. **What other kind of dwellings were built by the Anasazi?**

Native American Cultures Before 1500

1. Tepees were used by the Plains cultures.
2. Cultures in the Northeast Woodlands built longhouses.
3. Southwest cultures built pueblos.

Culture Groups

- Arctic
- Subarctic
- Northwest Coast
- Plateau
- Great Basin
- California
- Southwest
- Great Plains
- Northeast Woodlands
- Southeast

0   1,000 miles

0   1,000 kilometers

Azimuthal Equidistant projection

Geography *Skills*

1. **Region** To which culture group did the Apache and Hopi belong?
2. **Making Inferences** Based on the description of the dwellings, which cultures were nomadic?

The Mound Builders

The early cultures of Mexico and Central America appear to have influenced people living in lands to the north. In central North America, prehistoric Native Americans built thousands of mounds of earth that look very much like the stone pyramids of the Maya and the Aztec. Some of the mounds contained burial chambers. Some were topped with temples, as in the Mayan and Aztec cultures.

The mounds are dotted across the landscape from present-day Pennsylvania to the Mississippi River valley. They have been found as far north as the Great Lakes and as far south as Florida. Archaeologists think that the first mounds were built about 1000 B.C. They were not the work of a single group but of many different peoples, who are referred to as the **Mound Builders.**

Among the earliest Mound Builders were the **Adena,** hunters and gatherers who flourished in the Ohio Valley by 800 B.C. They were followed by the **Hopewell** people, who lived between 200 B.C. and A.D. 500. Farmers and traders, the Hopewell built huge burial mounds in the shape of birds, bears, and snakes. One of them, the **Great Serpent Mound,** looks like a giant snake winding across the ground. Archaeologists have found freshwater pearls, shells, cloth, and copper in the mounds. The objects indicate a widespread pattern of trade.

Cahokia

The largest settlement of the Mound Builders was **Cahokia** (kuh•HOH•kee•uh) in present-day Illinois. This city, built after A.D. 900 by a

Native American Population

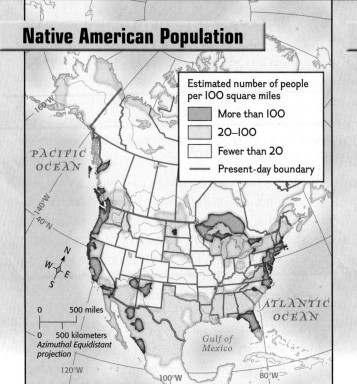

Estimated number of people per 100 square miles

- More than 100
- 20–100
- Fewer than 20
- — Present-day boundary

Hunters, Gatherers, and Fishers

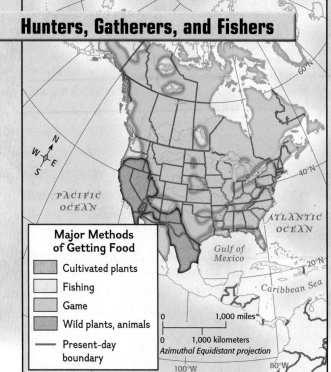

Major Methods of Getting Food

- Cultivated plants
- Fishing
- Game
- Wild plants, animals
- — Present-day boundary

people called the Mississippians, may have had 16,000 or more residents. The largest mound in Cahokia, the Monks Mound, rises nearly 100 feet (30 m). When it was built, it was probably the highest structure north of Mexico.

Cahokia resembled the great cities of Mexico, even though it was nearly 2,000 miles away. The city was dominated by the great pyramid-shaped mound. A temple crowned the summit—perhaps a place where priests studied the movements of the sun and stars or where the priest-ruler of Cahokia lived. A legend of the Natchez people, descendants of the Mississippians, hints of a direct link to Mexico:

66Before we came into this land we lived yonder under the sun [the speaker pointed southwest toward Mexico]. . . . Our nation extended itself along the great water [the Gulf of Mexico] where this large river [the Mississippi] loses itself.99

Reading Check **Identifying** In what area did the Anasazi live?

Other Native North Americans

Although the civilizations of the Hohokam, the Anasazi, and the Mound Builders eventually faded away, other Native American cultures arose to take their place. Around the time that Europeans began arriving, North America was home to many different societies.

Peoples of the North

The people who settled in the northernmost part of North America, in the lands around the Arctic Ocean, are called the **Inuit.** Some scientists think the Inuit were the last migrants to cross the land bridge into North America.

The Inuit had many skills that helped them survive in the cold Arctic climate. They may have brought some of these skills from northern Siberia, probably their original home. In the winter the Inuit built igloos, low-lying structures of snow blocks, which protected them from severe weather. Their clothing of furs and sealskins was both warm and waterproof. The Inuit were hunters and fishers. In the coastal waters, they pursued whales, seals, and walruses in small,

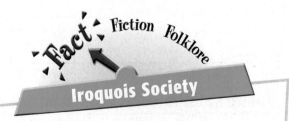

Iroquois Society

Powerful Iroquois Women did hold great power among the Iroquois people. Iroquois women owned houses, crops, and fields and chose the members of the Iroquois governing council.

skin-covered boats. On land they hunted caribou, large deerlike animals that lived in the far north. The Inuit made clothing from caribou skins and burned seal oil in lamps.

Peoples of the West

The mild climate and dependable food sources of the West Coast created a favorable environment for many different groups.

The peoples of the northwestern coast, such as the **Tlingit** (TLIHNG•kuht), **Haida,** and **Chinook,** developed a way of life that used the resources of the forest and the sea. They built wooden houses and made canoes, cloth, and baskets from tree bark. Using spears and traps, they fished for salmon along the coast and in rivers such as the Columbia. This large fish was the main food of the northwestern people. They preserved the salmon by smoking it over fires.

Salmon was also important for the people of the plateau region, the area between the Cascade Mountains and the Rocky Mountains. The **Nez Perce** (NEHZ PUHRS) and **Yakima** peoples fished the rivers, hunted deer in forests, and gathered roots and berries. The root of the camas plant, a relative of the lily, was an important part of their diet. The plateau peoples lived in earthen houses.

Present-day California was home to a great variety of cultures. Along the northern coast, Native Americans fished for their food. In the more barren environment of the southern deserts, nomadic groups wandered from place to place collecting roots and seeds. In the central valley, the **Pomo** gathered acorns and pounded them into flour. As in many Native American cultures, the women of the Pomo did most of the gathering and flour making.

In the Great Basin between the Sierra Nevada and the Rocky Mountains, Native Americans found ways to live in the dry climate. The soil was too hard and rocky for farming, so peoples such as the **Ute** (YOOT) and **Shoshone** (shuh•SHOHN) traveled in search of food. They ate small game, pine nuts, juniper berries, roots, and some insects. Instead of making permanent settlements, the Great Basin people created temporary shelters of branches and reeds.

Peoples of the Southwest

Descendants of the Anasazi formed the **Hopi,** the **Acoma,** and the **Zuni** peoples of the Southwest. They built their homes from a type of sun-dried mud brick called adobe. They raised corn or maize as their basic food. They also grew beans, squash, melons, pumpkins, and fruit. The people of the Southwest also took part in a sophisticated trade network that extended throughout the Southwest and into Mexico.

In the 1500s two new groups settled in the region—the **Apache** and the **Navajo.** Unlike the other peoples of the Southwest, the Apache and Navajo were hunters and gatherers. They hunted deer and other game. Eventually the Navajo settled into stationary communities and built square houses called hogans. In addition to hunting and gathering, they began to grow maize and beans. They also began raising sheep in the 1600s.

Peoples of the Plains

The peoples of the Great Plains were nomadic; villages were temporary, lasting only for a growing season or two. When the people moved from place to place, they dragged their homes—cone-shaped skin tents called tepees—behind them. The men hunted antelope, deer, and buffalo. The women tended plots of maize, squash, and beans.

When the Spanish brought horses to Mexico in the 1500s, some got loose. In time horses made their way north. Native Americans captured and tamed the wild horses, and the Comanche, the **Dakota,** and other Plains peoples became skilled riders. They learned to hunt on horseback and to use the horses in warfare, attacking their enemies with long spears, bows and arrows, clubs, and knives.

Citizenship
Peoples of the East and Southeast

The people who lived in the woodlands of eastern North America formed complex political systems to govern their nations. The **Iroquois** (IHR•uh•KWAWIH) and **Cherokee** had formal law codes and formed federations, governments that linked different groups.

The Iroquois lived near Canada in what is now northern New York State. There were five Iroquois groups or nations: the **Onondaga,** the **Seneca,** the **Mohawk,** the **Oneida,** and the **Cayuga.** These groups warred with each other until the late 1500s, when they joined to form the Iroquois League, also called the Iroquois Confederacy.

Iroquois women occupied positions of power in their communities. According to the constitution of the Iroquois League, women chose the 50 men who served on the league council.

The Iroquois constitution was written down after the Europeans came to North America. It describes the Iroquois peoples' desire for peace:

❝I am Dekanawidah and with the Five Nations' Confederate Lords I plant the Tree of Great Peace. . . . Roots have spread out from the Tree of the Great Peace, one to the north, one to the east, one to the south and one to the west. ❞

The Southeast was also a woodlands area, but with a warmer climate than the eastern woodlands. The Creek, Chickasaw, and Cherokee were among the region's Native American peoples. Many Creek lived in loosely knit farming communities in present-day Georgia and Alabama. There they grew corn, tobacco, squash, and other crops. The Chickasaw, most of whom lived farther west in what is now Mississippi, farmed the river bottomlands. The Cherokee farmed in the mountains of Georgia and the Carolinas.

Wherever they lived in North America, the first Americans developed ways of life that were well suited to their environments. In the 1500s, however, the Native Americans met people whose cultures, beliefs, and ways of life were different from anything they had known or ever seen. These newcomers were the Europeans, and their arrival would change the Native Americans' world forever.

✓ **Reading Check** **Describing** How did the use of the horse change the lifestyle of Native Americans on the Great Plains?

HISTORY Online

Student Web Activity
Visit taj.glencoe.com and click on **Chapter 1— Student Web Activities** for an activity on Native American cultures.

SECTION 3 ASSESSMENT

Checking for Understanding

1. **Key Terms** Use each of these terms in a complete sentence that will help explain its meaning: pueblo, drought, adobe, federation.
2. **Reviewing Facts** Identify clues that led archaeologists to believe that the Mound Builders were influenced by other cultures.

Reviewing Themes

3. **Culture and Traditions** What organization did the Iroquois form to promote peace among their people?

Critical Thinking

4. **Making Generalizations** Why was the environment of the West Coast favorable for settlement by so many groups of Native Americans?
5. **Comparing** Re-create the diagram below and explain how Native American cultures differed from one another by describing their locations and ways of living.

Culture	Region	Shelter
Tlingit		
Zuni		
Dakota		

Analyzing Visuals

6. **Geography Skills** Study the map on page 30. What groups lived in California? What groups lived in the Southeast?

Interdisciplinary Activity

Geography Create or sketch a model of a home that a Native American might have built. Use natural materials that exist in the area where you live and label the materials on your diagram. Consider the climate of your area in your design.

Chapter Summary

The First Americans

The first Americans begin to adapt to their surroundings.

Societies in South and Central America and in Mexico create powerful empires.

The Inca, Maya, and Aztec

- The **Inca** develop a complex political system. They also build a large network of paved roads.

- The **Maya** create a written language and develop new ways of farming.

- The **Aztec** build a large empire, stretching from north-central Mexico to the border of Guatemala, and from the Atlantic Ocean to the Pacific Ocean.

People of North America

- The people of North America do not develop empires as large as those of the Inca, Maya, and Aztec.

- Among the most advanced of the early cultures are the Hohokam and Anasazi of the Southwest and the Mound Builders of the Ohio River valley.

- People who settle in a particular region develop a common culture.

- In the **Southwest,** Native American peoples adapt to their harsh environment by improving techniques of irrigation to farm the land.

- Most of the people of the **Great Plains** were nomadic. They lived in tepees and used horses, spears, and bows and arrows to hunt deer, antelope, and buffalo.

- Native Americans of the Northeast form the **Iroquois League** to solve disputes.

Reviewing Key Terms

On a sheet of paper, define the following terms.

1. archaeology
2. artifact
3. Ice Age
4. nomad
5. carbon dating
6. culture
7. civilization
8. hieroglyphics
9. pueblo
10. federation

Reviewing Key Facts

11. For what reasons did Asians cross the land bridge to the Americas?
12. What regions did the land bridge connect?
13. What was the first crop raised by Native Americans in Mexico?
14. What does carbon dating measure?
15. What are hieroglyphics?
16. What regions were under Inca control?
17. What were two advantages of living in dwellings built into the side of cliffs?
18. What type of dwelling was common among the people of the Southwest?
19. In what region did the Tlingit, Haida, and the Chinook peoples live?
20. What groups formed the Iroquois League?

Critical Thinking

21. **Comparing** Re-create the diagram below and explain how the environment of Native Americans who lived in the Northwest differed from the environment of those who lived in the Southwest.

Location	Environment
Northwest	
Southwest	

22. **Analyzing Themes: Culture and Traditions** Religion was an important part of life in many Native American civilizations. What role did priests play in Mayan society?

23. **Analyzing Information** In what ways did the Inca and Aztec use war to increase their power?

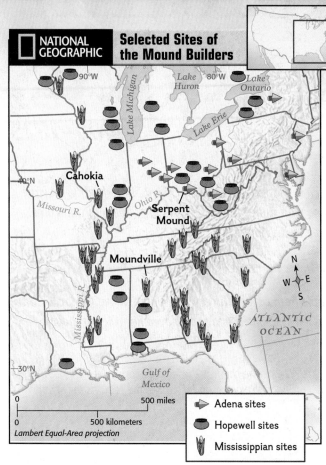

NATIONAL GEOGRAPHIC **Selected Sites of the Mound Builders**

90°W Lake Huron 80°W Lake Ontario
Lake Michigan Lake Erie
Cahokia
40°N Ohio R.
Missouri R. **Serpent Mound**
Moundville
Mississippi R.
ATLANTIC OCEAN
30°N Gulf of Mexico

N
W E
S

0   500 miles
0   500 kilometers
Lambert Equal-Area projection

Adena sites
Hopewell sites
Mississippian sites

 ## Geography and History Activity

Study the map above and answer the questions that follow.

24. **Location** Along what two major rivers did many of the Mound Builders settle?

25. **Place** Near which river did the Adena build most of their settlements?

26. **Movement** Of the Adena, Hopewell, and Mississippian cultures, which settled the farthest east?

Practicing Skills

Understanding the Parts of a Map *Use the key, compass rose, and scale bar on the map of Native American cultures on page 30 to answer these questions.*

27. What does the map key highlight?

28. About how far from the Gulf of Mexico did the Omaha people live?

29. Which Native American peoples settled in the Southwest region?

30. Which people lived farthest west—the Pawnee or the Miami?

 ## Technology Activity

31. **Using the Internet** Search the Internet for a Web site created by a modern Native American group. Based on information you find at the site, explain the group's goals.

Citizenship Cooperative Activity

32. **Research** Work with a partner to investigate the early history of your community using primary and secondary sources. Find out when and why it was founded. Who were the first settlers and early leaders? How did the government change over the years? Prepare a report for your class about what you have discovered.

Economics Activity

33. Create a cause-and-effect chart. Write on your chart: *Cause: The development of farming changed the way early nomads lived.* Then, describe at least two effects.

 ## Alternative Assessment

34. **Portfolio Writing Activity** Research information about one aspect of Aztec or Iroquois life. Present your information in a report to the other students.

 The Princeton Review
Standardized Test Practice

Directions: Choose the *best* answer to the following question.

Because the Mayan civilization was a theocracy, the most powerful Maya were

A   warriors.   C   priests.

B   craftsmen.   D   enslaved people.

Test-Taking Tip:

This question asks you to draw an inference. What is the meaning of the word *theocracy*? Understanding the definition will help to answer the question.

Exploring the Americas

1400–1625

Why It Matters

Although the English have been the major influence on United States history, they are only part of the story. Beginning with Native Americans and continuing through time, people from many cultures came to the Americas.

The Impact Today

The Americas today consist of people from cultures around the globe. Native Americans, Spanish, Africans, and others discussed in Chapter 2 have all played key roles in shaping the culture we now call American.

 The American Journey Video *The chapter 2 video, "Exploring the Americas," presents the challenges faced by European explorers, and discusses the reasons they came to the Americas.*

1513
• Balboa crosses the Isthmus of Panama

1492
• Christopher Columbus reaches America

1497
• John Cabot sails to Newfoundland

 The Americas

1400   1450   1500

World

1429
• Joan of Arc defeats the English at French town of Orléans

c. 1456
• Johannes Gutenberg uses movable metal type in printing

c. 1500
• Songhai Empire rises in Africa
• Rome becomes a major center of Renaissance culture

Founding of Maryland by **Emanuel Leutze** Native Americans lived in North America long before the Europeans arrived.

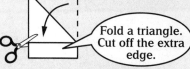
Evaluating Information Study Foldable
Make this foldable to help you learn about European exploration of the Americas.

Step 1 Fold the paper from the top right corner down so the edges line up. Cut off the leftover piece.

> Fold a triangle. Cut off the extra edge.

Step 2 Fold the triangle in half. Unfold.

> The folds will form an X dividing four equal sections.

Step 3 Cut up one fold line and stop at the middle. Draw an X on one tab and label the other three.

Step 4 Fold the X flap under the other flap and glue together.

> This makes a three-sided pyramid.

Reading and Writing As you read, ask yourself why England, France, and Spain were exploring the Americas. Write your questions under each appropriate pyramid wall.

1534
• Cartier claims Canada for France

c. 1570
• Iroquois form League of Five Nations

1607
• Jamestown settled

1620
• Pilgrims found Plymouth

1550

1600

1517
• Martin Luther promotes Church reform

1522
• Magellan's crew completes first world voyage

1588
• England defeats Spanish Armada

HISTORY Online

Chapter Overview
Visit taj.glencoe.com and click on **Chapter 2— Chapter Overviews** to preview chapter information.

A Changing World

Guide to Reading

Main Idea
New knowledge and ideas led Europeans to explore overseas.

Key Terms
classical, Renaissance, technology, astrolabe, caravel, pilgrimage, mosque

Reading Strategy
Determining Cause and Effect As you read the section, re-create the diagram below and identify three reasons Europeans increased overseas exploration.

Causes of European exploration

Read to Learn
- how technology made long sea voyages possible.
- how great civilizations flourished in Africa.

Section Theme
Culture and Traditions The spirit of the Renaissance changed the way Europeans thought about the world.

Preview of Events

1200	1300	1400
1271 Marco Polo travels to China from Italy	**1324** Mansa Musa makes a pilgrimage to Makkah	**c. 1400** Renaissance spreads throughout Europe

Marco Polo

A European Story

In 1271 Marco Polo set off from the city of Venice on a great trek across Asia to China. Only 17 years old at the time, Polo journeyed with his father and uncle, both Venetian merchants. Traveling on camels for more than three years, the merchants crossed almost 7,000 miles (11,265 km) of mountains and deserts. Finally they reached the palace of Kublai Khan (KOO•bluh KAHN), the Mongol emperor of China. There Marco Polo spent 17 years working for the Khan and learning much about China's advanced culture.

Expanding Horizons

For centuries after the fall of the Roman Empire, the people of western Europe were isolated from the rest of the world. Their world, dominated by the Catholic Church, was divided into many small kingdoms and city-states.

Meanwhile, the religion known as Islam swept across the Middle East and Africa. The followers of Islam are known as Muslims. As Muslim power grew,

European Christians became fearful of losing access to the Holy Land, the birthplace of Christianity, in what is now Israel.

Beginning in 1095, the Europeans launched the first of nine expeditions, known as the Crusades, to regain control of their holy sites. The Crusades brought west Europeans into contact with the Middle East. Arab merchants sold spices, sugar, silk and other goods from China and India to the Europeans. As European interest in Asia grew, Marco Polo returned from China. In 1296, he began writing an account of his trip describing the marvels of Asia. Polo's *Travels* was widely read in Europe. Little did he realize that 200 years later his book about the East would inspire Christopher Columbus and others to sail in the opposite direction to reach the same destination.

Ⓢ Economics

The Growth of Trade

Merchants could make a fortune selling goods from the Orient. Wealthy Europeans clamored for cinnamon, pepper, cloves, and other spices. They also wanted perfumes, silks, and precious stones.

Buying the goods from Arab traders in the Middle East, the merchants sent them overland by caravan to the **Mediterranean Sea** and then by ship to Italian ports. The cities of Venice, Genoa, and Pisa prospered and became centers of the growing East-West trade. The Arab merchants, however, charged very high prices. As demand for Asian goods increased, Europeans began looking for a route to the East that bypassed the Arab merchants.

The Growth of Ideas

In the 1300s a powerful new spirit emerged in the Italian city-states and spread throughout Europe. The development of banking and the expansion of trade with Asia made Italian merchants wealthy. These citizens were able to pursue an interest in the region's past and learn more about the glorious civilizations of ancient Rome and Greece.

Because they wanted to improve their knowledge of people and of the world, Italians studied the classical—ancient Greek and Roman—

works with new interest. Scholars translated Greek manuscripts on philosophy, poetry, and science. Many thinkers of this period began to take a more experimental approach to science; they tested new and old theories and evaluated the results.

Influenced by the classical texts, a great many authors began to write about the individual and the universe. Artists studied the sculpture and architecture of the classical world. They particularly admired the harmony and balance in Greek art, with its realistic way of portraying people.

The Renaissance

This period of intellectual and artistic creativity became known as the Renaissance (REH•nuh•SAHNTS). A French word meaning "rebirth," it refers to the renewed interest in classical Greek and Roman learning. Over the next two centuries, the Renaissance spread north, south, and west, reaching Spain and northern Europe in the 1400s.

The spirit of the Renaissance dramatically changed the way Europeans thought about themselves and the world. It encouraged them to pursue new ideas and set new goals; it paved the way for an age of exploration and discovery.

Reading Check **Describing** What cultures influenced the Renaissance?

Powerful Nations Emerge

During the 1400s the population of western Europe began to increase. Merchants and bankers in the growing cities wanted to expand their businesses through foreign trade. If they could buy spices and silks from the East directly, without going through the Arab and Italian cities, they could earn huge profits. They looked for alternatives to the overland route through the Middle East.

The development of large nation-states in western Europe helped expand trade and interest in overseas exploration. For many years Europe had been a patchwork of small states. Political power was divided among local lords, and few people traveled outside their region.

By the 1400s, however, a new type of centralized state was emerging in western Europe. Strong monarchs came to power in Spain, Portugal, England, and France. They began to establish national laws, courts, taxes, and armies to replace those of local lords. These ambitious kings and queens sought ways to increase trade and make their countries stronger and wealthier.

Reading Check **Explaining** What resulted from the emergence of large nation-states?

Linking Past & Present

Astrolabe to Satellite

"Land ho!" The tools that early explorers used to sail the uncharted seas were much different from the instruments used today. One early navigation tool was the astrolabe. A sailor held the astrolabe vertically, located a star through its sights, and measured the star's elevation above the horizon. A ship's approximate latitude could be identified this way.

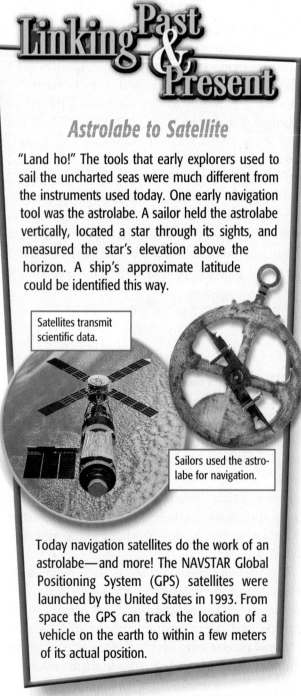

Satellites transmit scientific data.

Sailors used the astrolabe for navigation.

Today navigation satellites do the work of an astrolabe—and more! The NAVSTAR Global Positioning System (GPS) satellites were launched by the United States in 1993. From space the GPS can track the location of a vehicle on the earth to within a few meters of its actual position.

Technology's Impact

Advances in technology—the use of scientific knowledge for practical purposes—paved the way for European voyages of exploration. In the 1450s the introduction of movable type and the printing press made it much easier to print books. Now more people could have access to books and to new information. After its publication in print form in 1477, many Europeans read Marco Polo's *Travels*.

★ Geography
Better Maps

Maps were a problem for early navigators. Most maps were inaccurate because they were drawn from the often-mistaken impressions of traders and travelers. Little by little, cartographers, or mapmakers, gradually improved their skills.

Using the reports of explorers and information from Arab geographers, mapmakers made more accurate land and sea maps. These maps showed the direction of ocean currents. They also showed lines of latitude, which measured the distance north and south of the Equator.

Better instruments were developed for navigating the seas. Sailors could determine their latitude while at sea with an astrolabe, an instrument that measured the position of stars. Europeans also acquired the magnetic compass, a Chinese invention that began to be widely used in Europe and the Middle East in the 1200s. The compass allowed sailors to determine their direction when they were far from land.

Better Ships

Advances in ship design allowed shipbuilders to build sailing vessels capable of long ocean voyages. The stern rudder and the triangular sail made it possible for ships to sail into the wind. Both of these new features came from the Arabs. In the late 1400s, the Portuguese developed the three-masted caravel. The caravel sailed faster than earlier ships and carried more cargo and food supplies. It also could float in shallow water, which allowed sailors to explore inlets and to sail their ships up to the beach to make repairs. A Venetian sailor called the caravels "the best ships that sailed the seas."

By the mid-1400s the Italian ports faced increased competition for foreign trade. Powerful countries like Portugal and Spain began searching for sea routes to Asia, launching a new era of exploration. Portugal began its exploration by sending ships down the west coast of Africa, which Europeans had never visited before.

Reading Check **Explaining** How did the caravel affect overseas exploration in the fifteenth and sixteenth centuries?

African Kingdoms

Powerful kingdoms flourished in Africa south of the Sahara between 400 and 1600. The region was rich with natural resources. Africans mined gold, copper, and iron ore. Trade with Islamic societies in North Africa brought both wealth and Islamic ideas and customs to the West African kingdoms.

City-states on the east coast of Africa also benefited from trade. There Arab traders from the Middle East brought cotton, silk, and porcelain from India and China to exchange for ivory and metals from the African interior.

As the Portuguese sailed south along the African coastline in the mid-1400s, they set up trading posts. From these, they traded for gold and for slaves.

Ghana—A Trading Empire

Between 400 and 1100, a vast trading empire called **Ghana** emerged in West Africa. Well located between the salt mines of the Sahara and the gold mines to the south, Ghana prospered from the taxes the leaders of the empire imposed on trade.

Caravans with gold, ivory, and slaves from Ghana crossed the Sahara to North Africa. Muslim traders from North Africa loaded caravans

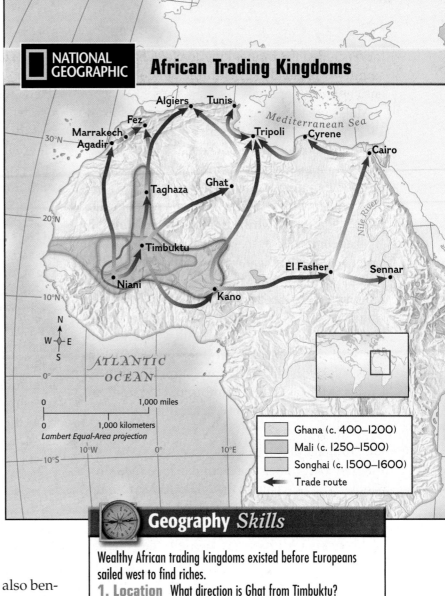

NATIONAL GEOGRAPHIC **African Trading Kingdoms**

Geography *Skills*

Wealthy African trading kingdoms existed before Europeans sailed west to find riches.
1. Location What direction is Ghat from Timbuktu?
2. Comparing What African kingdom covered the smallest area?

with salt, cloth, and brass and headed back to Ghana. As a result of their trading contacts, many West Africans became Muslims.

In 1076 people from North Africa called Almoravids attacked Ghana and disrupted its trade routes. While Ghana fought the Almoravids, new trade routes and gold mines opened up to the east, bypassing Ghana. Ghana then began to decline, and new states emerged in the region.

Mali—A Powerful Kingdom

Mali, one of the new states, grew into a powerful kingdom. The people of Mali developed their own trade routes across the desert to North Africa. By the late 1200s, Mali's expanded territory included the former kingdom of Ghana. The country was mainly agricultural, but gold mines enriched the kingdom.

Mali's greatest king, **Mansa Musa,** ruled from 1312 to 1337. He was described at the time as "the most powerful, the richest, the most fortunate, the most feared by his enemies, and the most able to do good to those around him."

In 1324 Musa, a Muslim, made a grand pilgrimage to the Muslim holy city of **Makkah** (also spelled Mecca) in western Saudi Arabia. A pilgrimage is a journey to a holy place. Arab writers reported that Musa traveled with a huge military escort. Ahead of him marched 500 royal servants who carried gold to distribute along the way. Musa returned to Mali with an Arab architect who built great mosques, Muslim houses of worship, in the capital of **Timbuktu.** Under Mansa Musa, Timbuktu became an important center of Islamic art and learning.

The Songhai Empire

Some years later the Songhai (SAWNG•hy) people, who lived along the **Niger River,** rose up against Mali rule. They built a navy to control the Niger and in 1468 captured Timbuktu. In the late 1400s, **Askìya Muhammad** brought the Songhai empire to the height of its power. Askìya strengthened his country and made it the largest in the history of West Africa. He built many schools and encouraged trade with Europe and Asia.

Plan of Government

Devoted to Islam, Askìya introduced laws based on the teachings of the holy book of Islam, the Quran. He appointed Muslim judges to uphold Islamic laws. Askìya also developed a sophisticated plan for his country's government. He divided Songhai into five provinces. For each province he appointed a governor, a tax collector, a court of judges, and a trade inspector. Everyone in Songhai used the same weights and measures and followed the same legal system.

In the late 1500s, the North African kingdom of Morocco sent an army across the Sahara to attack Songhai gold-trading centers. Armed with guns and cannons, the Moroccans easily defeated the Songhai.

✓ **Reading Check** **Identifying** Which African kingdom thrived between A.D. 400 and A.D. 1100?

HISTORY Online
Student Web Activity
Visit taj.glencoe.com and click on **Chapter 2— Student Web Activities** for an activity on African kingdoms.

SECTION 1 ASSESSMENT

Checking for Understanding

1. **Key Terms** Write sentences in which you use the following groups of terms: classical and Renaissance; technology, astrolabe, and caravel; pilgrimage and mosque.

2. **Reviewing Facts** Name three technological advances that furthered European exploration. Describe how these advances helped explorers.

Reviewing Themes

3. **Culture and Traditions** How did the Islamic religion spread to the early kingdoms of Africa? What is the name of the holy book of Islam?

Critical Thinking

4. **Drawing Conclusions** Why do you think the Renaissance began in Italy and not in another part of Europe?

5. **Comparing** Re-create the diagram below and compare three African kingdoms. In the outer spaces, describe each kingdom. In the shared space, identify similarities between them.

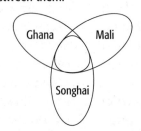

Analyzing Visuals

6. **Geography Skills** Review the map of the African trading kingdoms on page 41. Which of the trading kingdoms was established earliest? In which region of Africa did the three trading kingdoms develop?

Interdisciplinary Activity

Science Select a technological advance that has occurred during your lifetime. Compare its effects to the effects of one of the technological advances described in Section 1. Which has had the greater impact on society? Explain.

Early Exploration

Main Idea

In search of trade routes, Portuguese explorers ushered in an era of overseas exploration.

Key Terms

line of demarcation, strait, circumnavigate

Reading Strategy

Organizing Information As you read the section, re-create the diagram below and identify explorers, when they traveled, and where they went.

Explorer	Date(s)	Region

Read to Learn

- how Portugal led the way in overseas exploration.
- about Columbus's plan for sailing to Asia.

Section Theme

Geography and History In 1400 Europeans had a limited knowledge of the geography of the world.

Preview of Events

♦1000   ♦1200   ♦1400   ♦1600

c. 1000
Leif Eriksson lands in present-day Newfoundland

1488
Bartholomeu Dias reaches the Indian Ocean

1492
Columbus lands in the Americas

1498
Vasco da Gama reaches India

1519
Magellan begins circumnavigation of the world

Compass

A European Story

More than 150 years after the death of Marco Polo, a young Italian sea captain—Christopher Columbus—sat down to read Polo's *Travels* with interest. Columbus read what Polo had to say about the islands of Cipangu, or present-day Japan. According to Polo, Cipangu lay some 1,500 miles (2,414 km) off the eastern shore of Asia. Because the earth is round, Columbus reasoned, a person sailing west from Europe should quickly reach Cipangu. It could be much closer than anyone thought.

Unfortunately, Marco Polo—and therefore Columbus—was wrong.

Seeking New Trade Routes

The maps that Columbus and the first European explorers used did not include America. They showed three continents—Europe, Asia, and Africa—merged together in a gigantic landmass, or large area of land. This landmass was bordered by oceans. Some explorers thought that the Western (Atlantic) and Eastern (Pacific) Oceans ran together to form what they called the **Ocean Sea.** At the time, no one realized that another huge landmass was missing from the maps. They also did not realize that the oceans were as large as they are.

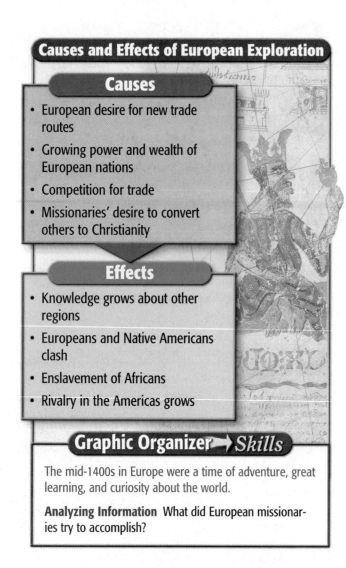

Causes and Effects of European Exploration

Causes

- European desire for new trade routes
- Growing power and wealth of European nations
- Competition for trade
- Missionaries' desire to convert others to Christianity

Effects

- Knowledge grows about other regions
- Europeans and Native Americans clash
- Enslavement of Africans
- Rivalry in the Americas grows

Graphic Organizer → Skills

The mid-1400s in Europe were a time of adventure, great learning, and curiosity about the world.

Analyzing Information What did European missionaries try to accomplish?

Portugal took the lead in exploring the boundaries of the known world. Because Portugal lacked a Mediterranean port, it could not be part of the profitable trade between Asia and Europe. The country's ambitious rulers wanted to find a new route to China and India.

The Portuguese also hoped to find a more direct way to get West African gold. The gold traveled by caravan across the desert to North Africa, then by ship across the Mediterranean. Portuguese traders needed a better route.

Early Portuguese Voyages

Prince Henry of Portugal laid the groundwork for a new era of exploration. He was fascinated by what lay beyond the known boundaries of the world. In about 1420 he set up a center for exploration on the southwestern tip of Portugal, "where endeth land and where

beginneth sea." Known as **Henry the Navigator,** the prince brought astronomers, geographers, and mathematicians to share their knowledge with Portuguese sailors and shipbuilders.

As Portuguese ships moved south along the coast of West Africa, they traded for gold and ivory and established trading posts. Because of its abundance of gold, the area came to be known as the **Gold Coast.** In the mid-1400s the Portuguese began buying slaves there as well.

King John II of Portugal launched new efforts to realize the Portuguese dream of a trading empire in Asia. If the Portuguese could find a sea route around Africa, they could trade directly with India and China. In the 1480s the king urged Portuguese sea captains to explore farther south along the African coast.

Bartholomeu Dias

In 1487 the king sent **Bartholomeu Dias** to explore the southernmost part of Africa. As Dias approached the area, he ran into a terrible storm that carried him off course and around the southern tip of Africa. Dias wrote that he had been around the "Cape of Storms." On learning of Dias's discovery, King John II renamed this southern tip of land the Cape of Good Hope—he hoped that the passage around Africa might lead to a new route to India.

Vasco da Gama

The first Portuguese voyages to India were made years later. In July 1497, after much preparation, **Vasco da Gama** set out from Portugal with four ships. Da Gama sailed down the coast of West Africa, rounded the Cape of Good Hope, and visited cities along the coast of East Africa. He engaged an Arab pilot who knew the Indian Ocean well. With the pilot's help, Da Gama sailed on to India. He reached the port of Calicut in 1498, completing the long-awaited eastern sea route to Asia.

The Portuguese Empire

Events moved quickly after that. Pedro Alvares Cabral, following Da Gama's route, swung so wide around Africa that he touched Brazil. By claiming the land for his king, he gave

Portugal a stake in the Americas. Meanwhile, Portuguese fleets began to make annual voyages to India returning with cargoes that made Lisbon the marketplace of Europe.

✓ Reading Check) **Analyzing** Why was Portugal interested in exploration?

Columbus Crosses the Atlantic

Christopher Columbus had a different plan for reaching Asia. He thought he could get there by sailing west. Born in Genoa, Italy, in 1451, Columbus became a sailor for Portugal. He had traveled as far north as the Arctic Circle and as far south as the Gold Coast.

In the 1400s most educated people believed the world was round. A more difficult matter was determining its size. Columbus was among those who based their estimates of the earth's size on the work of Ptolemy, an ancient Greek astronomer. Columbus believed Asia was about 2,760 miles (4,441 km) from Europe—a voyage of about two months by ship. Ptolemy, however, had underestimated the size of the world.

The Viking Voyages

Several centuries before Columbus, northern Europeans called **Vikings** had sailed west and reached North America. In the 800s and 900s, Viking ships visited Iceland and Greenland and established settlements. According to Norse

TECHNOLOGY & History

Spanish Galleon

In the late 1500s and early 1600s, Spanish galleons carried gold and silver from the West Indies to Spain. That's not all these ships carried, however. The threat of pirates prompted the Spanish galleons to carry weapons as part of their cargo. *What powered the Spanish galleons?*

The crow's nest served as a lookout.

1 Two or three sails on the **foremast** and **mainmast** allowed the ship to "catch the wind."

2 Elaborate living quarters for the captain were placed within the high **sterncastle.** The rest of the crew slept on deck.

3 Strong hands were needed to climb the rigging into the **crow's nest,** or lookout platform.

4 Stones and bricks provided **ballast** to keep the ship from tipping over. These stones would be replaced with cargo in the Americas. Many colonial streets and sidewalks were paved with ballast stones.

Spanish galleons were about 140 feet (43 meters) long.

5 Food and water were stored in the **hold.**

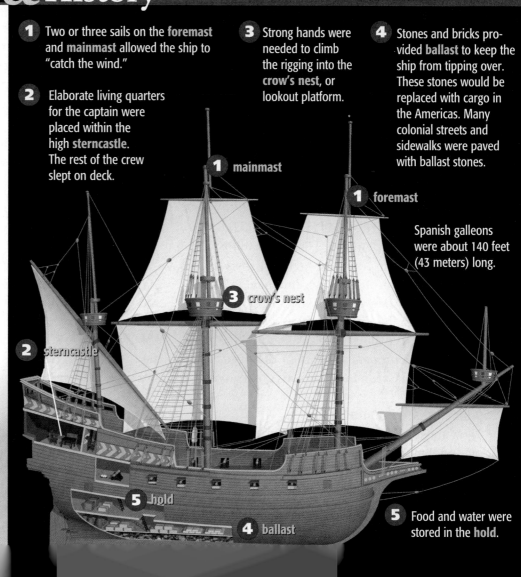

1 mainmast
1 foremast
3 crow's nest
2 sterncastle
5 hold
4 ballast

ing Portugal with envy. They, too, wanted to share in the riches of Asian trade. Columbus needed a sponsor to finance his ambitious project of a westward voyage to Asia. He visited many European courts looking for support. After years of frustration, he finally found a sponsor in Spain.

Queen Isabella, a devout Christian, was finally persuaded by her husband's minister of finance to support the expedition for two reasons. First, Columbus had promised to bring Christianity to any lands he found. Second, if he found a way to Asia, Spain would become very wealthy. She promised Columbus a share of any riches gained from lands he discovered on his way to Asia.

Columbus's First Voyage

On August 3, 1492, Columbus set out from Palos, Spain. He had two small ships, the *Niña* and the *Pinta*, and a larger one, the *Santa María*, carrying a total of about 90 sailors. The small fleet stopped at the Canary Islands for repairs and to stock up on supplies, then sailed westward into the unknown.

The ships had good winds, but after a month at sea the sailors began to worry. Columbus wrote that he was

> ❝having trouble with the crew . . . . I am told that if I persist in going onward, the best course of action will be to throw me into the sea.❞

Columbus, however, was determined. He told the men, "I made this voyage to go to the Indies, and [I] shall continue until I find them, with God's help." To convince the crew that they had not traveled too far from home, Columbus altered the distances in his ship's log. 📖 *(See page 959 of the Primary Sources Library for another log entry by Columbus.)*

"Tierra! Tierra!"

On October 12, 1492, at 2:00 in the morning, a lookout shouted, *"Tierra! Tierra!"*—"Land! Land!" He had spotted a small island, part of the group now called the Bahamas. Columbus went ashore, claimed the island for Spain, and named it San Salvador. Although he did not know it, Columbus had reached the Americas.

sagas, or traditional stories, a Viking sailor named Leif Eriksson explored a land west of Greenland known as Vinland about the year 1000. Other Norse sagas describe failed attempts by the Vikings to settle in Vinland. Historians think that Vinland was North America. Archaeologists have found the remains of a Viking settlement in Newfoundland. No one is sure what other parts of North America the Vikings explored.

The Viking voyages to other lands were not well known. Europeans did not "discover" the Americas until Columbus made his great voyage.

Spain Backs Columbus

For most of the 1400s, Spanish monarchs devoted their energy to driving the Muslims out of their country. With the fall of the last Muslim kingdom in southern Spain in 1492, **King Ferdinand** and **Queen Isabella** of Spain could focus on other goals. The Spanish had been watching the seafaring and trading successes of neighbor-

Columbus explored the area for several months, convinced he had reached the East Indies, the islands off the coast of Asia. Today the **Caribbean Islands** are often referred to as the **West Indies.** Columbus called the local people Indians. He noted that they regarded the Europeans with wonder and often touched them to find out "if they were flesh and bones like themselves."

When Columbus returned to Spain in triumph, Queen Isabella and King Ferdinand received him with great honor and agreed to finance his future voyages. Columbus had earned the title of Admiral of the Ocean Sea.

Columbus's Later Voyages

Columbus made three more voyages from Spain in 1493, 1498, and 1502. He explored the Caribbean islands of Hispaniola (present-day Haiti and the Dominican Republic), Cuba, and Jamaica, and he sailed along the coasts of Central America and northern South America. He claimed the new lands for Spain and established settlements.

Columbus originally thought the lands he had found were in Asia. Later explorations made it clear that Columbus had not reached Asia at all. He had found a part of the globe unknown to Europeans, Asians, and Africans. In the following years, the Spanish explored most of the Caribbean region. In time their voyages led to the establishment of the Spanish Empire in the Americas.

Dividing the World

Both Spain and Portugal wanted to protect their claims, and they turned to Pope Alexander VI for help. In 1493 the pope drew a line of demarcation, an imaginary line running down the

TWO VIEWPOINTS

Who Had the Right to Claim the Americas?

Who owned the land of the Americas before the Europeans arrived? Did it belong to the people who already lived there, or was it there to be taken by the Europeans? While reading the excerpts below, notice the difference in opinions about who owned the rights to the land of the Americas.

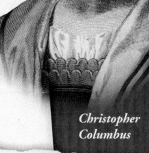

Christopher Columbus

Letter from Christopher Columbus to the King and Queen of Spain, March 4, 1493

. . . I come from the Indies with the armada Your Highnesses gave me . . . . I found innumerable [many] people and very many islands, of which I took possession in Your Highnesses' name, by royal crier and with Your Highnesses' royal banner unfurled, and it was not contradicted . . . .

And I continued to enter very many harbors, in each of which I placed a very large cross in the most appropriate spot, as I had done in all the other [harbors] of the other islands. . . .

Speech by Chief Red Jacket, leader of the Seneca Nation, to a white missionary, 1805

There was a time when our forefathers owned this great island. Their seats extended from the rising to the setting of the sun. The Great Spirit had made it for the use of Indians. He had created buffalo, the deer, and other animals for food. He had made the bear and beaver, and their skins served us for clothing . . . .

The white people, brother, had now found our country. Tidings were carried back and more came amongst us. Yet we did not fear them. We took them to be friends. . . .

Brother, our seats were once large, and yours were very small. You have now become a great people, and we have scarcely a place left to spread our blankets. You have got our country, but you are not satisfied. You want to force your religion upon us . . . .

Learning From History

1. According to Christopher Columbus, who owned the land that he explored in the Americas?
2. How did the relationship between Europeans and Native Americans seem to change as more and more Europeans came to America?

middle of the Atlantic from the North Pole to the South Pole. Spain was to control all the lands to the west of the line. Portugal was to have control of all lands to the east of the line. Portugal, however, protested that the division favored Spain. As a result, in 1494 the two countries signed the Treaty of Tordesillas (TOHR•day•SEE•yuhs), an agreement to move the line farther west. The treaty divided the entire unexplored world between Spain and Portugal.

✦Geography
Exploring America

In 1499 explorer Amerigo Vespucci began mapping South America's coastline. Vespucci concluded that South America was a continent, not part of Asia. By the early 1500s, European geographers had begun to call the continent America, in honor of Amerigo Vespucci. While European geographers discussed Vespucci's findings, others continued to explore America.

NATIONAL GEOGRAPHIC — European Voyages of Exploration

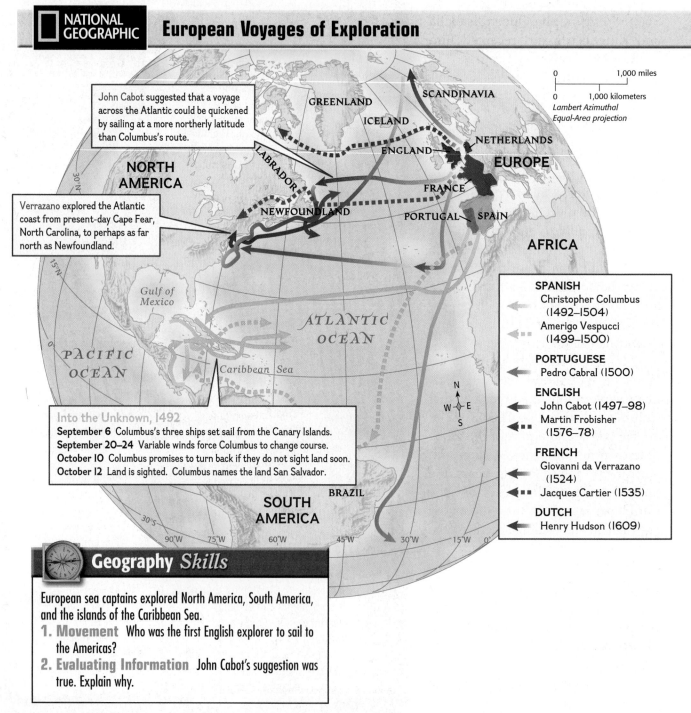

John Cabot suggested that a voyage across the Atlantic could be quickened by sailing at a more northerly latitude than Columbus's route.

Verrazano explored the Atlantic coast from present-day Cape Fear, North Carolina, to perhaps as far north as Newfoundland.

0   1,000 miles
0   1,000 kilometers
Lambert Azimuthal
Equal-Area projection

Into the Unknown, 1492
September 6 Columbus's three ships set sail from the Canary Islands.
September 20–24 Variable winds force Columbus to change course.
October 10 Columbus promises to turn back if they do not sight land soon.
October 12 Land is sighted. Columbus names the land San Salvador.

SPANISH
Christopher Columbus (1492–1504)
Amerigo Vespucci (1499–1500)

PORTUGUESE
Pedro Cabral (1500)

ENGLISH
John Cabot (1497–98)
Martin Frobisher (1576–78)

FRENCH
Giovanni da Verrazano (1524)
Jacques Cartier (1535)

DUTCH
Henry Hudson (1609)

Geography *Skills*

European sea captains explored North America, South America, and the islands of the Caribbean Sea.
1. **Movement** Who was the first English explorer to sail to the Americas?
2. **Evaluating Information** John Cabot's suggestion was true. Explain why.

Vasco Núñez de Balboa (bal•BOH•uh), governor of a Spanish town in present-day Panama, had heard stories of the "great waters" beyond the mountains. In 1513 he formed an exploring party and hiked through the steaming jungles. After many days of difficult travel, the Spaniard climbed a hill and saw a vast body of water. When he reached the water's edge, Balboa waded in and claimed it and the adjoining lands for Spain. Balboa was the first European to see the Pacific Ocean from the Americas.

Sailing Around the World

The Spanish wanted to find a sea route through or around South America to Asia. In 1519 they hired **Ferdinand Magellan,** a Portuguese mariner, to lead an expedition of five ships. Sailing from Spain, Magellan headed west across the Atlantic Ocean and then south along the eastern coast of South America.

By late November 1520, Magellan had found and sailed through the narrow, twisting sea passage to the Pacific. This strait still bears his name. At the end of the strait, Magellan exclaimed: "We are about to stand [go] into an ocean where no ship has ever sailed before." He named the ocean the Pacific, which means "peaceful."

Fact · Fiction · Folklore

America's Flags

Spanish banner, 1492 Christopher Columbus proudly carried the Spanish banner of Castile and León to the shores of the Bahamas. The flag's castle represented Queen Isabella. The lion symbolized her husband, King Ferdinand.

Magellan expected to reach Asia in just a few weeks after rounding South America, but the voyage across the Pacific lasted four months. The crew ran out of food and ate sawdust, rats, and leather to stay alive. Magellan was killed in a skirmish in the Philippines, but some of his crew continued. Their trip had taken almost three years. Only one of the five original ships and 18 of the more than 200 crew members completed the difficult journey. These men were the first to circumnavigate, or sail around, the world.

✓ **Reading Check** **Describing** Why did Spain finance Columbus's voyage?

SECTION 2 ASSESSMENT

Checking for Understanding

1. **Key Terms** Write a short paragraph in which you use the following terms: line of demarcation, strait, circumnavigate.
2. **Reviewing Facts** Who were the first Europeans to reach the Americas and when did they arrive?

Reviewing Themes

3. **Geography and History** What nations signed the Treaty of Tordesillas? What was the purpose of the line of demarcation? How did the treaty affect European exploration of the Americas?

Critical Thinking

4. **Making Inferences** For years, many history books have claimed that "Columbus discovered America." Why do you think Native Americans might disagree with the choice of the word "discovered" in this statement? What might be a better word?
5. **Organizing Information** Re-create the diagram below and identify the regions Columbus explored.

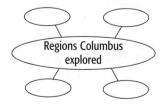

Regions Columbus explored

Analyzing Visuals

6. **Geography Skills** Review the map of European voyages of exploration on page 48; then answer the questions that follow. When did Verrazano make his voyage? For what country did he sail? How did Cabot's route to the Americas differ from that of Columbus?

Interdisciplinary Activity

Geography Draw a map of the world as you think Columbus might have seen it in 1492. Remember his error in calculating distance.

America's LITERATURE

Michael Dorris (1945–1997)

A Modoc Native American, Michael Dorris was an educator, a social activist, and an award-winning author. *Morning Girl,* his first book for young adults, portrays the lives of the Taino people of the Bahamas.

READ TO DISCOVER

Morning Girl is the fictional story of a young Native American woman who meets Columbus and his crew as they arrive in the Bahamas in 1492. While reading this passage, think about the ways that Morning Girl's life might change as a result of Columbus's visit.

READER'S DICTIONARY

backward: undeveloped
Morning Girl: a young Taino woman

Chief's chair, Taino people

Morning Girl

I swam closer to get a better look and had to stop myself from laughing. The strangers had wrapped every part of their bodies with colorful leaves and cotton. Some had decorated their faces with fur and wore shiny rocks on their heads. Compared to us, they were very round. Their canoe was short and square, and, in spite of all their dipping and pulling, it moved so slowly. What a **backward,** distant island they must have come from. But really, to laugh at guests, no matter how odd, would be impolite, especially since I was the first to meet them. If I was foolish, they would think they had arrived at a foolish place. . . .

I kicked toward the canoe and called out the simplest thing.

"Hello!". . .

The man stared at me as though he'd never seen a girl before, then shouted something to his relatives. They all stopped paddling and looked in my direction.

"Hello," I tried again. "Welcome to home. My name is **Morning Girl. . . .**"

All the fat people in the canoe began pointing at me and talking at once. In their excitement they almost turned themselves over, and I allowed my body to sink beneath the waves for a moment in order to hide my smile. . . .

When I came up they were still watching, the way babies do: wide eyed and with their mouths uncovered. They had much to learn about how to behave. . . . It was clear that they hadn't traveled much before.

From *Morning Girl* by Michael Dorris. Text © 1992 by Michael Dorris. Reprinted with permission from Hyperion Books for Children.

ANALYZING LITERATURE

1. **Recall and Interpret** How does Morning Girl describe the strangers' appearance?
2. **Evaluate and Connect** Are Morning Girl's impressions of the visitors positive or negative? Explain your reasoning.

Interdisciplinary Activity

Descriptive Writing Imagine that you are an explorer who arrived in America with Columbus. Describe the people and climate you encounter in America. Compare the way people live in America to your way of life in Europe.

Spain in America

Guide to Reading

Main Idea

In the sixteenth century, Spain established and governed a vast empire in the Americas.

Key Terms

conquistador, tribute, pueblo, mission, presidio, *encomienda*, plantation

Reading Strategy

Organizing Information As you read the section, re-create the diagram below and identify Spanish conquistadors, along with the regions they explored.

Conquistador	Region Explored

Read to Learn

• how the great Aztec and Inca Empires came to an end.
• how Spain governed its empire in the Americas.

Section Theme

Culture and Traditions The conquistadors conquered mighty empires in the Americas.

Preview of Events

♦1500   ♦1530   ♦1560

1519
Hernán Cortés lands in Mexico

1532
Francisco Pizarro captures Atahualpa

1541
De Soto crosses the Mississippi River

1565
Spain establishes fort at St. Augustine, Florida

AN American Story

Would you like to visit a place described in the following way? "A river . . . [stretched] two leagues wide, in which there were fishes as big as horses. . . . The lord of the country took his afternoon nap under a great tree on which were hung a great number of little gold bells. . . . The jugs and bowls were [made] of gold."

"[It was] a land rich in gold, silver, and other wealth . . . great cities . . . and civilized people wearing woolen clothes."

Conquistador's armor

Spanish Conquistadors

Stories of gold, silver, and kingdoms wealthy beyond belief greeted the early Spanish explorers in the Americas. The reports led them far and wide in search of fabulous riches.

Known as conquistadors (kahn•KEES•tuh•dawrs), these explorers received grants from the Spanish rulers. They had the right to explore and establish settlements in the Americas. In exchange they agreed to give the Spanish crown one-fifth of any gold or treasure discovered. This arrangement allowed Spanish rulers to launch expeditions with little risk. If a conquistador failed, he lost his own fortune. If he succeeded, both he and Spain gained wealth and glory.

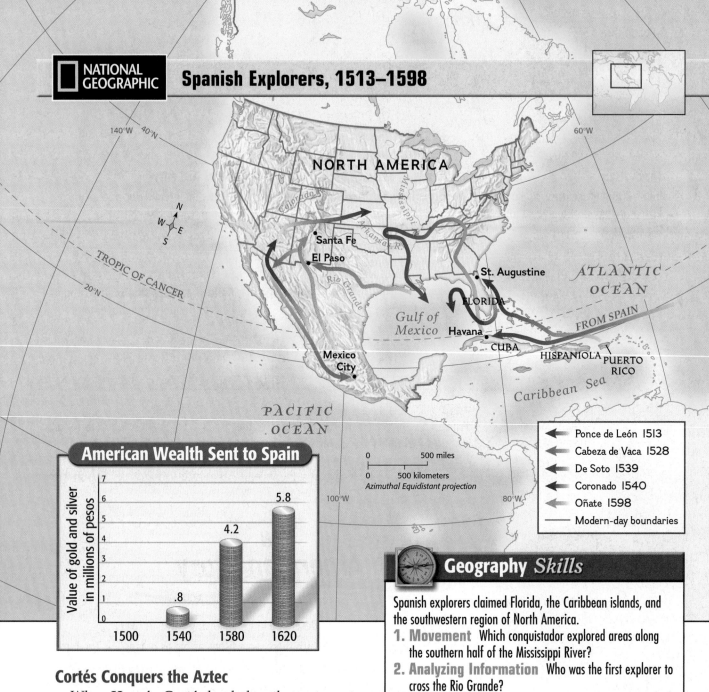

NORTH AMERICA

140°W 40°N

TROPIC OF CANCER

20°N

Colorado

Arkansas R.

Mississippi

Santa Fe

El Paso

Rio Grande

Gulf of Mexico

Mexico City

PACIFIC OCEAN

St. Augustine

FLORIDA

Havana

CUBA

HISPANIOLA   PUERTO RICO

Caribbean Sea

ATLANTIC OCEAN

FROM SPAIN

60°W

80°W

100°W

American Wealth Sent to Spain

Value of gold and silver in millions of pesos

1500	1540	1580	1620
	.8	4.2	5.8

0   500 miles
0   500 kilometers
Azimuthal Equidistant projection

◄── Ponce de León 1513
◄── Cabeza de Vaca 1528
◄── De Soto 1539
◄── Coronado 1540
◄── Oñate 1598
─── Modern-day boundaries

Geography *Skills*

Spanish explorers claimed Florida, the Caribbean islands, and the southwestern region of North America.
1. **Movement** Which conquistador explored areas along the southern half of the Mississippi River?
2. **Analyzing Information** Who was the first explorer to cross the Rio Grande?

Cortés Conquers the Aztec

When **Hernán Cortés** landed on the east coast of what we now know as Mexico in 1519, he was looking for gold and glory. He came with about 500 soldiers, some horses, and a few cannons. Cortés soon learned about the great Aztec Empire and its capital of Tenochtitlán.

In building their empire, the Aztec had conquered many cities in Mexico. These cities were forced to give crops, clothing, gold, and precious stones to the Aztec as tribute. Cortés formed alliances with nearby cities against the Aztec.

Cortés marched into Tenochtitlán in November with his small army and his Native American allies. The Aztec emperor **Montezuma** (MAHN •tuh•ZOO•muh)—also spelled Moctezuma—

welcomed Cortés and his soldiers and provided them with food and a fine palace. However, Cortés took advantage of the Aztec's hospitality and made Montezuma his prisoner.

In the spring of 1520, the Aztec rebelled against the Spanish. During the fighting Montezuma was hit by stones and later died. The battle lasted for days. Eventually, the Spanish were forced to leave Tenochtitlán. Cortés, however, was determined to retake the city. He waited until more Spanish troops arrived, then attacked and destroyed the Aztec capital in 1521. An Aztec poem describes the awful scene:

> 66Without roofs are the houses,
> And red are their walls with blood. . . .
> Weep, my friends,
> Know that with these disasters
> We have lost our Mexican nation.99

The Aztec Empire disintegrated, and Spain seized control of the region.

Pizarro Conquers Peru

The conquistador **Francisco Pizarro** sailed down the Pacific coast of South America with about 180 Spanish soldiers. Pizarro had heard tales of the incredibly wealthy Inca Empire in what is now Peru. In 1532 Pizarro captured the Inca ruler, **Atahualpa** (ah•tah•WAHL•pah), and destroyed much of the Incan army.

The following year, the Spanish falsely accused Atahualpa of crimes and executed him. The Inca were used to obeying commands from their rulers. Without leadership they were not able to fight effectively. Within a few years, Pizarro had gained control of most of the vast Inca Empire.

Why Spain Succeeded

The conquistadors' victories in Mexico and Peru were quick and lasting. How could Cortés and Pizarro, with only a few hundred Spanish soldiers, conquer such mighty empires?

First, the Spanish arrived with strange weapons—guns and cannons—and fearsome animals. They rode horses and had huge, ferocious dogs. To the Native Americans, the Spanish seemed almost like gods. Second, many Native Americans hated their Aztec overlords and assisted the conquistadors in overthrowing them.

Finally, disease played an extremely large role in the Spanish conquest. Native Americans had no immunity to the diseases the Europeans had, unknowingly, brought with them. Epidemics of smallpox and other diseases wiped out entire communities in the Americas and did much to weaken the resistance of the Aztec and Inca.

✓ **Reading Check** **Analyzing** How were the Spanish able to defeat mighty Native American empires?

Spain in North America

Mexico and Peru were rich in silver and gold. Hoping to find similar wealth to the north, conquistadors explored the southeastern and southwestern parts of North America.

Juan Ponce de León made the first Spanish landing on the mainland of North America, arriving on the east coast of present-day Florida in 1513. According to legend, Ponce de León hoped to find not only gold, but the legendary fountain of youth, "a spring of running water of such marvelous virtue" that drinking it "makes old men young again." Ponce de León's exploration led to the first Spanish settlement in what is now the United States. In 1565 the Spanish established a fort at **St. Augustine,** Florida.

The Seven Cities of Cibola

Many other conquistadors searched for quick riches. None ever achieved this goal, and several lost their lives trying. **Álvar Núñez Cabeza de Vaca** (cah•BAY•sah day VAH•cah) was part of a Spanish expedition to Florida in 1528.

After encountering troubles in Florida, the expedition, led by **Pánfilo de Narváez,** sailed along the coast toward Mexico. However, in November 1528, three of the five boats were lost in a storm. The two boats that survived went aground on an island near present-day Texas. Within a few months, only a handful of the shipwrecked explorers were still alive.

Fact ▸ **Fiction** ◂ Folklore

The First Thanksgiving

Who celebrated the first Thanksgiving? We all know that the Pilgrims celebrated the first Thanksgiving. Or did they? On April 30, 1598, long before the Pilgrims came to North America, Spanish colonists held a thanksgiving feast near present-day El Paso, Texas. Juan de Oñate had led 400 men and their families across the desert from Mexico. After they reached the Rio Grande, Oñate told them to feast and give thanks for the abundance of the new land.

People In History

Juana Inés de la Cruz 1651–1695

A Mexican nun, Juana Inés de la Cruz, may have been the first woman in the Americas to write about women's rights. What is remarkable about Sor Juana ("Sister" Juana) is that she was a famous writer at a time when most women were not taught to read. Her poems and stories were well known in Mexico; her plays were performed in the royal palace of Mexico, and her books were popular in Spain.

An archbishop of the Church, however, did not approve of women freely expressing their opinions. He threatened to put her on trial for violating Church rules unless she followed a strict vow of poverty and sold her books and belongings.

Although she gave the appearance of obedience, an unfinished poem found in her belongings after her death showed that she continued to exercise her talent.

To survive, Cabeza de Vaca and an enslaved African named **Estevanico** became medicine men. Cabeza de Vaca later wrote that their method of healing was "to bless the sick, breathing on them" and to recite Latin prayers.

In 1533 the Spaniards set off on foot on a great 1,000-mile journey across the Southwest. Arriving in Mexico in 1536, Cabeza de Vaca related tales he had heard of seven cities with walls of emerald and streets of gold.

The stories inspired **Hernando de Soto,** who led an expedition to explore Florida and lands to the west. For three years De Soto and his troops wandered around the southeastern area of the present-day United States, following stories of gold. As the Spaniards traveled, they took advantage of the native peoples. Their usual method was to enter a village, take the chief hostage, and demand food and supplies.

De Soto crossed the **Mississippi River** in 1541, describing it as "swift, and very deep." After traveling as far west as present-day Oklahoma, De Soto died of fever. His men buried him in the waters of the Mississippi.

Francisco Vásquez de Coronado also wanted to find the legendary "Seven Cities of Cibola." After traveling through areas of northern Mexico and present-day Arizona and New Mexico, the expedition reached a town belonging to the Zuni people in early summer 1540. They realized at once that there was no gold. Members of the expedition traveled west to the Colorado River and east into what is now Kansas. They found nothing but "windswept plains" and strange "shaggy cows" (buffalo). Disappointed, Coronado returned to Mexico.

✔ **Reading Check** **Explaining** How did stories of the "Seven Cities of Cibola" affect Spanish exploration?

Spanish Rule

Spanish law called for three kinds of settlements in the Americas—pueblos, missions, and presidios. Pueblos, or towns, were established as centers of trade. Missions were religious communities that usually included a small town, surrounding farmland, and a church. A presidio, or fort, was usually built near a mission.

Juan de Oñate (day ohn • YAH • tay) was sent from Mexico to gain control over lands to the north and to convert the inhabitants. In 1598 Oñate founded the province of New Mexico and introduced cattle and horses to the Pueblo people.

Social Classes

A class system developed in Spain's empire. The upper class consisted of people who had been born in Spain, called *peninsulares.* The *peninsulares* owned the land, served in the Catholic Church, and ran the local government. Below them were the creoles, people born in the Americas to Spanish parents. Lower in the class structure were the mestizos (meh•STEE•zohs), people with Spanish and Native American parents. Still lower were the Native Americans, most of whom lived in great poverty. At the very bottom were enslaved Africans.

In the 1500s the Spanish government granted each conquistador who settled in the Americas an *encomienda,* the right to demand taxes or labor from Native Americans living on the land. This system turned the Native Americans into slaves. Grueling labor in the fields and in the gold and silver mines took its toll. Many Native Americans died from malnutrition and disease.

A Spanish priest, **Bartolomé de Las Casas,** condemned the cruel treatment of the Native Americans. He pleaded for laws to protect them. Las Casas claimed that millions had died because the Spanish "made gold their ultimate aim, seeking to load themselves with riches in the shortest possible time."

Because of Las Casas's reports, in 1542 the Spanish government passed the New Laws, which forbade making slaves of Native Americans. Although not always enforced, the laws did correct the worst abuses.

The Plantation System

Some Spanish settlers made large profits by exporting crops and raw materials back to Spain. In the West Indies, the main exports were tobacco and sugarcane. To raise these crops, the Spanish developed the plantation system. A plantation was a large estate. The Spanish used Native Americans to work their plantations.

Las Casas suggested replacing them with enslaved Africans—a suggestion he bitterly regretted later. He thought the Africans could endure the labor better than the Native Americans.

By the mid-1500s the Spanish were bringing thousands from West Africa to the Americas. The Portuguese did the same in Brazil. The Africans who survived the brutal ocean voyage were sold to plantation owners. By the late 1500s, plantation slave labor was an essential part of the economy of the colonies.

Reading Check **Describing** Whom did Las Casas try to protect?

SECTION 3 ASSESSMENT

Checking for Understanding

1. **Key Terms** Write three true and three false statements using each of the following terms once: conquistador, tribute, pueblo, mission, presidio, plantation. Indicate which statements are false.

2. **Reviewing Facts** What three kinds of settlements did Spain establish in the Americas? How did they differ?

Reviewing Themes

3. **Culture and Traditions** What groups made up the class system in Spanish America?

Critical Thinking

4. **Analyzing Primary Sources** One conquistador explained, "We came to serve God and the king, and also to get rich." In what way do you think conquistadors planned to serve "God and the king"?

5. **Determining Cause and Effect** Re-create the diagram below and list causes of Spain's success in conquering Native American empires.

Spain's success

Analyzing Visuals

6. **Geography Skills** Review the map of Spanish exploration on page 52. What expedition traveled from Florida to the Mississippi River? Through what regions did the Coronado expedition travel?

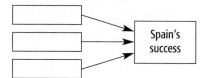

Interdisciplinary Activity

Geography Using cookbooks as references, create an all-American dinner menu that features only foods introduced to Europeans by Native Americans.

Using an astrolabe like this one to establish latitude, Father Kino carefully mapped the region.

Gila River

Santa Cruz River

San Pedro River

United States
Mexico

Gulf of California

Baja California

Magdalena River

Altar River

San Miguel River

Sonoita River

Nuestra Señora de los Dolores

N
W E
S

A typical Spanish mission surrounded a large open courtyard.

Crops

Living quarters

Workshop

Church

Granary

PADRE ON HORSEBACK

MISSIONARY AND EXPLORER Eusebio Kino (yoo•SAY•be•oh KEE•no) was an Italian who studied astronomy, mapmaking, and mathematics before becoming a Jesuit priest. In 1681 he went to Mexico with the Spaniards to map the area and convert Native Americans to Catholicism.

MISSIONARY IN THE PIMERÍA ALTA

After several years in Mexico City and Baja California, Father Kino was sent to establish missions in the "Pimería Alta"—the Upper Pima Country—part of present-day Sonora, Mexico, and southern Arizona.

In March 1687 Father Kino established his first mission, Nuestra Señora de los Dolores at Cosari. He helped start more than 20 missions along the San Miguel, Magdalena, and Altar rivers.

Father Kino and other missionaries changed the face of Pimería Alta forever. The priests converted thousands of Native Americans to Christianity. By introducing live-stock, wheat, European fruit, and other new crops, the missionaries altered the economy of the region.

EXPLORER AND MAPMAKER

Kino traveled so much he was known as the "padre on horse-back." He covered thousands of miles tending to the needs of his converts and exploring and mapping the Sonoran Desert and California.

Statue of Father Kino

Spaniards introduced wheat and other crops.

Father Kino's Missions

• • • Present–day boundary

🛕 Mission

0   50 miles
0   50 kilometers

To Mexico City

San Xavier del Bac, a mission started by Father Kino in 1700, still stands today outside of Tucson.

LEARNING *from* GEOGRAPHY

1. Where did Father Kino establish his missions? Why?

2. How did the introduction of food crops and domestic animals affect the development of the Southwest?

Exploring North America

Main Idea

Rivalries between countries, the search for a Northwest Passage to Asia, and early trading activities led to increased exploration of North America.

Key Terms

mercantilism, Columbian Exchange, Northwest Passage, coureur de bois

Reading Strategy

Determining Cause and Effect As you read the section, re-create the diagram below and provide an effect for each cause.

Exploration of North America	
Causes	Effects
Protestant Reformation	
Search for NW passage	
Early trading activities	

Read to Learn

- how the Protestant Reformation affected North America.
- why the activities of early traders encouraged exploration.

Section Theme

Global Connections European nations competed for overseas land and resources.

Preview of Events

♦1450	♦1500	♦1550	♦1600

1497
John Cabot lands in Newfoundland

1517
Martin Luther starts the Protestant Reformation

1535
Jacques Cartier sails up the St. Lawrence River to Montreal

1609
Henry Hudson sails the Hudson River

Martin Luther

A European Story

In 1517 Martin Luther, a German priest, nailed a list of complaints about the Catholic Church on the door of a local church. Luther declared that the Bible was the only true guide for Christians. He rejected many Church practices—even the authority of the pope—because they were not mentioned in the Bible. Luther also believed that faith rather than good deeds was the way to salvation.

Church officials tried to get Luther to take back his statements. "I cannot go against my conscience," he replied. "Here I stand. I cannot do otherwise. God help me."

A Divided Church

Martin Luther's actions led to incredible changes in Europe. Before he voiced his beliefs, the countries of Europe had their differences, but they were bound together by a common church. For centuries, Catholicism had been the main religion of western Europe. In the 1500s, however, Luther's opposition to the policies of the Roman Catholic Church emerged.

Within a few years, Luther had many followers. They broke away from Catholicism to begin their own Christian churches. Martin Luther's protests were the start of a great religious and historical movement known as the **Protestant Reformation.**

Protestantism Spreads in Europe

From Germany Luther's ideas spread rapidly. **John Calvin,** a French religious thinker, also broke away from the Catholic Church. Like Luther, Calvin rejected the idea that good works would ensure a person's salvation. He believed that God had already chosen those who would be saved.

In England, King Henry VIII also left the Catholic Church, but not for religious reasons. Pope Clement VII had refused Henry's request to declare his first marriage invalid. In 1534 the English Parliament, working with the king,

denied the authority of the pope and recognized the king as the head of the Church of England. During the rule of Henry's daughter, Queen Elizabeth I, further reforms firmly established England as a Protestant nation.

Religious Rivalries in the Americas

Throughout western Europe, people and nations divided into Catholics and Protestants. When these Europeans crossed the Atlantic, they took along their religious differences.

Spanish and French Catholics worked to spread their faith to the Native Americans. The Spanish settled in the southwestern and southeastern regions of North America, and the French settled in the northeast. Dutch and English Protestants established colonies in lands along the Atlantic coast between the French and the Spanish settlements. Some of the English settlements were founded by Protestants who wanted to practice their beliefs in peace.

✓ **Reading Check** **Explaining** What role did religion play in the exploration of North America?

Picturing **History**

In 1676 Kateri Tekakwitha, a 20-year-old Mohawk woman, accepted Christianity from French Catholic missionaries. **What region of North America was settled by the French?**

§ Economics

Economic Rivalry

Religion was only one of the factors that pushed European nations across the Atlantic Ocean. The promise of great wealth was equally strong, especially as other Europeans watched Spain gain riches from its colonies.

According to the economic theory of mercantilism, a nation's power was based on its wealth. Rulers tried to increase their nation's total wealth by acquiring gold and silver and by developing trade. Mercantilism provided great opportunities for individual merchants to make money. It also increased rivalry between nations.

Several countries in Europe competed for overseas territory that could produce wealth. They wanted to acquire colonies in the Americas that could provide valuable resources, such as gold and silver, or raw materials. The colonies would also serve as a place to sell European products.

MORE ABOUT...

The Columbian Exchange

Trade between the continents, known as the Columbian Exchange, changed life on both sides of the Atlantic.

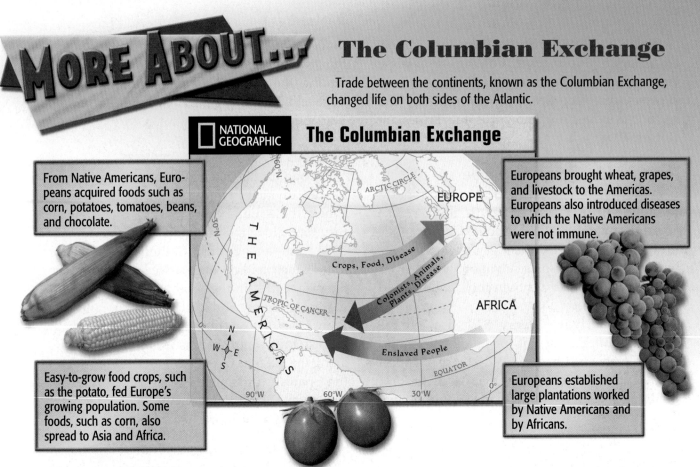

NATIONAL GEOGRAPHIC

The Columbian Exchange

From Native Americans, Europeans acquired foods such as corn, potatoes, tomatoes, beans, and chocolate.

Europeans brought wheat, grapes, and livestock to the Americas. Europeans also introduced diseases to which the Native Americans were not immune.

Easy-to-grow food crops, such as the potato, fed Europe's growing population. Some foods, such as corn, also spread to Asia and Africa.

Europeans established large plantations worked by Native Americans and by Africans.

The Columbian Exchange

The voyages of Columbus and other explorers brought together two parts of the globe that previously had had no contact: the continents of Europe, Asia, and Africa in one hemisphere and the Americas in the other. The contact led to an exchange of plants, animals, and diseases that altered life on both sides of the Atlantic. Scholars refer to this as the Columbian Exchange.

A Northwest Passage

The Treaty of Tordesillas had divided the Americas between Spain and Portugal. It did not allow for claims by other nations—so England, France, and the Netherlands ignored the treaty. During the 1500s and early 1600s, these countries sent explorers to chart the coast of North America. They wanted to profit from trade and colonization as well. The voyage to Asia—either around the southern tip of Africa or around South America—was long and difficult. For this reason, the three countries hoped to discover a Northwest Passage to Asia—a more direct water route through the Americas.

In 1497 England sent **John Cabot,** an Italian, to look for a northern route to Asia. Cabot prob-

ably landed on the coast of present-day Newfoundland. England used Cabot's voyage as the basis for its claims to North America.

In 1524 France hired an Italian, **Giovanni da Verrazano,** to look for the northern sea route. Verrazano explored the coast of North America from present-day Nova Scotia down to the Carolinas.

In 1535 French explorer **Jacques Cartier** (KAR•tyay) sailed up the St. Lawrence River hoping it would lead to the Pacific. He got as far as the Huron village of Hochelaga. Cartier wrote that from the mountain next to the village, "one sees a very great distance." He named the peak Mont-Royal, which means "royal mountain." This is the site of the city now called **Montreal.** Cartier had heard stories about gold, but he found neither gold nor a sea route to Asia.

Hudson's Discoveries

The Netherlands, too, wanted to find a passage through the Americas. They hired **Henry Hudson,** an English sailor, to explore. In 1609 he discovered the river that now bears his name. In his ship, the *Half Moon,* Hudson sailed north on the Hudson River as far as the site of present-day Albany. Deciding that he had not found a passage to India, he turned back. The following year Hudson tried again, this time sent by England.

Sailing almost due west from northern England, Henry Hudson and his crew discovered a huge bay, now called **Hudson Bay.** Hudson thought he had reached the Pacific Ocean. After months of searching for an outlet from the bay, however, the crew rebelled. Hudson, his son John, and a few sailors were set adrift in a small boat—and never seen again.

French Open Trading Posts

France had shown little interest in building an empire in the Americas. Its rulers were preoccupied by political and religious conflicts at home. The French viewed North America as an opportunity for profits from fishing and fur trading rather than as a place to settle.

Furs were popular in Europe, and traders could make large profits from beaver pelts acquired in North America. A group of French

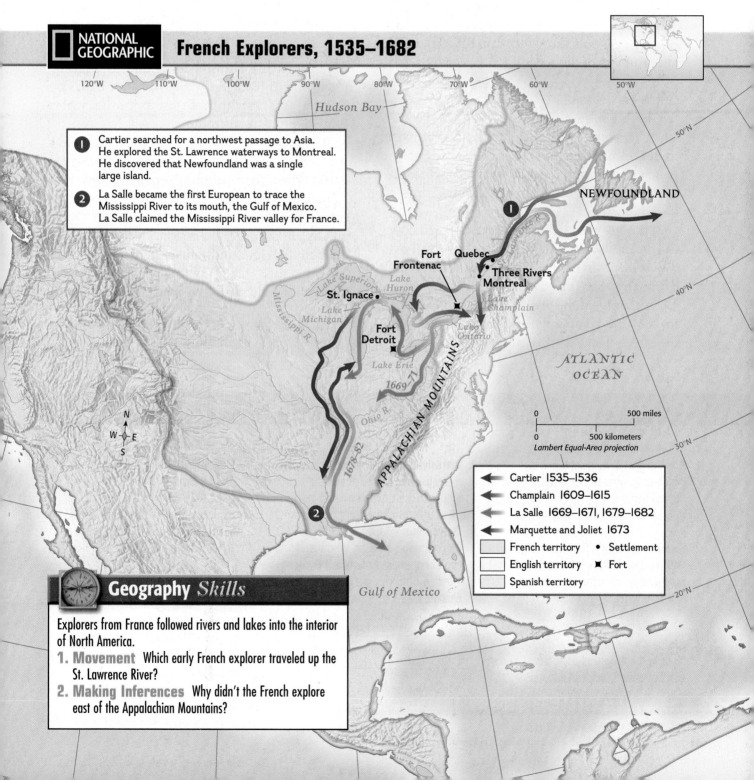

NATIONAL GEOGRAPHIC

French Explorers, 1535–1682

1. Cartier searched for a northwest passage to Asia. He explored the St. Lawrence waterways to Montreal. He discovered that Newfoundland was a single large island.

2. La Salle became the first European to trace the Mississippi River to its mouth, the Gulf of Mexico. La Salle claimed the Mississippi River valley for France.

Cartier 1535–1536
Champlain 1609–1615
La Salle 1669–1671, 1679–1682
Marquette and Joliet 1673
French territory • Settlement
English territory ✖ Fort
Spanish territory

Geography *Skills*

Explorers from France followed rivers and lakes into the interior of North America.

1. **Movement** Which early French explorer traveled up the St. Lawrence River?

2. **Making Inferences** Why didn't the French explore east of the Appalachian Mountains?

traders made an agreement with the Native Americans to trade fur. In 1608 the group sent **Samuel de Champlain** to establish a settlement in **Quebec** in what is now Canada. Champlain made several trips to the region and discovered Lake Champlain. He described the beautiful scenery and abundant wildlife and the Native Americans he met there.

From Quebec the French moved into other parts of Canada, where they built trading posts to collect furs gathered by Native Americans and French trappers. The trappers were called coureurs de bois (ku•RUHR duh BWAH), meaning "runners of the woods."

Dutch Settlements

Like other European countries, the Netherlands was also eager to claim its share of world trade. Until Hudson's voyage, there had been no Dutch exploration in North America. Hudson's voyage became the start for Dutch claims on the continent.

Although the Netherlands was a small country, its large fleet of trading ships sailed all over the world. In 1621 the Dutch West India Company set up a trading colony—New Netherland—in the area Hudson had explored. In 1624 the company sent 30 families to settle the area. They settled at Fort Orange (later

Fact · Fiction · Folklore

America's Flags

Flag of New France Settlers in New France often flew this flag of the French Royal Navy. They also flew the French Royal Banner, which was blue instead of white.

Albany) on the Hudson River and on Burlington Island in New Jersey. Shortly after that, Fort Nassau was established just opposite where Philadelphia stands today.

The center of the new colony was New Amsterdam, located on the tip of Manhattan Island where the Hudson River enters New York Harbor. In 1626 Peter Minuit, the governor of the colony, paid the Manhates people 60 Dutch guilders in goods for the island. The goods probably included cloth, and valuable tools such as axes, hoes, and awls. Like Portugal, Spain, and France, the Netherlands started colonies in the Americas.

✓ **Reading Check** **Analyzing** Why was the idea of a Northwest Passage important?

SECTION 4 ASSESSMENT

Checking for Understanding

1. **Key Terms** Write a sentence in which you correctly use each of the following terms: mercantilism, Columbian Exchange, Northwest Passage, coureur de bois
2. **Reviewing Facts** What were English, French, and Dutch explorers searching for while charting the coast of North America?

Reviewing Themes

3. **Global Connections** How did French goals in the Americas differ from the goals of other European nations?

Critical Thinking

4. **Identifying Central Issues** How did the economic theory of mercantilism influence the exploration and settlement of North America by Europeans?
5. **Determining Cause and Effect** Re-create the diagram below and explain how the Columbian Exchange affected both sides of the Atlantic Ocean.

Columbian Exchange	
Effects on the Americas	Effects on Europe

Analyzing Visuals

6. **Geography Skills** Review the map, *French Explorers, 1535–1682,* on page 61. Which of the French explorers traveled farthest south? Along what river did Marquette and Joliet travel?

Interdisciplinary Activity

Persuasive Writing Write a letter to one of the explorers who searched for a Northwest Passage. In the letter, explain why it is important for your nation to find a Northwest Passage.

Social Studies
SKILLBUILDER

Reading a Time Line

Why Learn this Skill?

Knowing the relationship of time to events is important in studying history. A time line is a visual way to show chronological order within a time period. Most time lines are divided into sections representing equal time intervals. For example, a time line showing 1,000 years might be divided into ten 100-year sections. Each event on a time line appears beside the date when the event took place.

Learning the Skill

To read a time line, follow these steps:
- Find the dates on the opposite ends of the time line to know the time span. Also note the intervals between dates on the time line.
- Study the order of events.
- Analyze relationships among events or look for trends.

Magellan

Practicing the Skill

Analyze the time line of Magellan's voyage below. Use it to answer the questions that follow.

❶ What time span is represented?

❷ How many years do each of the sections represent?

❸ Did Magellan's voyage to the Spice Islands occur before or after his voyage to the Philippines?

❹ How long did Magellan's voyage around the world take?

Applying the Skill

Making a Time Line List 10 key events that have occurred in your life and the dates on which these events occurred. Write the events in chronological order on a time line.

GO TO ▶ Glencoe's **Skillbuilder Interactive Workbook CD-ROM, Level 1,** provides instruction and practice in key social studies skills.

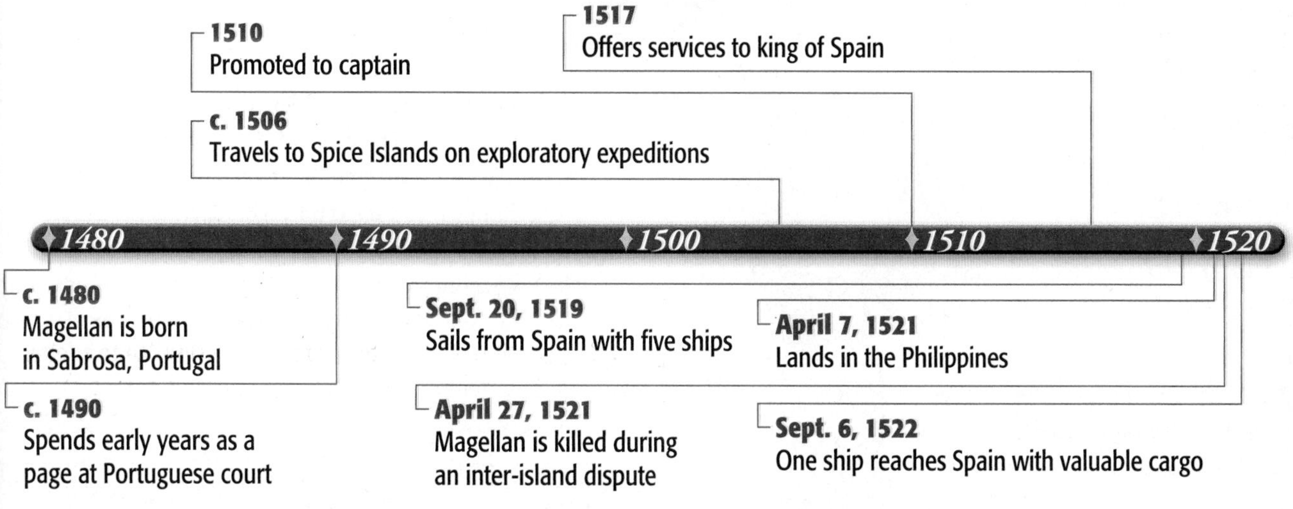

1510
Promoted to captain

1517
Offers services to king of Spain

c. 1506
Travels to Spice Islands on exploratory expeditions

◆1480   ◆1490   ◆1500   ◆1510   ◆1520

c. 1480
Magellan is born in Sabrosa, Portugal

Sept. 20, 1519
Sails from Spain with five ships

April 7, 1521
Lands in the Philippines

c. 1490
Spends early years as a page at Portuguese court

April 27, 1521
Magellan is killed during an inter-island dispute

Sept. 6, 1522
One ship reaches Spain with valuable cargo

Chapter Summary

Exploring the Americas

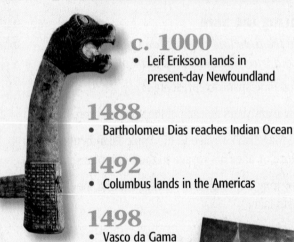

c. 1000
- Leif Eriksson lands in present-day Newfoundland

1488
- Bartholomeu Dias reaches Indian Ocean

1492
- Columbus lands in the Americas

1498
- Vasco da Gama reaches India

1519
- Magellan begins circum-navigation of the world
- Hernán Cortés lands in Mexico

1532
- Francisco Pizarro captures Atahualpa

1535
- Jacques Cartier sails up the St. Lawrence River to Montreal

1541
- De Soto crosses the Mississippi River

1565
- Spain establishes fort at St. Augustine, Florida

1609
- Henry Hudson sails the Hudson River

Reviewing Key Terms

Examine the groups of words below. Then write sentences explaining what each group has in common.

1. Renaissance, astrolabe, caravel
2. conquistador, mission, presidio
3. mercantilism, Northwest Passage

Reviewing Key Facts

4. Why were Europeans interested in Asia?
5. What three large African kingdoms south of the Sahara flourished between 300 and 1600?
6. What European leader set up a center for exploration in Portugal?
7. Where did the earliest Portuguese explorers sail?
8. Which country supported Columbus on his quest to find a water route to Asia?
9. List the major accomplishments of Vasco da Gama, Juan Ponce de León, and John Cabot.
10. What was the main reason the Spanish wanted to conquer the Aztec and the Inca?
11. How did the Spanish colonial system of *encomiendas* affect Native Americans?
12. What movement created religious rivalries in Europe that carried over into exploration of the Americas?
13. What were explorers searching for during their explorations of the North American coast?

Critical Thinking

14. **Analyzing Primary Sources** Read the Two Viewpoints on page 47. What does Red Jacket mean by "this great island"?
15. **Drawing Conclusions** Why do you think the Caribbean Islands are often referred to as the West Indies?
16. **Analyzing Information** Study the feature on the Columbian Exchange on page 60. What foods were shipped to Europe?
17. **Determining Cause and Effect** Re-create the diagram below and identify three reasons for voyages of exploration and three effects that resulted from the exploration.

Voyages of exploration

HISTORY *Online*

Self-Check Quiz
Visit taj.glencoe.com and click on **Chapter 2—Self-Check Quizzes** to prepare for the chapter test.

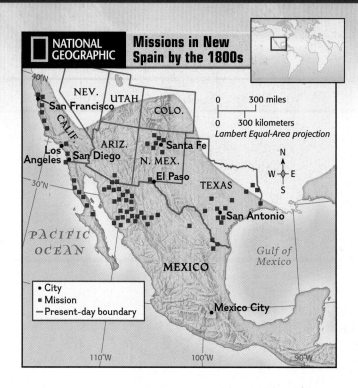

NATIONAL GEOGRAPHIC
Missions in New Spain by the 1800s

- • City
- ■ Mission
- — Present-day boundary

Geography and History Activity

Study the map above and answer the questions that follow.

18. **Place** In what present-day states were the Spanish missions located?

19. **Location** Near what city was the northernmost Spanish mission located?

20. **Location** In which direction would a traveler leaving Mexico City journey to reach San Diego?

Practicing Skills

Reading a Time Line *Study the time line on pages 36–37, then answer the following questions.*

21. What is the time span covered on this time line?

22. In which century does the greatest number of events take place on this time line?

23. What event occurred in 1522?

Technology Activity

24. **Using Word Processing Software** Search the library for information on boats and sailing. Using word processing software, prepare a report about a navigational instrument that is in use today. Describe how it would have been helpful to an explorer such as Magellan.

Citizenship Cooperative Activity

25. **Interviewing** In a group of three, find out if any people in your community have come from Great Britain, Spain, France, or other countries. Try to interview these people and ask them about the political system of the country they came from. Prepare an oral report for the class.

Economics Activity

26. Ask family members and other adults about prices paid for common products in years past. Ask about grocery items, haircuts, cars, and so on. Compare these prices with current prices. Share your findings with the class.

Alternative Assessment

27. **Portfolio Writing Activity** Choose an explorer discussed in this chapter. Use library resources to research the explorer's life and achievements. Prepare an interview with that explorer. Plan the questions to ask and the answers you would expect the explorer to give. Write the interview as a magazine article.

The Princeton Review

Standardized Test Practice

Directions: Choose the *best* answer to the following question.

Juana Inés de la Cruz was an unusual woman because she was famous as a

A writer.

B prince.

C farmer.

D warrior.

Test-Taking Tip:

Eliminate answers that don't make sense. For instance, a woman could not be a prince, so **B** could not be the correct answer.

UNIT
2 Colonial Settlement

1587–1770

Why It Matters

As you study Unit 2, you will learn
that in the 1600s and 1700s the English established colonies in the Americas—some for profit and others by
religious groups seeking freedom. In
time, a distinctly new American society
emerged.

Pewter pitcher,
Plymouth plantation

Primary Sources Library

See pages 960–961 for primary source
readings to accompany Unit 2.
Use the **American History
Primary Source Document Library
CD-ROM** to find additional primary
sources about the European colonies.

*Signing the
Mayflower Compact* by
Edward Percy Moran

"The Indians brought us great store both of Corne and bread ready made. . . ."

— John Smith, 1608

CHAPTER 3
Colonial America
1587–1770

Why It Matters

A new culture took root in North America. The values and beliefs of this new culture developed as people from several parts of the world migrated to the continent.

The Impact Today

The colonies influenced values and beliefs many Americans cherish today. For example:
- *Many people still come to the Americas in search of economic opportunity and religious freedom.*
- *Representative government remains an important part of the American political system.*

 The American Journey Video *The chapter 3 video, "The Lost Colony," examines the colony of Roanoke and how conditions were much harsher than settlers were led to believe.*

1607
- English establish first permanent settlement at Jamestown

1620
- Pilgrims land at Plymouth Rock

1630
- Puritans begin settling Massachusetts Bay

The Americas

1550   1600   1650

World

1588
- England defeats Spanish Armada

c. 1605
- Shakespeare writes *King Lear*

1660
- King Charles II is restored to the English throne

Pilgrims Going to Church by George Boughton George Boughton painted many scenes about American colonial life.

FOLDABLES
Study Organizer

Comparison Study Foldable When you group facts into categories, it is easier to make comparisons. Make this foldable to compare and contrast the 13 colonies and their regions.

Step 1 Collect 7 sheets of paper and place them about ½ inch apart.

> Keep the edges straight.

Step 2 Fold up the bottom edges of the paper to form 14 tabs.

> This makes all tabs the same size.

Step 3 When all the tabs are the same size, crease the paper to hold the tabs in place and staple the sheets together. Label each tab with the name of a colony and color-code each region.

The Thirteen Colonies	
Massachusetts	Northern
New Hampshire	
Rhode Island	
Connecticut	
New York	Middle
Delaware	
New Jersey	
Pennsylvania	
Virginia	Southern
Maryland	
North Carolina	
South Carolina	
Georgia	

> Staple together along the fold.

Reading and Writing As you read, write what you learn about each of the 13 colonies under each tab and compare the colonies.

1675
• King Philip's War begins

1718
• French establish port of New Orleans

1763
• British tighten enforcement of Navigation Acts

1769
• Mission of San Diego founded

1670
• Alafin Ajagbo founds Oyo Empire in Nigeria

1702
• England and France go to war

1700 *1750*

HISTORY
Online

Chapter Overview
Visit taj.glencoe.com and click on **Chapter 3— Chapter Overviews** to preview chapter information.

Early English Settlements

Guide to Reading

Main Idea
Jamestown became the first successfully established English colony in North America.

Key Terms
charter, joint-stock company, burgesses

Reading Strategy
Organizing Information As you read Section 1, re-create the diagram below and describe the economy and government of Jamestown.

Jamestown	Description
Economy	
Government	

Read to Learn
- what crop saved the people of Jamestown.
- how the colonists received political rights.

Section Theme
Economic Factors Many settlers journeyed to America with the hope of making a fortune.

Preview of Events

♦1580   ♦1590   ♦1600   ♦1610   ♦1620

1583
Sir Humphrey Gilbert claims Newfoundland for Queen Elizabeth

c. 1590
Settlers of Roanoke Island vanish

1607
Colonists settle at Jamestown

1619
House of Burgesses meets in Jamestown

A
European Story

In the summer of 1588, Spanish warships sailed toward the coast of England. King Philip II of Spain had sent the armada, or war fleet, of 132 ships to invade England. With 30,000 troops and 2,400 guns, the Spanish Armada was the mightiest naval force the world had ever seen. Yet the smaller, swifter English ships won the battle. The Spanish Armada fled north to Scotland, where violent storms destroyed and scattered the fleet. Only about one-half of the Spanish ships straggled home.

English soldier's helmet, Jamestown

England in America

England and Spain had been heading toward war for years. Trading rivalry and religious differences divided the two countries. King Philip II, who ruled Spain from 1556 to 1598, was a powerful monarch and a strong defender of the Catholic faith. He wanted to put a Catholic ruler on the throne of England and bring the country back to the Catholic Church. King Philip did not consider Queen Elizabeth, a Protestant, the rightful ruler of England.

Attacks on Spanish ships and ports by such English adventurers as **Sir Francis Drake** angered Philip. He thought that Queen Elizabeth should punish Drake for his raids. Instead, she honored Drake with a knighthood. Philip sent the Spanish Armada to conquer England—but it failed completely.

Although war between England and Spain continued until 1604, the defeat of the armada marked the end of Spanish control of the seas. Now the way was clear for England and other nations to start colonies in North America.

The Lost Colony of Roanoke

The English had made several attempts to establish a base on the other side of the Atlantic before their victory over Spain. In 1583 **Sir Humphrey Gilbert** claimed Newfoundland for Queen Elizabeth. Then he sailed south along the coast looking for a place to establish a colony. Before finding a site, he died at sea.

The following year, Queen Elizabeth gave **Sir Walter Raleigh** the right to claim land in North America. Raleigh sent an expedition to look for a good place to settle. His scouts returned with an enthusiastic report of **Roanoke Island,** off the coast of present-day North Carolina.

In 1585 Raleigh sent about 100 men to settle on Roanoke Island. After a difficult winter on the island, the unhappy colonists decided to return to England. In 1587 Raleigh tried again, sending 91 men, 17 women, and 9 children to Roanoke. **John White,** a mapmaker and artist, led the group. Shortly after arriving on the island, White's daughter gave birth. This baby, named **Virginia Dare,** was the first English child born in North America. White explored the area and drew pictures of what he saw. He and other explorers described the towns of the Native Americans who lived in the area:

> ❝Their towns are small and few . . . a village may contain but ten or twelve houses—some perhaps as many as twenty. . . . ❞

The new settlers began building a colony. They needed many supplies, however, and White sailed to England for the supplies and to recruit more settlers. Although he had hoped to be back within a few months, the war with Spain delayed his return for nearly three years.

When White finally returned to Roanoke, he found it deserted. The only clue to the fate of the settlers was the word *Croatoan* carved on a gatepost. White thought the colonists must have gone to Croatoan Island, about 50 miles to the south. Bad weather kept White from investigating. The Roanoke colonists were never seen again.

✓ **Reading Check** **Describing** Why did Raleigh choose Roanoke as the site for the colony?

Jamestown Settlement

Roanoke was Sir Walter Raleigh's last attempt to establish a colony. For a time his failure discouraged others from planning English colonies in North America. However, the idea emerged again in 1606. Several groups of merchants sought charters, the right to organize settlements in an area, from King James I.

The Virginia Company

One group of merchants, the Virginia Company of London, received a charter to "make habitation . . . into that part of America, commonly called Virginia." The Virginia Company was a joint-stock company. Investors bought stock, or part ownership, in the company in return for a share of its future profits.

The company acted quickly. In December 1606, it sent 144 settlers in 3 ships to build a new colony in North America. The settlers were supposed to look for gold and attempt to establish trade in fish and furs. Forty of them died during the voyage.

In April 1607, the ships entered **Chesapeake Bay** and then sailed up a river flowing into the bay. The colonists named the river the James and their new settlement **Jamestown** to honor their king. The settlers built Jamestown on a peninsula so they could defend it from attack. The site had major drawbacks, however. The swampy land swarmed with mosquitoes that carried disease. Jamestown also lacked good farmland.

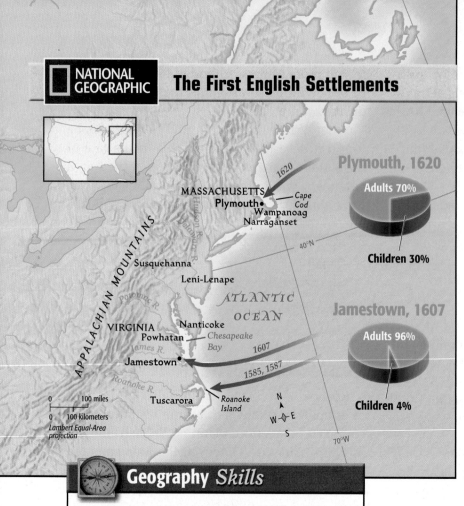

NATIONAL GEOGRAPHIC

The First English Settlements

Plymouth, 1620

Adults 70%

Children 30%

Jamestown, 1607

Adults 96%

Children 4%

MASSACHUSETTS
Plymouth • — Cape Cod
Wampanoag
Narraganset

Susquehanna

Leni-Lenape

ATLANTIC OCEAN

VIRGINIA   Nanticoke
Powhatan — Chesapeake Bay
Jamestown •   1607

1585, 1587

Tuscarora   Roanoke Island

APPALACHIAN MOUNTAINS

0   100 miles
0   100 kilometers
Lambert Equal-Area projection

Geography *Skills*

Many Native American groups lived near the first English settlements in the late 1500s and early 1600s.
1. **Location** Which colony was located farthest north?
2. **Location** Which Native American groups lived nearest to the Jamestown colonists?

The colonists faced more hardships over the next several months. Many of them were not accustomed to hard labor. Because the London investors expected a quick profit from their colony, the settlers searched for gold and silver when they should have been growing food. In addition, disease and hunger took a huge toll on the colonists. By spring 1608, when ships arrived with supplies and more settlers, only 38 of the Jamestown colonists remained alive.

Captain John Smith

Governing Jamestown was perhaps the biggest obstacle the colonists faced. The colony survived its first two years because of 27-year-old **Captain John Smith,** an experienced soldier and explorer. Smith forced the settlers to work, explored the area, and managed to get corn from the local Native Americans led by Chief Powhatan. In August 1609, 400 new settlers arrived. Two months later, John Smith returned to England. Without strong leadership, the colony could not feed so many people. The winter of 1609–1610 became known as "the starving time." Fighting broke out with the Native Americans. When more settlers arrived in the spring they found only 60 survivors.

💲Economics

Farming the Land

Although the Virginia colonists did not find any gold or silver, they did discover another way to make money for the investors. One colonist, **John Rolfe,** learned to grow a type of tobacco using seeds from the West Indies. The first crop was sold in England in 1614. Soon planters all along the James River were raising tobacco, and the colony of Virginia began to prosper and grow. Relations with the Native Americans also improved after Rolfe married **Pocahontas,** the daughter of Chief Powhatan.

In 1614 some of the colonists were allowed to rent plots of land. Most of what they grew on their plots was their own. This move toward private ownership encouraged the colonists to grow food crops to sell—and work harder. One of the colonists explained that the colonists often avoided work when

❝our people were fed out of the common store, and labored jointly together.❞

Now that the colonists could farm their own land and operate for profit in a competitive system, they made greater efforts to succeed.

Pocahontas

Private land ownership was expanded in 1618. All the colonists who had paid their own way to America were granted 100 acres of land. In order to attract more colonists, the company gave a land grant called a **headright** of 50 acres to those who paid their own way. A settler also received 50 acres for each family member over 15 years of age and for each servant brought to Virginia. This system convinced thousands of people to move to Virginia.

Citizenship

Representative Government

At first nearly all of Jamestown's settlers were men. They worked for the Virginia Company and lived under strict rules. As the colony grew, the settlers complained about taking orders from the Virginia Company in London. In 1619 the company agreed to let the colonists have some say in their government. Ten towns in the colony each sent two representatives called burgesses to an assembly. The assembly had the right to make local laws for the colony. On July 30, 1619, the **House of Burgesses** met for the first time in a church in Jamestown.

New Arrivals in Jamestown

In 1619 the Virginia Company sent 90 women to Jamestown. As a company report noted: "The plantation can never flourish till families be planted, and the respect of wives and children fix the people on the soil." Colonists who wanted to marry one of the women had to pay a fee of 120 pounds of tobacco. Men still outnumbered women in the colony, but marriage and children became a part of life in Virginia.

A Dutch ship brought another group of newcomers to Jamestown in 1619—twenty Africans who were sold to Virginia planters to labor in the tobacco fields. These first Africans may have come as servants—engaged to work for a set period of time—rather than as slaves.

Until about 1640 some African laborers in Jamestown were free and even owned property. William Tucker, the first African American born in the American colonies, was a free man. In the years to follow, however, many more shiploads of Africans would arrive in North America, and those unwilling passengers would be sold as slaves. Slavery was first recognized in Virginia law in the 1660s.

In the early 1620s, the Virginia Company faced financial troubles. The company had poured all its money into Jamestown, but little profit was returned. The colony also suffered an attack by the Native Americans. In 1624 King James canceled the company's charter and made Jamestown the first royal colony for England in America.

Reading Check **Analyzing** Why was the House of Burgesses important?

SECTION 1 ASSESSMENT

Checking for Understanding

1. **Key Terms** Write a short paragraph in which you use the following key terms: charter, burgesses, joint-stock company.
2. **Reviewing Facts** Why did the Virginia Company establish settlements in North America?

Reviewing Themes

3. **Economic Factors** What economic activity helped save the Jamestown settlement?

Critical Thinking

4. **Making Inferences** Why do you think the king of England was willing to let a group of merchants try to establish a colony in North America?
5. **Determining Cause and Effect** Re-create the diagram below and list two effects of Jamestown's growth.

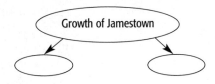

Growth of Jamestown

Analyzing Visuals

6. **Geography Skills** Study the map and graphs on page 72. What percentage of settlers in Plymouth were children?

Interdisciplinary Activity

Geography Create a poster that might have attracted early colonists to the area where you live. Focus on the location as well as natural features in your area such as good farmland, forests, waterways, and mineral resources.

FOOTHOLD IN THE NEW WORLD

JAMESTOWN: THE FIRST PERMANENT ENGLISH COLONY In the spring of 1607, three ships carrying more than a hundred English settlers sailed into the Chesapeake Bay to establish a colony and find gold. The settlers built a fort on a marshy island in the James River and named it in honor of King James I.

THE EXPEDITIONS

Captain John Smith emerged as a leader of the group. An avid explorer, he led four expeditions in the area:

- Shortly after arriving, he and Captain Christopher Newport sailed up the James River to search for gold. Powhatan's followers made them turn back at the falls.

- In December 1607 Smith and a small band of settlers set out looking for gold and food along the Chickahominy River. According to Smith, he was captured and about to be clubbed to death by Powhatan's followers when Pocahontas (the chief's daughter) saved him.

- In 1608 Smith headed up two voyages to explore the northern reaches of Chesapeake Bay. He searched futilely for gold and an outlet to the Pacific Ocean.

THE SETTLEMENT

The colonists endured many terrible hardships. Bad water, disease, starvation, and conflict with the Native Americans took a heavy toll. By early 1608 only 38 hardy souls remained alive.

Settlers learned to grow crops in the new land. When tobacco from the West Indies was introduced, it became a commercial success and guaranteed Jamestown's future.

LEARNING *from* GEOGRAPHY

1. Compare the dwellings of the colonists and the Native Americans.

2. How did the introduction of tobacco affect the development of the colony?

Jamestown

- ■ Native American settlement
- ▭ Powhatan's territory

Expeditions

- —— May 1607
- —— December 1607 – January 1608
- —— January – July 1608
- —— July – September 1608

0   25 miles

0   25 kilometers

Appalachian

The Native Americans taught the settlers to cultivate native crops such as corn, beans, and squash. Corn quickly became the staple food.

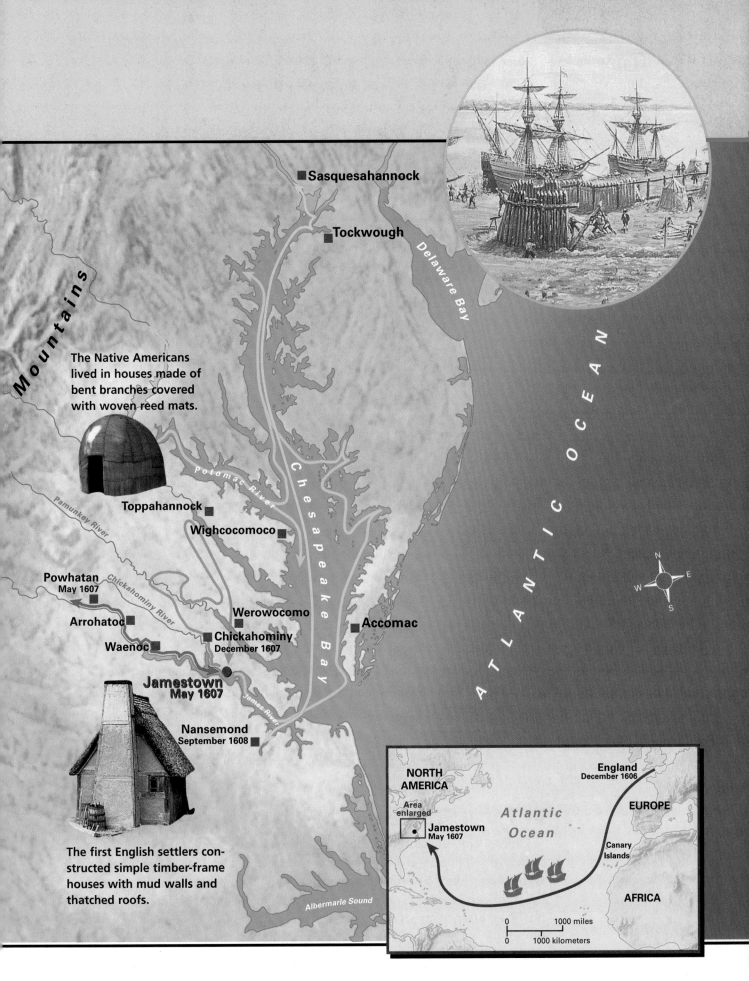

Sasquesahannock

Tockwough

Delaware Bay

Mountains

The Native Americans lived in houses made of bent branches covered with woven reed mats.

Pamunkey River

Potomac River

Toppahannock

Wighcocomoco

Chesapeake Bay

Powhatan
May 1607

Chickahominy River

Arrohatoc

Werowocomo

Waenoc

Chickahominy
December 1607

Accomac

Jamestown
May 1607

James River

Nansemond
September 1608

The first English settlers constructed simple timber-frame houses with mud walls and thatched roofs.

Albermarle Sound

ATLANTIC OCEAN

N
W   E
S

NORTH AMERICA

Area enlarged

Jamestown
May 1607

Atlantic Ocean

England
December 1606

EUROPE

Canary Islands

AFRICA

0   1000 miles
0   1000 kilometers

New England Colonies

Guide to Reading

Main Idea

Settlers begin to form the New England Colonies.

Key Terms

dissent, persecute, Puritan, Separatist, Pilgrim, Mayflower Compact, toleration

Reading Strategy

Classifying Information As you read Section 2, re-create the diagram below and explain why different colonies in New England were settled.

Colony	Reasons the colony was settled
Massachusetts	
Connecticut	
Rhode Island	

Read to Learn

- why the Pilgrims and the Puritans came to America.
- how the Connecticut, Rhode Island, and New Hampshire colonies began.

Section Theme

Civic Rights and Responsibilities Puritan and Pilgrim colonists settled in America in search of religious freedom.

Preview of Events

♦1620 — ♦1630 — ♦1640

1620
Pilgrims land at Plymouth

1630
Puritans settle the Massachusetts Bay Colony

1636
Thomas Hooker founds Hartford

1638
Anne Hutchinson founds Portsmouth

Shoes, Plymouth Colony

★ AN ★
American Story

The young man looked around at the other passengers aboard the *Mayflower*. He and the other passengers sailed to the new world not knowing what they would find. They had muskets but knew little about shooting. They planned to fish but knew nothing about fishing. They had hoped to settle in Virginia but instead landed in New England without enough supplies to last the winter. The only thing these people had plenty of was courage. They would need it.

Religious Freedom

Unlike the Jamestown settlers, the next wave of colonists would arrive in search of religious freedom. England had been a Protestant country since 1534, when King Henry VIII broke away from the Roman Catholic Church and formed the Anglican Church. Not everyone in England was happy with the new church, however. Many people dissented—they disagreed with the beliefs or practices of the Anglicans. English Catholics, for example, still considered the pope the head of the church, and they were often persecuted, or treated harshly, for that reason.

At the same time, some Protestants wanted to change—or reform—the Anglican Church, while others wanted to break away from it altogether. The Protestants who wanted to reform the Anglican Church were called Puritans. Those who wanted to leave and set up their own churches were known as Separatists.

The Separatists were persecuted in England, and some fled to the Netherlands. Though they found religious freedom there, the Separatists had difficulty finding work. They also worried that their children were losing their religious values and their English way of life.

The Pilgrims' Journey

Some Separatists in the Netherlands made an arrangement with the Virginia Company. The Separatists could settle in Virginia and practice their religion freely. In return they would give the company a share of any profits they made.

The Separatists considered themselves Pilgrims because their journey had a religious purpose. Only 35 of the 102 passengers who boarded the *Mayflower* in September 1620 were Pilgrims. The others were called "strangers." They were common people—servants, craftspeople, and poor farmers—who hoped to find a better life in America. Because Pilgrim beliefs shaped life in the Plymouth colony, however, all the early settlers are usually called Pilgrims.

The Mayflower Compact

The *Mayflower*'s passengers planned to settle in the Virginia colony. The first land they sighted was **Cape Cod,** well north of their target. Because it was November and winter was fast approaching, the colonists decided to drop anchor in Cape Cod Bay. They went ashore on a cold, bleak day in December at a place called Plymouth. **William Bradford,** their leader and historian, reported that "all things stared upon them with a weather-beaten face."

Plymouth was outside the territory of the Virginia Company and its laws. Before going ashore, the Pilgrims drew up a formal document called the Mayflower Compact. The compact pledged their loyalty to England and declared their intention of forming "a civil body politic,

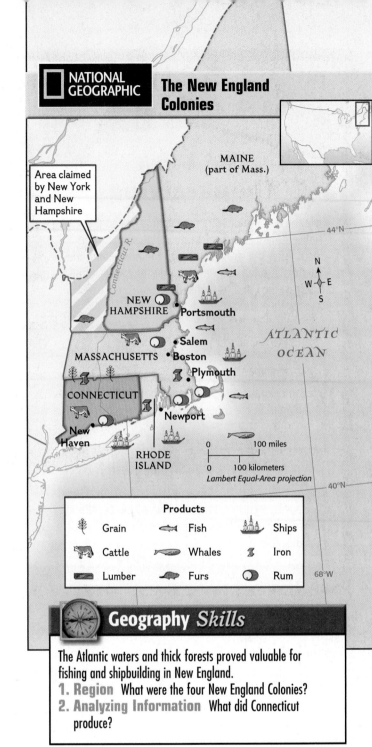

NATIONAL GEOGRAPHIC — The New England Colonies

Products

Grain	Fish	Ships
Cattle	Whales	Iron
Lumber	Furs	Rum

Geography *Skills*

The Atlantic waters and thick forests proved valuable for fishing and shipbuilding in New England.
1. **Region** What were the four New England Colonies?
2. **Analyzing Information** What did Connecticut produce?

for our better ordering and preservation." The signers also promised to obey the laws passed "for the general good of the colony." The Mayflower Compact was a necessary step in the development of representative government in America. *(See page 986 of the Appendix for the entire text of the Mayflower Compact.)*

Help From the Native Americans

Their first winter in America, almost half the Pilgrims died of malnutrition, disease, and

MORE ABOUT...

The First Thanksgiving

In the autumn of 1621 the Pilgrims invited the Native Americans to celebrate the peace between them. After the struggle through the first winter, the Pilgrims also felt relieved to be raising food. During the feast the Pilgrims thanked God for the harvest and for their survival.

First Thanksgiving by Jennie A. Brownscombe

Who took part? About 50 men, women, and children colonists and 90 Wampanoag Native Americans took part in the three-day feast.

What did they do? Dancing, singing, and playing games were part of the celebration. The Wampanoag demonstrated their skills with the bow and arrow.

When was it held? Exactly when the festival took place is uncertain, but it is believed the celebration occurred sometime between September 21 and November 9.

What did they eat? They most likely ate wild fowl, duck, and turkey shot by the colonists and deer provided by the Wampanoag.

cold. In the spring a few Native Americans approached the settlement. Two of them, **Squanto** and **Samoset,** befriended the colonists. Squanto was a Pawtuxet who had been kidnapped to Europe and had learned English.

Squanto and Samoset showed the Pilgrims how to grow corn, beans, and pumpkins and where to hunt and fish. Without their help the Pilgrims might not have survived. Squanto and Samoset also helped the Pilgrims make a treaty with the Wampanoag people who lived in the area. **Massasoit,** a Wampanoag leader, signed a treaty with the Pilgrims in March 1621, and the two groups lived in harmony.

✓ **Reading Check** **Summarizing** Why was the Mayflower Compact an important step toward representative government?

New Settlements

In 1625 the English throne passed to Charles I. Charles objected to the Puritans' calls for reform in the Anglican Church, and persecution of Puritans increased again. Some Puritans looked for a way to leave England.

In 1629 a group of Puritans formed the Massachusetts Bay Company and received a royal charter to establish a colony north of Plymouth. This was the Puritans' chance to create a new society in America—a society based on the Bible.

The company chose a well-educated Puritan named **John Winthrop** to be the colony's governor. In 1630 Winthrop led about 900 men, women, and children to **Massachusetts Bay.** Most of them settled in a place they called Boston.

🗣 Citizenship

Growth and Government

During the 1630s, more than 15,000 Puritans journeyed to Massachusetts to escape religious persecution and economic hard times in England. This movement of people became known as the **Great Migration.**

At first, John Winthrop and his assistants made the colony's laws. They were chosen by the General Court, which was made up of the colony's stockholders. In 1634, settlers demanded a larger role in the government. The General Court became an elected assembly. Adult male church members were allowed to vote for the governor and for their town's representatives to the General Court. In later years, they also had to own property to vote.

The Puritans came to America to put their religious beliefs into practice. The Puritans had little toleration—they criticized or persecuted people who held other religious views. This lack of toleration led to the creation of new colonies.

Connecticut and Rhode Island

The fertile Connecticut River valley, south of Massachusetts, was much better for farming than was the stony soil around Boston. In the 1630s colonists began to settle in this area.

A minister named Thomas Hooker became dissatisfied with Massachusetts. He did not like the way that Winthrop and the other Puritan leaders ran the colony. In 1636 Hooker led his congregation through the wilderness to Connecticut, where he founded the town of **Hartford.** Three years later Hartford and two other towns, Windsor and Wethersfield, agreed to form a colony. They adopted a plan of government called the **Fundamental Orders of Connecticut.** This was the first written constitution in America, and it described the organization of representative government in detail.

Good land drew colonists to Connecticut, but Rhode Island was settled by colonists who were forced out of Massachusetts. The first of these was **Roger Williams,** a minister. Williams felt that people should not be persecuted for their religious practices. In his view the government should not force people to worship in a certain way. Williams also believed it was wrong for settlers to take land away from the Native Americans.

The ideas of Roger Williams caused Massachusetts leaders to banish him in 1635. He took refuge with the Narraganset people, who later

People In History

Anne Hutchinson 1591–1643

Anne Hutchinson came to Massachusetts with her husband in 1634. She began questioning the religious authority of the colony's ministers.

As Hutchinson gained followers, she was seen as a danger to the colony's stability. In 1637 the Massachusetts leaders put her on trial for speaking false ideas.

Hutchinson defended herself well, but she claimed God spoke to her directly. This disagreed with Puritan beliefs that God spoke only through the Bible. Her accusers found her guilty and ordered her to leave the colony. With her family and some followers, Hutchinson moved to Rhode Island.

sold Williams land where he founded the town of Providence. Williams received a charter in 1644 for a colony east of Connecticut called **Rhode Island and Providence Plantations.** With its policy of religious toleration, Rhode Island became a safe place for dissenters. It was the first place in America where people could worship freely.

Others followed Williams's example, forming colonies where they could worship as they pleased. In 1638 **John Wheelwright** led a group of dissidents from Massachusetts to the north. They founded the town of Exeter in **New Hampshire.** The same year, a group of Puritans settled Hampton. The colony of New Hampshire became fully independent of Massachusetts in 1679.

Conflict With Native Americans

Native Americans helped the settlers adapt to the land. They also traded with the settlers, exchanging furs for goods such as iron pots, blankets, and guns. In Virginia the colonists had frequent encounters with the many tribes of the Powhatan confederacy. In New England the settlers met the Wampanoags, Narragansets, and other groups.

Conflicts arose, however. Usually settlers moved onto Native American lands without permission or payment. Throughout the colonial period, English settlers and Native Americans competed fiercely for control of the land.

HISTORY Online

Student Web Activity
Visit taj.glencoe.com and click on **Chapter 3— Student Web Activities** for an activity on King Philip's War.

In 1636 war broke out between the settlers and the Pequot people. After two traders were killed in Pequot territory, Massachusetts sent troops to punish the Pequot. The Pequot then attacked a town in Connecticut killing nine people. In May 1637, troops from Connecticut attacked the main Pequot fort with the help of the Narraganset people. They burned the fort, killing hundreds.

In 1675 New England went to war against the Wampanoag people and their allies. Metacomet, the Wampanoag chief, was known to settlers as King Philip. He wanted to stop the settlers from moving onto Native American lands. The war began after settlers executed three Wampanoags for murder. Metacomet's forces attacked towns across the region, killing hundreds of people.

The settlers and their Native American allies fought back. King Philip's War, as the conflict was called, ended in defeat for the Wampanoag and their allies. The war destroyed the power of the Native Americans in New England, leaving the colonists free to expand their settlements.

✓ **Reading Check** **Evaluating** Describe the significance of the Fundamental Orders of Connecticut.

SECTION 2 ASSESSMENT

Checking for Understanding

1. **Key Terms** Write a short paragraph in which you use the following terms: dissent, persecute, Puritan, Separatist, Pilgrim, Mayflower Compact, toleration.

2. **Reviewing Facts** Identify the reasons why the Separatists left Europe for the Americas.

Reviewing Themes

3. **Civic Rights and Responsibilities** What freedom did Rhode Island offer that other colonies did not?

Critical Thinking

4. **Comparing** What did the Mayflower Compact and the Fundamental Orders of Connecticut have in common?

5. **Determining Cause and Effect** Re-create the diagram below and describe the effects as colonists interacted with Native Americans.

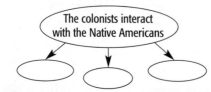
The colonists interact with the Native Americans

Analyzing Maps

6. **Geography Skills** Study the map on page 77. What products came from New Hampshire?

Interdisciplinary Activity

Music Create a song that the Pilgrims might have sung as they crossed the Atlantic on the Mayflower. Create the lyrics for the song by using what you have learned about why the Pilgrims sailed to New England. Teach your song to your class.

Social Studies
SKILLBUILDER

Reading a Bar Graph

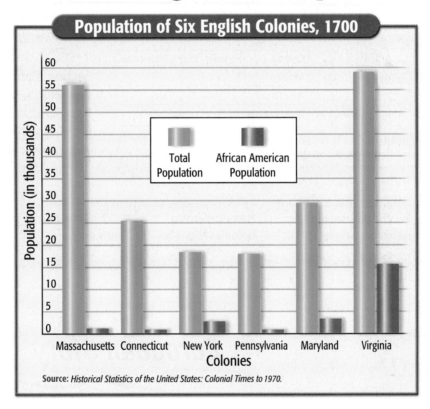

Population of Six English Colonies, 1700

Source: *Historical Statistics of the United States: Colonial Times to 1970.*

Why Learn This Skill?

A bar graph presents numerical information in a visual way. Bars of various lengths stand for different quantities. A bar graph lets you see a lot of information in an organized way. Bars may be drawn vertically—up and down—or horizontally—left to right. Labels along the left axis and the bottom axis explain what the bars represent.

Learning the Skill

To read a bar graph:
• Read the title to learn the subject of the graph.
• Look at the horizontal and vertical axes to find out what information the graph presents.
• Compare the lengths of the bars on the graph.

Practicing the Skill

Study the bar graph on this page and answer the following questions.

❶ Which colony had the largest total population in 1700? The smallest?

❷ Did Virginia or Maryland have a larger African American population?

Applying the Skill

Reading a Bar Graph Create a bar graph to represent the number of students in each American history class in your school.

 Glencoe's **Skillbuilder Interactive Workbook CD-ROM, Level 1,** provides instruction and practice in key social studies skills.

Guide to Reading

Main Idea
People from many different countries settled in the Middle Colonies for a variety of reasons, including religious freedom.

Key Terms
patroon, proprietary colony, pacifist

Reading Strategy
Classifying Information As you read the section, re-create the diagram below and describe how the Middle Colonies were founded.

Colony	Founder	Why settlers came
New York		
New Jersey		
Pennsylvania		

Read to Learn
• why the Middle Colonies had the most diverse populations in colonial America.
• who was America's first town planner.

Section Theme
Individual Action Leaders such as Peter Stuyvesant and William Penn helped the Middle Colonies grow.

Preview of Events

♦1600   ♦1650   ♦1700

1626
Manhattan Island purchased from the Manhates people

1664
New Amsterdam becomes New York

1681
William Penn founds Pennsylvania

1702
New Jersey becomes a royal colony

English royal plate

A European Story

In 1649, 17-year-old Philip Henry stood near the back of the crowd gathered around a public platform near Whitehall Palace in London. There he watched Charles I, the king of England, prepare to die. The king made a short speech, prayed silently, and then knelt with his head on the block.

With just one blow, the executioner severed the king's head from his body. At that moment, the crowd uttered "such a groan as I never heard before, and desire I may never hear again," Henry wrote in his diary.

England and the Colonies

In England the Puritans who controlled Parliament were engaged in a struggle for power against King Charles I. In 1642 a civil war began. Led by Oliver Cromwell, a Puritan, the Parliamentary forces defeated the king. Charles I was beheaded in 1649 after a parliamentary court declared him guilty of treason.

A new government was established with Cromwell as Protector. During these years of unrest, many Puritans left New England and returned to England to fight with Parliament's forces. After the war ended, English men and women loyal to the king went to royal colonies like Virginia.

After Cromwell died in 1658, Parliament brought back the monarchy, but placed new limits on the ruler's powers. Charles II, son of Charles I, became king in 1660. His reign is called the *Restoration* because the monarchy had been restored.

In 1660 England had two clusters of colonies in what is now the United States—Massachusetts, New Hampshire, Connecticut, and Rhode Island in the north and Maryland and Virginia in the south. Between the two groups of English colonies were lands that the Dutch controlled.

In 1621 a group of Dutch merchants had formed the Dutch West India Company to trade in the Americas. Their posts along the Hudson River grew into the colony of New Netherland. The main settlement of the colony was **New Amsterdam,** located on **Manhattan Island.** In 1626 the company bought Manhattan from the Manhates people for small quantities of beads and other goods. Blessed with a good seaport, the city of New Amsterdam soon became a center of shipping to and from the Americas.

To increase the number of permanent settlers in its colony, the Dutch West India Company sent over families from the Netherlands, Germany, Sweden, and Finland. The company gave a large estate to anyone who brought at least 50 settlers to work the land. The wealthy landowners who acquired these riverfront estates were called patroons. The patroons ruled like kings. They had their own courts and laws. Settlers owed the patroon labor and a share of their crops.

England Takes Over

New Netherland boasted an excellent harbor and thriving river trade. The English wanted to acquire the valuable Dutch colony that lay between England's New England and Southern Colonies. In 1664 the English sent a fleet to attack New Amsterdam.

At the time **Peter Stuyvesant** was governor of the colony. His strict rule and heavy taxes turned many of the people in New Netherland against him. When the English ships sailed into New Amsterdam's harbor, the governor was unprepared for a battle and surrendered the colony to the English forces.

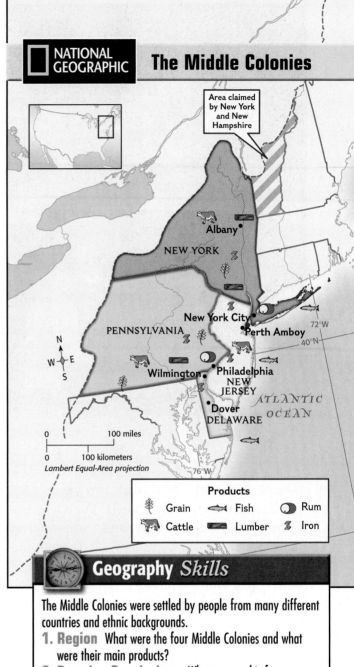

The Middle Colonies

Area claimed by New York and New Hampshire

Albany

NEW YORK

New York City
Perth Amboy

PENNSYLVANIA

72°W
40°N

Wilmington
Philadelphia
NEW JERSEY

Dover
DELAWARE

ATLANTIC OCEAN

0   100 miles

0   100 kilometers
Lambert Equal-Area projection
76°W

Products

Grain   Fish   Rum

Cattle   Lumber   Iron

Geography *Skills*

The Middle Colonies were settled by people from many different countries and ethnic backgrounds.

1. **Region** What were the four Middle Colonies and what were their main products?
2. **Drawing Conclusions** What geographic features made Philadelphia and New York City centers for trade?

King Charles II gave the colony to his brother, the **Duke of York,** who renamed it **New York.** New York was a proprietary colony, a colony in which the owner, or proprietor, owned all the land and controlled the government. It differed from the New England Colonies where voters elected the governor and an assembly.

Most of New York's settlers lived in the Hudson River valley. The Duke of York promised the diverse colonists freedom of religion and allowed them to keep their property. As a result,

Penn's Treaty with the Indians In 1682 William Penn made his first treaty with the Delaware people. **Why did Penn see Pennsylvania as a "holy experiment"?**

most of the Dutch colonists decided to remain in New York. In 1664 New York had about 8,000 inhabitants. Most were Dutch, but Germans, Swedes, Native Americans, and Puritans from New England lived there as well. The population also included at least 300 enslaved Africans. New Amsterdam, which was later called New York City, was one of the fastest-growing locations in the colony.

By 1683 the colony's population had swelled to about 12,000 people. A governor and council appointed by the Duke of York directed the colony's affairs. The colonists demanded a representative government like the governments of the other English colonies. The duke resisted the idea, but the people of New York would not give up. Finally, in 1691, the English government allowed New York to elect a legislature.

New Jersey

The Duke of York gave the southern part of his colony, between the Hudson and Delaware Rivers, to **Lord John Berkeley** and **Sir George Carteret.** The proprietors named their colony New Jersey after the island of Jersey in the English Channel, where Carteret was born.

To attract settlers, the proprietors offered large tracts of land and generous terms. They also promised freedom of religion, trial by jury, and a representative assembly. The assembly would make local laws and set tax rates.

Like New York, New Jersey was a place of ethnic and religious diversity. Because New Jersey had no natural harbors, however, it did not develop a major port or city like New York.

The proprietors of New Jersey did not make the profits they had expected. Berkeley sold his share, West Jersey, in 1674. Carteret's share, East Jersey, was sold in 1682.

By 1702 New Jersey had passed back into the hands of the king, becoming a royal colony. The colonists still continued to make local laws.

Reading Check **Explaining** Why did no major port develop in New Jersey?

Pennsylvania

In 1680 **William Penn,** a wealthy English gentleman, presented a plan to King Charles. Penn's father had once lent the king a great deal of money. Penn had inherited the king's promise to repay the loan. Instead of money, however, Penn asked for land in America. Pleased to get rid of his debt so easily, the king gave Penn a tract of land stretching inland from the Delaware River. The new colony, named Pennsylvania, was nearly as large as England.

William Penn belonged to a Protestant group of dissenters called the Society of Friends, or **Quakers.** The Quakers believed that every individual had an "inner light" that could guide him or her to salvation. Each person could experience religious truth directly, which meant that church services and officials were unnecessary. Everyone was equal in God's sight. Though firm in their beliefs, the Quakers were tolerant of the views of others.

Many people in England found the Quakers' ideas a threat to established traditions. Quakers would not bow or take off their hats to lords and ladies because of their belief that everyone was equal. In addition they were pacifists, people who refuse to use force or to fight in wars. Quakers were fined, jailed, and even executed for their beliefs.

William Penn saw Pennsylvania as a "holy experiment," a chance to put the Quaker ideals of toleration and equality into practice. In 1682 he sailed to America to supervise the building of **Philadelphia,** the "city of brotherly love." Penn believed that

66any government is free to the people under it . . . where the laws rule, and the people are a party to those laws.99

Penn had designed the city himself, making him America's first town planner. Penn also wrote Pennsylvania's first constitution.

Penn believed that the land belonged to the Native Americans and that settlers should pay for it. In 1682 he negotiated the first of several treaties with local Native Americans.

To encourage European settlers to come to Pennsylvania, Penn advertised the colony throughout Europe with pamphlets in several languages. By 1683 more than 3,000 English, Welsh, Irish, Dutch, and German settlers had arrived. In 1701, in the Charter of Liberties, Penn granted the colonists the right to elect representatives to the legislative assembly.

The southernmost part of Pennsylvania was called the Three Lower Counties. Settled by Swedes in 1638, the area had been taken over by the Dutch and the English before becoming part of Pennsylvania. The Charter of Privileges allowed the lower counties to form their own legislature, which they did in 1704. Thereafter the counties functioned as a separate colony known as Delaware, supervised by Pennsylvania's governor.

✓**Reading Check** **Summarizing** How did William Penn encourage self-government?

SECTION 3 ASSESSMENT

Checking for Understanding

1. **Key Terms** Write a short paragraph in which you use the following key terms: patroon, proprietary colony, pacifist

2. **Reviewing Facts** What did the Charter of Liberties grant to Pennsylvania colonists?

Reviewing Themes

3. **Individual Action** How did William Penn earn the respect of Native Americans?

Critical Thinking

4. **Compare and Contrast** How was the Quaker religion different from that of the Puritans?

5. **Organizing Information** Re-create the diagram below and describe how each of the Middle Colonies was governed.

Colony	Type of government
New York	
New Jersey	
Pennsylvania	

Analyzing Visuals

6. **Geography Skills** Review the map on page 83. What is the title of the map? What items are shown in the key? What products were important to Pennsylvania?

Interdisciplinary Activity

Art Design a flag for one of the Middle Colonies. Decide what symbols and colors would be appropriate to represent that colony. Display your flags in class.

Guide to Reading

Main Idea
The Southern Colonies relied on cash crops to survive, while the French and Spanish tried to establish their own settlements.

Key Terms
indentured servant, constitution, debtor, tenant farmer, mission

Reading Strategy
Classifying Information As you read the section, re-create the diagram below and identify the main crops of three of the Southern Colonies.

Colony	Main crop
Maryland	
North Carolina	
South Carolina	

Read to Learn
• how the Southern Colonies were established.
• how French and Spanish colonies differed from the English colonies.

Section Theme
Groups and Institutions Spanish and French settlements developed in different ways from English settlements.

Preview of Events

♦1600	♦1650	♦1700	♦1750

c. 1610
Spanish establish
Santa Fe

1676
Bacon's Rebellion
occurs

1718
French establish city
of New Orleans

1733
First settlers
arrive in Georgia

*Slave drum,
Virginia*

AN American Story

How did it feel to be enslaved on the plantations of the South? In the 1930s, interviewers put this question to African Americans once under slavery. Many of them were approaching 100 years old, and some still carried deep scars on their backs from whippings. To be a slave meant to have no human rights. Elderly Roberta Mason remembered, "Once they whipped my father 'cause he looked at a slave they killed, and cried."

Coming to America

By 1660, while tobacco prices fell, large plantations continued to prosper because they were better able to maintain high profits than were small farms. Along with the growth of plantations, there was an increasing need for workers in the newly settled Southern Colonies.

Establishing colonies in North America involved a great deal of work. The settlers had to clear the land, construct homes and churches, plant crops, and tend the fields. As the colonies expanded, the demand for capable workers grew.

Not all people came to work in the colonies of their own free will. English criminals and Scottish and Irish prisoners of war were also shipped to the colonies. They could earn their release by working for a period of time—often seven years. Some colonists complained that their settlements were dumping grounds for "His Majesty's seven-year passengers." African rulers took prisoners during wars and raids. They enslaved the captives and sold them to European slave traders who took them to the colonies. Many people came to the colonies as indentured servants. To pay for their passage to America, they agreed to work without pay for a certain period of time.

Establishing Maryland

Maryland arose from the dream of **Sir George Calvert, Lord Baltimore,** a Catholic. Calvert wanted to establish a safe place for his fellow Catholics, who were being persecuted in England. He also hoped that a colony would bring him a fortune.

Calvert's dream came true in 1632 when King Charles I gave him a proprietary colony north of Virginia. Calvert died before receiving the grant. His son Cecilius Calvert inherited the colony. It was named Maryland either after the English queen, Henrietta Maria, or after the Virgin Mary.

The younger Calvert—the new Lord Baltimore—never lived in Maryland. Instead, he sent two of his brothers to run the colony. They reached America in 1634 with two ships and more than 200 settlers. Entering the Chesapeake Bay, they sailed up the **Potomac River** through fertile countryside. A priest in the party described the Potomac as "the sweetest and greatest river I have ever seen." The colonists chose a site for their settlement, which they called St. Marys.

Knowing that tobacco had saved the Virginia colony, the Maryland colonists turned first to tobacco farming. To keep the colony from becoming too dependent on one crop, however, a Maryland law declared that "every person planting tobacco shall plant and tend two acres of corn." In addition to corn, most Maryland tobacco farmers produced wheat, fruit, vegetables, and livestock to feed their families and

their workers. **Baltimore,** founded in 1729, was Maryland's port. Before long Baltimore became the colony's largest settlement.

Aristocrats and Farmers

Lord Baltimore gave large estates to his relatives and other English aristocrats. By doing so he created a wealthy and powerful class of landowners in Maryland.

The colony needed people to work in the plantation fields. To bring settlers to the colony, Lord Baltimore promised land—100 acres to each

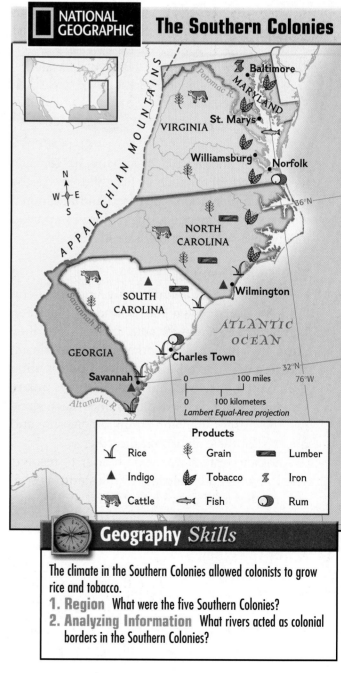

NATIONAL GEOGRAPHIC The Southern Colonies

Products

Rice	Grain	Lumber
Indigo	Tobacco	Iron
Cattle	Fish	Rum

Geography *Skills*

The climate in the Southern Colonies allowed colonists to grow rice and tobacco.
1. **Region** What were the five Southern Colonies?
2. **Analyzing Information** What rivers acted as colonial borders in the Southern Colonies?

Margaret Brent c.1601—1671

PARLOR

Born in England, Margaret Brent moved to Maryland in 1638. She quickly accumulated several thousand acres of land and became one of the largest landowners. According to colonial records, she was also the first woman to own land in her own name.

Brave and forceful, Brent helped to put down a rebellion from neighboring Virginia, and she took charge of paying Maryland's troops. Refusing to follow the restricted life of most colonial women, she later served as attorney for Lord Baltimore, Maryland's proprietor.

In January 1648 Brent came into conflict with the colonial government when she appeared before the assembly. She demanded two votes, one for herself as a landowner and one as Lord Baltimore's legal representative. After the government denied her claim, she moved to a large plantation in Virginia. There, America's first woman lawyer lived the rest of her life.

male settler, another 100 for his wife, 100 for each servant, and 50 for each of his children. As the number of plantations increased and additional workers were needed, the colony imported indentured servants and enslaved Africans.

The Mason-Dixon Line

For years the Calvert family and the Penn family argued over the boundary between Maryland and Pennsylvania. In the 1760s they hired two British astronomers, Charles Mason and Jeremiah Dixon, to map the line dividing the colonies. It took the two scientists many years to lay out the boundary stones. Each stone had the crest of the Penn family on one side and the crest of the Calverts on the other.

Another conflict was even harder to resolve. The Calverts had welcomed Protestants as well as Catholics in Maryland. Protestant settlers outnumbered Catholics from the start.

Act of Toleration

To protect the Catholics from any attempt to make Maryland a Protestant colony, Baltimore passed a law called the **Act of Toleration** in 1649. The act granted Protestants and Catholics the right to worship freely, but tensions contin-

ued between Protestants and Catholics. In 1692, with the support of the English government, the Protestant-controlled assembly made the Anglican Church the official church in Maryland, and imposed the same restrictions on Catholics that existed in England.

Reading Check Explaining Why did George Calvert establish the colony of Maryland?

Virginia Expands

While other colonies were being founded, Virginia continued to grow. Wealthy tobacco planters held the best land near the coast, so new settlers pushed inland. As the settlers moved west, they found the lands inhabited by Native Americans. In the 1640s, to avoid conflicts, Virginia's governor William Berkeley worked out an arrangement with the Native Americans. In exchange for a large piece of land, he agreed to keep settlers from pushing farther into their lands.

Bacon's Rebellion

Nathaniel Bacon, a wealthy young planter, was a leader in the western part of Virginia. He and other westerners opposed the colonial government because it was dominated by easterners. Many of the westerners resented Governor Berkeley's pledge to stay out of Native American territory. Some of them settled in the forbidden lands and then blamed the government in Jamestown for not protecting them from Native American raids.

In 1676 Bacon led the angry westerners in attacks on Native American villages. Governor Berkeley declared Bacon "the greatest rebel that ever was in Virginia." Bacon's army marched to Jamestown, set fire to the capital, and drove Berkeley into exile. Only Bacon's sudden illness and death kept him from taking charge of Virginia. England then recalled Berkeley and sent troops to restore order.

Bacon's Rebellion had shown that the settlers were not willing to be restricted to the coast. The colonial government created a militia force to control the Native Americans and opened up more land to settlement.

✓ **Reading Check** **Analyzing** Why did Bacon oppose the colonial government?

Settling the Carolinas

In 1663 King Charles II created a large proprietary colony south of Virginia. The colony was called Carolina, which means "Charles's land" in Latin. The king gave the colony to a group of eight prominent members of his court who had helped him regain his throne.

The Carolina proprietors carved out large estates for themselves and hoped to make money by selling and renting land. The proprietors provided money to bring colonists over from England. Settlers began arriving in Carolina in 1670. By 1680 they had founded a city, which they called Charles Town after the

Nathaniel Bacon

king. The name later became **Charleston.**

John Locke, an English political philosopher, wrote a constitution for the Carolina colony. This constitution, or plan of government, covered such subjects as land distribution and social ranking. Locke was concerned with principles and rights. He argued that

❝every man has a property in his own person. This nobody has any right to but himself. The labour of his body, and the work of his hands, we may say, are properly his. . . .❞

Carolina, however, did not develop according to plan. The people of northern and southern Carolina soon went their separate ways, creating two colonies.

💲 Economics
Northern and Southern Carolina

The northern part of Carolina was settled mostly by farmers from Virginia's backcountry. They grew tobacco and sold forest products such as timber and tar. Because the northern Carolina coast did not have a good harbor, the farmers relied on Virginia's ports and merchants to conduct their trade.

The southern part of the Carolinas was more prosperous, thanks to fertile farmland and a good harbor at Charles Town. Settlements spread, and the trade in deerskin, lumber, and beef flourished. In the 1680s planters discovered that rice grew well in the wet coastal lowlands. Rice soon became the colony's leading crop.

In the 1740s a young Englishwoman named **Eliza Lucas** developed another important Carolina crop—indigo. Indigo, a blue flowering plant, was used to dye textiles. After experimenting with seeds from the West Indies, Lucas succeeded in growing and processing indigo, the "blue gold" of Carolina.

Slave Labor in the Carolinas

Most of the settlers in southern Carolina came from another English colony—the island of Barbados in the West Indies. In Barbados the colonists used enslaved Africans to produce sugar. The colonists brought these workers with them.

Many enslaved Africans who arrived in the Carolinas worked in the rice fields. Some of them knew a great deal about rice cultivation because they had come from the rice-growing areas of West Africa. Growing rice required much labor, so the demand for slaves increased. By 1708 more than half the people living in southern Carolina were enslaved Africans.

By the early 1700s, Carolina's settlers were angry at the proprietors. They wanted a greater role in the colony's government. In 1719 the settlers in southern Carolina seized control of the colony from its proprietors. In 1729 Carolina became two royal colonies—North and South Carolina.

✓ **Reading Check** **Explaining** Who was John Locke? What did he do for Carolina?

Picturing **History**

A rice plantation included the owner's large house surrounded by the small dwellings of enslaved Africans. **Why did rice cultivation increase the demand for enslaved labor?**

Georgia

Georgia, the last of the British colonies in America to be established, was founded in 1733. A group led by General **James Oglethorpe** received a charter to create a colony where English debtors and poor people could make a fresh start. In Great Britain, debtors—those who are unable to repay their debts—were generally thrown into prison.

The British government had another reason for creating Georgia. This colony could protect the other British colonies from Spanish attack. Great Britain and Spain had been at war in the early 1700s, and new conflicts over territory in North America were always breaking out. Located between Spanish Florida and South Carolina, Georgia could serve as a military barrier.

Oglethorpe's Town

Oglethorpe led the first group of "sober, industrial, and moral persons" to Georgia in 1733. They built a town called **Savannah,** as well as forts to defend themselves from the Spanish.

Oglethorpe wanted the people of Georgia to be hardworking, independent, and Protestant. He kept the size of farms small and banned slavery, Catholics, and rum.

Colony	1st Permanent Settlement	Reasons Founded	Founders or Leaders
New England Colonies			

Massachusetts
  Plymouth
  Mass. Bay Colony
	
	1620
	1630
		
		Religious freedom
		Religious freedom
			John Carver, William Bradford, John Winthrop

New Hampshire	c. 1620	Profit from trade and fishing	Ferdinando Gorges, John Mason
Rhode Island	1636	Religious freedom	Roger Williams
Connecticut	1635	Profit from fur trade, farming; religious and political freedom	Thomas Hooker
Middle Colonies			
New York	1624	Expand trade	Dutch settlers
Delaware	1638	Expand trade	Swedish settlers
New Jersey	1638	Profit from selling land	John Berkeley, George Carteret
Pennsylvania	1682	Profit from selling land; religious freedom	William Penn
Southern Colonies			
Virginia	1607	Expand trade	John Smith
Maryland	1634	To sell land; religious freedom	Cecil Calvert
North Carolina	c. 1660s	Profit from trade and selling land	Group of eight aristocrats
South Carolina	1670	Profit from trade and selling land	Group of eight aristocrats
Georgia	1733	Religious freedom; protection against Spanish Florida; safe home for debtors	James Oglethorpe

NOVA BRITANNIA.
OFFERING MOST
Excellent fruites by Planting in
VIRGINIA.
Exciting all such as be well affected
to further the same.

LONDON
Printed for SAMVEL MACHAM, and are to be sold at
his Shop in Pauls Church-yard, at the
Signe of the Bul-head.
1609.

Chart Skills

The thirteen colonies were founded over a span of 125 years.

Sequencing What colony was the first to be settled? Which was the last?

Although Georgia had been planned as a debtors' colony, it actually received few debtors. Hundreds of poor people came from Great Britain. Religious refugees from Germany and Switzerland and a small group of Jews also settled there. Georgia soon had a higher percentage of non-British settlers than any other British colony in the Americas.

The Colony Changes

Many settlers complained about the limits on the size of landholdings and the law banning slave labor. They also objected to the many rules Oglethorpe made regulating their lives. The colonists referred to Oglethorpe as "our perpetual dictator."

Oglethorpe grew frustrated by the colonists' demands and the colony's slow growth. He agreed to let people have larger landholdings and lifted the bans against slavery and rum. In 1751 he gave up altogether and turned the colony back over to the king.

By that time British settlers had been in what is now the eastern United States for almost a century and a half. They had lined the Atlantic coast with colonies.

Reading Check **Explaining** How did Georgia serve as protection for the English colonies?

New France

The British were not the only Europeans who were colonizing North America, however. Elsewhere on the continent, the Spanish and the French had built settlements of their own.

The French had founded **Quebec** in 1608. At first they had little interest in large-scale settlement in North America. They were mainly concerned with fishing and trapping animals for their fur. French trappers and missionaries went far into the interior of North America. French fur companies built forts and trading posts to protect their profitable trade.

In 1663 **New France** became a royal colony. King Louis XIV limited the privileges of the fur companies. He appointed a royal governor who strongly supported new explorations.

Down the Mississippi River

In the 1670s two Frenchmen—a fur trader, **Louis Joliet,** and a priest, **Jacques Marquette**—explored the Mississippi River by canoe. Joliet and Marquette hoped to find gold, silver, or other precious metals. They were also looking for a water passage to the Pacific Ocean. The two explorers reached as far south as the junction of the Arkansas and Mississippi Rivers. When they realized that the Mississippi flowed south into the Gulf of Mexico rather than west into the Pacific, they turned around and headed back upriver.

A few years later, **René-Robert Cavelier, Sieur de La Salle,** followed the Mississippi River all the way to the Gulf of Mexico. La Salle claimed the region around the river for France. He called this territory Louisiana in honor of King Louis XIV. In 1718 the French governor founded the port of **New Orleans** near the mouth of the Mississippi River. Later French explorers, traders, and missionaries traveled west to the Rocky Mountains and southwest to the Rio Grande.

Growth of New France

French settlement in North America advanced very slowly. Settlement in New France consisted of a system of estates along the St. Lawrence River. The estate holders received land in exchange for bringing settlers to the colony. Known as tenant farmers, the settlers paid their lord an annual rent and worked for him for a fixed number of days each year.

The French had better relations with the Native Americans than did other Europeans. French trappers and missionaries traveled deep into Indian lands. They lived among the Native American peoples, learned their languages, and respected their ways.

Although the missionaries had come to convert Native Americans to Catholicism, they did not try to change the Indians' customs. Most important, the French colony grew so slowly that Native Americans were not pushed off their lands.

✓**Reading Check** **Describing** What region did La Salle explore?

New Spain

In the early 1600s, England, France, and the Netherlands began their colonization of North America. The Spanish, however, still controlled most of Mexico, the Caribbean, and Central and South America. They also expanded into the western and southern parts of what would one day be the United States.

Spain was determined to keep the other European powers from threatening its empire in America. To protect their claims, the Spanish sent soldiers, missionaries, and settlers north into present-day New Mexico.

In late 1609 or early 1610, Spanish missionaries, soldiers, and settlers founded **Santa Fe.** Another group of missionaries and settlers went to what is now Arizona in the late 1600s. When France began exploring and laying claim to lands around the Mississippi River, the Spanish moved into what is now Texas. Spain wanted to control the area between the French territory and their own colony in Mexico. In the early 1700s, Spain established San Antonio and seven other military posts in Texas.

Missions in California

Spanish priests built a string of missions along the Pacific coast. Missions are religious settlements established to convert people to a particular faith. The missions enabled the Spanish to lay claim to California.

The Spanish did more than convert Native Americans to Christianity. Spanish missionaries and soldiers also brought them to the missions—often by force—to serve as laborers in fields and workshops.

In 1769 **Junípero Serra,** a Franciscan monk, founded a mission at **San Diego.** Over the next 15 years, Father Serra set up eight more missions in California along a route called *El Camino Real* (The Royal Highway)—missions that would grow into such cities as Los Angeles and Monterey.

The distance from one mission to the next was usually a day's walk, and Serra traveled on foot to visit each one and advise the missionaries. Serra also championed the rights of the Native Americans. He worked to prevent Spanish army commanders in the region from mistreating them.

European Conflicts in North America

The rivalries between European nations carried over into the Americas. Britain and France fought several wars in the 1700s. When the two countries were at war in Europe, fighting often broke out between British colonists in America and French colonists in New France.

"[The natives] treated us with much confidence and good-will."

—*Junípero Serra, 1769*

France and Great Britain were the principal rivals of the colonial period. Both nations were expanding their settlements in North America. In the late 1700s and early 1800s, wars in Europe between the British and the French would shape events across the Atlantic even more decisively.

Reading Check **Explaining** Why did Spain establish missions in California?

SECTION 4 ASSESSMENT

Checking for Understanding

1. **Key Terms** Write a short paragraph in which you use all of the following terms: indentured servant, constitution, debtor, tenant farmer, mission.
2. **Reviewing Facts** Explain why French settlement in North America was slower than in the English colonies.

Reviewing Themes

3. **Groups and Institutions** What role did Margaret Brent play in the government and economy of Maryland?

Critical Thinking

4. **Analyzing Information** Do you think uprisings such as Bacon's Rebellion were a sign of more unrest to come? Explain your answer.
5. **Organizing Information** Re-create the diagram below and describe the regions that these countries controlled in North America.

Country	Region
Spain	
France	

Analyzing Visuals

6. **Geography Skills** Review the map on page 87. Which of the Southern Colonies included the city of Norfolk? What were the main products in Georgia? What was the major city in South Carolina?

Interdisciplinary Activity

Art Work with a group to create a bulletin board display titled "The Southern Colonies." Include slogans and pictures to show the colonies' origins, climate, natural resources, and products.

ASSESSMENT and ACTIVITIES

Chapter Summary
Colonial America

1587–1650

- English settle Roanoke Island, 1587
- First permanent English colony at Jamestown, 1607
- Champlain founds Quebec, 1608
- Spanish settlers found Santa Fe, c. 1610
- House of Burgesses meet, 1619
- First Africans arrive at Jamestown, 1619

- Mayflower Compact signed, 1620
- Puritans settle Massachusetts Bay Colony, 1630
- Thomas Hooker founds Hartford, 1636
- Anne Hutchinson founds Portsmouth, 1638
- Maryland passes religious Toleration Act, 1649

1650–1700

- Marquette and Joliet explore Mississippi River, 1673
- King Philip's War, 1675
- Bacon's Rebellion, 1676
- William Penn receives charter for Pennsylvania, 1681

1700–1769

- French found city of New Orleans, 1718
- Carolina is divided into separate colonies, 1729
- Georgia settled, last of 13 English colonies, 1733
- Father Serra establishes mission at San Diego, 1769

Reviewing Key Terms

Examine the pairs of words below. Then write a sentence explaining what each of the pairs have in common.

1. charter, joint-stock company
2. dissent, persecute
3. patroon, proprietary colony
4. indentured servant, debtor
5. Pilgrim, Mayflower Compact

Reviewing Key Facts

6. Why did settlers choose a peninsula on which to build Jamestown?
7. Why did the Virginia Company create the House of Burgesses?
8. How did the Puritans' and the Pilgrims' view of the Anglican Church differ?
9. How did the Native Americans help the Pilgrims?
10. What is important about the year 1607?
11. Name two things that colonial leaders offered to attract settlers.
12. What were Sir George Calvert's two main reasons for establishing Maryland?
13. Why was there a high demand for slave labor in the Carolinas?
14. Describe the relationship between the French and the Native Americans.
15. Why did Spain send missionaries to the Pacific coast and the Southwest?

Critical Thinking

16. **Comparing** How did the economic activities of the French differ from those of the English in North America?
17. **Analyzing Themes: Civic Rights and Responsibilities** What role did religious freedom play in the founding of Rhode Island and Pennsylvania?
18. **Synthesizing Information** Re-create the diagram below. List three religious groups that left England and describe their beliefs.

Religious groups

94

Geography and History Activity

Study the map below and answer the questions that follow.

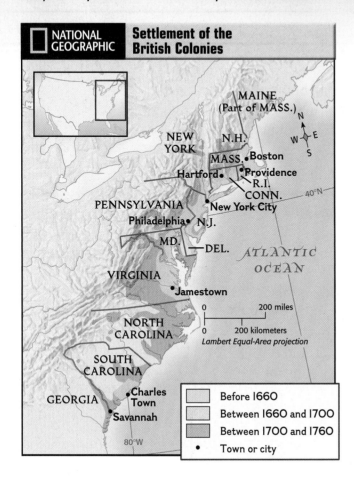

NATIONAL GEOGRAPHIC **Settlement of the British Colonies**

MAINE (Part of MASS.)

NEW YORK
N.H.
MASS. •Boston
Hartford• •Providence
R.I.
CONN.
40°N
PENNSYLVANIA •New York City
Philadelphia• N.J.
MD.
—DEL.
ATLANTIC OCEAN
VIRGINIA
•Jamestown

0   200 miles
0   200 kilometers
Lambert Equal-Area projection

NORTH CAROLINA

SOUTH CAROLINA

GEORGIA •Charles Town
•Savannah
80°W

	Before 1660
	Between 1660 and 1700
	Between 1700 and 1760
•	Town or city

19. **Location** Which colonies had the largest areas of settlement before 1660?

20. **Place** During what time period was Boston settled?

Practicing Skills

Reading a Bar Graph *Study the bar graph on page 81; then answer these questions:*

21. Which colonies had passed 35,000 in population by 1700?

22. Which colony had the largest African American population?

 ## Technology Activity

23. **Using the Internet** Search the Internet for information about the Canadian cities of Quebec and Montreal. Find historical sites that show the French presence in these cities. Then, create a travel brochure.

Citizenship Cooperative Activity

24. When you become 18 years old, you can begin to exercise one of your most important rights—the right to vote. First, however, you must register. Work with a partner to find out where you can obtain a voter registration card. Make a list of the information you will need for the card. Share your information with the class.

Economics Activity

25. Most societies use a medium of exchange—something accepted in return for goods and services. Money is one medium of exchange. In the colonies, however, the people never had a form of money that had the same value everywhere and was accepted by everyone. Since using money presented problems, colonists often traded goods without the use of money. This is called barter. Research to find out more about barter. Then answer: What are the advantages of barter?

 ## Alternative Assessment

26. **Portfolio Writing Activity** Examine the painting on page 84. What ideas is the artist presenting? Write a paragraph that answers the question.

The Princeton Review

Standardized Test Practice

Directions: Choose the *best* answer to the following question.

Which colony was founded to put Quaker ideas into practice?

A Plymouth   C Georgia
B Virginia   D Pennsylvania

Test-Taking Tip:

As you read the stem of each multiple-choice question, try to anticipate the answer before you look at the choices. If your answer is one of the choices, it is probably correct.

Making a Compass

Imagine standing on board your ship. As captain of the ship, you are in charge of the lives of about 150 crewmembers. Now your ship is in the middle of the ocean, and you are looking all around you. All you can see is water—water everywhere. How in the world will you know where to find land? You are facing the same problem that Marco Polo, Christopher Columbus, Vasco da Gama, and other explorers faced. What is the solution? Use a compass to find direction.

The Way It Was

Chinese sailors probably first developed and used the compass in the early 1000s or 1100s to guide their ships. The Arabs then used this technology and passed it on to the Europeans. The Europeans improved the magnetic compass, and during the age of exploration European sailors used it to figure out where they were and how far they were from land.

Believe It or Not

In the late 1800s, some shipbuilders built ships with iron and steel. However, these metals interfered with the magnetic compasses sailors used. Eventually navigators learned to make the necessary adjustments to the compass so it would work properly.

Compasses come in many shapes and sizes.

Materials

✓ a paper clip (straightened)

✓ a small bar magnet (a refrigerator magnet will work if you don't have a bar magnet)

✓ a small piece of cork (or Styrofoam)

✓ a small cup or bowl of water on which to float the cork and paper clip

✓ a sheet of plain paper and a pen

What To Do

After your teacher has organized you into groups of three or four, follow the directions below.

1 Make sure that the paper clip has been straightened. Then, run the magnet over the paper clip a few times, always in the same direction. By doing this, you are magnetizing the paper clip.

2 Carefully push one end of the paper clip into one end of the cork (or Styrofoam). Carefully drive the paper clip through the length of the cork, stopping when it is securely attached to the cork.

3 Float the cork and paper clip in the cup or bowl of water. (The paper clip should be above the water, not touching it.) Next, cut out a ring of paper to place outside of the bowl. On the paper ring, mark the compass directions N, E, S, and W. Your compass is now complete.

4 Place your compass on a stable surface, such as a table. What happens?

5 Experiment further by placing the magnet near your compass, and observing what happens.

6 Turn your compass to face each of the room's four walls. Read your compass to determine how accurately it indicates the north, south, east, and west sides of the classroom.

Project Report

1. Why did European explorers use compasses? Why would sailors today use compasses?

2. How do compasses work? Why must compass needles be magnetized?

3. What happened to your compass when you placed it on the table? What direction did it point? Why?

4. **Drawing Conclusions** What would occur if you moved a magnet around your compass? Why would this happen?

Go a Step Further

Put your compass to use! Choose a partner. While your partner is out of the room, hide a scrap of paper with a message on it somewhere in the room. When your partner returns to the room, give directions on how to find the paper using the compass. Try following the directions yourself first to make sure they work.

CHAPTER 4

The Colonies Grow

1607–1770

Why It Matters

Independence was a spirit that became evident early in the history of the American people. The spirit of independence contributed to the birth of a new nation, one with a new government and a culture that was distinct from those of other countries.

The Impact Today

Americans continue to value independence. For example:
* *The right to practice one's own religion freely is safeguarded.*
* *Americans value the right to express themselves freely and to make their own laws.*

The American Journey *Video* *The chapter 4 video, "Middle Passage: Voyages of the Slave Trade," examines the beginnings of the slave trade, focusing on the Middle Passage.*

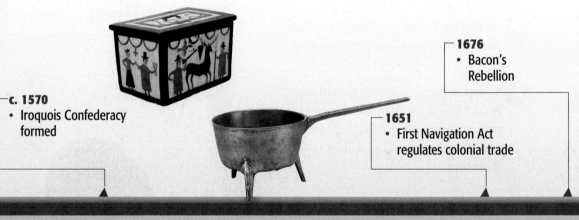

c. 1570
* Iroquois Confederacy formed

1651
* First Navigation Act regulates colonial trade

1676
* Bacon's Rebellion

The Americas

| 1550 | 1600 | 1650 |

World

1603
* Tokugawa Shogunate emerges in Japan

1610
* Galileo observes planets and stars with telescope

1644
* Qing Dynasty established in China

The South Side of St. John's Street by **Joseph B. Smith** This painting shows a quiet neighborhood in New York City during the late 1760s.

FOLDABLES™
Study Organizer

Compare-Contrast Study Foldable Make the following (Venn diagram) foldable to compare and contrast the peoples involved in the French and Indian War.

Step 1 Fold a sheet of paper from side to side, leaving a 2-inch tab uncovered along the side.

> Fold it so the left edge lies 2 inches from the right edge.

Step 2 Turn the paper and fold into thirds.

Step 3 Unfold and cut along the two inside fold lines.

> Cut along the two folds on the front flap to make 3 tabs.

Step 4 Label the foldable as shown.

The French and Indian War
French and Native Americans | Both | British and Colonists

Reading and Writing As you read about the participants of the war, write facts about them under the appropriate tabs of your foldable.

1700s
- Enslaved Africans brought to America

c. 1740
- Great Awakening peaks

1754
- French and Indian War begins

1763
- Proclamation of 1763

1700

1750

1689
- English Bill of Rights signed

1690
- Locke's *Two Treatises of Government*

1702
- England and France at war

1748
- Montesquieu's *The Spirit of Laws*

HISTORY
Online

Chapter Overview
Visit taj.glencoe.com and click on **Chapter 4— Chapter Overviews** to preview chapter information.

Life in the Colonies

Guide to Reading

Main Idea
Each region developed a unique way of life.

Key Terms
subsistence farming, triangular trade, cash crop, diversity, Tidewater, backcountry, overseer

Reading Strategy
Classifying Information As you read Section 1, re-create the diagram below and describe the differences in the economies of the New England, Middle, and Southern Colonies.

Economic Development		
New England	Middle Colonies	Southern Colonies

Read to Learn
- what the triangular trade was and how it affected American society.
- how the regions in the colonies differed from one another.
- why the use of enslaved workers increased in the colonies.

Section Theme
Economic Factors Ways of earning a living varied among the colonies.

Preview of Events

◆1700   ◆1750   ◆1800

1700s
Thousands of enslaved Africans are brought to America

1750
South Carolina and Georgia have the fastest-growing colonial economies

c. 1760
New York City's population reaches 18,000

Colonial spinning wheel

★AN★
American Story

    In 1760 Englishman Andrew Burnaby traveled throughout the North American colonies, observing American life. He could not imagine that these colonies would ever join in union for they were as different from one another as "fire and water," and each colony was jealous of the other. "In short, such is the difference of character, of manners, of religion, of interest, of the different colonies, that I think . . . were they left to themselves, there would soon be a civil war, from one end of the continent to the other."

New England Colonies

    Although Burnaby believed that the colonies would never unite, the colonies continued to grow. The number of people living in the colonies rose from about 250,000 in 1700 to approximately 2.5 million by the mid-1770s. The population of African Americans increased at an even faster rate—from about 28,000 to more than 500,000.

Immigration was important to this growth. Between 1607 and 1775, almost a million people—an estimated 690,000 Europeans and 278,000 Africans—came to live in the colonies.

Another reason for the growing population was that colonial women tended to marry early and have large families. It was not unusual for a woman to have seven or more children. In addition America, especially New England, turned out to be an unusually healthy place to live. Many babies survived the diseases of childhood to become adults, and many adults lived to an old age.

Most people in New England lived in well-organized towns. In the center of the town stood the meetinghouse, a building used for both church services and town meetings. The meetinghouse faced a piece of land called the green, or common, where cows grazed and the citizen army trained. Farmers lived in the town and worked in fields on its outskirts.

Farming was the main economic activity in all the colonies, but New England farms were smaller than those farther south. Long winters and thin, rocky soil made large-scale farming difficult. Farmers in New England practiced subsistence farming, which means that they generally produced just enough to meet the needs of their families, with little left over to sell or exchange. Most Northern farmers relied on their children for labor. Everyone in the family worked—spinning yarn, preserving fruit, milking cows, fencing in fields, and sowing and harvesting grain.

$ Economics
Commerce in New England

New England also had many small businesses. Some people used the waterpower from the streams on their land to run mills for grinding grain or sawing lumber. Women who made cloth, garments, candles, or soap for their families sometimes made enough of these products to sell or trade. Large towns attracted skilled craftspeople who set themselves up as blacksmiths, shoemakers, furniture makers, gunsmiths, metalsmiths, and printers.

Shipbuilding was an important industry. The lumber for building ships came from the forests of New England and was transported down rivers to the shipyards in coastal towns.

America's *Architecture*

A house design called a "salt box" became popular in many areas. The design featured a square or rectangular house, often with an addition in the back that provided more living space. These houses were called salt boxes because they were similar in shape to the wooden box in which salt was kept in colonial kitchens. **Where was the meetinghouse located in many towns?**

Pineapples symbolized hospitality in colonial America.

The region also relied on fishing. New Englanders fished for cod, halibut, crabs, oysters, and lobsters. Some ventured far out to sea to hunt whales for oil and whalebone.

Colonial Trade

As the center of the shipping trade in America, northern coastal cities linked the northern colonies with the Southern Colonies, and linked America to other parts of the world. New England ships sailed south along the Atlantic coast, trading with the colonies and with islands in the **West Indies.** They crossed the Atlantic carrying fish, furs, and fruit to trade for manufactured goods in England and Europe.

These colonial merchant ships followed many different trading routes. Some went directly to England and back. Others followed routes that came to be called the triangular trade because the routes formed a triangle. On one leg of such a route, ships brought sugar and molasses from the West Indies to the New England colonies. In New England, the molasses would be made into rum. Next, the rum and other goods were shipped to West Africa and traded for enslaved

Africans. Slavery was widely practiced in West Africa. Many West African kingdoms enslaved those they defeated in war. Some of the enslaved were sold to Arab slave traders. Others were forced to mine gold or work in farm fields. With the arrival of the Europeans, enslaved Africans also began to be shipped to America in exchange for trade goods.

The Middle Passage

The inhumane part of the triangular trade, shipping enslaved Africans to the West Indies, was known as the **Middle Passage.** Olaudah Equiano, a young African forced onto a ship to America, later described the voyage:

66 I was soon put down under the decks. . . . The closeness of the place, and the heat of the climate, added to the number in the ship, which was so crowded that each had scarcely room to turn himself, almost suffocated us. . . . The shrieks of the women, and the groans of the dying, rendered [made] the whole a scene of horror. 99

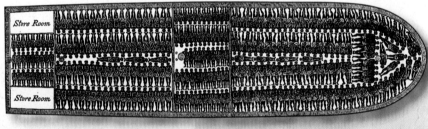

Slaves packed in a ship

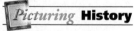

Picturing **History**

A deck plan (above) reveals tightly packed ranks of slaves on a ship bound from Africa to the Americas. Once docked, the ship's human cargo was replaced with rum or molasses. **What does the term "Middle Passage" refer to?**

102

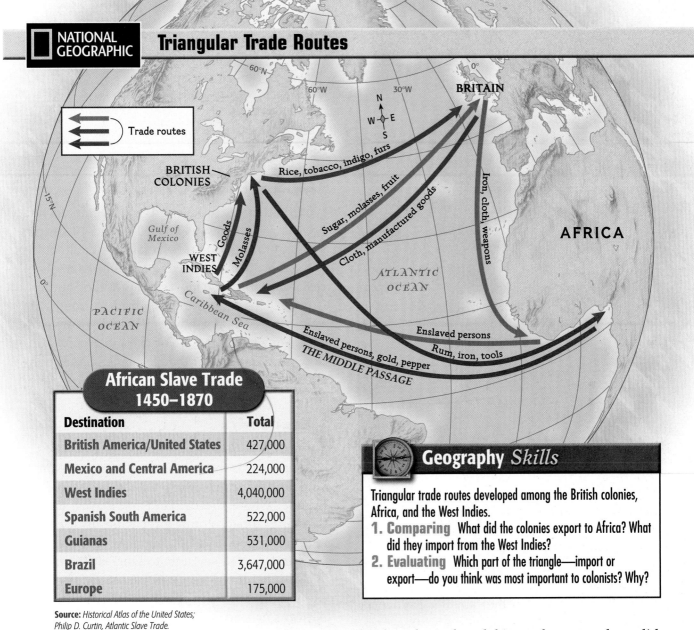

Trade routes

Rice, tobacco, indigo, furs

Sugar, molasses, fruit

Cloth, manufactured goods

Iron, cloth, weapons

Goods

Molasses

Enslaved persons, gold, pepper
THE MIDDLE PASSAGE

Enslaved persons

Rum, iron, tools

BRITAIN

AFRICA

BRITISH COLONIES

Gulf of Mexico

WEST INDIES

Caribbean Sea

PACIFIC OCEAN

ATLANTIC OCEAN

African Slave Trade 1450–1870	
Destination	**Total**
British America/United States	427,000
Mexico and Central America	224,000
West Indies	4,040,000
Spanish South America	522,000
Guianas	531,000
Brazil	3,647,000
Europe	175,000

Source: *Historical Atlas of the United States;*
Philip D. Curtin, Atlantic Slave Trade.

Geography *Skills*

Triangular trade routes developed among the British colonies, Africa, and the West Indies.

1. **Comparing** What did the colonies export to Africa? What did they import from the West Indies?
2. **Evaluating** Which part of the triangle—import or export—do you think was most important to colonists? Why?

With its trade, shipbuilding, and fishing, New England's economy flourished. Although good farmland was lacking in much of the region, New England's population grew and towns and cities developed.

Reading Check **Explaining** Where was the shipping hub in America?

The Middle Colonies

The Middle Colonies enjoyed fertile soil and a slightly milder climate than New England's. Farmers in this region cultivated larger areas of land and produced bigger harvests than did New Englanders. In New York and Pennsylvania, farmers grew large quantities of wheat and other cash crops, crops that could be sold easily in markets in the colonies and overseas.

Farmers sent cargoes of wheat and livestock to New York City and Philadelphia for shipment, and these cities became busy ports. By the 1760s New York, with 18,000 people, and Philadelphia, with 24,000 people, were the largest cities in the American colonies.

Industries of the Middle Colonies

Like the New England Colonies, the Middle Colonies also had industries. Some were home-based crafts such as carpentry and flour

making. Others included larger businesses such as lumbering, mining, and small-scale manufacturing.

One iron mill in northern New Jersey employed several hundred workers, many of them from Germany. Other smaller ironworks operated in New Jersey and Pennsylvania.

German Immigrants

Most of the nearly 100,000 German immigrants who came to America in the colonial era settled in Pennsylvania. Using agricultural methods developed in Europe, these immigrants became successful farmers.

The Germans belonged to a number of Protestant groups. Together with the Dutch, Swedish, and other non-English immigrants, they gave the Middle Colonies a cultural diversity, or variety, that was not found in New England. With the diversity came tolerance for religious and cultural differences.

✔ **Reading Check** **Explaining** What are cash crops?

The Southern Colonies

With their rich soil and warm climate, the Southern Colonies were well suited to certain kinds of farming. Southern farmers could cultivate large areas of land and produce harvests of cash crops. Because most settlers in the Southern Colonies made their living from farming the land, they did not have the need to develop commerce or industry. For the most part, London merchants rather than local merchants managed Southern trade.

ⓢ Economics

Tobacco and Rice

Tobacco was the principal cash crop of Maryland and Virginia. Most tobacco was sold in Europe, where the demand for it was strong. Growing tobacco and preparing it for sale required a good deal of labor. At first planters used indentured servants to work in the fields. When indentured servants became scarce and expensive, Southern planters used enslaved Africans instead.

Slaveholders with large properties became rich on tobacco. Sometimes, however, a surplus, or extra amounts, of tobacco on the market caused prices to fall and then the growers' profits also fell. In time, some tobacco planters switched to growing other crops such as corn and wheat.

The main cash crop in South Carolina and Georgia was rice. In low-lying areas along the coast, planters built dams to create rice fields, called paddies. These fields were flooded when the rice was young and drained when the rice was ready to harvest. Work in the rice paddies involved standing knee-deep in the mud all day with no protection from the blazing sun or the biting insects.

Because rice harvesting required so much strenuous work, rice growers relied on slave labor. Rice proved to be even more profitable than tobacco. As it became popular in southern Europe, the price of rice rose steadily. By the 1750s South Carolina and Georgia had the fastest-growing economies in the colonies.

Tidewater and Backcountry

Most of the large Southern plantations were located in the Tidewater, a region of flat, low-lying plains along the seacoast. Plantations, or large farms, were often located on rivers so crops could be shipped to market by boat.

Each plantation was a self-contained community with fields stretching out around a cluster of buildings. The planter's wife supervised the main house and the household servants. A plantation also included slave cabins, barns and stables, and outbuildings such as carpenter and blacksmith shops and storerooms. Even kitchens were in separate buildings. A large plantation might also have its own chapel and school.

West of the Tidewater lay a region of hills and forests climbing up toward the **Appalachian Mountains.** This region was known as the backcountry and was settled in part by hardy newcomers to the colonies. The backcountry settlers grew corn and tobacco on small farms. They usually worked alone or with their families, although some had one or two enslaved Africans to help.

In the Southern Colonies, the independent small farmers of the backcountry outnumbered the large plantation owners. The plantation owners, however, had greater wealth and more influence. They controlled the economic and political life of the region.

Reading Check **Comparing** How were the settlers of the Tidewater different from those of the backcountry?

History *Through Art*

The Old Plantation by an unknown artist
This watercolor from the 1700s shows a traditional African celebration on a Southern plantation. **Where would you be more likely to find enslaved African laborers—in the Tidewater or backcountry? Why?**

Slavery

Most enslaved Africans lived on plantations. Some did housework, but most worked in the fields and often suffered great cruelty. The large plantation owners hired overseers, or bosses, to keep the slaves working hard.

By the early 1700s, many of the colonies had issued **slave codes,** strict rules governing the behavior and punishment of enslaved Africans. Some codes did not allow slaves to leave the plantation without written permission from the master. Some made it illegal to teach enslaved people to read or write. They usually allowed slaves to be whipped for minor offenses and hanged or burned to death for serious crimes. Those who ran away were often caught and punished severely.

African Traditions

Although the enslaved Africans had strong family ties, their families were often torn apart. Slaveholders could sell a family member to another slaveholder. Slaves found a source of strength in their African roots. They developed a culture that drew on the languages and customs of their West African homelands.

Some enslaved Africans learned trades such as carpentry, blacksmithing, or weaving. Skilled

Banning Slavery

Slavery was first outlawed in the northern colonies. This is not true. Slavery was first outlawed in the colony of Georgia in 1735. Georgia eventually made slavery legal again.

workers could sometimes set up shops, sharing their profits with the slaveholders. Those lucky enough to be able to buy their freedom joined the small population of free African Americans.

Criticism of Slavery

Although the majority of white Southerners were not slaveholders, slavery played an important role in the economic success of the Southern Colonies. That success, however, was built on the idea that one human being could own another. Some colonists did not believe in slavery. Many Puritans refused to hold enslaved people. In Pennsylvania, Quakers and Mennonites condemned slavery. Eventually the debate over slavery would erupt in a bloody war, pitting North against South.

✓ **Reading Check** **Describing** What did slave codes do?

SECTION 1 ASSESSMENT

Checking for Understanding

1. **Key Terms** Use each of these terms in a sentence that will help explain its meaning: subsistence farming, triangular trade, cash crop.
2. **Reviewing Facts** Identify the various economic activities carried on in the Middle Colonies.

Reviewing Themes

3. **Economic Factors** How did New England's natural resources help its commerce?

Critical Thinking

4. **Comparing** How did farming in New England compare with farming in the Southern Colonies? Use a chart like the one below to answer the question.

	Similarities	Differences
New England		
Southern Colonies		

5. **Making Inferences** How do you think plantation owners in the Southern Colonies justified their use of enslaved Africans?

Analyzing Visuals

6. **Geography Skills** Study the map on page 103. What goods were traded from the British Colonies to Great Britain? From the West Indies to the British Colonies?

Interdisciplinary Activity

Informative Writing Imagine you live in New England in the 1750s and are visiting cousins on a farm in the Carolinas. Write a letter to a friend at home describing your visit to the farm.

America's LITERATURE

Olaudah Equiano
(c. 1750–1797)

Olaudah Equiano was 11 years old when he and his sister were kidnapped by slavetraders. Olaudah was taken to the West Indies and sold into slavery. His life story includes memories of his childhood in Africa. He wrote his story after receiving the name Gustavus Vassa from one of his masters and buying his freedom. Published during the time of the movement to end slavery, Equiano's work became a best-seller.

READ TO DISCOVER

This selection begins after Olaudah has been kidnapped and forced to endure the terrifying trip across the Atlantic Ocean aboard a slave ship. As you read, think about what life must have been like for Africans who were sold into slavery.

READER'S DICTIONARY

parcel: group
lots: groups
toil: work

The Kidnapped Prince

Right away we were taken to a merchant's yard, where we were all penned up together like so many sheep. When I looked out at the town, everything was new to me. The houses were built with bricks, in stories, and were completely different from any I had seen in Africa. I was still more astonished at seeing people on horseback. . . .

We were not many days in the merchant's custody before we were sold—like this:

Someone beat a drum. Then all the buyers rushed at once into the yard where we were penned to choose the **parcel** of us that they liked best. They rushed from one group of us to another, with tremendous noise and eager faces, terrifying us all.

Three men who were sold were brothers. They were sold in different **lots.** I still remember how they cried when they were parted. Probably they never saw each other again.

I didn't know it, but this happened all the time in slave sales. Parents lost their children; brothers lost their sisters. Husbands lost their wives.

We had already lost our homes, our countries, and almost everyone we loved. The people who did the selling and buying could have done

it without separating us from our very last relatives and friends. They already could live in riches from our misery and **toil.** What possible advantage did they gain from this refinement of cruelty?

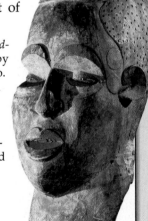

From *The Kidnapped Prince* by Olaudah Equiano. Adapted by Ann Cameron. Copyright © 1995 by Ann Cameron. Reprinted by permission of Alfred A. Knopf, Inc.

ANALYZING LITERATURE

1. **Recall and Interpret** How did the Africans feel as they were being sold?
2. **Evaluate and Connect** Do you think Olaudah Equiano supports slavery? Explain.

Interdisciplinary Activity

Descriptive Writing Re-read the excerpt and think about what it must have been like to be separated from family members. Write a dialogue you think might occur between two family members as they are about to be separated from each other.

Government, Religion, and Culture

Guide to Reading

Main Idea
The ideals of American democracy and freedom of religion took root during the colonial period.

Key Terms
mercantilism, export, import, smuggling, charter colony, proprietary colony, royal colony, apprentice, literacy

Reading Strategy
Organizing Information As you read the section, re-create the diagram below and identify the three types of English colonies.

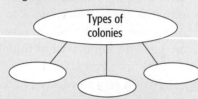

Types of colonies

Read to Learn
• why the Navigation Acts angered the colonists.
• who had the right to vote in colonial legislatures.

Section Theme
Continuity and Change The roots of American democracy, freedom of religion, and public education are found in the American colonial experience.

Preview of Events

♦1630   ♦1670   ♦1710   ♦1750

1636
Harvard College is established

1693
College of William and Mary is founded

1732
Benjamin Franklin publishes *Poor Richard's Almanack*

c. 1740
Great Awakening sweeps through the colonies

From Poor Richard's Almanack

AN American Story

"Fish and Visitors stink after three days."

"Beware of little Expenses: a small Leak will sink a great Ship."

"No gains without pains."

Benjamin Franklin wrote these and other witty sayings for his annual book, *Poor Richard's Almanack*. The last saying—"No gains without pains"—was particularly true in the American colonies in the late 1600s.

English Colonial Rule

In his writings, Benjamin Franklin celebrated a new American spirit. This spirit signaled that Americans were beginning to view themselves differently from the way Great Britain viewed them.

Trouble was brewing in England—and in the colonies—during the mid-1600s. England's monarchy had been restored with Charles II on the throne, but many people were not satisfied with his rule. James II, Charles's successor, attempted to take back the powers Parliament had won during the English Civil War. He also tried to tighten royal control over the colonies.

In 1688 Parliament took action. It forced out James and placed his daughter Mary and her Dutch husband, William of Orange, on the throne. This change, which showed the power of the elected representatives over the monarch, came to be known as the **Glorious Revolution.**

William and Mary signed an **English Bill of Rights** in 1689 guaranteeing certain basic rights to all citizens. This document became part of the heritage of English law that the American colonists shared. It later inspired the people who created the American Bill of Rights.

England viewed its North American colonies as an economic resource. The colonies provided England with raw materials. English manufacturers used these materials to produce finished goods, which they sold to the colonists. This process followed an economic theory called mercantilism. This theory states that as a nation's trade grows, its gold reserves increase, and the nation becomes more powerful. To make money from its trade, England had to export, or sell abroad, more goods than it imported, or bought from foreign markets.

To make certain that only England benefited from trade with the colonies, Parliament passed a series of laws between 1651 and 1673. These laws, called the **Navigation Acts**, directed the flow of goods between England and the colonies. Colonial merchants who had goods to send to England could not use foreign ships— even if those ships offered cheaper rates. The Navigation Acts also prevented the colonists from sending certain products, such as sugar or tobacco, outside England's empire.

Some colonists ignored these laws and began smuggling, or trading illegally with other nations. Controls on trade would later cause even more conflict between the American colonies and England.

✓ Reading Check **Examining** Under mercantilism, who controlled trade and who supplied raw materials?

People In History

Benjamin Franklin 1706–1790

Ben Franklin learned the printer's trade as a young man. By the time he was 23, he owned his own newspaper in Philadelphia. Soon afterward he began publishing *Poor Richard's Almanack*, a calendar filled with advice, philosophy, and wise sayings, such as "Early to bed, early to rise, makes a man healthy, wealthy, and wise."

Franklin was deeply interested in science. He invented the lightning rod, bifocal eyeglasses, and the Franklin stove for heating. Energetic and open-minded, Franklin served in the Pennsylvania Assembly for many years. He founded a hospital, a fire department, America's first lending library, and an academy of higher learning that later became the University of Pennsylvania.

Franklin's greatest services to his fellow Americans would come during the 1770s. As a statesman and patriot, Franklin would help guide the colonies toward independence.

Causes and Effects of the Great Awakening

The Great Awakening

The Great Awakening is the name for the powerful religious revival that swept over the colonies beginning in the 1720s. Christian ministers such as George Whitefield and Jonathan Edwards preached throughout the colonies, drawing huge crowds. The Great Awakening had a lasting effect on the way in which the colonists viewed themselves, their relationships with one another, and their faith.

Causes

- Jonathan Edwards, George Whitefield, and others preach of the need for a revival of religious belief.
- Awareness of the importance of religion in people's lives grows.
- A religious revival sweeps through America in the mid-1700s.

Jonathan Edwards

🔲 Citizenship

Colonial Government

The English colonists brought with them ideas about government that had been developing in England for centuries. By the 1600s the English people had won political liberties, such as trial by jury, that were largely unknown elsewhere. At the heart of the English system were two principles of government. These principles—limited government and representative government—greatly influenced the development of the United States.

By the time the first colonists reached North America, the idea that government was not all-powerful had become an accepted part of the English system of government. The idea first appeared in the Magna Carta that King John was forced to sign in 1215. The Magna Carta established the principle of limited government, in which the power of the king, or government, was limited. This document provided for protection against unjust punishment and against the loss of life, liberty, and property, except according to law. 📖 *(See page 985 of the Appendix for excerpts from the Magna Carta.)*

As the colonies grew, they relied more and more on their own governments to make local laws. By the 1760s there were three types of colonies in America—charter colonies, proprietary colonies, and royal colonies.

Charter Colonies

Connecticut and Rhode Island, the charter colonies, were established by settlers who had been given a charter, or a grant of rights and privileges. These colonists elected their own governors and the members of the legislature. Great Britain had the right to approve the governor, but the governor could not veto the acts of the legislature.

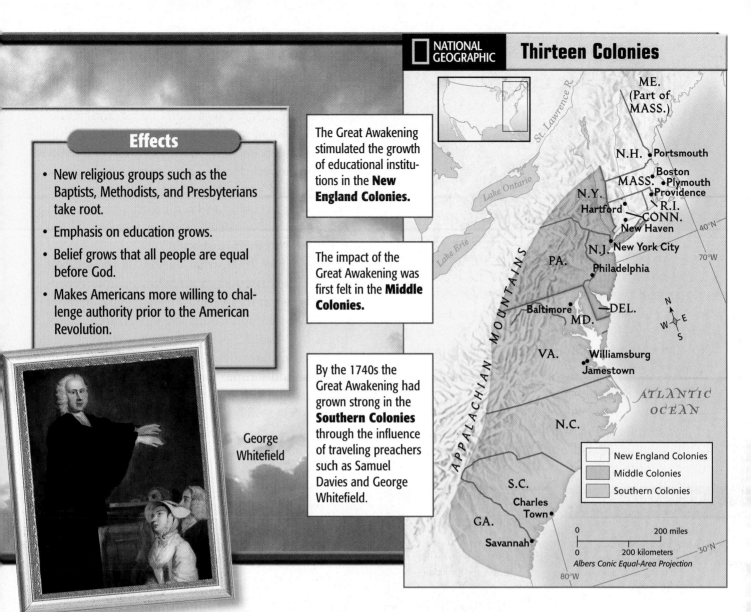

Effects

- New religious groups such as the Baptists, Methodists, and Presbyterians take root.
- Emphasis on education grows.
- Belief grows that all people are equal before God.
- Makes Americans more willing to challenge authority prior to the American Revolution.

George Whitefield

The Great Awakening stimulated the growth of educational institutions in the **New England Colonies.**

The impact of the Great Awakening was first felt in the **Middle Colonies.**

By the 1740s the Great Awakening had grown strong in the **Southern Colonies** through the influence of traveling preachers such as Samuel Davies and George Whitefield.

ME. (Part of MASS.)

N.H. Portsmouth

MASS. Boston Plymouth Providence

N.Y. Hartford R.I. CONN. New Haven

N.J. New York City

PA. Philadelphia

Baltimore DEL. MD.

VA. Williamsburg Jamestown

N.C.

S.C. Charles Town

GA. Savannah

ATLANTIC OCEAN

APPALACHIAN MOUNTAINS

Lake Ontario

Lake Erie

St. Lawrence R.

40°N

70°W

30°N

80°W

New England Colonies
Middle Colonies
Southern Colonies

0   200 miles
0   200 kilometers
Albers Conic Equal-Area Projection

Proprietary Colonies

The proprietary colonies—Delaware, Maryland, and Pennsylvania—were ruled by proprietors. These were individuals or groups to whom Britain had granted land. Proprietors were generally free to rule as they wished. They appointed the governor and members of the upper house of the legislature, while the colonists elected the lower house.

Royal Colonies

By the 1760s Georgia, Massachusetts, New Hampshire, New Jersey, New York, North Carolina, South Carolina, and Virginia were royal colonies. Britain directly ruled all royal colonies. In each, the king appointed a governor and council, known as the upper house. The colonists elected an assembly, called the lower house. The governor and members of the council usually did what the British leaders told them to do. However, this often led to conflict with the colonists in the assembly, especially when officials tried to enforce tax laws and trade restrictions.

Voting Rights

Colonial legislatures gave only some people a voice in government. Generally, white men who owned property had the right to vote; however, most women, indentured servants, landless poor, and African Americans could not vote. In spite of these limits, a higher proportion of people was involved in government in the colonies than anywhere in the European world. This strong participation gave Americans training that was valuable when the colonies became independent.

Reading Check **Drawing Inferences** How did the Magna Carta affect government in the colonies?

An Emerging Culture

From the 1720s through the 1740s, a religious revival called the **Great Awakening** swept through the colonies. In New England and the Middle Colonies, ministers called for "a new birth," a return to the strong faith of earlier days. One of the outstanding preachers was **Jonathan Edwards** of Massachusetts. People thought that his sermons were powerful and convincing.

The English preacher **George Whitefield,** who arrived in the colonies in 1739, helped spread the religious revival. Whitefield inspired worshipers in churches and open fields from New England to Georgia. The Great Awakening led to the formation of many new churches.

Family Roles

Throughout the colonies, people adapted their traditions to the new conditions of life in America. Religion, education, and the arts contributed to a new American culture. The family formed the foundation of colonial society.

A colonial farm was both home and workplace. Mothers and fathers cared for their children. Women cooked, made butter and cheese, and preserved food. They spun yarn, made clothes, and tended chickens and cows. Men worked in the fields and built barns, houses, and fences. In many areas, women worked in the fields next to their husbands.

Men were the formal heads of the households. They managed the farms and represented the family in community affairs. In most churches, women could attend church meetings, but could not speak, vote, or serve as clergy. Families often arranged for their sons to work as indentured servants for farmers or to serve as apprentices, or learning assistants, to craft workers who taught them a trade. Married women were considered under their husbands' authority and had few rights.

TECHNOLOGY & History

Colonial Printing Press

Life in the colonies often revolved around local printers who produced pamphlets, small flyers, books, and newspapers. The first printing press in the American colonies was established by Stephen Daye in 1639.

Type is made up of large numbers of single letters that can be moved and reused.

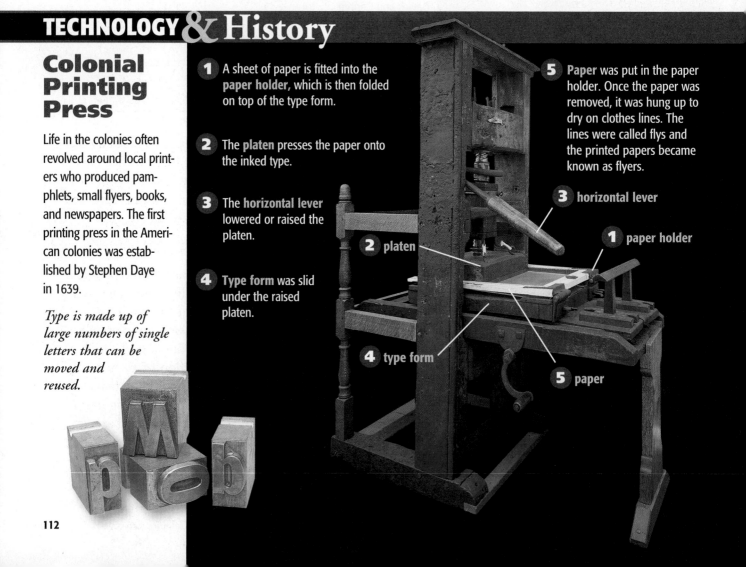

1 A sheet of paper is fitted into the **paper holder,** which is then folded on top of the type form.

2 The **platen** presses the paper onto the inked type.

3 The **horizontal lever** lowered or raised the platen.

4 **Type form** was slid under the raised platen.

5 **Paper** was put in the paper holder. Once the paper was removed, it was hung up to dry on clothes lines. The lines were called flys and the printed papers became known as flyers.

3 horizontal lever

1 paper holder

2 platen

4 type form

5 paper

Women in cities and towns sometimes held jobs outside the home. Young unmarried women might work for wealthy families as maids, cooks, and nurses. Widows might work as teachers, nurses, and seamstresses. They also opened shops and inns. Widows and women who had never married could run businesses and own property, even though they could not vote. 📖 *(See page 960 of the Primary Sources Library for the selection, "What is an American?")*

Education

Most colonists valued education. Children were often taught to read and write at home by their parents. In New England and Pennsylvania, in particular, school systems were set up to make sure that everyone could read and study the Bible. In 1647 the Massachusetts Puritans passed a public education law. Each community with 50 or more households had to have a school supported by taxes. Although some communities did not set up schools, most did.

By 1750, New England had a very high level of literacy, the ability to read and write. Approximately 85 percent of the men and about half of the women could read. Many learned to read from *The New England Primer,* which combined lessons in good conduct with reading and writing.

Many colonial schools were run by widows or unmarried women. In the Middle Colonies, some schools were run by Quakers and other religious groups. In the towns and cities, craftspeople set up night schools for their apprentices.

The colonies' early colleges were founded to train ministers. The first was Harvard College, established in 1636 by the Puritans in Cambridge, Massachusetts. Anglicans founded William and Mary College in Virginia in 1693.

The Enlightenment

By the middle of the 1700s, many educated colonists were influenced by the **Enlightenment.** This movement, which began in Europe, spread the idea that knowledge, reason, and science could improve society. In the colonies, the Enlightenment increased interest in science. People observed nature, staged experiments, and published their findings. The best known American scientist was Benjamin Franklin.

Freedom of the Press

In 1735 John Peter Zenger of the *New York Weekly Journal* faced charges of libel for printing a critical report about the royal governor of New York. Andrew Hamilton argued that free speech was a basic right of English people. He defended Zenger by asking the jury to base its decision on whether Zenger's article was true, not whether it was offensive. The jury found Zenger not guilty. At the time the case attracted little attention, but today it is regarded as an important step in the development of a free press in America.

✓ **Reading Check** **Analyzing** What was the impact of the Great Awakening?

SECTION 2 ASSESSMENT

Checking for Understanding

1. **Key Terms** Use each of these terms in a complete sentence that will help explain its meaning: export, charter colony, proprietary colony, apprentice, literacy.
2. **Reviewing the Facts** Identify some contributions of women inside and outside the home.

Reviewing Themes

3. **Continuity and Change** Why did the Navigation Acts anger the colonists?

Critical Thinking

4. **Drawing Conclusions** Why did Andrew Hamilton defend John Peter Zenger and free speech?
5. **Determining Cause and Effect** Re-create the diagram below and describe the effects of the Great Awakening.

```
           ⟨⟩
Great ───── ⟨⟩
Awakening
           ⟨⟩
```

Analyzing Visuals

6. **Picturing History** Examine the printing press on page 112. Who established the first printing press in the colonies? How do you think the colonists communicated their ideas before printed material was widely used?

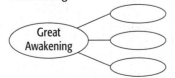

Interdisciplinary Activity

Government Draw a chart that shows the structure of a royal colony, a proprietary colony, and a charter colony.

What were people's lives like in the past?

What—and who—were people talking about? What did they eat? What did they do for fun? These two pages will give you some clues to everyday life in the U.S. as you step back in time with TIME Notebook.

Profile

EDWARD WINSLOW *was 25 when he sailed on the* Mayflower *to Massachusetts. Winslow helped found Plymouth Colony, served as the colony's governor three times—and still found time to sit down to the very first Thanksgiving celebrated in the British colonies in the fall of 1621. Here's part of what he wrote about the first big feast:*

"OUR HARVEST BEING GOTTEN IN, OUR GOVERNOR sent four men on the fowling (*hunt for fowl*), that we might … rejoice together after we had gathered the fruits of our labors. In one day, they killed as much fowl as … served the company almost a week. At which time, … many of the Indians came amongst us … with some ninety men whom for three days we entertained and feasted…."

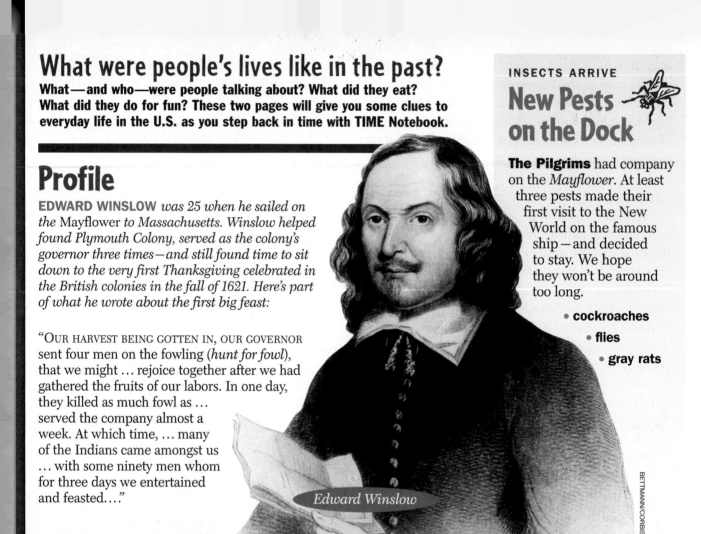

Edward Winslow

INSECTS ARRIVE
New Pests on the Dock

The Pilgrims had company on the *Mayflower*. At least three pests made their first visit to the New World on the famous ship—and decided to stay. We hope they won't be around too long.

- cockroaches
- flies
- gray rats

COLONIAL EVENTS

Virginia Is Number 1

Here's a list of events that happened first in 1619 in Virginia. One of the facts is wrong. Can you figure out the one that doesn't belong?

1 First boatload of African slaves

2 First labor strike

3 First elected lawmakers

4 First time English settlers can own land

5 First daily newspaper

6 First boatload of women who agreed to marry colonists in exchange for a ticket across the Atlantic

answer: 5

POPULAR FOOD

Have Your Corn Cake – and Eat It Too!

This New World meal is all the rage in the colonies.

Stir one cup of coarse cornmeal grits into three cups of water.

Place on stove. Simmer.

Remove from heat when all the water is absorbed. Let it cool.

Shape the mixture into two round, flat cakes on a floured work surface.

Bake it in a hot oven for 45 minutes.

Serve warm or cold with freshly churned butter.

VERBATIM

WHAT PEOPLE ARE SAYING

❝…I found some black people about me, and I believe some were those who had brought me on board and had been receiving their pay….I asked them if we were not to be eaten by those white men with horrible looks, red faces, and long hair.❞

OLAUDAH EQUIANO,
11-year-old kidnapped from his home in what is now Nigeria and brought to America as an enslaved person, on his first day on the slave ship

❝For pottage and puddings and custards and pies / Our pumpkins and parsnips are common supplies. We have pumpkins at morning and pumpkins at noon, / If it were not for pumpkin, / We should be undone.❞

AMERICAN FOLK SONG,
a tribute to the pumpkin

NUMBERS

THE COLONIES AT THE TIME

1,500 Number of English children in 1627 who were kidnapped and sent to work as servants in Virginia

80% Percentage of colonists who died in Jamestown, Virginia, during the winter of 1609–10 after getting so hungry they ate rats, snakes, and horsehide

65% Percentage of colonists who could read in 1620

2,500 Number of trees needed to build a ship the size of the *Mayflower*

NORTH WIND PICTURES

0 Number of chairs set at the dinner table for children— only adults sat while eating

50 Number of pounds of tobacco colonists in Virginia were fined if they did not go to church in the early 1600s

France and Britain Clash

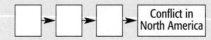
Guide to Reading

Main Idea
Rivalry between Great Britain and France led to a long-lasting conflict.

Key Terms
Iroquois Confederacy, militia

Reading Strategy
Organizing Information As you read the section, re-create the diagram below and describe the events that led to conflict in North America.

☐ → ☐ → ☐ → Conflict in North America

Read to Learn
• how wars in Europe spread to the American colonies.
• about the purpose of the Albany Plan of Union.

Section Theme
Continuity and Change American colonists and Native American groups were drawn into the clash between France and Britain.

Preview of Events

♦1740   ♦1750   ♦1760

1745
New England troops seize Fort Louisbourg from France

1753
George Washington sent to Ohio country to protest French actions

1754
Benjamin Franklin proposes Albany Plan of Union

Powderhorn, French and Indian War

AN American Story

In 1689 England and France began competing to be the most powerful nation in Europe. This contest for power went on for generations, with only short intervals of peace. In 1758 writer Nathaniel Ames noted, "The parts of North America which may be claimed by Great Britain or France are of as much worth as either kingdom. That fertile country to the west of the Appalachian Mountains [is the] 'Garden of the World'!"

British-French Rivalry

Britain and France had been competing for wealth for centuries. By 1700 they were two of the strongest powers in Europe. Their long rivalry aroused bitter feelings between British and French colonists in North America.

As the growing population of the American colonies pushed up against French-held territory, hostility between England and France increased. At the same time, some land companies wanted to explore opportunities in the **Ohio River valley.** However, the French, who traded throughout the Ohio country, regarded this territory as their own. They had no intention of letting British colonists share in their profitable fur trade.

In the 1740s British fur traders went into the Ohio country. They built a fort deep in the territory of the Miami people at a place called Pickawillany. Acting quickly, the French attacked Pickawillany and drove the British traders out of Ohio. The French then built a string of forts along the rivers of the upper Ohio Valley, closer to the British colonies than ever before. Two mighty powers—Great Britain and France—were headed for a showdown in North America.

In the early 1700s, Britain had gained control of Nova Scotia, Newfoundland, and the Hudson Bay region. In the 1740s French troops raided towns in Maine and New York. In response a force of New Englanders went north and captured the important French fortress at **Louisbourg** on Cape Breton Island, north of Nova Scotia. Later Britain returned Louisbourg to France, much to the disgust of the New England colonists.

Native Americans Take Sides

The French traders and the British colonists knew that Native American help would make a difference in their struggle for North America. The side that received the best trade terms from Native Americans and the most help in the war would probably win the contest for control of North America.

The French had many Native American allies. Unlike the British, the French were interested mainly in trading for furs—not in taking over Native American land. The French also had generally better relations with Native Americans. French trappers and fur traders often married Native American women and followed their customs. French missionaries traveled through the area, converting many Native Americans to Catholicism.

During the wars between Great Britain and France, Native Americans often helped the French by raiding British settlements. In 1704, for example, the Abenaki people joined the French in an attack on the British frontier outpost at Deerfield, Massachusetts, in which almost 50 settlers were killed.

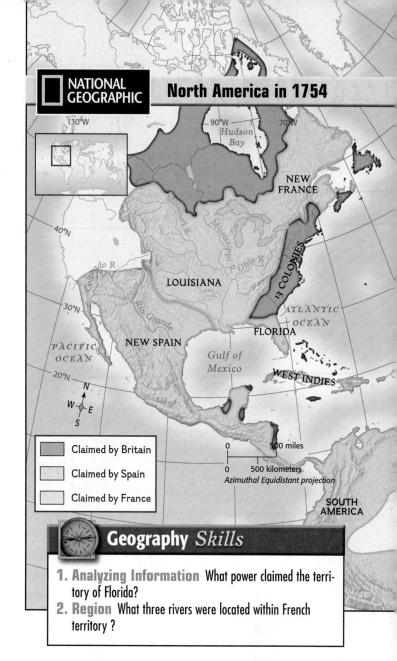

NATIONAL GEOGRAPHIC **North America in 1754**

Claimed by Britain
Claimed by Spain
Claimed by France

0   500 miles
0   500 kilometers
Azimuthal Equidistant projection

Geography *Skills*

1. **Analyzing Information** What power claimed the territory of Florida?
2. **Region** What three rivers were located within French territory?

The Iroquois Confederacy

The most powerful group of Native Americans in the East was the Iroquois Confederacy, based in New York. When the confederacy was first formed in about 1570, it included five nations—the Mohawk, Seneca, Cayuga, Onondaga, and Oneida. Other groups later joined or were conquered by the Iroquois.

The Iroquois managed to remain independent by trading with both the British and the French. By skillfully playing the British and French against each other, the Iroquois dominated the area around the Great Lakes.

By the mid-1700s, however, the Iroquois came under greater pressure as the British moved into the Ohio Valley. Eventually the leaders of the confederacy gave certain trading rights to the

TWO VIEWPOINTS

I Claim This Land!

In the sixteenth century, Europeans became aware of a larger world around them—a world where they could claim new lands and profits. Soon a desire arose in England and France to conquer these lands and the people in them, and a race began to be the first to make those claims.

Drake Claims South and North America for England, June 1579

This country our general named Albion, and that for two causes; the one in respect of the white banks and cliffs, . . . that it might have some affinity [similarity], even in name also, with our own country, which was sometime so called.

Before we went from there, our general caused to be set up, a monument of our being there; as also of her majesties, and successors right and title to that kingdom, namely, a plate of brass, fast nailed to a great and firm post; whereon is [carved] her graces name, and the day and year of our arrival there, and of the free giving up, of the province and kingdom, both by the king and people, into her majesties hands. . . .

Sieur de St. Lusson Claims West and Northwest America for France, 1671

In the name of the Most High, Mighty, and Redoubted Monarch, Louis the Fourteenth of that name, Most Christian King of France and Navarre, I take possession of this place, Ste. Marie of the Sault, as also of Lakes Huron and Superior, the Island of Manitoulin, and all countries, rivers, lakes, and streams . . . both those which have been discovered and those which may be discovered hereafter, in all their length and breadth, bounded on the one side by the seas of the North and of the West, and on the other by the South Sea: Declaring to the nations thereof that from this time forth they are vassals [servants] of his Majesty, bound to obey his laws and follow his customs. . . .

Francis Drake

Learning From History

1. How are the two accounts similar?
2. Why do you think these men held such formal ceremonies when claiming a piece of land?

British and reluctantly became their allies. By taking this step, the Iroquois upset the balance of power between the French and British that had been so difficult to establish.

> **Reading Check** **Explaining** Why were Native Americans more likely to help the French than help the British?

American Colonists Take Action

A group of Virginians had plans for settling the Ohio Valley. In the fall of 1753 Governor Robert Dinwiddie of Virginia sent a 21-year-old planter and surveyor named **George Washington** into the Ohio country. Washington's mission was to tell the French that they were trespassing on territory claimed by Great Britain and demand that they leave.

Washington delivered the message, but it did no good. "The French told me," Washington said later, "that it was their absolute design to take possession of the Ohio, and by God they would do it."

Washington's First Command

In the spring of 1754, Dinwiddie made Washington a lieutenant colonel and sent him back to the Ohio country with a militia—a group of civilians trained to fight in emergencies—of 150 men. The militia had instructions to build a fort where the Allegheny and Monongahela Rivers meet to form the Ohio River—the site of present-day Pittsburgh. When Washington and his troops arrived, they found the French were already building Fort Duquesne (doo•KAYN) on that spot.

Washington established a small post nearby called **Fort Necessity.** Although greatly outnumbered, the forces of the inexperienced Washington attacked a French scouting party. The French surrounded Washington's soldiers and forced them to surrender, but the soldiers were later released and they returned to Virginia. Washington's account of his experience in the Ohio country was published, and his fame spread throughout the colonies and Europe. In spite of his defeat, the colonists regarded Washington as a hero who struck the first blow against the French.

The Albany Plan of Union

While Washington struggled with the French, representatives from New England, New York, Pennsylvania, and Maryland met to discuss the threat of war. In June 1754, the representatives gathered in Albany, New York. They wanted to find a way for the colonies to defend themselves against the French. They also hoped to persuade the Iroquois to take their side against the French.

The representatives adopted a plan suggested by Benjamin Franklin. Known as the **Albany Plan of Union,** Franklin's plan called for "one general government" for 11 of the American colonies. An elected legislature would govern these colonies and would have the power to collect taxes, raise troops, and regulate trade. Not a single colonial assembly approved the plan. None of the colonies were willing to give up any

Fact Fiction Folklore

The Albany Plan

The Albany Plan was the first colonial constitution. Actually it was not the first. In 1639, settlers in Connecticut drew up America's first formal constitution, or charter, called the Fundamental Orders of Connecticut. This document laid out a plan for government that gave the people the right to elect the governor, judges, and representatives to make laws.

of their power. The Albany meeting failed to unite the colonists to fight the French. Disappointed, Franklin wrote,

66Everyone cries, a union is necessary, but when they come to the manner and form of the union, their weak noodles [brains] are perfectly distracted.99

Washington's defeat at Fort Necessity marked the start of a series of clashes and full-scale war. The colonists called it the French and Indian War because they fought two enemies—the French and their Native American allies.

☑ **Reading Check** **Analyzing** What was the purpose of the Albany Plan of Union?

SECTION 3 ASSESSMENT

Checking for Understanding

1. **Key Terms** Write a short paragraph that uses the terms Iroquois Confederacy and militia.
2. **Reviewing Facts** List two reasons the French felt threatened by British interest in the Ohio River valley.

Reviewing Themes

3. **Continuity and Change** Why did colonists consider George Washington a hero, even after he was defeated by the French?

Critical Thinking

4. **Analyzing Primary Sources** Re-read Benjamin Franklin's quote on this page. What was his reaction to the colonies' refusal to accept the Albany Plan of Union?
5. **Evaluating Information** Re-create the diagram below and explain the powers the legislature would have under the Albany Plan.

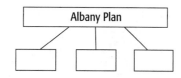

Analyzing Visuals

6. **Geography Skills** Study the map on page 117. What countries claimed land in North America? What power controlled most of what is present-day Canada? If you live in North America, what country controlled the region in which you live?

Interdisciplinary Activity

Expository Writing Make a list of five questions that a reporter might have asked Iroquois leaders after they reluctantly sided with the British.

Critical Thinking SKILLBUILDER

Understanding Cause and Effect

Why Learn This Skill?

You know that if you watch television instead of completing your homework you will receive poor grades. This is an example of a cause-and-effect relationship. The cause—watching television instead of doing homework—leads to an effect—poor grades.

Learning the Skill

A *cause* is any person, event, or condition that makes something happen. What happens as a result is known as an *effect*. These guidelines will help you identify cause and effect.

- Identify two or more events.
- Ask questions about why events occur.
- Look for "clue words" that alert you to cause and effect, such as *because, led to, brought about, produced,* and *therefore.*
- Identify the outcome of events.

Practicing the Skill

Study the cause-and-effect chart about the slave trade on this page. Think about the guidelines listed above. Then answer the questions below.

1 What were some causes of the development of slavery in the colonies?

2 What were some of the short-term effects of enslaving Africans?

3 What was the long-term effect of the development of slavery?

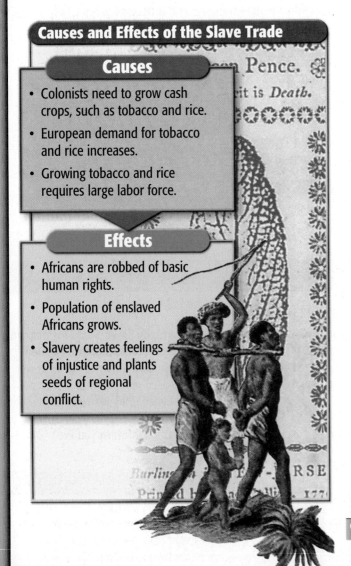

Causes and Effects of the Slave Trade

Causes

- Colonists need to grow cash crops, such as tobacco and rice.
- European demand for tobacco and rice increases.
- Growing tobacco and rice requires large labor force.

Effects

- Africans are robbed of basic human rights.
- Population of enslaved Africans grows.
- Slavery creates feelings of injustice and plants seeds of regional conflict.

Applying the Skill

Understanding Cause and Effect Read an account of a recent event or chain of events in your community newspaper. Determine at least one cause and one effect of that event. Show the cause-and-effect relationship in a chart.

 GO TO

Glencoe's **Skillbuilder Interactive Workbook CD-ROM, Level 1,** provides instruction and practice in key social studies skills.

SECTION 4 The French and Indian War

Guide to Reading

Main Idea
England and France fought for control of North America. The French and Indian War resulted from this struggle.

Key Terms
alliance, speculator

Reading Strategy
Organizing Information As you read the section, re-create the diagram below and describe the effects these events had on the conflict between France and Britain.

Turning point	Effect
Pitt takes charge	
Quebec falls	

Read to Learn
- how British fortunes improved after William Pitt took over direction of the war.
- how Chief Pontiac united his people to fight for their land.

Section Theme
Individual Action Victory or loss in war often depended on the actions of a single leader.

Preview of Events

◆1750   ◆1755   ◆1760   ◆1765

1754
French and Indian War begins

1758
French forces driven out of Fort Duquesne

1759
British forces capture Quebec

1763
Proclamation of 1763 established

Native American maize mask

AN American Story

"These lakes, these woods, and mountains were left [to] us by our ancestors. They are our inheritances, and we will part with them to no one. . . . [Y]ou ought to know that He, the Great Spirit and Master of Life, has provided food for us in these spacious lakes and on the woody mountains. . . ."

These words, spoken by Chief Pontiac, served as a warning to the British colonists who wanted to take Native American lands.

The British Take Action

During the French and Indian War, some Native Americans fought on the side of the British. Many others fought against the British. The war that raged in North America through the late 1750s and early 1760s was one part of a larger struggle between England and France for control of world trade and power on the seas.

In 1754 the governor of Massachusetts announced to the colonial assembly that the French were on the way to "making themselves masters of this Continent."

The British colonists knew that the French were building well-armed forts throughout the Great Lakes region and the Ohio River valley. Their network of **alliances**, or unions, with Native Americans allowed the French to control large areas of land, stretching from the St. Lawrence River in Canada all the way south to New Orleans. The French and their Native American allies seemed to be winning control of the American frontier. The final showdown was about to begin.

During the early stages of the French and Indian War, the British colonists fought the French and the Native Americans with little help from Britain. In 1754, however, the government in London decided to intervene in the conflict. It was alarmed by the new forts the French were building and by George Washington's defeat at Fort Necessity. In the fall of 1754, Great Britain appointed **General Edward Braddock** commander in chief of the British forces in America and sent him to drive the French out of the Ohio Valley.

Braddock Marches to Duquesne

In June 1755, Braddock set out from Virginia with about 1,400 red-coated British soldiers and a smaller number of blue-coated colonial militia. George Washington served as one of his aides. It took Braddock's army several weeks to trek through the dense forest to **Fort Duquesne.** Washington reported that Braddock

❝halted to level every mole-hill and to erect bridges over every brook, by which means we were four days in getting twelve miles.❞

Washington tried to tell Braddock that his army's style of marching was not well suited to fighting in frontier country. Lined up in columns and rows, the troops made easy targets. Braddock ignored the advice.

On July 9 a combined force of Native American warriors and French troops ambushed the British. The French and Native Americans were hidden, firing from behind trees and aiming at the bright uniforms. The British, confused and frightened, could not even see their attackers. One of the survivors of Braddock's army, Captain Orne, later described the "great confusion"

Picturing **History**

Native American warriors and French troops, protected by rocks and trees, fire into General Braddock's army, who were crammed together on a forest trail. **What weakness of the British army contributed to Braddock's defeat?**

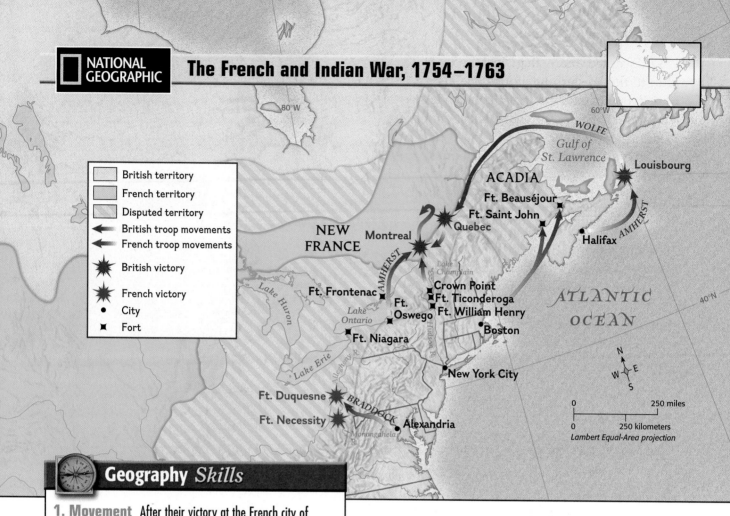

The French and Indian War, 1754–1763

NATIONAL GEOGRAPHIC

Geography Skills

1. **Movement** After their victory at the French city of Quebec, in what direction did the British troops advance?
2. **Drawing Conclusions** Why would Ft. Duquesne be a valuable fort to control?

that overcame Braddock's troops when they were attacked. Braddock called for an orderly retreat, "but the panic was so great he could not succeed." Braddock was killed, and the battle ended in a bitter defeat for the British, who suffered nearly 1,000 casualties. Washington led the survivors back to Virginia.

Britain Declares War on France

The fighting in America helped start a new war in Europe, known as the **Seven Years' War.** After arranging an alliance with Prussia, Britain declared war on France in 1756. Prussia fought France and its allies in Europe while Britain fought France in the Caribbean, India, and North America.

The first years of the war were disastrous for the British and their American colonies. French troops captured several British forts, and their Native American allies began staging raids on frontier farms from New York to Pennsylvania. They killed settlers, burned farmhouses and crops, and drove many families back toward the coast. French forces from Canada captured British forts at Lake Ontario and at Lake George.

Pitt Takes Charge

Great Britain's prospects in America improved after **William Pitt** came to power as secretary of state and then as prime minister. An outstanding military planner, Pitt knew how to pick skilled commanders. He oversaw the war effort from London.

To avoid having to deal with constant arguments from the colonies about the cost of the war, Pitt decided that Great Britain would pay for supplies needed in the war—no matter the cost. In doing so Pitt ran up an enormous debt. After the French and Indian War, the British raised the colonists' taxes to help pay this debt. Pitt had only delayed the moment when the colonists had to pay their share of the bill.

Pitt wanted more than just a clear path to the Western territories. He also intended to conquer French Canada. He sent British troops to North America under the command of such energetic officers as **Jeffrey Amherst** and **James Wolfe.**

In 1758 Amherst and Wolfe led a British assault that recaptured the fortress at Louisbourg. That same year a group of New Englanders, led by British officers, captured Fort Frontenac at Lake Ontario. Still another British force marched across Pennsylvania and forced the French to abandon Fort Duquesne, which was renamed Fort Pitt.

☑ **Reading Check** **Describing** What abilities did William Pitt bring to the post of prime minister?

The Fall of New France

The year 1759 brought so many British victories that people said the church bells of London wore thin with joyous ringing. The British captured several French islands in the West Indies and the city of Havana in Cuba. They defeated the French in India, and destroyed a French fleet that had been sent to reinforce Canada. The greatest victory of the year, though, took place in the heart of New France.

The Battle of Quebec

Perched high on a cliff overlooking the St. Lawrence River, **Quebec,** the capital of New France, was thought to be impossible to attack. In September 1759, British general James Wolfe found a way.

One of Wolfe's scouts spotted a poorly guarded path up the back of the cliff. Wolfe's soldiers overwhelmed the guards posted on the path and then scrambled up the path during the night. The British troops assembled outside the fortress of Quebec on a field called the **Plains of Abraham.** There they surprised and defeated the French army. James Wolfe died in the battle. The French commander, the Marquis de Montcalm, was wounded and died the next day.

"If you are French . . . join us. If you are English, we declare war against you. Let us have your answer."

—*Pontiac, 1763*

The Treaty of Paris

The fall of Quebec and General Amherst's capture of Montreal the following year brought the fighting in North America to an end. In the **Treaty of Paris** of 1763, France was permitted to keep some of its sugar-producing islands in the West Indies, but it was forced to give Canada and most of its lands east of the Mississippi River to Great Britain. From Spain, France's ally, Great Britain gained Florida. In return, Spain received French lands west of the Mississippi River—the Louisiana Territory—as well as the port of New Orleans.

The Treaty of Paris marked the end of France as a power in North America. The continent was now divided between Great Britain and Spain, with the Mississippi River marking the boundary. While the Spanish and British were working out a plan for the future of North America, many Native Americans still lived on the lands covered by the European agreement.

☑ **Reading Check** **Summarizing** What lands did Spain receive under the Treaty of Paris?

Trouble on the Frontier

The British victory over the French dealt a blow to the Native Americans of the Ohio River valley. They had lost their French allies and trading partners. Although they continued to trade with the British, the Native Americans regarded them as enemies. The British raised the prices of their goods and, unlike the French, refused to pay the Native Americans for the use of their land. Worst of all, British settlers began moving into the valleys of western Pennsylvania.

Pontiac's War

Pontiac, chief of an Ottawa village near Detroit, recognized that the British settlers threatened the Native American way of life. Just as Benjamin Franklin had tried to bring the colonies together with the Albany Plan, Pontiac wanted to join Native American groups to fight the British.

In the spring of 1763, Pontiac put together an alliance. He attacked the British fort at Detroit while other war parties captured most of the other British outposts in the Great Lakes region. That summer Native Americans killed settlers along the Pennsylvania and Virginia frontiers in a series of raids called **Pontiac's War.**

The Native Americans, however, failed to capture the important strongholds of Niagara, Fort Pitt, and Detroit. The war ended in August 1765, after British troops defeated Pontiac's allies, the Shawnee and Delaware people. In July 1766, Pontiac signed a peace treaty and was pardoned by the British.

HISTORY Online

Student Web Activity
Visit taj.glencoe.com and click on **Chapter 4— Student Web Activities** for an activity on the French and Indian War.

★ Geography
The Proclamation of 1763

To prevent more fighting, Britain called a halt to the settlers' westward expansion. In the **Proclamation of 1763,** King George III declared that the Appalachian Mountains were the temporary western boundary for the colonies. The proclamation angered many people, especially those who owned shares in land companies. These speculators, or investors, had already bought land west of the mountains. They were furious that Britain ignored their land claims.

Although the end of the French and Indian War brought peace for the first time in many years, the Proclamation of 1763 created friction. More conflicts would soon arise between Britain and the colonists in North America.

✓ **Reading Check** **Examining** Why were many colonists angered by the Proclamation of 1763?

SECTION 4 ASSESSMENT

Checking for Understanding

1. **Key Terms** Use the terms alliance and speculator in a short paragraph to explain their meaning.
2. **Reviewing the Facts** Name the three nations that were involved in the Seven Years' War.

Reviewing Themes

3. **Individual Action** How did Pontiac plan to defend Native Americans from British settlers? Was his plan successful?

Critical Thinking

4. **Analyzing Information** What did the British hope to gain by issuing the Proclamation of 1763?
5. **Analyzing Information** What actions do you think General Braddock could have taken to increase his army's chances of defeating the French? Re-create the diagram below to organize your answer.

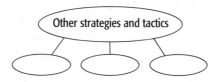

Other strategies and tactics

Analyzing Visuals

6. **Geography Skills** Study the map of the French and Indian War on page 123. What was the result of the battle at Fort Duquesne? What route did British General Wolfe take to reach Quebec?

Interdisciplinary Activity

Geography Sketch a map showing the land claims of Great Britain, France, and Spain in North America after the Treaty of Paris.

Chapter Summary

The Colonies Grow

- Between the 1600s and early 1700s, thirteen American colonies are established—some for profit and others by religious groups seeking freedom.

- New England, the Middle Colonies, and the Southern Colonies develop diverse economies.

- Although many different people live in the colonies, their values and beliefs, government, and educational institutions grow out of English traditions.

- Between 1650 and 1750, Parliament passes laws regulating colonial trade.

- In 1754 the French and Indian War begins.

- From 1689 to 1763, France and Britain fight a series of wars.

- Under the terms of the Treaty of Paris, Britain obtains control of much of the continent.

- North America is divided between Great Britain and Spain.

Reviewing Key Terms

Use all the terms below in one of three paragraphs, each about one of the following: trade, farming, organization of the colonies.

1. subsistence farming
2. cash crop
3. export
4. mercantilism
5. charter colony
6. proprietary colony
7. import

Reviewing Key Facts

8. Why did the colonial population grow rapidly?
9. What differences existed between the Tidewater planters and the backcountry farmers of the South?
10. What was the Great Awakening?
11. What immigrant groups settled in Pennsylvania?
12. How did the soil in the Middle Colonies differ from that in New England? What did that mean for the two regions?
13. What was the Iroquois Confederacy?
14. What was England's reason for the Navigation Acts?
15. What was the Enlightenment?
16. What North American land claims were the French forced to give up in the Treaty of Paris?
17. Why did the Proclamation of 1763 cause friction?

Critical Thinking

18. **Comparing** How did the economies of the New England and Southern Colonies differ? Re-create the chart below to answer the question.

Northern economy	Southern economy

19. **Drawing Conclusions** Re-read the People in History feature on page 109. In what ways did Benjamin Franklin represent the Enlightenment way of thinking?
20. **Determining Cause and Effect** How did the French relationship with Native Americans help them in their conflicts with the British?
21. **Analyzing Information** Re-read the Two Viewpoints feature on page 118. Why did Drake give the name 'Albion' to the land?

Geography and History Activity

Study the map of North America in 1754 on page 117; then answer these questions.

22. What countries controlled land on the continent?
23. What regions were under Spain's control?
24. Who controlled the land that is now Mexico?
25. What nation controlled the Mississippi River?

Practicing Skills

Determining Cause and Effect *Each of the following three sentences illustrates a cause-and-effect relationship. On a separate sheet of paper, identify the cause(s) and effect(s) in each sentence.*

26. During the 1700s the population of the English colonies grew dramatically as a result of high immigration.
27. To make certain that only England benefited from trade with the colonies, Parliament passed the Navigation Acts.
28. Because worship was so central to the Puritans, they built their towns around the church.

Citizenship Cooperative Activity

29. **Community Volunteers** Work with a partner to make a list of places in your community that need the services of volunteers. These can include libraries, nursing homes, and day care centers. Call each place and ask what the volunteers do, what times of the day and week they are needed, and how a volunteer can get started. Share your findings with the class. Then volunteer some of your time at one of the places you contacted.

Economics Activity

30. Working with a partner, create a map showing a trade route that colonial merchants might use. To get started, examine maps and information from your text and from encyclopedias and historical atlases. Include the physical features that the colonial merchants had to face, including rivers, mountains, lakes, and so on.

Alternative Assessment

31. **Expressive Writing** Review the chapter for details on the experiences of enslaved Africans and record them in your journal. Use these details to help you write a poem describing the feelings of an enslaved African who is about to board a ship for the Americas.

Self-Check Quiz
Visit taj.glencoe.com and click on **Chapter 4—Self-Check Quizzes** to prepare for the chapter test.

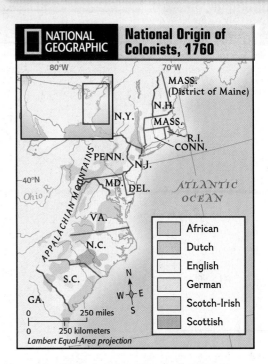

NATIONAL GEOGRAPHIC **National Origin of Colonists, 1760**

Key:
- African
- Dutch
- English
- German
- Scotch-Irish
- Scottish

Lambert Equal-Area projection

Standardized Test Practice

Directions: Use the map above to answer the following question.

According to the map, which of the following statements is true?

F The Appalachian Mountains divided North Carolina and South Carolina.

G Virginia had the largest population.

H Most of Delaware's people were English.

J Dutch communities were widespread throughout South Carolina.

Test-Taking Tip:
Make sure that you look at the map's *title* and *key* so that you understand what it represents. Since the map does not show *total population* of the colonies, you can eliminate answer **G**.

UNIT 3

Creating a Nation

1763–1791

Why It Matters

As you study Unit 3, you will learn that the purpose of the Declaration of Independence was to justify the American Revolution and to explain the founding principles of the new nation. You will also learn that the Constitution established a republic, in which power is held by voting citizens through their representatives.

American flag, Revolutionary War

Primary Sources Library

See pages 962–963 for primary source readings to accompany Unit 3.

Use the **American History Primary Source Document Library CD-ROM** to find additional primary sources about the American move toward independence.

Washington Crossing the Delaware by Emanuel Gottlieb Leutze

"Give me
liberty, or give
me death!"

—Patrick Henry, 1775

Why It Matters

A spirit of independence became evident early in the history of the American people. Far from the established rules and restrictions they had faced in their home countries, the new settlers began to make their own laws and develop their own ways of doing things.

The Impact Today

The ideals of revolutionary America still play a major role in shaping the society we live in. For example:

- *Americans still exercise their right to protest laws they view as unfair.*
- *Citizens have the right to present their views freely.*

The American Journey Video *The chapter 5 video, "Loyalists and Tories," portrays events leading up to the Revolutionary War from a Loyalist's point of view, as well as a Patriot's.*

The Americas

1763
- Treaty of Paris

1765
- Stamp Act protests

1770
- Boston Massacre

1763　　　　　　*1766*　　　　　　*1769*

World

1762
- Rousseau publishes *The Social Contract*

1764
- Mozart (aged eight) writes first symphony

1769
- Watt patents steam engine

1770
- Russians destroy Ottoman fleet

Bunker Hill by Don Troiani Low on ammunition, Colonel William Prescott gives the order, "Don't fire until you see the whites of their eyes."

1773
• Boston Tea Party

1774
• First Continental Congress meets

1776
• Declaration of Independence signed

1775
• Battles fought at Lexington and Concord

1772

1775

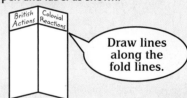

1772
• Poland partitioned among Russia, Prussia, and Austria

1774
• Louis XVI becomes king of France

HISTORY Online

Chapter Overview
Visit taj.glencoe.com and click on **Chapter 5— Chapter Overviews** to preview chapter information.

Taxation Without Representation

Preview of Events

♦1760 ♦1765 ♦1770

1763
Proclamation of 1763

1764
Parliament passes Sugar Act

1765
Parliament enacts Stamp Act

1767
Townshend Acts tax colonial imports

St. Edward's crown, worn by George III

AN
American Story

Huron and Ottawa warriors silently peered from the woods. They watched about 100 British soldiers camped on Lake Erie's shore. The soldiers—sent by the British Crown—had just stopped to rest on their way to Fort Detroit. They were worried about rumors of Native Americans planning war.

Suddenly the warriors rushed from the forest. The British managed to escape in two boats. War raged on the frontier—and the British were in the thick of it!

Relations with Britain

After winning the French and Indian War, Great Britain controlled a vast territory in North America. To limit settlement of this territory, Britain issued the Proclamation of 1763. Parts of the land acquired through the Treaty of Paris became the provinces of Quebec, East Florida, West Florida, and Grenada (a combination of several Caribbean islands). Most importantly, the Proclamation prohibited colonists from moving west of the Appalachian Mountains.

Stopping western settlement provided several advantages for Britain. It allowed the British government, not the colonists, to control westward movement. In this way, westward expansion would go on in an orderly way, and conflict with Native Americans might be avoided. Slower western settlement would also slow colonists moving away from the colonies on the coast—where Britain's important markets and investments were. Finally, closing western settlement protected the interests of British officials who wanted to control the lucrative fur trade. The British planned to keep 10,000 troops in America to protect their interests.

These plans alarmed the colonists. Many feared that the large number of British troops in North America might be used to interfere with their liberties. They saw the Proclamation of 1763 as a limit on their freedom. These two measures contributed to the feeling of distrust that was growing between Great Britain and its colonies.

The financial problems of Great Britain complicated the situation. The French and Indian War left Britain with a huge public debt. Desperate for new revenue, or incoming money, the king and Parliament felt it was only fair that the colonists pay part of the cost. They began plans to tax them. This decision set off a chain of events that enraged the American colonists and surprised British authorities.

Britain's Trade Laws

In 1763 **George Grenville** became prime minister of Britain. He was determined to reduce Britain's debt. He decided to take action against smuggling in the colonies. When the colonists smuggled goods to avoid taxes, Britain lost revenue that could be used to pay debts.

Grenville knew that American juries often found smugglers innocent. In 1763 he convinced Parliament to pass a law allowing smugglers to be sent to vice-admiralty courts. Vice-admiralty courts were run by officers and did not have juries. In 1767 Parliament decided to authorize writs of assistance. These legal documents allowed customs officers to enter any location to search for smuggled goods.

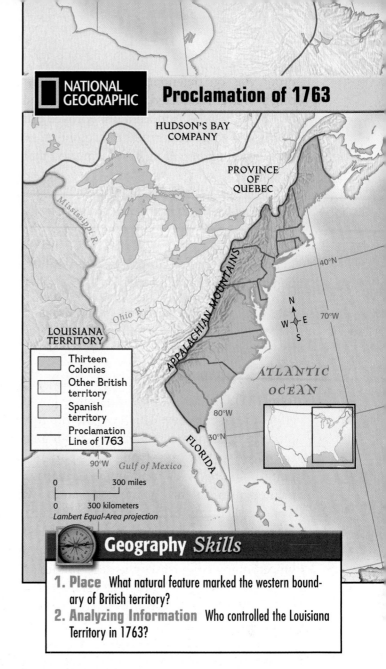

Proclamation of 1763

Geography Skills

1. **Place** What natural feature marked the western boundary of British territory?
2. **Analyzing Information** Who controlled the Louisiana Territory in 1763?

The Sugar Act

With a new law in place to stop smuggling, Grenville tried to increase tax revenue. In 1764 Parliament passed the **Sugar Act.** The act lowered the tax on molasses imported by the colonists. Grenville hoped the lower tax would convince the colonists to pay the tax instead of smuggling. The act also let officers seize goods from smugglers without going to court.

The Sugar Act and the new laws to control smuggling angered the colonists. They believed their rights as Englishmen were being violated. Writs of assistance violated their right to be secure in their home. Vice-admiralty courts violated their right to a jury trial. Furthermore, in trials at vice-admiralty courts, the burden of proof was on defendants to prove their innocence. This contradicted British law, which states that the accused is "innocent until proved guilty."

These measures alarmed the colonists. **James Otis,** a young lawyer in Boston, argued that

> 66no parts of [England's colonies] can be taxed without their consent . . . every part has a right to be represented.99

In his speeches and pamphlets, Otis defined and defended colonial rights.

✓ **Reading Check** **Analyzing** Why did Parliament pass the Sugar Act?

The Stamp Act

In 1765 Parliament passed another law in an effort to raise money. This law, the **Stamp Act,** placed a tax on almost all printed material in the colonies—everything from newspapers and pamphlets to wills and playing cards. All printed material had to have a stamp, which was applied by British officials. Because so many items were taxed, it affected almost everyone in the colonial cities. The Stamp Act convinced many colonists of the need for action.

Opposition to the Stamp Act centered on two points. Parliament had interfered in colonial affairs by taxing the colonies directly. In addition, it taxed the colonists without their consent. In passing the Stamp Act without consulting the colonial legislatures, Parliament ignored the colonial tradition of self-government.

Protesting the Stamp Act

A young member of the Virginia House of Burgesses, **Patrick Henry,** persuaded the burgesses to take action against the Stamp Act. According to tradition, when he was accused of treason, Henry replied,

> 66If this be treason, make the most of it!99

The Virginia assembly passed a resolution—a formal expression of opinion—declaring it had "the only and sole exclusive right and power to lay taxes" on its citizens.

In Boston **Samuel Adams** helped start an organization called the **Sons of Liberty.** Members took to the streets to protest the Stamp Act. People in other cities also organized Sons of Liberty groups.

Throughout the summer of 1765, protesters burned effigies—rag figures—representing unpopular tax collectors. They also raided and destroyed houses belonging to royal officials and marched through the streets shouting that only Americans had the right to tax Americans.

The Stamp Act Congress

In October delegates from nine colonies met in New York at the **Stamp Act Congress.** They drafted a petition to the king and Parliament declaring that the colonies could not be taxed except by their own assemblies.

In the colonial cities, people refused to use the stamps. They urged merchants to boycott—refuse to buy—British and European goods in protest. Thousands of merchants, artisans, and farmers signed nonimportation agreements. In these agreements they pledged not to buy or use goods imported from Great Britain. As the boycott spread, British merchants lost so much business that they begged Parliament to repeal, or cancel, the Stamp Act.

Revenue stamp

The Act Is Repealed

In March 1766, Parliament gave in to the colonists' demands and repealed the Stamp Act. Yet the colonists' trust in the king and Parliament was never fully restored.

While the colonists celebrated their victory over the Stamp Act, Parliament passed another act on the same day it repealed the Stamp Act. The **Declaratory Act** of 1766 stated that Parliament had the right to tax and make decisions for the British colonies "in all cases." The colonists might have won one battle, but the war over making decisions for the colonies had just begun.

✓ **Reading Check** **Evaluating** What role did Samuel Adams play in colonial protests?

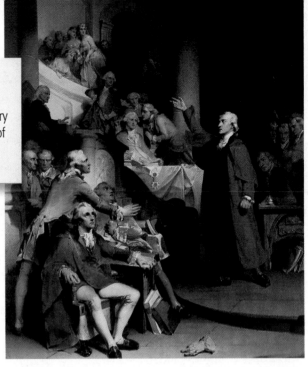

History *Through Art*

Patrick Henry Before the Virginia House of Burgesses by Peter F. Rothermel Patrick Henry gave a fiery speech before the Virginia House of Burgesses in 1765. **Why did Henry deliver the speech?**

New Taxes

Soon after the Stamp Act crisis, Parliament passed a set of laws in 1767 that came to be known as the **Townshend Acts.** In these acts the British leaders tried to avoid some of the problems the Stamp Act caused. They understood that the colonists would not tolerate internal taxes—those levied or paid inside the colonies. As a result the new taxes applied only to imported goods, with the tax being paid at the port of entry. The goods taxed, however, included basic items—such as glass, tea, paper, and lead—that the colonists had to import because they did not produce them.

By this time the colonists were outraged by *any* taxes Parliament passed. They believed that only their own representatives had the right to levy taxes on them. The colonists responded by bringing back the boycott that had worked so well against the Stamp Act. The boycott proved to be even more widespread this time.

Women took an active role in the protest against the Townshend Acts. In towns throughout the colonies, women organized groups to support the boycott of British goods, sometimes calling themselves the **Daughters of Liberty.** They urged Americans to wear homemade fabrics and produce other goods that were available only from Britain before. They believed this would help the American colonies become economically independent.

✓**Reading Check** **Comparing** How did the Townshend Acts differ from the Stamp Act?

SECTION 1 ASSESSMENT

Checking for Understanding

1. **Key Terms** Write sentences or short paragraphs in which you use the following groups of terms correctly: (1) revenue and writs of assistance; (2) resolution, effigy, boycott, nonimportation, and repeal.

2. **Reviewing Facts** State two reasons for the deterioration of relations between the British and the colonists.

Reviewing Themes

3. **Civic Rights and Responsibilities** Why did the colonists think the writs of assistance violated their rights?

Critical Thinking

4. **Identifying Central Issues** Why did British policies following the French and Indian War lead to increased tensions with American colonists?

5. **Determining Cause and Effect** Re-create the diagram below and describe the effects of these British actions.

British Actions	Effects
Sugar Act ⇨	
Stamp Act ⇨	
Townshend Acts ⇨	

Analyzing Visuals

6. **Geography Skills** Review the map on page 133. The Proclamation of 1763 banned colonists from settling west of the Appalachian Mountains. Why did the British government want to halt western movement?

Interdisciplinary Activity

Persuasive Writing Write a letter to the editor of a colonial newspaper in which you attempt to persuade fellow colonists to boycott British goods. Use standard grammar, spelling, sentence structure and punctuation.

SECTION 2 Building Colonial Unity

Guide to Reading

Main Idea
As tensions between colonists and the British government increased, protests grew stronger.

Key Terms
propaganda, committee of correspondence

Reading Strategy
Organizing Information As you read the section, re-create the diagram below and describe how the Intolerable Acts changed life for colonists.

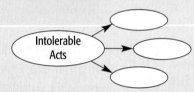

Read to Learn
• why Boston colonists and British soldiers clashed, resulting in the Boston Massacre.
• how the British government tried to maintain its control over the colonies.

Section Theme
Groups and Institutions Colonists banded together to protest British laws.

Preview of Events

♦1770   ♦1773   ♦1776

1770
Boston Massacre takes place

1772
Samuel Adams sets up a committee of correspondence

1773
Boston Tea Party occurs

1774
Parliament passes the Intolerable Acts

DON'T TREAD ON ME

American protest banner

AN
American Story

In the spring of 1768, British customs officials in Boston seized the *Liberty,* a ship belonging to John Hancock, a merchant and protest leader. The ship had docked in Boston Harbor to unload a shipment of wine and take on new supplies. The customs officials, however, charged that Hancock was using the ship for smuggling. As news of the ship's seizure spread through Boston, angry townspeople filled the streets. They shouted against Parliament and the taxes it had imposed on them. The *Liberty* affair became one of the events that united the colonists against British policies.

Trouble in Boston

Protests like the *Liberty* affair made British colonial officials nervous. In the summer of 1768, worried customs officers sent word back to Britain that the colonies were on the brink of rebellion. Parliament responded by sending two regiments of troops to Boston. As angry Bostonians jeered, the newly arrived "redcoats" set up camp right in the center of the city.

Many colonists, especially those living in Boston, felt that the British had pushed them too far. First the British had passed a series of laws that violated colonial rights. Now they had sent an army to occupy colonial cities.

To make matters worse, the soldiers stationed in Boston acted rudely and sometimes even violently toward the colonists. Mostly poor men, the redcoats earned little pay. Some of them stole goods from local shops or scuffled with boys who taunted them in the streets. The soldiers competed off-hours for jobs that Bostonians wanted. The townspeople's hatred for the soldiers grew stronger every day.

The Boston Massacre

Relations between the redcoats and the Boston colonists grew more tense. Then on March 5, 1770, the tension finally reached a peak. That day a fight broke out between townspeople and soldiers. While some British officers tried to calm the crowd, one man shouted,

❝We did not send for you. We will not have you here. We'll get rid of you, we'll drive you away!❞

The angry townspeople moved through the streets, picking up any weapon they could find—sticks, stones, shovels, and clubs. They pushed forward toward the customshouse on King Street.

As the crowd approached, the sentry on duty panicked and called for help. The crowd responded by throwing stones, snowballs, oyster shells, and pieces of wood at the soldiers. "Fire, you bloodybacks, you lobsters," the crowd screamed. "You dare not fire."

After one of the soldiers was knocked down, the nervous and confused redcoats did fire. Several shots rang out, killing five colonists. One Bostonian cried out:

❝Are the inhabitants to be knocked down in the streets? Are they to be murdered in this manner?❞

Among the dead was **Crispus Attucks,** a dockworker who was part African, part Native American. The colonists called the tragic encounter the **Boston Massacre.**

The Word Spreads

Colonial leaders used news of the killings as propaganda—information designed to influence opinion—against the British. Samuel Adams put up posters describing the "Boston Massacre" as a slaughter of innocent Americans by bloodthirsty redcoats. An engraving by Paul Revere showed a British officer giving the order to open fire on an orderly crowd. Revere's powerful image strengthened anti-British feeling.

The Boston Massacre led many colonists to call for stronger boycotts on British goods. Aware of the growing opposition to its policies, Parliament repealed all the Townshend Acts taxes except the one on tea. Many colonists believed they had won another victory. They ended their boycotts, except on the taxed tea, and started to trade with British merchants again.

Some colonial leaders, however, continued to call for resistance to British rule. In 1772 Samuel Adams revived the Boston committee of correspondence, an organization used in earlier protests. The committee circulated writings about colonists' grievances against Britain. Soon other committees of correspondence sprang up throughout the colonies, bringing together protesters opposed to British measures. 📖 *(See page 962 of the Primary Sources Library for readings about colonial resistance.)*

✓**Reading Check** **Explaining** How did the Boston Massacre contribute to the repeal of the Townshend Acts?

The Boston Massacre

The British soldiers never stood trial for the massacre. Eight soldiers and the commanding officer at the Boston Massacre *were* jailed and tried for murder. Many Patriots thought it was an act of disloyalty to defend the soldiers. The soldiers' hopes for justice rested in the hands of John Adams, who believed that even the enemy should be given a fair trial. Two of the soldiers were found guilty of manslaughter. The others were found not guilty on grounds of self-defense. Some Patriots questioned Adams's loyalty; others argued that the trial showed even the hated redcoats could receive a fair trial.

MORE ABOUT...

The Boston Tea Party

The Boston Tea Party is one of the significant events leading ultimately to American independence.

Most of the Townshend Acts are repealed. The tax on tea remains.

In November 1773, the citizens of Boston refuse to allow three British ships to unload 342 chests of tea.

On the evening of December 16, Boston citizens disguised as Native Americans board the ships and empty the tea into Boston Harbor.

King George III and Parliament respond by closing the city port.

"Fellow countrymen, we cannot afford to give a single inch! If we retreat now, everything we have done becomes useless!"

— *Samuel Adams,*
December 1773

A Crisis Over Tea

In the early 1770s, some Americans considered British colonial policy a "conspiracy against liberty." The British government's actions in 1773 seemed to confirm that view.

The British East India Company faced ruin. To save the East India Company, Parliament passed the **Tea Act** of 1773. This measure gave the company the right to ship tea to the colonies without paying most of the taxes usually placed on tea. It also allowed the company to bypass colonial merchants and sell its tea directly to shopkeepers at a low price. This meant that East India Company tea was cheaper than any other tea in the colonies. The Tea Act gave the company a very favorable advantage over colonial merchants.

Colonial Demands

Colonial merchants immediately called for a new boycott of British goods. Samuel Adams and others denounced the British monopoly. The Tea Act, they argued, was just another attempt to crush the colonists' liberty.

At large public meetings in Boston and Philadelphia, colonists vowed to stop the East India Company's ships from unloading. The Daughters of Liberty issued a pamphlet declaring that rather than part with freedom, "we'll part with our tea."

Parliament ignored warnings that another crisis was brewing. The East India Company shipped tea to Philadelphia, New York, Boston, and Charles Town. The colonists forced the ships sent to New York and Philadelphia to turn back. The tea sent to Charles Town was seized and stored in a warehouse. In Boston, a showdown began.

The Boston Tea Party

Three tea ships arrived in Boston Harbor in late 1773. The royal governor, whose house had been destroyed by Stamp Act protesters, refused to let the ships turn back. When he ordered the tea unloaded, Adams and the Boston Sons of Liberty acted swiftly. On December 16, a group of men disguised as Mohawks and armed with hatchets marched to the wharves. At midnight they boarded the ships and threw 342 chests of tea overboard, an event that became known as the **Boston Tea Party.**

Word of this act of defiance spread throughout the colonies. Men and women gathered in the streets to celebrate the bravery of the Boston Sons of Liberty. Yet no one spoke of challenging British rule, and colonial leaders continued to think of themselves as members of the British empire.

The Intolerable Acts

When news of the Boston Tea Party reached London, the reaction was quite different. King **George III** realized that Britain was losing control of the colonies. "We must master them or totally leave them alone." Not prepared to give up, the king and Parliament vowed to punish Boston. In the spring of 1774, Parliament passed the **Coercive Acts,** very harsh laws intended to punish the people of Massachusetts for their resistance.

The Coercive Acts closed Boston Harbor until the Massachusetts colonists paid for the ruined tea. This action prevented the arrival of food and other supplies that normally came by ship. Worse, the laws took away certain rights of the Massachusetts colonists. For example, the laws banned most town meetings, an important form of self-government in New England. Another provision permitted royal officers to be tried in other colonies or in Britain when accused of crimes.

The Coercive Acts also forced Bostonians to shelter soldiers in their own homes. Parliament planned to isolate Boston with these acts. Instead the other colonies sent food and clothing to demonstrate their support for Boston. The colonists maintained that the Coercive Acts violated their rights as English citizens. These included the rights to no quartering of troops in private homes and no standing army in peacetime without their consent.

The Quebec Act, passed shortly after the Coercive Acts, further angered the colonists. This act set up a permanent government for Quebec and granted religious freedom to French Catholics. Colonists strongly objected to the provision that gave Quebec the area west of the Appalachians and north of the Ohio River. This provision ignored colonial claims to the area. The feelings of the colonists were made clear by *their* name for the new laws—the Intolerable Acts.

Reading Check **Summarizing** List the effects of the Coercive Acts on the citizens of Boston.

SECTION 2 ASSESSMENT

Checking for Understanding

1. **Key Terms** Use these terms in sentences that relate to the Boston Massacre: propaganda, committee of correspondence.
2. **Reviewing Facts** How did colonial leaders use the Boston Massacre to their advantage?

Reviewing Themes

3. **Groups and Institutions** Why were the committees of correspondence powerful organizations?

Critical Thinking

4. **Drawing Conclusions** Do you think the Boston Tea Party was a turning point in the relationship between the British and the colonists? Explain.
5. **Organizing Information** Re-create the diagram below and describe how colonists showed their opposition to British policies.

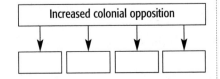

Analyzing Visuals

6. **Picturing History** Examine the material about the Boston Tea Party on page 138. What artifacts are shown? When did the "tea party" take place?

Interdisciplinary Activity

Art Draw a cartoon strip showing the story of the Boston Tea Party. Use at least four cartoon frames to present the sequence of events from your point of view. Compare your cartoon to a classmate's and describe his or her point of view.

America's LITERATURE

Esther Forbes (1891–1967)

Esther Forbes wrote a number of books; among them is the prize-winning biography *Paul Revere and the World He Lived In*. As she researched Paul Revere's life, Forbes learned that many young apprentices played a role in the American Revolution. *Johnny Tremain*, a fictional work, tells the story of such an apprentice.

READ TO DISCOVER

In this passage from *Johnny Tremain*, 14-year-old Johnny and his friend Rab have disguised themselves as Mohawks. They join the crowd at Griffin's Wharf in Boston Harbor, where three English ships carrying tea are docked and are unable to leave or unload their cargo.

READER'S DICTIONARY

boatswain: officer on a ship
warped: roped
jargon: strange language
hold: place where cargo is stored on a ship
winch: machine for hauling

Johnny Tremain

There was a **boatswain's** whistle, and in silence one group boarded the *Dartmouth*. The *Eleanor* and the *Beaver* had to be **warped** in to the wharf. Johnny was close to Mr. Revere's heels. He heard him calling for the captain, promising him, in the **jargon** everyone talked that night, that not one thing should be damaged on the ship except only the tea, but the captain and all his crew had best stay in the cabin until the work was over.

Captain Hall shrugged and did as he was told, leaving his cabin boy to hand over the keys to the **hold.** The boy was grinning with pleasure. The "tea party" was not unexpected. . . .

The **winches** rattled and the heavy chests began to appear—one hundred and fifty of them. As some men worked in the hold, others broke open the chests and flung the tea into the harbor. But one thing made them unexpected difficulty. The tea inside the chests was wrapped in heavy canvas. The axes went through the wood easily enough—the canvas made endless trouble. Johnny had never worked so hard in his life.

Then Mr. Revere called the captain to come up and inspect. The tea was utterly gone, but Captain Hall agreed that beyond that there had not been the slightest damage.

It was close upon dawn when the work on all three ships was done. And yet the great, silent audience on the wharf, men, women, and children, had not gone home. As the three groups came off the ships, they formed in fours along the wharf, their axes on their shoulders. Then a hurrah went up and a fife began to play.

Paul Revere

Excerpt from *Johnny Tremain* by Esther Forbes. Copyright © 1943 by Esther Forbes Hoskins, © renewed 1971 by Linwood M. Erskine, Jr., Executor of the Estate of Esther Forbes Hoskins. Reprinted by permission of Houghton Mifflin Co. All rights reserved.

ANALYZING LITERATURE

1. **Recall and Interpret** Why was the "tea party" expected?
2. **Evaluate and Connect** What does the conduct of the "tea party" participants suggest about the protest? Explain your answer.

Interdisciplinary Activity

Expository Writing Write a one-page paper about how you think you would react in Johnny's situation.

SECTION 3 A Call to Arms

Guide to Reading

Main Idea
Colonial leaders met at Philadelphia in 1774 to discuss a united response to British policies. Seven months later American and British troops met in battle for the first time.

Key Terms
militia, minutemen, Loyalist, Patriot

Reading Strategy
Sequencing Information As you read the section, re-create the diagram below and list six events leading to the Battle of Bunker Hill.

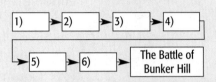

1) ➤ 2) ➤ 3) ➤ 4)
➤ 5) ➤ 6) ➤ The Battle of Bunker Hill

Read to Learn
• what happened at the Continental Congress in Philadelphia.
• how the colonists met British soldiers in the first battle.

Section Theme
Groups and Institutions With the establishment of the Continental Congress, the colonies continued to protest.

Preview of Events

♦1774   ♦1775   ♦1776

September 1774
First Continental Congress meets

April 19, 1775
Battles of Lexington and Concord are fought

May 10, 1775
Ethan Allen captures Fort Ticonderoga

June 17, 1775
Battle of Bunker Hill is fought

Revolutionary War drum and fife

AN
American Story

At first few colonists wanted a complete break with Britain. One of the most popular songs of the time, "The Bold Americans," called for *both* liberty and continued loyalty to the British king:

> We'll honor George, our sovereign, while he sits on the throne.
> If he grants us liberty, no other king we'll own.
> If he will grant us liberty, so plainly shall you see,
> We are the boys that fear no noise! Success to liberty.

As tensions mounted, however, a peaceful compromise was no longer possible.

The Continental Congress

Colonial leaders realized they needed more than boycotts to gain the liberty they sang about in "The Bold Americans." They needed the colonies to act together in their opposition to British policies.

In September 1774, 55 men arrived in the city of Philadelphia. Sent as delegates from all the colonies except Georgia, these men had come to establish a political body to represent American interests and challenge British control. They called the new organization the **Continental Congress.**

Delegates to the Congress

Major political leaders from all the colonies attended the Congress. Massachusetts sent fiery Samuel Adams and his younger cousin **John Adams,** a successful lawyer. New York sent **John Jay,** another lawyer. From Virginia came **Richard Henry Lee** and **Patrick Henry,** two of the most outspoken defenders of colonial rights, as well as **George Washington.**

Patrick Henry summed up the meaning of the gathering:

66The distinctions between Virginians, Pennsylvanians, New Yorkers, and New Englanders are no more. . . . I am not a Virginian, but an American.99

Decisions of the Congress

Although the delegates were hardly united in their views, they realized they needed to work together. First they drafted a statement of grievances calling for the repeal of 13 acts of Parliament passed since 1763. They declared that these laws violated the colonists' rights. Their rights were based on the "laws of nature, the principles of the English constitution, and the several charters" of the colonies. The delegates also voted to boycott all British goods and trade. No British products could be brought into or consumed in the colonies, and no colonial goods could be shipped to Britain.

One of Congress's major decisions was to endorse the Suffolk Resolves. These resolutions had been prepared by Bostonians and others who lived in Suffolk County, Massachusetts. They called on the people of Suffolk County to arm themselves against the British. The people responded by forming militias—groups of citizen soldiers. Many wondered if war was coming. The answer came the following spring.

Reading Check **Explaining** What was the purpose of the Continental Congress?

The First Battles

Colonists expected that if fighting against the British broke out, it would begin in New England. Militia companies in Massachusetts held frequent training sessions, made bullets, and stockpiled rifles and muskets. Some companies, known as minutemen, boasted they would be ready to fight on a minute's notice. In the winter of 1774–1775, a British officer stationed in Boston noted in his diary:

66The people are evidently making every preparation for resistance. They are taking every means to provide themselves with arms.99

Britain Sends Troops

The British also prepared for conflict. King George announced to Parliament that the New England colonies were "in a state of rebellion" and said that "blows must decide" who would control America. By April 1775, British general Sir Thomas Gage had several thousand soldiers under his command in and around Boston, with many more on the way.

Gage had instructions to take away the weapons of the Massachusetts militia and arrest the leaders.

Gage learned that the militia was storing arms and ammunition at **Concord,** a town about 20 miles northwest of Boston. He ordered 700 troops under Lieutenant-Colonel Francis Smith to march

> **❝**to Concord, where you will seize and destroy all the artillery and ammunition you can find.**❞**

Alerting the Colonists

On the night of April 18, 1775, Dr. Joseph Warren walked the streets of Boston, looking for any unusual activity by the British army. He saw a regiment form ranks in Boston Common and then begin to march out of the city.

Warren rushed to alert **Paul Revere** and **William Dawes,** leading members of the Sons of Liberty. Revere and Dawes rode to Lexington, a town east of Concord, to warn Samuel Adams and John Hancock that the British were coming.

Revere galloped off across the moonlit countryside, shouting, "The regulars are out!" to the people and houses he passed along the way. When he reached Lexington, he raced to tell Adams and Hancock his news. Adams could barely control his excitement. "What a glorious morning this is!" Adams was ready to fight for American independence.

Fighting at Lexington and Concord

At dawn the redcoats approached Lexington. When they reached the center of the town they discovered a group of about 70 minutemen who had been alerted by Revere and Dawes. Led by Captain John Parker, the minutemen had positioned themselves on the town common with muskets in hand. A minuteman reported,

> **❝**There suddenly appeared a number of the King's troops, about a thousand . . . the foremost of which cried, 'Throw down your arms, ye villains, ye rebels.'**❞**

A shot was fired, and then both sides let loose with an exchange of bullets. When the fighting was over, eight minutemen lay dead.

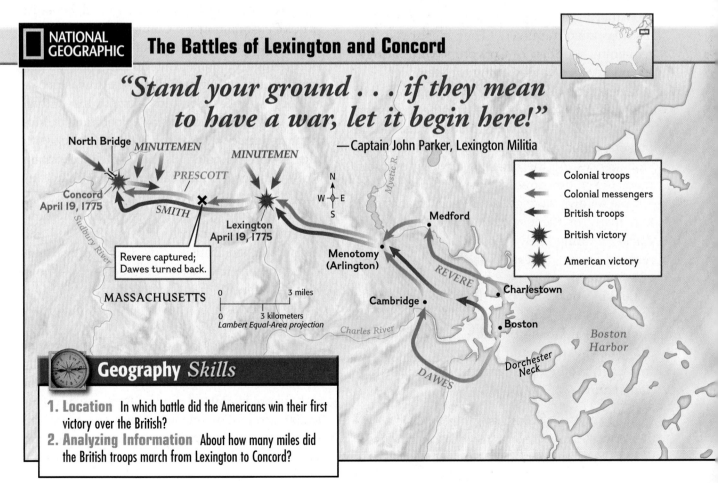

NATIONAL GEOGRAPHIC   **The Battles of Lexington and Concord**

"Stand your ground . . . if they mean to have a war, let it begin here!"
—Captain John Parker, Lexington Militia

Colonial troops
Colonial messengers
British troops
British victory
American victory

North Bridge   MINUTEMEN
MINUTEMEN
PRESCOTT
Concord
April 19, 1775
SMITH
Revere captured;
Dawes turned back.
Lexington
April 19, 1775
MASSACHUSETTS
Sudbury River
Mystic R.
Medford
Menotomy
(Arlington)
REVERE
Charlestown
Cambridge
Boston
Charles River
DAWES
Dorchester
Neck
Boston
Harbor

0   3 miles
0   3 kilometers
Lambert Equal-Area projection

Geography *Skills*

1. **Location** In which battle did the Americans win their first victory over the British?
2. **Analyzing Information** About how many miles did the British troops march from Lexington to Concord?

A View of the Town of Concord, 1775 by an unknown artist Two British officers (left) search for fleeing minutemen, while British troops march through Concord. **Why did the British march to Lexington and Concord?**

The British troops continued their march to Concord. When they arrived there, they discovered that most of the militia's gunpowder had already been removed. They destroyed the remaining supplies. At Concord's North Bridge, the minutemen were waiting for them.

Messengers on horseback had spread word of the British movements. All along the road from Concord to Boston, farmers, blacksmiths, saddle makers, and clerks hid behind trees, rocks, and stone fences. As the British marched down the road, the militia fired. A British officer wrote, "These fellows were generally good marksmen, and many of them used long guns made for duck shooting." By the time the redcoats reached Boston, at least 174 were wounded and 73 were dead.

Looking back, the poet Ralph Waldo Emerson wrote in "The Concord Hymn" that the Americans at Lexington and Concord had fired the "shot heard 'round the world." The battle for America's independence from Great Britain had begun.

Reading Check **Describing** What tactics did the colonists use against the British troops on their march back from Concord to Boston?

More Military Action

Shortly after Lexington and Concord, Benedict Arnold, a captain in the Connecticut militia, was authorized to raise a force of 400 to seize Fort Ticonderoga on Lake Champlain. Ticonderoga was not only strategically located but was rich in military supplies. Arnold learned that Ethan Allen was also mounting an expedition in Vermont to attack the fort. Arnold joined with Allen's force, known as the Green Mountain Boys, and together they caught the British by surprise. The garrison surrendered on May 10, 1775.

Later during the war, Arnold conspired to surrender the key fort of West Point to the British and led British raids against the Americans in Virginia and Connecticut. Arnold became a general in the British army.

Building Forces

After the battles of Lexington and Concord, the committees of correspondence sent out calls for volunteers to join the militias. Soon the colonial militia assembled around Boston was about 20,000 strong. For several weeks, the American and British armies waited nervously to see who would make the next move.

The Battle of Bunker Hill

On June 16, 1775, about 1,200 militiamen under the command of Colonel William Prescott set up fortifications at Bunker Hill and nearby Breed's Hill, across the harbor from Boston.

The British decided to drive the Americans from their strategic locations overlooking the city. The next day the redcoats crossed the harbor and assembled at the bottom of Breed's Hill. Bayonets drawn, they charged up the hill. With his forces low on ammunition, Colonel Prescott reportedly shouted the order, "Don't fire until you see the whites of their eyes." The Americans opened fire, forcing the British to retreat. The redcoats charged two more times, receiving furious fire. In the end the Americans ran out of gunpowder and had to withdraw.

The British won the **Battle of Bunker Hill** but suffered heavy losses—more than 1,000 dead and wounded. As one British officer wrote in his diary, "A dear bought victory, another such would have ruined us." The British had learned that defeating the Americans on the battlefield would not be quick or easy.

Choosing Sides

As American colonists heard about these battles, they faced a major decision. Should they join the rebels or remain loyal to Britain? Those who

Fact Fiction Folklore

The Battle of Bunker Hill

The Battle of Bunker Hill was fought on Breed's Hill. Most of the fighting did actually take place on Breed's Hill. The Patriot soldiers received instructions to set up defensive positions on Bunker Hill. For reasons that are unclear, they set up the positions on nearby Breed's Hill.

chose to stay with Britain, the Loyalists, did not consider unfair taxes and regulations good reasons for rebellion. Some remained loyal to the king because they were officeholders who would lose their positions as a result of the Revolution. Others were people who lived in relative isolation and who had not been part of the wave of discontent that turned so many Americans against Britain. Still others expected Britain to win the war and wanted to gain favor with the British. The Patriots, on the other hand, were determined to fight the British to the end—until American independence was won.

☑ **Reading Check** **Describing** What did the British learn from the Battle of Bunker Hill?

SECTION 3 ASSESSMENT

Checking for Understanding

1. **Key Terms** One of the following terms does not belong with the other three. Identify the term that does not belong and explain why. Terms: militia, minutemen, Loyalist, Patriots.
2. **Reviewing Facts** What decisions were made by the First Continental Congress?

Reviewing Themes

3. **Groups and Institutions** Why did the Continental Congress pass a resolution to form militias?

Critical Thinking

4. **Making Inferences** What reasons might Loyalists have had to support Great Britain?
5. **Comparing** Re-create the diagram below and list the differing beliefs of Patriots and Loyalists and those shared by both.

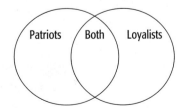

Analyzing Visuals

6. **Chart Skills** Review the cause-and-effect chart on page 142. What event in 1763 was significant to the independence movement?

Interdisciplinary Activity

Expressive Writing Write a one-act play in which a small group of ordinary men, women, and children in a small town react to news of the Battle of Lexington. Remember that reactions varied from colony to colony and that not all colonists wanted independence from Great Britain.

Critical Thinking
SKILLBUILDER

Distinguishing Fact From Opinion

Why Learn This Skill?

Suppose a friend says, "Our school's basketball team is awesome. That's a fact." Actually, it is not a fact; it is an opinion. Knowing how to tell the difference between a fact and an opinion can help you analyze the accuracy of political claims, advertisements, and many other kinds of statements.

Paul Revere's ride

Learning the Skill

A **fact** answers a specific question such as: What happened? Who did it? When and where did it happen? Why did it happen? Statements of fact can be checked for accuracy and proven.

An **opinion,** on the other hand, expresses beliefs, feelings, and judgments. Although it may reflect someone's thoughts, we cannot prove or disprove it.

An opinion often begins with phrases such as *I believe, I think, probably, it seems to me,* or *in my opinion.* It often contains words such as *might, could, should,* and *ought* and superlatives such as *best, worst,* and *greatest.* Judgment words that express approval or disapproval—such as *good, bad, poor,* and *satisfactory*—also usually indicate an opinion.

To distinguish between facts and opinions, ask yourself these questions:

• Does this statement give specific information about an event?
• Can I check the accuracy of this statement?
• Does this statement express someone's feelings, beliefs, or judgment?
• Does it include phrases such as *I believe,* superlatives, or judgment words?

Practicing the Skill

Read each numbered statement below. Tell whether each is a fact or an opinion, and explain how you arrived at your answer.

1. Paul Revere rode to Lexington with the news that the British redcoats were coming.

2. The redcoats were the most feared soldiers in the world at that time.

3. The Daughters of Liberty opposed the Tea Act of 1773.

4. The Boston Tea Party raiders should have sunk the tea ships.

5. George III was a foolish king.

Applying the Skill

Distinguishing Fact from Opinion Analyze 10 advertisements. List at least three facts and three opinions presented in the ads.

 GO TO Glencoe's **Skillbuilder Interactive Workbook CD-ROM, Level 1,** provides instruction and practice in key social studies skills.

SECTION 4 Moving Toward Independence

Guide to Reading

Main Idea
The Second Continental Congress voted to approve the Declaration of Independence.

Key Terms
petition, preamble

Reading Strategy
Organizing Information As you read the section, re-create the diagram below and describe the parts of the Declaration of Independence.

Parts of the Declaration of Independence

Read to Learn
- what happened at the Second Continental Congress.
- why the colonists drafted the Declaration of Independence.

Section Theme
Government and Democracy The Declaration of Independence declared the colonies free and independent.

Preview of Events

◆1775	◆1776	◆1777

May 10, 1775
Second Continental Congress meets

July 1775
The Congress sends Olive Branch Petition to George III

March 1776
George Washington takes Boston from the British

July 4, 1776
Declaration of Independence is approved

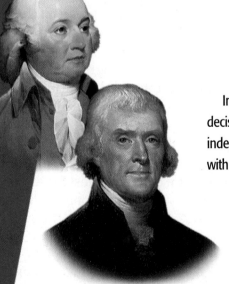

★★★★★★★★★★ AN American Story

In June 1776, delegates to the Second Continental Congress came to a momentous decision. They agreed to have a committee draw up a document declaring America's independence from Great Britain. Many years later John Adams recalled a conversation with Thomas Jefferson about the writing of the document.

Jefferson: You should do it.

Adams: Oh! no.

Jefferson: Why will you not? You ought to do it. . . .

Adams: You can write ten times better than I can.

Jefferson: Well, if you are decided, I will do as well as I can.

Adams and Jefferson

Colonial Leaders Emerge

On May 10, 1775, the **Second Continental Congress** assembled for the first time, declaring independence was a long way off. The conversation between Jefferson and Adams did not occur until more than a year after that first meeting.

The Second Continental Congress acted as a central government for the colonies.

The delegates to the Second Continental Congress included some of the greatest political leaders in America. Among those attending were John and Samuel Adams, Patrick Henry, Richard Henry Lee, and George Washington—all delegates to the First Continental Congress held in 1774. Several distinguished new delegates came as well.

Benjamin Franklin, one of the most accomplished and respected men in the colonies, had been an influential member of the Pennsylvania legislature. In 1765, during the Stamp Act Crisis, he represented the colonies in London and helped secure the repeal of the act.

Fact **Fiction** **Folklore**

America's Flags

Continental Colors, 1775–1777 The Continental Colors, or Grand Union flag, was the first to represent all the colonies. Its 13 stripes stood for the thirteen colonies. The crosses represented the British flag and symbolized the colonists' loyalty to Great Britain at that time.

John Hancock of Massachusetts, 38 years old, was a wealthy merchant. He funded many Patriot groups, including the Sons of Liberty. The delegates chose Hancock as president of the Second Continental Congress.

Thomas Jefferson, only 32 when the Congress began, had already acquired a reputation as a brilliant thinker and writer. As a member of the Virginia House of Burgesses, Jefferson had become associated with the movement toward independence.

The Second Continental Congress began to govern the colonies. It authorized the printing of money and set up a post office with Franklin in charge. It established committees to communicate with Native Americans and with other countries. Most important, the Congress created the **Continental Army** to fight against Britain in a more organized way than the colonial militias could. On John Adams's recommendation, the Congress unanimously chose George Washington to be the army's commander.

After Washington left to take charge of the colonial forces in Boston, the delegates offered Britain one last chance to avoid all-out war. In July the Congress sent a petition, or formal request, to George III. Called the **Olive Branch Petition,** it assured the king of the colonists' desire for peace. It asked the king to protect the colonists' rights, which Parliament seemed determined to destroy. George III refused to receive the Olive Branch Petition. Instead he prepared for war, hiring more than 30,000 German troops to send to America and fight beside British troops.

The Colonies Take the Offensive

Meanwhile the Congress learned that British troops stationed in what is now Canada were planning to invade New York. The Americans decided to strike first. Marching north from Fort Ticonderoga, a Patriot force captured Montreal in November. An American attack on Quebec led by Benedict Arnold failed, however. The American forces stayed outside the city of Quebec through the long winter and returned to Fort Ticonderoga in 1776.

Washington reached Boston in July 1775, a few weeks after the Battle of Bunker Hill. He found the members of the militia growing in number every day, but he realized they lacked discipline, organization, and leadership. He began the hard work of shaping these armed civilians into an army.

By March 1776, Washington judged the Continental Army ready to fight. He positioned the army in a semicircle around Boston and gave the order for its cannons to bombard the British forces. The redcoats, under Sir William Howe, hurriedly withdrew from the city and boarded their ships. On March 17 Washington led his jubilant troops into Boston. The British troops sailed to Halifax, Nova Scotia.

Moving Toward Independence

Throughout the colonies in late 1775 and early 1776, some Americans still hoped to avoid a complete break with Britain. Support for the position of absolute independence was growing, however.

In January 1776, **Thomas Paine** published a pamphlet called *Common Sense* that captured the attention of the American colonists. In bold language, Paine called for complete independence from Britain. He argued that it was simply

HISTORY Online

Student Web Activity
Visit taj.glencoe.com and click on **Chapter 5— Student Web Activities** for an activity on the Declaration of Independence.

People In History

Abigail Adams 1744–1818

Born into a comfortable Massachusetts household, Abigail Smith spent her youth reading and studying. At age 19 she married 28-year-old lawyer John Adams, who became a leader in the independence movement. Through her letters to family and friends, Abigail left us a record of her thoughts about the

revolution as it developed. She also shared her hopes for the new nation.

As Congress considered a declaration of independence, she teasingly —but seriously—wrote to her husband:

"I long to hear that you have declared an independency . . . I desire you would Remember the

Ladies, and be more generous and favorable to them than your ancestors."

Their correspondence during the times they spent apart showed a thoughtful exchange of ideas and a strong respect for one another. Abigail Adams would later become the second of the new nation's first ladies.

Thomas Jefferson prepared the draft of the Declaration, while Benjamin Franklin and John Adams made suggestions. **Why is July 2, 1776, a historic day?**

"common sense" to stop following the "royal brute," King George III. Paine told the colonists their cause was not just a squabble over taxes but a struggle for freedom—"in a great measure the cause of all mankind." *Common Sense* inspired thousands of Americans. 📖 *(See page 962 of the Primary Sources Library for another excerpt from* Common Sense.*)*

Reading Check **Explaining** Why was Thomas Paine important to the independence movement?

The Colonies Declare Independence

At the Second Continental Congress in Philadelphia, the meeting hall was filled with spirited debate. One central issue occupied the delegates: Should the colonies declare themselves an independent nation, or should they stay under British rule?

In April 1776, North Carolina instructed its delegates to support independence. On June 7 Virginia's Richard Henry Lee proposed a bold resolution:

❝That these United Colonies are, and of right ought to be, free and independent States . . . and that all political connection between them and the State of Great Britain is, and ought to be, totally dissolved.❞

The Congress debated the resolution. Some delegates still thought the colonies were not ready to form a separate nation. Others argued that war already had begun and a large portion of the American population wanted to separate from Great Britain. Still others feared Great Britain's power to hold down the rebellion.

While the delegates debated the issue, the Congress chose a committee to draft a **Declaration of Independence.** Jefferson was selected to write the historic document. Jefferson drew on the ideas of thinkers such as English philosopher John Locke to set out the colonies' reasons for proclaiming their freedom. Locke wrote that people were born with certain natural rights to life, liberty, and property; that people formed governments to protect these rights; and that a government interfering with these rights might rightfully be overthrown.

On July 2, 1776, the Congress finally voted on Lee's resolution for independence. Twelve colonies voted for it. New York did not vote but later announced its support. Next the delegates took up Jefferson's draft of the Declaration of Independence. After making some changes, they approved the document on July 4, 1776.

John Hancock, the president of the Congress, was the first to sign the Declaration of Independence. Hancock remarked that he wrote his name large enough for King George to read it without his glasses. Hancock's bold signature stands out on the original document. Eventually 56 delegates signed the paper announcing the birth of the United States.

Copies of the Declaration went out to the newly declared states. Washington had it read to his troops on July 9. In New York American soldiers tore down a statue of George III in celebration. In Worcester, Massachusetts, the reading of the Declaration of Independence was followed by "repeated [cheers], firing of musketry and cannon, bonfires, and other demonstrations of joy."

The Declaration of Independence

The Declaration has four major sections. The **preamble,** or introduction, states that people who wish to form a new country should explain their reasons for doing so. The next two sections list the rights the colonists believed they should have and their complaints against Britain. The final section proclaims the existence of the new nation.

The Declaration of Independence states what Jefferson and many Americans thought were universal principles. It begins with a description of traditional English political rights.

> **❝** We hold these truths to be self-evident, that all men are created equal, that they are endowed by their Creator with certain unalienable Rights, that among these are Life, Liberty, and the pursuit of Happiness. **❞**

The Declaration states that government exists to protect these rights. If it does not, it goes on to state that "it is the Right of the People to alter or to abolish it and to institute new Government."

The Declaration goes on to list the many grievances Americans held against the king and Parliament. The crimes of George III included "cutting off our trade with all parts of the world" and "imposing taxes on us without our

Independence Day

Congress voted for independence on July 4, 1776. Actually, Congress voted for independence on July 2, 1776. Why, then, is Independence Day celebrated on the fourth? On that day the delegates voted to accept Jefferson's statement, the Declaration of Independence, as the reason why they had voted for independence two days earlier.

consent." Americans, the Declaration says, had "Petitioned for Redress" of these grievances. These petitions, however, were ignored or rejected by Britain.

The Declaration ends by announcing America's new status. Now pledging "to each other our Lives, our Fortunes, and our sacred Honor," the Americans declared themselves a new nation. The struggle for American independence—the American Revolution—had begun. 📖 *(See pages 154–157 for the entire text of the Declaration of Independence.)*

✓ **Reading Check** **Summarizing** What grievances against King George III were included in the Declaration of Independence?

SECTION 4 ASSESSMENT

Checking for Understanding

1. **Key Terms** Connect the terms below with the proper document. Then write a sentence in which you use each term. Terms: **petition, preamble.** Documents: Declaration of Independence, Olive Branch Petition
2. **Reviewing Facts** What was King George III's response to the Olive Branch Petition?

Reviewing Themes

3. **Government and Democracy** Why was the Second Continental Congress more like a government than the First Continental Congress?

Critical Thinking

4. **Analyzing Primary Sources** Based on the quote from the Declaration of Independence on this page, what are the "unalienable Rights" to which Jefferson referred? Give examples.
5. **Organizing Information** Re-create the diagram below and describe each individual's role in the movement toward independence.

	Role
Thomas Jefferson	
Thomas Paine	
Samuel Adams	
Benjamin Franklin	

Analyzing Visuals

6. **Picturing History** Compare the flag on page 148 with the flag on page 128. How are the two flags similar? How are they different? Which of the flags more closely resembles the American flag of today?

Interdisciplinary Activity

Expository Writing Prepare a help-wanted ad to locate a person qualified to write the Declaration of Independence. Describe the responsibilities of the job as well as the experience and character traits that are needed.

EVE OF REVOLUTION

IN THE EARLY 1770s most colonists thought of themselves as British subjects. However, they also thought of themselves as Virginians or Georgians or New Yorkers. It wasn't until colonists began to unite in opposition to harsh British policies that they began to consider themselves Americans.

STIRRINGS OF REVOLT

In 1772 Samuel Adams convinced a group of Bostonians to join a Committee of Correspondence to communicate with other towns in Massachusetts. Soon, the idea spread. In colony after colony, Americans joined Committees of Correspondence. In this era before radios or telephones, the committees spread opposition to British policies into nearly every county, town, and city.

In 1774 delegates gathered at the Continental Congress in Philadelphia to form an organization to represent their interests as Americans. In addition to stating their grievances and voting to boycott British products, the Patriots decided to organize their own militias.

THE SHOT HEARD 'ROUND THE WORLD

The Revolution's first blow fell early on the morning of April 19, 1775. British redcoats clashed with colonial minutemen at Lexington and Concord. This clash, later called the "shot heard 'round the world," was the first battle of the Revolutionary War. The Battle of Bunker Hill in June showed that the war would be hard, long, and expensive on both sides.

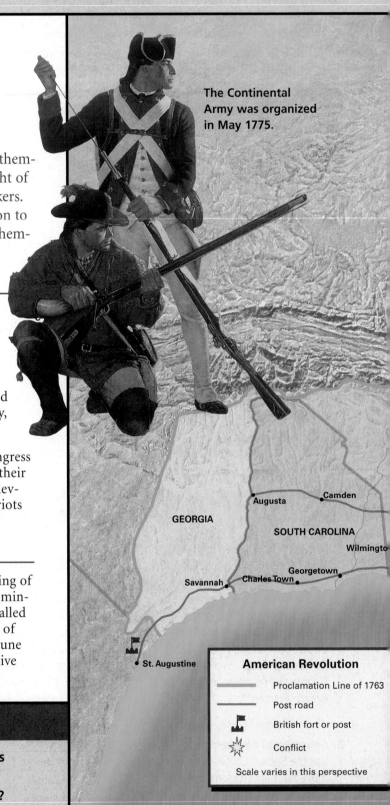

The Continental Army was organized in May 1775.

GEORGIA

Augusta   Camden

SOUTH CAROLINA

Wilmingto

Georgetown

Savannah   Charles Town

St. Augustine

American Revolution

——— Proclamation Line of 1763

——— Post road

⚑ British fort or post

✴ Conflict

Scale varies in this perspective

LEARNING *from* GEOGRAPHY

1. **How do you think the geography of the colonies made communication difficult?**

2. **Near what cities did the early battles take place?**

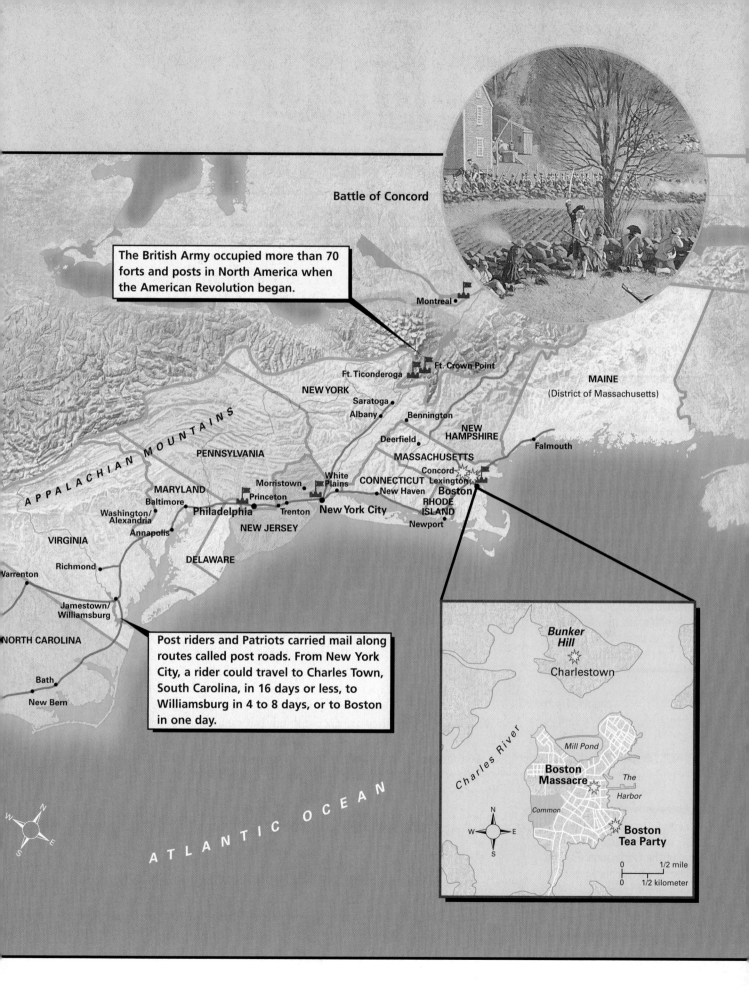

Battle of Concord

The British Army occupied more than 70 forts and posts in North America when the American Revolution began.

Montreal

Ft. Ticonderoga
Ft. Crown Point

MAINE
(District of Massachusetts)

NEW YORK

Saratoga
Albany   Bennington

NEW
HAMPSHIRE

Deerfield

Falmouth

APPALACHIAN MOUNTAINS

PENNSYLVANIA

MASSACHUSETTS

Concord
Lexington

MARYLAND

Morristown
White
Plains

CONNECTICUT
New Haven

Boston

Princeton

Baltimore

RHODE
ISLAND

Philadelphia

Trenton

New York City

Newport

Washington/
Alexandria

Annapolis

NEW JERSEY

VIRGINIA

DELAWARE

Richmond

Warrenton

Jamestown/
Williamsburg

Post riders and Patriots carried mail along routes called post roads. From New York City, a rider could travel to Charles Town, South Carolina, in 16 days or less, to Williamsburg in 4 to 8 days, or to Boston in one day.

NORTH CAROLINA

Bath

New Bern

ATLANTIC OCEAN

N
W   E
S

Bunker
Hill

Charlestown

Charles River

Mill Pond

Boston
Massacre

The
Harbor

Common

Boston
Tea Party

N
W   E
S

0   1/2 mile
0   1/2 kilometer

The Declaration of Independence

In Congress, July 4, 1776. The unanimous Declaration of the thirteen united States of America,

[Preamble]

What It Means
The Preamble The Declaration of Independence has four parts. The Preamble explains why the Continental Congress drew up the Declaration.

impel *force*

When in the Course of human events, it becomes necessary for one people to dissolve the political bands which have connected them with another, and to assume among the Powers of the earth, the separate and equal station to which the Laws of Nature and of Nature's God entitle them, a decent respect to the opinions of mankind requires that they should declare the causes which **impel** them to the separation.

[Declaration of Natural Rights]

What It Means
Natural Rights The second part, the Declaration of Natural Rights, lists the rights of the citizens. It goes on to explain that, in a republic, people form a government to protect their rights. The Declaration refers to these rights as *unalienable rights.* The word unalienable means non-transferable. An unalienable right is a right that cannot be surrendered.

endowed *provided*

despotism *unlimited power*

We hold these truths to be self-evident, that all men are created equal, that they are **endowed** by their Creator with certain unalienable Rights, that among these are Life, Liberty, and the pursuit of Happiness.

That to secure these rights, Governments are instituted among Men, deriving their just powers from the consent of the governed,

That whenever any Form of Government becomes destructive of these ends, it is the Right of the People to alter or to abolish it, and to institute new Government, laying its foundation on such principles and organizing its powers in such form, as to them shall seem most likely to effect their Safety and Happiness. Prudence, indeed, will dictate that Governments long established should not be changed for light and transient causes; and accordingly all experience hath shown, that mankind are more disposed to suffer, while evils are sufferable, than to right themselves by abolishing the forms to which they are accustomed. But when a long train of abuses and usurpations, pursuing invariably the same Object evinces a design to reduce them under absolute **Despotism,** it is their right, it is their duty, to throw off such Government, and to provide new Guards for their future security.

[List of Grievances]

What It Means
List of Grievances The third part of the Declaration lists the colonists' complaints against the British government. Notice that King George III is singled out for blame.

usurpations *unjust uses of power*

Such has been the patient sufferance of these Colonies; and such is now the necessity which constrains them to alter their former Systems of Government. The history of the present King of Great Britain is a history of repeated injuries and **usurpations,** all having in direct object the establishment of an absolute Tyranny over these States. To prove this, let Facts be submitted to a candid world.

He has refused his Assent to Laws, the most wholesome and necessary for the public good.

He has forbidden his Governors to pass Laws of immediate and pressing importance, unless suspended in their operation till his Assent should be obtained; and when so suspended, he has utterly neglected to attend to them.

He has refused to pass other Laws for the accommodation of large districts of people, unless those people would **relinquish** the right of Representation in the Legislature, a right **inestimable** to them and formidable to tyrants only.

He has called together legislative bodies at places unusual, uncomfortable, and distant from the depository of their Public Records, for the sole purpose of fatiguing them into compliance with his measures.

He has dissolved Representative Houses repeatedly, for opposing with manly firmness his invasions on the rights of the people.

He has refused for a long time, after such dissolutions, to cause others to be elected; whereby the Legislative Powers, incapable of **Annihilation,** have returned to the People at large for their exercise; the State remaining in the mean time exposed to all the dangers of invasion from without, and **convulsions** within.

He has endeavoured to prevent the population of these States; for that purpose obstructing the Laws for **Naturalization of Foreigners;** refusing to pass others to encourage their migrations hither, and raising the conditions of new Appropriations of Lands.

He has obstructed the Administration of Justice, by refusing his Assent to Laws for establishing Judiciary Powers.

He has made Judges dependent on his Will alone, for the **tenure** of their offices, and the amount and payment of their salaries.

He has erected a multitude of New Offices, and sent hither swarms of Officers to harass our people, and eat out their substance.

relinquish *give up*
inestimable *priceless*

annihilation *destruction*

convulsions *violent disturbances*

Naturalization of Foreigners *process by which foreign-born persons become citizens*

tenure *term*

He has kept among us, in times of peace, Standing Armies without the Consent of our legislature.

He has affected to render the Military independent of and superior to the Civil Power.

He has combined with others to subject us to a jurisdiction foreign to our constitution, and unacknowledged by our laws; giving his Assent to their acts of pretended legislation:

quartering *lodging*

For **quartering** large bodies of troops among us:

For protecting them, by a mock Trial, from Punishment for any Murders which they should commit on the Inhabitants of these States:

For cutting off our Trade with all parts of the world:

For imposing taxes on us without our Consent:

For depriving us in many cases, of the benefits of Trial by Jury:

For transporting us beyond Seas to be tried for pretended offences:

For abolishing the free System of English Laws in a neighbouring Province, establishing therein an Arbitrary government, and enlarging its

render *make*

Boundaries so as to **render** it at once an example and fit instrument for introducing the same absolute rule into these Colonies:

For taking away our Charters, abolishing our most valuable Laws, and altering fundamentally the Forms of our Governments:

For suspending our own Legislature, and declaring themselves invested with Power to legislate for us in all cases whatsoever.

abdicated *given up*

He has **abdicated** Government here, by declaring us out of his Protection and waging War against us.

He has plundered our seas, ravaged our Coasts, burnt our towns, and destroyed the lives of our people.

He is at this time transporting large armies of foreign mercenaries to compleat the works of death, desolation and tyranny, already begun with circumstances of Cruelty & **perfidy** scarcely paralleled in the most bar-

perfidy *violation of trust*

barous ages, and totally unworthy the Head of a civilized nation.

He has constrained our fellow Citizens taken Captive on the high Seas to bear Arms against their Country, to become the executioners of their friends and Brethren, or to fall themselves by their Hands.

insurrections *rebellions*

He has excited domestic **insurrections** amongst us, and has endeavoured to bring on the inhabitants of our frontiers, the merciless Indian Savages, whose known rule of warfare, is an undistinguished destruction of all ages, sexes and conditions.

petitioned for redress *asked formally for a correction of wrongs*

In every stage of these Oppressions We have **Petitioned for Redress** in the most humble terms: Our repeated Petitions have been answered only by repeated injury. A Prince, whose character is thus marked by every act which may define a Tyrant, is unfit to be the ruler of a free People.

Nor have We been wanting in attention to our British brethren. We have warned them from time to time of attempts by their legislature to extend an

unwarrantable jurisdiction *unjustified authority*

unwarrantable jurisdiction over us. We have reminded them of the circumstances of our emigration and settlement here. We have appealed to their native justice and magnanimity, and we have conjured them by the ties of our common kindred to disavow these usurpations, which, would inevitably interrupt our connections and correspondence. They too have been deaf to the voice of justice and of **consanguinity**. We must, therefore,

consanguinity *originating from the same ancestor*

acquiesce in the necessity, which denounces our Separation, and hold them, as we hold the rest of mankind, Enemies in War, in Peace Friends.

[Resolution of Independence by the United States]

We, therefore, the Representatives of the united States of America, in General Congress, Assembled, appealing to the Supreme Judge of the world for the **rectitude** of our intentions, do, in the Name, and by Authority of the good People of these Colonies, solemnly publish and declare, That these United Colonies are, and of Right ought to be Free and Independent States; that they are Absolved from all Allegiance to the British Crown, and that all political connection between them and the State of Great Britain, is and ought to be totally dissolved; and that as Free and Independent States, they have full Power to levy War, conclude Peace, contract Alliances, establish Commerce, and to do all other Acts and Things which Independent States may of right do.

And for the support of this Declaration, with a firm reliance on the Protection of Divine Providence, we mutually pledge to each other our Lives, our Fortunes and our sacred Honor.

John Hancock
  President from
  Massachusetts

Georgia
Button Gwinnett
Lyman Hall
George Walton

North Carolina
William Hooper
Joseph Hewes
John Penn

South Carolina
Edward Rutledge
Thomas Heyward, Jr.
Thomas Lynch, Jr.
Arthur Middleton

Maryland
Samuel Chase
William Paca
Thomas Stone
Charles Carroll
  of Carrollton

Virginia
George Wythe
Richard Henry Lee
Thomas Jefferson
Benjamin Harrison
Thomas Nelson, Jr.
Francis Lightfoot Lee
Carter Braxton

Pennsylvania
Robert Morris
Benjamin Rush
Benjamin Franklin
John Morton
George Clymer
James Smith
George Taylor
James Wilson
George Ross

Delaware
Caesar Rodney
George Read
Thomas McKean

New York
William Floyd
Philip Livingston
Francis Lewis
Lewis Morris

New Jersey
Richard Stockton
John Witherspoon
Francis Hopkinson
John Hart
Abraham Clark

New Hampshire
Josiah Bartlett
William Whipple
Matthew Thornton

Massachusetts
Samuel Adams
John Adams
Robert Treat Paine
Elbridge Gerry

Rhode Island
Stephen Hopkins
William Ellery

Connecticut
Samuel Huntington
William Williams
Oliver Wolcott
Roger Sherman

What It Means
Resolution of Independence The Final section declares that the colonies are "Free and Independent States" with the full power to make war, to form alliances, and to trade with other countries.

rectitude *rightness*

What It Means
Signers of the Declaration The signers, as representatives of the American people, declared the colonies independent from Great Britain. Most members signed the document on August 2, 1776.

Chapter Summary

Road to Independence

Follow the arrows to review the causes and the effects that led to the colonies declaring independence.

Cause: French and Indian War leaves Great Britain in debt

Effect: Britain taxes colonies; Parliament passes Sugar Act and Stamp Act → **Becomes Cause**

Effect: Colonists boycott British goods → **Becomes Cause**

Effect: British send troops to Boston, resulting in the Boston Massacre → **Becomes Cause**

Effect: British repeal import taxes → **Becomes Cause**

Effect: Colonists respond with Boston Tea Party → **Becomes Cause**

Effect: Parliament passes the Coercive Acts → **Becomes Cause**

Effect: First Continental Congress drafts a statement of grievances → **Becomes Cause**

Effect: British troops fight colonists at battles of Lexington and Concord; British defeat colonial forces at Bunker Hill

Congress signs Declaration of Independence

Reviewing Key Terms

Write five true and four false statements using the terms below. Use only one term in each statement. Indicate which statements are true and which are false. Below each false statement explain why it is false.

1. revenue
2. boycott
3. repeal
4. propaganda
5. militia
6. minutemen
7. Patriot
8. preamble
9. unalienable rights

Reviewing Key Facts

10. What did the British do to keep colonists from moving westward?
11. How did the British government use the colonies to raise revenue? Why did this anger the colonists?
12. What incident caused the British Parliament to pass the Coercive Acts?
13. What was the purpose of the First Continental Congress?
14. How did the events of 1776 move the colonists closer to self-government?
15. According to the Declaration of Independence, if a government does not protect the basic rights of the people it governs, what do people have the right to do?
16. Identify the four sections of the Declaration of Independence.

Critical Thinking

17. **Drawing Conclusions** Why did the colonists think that the Stamp Act ignored the colonial tradition of self-government?
18. **Organizing Information** Re-create the diagram below and show ways the colonists, by working in groups, resisted the British during the revolutionary period.

Group action by colonists

19. **Analyzing Primary Sources** What did Patrick Henry mean when he said, "I am not a Virginian, but an American"?
20. **Analyzing Information** According to the Declaration of Independence, what are the three basic freedoms to which every person is entitled?

Practicing Skills

Distinguishing Fact From Opinion *Read the following statements. Tell whether each is a fact or an opinion.*

21. Great Britain should not have tried to stop the colonists from settling west of the Appalachians.

22. The Stamp Act placed a tax on almost all printed material in the colonies.

23. The Daughters of Liberty urged Americans to wear home-made fabrics.

24. Thomas Jefferson was a better writer than John Adams.

Geography and History Activity

Study the map on page 133; then answer the following questions.

25. What bodies of water did the Proclamation of 1763 prevent colonists from reaching?

26. What nation claimed the land west of the Mississippi River?

27. The land west of the Appalachian Mountains became part of what province?

28. What natural feature was cited in the Proclamation of 1763 as an approximate boundary?

Citizenship Cooperative Activity

29. Work with a group of classmates to create your own "Declaration of Independence." Use the original Declaration of Independence on pages 154–157 as a guide to create your document. Outline the basic freedoms that you expect to have as a citizen and describe why these freedoms are important to you. Then write at least three responsibilities and/or sacrifices that citizens should be willing to make to enjoy the freedoms you listed. After your group has completed its Declaration of Independence, have the groups come together as a class. Share all the groups' documents and compare the ideas expressed in each.

Technology Activity

30. **Using the Internet** On the Internet, locate the computer address for the National Archives or the Library of Congress in Washington, D.C. Search each site for documents concerning the drafting of the Declaration of Independence and/or photos of pamphlets produced by the colonies in the 1700s. Print a copy of what you find or sketch a likeness to share with the class.

Self-Check Quiz
Visit taj.glencoe.com and click on **Chapter 5—Self-Check Quizzes** to prepare for the chapter test.

Economics Activity

31. How did laws passed by the British after 1763 affect American trade and industry? Write your answer in a one-page paper.

Alternative Assessment

32. **Persuasive Writing** What do you think a good citizen is? Is it someone who follows the law? Or might it be someone who breaks the law in order to stand up for an ideal? Do you think that people like the Sons of Liberty acted as good citizens? Write a persuasive paper explaining your views.

The Princeton Review

Standardized Test Practice

Read the following passage and choose the *best* answer to the question that follows.

An English philosopher named John Locke wrote about his belief that people had natural rights. These included the right to life, liberty, and property. In *Two Treatises of Government,* Locke wrote that people created government to protect natural rights. If a government failed in its basic duty of protecting natural rights, people had the right to overthrow the government.

Locke's ideas contributed to the

A Proclamation of 1763.

B Intolerable Acts.

C Declaration of Independence.

D Articles of Confederation.

Test-Taking Tip:

Look for clues in the passage to support your answer. For example, the passage refers to *life, liberty and property.* It also states that *people had the right to overthrow the government.* Which answer does this information best support?

The American Revolution

1776–1783

Why It Matters

Although the United States declared its independence in 1776, no country recognized it as an independent nation at that time. It took a war and the efforts of American diplomats to win this recognition.

The Impact Today

In fighting for the principles set forth in the Declaration of Independence, the American Patriots laid the foundation for the United States of America we know today.

 The American Journey *Video The chapter 6 video, "The American Revolution," details how the American Patriots were able to defeat a powerful British military.*

1778
- France and U.S. form an alliance

1777
- Battle of Saratoga

1777–1778
- Patriot troops winter at Valley Forge

1776
- U.S. Declaration of Independence written

The Americas

1774   1776   1778

World

1774
- Joseph Priestley discovers oxygen

1776
- Adam Smith's *Wealth of Nations* published

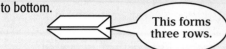

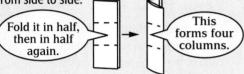

Organizing Information Study Foldable

When you group information into categories on a table, it is easier to compare characteristics of items. Make this foldable to help you compare the attitudes and actions of the Patriots and Loyalists.

Step 1 Fold a sheet of paper into thirds from top to bottom.

> This forms three rows.

Step 2 Open the paper and refold it into fourths from side to side.

> Fold it in half, then in half again.

> This forms four columns.

Step 3 Unfold, turn the paper, and draw lines along the folds.

Step 4 Label your table as shown.

The American Revolution	Patriots	Loyalists
Beginning		
Middle		
End		

Reading and Writing As you read about the American Revolution, write down facts about the attitudes and actions of the Patriots and Loyalists at different times during the war.

Molly Pitcher at the Battle of Monmouth by Dennis Malone Carter
According to legend, when her husband collapsed, Molly Pitcher immediately took his place in the gun crew and continued firing his cannon.

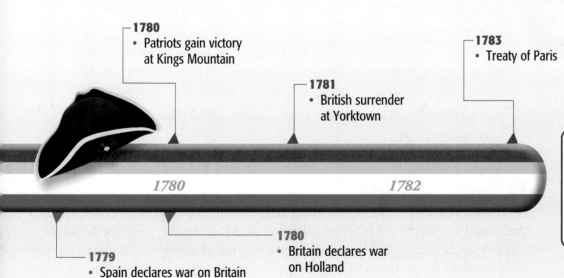

1780
• Patriots gain victory at Kings Mountain

1781
• British surrender at Yorktown

1783
• Treaty of Paris

1780   1782

1779
• Spain declares war on Britain

1780
• Britain declares war on Holland

HISTORY
Online

Chapter Overview
Visit taj.glencoe.com and click on Chapter 6—Chapter Overviews to preview chapter information.

The Early Years

Main Idea

The British and the Americans each had advantages and disadvantages as they faced one another in war.

Key Terms

neutral, mercenary, recruit

Reading Strategy

Classifying Information As you read the section, re-create the chart below and describe British and American advantages and disadvantages in the spaces provided.

	Advantages	Disadvantages
British		
American		

Read to Learn

- why some Americans supported the British.
- how the Battle of Saratoga marked a turning point of the war.

Section Theme

Groups and Institutions Although British forces won several battles early in the war, Patriot victories slowed their progress.

Preview of Events

♦1776   ♦1777   ♦1778

July 1776
American colonies declare independence

December 1776
Patriots capture Hessians at Trenton

October 1777
Burgoyne surrenders at Saratoga

1778
African American regiment forms in Rhode Island

✶✶✶✶✶✶✶✶✶
AN
American Story

The mighty British troops sailed to America, confident that they would quickly and easily crush the rebellious colonists. A British officer wrote to his friend, describing a military skirmish:

> September 3, 1776
> We landed on Long-Island. . . . [I]t was a fine sight to see with what [eagerness] they dispatched the Rebels with their bayonets after we had surrounded them so that they could not resist. . . . The island is all ours, and we shall soon take New-York, for the Rebels dare not look us in the face. I expect the affair will be over [after] this campaign. . . .

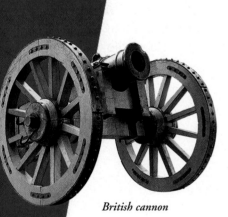

British cannon

The Opposing Sides

Following years of disagreement and negotiation, the tensions between the colonies and England had reached a critical point. After the colonies declared independence from England in July 1776, the war for freedom was unavoidable.

Both the British and the Americans expected the war for independence to be short. The British planned to crush the rebellion by force. Most of the Patriots—Americans who supported independence—believed the British would give up after losing one or two major battles. Few Patriots believed John Adams when he predicted in April 1776:

> 66We shall have a long . . . and bloody war to go through.99

At first glance the British had an overwhelming advantage in the war. They had the strongest navy in the world; an experienced, well-trained army; and the wealth of a worldwide empire. Britain also had a much larger population than the United States—over 8 million people in Britain compared to only 2.5 million in the United States.

The colonists suffered serious disadvantages. They lacked a regular army and a strong navy. American soldiers also lacked military experience, and weapons and ammunition were in short supply. Many Patriots belonged to militia groups—local forces—but they were volunteer soldiers who fought for short periods of time before returning home.

The Patriots faced another obstacle. Not all Americans supported the struggle for independence. Some people were neutral, taking neither side in the conflict. The Quakers, for example, would not participate in the war because they opposed all armed conflict. Still other Americans remained loyal to Britain.

The Loyalists

Those who remained loyal to Britain and opposed the war for independence were called Loyalists or Tories. At least one American in five was a Loyalist—perhaps as many as one in three. Some people changed sides during the war, depending on which army was closer. Loyalist strength varied

TWO VIEWPOINTS

The War Between Americans

The American Revolution was not only a war between the British and the Americans. It also divided Americans themselves. While American Patriots fought passionately for independence, Loyalists fought just as fiercely for their British king.

Loyalist Views
The Congress—1776 song

Ye Tories all rejoice and sing
Success to George our gracious King,
The faithful subjects tribute bring
And [denounce] the Congress.

Prepare, prepare, my friends prepare
For scenes of blood, the field of war;
To royal standard we'll repair,
And curse the haughty Congress.

Huzza! Huzza! and thrice Huzza!
Return peace, harmony and law!
Restore such times as once we saw
And bid adieu to Congress.

Patriot Views
Patrick Henry of Virginia, 1775 —

"Has Great Britain any enemy in this quarter of the world, to call for all this accumulation of navies and armies? No, sir, she has none. They are meant for us; they can be meant for no other. They are sent over to bind and rivet upon us those chains which the British ministry have been so long forging. And what have we to oppose to them? Shall we try argument? Sir, we have been trying that for the last ten years . . . but it has been all in vain."

Learning From History

1. Why did Patrick Henry believe that war was necessary?
2. Which argument—Loyalist or Patriot—would convince you if you had been an American at this time? Explain your answer.

163

Linking Past & Present

Women in War

Molly Pitcher and Deborah Sampson were two of the few women who actually fought in the Revolution. Other colonial women, along with their families, followed the armies to cook and clean for their husbands. Today women make up over 14 percent of the armed forces of the United States. Women soldiers served in Panama in 1989 and in the Persian Gulf War of 1991. Thousands more served in peacekeeping missions in Somalia, Bosnia, and Haiti.

Past
Molly Pitcher

Present
Women marines served in the Gulf War.

from region to region. In general it was strongest in the Carolinas and Georgia and weakest in New England.

Loyalists supported Britain for different reasons. Some remained loyal because they were members of the Anglican Church, headed by the British king. Some depended on the British for their jobs. Many feared the disorder that would come from challenging the established government. Others simply could not understand what all the commotion was about. No other country, one Loyalist complained, "faced a rebellion arising from such trivial causes."

The issue of independence disrupted normal relations. Friends and families were divided over their loyalty to Britain. For example, William Franklin, son of Patriot Benjamin Franklin, was a Loyalist who had served as a royal governor. As one Connecticut Loyalist observed:

66Neighbor was against neighbor, father against son and son against father. He that would not thrust his own blade through his brother's heart was called an infamous villain.99

African Americans in the War

Some African Americans also sided with the Loyalists. At the start of the war, the British appealed to enslaved Africans to join them. Lord Dunmore, the royal governor of Virginia, announced that enslaved people who fought on the British side would be freed, and many men answered his call. Eventually some of them ended up free in Canada, and others settled the British colony of Sierra Leone in Africa.

Patriot Advantages

The Americans possessed some advantages. They were fighting on their own ground and fought with great determination to protect it. The British, on the other hand, had to wage war in a faraway land and were forced to ship soldiers and supplies thousands of miles across the Atlantic Ocean.

The makeup of the British army in America also helped the Patriots. The British relied on mercenaries—hired soldiers—to fight. The Americans called the mercenaries **Hessians,** after the region in Germany where most of them lived. To gain support for the war effort, Patriots compared their own troops, who were fighting for the freedom of their own land, to the Hessians, who fought for money. The Patriots had a much greater stake in winning the war than the hired soldiers did. This personal stake gave the Americans an edge over the Hessians in battle.

The Americans' greatest advantage was probably their leader, George Washington. Few could match him for courage, honesty, and determination. The war might have taken a different turn without Washington steering its course.

Raising an Army

The Americans placed great value on liberty and personal freedom for citizens. After throwing off the rule of the British Parliament, they were unwilling to transfer power to their own Continental Congress. In some ways the American Revolution was really 13 separate wars, with each state pursuing its own interests. As a result Congress experienced difficulty enlisting soldiers and raising money to fight the war.

Although the militia played an essential role in the Patriots' forces, the Americans also needed a regular army—well-trained soldiers who could fight anywhere in the colonies. The Congress established the Continental Army but depended on the states to recruit, or enlist, soldiers.

At first soldiers signed up for one year of army service. General Washington appealed for longer terms. "If we ever hope for success," he said, "we must have men enlisted for the whole term of the war." Eventually the Continental Congress offered enlistments for three years or for the length of the war. Most soldiers, however, still signed up for only a year.

Women also fought with the Patriot forces. **Margaret Corbin** of Pennsylvania accompanied her husband when he joined the Continental Army. After he died in battle, she took his place. Mary Ludwig Hays McCauley also accompanied her husband in battle. The soldiers called her "Moll of the Pitcher," or **Molly Pitcher,** because she carried water pitchers to the soldiers. As a teenager, **Deborah Sampson** of Massachusetts watched her brothers and their friends go off to war. Moved by a sense of adventure, she disguised herself as a boy and enlisted.

Reading Check **Summarizing** What disadvantages did the Patriots face?

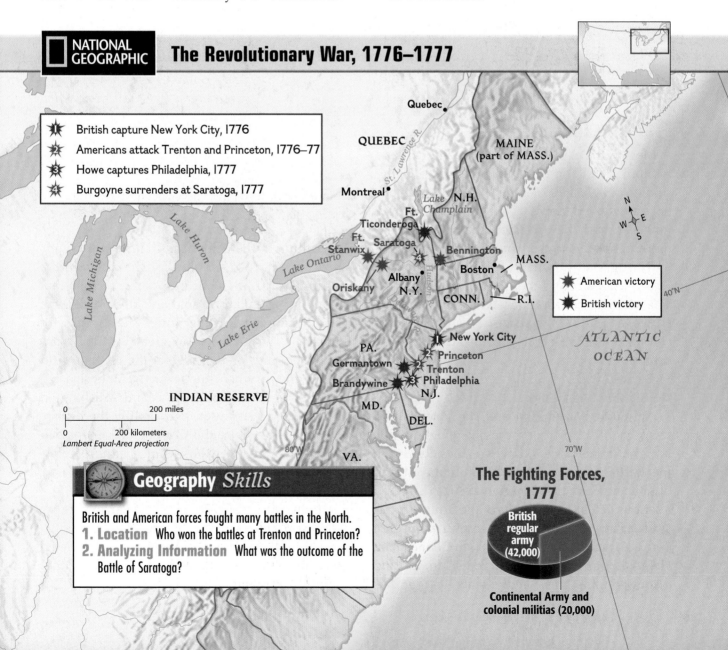

NATIONAL GEOGRAPHIC   The Revolutionary War, 1776–1777

- ✸ British capture New York City, 1776
- ✸ Americans attack Trenton and Princeton, 1776–77
- ✸ Howe captures Philadelphia, 1777
- ✸ Burgoyne surrenders at Saratoga, 1777

Quebec

QUEBEC

MAINE (part of MASS.)

Montreal

Lake Champlain

N.H.

Ft. Ticonderoga

Ft. Stanwix   Saratoga

Bennington

MASS.

Boston

Oriskany

Albany

N.Y.

CONN.

R.I.

✸ American victory

✸ British victory

40°N

New York City

ATLANTIC OCEAN

PA.

Princeton

Germantown   Trenton

Brandywine   Philadelphia

N.J.

INDIAN RESERVE

MD.

DEL.

VA.

0   200 miles

0   200 kilometers

Lambert Equal-Area projection

80°W

70°W

Geography *Skills*

British and American forces fought many battles in the North.

1. **Location** Who won the battles at Trenton and Princeton?
2. **Analyzing Information** What was the outcome of the Battle of Saratoga?

The Fighting Forces, 1777

British regular army (42,000)

Continental Army and colonial militias (20,000)

People In History

Thomas Paine 1737–1809

In early 1776 Thomas Paine published a pamphlet titled *Common Sense*. The pamphlet moved many American colonists toward independence. After taking part in the retreat across New York and New Jersey, Paine published another pamphlet to help boost Americans' lagging spirits. In *The American Crisis*, written in December 1776, he warned: "These are the times that try men's souls. The summer soldier and the sunshine patriot will in this crisis shrink from the service of their country; but he that stands it now deserves the love and thanks of man and woman."

He reminded Americans that "the harder the conflict, the more glorious the triumph."

Washington had Paine's stirring words read to his troops to inspire them to continue the fight for independence. Throughout the colonies people passed copies of *The American Crisis* from hand to hand and discussed Paine's patriotic ideas.

Fighting in New York

Most of the early battles involved few troops. At Bunker Hill, for example, about 2,200 British soldiers fought 1,200 Americans. The British had not yet won a decisive victory over the Patriots, however, and they realized they would need more troops to end the war quickly.

During the summer of 1776, Britain sent 32,000 troops across the Atlantic to New York. The British commander, **General William Howe,** hoped the sheer size of his army would convince the Patriots to give up. He was soon disappointed.

Defeat on Long Island

Although Washington and the Patriots had fewer than 20,000 troops, they were determined to fight. In late August the two sides clashed in the **Battle of Long Island.** Outnumbered and outmaneuvered, the Continental Army suffered a serious defeat at the hands of the British forces.

One Patriot, **Nathan Hale,** proved himself a hero at Long Island. A teacher from Connecticut, Hale volunteered to spy on British troops and disguised himself as a Dutch schoolteacher. The British discovered his true identity, however, and hanged him. According to tradition, just before his hanging, Hale's last words were,

> **"**I only regret that I have but one life to lose for my country.**"**

Although the Americans showed bravery, they ran short of supplies for the army. In the autumn of 1776, a British officer wrote that many of the Patriot soldiers killed on Long Island had not been wearing shoes, socks, or jackets. "They are also in great want of blankets," he said, predicting that the rebels would suffer greatly when "the severe weather sets in."

After the defeat on Long Island, Washington retreated to Manhattan, pursued by the British. By late November, the Continental Army had retreated across New Jersey into Pennsylvania.

A Low Point

In the winter of 1776–1777, the Patriots' cause was near collapse. The size of the Continental Army had dwindled. Some soldiers completed their terms of service and went home. Other soldiers ran away.

Washington wrote his brother that, if new soldiers were not recruited soon, "I think the game is pretty near up." Still, Washington could not believe that the fight for liberty would truly fail.

✓ **Reading Check** **Describing** Why was the total number of soldiers in the Continental Army decreasing?

Patriot Gains

Washington pleaded with the Continental Congress for more troops. He asked the Congress to enlist free African Americans. Early in the war, the Southern states had persuaded the Congress to not allow African Americans in the Continental Army. Many white people in the South felt uncomfortable about giving guns to African Americans and allowing them to serve as soldiers. In Southern states with large enslaved populations, whites feared revolts.

African Americans Join the Fight

As the need for soldiers grew, some states ignored the ban and enlisted African Americans. Rhode Island raised an all-African American regiment in 1778. By the war's end, every state except South Carolina enlisted African Americans to fight.

Historians estimate that as many as 5,000 African Americans joined the Patriots. Among them were **Lemuel Hayes** and **Peter Salem,** who fought at Concord. African Americans fought for the same reasons as other Americans. They believed in the Patriot cause or they needed the money. Some soldiers were enslaved Africans who had run away from slaveholders. Others fought to earn their freedom.

American Victories in New Jersey

The British army settled in New York for the winter of 1776, leaving some troops in New Jersey at **Trenton** and **Princeton.** Armies usually called a halt to their wars during the winter, and the British did not expect to fight.

Stationed across the Delaware River from the British camp in New Jersey, Washington saw a chance to catch the British off guard. On Christmas night 1776, Washington took 2,400 troops

Fact · Fiction · Folklore

America's Flags

First Stars and Stripes, 1777–1795 On June 14, 1777, the Continental Congress designed the first Stars and Stripes. The Congress determined that "the Flag of the United States be 13 stripes, alternate red and white; that the Union be 13 stars, white in a blue field representing a new constellation." For Americans past and present, the color red symbolizes courage; white, purity of ideals; and blue, strength and unity of the states.

across the icy river and surprised the enemy at Trenton the next day. The Americans captured more than 900 Hessians. The British sent reinforcements under Lord Charles Cornwallis, but Washington led his troops away from Cornwallis's men. Washington then marched the army to Princeton, where they drove away the British. One discouraged British soldier wrote in his diary,

❝A few days ago [the Americans] had given up the cause for lost. Their late successes have turned the scale and now they are all liberty mad again.❞

✓ **Reading Check** **Explaining** What was the outcome of the battle at Trenton?

A British Plan for Victory

The British worked out a battle plan for 1777. They would take Albany, New York, and gain control of the Hudson River. This would separate New England from the Middle Colonies.

The plan involved a three-pronged attack. General John Burgoyne would lead nearly 8,000 troops south from Canada. A second force, under Lieutenant Colonel Barry St. Leger, would move east from Lake Ontario. A third group, under General Howe, would move north from New York City. The three British forces would meet at Albany and destroy the Patriot troops.

The British Capture Philadelphia

Howe planned to take Philadelphia, the American capital, before marching to Albany. After winning battles in September 1777 at Brandywine and Paoli near Philadelphia, Howe's troops captured the city itself, forcing the Continental Congress to flee. In early October Washington attacked the main British camp at nearby Germantown, but he was forced to withdraw. Howe postponed the move north to Albany and decided to spend the winter in Philadelphia.

Patriots Slow the British

Meanwhile problems delayed the British plans to take Albany. In August American soldiers halted St. Leger's advance at Fort Stanwix, New York. Led by **Benedict Arnold,** the Americans forced the British to retreat.

General Burgoyne's army was not making much progress toward Albany either. In July Burgoyne captured Fort Ticonderoga, but trouble followed. Burgoyne, a dashing general who enjoyed good food and fine clothes, traveled with 30 wagons of luxury goods. Loaded down with this heavy baggage, Burgoyne's army moved slowly through the dense forests. To make matters worse, the Americans blocked the British by chopping down trees across their path.

In need of food and supplies, Burgoyne sent 800 troops and Native Americans to capture the American supply base at Bennington, Vermont.

The British troops' brightly colored uniforms made the soldiers easy targets in the woods. A local militia group, the **Green Mountain Boys,** attacked and defeated them. Having lost part of his army and desperately short of supplies, Burgoyne retreated in October to the town of **Saratoga** in New York.

The Battle of Saratoga

At Saratoga Burgoyne faced serious trouble. He expected British forces from the west and south to join him, but they had not arrived. The Americans had stopped St. Leger's army at Fort Stanwix, and Howe's forces were still in Philadelphia. In addition, American troops under the command of **General Horatio Gates** blocked his path to the south. Burgoyne found himself surrounded by an army about three times as large as his own. Burgoyne made a last desperate attack on October 7, but the Americans held firm.

On October 17, 1777, General Burgoyne surrendered. As a Patriot band played "Yankee Doodle," over 5,700 British soldiers handed their weapons to the Americans. The British plan to separate New England from the Middle Colonies had failed. Soon afterward, General Howe resigned as commander of the British troops in America. He was replaced by General Henry Clinton.

✔️ **Reading Check** **Analyzing** Why was the Battle of Saratoga an important victory for the Americans?

SECTION 1 ASSESSMENT

Checking for Understanding

1. **Key Terms** Write a short paragraph in which you define the following terms: neutral, mercenary, recruit.
2. **Reviewing Facts** Compare the strengths of the British and American military forces.

Reviewing Themes

3. **Groups and Institutions** What problems did the Continental Congress face in raising an army to fight during the American Revolution?

Critical Thinking

4. **Analyzing Information** Explain why African Americans were willing to enlist in the Continental Army.
5. **Organizing Information** Re-create the chart below and describe each battle, including its outcome, in the space provided.

Battle	Description
Long Island	
Trenton/Princeton	

Analyzing Visuals

6. **Geography Skills** Examine the map on page 165. Which event came first—the British capture of New York or the British capture of Philadelphia?

Interdisciplinary Activity

Descriptive Writing Write a newspaper article that describes the Battle of Saratoga. Include details about British and American strategies and troop movements.

Reading a Military Map

Why Learn This Skill?

In your study of American history, you often have to read maps. A military map shows the areas where battles occurred, routes soldiers took, who won the battles, and who controlled various sites.

Learning the Skill

Military maps use colors, symbols, and arrows to show major battles, troop movements, and defensive positions during a particular battle or over a period of time.

When reading a military map, follow these steps:

- Read the map title. This will indicate the location and time period covered on the map.

- Read the map key. This tells what the symbols on the map represent. For example, battle sites may be symbolized by crossed swords, a burst shell, or a star.

- Study the map itself. This will reveal the actual events or sequence of events that took place. Notice the geography of the area and try to determine how it could affect military strategy.

Practicing the Skill

Analyze the information on the map on this page; then answer the following questions.

1 What troops surrounded Boston Harbor? How do you know this?

2 What action did the American forces take after fighting the Battle of Bunker Hill?

3 Which commander led the British troops to Breed's Hill?

4 In which direction did the British forces move when they left Boston? What parts of the map help you find this information?

NATIONAL GEOGRAPHIC

Battle of Bunker Hill, June 17, 1775

0   1 mile
0   1 kilometer
Lambert Equal-Area projection

Bunker Hill

Breed's Hill

GAGE

Charlestown

Boston Harbor

Boston (occupied by British)

N
W–E
S

Charles River

Dorchester Neck

← American forces
▬ American lines
← British forces
⌐⌐⌐⌐⌐ Ridge

Applying the Skill

Reading a Military Map Find a map of a specific battle of the American Revolution in an encyclopedia or other reference book. Create a three-dimensional model of the battle and use moveable pieces to represent troops. Then demonstrate troop movements over the course of the battle.

GO TO

Glencoe's **Skillbuilder Interactive Workbook CD-ROM, Level 1,** provides instruction and practice in key social studies skills.

What were people's lives like in the past?

What—and who—were people talking about? What did they eat? What did they do for fun? These two pages will give you some clues to everyday life in the U.S. as you step back in time with TIME Notebook.

BETTMANN/CORBIS

Eyewitness
The Boston Tea Party

GEORGE HEWES *is one of hundreds of people roused by Sam Adams on December 16, 1773. Adams whipped the crowd into a rage, resulting in the dumping of 342 cases of untaxed British tea into Boston Harbor. Hewes boarded one of the ships that night and here is what he remembers:*

"IT WAS NOW EVENING, AND I IMMEDIATELY DRESSED MYSELF IN THE costume of an Indian, equipped with a small hatchet . . . and a club, with which, after having painted my face and hands with coal dust in the shop of a blacksmith, I [went] to Griffin's Wharf, where the ships lay that contained the tea. . . .I fell in with many who were dressed, equipped and painted as I was, and who fell in with me and marched in order to the place of our destination. . . .We then were ordered by our commander to open the hatches and take out all the chests of tea and throw them overboard, and we immediately proceeded to execute his orders, first cutting and splitting the chests with our tomahawks, so as to thoroughly expose them to the effects of the water."

1770s WORD PLAY

What's In A Name?

Match the nickname with the person or thing to the right.

1. Sable Genius

2. Molly Pitcher

3. Battalia Pie

4. Brown Bess

a. Mary Hays gave American soldiers water and fired a cannon in the war

b. Benjamin Banneker, African American, built the first American clock

c. Most famous type of gun used in the 1700s

d. Meal made of pigeon, rabbit, sheep tongues, and the red growth on the heads of roosters

Benjamin Banneker

NORTH WIND PICTURES

answers: 1. b; 2. a; 3. d; 4. c

How to Load and Shoot a Cannon

Here are the steps that soldiers follow before firing their cannons at the British:

1 As the officer in charge, you must be loud enough to be heard above the noise of cannon shot.

2 Have six or seven strong people help you as the cannon is difficult to load and shoot. Then you must call out the following commands:

"WORM!" The **wormer**, a soldier with a long piece of iron, must step forward to clean out the barrel of the cannon.

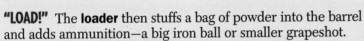

"SPONGE!" The **sponger** must stick a wet sheepskin into the cannon barrel to cool it off and put out any sparks from the last use.

BROWN BROTHERS

"LOAD!" The **loader** then stuffs a bag of powder into the barrel and adds ammunition—a big iron ball or smaller grapeshot.

"RAM!" The **rammer** will push and pack the ammunition down the barrel with a pole.

"PICK AND PRIME!" The **gunner** must now open a bag of gun powder. He puts a little powder in a vent hole.

"GIVE!" The **gunner** must light a fuse.

"FIRE!" The **gunner** lights the powder on top of the barrel with the fuse. The flame jumps through the air vent and ignites the powder inside the cannon.

"STAND BACK!" The **cannon ball** will explode out of the barrel at about 1,000 feet per second.

NUMBERS

THE COLONIES AT THE TIME

60 Seconds it takes a Minuteman soldier to get ready to fight

16 Age of Sibyl Ludington, who in 1777 made a 40-mile midnight ride like Paul Revere's, shouting "The British are coming!"

10,000 The approximate number of enslaved persons who earned their freedom by fighting against the British

200 Number of American doctors with actual medical degrees in 1776

COLONIAL GAMES

Nine Man Morris Scores a Ten!

What are all the colonial kids playing?
It's that entertaining game **Nine Man Morris**.

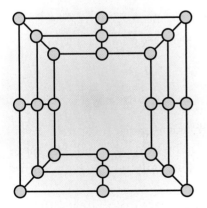

1. Get nine copper coins, nine silver coins, and a friend to play with you.

2. Make a drawing like the one shown on a piece of paper.

3. Give yourself the copper coins and your friend the silver ones.

4. Take turns placing your coins on the dots in the drawing.

5. Be the first to line up three of your coins in a row.

6. Capture one of the other player's coins when you get three in a row.

7. Keep playing until one player is down to two coins. The other player wins!

The War Continues

Guide to Reading

Main Idea
As the Revolutionary War continued, the Americans received support from European countries.

Key Terms
desert, inflation

Reading Strategy
Classifying Information As you read the section, re-create the chart below and describe how each person helped the Americans fight for independence.

Person	Contribution
Lafayette	
Pulaski	
Von Steuben	
De Miralles	

Read to Learn
• why other nations helped the Patriots.
• how Washington's troops survived the winter at Valley Forge.
• what challenges Americans faced at home as a result of the war.

Section Theme
Groups and Institutions Patriots faced hardships but were encouraged by help from Europeans.

Preview of Events

♦1777   ♦1778   ♦1779

October 1777
Americans win
Battle of Saratoga

Winter 1777–1778
Patriot troops suffer
at Valley Forge

February 1778
France and U.S.
form an alliance

1779
Spain declares
war on Britain

*French medal showing
Benjamin Franklin*

★ AN ★
American Story

The Continental Congress sent Jonathan Austin of Boston to France to deliver the news of the American victory at Saratoga. Benjamin Franklin was already in France trying to get that country to help the Americans against the British. As soon as Austin arrived, Franklin nervously inquired, "Is Philadelphia taken?" Austin answered, "It is, sir. But, sir, I have greater news than that. General Burgoyne and his whole army are prisoners of war."

Gaining Allies

The victory at Saratoga in October 1777 boosted American spirits. Even more, Saratoga marked a turning point in the war. The European nations, especially France, realized that the United States might actually win its war against Great Britain.

Now was the time for the Americans to seek support from Great Britain's rivals. By late 1777 Benjamin Franklin had been in Paris for a year, trying to get the French to support the Americans' fight for independence. With his skill and charm, Franklin gained many friends for the United States. The French gave the Americans money secretly, but they had not committed to an alliance.

France

News of the American victory at Saratoga caused a shift in France's policy. Realizing that the Americans had a chance of defeating Britain, the French announced support for the United States openly. In February 1778, the French and the Americans worked out a trade agreement and an alliance. France declared war on Britain and sent money, equipment, and troops to aid the American Patriots.

Spain

Other European nations also helped the American cause, mostly because they hated the British. Although Spain did not recognize American independence until after the Revolution, Spain declared war on Britain in 1779. The Spanish governor of Louisiana, **Bernardo de Gálvez** (GAHL•vez), raised an army. Gálvez's soldiers forced British troops from Baton Rouge and Natchez. Then the army captured British forts at Mobile in 1780 and Pensacola in 1781. Gálvez's campaign through hundreds of miles of wilderness diverted British troops from other fronts.

Winter at Valley Forge

Word of the French-American alliance did not reach the United States until the spring of 1778. Meanwhile British general Howe and his forces spent the winter in comfort in Philadelphia. Washington set up camp at **Valley Forge,** about 20 miles to the west of the British. Washington and his troops endured a winter of terrible suffering, lacking decent food, clothing, and shelter. Washington's greatest challenge at Valley Forge was keeping the Continental Army together.

Joseph Martin, a young private from Connecticut, spent the winter at Valley Forge. "We had a hard duty to perform," he wrote years later, "and little or no strength to perform it with." Most of the men lacked blankets, shoes, and shirts. Martin made a rough pair of moccasins for himself out of a scrap of cowhide. Although the moccasins hurt his feet, they were better than going barefoot, "as hundreds of my companions had to do, till they might be tracked by their bloods upon the rough, frozen ground."

📖 (See page 963 for more accounts of the winter at Valley Forge.)

Not surprisingly, many men deserted, or left without permission, while the Continental Army was camped at Valley Forge. Some officers resigned. The army seemed to be falling apart.

History *Through Art*

The March to Valley Forge by William B.T. Trego
While waiting for French aid, American soldiers spent a brutal winter at Valley Forge, Pennsylvania. **What were the soldiers' living conditions at Valley Forge?**

Yet somehow, with strong determination, the Continental Army survived the winter, and conditions gradually improved. The troops built huts and gathered supplies from the countryside. Volunteers—including Washington's wife, Martha—made clothes for the troops and cared for the sick. Washington declared that no army had ever suffered "such uncommon hardships" with such "patience and fortitude." New soldiers joined the ranks in the spring.

66The army grows stronger every day," one officer wrote. "There is a spirit of discipline among the troops that is better than numbers.99

In April 1778 Washington told his troops of the Patriots' alliance with France. Everyone's spirits rose at the thought of help from overseas. The Continental Army celebrated with a religious service and a parade.

Help From Overseas

Among the hardy soldiers who spent the winter at Valley Forge was a French nobleman, the **Marquis de Lafayette** (lah•fay•EHT). Filled with enthusiasm for the ideas expressed in the Declaration of Independence, Lafayette had bought a ship and set sail for America. He rushed to join the battle for freedom. Lafayette wrote to his wife and children in France,

66The future of America is closely bound up with the future of all mankind.99

Upon his arrival in Philadelphia, Lafayette offered his services and those of his followers to General Washington. Lafayette became a trusted aide to Washington.

Other Europeans also volunteered to work for the Patriot cause. Two Poles—Thaddeus Kosciusko (kawsh•CHUSH•koh), an engineer, and Casimir Pulaski, a cavalry officer—contributed to the American efforts. Pulaski died in 1779, fighting for the Continental Army.

Friedrich von Steuben (STOO•buhn), a former army officer from Germany, also came to help Washington. Von Steuben drilled the Patriot troops at Valley Forge, teaching them military discipline. He turned the ragged Continental Army into a more effective fighting force.

Juan de Miralles (mee•RAH•yays) arrived in Philadelphia in 1778 as a representative of Spain. At his urging, Spain, Cuba, and Mexico sent financial aid to the colonies. Miralles befriended many Patriot leaders and lent money to the cause.

$ Economics
Money Problems

Getting money to finance the war was a major problem. The Continental Congress had no power to raise money through taxes. Although

Causes and Effects of French-American Alliance in 1778

Causes
- Longstanding hostility between Britain and France
- Conflict between Britain and France during French and Indian War
- Victory at Saratoga boosts French confidence in Patriots

Effects
- France lends money to the Continental Congress
- France sends soldiers and ships to help American forces
- Americans win independence

Graphic Organizer → Skills

In 1777 Benjamin Franklin negotiated with French leaders for money and support for the American cause.

Drawing Conclusions Why was it important for France to recognize the independence of the American colonies?

the Congress received some money from the states and from foreign countries, much more money was needed.

To pay for the war, the Congress and the states printed hundreds of millions of dollars worth of paper money. These bills quickly lost their value, however, because the amount of bills in circulation grew faster than the supply of gold and silver backing them. This led to inflation, which means that it took more and more money to buy the same amount of goods. The Congress stopped issuing the paper money because no one would use it. However, the Americans had no other way to finance the fighting of their war for independence.

☑ **Reading Check** **Describing** How did Lafayette help the Patriot cause?

Picturing **History**

Paper notes issued by the Congress and the states rapidly declined in value. By the time these South Carolina bills were printed, their real value was only 10 percent of their face value. **Why did American notes quickly decline in value?**

Life on the Home Front

The war changed the lives of all Americans, even those who stayed at home. With thousands of men away in military service, women took over the duties that had once been the responsibility of their husbands or fathers. Other women ran their husbands' or their own businesses.

Changing Attitudes

The ideals of liberty and freedom that inspired the American Revolution caused some women to question their place in society. In an essay on education, **Judith Sargeant Murray** of Massachusetts argued that women's minds are as good as men's. Girls, therefore, should get as good an education as boys. At a time when most girls received little schooling, this was a radical idea.

Abigail Adams also championed women's interests. She wrote to her husband, John Adams, who was a member of the Second Continental Congress:

❝I cannot say that I think you are very generous to the ladies, for, whilst you are proclaiming peace and good will to men, emancipating all nations, you insist upon retaining an absolute power over wives.❞

Treatment of Loyalists

Every state had some Loyalists. Thousands of them fought with the British against the Patriots. To prove their loyalty to Britain, some Loyalists spied and informed on the Patriots.

Many Loyalists, however, fled the American colonies during the Revolutionary War. They packed their belongings and sold whatever they could. Some left hurriedly for England. Others took off for Florida. Still others journeyed to the frontier beyond the Appalachian Mountains and to Canada.

Loyalists who remained in the United States faced difficult times. Their neighbors often shunned them. Some became victims of mob violence. Loyalists who actively helped the British could be arrested and tried as traitors. Patriots executed a few Loyalists, but such extreme measures were unusual.

▣ Citizenship

Hopes for Equality

The Revolutionary War ideals of freedom and liberty inspired some white Americans to question slavery. As early as the Stamp Act crisis,

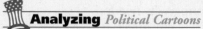
religious groups and other groups had voted to condemn slavery. In 1778 Governor William Livingston of New Jersey asked the legislature to free all enslaved people in the state. Slavery, Livingston said, was "utterly inconsistent with the principles of Christianity and humanity."

African Americans made similar arguments. In New Hampshire enslaved Africans asked the legislature for their freedom

66so that the name of *slave* may not be heard in a land gloriously contending for the sweets of freedom.99

From the beginning of the war—at Lexington, Concord, and Bunker Hill—African American soldiers fought for the American cause. To some fighting for freedom, both African American and white, the Revolution seemed to bring nearer the day when slavery would be abolished. Vermont, New Hampshire, Massachusetts, and Pennsylvania attempted to end slavery in their states. The issue of slavery would remain unsettled for many years, however.

Reading Check **Explaining** What contributions did women make during the war?

SECTION 2 ASSESSMENT

Checking for Understanding

1. **Key Terms** Write a short paragraph in which you define the terms desert and inflation correctly. Use standard sentence structure and spelling in your paragraph.
2. **Reviewing Facts** Explain why the French did not publicly support the Americans until after the Battle of Saratoga.

Reviewing Themes

3. **Groups and Institutions** How were the Loyalists treated by the Patriots during the war?

Critical Thinking

4. **Making Inferences** The Americans claimed to fight for liberty and freedom. How did these ideals make women and enslaved Africans question their positions in society?
5. **Determining Cause and Effect** Re-create the diagram below and describe what happened when the Continental Congress tried to finance the war by printing money.

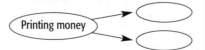

Analyzing Visuals

6. **Graphic Organizer Skills** Study the cause-and-effect chart on page 174. In what ways did France help the Americans in their fight for independence? What event led France to aid the Americans in the first place?

Interdisciplinary Activity

Expository Writing Why was Washington such an effective leader? Write a one-page paper describing both his personal and professional characteristics.

The War Moves West and South

Guide to Reading

Main Idea
Revolutionary War fighting spreads to the West and South.

Key Terms
blockade, privateer, guerrilla warfare

Reading Strategy
Organizing Information As you read the section, re-create the chart below and describe the significance of key battles in the West and South.

Battle	Significance
Vincennes	
Camden	
Kings Mountain	
Guilford Courthouse	

Read to Learn
• how the war involved Native Americans.
• how a new kind of fighting developed in the South.

Section Theme
Geography and History As the war continued, Patriot victories were won in the West, in the South, and at sea.

Preview of Events

♦1778   ♦1779   ♦1780   ♦1781

July 1778
George Rogers Clark captures Vincennes

September 1779
The *Serapis* surrenders to John Paul Jones

May 1780
British troops take Charles Town

January 1781
Patriots defeat British at Cowpens

*The Swamp Fox
and his troops*

AN American Story

Francis Marion organized a small but expert fighting force in South Carolina. Living off the land, Marion's soldiers harassed British troops by staging daring surprise attacks, sabotaging communication and supply lines, and rescuing American prisoners. After these attacks, Marion withdrew his men to swamps and forests. His habit of disappearing into the swamps to get away from the British earned him his nickname, the Swamp Fox.

War in the West

At the same time Francis Marion was staging his daring raids in the South, important battles of the Revolutionary War were taking place along the western frontier. Much of this fighting involved Native Americans. Although some helped the Patriots, more sided with the British. For many Native Americans, the British seemed to present less of a threat than the Americans did.

West of the Appalachian Mountains, the British and their Native American allies were raiding American settlements. Mohawk chief **Joseph Brant** led a number of brutal attacks in southwestern New York and northern Pennsylvania. After the war, Brant served as a representative of the Mohawk people to the Continental Congress and tried to get a fair land settlement for his people. Unable to reach an agreement, Brant and his people moved to Canada.

Henry Hamilton commanded Detroit, the main British base in the West. Some called Hamilton the "hair buyer" because he paid Native Americans for the scalps of settlers.

★ Geography
Victory at Vincennes

George Rogers Clark, a lieutenant colonel in the Virginia militia, set out to end the British attacks on western settlers. In July 1778, Clark and 175 soldiers sailed down the Ohio River to the mouth of the Tennessee River. After marching about 120 miles, the Patriots seized the British post at Kaskaskia (ka•SKAS•kee•uh) in present-day Illinois. Then, in July 1778, they captured the British town of **Vincennes** (vihn•SEHNZ) in present-day Indiana.

During Clark's absence in December, British troops under Henry Hamilton's command recaptured Vincennes. Clark vowed to get it back. In February 1779, after marching for days through countrysides flooded with icy waters, Clark and his troops surprised the British, forcing Hamilton to surrender. George Rogers Clark's victory at Vincennes strengthened the American position in the West.

✓ **Reading Check** **Explaining** What British outposts did George Rogers Clark's troops capture?

Glory at Sea

As fighting continued on the western frontier, other battles raged at sea. Great Britain used its powerful navy to patrol American waterways,

What If...

Washington Had Stepped Down?

Throughout the Revolutionary War, Washington succeeded in holding his army together, despite many difficulties. He had to deal with low morale among soldiers who lived on poor rations and received low pay. The Continental Congress often interfered with his conduct of military operations. During the gloomy winter at Valley Forge, some congressmen and army officers plotted to replace Washington as commander in chief.

One of his critics was Dr. Benjamin Rush, who served for a time as surgeon general of the Continental Army. In a letter to John Adams, Rush compared Washington unfavorably to the hero of Saratoga, Horatio Gates.

❝I am more convinced than ever of the necessity of discipline and system in the management of our affairs. I have heard several officers who have served under General Gates compare his army to a well-regulated family. The same gentlemen have compared Gen'l Washington's imitation of an army to an unformed mob. Look at the characters of both! The one [Gates] on the pinnacle of military glory—exulting in the success of schemes planned with wisdom, and executed with vigor and bravery. . . . See the other [Washington] outgeneraled and twice beaten. . . .❞

—Dr. Benjamin Rush, October 21, 1777

keeping the ships of the Patriots and the ships of their allies from entering or leaving American harbors. This British blockade prevented supplies and reinforcements from reaching the Continental Army.

Privateers

To break the British naval blockade, the Second Continental Congress ordered the construction of 13 American warships. Only two of these, however, sailed to sea. The Americans destroyed four of their own ships to keep them out of British hands. Others were quickly captured by the British. Several states maintained their own small fleets, but the American navy was too weak to operate effectively.

American privateers captured more British vessels at sea than did the American navy. The privateers were privately owned merchant ships equipped with weapons. The Congress authorized approximately 2,000 ships to sail as privateers and attack enemy shipping. Finding crews for these ships was not difficult. Sailors

from the whaling and fishing ports of New England signed on eagerly for the profitable privateering trade.

John Paul Jones

A daring American naval officer, **John Paul Jones,** began raiding British ports in 1777. He sailed in an old French ship that Benjamin Franklin had obtained for him. Jones gave the ship a French name, *Bonhomme Richard,* in honor of Franklin's *Poor Richard's Almanack.*

Sailing near the coast of Great Britain in September 1779, the *Bonhomme Richard* met a large fleet of British merchant ships escorted by the warship *Serapis.* The *Bonhomme Richard* moved close to the *Serapis* before attacking. The two ships fought for more than three hours. At one point Jones's ship was so badly damaged that the British captain asked whether Jones wished to surrender. Jones is said to have answered, "I have not yet begun to fight."

In the end the *Serapis* surrendered, but the *Bonhomme Richard* sank not long after the battle. Still, his victory made John Paul Jones a naval hero to the American Patriots.

☑ **Reading Check** **Describing** How did John Paul Jones contribute to the war effort?

Struggles in the South

In the early years of the war, the Americans had won some battles in the South. In 1776 they had crushed Loyalists at the Battle of Moore's Creek, near Wilmington, North Carolina, and had saved **Charles Town,** South Carolina, from the British. Although a small battle, its impact was great.

By 1778 the British realized that bringing the American colonies back into the empire would not be easy. As a result they changed their strategy and planned a hard-hitting offensive to finish the war.

The British concentrated their efforts in the South, where there were many Loyalists. They hoped to use British sea power and the support of the Loyalists to win decisive victories in the Southern states. Initially the strategy worked.

What might have happened?

1. How do you think the soldiers might have reacted to Washington stepping down?

2. Washington wrote that he would resign his post if he could not count on support. Would the American Revolution have taken a different course with another commander? Explain your answer.

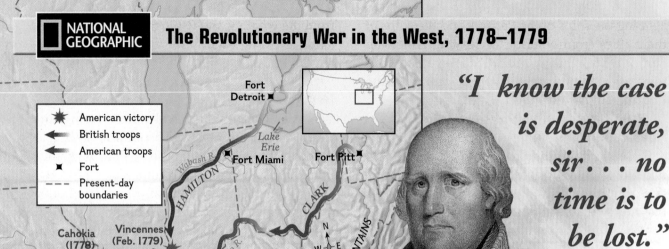

The Revolutionary War in the West, 1778–1779

American victory
British troops
American troops
Fort
Present-day boundaries

Fort Detroit

Lake Erie

Wabash R.

HAMILTON

Fort Miami

Fort Pitt

CLARK

Ohio R.

APPALACHIAN MOUNTAINS

Cahokia (1778)

Vincennes (Feb. 1779)

Kaskaskia (July 1778)

N W E S

0   200 miles
0   200 kilometers
Lambert Equal-Area projection

"I know the case is desperate, sir . . . no time is to be lost."

—letter to Patrick Henry, February 1779

Geography Skills

The Revolutionary War spread west of the Appalachian Mountains where American troops won key victories.

1. **Region** What victories did the American forces win in the West?
2. **Analyzing Information** From what fort did Clark's troops set out?

George Rogers Clark captured the key points of Kaskaskia, Cahokia, and Vincennes, saving the west region for the United States.

British Victories

In late 1778 General Henry Clinton sent 3,500 British troops from New York to take Savannah, on the coast of Georgia. The British occupied the city and overran most of the state.

Clinton himself headed south with a large army in early 1780 to attack the port of Charles Town, South Carolina. Charles Town surrendered in May, and the British took thousands of prisoners. It marked the worst American defeat of the war. A member of Britain's Parliament gloated, "We look on America as at our feet."

Clinton returned to New York, leaving **General Charles Cornwallis** in command of British forces in the South. The Continental Congress sent forces under General Horatio Gates to face Cornwallis. The two armies met at **Camden,** South Carolina, in August 1780. Although the British won, Cornwallis soon found that he could not control the area he had conquered. He and his troops faced a new kind of warfare.

Guerrilla Warfare

The British received less help than they had expected from Loyalists in Southern states. Instead, as British troops moved through the countryside, small forces of Patriots attacked them. These bands of soldiers appeared suddenly, struck their blows, and then disappeared. This hit-and-run technique of guerrilla warfare caught the British off guard.

One successful guerrilla leader, **Francis Marion,** operated out of the swamps of eastern South Carolina. Known as the Swamp Fox, Marion was quick and smart. One British colonel grumbled that "the devil himself" could not catch Marion.

Help From Spain

When 30-year-old Bernardo de Gálvez became governor of the Spanish territory of Louisiana in January 1777, Spain was neutral. That did not stop Gálvez from helping the colonists. He loaned thousands of dollars to the Americans and opened the port of New Orleans to free trade on the part of the colonists. Gálvez also organized the shipment of tons of supplies and ammunition up the Mississippi River to the army of George Rogers Clark in the Northwest Territory. With this help from Gálvez, Clark was able to capture the key points of Kaskaskia, Cahokia, and Vincennes.

In the summer of 1779, Spain declared war on Britain. Gálvez raised an army of Spanish soldiers along with Creoles, Native Americans, and African Americans and marched on British posts along the lower Mississippi. Striking quickly, he captured British forts at Baton Rouge and Natchez. Then, in March 1780, Gálvez forced British Mobile to surrender. In May 1781 he took Pensacola, the British capital of West Florida.

These victories opened supply lines for military goods from Spain, France, Cuba, and Mexico. According to historian Buchanan Parker Thomson, Gálvez had given

❝the most vital aid contributed by any one man to the struggling American colonies. In winning this triumphant victory over the last great British outpost, he had not only served his King to the limit of his strength but had made to the United States the most important gift an ally could offer: the security of their southeastern and western frontiers.❞

NATIONAL GEOGRAPHIC
The Revolutionary War in the South, 1778–1781

1 British capture Savannah, 1778

2 British capture Charles Town and Camden, but are defeated at Kings Mountain in October 1780 and at Cowpens in January 1781

3 Washington and Rochambeau rush toward Virginia, August 1781

4 French Admiral De Grasse keeps British ships away

5 Cornwallis trapped; the British surrender at Yorktown, 1781

Legend:
→ American and allied forces
← British forces
✸ American victory
✹ British victory
■ Fort

Geography Skills

Most of the fighting took place in the South during the latter years of the Revolutionary War.
1. **Location** What British general was trapped at Yorktown, Virginia?
2. **Drawing Conclusions** How did the French navy help the Americans win the war?

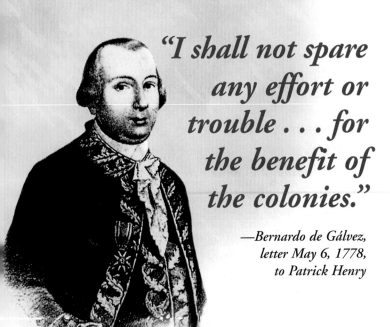

> *"I shall not spare any effort or trouble . . . for the benefit of the colonies."*
>
> —Bernardo de Gálvez,
> letter May 6, 1778,
> to Patrick Henry

Patriot Victories

After the British victory at Camden, South Carolina, the British moved northward through the Carolinas in September 1780. At **Kings Mountain,** a British officer and more than 1,000 Loyalists defended an outpost against the attack of Patriot sharpshooters. The Patriots forced the British to retreat. The victory brought new support for independence from Southerners. They wanted to see an end to the war that was destroying their homes and farms.

In October 1780, **Nathanael Greene** replaced Gates as commander of the Continental forces in the South. Rather than lead an all-out attack on Cornwallis's forces, Greene split his army in two. In January 1781, one section of the army, led by General Daniel Morgan, defeated the British at **Cowpens,** South Carolina. Another section joined Marion's guerrilla raids. In March Greene reunited his forces to meet Cornwallis's army at **Guilford Courthouse,** in present-day Greensboro, North Carolina. Greene's army was forced to retreat, but the British sustained great losses in the process. General Cornwallis abandoned the Carolina campaign.

British Retreat

Cornwallis decided to march north to Virginia in April 1781. His troops carried out raids throughout the state, nearly capturing Governor Thomas Jefferson and the Virginia legislature in June. Jefferson fled on horseback, just ahead of the advancing British troops.

General Washington sent Lafayette and General Anthony Wayne south to fight Cornwallis. Meanwhile Cornwallis set up camp at Yorktown, which was located on the Virginia coast, and awaited further orders from Clinton in New York. The battle for control of the South was entering its final phase.

Reading Check **Evaluating** What effect did the Patriot victory at Kings Mountain produce?

SECTION 3 ASSESSMENT

Checking for Understanding

1. **Key Terms** Write a short paragraph in which you use the following terms: blockade, privateer, guerrilla warfare.

2. **Reviewing Facts** Explain why most Native Americans sided with the British in the conflict.

Reviewing Themes

3. **Geography and History** How did the British navy use the location of the colonies to their advantage?

Critical Thinking

4. **Drawing Conclusions** Why was guerrilla warfare effective against the British?

5. **Analyzing Information** Re-create the diagram below and describe the results of the battle at Guilford Courthouse.

Analyzing Visuals

6. **Geography Skills** Study the maps on pages 180 and 181. Who won the battle at Cowpens, South Carolina? At Kings Mountain, South Carolina? Whose forces did George Rogers Clark face at Vincennes?

Interdisciplinary Activity

Art Create a symbol or emblem that captures the spirit of the Patriot soldiers.

The War Is Won

Guide to Reading

Main Idea
The American colonies overcame many disadvantages to win independence.

Key Terms
ratify, ambush

Reading Strategy
Organizing Information As you read the section, re-create the diagram below and list the reasons why the Americans were able to defeat the British in the Revolutionary War.

Reasons for the British defeat

Read to Learn
• how George Washington changed his military strategy.
• why the Americans won the Revolutionary War despite many disadvantages.

Section Theme
Groups and Institutions A combined Patriot force secured final victory, ensuring an independent United States.

Preview of Events

♦1780   ♦1781   ♦1782   ♦1783

July 1780
French troops arrive in colonies

August 1781
Washington advances toward British at Yorktown

October 1781
Cornwallis surrenders at Yorktown

September 1783
Treaty of Paris is signed

General Rochambeau, French commander

★ AN ★ American Story

A popular children's tune in eighteenth-century Britain went like this:
> *"If ponies rode men and if grass ate the cows,*
> *And cats should be chased into holes by the mouse . . .*
> *If summer were spring and the other way 'round,*
> *Then all the world would be upside down."*

This song would hold special meaning for the British troops in America as the Revolution reached its peak.

Victory at Yorktown

The Revolutionary War was at a critical point. Both armies needed a victory to win the war. While General Washington made plans to attack the British at Yorktown, Virginia, rather than New York City, the Patriots hoped for help from the French.

In July 1780, French warships appeared in the waters off **Newport,** Rhode Island. The ships carried more than 5,000 soldiers under the command of the French general, the **Comte de Rochambeau** (ROH•SHAM•BOH). Cheering crowds greeted the French soldiers, who were well armed and clad in colorful uniforms and plumed caps. The promised French aid had arrived at last. Unfortunately the British fleet arrived soon afterward and trapped the French ships in Newport.

In the autumn of 1780, Washington camped north of New York City waiting for a second fleet of French ships. From this position he could keep a close eye on the British army based in New York that General Clinton commanded. Washington planned to attack Clinton's army as soon as this second French fleet arrived from the West Indies. He had to wait a year to put his plan into action, however, because the fleet did not set sail for America until the summer of 1781.

Change in Plans

Washington had followed reports of the fighting in the South during 1780 and 1781. He knew that the British army commanded by Cornwallis was camped in **Yorktown,** Virginia. Washington also knew that Patriot forces under the Marquis de Lafayette were keeping Cornwallis and his troops bottled up on the Yorktown peninsula.

In August 1781, Washington learned that **Admiral François de Grasse,** the French naval

commander, was heading toward Chesapeake Bay instead of New York. Washington quickly changed his plans. He would advance on the British at Yorktown rather than at New York City.

Washington took steps to keep the new American strategy secret. He wanted Clinton to think the Patriots still planned to attack New York. This, he hoped, would keep Clinton from sending aid to Cornwallis.

General Rochambeau had marched his troops from Newport to join General Washington in July. Washington and Rochambeau then rushed south with their armies. The secrecy was so strict that most of the soldiers did not know where they were going. One soldier wrote,

> ❝We do not know the object of our march, and are in perfect ignorance whether we are going against New York, or . . . Virginia.❞

Washington's troops marched 200 miles in 15 days. General Clinton in New York did not detect the forces heading south to Virginia. Three groups—Lafayette's troops, Washington's and Rochambeau's main American-French army, and the French fleet under Admiral De Grasse—would meet at Yorktown.

The Siege of Yorktown

Washington wondered whether his complicated plan had fooled Clinton, and whether the French fleet would reach Yorktown in time. On September 5, to his great relief, Washington received news that Admiral De Grasse's ships were nearing Yorktown.

The plan worked perfectly, and the British were thoroughly confused. By the end of September, 14,000 American and French troops had trapped Cornwallis's 7,500 British and Hessian troops at Yorktown. Meanwhile, De Grasse's

Picturing **History**

The Marquis de Lafayette (left) relied on James Armistead (right), an enslaved African American, to gather military information about the British. Armistead was later freed and took the name James Armistead Lafayette.
How did the French help the Patriots win the war?

History *Through Art*

Surrender of Lord Cornwallis by **John Trumbull** Trapped by American and French forces, General Charles Cornwallis surrendered at Yorktown. The victory would guarantee America's independence. **What were the two major terms of the Treaty of Paris?**

fleet kept Cornwallis from escaping by sea. General Clinton and the rest of the British army waited in New York, unable to help Cornwallis.

Cornwallis's Defeat

On October 9 the Americans and French began a tremendous bombardment. A Hessian soldier described the dreadful scene in his diary:

> ❝One saw men lying nearly everywhere who were mortally wounded and whose heads, arms, and legs had been shot off. . . . Likewise on watch and on post in the lines, on trench and work details, they were wounded by the fearfully heavy fire.❞

British supplies began running low, and many soldiers were wounded or sick. Cornwallis realized the hopelessness of his situation. On October 19 he surrendered. The Patriots had won the **Battle of Yorktown.**

Handing over their weapons, the British marched between rows of French and American troops—the French in fancy white uniforms on one side and the raggedly clothed Continental Army on the other. A French band played "Yankee Doodle," and a British band responded with a children's tune called "The World Turned Upside Down." Indeed it had.

✓**Reading Check** **Explaining** Why did Washington decide to advance on the British camp at Yorktown?

Independence

The fighting did not really end with Yorktown. The British still held Savannah, Charles Town, and New York, and a few more clashes took place on land and sea. The Patriot victory at Yorktown, however, convinced the British that the war was too costly to pursue.

The two sides sent delegates to Paris to work out a treaty. **Benjamin Franklin, John Adams,** and **John Jay** represented the United States. The American Congress ratified, or approved, the preliminary treaty in April 1783. The final **Treaty of Paris** was signed on September 3, 1783. By that time Britain had also made peace with France and Spain.

The Treaty of Paris was a triumph for the Americans. Great Britain recognized the United States as an independent nation. The territory that the new nation claimed extended from the Atlantic Ocean west to the Mississippi River and from Canada in the north to Spanish Florida in the south. The British promised to withdraw all their troops from American territory. They also agreed to give Americans the right to fish in the waters off the coast of Canada.

The United States, in turn, agreed that British merchants could collect

HISTORY *Online*

Student Web Activity
Visit taj.glencoe.com and click on **Chapter 6— Student Web Activities** for an activity on the Battle of Yorktown.

People In History

Peter Francisco 1760–1831

Peter Francisco was found abandoned in Colonial America in 1765 when he was about five years old. It was later learned that he was from an island in the Portuguese Azores. The abandoned boy was adopted by an uncle of Patrick Henry.

When the Revolution began, 16-year-old Francisco joined the Tenth Virginia Regiment and earned a reputation for bravery and dedication to the revolutionary cause. George Washington was reported to have said about Francisco, "Without him we would have lost two crucial battles, perhaps the war, and with it our freedom. He was truly a one-man army."

After the war, Francisco served as sergeant at arms in the Virginia House of Delegates. In 1974 the Portuguese Continental Union of the United States of America began bestowing a "Peter Francisco Award" upon distinguished Americans who have contributed to the Portuguese cause.

---

debts owed by Americans. The treaty also stated that the Congress would advise the states that property taken from Loyalists was to be returned to them.

The Newburgh Conspiracy

After the British surrender, Washington maintained a strong army with headquarters at Newburgh, New York, planning to disband it when the peace treaty was signed. The period following the British surrender at Yorktown was not easy for American soldiers. Anger mounted when Congress refused to fund their pensions and failed to provide other pay. In disgust some officers circulated a letter in March 1783. If their demands were not met, the letter said, the army should refuse to disband.

Shocked and worried, General Washington realized that such an action could lead to a revolt that would threaten to destroy the new nation. He persuaded the angry officers to be patient with Congress. Then he urged Congress to meet the soldiers' just demands: "If, retiring from the field, they [the officers] are to grow old in poverty...then shall I have learned what ingratitude is."

Washington's leadership ended the threat to the new nation, and Congress soon acted on the demands.

Washington's Farewell

British troops left New York City in late November 1783. The war had truly ended, and George Washington could at last give up his command. On December 4 Washington said farewell to his officers at Fraunces' Tavern in Manhattan. "With a heart full of love and gratitude, I now take my leave of you."

Nearly three weeks later Washington formally resigned from the army at a meeting of the Second Continental Congress in Annapolis, Maryland. A witness described the scene: "The spectators all wept, and there was hardly a member of Congress who did not drop tears." Washington said,

> 66 Having now finished the work assigned me I retire . . . and take my leave of all the employments of public life. 99

He returned to his home, Mount Vernon, in time for Christmas. There he planned to live quietly with his family.

Why the Americans Won

How had the Americans managed to win the Revolutionary War? How had they defeated Britain, the world's strongest power?

The Americans had several advantages in the war. They fought on their own land, while the British had to bring troops and supplies from thousands of miles away. The siege of Yorktown showed how the British depended on support from the sea. When their ships were blocked, the British troops were without support.

The British succeeded in occupying cities but had difficulty controlling the countryside. They had not been successful at Saratoga or in the Carolinas. The Patriots, however, knew the local terrain and where to lay an ambush—a surprise attack.

Help from other nations contributed to the American victory. The success at Yorktown would not have been possible without French soldiers and ships. Loans from France helped the Americans win the war. The Spanish also aided the Patriots by attacking the British in the Mississippi Valley and along the Gulf of Mexico.

Perhaps most important, the American Revolution was a people's movement. Its outcome depended not on any one battle or event but on the determination and spirit of all the Patriots. As the Continental Army marched from New York to Yorktown, crowds came out to watch and wish the troops well. Washington pointed to the crowd and said,

> ❝We may be beaten by the English . . . but here is an army they will never conquer.❞

The Influence of the American Revolution

In 1776 the American colonists began a revolution, making clear the principles of freedom and rights outlined in the Declaration of Independence. These ideas bounded back across the Atlantic to influence the French Revolution. French rebels in 1789 fought in defense of "Liberty, Equality, and Fraternity." French revolutionaries repeated the principles of the American Declaration of Independence: "Men are born and remain free and equal in rights."

In 1791 the ideals of the American and French Revolutions traveled across the Caribbean and the Atlantic to the French-held island colony of Saint Domingue. Inspired by talk of freedom, enslaved Africans took up arms. Led by Toussaint-Louverture, they shook off French rule. In 1804, Saint Domingue—present-day Haiti—became the second nation in the Americas to achieve independence from colonial rule. "We have asserted our rights," declared the revolutionaries. "We swear never to yield them to any power on earth."

Reading Check **Summarizing** What were three reasons the Americans were successful in their fight?

SECTION 4 ASSESSMENT

Checking for Understanding

1. **Key Terms** Use each of these terms in a sentence that will help explain its meaning: ratify, ambush.
2. **Reviewing Facts** Describe how the French navy helped George Washington at Yorktown.

Reviewing Themes

3. **Groups and Institutions** What influence did the American Revolution have around the world?

Critical Thinking

4. **Predicting Consequences** What might have happened if the French fleet had not arrived at Yorktown?
5. **Organizing Information** Re-create the diagram below and describe the terms that the Americans agreed to in the Treaty of Paris.

```
        Treaty of Paris
         /         \
       ( )         ( )
```

Analyzing Visuals

6. **Picturing History** Look at the painting on page 185. How does the artist focus attention on the figures in the center of the painting?

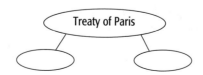

Interdisciplinary Activity

Geography Create a map of the United States that shows the boundaries of the country at the time of the Treaty of Paris. Use colored pencils to show the lands that the British gave to the Americans.

Chapter Summary
The American Revolution

1776
- Thomas Paine writes the inspiring *Common Sense.*
- The Continental Army is defeated at the Battle of Long Island.
- George Washington leads troops across the Delaware River to surprise the British at Trenton.

1777
- The Patriots defeat the British at Saratoga, New York.
- The British capture Philadelphia.

1778
- France provides money, troops, and equipment to the Patriots.
- The Continental Army suffers from the lack of supplies at Valley Forge.

1779
- John Paul Jones forces the surrender of the British warship *Serapis.*

1780
- The British capture Charles Town and take thousands of prisoners.

1781
- The Americans win the Battle of Yorktown.

1783
- The Treaty of Paris is signed, marking the end of the Revolution.

Reviewing Key Terms

Examine the pairs of words below. Then write a sentence explaining what each of the pairs has in common.

1. mercenary, recruit
2. blockade, privateer
3. guerrilla warfare, ambush

Reviewing Key Facts

4. Why did the British think their military forces were superior to those of the Americans?
5. Why did Loyalists support Britain?
6. How did Thomas Paine help the Patriots during the Revolutionary War?
7. What European nations fought with the Americans against the British?
8. What were some of the problems that troops faced during the winter at Valley Forge?
9. What ideas did Judith Sargeant Murray promote about education?
10. Why did many Native Americans give their support to the British?
11. What fighting method did the Americans use to keep the British from taking the Southern Colonies?
12. Which battle convinced the British that fighting the Americans was too costly?
13. Why was fighting on their own land an advantage for the Patriots?

Critical Thinking

14. **Compare and Contrast** What advantage did the Patriots have over the British mercenaries?
15. **Analyzing Information** How did women help in the war effort?
16. **Drawing Conclusions** Why do you think the British found it easier to capture American cities than to take over the American countryside?
17. **Determining Cause and Effect** Re-create the diagram below and describe two ways America's fight for independence influenced other countries.

Independence

Geography and History Activity

The Treaty of Paris in 1783 established the boundaries of the new United States. The newly independent nation shared land claims on the North American continent with several nations. Study the map below and answer the questions that follow.

18. Location What natural landmark formed the new western boundary of the United States?

19. Region Which country claimed the most land in North America in 1783? The least land?

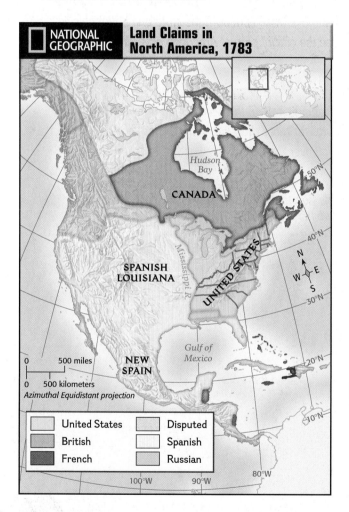

NATIONAL GEOGRAPHIC
Land Claims in North America, 1783

Hudson Bay

CANADA

SPANISH LOUISIANA

Mississippi R.

UNITED STATES

Gulf of Mexico

NEW SPAIN

0   500 miles
0   500 kilometers
Azimuthal Equidistant projection

☐ United States	☐ Disputed
☐ British	☐ Spanish
☐ French	☐ Russian

Practicing Skills

Reading a Military Map *Study the military map on page 181. Then answer the questions that follow.*

20. What color symbolizes British troop movement?

21. What symbol represents battles?

22. When did the British capture the city of Savannah?

23. Who was victorious at the Battle of Cowpens?

HISTORY Online
Self-Check Quiz
Visit taj.glencoe.com and click on **Chapter 6—Self-Check Quizzes** to prepare for the chapter test.

Citizenship Cooperative Activity

24. Expository Writing As citizens, we have responsibilities to our communities. For a community to be successful, its citizens must take an active role in it. Write a one-page paper in which you discuss the topic, "My responsibilities to my community."

Economics Activity

25. Look up the word *inflation* in a dictionary or another reference book. Write a definition of the term in your own words. Then write answers to these questions:

- What happens to the price of goods during periods of inflation?

- How would inflation affect your standard of living?

Alternative Assessment

26. Portfolio Writing Activity Scan the chapter for details about people who came to the United States from other countries to help in the war effort. Record the names in your journal. Then create a chart that shows the people's names, their home countries, and what they did to aid the Americans.

The Princeton Review
Standardized Test Practice

Directions: Choose the *best* answer to the following question.

What American victory convinced the French to form an alliance with the United States?
A Saratoga   **C** Bunker Hill
B Ticonderoga   **D** Trenton

Test-Taking Tip

Remember to eliminate answers that you know are wrong. For example, the Patriots did not win the battle of Bunker Hill; therefore, choice **C** is not correct.

A More Perfect Union

1777–1790

Why It Matters

When the American colonies broke their political ties with Great Britain, they faced the task of forming independent governments at both the state and national levels. In 1788 the Constitution became the official plan of American government.

The Impact Today

Created to meet the needs of a changing nation, the Constitution has been the fundamental law of the United States for more than 200 years. It has served as a model for many constitutions all over the world.

The American Journey *Video* *The chapter 7 video, "Discovering Our Constitution," examines how the Constitution has preserved our government and the rights of citizens for over two hundred years.*

1777
• Articles of Confederation written

1783
• Treaty of Paris

United States
PRESIDENTS

1776   *1779*   *1782*

World

1778
• France goes to war against Britain

1780
• League of Armed Neutrality formed

1784
• Russians found colony on Kodiak Island, Alaska

Compare-Contrast Study Foldable Make this foldable to help you compare the Articles of Confederation to the U.S. Constitution.

Step 1 Fold a sheet of paper from side to side, leaving a 2-inch tab uncovered along the side.

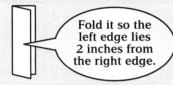

Fold it so the left edge lies 2 inches from the right edge.

Step 2 Turn the paper and fold it into thirds.

Step 3 Unfold and cut along the two inside fold lines.

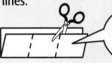

Cut along the two folds on the front flap to make 3 tabs.

Step 4 Label the foldable as shown.

A More Perfect Union
Articles of Confederation | Both | U.S. Constitution

Reading and Writing As you read the chapter, write what you learn about these documents under the appropriate tabs.

George Washington Addressing the Constitutional Convention by J.B. Stearns The Constitution created the basic form of American government.

1787
- Shays's Rebellion
- U.S. Constitution signed
- Northwest Ordinance passed

1788
- U.S. Constitution ratified

Washington 1789–1797

1785

1788

1791

1785
- First hot air balloon crosses English Channel

1788
- British establish penal colony in Australia

1789
- French Revolution begins

HISTORY
Online

Chapter Overview
Visit taj.glencoe.com and click on **Chapter 7— Chapter Overviews** to preview chapter information.

The Articles of Confederation

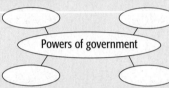

Phillis Wheatley

AN American Story

Many Americans, from colonial times on, spoke out for liberty. One who lent her voice to the pursuit of freedom was poet Phillis Wheatley. Celebrated as the founder of the African American literary tradition, Wheatley wrote many poems supporting the colonists in the Revolutionary War. For many Americans, like Wheatley, the end of the Revolution was a reason for joy. American liberty had survived the challenge of war. But could it meet the demands of peace?

Thirteen Independent States

Although the Americans won their independence, they had trouble winning Britain's respect. Ignoring the terms of the Treaty of Paris, the British kept troops at frontier posts in American territory. The British believed the new American government was weak and ineffective. While Americans were fighting for their independence on the battlefield, they were also creating new governments. After rejecting British rule, they needed to establish their own political institutions.

State Constitutions

In May 1776 the Continental Congress asked the states to organize their governments, and each moved quickly to adopt a state constitution, or plan of government. By the end of 1776, eight states had drafted constitutions. New York and Georgia followed suit in 1777, and Massachusetts in 1780. Connecticut and Rhode Island retained their colonial charters as state constitutions.

Their experience with British rule made Americans cautious about placing too much power in the hands of a single ruler. For that reason the states adopted constitutions that limited the power of the governor. Pennsylvania even replaced the office of governor with an elected council of 12 members.

Limiting Power

The states took other measures against concentration of power. They divided government functions between the governor (or Pennsylvania's council) and the legislature. Most states established two-house, or bicameral, legislatures to divide the power even further.

The writers of the constitutions not only wanted to prevent abuses of power in the states, but they also wanted to keep power in the hands of the people. State legislators were popularly elected, and elections were frequent. In most states, only white males who were at least 21 years old could vote. These citizens also had to own a certain amount of property or pay a certain amount of taxes. Some states allowed free African American males to vote.

The state constitutions restricted the powers of the governors, which made the legislatures the most powerful branch of government. The state legislatures struggled to make taxes more fair, but there were many disagreements. Going from dependent colonies to self-governing states brought new challenges.

✔ **Reading Check** **Explaining** Why did some states choose a bicameral legislature?

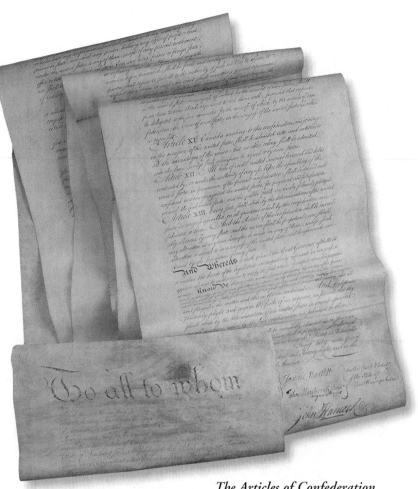

The Articles of Confederation

Forming a Republic

For Americans, establishing separate state governments was a much easier task than creating a central government. They agreed that their country should be a republic, a government in which citizens rule through elected representatives. They could not agree, however, on the organization and powers of their new republic.

At first most Americans favored a weak central government. They assumed the states would be very much like small, independent countries—similar to the way that the colonies had been set up. The states would act independently on most issues, working together through a central government only to wage war and handle relations with other nations.

Planning a New Government

In 1776 the Second Continental Congress appointed a committee to draw up a plan for a new government. The delegates in the Congress realized they needed a central government to coordinate the war effort against Britain. After much debate the Congress adopted the committee's plan, the **Articles of Confederation,** in November 1777.

The Articles, America's first constitution, provided for a new central government under which the states gave up little of their power. For the states, the Articles of Confederation were "a firm league of friendship" in which each state retained "its sovereignty, freedom and independence."

Under the Articles of Confederation, the government—consisting of the Congress—had the authority to conduct foreign affairs, maintain armed forces, borrow money, and issue currency. Yet it could not regulate trade, force citizens to join the army, or impose taxes. If Congress needed to raise money or troops, it had to ask the state legislatures—but the states were not required to contribute. In addition the govern-

ment lacked a chief executive. The Confederation government carried on much of its business, such as selling western lands, through congressional committees.

Under the new plan, each state had one vote in Congress, regardless of its population, and all states had to approve the Articles as well as any amendments. Despite this arrangement, the larger states believed that their population warranted having more votes. The states were also divided by whether or not they claimed land in the West. Maryland refused to approve the Articles until New York, Virginia, and other states abandoned claims to lands west of the Appalachian Mountains. Finally the states settled their differences. With Maryland's ratification, all 13 states had approved the Articles. On March 1, 1781, the Confederation formally became the government of the United States.

Why It Matters

Surveying the Land

When the Revolution began, only a few thousand white settlers lived west of the Appalachian Mountains. By the 1790s their numbers had increased to about 120,000. Through the Ordinance of 1785, Congress created a system for surveying—taking a detailed measurement of an area of land—and selling the western lands.

The Ordinance at first applied only to what was then called the Northwest Territory—present-day Ohio, Indiana, Michigan, Illinois, and Wisconsin. It established a system of land survey and settlement that we still use today.

The Land Ordinance led to the sale of large amounts of land and speeded settlement of the Northwest Territory.

The Confederation Government

The years between 1781 and 1789 were a critical period for the young American republic. The Articles of Confederation did not provide a government strong enough to handle the problems facing the United States. The Congress had limited authority. It could not pass a law unless nine states voted in favor of it. Any attempt to change the Articles required the consent of all 13 states, making it difficult for the Congress to pass laws when there was any opposition. Despite its weaknesses, the Confederation did accomplish some important things. Under the Confederation government, Americans won their independence and expanded foreign trade. The Confederation also provided for settling and governing the nation's western territories.

Reading Check **Explaining** What powers did the Confederation government have?

New Land Policies

At the beginning of the Revolutionary War, only a few thousand settlers lived west of the Appalachian Mountains. By the 1790s the number was approaching 120,000. These western settlers hoped to organize their lands as states and join the union, but the Articles of Confederation contained no provision for adding new states. Congress realized that it had to extend its national authority over the frontier and bring order to this territory.

During the 1780s all of the states except Georgia gave up their claims to lands west of the Appalachians, and the central government took control of these lands. In 1784 Congress, under a

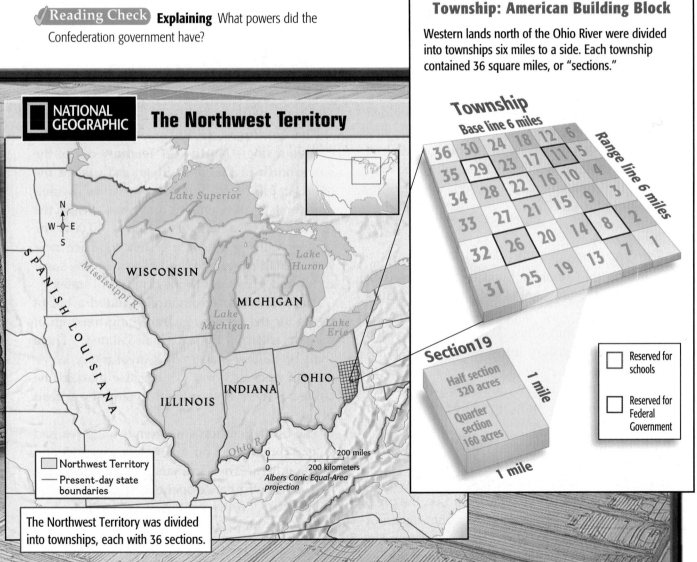

NATIONAL GEOGRAPHIC The Northwest Territory

The Northwest Territory was divided into townships, each with 36 sections.

- Northwest Territory
- Present-day state boundaries

0 — 200 miles
0 — 200 kilometers
Albers Conic Equal-Area projection

Township: American Building Block

Western lands north of the Ohio River were divided into townships six miles to a side. Each township contained 36 square miles, or "sections."

Township
Base line 6 miles
Range line 6 miles

Section 19
Half section 320 acres
Quarter section 160 acres
1 mile
1 mile

☐ Reserved for schools
☐ Reserved for Federal Government

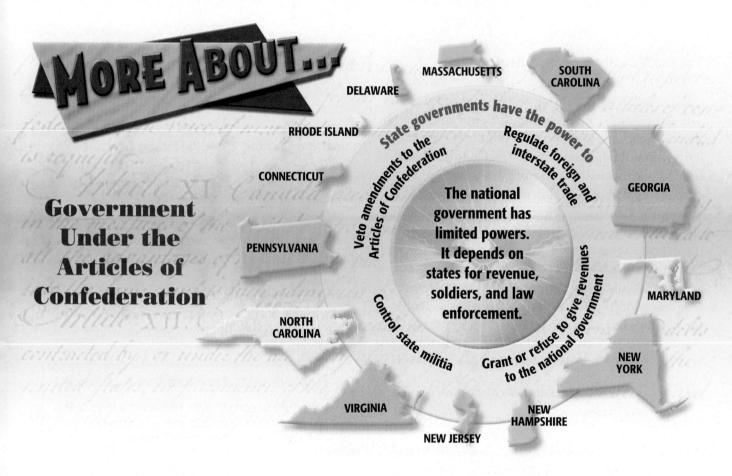

Government Under the Articles of Confederation

State governments have the power to
- Regulate foreign and interstate trade
- Grant or refuse to give revenues to the national government
- Control state militia
- Veto amendments to the Articles of Confederation

The national government has limited powers. It depends on states for revenue, soldiers, and law enforcement.

DELAWARE
MASSACHUSETTS
SOUTH CAROLINA
RHODE ISLAND
CONNECTICUT
GEORGIA
PENNSYLVANIA
MARYLAND
NORTH CAROLINA
NEW YORK
VIRGINIA
NEW HAMPSHIRE
NEW JERSEY

plan proposed by Thomas Jefferson, divided the western territory into self-governing districts. When the number of people in a district reached the population of the smallest existing state, that district could petition, or apply to, Congress for statehood.

The Ordinance of 1785

In 1785 the Confederation Congress passed an ordinance, or law, that established a procedure for surveying and selling the western lands north of the Ohio River. The new law divided this massive territory into townships six miles long and six miles wide. These townships were to be further divided into 36 sections of 640 acres each that would be sold at public auction for at least a dollar an acre.

Land speculators viewed the law as an opportunity to cheaply accumulate large tracts of land. Concerned about lawless people moving into western lands, Richard Henry Lee, the president of Congress, urged that "the rights of property be clearly defined" by the government. Congress drafted another ordinance to protect the interests of hard-working settlers.

The Northwest Ordinance

The Northwest Ordinance, passed in 1787, created a single **Northwest Territory** out of the lands north of the Ohio River and east of the Mississippi River. The lands were to be divided into three to five smaller territories. When the population of a territory reached 60,000, the people could petition for statehood. Each new state would come into the Union with the same rights and privileges as the original 13 states.

The Northwest Ordinance included a bill of rights for the settlers, guaranteeing freedom of religion and trial by jury. It also stated, "There shall be neither slavery nor involuntary servitude in said territory." This clause marked the United States's first attempt to stop the spread of slavery.

The Confederation's western ordinances had an enormous effect on American expansion and development. The Ordinance of 1785 and the Northwest Ordinance opened the way for settlement of the Northwest Territory in a stable and orderly manner.

Reading Check Explaining What was the purpose of the Northwest Ordinance?

Trouble on Two Fronts

Despite its accomplishments, the Confederation government had so little power that it could not deal with the country's financial problems. It also failed to resolve problems with Britain and Spain.

§Economics
Financial Problems

By 1781 the money printed during the Revolutionary War had depreciated, or fallen in value, so far that it was almost worthless. Unable to collect taxes, both the Continental Congress and the states had printed their own paper money. No gold or silver backed up these bills. The value of the bills plummeted, while the price of food and other goods soared. Between 1779 and 1781, the number of Continental dollars required to buy one Spanish silver dollar rose from 40 to 146. In Boston and some other areas, high prices led to food riots.

Fighting the war left the Continental Congress with a large debt. Congress had borrowed money from American citizens and foreign governments during the war. It still owed the Revolutionary soldiers their pay for military service. Lacking the power to tax, the Confederation could not pay its debts. It requested funds from the states, but the states contributed only a small portion of the money needed.

Robert Morris's Import Tax

In 1781, faced with a total collapse of the country's finances, Congress created a department of finance under Philadelphia merchant **Robert Morris.** While serving in Congress, Morris had proposed a 5 percent tax on imported goods to help pay the national debt.

The plan required that the Articles of Confederation be changed to give Congress the power to levy the tax. Although 12 states approved the plan, Rhode Island's opposition killed the measure. A second effort in 1783 also failed to win unanimous approval. The financial crisis only worsened.

Problems with Britain

The weaknesses of the new American government became more evident as the United States encountered problems with other countries. In the Treaty of Paris of 1783, Britain had promised to withdraw from the lands east of the Mississippi River. Yet British troops continued to occupy several strategic forts in the Great Lakes region.

Picturing **History**

Pennsylvania merchant and banker Robert Morris became Superintendent of Finance in May 1781. **What reform did Morris propose to help the nation's finances?**

Continental currency

Robert Morris

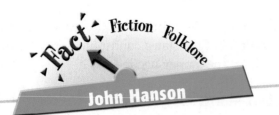

Fact · Fiction · Folklore

John Hanson

The Forgotten President? Who was the first president of the United States? Was it George Washington—or John Hanson? Some historians consider Hanson the first United States president because he was the first to serve in the office in 1781 under the Articles of Confederation. Other historians argue that Hanson was the head of Congress, but not until George Washington began his term in 1789 did the nation have a "true" president.

British trade policy caused other problems. American merchants complained that the British were keeping Americans out of the West Indies and other profitable British markets.

In 1785 Congress sent **John Adams** to London to discuss these difficulties. The British, however, were not willing to talk. They pointed to the failure of the United States to honor *its* promises made in the Treaty of Paris. The British claimed that Americans had agreed to pay Loyalists for the property taken from them during the Revolutionary War. The Congress had, in fact, recommended that the states pay the Loyalists, but the states had refused.

Problems With Spain

If American relations with Great Britain were poor, affairs with Spain were worse. Spain, which held Florida as well as lands west of the Mississippi River, was anxious to halt American expansion into the territory it claimed. As a result, Spain closed the lower Mississippi River to American shipping in 1784. Western settlers depended on the Mississippi River for commerce. As **John Jay,** the American secretary of foreign affairs, had noted a few years earlier:

> ❝The Americans, almost to a man, believed that God Almighty had made that river a highway for the people of the upper country to go to sea by.❞

In 1786 American diplomats reached an agreement with Spain. Representatives from the Southern states, however, blocked the agreement because it did not include the right to use the Mississippi River.

The weakness of the Confederation and its inability to deal with problems worried many leaders. George Washington described the government as "little more than the shadow without the substance." Many Americans began to agree that the country needed a stronger government.

✓Reading Check **Analyzing** Why did Spain close the lower Mississippi River to American trade?

SECTION 1 ASSESSMENT

Checking for Understanding

1. **Key Terms** Use each of these terms in a complete sentence that will help explain its meaning: constitution, bicameral, republic, petition, ordinance, depreciate.
2. **Reviewing Facts** Describe the country's financial problems after the Revolutionary War.

Reviewing Themes

3. **Government and Democracy** Why did most states limit the power of their governors and divide the legislature into two bodies?

Critical Thinking

4. **Predicting Consequences** What effect do you think the Northwest Ordinance had on Native Americans?
5. **Organizing Information** Re-create the diagram below and summarize the strengths and weaknesses of the Confederation government.

The Articles of Confederation	
Strengths	Weaknesses

Analyzing Visuals

6. **Geography Skills** Study the material on pages 194 and 195 about the Ordinance of 1785. Then answer these questions. What present-day states were created from the Northwest Territory? How many sections are in a township?

Interdisciplinary Activity

Citizenship Imagine you are an American citizen in the 1780s. Create a poster that defends the Articles of Confederation. Be sure to include reasons the Confederation Congress is needed.

Convention and Compromise

Guide to Reading

Main Idea
The new Constitution corrected the weaknesses of government under the Articles of Confederation.

Key Terms
depression, manumission, proportional, compromise

Reading Strategy
Organizing Information As you read the section, re-create the diagram below. In the boxes, describe the role each individual played in creating the new plan of government.

	Role
Edmund Randolph	
James Madison	
Roger Sherman	

Read to Learn
• how the Constitutional Convention broke the deadlock over the form the new government would take.
• how the delegates answered the question of representation.

Section Theme
Groups and Institutions National leaders worked to produce a new constitution for the United States.

Preview of Events

♦1783	♦1785	♦1787	♦1789
1784 Rhode Island passes plan to end slavery	**September 1786** Daniel Shays leads rebellion	**May 1787** Delegates meet to revise Articles of Confederation	**September 1787** Delegates sign draft of Constitution

George Washington

AN American Story

By 1786 many Americans observed that the Confederation was not working. George Washington himself agreed that the United States was really "thirteen Sovereignties pulling against each other."

In the spring of 1787, Washington joined delegates from Virginia and 11 other states who gathered in Philadelphia to address this problem. Rhode Island decided not to participate. The delegates came "for the sole and express purpose of revising the Articles of Confederation."

Economic Depression

The call to revise the Articles of Confederation came while the young nation faced difficult problems. Many Americans believed that the Confederation government was too weak to deal with these challenges.

After the Revolutionary War ended, the United States went through a depression, a period when economic activity slowed and unemployment

Picturing History

Only through donations was Massachusetts able to raise a militia to defeat Shays. **Why did Shays's Rebellion frighten many Americans?**

increased. Southern plantations had been damaged during the war, and rice exports dropped sharply. Trade also fell off when the British closed the profitable West Indies (Caribbean) market to American merchants. What little money there was went to pay foreign debts, and a serious currency shortage resulted.

Difficult Times for Farmers

American farmers suffered because they could not sell their goods. They had problems paying the requests for money that the states levied to meet Revolutionary War debts. As a result state officials seized farmers' lands to pay their debts and threw many farmers into jail. Grumblings of protest soon grew into revolt.

Shays's Rebellion

Resentment grew especially strong in Massachusetts. Farmers viewed the new government as just another form of tyranny. They wanted the government to issue paper money and make new policies to relieve debtors. In a letter to state officials, some farmers proclaimed:

> **❝**Surely your honours are not strangers to the distresses [problems] of the people but . . . know that many of our good inhabitants are now confined in [jail] for debt and taxes.**❞**

In 1786 angry farmers lashed out. Led by **Daniel Shays,** a former Continental Army captain, they forced courts in western Massachusetts to close so judges could not confiscate farmers' lands.

In January 1787 Shays led more than 1,000 farmers toward the federal arsenal in **Springfield,** Massachusetts, for arms and ammunition. The state militia ordered the advancing farmers to halt, then fired over their heads. The farmers did not stop, and the militia fired again, killing four rebels. Shays and his followers scattered, and the uprising was over.

Shays's Rebellion frightened many Americans. They worried that the government could not control unrest and prevent violence. On hearing of the rebellion, George Washington wondered whether "mankind, when left to themselves, are unfit for their own government." Thomas Jefferson, minister to France at the time, had a different view. "A little rebellion, now and then," he wrote, "is a good thing."

The Issue of Slavery

The Revolutionary War brought attention to the contradiction between the American battle for liberty and the practice of slavery. Between 1776 and 1786, 11 states—all except South Carolina and Georgia—outlawed or heavily taxed the importation of enslaved people.

Although slavery was not a major source of labor in the North, it existed and was legal in all the Northern states. Many individuals and groups began to work to end the institution of slavery. In 1774 Quakers in Pennsylvania organized the first American antislavery society. Six years later Pennsylvania passed a law that provided for the gradual freeing of enslaved people.

Between 1783 and 1804, Connecticut, Rhode Island, New York, and New Jersey passed laws that gradually ended slavery. Still, free African Americans faced discrimination. They were barred from many public places. Few states gave free African Americans the right to vote. The children of most free blacks had to attend separate schools. Free African Americans established their own institutions—churches, schools, and mutual-aid societies—to seek opportunity.

The states south of Pennsylvania clung to the institution of slavery. The plantation system of the South had been built on slavery, and many Southerners feared that their economy could not survive without it. Nonetheless, an increasing number of slaveholders began freeing the enslaved people that they held after the war. Virginia passed a law that encouraged manumission, the freeing of individual enslaved persons, and the state's population of free African Americans grew.

The abolition of slavery in the North divided the new country on the critical issue of whether people should be allowed to hold other human beings in bondage. This division came at the time when many American leaders had decided that the Articles of Confederation needed strengthening. In the summer of 1787, when state representatives assembled to plan a new government, they compromised on this issue. It would take years of debate, bloodshed, and ultimately a war to settle the slavery question.

✓ **Reading Check** **Explaining** Why did Southern states support slavery?

A Call for Change

The American Revolution had led to a union of 13 states, but it had not yet created a nation. Some leaders were satisfied with a system of independent state governments that resembled the old colonial governments. Others saw a

strong national government as the solution to America's problems. They demanded a reform of the Articles of Confederation.

Two Americans active in the movement for change were **James Madison,** a Virginia planter, and **Alexander Hamilton,** a New York lawyer. In September 1786, Hamilton proposed calling a convention in Philadelphia to discuss trade issues. He also suggested that this convention consider what possible changes were needed to make

❝the Constitution of the Federal Government adequate to the exigencies [needs] of the Union.❞

At first George Washington was not enthusiastic about the movement to revise the Articles of Confederation. When he heard the news of Shays's Rebellion, Washington changed his mind. After Washington agreed to attend the Philadelphia convention, the meeting took on greater significance.

✓ **Reading Check** **Evaluating** Why did Madison and Hamilton call for a convention in 1787?

Picturing **History**

Philadelphia preachers Richard Allen (left) and Absalom Jones (right) founded the Free African Society and later set up the first African American churches. **What challenges did free African Americans face?**

The Constitutional Convention

The Philadelphia meeting began in May 1787 and continued through one of the hottest summers on record. The 55 delegates included planters, merchants, lawyers, physicians, generals, governors, and a college president. Three of the delegates were under 30 years of age, and one, Benjamin Franklin, was over 80. Many were well educated. At a time when only one white man in 1,000 went to college, 26 of the delegates had college degrees. Native Americans, African Americans, and women were not considered part of the political process, so none attended.

Several men stood out as leaders. The presence of George Washington and Benjamin Franklin ensured that many people would trust the Convention's work. Two Philadelphians also played key roles. James Wilson often read Franklin's speeches and did important work on the details of the Constitution. Gouverneur Morris, a powerful speaker and writer, wrote the final draft of the Constitution.

From Virginia came Edmund Randolph and James Madison. Both were keen supporters of a strong national government. Madison's careful notes are the major source of information about the Convention's work. Madison is often called the **Father of the Constitution** because he was the author of the basic plan of government that the Convention adopted.

Organization

The Convention began by unanimously choosing George Washington to preside over the meetings. It also decided that each state would have one vote on all questions. A simple majority vote of those states present would make decisions. No meetings could be held unless delegates from at least seven of the 13 states were present. The delegates decided to close their doors to the public and keep the sessions secret. This was a key decision because it made it possible for the delegates to talk freely.

The Virginia Plan

After the rules were adopted, the Convention opened with a surprise. It came from the Virginia delegation. Edmund Randolph proposed

America's *Architecture*

Independence Hall The Pennsylvania State House, later known as Independence Hall, was the site of the signing of the Declaration of Independence and of the Constitutional Convention. Independence Hall was restored in 1950 and is now maintained as a museum. **Why do you think this site was used for many important events?**

People In History

James Madison 1751–1836

James Madison, only 36 at the time of the Constitutional Convention, was the best prepared of the delegates. In the months before the convention, he had made a detailed study of government. He read hundreds of books on history, politics, and economics. He also corresponded with Thomas Jefferson.

Madison looked for ways to build a strong but fair system of government. He knew that republics were considered weaker than monarchies because kings or queens could use their authority to act quickly and decisively. Who would provide the same leadership in a republic? At the same time, Madison was con-

cerned about protecting the people from misuse of power. As he searched for solutions, Madison worked out a new plan that included a system of balances among different functions of government. The delegates adopted many of Madison's ideas in what would become the United States Constitution.

---

that the delegates create a strong national government instead of revising the Articles of Confederation. He introduced the **Virginia Plan,** which was largely the work of James Madison. The plan called for a two-house legislature, a chief executive chosen by the legislature, and a court system. The members of the lower house of the legislature would be elected by the people. The members of the upper house would be chosen by the lower house. In both houses the number of representatives would be proportional, or corresponding in size, to the population of each state. This would give Virginia many more delegates than Delaware, the state with the smallest population.

Delegates from Delaware, New Jersey, and other small states immediately objected to the plan. They preferred the Confederation system in which all states were represented equally.

Delegates unhappy with the Virginia Plan rallied around **William Paterson** of New Jersey. On June 15 he presented an alternative plan that revised the Articles of Confederation, which was all the convention was empowered to do.

The New Jersey Plan

The **New Jersey Plan** kept the Confederation's one-house legislature, with one vote for each state. Congress, however, could set taxes and regulate trade—powers it did not have under the Articles. Congress would elect a weak executive branch consisting of more than one person.

Paterson argued that the Convention should not deprive the smaller states of the equality they had under the Articles. Thus, his plan was designed simply to amend the Articles.

✔ **Reading Check** **Explaining** Why did some delegates criticize the Virginia Plan?

Compromise Wins Out

The convention delegates had to decide whether they were simply revising the Articles of Confederation or writing a constitution for a new national government. On June 19 the states voted to work toward a national government based on the Virginia Plan, but they still had to resolve the thorny issue of representation that divided the large and small states.

Picturing **History**

Delegates to the Constitutional Convention met in this room at Independence Hall. **How many states had to ratify the Constitution before it went into effect?**

Discussion and Disagreement

As the convention delegates struggled to deal with difficult questions, tempers and temperatures grew hotter. How were the members of Congress to be elected? How would state representation be determined in the upper and lower houses? Were enslaved people to be counted as part of the population on which representation was based?

🔲Citizenship
The Great Compromise

Under Franklin's leadership, the convention appointed a "grand committee" to try to resolve their disagreements. **Roger Sherman** of Connecticut suggested what came to be known as the **Great Compromise.** A compromise is an agreement between two or more sides in which each side gives up some of what it wants.

Sherman proposed a two-house legislature. In the lower house—the House of Representatives—the number of seats for each state would vary according to the state's population. In the upper house—the Senate—each state would have two members.

The Three-Fifths Compromise

Another major compromise by the delegates dealt with counting enslaved people. Southern states wanted to include the enslaved in their population counts to gain delegates in the House of Representatives. Northern states objected to this idea because enslaved people were legally considered property. Some delegates from Northern states argued that the enslaved, as property, should be counted for the purpose of taxation but not representation. However, neither side considered giving enslaved people the right to vote.

The committee's solution, known as the **Three-Fifths Compromise,** was to count each enslaved person as three-fifths of a free person for both taxation and representation. In other words, every five enslaved persons would equal three free persons. On July 12 the convention delegates voted to approve the Three-Fifths Compromise. Four days later, they agreed that each state should elect two senators.

Slave Trade

The convention needed to resolve another difficult issue that divided the Northern and Southern states. Having banned the slave trade within their borders, Northern states wanted to prohibit it throughout the nation. Southern states considered slavery and the slave trade essential to their economies. To keep the Southern states in the nation, Northerners agreed that the Congress could not interfere with the slave trade until 1808. Beginning that year Congress could limit the slave trade if it chose to.

Bill of Rights

George Mason of Virginia proposed a bill of rights to be included in the Constitution. Some delegates worried that without the protection of a bill of rights the new national government might abuse its power. However, most of the delegates believed that the Constitution, with its carefully defined listing of government powers, provided adequate protection of individual rights. Mason's proposal was defeated.

Approving the Constitution

The committees finished their work on the Constitution in late summer. On September 17, 1787, the delegates assembled in the Philadelphia State House to sign the document. Franklin made a final plea for approval:

> 66 I consent to this Constitution because I expect no better, and because I am not sure, that it is not the best. 99

Three delegates refused to sign—Elbridge Gerry of Massachusetts, and Edmund Randolph and George Mason of Virginia. Gerry and Mason would not sign without a bill of rights.

The Confederation Congress then sent the approved draft of the Constitution to the states for consideration. To amend the Articles of Confederation had required unanimous approval of the states. Getting a unanimous vote had proved slow and frustrating. Therefore, the delegates agreed to change the approval process for the Constitution. When 9 of the 13 states had approved, the new government of the United States would come into existence. *(See pages 232–253 for the entire text of the Constitution.)*

✓ **Reading Check** **Analyzing** Who refused to sign the Constitution? Explain why.

HISTORY Online

Student Web Activity
Visit taj.glencoe.com and click on **Chapter 7— Student Web Activities** for an activity on the Constitutional Convention.

SECTION 2 ASSESSMENT

Checking for Understanding

1. **Key Terms** Use the terms that follow to write a newspaper article about the main events of the Constitutional Convention: depression, manumission, proportional, compromise.
2. **Reviewing Facts** Explain what caused Shays's Rebellion. What was one effect?

Reviewing Themes

3. **Groups and Institutions** How did the Great Compromise satisfy both the small and the large states on the question of representation?

Critical Thinking

4. **Summarizing Information** You are asked to write a 30-second news broadcast to announce the agreement made in the Great Compromise. What would you include in the broadcast?
5. **Analyzing Information** Re-create the diagram below and identify arguments for and against ratifying the Constitution.

Ratification	
Arguments for	Arguments against

Analyzing Visuals

6. **Picturing History** Examine the images that appear on pages 202 and 204. What do they show? Where are they located? Why are these places important in the nation's history?

Interdisciplinary Activity

Government Create a political cartoon that illustrates the view of either the Northern states or the Southern states on how enslaved people should be counted for representation.

Critical Thinking SKILLBUILDER

Making Comparisons

Why Learn This Skill?

Suppose you want to buy a portable compact disc (CD) player, and you must choose among three models. You would probably compare characteristics of the three models, such as price, sound quality, and size, to figure out which model is best for you. When you study American history, you often compare people or events from one time period with those from a different time period.

Learning the Skill

When making comparisons, you examine two or more groups, situations, events, or documents. Then you identify similarities and differences. For example, the chart on this page compares two documents, specifically the powers each gave the federal government. The Articles of Confederation were implemented before the United States Constitution, which replaced the Articles.

When making comparisons, you first decide what items will be compared and determine which characteristics you will use to compare them. Then you identify similarities and differences in these characteristics.

Practicing the Skill

Analyze the information on the chart on this page. Then answer the following questions.

1 What items are being compared?

2 Which document allowed the government to organize state militias?

3 Which document allowed the government to coin money? Regulate trade?

4 In what ways are the two documents different?

5 In what ways are the two documents similar?

Powers of the Federal Government

	Articles of Confederation	United States Constitution
Declare war; make peace	✔	✔
Coin money	✔	✔
Manage foreign affairs	✔	✔
Establish a postal system	✔	✔
Impose taxes		✔
Regulate trade		✔
Organize a court system		✔
Call state militias for service		✔
Protect copyrights		✔
Take other necessary actions to run the federal government		✔

Applying the Skill

Making Comparisons On the editorial page of your local newspaper, find two letters to the editor that express different viewpoints on the same issue. Read the letters and identify the similarities and differences between the two points of view.

 Glencoe's **Skillbuilder Interactive Workbook CD-ROM, Level 1,** provides instruction and practice in key social studies skills.

A New Plan of Government

Guide to Reading

Main Idea
The United States system of government rests on the Constitution.

Key Terms
Enlightenment, federalism, article, legislative branch, executive branch, Electoral College, judicial branch, checks and balances, ratify, Federalist, Antifederalist, amendment

Reading Strategy
Organizing Information Re-create the diagram below. In the boxes explain how the system of checks and balances works.

	Has check or balance over:	Example
President		
Congress		
Supreme Court		

Read to Learn
• about the roots of the Constitution.
• how the Constitution limits the power of government.

Section Theme
Civic Rights and Responsibilities
The Constitution outlines the responsibilities and the limits of the three branches of the national government.

Preview of Events

♦1680	♦1720	♦1760	♦1800

1689
English Bill of Rights established

1690
Locke publishes *Two Treatises of Civil Government*

1748
Montesquieu writes *The Spirit of Laws*

1787
Constitutional Convention meets in Philadelphia

AN American Story

As Benjamin Franklin was leaving the last session of the Constitutional Congress, a woman asked, "What kind of government have you given us, Dr. Franklin? A republic or a monarchy?" Franklin answered, "A republic, Madam, if you can keep it." Franklin's response indicated that a republic—a system of government in which the people elect representatives to exercise power for them—requires citizens to take an active role.

Washington's chair, Constitutional Convention

Roots of the Constitution

After four long and difficult months, Franklin and the other delegates had produced a new constitution. The document provided the framework for a strong central government for the United States.

Although a uniquely American document, the Constitution has roots in many other civilizations. The delegates had studied and discussed the history of political development at length—starting with ancient Greece—so that their new government could avoid the mistakes of the past.

Many ideas embedded in the Constitution came from the study of European political institutions and political writers. British ideas and institutions particularly influenced the delegates.

The Framers who shaped the document were familiar with the parliamentary system of Britain, and many had participated in the colonial assemblies or their state assemblies. They valued the individual rights guaranteed by the British judicial system. Although the Americans had broken away from Britain, they respected many British traditions.

British System of Government

The **Magna Carta** (1215) had placed limits on the power of the monarch. England's lawmaking body, Parliament, emerged as a force that the king had to depend on to pay for wars and to finance the royal government. Like Parliament, the colonial assemblies controlled their colony's funds. For that reason the assemblies had some control over colonial governors.

The English Bill of Rights of 1689 provided another important model for Americans. Many Americans felt that the Constitution also needed a bill of rights.

Framers of the Constitution got many ideas on the nature of people and government from European writers of the Enlightenment. The Enlightenment was a movement of the 1700s that promoted knowledge, reason, and science as the means to improve society. James Madison and other architects of the Constitution were familiar with the work of **John Locke** and **Baron de Montesquieu** (MAHN•tuhs•KYOO), two important philosophers.

Locke, an English philosopher, believed that all people have **natural rights.** These natural rights include the rights to life, liberty, and property. In his *Two Treatises of Civil Government* (1690), he wrote that government is based on an agreement, or contract, between the people and the ruler. Many Americans interpreted natural rights to mean the rights of Englishmen defined in the Magna Carta and the English Bill of Rights. The Framers viewed the Constitution as a contract between the American people and their government. The contract protected the people's natural rights by limiting the government's power.

> ## "[E]very man has a property in his own person. This nobody has any right to but himself."
>
> —*John Locke,* **The Second Treatise of Government** *(1690)*

In *The Spirit of Laws* (1748), the French writer Montesquieu declared that the powers of government should be separated and balanced against each other. This separation would keep any one person or group from gaining too much power. The powers of government should also be clearly defined and limited to prevent abuse. Following the ideas of Montesquieu, the Framers of the Constitution carefully specified and divided the powers of government.

✔ **Reading Check** **Describing** How did the English Bill of Rights influence Americans?

The Federal System

The Constitution created a federal system of government that divided powers between the national, or federal, government and the states. Under the Articles of Confederation the states retained their sovereignty. Under the Constitution the states gave up some of their powers to the federal government while keeping others.

Shared Powers

Federalism, or sharing power between the federal and state governments, is one of the distinctive features of the United States government.

Under the Constitution, the federal government gained broad powers to tax, regulate trade, control the currency, raise an army, and declare war. It could also pass laws that were "necessary and proper" for carrying out its responsibilities.

However, the Constitution left important powers in the hands of the states. The states had the power to pass and enforce laws and regulate trade within their borders. They could also establish local governments, schools, and other institutions affecting the welfare of their citizens. Both federal and state governments also had the power to tax and to build roads.

The Constitution Becomes Supreme Law of the Land

The Constitution and the laws that Congress passed were to be "the supreme law of the land." No state could make laws or take actions that went against the Constitution. Any dispute between the federal government and the states was to be settled by the federal courts on the basis of the Constitution. Under the new federal system, the Constitution became the final and supreme authority.

Reading Check **Describing** What is the principle of federalism?

The Organization of Government

Influenced by Montesquieu's idea of a division of powers, the Framers divided the federal government into three branches—legislative, executive, and judicial. The first three articles, or parts, of the Constitution describe the powers and responsibilities of each branch.

America's *Architecture*

The Old Senate Chamber The U.S. Senate met in the Old Senate Chamber from 1810 until 1859. The two-story chamber is semicircular in shape and measures 75 feet long and 50 feet wide. Two visitors galleries overlook the chamber. After the Senate moved to its present location, the room was occupied by the Supreme Court, from 1860 to 1935. **What branches of government conducted business in the chamber?**

The Legislative Branch

Article I of the Constitution establishes Congress, the legislative branch, or lawmaking branch, of the government. Congress is composed of the House of Representatives and the Senate. As a result of the Great Compromise between large and small states, each state's representation in the House is proportional to its population. Representation in the Senate is equal—two senators for each state.

The powers of Congress include collecting taxes, coining money, and regulating trade. Congress can also declare war and "raise and support armies." Finally it makes all laws needed to fulfill the functions given to it as stated in the Constitution.

The Executive Branch

Memories of King George III's rule made some delegates reluctant to establish a powerful executive, or ruler. Others believed that the

Confederation had failed, in part, because it lacked an executive branch or president. They argued that a strong executive would serve as a check, or limit, on Congress.

Article II of the Constitution established the executive branch, headed by the president, to carry out the nation's laws and policies. The president serves as commander in chief of the armed forces and conducts relations with foreign countries.

The president and a vice president are elected by a special group called the Electoral College, made up of presidential electors. Each state's voters select electors to cast their votes for the president and vice president. Each state has as many electors as it has senators and representatives in Congress. The president and vice president chosen by the electors serve a four-year term.

The Judicial Branch

Article III of the Constitution deals with the judicial branch, or court system, of the United States. The nation's judicial power resides in "one supreme Court" and any other lower federal courts that Congress might establish. The Supreme Court and the federal courts hear cases involving the Constitution, laws passed by Congress, and disputes between states.

System of Checks and Balances

The most distinctive feature of the United States government is the separation of powers. The Constitution divides government power among the legislative, executive, and judicial branches. To keep any one branch from gaining too much power, the Framers built in a system of checks and balances. The three branches of government have roles that check, or limit, the others so that no single branch can dominate the government.

Both the House and the Senate must pass a bill for it to become law. The president can check Congress by vetoing, or rejecting, the bill. However, Congress can then check the president by overriding, or voting down, the veto. To override a veto, two-thirds of the members of both houses of Congress must vote for the bill.

The system of checks and balances also applies to the Supreme Court. The president appoints Supreme Court justices, and the Senate must approve the appointments.

Over time, the Court became a check on Congress and the president by ruling on the constitutionality of laws and presidential acts. The system has been successful in maintaining a balance of power among the branches of the federal government and limiting abuses of power.

National Citizens

The Constitution created citizens of the United States. It set up a government in which the people choose their officials—directly or indirectly. Officials answer to the people rather than to the states. The new government pledged to protect the personal freedoms of its citizens.

With these revolutionary changes, Americans showed the world that it was possible for a people to change its form of government through discussion and choice—rather than through chaos, force, or war. The rest of the world watched the new nation with interest to see whether its experiment in self-government would really work.

Reading Check **Explaining** Why does the Constitution divide government power among the legislative, executive, and judicial branches?

Citizenship

The Constitutional Debate

The delegates at Philadelphia had produced the Constitution, but its acceptance depended upon the will of the people. Gaining approval of the Constitution, with its radical new plan of government, was not going to be easy. Supporters and opponents prepared to defend their positions.

Before the Constitution could go into effect, nine states needed to ratify, or approve, it. State legislatures set up special ratifying conventions to consider the document. By late 1787 these conventions started to meet. Rhode Island stood apart. Its leaders opposed the Constitution from the beginning and therefore did not call a convention to approve it.

A great debate now took place throughout the country. In newspapers, at public meetings, and in ordinary conversations, Americans discussed the arguments for and against the new Constitution.

Linking Past & Present

Great Seal of the United States

The Great Seal of the United States is the official seal of the United States government. The seal appears on important government documents. First adopted in 1782, it remains in use today. The face of the seal shows an American eagle with its wings spread. The seal also includes the motto *E pluribus unum* ("From many, one"). Most Americans don't know it, but they often carry around the seal. The one-dollar bill has both sides of the Great Seal on its back.

The United States has had several versions of the Great Seal.

The Great Seal and the number thirteen

On the Great Seal are

13 stars in the crest above the eagle

13 stripes on the eagle's shield

13 arrows in the eagle's left claw

13 olives and leaves in the eagle's right claw

13 letters in *E Pluribus Unum*

13 letters in the motto above the eye, *Annuit Coeptis*

Federalists

Supporters of the new Constitution were called Federalists. Better organized than their opponents, Federalists enjoyed the support of two of the most respected men in America— George Washington and Benjamin Franklin.

Three of the nation's most gifted political thinkers—James Madison, Alexander Hamilton, and **John Jay**—also backed the Constitution.

Madison, Hamilton, and Jay teamed up to write a series of essays explaining and defending the Constitution. These essays appeared in newspapers around the country and were widely read by Americans of every persuasion. Called *The Federalist Papers,* they were later published as a book and sent to delegates at the remaining ratifying conventions. 📖 *(See page 986 of the Appendix for an excerpt from* The Federalist Papers.*)* Jefferson described the series of essays as

❝the best commentary on the principles of government which was ever written.❞

Antifederalists

The Federalists called those who opposed ratification Antifederalists. Although not as well organized as the Federalists, the Antifederalists

had some dedicated supporters. They responded to the Federalists with a series of their own essays, now known as the *Antifederalist Papers.* Their main argument was that the new Constitution would take away the liberties Americans had fought to win from Great Britain. The Constitution would create a strong central government, ignore the will of the states and the people, and favor the wealthy few over the common people. Antifederalists preferred local government close to the people. An energetic central government, they feared, would be government by a small, educated group of individuals. They agreed with Patrick Henry, who warned that the Constitution was "incompatible with the genius of republicanism."

Protecting Rights

Perhaps the strongest criticism of the Constitution was that it lacked a bill of rights to protect individual freedoms. Antifederalists believed that no government could be trusted to protect the freedom of its citizens. Several state conventions took a stand and announced that they would not ratify the Constitution without the addition of a bill of rights.

Mercy Otis Warren, a Massachusetts opponent of the Constitution, expressed the problem faced by many Antifederalists. She admitted the need for a strong government but feared it.

❝We have struggled for liberty and made costly sacrifices . . . and there are still many among us who [value liberty] too much to relinquish . . . the rights of man for the dignity of government.❞

In many ways the debate between Federalists and Antifederalists came down to their different fears. Federalists feared disorder without a strong central government. They believed that more uprisings like Shays's Rebellion would occur. They looked to the Constitution to create a national government capable of maintaining order. The Antifederalists feared oppression more than disorder. They worried about the concentration of power that would result from a strong national government.

✓ **Reading Check** **Explaining** According to the Antifederalists, why was a bill of rights important?

A cartoon published in 1788 celebrates New Hampshire becoming the ninth state to ratify the Constitution. **From the cartoon, which was the first state to ratify?**

Adopting the Constitution

On December 7, 1787, Delaware became the first state to approve the Constitution. On June 21, 1788, the ninth state—New Hampshire—ratified it. In theory that meant that the new government could go into effect. However, without the support of the two largest states—New York and Virginia—the future of the new government was not promising. Neither state had ratified yet, and both had strong Antifederalist groups.

In Virginia, **Patrick Henry** gave fiery speeches against the proposed Constitution. It did not, he charged, sufficiently limit the power of the federal government. Still, Virginia ratified the Constitution at the end of June 1788, after being assured that the Constitution would include a bill of rights amendment. An amendment is something added to a document.

That left three states—New York, North Carolina, and Rhode Island—to ratify. In July 1788, New York finally ratified it by a narrow margin. North Carolina ratified in November 1789, and Rhode Island ratified in May 1790.

After ratification came the celebrations. Boston, New York, and Philadelphia held big parades accompanied by cannon salutes and ringing church bells. Smaller celebrations took place in hundreds of American towns.

The task of creating the Constitution had ended. The Bill of Rights would be added in 1791, after the new government took office. Now it was time for the nation to elect leaders and begin the work of government.

✓ **Reading Check** **Explaining** Why was the support of New York and Virginia vital to ratifying the Constitution?

SECTION 3 ASSESSMENT

Checking for Understanding

1. **Key Terms** Define the following terms: Enlightenment, federalism, article, Electoral College, checks and balances, ratify, Federalist, Antifederalist, amendment.

2. **Reviewing Facts** What influence did John Locke have on American government?

Reviewing Themes

3. **Civic Rights and Responsibilities** Why did the Framers of the Constitution believe that a division of powers and a system of checks and balances were necessary in a government?

Critical Thinking

4. **Finding the Main Idea** What do you think was the most important reason for establishing a strong central government under the Constitution?

5. **Comparing** Re-create the diagram below. Describe the differences between Hamilton's and Henry's views on the Constitution.

Views on the Constitution	
Hamilton	Henry

Analyzing Visuals

6. **Political Cartoons** Study the political cartoon on this page. Then answer the questions that follow. What do the pillars represent? How do the last two pillars appear?

Interdisciplinary Activity

Citizenship Refer to the Bill of Rights on pages 244–245. Collect photographs from newspapers or magazines that illustrate the freedoms guaranteed in the Bill of Rights. Put your photos on a poster entitled "Pictures of Liberty."

Chapter Summary

A More Perfect Union

1777
- Congress adopts the Articles of Confederation to coordinate the war effort against Britain.

1781
- The Articles of Confederation formally become the government of the United States.

1784
- Spain closes the lower Mississippi River to American shipping.

1785
- The Land Ordinance provides a method for settlement of public lands north of the Ohio River.

1787
- Congress provides for the organization of the Northwest Territory and outlines the steps that a territory must take in order to become a state.
- Delegates meet in Philadelphia and draft the Constitution.
- Delaware becomes the first state to ratify the Constitution.

1788
- New Hampshire becomes the ninth state to vote for ratification.

1790
- The last of the 13 states—Rhode Island—votes for ratification.

1791
- Bill of Rights is added to the Constitution.

Reviewing Key Terms

For each of the pairs of terms below, write a sentence or short paragraph showing how the two are related.

1. constitution, ratify
2. bicameral, legislative branch
3. executive branch, Electoral College

Reviewing Key Facts

4. Summarize the strengths and weaknesses of the Articles of Confederation.
5. What caused the depression after the Revolution?
6. How did the Northwest Ordinance provide for the country's expansion?
7. According to the Virginia Plan, how was the legislature to be set up?
8. Who supported the New Jersey Plan?
9. What was the Three-Fifths Compromise?
10. What powers did the Constitution leave in the hands of the state governments?
11. Why did some states want a bill of rights added to the Constitution?
12. How did the *Federalist Papers* and the *Antifederalist Papers* influence ideas on systems of U.S. government?
13. How does the system of checks and balances work?

Critical Thinking

14. **Comparing** Who had the most power under the Articles of Confederation? Re-create the diagram below. In the boxes, describe the powers given to the state and national governments.

State Governments	National Government

15. **Analyzing Themes: Groups and Institutions** Were the people who attended the Constitutional Convention representative of the American public? Explain.
16. **Drawing Conclusions** Why was a system of checks and balances built into the Constitution?
17. **Analyzing Information** Refer to the grievances listed in the Declaration of Independence on pages 154–157. How were these grievances addressed in the Constitution?

HISTORY Online

Self-Check Quiz
Visit taj.glencoe.com and click on **Chapter 7—Self-Check Quizzes** to prepare for the chapter test.

Geography and History Activity

Examine the map of the Northwest Territory on page 195. Then answer the questions that follow.

18. How many miles long and wide was a township?

19. How many miles long and wide was a section?

20. How many acres were in a section?

Practicing Skills

Making Comparisons   *The two statements that follow reflect the opinions of an Antifederalist and a Federalist toward the ratification of the Constitution. Read the opinions; then answer the questions.*

"These lawyers and men of learning, and moneyed men . . . make us poor illiterate people swallow down the pill, expect to get into Congress themselves; they expect to be the managers of this Constitution, and get all the power and all the money into their own hands, and then they will swallow up all of us little folks. . . . This is what I am afraid of."

— Amos Singletary, farmer

"I am a plain man, and get my living by the plough. . . . I did not go to any lawyer, to ask his opinion; I formed my own opinion, and was pleased with this Constitution. . . . I don't think the worse of the Constitution because lawyers, and men of learning, and moneyed men, are fond of it."

— Jonathan Smith, farmer

21. Who is the Antifederalist? How do you know?

22. How are the two opinions similar? How are they different?

23. In your opinion, does the Antifederalist or the Federalist make the stronger argument? Explain.

Citizenship Cooperative Activity

24. **Interviewing** In groups of three, interview students from your school and adults from your community to find out what they know about the powers of government specified in the Constitution. Prepare a list of questions to use in your interviews. To keep the interviews brief, you might use yes/no questions, such as "Does the Constitution give the government the power to regulate highways?" Compile the answers and present a report to your class.

Economics Activity

25. For a week, keep track of the number of times that you read about or hear about the topics of unemployment and inflation. Write down the source from which you heard or read this information. After each entry, indicate whether the economic news was good.

Alternative Assessment

26. **Portfolio Writing Activity** Review the Bill of Rights to the Constitution (first 10 amendments) on pages 244–245. Summarize each in your journal. Next, choose the amendment from the Bill of Rights that you think is the most important. Write a paragraph in which you explain your choice. Finally, knowing what you know about today's society, write a short description of a right you think the Framers of the Constitution should have included.

Standardized Test Practice

Directions: Choose the *best* answer to the following multiple choice question.

Each of the states enacted state constitutions in the late 1700s. All state constitutions

A established equal rights for all persons living in the state.

B set up legislative and executive branches of state government.

C granted women the right to vote.

D agreed that states would be supervised by the federal government.

Test-Taking Tip:

Eliminate answers that do not make sense. For example, *equal rights for all* (choice A) is a fairly new concept. During the 1700s, women and enslaved people had few rights.

Civics in Action
A Citizenship Handbook

The Constitution

Guide to Reading

Main Idea

For more than 200 years, the Constitution has provided the framework for the United States government and has helped preserve the basic rights of American citizens.

Key Terms

preamble, domestic tranquility, popular sovereignty, republicanism, federalism, enumerated powers, reserved powers, concurrent powers, amendment, implied powers, judicial review

Read to Learn

- why the Constitution is the nation's most important document.
- the goals of the Constitution.
- the principles that form the basis of the Constitution.

Goals of the Constitution

The Preamble, or introduction, to the Constitution reflects the basic principle of American government—the right of the people to govern themselves. It also lists six goals for the United States government:

> 66...to form a more perfect Union, establish Justice, insure domestic Tranquility, provide for the common defence [defense], promote the general Welfare, and secure the Blessings of Liberty to ourselves and our Posterity. 99

These goals guided the Constitution's Framers as they created the new government. They remain as important today as they were when the Constitution was written.

To Form a More Perfect Union Under the Articles of Confederation, the states functioned almost like independent nations. For the most part, they did not work together on important matters such as defense and finances. This lack of unity could have been dangerous for the nation during times of crisis. To form "a more perfect Union" the Framers believed the states needed to agree to operate as a single country and cooperate on major issues.

To Establish Justice For the Framers, treating each citizen equally was one of the fundamental principles on which to build the new nation.

The Constitution provides a national system of courts to protect the people's rights, and to hear cases involving violations of federal law and disputes between the states.

To Insure Domestic Tranquility Shays's Rebellion began in 1786 and shocked Americans. The United States had become a self-governing nation, yet a group of people had resorted to violence to express their anger over government policies. The Constitution provides a strong central government to "insure domestic Tranquility"—that is, to keep peace among the people.

To Provide for the Common Defense The Articles of Confederation required nine states to approve any decision by the Confederation Congress to build an army or navy. The Constitution gives the federal government the power to maintain armed forces to protect the country and its citizens from attack.

To Promote the General Welfare The Declaration of Independence states that the purpose of government is to promote "Life, Liberty, and the pursuit of Happiness" for the people of the nation. The Constitution includes ways to "promote the general Welfare"—or well-being—of the people by maintaining order, protecting individual liberties, regulating commerce and bankruptcies, and promoting science and technology by granting patents.

To Secure the Blessings of Liberty The American colonists fought the Revolutionary War to gain their liberty. The Framers believed that preserving liberty should also be a major goal of the Constitution. The Constitution guarantees that no American's basic rights will be taken away now or for posterity (generations not yet born).

✓ **Reading Check** Analyzing What is the purpose of the Preamble?

Major Principles

The principles outlined in the Constitution were the Framers' solution to the problems of a representative government. The Constitution rests on seven major principles: (1) popular sovereignty, (2) republicanism, (3) limited government, (4) federalism, (5) separation of powers, (6) checks and balances, and (7) individual rights.

Popular Sovereignty The Declaration of Independence states that governments derive their powers from "the consent of the governed." The opening words of the Constitution, "We the people," reinforce this idea of popular sovereignty—or "authority of the people."

Republicanism Under republicanism, voters hold sovereign power. The people elect representatives and give them the responsibility to make laws and conduct government. For most Americans today, the terms *republic* and *representative democracy* mean the same thing: a system of limited government where the people are the ultimate source of governmental power.

Limited Government The Framers saw both benefits and risks in creating a powerful national government. They agreed that the nation needed strong central authority but feared misuse of power. They wanted to prevent the government from using its power to give one

Voting is a basic political right of all citizens.

Major Principles of the Constitution

Popular Sovereignty	People are the source of the government's power.
Republicanism	People elect their political representatives.
Limited Government	The Constitution limits the actions of government by specifically listing powers it does and does not have.
Federalism	In this government system, power is divided between national and state governments.
Separation of Powers	Each of the three branches of government has its own responsibilities.
Checks and Balances	Each branch of government holds some control over the other two branches.
Individual Rights	Basic liberties and rights of all citizens are guaranteed in the Bill of Rights.

Chart *Skills*

The Principles outlined in the Constitution were the Framers' solution to the complex problems presented by a representative government.

Analyzing Information What is the relationship between checks and balances and separation of powers?

REGISTER TO
VOTE HERE

The Federal System

National Government

Enumerated Powers
- Regulate trade
- Coin Money
- Provide an army and navy
- Conduct Foreign affairs
- Set up federal courts

National & State Governments

Concurrent Powers
- Enforce the laws
- Establish courts
- Collect taxes
- Borrow money
- Provide for the general welfare

State Governments

Reserved Powers
- Regulate trade within the state
- Establish local government systems
- Conduct elections
- Establish public school systems

group special advantages or to deprive another group of its rights. By creating a limited government, they made certain the government would have only those powers granted by the people.

Article I of the Constitution states the powers that the government has and the powers that it does not have. Other limits on government appear in the Bill of Rights, which guarantees certain rights and liberties to the people.

Limited government can be described as the "rule of law." No people or groups are above the law. Government officials must obey the law.

Federalism When the states banded together under the Constitution, they gave up some independence. States could no longer print their own money or tax items imported from other states. Nevertheless, each state governed itself much as it had in the past.

This system, in which the power to govern is shared between the national government and the states, is called the federal system, or federalism. Our federal system allows the people of each state to deal with their needs in their own way. At the same time, it lets the states act together to deal with matters that affect all Americans.

The Constitution defines three types of government powers. Enumerated powers belong only to the federal government. These include the power to coin money, regulate interstate and foreign trade, maintain the armed forces, and create federal courts (Article I, Section 8).

The second kind of powers are those retained by the states, known as reserved powers. They include such rights as the power to establish schools, pass marriage and divorce laws, and regulate trade within a state. Although reserved powers are not listed specifically in the Constitution, the Tenth Amendment says that all powers not specifically granted to the federal government "are reserved to the States."

The third set of powers defined by the Constitution are concurrent powers—powers shared by the state and federal governments. Among these powers are the right to raise taxes, borrow money, provide for public welfare, and administer criminal justice.

When conflicts arise between state law and federal law, the Constitution declares that the Constitution is "the supreme Law of the Land." Conflicts between state law and federal law must be settled in a federal court.

Separation of Powers To prevent any single group or institution in government from gaining too much authority, the Framers divided the federal government into three branches: **legislative, executive,** and **judicial.** Each branch has its own functions and powers. The legislative branch, Congress, makes the laws. The executive branch, headed by the president, carries out the laws. The judicial branch, consisting of the Supreme Court and other federal courts, interprets and applies the laws.

Checks and Balances As an additional safeguard, the Framers established a system of **checks and balances** in which each branch of government can check, or limit, the power of the other branches. This system helps maintain a

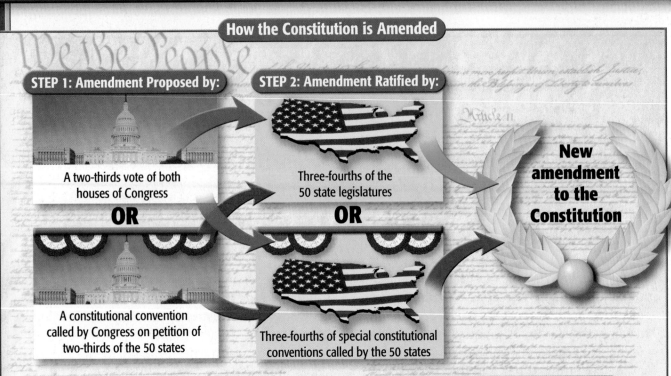

How the Constitution is Amended

STEP 1: Amendment Proposed by:

A two-thirds vote of both houses of Congress

OR

A constitutional convention called by Congress on petition of two-thirds of the 50 states

STEP 2: Amendment Ratified by:

Three-fourths of the 50 state legislatures

OR

Three-fourths of special constitutional conventions called by the 50 states

New amendment to the Constitution

Graphic Organizer → Skills

Amending the Constitution allows it to be able to adapt to changing times.

Analyzing Information What role do the states play in the amendment process?

balance in the power of the three branches. For example, Congress can pass a law. Then the president can reject the law by vetoing it. However, Congress can override, or reverse, the president's veto if two-thirds of the members of both houses vote again to approve the law.

Over the years, the Supreme Court has acquired the power to determine the meaning of the Constitution and to declare that a law or a government policy goes against the Constitution. In doing so, the Court provides a check on the powers of Congress and the president. Judicial decisions—those made by the courts—can be overruled by amending the Constitution. The president and the Senate provide a check on the judicial branch through their power to appoint and approve federal judges. Congress can also change a law so that it no longer conflicts with the Constitution, or it can amend the Constitution. The Fourteenth Amendment, passed by Congress in 1866, overturned the Supreme Court's ruling in the *Dred Scott* decision, which had ruled that enslaved African Americans were not citizens.

Individual Rights The Bill of Rights became part of the Constitution in 1791. These first 10 amendments protect basic liberties and rights that you may take for granted—including freedom of speech, freedom of the press, freedom of assembly, freedom of religion, and the right to a trial by jury.

The 17 amendments that follow the Bill of Rights expand the rights of Americans and adjust certain provisions of the Constitution. Included among them are amendments that abolish slavery, define citizenship, guarantee the right to vote to all citizens, authorize an income tax, and set a two-term limit on the presidency.

Reading Check **Explaining** What is popular sovereignty?

A Living Constitution

Two years after the Constitutional Convention, Benjamin Franklin wrote, "Our Constitution is in actual operation; everything appears to promise that it will last; but in this world nothing is certain but death and taxes."

Despite Franklin's uncertainty about the Constitution's future, it is still very much alive today. The Constitution has survived because the Framers wrote a document that the nation could alter and adapt to meet changing needs. The result is a flexible document that can be interpreted in different ways in keeping with the conditions of a particular time. The Constitution's flexibility allows the government to deal with matters the Framers never anticipated—such as regulating nuclear power plants or developing a space program. In addition the Constitution contains a provision for amending—changing or adding to—the document.

Amending the Constitution The Framers intentionally made the amendment process difficult to discourage minor or frequent changes being made. Although thousands of amendments—changes to the Constitution—have been proposed since 1788, only 27 of them have actually become part of the Constitution.

An amendment may be proposed in two ways: by the vote of two-thirds of both houses of Congress or by two-thirds of the state legislatures asking for a special convention on the amendment. The second method has never been used. Ratification of an amendment requires approval by three-fourths of the states. The Constitution can be ratified by the approval of state legislatures or by special state conventions.

Only the Twenty-first Amendment—which repealed the Eighteenth Amendment, banning the sale of alcoholic beverages—was ratified by state conventions. Voters in each state chose the delegates to the special conventions.

Interpreting the Constitution The Constitution includes two provisions that give Congress the power to act as needed to meet changing conditions. The first of these provisions is what is known as the "elastic clause" (Article I, Section 8). It directs Congress to "make all Laws which shall be necessary and proper" for executing all the powers of government. Congress has interpreted this clause to mean that it has certain implied powers, powers not specifically defined in the Constitution. Over the years,

Congress has drawn on its implied powers to pass laws to deal with the needs of society.

The second provision used to expand congressional authority, the "commerce clause" (Article I, Section 8), gives Congress the power to "regulate Commerce with foreign Nations, and among the several States." Congress has used this clause to expand its powers into a number of areas, such as regulation of the airline industry, radio and television, and nuclear energy.

Powers of the Presidency The Constitution describes the role and the powers of the president in general terms. This has allowed the executive branch to extend its powers. In 1803, for example, President Thomas Jefferson approved a treaty with France that enabled the United States to buy an enormous tract of land.

The Bill of Rights

1	Guarantees freedom of religion, speech, assembly, and press, and the right of people to petition the government
2	Protects the rights of states to maintain a militia and of citizens to bear arms
3	Restricts quartering of troops in private homes
4	Protects against "unreasonable searches and seizures"
5	Assures the right not to be deprived of "life, liberty, or property, without due process of law"
6	Guarantees the right to a speedy and public trial by an impartial jury
7	Assures the right to a jury trial in cases involving the common law (the law established by previous court decisions)
8	Protects against excessive bail, or cruel and unusual punishment
9	Provides that people's rights are not restricted to those specified in the first eight Amendments
10	Restates the Constitution's principle of federalism by providing that powers not granted to the national government nor prohibited to the states are reserved to the states and to the people

"I have finally been included in 'We the people.'"

—Barbara Jordan, U.S. representative from Texas, 1972–1978

The Courts The role of the judicial branch has also grown as powers implied in the Constitution have been put into practice. In 1803 Chief Justice John Marshall expanded the powers of the Supreme Court by striking down an act of Congress in the case of *Marbury* v. *Madison*. In that decision the Court defined its right to determine whether a law violates the Constitution. Although not mentioned in the Constitution, judicial review has become a major power of the judicial branch.

The process of amending the Constitution and applying its principles in new areas helps keep our government functioning well. In 1974 Barbara Jordan, an African American member of Congress and a constitutional scholar, spoke in ringing tones of her faith in the Constitution:

❝I felt somehow for many years that George Washington and Alexander Hamilton just left me out by mistake. But through the process of amendment, interpretation, and court decision I have finally been included in 'We the people.'**❞**

✔️**Reading Check** **Explaining** What are implied powers?

SECTION 1 ASSESSMENT

Checking for Understanding

1. **Key Terms** Write complete sentences using each group of terms below. Group 1: republicanism, federalism. Group 2: enumerated powers, concurrent powers. Group 3: preamble, amendment.
2. **Reviewing Facts** Explain the origin of judicial review.

Reviewing Themes

3. **Government and Democracy** What is the importance of federalism in the Constitution?

Critical Thinking

4. **Analyzing Information** Why was it so important for basic freedoms to be guaranteed in the Constitution?
5. **Comparing** Re-create the diagram below and describe how each branch of government has power over another branch.

Branch	Power
Legislative	
Executive	
Judicial	

Analyzing Visuals

6. **Reading a Table** Refer to the table on page 218. How are popular sovereignty and republicanism related?

Interdisciplinary Activity

Civics The Bill of Rights guarantees certain basic rights to all Americans. Select one of the 10 amendments that make up the Bill of Rights (see page 221) and research its history. Present your findings in a one-page essay.

SECTION 2 The Federal Government

Guide to Reading

Main Idea
The government of the United States has three branches: the legislative branch, the executive branch, and the judicial branch.

Key Terms
appropriate, impeach, constituents

Read to Learn
- the goals of the three branches of the government.
- the powers of the three branches of the government.

The Legislative Branch

Congress, the legislative branch of the government, makes the nation's laws. It also has the power to "lay and collect taxes" and to declare war. Congress has two houses, the House of Representatives and the Senate.

The House and Senate Today the House of Representatives has 435 voting members and five nonvoting delegates from the District of Columbia, Puerto Rico, Guam, American Samoa, and the Virgin Islands. The number of representatives from each state is determined by the state's population. Representatives, who must be at least 25 years old, serve two-year terms.

The Senate consists of 100 senators, two from each state. Senators, who must be at least 30 years old, serve six-year terms. The senators' terms are staggered, which means that one-third of the Senate seats come up for election every two years.

Seal of the U.S. Congress

The Role of Congress Congress has two primary functions: to make the nation's laws and to control government spending. The government cannot spend any money unless Congress appropriates, or sets aside, funds. All tax and spending bills must originate in the House of Representatives and gain approval in both the House and the Senate before moving on to the president for signature.

Congress also serves as a watchdog over the executive branch, monitoring its actions and investigating possible abuses of power. The House of Representatives can impeach, or bring formal charges against, any federal official it suspects of wrongdoing or misconduct. If an official is impeached, the Senate acts as a court and tries the accused official. Officials who are found guilty may be removed from office.

The Senate also holds certain special powers. Only the Senate can ratify treaties made by the president and confirm presidential appointments of federal officials, such as department heads, ambassadors, and federal judges.

All members of Congress have the responsibility of representing their constituents, the people of their home states and districts. As a constituent you can expect your senators and representatives to promote and protect your state's interests as well as those of the nation.

Congress at Work Thousands of **bills**, or proposed laws, are introduced in Congress every year. Because individual members of Congress

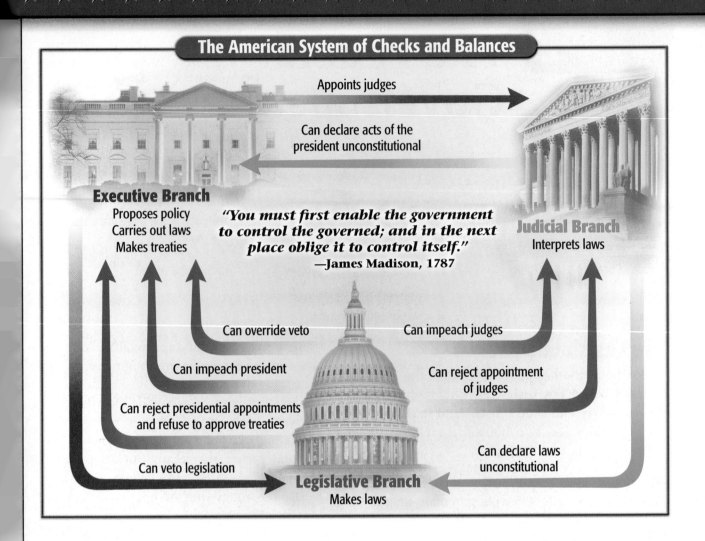

The American System of Checks and Balances

Appoints judges

Can declare acts of the president unconstitutional

Executive Branch
Proposes policy
Carries out laws
Makes treaties

"You must first enable the government to control the governed; and in the next place oblige it to control itself."
—James Madison, 1787

Judicial Branch
Interprets laws

Can override veto

Can impeach judges

Can impeach president

Can reject appointment of judges

Can reject presidential appointments and refuse to approve treaties

Can veto legislation

Can declare laws unconstitutional

Legislative Branch
Makes laws

---

cannot possibly study all these bills carefully, both houses use committees of selected members to evaluate proposed legislation.

Standing committees are permanent committees in both the House and the Senate that specialize in a particular topic, such as agriculture, commerce, or veterans' affairs. These committees usually are broken down into **subcommittees** that focus on a particular aspect of a problem or issue.

The House and the Senate sometimes form temporary **select committees** to deal with issues requiring special attention. These committees meet only until they complete their task.

Occasionally the House and the Senate form **joint committees** with members from both houses. These committees meet to consider specific issues, such as the system of federal taxation. One type of joint committee, a **conference committee,** has a special function. If the House

and the Senate pass different versions of the same bill, a conference committee tries to work out a compromise bill acceptable to both houses.

When it receives a bill, a committee can kill it by rejecting it outright, "pigeonhole" it by setting it aside without reviewing it, or prepare it for consideration by the full House or Senate. While preparing bills, committees hold public hearings at which citizens can present arguments and documents supporting or opposing the bills.

Once a bill is approved by a committee in either house of Congress, it is sent to the full Senate or House for debate. After debate the bill may be passed, rejected, or returned to committee for further changes.

When both houses pass a bill, the bill goes to the president. If the president approves the bill and signs it, it becomes law. If the president vetoes the bill, it does not become law, unless Congress **overrides** (cancels) the presidential veto by a vote of two-thirds of the members in each house.

✓**Reading Check** **Sequencing** List the basic steps of how a bill becomes a law.

The Executive Branch

The executive branch of government includes the president, the vice president, and various executive offices, departments, and agencies. The executive branch carries out the laws that Congress passes.

Chief Executive The president plays a number of different roles in government, each of which has specific powers and responsibilities. These roles include the nation's chief executive, chief diplomat, commander in chief, chief of state, and legislative leader.

As chief executive, the president is responsible for carrying out the nation's laws. Many executive departments and agencies assist the president in this job.

Chief Diplomat As chief diplomat, the president directs foreign policy, appoints ambassadors, and negotiates treaties with other nations. Treaties must be approved by a two-thirds vote of the Senate before they go into effect.

Commander in Chief As commander in chief of the armed forces, the president can use the military to intervene or offer assistance in crises at home and around the world. The president cannot declare war; only Congress holds this power. The president can send troops to other parts of the world for up to 60 days but must notify Congress when doing so. The troops may remain longer only if Congress gives approval or declares war.

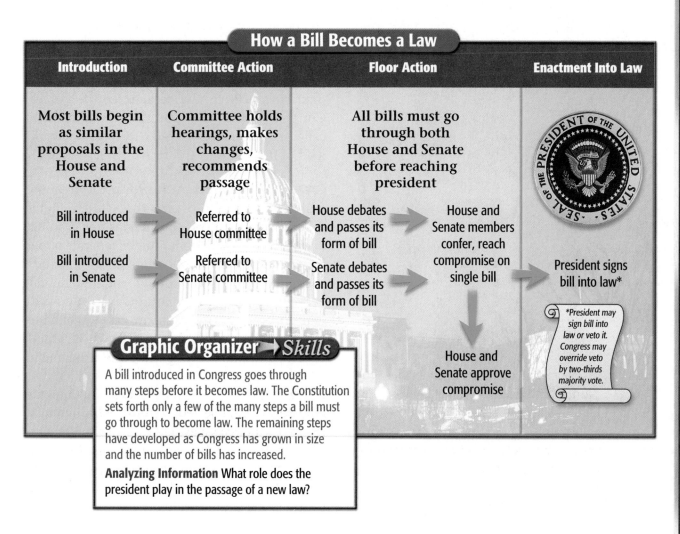

How a Bill Becomes a Law

Introduction	Committee Action	Floor Action	Enactment Into Law
Most bills begin as similar proposals in the House and Senate	Committee holds hearings, makes changes, recommends passage	All bills must go through both House and Senate before reaching president	
Bill introduced in House →	Referred to House committee →	House debates and passes its form of bill →	House and Senate members confer, reach compromise on single bill →
Bill introduced in Senate →	Referred to Senate committee →	Senate debates and passes its form of bill →	President signs bill into law*
		House and Senate approve compromise	*President may sign bill into law or veto it. Congress may override veto by two-thirds majority vote.

Graphic Organizer → Skills

A bill introduced in Congress goes through many steps before it becomes law. The Constitution sets forth only a few of the many steps a bill must go through to become law. The remaining steps have developed as Congress has grown in size and the number of bills has increased.

Analyzing Information What role does the president play in the passage of a new law?

Chief of State As chief of state, the president serves a symbolic role as the representative of all Americans. The president fulfills this role when receiving foreign ambassadors or heads of state, visiting foreign nations, or bestowing honors on Americans.

Legislative Leader The president serves as a legislative leader by proposing laws to Congress and working to see that they are passed. In the annual State of the Union address, the president presents goals for legislation.

The Executive Branch at Work Many executive offices, departments, and independent agencies help the president carry out and enforce the nation's laws. The Executive Office of the President (EOP) is made up of individuals and agencies that directly assist the president. Presidents rely heavily on the EOP for advice and for gathering information.

The executive branch also includes 14 executive departments, each responsible for a different area of government. For example, the

Department of State plans and carries out foreign policy, and the Department of the Interior manages and protects the nation's public lands and natural resources. The heads, or secretaries, of these departments are members of the president's **cabinet,** a group that helps the president make decisions and set government policy.

The independent agencies manage federal programs in many fields. These include aeronautics and space, banking, communications, farm credit, and trade. Government corporations are government agencies that are run like privately owned businesses. One government corporation whose services you may often use is the United States Postal Service.

✓**Reading Check** **Describing** What is the president's cabinet?

The Judicial Branch

Article III of the Constitution called for the creation of a Supreme Court and "such inferior [lower] courts as Congress may from time to time ordain and establish." In 1789 Congress passed a **Judiciary Act,** which added a series of district courts to the federal court system. Congress added appeals courts, sometimes called circuit courts, in 1891 to ease the workload of the Supreme Court.

Lower Federal Courts At the lowest level of the federal court system are the United States **district courts.** These courts consider criminal and civil cases that come under federal, rather than state, authority. The criminal cases include such offenses as kidnapping and federal tax evasion. Civil cases cover claims against the federal government and cases involving constitutional rights, such as free speech. There are 91 district courts in the nation, with at least one in every state.

The next level of federal courts, the **appeals courts,** reviews district court decisions in which the losing side has asked for a review of the verdict. If an appeals court disagrees with the lower court's decision, it can either overturn the verdict or order a retrial. There are 14 appeals courts in the United States.

The Supreme Court The **Supreme Court** stands at the top of the American legal system. Article III of the Constitution created the Supreme Court as one of three coequal branches of the national government, along with Congress and the president.

The Supreme Court is composed of nine justices: the chief justice of the United States and eight associate justices. Congress sets this number and has the power to change it. Over the years it has varied from 5 to 10, but it has been 9 since 1869.

The Constitution does not describe the duties of the justices. Instead, the duties have developed from laws, through tradition, and as the needs and circumstances of the nation have developed. The main duty of the justices is to hear and rule on cases. This duty involves them in three decision-making tasks: deciding which cases to hear from among the thousands appealed to the Court each year; deciding the case itself; and determining an explanation for the decision, called the Court's **opinion.**

Shaping Public Policy The Supreme Court is both a political and a legal institution. It is a legal institution because it is responsible for settling disputes and interpreting the meaning of laws. The Court is a political institution because when it applies the law to specific disputes, it often determines what national policy will be. For example, when the Court rules that certain parts of the Social Security Act must apply to men and women equally, it is determining government policy.

Judicial Review As you have read, the Supreme Court's power to examine the laws and actions of local, state, and national governments and to cancel them if they violate the Constitution is called judicial review. The Supreme Court first assumed the power of judicial review in the case of *Marbury* v. *Madison* (1803). Since then, the Court has invalidated, or canceled, nearly 200 provisions of federal law.

The Supreme Court may also review presidential policies. In the case of *Ex parte Milligan* (1866), the Court ruled President Lincoln's suspension of certain civil rights during the Civil War was unconstitutional.

Judicial review of state laws and actions may have as much significance as the Court's activities at the federal level. In *Brown* v. *Board of Education of Topeka* (1954), the Court held that laws requiring or permitting racially segregated schools in four states were unconstitutional. The *Brown* decision cleared the way for the end of segregated schools throughout the nation.

✓ **Reading Check** **Describing** How was the court system set up?

SECTION 2 ASSESSMENT

Checking for Understanding

1. **Key Terms** Use each of these terms in a complete sentence that helps explain its meaning: appropriate, impeach, constituents.

2. **Reviewing Facts** List three responsibilities of the president.

Reviewing Themes

3. **Government and Democracy** Why is Congress's power to appropriate money important?

Critical Thinking

4. **Analyzing Information** Which branch of government do you think is most powerful? Explain why you think so.

5. **Analyzing Information** Re-create the diagram below and provide five different kinds of Congressional committees.

Committees

Analyzing Visuals

6. **Reading a Flowchart** Refer to the flowchart on page 225. What do committees do to a bill?

Interdisciplinary Activity

Current Events Research in newspapers and news magazines about bills that are being debated in Congress. Find out what the bill will do if it is passed. Write a one-page paper about the bill and what has happened to it as it has gone through Congress.

SECTION 3 Citizens' Rights and Responsibilities

The Rights of American Citizens

66We hold these truths to be self-evident, that all men are created equal, that they are endowed by their Creator with certain unalienable Rights, that among these are Life, Liberty, and the pursuit of Happiness.99

These words from the Declaration of Independence continue to inspire Americans. They have encouraged Americans to pursue the ideals expressed in the Declaration and to create a Constitution and a Bill of Rights that protect these rights. The rights of Americans fall into three broad categories: the right to be protected from unfair actions of the government, to have equal treatment under the law, and to have basic freedoms.

Due Process The Fifth Amendment states that no person shall "be deprived of life, liberty, or property, without due process of law." Due process of law means that the government must follow procedures established by law and guaranteed by the Constitution, treating all people according to these principles.

Equal Protection All Americans, regardless of race, religion, or political beliefs, have the right to be treated the same under the law. The Fourteenth Amendment requires every state to grant its citizens "equal protection of the laws."

Basic Freedoms The basic freedoms involve the liberties outlined in the First Amendment—freedom of speech, freedom of religion, freedom of the press, freedom of assembly, and the right to petition. In a democratic society, power exists in the hands of the people. Therefore, its citizens must be free to exchange ideas freely.

The First Amendment allows citizens to criticize the government, in speech or in the press, without fear of punishment. It also states that the government cannot endorse a religion, nor can it prohibit citizens from practicing a religion if they choose to do so. In addition, the Ninth Amendment states that the rights of Americans are not limited to those mentioned in the Constitution. This has allowed basic freedoms to expand over the years through the passage of other amendments and laws. The Twenty-sixth Amendment, for example, extends the right to vote to American citizens 18 years of age.

Limits on Rights Our rights are not unlimited. The government can establish laws or rules to restrict certain standards to protect the health, safety, security, and moral standards of a community. Moreover, rights may be limited to prevent one person's rights from interfering with the rights of others. The restrictions of rights, however, must be reasonable and must apply to everyone equally.

✓**Reading Check** **Summarizing** What is due process of law?

Citizen Participation

A citizen is a person who owes loyalty to and is entitled to the protection of a state or nation. How do you become an American citizen? Generally, citizenship is granted to anyone born within the borders of the United States. Citizenship is also granted to anyone born outside the United States if one parent is a United States citizen. A person of foreign birth can also become a citizen through the process of naturalization.

To qualify, applicants must be at least 18 years old. They must have been lawfully admitted for permanent residence and have lived in the United States for at least five years. They must possess good moral character and accept the principles of the Constitution. Applicants must also understand English and demonstrate an understanding of the history and principles of the government of the United States. Before being admitted to citizenship, applicants must be willing to give up any foreign allegiance and must promise to obey the Constitution and the laws of the United States.

As citizens of the United States, we are expected to carry out certain duties and responsibilities. **Duties** are things we are required to do by law. **Responsibilities** are things we should do. Fulfilling both our duties and our responsibilities helps ensure that we have a good government and that we continue to enjoy our rights.

Duties

One of the duties of all Americans is to obey the law. Laws serve three important functions. They help maintain order; they protect the health, safety, and property of all citizens; and they make it possible for people to live together peacefully. If you disobey laws, for example, you endanger others and interfere with the smooth functioning of society. If you believe a law needs to be changed, you can work through your elected representatives to improve it.

Americans also have a duty to pay taxes. The government uses tax money to defend the nation, provide health insurance for people over 65, and build roads and bridges. Americans benefit from services provided by the government.

Flag Etiquette

★ The flag should be raised and lowered by hand and displayed only from sunrise to sunset. On special occasions, it may be displayed at night.

★ The flag may be displayed on all days, weather permitting, particularly on national and state holidays and on historic and special occasions.

★ No flag should be flown above the American flag or to the right of it at the same height.

★ The flag may be flown at half-mast to mourn the death of public officials.

★ The flag should never touch the ground or floor beneath it.

★ The flag may be flown upside down only to signal distress.

★ When the flag becomes old and tattered, it should be destroyed by burning. According to an approved custom, the Union (the white stars on the blue field) is first cut from the flag; then the two pieces, which no longer form a flag, are burned.

Another duty of citizens is to defend the nation. All males aged 18 and older must register with the government in case they are needed for military service. The nation no longer has a **draft,** or required military service, but a war could make the draft necessary again.

The Constitution guarantees all Americans the right to a trial by a jury of their peers (equals). For this reason you should be prepared to serve on a jury when you become eligible at the age of 18. Having a large group of jurors on hand is necessary to guarantee the right to a fair and speedy trial. You also have a duty to serve as a witness at a trial if called to do so.

Responsibilities

The responsibilities of citizens are not as clear-cut as their duties. Because responsibilities are voluntary, people are not arrested or punished if they do not fulfill these obligations. The quality of our government and of our lives will diminish, however, if our responsibilities are not carried out.

Keep in mind that government exists to serve you. Therefore, one of your responsibilities as a citizen is to know what the government is doing and to voice your opinion when you feel strongly about something the government has done or has failed to do. When the government learns that most people favor or oppose an action, it usually follows their wishes.

You also need to be informed about your rights and to exercise them when necessary. Knowing your rights helps preserve them. Other responsibilities include respecting diversity, accepting responsibility for your actions, and supporting your family.

Citizens taking part in a town meeting

Vote, Vote, Vote! Perhaps your most important responsibility as an American citizen will be to vote when you reach the age of 18. Voting allows you to participate in government and guide its direction. When you vote for people to represent you in government, you will be exercising your right of self-government. If you disapprove of the job your representatives are doing, it will be your responsibility to help elect other people in the next election. You can also let your representatives know how you feel about issues through letters, telephone calls, and petitions.

While not everyone holds public office, everyone can participate in government in other ways. Working on a political campaign, volunteering to help in a hospital or a library, and participating in a local park cleanup are all ways to take responsibility and to make a contribution to good government and a well-run community.

Respecting Others' Rights To enjoy your rights to the fullest, you must be prepared to respect the rights of others. Respecting the rights of others also means respecting the rights of people with whom you disagree. Respecting and accepting others regardless of race, religion, beliefs, or other differences is essential in a democracy. All Americans are entitled to the same respect and good treatment.

✓ **Reading Check** **Identifying** What is naturalization?

SECTION 3 ASSESSMENT

Checking for Understanding

1. **Key Terms** Use each of these terms in a complete sentence that helps explain its meaning: due process of law, citizen, naturalization.

2. **Reviewing Facts** Why are personal responsibilities important?

Reviewing Themes

3. **Government and Democracy** Summarize three of the freedoms granted in the First Amendment.

Critical Thinking

4. **Analyzing Information** The Fifth Amendment states that people have the right of "due process of law." Why is this phrase important?

5. **Analyzing Information** Re-create the diagram below and provide the three categories of American rights.

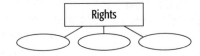

Analyzing Visuals

6. **Analyzing a Chart** Refer to the chart on page 229. For what reason may the flag be flown at half-mast?

Interdisciplinary Activity

Civics One responsibility of being an American citizen is to become involved in the democratic system. Make a poster showing how students can get involved in their community's democracy. Display your poster in a prominent place in school.

Handbook Assessment

✓ Reviewing Key Terms

Write the key term that completes each sentence. Then write a sentence for each term not chosen.

a. popular sovereignty   **d.** amendment

b. enumerated powers   **e.** implied powers

c. reserved powers   **f.** judicial review

1. A(n)_____ is a change to the Constitution.

2. Those powers that are suggested but not directly stated in the Constitution are called _____.

3. _____ is the Supreme Court's power to review all congressional acts and executive actions.

4. Those powers mentioned specifically in the Constitution are called _____.

✓ Reviewing Key Facts

5. List the six goals of government stated in the Preamble.

6. How does one become a naturalized citizen?

7. Explain why the amendment process is so difficult.

8. Explain why responsible citizenship is important. Provide examples of responsible citizenship.

9. How does the Constitution protect individual rights?

10. Summarize the basic freedoms outlined in the First Amendment.

✓ Critical Thinking

11. **Analyzing Information** Analyze how limited government, republicanism, and popular sovereignty are important parts of the Constitution.

12. **Identifying Options** Describe five possible ways a person can fulfill his or her responsibilities in society and at home.

13. **Comparing** Some people argue that there should be a limit on the number of terms a senator or representative can serve. What are some of the advantages of the present system, which does not limit these terms? What are some of the disadvantages?

14. **Predicting Consequences** Re-create the diagram below and predict what might have happened to the U.S. if the Framers had not provided for a system of checks and balances.

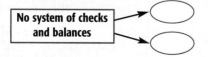

✓ Citizenship Cooperative Activity

15. **Examining Citizens' Rights** Working with a partner, choose one of the following rights and trace its historical development in the United States from the time the Constitution was ratified to the present:

     suffrage   freedom of speech

     freedom of religion   equal protection of law

16. **Civic Planning** Constitutions provide a plan for organizing and operating governments. What plan provides the rules for your local government? Contact a local government official to find out about the basic plan of your city or town. Share your findings with the class.

✓ Alternative Assessment

17. **Portfolio Writing Activity** Part of your responsibility as an American citizen is to be informed about what the government is doing and to voice your opinion about its actions. Compose a letter to the editor of your local newspaper. In your letter, express your opinion about an issue in your community.

Standardized Test Practice

Directions: Choose the *best* answer to the following question.

Under the Constitution, the president chooses judges to serve on the Supreme Court, but each choice must be approved by the Senate. This is an example of what principle of government?

A   Checks and balances

B   Federalism

C   Separation of powers

D   Judicial Review

Test-Taking Tip:

What do you think would happen if the president could choose all judges without anyone else's approval? The writers of the Constitution wanted to make sure that none of the three branches of government became too powerful. Which answer shows this idea?

The Constitution of the United States

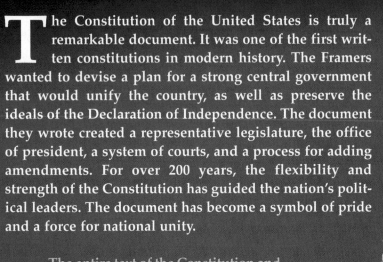

The Constitution of the United States is truly a remarkable document. It was one of the first written constitutions in modern history. The Framers wanted to devise a plan for a strong central government that would unify the country, as well as preserve the ideals of the Declaration of Independence. The document they wrote created a representative legislature, the office of president, a system of courts, and a process for adding amendments. For over 200 years, the flexibility and strength of the Constitution has guided the nation's political leaders. The document has become a symbol of pride and a force for national unity.

The entire text of the Constitution and its amendments follows. Those passages that have been set aside, outdated by the passage of time, or changed by the adoption of amendments are printed in blue. Also included are explanatory notes that will help clarify the meaning of each article and section.

James Madison, author of the Constitution

Preamble

We the People of the United States, in Order to form a more perfect Union, establish Justice, insure domestic Tranquility, provide for the common defence, promote the general Welfare, and secure the Blessings of Liberty to ourselves and our Posterity, do ordain and establish this Constitution for the United States of America.

Article I

Section 1

All legislative Powers herein granted shall be vested in a Congress of the United States, which shall consist of a Senate and House of Representatives.

Section 2

[1.] The House of Representatives shall be composed of Members chosen every second Year by the People of the several States, and the Electors in each State shall have the Qualifications requisite for Electors of the most numerous Branch of the State Legislature.

[2.] No person shall be a Representative who shall not have attained to the Age of twenty five Years, and been seven Years a Citizen of the United States, and who shall not, when elected, be an Inhabitant of that State in which he shall be chosen.

[3.] Representatives and direct Taxes shall be apportioned among the several States which may be included within this Union, according to their respective Numbers, which shall be determined by adding to the whole Number of free Persons, including those bound to Service for a Term of Years, and excluding Indians not taxed, three fifths of all other Persons. The actual Enumeration shall be made within three Years after the first Meeting of the Congress of the United States, and within every subsequent Term of ten Years, in such Manner as they shall by Law direct. The Number of Representatives shall not exceed one for every thirty Thousand, but each State shall have at Least one Representative; and until such enumeration shall be made, the State of New Hampshire shall be entitled to chuse three; Massachusetts eight, Rhode-Island and Providence Plantations one, Connecticut five, New-York six, New Jersey four, Pennsylvania eight, Delaware one, Maryland six, Virginia ten, North Carolina five, South Carolina five, and Georgia three.

[4.] When vacancies happen in the Representation from any State, the Executive Authority thereof shall issue Writs of Election to fill such Vacancies.

[5.] The House of Representatives shall chuse their Speaker and other Officers; and shall have the sole Power of Impeachment.

The Preamble introduces the Constitution and sets forth the general purposes for which the government was established. The Preamble also declares that the power of the government comes from the people.

The printed text of the document shows the spelling and punctuation of the parchment original.

Article I. The Legislative Branch

The Constitution contains seven divisions called articles. Each article covers a general topic. For example, Articles I, II, and III create the three branches of the national government—the legislative, executive, and judicial branches. Most of the articles are divided into sections.

Section 2. House of Representatives

Division of Representatives Among the States The number of representatives from each state is based on the size of the state's population. Each state is entitled to at least one representative. *What are the qualifications for members of the House of Representatives?*

Vocabulary

preamble: *introduction*
constitution: *principles and laws of a nation*
enumeration: *census or population count*
impeachment: *bringing charges against an official*

The Constitution of the United States   **233**

Section 3. The Senate

Number of Members, Terms of Office, and Voting Procedure Originally, senators were chosen by the state legislators of their own states. The Seventeenth Amendment changed this, so that senators are now elected by the people. There are 100 senators, 2 from each state. The vice president serves as president of the Senate.

John Adams, the first vice president

Section 3. The Senate

Trial of Impeachment One of Congress's powers is the power to impeach—to accuse government officials of wrongdoing, put them on trial, and if necessary remove them from office. *Which body has the power to decide the official's guilt or innocence?*

Vocabulary

president pro tempore: *presiding officer of Senate who serves when the vice president is absent*
indictment: *charging a person with an offense*
quorum: *minimum number of members that must be present to conduct sessions*
adjourn: *to suspend a session*
immunity privilege: *members cannot be sued or prosecuted for anything they say in Congress*
emoluments: *salaries*
bill: *draft of a proposed law*
revenue: *income raised by government*

Section 3

[1.] The Senate of the United States shall be composed of two Senators from each State, chosen by the Legislature thereof, for six Years; and each Senator shall have one Vote.

[2.] Immediately after they shall be assembled in Consequence of the first Election, they shall be divided as equally as may be into three Classes. The Seats of the Senators of the first Class shall be vacated at the Expiration of the second Year, of the second Class at the Expiration of the fourth Year, and of the third Class at the Expiration of the sixth Year, so that one third may be chosen every second Year; and if Vacancies happen by Resignation, or otherwise, during the Recess of the Legislature of any State, the Executive thereof may make temporary Appointments until the next Meeting of the Legislature, which shall then fill such Vacancies.

[3.] No Person shall be a Senator who shall not have attained to the Age of thirty Years, and been nine Years a Citizen of the United States, and who shall not, when elected, be an Inhabitant of that State for which he shall be chosen.

[4.] The Vice President of the United States shall be President of the Senate, but shall have no Vote, unless they be equally divided.

[5.] The Senate shall chuse their other Officers, and also a President pro tempore, in the Absence of the Vice President, or when he shall exercise the Office of the President of the United States.

[6.] The Senate shall have the sole Power to try all Impeachments. When sitting for that Purpose, they shall be on Oath or Affirmation. When the President of the United States is tried, the Chief Justice shall preside: And no Person shall be convicted without the Concurrence of two thirds of the Members present.

[7.] Judgment in Cases of Impeachment shall not extend further than to removal from Office, and disqualification to hold and enjoy any Office of honor, Trust or Profit under the United States: but the Party convicted shall nevertheless be liable and subject to Indictment, Trial, Judgment and Punishment, according to Law.

Section 4

[1.] The Times, Places and Manner of holding Elections for Senators and Representatives, shall be prescribed in each State by the Legislature thereof; but the Congress may at any time by Law make or alter such Regulations, except as to the Places of chusing Senators.

[2.] The Congress shall assemble at least once in every Year, and such Meeting shall be on the first Monday in December, unless they shall by Law appoint a different Day.

Section 5

[1.] Each House shall be the Judge of the Elections, Returns and Qualifications of its own Members, and a Majority of each shall constitute a Quorum to do Business; but a smaller Number may adjourn from day to day, and may be authorized to compel the Attendance of absent Members, in such Manner, and under such Penalties as each House may provide.

[2.] Each House may determine the Rules of its Proceedings, punish its Members for disorderly Behaviour, and, with the Concurrence of two thirds, expel a Member.

[3.] Each House shall keep a Journal of its Proceedings, and from time to time publish the same, excepting such Parts as may in their Judgment require Secrecy; and the Yeas and Nays of the Members of either House on any question shall, at the Desire of one fifth of those Present, be entered on the Journal.

[4.] Neither House, during the Session of Congress, shall, without the Consent of the other, adjourn for more than three days, nor to any other Place than that in which the two Houses shall be sitting.

Section 6

[1.] The Senators and Representatives shall receive a Compensation for their Services, to be ascertained by Law, and paid out of the Treasury of the United States. They shall in all Cases, except Treason, Felony and Breach of the Peace, be privileged from Arrest during their Attendance at the Session of their respective Houses, and in going to and returning from the same; and for any Speech or Debate in either House, they shall not be questioned in any other Place.

[2.] No Senator or Representative shall, during the Time for which he was elected, be appointed to any civil Office under the Authority of the United States, which shall have been created, or the Emoluments whereof shall have been encreased during such time; and no Person holding any Office under the United States, shall be a Member of either House during his Continuance in Office.

Section 7

[1.] All Bills for raising Revenue shall originate in the House of Representatives; but the Senate may propose or concur with Amendments as on other Bills.

[2.] Every Bill which shall have passed the House of Representatives and the Senate, shall, before it become a Law, be presented to the President of the United States; If he approve he shall sign it, but if not he shall return it, with his Objections to that House in which it shall have originated, who shall enter the Objections at large on their Journal, and proceed to reconsider it. If after such Reconsideration two thirds of that House shall agree to pass the Bill, it shall be sent, together with the Objections, to the other House, by which it shall likewise be reconsidered, and if approved by two thirds

Senate gavel

Section 6. Privileges and Restrictions

Pay and Privileges To strengthen the federal government, the Founders set congressional salaries to be paid by the United States Treasury rather than by members' respective states. Originally, members were paid $6 per day. In 2002, all members of Congress received a base salary of $150,000.

Section 7. Passing Laws

Revenue Bills All tax laws must originate in the House of Representatives. This ensures that the branch of Congress that is elected by the people every two years has the major role in determining taxes.

Section 7. Passing Laws

How Bills Become Laws A bill may become a law only by passing both houses of Congress and by being signed by the president. The president can check Congress by rejecting—vetoing—its legislation. *How can Congress override the president's veto?*

of that House, it shall become a Law. But in all such Cases the Votes of both Houses shall be determined by yeas and Nays, and the Names of the Persons voting for and against the Bill shall be entered on the Journal of each House respectively. If any Bill shall not be returned by the President within ten Days (Sundays excepted) after it shall have been presented to him, the Same shall be a Law, in like Manner as if he had signed it, unless the Congress by their Adjournment prevent its Return, in which Case it shall not be a Law.

[3.] Every Order, Resolution, or Vote to which the Concurrence of the Senate and House of Representatives may be necessary (except on a question of Adjournment) shall be presented to the President of the United States; and before the Same shall take Effect, shall be approved by him, or being disapproved by him, shall be repassed by two thirds of the Senate and House of Representatives, according to the Rules and Limitations prescribed in the Case of a Bill.

Section 8

[1.] The Congress shall have the Power To lay and collect Taxes, Duties, Imposts and Excises, to pay the Debts and provide for the common Defence and general Welfare of the United States; but all Duties, Imposts and Excises shall be uniform throughout the United States;

[2.] To borrow Money on the credit of the United States;

[3.] To regulate Commerce with foreign Nations, and among the several States, and with the Indian Tribes;

[4.] To establish an uniform Rule of Naturalization, and uniform Laws on the subject of Bankruptcies throughout the United States;

[5.] To coin Money, regulate the Value thereof, and of foreign Coin, and fix the Standard of Weights and Measures;

[6.] To provide for the Punishment of counterfeiting the Securities and current Coin of the United States;

[7.] To establish Post Offices and post Roads;

[8.] To promote the Progress of Science and useful Arts, by securing for limited Times to Authors and Inventors the exclusive Right to their respective Writings and Discoveries;

[9.] To constitute Tribunals inferior to the supreme Court;

[10.] To define and punish Piracies and Felonies committed on the high Seas, and Offences against the Law of Nations;

[11.] To declare War, grant Letters of Marque and Reprisal, and make Rules concerning Captures on Land and Water;

Section 8. Powers Granted to Congress

Expressed Powers Expressed powers are those powers directly stated in the Constitution. Most of the expressed powers of Congress are listed in Article I, Section 8. These powers are also called enumerated powers because they are numbered 1–18. *Which clause gives Congress the power to declare war?*

Civil War money

Vocabulary

resolution: *legislature's formal expression of opinion*

naturalization: *procedure by which a citizen of a foreign nation becomes a citizen of the United States*

tribunal: *a court*

letter of marque: *authority given to a citizen to outfit an armed ship and use it to attack enemy ships in time of war*

reprisal: *taking by force property or territory belonging to another country or to its citizens*

insurrection: *rebellion*

[12.] To raise and support Armies, but no Appropriation of Money to that Use shall be for a longer Term than two Years;

[13.] To provide and maintain a Navy;

[14.] To make Rules for the Government and Regulation of the land and naval Forces;

[15.] To provide for calling forth the Militia to execute the Laws of the Union, suppress Insurrections and repel Invasions;

[16.] To provide for organizing, arming, and disciplining, the Militia, and for governing such Part of them as may be employed in the Service of the United States, reserving to the States respectively, the Appointment of the Officers, and the Authority of training the Militia according to the discipline prescribed by Congress;

[17.] To exercise exclusive Legislation in all Cases whatsoever, over such District (not exceeding ten Miles square) as may, by Cession of particular States, and the Acceptance of Congress, become the Seat of Government of the United States, and to exercise like Authority over all Places purchased by the Consent of the Legislature of the State in which the Same shall be, for the Erection of Forts, Magazines, Arsenals, dock-Yards, and other needful Buildings;—And

[18.] To make all Laws which shall be necessary and proper for carrying into Execution the foregoing Powers, and all other Powers vested by this Constitution in the Government of the United States, or in any Department or Officer thereof.

Section 9

[1]. The Migration or Importation of such Persons as any of the States now existing shall think proper to admit, shall not be prohibited by the Congress prior to the Year one thousand eight hundred and eight, but a Tax or duty may be imposed on such Importation, not exceeding ten dollars for each Person.

[2.] The Privilege of the Writ of Habeas Corpus shall not be suspended, unless when in Cases of Rebellion or Invasion the public Safety may require it.

[3.] No Bill of Attainder or ex post facto Law shall be passed.

[4.] No Capitation, or other direct, Tax shall be laid, unless in Proportion to the Census or Enumeration herein before directed to be taken.

[5.] No Tax or Duty shall be laid on Articles exported from any State.

[6.] No Preference shall be given by any Regulation of Commerce or Revenue to the Ports of one State over those of another: nor shall Vessels bound to, or from, one State, be obliged to enter, clear, or pay Duties in another.

Seal of the U.S. Navy

Section 8. Powers Granted to Congress

Elastic Clause The final enumerated power is often called the "elastic clause." This clause gives Congress the right to make all laws "necessary and proper" to carry out the powers expressed in the other clauses of Article I. It is called the elastic clause because it lets Congress "stretch" its powers to meet situations the Founders could never have anticipated.

What does the phrase "necessary and proper" in the elastic clause mean? Almost from the beginning, this phrase was a subject of dispute. The issue was whether a strict or a broad interpretation of the Constitution should be applied. The dispute was first addressed in 1819, in the case of *McCulloch* v. *Maryland*, when the Supreme Court ruled in favor of a broad interpretation.

Section 9. Powers Denied to the Federal Government

Habeas Corpus A writ of habeas corpus issued by a judge requires a law official to bring a prisoner to court and show cause for holding the prisoner. A bill of attainder is a bill that punished a person without a jury trial. An "ex post facto" law is one that makes an act a crime after the act has been committed. *What does the Constitution say about bills of attainder?*

[7.] No Money shall be drawn from the Treasury, but in Consequence of Appropriations made by Law; and a regular Statement and Account of the Receipts and Expenditures of all public Money shall be published from time to time.

[8.] No Title of Nobility shall be granted by the United States: And no Person holding any Office of Profit or Trust under them, shall, without the Consent of the Congress, accept of any present, Emolument, Office, or Title, of any kind whatever, from any King, Prince, or foreign State.

Section 10

[1.] No State shall enter into any Treaty, Alliance, or Confederation; grant Letters of Marque and Reprisal; coin Money; emit Bills of Credit; make any Thing but gold and silver Coin a Tender in Payment of Debts; pass any Bill of Attainder, ex post facto Law, or Law impairing the Obligation of Contracts, or grant any Title of Nobility.

[2.] No State shall, without the Consent of the Congress, lay any Imposts or Duties on Imports or Exports, except what may be absolutely necessary for executing it's inspection Laws: and the net Produce of all Duties and Imposts, laid by any State on Imports and Exports, shall be for the Use of the Treasury of the United States; and all such Laws shall be subject to the Revision and Controul of the Congress.

[3.] No State shall, without the Consent of Congress, lay any Duty of Tonnage, keep Troops, or Ships of War in time of Peace, enter into any Agreement or Compact with another State, or with a foreign Power, or engage in War, unless actually invaded, or in such imminent Danger as will not admit of delay.

Section 10. Powers Denied to the States

Limitations on Power Section 10 lists limits on the states. These restrictions were designed, in part, to prevent an overlapping in functions and authority with the federal government.

United States coins

Article II. The Executive Branch

Article II creates an executive branch to carry out laws passed by Congress. Article II lists the powers and duties of the presidency, describes qualifications for office and procedures for electing the president, and provides for a vice president.

Article II

Section 1

[1.] The executive Power shall be vested in a President of the United States of America. He shall hold his Office during the Term of four Years, and, together with the Vice President, chosen for the same Term, be elected, as follows

[2.] Each State shall appoint, in such Manner as the Legislature thereof may direct, a Number of Electors, equal to the whole Number of Senators and Representatives to which the State may be entitled in the Congress: but no Senator or Representative, or Person holding an Office of Trust or Profit under the United States, shall be appointed an Elector.

[3.] The Electors shall meet in their respective States, and vote by Ballot for two Persons, of whom one at least shall not be an Inhabitant of the same State with

Vocabulary

appropriations: *funds set aside for a specific use*
emolument: *payment*
impost: *tax*
duty: *tax*

themselves. And they shall make a List of all the Persons voted for, and of the Number of Votes for each; which List they shall sign and certify, and transmit sealed to the Seat of the Government of the United States, directed to the President of the Senate. The President of the Senate shall, in the Presence of the Senate and House of Representatives, open all the Certificates, and the Votes shall then be counted. The Person having the greatest Number of Votes shall be the President, if such Number be a Majority of the whole Number of Electors appointed; and if there be more than one who have such Majority, and have an equal Number of Votes, then the House of Representatives shall immediately chuse by Ballot one of them for President; and if no person have a Majority, then from the five highest on the List the said House shall in like Manner chuse the President. But in chusing the President, the Votes shall be taken by States, the Representation from each State having one Vote; A quorum for this Purpose shall consist of a Member or Members from two thirds of the States, and a Majority of all the States shall be necessary to a Choice. In every Case, after the Choice of the President, the Person having the greatest Number of Votes of the Electors shall be the Vice President. But if there should remain two or more who have equal Votes, the Senate shall chuse from them by Ballot the Vice President.

[4.] The Congress may determine the Time of chusing the Electors, and the Day on which they shall give their Votes; which Day shall be the same throughout the United States.

[5.] No Person except a natural born Citizen, or a Citizen of the United States, at the time of the Adoption of this Constitution, shall be eligible to the Office of President; neither shall any Person be eligible to that Office who shall not have attained to the Age of thirty five Years, and been fourteen Years a Resident within the United States.

[6.] In Case of the Removal of the President from Office, or of his Death, Resignation, or Inability to discharge the Powers and Duties of the said Office, the Same shall devolve on the Vice President, and the Congress may by Law provide for the Case of Removal, Death, Resignation or Inability, both of the President and Vice President, declaring what Officer shall then act as President, and such Officer shall act accordingly, until the Disability be removed, or a President shall be elected.

[7.] The President shall, at stated Times, receive for his Services, a Compensation, which shall neither be increased nor diminished during the Period for which he shall have been elected, and he shall not receive within that Period any other Emolument from the United States, or any of them.

[8.] Before he enter on the Execution of his Office, he shall take the following Oath or Affirmation:—"I do solemnly swear (or affirm) that I will faithfully execute the Office of President of the United States, and will to the best of my Ability, preserve, protect and defend the Constitution of the United States."

Section 1. President and Vice President

Former Method of Election The Twelfth Amendment, added in 1804, changed the method of electing the president stated in Article II, Section 1, paragraph 3. The Twelfth Amendment requires that the electors cast separate ballots for president and vice president.

George Washington, the first president

Section 1. President and Vice President

Qualifications The president must be a citizen of the United States by birth, at least 35 years of age, and a resident of the United States for 14 years.

Section 1. President and Vice President

Vacancies If the president dies, resigns, is removed from office by impeachment, or is unable to carry out the duties of the office, the vice president assumes the duties of the president. The Twenty-Fifth Amendment sets procedures for presidential succession.

Section 1. President and Vice President

Salary Originally, the president's salary was $25,000 per year. The president's current salary is $400,000 plus a $50,000 nontaxable expense account per year. The president also receives living accommodations in two residences—the White House and Camp David.

Section 2. Powers of the President

Military, Cabinet, Pardons Mention of "the principal officer in each of the executive departments" is the only suggestion of the president's cabinet to be found in the Constitution. The cabinet is an advisory body, and its power depends on the president. Section 2, Clause 1 also makes the president—a civilian—the head of the armed services. This established the principle of civilian control of the military.

Section 2. Powers of the President

Treaties and Appointments An executive order is a command issued by a president to exercise a power which he has been given by the U.S. Constitution or by a federal statute. In times of emergency, presidents sometimes have used the executive order to override the Constitution of the United States and the Congress. During the Civil War, President Lincoln suspended many fundamental rights guaranteed in the Constitution and the Bill of Rights. He closed down newspapers that opposed his policies and imprisoned some who disagreed with him. Lincoln said that these actions were justified to preserve the Union.

Impeachment ticket

Article III. The Judicial Branch

The term *judicial* refers to courts. The Constitution set up only the Supreme Court but provided for the establishment of other federal courts. The judiciary of the United States has two different systems of courts. One system consists of the federal courts, whose powers derive from the Constitution and federal laws. The other includes the courts of each of the 50 states, whose powers derive from state constitutions and laws.

Section 2

[1.] The President shall be Commander in Chief of the Army and Navy of the United States, and of the Militia of the several States, when called into the actual Service of the United States; he may require the Opinion, in writing, of the principal Officer in each of the executive Departments, upon any Subject relating to the Duties of their respective Offices, and he shall have Power to grant Reprieves and Pardons for Offences against the United States, except in Cases of Impeachment.

[2.] He shall have Power, by and with the Advice and Consent of the Senate, to make Treaties, provided two thirds of the Senators present concur; and he shall nominate, and by and with the Advice and Consent of the Senate, shall appoint Ambassadors, other public Ministers and Consuls, Judges of the supreme Court, and all other Officers of the United States, whose Appointments are not herein otherwise provided for, and which shall be established by Law: but the Congress may by Law vest the Appointment of such inferior Officers, as they think proper, in the President alone, in the Courts of Law, or in the Heads of Departments.

[3.] The President shall have Power to fill up all Vacancies that may happen during the Recess of the Senate, by granting Commissions which shall expire at the End of their next Session.

Section 3

He shall from time to time give to the Congress Information of the State of the Union, and recommend to their Consideration such Measures as he shall judge necessary and expedient; he may, on extraordinary Occasions, convene both Houses, or either of them, and in Case of Disagreement between them, with Respect to the Time of Adjournment, he may adjourn them to such Time as he shall think proper; he shall receive Ambassadors and other public Ministers; he shall take Care that the Laws be faithfully executed, and shall Commission all the Officers of the United States.

Section 4

The President, Vice President and all civil Officers of the United States, shall be removed from Office on Impeachment for, and Conviction of, Treason, Bribery, or other high Crimes and Misdemeanors.

Article III

Section 1

The judicial Power of the United States, shall be vested in one supreme Court, and in such inferior Courts as the Congress may from time to time ordain and establish. The Judges, both of the supreme and inferior Courts, shall hold their Offices during good Behaviour, and shall, at stated Times, receive for their Services, a Compensation, which shall not be diminished during their Continuance in Office.

Section 2

[1.] The judicial Power shall extend to all Cases, in Law and Equity, arising under this Constitution, the Laws of the United States, and Treaties made, or which shall be made, under their Authority;—to all Cases affecting Ambassadors, other public Ministers and Consuls;—to all Cases of admiralty and maritime Jurisdiction;—to Controversies to which the United States shall be a Party;—to Controversies between two or more States;—between a State and Citizens of another State;—between Citizens of different States,—between Citizens of the same State claiming Lands under Grants of different States, and between a State, or the Citizens thereof, and foreign States, Citizens or Subjects.

[2.] In all Cases affecting Ambassadors, other public Ministers and Consuls, and those in which a State shall be Party, the supreme Court shall have original Jurisdiction. In all the other Cases before mentioned, the supreme Court shall have appellate Jurisdiction, both as to Law and Fact, with such Exceptions, and under such Regulations as the Congress shall make.

[3.] The Trial of all Crimes, except in Cases of Impeachment, shall be by Jury; and such Trial shall be held in the State where the said Crimes shall have been committed; but when not committed within any State, the Trial shall be at such Place or Places as the Congress may by Law have directed.

Section 3

[1.] Treason against the United States, shall consist only in levying War against them, or in adhering to their Enemies, giving them Aid and Comfort. No Person shall be convicted of Treason unless on the Testimony of two Witnesses to the same overt Act, or on Confession in open Court.

[2.] The Congress shall have Power to declare the Punishment of Treason, but no Attainder of Treason shall work Corruption of Blood, or Forfeiture except during the Life of the Person attainted.

Article IV

Section 1

Full Faith and Credit shall be given in each State to the public Acts, Records, and judicial Proceedings of every other State. And the Congress may by general Laws prescribe the Manner in which such Acts, Records and Proceedings shall be proved, and the Effect thereof.

Section 2. Jurisdiction
Statute Law Federal courts deal mostly with "statute law," or laws passed by Congress, treaties, and cases involving the Constitution itself.

Section 2. Jurisdiction
The Supreme Court A Court with "original jurisdiction" has the authority to be the first court to hear a case. The Supreme Court primarily has "appellate jurisdiction" and mostly hears cases appealed from lower courts.

Article IV. Relations Among the States

Article IV explains the relationship of the states to one another and to the national government. This article requires each state to give citizens of other states the same rights as its own citizens, addresses admitting new states, and guarantees that the national government will protect the states.

Vocabulary

original jurisdiction: *authority to be the first court to hear a case*

appellate jurisdiction: *authority to hear cases that have been appealed from lower courts*

treason: *violation of the allegiance owed by a person to his or her own country, for example, by aiding an enemy*

Section 2

[1.] The Citizens of each State shall be entitled to all Privileges and Immunities of Citizens in the several States.

[2.] A Person charged in any State with Treason, Felony, or other Crime, who shall flee from Justice, and be found in another State, shall on Demand of the executive Authority of the State from which he fled, be delivered up, to be removed to the State having Jurisdiction of the Crime.

[3.] No Person held to Service of Labour in one State, under the Laws thereof, escaping into another, shall, in Consequence of any Law or Regulation therein, be discharged from such Service or Labour, but shall be delivered up on Claim of the Party to whom such Service or Labour may be due.

Section 3. New States and Territories

New States Congress has the power to admit new states. It also determines the basic guidelines for applying for statehood. Two states, Maine and West Virginia, were created within the boundaries of another state. In the case of West Virginia, President Lincoln recognized the West Virginia government as the legal government of Virginia during the Civil War. This allowed West Virginia to secede from Virginia without obtaining approval from the Virginia legislature.

Section 3

[1.] New States may be admitted by the Congress into this Union; but no new State shall be formed or erected within the Jurisdiction of any other State; nor any State be formed by the Junction of two or more States, or Parts of States, without the Consent of the Legislatures of the States concerned as well as of the Congress.

[2.] The Congress shall have Power to dispose of and make all needful Rules and Regulations respecting the Territory or other Property belonging to the United States; and nothing in this Constitution shall be so construed as to Prejudice any Claims of the United States, or of any particular State.

Section 4. Federal Protection for States

Republic Government can be classified in many different ways. The ancient Greek philosopher Aristotle classified government based on the question: Who governs? According to Aristotle, all governments belong to one of three major groups: (1) autocracy—rule by one person; (2) oligarchy—rule by a few persons; or (3) democracy—rule by many persons. A republic is a form of democracy in which the people elect representatives to make laws and conduct government.

Section 4

The United States shall guarantee to every State in this Union a Republican Form of Government, and shall protect each of them against Invasion; and on Application of the Legislature, or of the Executive (when the Legislature cannot be convened) against domestic Violence.

Article V. The Amendment Process

Article V spells out the ways that the Constitution can be amended, or changed. All of the 27 amendments were proposed by a two-thirds vote of both houses of Congress. Only the Twenty-first Amendment was ratified by constitutional conventions of the states. All other amendments have been ratified by state legislatures. *What is an amendment?*

Article V

The Congress, whenever two thirds of both Houses shall deem it necessary, shall propose Amendments to this Constitution, or, on the Application of the Legislatures of two thirds of the several States, shall call a Convention for proposing Amendments, which, in either Case, shall be valid to all Intents and Purposes, as Part of this Constitution, when ratified by the Legislatures of three fourths of the several States, or by Conventions in three fourths thereof, as the one or the other Mode of Ratification may be proposed by the Congress; Provided that no Amendment which may be made prior to the Year One thousand eight hundred and eight shall in any Manner affect the first and fourth Clauses in the Ninth Section of the first Article; and that no State, without its Consent, shall be deprived of its equal Suffrage in the Senate.

Vocabulary

extradition: *surrender of a criminal to another authority*

amendment: *a change to the Constitution*

ratification: *process by which an amendment is approved*

Article VI

[1.] All Debts contracted and Engagements entered into, before the Adoption of this Constitution, shall be as valid against the United States under this Constitution, as under the Confederation.

[2.] This Constitution, and the Laws of the United States which shall be made in Pursuance thereof; and all Treaties made, or which shall be made, under the Authority of the United States, shall be the supreme Law of the Land; and the Judges in every State shall be bound thereby, any Thing in the Constitution or Laws of any State to the Contrary notwithstanding.

[3.] The Senators and Representatives before mentioned, and the Members of the several State Legislatures, and all executive and judicial Officers, both of the United States and of the several States, shall be bound by Oath or Affirmation, to support this Constitution; but no religious Test shall ever be required as a Qualification to any Office or public Trust under the United States.

Article VII

The Ratification of the Conventions of nine States, shall be sufficient for the Establishment of this Constitution between the States so ratifying the Same.

Done in Convention by the Unanimous Consent of the States present the Seventeenth Day of September in the Year of our Lord one thousand seven hundred and Eighty seven and of the Independence of the United States of America the Twelfth. In witness whereof We have hereunto subscribed our Names,

Article VI. National Supremacy

Article VI contains the "supremacy clause." This clause establishes that the Constitution, laws passed by Congress, and treaties of the United States "shall be the supreme Law of the Land." The "supremacy clause" recognized the Constitution and federal laws as supreme when in conflict with those of the states.

Article VII. Ratification

Article VII addresses ratification and declares that the Constitution would take effect after it was ratified by nine states.

Signers

George Washington, **President and Deputy from Virginia**

New Hampshire
John Langdon
Nicholas Gilman

Massachusetts
Nathaniel Gorham
Rufus King

Connecticut
William Samuel Johnson
Roger Sherman

New York
Alexander Hamilton

New Jersey
William Livingston
David Brearley
William Paterson
Jonathan Dayton

Pennsylvania
Benjamin Franklin
Thomas Mifflin
Robert Morris
George Clymer
Thomas FitzSimons
Jared Ingersoll
James Wilson
Gouverneur Morris

Delaware
George Read
Gunning Bedford, Jr.
John Dickinson
Richard Bassett
Jacob Broom

Maryland
James McHenry
Daniel of St. Thomas Jenifer
Daniel Carroll

Virginia
John Blair
James Madison, Jr.

North Carolina
William Blount
Richard Dobbs Spaight
Hugh Williamson

South Carolina
John Rutledge
Charles Cotesworth Pinckney
Charles Pinckney
Pierce Butler

Georgia
William Few
Abraham Baldwin

Attest: William Jackson, **Secretary**

Bill of Rights

The first 10 amendments are known as the Bill of Rights (1791). These amendments limit the powers of government. The First Amendment protects the civil liberties of individuals in the United States. The amendment freedoms are not absolute, however. They are limited by the rights of other individuals. *What freedoms does the First Amendment protect?*

Amendment 2

Right to Bear Arms This amendment is often debated. Originally, it was intended to prevent the national government from repeating the actions of the British, who tried to take weapons away from the colonial militia, or armed forces of citizens. This amendment seems to support the right of citizens to own firearms, but the Supreme Court has ruled that it does not prevent Congress from regulating the interstate sale of weapons. *Why is the Second Amendment's meaning debated?*

Amendment 5

Rights of Accused Persons This amendment contains important protections for people accused of crimes. One of the protections is that government may not deprive any person of life, liberty, or property without due process of law. This means that the government must follow proper constitutional procedures in trials and in other actions it takes against individuals. *According to Amendment V, what is the function of a grand jury?*

Vocabulary

quarter: *to provide living accommodations*
probable cause: *police must have a reasonable basis to believe a person is linked to a crime*
warrant: *document that gives police particular rights or powers*
common law: *law established by previous court decisions*
bail: *money that an accused person provides to the court as a guarantee that he or she will be present for a trial*

Amendment I

Congress shall make no law respecting an establishment of religion, or prohibiting the free exercise thereof; or abridging the freedom of speech, or of the press; or the right of the people peaceably to assemble, and to petition the Government for a redress of grievances.

Amendment II

A well regulated Militia, being necessary to the security of a free State, the right of the people to keep and bear Arms, shall not be infringed.

Amendment III

No Soldier shall, in time of peace be quartered in any house, without the consent of the Owner, nor in time of war, but in a manner to be prescribed by law.

Amendment IV

The right of the people to be secure in their persons, houses, papers, and effects, against unreasonable searches and seizures, shall not be violated, and no Warrants shall issue, but upon probable cause, supported by Oath or affirmation, and particularly describing the place to be searched, and the persons or things to be seized.

Amendment V

No person shall be held to answer for a capital, or otherwise infamous crime, unless on a presentment or indictment of a Grand Jury, except in cases arising in the land or naval forces, or in the Militia, when in actual service in time of War or public danger; nor shall any person be subject for the same offence to be twice put in jeopardy of life or limb; nor shall be compelled in any criminal case to be a witness against himself, nor be deprived of life, liberty, or property, without due process of law; nor shall private property be taken for public use without just compensation.

Amendment VI

In all criminal prosecutions, the accused shall enjoy the right to a speedy and public trial, by an impartial jury of the State and district wherein the crime shall have been committed, which district shall have been previously ascertained by law, and to be informed of the nature and cause of the accusation; to be confronted with the witnesses against him; to have compulsory process for obtaining Witnesses in his favor, and to have the assistance of counsel for his defence.

Amendment 6

Right to a Speedy, Fair Trial A basic protection is the right to a speedy, public trial. The jury must hear witnesses and evidence on both sides before deciding the guilt or innocence of a person charged with a crime. This amendment also provides that legal counsel must be provided to a defendant. In 1963, the Supreme Court ruled, in *Gideon* v. *Wainwright*, that if a defendant cannot afford a lawyer, the government must provide one to defend him or her. *Why is the right to a "speedy" trial important?*

Amendment VII

In Suits at common law, where the value in controversy shall exceed twenty dollars, the right of trial by jury shall be preserved, and no fact tried by a jury, shall be otherwise reexamined in any Court of the United States, than according to the rules of common law.

Amendment VIII

Excessive bail shall not be required, nor excessive fines imposed, nor cruel and unusual punishments inflicted.

Amendment IX

The enumeration in the Constitution, of certain rights, shall not be construed to deny or disparage others retained by the people.

Amendment 9

Powers Reserved to the People This amendment prevents government from claiming that the only rights people have are those listed in the Bill of Rights.

Amendment X

The powers not delegated to the United States by the Constitution, nor prohibited by it to the States, are reserved to the States respectively, or to the people.

Amendment 10

Powers Reserved to the States The final amendment of the Bill of Rights protects the states and the people from an all-powerful federal government. It establishes that powers not given to the national government—or denied to the states—by the Constitution belong to the states or to the people.

Amendment XI

The Judicial power of the United States shall not be construed to extend to any suit in law or equity, commenced or prosecuted against one of the United States by Citizens of another State, or by Citizens or Subjects of any Foreign State.

Amendment 11

Suits Against States The Eleventh Amendment (1795) limits the jurisdiction of the federal courts. The Supreme Court had ruled that a federal court could try a lawsuit brought by citizens of South Carolina against the state of Georgia. This case, *Chisholm* v. *Georgia*, decided in 1793, raised a storm of protest, leading to passage of the Eleventh Amendment.

Amendment 12
Election of President and Vice President The Twelfth Amendment (1804) corrects a problem that had arisen in the method of electing the president and vice president. This amendment provides for the Electoral College to use separate ballots in voting for president and vice president. *If no candidate receives a majority of the electoral votes, who elects the president?*

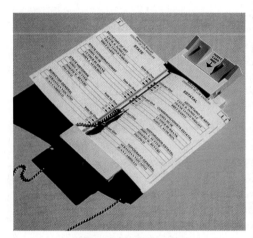

Ballot and ballot marker

Amendment 13
Abolition of Slavery Amendments Thirteen (1865), Fourteen (1868), and Fifteen (1870) often are called the Civil War amendments because they grew out of that great conflict. The Thirteenth Amendment outlaws slavery.

Vocabulary

majority: *more than half*
devolve: *to pass on*
abridge: *to reduce*
insurrection: *rebellion against the government*
emancipation: *freedom from slavery*

Amendment XII

The electors shall meet in their respective states and vote by ballot for President and Vice-President, one of whom, at least, shall not be an inhabitant of the same state with themselves; they shall name in their ballots the person voted for as President, and in distinct ballots the person voted for as Vice-President, and they shall make distinct lists of all persons voted for as President, and of all persons voted for as Vice-President, and of the number of votes for each, which lists they shall sign and certify, and transmit sealed to the seat of the government of the United States, directed to the President of the Senate;—The President of the Senate shall, in the presence of the Senate and House of Representatives, open all the certificates and the votes shall then be counted;—The person having the greatest number of votes for President, shall be the President, if such number be a majority of the whole number of Electors appointed; and if no person have such majority, then from the persons having the highest numbers not exceeding three on the list of those voted for as President, the House of Representatives shall choose immediately, by ballot, the President. But in choosing the President, the votes shall be taken by states, the representation from each state having one vote; a quorum for this purpose shall consist of a member or members from two-thirds of the states, and a majority of all the states shall be necessary to a choice. And if the House of Representatives shall not choose a President whenever the right of choice shall devolve upon them, before the fourth day of March next following, then the Vice-President shall act as President, as in the case of the death or other constitutional disability of the President. The person having the greatest number of votes as Vice-President, shall be the Vice-President, if such number be a majority of the whole number of Electors appointed, and if no person have a majority, then from the two highest numbers on the list, the Senate shall choose the Vice-President; a quorum for the purpose shall consist of two-thirds of the whole number of Senators, and a majority of the whole number shall be necessary to a choice. But no person constitutionally ineligible to the office of President shall be eligible to that of Vice-President of the United States.

Amendment XIII

Section 1

Neither slavery nor involuntary servitude, except as a punishment for crime whereof the party shall have been duly convicted, shall exist within the United States, or any place subject to their jurisdiction.

Section 2

Congress shall have power to enforce this article by appropriate legislation.

Amendment XIV

Section 1

All persons born or naturalized in the United States, and subject to the jurisdiction thereof, are citizens of the United States and of the State wherein they reside. No State shall make or enforce any law which shall abridge the privileges or immunities of citizens of the United States; nor shall any State deprive any person of life, liberty, or property, without due process of law; nor deny to any person within its jurisdiction the equal protection of the laws.

Section 2

Representatives shall be apportioned among the several States according to their respective numbers, counting the whole number of persons in each State, excluding Indians not taxed. But when the right to vote at any election for the choice of electors for President and Vice President of the United States, Representatives in Congress, the Executive and Judicial officers of a State, or the members of the Legislature thereof, is denied to any of the male inhabitants of such State, being twenty-one years of age, and citizens of the United States, or in any way abridged, except for participation in rebellion, or other crime, the basis of representation therein shall be reduced in the proportion which the number of such male citizens shall bear to the whole number of male citizens twenty-one years of age in such State.

Section 3

No person shall be a Senator or Representative in Congress, or elector of President and Vice President, or hold any office, civil or military, under the United States, or under any State, who, having previously taken an oath, as a member of Congress, or as an officer of the United States, or as a member of any State legislature, or as an executive or judicial officer of any State, to support the Constitution of the United States, shall have engaged in insurrection or rebellion against the same, or given aid or comfort to the enemies thereof. But Congress may by a vote of two-thirds of each House, remove such disability.

Section 4

The validity of the public debt of the United States, authorized by law, including debts incurred for payment of pensions and bounties for service in suppressing insurrection or rebellion, shall not be questioned. But neither the United States nor any State shall assume or pay any debt or obligation incurred in aid of insurrection or rebellion against the United States, or any claim for the loss or emancipation of any slave; but all such debts, obligations and claims shall be held illegal and void.

Amendment 14

Rights of Citizens The Fourteenth Amendment (1868) originally was intended to protect the legal rights of the freed slaves. Today it protects the rights of citizenship in general by prohibiting a state from depriving any person of life, liberty, or property without "due process of law." In addition, it states that all citizens have the right to equal protection of the law in all states.

Amendment 14. Section 2

Representation in Congress This section reduced the number of members a state had in the House of Representatives if it denied its citizens the right to vote. Later civil rights laws and the Twenty-Fourth Amendment guaranteed the vote to African Americans.

Amendment 14. Section 3

Penalty for Engaging in Insurrection The leaders of the Confederacy were barred from state or federal offices unless Congress agreed to remove this ban. By the end of Reconstruction all but a few Confederate leaders were allowed to return to public life.

Amendment 14. Section 4

Public Debt The public debt acquired by the federal government during the Civil War was valid and could not be questioned by the South. However, the debts of the Confederacy were declared to be illegal. *Could former slaveholders collect payment for the loss of their slaves?*

Amendment 15

Right to Vote The Fifteenth Amendment (1870) prohibits the government from denying a person's right to vote on the basis of race. Despite the law, many states denied African Americans the right to vote by such means as poll taxes, literacy tests, and white primaries. During the 1950s and 1960s, Congress passed successively stronger laws to end racial discrimination in voting rights.

Internal Revenue Service

Amendment 17

Direct Election of Senators The Seventeenth Amendment (1913) states that the people, instead of state legislatures, elect United States senators. *How many years are in a Senate term?*

Vocabulary

apportionment: *distribution of seats in House based on population*
vacancy: *an office or position that is unfilled or unoccupied*

Section 5

The Congress shall have power to enforce, by appropriate legislation, the provisions of this article.

Amendment XV

Section 1

The right of citizens of the United States to vote shall not be denied or abridged by the United States or by any State on account of race, color, or previous condition of servitude.

Section 2

The Congress shall have power to enforce this article by appropriate legislation.

Amendment XVI

The Congress shall have power to lay and collect taxes on incomes, from whatever source derived, without apportionment among the several States and without regard to any census or enumeration.

Amendment XVII

Section 1

The Senate of the United States shall be composed of two Senators from each State, elected by the people thereof, for six years; and each Senator shall have one vote. The electors in each State shall have the qualifications requisite for electors of the most numerous branch of the State legislatures.

Section 2

When vacancies happen in the representation of any State in the Senate, the executive authority of such State shall issue writs of election to fill such vacancies: *Provided,* That the legislature of any State may empower the executive thereof to make temporary appointments until the people fill the vacancies by election as the legislature may direct.

Section 3

This amendment shall not be so construed as to affect the election or term of any Senator chosen before it becomes valid as part of the Constitution.

Amendment XVIII

Section 1

After one year from ratification of this article, the manufacture, sale, or transportation of intoxicating liquors within, the importation thereof into, or the exportation thereof from the United States and all territory subject to the jurisdiction thereof for beverage purposes is hereby prohibited.

Section 2

The Congress and the several States shall have concurrent power to enforce this article by appropriate legislation.

Section 3

This article shall be inoperative unless it shall have been ratified as an amendment to the Constitution by the legislatures of the several States, as provided in the Constitution, within seven years from the date of the submission hereof to the States by the Congress.

Amendment XIX

Section 1

The right of citizens of the United States to vote shall not be denied or abridged by the United States or by any State on account of sex.

Section 2

Congress shall have power by appropriate legislation to enforce the provisions of this article.

Amendment XX

Section 1

The terms of the President and Vice President shall end at noon on the 20th day of January, and the terms of the Senators and Representatives at noon on the 3d day of January, of the years in which such terms would have ended if this article had not been ratified; and the terms of their successors shall then begin.

Section 2

The Congress shall assemble at least once in every year, and such meeting shall begin at noon on the 3d day of January, unless they shall by law appoint a different day.

Amendment 18

Prohibition of Alcoholic Beverages The Eighteenth Amendment (1919) prohibited the production, sale, or transportation of alcoholic beverages in the United States. Prohibition proved to be difficult to enforce. This amendment was later repealed by the Twenty-first Amendment.

Amendment 19

Woman Suffrage The Nineteenth Amendment (1920) guaranteed women the right to vote. By then women had already won the right to vote in many state elections, but the amendment put their right to vote in all state and national elections on a constitutional basis.

Amendment 20

"Lame-Duck" Amendment The Twentieth Amendment (1933) sets new dates for Congress to begin its term and for the inauguration of the president and vice president. Under the original Constitution, elected officials who retired or who had been defeated remained in office for several months. For the outgoing president, this period ran from November until March. Such outgoing officials had little influence and accomplished little, and they were called lame ducks because they were so inactive. *What date was fixed as Inauguration Day?*

> ### Amendment 20. Section 3
> **Succession of President and Vice President** This section provides that if the president-elect dies before taking office, the vice president-elect becomes president.

John Tyler was the first vice president to become president when a chief executive died.

> ### Amendment 21
> **Repeal of Prohibition Amendment** The Twenty-first Amendment (1933) repeals the Eighteenth Amendment. It is the only amendment ever passed to overturn an earlier amendment. It is also the only amendment ratified by special state conventions instead of state legislatures.

Vocabulary

president-elect: *individual who is elected president but has not yet begun serving his or her term*
District of Columbia: *site of nation's capital, occupying an area between Maryland and Virginia*

Section 3
If, at the time fixed for the beginning of the term of the President, the President elect shall have died, the Vice President elect shall become President. If a President shall not have been chosen before the time fixed for the beginning of his term, or if the President elect shall have failed to qualify, then the Vice President elect shall act as President until a President shall have qualified; and the Congress may by law provide for the case wherein neither a President elect nor a Vice President elect shall have qualified, declaring who shall then act as President, or the manner in which one who is to act shall be selected, and such person shall act accordingly until a President or Vice President shall have qualified.

Section 4
The Congress may by law provide for the case of the death of any of the persons from whom the House of Representatives may choose a President whenever the right of choice shall have devolved upon them, and for the case of the death of any of the persons from whom the Senate may choose a Vice President whenever the right of choice shall have devolved upon them.

Section 5
Sections 1 and 2 shall take effect on the 15th day of October following the ratification of this article.

Section 6
This article shall be inoperative unless it shall have been ratified as an amendment to the Constitution by the legislatures of three-fourths of the several States within seven years from the date of its submission.

Amendment XXI

Section 1
The eighteenth article of amendment to the Constitution of the United States is hereby repealed.

Section 2
The transportation or importation into any State, Territory, or possession of the United States for delivery or use therein of intoxicating liquors, in violation of the laws thereof, is hereby prohibited.

Section 3
This article shall be inoperative unless it shall have been ratified as an amendment to the Constitution by conventions in the several States, as provided in the Constitution, within seven years from the date of the submission hereof to the States by the Congress.

Amendment XXII

Section 1

No person shall be elected to the office of the President more than twice, and no person who had held the office of President, or acted as President, for more than two years of a term to which some other person was elected President shall be elected to the office of the President more than once. But this Article shall not apply to any person holding the office of President when this Article was proposed by the Congress, and shall not prevent any person who may be holding the office of President, or acting as President, during the term within which this Article becomes operative from holding the office of President or acting as President during the remainder of such term.

Section 2

This article shall be inoperative unless it shall have been ratified as an amendment to the Constitution by the legislatures of three-fourths of the several States within seven years from the date of its submission to the States by the Congress.

Amendment XXIII

Section 1

The District constituting the seat of Government of the United States shall appoint in such manner as the Congress may direct:

A number of electors of President and Vice President equal to the whole number of Senators and Representatives in Congress to which the District would be entitled if it were a State, but in no event more than the least populous State; they shall be in addition to those appointed by the States, but they shall be considered, for the purposes of the election of President and Vice President, to be electors appointed by a State; and they shall meet in the District and perform such duties as provided by the twelfth article of amendment.

Section 2

The Congress shall have power to enforce this article by appropriate legislation.

Amendment 22

Limit on Presidential Terms The Twenty-second Amendment (1951) limits presidents to a maximum of two elected terms. It was passed largely as a reaction to Franklin D. Roosevelt's election to four terms between 1933 and 1945.

Presidential campaign buttons

Amendment 23

Presidential Electors for the District of Columbia The Twenty-third Amendment (1961) allows citizens living in Washington, D.C., to vote for president and vice president, a right previously denied residents of the nation's capital. The District of Columbia now has three presidential electors, the number to which it would be entitled if it were a state.

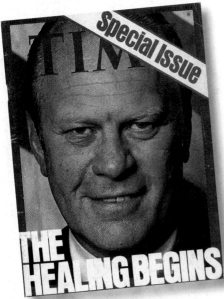

President Gerald Ford

Amendment XXIV

Section 1

The right of citizens of the United States to vote in any primary or other election for President or Vice President, for electors for President or Vice President, or for Senator or Representative in Congress, shall not be denied or abridged by the United States or any State by reason of failure to pay any poll tax or other tax.

Section 2

The Congress shall have power to enforce this article by appropriate legislation.

Amendment XXV

Section 1

In case of the removal of the President from office or his death or resignation, the Vice President shall become President.

Section 2

Whenever there is a vacancy in the office of the Vice President, the President shall nominate a Vice President who shall take the office upon confirmation by a majority vote of both Houses of Congress.

Section 3

Whenever the President transmits to the President pro tempore of the Senate and the Speaker of the House of Representatives his written declaration that he is unable to discharge the powers and duties of his office, and until he transmits to them a written declaration to the contrary, such powers and duties shall be discharged by the Vice President as Acting President.

Section 4

Whenever the Vice President and a majority of either the principal officers of the executive departments or of such other body as Congress may by law provide, transmit to the President pro tempore of the Senate and the Speaker of the House of Representatives their written declaration that the President is unable to discharge the powers and duties of his office, the Vice President shall immediately assume the power and duties of the office of Acting President.

Thereafter, when the President transmits to the President pro tempore of the Senate and the Speaker of the House of Representatives his written declaration that no inability exists, he shall resume the powers and duties of his office unless the Vice President and a majority of either the principal officers of the executive department or of such other body as Congress may by law provide, transmit within four days to the President pro tempore of the Senate and the Speaker of the House of Representatives their written declaration that the President is unable to discharge the powers and duties of his office. Thereupon Congress shall decide the issue, assembling within forty-eight hours for that purpose if not in session. If the Congress, within twenty-one days after receipt of the latter written declaration, or, if Congress is not in session, within twenty-one days after Congress is required to assemble, determines by two-thirds vote of both Houses that the President is unable to discharge the powers and duties of his office, the Vice President shall continue to discharge the same as Acting President; otherwise, the President shall resume the power and duties of his office.

Amendment XXVI

Section 1
The right of citizens of the United States, who are eighteen years of age or older, to vote shall not be denied or abridged by the United States or by any State on account of age.

Section 2
The Congress shall have power to enforce this article by appropriate legislation.

Amendment XXVII
No law, varying the compensation for the services of Senators and Representatives, shall take effect, until an election of representatives shall have intervened.

Amendment 26
Eighteen-Year-Old Vote The Twenty-sixth Amendment (1971) guarantees the right to vote to all citizens 18 years of age and older.

Amendment 27
Restraint on Congressional Salaries The Twenty-seventh Amendment (1992) makes congressional pay raises effective during the term following their passage. James Madison offered the amendment in 1789, but it was never adopted. In 1982 Gregory Watson, then a student at the University of Texas, discovered the forgotten amendment while doing research for a school paper. Watson made the amendment's passage his crusade.

Joint meeting of Congress

UNIT
4
The
New
Republic

1789–1825

Pitcher honoring
Washington's
inauguration, 1789

Why It Matters

*As you study Unit 4, you will learn
how the young United States chose its
leaders and established its policies.
The following resources offer more
information about this period in
American history.*

Primary Sources Library

*See pages 964–965 for primary source
readings to accompany Unit 4.*

💿 *Use the **American History
Primary Source Document Library
CD-ROM** to find additional primary
sources about the new republic.*

*Daniel Boone Escorting
Settlers Through the
Cumberland Gap by
George Caleb Bingham*

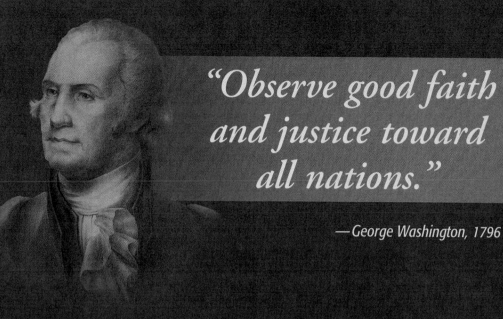

"*Observe good faith and justice toward all nations.*"

—*George Washington, 1796*

A New Nation

1789–1800

Why It Matters

George Washington's administration faced the huge task of making the new government work. The Constitution had created the office of the presidency, but Washington established many procedures and customs.

The Impact Today

President Washington set many examples that presidents still follow. These include creating a cabinet, directing foreign affairs, and serving as chief legislator.

The American Journey *Video* *The chapter 8 video, "George Washington," examines the issues that arose upon the establishment of the office of president.*

1789
- Washington becomes first president
- Judiciary Act passed

1791
- Bill of Rights added to Constitution

1794
- Whiskey Rebellion

 United States
Washington 1789–1797

PRESIDENTS

1790

1792

1794

 World

1792
- France declares war on Austria

1793
- Louvre opens as public museum in Paris

1794
- Slavery abolished in all French colonies

FOLDABLES
Study Organizer

Summarizing Study Foldable Make this foldable and use it as a journal to help you record the major events that occurred as the new nation of the United States formed.

Step 1 Fold a sheet of paper from top to bottom.

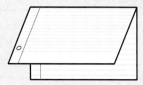

Step 2 Then fold it in half from side to side.

Step 3 Label the foldable as shown.

Journal of American Firsts

Reading and Writing As you read the chapter, find the "firsts" experienced by the new nation, and record them in your foldable journal. For example, list the precedents set by President Washington and identify the first political parties.

Boston Harbor as Seen from Constitution Wharf by Robert Salmon
Salmon recorded the emerging cities and scenic harbors of the young nation.

1795
- Nation's first chief justice, John Jay, retires from court

Adams
1797–1801

1798
- Alien and Sedition Acts passed
- XYZ affair

1800
- Convention of 1800 resolves U.S./French conflicts

1796

1798

1796
- Jenner develops smallpox vaccine

1799
- Rosetta stone discovered

HISTORY
Online

Chapter Overview
Visit <u>taj.glencoe.com</u> and click on **Chapter 8—Chapter Overviews** to preview chapter information.

The First President

Main Idea

President Washington and the first Congress tackled the work of establishing a new government.

Key Terms

precedent, cabinet, national debt, bond, speculator, unconstitutional, tariff

Reading Strategy

Classifying Information As you read the section, re-create the diagram below and list the actions taken by Congress and Washington's first administration.

Actions	
Washington	Congress

Read to Learn

• what actions were taken to launch the new government.
• how Hamilton proposed to strengthen the economy.

Section Theme

Government and Democracy President Washington and Congress took actions that shaped the future of government in our nation.

Preview of Events

♦1789	♦1790	♦1791	♦1792

April 6, 1789
George Washington is elected president

April 30, 1789
Washington takes the oath of office

September 1789
Judiciary Act sets up federal court system

December 1791
Bill of Rights added to the Constitution

AN American Story

Celebrations erupted in the streets of Philadelphia, New York, Boston, and Charleston in 1789. News of the Constitution's ratification was greeted with relief and enthusiasm. All that was needed now was a leader to guide the new nation.

On April 6 the new Senate counted the presidential ballots. To no one's surprise, the votes were unanimous. Senator John Langdon wrote to General George Washington: "Sir, I have the honor to transmit to Your Excellency the information of your unanimous election to the office of President of the United States of America." Washington was ready to begin the difficult task of leading the country.

February 22nd, 1732
December 14th, 1799

Washington banner

President Washington

The 57-year-old president-elect made his way slowly toward New York City, then the nation's capital. After the Constitutional Convention, George Washington had looked forward to a quiet retirement. Instead his fellow citizens elected him to the highest office in the land. On April 30, 1789, Washington took the oath of office as the first president of the United States under the federal Constitution (there had been several presidents under the Articles of Confederation). John Adams became vice president. 📖 *(See page 964 of the Primary Sources Library for an excerpt of an account of Washington's First Inaugural.)*

Perhaps no office in the new government created more suspicion among the people than the office of president. Many Americans feared that a president would try to become king, but they trusted Washington. They believed that his leadership had brought them victory in the Revolutionary War.

Washington was aware of the difficulties he faced. He knew that the precedents, or traditions, he established as the nation's first president would shape the future of the United States. "No slip will pass unnoticed," he remarked. One precedent he established concerned the way people should address him. Vice President Adams supported "His Highness the President of the United States," but ultimately it was decided that "Mr. President" would be more appropriate.

Washington and the new Congress also had many decisions to make about the structure of government. For example, the Constitution gave Congress the power to establish executive departments, but it did not state whether the department heads would report to the president or to Congress.

The First Congress

During the summer of 1789, Congress set up three departments in the executive branch of government. The State Department would handle relations with other nations, the Treasury Department would deal with financial matters, and the War Department would provide for the nation's defense. Congress also created the office of attorney general to handle the government's legal affairs and the office of postmaster general to direct the postal service.

To head the departments, Washington chose prominent political figures of the day—**Thomas Jefferson** as secretary of state, **Alexander Hamilton** as secretary of the treasury, and **Henry Knox** as secretary of war. He appointed **Edmund Randolph** as attorney general. Washington met regularly with the three department heads and the attorney general, who together became known as the cabinet.

Congress created the executive departments; opinion was divided, however, on how much power the president should have over them. For example, should the president be able to replace an official that he had appointed and the Senate had confirmed? Senators were evenly divided in voting on the issue.

Vice President Adams broke the tie by voting to allow the president the authority to dismiss cabinet officers without the Senate's approval. This decision strengthened the president's position. It also helped create a greater separation between the legislative and executive branches of government by establishing the president's authority over the executive branch.

Judiciary Act

The first Congress also had to decide how to set up the nation's court system. The Constitution briefly mentioned a supreme court but had left further details about the courts to Congress.

Disagreements arose between those favoring a uniform, national legal system and those favoring state courts. The two groups reached a compromise in the **Judiciary Act of 1789.** With this act, Congress established a federal court system with 13 district courts and three circuit courts to serve the nation. State laws would remain, but the federal courts would have the power to reverse state decisions.

The Supreme Court would be the final authority on many issues. Washington nominated **John Jay** to lead the Supreme Court as chief justice, and the Senate approved Jay's nomination. With the Judiciary Act, Congress had taken the first steps toward creating a strong and independent national judiciary.

Betsy Ross Flag Legend holds that Philadelphia seamstress Betsy Ross stitched the first Stars and Stripes in 1776. Historical record does not support this account, however. The popular "Betsy Ross flag," with 13 stars arranged in a circle, did not appear until the early 1790s.

People In History

Benjamin Banneker 1731–1806

Benjamin Banneker

Black Heritage USA 15c

Benjamin Banneker was born into a free African American family in Maryland. He attended a private Quaker school, but was largely self-educated. When his father died, Banneker sold the family farm and devoted the rest of his life to mathematics and natural sciences.

Banneker's skill in mathematics prompted Thomas Jefferson to give him a job surveying the land for the new national capital at Washington, D.C. When French architect Pierre L'Enfant was removed from the project, he took his detailed maps with him. Banneker amazed everyone

by redrawing the missing maps from memory! From 1792 to 1802 he made astronomical and tide calculations for a yearly almanac. Banneker became a symbol for racial justice in a land not yet ready to grant him the rights of citizenship, granted to others in the Bill of Rights.

The Bill of Rights

Americans had long feared strong central governments. They had fought a revolution to throw off one and did not want to replace it with another. Many people insisted the Constitution needed to include guarantees of personal liberties. Some states had supported the Constitution on the condition that a bill of rights be added.

To fulfill the promises made during the fight for ratification of the Constitution, James Madison introduced a set of amendments during the first session of Congress. Congress passed 12 amendments, and the states ratified 10 of them. In December 1791, these 10 amendments were added to the Constitution and became known as the **Bill of Rights.**

The Bill of Rights limits the powers of government. Its purpose is to protect the rights of individual liberty, such as freedom of speech, and rights of persons accused of crimes, including trial by jury. The Tenth Amendment protects the rights of states and individuals by saying that powers not specifically given to the federal government "are reserved to the States

respectively, or to the people." With the Tenth Amendment, Madison hoped to use the states as an important line of defense against a too-powerful national government. 📖 *(See pages 244–245 for the entire text of the Bill of Rights.)*

(See pages 244–245 for the entire text of the Bill of Rights.)

✔ **Reading Check** **Describing** Why was the Bill of Rights created?

💲Economics

Financial Problems

Washington himself rarely proposed laws, and he almost always approved the bills that were passed by Congress. The first president concentrated on foreign affairs and military matters and left the government's economic policies to his dynamic secretary of the treasury, Alexander Hamilton.

The new nation faced serious financial problems. The national debt—the amount the nation's government owed—was growing. Hamilton tried to find a way to improve the government's financial reputation and to strengthen the nation at the same time.

Hamilton's Plan

In 1790 Hamilton proposed that the new government pay off the millions of dollars in debts owed by the Confederation government to other countries and to individual American citizens. The states had fought for the nation's independence, Hamilton argued, so the national government should pay for the cost of their help. Hamilton also believed that federal payment of state debts would give the states a strong interest in the success of the national government.

Opposition to the Plan

Congress agreed to pay money owed to other nations, but Hamilton's plan to pay off the debt to American citizens unleashed a storm of protest. When the government had borrowed money during the American Revolution, it had issued bonds—paper notes promising to repay the money in a certain length of time. While waiting for the payment, many of the original bond owners—shopkeepers, farmers, and soldiers—had sold the bonds for less than their value. They were purchased by speculators, people who risk money in order to make a larger profit. Hamilton proposed that these bonds be paid off at their original value. Opponents believed that Hamilton's plan would make speculators rich, and

❝established at the expense of national justice, gratitude, and humanity.❞

The original bond owners felt betrayed by the government because they had lost money on their bonds while new bond owners profited.

Even stronger opposition came from the Southern states, which had accumulated much less debt than the Northern states. Southern states complained that they would have to pay more than their share under Hamilton's plan.

Compromise Results in a Capital

To win support for his plan, Hamilton compromised. He agreed to a proposal from Southern leaders to locate the new nation's capital in the South after moving to Philadelphia while workmen prepared the new city for the federal government. A special district would be laid out between Virginia and Maryland along the banks of the Potomac River. This district became **Washington, D.C.** In return, Southerners supported his plan to pay off the state debts.

Reading Check **Explaining** Why did Hamilton's plan to pay off the debt to American citizens cause such a storm of protest?

America's *Architecture*

The Capitol is the seat of the United States Congress in Washington, D.C. Built on a hill popularly called Capitol Hill, the Capitol contains floor space equivalent to over 16 acres. The dome of the United States Capitol, finished in 1863, is one of the most famous landmarks in the United States. Other important parts of the Capitol include the Rotunda directly under the dome, the Senate Chamber in the north wing, the House Chamber in the south wing, and the National Statuary Hall.

Building the Economy

Hamilton made other proposals for building a strong national economy. He asked Congress to create a national bank, the Bank of the United States. Both private investors and the national government would own the Bank's stock.

The Fight Over the Bank

In 1792 there were only eight other banks in the nation. All eight had been established by state governments. Madison and Jefferson opposed the idea of a national bank. They believed it would benefit the wealthy. They also charged that the Bank was unconstitutional—that it was inconsistent with the Constitution. Hamilton argued that although the Constitution did not specifically say that Congress could create a bank, Congress still had the power to do so. In the end the president agreed with Hamilton and signed the bill creating the national bank.

Tariffs and Taxes

At the time, most Americans earned their living by farming. Hamilton thought the development of manufacturing would make America's economy stronger. He proposed a tariff—a tax on imports—to encourage people to buy American products. This protective tariff would protect American industry from foreign competition.

The South, having little industry to protect, opposed protective tariffs. Hamilton did win support in Congress for some low tariffs to raise money rather than to protect industries. By the 1790s the revenue from tariffs provided 90 percent of the national government's income.

The final portion of Hamilton's economic program concerned the creation of national taxes. The government needed additional funds to operate and to make interest payments on the national debt. At Hamilton's request Congress approved a variety of taxes, including one on whiskey distilled in the United States.

Hamilton's economic program gave the national government new financial powers. However, his proposals split Congress and the nation. The opponents—including Jefferson and Madison—feared a national government with strong economic powers dominated by the wealthy class. They had a very different vision of what America should become.

✓ **Reading Check** **Comparing** Summarize the arguments for and against protective tariffs.

SECTION 1 ASSESSMENT

Checking for Understanding

1. **Key Terms** Write a paragraph for each group of terms below. Group 1: precedent, cabinet. Group 2: national debt, bond, speculator. Group 3: unconstitutional, tariff.
2. **Reviewing Facts** Name three things that Hamilton wanted to do to create a stable economic system and strengthen the economy.

Reviewing Themes

3. **Government and Democracy** What compromise did Congress reach in establishing a court system?

Critical Thinking

4. **Analyzing Primary Sources** Hamilton said about Washington, "He consulted much, pondered much, resolved slowly, resolved surely." Did this make Washington a good first president? Explain.
5. **Comparing** Re-create the diagram below. Compare the views of Hamilton and Jefferson. In the boxes, write "for" or "against" for each issue.

Issue	Hamilton	Jefferson
National bank		
Protective tariff		
National taxes		

Analyzing Visuals

6. **Picturing History** Examine the picture of the U.S. Capitol on page 261. The Capitol is one of the most widely recognized buildings in the world. What members of the government serve in the Capitol? What does the U.S. Capitol symbolize to you?

Interdisciplinary Activity

Expository Writing You have been given the task of choosing the first cabinet members. Write a job description for the secretaries of state, treasury, and war. Then interview classmates to see who would be best suited for each position.

Early Challenges

Guide to Reading

Main Idea
In the 1790s, the new government struggled to keep peace at home and avoid war abroad.

Key Terms
neutrality, impressment

Reading Strategy
Classifying Information As you read the section, re-create the diagram below and list results of government actions during the early Republic.

Government action	Results
Treaty of Greenville	
Proclamation of Neutrality	
Jay's Treaty	
Pinckney's Treaty	

Read to Learn
- how the federal government asserted its power in the West.
- how the United States tried to stay out of European conflicts.

Section Theme
Geography and History The new government clashed over control of the Northwest Territory.

Preview of Events

♦1790   ♦1792   ♦1794   ♦1796

November 1791
Little Turtle defeats St. Clair's forces

March 1793
Washington begins second term

July 1794
Western farmers revolt in Whiskey Rebellion

August 1794
Battle of Fallen Timbers occurs

October 1795
Spain opens Mississippi River to American shipping

AN American Story

Far removed from the bustle of trade and shipping along the Atlantic coast, farmers on the western frontier lived quite differently. In fact, western ways seemed almost primitive to travelers from the East. They seemed to notice only the poor roads and the boring diet of corn and salted pork. Living in scattered, isolated homesteads, frontier farmers were proud of their self-reliance. They wanted no "eastern" tax collectors heading their way.

Drawing of tax collector

The Whiskey Rebellion

Hamilton's taxes led to rebellion in western Pennsylvania. The farmers were in an uproar over having to pay a special tax on the whiskey they made from surplus corn. In the backcountry most farmers lived by bartering—exchanging whiskey and other items they produced for goods they needed. They rarely had cash. How could they pay a tax on whiskey?

The farmers' resistance was mostly peaceful—until July 1794, when federal officers stepped up efforts to collect the tax. Then a large mob of people armed with swords, guns, and pitchforks attacked tax collectors and burned down buildings.

The armed protest, called the **Whiskey Rebellion,** alarmed government leaders. President Washington and his advisers decided to crush the challenge. The rebellion collapsed as soon as the army crossed the Appalachian Mountains.

By his action, Washington served notice to those who opposed government actions. If citizens wished to change the law, they had to do so peacefully, through constitutional means. Government would use force when necessary to maintain the social order.

☑ **Reading Check** **Explaining** How did the Whiskey Rebellion affect the way government handled protesters?

★ Geography

Struggle Over the West

The new government faced difficult problems in the West. The Native Americans who lived between the Appalachian Mountains and the Mississippi River denied that the United States had any authority over them. On many occasions Native Americans turned to Britain and Spain to help them in their cause. Both countries welcomed the opportunity to prevent American settlement of the region.

Washington worried about European ambitions in the Northwest Territory. He hoped that signing treaties with the Native American tribes in the area would lessen the influence of the British and Spanish. American settlers ignored the treaties and continued to move onto lands promised to the Native Americans. Fighting broke out between the two groups.

Washington sent an army under General Arthur St. Clair to restore order in the Northwest Territory. In November 1791, St. Clair's forces were badly beaten by Little Turtle, chief of the Miami people. More than 600 American soldiers died in a battle by the Wabash River.

Many Americans believed that an alliance with France would enable them to defeat the combined forces of the British, Spanish, and Native Americans in the West. The British, who still had forts in the region, wanted to hold on to the profitable fur trade. The possibility of French involvement in the region pushed the British to make a bold bid for control of the West. In 1794 the British government urged Native Americans to destroy American settlements west of the Appalachians. The British also began building a new fort in Ohio.

Battle of Fallen Timbers

The Native Americans demanded that all settlers north of the Ohio River leave the territory. Washington sent another army headed by Anthony Wayne, a former Revolutionary War general, to challenge their demands. In August 1794 his army defeated over 1,000 Native Americans under Shawnee chief Blue Jacket at the **Battle of Fallen Timbers** (near present-day Toledo, Ohio). The Battle of Fallen Timbers crushed the Native Americans' hopes of keeping their land. In the **Treaty of Greenville** (1795), the Native Americans agreed to surrender most of the land in present-day Ohio.

☑ **Reading Check** **Describing** What did Native American groups do to fight more effectively in the Northwest?

Problems With Europe

Shortly after Washington was inaugurated in 1789, the French Revolution began. At first most Americans cheered upon hearing the news. The French had helped the Americans in their struggle for independence, and their revolution seemed to embody many of the ideals of the American Revolution.

By 1793 the French Revolution had turned bloody. The leaders had executed the king and queen of France and thousands of French citizens. Public opinion in the United States started to divide. The violence of the French Revolution, as well as its attack on religion and disregard of individual liberties, offended many Americans. Others hailed the new republic as a copy of the United States.

When Britain and France went to war in 1793, some Americans, particularly in the South, sympathized with France. Others, especially manufacturers and merchants who traded with the British, favored Britain. Hamilton, Adams, and their supporters generally sided with the

British. Jefferson was pro-French. A French victory, Jefferson reasoned, would help drive the British out of North America.

Washington hoped that the nation could maintain its neutrality—that is, that it would not take sides in the conflict between France and Britain. As time went on, however, neutrality became increasingly difficult.

Washington Proclaims Neutrality

The French tried to involve the United States in their conflict with Britain. In April 1793, they sent diplomat **Edmond Genêt** (zhuh•NAY) to the United States. His mission was to recruit American volunteers to attack British ships.

President Washington took action to discourage American involvement. On April 22 he issued a **Proclamation of Neutrality.** It prohibited American citizens from fighting in the war and barred French and British warships from American ports. Genêt's plans eventually failed, but he did manage to sign up a few hundred Americans to serve on French ships. These ships seized British vessels and stole their cargoes before Washington ended their adventures by closing American ports.

Outraged by the French attacks at sea, the British began capturing American ships that traded with the French. The British also stopped American merchant ships and forced their crews into the British navy. This practice, known as impressment, infuriated the Americans. British attacks on American ships and sailors, along with the challenge in the West, pushed the nation closer to war with Great Britain.

A Controversial Treaty

President Washington decided to make one last effort to come to a peaceful solution with Britain. He sent John Jay, chief justice of the Supreme Court, to negotiate.

The British were willing to listen to Jay's proposals. War with the United States would only make it harder to carry on the war with France, and the United States was Britain's best market.

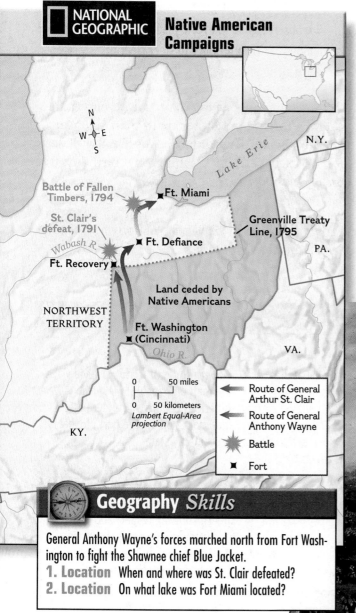

NATIONAL GEOGRAPHIC

Native American Campaigns

Battle of Fallen Timbers, 1794

Ft. Miami

St. Clair's defeat, 1791

Wabash R.

Ft. Defiance

Ft. Recovery

Lake Erie

N.Y.

Greenville Treaty Line, 1795

PA.

Land ceded by Native Americans

NORTHWEST TERRITORY

Ft. Washington (Cincinnati)

Ohio R.

VA.

KY.

0   50 miles
0   50 kilometers
Lambert Equal-Area projection

← Route of General Arthur St. Clair
← Route of General Anthony Wayne
✹ Battle
▪ Fort

Geography *Skills*

General Anthony Wayne's forces marched north from Fort Washington to fight the Shawnee chief Blue Jacket.
1. Location When and where was St. Clair defeated?
2. Location On what lake was Fort Miami located?

Picturing **History**

Upon signing the Treaty of Greenville, 12 Native American nations received $20,000 worth of goods to share. **How did the treaty affect white settlement?**

Chief Justice John Jay

In **Jay's Treaty** the British agreed to withdraw from American soil, to pay damages for ships they had seized, and to allow some American ships to trade with British colonies in the Caribbean. The treaty also provided for settlement of debts from before 1776.

Despite these gains few Americans approved of Jay's Treaty. They protested that the treaty did not deal with the issue of impressment and did not mention British interference with American trade. Although Washington found fault with the treaty, he realized it would end an explosive crisis with Great Britain. He sent the treaty to the Senate, which narrowly approved it after a fierce debate.

Treaty With Spain

When Jay's Treaty was made, Spanish leaders realized that the United States and Great Britain could work together against the Spanish Empire in North America. Thomas Pinckney was sent to Spain to try to settle the differences between the two nations. In 1795 **Pinckney's Treaty** gave the Americans free navigation of the Mississippi River and the right to trade at New Orleans.

Reading Check **Describing** Why did many Americans protest Jay's Treaty?

Washington's Farewell

In September 1796, Washington announced he would not seek a third term. By choosing to serve only two terms, Washington set a precedent that later presidents would follow.

Plagued with a variety of ailments, the 64-year-old president looked forward to retirement at Mount Vernon. He also felt troubled over the divisions that had developed in American politics and with what he considered a grave danger to the new nation—the growth of political parties.

Washington's "Farewell Address" was published in a Philadelphia newspaper. In it he attacked the evils of political parties and entanglement in foreign affairs. He also urged his fellow citizens to

❝observe good faith and justice toward all nations . . . Tis our policy to steer clear of permanent alliances.❞

Washington's parting words influenced the nation's foreign policy for more than 100 years. The text is still read aloud in the United States Senate each year on Washington's birthday. 📖
(See page 987 of the Appendix for an excerpt from Washington's Farewell Address.)

Reading Check **Explaining** What was the impact of Washington's Farewell Address?

SECTION 2 ASSESSMENT

Checking for Understanding

1. **Key Terms** Use the terms neutrality and impressment in a sentence about Washington's administration.
2. **Reviewing Facts** What message was Washington sending to the American people when he used force to stop the Whiskey Rebellion?

Reviewing Themes

3. **Geography and History** How did the Treaty of Greenville affect the land claims of Native Americans in the Northwest Territory?

Critical Thinking

4. **Predicting Consequences** What did the United States have to gain by remaining neutral in foreign affairs?
5. **Determining Cause and Effect** Re-create the diagram below. In the boxes, list the cause and effects of the Whiskey Rebellion.

Cause	Cause/Effect	Effects
	Whiskey Rebellion	

Analyzing Visuals

6. **Geography and History** Review the map on page 265. The Native American nations surrendered land that makes up a large part of what present-day state?

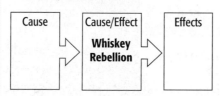

Descriptive Writing A tribute is a speech showing respect and gratitude. Write a one-paragraph tribute that you might have delivered if you had been asked to speak at George Washington's funeral.

The First Political Parties

Main Idea

By the election of 1796, two distinct political parties with different views about the role of the national government had formed.

Key Terms

partisan, implied powers, caucus, alien, sedition, nullify, states' rights

Reading Strategy

Classifying Information As you read Section 3, create a diagram like the one below and list the differences between the Federalists and the Democratic-Republicans.

Issue	Federalists	Democratic-Republicans
Role of federal government		

Read to Learn

- how political parties got started and what positions they supported.
- how John Adams and Thomas Jefferson became candidates of opposing parties in the election of 1796.

Section Theme

Government and Democracy Different values fueled the rise of the nation's first political parties.

Preview of Events

◆1796   ◆1798   ◆1800

1796
Federalists nominate Adams for president; Democratic-Republicans nominate Jefferson

1797
John Adams becomes president

1798
Congress passes Alien and Sedition Acts

1800
Convention of 1800

George Washington

AN American Story

The Washington presidency was known for its dignity and elegance. The president rode in a coach drawn by horses and accompanied by mounted attendants. He and his wife, Martha, lived in the finest house in Philadelphia, the new nation's capital. They entertained a great deal, holding weekly receptions. Each year a ball was held on Washington's birthday. The president wore a black velvet suit with gold buckles, yellow gloves, powdered hair, an ostrich plume in his hat, and a sword in a white leather sheath. Despite these extravagances, Washington's character and military record were admired by most Americans.

Opposing Views

Although hailed by Americans as the nation's greatest leader, George Washington did not escape criticism during his two terms as president. From time to time, harsh attacks on his policies and on his personality appeared in newspapers. One paper even called Washington "the scourge and the misfortune of his country."

Causes

- Different philosophies of government
- Conflicting interpretations of the Constitution
- Different economic and regional interests
- Disagreement over foreign affairs

Effects

- Federalists and Democratic-Republicans propose different solutions
- The two parties nominate candidates
- Political parties become a way of American life

Graphic Organizer → Skills

Thomas Jefferson and Alexander Hamilton emerged as the leaders of the two opposing parties.

Analyzing Information How did the first two political parties emerge?

Most attacks on Washington had come from supporters of Thomas Jefferson. They were trying to discredit the policies of Washington and Hamilton by attacking the president. By 1796 Americans were beginning to divide into opposing groups and to form political parties.

At that time, many Americans considered political parties harmful. Parties—or "factions" as they were called—were to be avoided as much as strong central government. The nation's founders did not even mention political parties in the Constitution.

Washington had denounced political parties and warned that they would divide the nation. To others it seemed natural that people would disagree about issues and that those who held similar views would band together.

In Washington's cabinet Hamilton and Jefferson often took opposing sides on issues. They disagreed on economic policy and foreign relations, on the power of the federal government, and on interpretations of the Constitution. Even

Washington had been partisan—favoring one side of an issue. Although he believed he stood above politics, Washington usually supported Hamilton's positions.

Political Parties Emerge

In Congress and the nation at large, similar differences existed. By the mid-1790s, two distinct political parties had taken shape.

The name **Federalist** had first described someone who supported ratification of the Constitution. By the 1790s the word was applied to the group of people who supported the policies of the Washington administration.

Generally Federalists stood for a strong federal government. They admired Britain because of its stability and distrusted France because of the violent changes following the French Revolution. Federalist policies tended to favor banking and shipping interests. Federalists received the strongest support in the Northeast, especially in New England, and from wealthy plantation owners in the South.

Efforts to turn public opinion against Federalist policies began seriously in late 1791 when Philip Freneau (Freh•NOH) began publishing the *National Gazette.* Jefferson, then secretary of state, helped the newspaper get started. Later he and Madison organized people who disagreed with Hamilton. They called their party the **Republicans,** or the **Democratic-Republicans.**

The Republicans wanted to limit government's power. They feared that a strong federal government would endanger people's liberties. They supported the French and condemned what they regarded as the Washington administration's pro-British policies. Republican policies appealed to small farmers and urban workers, especially in the Middle Atlantic states and the South.

🔲 Citizenship

Views of the Constitution

One difference between Federalists and Republicans concerned the basis of government power. In Hamilton's view the federal government had implied powers, powers that were not expressly forbidden in the Constitution.

Hamilton used the idea of implied powers to justify a national bank. He argued that the Constitution gave Congress the power to issue money and regulate trade, and a national bank would clearly help the government carry out these responsibilities. Therefore, creating a bank was within the constitutional power of Congress.

Jefferson and Madison disagreed with Hamilton. They believed in a strict interpretation of the Constitution. They accepted the idea of implied powers, but in a much more limited sense than Hamilton did: Implied powers are those powers that are "absolutely necessary" to carry out the expressed powers.

The People's Role

The differences between the parties, however, went even deeper. Federalists and Republicans had sharply opposing views on the role ordinary people should play in government.

Federalists supported representative government, in which elected officials ruled in the people's name. They did not believe that it was wise to let the public become too involved in politics. Hamilton said:

> 66 The people are turbulent and changing. . . . They seldom judge or determine right. 99

Public office, Federalists thought, should be held by honest and educated men of property who would protect everyone's rights. Ordinary people were too likely to be swayed by agitators.

In contrast, the Republicans feared a strong central government controlled by a few people. They believed that liberty would be safe only if ordinary people participated in government. As Jefferson explained:

> 66 I am not among those who fear the people; they, and not the rich, are our dependence [what we depend on] for continued freedom. 99

Washington's Dilemma

Washington tried to get his two advisers to work out their differences. Knowing Jefferson was discontented, Washington wrote:

> 66 I have a great sincere esteem and regard for you both, and ardently wish that some line could be marked out by which both [of] you could walk. 99

Nevertheless, by 1793 Jefferson was so unhappy that he resigned as secretary of state. In 1795, Alexander Hamilton resigned, too, as secretary of the treasury. The rival groups and their points of view moved further apart.

The Election of 1796

In the presidential election of 1796, candidates sought office for the first time as members of a party. To prepare for the election, the Federalists and the Republicans held meetings called caucuses. At the caucuses members of

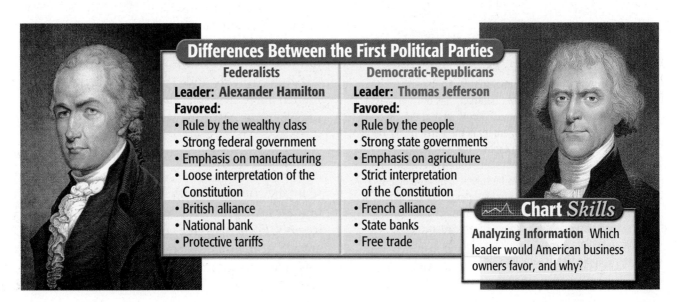

Differences Between the First Political Parties

Federalists	Democratic-Republicans
Leader: Alexander Hamilton	**Leader: Thomas Jefferson**
Favored:	**Favored:**
• Rule by the wealthy class	• Rule by the people
• Strong federal government	• Strong state governments
• Emphasis on manufacturing	• Emphasis on agriculture
• Loose interpretation of the Constitution	• Strict interpretation of the Constitution
• British alliance	• French alliance
• National bank	• State banks
• Protective tariffs	• Free trade

Chart Skills

Analyzing Information Which leader would American business owners favor, and why?

Student Web Activity
Visit taj.glencoe.com and click on **Chapter 8— Student Web Activities** for an activity on the first political parties.

Congress and other leaders chose their party's candidates for office.

The Federalists nominated Vice President John Adams as their candidate for president and Charles Pinckney for vice president. The Republicans put forth former secretary of state Jefferson for president and Aaron Burr for vice president. Adams and Jefferson, who had been good friends, became rivals. The Federalists expected to carry New England. The Republicans' strength lay in the South, which would give most of its votes to Jefferson.

In the end Adams received 71 electoral votes, winning the election. Jefferson finished second with 68 votes. Under the provisions of the Constitution at that time, the person with the second-highest number of electoral votes became vice president. Jefferson therefore became the new vice president. The administration that took office on March 4, 1797, had a Federalist president and a Republican vice president.

✓ **Reading Check** **Explaining** Which political party would a Boston factory owner most likely support?

American Heroes

Did Johnny Appleseed scatter apple seeds in the wilderness? There was a real Johnny Appleseed. Johnny, whose real name was John Chapman, was born in Massachusetts in 1774. When the rich lands west of the Ohio River were opened for settlement in the early 1800s, he was the among the first to explore the new territory. Johnny Appleseed did not scatter seeds as he wandered, as many people believe. As he traveled, he would spot good sites for planting. There he would clear the land and plant the seeds. His orchards varied in size. Some covered about an acre. Others covered many acres. When settlers arrived, they found Johnny Appleseed's young apple trees ready for sale.

President John Adams

John Adams had spent most of his life in public service. One of Massachusetts's most active patriots, he later became ambassador to France and to Great Britain. He helped to negotiate the Treaty of Paris that ended the Revolution. Under Washington, he served two terms as vice president.

The XYZ Affair

When Adams took office, he inherited the dispute with France. The French regarded Jay's Treaty, signed in 1794, as an American attempt to help the British in their war with France. To punish the United States, the French seized American ships that carried cargo to Britain.

Adams wanted to avoid war with France. In the fall of 1797, he sent a delegation to Paris to try to resolve the dispute. French foreign minister **Charles de Talleyrand,** however, refused to meet with the Americans. Instead, Talleyrand sent three agents who demanded a bribe and a loan for France from the Americans. "Not a sixpence," the Americans replied and sent a report of the incident to the United States. Adams was furious. Referring to the three French agents as X, Y, and Z, the president urged Congress to prepare for war. The incident became known as the **XYZ affair.**

Undeclared War With France

Congress responded with a program to strengthen the armed forces. It established the Navy Department in April 1798 and set aside money for building warships. Congress also increased the size of the army. George Washington was appointed commanding general.

Between 1798 and 1800, United States and French naval vessels clashed on a number of occasions, although war was not formally declared. Adams's representatives negotiated an agreement with France in September 1800 that ensured peace.

In the view of most Americans, France had become an enemy. The Republican Party, friendly toward France in the past, hesitated to turn around and condemn France. As a result, in the 1798 elections, Americans voted some Republicans out of office.

More About... The Alien and Sedition Acts

Naturalization Act
Required that aliens be residents for 14 years instead of 5 years before they became eligible for U.S. citizenship.

Alien Acts
Allowed the president to imprison aliens, or send those he considered dangerous out of the country.

Sedition Act
Made it a crime to speak, write, or publish "false, scandalous, and malicious" criticisms of the government.

Why they were passed
The Federalist-controlled Congress wanted to:
• strengthen the federal government.
• silence Republican opposition.

Results
• Discouraged immigration and led some foreigners already in the country to leave.
• Convicted 10 Republican newspaper editors who had criticized the Federalists in government.

Reaction
• Opposition to Federalist party grows.
• Led to movement to allow states to overturn federal laws.

Alien and Sedition Acts

The threat of war with France made Americans more suspicious of aliens, immigrants living in the country who were not citizens. Many Europeans who came to the United States in the 1790s supported the ideals of the French Revolution. Some Americans questioned whether these aliens would remain loyal if the United States went to war with France.

Federalists in Congress responded with strict laws to protect the nation's security. In 1798 they passed a group of measures known as the **Alien and Sedition Acts.** Sedition refers to activities aimed at weakening established government.

Citizenship

Domestic and Foreign Affairs

For some Americans, fears of a strong central government abusing its power seemed to be coming true. The Republicans looked to the states to preserve the people's liberties and stand up to what they regarded as Federalist tyranny. Madison and Jefferson drafted documents of protest that were passed by the Virginia and Kentucky legislatures.

The Virginia and Kentucky Resolutions of 1798 and 1799 claimed that the Alien and Sedition Acts could not be put into action because they violated the Constitution. The Kentucky Resolutions further suggested that states might nullify—legally overturn—federal laws considered unconstitutional.

The resolutions affirmed the principle of states' rights—limiting the federal government to those powers clearly assigned to it by the Constitution and reserving to the states all other powers not expressly forbidden to them. The issue of states' rights would arise again and again in the nation's early history.

As the election of 1800 approached, the Federalists found themselves under attack. They urged Adams to step up the war with France. They hoped to benefit politically from the

Fighting in Congress The Sedition Act led to hard feelings, even violence. This cartoon provides a humorous look at a fight in Congress. Federalist Roger Griswold attacks Republican Matthew Lyon with a cane. Lyon seizes a pair of fire tongs and fights back. On the wall is a painting named "Royal Sport" showing animals fighting. **How are the other members of Congress reacting to the fight?**

1 Matthew Lyon   **2** Roger Griswold   **3** painting

patriotic feelings that war would unleash. Adams refused to rush to war, especially for his own political gain. Instead he appointed a new commission to seek peace with France.

In 1800 the French agreed to a treaty and stopped attacks on American ships. Although the agreement with France was in the best interest of the United States, it hurt Adams's chance for re-election. Rather than applauding the agreement, Hamilton and his supporters now opposed their own president. With the Federalists split, the Republican prospects for capturing the presidency improved. The way was prepared for Thomas Jefferson in the election of 1800.

Reading Check **Summarizing** How did the peace agreement with France affect the Federalists?

SECTION 3 ASSESSMENT

Checking for Understanding

1. **Key Terms** Write a short newspaper article about the election of 1796 in which you use the following terms: partisan, implied powers, caucus.

2. **Reviewing Facts** Who was elected president in 1796, and who became vice president?

Reviewing Themes

3. **Government and Democracy** How were the Federalists different from the Republicans in how they felt about a powerful central government?

Critical Thinking

4. **Drawing Conclusions** Do you think the development of political parties was necessary? Why or why not?

5. **Classifying Information** Re-create the diagram below. Provide information about the election of 1796 in the spaces provided.

Presidential Election of 1796		
Candidate		
Party		
Electoral votes		
Winner (check column)		
Vice President (check column)		

Analyzing Visuals

6. **Graphic Organizer Skills** Study the diagram on page 271. Who are aliens? Why were the Alien and Sedition Acts passed? How did their passage affect the Federalist Party?

Interdisciplinary Activity

Art Choose the presidential candidate for whom you would have voted in 1796. Design a campaign poster or button using words and illustrations to help promote your candidate.

Social Studies
SKILLBUILDER

Reading a Flowchart

Why Learn This Skill?

Sometimes determining a sequence of events can be confusing, particularly when many events occur at the same time. A flowchart can help you understand what is going on in a series of events.

Learning the Skill

Flowcharts show the steps in a process or a sequence of events. For example, a flowchart could be used to show the movement of goods through a factory, of people through a training program, or of a bill through Congress. The following steps explain how to read a flowchart:

- Read the title or caption of the flowchart to find out what you are studying.
- Read all of the labels or sentences on the flowchart.
- Look for numbers indicating a sequence, or arrows showing the direction of movement.

Practicing the Skill

Read the flowchart on this page. It shows a sequence of events that took place in the Northwest Territory. Analyze the information in the flowchart; then answer the following questions.

1 What symbol is used to show the sequence of the events?

2 What actions taken by the British set off the sequence of events that are reflected in the title of the chart?

3 What action did Washington take in response to trouble in the Ohio Valley?

4 What information from the chapter could you add to the flowchart to continue the sequence of events?

Conflicts in the Northwest Territory

1790s
Great Britain holds forts in the Ohio Valley.

British stir up trouble between Native Americans and American settlers in the Ohio Valley.

President Washington sends troops into the Northwest Territory.

Federal troops are defeated by Miami chief Little Turtle.

Applying the Skill

Making a Flowchart Imagine that a student who is new to your school asks you how to sign up for a sport or social club. Draw a flowchart outlining the steps the student should follow.

 Glencoe's **Skillbuilder Interactive Workbook CD-ROM, Level 1,** provides instruction and practice in key social studies skills.

Chapter Summary

A New Nation

Federal Government

- First Congress establishes three executive departments
- Judiciary Act of 1789 passes
- Bill of Rights added to the Constitution
- Nation's capital moves to Washington, D.C.
- National bank created
- Congress approves tariffs

Early Challenges

- Whiskey Rebellion put down
- Force and treaties slow Native American resistance to settlement
- Washington maintains American neutrality
- Treaty with Spain allows access to the Mississippi River

The New Nation

First Political Parties

- Federalists emerge, promoting a strong central government
- Republicans want to leave more power in the hands of the states.

President John Adams

- Federalist John Adams becomes second president
- American and French naval forces fight an undeclared war
- Federalists in Congress pass the Alien and Sedition Acts
- Virginia and Kentucky Resolutions advocate states' rights

Reviewing Key Terms

On graph paper, create a word search puzzle using the following terms. Crisscross the terms vertically and horizontally, then fill in the remaining squares with extra letters. List the definition of each term below the puzzle as clues. Share your puzzle with a classmate.

1. precedent
2. cabinet
3. tariff
4. neutrality
5. impressment
6. caucus
7. sedition
8. states' rights

Reviewing Key Facts

9. Why did Hamilton want national taxes? Why did some oppose the taxes?
10. What was the importance of the Judiciary Act of 1789?
11. What caused farmers in western Pennsylvania to revolt during the Whiskey Rebellion?
12. According to Hamilton, what are implied powers?
13. What actions by France led to an undeclared war with the United States?
14. Who was elected president in 1796? Who was elected vice president?

Critical Thinking

15. **Analyzing Themes: Government and Democracy** Refer to the grievances listed in the Declaration of Independence. How were these grievances addressed in the Bill of Rights?
16. **Analyzing Information** What did President Washington say in his Farewell Address about political parties and foreign policy?
17. **Comparing** Re-create the diagram below. Compare the positions of the Federalists and Democratic-Republicans on the national bank. In the boxes list the leaders and their positions.

National Bank	
Federalists	**Democratic-Republicans**
Leader:	Leader:
Position:	Position:

Practicing Skills

Reading a Flowchart *Alexander Hamilton promoted the creation of a national bank. Study the flowchart below. Then answer the questions that follow.*

How Banks Work Today

Workers receive payment for work.

People deposit savings in banks and receive interest.

Banks loan money to businesses and receive interest.

Businesses use loan money to make products and pay workers.

18. What is used to show the sequence of events?

19. What happens after workers receive payment for work?

20. What two parts on this flowchart show who receives interest on their money?

 Geography and History Activity

Study the map on page 265. Then answer the questions that follow.

21. **Movement** In which direction did St. Clair's troops move?

22. **Location** Along what river was Ft. Washington located?

Citizenship Cooperative Activity

23. **Researching** Work in groups of four to discuss and develop answers to these questions:
    - How does the Bill of Rights reflect the principle of limited government?
    - What are two individual rights protected in the Bill of Rights?
    - Why would it be necessary to change the Constitution?

Self-Check Quiz
Visit taj.glencoe.com and click on **Chapter 8— Self-Check Quizzes** to prepare for the chapter test.

Economics Activity

24. **Math Practice** When you deposit money in a bank, you receive interest—a payment for lending money to the bank. To figure simple interest, you need to know what the interest rate is. Say, for example, a local bank is offering simple interest on savings accounts at 6 percent per year. If you deposit $100, how much will you have in the account at the end of one year? At the end of four years?

 Technology Activity

25. **Using a Computerized Card Catalog** Search your local library's computerized card catalog for sources on Mount Vernon, George Washington's home. Find the sources on the library shelves, then use the information you found to write a two-paragraph description that Washington might have written if he had ever wanted to sell his home.

 Alternative Assessment

26. Review the chapter and make a list of the differences between the Federalist and Republican parties. Based on your list, create a symbol to represent each of the parties.

 Standardized Test Practice
The Princeton Review

Directions: Choose the *best* answer to the following question.

Certain grievances listed in the Declaration of Independence were addressed in the Bill of Rights. Which amendment addressed the quartering of troops?

A 1st Amendment   C 8th Amendment

B 3rd Amendment   D 12th Amendment

Test-Taking Tip

Read the question carefully. The 12th Amendment was not part of the Bill of Rights, so it can be eliminated as a possibility.

The Jefferson Era

1800–1816

Why It Matters

In 1801 the Democratic-Republican Party took control of the nation's government. The Federalists—the party of Alexander Hamilton and John Adams—were now on the sidelines and played the role of critics to the Republican administration.

The Impact Today

Politicians today operate within the party system that took shape at that time.

• While the two main parties have changed, each still works to win votes and gain power.

• If the people vote to change the party in power, the newly elected representatives take office peacefully and the government continues.

The American Journey *Video* *The chapter 9 video, "The True Story of Sacagawea," tells the story of the Shoshone woman who helped guide the Lewis and Clark expedition.*

1803
• Supreme Court establishes judicial review

1804
• Lewis and Clark begin expedition

1807
• Congress passes Embargo Act

United States PRESIDENTS

Jefferson 1801–1809

1800

1804

1808

World

1804
• Napoleon names himself emperor of France

1808
• Beethoven's *Fifth Symphony* performed

Battle of North Point by Don Troiani American soldiers battled
British forces advancing on Baltimore.

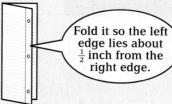
1811
• Battle of
  Tippecanoe

1812
• U.S. declares
  war on Britain

1815
• Battle of
  New Orleans

Madison
1809–1817

1812   1816

1812
• Napoleon
  invades Russia

1814
• Congress of
  Vienna meets

1815
• Napoleon
  defeated at
  Waterloo

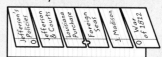

HISTORY
Online

Chapter Overview
Visit taj.glencoe.com and
click on **Chapter 9—
Chapter Overviews** to preview chapter information.

The Republicans Take Power

Guide to Reading

Main Idea
The election of 1800 marked the transfer of power from one political party to another through a democratic election.

Key Terms
laissez-faire, customs duties, judicial review

Reading Strategy
Organizing Information As you read the section, use a diagram like the one shown here to identify ways Republicans tried to reduce the role of government.

Ways the Republicans reduced government

Read to Learn
- how the election deadlock of 1800 was resolved.
- how John Marshall strengthened the Supreme Court.

Section Theme
Government and Democracy Jefferson believed that a large federal government threatened liberty.

Preview of Events

♦1800   ♦1801   ♦1802   ♦1803

1800
Thomas Jefferson and John Adams contend for presidency

1801
Judiciary Act expands court system

March 1801
Jefferson is inaugurated

1803
Marbury v. *Madison* sets precedent for judicial review

AN American Story

Abigail Adams in the unfinished White House

In 1801 Washington, D.C., was slowly rising from a swampy site on the Potomac River. The nation's new capital had only two noteworthy buildings—the president's mansion (later called the White House) and the still-unfinished Capitol. Between them stretched about two miles of muddy streets on which pigs and chickens roamed freely.

Very few people liked being in Washington. It was hot and steamy in the summer, and the river and swamps were a breeding ground for mosquitoes. Abigail Adams called the new capital "the very dirtiest Hole."

The Election of 1800

The Federalist and Republican parties fought a bitter election campaign in 1800. Federalists supported President Adams for a second term and Charles Pinckney of South Carolina for vice president. Republicans nominated **Thomas Jefferson** for president and **Aaron Burr** of New York as his running mate.

The election campaign of 1800 differed greatly from campaigns of today. Neither Adams nor Jefferson traveled around the country making speeches about why he should be elected. That would have been considered in bad taste. Instead the candidates and their allies wrote hundreds of letters to leading citizens and friendly newspapers to publicize their views. The letter-writing campaign, however, was not polite.

Federalists charged the Republican Jefferson, who believed in freedom of religion, as being "godless." Republicans warned that the Federalists would bring back monarchy. Federalists, they claimed, represented the interests of wealthy people with property.

Election Deadlock

When members of the Electoral College voted, Jefferson and Burr each received 73 votes. Because of this tie, the House of Representatives had to decide the election. At the time the electors voted for each presidential and vice-presidential candidate individually rather than voting for a party's candidates as a team.

In the House, Federalists saw a chance to prevent the election of Jefferson by supporting Burr. For 35 ballots, the election remained tied. Finally, at Alexander Hamilton's urging, one Federalist decided not to vote for Burr. Jefferson became president, and Burr became vice president.

To prevent another showdown between a presidential and a vice-presidential candidate, Congress passed the Twelfth Amendment to the Constitution in 1803. This amendment, ratified in 1804, requires electors to vote for the president and vice president on separate ballots. 📖
(See page 246 for the entire text of the Twelfth Amendment.)

Jefferson's Inauguration

On March 4, 1801, the day of the inauguration, Jefferson dressed in everyday clothes. He left his boardinghouse and walked to the Senate to be sworn in as president. President Adams did not attend the ceremony. He had slipped out of the presidential mansion and left the city so he would not have to watch Thomas Jefferson become president.

In his Inaugural Address, Jefferson tried to bridge the gap between the developing political parties and reach out to Federalists with healing words. "We are all Republicans, we are all Federalists," he said. Then he outlined some of his goals, which included "a wise and frugal government" and "the support of state governments in all their rights." Jefferson had long been a supporter of states' rights. He believed that a large federal government threatened liberty and that vigilant states could best protect freedom.

Jefferson believed in reducing the power and size of the federal government. These ideas were similar to the French philosophy of **laissez-faire** (leh•say FEHR), which means "let (people) do (as they choose)."

✓ **Reading Check** **Describing** What does the Twelfth Amendment to the Constitution require?

America's *Architecture*

Monticello Thomas Jefferson had many talents, including being a skilled architect. He designed buildings at the University of Virginia and his home at Monticello. Construction on Monticello began in 1769, following Jefferson's first design. Remodeling and enlarging the house began in 1796 and was completed by 1809.

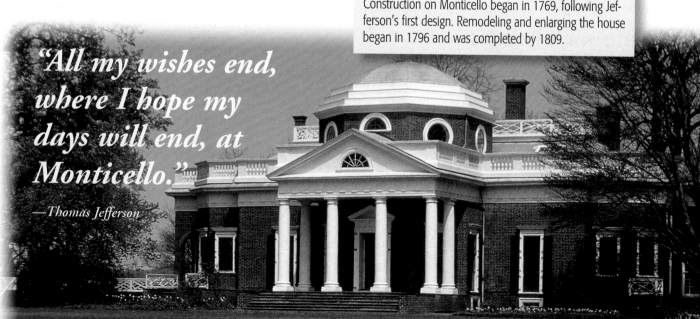

"All my wishes end, where I hope my days will end, at Monticello."

—*Thomas Jefferson*

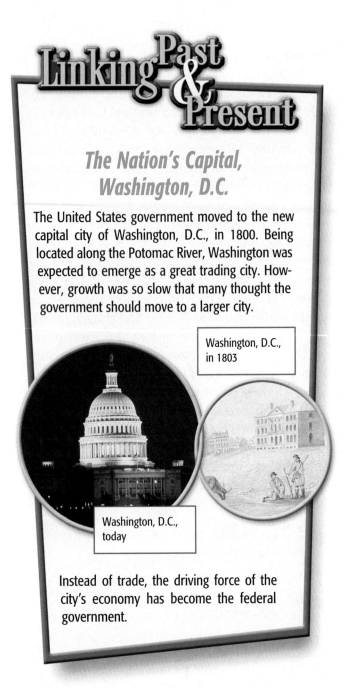

Linking Past & Present

The Nation's Capital, Washington, D.C.

The United States government moved to the new capital city of Washington, D.C., in 1800. Being located along the Potomac River, Washington was expected to emerge as a great trading city. However, growth was so slow that many thought the government should move to a larger city.

Washington, D.C., in 1803

Washington, D.C., today

Instead of trade, the driving force of the city's economy has become the federal government.

Jefferson's Policies

Thomas Jefferson had strong ideas about how to make the United States a success. He believed that the strength of the United States was its independent farmers. As long as most people owned their own property, they would fight to protect their rights and to preserve the republic. For this reason, Jefferson favored expanding the nation westward to acquire more land. He also believed the federal government should be kept small. He distrusted standing armies and wanted to reduce the size of the military.

Jefferson's Cabinet

When Jefferson entered office, he surrounded himself with men who shared his Republican principles. His secretary of state was his friend and fellow Virginian, James Madison. For secretary of the treasury, he chose **Albert Gallatin.** This Pennsylvanian had a grasp of financial matters that equaled Alexander Hamilton's.

The new government soon ended two unpopular Federalist measures. It allowed the Alien and Sedition acts to expire and repealed the Naturalization Act. For Republicans both acts were symbols of a federal government that threatened individual liberties.

Cutting Costs

Jefferson and Gallatin aimed to reduce the national debt that the Federalists had left. They scaled down military expenses. They cut the army by one-third and reduced the navy from 25 to 7 ships. By slashing spending Jefferson and Gallatin significantly lowered the national debt within a few years.

Jefferson and Gallatin also persuaded Congress to repeal all federal internal taxes, including the hated whiskey tax. At that point government funds would come only from customs duties—taxes on foreign imported goods—and from the sale of western lands.

The entire federal government in 1801 consisted of only a few hundred people. This was exactly how Jefferson thought it should be. In his view the responsibilities of the national government should be limited to delivering the mail, collecting customs duties, and conducting a census every 10 years.

Reading Check **Explaining** How did the changes that Jefferson made when he became president reflect his views about government?

Jefferson and the Courts

Jefferson hoped that some Federalists would support his policies. However, bitter feelings between the parties continued during his administration. Much of the ill will resulted from a fight over control of the federal courts.

Student Web Activity
Visit taj.glencoe.com and click on **Chapter 9—Student Web Activities** for an activity on the history of the Supreme Court.

Judiciary Act of 1801

Before Jefferson took office, the Federalists passed the Judiciary Act of 1801. The act set up regional courts for the United States with 16 judges and many other judicial officials. In his last days as president, John Adams made hundreds of appointments to these positions, and the Federalist-controlled Congress approved them. Adams also asked **John Marshall,** his secretary of state, to serve as chief justice of the United States. By these actions Adams shut President-elect Jefferson out of the appointment process and ensured that Federalists would control the courts.

Adams and Marshall worked around the clock in the final hours of the Federalist government, processing the papers for these judicial appointments. The appointments could not take effect, however, until the papers (commissions) for these last-minute "midnight judges" were delivered. When Jefferson became president on March 4, a few of the commissions had not yet been delivered. He told Secretary of State Madison not to deliver them. One commission was addressed to William Marbury.

Marbury v. *Madison*

To force the delivery of his commission, Marbury took his case directly to the Supreme Court, which he claimed had jurisdiction as a result of the Judiciary Act of 1789. John Marshall wrote an opinion turning down Marbury's claim. He noted that the Constitution did not give the Court jurisdiction to decide Marbury's case.

In his opinion, Marshall set out three principles of judicial review: (a) The Constitution is the supreme law of the land. (b) When there is a conflict between the Constitution and any other law, the Constitution must be followed. (c) The judicial branch has a duty to uphold the Constitution. It must be able to determine when a federal law conflicts with the Constitution and to nullify, or cancel, unconstitutional laws.

Marshall not only extended the power of the Court, he also broadened federal power at the expense of the states. In *McCulloch* v. *Maryland* (1819), the Court held that the elastic clause allows Congress to do more than the Constitution expressly authorizes it to do. In *Gibbons* v. *Ogden* (1824) the Court held that federal law takes precedence over state law in interstate transportation. *(See the Supreme Court Case Summaries beginning on page 997 for more on these cases.)*

✓ **Reading Check** **Summarizing** Summarize the court case that established judicial review.

SECTION 1 ASSESSMENT

Checking for Understanding

1. **Key Terms** Write a short paragraph in which you explain the terms laissez-faire, customs duties, and judicial review.
2. **Reviewing Facts** Explain how Jefferson cut government spending.

Reviewing Themes

3. **Government and Democracy** How did the judicial branch under Jefferson serve as a check on the executive and legislative branches?

Critical Thinking

4. **Identifying Central Issues** How was the deadlock in the presidential election of 1800 finally resolved?
5. **Determining Cause and Effect** Re-create the diagram below. In the boxes list the effects that came from the appointment of the "midnight judges."

Adams appoints judges → □ → □ → □

Analyzing Visuals

6. **Analyzing Architecture** Examine the photograph of Monticello on page 279. Who lived there? What do you think gives Monticello its unique look? Explain.

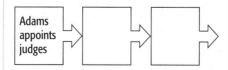

Interdisciplinary Activity

Expository Writing A letter of recommendation is written to discuss the positive qualities of a person. Write a letter from John Adams to Thomas Jefferson about John Marshall. Address Marshall's skills and leadership qualities.

SECTION 2 The Louisiana Purchase

Main Idea
The Louisiana Purchase opened a vast area to exploration and settlement.

Key Terms
Conestoga wagon, secede

Reading Strategy
Classifying Information As you read, re-create the diagram below and describe the areas that Lewis and Clark, and Zebulon Pike explored.

Explorer	Region explored
Meriwether Lewis and William Clark	
Zebulon Pike	

Read to Learn
- how the United States expanded in the early 1800s.
- how Lewis and Clark led an expedition to explore the Louisiana Territory.

Section Theme
Geography and History The purchase of the Louisiana Territory doubled the nation's size.

Preview of Events

♦1804	♦1805	♦1806	♦1807
October 1803 Senate ratifies Louisiana Purchase treaty	**May 1804** Lewis and Clark begin expedition	**September 1806** Lewis and Clark return to St. Louis	**November 1806** Zebulon Pike sights Pikes Peak

AN American Story

Why did Americans risk everything they had to travel west? An English visitor, Harriet Martineau, observed: "The pride and delight of Americans is in their quantity of land. . . . The possession of land is the aim of all action . . . and the cure for all social evils. . . . If a man is disappointed in politics or love, he goes and buys land. If he disgraces himself, he betakes himself to a lot in the West. . . ."

Conestoga wagon

Western Territory

During the early 1800s, more and more Americans moved west in search of land and adventure. These pioneers headed over the mountains into Kentucky and Tennessee and the less settled areas of the Northwest Territory. Most of these pioneers were farmers. They made a long and exhausting journey over the Appalachian Mountains. Pioneers had to trudge along crude, muddy roads or cut their way through dense forests.

Settlers loaded their household goods into Conestoga wagons, sturdy vehicles topped with white canvas. For these westward-bound pioneers, their two most valued possessions were a rifle for protection and hunting and an ax to hack their way through the dense forests.

In 1800 the territory of the United States extended only as far west as the Mississippi River. The area to the west of the river—known as the **Louisiana Territory**—belonged to Spain. It was an enormous area of land, anchored to the south by the city of New Orleans and extending west to the Rocky Mountains. Its northern boundaries remained undefined.

Many of the pioneers settled down and established farms along rivers that fed into the upper Mississippi River. They needed the river to ship their crops to markets. The Spanish allowed the Americans to sail on the lower Mississippi and trade in **New Orleans.** For the western farmers, this right was vital. The goods they sent downriver were unloaded in New Orleans and sent by ship to markets on the East Coast.

The French Threat

In 1802 the Spanish suddenly changed their policy. They refused to allow American goods to move into or past New Orleans. That same year, President Jefferson confirmed that Spain and France had made a secret agreement that transferred the Louisiana Territory to France.

This agreement posed a serious threat for the United States. France's leader, **Napoleon Bonaparte,** had plans for empires in Europe and the Americas. Jefferson was alarmed. He believed French control would jeopardize American trade on the Mississippi River. Jefferson authorized Robert Livingston, the new minister to France, to offer as much as $10 million for New Orleans and West Florida in order to gain control of the territory. Jefferson believed that France had gained Florida as well as Louisiana in its secret agreement with Spain.

Revolt in Santo Domingo

Napoleon had recognized the importance of Santo Domingo as a Caribbean naval base from which he could control an American empire. Events in Santo Domingo ended Napoleon's dream of a Western empire. Inspired by the ideas of the French Revolution, enslaved Africans and other laborers in Santo Domingo had revolted against the island's plantation owners. After fierce and bitter fighting, the rebels, led by **Toussaint-Louverture** (TOO•SA LOO•vuhr•TYUR), declared the colony an independent republic. Toussaint set up a new government.

In 1802 Napoleon sent troops to regain control. The French captured Toussaint but could not regain control of the island. By 1804, the French were driven out of Santo Domingo and the country regained its original name of Haiti.

Reading Check **Explaining** Why was the Mississippi River important to western farmers?

The Nation Expands

Without Santo Domingo, Napoleon had little use for Louisiana. The French also needed money to finance Napoleon's plans for war against Britain. The French believed they had something to sell that the United States might want to buy.

French foreign minister Charles de Talleyrand informed the American diplomats that the entire Louisiana Territory was for sale. Livingston and James Monroe, Jefferson's new special representative, were taken completely by surprise. Accepting the offer went far beyond what they were authorized to do, but the deal was too good to pass up. After a few days of negotiation, the parties agreed on a price of $15 million.

The Louisiana Purchase pleased Jefferson. The new territory would provide cheap and abundant land for farmers for generations to come. He worried, however, whether the purchase was legal. The Constitution said nothing about acquiring new territory. By what authority could he justify the purchase? Livingston wrote from Paris, urging Jefferson to accept the deal before Napoleon changed his mind. Jefferson decided the government's treaty-making powers allowed the purchase of the new territory. The Senate gave its approval in October 1803. With the ratification of the treaty, the size of the United States doubled.

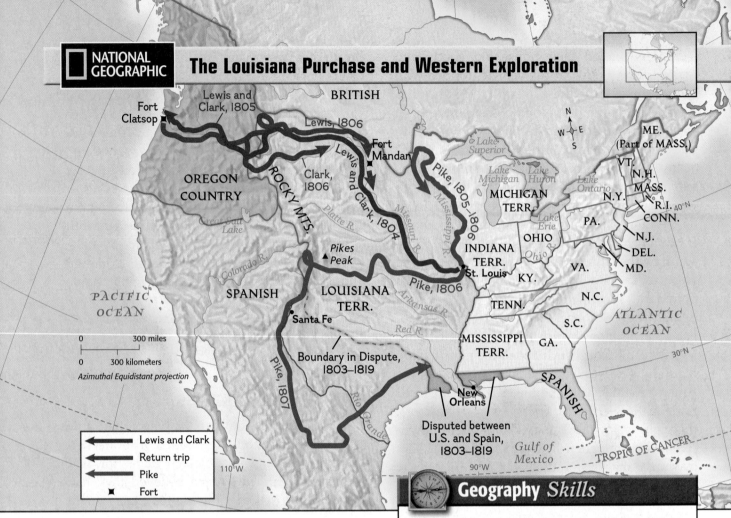

NATIONAL GEOGRAPHIC

The Louisiana Purchase and Western Exploration

Fort Clatsop

Lewis and Clark, 1805

BRITISH

Lewis, 1806

Fort Mandan

Pike, 1805–1806

OREGON COUNTRY

ROCKY MTS.

Clark, 1806

Lewis and Clark, 1804

Great Salt Lake

MICHIGAN TERR.

Lake Superior

Lake Michigan

Lake Huron

Lake Ontario

ME. (Part of MASS.)

VT.

N.H.

MASS.

N.Y.

R.I.

CONN.

40°N

PA.

N.J.

DEL.

MD.

Platte R.

Missouri R.

Mississippi R.

INDIANA TERR.

OHIO

Ohio R.

St. Louis

Pike, 1806

KY.

VA.

Pikes Peak

Colorado R.

PACIFIC OCEAN

SPANISH

LOUISIANA TERR.

Santa Fe

Arkansas R.

Red R.

Boundary in Dispute, 1803–1819

TENN.

N.C.

S.C.

MISSISSIPPI TERR.

GA.

ATLANTIC OCEAN

30°N

Pike, 1807

Rio Grande

New Orleans

Disputed between U.S. and Spain, 1803–1819

SPANISH

Gulf of Mexico

TROPIC OF CANCER

110°W

90°W

N
W E
S

Legend:
Lewis and Clark
Return trip
Pike
Fort

0 — 300 miles
0 — 300 kilometers
Azimuthal Equidistant projection

Geography Skills

The purchase of the Louisiana Territory doubled the size of the United States. Americans quickly set out to explore the region and lands farther west.

1. **Place** What geographical barrier did Lewis and Clark have to cross in order to reach the Pacific Ocean?
2. **Region** What rivers flowed through the Louisiana Territory?

Geography

Lewis and Clark

Jefferson wanted to know more about the mysterious lands west of the Mississippi. Even before the Louisiana Purchase was complete, he persuaded Congress to sponsor an expedition to explore the new territory. Jefferson was particularly interested in the expedition as a scientific venture. Congress was interested in commercial possibilities and in sites for future forts.

To head the expedition, Jefferson chose his private secretary, 28-year-old **Meriwether Lewis.** Lewis was well qualified to lead this journey of exploration. He had joined the militia during the Whiskey Rebellion and had been in the army since that time. The expedition's co-leader was **William Clark,** 32, a friend of Lewis's from military service. Both Lewis and Clark were knowledgeable amateur scientists and had conducted business with Native Americans. Together they assembled a crew that included expert river men, gunsmiths, carpenters, scouts, and a cook. Two

men of mixed Native American and French heritage served as interpreters. An African American named York rounded out the group.

The expedition left **St. Louis** in the spring of 1804 and slowly worked its way up the **Missouri River.** Lewis and Clark kept a journal of their voyage and made notes on what they saw and did.

Along their journey they encountered Native American groups. One young Shoshone woman named **Sacagawea** (SA•kuh•juh•WEE•uh) joined their group as a guide. After 18 months and nearly 4,000 miles, Lewis and Clark reached the Pacific Ocean. After spending the winter there, both explorers headed back east along separate routes.

When the expedition returned in September 1806, it had collected valuable information on people, plants, animals, and the geography of the West. Perhaps most important, the journey provided inspiration to a nation of people eager to move westward.

Pike's Expedition

Even before Lewis and Clark returned, Jefferson sent others to explore the wilderness. Lieutenant **Zebulon Pike** led two expeditions between 1805 and 1807, traveling through the upper Mississippi River valley and into the region that is now the state of Colorado. In Colorado he found a snow-capped mountain he called Grand Peak. Today this mountain is known as Pikes Peak. During his expedition Pike was captured by the Spanish but was eventually released.

Federalists Plan to Secede

Many Federalists opposed the Louisiana Purchase. They feared that the states carved out of the new territory would become Republican, reducing the Federalists' power. A group of Federalists in Massachusetts plotted to secede—withdraw—from the Union. They wanted New England to form a separate "Northern Confederacy."

The plotters realized that to have any chance of success, the Northern Confederacy would have to include New York as well as New England. The Massachusetts Federalists needed a powerful friend in that state who would back their plan. They turned to Aaron Burr, who had been cast aside by the Republicans for his refusal to withdraw from the 1800 election. The Federalists gave Burr their support in 1804, when he ran for governor of New York.

Burr and Hamilton

Alexander Hamilton had never trusted Aaron Burr. Now Hamilton was concerned about rumors that Burr had secretly agreed to lead New York out of the Union. Hamilton accused Burr of plotting treason. When Burr lost the election for governor, he blamed Hamilton and challenged him to a duel. In July 1804, the two men—armed with pistols—met in Weehawken, New Jersey. Hamilton hated dueling and pledged not to shoot at his rival. Burr, however, did fire and aimed to hit Hamilton. Seriously wounded, Hamilton died the next day. Burr fled to avoid arrest.

Reading Check **Summarizing** Why did France sell the Louisiana Territory to the United States?

SECTION 2 ASSESSMENT

Checking for Understanding

1. **Key Terms** Write a short paragraph in which you describe the terms Conestoga wagon and secede.
2. **Reviewing Facts** What European countries controlled the Louisiana Territory up until 1800?

Reviewing Themes

3. **Geography and History** Why were the Mississippi River and New Orleans important to the United States?

Critical Thinking

4. **Determining Cause and Effect** How do you think the Lewis and Clark expedition helped to prepare people who wanted to move west?
5. **Organizing Information** Create a diagram like the one below that lists the benefits of acquiring the Louisiana Territory.

Benefits

Analyzing Visuals

6. **Geography Skills** Review the map on page 284. What was the farthest western point that the Lewis and Clark expedition reached? What is the straight-line distance between St. Louis and Pikes Peak?

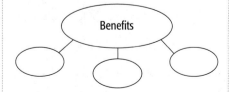

Interdisciplinary Activity

Descriptive Writing Accurate descriptions and drawings in their journals made Lewis and Clark's observations valuable. Find an example of plants or animals nearby. Carefully draw and describe what you see.

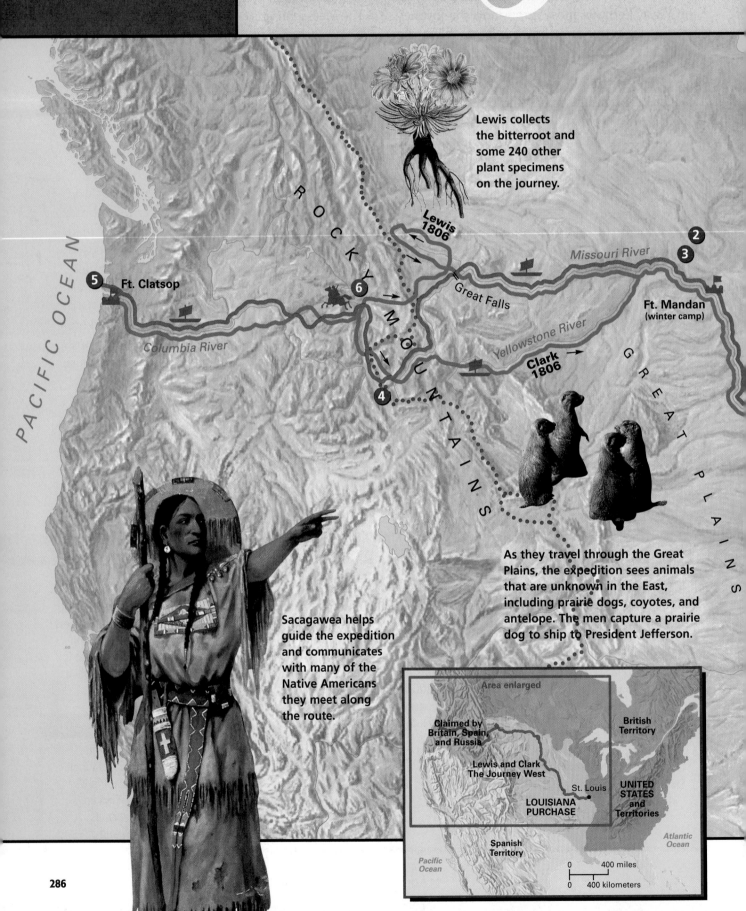

Lewis collects the bitterroot and some 240 other plant specimens on the journey.

ROCKY MOUNTAINS

Lewis 1806

②
③

Missouri River

Great Falls

Ft. Mandan (winter camp)

Yellowstone River

Clark 1806

GREAT PLAINS

⑤ **Ft. Clatsop**

⑥

④

Columbia River

PACIFIC OCEAN

As they travel through the Great Plains, the expedition sees animals that are unknown in the East, including prairie dogs, coyotes, and antelope. The men capture a prairie dog to ship to President Jefferson.

Sacagawea helps guide the expedition and communicates with many of the Native Americans they meet along the route.

Area enlarged

Claimed by Britain, Spain, and Russia

British Territory

Lewis and Clark The Journey West

St. Louis

UNITED STATES and Territories

LOUISIANA PURCHASE

Spanish Territory

Pacific Ocean

Atlantic Ocean

| 0 | | 400 miles |
| 0 | | 400 kilometers |

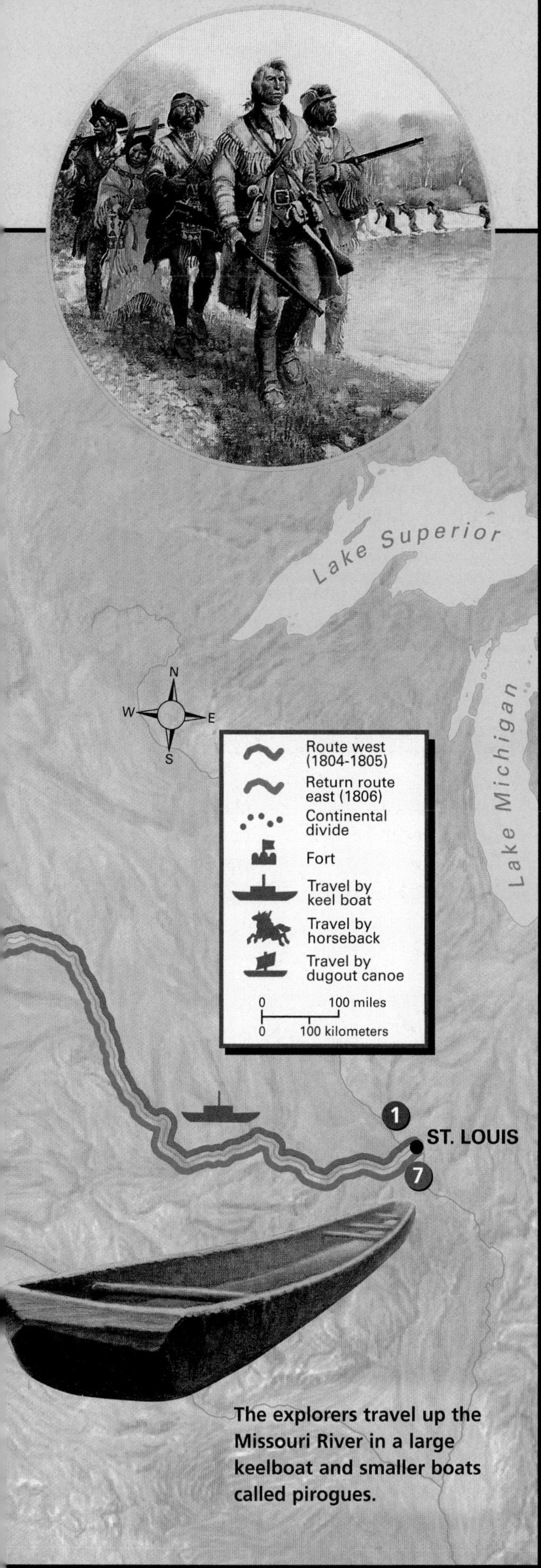

INTO THE UNKNOWN

LEWIS AND CLARK In 1803 President Jefferson set up the Corps of Discovery to find a water route to the Pacific and explore the recently acquired Louisiana Purchase. In the spring of 1804, William Clark and Meriwether Lewis, with a company of recruits, set off from St. Louis.

1804 THE JOURNEY WEST

1 MAY 14 The members of the Corps of Discovery, which number over 45, embark on the expedition, which would eventually cover over 7,700 miles.

2 NOVEMBER The explorers set up a winter camp near the villages of the Mandans and Hidatsas. Sacagawea, a Shoshone woman who had been kidnapped by the Hidatsa, joins the expedition.

1805

3 APRIL 7 Lewis and Clark send a group back on the keelboat with reports and specimens of some of the plants and animals that were unknown in the East. The expedition continues in smaller boats.

4 AUGUST 12 Lewis realizes that there is no Northwest Passage—or river route—to the Pacific. The Corps continues on horseback.

5 DECEMBER 25 The expedition celebrates Christmas in its new winter quarters, Fort Clatsop.

1806 THE RETURN TRIP

6 JULY 3 The expedition splits into smaller units to explore more of the Louisiana Territory. They reunite on August 12.

7 SEPTEMBER 23 The Corps of Discovery finally arrives back in St. Louis. The explorers had established peaceful contact with many Native Americans and accumulated a wealth of geographic information. Fur traders and others, armed with the new knowledge, soon start heading west.

Map Legend

- Route west (1804-1805)
- Return route east (1806)
- Continental divide
- Fort
- Travel by keel boat
- Travel by horseback
- Travel by dugout canoe

0 — 100 miles
0 — 100 kilometers

Lake Superior

Lake Michigan

ST. LOUIS

The explorers travel up the Missouri River in a large keelboat and smaller boats called pirogues.

LEARNING from GEOGRAPHY

1. What obstacles do you think would have been the most difficult for the expedition?

2. Write a paragraph that describes the importance of teamwork in helping the Corps of Discovery reach its goals.

287

A Time of Conflict

Guide to Reading

Main Idea
Between 1800 and 1815 the United States experienced rapid expansion as well as the challenge of war.

Key Terms
tribute, neutral rights, impressment, embargo, War Hawks, nationalism

Reading Strategy
Organizing Information As you read the section, re-create the diagram below and describe in the box the actions the United States took in each of these situations.

U.S. actions
— Demand for tribute
— Attack on *Chesapeake*
— Tecumseh's confederation

Read to Learn
• why Tecumseh built a confederacy among Native American nations.
• why the War Hawks wanted to go to war.

Section Theme
Global Connections The nation's neutrality was challenged.

Preview of Events

♦ 1804	♦ 1808	♦ 1812

1804
Barbary pirates seize the U.S. warship *Philadelphia*

1807
The British navy attacks the American vessel *Chesapeake*; Congress passes the Embargo Act

1811
Harrison defeats the Prophet at Tippecanoe

1812
Madison asks Congress to declare war on Britain

AN American Story

American sailors

The floors of the oceans are littered with the remains of once-mighty ships and the unmarked graves of unlucky sailors who sank with them in the 1700s. Seafarer Francis Rogers described the terror of a storm in this journal entry: "The sky seemed all on fire and [all around] were such swift darting rays of lightning, flying in long bright veins, with inexpressible fury as was very frightful."

Americans in Foreign Seas

Despite the dangers of sea travel in the early 1800s, the livelihoods of many Americans depended on trade with foreign nations. In 1785 the American ship *Empress of China* returned to New York from China with a highly prized cargo of tea and silk. The goods sold for a fabulous profit. Soon ships from New York, Philadelphia, and especially New England were sailing regularly to China and India carrying furs and other goods. In the following years, American merchant ships sailed far and wide, making calls in South America, Africa, and lands along the Mediterranean Sea.

War between the French and British in the mid-1790s gave an additional boost to American shipping. Rather than risk capture or destruction by the enemy, many French and British merchant ships remained at home. American shippers profited from the situation and increased their trade. By 1800 the United States had almost 1,000 merchant ships trading around the world.

Barbary Pirates

Sailing in foreign seas was not without danger. In the Mediterranean, for example, ships had to be on guard for pirates from Tripoli and the other **Barbary Coast states** of North Africa. For years these Barbary pirates had been terrorizing the Mediterranean. They demanded tribute, or protection money, from European governments to let their ships pass safely.

War With Tripoli

The United States, too, had paid tribute for safe passage—but not enough. In 1801 the ruler of Tripoli asked for more money from the United States. When President Jefferson refused, the ruler chopped down the flagpole of the American consulate—a declaration of war. Jefferson sent ships to the Mediterranean and blockaded, or closed off, Tripoli. The American fleet, however, was not powerful enough to defeat the Barbary pirates, and the conflict continued.

In 1804 the pirates seized the U.S. warship *Philadelphia* and towed it into Tripoli Harbor. They threw the captain and crew into jail. **Stephen Decatur,** a 25-year-old United States Navy captain, took action. Slipping into the heavily guarded harbor with a small raiding party, Decatur burned the captured ship to prevent the pirates from using it. A British admiral praised the deed as the "most bold and daring act of the age."

Negotiations finally ended the conflict with Tripoli in June 1805. Tripoli agreed to stop demanding tribute, but the United States had to pay a ransom of $60,000 for the release of the American prisoners.

Reading Check **Explaining** Why did Tripoli declare war on the United States?

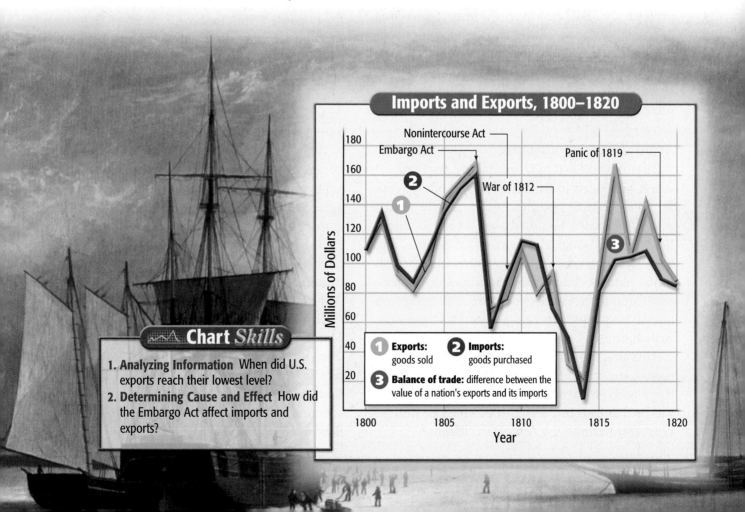

Chart Skills

1. **Analyzing Information** When did U.S. exports reach their lowest level?
2. **Determining Cause and Effect** How did the Embargo Act affect imports and exports?

Imports and Exports, 1800–1820

Millions of Dollars

Noninterourse Act
Embargo Act
War of 1812
Panic of 1819

❶ **Exports:** goods sold ❷ **Imports:** goods purchased ❸ **Balance of trade:** difference between the value of a nation's exports and its imports

Year

Freedom of the Seas

Riding the wave of four successful years as president, Jefferson won reelection easily in 1804. Jefferson received 162 electoral votes to only 14 for his Federalist opponent, Charles Pinckney. His second term began with the nation at peace. Across the sea, however, Great Britain and France were already involved in a war that threatened to interfere with American trade.

The thriving foreign trade of the United States depended on being able to sail the seas freely. The nation had resolved the threat from the Barbary pirates. Now it was challenged at sea by the two most powerful nations in Europe.

Neutral Rights Violated

When Britain and France went to war in 1803, America enjoyed a prosperous commerce with both countries. As long as the United States remained neutral, shippers could continue doing business. A nation not involved in a conflict had neutral rights—the right to sail the seas and not take sides.

For two years American shipping continued to prosper. By 1805, however, the warring nations had lost patience with American "neutrality." Britain blockaded the French coast and threatened to search all ships trading with France. France later announced that it would search and seize ships caught trading with Britain.

American Sailors Kidnapped

The British needed sailors for their naval war. Conditions in the British Royal Navy were terrible. British sailors were poorly paid, poorly fed, and badly treated. Many of them deserted. Desperately in need of sailors, the British often used force to get them. British naval patrols claimed the right to stop American ships at sea and search for any sailors on board suspected of being deserters from the British navy.

This practice of forcing people to serve in the navy was called impressment. While some of those taken were deserters from the British navy, the British also impressed thousands of native-born and naturalized American citizens.

Attack on the *Chesapeake*

Quite often the British would lie in wait for American ships outside an American harbor. This happened in June 1807 off the coast of **Virginia.** A British warship, the *Leopard,* intercepted the American vessel *Chesapeake* and demanded to search the ship for British deserters. When the *Chesapeake*'s captain refused, the British opened fire, killing 3, wounding 18, and crippling the American ship.

As news of the attack spread, Americans reacted with an anti-British fury not seen since the Revolutionary War. Secretary of State **James Madison** called the attack an outrage. Many demanded war against Britain. Although President Jefferson did not intend to let Great Britain's actions go unanswered, he sought a course of action other than war.

A Disastrous Trade Ban

Britain's practice of impressment and its violation of America's neutral rights had led Jefferson to ban some trade with Britain. The attack on the *Chesapeake* triggered even stronger measures. In December 1807, the Republican Congress passed the **Embargo Act.** An embargo prohibits trade with another country. Although Great Britain was the target of this act, the embargo banned imports from and exports to *all* foreign countries. Jefferson wanted to prevent Americans from using other countries as go-betweens in the forbidden trade.

With the embargo, Jefferson and Madison hoped to hurt Britain but avoid war. They believed the British depended on American agricultural products. As it turned out, the embargo of 1807 was a disaster. The measure wiped out all American commerce with other nations. Worse, it proved ineffective against Britain. The British simply traded with Latin America for its agricultural goods.

The embargo clearly had not worked. On March 1, 1809, Congress repealed it. In its place Congress enacted the much weaker **Nonintercourse Act.** The new act prohibited trade only with Britain and France and their colonial possessions. It was no more popular or successful than the Embargo Act.

Jefferson Leaves Office

Following Washington's precedent, Jefferson made it clear in mid-1808 that he would not be a candidate for a third term. With Jefferson's approval the Republicans chose James Madison as their candidate for president. The Federalists nominated Charles Pinckney and hoped that anger over the embargo would help their party. Pinckney carried most of New England, but the Federalist ticket collected little support from the other regions. Madison won with 122 electoral votes to Pinckney's 47 votes.

✓ **Reading Check** **Evaluating** How effective was the Embargo Act?

War Fever

James Madison did not take office as president under the most favorable conditions. At home and abroad, the nation was mired in the embargo crisis. Meanwhile Britain continued to claim the right to halt American ships, and cries for war with Britain grew louder.

Closer to War

In 1810 Congress passed a law permitting direct trade with either France or Britain, depending on which country first lifted its trade restrictions against America. Napoleon seized the opportunity and promised to end France's trade restrictions.

Unfortunately for Madison, Napoleon had tricked the American administration. The French continued to seize American ships, selling them and pocketing the proceeds. Americans were deeply divided. To some it seemed as if the nation was on the verge of war—but it was hard to decide if the enemy should be Britain or France. Madison knew that France had tricked him, but he continued to see Britain as the bigger threat to the United States.

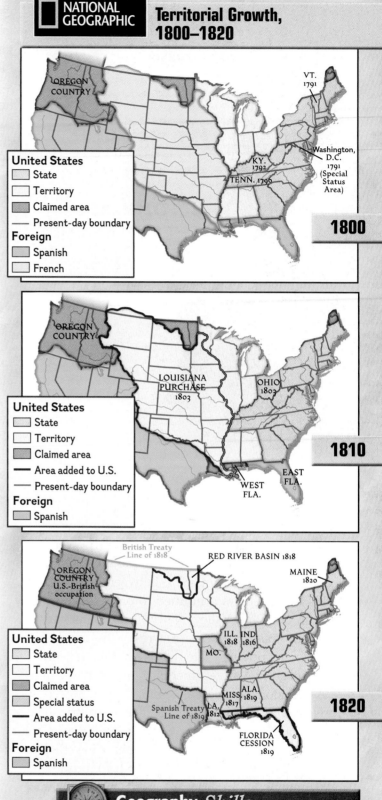

NATIONAL GEOGRAPHIC **Territorial Growth, 1800–1820**

1800

United States
- State
- Territory
- Claimed area
- Present-day boundary

Foreign
- Spanish
- French

1810

United States
- State
- Territory
- Claimed area
- Area added to U.S.
- Present-day boundary

Foreign
- Spanish

1820

United States
- State
- Territory
- Claimed area
- Special status
- Area added to U.S.
- Present-day boundary

Foreign
- Spanish

Geography *Skills*

Between 1790 and 1820, the United States doubled its size and added 10 new states.

1. **Region** When did Indiana become part of the United States?
2. **Human-Environment Interaction** Describe the changes in French territory between 1800 and 1820.

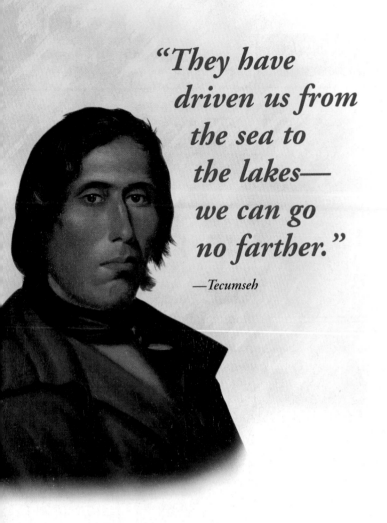

"They have driven us from the sea to the lakes— we can go no farther."

—*Tecumseh*

Frontier Conflicts

While Madison was trying to decide how to resolve the difficulties with European powers, news arrived about problems in the West. **Ohio** had become a state in 1803. Between 1801 and 1810, white settlers continued to press for more land in the Ohio Valley. Native Americans had given up many millions of acres. Now the settlers were moving onto lands that had been guaranteed to Native Americans by treaty.

As tensions increased, some Native Americans began renewing their contacts with British agents and fur traders in Canada. Others pursued a new strategy. A powerful Shawnee chief named **Tecumseh** (tuh•KUHM•suh) built a confederacy among Native American nations in the Northwest. Tecumseh believed that a strong alliance—with the backing of the British in Canada—could put a halt to white movement onto Native American lands.

A commanding speaker, Tecumseh possessed great political skills. In his view, the United States

government's treaties with separate Native American nations were worthless. "The Great Spirit gave this great island to his red children," he said. No one nation had the right to give it away.

Tecumseh had a powerful ally—his brother, known as **the Prophet.** The Prophet urged Native Americans everywhere to return to the customs of their ancestors. They should, he said, give up practices learned from the white invaders—wearing western dress, using plows and firearms, and especially drinking alcohol. The Prophet attracted a huge following among Native Americans. He founded a village at a site in northern Indiana, near present-day Lafayette, where the Tippecanoe and Wabash Rivers meet. It was called Prophetstown.

A Meeting With Harrison

The American governor of the Indiana Territory, **General William Henry Harrison,** became alarmed by the growing power of the two Shawnee brothers. He feared they would form an alliance with the British.

In a letter to Tecumseh, Harrison warned that the United States had many more warriors than all the Indian nations could put together. "Do not think that the redcoats can protect you; they are not able to protect themselves." Tecumseh sent word that he would reply in person.

A few weeks later, Tecumseh came to Harrison and spoke to the white people assembled there:

❝Brothers: Since the peace was made, you have killed some of the Shawnees, Winnebagoes, Delawares, and Miamis, and you have taken our land from us; and I do not see how we can remain at peace if you continue to do so. You try to force the red people to do some injury; it is you who are pushing them on to do mischief. You try to keep the tribes apart, and make distinctions among them. You wish to prevent the Indians from uniting.❞

The Battle of Tippecanoe

In 1811 while Tecumseh was in the South trying to expand his confederacy, Harrison decided to attack Prophetstown on the

Tippecanoe River. After more than two hours of battle, the Prophet's forces fled the area in defeat. The **Battle of Tippecanoe** was proclaimed a glorious victory for the Americans. Harrison acquired the nickname "Tippecanoe" and used it as a patriotic rallying cry when he ran for president in 1840.

Harrison's victory at the Battle of Tippecanoe, however, resulted in something the American people had hoped to prevent. Tecumseh now joined forces with the British troops. White settlers in the region claimed that the British had supplied Tecumseh's confederacy with guns. As a result, the rallying cry of the settlers became "On to Canada!"

War Hawks

Back in the nation's capital, President Madison faced demands for a more aggressive policy toward the British. The most insistent voices came from a group of young Republicans elected to Congress in 1810. Known as the War Hawks, they came from the South and the West. The War Hawks pressured the president to declare war against Britain.

While the War Hawks wanted to avenge British actions against Americans, they were also eager to expand the nation's power. Their nationalism—or loyalty to their country—appealed to a renewed sense of American patriotism. The leading War Hawks were **Henry**

TECHNOLOGY & History

The Conestoga Wagon

By the mid-1700s, sturdy Conestoga wagons transported settlers and their freight over the Appalachian Mountains. These wagons were first built in the Conestoga Creek region of Lancaster, Pennsylvania. As people pushed even farther westward, the Conestoga was seen rolling across the plains toward Oregon and California. *Why did Conestoga wagons have a high front and back?*

1 Six to eight draft horses or a dozen oxen pull the wagon. The driver rides or walks beside the animals.

2 The boat-shaped wagon's high front and back keep goods from falling out on steep mountain trails.

3 A **toolbox** attached to the side of the wagon holds spare parts for needed repairs.

4 A white canvas cloth stretches over the hoops, or **wagon bows**. This cover protects passengers and cargo from heat, rain, and snow.

5 Broad **wheels** help keep the heavy wagon from being mired in the mud.

The average Conestoga wagon was 21 feet long, 11 feet high, and 4 feet in width and depth. It could carry up to 12,000 pounds of cargo.

Clay from Kentucky and **John Calhoun** from South Carolina, both in their 30s. Hunger for land heightened war fever. Westerners wanted to move north into the fertile forests of southern Canada. A war with Britain might make Canadian land available. Southerners wanted Spanish Florida.

The War Hawks urged major military spending. Through their efforts Congress quadrupled the army's size. The Federalists in the Northeast, however, remained strongly opposed to the war.

Declaring War

By the spring of 1812, Madison concluded that war with Britain was inevitable. In a message to Congress on June 1, he cited "the spectacle of injuries and indignities which have been heaped on our country" and asked for a declaration of war.

In the meantime the British had decided to end their policy of search and seizure of American ships. Unfortunately, because of the amount of time it took for news to travel across the Atlantic, this change in policy was not known in Washington. Word of the breakthrough arrived too late. Once set in motion, the war machine could not be stopped.

Reading Check **Explaining** Why did the War Hawks call for war with Britain?

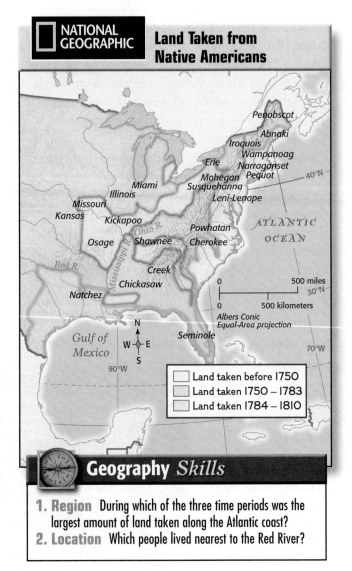

NATIONAL GEOGRAPHIC   Land Taken from Native Americans

Land taken before 1750
Land taken 1750 – 1783
Land taken 1784 – 1810

Geography *Skills*

1. **Region** During which of the three time periods was the largest amount of land taken along the Atlantic coast?
2. **Location** Which people lived nearest to the Red River?

SECTION 3 ASSESSMENT

Checking for Understanding

1. **Key Terms** Write two paragraphs in which you use all of the following terms: tribute, neutral rights, impressment, embargo, War Hawks, nationalism.
2. **Reviewing Facts** Describe the negotiations that ended the war between the United States and Tripoli.

Reviewing Themes

3. **Global Connections** How did the conflict in Europe help the American shipping industry prosper?

Critical Thinking

4. **Determining Cause and Effect** How did frontier battles with Native Americans intensify Americans' anti-British feelings?
5. **Sequencing Information** Re-create the diagram below and list key events in the nation's effort to remain neutral in the war between France and Britain.

```
         June          Dec.
1805     1807          1807          1809
  |        |             |             |
```

Analyzing Visuals

6. **Geography Skills** Examine the maps that appear on page 291. When did Tennessee gain statehood? Which of the maps shows the territory gained from the Louisiana Purchase? In what year was Florida ceded to the United States?

Interdisciplinary Activity

Art Choose a side in the argument about war with Great Britain. Draw a political cartoon supporting your point of view.

America's LITERATURE

Ignatia Broker (1919–1987)

Ignatia Broker was born on the White Earth Ojibway Reservation in Minnesota. She grew up hearing the stories of her people. She decided that one day she would tell others about Ojibway traditions. Through her writing, Broker passed on many Ojibway tales about "the purity of man and nature and keeping them in balance."

READ TO DISCOVER

Night Flying Woman tells the story of Oona, Ignatia Broker's great-great-grandmother. Oona was still a child when the Ojibway were forced to leave their land and find a new home. As you read, look for the ways in which Oona overcomes her fear of her latest home. What gives the Ojibway people faith that they will continue as a people?

READER'S DICTIONARY

fretful: worrisome, anxious, uneasy

A-wa-sa-si: a storyteller traveling with Oona's people

Ojibway: a Native American nation

Night Flying Woman

The next morning, very early, Grandfather, Oldest Uncle, and Father walked into the thick forest. Oona did not see them leave, for she was sleeping soundly. When Mother told her that they were gone, Oona looked at the forest fearfully. It seemed very unfriendly. She thought, "It has swallowed up my grandfather and father." She became **fretful.**

Mother said, "Daughter, look at the forest again but do not look and see only the dark and shadows. Instead, look at the trees, each one, as many as you can. Then tell me what you think.". . .

As Oona looked at the trees, she heard the si-si-gwa-d—the murmuring that the trees do when they brush their branches together. It was a friendly sound, and the sun sent sparkles through the si-si-gwa-d that chased the shadows. Suddenly the forest seemed different to Oona, and she knew that Grandfather, Oldest Uncle, and Father had gone into a friendly place. . . .

A-wa-sa-si said, "The forests have never failed the **Ojibway.** . . . As long as the Ojibway are beneath, the trees will murmur with contentment. When the Ojibway and the Animal Brothers are gone, the forest will weep and this will be reflected in the sound of the si-si-gwa-d. . . . In each generation of

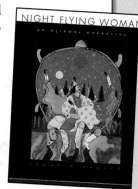

Ojibway there will be a person who will hear the si-si-gwa-d, who will listen and remember and pass it on to the children. Remembering our past and acting accordingly will ensure that we, the Ojibway, will always people the earth. The trees have patience and so they have stood and have seen many generations of Ojibway. Yet will there be more, and yet will they see more."

From *Night Flying Woman: An Ojibway Narrative* by Ignatia Broker. Copyright © 1983 by the Minnesota Historical Society. Reprinted by permission.

ANALYZING LITERATURE

1. **Recall and Interpret** What sound did Oona hear in the forest? How did the sound affect Oona's feelings about the forest?
2. **Evaluate and Connect** What does Ignatia Broker in *Night Flying Woman* say about the importance of the past? Explain your answer.

Interdisciplinary Activity

Art Create a painting or drawing that shows the forest as Oona saw it. Use symbols to hint at the coming of the Europeans.

The War of 1812

Guide to Reading

Main Idea
Beginning in 1812 the United States was at war with Britain. Fighting took place in the United States, in Canada, and at sea.

Key Terms
frigate, privateer

Reading Strategy
Taking Notes As you read the section, re-create the diagram below and in the boxes describe each battle's outcome.

Battle	Outcome
Lake Erie	
Washington, D.C.	
New Orleans	

Read to Learn
- how the British seized and set fire to Washington, D.C.
- why Andrew Jackson fought a battle after the war was over.

Section Theme
Government and Democracy The end of the War of 1812 produced a new spirit of nationalism.

Preview of Events

♦1812 ♦1813 ♦1814 ♦1815

June 1812
United States declares war on Britain

September 1813
Perry defeats the British navy on Lake Erie

August 1814
The British burn Washington, D.C.

January 1815
American forces win the Battle of New Orleans

Madison peace medal

AN American Story

While President Madison awarded peace medals to Native Americans who supported the United States against the British, Congressional War Hawks could be heard singing:

> Ye Parliaments of England,
> Ye lords and commons, too,
> Consider well what you're about,
> And what you're goin' to do;

> You're now at war with Yankees,
> And I'm sure you'll rue the day
> Ye roused the sons of liberty,
> In North Americay.

War Begins

Despite their swaggering songs, the War Hawks did not achieve the quick victory they boldly predicted. The Americans committed a series of blunders that showed how unprepared they were for war. The regular army now consisted of fewer than 7,000 troops. The states had between 50,000 and 100,000 militia, but the units were poorly trained, and many states opposed "Mr. Madison's war." The military commanders, veterans of the American Revolution, were too old for warfare, and the government in Washington provided no leadership. The Americans also underestimated the strength of the British and their Native American allies.

The war started in July 1812, when **General William Hull** led the American army from **Detroit** into Canada. Hull was met by Tecumseh and his warriors. Fearing a massacre by the Native Americans, Hull surrendered Detroit to a small British force in August. Another attempt by General William Henry Harrison was unsuccessful as well. Harrison decided that the Americans could make no headway in Canada as long as the British controlled Lake Erie.

Naval Battles

Oliver Hazard Perry, commander of the **Lake Erie** naval forces, had his orders. He was to assemble a fleet and seize the lake from the British. From his headquarters in Put-in-Bay, Ohio, Perry could watch the movements of the enemy ships. The showdown came on September 10, 1813, when the British ships sailed out to face the Americans. In the bloody battle that followed, Perry and his ships defeated the British naval force. After the battle, Perry sent General William Henry Harrison the message, "We have met the enemy and they are ours."

With Lake Erie in American hands, the British and their Native American allies tried to pull back from the Detroit area. Harrison and his troops cut them off. In the fierce **Battle of the Thames** on October 5, the great leader Tecumseh was killed.

The Americans also attacked the town of York (present-day Toronto, Canada), burning the parliament buildings. Canada remained unconquered, but by the end of 1813 the Americans had won some victories on land and at sea.

To lower the national debt, the Republicans had reduced the size of the navy. However, the navy still boasted three of the fastest frigates, or warships, afloat. Americans exulted when the *Constitution,* one of these frigates, destroyed two British vessels—the *Guerrière* in August 1812 and the *Java* four months later. After seeing a shot bounce off the *Constitution*'s hull during battle, a sailor nicknamed the ship "Old Ironsides."

American privateers, armed private ships, also staged spectacular attacks on British ships and captured numerous vessels. These victories were more important for morale than for their strategic value.

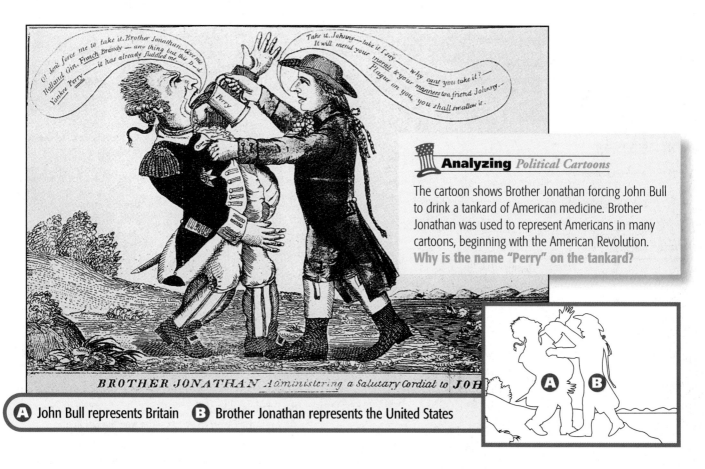

BROTHER JONATHAN Administering a Salutary Cordial to JOH...

Analyzing *Political Cartoons*

The cartoon shows Brother Jonathan forcing John Bull to drink a tankard of American medicine. Brother Jonathan was used to represent Americans in many cartoons, beginning with the American Revolution. **Why is the name "Perry" on the tankard?**

Ⓐ John Bull represents Britain   Ⓑ Brother Jonathan represents the United States

Setbacks for Native Americans

With the death of Tecumseh in 1813, hopes for a Native American confederation died. In his travels two years before his death, Tecumseh had discussed plans for a confederation with the Creeks in the Mississippi Territory.

In March 1814, a lanky Tennessee planter named **Andrew Jackson** attacked the Creeks. Jackson's forces slaughtered more than 550 of the Creek people. Known as the **Battle of Horseshoe Bend,** the defeat broke the Creeks' resistance and forced them to give up most of their lands to the United States.

☑ **Reading Check** **Evaluating** Do you think the United States was prepared to wage war? Explain.

The British Offensive

British fortunes improved in the spring of 1814. They had been fighting a war with Napoleon and had won. Now they could send more forces to America.

Attack on Washington, D.C.

In August 1814, the British sailed into Chesapeake Bay. Their destination was Washington, D.C. On the outskirts of Washington, D.C., the British troops quickly overpowered the American militia and then marched into the city. "They proceeded, without a moment's delay, to burn and destroy everything in the most distant degree connected with government," reported a British officer.

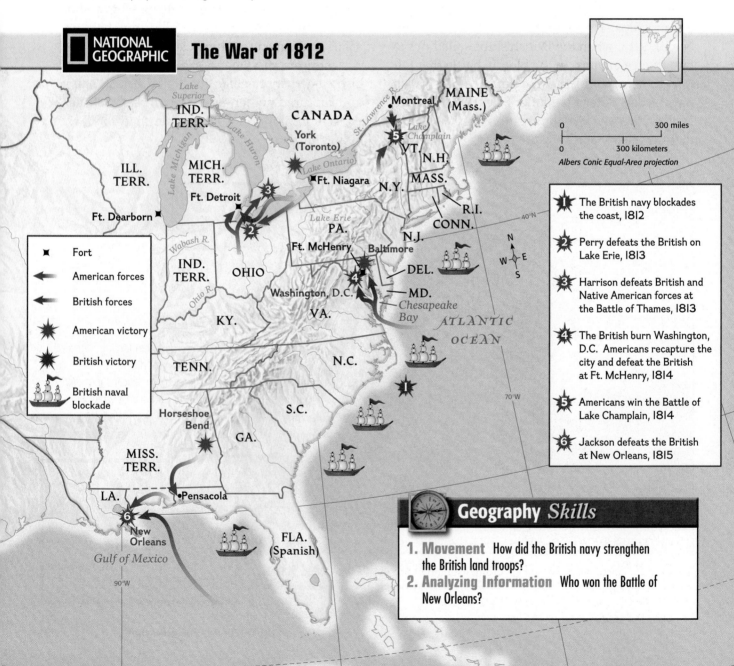

NATIONAL GEOGRAPHIC **The War of 1812**

Map legend:
- ✶ Fort
- American forces
- British forces
- ✶ American victory
- ✶ British victory
- British naval blockade

1. The British navy blockades the coast, 1812
2. Perry defeats the British on Lake Erie, 1813
3. Harrison defeats British and Native American forces at the Battle of Thames, 1813
4. The British burn Washington, D.C. Americans recapture the city and defeat the British at Ft. McHenry, 1814
5. Americans win the Battle of Lake Champlain, 1814
6. Jackson defeats the British at New Orleans, 1815

Geography *Skills*

1. **Movement** How did the British navy strengthen the British land troops?
2. **Analyzing Information** Who won the Battle of New Orleans?

People In History

Dolley Madison 1768–1849

Born in North Carolina, Dolley Payne grew up in Virginia until, at age 15, her family moved to Philadelphia. There she married John Todd, Jr. As Dolley Todd, she gave birth to two children, but lost her husband and one child in 1793 during a yellow fever epidemic.

The following year she married James Madison. While her husband was secretary of state, Dolley Madison served as unofficial first lady for the widower president, Thomas Jefferson. She became the nation's official first lady when James Madison was elected president in 1808. During the War of 1812

she showed remarkable bravery. In 1814, as the British approached the capital, she refused to leave the executive mansion until she had packed up many valuable government documents, a painting of George Washington, and other priceless valuables.

The Capitol and the president's mansion were among the buildings burned. Watching from outside the city, President Madison and his cabinet saw the night sky turn orange. Fortunately a violent thunderstorm put out the fires before they could do more damage. August 24, 1814, was a low point for the Americans.

Baltimore Holds Firm

Much to everyone's surprise, the British did not try to hold Washington. They left the city and sailed north to Baltimore. Baltimore, however, was ready and waiting—with barricaded roads, a blocked harbor, and some 13,000 militiamen. The British attacked in mid-September. They were kept from entering the town by a determined defense and ferocious bombardment from Fort McHenry in the harbor.

During the night of September 13–14, a young attorney named **Francis Scott Key** watched as the bombs burst over Fort McHenry. Finally "by the dawn's early light," Key was able to see that the American flag still flew over the fort. Deeply moved by patriotic feeling, Key wrote a poem called "The Star-Spangled Banner." In 1931, Congress designated "The Star-Spangled Banner" as the National Anthem. 📖 *(See page 987 of the Appendix for an excerpt from "The Star-Spangled Banner.")*

Defeat at Plattsburgh

Meanwhile, in the north, General Sir George Prevost led more than 10,000 British troops into New York State from Canada. The first British goal was to capture Plattsburgh, a key city on the shore of Lake Champlain. The invasion was stopped when an American naval force on Lake Champlain defeated the British fleet on the lake in September 1814. Knowing the American ships could use their control of the lake to bombard them and land troops behind them, the British retreated to Canada.

After the Battle of Lake Champlain, the British decided the war in North America was too costly and unnecessary. Napoleon had been defeated in Europe. To keep fighting the United States would gain little and was not worth the effort.

The War Ends

American and British representatives signed a peace agreement in December 1814 in Ghent, Belgium. The **Treaty of Ghent** did not change any existing borders. Nothing was mentioned about the impressment of sailors, but, with Napoleon's defeat, neutral rights had become a dead issue.

Before word of the treaty had reached the United States, one final—and ferocious—battle occurred at New Orleans. In December 1814, British army troops moved toward New Orleans. Awaiting them behind earthen fortifications was an American army led by Andrew Jackson.

On January 8, 1815, the British troops advanced. The redcoats were no match for Jackson's soldiers, who shot from behind bales of cotton. In a short but gruesome battle, hundreds of British soldiers were killed. At the **Battle of New Orleans,** Americans achieved a decisive victory. Andrew Jackson became a hero, and his fame helped him win the presidency in 1828.

American Nationalism

New England Federalists had opposed "Mr. Madison's war" from the start. In December 1814, unhappy New England Federalists gathered in Connecticut at the **Hartford Convention.** A few favored secession. Most wanted to remain within the Union, however. To protect their interests, they drew up a list of proposed amendments to the Constitution.

After the convention broke up, word came of Jackson's spectacular victory at New Orleans, followed by news of the peace treaty. In this moment of triumph, the Federalist grievances seemed unpatriotic. The party lost respect in the eyes of the public. Most Americans felt proud and self-confident at the end of the War of 1812.

America's Flags

The First Star-Spangled Banner, 1779–1818 The Stars and Stripes flag gained two more stars and two more stripes in 1795, after Kentucky and Vermont joined the Union.

Congress realized that the flag would become too large if a stripe were added for every new state. It decided in 1818 to keep the stripes at 13—for the thirteen original colonies—and to add a star for each new state.

The young nation had gained new respect from other nations in the world. Americans felt a new sense of patriotism and a strong national identity.

Although the Federalist Party weakened, its philosophy of strong national government was carried on by the War Hawks who were part of the Republican Party. They favored trade, western expansion, the energetic development of the economy, and a strong army and navy.

Reading Check **Analyzing** Did the Treaty of Ghent resolve any major issues? Explain.

SECTION 4 ASSESSMENT

Checking for Understanding

1. **Key Terms** Write a short paragraph in which you use the terms frigate and privateer.
2. **Reviewing Facts** Who won the Battle of Lake Champlain? Why was it an important victory?

Reviewing Themes

3. **Government and Democracy** Why did the Federalist Party lose support after the War of 1812?

Critical Thinking

4. **Drawing Conclusions** Why did people from the North, South, and the West feel differently about going to war with Britain?
5. **Determining Cause and Effect** Recreate the diagram below. In the ovals, list four effects that the War of 1812 had on the United States.

Effects of the War of 1812

Analyzing Visuals

6. **Geography Skills** Study the map on page 298. On what lake did Perry defeat the British? Which battle— Lake Champlain or Thames—took place later in time?

Interdisciplinary Activity

Music Imagine if Francis Scott Key had been at the Battle of New Orleans instead of in Baltimore. Rewrite the first verse of "The Star-Spangled Banner" based on what occurred in that battle.

Writing a Journal

Why Learn This Skill?

Journal writing is personal writing with a casual style. What you write *on* is not as important as what you write *about*—your experiences, interests, and even your feelings.

Learning the Skill

A journal is a written account that records what you have learned or experienced. In the journal you can express your feelings about a subject, summarize key topics, describe difficulties or successes in solving particular problems, and draw maps or other visuals. To help you get started writing in your journal, follow these steps:

- As you read your textbook, jot down notes or questions about a specific topic or event. Then look for details and answers about it as you continue reading.
- Describe your feelings as you read a selection or look at a photograph. Are you angry, happy, frustrated, sad? Explain why.
- Ask yourself if drawing a map or flowchart would help you understand an event better. If so, draw in your journal.

Practicing the Skill

The following excerpt describes the burning of Washington, D.C., during the War of 1812. Read the excerpt, then use the following questions to help you write entries in your own journal.

66 [T]his was a night of dismay to the inhabitants of Washington. They were taken completely by surprise. . . . The first impulse of course tempted them to fly. . . . [T]he streets were . . . crowded with soldiers and senators, men, women, and children, horses, carriages, and carts loaded with household furniture, all hastening towards a wooden bridge which crosses the Potomac. The confusion . . . was terrible, and the crowd upon the bridge was such to endanger its giving way. 99

1 What is particularly interesting about this description?

2 What are your feelings as you read the excerpt?

3 Draw a map or other visual to help you understand the situation described here.

William Clark's journal

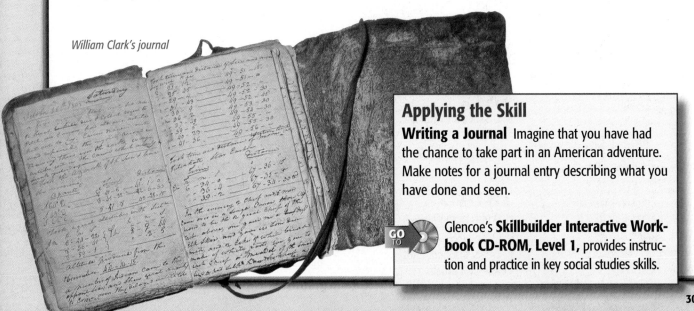

Applying the Skill

Writing a Journal Imagine that you have had the chance to take part in an American adventure. Make notes for a journal entry describing what you have done and seen.

GO TO Glencoe's **Skillbuilder Interactive Workbook CD-ROM, Level 1,** provides instruction and practice in key social studies skills.

Chapter Summary

The Jefferson Era

1801
- Thomas Jefferson inaugurated as third president

1803
- *Marbury* v. *Madison* sets precedent for judicial review
- Louisiana Territory purchased from France
- Ohio becomes a state

1804
- Twelfth Amendment ratified
- Lewis and Clark expedition sets off from St. Louis
- Thomas Jefferson wins reelection

1807
- American ship *Chesapeake* attacked by British navy
- Congress passes the Embargo Act

1809
- James Madison becomes president

1811
- Harrison defeats the Prophet at Tippecanoe

1812
- U.S. declares war on Britain
- British navy blockades coast

1813
- Perry defeats British navy on Lake Erie
- Tecumseh killed at the Battle of the Thames

1814
- British burn Washington, D.C.
- Treaty of Ghent ends war with Britain

302

Reviewing Key Terms

On a sheet of paper, use all of the following terms to write several short, historically accurate paragraphs related to the information in the chapter. Use standard grammar and punctuation.

1. laissez-faire
2. impressment
3. embargo
4. nationalism
5. judicial review
6. secede

Reviewing Key Facts

7. What did Congress do to prevent a deadlock in presidential elections?
8. How did events in Santo Domingo (Haiti) influence American expansion?
9. How did the Embargo Act of 1807 hurt the United States?
10. Who were the War Hawks?
11. What effect did Tecumseh's death have on Native Americans?

Critical Thinking

12. **Analyzing Themes: Government and Democracy** Summarize the importance of the *Marbury* v. *Madison* decision.
13. **Analyzing Information** What were the boundaries of the Louisiana Territory?
14. **Comparing** Re-create the diagram below. In the boxes, describe the differences between the War Hawks and Federalists in their views of the War of 1812.

War of 1812	
View of War Hawks	View of Federalists

Geography and History Activity

Study the maps of territorial growth on page 291 and answer the following questions.

15. **Location** In what year did Mississippi become a state?
16. **Region** What three Southern states were admitted to the nation between 1810 and 1820?

Practicing Skills

17. Writing a Journal By the late 1700s, more than 55,000 Americans had crossed the mountains into Kentucky and Tennessee. Write entries for a journal for such a trip. Explain why you are enduring such hardships to move to new land.

Citizenship Cooperative Activity

18. Analyzing Current Events With a partner, choose a recent event for which you will be able to locate primary and secondary sources of information. Compare the primary source with one secondary source. Prepare a report for the class in which you describe the event and compare the information in the primary and secondary sources.

Economics Activity

19. Work in small groups to prepare an international trade map. Your map should show United States imports during the early 1800s from each of the major continents. What major ports were merchants sailing to during this time? What products were they bringing back to the United States? Your map should include the names of important ports, the countries where they were located, symbols to represent the different products, a map key to explain the symbols, and other information such as distances or major shipping routes.

 Technology Activity

20. Using a Spreadsheet Search the library for information about the modern city of New Orleans. Make a database using the spreadsheet. Beginning in column B, label four columns as follows: 1) Street names; 2) Buildings; 3) Foods; 4) Sites. Beginning in row two, label rows as follows: 1) Spanish; 2) French. Fill in the spreadsheet with the information you find.

 Alternative Assessment

21. Portfolio Writing Activity Review the chapter for information about the expedition of Lewis and Clark. Imagine that you had the chance to accompany them on their adventure. Write a letter home describing what you have done and seen. Be sure to include how you were affected by the land and the people you encountered.

Self-Check Quiz
Visit taj.glencoe.com and click on **Chapter 9—Self-Check Quizzes** to prepare for the chapter test.

 Standardized Test Practice

Use the map below to choose the *best* answer to the question.

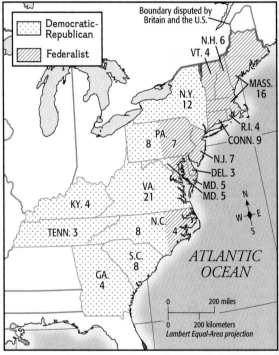

Which of the following statements about the election of 1800 is true?

F Federalists won Georgia's electoral votes.

G New Hampshire supported the Democratic-Republican ticket.

H Connecticut had seven electoral votes.

J Pennsylvania was one of the states that split its votes.

Test-Taking Tip:

Double-check all answer choices to make sure that you have chosen the best answer. Make sure that your answer choice is supported by information on the map. Check each choice against the map. Only one is correct.

Growth and Expansion

1790–1825

Why It Matters

During the early 1800s, manufacturing took on a stronger role in the American economy. During the same period, people moved westward across the continent in larger and larger numbers. In 1823 the United States proclaimed its dominant role in the Americas with the Monroe Doctrine.

The Impact Today

These developments were important factors in shaping the nation. Today the United States is one of the leading economic and military powers in the world.

The American Journey Video *The chapter 10 video, "The One-Room Schoolhouse," depicts a typical school day in the nineteenth century.*

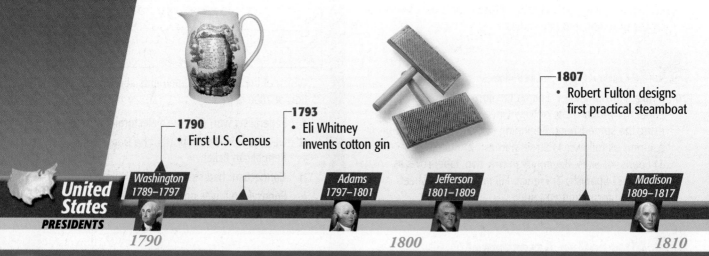

1807
• Robert Fulton designs first practical steamboat

1793
• Eli Whitney invents cotton gin

1790
• First U.S. Census

United States PRESIDENTS	Washington 1789–1797	Adams 1797–1801	Jefferson 1801–1809	Madison 1809–1817

1790   1800   1810

World

1804
• Haiti claims independence from France

1792
• Russia invades Poland

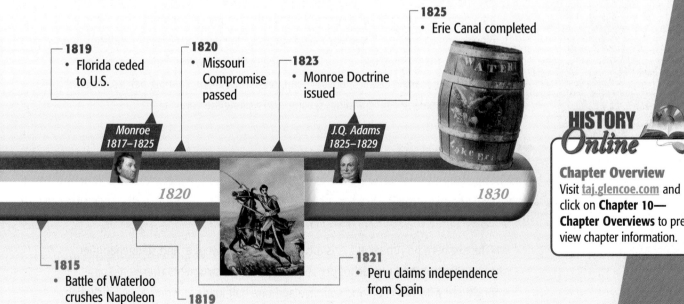

Valley of the Yosemite by Albert Bierstadt Bierstadt's panoramic scenes of the American West capture the vastness of the landscape.

1825
• Erie Canal completed

1819
• Florida ceded to U.S.

1820
• Missouri Compromise passed

1823
• Monroe Doctrine issued

Monroe 1817–1825

J.Q. Adams 1825–1829

1820

1830

1815
• Battle of Waterloo crushes Napoleon

1819
• Bolívar defeats Spanish forces at Boyacá

1821
• Peru claims independence from Spain

HISTORY
Online

Chapter Overview
Visit taj.glencoe.com and click on **Chapter 10— Chapter Overviews** to preview chapter information.

Economic Growth

Main Idea
The rise of industry and trade led to the growth of cities.

Key Terms
Industrial Revolution, capitalism, capital, free enterprise, technology, cotton gin, patent, factory system, interchangeable parts

Reading Strategy
Organizing Information As you read the section, re-create the diagram below and describe in the ovals changes brought about by the Industrial Revolution.

Industrial Revolution

Read to Learn
- how the Industrial Revolution began in the United States.
- how the United States changed as it became more economically independent.

Section Theme
Economic Factors The Industrial Revolution changed the way goods were made.

Preview of Events

♦1790   ♦1800   ♦1810   ♦1820

1793
Eli Whitney invents the cotton gin

1807
Congress passes Embargo Act

1814
Francis Lowell opens textile plant in Massachusetts

1816
Second National Bank is chartered

American blacksmith, early 1800s woodcut

★★★★★ AN
American Story

Both men and women in the early 1800s valued hard work. An English journalist described the farmers of Long Island in 1818: "Every man can use an axe, a saw, and a hammer. Scarcely one who cannot do any job at rough carpentering, and mend a plough and wagon. . . . " Another European noted the daily activities of American women in 1823: "They take care of everything pertaining to the domestic economy, for example, making candles, boiling soap, preparing starch, canning berries, fruit and cucumbers, baking, and spinning, sewing, and milking the cows."

The Growth of Industry

During the colonial era, workers were in short supply. Americans learned to develop tools that made work easier and more efficient. American methods and inventions won the admiration of Europeans. One observer exclaimed:

❝The axe here [in America] . . . is a combination axe, wedge, and sledgehammer; what an accomplished woodchopper can do with this instrument! There are some among them who can chop and split five and one-half loads of wood a day, including stacking them.❞

People working in their homes or in workshops made cloth and most other goods. Using hand tools, they produced furniture, farm equipment, household items, and clothing.

In the mid-1700s, however, the way goods were made began to change. These changes appeared first in Great Britain. British inventors created machinery to perform some of the work involved in cloth making, such as spinning. The machines ran on waterpower, so British cloth makers built mills along rivers and installed the machines in these mills. People left their homes and farms to work in the mills and earn wages. The changes this system brought about were so great that this historic development is known as the **Industrial Revolution.**

The Industrial Revolution in New England

The Industrial Revolution began to take root in the United States around 1800, appearing first in New England—Massachusetts, Rhode Island, Connecticut, Vermont, and New Hampshire. New England's soil was poor, and farming was difficult. As a result, people were willing to leave their farms to find work elsewhere. Also, New England had many rushing rivers and streams. These provided the waterpower necessary to run the machinery in the new factories.

New England's geographic location also proved to be an advantage. It was close to other resources, including coal and iron from nearby Pennsylvania. New England also had many ports. Through these ports passed the cotton

TECHNOLOGY & History

Textile Mill

The Lowell factory system was designed to bring work and workers together. A typical Lowell textile mill in 1830 housed 4,500 spindles, 120 power looms, and more than 200 employees under one roof. *What type of energy powered the mills?*

Gears

1. The first steps in textile production **clean** the raw cotton and turn loose cotton into crude yarn.

2. The **spinning** process transforms the yarn into thread.

3. At the **weaving** stage, power **looms** interlace the threads into coarse cloth or fabric.

4. Fabric is measured and batched for **dyeing**. Vegetable dyes were the earliest known dyes.

3 weaving looms

4 dyeing

2 spinning

1 clean

shipped from Southern states to New England factories, as well as the finished cloth bound for markets throughout the nation.

Also necessary to strong industrial growth is an economic system that allows competition to flourish with a minimum of government interference. The economic system of the United States is called capitalism. Under capitalism, individuals put their capital, or money, into a business in hopes of making a profit.

Free enterprise is another term used to describe the American economy. In a system of free enterprise, people are free to buy, sell, and produce whatever they want. They can also work wherever they wish. The major elements of free enterprise are competition, profit, private property and economic freedom. Business owners have the freedom to produce the products that they think will be the most profitable. Buyers also compete to find the best products at the lowest prices.

New Technology

Workers, waterpower, location, and capital all played roles in New England's Industrial Revolution. Yet without the invention of new machines and technology—scientific discoveries that simplify work—the Industrial Revolution could not have taken place.

Inventions such as the spinning jenny and the water frame, which spun thread, and the power loom, which wove the thread into cloth, made it possible to perform many steps in making cloth by machine, saving time and money. Because these new machines ran on waterpower, most mills were built near rivers. In 1785, for the first time, a steam engine provided power for a cotton mill.

In 1793 **Eli Whitney** of Massachusetts invented the cotton gin, a simple machine that quickly and efficiently removed the seeds from the cotton fiber. The cotton gin enabled one worker to clean cotton as fast as 50 people working by hand.

In 1790 Congress passed a patent law to protect the rights of those who developed "useful and important inventions." A patent gives an inventor the sole legal right to the invention and

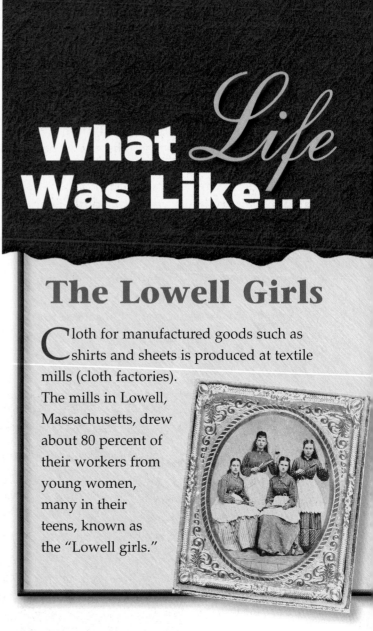

What Life Was Like...

The Lowell Girls

Cloth for manufactured goods such as shirts and sheets is produced at textile mills (cloth factories). The mills in Lowell, Massachusetts, drew about 80 percent of their workers from young women, many in their teens, known as the "Lowell girls."

its profits for a certain period of time. One of the first patents went to Jacob Perkins for a machine to make nails.

Reading Check **Analyzing** Why were the first mills in Great Britain built near rivers?

New England Factories

The British tried to keep their new industrial technology a secret. They even passed laws prohibiting their machinery as well as their skilled mechanics from leaving the country. However, a few enterprising workers managed to slip away to the United States.

In Britain **Samuel Slater** had worked in a factory that used machines invented by Richard Arkwright for spinning cotton threads. Slater

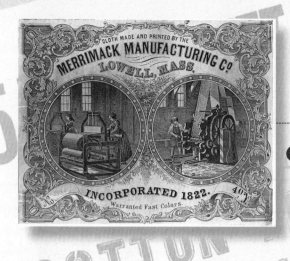
CLOTH MADE AND PRINTED BY THE
MERRIMACK MANUFACTURING CO.
LOWELL, MASS.
INCORPORATED 1822.
Warranted Fast Colors.

Working Conditions

The young women who worked in Lowell's mills endured difficult working conditions. They put in long hours—from sunrise to sunset—for low wages. The volume of the factory machinery was earsplitting and the work was monotonous. The women usually performed one task over and over again.

Magazine

The Lowell Offering was a magazine written for and about the mill girls.

On the Job

Lucy Larcom started working in the mills when she was 11 years old. She later recalled her life at Waltham:

66 We did not call ourselves ladies. We did not forget that we were working girls, wearing aprons suitable to our work, and that there was some danger of our becoming drudges. 99

memorized the design of Arkwright's machines and slipped out of Britain in 1789. Once in the United States, Slater took over the management of a cotton mill in Pawtucket, Rhode Island. There he duplicated Arkwright's machines. Using these machines the mill made cotton thread. Women working in their homes wove the thread into cloth. Slater's mill marked an important step in the Industrial Revolution in America.

In 1814 **Francis Cabot Lowell** opened a textile plant in Waltham, Massachusetts. The plan he implemented went several steps beyond Slater's mill. For the first time, all the stages of cloth making were performed under one roof. Lowell's mill launched the factory system, a system bringing manufacturing steps together in one place to increase efficiency. The factory system

was a significant development in the way goods were made—and another important part of the Industrial Revolution.

Interchangeable Parts

The inventor Eli Whitney started the use of interchangeable parts. These were identical machine parts that could be quickly put together to make a complete product. Because all the parts were alike, they could be manufactured with less-skilled labor, and they made machine repair easier. Interchangeable parts opened the way for producing many different kinds of goods on a mass scale and for reducing the price of the goods.

✓**Reading Check** **Describing** How did the factory system work?

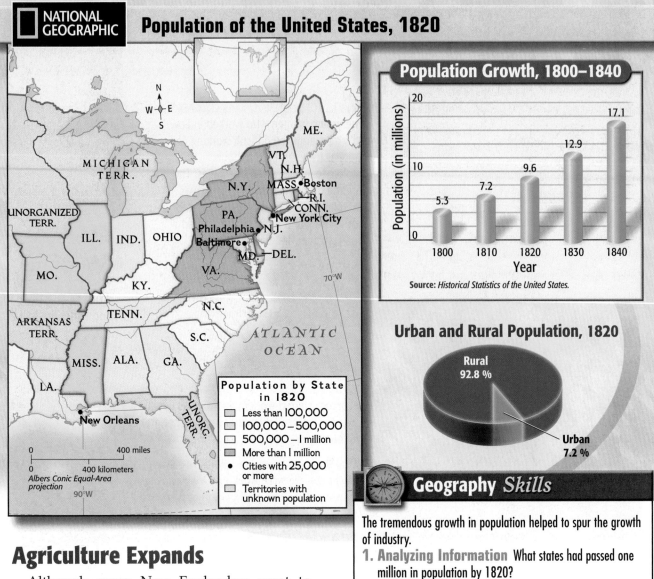

Population of the United States, 1820

Population Growth, 1800–1840

Population (in millions)

- 1800: 5.3
- 1810: 7.2
- 1820: 9.6
- 1830: 12.9
- 1840: 17.1

Year

Source: *Historical Statistics of the United States.*

Urban and Rural Population, 1820

Rural 92.8 %

Urban 7.2 %

Population by State in 1820

- ☐ Less than 100,000
- ☐ 100,000 – 500,000
- ☐ 500,000 – 1 million
- ☐ More than 1 million
- • Cities with 25,000 or more
- ☐ Territories with unknown population

0 — 400 miles
0 — 400 kilometers
Albers Conic Equal-Area projection

Geography *Skills*

The tremendous growth in population helped to spur the growth of industry.

1. **Analyzing Information** What states had passed one million in population by 1820?
2. **Comparing** Which state had the larger population—Missouri or Alabama?

Agriculture Expands

Although many New Englanders went to work in factories, most Americans still lived and worked on farms. In the 1820s more than 65 percent of Americans were farmers.

In the Northeast, farms tended to be small, and the produce was usually marketed locally. In the South, cotton production increased dramatically. The demand for cotton had grown steadily with the development of the textile industries of New England and Europe. Southern plantation owners used enslaved workers to plant, tend, and pick the cotton. The cotton gin—which made it possible to clean the cotton faster and less expensively than by hand—encouraged the planters to raise larger crops. Between 1790 and 1820, cotton production soared from 3,000 to more than 300,000 bales a year.

In the West, agriculture also expanded. Southern farmers seeking new land moved west to plant cotton. Western farmers north of the Ohio River concentrated on raising pork and cash crops such as corn and wheat.

Reading Check **Describing** How was the Northeast different from the South in what it produced?

Economic Independence

Most new industries were financed by small investors—merchants, shopkeepers, and farmers. These people invested some of their money in the hope of earning profits if the new businesses succeeded. Low taxes, few government regulations, and competition encouraged people to invest in new industries.

Large businesses called **corporations** began to develop rapidly in the 1830s, when some legal obstacles to their formation were removed. The rise of these new corporations made it easier to sell **stock**—shares of ownership in a company—to finance improvement and development.

The charter of the First Bank of the United States had expired in 1811. In 1816 Congress chartered the **Second Bank of the United States,** also chartered for 20 years. The Bank had the power to make large loans to businesses. State banks and frontier people criticized the Bank on the grounds that it was a monopoly used by the rich and powerful for their own gain. Those who believed in strict interpretation of the Constitution also criticized it because they believed Congress did not have the power to charter such a bank.

Cities Come of Age

The growth of factories and trade spurred the growth of towns and cities. The new industrial towns grew quickest. Many developed along rivers and streams to take advantage of the waterpower. Older cities like New York, Boston, and Baltimore also grew as centers of commerce and trade. In the West, towns like Pittsburgh, Cincinnati, and Louisville profited from their locations on major rivers. As farmers in the West shipped more and more of their products by water, these towns grew rapidly.

Cities and towns looked quite different from modern urban areas. Buildings were made of wood or brick. Streets and sidewalks were unpaved, and barnyard animals often roamed freely. There were no sewers to carry waste and dirty water away, so the danger of diseases such as cholera and yellow fever was very real. In 1793, for example, a yellow fever epidemic in Philadelphia killed thousands of people.

Fire posed another threat to cities. Sparks from a fireplace or chimney could easily ignite a wooden building and spread to others. Few towns or cities had organized fire companies, and fires could be disastrous.

Cities and towns of the period also had advantages, however. Some people left farming because cities and towns offered a variety of jobs and steady wages. As cities grew they added libraries, museums, and shops that were unavailable in the countryside. For many, the jobs and attractions of city life outweighed any of the dangers.

✓ **Reading Check** **Analyzing** Why did cities such as Pittsburgh and Louisville grow?

SECTION 1 ASSESSMENT

Checking for Understanding

1. **Key Terms** Use each of these terms in a sentence that will help explain its meaning: Industrial Revolution, capital, technology, cotton gin, patent, factory system, interchangeable parts.

2. **Reviewing Facts** Describe the reasons New England was ideal for the development of factories.

Reviewing Themes

3. **Economic Factors** How did the cotton gin affect cotton production?

Critical Thinking

4. **Categorizing Information** Re-create the diagram below and describe the major elements of the free enterprise system.

```
        ⬭           ⬭
         \         /
          ( Free enterprise )
          (    system      )
         /         \
        ⬭           ⬭
```

5. **Determining Cause and Effect** Was new technology necessary for the Industrial Revolution? Explain.

Analyzing Visuals

6. **Geography Skills** Study the map and the graphs on page 310. What do the cities shown on the map have in common? Which state had the larger population in 1820—Georgia or Ohio?

Interdisciplinary Activity

Expository Writing Study the map and graphs on page 310. Create a quiz for your classmates based on the information presented. Trade quizzes with a classmate and answer those questions.

TIME NOTEBOOK

What were people's lives like in the past?

What—and who—were people talking about? What did they eat? What did they do for fun? These two pages will give you some clues to everyday life in the U.S. as you step back in time with TIME Notebook.

Profile

SAGOYEWATHA *is the great Iroquois leader some call Red Jacket. Why? Because he fought with the British in the Revolutionary War. Sagoyewatha means "He Causes Them to Be Awake." Below is part of a speech Sagoyewatha delivered in 1805 to a group of religious leaders from Boston:*

"BROTHERS, OUR (*NATIVE AMERICAN*) SEATS were once large and yours (colonists) were small. You have now become a great people, and we have scarcely a place left to spread our blankets. You have got our country but are not satisfied; you want to force your religion upon us....

Brothers, continue to listen. You say there is but one way to worship and serve the Great Spirit. If there is but one religion, why do you white people differ so much about it?...

Brothers, we...also have a religion which was given to our forefathers and has been handed down to us, their children...."

Sagoyewatha

VERBATIM

WHAT PEOPLE ARE SAYING

"We are one."

"Mind your business."

FIRST OFFICIAL U.S. COIN,
sayings are on the front and back of the coin minted in 1787

"I die hard, but I am not afraid to go."

GEORGE WASHINGTON,
on his deathbed in 1799

"My mother and myself begged Mr. Carter not to sell this child out of Fredg [*plantation*], he gave us his word and honor that he would not, but as soon as we left him, he sold the child."

JAMES CARTER,
African American slave of Landon Carter, writing around 1790 about his sister, whom he never saw again

"May the Lord bless King George, convert him, and take him to heaven, as we want no more of him."

REVEREND JOHN GRUBER,
to his Baltimore congregation during the War of 1812

1790s WORD PLAY
Ahoy There!

The U.S.S. *Constitution,* the world's largest frigate, or warship, was launched in 1797 with a crew of 450 and 54 cannons. Want to join the crew? First, you must prove you can understand a sailor's vocabulary. Match each word or phrase in the first column with its original meaning.

1 Keel over

2 Try a new tack

3 Let the cat out of the bag

4 Mind your p's and q's

5 Shipshape

a. Sailors who do wrong are disciplined with a cat-o'-nine-tails whip that's kept in a red sack

b. Putting a ship in for repair

c. Bartenders keep track of what sailors drink and owe by marking numbers under "pints" and "quarts"

d. The course or direction boats take into the wind

e. Good condition

answers: 1. b; 2. d; 3. a; 4. c; 5. e

NATIVE AMERICAN LIFE
Sports Story

GEORGE CATLIN *is a white man with a strong interest in Native American life. This lawyer has made a name for himself as an artist, painting portraits of Native American leaders, families, and everyday Western life. Here he paints with words, telling us about a game (one the French call lacrosse) played by Choctaw men:*

"EACH PARTY (TEAM) HAD THEIR GOAL MADE WITH TWO UPRIGHT POSTS, about 25 feet high and six feet apart, set firm in the ground, with a pole across at the top. These goals were about 40 to 50 rods (660–825 feet) apart. At a point just halfway between was another small stake, driven down, where the ball was to be thrown up at the firing of a gun, to be struggled for by the players ... who were some 600 or 700 in numbers, and were (trying) to catch the ball in their sticks, and throw it home and between their respective stakes....For each time that the ball was passed between the stakes of either party, one was counted for their game...until the successful party arrived to 100, which was the limit of the game, and accomplished at an hour's sun."

RIGHT: George Catlin *painted this picture of a 15-year-old Native American girl. Her name, Ka-te-qua, means "female eagle."*

BELOW: *Painting by* **George Catlin** *of* **Choctaw athletes** *playing their version of lacrosse.*

NATIONAL GALLERY OF ART

NY PUBLIC LIBRARY/TIME INC. PICTURE COLLECTION

NUMBERS
U.S. AT THE TIME

30 Number of treaties that took away Native American land or moved their borders. The treaties were between the U.S. and the Creeks, Choctaws, and Chickasaws between 1789 and 1825

$158 million
The price the U.S. spent to fight the War of 1812

First Elizabeth Seton founds the Sisters of Charity, a Roman Catholic order, in 1809

First Mary Kies becomes the first woman to receive a U.S. patent in 1809 for a method of weaving straw with silk

$3,820.33 Amount paid to Paul Revere for providing the U.S.S. *Constitution* with copper parts and a ship's bell in 1797

45 feet Length of the dinosaur dug up by Lewis and Clark on their 1804 expedition

Westward Bound

Guide to Reading

Main Idea
The huge amount of territory added to the United States during the early 1800s gave the country a large store of natural resources and provided land for more settlers.

Key Terms
census, turnpike, canal, lock

Reading Strategy
Taking Notes As you read the section, re-create the diagram below and describe why each was important to the nation's growth.

	Significance
National Road	
John Fitch	
Erie Canal	

Read to Learn
• how land and water transportation improved in the early 1800s.
• how settlements in the West affected the nation's economy and politics.

Section Theme
Science and Technology Expansion of transportation systems helped settlement spread westward.

Preview of Events

♦1800	♦1810	♦1820	♦1830
1806 Congress approves funds for national road	**1807** Fulton's *Clermont* steams to Albany	**1820** U.S. population stands at 9.6 million	**1825** Erie Canal is completed

AN American Story

Pioneer homestead, Smoky Mountains

During the 1800s, settlers poured into the frontier west of the Appalachians. The typical frontier family moved from place to place as the line of settlement pushed ever westward. Their home often consisted of a three-sided shack or a log cabin with a dirt floor and no windows or door. A pile of leaves in the loft of the cabin often served as a bed. Loneliness, poverty, and an almost primitive lifestyle were daily companions to many frontier people.

Moving West

The first census—the official count of a population—of the United States in 1790 revealed a population of nearly four million. Most of the Americans counted lived east of the Appalachian Mountains and within a few hundred miles of the Atlantic coast.

Within a few decades this changed. The number of settlers heading west increased by leaps and bounds. In 1811 a Pennsylvania resident reported seeing 236 wagons filled with people and their possessions on the road to Pittsburgh. A man in Newburgh, New York, counted 60 wagons rolling by in a single day. In 1820, just 30 years after the first census, the population of the

United States had more than doubled, to about 10 million people, with nearly 2 million living west of the Appalachians.

Traveling west was not easy in the late 1790s and early 1800s. The 363-mile trip from **New York City** to **Buffalo** could take as long as three weeks. A pioneer family heading west with a wagonload of household goods faced hardship and danger along the way.

Roads and Turnpikes

The nation needed good inland roads for travel and for the shipment of goods. Private companies built many turnpikes, or toll roads. The fees travelers paid to use those roads helped to pay for construction. Many of the roads had a base of crushed stone. In areas where the land was often muddy, companies built "corduroy roads," consisting of logs laid side by side, like the ridges of corduroy cloth. 📖 *(See page 965 of the Primary Sources Library for an account of a typical stagecoach journey.)*

When Ohio joined the Union in 1803, the new state asked the federal government to build a road to connect it with the East. In 1806 Congress approved funds for a **National Road** to the West and five years later agreed on the route. Because work on the road stopped during the War of 1812, the first section, from Maryland to western Virginia, did not open until 1818. In later years the National Road reached Ohio and continued on to Vandalia, Illinois. Congress viewed the National Road as a military necessity, but it did not undertake other road-building projects.

⭐Geography
River Travel

River travel had definite advantages over wagon and horse travel. It was far more comfortable than travel over the bumpy roads, and pioneers could load all their goods on river barges—if they were heading downstream in the direction of the current.

River travel had two problems, however. The first related to the geography of the eastern United States. Most major rivers in the region flowed in a north-south direction, not east to west, where most people and goods were headed. Second, traveling upstream by barge against the current was extremely difficult and slow.

People In History

Robert Fulton 1765–1815

Robert Fulton grew up in Lancaster, Pennsylvania. At an early age he created his own lead pencils and rockets. While living in Europe in the late 1790s, Fulton designed and built a submarine called the *Nautilus* to be used in France's war against Britain. Submarine warfare became common later.

Fulton returned to the United States and developed a steamboat engine that was more powerful and provided a smoother ride than previous engines. On August 17, 1807, Fulton's *Clermont* made its first successful run. By demonstrating the usefulness of two-way river travel, Fulton launched the steamboat

era. Although his engine was considered a great success, trouble followed after Fulton received a monopoly and government money. Eventually, the collapse of the monopoly led to lower prices, growth of competition, and introduction of new technology to improve the steamboat.

Steam engines were already being used in the 1780s and 1790s to power boats in quiet waters. Inventor James Rumsey equipped a small boat on the Potomac River with a steam engine. John Fitch, another inventor, built a steamboat that navigated the Delaware River. Neither boat, however, had enough power to withstand the strong currents and winds found in large rivers or open bodies of water.

In 1802 Robert Livingston, a political and business leader, hired **Robert Fulton** to develop a steamboat with a powerful engine. Livingston wanted the steamboat to carry cargo and passengers up the **Hudson River** from New York City to **Albany.**

In 1807 Fulton had his steamboat, the *Clermont,* ready for a trial. Powered by a newly designed engine, the *Clermont* made the 150-mile trip from New York to Albany in the unheard-of time of 32 hours. Using only sails, the trip would have taken four days.

About 140-feet long and 14-feet wide, the *Clermont* offered great comforts to its passengers. They could sit or stroll about on deck, and at

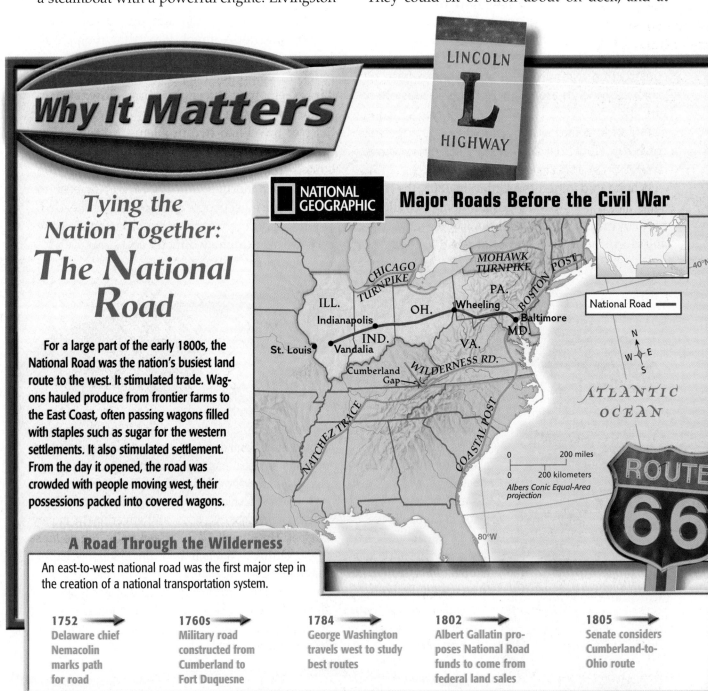

Why It Matters

Tying the Nation Together:
The National Road

For a large part of the early 1800s, the National Road was the nation's busiest land route to the west. It stimulated trade. Wagons hauled produce from frontier farms to the East Coast, often passing wagons filled with staples such as sugar for the western settlements. It also stimulated settlement. From the day it opened, the road was crowded with people moving west, their possessions packed into covered wagons.

NATIONAL GEOGRAPHIC — Major Roads Before the Civil War

National Road ———

A Road Through the Wilderness

An east-to-west national road was the first major step in the creation of a national transportation system.

1752	1760s	1784	1802	1805
Delaware chief Nemacolin marks path for road	Military road constructed from Cumberland to Fort Duquesne	George Washington travels west to study best routes	Albert Gallatin proposes National Road funds to come from federal land sales	Senate considers Cumberland-to-Ohio route

night they could relax in the sleeping compartments below deck. The engine was noisy, but its power provided a fairly smooth ride.

Steamboats ushered in a new age in river travel. They greatly improved the transport of goods and passengers along major inland rivers. Shipping goods became cheaper and faster. Steamboats also contributed to the growth of river cities like Cincinnati and St. Louis.

✓ **Reading Check** **Comparing** What advantages did steamboat travel have over wagon and horse travel?

Canals

Although steamboats represented a great improvement in transportation, their routes depended on the existing river system. Steamboats could not effectively tie the eastern and western parts of the country together.

In New York, business and government officials led by De Witt Clinton came up with a plan to link New York City with the Great Lakes

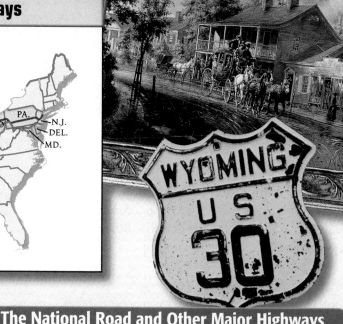

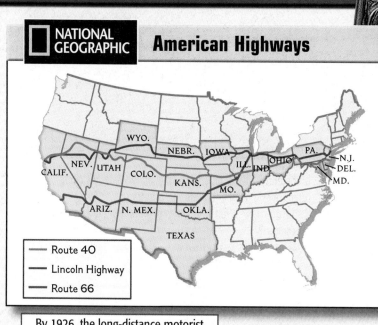

NATIONAL GEOGRAPHIC **American Highways**

Legend:
— Route 40
— Lincoln Highway
— Route 66

By 1926, the long-distance motorist could use transcontinental highways for car travel.

The National Road and Other Major Highways

	Official Status	From/To	Length in miles/km
National Road	1806	Cumberland, Md./Vandalia, Ill.	780/1,255
Lincoln Highway*	1913	New York City/San Francisco	3,390/5,456
Route 40	1926	Atlantic City, N.J./San Francisco	3,020/4,860
Route 66	1926	Chicago/Santa Monica, Calif.	2,450/3,943

*first transcontinental road for automobiles

1811 ➡️
Construction begins at Cumberland

1818 ➡️
Cumberland-to-Wheeling section completed

1825 ➡️
Construction in Ohio begins

1833 ➡️
Route to Columbus, Ohio, completed

1850 ➡️
National Road stops at Vandalia

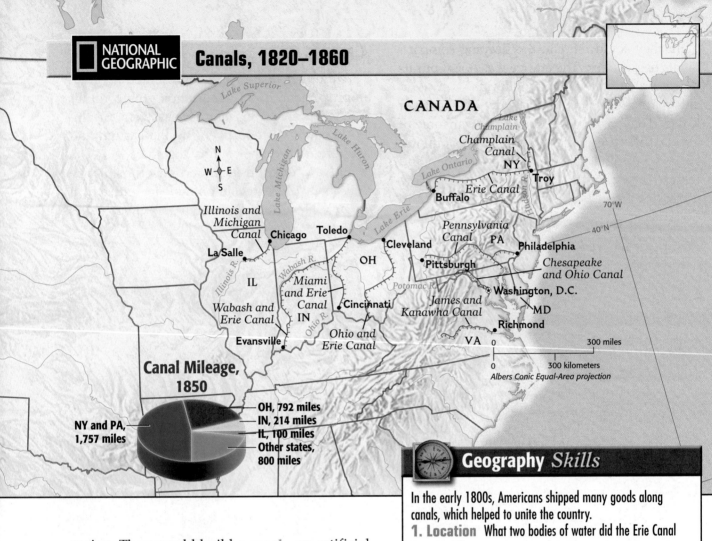

CANADA

N W E S

Lake Superior

Lake Michigan

Lake Huron

Lake Ontario

Lake Erie

Lake Champlain

Champlain Canal

NY • Troy

Erie Canal

Hudson R.

• Buffalo

70°W

40°N

Illinois and Michigan Canal • Chicago

Toledo •

• Cleveland

La Salle •

Pennsylvania Canal PA

• Philadelphia

IL

Wabash R.

OH

• Pittsburgh

Chesapeake and Ohio Canal

Miami and Erie Canal

Potomac R.

✷ Washington, D.C.

Wabash and Erie Canal

IN

Ohio R.

• Cincinnati

James and Kanawha Canal

MD

• Evansville

Ohio and Erie Canal

• Richmond

VA

0   300 miles

0   300 kilometers
Albers Conic Equal-Area projection

Canal Mileage, 1850

NY and PA, 1,757 miles

OH, 792 miles
IN, 214 miles
IL, 100 miles
Other states, 800 miles

Geography *Skills*

In the early 1800s, Americans shipped many goods along canals, which helped to unite the country.
1. **Location** What two bodies of water did the Erie Canal connect?
2. **Analyzing Information** About how many miles long was the Erie Canal?

region. They would build a canal—an artificial waterway—across New York State, connecting Albany on the Hudson River with Buffalo on **Lake Erie.**

Building the Erie Canal

Thousands of laborers, many of them Irish immigrants, worked on the construction of the 363-mile **Erie Canal.** Along the canal they built a series of locks—separate compartments where water levels were raised or lowered. Locks provided a way to raise and lower boats at places where canal levels changed.

After more than two years of digging, the Erie Canal opened on October 26, 1825. Clinton boarded a barge in Buffalo and journeyed on the canal to Albany. From there, he headed down the Hudson River to New York City. As crowds cheered, the officials poured water from Lake Erie into the Atlantic. The East and Midwest were joined.

In its early years, the canal did not allow steamboats because their powerful engines could

damage the earthen embankments along the canal. Instead, teams of mules or horses hauled the boats and barges. A two-horse team pulled a 100-ton barge about 24 miles in one day—astonishingly fast compared to travel by wagon. In the 1840s the canal banks were reinforced to accommodate steam tugboats pulling barges.

The success of the Erie Canal led to an explosion in canal building. By 1850 the United States had more than 3,600 miles of canals. Canals lowered the cost of shipping goods. They brought prosperity to the towns along their routes. Perhaps most important, they helped unite the growing country.

✓ **Reading Check** **Identifying** What two cities did the Erie Canal connect?

Western Settlement

Americans moved westward in waves. The first wave began before the 1790s and led to the admission of four new states between 1791 and 1803—Vermont, Kentucky, Tennessee, and Ohio. A second wave of westward growth began between 1816 and 1821. Five new western states were created—Indiana, Illinois, Mississippi, Alabama, and Missouri.

The new states reflected the dramatic growth of the region west of the Appalachians. Ohio, for example, had only 45,000 settlers in 1800. By 1820 it had 581,000.

Pioneer families tended to settle in communities along the great rivers, such as the Ohio and the Mississippi, so that they could ship their crops to market. The expansion of canals, which crisscrossed the land in the 1820s and 1830s, allowed people to live farther away from the rivers.

People also tended to settle with others from their home communities. Indiana, for example, was settled mainly by people from Kentucky and Tennessee, while Michigan's pioneers came mostly from New England.

Western families often gathered together for social events. Men took part in sports such as wrestling. Women met for quilting and sewing parties. Both men and women participated in cornhuskings—gatherings where farm families

Legendary Heroes

Paul Bunyan and John Henry Legends have grown around mythical figures like Paul Bunyan. Imaginary stories were passed along about how this giant lumberjack dug the Mississippi River and performed other incredible feats. Yet some of the famous characters in American folklore were real people. There was a John Henry who worked on the railroads. He was an African American renowned for his strength and skill in driving the steel drills into solid rock. He is best remembered for something that probably never happened. According to legend, John Henry defeated a steel-driving machine, but the effort killed him.

shared the work of stripping the husks from ears of corn.

Life in the West did not include the conveniences of Eastern town life, but the pioneers had not come west to be pampered. They wanted to make a new life for themselves and their families. America's population continued to spread westward in the years ahead.

✓ **Reading Check** **Identifying** What states were formed between 1791 and 1803?

SECTION 2 ASSESSMENT

Checking for Understanding

1. **Key Terms** Use the following terms to write a short newspaper article about the opening of the Erie Canal: turnpike, canal, lock.
2. **Reviewing Facts** Describe the improvements for transportation in the westward expansion during the early 1800s.

Reviewing Themes

3. **Science and Technology** How did steam-powered boats improve river travel?

Critical Thinking

4. **Drawing Conclusions** How did better transportation affect westward expansion?
5. **Comparing** What forms of communication and transportation linked East to West in the early 1800s? What links exist today? Re-create the diagram below and compare the links.

Links	
Early 1800s	Today

Analyzing Visuals

6. **Geography Skills** Study the information on the National Road on pages 316 and 317. When did construction of the National Road begin? To what city did it extend? How long was the National Road?

Interdisciplinary Activity

Geography Create a chart that lists the major means of transportation that helped the United States grow. Include the advantages and disadvantages of each type of transportation.

SKILLBUILDER

Reading a Diagram

Why Learn This Skill?

Suppose you buy a new bicycle and discover that you must assemble the parts before you can ride it. A *diagram*, or a drawing that shows how the parts fit together, would make this job much easier.

Learning the Skill

To read a diagram, follow these steps:
- Read the title to find out what the diagram shows.
- Read all labels carefully to clearly determine their meanings.
- Read the legend and identify symbols and colors used in the diagram.
- Look for numbers indicating a sequence of steps, or arrows showing movement.

Practicing the Skill

Analyze the diagram of the Clermont, *then answer the following questions.*

1. What type of energy was used to power this ship?

2. What was the purpose of the paddle wheels?

Applying the Skill

Making a Diagram Draw a diagram showing either how to make macaroni and cheese or how to tie a pair of shoes. Label your diagram.

 Glencoe's **Skillbuilder Interactive Workbook CD-ROM, Level 1,** provides instruction and practice in key social studies skills.

The *Clermont* Steamboat

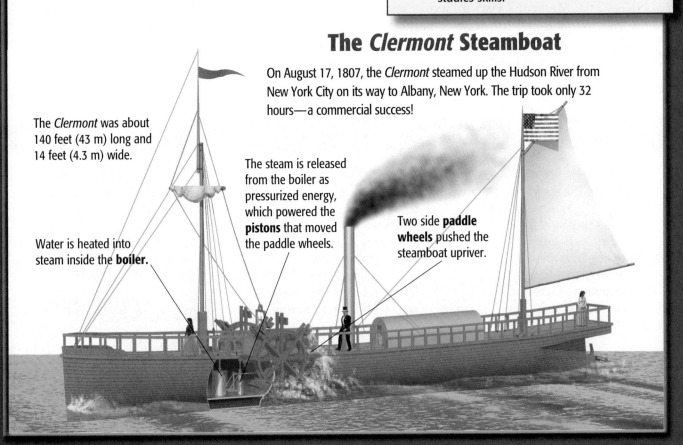

On August 17, 1807, the *Clermont* steamed up the Hudson River from New York City on its way to Albany, New York. The trip took only 32 hours—a commercial success!

The *Clermont* was about 140 feet (43 m) long and 14 feet (4.3 m) wide.

The steam is released from the boiler as pressurized energy, which powered the **pistons** that moved the paddle wheels.

Water is heated into steam inside the **boiler.**

Two side **paddle wheels** pushed the steamboat upriver.

Unity and Sectionalism

Guide to Reading

Main Idea
As the nation grew, differences in economic activities and needs increased sectionalism.

Key Terms
sectionalism, internal improvements, American System, disarmament, demilitarize, court-martial

Reading Strategy
Organizing Information As you read the section, re-create the diagram below and list four issues that created sectional conflict.

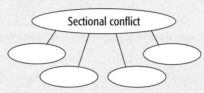

Sectional conflict

Read To Learn
- why sectional differences grew in the 1820s.
- what effect the Monroe Doctrine had on foreign policy.

Section Theme
Individual Action Senators Calhoun, Webster, and Clay represented different regions and different interests.

Preview of Events

♦1815	♦1820	♦1825
1816 James Monroe elected president	**1820** Missouri Compromise passed	**1823** Monroe Doctrine issued

James Monroe pocket watch

★★★★★★★
AN
American Story

Following the War of 1812, Americans felt buoyed by a new sense of pride and faith in the United States. In his Inaugural Address on March 4, 1817, President James Monroe expressed this feeling of proud nationalism: "If we look to the history of other nations, ancient or modern, we find no example of a growth so rapid, so gigantic, of a people so prosperous and happy."

The Era of Good Feelings

The absence of major political divisions after the War of 1812 helped forge a sense of national unity. In the 1816 presidential election, James Monroe, the Republican candidate, faced almost no opposition. The Federalists, weakened by doubts of their loyalty during the War of 1812, barely existed as a national party. Monroe won the election by an overwhelming margin.

Although the Federalist Party had almost disappeared, many of its programs gained support. Republican president James Madison, Monroe's predecessor, had called for tariffs to protect industries, for a national bank, and for other programs.

Political differences seemed to fade away, causing a Boston newspaper to call these years the **Era of Good Feelings.** The president himself symbolized these good feelings.

Monroe had been involved in national politics since the American Revolution. He wore breeches and powdered wigs—a style no longer in fashion. With his sense of dignity, Monroe represented a united America, free of political strife.

Early in his presidency, Monroe toured the nation. No president since George Washington had done this. He paid his own expenses and tried to travel without an official escort. Everywhere Monroe went, local officials greeted him and celebrated his visit.

Monroe arrived in Boston, the former Federalist stronghold, in the summer of 1817. About 40,000 well-wishers cheered him, and John Adams, the second president, invited Monroe to his home. Abigail Adams commended the new president's "unassuming manner."

Monroe did not think the demonstrations were meant for him personally. He wrote Madison that they revealed a "desire in the body of the people to show their attachment to the union."

Two years later Monroe continued his tour, traveling as far south as Savannah and as far west as Detroit. In 1820 President Monroe won reelection, winning all but one electoral vote.

Reading Check **Describing** Why was this period called the Era of Good Feelings?

Sectionalism Grows

The Era of Good Feelings did not last long. Regional differences soon came to the surface, ending the period of national harmony.

Most Americans felt a strong allegiance to the region where they lived. They thought of themselves as Westerners or Southerners or Northerners. This sectionalism, or loyalty to their region, became more intense as differences arose over national policies.

The conflict over slavery, for example, had always simmered beneath the surface. Most white Southerners believed in the necessity and value of slavery. Northerners increasingly opposed it. To protect slavery, Southerners stressed the importance of states' rights. States' rights are provided in the Constitution. Southerners believed they had to defend these rights against the federal government infringing on them.

The different regions also disagreed on the need for tariffs, a national bank, and internal improvements. Internal improvements were federal, state, and privately funded projects, such as canals and roads, to develop the nation's transportation system. Three powerful voices emerged in Congress in the early 1800s as spokespersons for their regions: John C. Calhoun, Daniel Webster, and Henry Clay.

John C. Calhoun

John C. Calhoun, a planter from South Carolina, was one of the War Hawks who had called for war with Great Britain in 1812. Calhoun remained a nationalist for some time after the war. He favored support for internal improvements and developing industries, and he backed a national bank. At the time, he believed these programs would benefit the South.

In the 1820s, however, Calhoun's views started to change, and he emerged as one of the chief supporters of **state sovereignty,** the idea that states have autonomous power. Calhoun

Fact · Fiction · Folklore

America's Flags

Flag of 1818 By 1818 the number of states had reached 20. In April President Monroe signed a bill that set the basic design of the flag. Each newly admitted state added a star to the field of blue. The addition of a new star took place on the Fourth of July following the state's year of entry.

The Great Star Flag Congress did not state how the stars should be arranged, so flagmakers used various designs. The Great Star Flag placed the stars in the form of a five-pointed star.

The Missouri Compromise, 1820

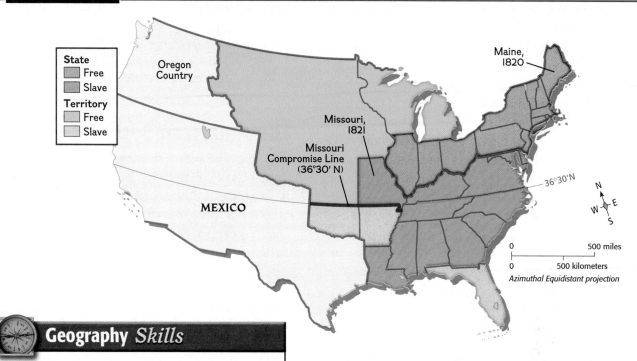

State
Free
Slave
Territory
Free
Slave

Oregon Country

Maine, 1820

Missouri, 1821

Missouri Compromise Line (36°30' N)

MEXICO

36°30'N

N W E S

0   500 miles
0   500 kilometers
Azimuthal Equidistant projection

Geography *Skills*

After 1820 all new states north of 36°30'N were to be admitted as free states.
1. **Region** Did Missouri enter the Union as a free state or a slave state?
2. **Analyzing Information** Was Maine a slave state or a free state in 1820?

became a strong opponent of nationalist programs such as high tariffs. Calhoun and other Southerners argued that tariffs raised the prices that they had to pay for the manufactured goods they could not produce for themselves. They also argued that high tariffs protected inefficient manufacturers.

Daniel Webster

First elected to Congress in 1812 to represent his native New Hampshire, **Daniel Webster** later represented Massachusetts in both the House and the Senate. Webster began his political career as a supporter of free trade and the shipping interests of New England. In time, Webster came to favor the Tariff of 1816—which protected American industries from foreign competition—and other policies that he thought would strengthen the nation and help the North.

Webster gained fame as one of the greatest orators of his day. As a United States senator, he spoke eloquently in defense of the nation as a whole against sectional interests. In one memorable speech Webster declared, "Liberty and Union, now and forever, one and inseparable!"

Henry Clay

Another leading War Hawk, **Henry Clay** of Kentucky, became Speaker of the House of Representatives in 1811 and a leader who represented the interests of the Western states. He also served as a member of the delegation that negotiated the Treaty of Ghent, ending the War of 1812. Above all, Henry Clay became known as the national leader who tried to resolve sectional disputes through compromise.

The Missouri Compromise

Sectional tension reached new heights in 1820 over the issue of admitting new states to the Union. The problem revolved around slavery. The South wanted Missouri, part of the Louisiana Purchase, admitted as a slave state. Northerners wanted Missouri to be free of slavery. The issue became the subject of debate throughout the country, exposing bitter regional divisions that would plague national politics for decades.

While Congress considered the Missouri question, Maine—still part of Massachusetts—also applied for statehood. The discussions about Missouri now broadened to include Maine.

Some observers feared for the future of the Union. Eventually Henry Clay helped work out a compromise that preserved the balance between North and South. The **Missouri Compromise,** reached in March 1820, provided for the admission of Missouri as a slave state and Maine as a free state. The agreement banned slavery in the remainder of the Louisiana Territory north of the 36°30'N parallel.

Reading Check **Identifying** What issue did the Missouri Compromise address? How did the Northern and Southern attitudes towards slavery differ?

The American System

Though he was a spokesperson for the West, Henry Clay believed his policies would benefit *all* sections of the nation. In an 1824 speech, he called his program the "American System." The American System included a protective tariff; a program of internal improvements, especially the building of roads and canals, to stimulate trade; and a national bank to control inflation and to lend money to build developing industries.

Clay believed that the three parts of his plan would work together. The tariff would provide the government with money to build roads and canals. Healthy businesses could use their profits to buy more agricultural goods from the South, then ship these goods northward along the nation's efficient new transportation system.

Not everyone saw Clay's program in such positive terms. Former president Jefferson believed the American System favored the wealthy manufacturing classes in New England. Many people in the South agreed with Jefferson. They saw no benefits to the South from the tariff or internal improvements.

In the end, little of Clay's American System went into effect. Congress eventually adopted some internal improvements, though not on the scale Clay had hoped for. Congress had created the Second National Bank in 1816, but it remained an object of controversy.

McCulloch v. Maryland

The Supreme Court also became involved in sectional and states' rights issues at this time. The state of Maryland imposed a tax on the Baltimore branch of the Second Bank of the United States—a federal institution. The Bank refused to pay the state tax, and the case, *McCulloch v. Maryland,* reached the Court in 1819.

Linking Past & Present

"Modern" Medicine

Past

Cuticura Plaster

In the mid-1800s, a visit to the doctor's office was viewed with suspicion. Faced with "cures" that were often fatal, people started using patent medicines—those they could buy in stores. One popular remedy, Snake Oil, was a mixture of wintergreen and white gasoline.

Today artificial hearts, cameras that move through veins, and other products have greatly improved Americans' health.

Present
Genetic engineer

Speaking for the Court, Chief Justice **John Marshall** ruled that Maryland had no right to tax the Bank because it was a federal institution. He argued that the Constitution and the federal government received their authority directly from the people, not by way of the state governments. Those who opposed the *McCulloch* decision argued that it was a "loose construction" of the Constitution, which says that the federal government can "coin" money—gold, silver, and other coins—but the Constitution does not mention paper money. In addition, the Constitutional Convention had voted *not* to give the federal government the authority to charter corporations, including banks. *(See page 998 of the Appendix for a summary of McCulloch v. Maryland.)*

Gibbons v. Ogden

Another Supreme Court case, *Gibbons* v. *Ogden,* established that states could not enact legislation that would interfere with Congressional power over interstate commerce. The Supreme Court's rulings strengthened the national government. They also contributed to the debate over sectional issues. People who supported states' rights believed that the decisions increased federal power at the expense of state power. Strong nationalists welcomed the rulings' support for national power. *(See page 997 of the Appendix for a summary of Gibbons v. Ogden.)*

Reading Check **Examining** Why was the Court's decision in *Gibbons* v. *Ogden* significant?

Foreign Affairs

The War of 1812 heightened Americans' pride in their country. Abigail Adams, wife of John Adams, wrote from England to her sister back in Massachusetts:

❝Do you know that European birds have not half the melody of ours? Nor is their fruit half so sweet, nor their flowers half so fragrant, nor their manners half so pure, nor their people half so virtuous.❞

At the same time, many Americans realized that the United States needed peace with Britain to grow and develop. It had to put differences aside and establish a new relationship with the "Old World."

Relations With Britain

In the years following the War of 1812, President Monroe and his secretary of state, John Quincy Adams, moved to resolve long-standing disputes with Great Britain and Spain.

In 1817, in the **Rush-Bagot Treaty,** the United States and Britain agreed to set limits on the number of naval vessels each could have on the Great Lakes. The treaty provided for the disarmament—the removal of weapons—along an important part of the border between the United States and British **Canada.**

The second agreement with Britain, the **Convention of 1818,** set the boundary of the Louisiana Territory between the United States and Canada at the 49th parallel. The convention created a secure and demilitarized border—a border without armed forces. Through Adams's efforts, Americans also gained the right to settle in the **Oregon Country.**

Relations With Spain

Spain owned East Florida and also claimed West Florida. The United States contended that West Florida was part of the Louisiana Purchase. In 1810 and 1812, Americans simply added parts of West Florida to Louisiana and Mississippi. Spain objected but took no action.

In April 1818, General **Andrew Jackson** invaded Spanish East Florida, seizing control of two Spanish forts. Jackson had been ordered to stop Seminole raids on American territory from Florida. In capturing the Spanish forts, however, Jackson went beyond his instructions.

Luis de Onís, the Spanish minister to the United States, protested forcefully and demanded the punishment of Jackson and his officers. Secretary of War Calhoun said that Jackson should be court-martialed—tried by a military court—for overstepping instructions. Secretary of State John Quincy Adams disagreed.

★Geography
Adams-Onís Treaty

Although Secretary of State Adams had not authorized Jackson's raid, he did nothing to stop it. Adams guessed that the Spanish did not want war and that they might be ready to settle the Florida dispute. He was right. For the Spanish the raid had demonstrated the military strength of the United States.

Already troubled by rebellions in **Mexico** and South America, Spain signed the **Adams-Onís Treaty** in 1819. Spain gave East Florida to the United States and abandoned all claims to West Florida. In return the United States gave up its claims to Spanish Texas and took over responsibility for paying the $5 million that American citizens claimed Spain owed them for damages.

The two countries also agreed on a border between the United States and Spanish possessions in the West. The border extended northwest from the Gulf of Mexico to the 42nd parallel and then west to the Pacific, giving the United States a large piece of territory in the Pacific Northwest. America had become a transcontinental power.

✔ **Reading Check** **Identifying** What areas did the United States obtain from Spain?

Latin American Republics

While the Spanish were settling territorial disputes with the United States, they faced a series of challenges within their empire. In the early

Miguel Hidalgo

1800s, Spain controlled a vast colonial empire that included what is now the southwestern United States, Mexico and Central America, and all of South America except Brazil.

In the fall of 1810 a priest, **Miguel Hidalgo** (ee• DAHL• goh), led a rebellion against the Spanish government of Mexico. Hidalgo called for racial equality and the redistribution of land. The Spanish defeated the revolutionary forces and executed Hidalgo. In 1821 Mexico gained its independence, but independence did not bring social and economic change.

Bolívar and San Martín

Independence in South America came largely as a result of the efforts of two men. **Simón Bolívar,** also known as "the Liberator," led the movement that won freedom for the present-day countries of Venezuela, Colombia, Panama, Bolivia, and Ecuador. **José de San Martín** successfully achieved independence for Chile and Peru. By 1824 the revolutionaries' military victory was complete, and most of South America had liberated itself from Spain. Portugal's large colony of Brazil gained its independence peacefully in 1822. Spain's empire in the Americas had shrunk to Cuba, Puerto Rico, and a few other islands in the Caribbean.

The Monroe Doctrine

In 1822 Spain had asked France, Austria, Russia, and Prussia— the Quadruple Alliance —for help in its fight against revolutionary forces in South America. The possibility of increased European involvement in North America led President Monroe to take action.

HISTORY Online

Student Web Activity
Visit taj.glencoe.com and click on **Chapter 10— Student Web Activities** for an activity on the democratic movements in the Americas.

The president issued a statement, later known as the **Monroe Doctrine,** on December 2, 1823. While the United States would not interfere with any existing European colonies in the Americas, Monroe declared, it would oppose any new ones. North and South America "are henceforth not to be considered as subjects for future colonization by any European powers."

In 1823 the United States did not have the military power to enforce the Monroe Doctrine. The Monroe Doctrine nevertheless became an important element in American foreign policy and has remained so for more than 170 years. *(See page 988 of the Appendix for an excerpt from the Monroe Doctrine.)*

Reading Check **Evaluating** How did the Monroe Doctrine affect foreign policy?

SECTION 3 ASSESSMENT

Checking for Understanding

1. **Key Terms** Write a short paragraph in which you use the following key terms: sectionalism, internal improvements, American System, disarmament, demilitarize.
2. **Reviewing Facts** Describe the disagreement between the North and South that resulted in the Missouri Compromise.

Reviewing Themes

3. **Individual Action** What action did Daniel Webster take that shows he placed his concerns for the nation above his sectional interests?

Critical Thinking

4. **Identifying Central Issues** Explain the debate involved in *Gibbons* v. *Ogden* and the final decision.
5. **Determining Cause and Effect** Describe the chain of events in Latin America and Europe that led to the adoption of the Monroe Doctrine. Show your answers in a diagram like the one below.

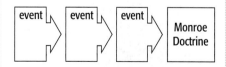

Analyzing Visuals

6. **Geography Skills** Use the map on page 323 to answer these questions. Which parallel did the Missouri Compromise line follow? How many slave states were there in 1820? How many free states?

Interdisciplinary Activity

Art Design a flag to represent either the North, South, or West during the early 1800s. Use photos, symbols, or mottoes that might have been popular with the people who lived in these regions.

Chapter Summary

Growth and Expansion

1790
- Samuel Slater builds first cotton mill in America

1793
- Eli Whitney invents the cotton gin

1801
- John Marshall is appointed chief justice of the Supreme Court

1807
- Robert Fulton builds the *Clermont*

1811
- National Road is begun

1816
- James Monroe elected president
- Second National Bank is chartered

1817
- Rush-Bagot Treaty is signed

1818
- Convention of 1818 agreement is signed

1819
- Adams-Onís Treaty is signed
- Supreme Court rules on *McCulloch* v. *Maryland*

1820
- Missouri Compromise is adopted

1823
- Monroe Doctrine is announced

1825
- Erie Canal is opened

Reviewing Key Terms

On a sheet of paper, create a crossword puzzle using the following terms. Use the terms' definitions as your crossword clues.

1. Industrial Revolution
2. factory system
3. sectionalism
4. disarmament
5. demilitarize
6. court-martial

Reviewing Key Facts

7. What problems did cities face as a result of rapid growth during the Industrial Revolution?
8. How did the landscape of New England affect how and where people lived in the late 1700s and early 1800s?
9. How did canals boost the economy of the Great Lakes region?
10. How did North and South differ on the issue of tariffs?
11. What had happened to the Federalist Party by the time James Monroe became president?
12. What was the American System?
13. Explain the debate involved in *McCulloch* v. *Maryland* and the final decision in the case. Why was the decision significant?
14. Describe the provisions of the Monroe Doctrine.

Critical Thinking

15. **Analyzing Themes: Economic Factors** How did the Industrial Revolution help to make the United States more economically independent in the early 1800s?
16. **Analyzing Themes: Global Connections** Why did Secretary of State John Quincy Adams allow General Jackson's invasion into Spanish East Florida in 1818?
17. **Determining Cause and Effect** How did the development of roads boost the growth of the United States? Use a diagram like the one shown to organize your answer.

Roads

Geography and History Activity

In 1819 Spain ceded Florida to the United States in the Adams-Onís Treaty. The Spanish had established colonies in Florida beginning in the 1500s. Study the map and answer the questions that follow.

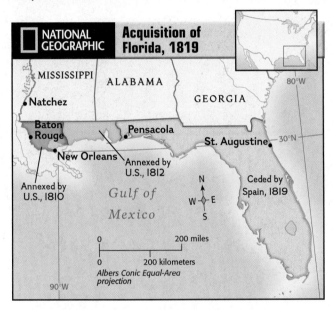

NATIONAL GEOGRAPHIC
Acquisition of Florida, 1819

MISSISSIPPI
ALABAMA
GEORGIA
80°W
Natchez
Baton Rouge
Pensacola
St. Augustine
30°N
New Orleans
Annexed by U.S., 1812
Gulf of Mexico
Annexed by U.S., 1810
Ceded by Spain, 1819
N
W E
S
90°W

0   200 miles
0   200 kilometers
Albers Conic Equal-Area projection

18. **Region** When was the largest portion of Florida acquired from Spain?

19. **Location** What body of water blocked further expansion of Florida to the west?

20. **Movement** In what direction did the United States acquire the various parts of Florida?

Practicing Skills

Reading a Diagram *Study the diagram of the textile mill on page 307. Use the diagram to answer these questions.*

21. What is the first step in the production of textiles?

22. At what stage does the thread become cloth?

23. What process turns the yarn into thread?

24. When would a cotton gin be necessary in this process?

25. Now choose one of the inventions mentioned in the chapter. Prepare a diagram that traces the development of that invention to a similar device in use today. For example, you might diagram the development of a modern cruise ship, showing all the improvements made from start to finish.

HISTORY Online

Self-Check Quiz
Visit taj.glencoe.com and click on **Chapter 10— Self-Check Quizzes** to prepare for the chapter test.

Citizenship Cooperative Activity

26. **Exploring Your Community's Past** Working with two other students, contact a local historical society to learn about your community's history. Then interview people in your neighborhood to learn about their roots in the community. Find out when their families first settled there. Write a history of the community and give a copy of it to the historical society.

Economics Activity

27. **Using the Internet** Search the Internet for information about how to apply for a patent for an invention. Create a step-by-step list of directions describing the process.

 ## Alternative Assessment

28. **Portfolio Writing Activity** Review Section 2 of the chapter for information about what it was like to live in the West in the early 1800s. Record your notes in your journal. Use your notes to write a postcard to a friend describing your social life.

The Princeton Review
Standardized Test Practice

Directions: Choose the *best* answer to the following question.

The South opposed protective tariffs for which reason?

A They thought tariffs would not work.

B They had very little industry to protect.

C They thought foreign goods were better.

D Their main business was smuggling.

Test-Taking Tip:

Eliminate answers that do not make sense. For example, it is not realistic that the main business for the entire South was smuggling. Therefore, answer **D** cannot be correct.

UNIT
5 The Growing Nation

1820–1860

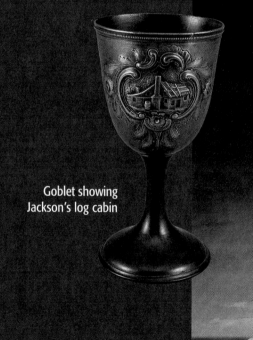

Goblet showing
Jackson's log cabin

Why It Matters

As you study Unit 5, you will learn how growth, migration, and conflict increased following the Industrial Revolution. The following resources offer more information about this period in American history.

Primary Sources Library

See pages 966–967 for primary source readings to accompany Unit 5.

💿 *Use the **American History Primary Source Document Library CD-ROM** to find additional primary sources about the developing nation.*

Advice on the Prairie
by William T. Ranney

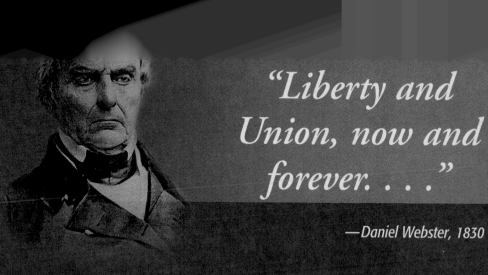

"Liberty and Union, now and forever. . . ."

—Daniel Webster, 1830

CHAPTER 11

The Jackson Era

1824–1845

Why It Matters

The struggle for political rights took shape in the 1820s and 1830s, when many people questioned the limits of American democracy.

The Impact Today

In the years since the Jackson era:
- *Women, African Americans, and other minorities have won the right to vote and to participate in the political process.*
- *Today every United States citizen aged 18 or older, regardless of gender, race, or wealth, has the right to vote.*

The American Journey Video *The chapter 11 video, "Old Hickory," chronicles events in Andrew Jackson's military and political careers.*

1833
- Force Bill passed

1823
- President Monroe outlines Monroe Doctrine

1830
- Indian Removal Act passed
- Webster-Hayne debate

United States PRESIDENTS

 Monroe 1817–1825

 J. Q. Adams 1825–1829

 Jackson 1829–1837

1820   *1825*   *1830*

World

1822
- Brazil gains independence from Portugal

1826
- French scientist Niépce produces first photograph

1829
- Louis Braille publishes reading system for the blind

1833
- Slavery abolished in British colonies

Stump Speaking by George Caleb Bingham Bingham's series of election paintings expressed faith in the growth of democracy.

FOLDABLES™
Study Organizer

Evaluating Information Study Foldable
Make this foldable to help you ask and answer questions about the Jackson era.

Step 1 Fold a sheet of paper in half from side to side, leaving a $\frac{1}{2}$ inch tab along the side.

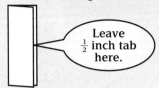

Leave $\frac{1}{2}$ inch tab here.

Step 2 Turn the paper and fold it into fourths.

Fold in half, then fold in half again.

Step 3 Unfold and cut up along the three fold lines.

Make four tabs.

Step 4 Label your foldable as shown.

Who? What? When? Why?

Reading and Writing As you read, ask yourself "who" Andrew Jackson was, "what" he did, "when" he did it, and "why" it happened. Write your thoughts and facts under each appropriate tab.

1834
• Indian Territory created by Congress

1837
• Panic of 1837

1838
• Cherokee forced to move west

1840
• Harrison elected president

Van Buren 1837–1841

W. H. Harrison 1841

Tyler 1841–1845

THE HERO OF TIPPECANOE

1835   *1840*   *1845*

1839
• Scottish blacksmith, Kirkpatrick Macmillian, produces first bicycle

1843
• Charles Dickens writes "A Christmas Carol"

1845
• Deadly fungus destroys much of Ireland's potato crop

HISTORY Online

Chapter Overview
Visit taj.glencoe.com and click on **Chapter 11— Chapter Overviews** to preview chapter information.

Jacksonian Democracy

Guide to Reading

Main Idea
The United States's political system changed under Andrew Jackson.

Key Terms
favorite son, majority, plurality, mudslinging, landslide, suffrage, bureaucracy, spoils system, caucus, nominating convention, tariff, nullify, secede

Reading Strategy
As you read Section 1, create a chart like the one below and in the boxes describe the political parties in 1828.

	Candidate	Views
Democratic Republicans		
National Republicans		

Read to Learn
• why the nation's sixth president was chosen by the House.
• what political changes came under President Jackson.

Section Theme
Continuity and Change James Monroe's decision not to seek a third term was followed by two hotly contested presidential elections.

Preview of Events

♦1825   ♦1830   ♦1835

1825
John Quincy Adams wins presidency in House election

1828
Andrew Jackson elected president

1830
Webster and Hayne debate

1832
South Carolina threatens to secede

Jackson sewing box

AN American Story

The presidential campaign of 1828 was one of the most vicious in American history. Supporters of John Quincy Adams in Philadelphia distributed a pamphlet titled "Some Account of Some of the Bloody Deeds of General Jackson." One illustration in the pamphlet showed a ferocious-looking Andrew Jackson plunging his sword through the body of a helpless civilian. Meanwhile Jackson's supporters falsely accused John Quincy Adams of kidnapping a young American girl and selling her to the ruler of Russia.

The Election of 1824

From 1816 to 1824, the United States had only one political party, the Jeffersonian Republicans. Within the party, however, differences arose among various groups that had their own views and interests. In 1824 James Monroe was finishing his second term as president but declined to run for a third term. Four candidates from the Republican Party competed for the presidency.

The four candidates' opinions differed on the role of the federal government. They also spoke for different parts of the country. The Republican Party nominated **William H. Crawford,** a former congressman from Georgia. However, Crawford's poor health weakened him as a candidate.

The other three Republicans in the presidential race were favorite son candidates, meaning they received the backing of their home states rather than that of the national party. Two of these candidates—**Andrew Jackson** and **Henry Clay**—came from the West. Clay, of Kentucky, was Speaker of the House of Representatives. He fought for his program of internal improvements, high tariffs, and a stronger national bank.

General Andrew Jackson of Tennessee was not a Washington politician, but he was a hero of the War of 1812. Raised in poverty, he claimed to speak for the Americans who had been left out of politics.

John Quincy Adams of Massachusetts, son of former president John Adams, received support from merchants of the Northeast.

Striking a Bargain

In the election Jackson received the largest number of popular votes. However, no candidate received a majority, or more than half, of the electoral votes. Jackson won 99 electoral votes, which gave him a plurality, or largest single share. Under the terms of the Twelfth Amendment to the Constitution, when no candidate receives a majority of electoral votes, the House of Representatives selects the president.

While the House was preparing to vote on the next president, Henry Clay met with Adams. Clay agreed to use his influence as Speaker of the House to defeat Jackson. In return Clay may have hoped to gain the position of secretary of state.

With Clay's help Adams was elected president in the House. Adams quickly named Clay as secretary of state, traditionally the stepping-stone to the presidency. Jackson's followers accused the two men of making a **"corrupt bargain"** and stealing the election.

The Adams Presidency

In **Washington, D.C.,** the "corrupt bargain" had cast a shadow over Adams's presidency. Outside the capital Adams's policies ran against popular opinion. Adams wanted a stronger navy and government funds for scientific expeditions. Adams also wanted the federal government to direct economic growth.

Such ideas horrified those who desired a more limited role for the federal government, and Congress turned down many of Adams's proposals. This was especially true after the congressional elections of 1826, when enemies of Adams controlled both the House and Senate.

✓ **Reading Check** **Describing** Why were Adams and Clay accused of making a "corrupt bargain"?

The Election of 1828

By the election of 1828, the party had divided into two separate parties: the **Democratic-Republicans,** who supported Jackson, and the **National Republicans,** who supported Adams. Jackson's Democratic-Republicans, or Democrats, favored states' rights and mistrusted

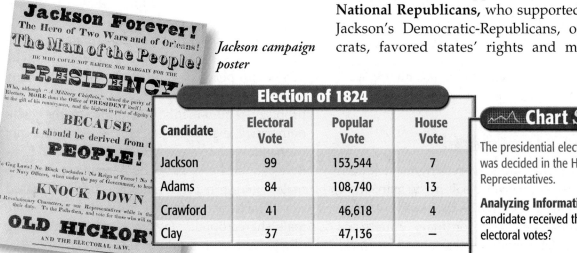

Jackson campaign poster

Election of 1824			
Candidate	**Electoral Vote**	**Popular Vote**	**House Vote**
Jackson	99	153,544	7
Adams	84	108,740	13
Crawford	41	46,618	4
Clay	37	47,136	—

Chart *Skills*

The presidential election of 1824 was decided in the House of Representatives.

Analyzing Information Which candidate received the most electoral votes?

strong central government. Many Democrats were individualists from the frontier, immigrants, or laborers in the big cities.

The National Republicans wanted a strong central government. They supported federal measures, such as road building and the Bank of the United States, that would shape the nation's economy. Many were merchants or farmers.

During the campaign both parties resorted to mudslinging, attempts to ruin their opponent's reputation with insults. The Democratic-Republicans accused Adams of betraying the people. They put out a handbill calling the election a contest "between an honest patriotism, on the one side, and an unholy, selfish ambition, on the other."

The National Republicans fought back. They created a vicious campaign song to play up embarrassing incidents in Jackson's life. One involved Jackson's order in the War of 1812 to execute several soldiers who had deserted.

Mudslinging was not the only new element introduced in the 1828 campaign. Election slogans, rallies, buttons, and events such as barbecues were also used to arouse enthusiasm. All of these new features became a permanent part of American political life.

Jackson Triumphs

In the election of 1828, Jackson received most of the votes cast by voters of the new frontier states. He also received many votes in the South, where his support for states' rights was popular. John C. Calhoun of South Carolina, who had served as Adams's vice president, switched parties to run with Jackson. Calhoun also championed states' rights. Jackson won the election in a landslide, an overwhelming victory, with 56 percent of the popular vote and 178 electoral votes.

✓ **Reading Check** **Summarizing** How did Jackson try to get the support of people in the election of 1828?

Jackson as President

Andrew Jackson was everything most Americans admired—a patriot, a self-made man, and a war hero. On March 4, 1829, thousands of farmers, laborers, and other ordinary Americans crowded into the nation's capital to hear Jackson's Inaugural Address. After Jackson's speech a crowd joined him at a White House reception. They filled the elegant rooms of the mansion, trampling on the carpets with muddy shoes, spilling food on sofas and chairs. They were there to shake the hand of the general who seemed just like them.

"Old Hickory"

Like many of his supporters, Andrew Jackson had been born in a log cabin. His parents, poor farmers, died before he was 15. As a teenager Jackson fought with the Patriots in the American Revolution. Before he was 30, he was elected to Congress from Tennessee.

Jackson gained fame during the War of 1812. He defeated the Creek Nation in the Battle of Horseshoe Bend and defeated the British at the Battle of New Orleans. His troops called him "Old Hickory" because he was as tough as a hickory stick.

Small farmers, craft workers, and others who felt left out of the expanding American economy loved Jackson. They felt that his rise from a log cabin to the White House demonstrated the American success story. His popularity with the common man changed politics in Washington, D.C.

🏛 Citizenship
New Voters

President Andrew Jackson promised "equal protection and equal benefits" for all Americans—at least for all white American men. During his first term, a spirit of equality spread through American politics.

In the nation's early years, most states had limited suffrage, or the right to vote, for men who owned property or paid taxes. By 1815 many states had loosened or soon would loosen the property requirements for voting. In the 1820s democracy expanded as people who had not been allowed to vote voted for the first time. Between 1824 and 1828, the percentage of white males voting in presidential elections increased from 26.9 to 57.6 percent. For the first time, white male sharecroppers, factory workers, and many others were brought into the political process.

A Andrew Jackson **B** Nicholas Biddle **C** Henry Clay **D** John C. Calhoun

The expansion of suffrage continued, and in 1840 more than 80 percent of white males voted in the presidential election. However, women still could not vote, and African Americans and Native Americans had few rights of any kind.

Another development in the broadening of democracy involved presidential electors. By 1828, 22 of the 24 states changed their constitutions to allow the people, rather than the state legislatures, to choose presidential electors.

The Spoils System

Democrats carried the spirit of democracy into government. They wanted to open up government jobs to people from all walks of life. They were disturbed that the federal government had become a bureaucracy, a system in which nonelected officials carry out laws. Democrats argued that ordinary citizens could handle any government job.

President Jackson fired many federal workers and replaced them with his supporters. The discharged employees protested vehemently. They charged that Jackson was acting like a tyrant, hiring and firing people at will. Jackson responded that a new set of federal employees would be good for democracy.

One Jackson supporter explained it another way: "To the victors belong the spoils." In other words, because the Jacksonians had won the election, they had the right to the spoils—benefits of victory—such as handing out government jobs to supporters. The practice of replacing government employees with the winning candidate's supporters became known as the spoils system.

Electoral Changes

Jackson's supporters worked to make the political system more democratic as well. They abandoned the unpopular caucus system. In this system major political candidates were chosen by committees made up of members of Congress. The caucuses were replaced by nominating conventions in which delegates from the states selected the party's presidential candidate.

The Democrats held their first national party convention in 1832 in **Baltimore, Maryland.** The convention drew delegates from each state in the Union. The delegates decided to nominate the candidate who could gather two-thirds of the vote, and Jackson won the nomination. This system allowed many people to participate in the selection of political candidates.

Reading Check **Describing** What is a caucus system?

Analyzing *Political Cartoons*

King Andrew Some people called Andrew Jackson "a man of the people." Others called him a power-hungry ruler. **What symbols does the cartoonist use to suggest items of royalty?**

$ Economics

The Tariff Debate

Americans from different parts of the country disagreed strongly on some issues. One such issue was the tariff, a fee paid by merchants who imported goods. While president, Jackson faced a tariff crisis that tested the national government's powers.

In 1828 Congress passed a very high tariff on manufactured goods from Europe. Manufacturers in the United States—mostly in the Northeast—welcomed the tariff. Because tariffs made European goods more expensive, American consumers were more likely to buy American-made goods.

Southerners, however, hated the new tariff. They called it the Tariff of Abominations— something hateful. These critics argued that, while tariffs forced consumers to buy American goods, tariffs also meant higher prices.

The South Protests

Southern politicians and plantation owners were ready to act. Vice President John C. Calhoun argued that a state or group of states had the right to nullify, or cancel, a federal law it considered against state interests. Some Southerners called for the Southern states to secede, or break away, from the United States and form their own government. When Calhoun explored this idea, troubling questions arose. The United States had been a nation for nearly 50 years. What if a state disagreed with the federal government? Did a state have the right to go its own way?

Calhoun drew from the ideas that Madison and Jefferson wrote in the Virginia and Kentucky Resolutions of 1798–1799. Calhoun argued that since the federal government was a creation of the states, the states themselves are the final authority of the constitutionality of federal laws. The alternative to state sovereignty, Calhoun pointed out, is to allow the Supreme Court or Congress to tell the people what our Constitution means and what orders we must obey.

The Webster–Hayne Debate

In January 1830, Senator Daniel Webster delivered a stinging attack on nullification. Webster stood on the floor of the Senate to challenge a speech given by Robert Hayne, a young senator from South Carolina. Hayne had defended the idea that the states had a right to nullify acts of the federal government, and even to secede.

In his response, Webster defended the Constitution and the Union. He argued that nullification could only mean the end of the Union. Webster closed with the ringing statement, "Liberty and Union, now and forever, one and inseparable!"

Jackson Takes a Stand

Nobody knew exactly where President Jackson stood on the issue of nullification. Many Southerners hoped that Jackson might side with them. In April 1830 supporters of states' rights invited the president to speak at a dinner. The guests, including Calhoun, waited anxiously for Jackson to speak. Finally, the president rose to his feet and spoke directly to Calhoun.

66Our federal union . . . must be preserved!99

The states' rights supporters were shocked and disappointed, but Calhoun answered the president's challenge. He raised his glass and said,

66The Union—next to our liberty, most dear.99

He meant that the fate of the Union must take second place to a state's liberty to overrule the Constitution if its interests were threatened.

Calhoun realized that Jackson would not change his views. Wishing to return to Congress to speak for Southern interests, Calhoun won election to the Senate in December 1832. Not long after, he resigned the vice presidency.

The Nullification Crisis

Southern anger over the tariff continued to build. The Union seemed on the verge of splitting apart. In 1832 Congress passed a new, lower tariff, hoping that the protest in the South would die down. It did not.

South Carolina, Calhoun's home state, had led the fight against the so-called Tariff of Abominations. Now South Carolina took the battle one step further. The state legislature passed the **Nullification Act,** declaring that it would not pay the "illegal" tariffs of 1828 and 1832. The South Carolina legislators threatened to secede from the Union if the federal government tried to interfere with their actions.

To ease the crisis, Jackson supported a compromise bill proposed by Henry Clay that would gradually lower the tariff over several years. At the same time, Jackson made sure that the South would accept Clay's compromise. Early in 1833 he persuaded Congress to pass the **Force Bill,** which allowed the president to use the United States military to enforce acts of Congress.

In response, South Carolina accepted the new tariff. However, to show that they had not been defeated, state leaders voted to nullify the Force Act. Calhoun and his followers claimed a victory for nullification, which had, they insisted, forced the revision of the tariff. For the time being, the crisis between a state and the federal government was over. Yet South Carolina and the rest of the South would remember the lesson of the nullification crisis—that the federal government would not allow a state to go its own way without a fight.

✓ **Reading Check** **Summarizing** Why did South Carolina pass the Nullification Act?

SECTION 1 ASSESSMENT

Check for Understanding

1. **Key Terms** Use each of these terms in a complete sentence that will help explain its meaning: favorite son, majority, plurality, mudslinging, landslide, suffrage, spoils system, secede.

2. **Reviewing Facts** Why did the House of Representatives select the president in the 1824 presidential election?

Reviewing Themes

3. **Continuity and Change** What election practices used in the 1828 presidential campaign are still used today?

Critical Thinking

4. **Drawing Conclusions** What was the main reason President Adams was not popular with the Democratic-Republicans?

5. **Organizing Information** Re-create the diagram below and describe the changes that took place in the political system under Andrew Jackson.

Changes

Analyzing Visuals

6. **Analyzing Political Cartoons** Look at the cartoon on page 338. What symbols are used to represent the United States? How does the cartoonist use labels? What does the cartoonist want readers to think of President Jackson?

Interdisciplinary Activity

Interviewing Prepare a list of five questions that you might have asked President Jackson if you had interviewed him.

Study & Writing
SKILLBUILDER

Analyzing Primary Sources

Why Learn This Skill?

Historians determine what happened in the past by combing through bits of evidence to reconstruct events. This evidence—both written and illustrated—is called *primary sources.* Examining primary sources can help you understand history.

Choctaw forced from their land

Learning the Skill

Primary sources are records of events made by the people who witnessed them. They include letters, diaries, photographs and pictures, news articles, and legal documents. To analyze primary sources, follow these steps:

- Identify when and where the document was written.
- Read the document for its content and try to answer the five "W" questions: <u>W</u>ho is it about? <u>W</u>hat is it about? <u>W</u>hen did it happen? <u>W</u>here did it happen? <u>W</u>hy did it happen?
- Identify the author's opinions.

Practicing the Skill

The primary source that follows comes from Speckled Snake, an elder of the Creek Nation, in 1829. He was more than 100 years old at the time

he said these words. Read the quote, then answer the questions that follow.

“Brothers! I have listened to many talks from our Great Father. When he first came over the wide waters, he was but a little man. . . . But when the white man had warmed himself before the Indians' fire and filled himself with their hominy, he became very large. With a step he bestrode the mountains and his feet covered the plains and the valleys. His hand grasped the eastern and the western sea, and his head rested on the moon. Then he became our Great Father. Brothers, I have listened to a great many talks from our Great Father. But they always began and ended in this—'Get a little further; you are too near me.'”

❶ What events are described?

❷ Who was affected by these events?

❸ What is the general feeling of the person who stated this opinion?

Applying the Skill

Analyzing Primary Sources Find a primary source from your past—a photograph, a report card, an old newspaper clipping, or your first baseball card. Bring this source to class and explain what it shows about that time in your life.

GO TO

Glencoe's **Skillbuilder Interactive Workbook CD-ROM, Level 1,** provides instruction and practice in key social studies skills.

Conflicts Over Land

Guide to Reading

Main Idea

As more white settlers moved into the Southeast, conflict arose between the Native Americans who lived there and the United States government.

Key Terms

relocate, guerrilla tactics

Reading Strategy

As you read Section 2, create a chart like the one below that describes what happened to each group of Native Americans as the United States expanded.

	Description
Cherokee	
Sauk/Fox	
Seminole	

Read to Learn

- how Native American peoples were forced off their lands in the Southeast.
- how President Jackson defied the Supreme Court.

Section Theme

Groups and Institutions In the 1830s many Native American peoples were forced to relocate.

Preview of Events

◆1830　　　◆1833　　　◆1836　　　◆1839

1830 Congress passes the Indian Removal Act

1832 Black Hawk leads Sauk and Fox people to Illinois

1835 Seminole refuse to leave Florida

1838 Cherokee driven from their homelands on the Trail of Tears

Sequoya

AN American Story

The Cherokee held their land long before European settlers arrived. Through treaties with the United States government, the Cherokee became a sovereign nation within Georgia. By the early 1800s the Cherokee had their own schools, their own newspaper, and their own written constitution. Sequoya's invention of a Cherokee alphabet enabled many of the Cherokee to read and write in their own language. The Cherokee farmed some of Georgia's richest land, and in 1829 gold was discovered there. Settlers, miners, and land speculators began trespassing on Cherokee territory in pursuit of riches.

Moving Native Americans

While the United States had expanded westward by the 1830s, large numbers of Native Americans still lived in the eastern part of the country. In Georgia, Alabama, Mississippi, and Florida lived the "Five Civilized Tribes"—the Cherokee, Creek, Seminole, Chickasaw, and Choctaw. The tribes had established farming societies with successful economies.

Because the area west of the Mississippi was dry and seemed unsuitable for farming, few white Americans lived there. Many settlers wanted the federal government to relocate Native Americans living in the Southeast. They proposed to force the Native Americans to leave their land and move west of the Mississippi River. President Andrew Jackson, a man of the frontier himself, supported the settlers' demand for Native American land.

Indian Removal Act

Congress responded by passing the **Indian Removal Act** in 1830. The act allowed the federal government to pay Native Americans to move west. Jackson then sent officials to negotiate treaties with Native Americans of the Southeast. Most felt compelled to accept payment for their lands. In 1834 Congress created the **Indian Territory,** an area in present-day Oklahoma, for Native Americans from the Southeast.

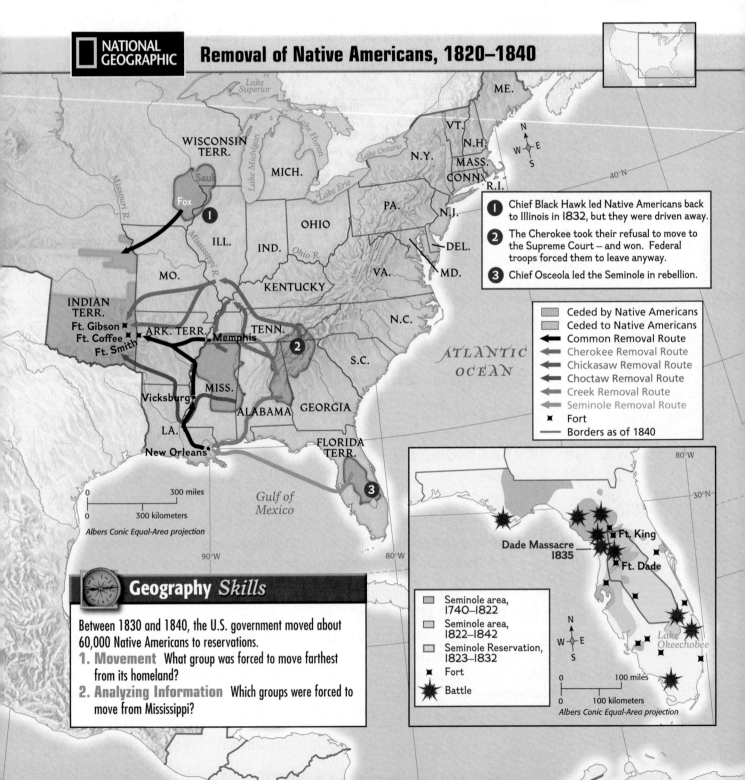

NATIONAL GEOGRAPHIC
Removal of Native Americans, 1820–1840

1. Chief Black Hawk led Native Americans back to Illinois in 1832, but they were driven away.

2. The Cherokee took their refusal to move to the Supreme Court — and won. Federal troops forced them to leave anyway.

3. Chief Osceola led the Seminole in rebellion.

Ceded by Native Americans
Ceded to Native Americans
Common Removal Route
Cherokee Removal Route
Chickasaw Removal Route
Choctaw Removal Route
Creek Removal Route
Seminole Removal Route
■ Fort
Borders as of 1840

Dade Massacre 1835
Ft. King
Ft. Dade
Lake Okeechobee

Seminole area, 1740–1822
Seminole area, 1822–1842
Seminole Reservation, 1823–1832
■ Fort
✶ Battle

100 miles
100 kilometers
Albers Conic Equal-Area projection

Geography *Skills*

Between 1830 and 1840, the U.S. government moved about 60,000 Native Americans to reservations.

1. **Movement** What group was forced to move farthest from its homeland?

2. **Analyzing Information** Which groups were forced to move from Mississippi?

Trail of Tears by Robert Lindneux Native Americans who were forced from their land traveled west in the 1830s. **Why was the forced march called the "Trail of Tears"?**

The Cherokee Nation

The Cherokee Nation, however, refused to give up its land. In treaties of the 1790s, the federal government had recognized the Cherokee people in the state of Georgia as a separate nation with their own laws. Georgia, however, refused to recognize Cherokee laws.

The Cherokee sued the state government and eventually took their case to the Supreme Court. In *Worcester* v. *Georgia* (1832), Chief Justice John Marshall ruled that Georgia had no right to interfere with the Cherokee. Only the federal government had authority over matters involving the Cherokee. 📖 *(See page 1000 of the Appendix for a summary of* Worcester v. Georgia.*)*

President Jackson had supported Georgia's efforts to remove the Cherokee. He vowed to ignore the Supreme Court's ruling. "John Marshall has made his decision," Jackson reportedly said. "Now let him enforce it."

The Trail of Tears

In 1835 the federal government persuaded a few Cherokee to sign a treaty giving up their people's land. Yet most of the 17,000 Cherokee refused to honor the treaty. They wrote a protest letter to the government and people of the United States.

❝We are aware that some persons suppose it will be for our advantage to [re]move beyond the Mississippi. . . . Our people universally think otherwise. . . . We wish to remain on the land of our fathers.❞

The Cherokee plea for understanding did not soften the resolve of President Jackson or the white settlers of the area. In 1838 **General Winfield Scott** and an army of 7,000 federal troops came to remove the Cherokee from their homes and lead them west. 📖 *(See page 988 of the Appendix for additional text of the Cherokee protest.)*

Scott threatened to use force if the Cherokee did not leave. He told them he had positioned troops all around the country so that resistance and escape were both hopeless. "Chiefs, head men, and warriors—Will you then, by resistance, compel us to resort to arms?" The Cherokee knew that fighting would only lead to their destruction. Filled with sadness and anger, their leaders gave in, and the long march to the West began. One man in Kentucky wrote of seeing hundreds of Cherokee marching by:

People In History

Osceola 1804–1838

Osceola was born in 1804. His ancestors were Creek, African American, British, Irish, and Scottish. After President Jackson signed the Indian Removal Act in 1830, Osceola became the leader of the Seminoles and led successful attacks on United States forts. Hiding in the swampy lands of the Everglades, the Seminoles grew tired, sick, and hungry. Osceola attempted to surrender but was captured. He and his family were imprisoned at Fort Moultrie, South Carolina, where he died of a throat infection in 1838. Although he had waged a war against the United States, the public considered Osceola an honorable hero and a victim of trickery, and he was given a funeral with full military honors.

66Even [the] aged . . . nearly ready to drop in the grave, were traveling with heavy burdens attached to their backs, sometimes on frozen ground and sometimes on muddy streets, with no covering for their feet.99

Brutal weather along the way claimed thousands of Cherokee lives. Their forced journey west became known to the Cherokee people as the Trail Where They Cried. Historians call it the **Trail of Tears.**

✓ **Reading Check** **Explaining** What was the purpose of the Indian Removal Act?

Native American Resistance

In 1832 the Sauk chieftain, **Black Hawk,** led a force of Sauk and Fox people back to Illinois, their homeland. They wanted to recapture this area, which had been given up in a treaty. The Illinois state militia and federal troops responded with force, gathering nearly 4,500 soldiers. They chased the Fox and Sauk to the Mississippi River and slaughtered most of the Native Americans as they tried to flee westward into present-day Iowa.

The Seminole people of Florida were the only Native Americans who successfully resisted their removal. Although they were pressured in the early 1830s to sign treaties giving up their land, the Seminole chief, **Osceola,** and some of his people refused to leave Florida. The Seminole decided to go to war against the United States instead.

In 1835 the Seminole joined forces with a group of African Americans who had run away to escape slavery. Together they attacked white settlements along the Florida coast. They used guerrilla tactics, making surprise attacks and then retreating back into the forests and swamps. In December 1835, Seminole ambushed soldiers under the command of Major Francis Dade. Only a few of the 110 soldiers survived the attack. The Dade Massacre pressured the call for more troops and equipment to fight the Seminole.

By 1842 more than 1,500 American soldiers had died in the Seminole wars. The government gave up and allowed some of the Seminole to remain in Florida. Many Seminole, however,

HISTORY Online
Student Web Activity
Visit taj.glencoe.com and click on **Chapter 11— Student Web Activities** for an activity on the Trail of Tears.

"We told them to let us alone and keep away from us; but they followed on."

—Black Hawk, Sauk leader (far right), pictured here with his son, Whirling Thunder

had died in the long war, and many more were captured and forced to move westward. After 1842 only a few scattered groups of Native Americans lived east of the Mississippi. Most had been removed to the West. Native Americans had given up more than 100 million acres of eastern land to the federal government. They had received in return about $68 million and 32 million acres in lands west of the Mississippi River. There they lived, divided by tribes, in reservations. Eventually, these reservations, too, would face intrusion from white civilization.

The area of present-day Oklahoma became part of the United States in 1803 with the Louisiana Purchase. The United States set aside this area as the home for various Native American groups.

The Five Civilized Tribes were relocated in the eastern half of present-day Oklahoma on lands claimed by several Plains groups, including the Osage, Comanche, and Kiowa. United States Army leaders got agreements from the Plains groups to let the Five Civilized Tribes live in peace. Settled in their new homes, the Five Tribes developed their governments, improved their farms, and built schools. The Five Tribes also developed a police force called the Lighthorsemen. This law enforcement unit maintained safety for the region.

Reading Check **Comparing** How was the response of the Seminoles different from that of the Cherokee when they were removed from their lands?

SECTION 2 ASSESSMENT

Checking for Understanding

1. **Key Terms** Use the terms relocate and guerrilla tactics in complete sentences that will explain their meanings.
2. **Analyzing** Analyze how President Jackson reacted to the Supreme Court decision supporting the Cherokees' rights.

Reviewing Themes

3. **Groups and Institutions** How were the Seminole able to resist relocation?

Critical Thinking

4. **Drawing Conclusions** How was Georgia's policy toward the Cherokee different from the previous federal policy?
5. **Organizing Information** Re-create the diagram below to show how the Cherokee were eventually removed from their land.

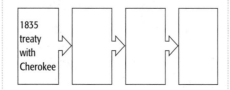

Analyzing Visuals

6. **Geography Skills** Study the maps on page 342. Which groups of Native Americans were located in Alabama? What does the inset map show? In what area of Florida was the Seminole reservation?

Interdisciplinary Activity

Persuasive Writing Write a letter to Andrew Jackson telling him why the Native Americans should or should not be allowed to stay in their homelands.

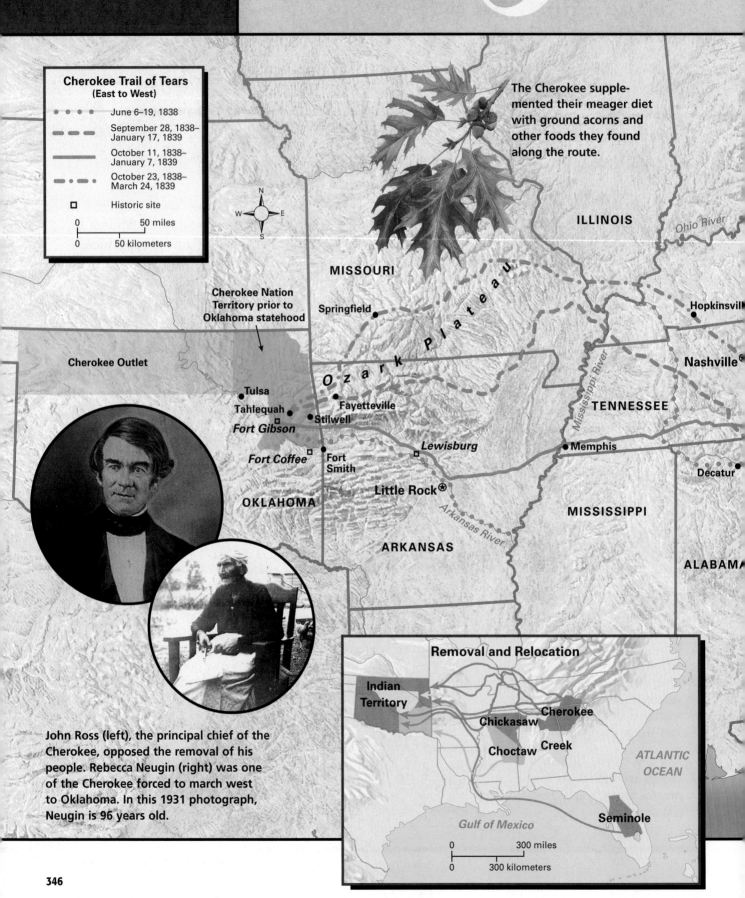

Cherokee Trail of Tears
(East to West)

- · · · · June 6–19, 1838
- – – – September 28, 1838– January 17, 1839
- ——— October 11, 1838– January 7, 1839
- –·–·– October 23, 1838– March 24, 1839
- □ Historic site

0 ————— 50 miles
0 ————— 50 kilometers

The Cherokee supplemented their meager diet with ground acorns and other foods they found along the route.

ILLINOIS

Ohio River

Cherokee Nation Territory prior to Oklahoma statehood

MISSOURI

Springfield

Hopkinsvill

Ozark Plateau

Nashville

Cherokee Outlet

Tulsa

Tahlequah
Fort Gibson
Stilwell

Fayetteville

TENNESSEE

Mississippi River

Fort Coffee

Fort Smith

Lewisburg

Memphis

Decatur

Little Rock

OKLAHOMA

Arkansas River

MISSISSIPPI

ARKANSAS

ALABAMA

John Ross (left), the principal chief of the Cherokee, opposed the removal of his people. Rebecca Neugin (right) was one of the Cherokee forced to march west to Oklahoma. In this 1931 photograph, Neugin is 96 years old.

Removal and Relocation

Indian Territory

Chickasaw

Cherokee

Choctaw

Creek

ATLANTIC OCEAN

Gulf of Mexico

Seminole

0 ————— 300 miles
0 ————— 300 kilometers

TRAIL OF TEARS

LONG BEFORE EUROPEAN EXPLORERS ARRIVED, the Cherokee, Chickasaw, Choctaw, Creek, and Seminole were living in eastern North America. The Native Americans built permanent communities, practiced agriculture, and developed complex tribal governments—thereby earning the name of Five Civilized Tribes.

REMOVAL

As white settlers moved into the southeastern states, they began demanding the land held by Native Americans. In 1830, Congress passed the Indian Removal Act to move the Five Civilized Tribes west of the Mississippi. Under pressure, the Choctaw, Chickasaw, and Creek moved west while the Cherokee and the Seminole resisted.

RESISTANCE

Despite protests from the Cherokee people, they were forced to march west. In 1838, 13 ragged groups trekked to Fort Gibson in the newly created Indian Territory (see maps). Along the journey, which became known as the "Trail of Tears," 4,000 Cherokee died of cold, hunger, or disease.

Some of the Seminole refused to abandon their homeland and waged a guerrilla war in the Florida Everglades until the government gave up its efforts to resettle them in 1842.

KENTUCKY

APPALACHIAN MOUNTAINS

NORTH CAROLINA

Cherokee

Fort Cass

Chattanooga

New Echota

SOUTH CAROLINA

Fort Payne

Atlanta

GEORGIA

Most Cherokee farmers lived in log cabins.

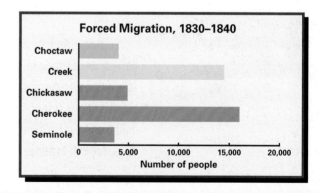

Forced Migration, 1830–1840

	Number of people
Choctaw	
Creek	
Chickasaw	
Cherokee	
Seminole	

0   5,000   10,000   15,000   20,000

LEARNING from GEOGRAPHY

1. To what present-day state were the Five Civilized Tribes forced to move?

2. Through what cities did the Cherokee travel during the removal that began on June 6, 1838?

SECTION 3 Jackson and the Bank

Main Idea
Economic issues affected the presidencies of Andrew Jackson and Martin Van Buren.

Key Terms
veto, depression, laissez-faire, log cabin campaign

Reading Strategy
Sequencing Information As you read the section, re-create the diagram below. In the spaces provided, describe the steps Andrew Jackson took that put the Bank of the United States out of business.

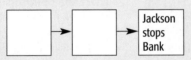

Jackson stops Bank

Read to Learn
• why Jackson wanted to destroy the Bank of the United States.
• how the Whigs came to power in 1840.

Section Theme
Economic Factors Economic issues influenced politics in the mid-1800s.

Preview of Events

♦ 1830	♦ 1835	♦ 1840	♦ 1845

1832
Andrew Jackson challenges the Bank of the United States

1836
Martin Van Buren is elected president

1837
Panic of 1837 strikes the nation

1841
Vice President John Tyler becomes president

Bank note issued in the mid-1800s

AN American Story

President Andrew Jackson made many enemies. His most outspoken rivals, the Whigs, were strong in Congress. They accused "King Andrew" of increasing his power and spreading corruption with the spoils system. In response, Jackson declared that the president was responsible for the protection of "the liberties and rights of the people and the integrity of the Constitution against the Senate, or the House of Representatives, or both together."

War Against the Bank

Jackson had another great battle during his presidency. For years, he had attacked the Bank of the United States as being an organization of wealthy Easterners over which ordinary citizens had no control. The Bank of the United States was a powerful institution. It held the federal government's money and controlled much of the country's money supply. Although the Bank had been chartered by Congress, it was run by private bankers rather than elected officials.

The Bank's president, **Nicholas Biddle,** represented everything Jackson disliked. Jackson prided himself on being a self-made man who started with nothing. Biddle, on the other hand, came from a wealthy family and had a good education and social standing.

In 1832 Jackson's opponents gave him the chance to take action against the Bank. Senators **Henry Clay** and **Daniel Webster,** friends of Biddle, planned to use the Bank to defeat Jackson in the 1832 presidential election. They persuaded Biddle to apply early for a new charter—a government permit to operate the Bank—even though the Bank's current charter did not expire until 1836.

Clay and Webster believed the Bank had popular support. They thought that an attempt by Jackson to veto its charter would lead to his defeat and allow Henry Clay to be elected president.

When the bill to renew the Bank's charter came to Jackson for signature, he was sick in bed. Jackson told his friend **Martin Van Buren,** "The bank, Mr. Van Buren, is trying to kill me. But I will kill it!" Jackson vetoed, or rejected, the bill.

Jackson, like many others, still felt the Bank was unconstitutional despite the Supreme Court's decision to the contrary in *McCulloch* v. *Maryland* (1819). In a message to Congress, Jackson angrily denounced the Bank, arguing that

> 66 . . . when laws . . . make the rich richer and the potent more powerful, the humble members of society—the farmers, mechanics, and laborers—who have neither the time nor the means of securing like favors to themselves, have a right to complain of the injustice of their Government. 99

The Election of 1832

Webster and Clay were right about one thing. The Bank of the United States did play a large part in the campaign of 1832. Their strategy for

Analyzing *Political Cartoons*

Many cartoons from the period depicted Jackson's battle against the Second Bank of the United States. **Does this cartoon support the president or the Bank? Explain.**

A The Bank   **B** President Jackson   **C** American people

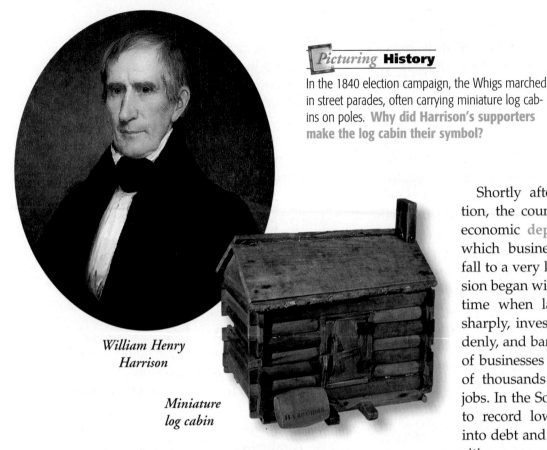

Picturing **History**

In the 1840 election campaign, the Whigs marched in street parades, often carrying miniature log cabins on poles. **Why did Harrison's supporters make the log cabin their symbol?**

*William Henry
Harrison*

*Miniature
log cabin*

gaining support for Clay as president, however, backfired. Most people supported Jackson's veto of the bank charter bill. Jackson was re-elected, receiving 55 percent of the popular vote and collecting 219 electoral votes to Clay's 49. Martin Van Buren was elected vice president.

Once re-elected, Jackson decided on a plan to "kill" the Bank ahead of the 1836 schedule. He ordered the withdrawal of all government deposits from the Bank and placed the funds in smaller state banks. In 1836 he refused to sign a new charter for the Bank, and it closed.

Economics

The Panic of 1837

When Jackson decided not to run for a third term in 1836, the Democrats selected Martin Van Buren of New York, Jackson's friend and vice president, as their candidate. Van Buren faced bitter opposition from the Whigs, a new political party that included former National Republicans and other anti-Jackson forces. Jackson's great popularity and his personal support helped Van Buren easily defeat several Whig opponents. Van Buren was inaugurated in 1837.

Shortly after Van Buren's election, the country entered a severe economic depression, a period in which business and employment fall to a very low level. The depression began with the Panic of 1837, a time when land values dropped sharply, investments declined suddenly, and banks failed. Thousands of businesses closed and hundreds of thousands of people lost their jobs. In the South, cotton prices fell to record lows. Farmers plunged into debt and lost their land. In the cities, many people could not afford food or rent. In February 1837, people in New York put up signs voicing their anger:

❝Bread, Meat, Rent, and Fuel!
Their prices must come down!
The Voice of the People shall be heard
and will prevail!❞

President Van Buren believed in the principle of laissez-faire—that government should interfere as little as possible in the nation's economy. Van Buren did persuade Congress to establish an independent federal treasury in 1840. The government would no longer deposit its money with private individual banks as it had started to do during President Jackson's war with the Bank of the United States. Instead the government would store its money in the federal treasury. The private banks had used government funds to back their banknotes. The new treasury system would prevent banks from using government funds in this way and so help guard against further bank crises.

Van Buren and his supporters hailed the new law as a "second declaration of independence." However, criticism of the act came from members of Van Buren's own Democratic Party as well as from Whigs. The split in the Democratic Party meant the Whigs had a chance to win the presidency in 1840.

✓ **Reading Check** **Explaining** What was the new treasury system supposed to prevent?

The Whigs Come to Power

The Democrats had controlled the presidency for 12 years. However, with the country still in the depths of depression, the Whigs thought they had a chance to win the election in 1840. They nominated **William Henry Harrison,** a hero of the War of 1812, to run against President Van Buren. **John Tyler**, a planter from Virginia, was Harrison's running mate. Because Harrison had gained national fame defeating Tecumseh's followers in the Battle of Tippecanoe, the Whigs' campaign slogan was "Tippecanoe and Tyler Too."

To win the election, Harrison had to gain the support of the laborers and farmers who had voted for Jackson. The Whigs adopted a log cabin as their symbol. Political cartoons in newspapers showed Harrison, a wealthy man from Virginia, in front of a log cabin. The Whigs wanted to show that their candidate was a "man of the people."

The Whigs also ridiculed Van Buren as "King Martin," a wealthy snob who had spent the people's money on fancy furniture for the White House. The log cabin campaign seemed to work, and Harrison went on to defeat Van Buren by a wide margin.

William Henry Harrison was inaugurated in 1841 as the first Whig president. The Whigs were still celebrating their victory when Harrison died of pneumonia on April 4, 1841. John Tyler of Virginia became the first vice president to gain the presidency because the elected president died in office.

Although Tyler had been elected vice president as a Whig, he had once been a Democrat. As president, Tyler, a strong supporter of states' rights, vetoed several bills sponsored by Whigs in Congress, including a bill to recharter the Bank of the United States. His lack of party loyalty outraged Whigs. Most of Tyler's cabinet resigned, and Whig leaders in Congress expelled Tyler from the party.

It seemed that the Whigs could not agree on their party's goals. Increasingly, Whigs voted according to sectional ties—North, South, and West—not party ties. This division may explain why the Whig candidate, Henry Clay, lost the election of 1844 to Democratic candidate **James Polk.** After only four years, the Whigs were out of power again.

✓ **Reading Check** **Describing** How did John Tyler become president?

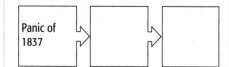

SECTION 3 ASSESSMENT

Checking for Understanding

1. **Key Terms** Use each of these terms in a complete sentence that will help explain its meaning: veto, depression, laissez-faire, log cabin campaign.
2. **Reviewing Facts** List Jackson's reasons for wanting to "kill" the Bank of the United States.

Reviewing Themes

3. **Economic Factors** Why did President Van Buren do little to solve the nation's economic problems during the depression?

Critical Thinking

4. **Analyzing Information** What tactics did the Whigs borrow from Jackson's campaign to win the election of 1840?
5. **Organizing Information** Re-create the diagram below to show how the Panic of 1837 affected the presidency of Martin Van Buren.

```
┌────────┐     ┌────────┐     ┌────────┐
│ Panic of│ ──▷ │        │ ──▷ │        │
│ 1837   │     │        │     │        │
└────────┘     └────────┘     └────────┘
```

Analyzing Visuals

6. **Analyzing Political Cartoons** Study the cartoon on page 349. Do you think the Bank of the United States is portrayed positively or negatively? Explain your answer.

Interdisciplinary Activity

Art Write a campaign slogan for Van Buren or Harrison in the election of 1840. Then design a campaign button that incorporates your slogan.

Chapter Summary

The Jackson Era

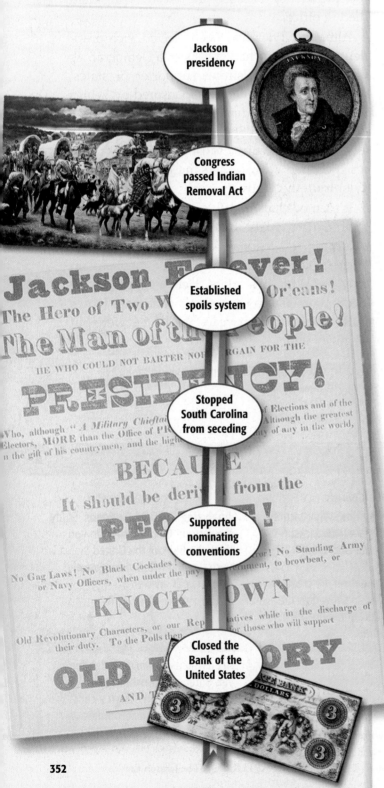

Jackson presidency

Congress passed Indian Removal Act

Established spoils system

Stopped South Carolina from seceding

Supported nominating conventions

Closed the Bank of the United States

Reviewing Key Terms

On graph paper, create a word search puzzle using the following terms. Crisscross the terms vertically and horizontally. Then fill in the remaining squares with extra letters. List the definitions below the puzzle as clues. Share your puzzle with a classmate.

1. plurality
2. landslide
3. suffrage
4. majority
5. nullify
6. secede
7. depression

Reviewing Key Facts

8. How did the supporters of Jackson and Adams differ in their beliefs?

9. What were some of the political tactics used by Democratic-Republicans and the National Republicans in the election of 1828?

10. Which Americans were prohibited from voting in most states before the 1800s?

11. How did nominating conventions make the selection of political candidates more democratic?

12. Why was the South against high tariffs?

13. Who did the Seminoles join forces with as they fought against forced removal from their land?

14. How did the Panic of 1837 affect the nation's economy?

15. Why was Harrison's log cabin campaign successful?

Critical Thinking

16. **Drawing Conclusions** President Andrew Jackson promised "equal protection and equal benefits" for all Americans. Do you think he included Native Americans in his promise? Why or why not?

17. **Analyzing Themes: Groups and Institutions** What agreement did the Cherokee Nation make with the federal government that Georgia refused to recognize?

18. **Organizing Information** Re-create the chart below. List the issues that Jackson dealt with during his presidency. Then describe how he responded to each issue.

Issues	Jackson's response

Geography and History Activity

The issue of states' rights was debated in the election of 1828. Study the map below and answer the questions that follow.

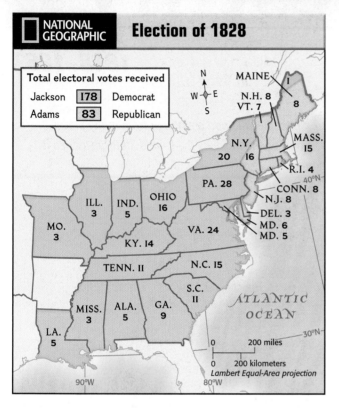

NATIONAL GEOGRAPHIC **Election of 1828**

Total electoral votes received

| Jackson | 178 | Democrat |
| Adams | 83 | Republican |

MAINE
N.H. 8
VT. 7
8

MASS. 15
N.Y. 20 16
R.I. 4
40°N
CONN. 8
PA. 28
N.J. 8
DEL. 3
MD. 6
MD. 5

ILL. 3   IND. 5   OHIO 16

MO. 3
VA. 24
KY. 14

TENN. 11   N.C. 15

S.C. 11

MISS. 3   ALA. 5   GA. 9

LA. 5

ATLANTIC OCEAN

30°N

0   200 miles
0   200 kilometers
Lambert Equal-Area projection

90°W   80°W

19. Region Which general areas of the United States voted for Andrew Jackson in the election of 1828?

20. Location Which candidate won more votes in Adams's home state of Massachusetts?

21. Place Which three states divided their total electoral count between the two candidates?

Practicing Skills

Analyzing Primary Sources *In an annual message to Congress in 1835, President Andrew Jackson spoke the words below. Read the excerpt and answer the questions that follow.*

> ❝All preceding experiments for the improvement of the Indians have failed. It seems now to be an established fact that they cannot live in contact with a civilized community and prosper. . . .
> A country west of Missouri and Arkansas has been assigned to them, into which the white settlements are not to be pushed.❞

22. Whose opinion is stated in the excerpt?

23. What is the speaker's attitude toward Native Americans?

24. According to the speaker, why should Native Americans be assigned to a country west of Missouri and Arkansas?

Citizenship Cooperative Activity

25. Becoming an Informed Voter With a partner, choose an election in your community. Outline how you would become informed on the candidates and/or the issues. Then follow your outline and become an informed voter. Share your outline and your findings with the class.

Economics Activity

26. Look in a dictionary to find definitions of "recession" and "depression." Write a paragraph to explain the difference between the two.

The Princeton Review **Standardized Test Practice**

Directions: Choose the *best* answer to the following question.

Which of the following statements expresses an opinion about Andrew Jackson?

A Jackson served two terms as president.

B He spoke out against South Carolina's Nullification Act.

C Because of Jackson, the United States has the best system of filling government positions.

D Jackson supported the Indian Removal Act.

Test-Taking Tip

An opinion is a person's belief. It is not a proven fact (such as answer A). Opinions often contain subjective words, like *easier* or *best.*

Manifest Destiny

1818–1853

Why It Matters

The United States was made up of people who had emigrated from many places in the world. Many Americans remained on the move as the United States extended its political borders and grew economically.

The Impact Today

The United States grew in size and wealth, setting the stage for the nation's rise to great economic and political power.

 The American Journey Video *The chapter 12 video, "Whose Destiny?," chronicles the influence of Manifest Destiny on the history of Texas.*

1820
• Missouri Compromise

1809
• Elizabeth Ann Seton founds Sisters of Charity

1824
• Russia surrenders land south of Alaska

United States
PRESIDENTS

| Madison 1809–1817 | Monroe 1817–1825 | J.Q. Adams 1825–1829 | Jackson 1829–1837 |

1810   *1820*   *1830*

World

1821
• Mexico declares independence from Spain

1828
• Russia declares war on Ottoman Empire

1830
• France occupies Algeria

War News from Mexico by Richard Caton Woodville Many of Woodville's paintings show scenes of everyday life.

1845
• U.S. annexes Texas

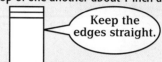

1848
• Treaty of Guadalupe Hidalgo signed

1846
• Congress declares war on Mexico

1850
• California becomes a state

1836
• Battle of the Alamo

| Van Buren 1837–1841 | W.H. Harrison 1841 | Tyler 1841–1845 | Polk 1845–1849 | Taylor 1849–1850 |

1840

1850

1839
• Opium War between Britain and China

1844
• The Dominican Republic secedes from Haiti

1846
• The planet Neptune is discovered

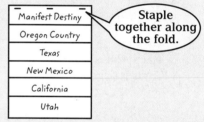

HISTORY Online

Chapter Overview
Visit taj.glencoe.com and click on **Chapter 12—Chapter Overviews** to preview chapter information.

The Oregon Country

Guide to Reading

Main Idea
Manifest Destiny is the idea that the United States was meant to extend its borders from the Atlantic Ocean to the Pacific Ocean.

Key Terms
joint occupation, mountain man, rendezvous, emigrant, Manifest Destiny

Reading Strategy
Sequencing Information As you read Section 1, re-create the diagram below and in the boxes list key events that occurred.

1819	1825	1836	1846

Read to Learn
• why large numbers of settlers headed for the Oregon country.
• how the idea of Manifest Destiny contributed to the nation's growth.

Section Theme
Economic Factors Many fur traders and pioneers moved to Oregon for economic opportunities.

Preview of Events

♦1820	♦1830	♦1840	♦1850
1819 Adams-Onís Treaty is signed	**1836** Marcus Whitman builds mission in Oregon	**1840s** "Oregon fever" sweeps through Mississippi Valley	**1846** U.S. and Britain set the Oregon Boundary at 49°N

AN American Story

On an April morning in 1851, 13-year-old Martha Gay said good-bye to her friends, her home, and the familiar world of Springfield, Missouri. She and her family were beginning a long, hazardous journey. The townsfolk watched as the Gays left in four big wagons pulled by teams of oxen. "Farewell sermons were preached and prayers offered for our safety," Martha wrote years later. "All places of business and the school were closed . . . and everybody came to say good-bye to us." This same scene occurred many times in the 1840s and 1850s as thousands of families set out for the Oregon country.

Doll owned by a young pioneer

Rivalry in the Northwest

The **Oregon country** was the huge area that lay between the Pacific Ocean and the Rocky Mountains north of **California.** It included all of what is now Oregon, Washington, and Idaho plus parts of Montana and Wyoming. The region also contained about half of what is now the Canadian province of British Columbia.

In the early 1800s, four nations laid claim to the vast, rugged land known as the Oregon country. The United States based its claim on Robert Gray's discovery of the **Columbia River** in 1792 and on the Lewis and Clark expedition. Great Britain based its claim on British explorations of the Columbia River. Spain, which had also explored the Pacific coast in the late 1700s, controlled California to the south. Russia had settlements that stretched south from **Alaska** into Oregon.

Adams-Onís Treaty

Many Americans wanted control of the Oregon country to gain access to the Pacific Ocean. Secretary of State **John Quincy Adams** played a key role in promoting this goal. In 1819 he negotiated the **Adams-Onís Treaty** with Spain. In the treaty the Spanish agreed to set the limits of their territory at what is now California's northern border and gave up any claim to Oregon. In 1824 Russia also surrendered its claim to the land south of Alaska. Only Britain remained to challenge American control of Oregon.

In 1818 Adams had worked out an agreement with Britain for joint occupation of the area. This meant that people from both the United States and Great Britain could settle there. When Adams became president in 1825, he proposed that the two nations divide Oregon along the 49°N line of latitude. Britain refused, insisting on a larger share of the territory. Unable to resolve their dispute, the two countries agreed to extend the joint occupation. In the following years, thousands of Americans streamed into Oregon, and they pushed the issue toward resolution.

Mountain Men

The first Americans to reach the Oregon country were not farmers but fur traders. They had come to trap beaver, whose skins were in great demand in the eastern United States and in Europe. The British established several trading posts in the region, as did merchant **John Jacob Astor** of New York. In 1808 Astor organized the American Fur Company. The American Fur Company soon became the most powerful of the fur companies in America. It allowed him to build up trade with the East Coast, the Pacific Northwest, and China.

At first the merchants traded for furs that the Native Americans supplied. Gradually American adventurers joined the trade. These people, who spent most of their time in the Rocky Mountains, came to be known as mountain men.

The tough, independent mountain men made their living by trapping beaver. Many had Native American wives and adopted Native American ways. They lived in buffalo-skin lodges and dressed in fringed buckskin pants, moccasins, and beads.

Some mountain men worked for fur-trading companies; others sold their furs to the highest bidder. Throughout the spring and early summer they ranged across the mountains, setting traps and then collecting the beaver pelts. In late summer they gathered for a rendezvous (RAHN•dih•voo), or meeting.

For the mountain men, the annual rendezvous was the high point of the year. They met with the trading companies to exchange their "hairy

"To explore unknown regions . . . was [the mountain men's] chief delight."

—*Clerk in a fur trade company*

banknotes"—beaver skins—for traps, guns, coffee, and other goods. They met old friends and exchanged news. They relaxed by competing in races and various other contests—including swapping stories about who had been on the most exciting adventures.

As they roamed searching for beaver, the mountain men explored the mountains, valleys, and trails of the West. Jim Beckwourth, an African American from Virginia, explored Wyoming's Green River. Robert Stuart and Jedediah Smith both found the **South Pass,** a broad break through the Rockies. South Pass later became the main route that settlers took to Oregon.

To survive in the wilderness, a mountain man had to be skillful and resourceful. Trapper Joe Meek told how, when faced with starvation, he once held his hands "in an anthill until they were covered with ants, then greedily licked them off." The mountain men took pride in joking about the dangers they faced.

In time the mountain men killed off most of the beaver and could no longer trap. Some went to settle on farms in Oregon. With their knowledge of the western lands, though, some mountain men found new work. Jim Bridger, Kit Carson, and others acted as guides to lead the parties of settlers now streaming west.

Reading Check **Identifying** What North American territories did Russia control in the early 1800s?

Alaska

Is Alaska the largest state? If you calculate by area, Alaska is far and away the largest state, with more than 570,000 square miles. It is approximately 2,000 miles from east to west. If placed on top of the mainland area of the United States, it would stretch from Atlanta to Los Angeles. Population is another matter. Alaska's population of 626,932 makes it the third least populous state. There is about 1.0 person per square mile in Alaska, compared to more than 79 people per square mile for the rest of the United States.

Settling Oregon

Americans began traveling to the Oregon country to settle in the 1830s. Reports of the fertile land persuaded many to make the journey. Economic troubles at home made new opportunities in the West look attractive.

The Whitman Mission

Among the first settlers of the Oregon country were missionaries who wanted to bring Christianity to the Native Americans. Dr. Marcus Whitman and his wife, Narcissa, went to Oregon in 1836 and built a mission among the Cayuse people near the present site of Walla Walla, Washington.

New settlers unknowingly brought measles to the mission. An epidemic killed many of the Native American children. Blaming the Whitmans for the sickness, the Cayuse attacked the mission in November 1847 and killed them and 11 others. Despite this, the flood of settlers continued into Oregon.

The Oregon Trail

In the early 1840s, "Oregon fever" swept through the Mississippi Valley. The depression caused by the Panic of 1837 had hit the region hard. People formed societies to gather information about Oregon and to plan and make the long trip. The "great migration" had begun. Tens of thousands of people made the trip. These pioneers were called emigrants because they left the United States to go to Oregon.

Before the difficult 2,000-mile journey, these pioneers stuffed their canvas-covered wagons, called **prairie schooners,** with supplies. From a distance these wagons looked like schooners (ships) at sea. Gathering in Independence or other towns in Missouri, they followed the **Oregon Trail** across the Great Plains, along the Platte River, and through the South Pass of the Rocky Mountains. On the other side, they took the trail north and west along the Snake and Columbia Rivers into the Oregon country.

Reading Check **Explaining** How did most pioneers get to Oregon?

MORE ABOUT...

The Oregon Trail

The Importance of the Trail The Oregon Trail was much more than just a trail to Oregon. It served as the most practical route to the western United States. The pioneers traveled in large groups, often of related families. Some went all the way to Oregon in search of farmland. Many others split off for California in search of gold.

The Journey The trip west lasted five or six months. The pioneers had to start in the spring and complete the trip before winter snows blocked the mountain passes. The trail crossed difficult terrain. The pioneers walked across seemingly endless plains, forded swift rivers, and labored up high mountains.

"We are creeping along slowly, one wagon after another, the same old gait, the same thing over, out of one mud hole into another all day."

—Amelia Stewart Knight, 1853

Problems Along the Way Although the pioneers feared attacks by Native Americans, such attacks did not often occur. More often Native Americans assisted the pioneers, serving as guides and trading necessary food and supplies. About 1 in 10 of the pioneers died on the trail, perishing from disease, overwork, hunger, or accidents.

"After Laramie we entered the great American desert, which was hard on the teams. Sickness became common. . . ."

—Catherine Sager Pringle, 1844

When did use of the trail stop? With the building of a transcontinental railroad in 1869, the days of using the Oregon Trail as a corridor to the West were over.

The Division of Oregon

Most American pioneers headed for the fertile **Willamette Valley** south of the Columbia River. Between 1840 and 1845, the number of American settlers in the area increased from 500 to 5,000, while the British population remained at about 700. The question of ownership of Oregon arose again.

Expansion of Freedom

Since colonial times many Americans had believed their nation had a special role to fulfill. For years people thought the nation's mission should

be to serve as a model of freedom and democracy. In the 1800s that vision changed. Many believed that the United States's mission was to spread freedom by occupying the entire continent. In 1819 John Quincy Adams expressed what many Americans were thinking when he said expansion to the Pacific was as inevitable "as that the Mississippi should flow to the sea."

Manifest Destiny

In the 1840s New York newspaper editor John O'Sullivan put the idea of a national mission in more specific words. O'Sullivan declared it was

Fact **Fiction** **Folklore**

The Presidency

Who was the first "dark horse" president? A dark horse is a little-known contender who unexpectedly wins. In 1844 the Democrats passed over Martin Van Buren, John C. Calhoun, and other party leaders. Instead, they nominated James K. Polk, the governor of Tennessee. The Whigs were confident that their candidate, the celebrated Henry Clay, would win the election easily. Contrary to all expectations, Polk won the election, becoming at age 49 the youngest president in American history up to that time.

America's "Manifest Destiny to overspread and to possess the whole of the continent which Providence has given us." O'Sullivan meant that the United States was clearly destined—set apart for a special purpose—to extend its boundaries all the way to the Pacific.

"Fifty-four Forty or Fight"

The settlers in Oregon insisted that the United States should have sole ownership of the area. More and more Americans agreed. As a result Oregon became a significant issue in the 1844 presidential election.

James K. Polk received the Democratic Party's nomination for president, partly because he supported American claims for sole ownership of Oregon. Democrats campaigned using the slogan "Fifty-four Forty or Fight." The slogan referred to the line of latitude that Democrats believed should be the nation's northern border in Oregon.

Henry Clay of the Whig Party, Polk's principal opponent, did not take a strong position on the Oregon issue. Polk won the election because the antislavery Liberty Party took so many votes from Clay in New York that Polk won the state. Polk won 170 electoral votes to 105 for Clay.

Reaching a Settlement

Filled with the spirit of Manifest Destiny, President Polk was determined to make Oregon part of the United States. Britain would not accept a border at "Fifty-four Forty," however. To do so would have meant giving up its claim entirely. Instead, in June 1846, the two countries compromised, setting the boundary between the American and British portions of Oregon at latitude 49°N.

During the 1830s Americans sought to fulfill their Manifest Destiny by looking much closer to home than Oregon. At that time much attention was also focused on Texas.

✓ **Reading Check** **Explaining** In what way did some people think of Manifest Destiny as a purpose?

SECTION 1 ASSESSMENT

Checking for Understanding

1. **Key Terms** Use each of these terms in a complete sentence that will help explain its meaning: joint occupation, mountain man, rendezvous, emigrant, Manifest Destiny.
2. **Reviewing Facts** Name the four countries that claimed parts of the Oregon country.

Reviewing Themes

3. **Economic Factors** How did the fur trade in Oregon aid Americans who began settling there?

Critical Thinking

4. **Making Generalizations** How did the idea of Manifest Destiny help Americans justify their desire to extend the United States to the Pacific Ocean?
5. **Determining Cause and Effect** Re-create the diagram below. In the box, describe how the fur trade led to interest in Oregon.

Cause
The fur trade develops

Analyzing Visuals

6. **Picturing History** Study the painting on page 359. Do you think it provides a realistic portrayal of the journey west?

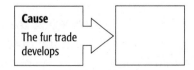

Informative Writing Imagine you and your family are traveling to the Oregon country in the 1840s. A friend will be making the same trip soon. Write a letter telling your friend what to expect on the journey.

Understanding Latitude and Longitude

Why Learn This Skill?

Your new friend invites you to her house. In giving directions, she says, "I live on Summit Street at the southwest corner of Indiana Avenue." She has pinpointed her exact location. We use a similar system of lines of latitude and longitude to pinpoint locations on maps and globes.

Learning the Skill

The imaginary horizontal lines that circle the globe from east to west are called lines of **latitude.** Because the distance between the lines of latitude is always the same, they are also called *parallels.* The imaginary vertical lines that intersect the parallels are lines of **longitude,** also called *meridians.*

Lines of longitude run from the North Pole to the South Pole. They are numbered in degrees east or west of a starting line called the Prime Meridian, which is at 0° longitude. On the opposite side of the earth from the Prime Meridian is the International Date Line, or 180° longitude.

The point at which parallels and meridians intersect is the grid address, or coordinates, of an exact location. The coordinates for Salt Lake City, for example, are 41°N and 112°W.

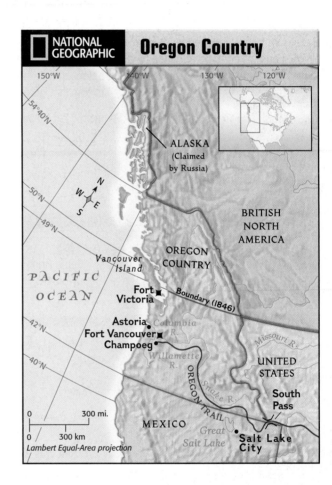

NATIONAL GEOGRAPHIC — Oregon Country

Practicing the Skill

Analyze the information on the map on this page, then answer the following questions.

1. What are the approximate coordinates of Fort Victoria?

2. At what line of latitude was the Oregon country divided between the United States and Britain?

3. What geographic feature lies at about 42°N and 115°W?

Applying the Skill

Understanding Latitude and Longitude Turn to the atlas map of the United States on pages RA2 and RA3. Find your city or the city closest to it. Identify the coordinates as closely as possible. Now list the coordinates of five other cities and ask a classmate to find the cities based on your coordinates.

 GO TO Glencoe's **Skillbuilder Interactive Workbook CD-ROM, Level 1,** provides instruction and practice in key social studies skills.

Independence for Texas

Davy Crockett

AN American Story

Davy Crockett was a backwoodsman from Tennessee. His skill as a hunter and story-teller helped get him elected to three terms in Congress. But when he started his first political campaign, Crockett was doubtful about his chances of winning. "The thought of having to make a speech made my knees feel mighty weak and set my heart to fluttering." Fortunately for Crockett, the other candidates spoke all day and tired out the audience. "When they were all done," Crockett boasted, "I got up and told some laughable story, and quit. . . . I went home, and didn't go back again till after the election was over." In the end, Crockett won the election by a wide margin.

A Clash of Cultures

Davy Crockett of Tennessee won notice for his frontier skills, his sense of humor, and the shrewd common sense he often displayed in politics. When he lost his seat in Congress in 1835, he did not return to Tennessee. Instead he went southwest to Texas.

Crockett thought he could make a new start there. He also wanted to help the Texans win their independence from Mexico. Little did he know his deeds in Texas would bring him greater fame than his adventures on the frontier or his years in Congress.

Conflict over Texas began in 1803, when the United States bought the Louisiana Territory from France. Americans claimed that the land in present-day Texas was part of the purchase. Spain protested. In 1819, in the **Adams-Onís Treaty,** the United States agreed to drop any further claim to the region.

Land Grants

At the time, few people lived in Texas. Most residents—about 3,000—were Tejanos (teh•HAH•nohs), or Mexicans who claimed Texas as their home. Native Americans including Comanches, Apaches, and Kiowas, also lived in the area.

Because the Spanish wanted to promote the growth of Texas, they offered vast tracts of land to people who agreed to bring families to settle on the land. The people who obtained these grants from the government and recruited the settlers were called empresarios.

Moses Austin, a businessman who had developed a mining operation in Missouri, applied for and received the first land grant in 1821. Before he could establish his colony, however, Moses contracted pneumonia and died. After Mexico declared independence from Spain, Austin's son, **Stephen F. Austin,** asked the Mexican government to confirm his father's land grant. Once he received confirmation, he began to organize the colony.

Stephen F. Austin recruited 300 American families to settle the fertile land along the Brazos River and the Colorado River of Texas. The first settlers came to be called the **Old Three Hundred.** Many received 960 acres, with additional acres for each child. Others received larger ranches. Austin's success made him a leader among the American settlers in Texas.

From 1823 to 1825, Mexico passed three colonization laws. All these laws offered new settlers large tracts of land at extremely low prices and

People In History

Stephen F. Austin 1793–1836

Stephen F. Austin earned the name "Father of Texas" because of his leadership in populating the Mexican territory of Texas. After attending college he worked as a businessperson. Austin organized the first land grant colony in Texas in 1821. Austin offered large tracts of land to settlers, and his colony grew quickly.

Austin often played the role of spokesperson with the Mexican government, sometimes on behalf of colonists who were not part of his settlement. He served as their advocate, even when he disagreed with their opinions. For example, he negotiated for permission to continue slavery in the province of Texas after it was banned by Mexican law. He also served

nearly a year in prison for promoting independence for the Texans.

After Texas won its war for independence, Austin ran for the office of president. He was defeated but was appointed secretary of state. He died just a few months later. The state of Texas honored Stephen F. Austin by naming its capital city—Austin—after its founding father.

What If...

The Defenders Had Not Stayed at the Alamo?

William Travis and almost 200 other defenders were determined to hold the Alamo. Travis wrote several messages to the people of Texas and the United States asking them for assistance. Travis's appeal was unsuccessful. Texas military forces were not yet well organized and were badly scattered. Travis's letter of February 24, 1836, is one of the finest statements of courage in American history.

The defenders—mostly volunteers—were free to leave whenever they chose. But they decided to defend the Alamo for a cause in which they believed.

Santa Anna hoped the fall of the Alamo would convince other Texans that it was useless to resist his armies. Instead, the heroism of those in the Alamo inspired other Texans to carry on the struggle. "Remember the Alamo!" became the battle cry of Houston's army.

Travis's Appeal for Aid at the Alamo,
February 24, 1836

To the People of Texas and All Americans in the World—

Fellow Citizens and Compatriots:

I am besieged by a thousand or more of the Mexicans under Santa Anna. I have sustained a continual Bombardment & cannonade for 24 hours & have not lost a man. The enemy has demanded a surrender at discretion, otherwise the garrison are to be put to the sword if the fort is taken. I have answered the demand with a cannon shot, and our flag still waves proudly from the walls. I shall never surrender or retreat.

Then, I call on you in the name of Liberty, of patriotism, & of everything dear to the American character, to come to our aid with all dispatch. The enemy is receiving reinforcements daily & will no doubt increase to three or four thousand in four or five days. If this call is neglected I am determined to sustain myself as long as possible & die like a soldier who never forgets what is due to his honor & that of his country.

Victory or Death
William Barret Travis
Lt. Col. Comdt.

---

reduced or no taxes for several years. In return the colonists agreed to learn Spanish, become Mexican citizens, convert to Catholicism—the religion of Mexico—and obey Mexican law.

Mexican leaders hoped to attract settlers from all over, including other parts of Mexico. Most Texas settlers, however, came from the United States.

Growing Tension

By 1830 Americans in Texas far outnumbered Mexicans. Further, these American colonists had not adopted Mexican ways. In the meantime the United States had twice offered to buy Texas from Mexico.

The Mexican government viewed the growing American influence in Texas with alarm. In 1830 the Mexican government issued a decree, or official order, that stopped all immigration

from the United States. At the same time, the decree encouraged the immigration of Mexican and European families with generous land grants. Trade between Texas and the United States was discouraged by placing a tax on goods imported from the United States.

These new policies angered the Texans. The prosperity of many citizens depended on trade with the United States. Many had friends and relatives who wanted to come to Texas. In addition, those colonists who held slaves were uneasy about the Mexican government's plans to end slavery.

Attempt at Reconciliation

Some of the American settlers called for independence. Others hoped to stay within Mexico but on better terms. In 1833 **General Antonio López de Santa Anna** became president of

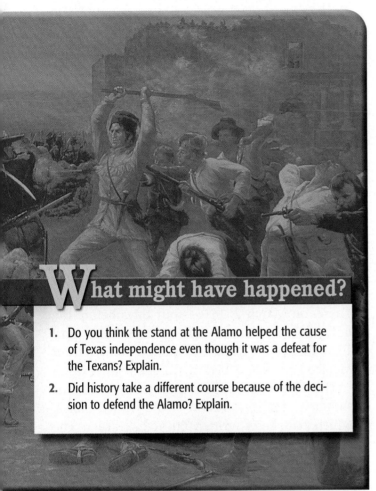

What might have happened?

1. Do you think the stand at the Alamo helped the cause of Texas independence even though it was a defeat for the Texans? Explain.

2. Did history take a different course because of the decision to defend the Alamo? Explain.

Mexico. Stephen F. Austin traveled to Mexico City with the Texans' demands, which were to remove the ban on American settlers and to make Texas a separate state.

Santa Anna agreed to the first request but refused the second. Austin sent a letter back to Texas, suggesting that plans for independence get underway. The Mexican government intercepted the letter and arrested Austin. While Austin was in jail, Santa Anna named himself dictator and overthrew Mexico's constitution of 1824. Without a constitution to protect their rights, Texans felt betrayed. Santa Anna reorganized the government, placing greater central control over Texas. This loss of local power dismayed many people.

Reading Check **Explaining** What role did empresarios play in colonization?

The Struggle for Independence

During 1835 unrest grew among Texans and occasionally resulted in open conflict. Santa Anna sent an army into Texas to punish the Texans for criticizing him. In October some Mexican troops tried to seize a cannon held by Texans at the town of **Gonzales.** During the battle the Texans decorated the front of the cannon with a white flag that bore the words "Come and Take It." After a brief struggle, Texans drove back the Mexican troops. Texans consider this to be the first fight of the Texan Revolution.

The Texans called on volunteers to join their fight. They offered free land to anyone who would help. Davy Crockett and many others—including a number of African Americans and Tejanos—answered that call.

In December 1835, the Texans scored an important victory. They liberated **San Antonio** from the control of a larger Mexican force. The Texas army at San Antonio included more than 100 Tejanos. Many of them served in a scouting company commanded by Captain Juan Seguín. Born in San Antonio, Seguín was an outspoken champion of the Texans' demand for independence.

Despite these victories, the Texans encountered problems. With the Mexican withdrawal, some Texans left San Antonio, thinking the war was won. Various groups argued over who was in charge and what course of action to follow. In early 1836, when Texas should have been making preparations to face Santa Anna, nothing was being done.

The Battle of the Alamo

Santa Anna marched north, furious at the loss of San Antonio. When his army reached San Antonio in late February 1836, it found a small Texan force barricaded inside a nearby mission called the **Alamo.**

Although the Texans had cannons, they lacked gunpowder. Worse, they had only about 180 soldiers to face Santa Anna's army of several thousand. The Texans did have brave leaders, though, including Davy Crockett, who had arrived with a band of sharpshooters from Tennessee, and a tough Texan named Jim Bowie. The commander, William B. Travis, was only 26

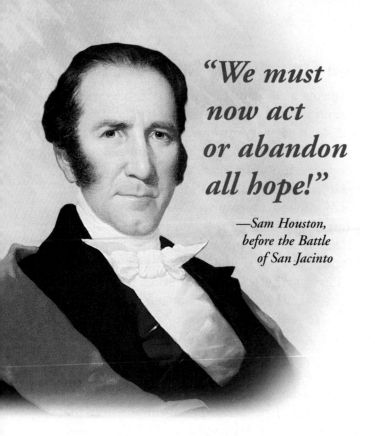

"We must now act or abandon all hope!"

—*Sam Houston, before the Battle of San Jacinto*

open land and tried to mount the Alamo's walls. The Mexicans were too numerous to hold back, however, and they finally entered the fortress, killing William Travis, Davy Crockett, Jim Bowie, and all the other defenders. Only a few women and children and some servants survived to tell of the battle.

In the words of Santa Anna's aide, "The Texans fought more like devils than like men." The defenders of the Alamo had killed hundreds of Mexican soldiers. But more important, they had bought Texans some much needed time.

Texas Declares Its Independence

During the siege of the Alamo, Texan leaders were meeting at Washington-on-the-Brazos, where they were drawing up a new constitution. There, on March 2, 1836—four days before the fall of the Alamo—American settlers and Tejanos firmly declared independence from Mexico and established the Republic of Texas.

The Texas Declaration of Independence was similar to the Declaration of the United States, which had been written 60 years earlier. The Texas Declaration stated that the government of Santa Anna had violated the liberties guaranteed under the Mexican Constitution. The declaration charged that Texans had been deprived of freedom of religion, the right to trial by jury, the right to bear arms, and the right to petition. It noted that the Texans' protests against these policies were met with force. The Mexican government had sent a large army to drive Texans from their homes. Because of these grievances, the declaration proclaimed the following:

years old, but he was determined to hold his position. Travis managed to send messages out through Mexican lines. He wrote several messages to the people of Texas and the United States, asking them for assistance. In his last message, Travis described the fighting that had already taken place and repeated his request for assistance. He warned that

66the power of Santa Anna is to be met here, or in the colonies; we had better meet them here than to suffer a war of devastation to rage in our settlements.99

Travis concluded with the statement that he and his troops were determined to hold the Alamo.

For 12 long days, the defenders of the Alamo kept Santa Anna's army at bay with rifle fire. The Mexicans launched two assaults but had to break them off. During the siege, 32 volunteers from Gonzales slipped through the Mexican lines to join the Alamo's defenders.

On March 6, 1836, Mexican cannon fire smashed the Alamo's walls, and the Mexicans launched an all-out attack. The Alamo defenders killed many Mexican soldiers as they crossed

66The people of Texas, in solemn convention assembled, appealing to a candid world for the necessities of our condition, do hereby resolve and declare that our political connection with the Mexican nation has forever ended; and that the people of Texas do now constitute a free, sovereign, and independent republic....99

HISTORY Online

Student Web Activity
Visit taj.glencoe.com and click on **Chapter 12—Student Web Activities** for an activity on the fight for Texas independence.

With Mexican troops in Texas, it was not possible to hold a general election to ratify the constitution and vote for leaders of the new republic. Texas leaders set up a temporary government. They selected officers to serve until regular elections could be held.

David G. Burnet, an early pioneer in Texas, was chosen president and Lorenzo de Zavala, vice president. De Zavala had worked to establish a democratic government in Mexico. He moved to Texas when it became clear that Santa Anna would not make reforms.

The government of the new republic named **Sam Houston** as commander in chief of the Texas forces. Houston had come to Texas in 1832. Raised among the Cherokee people, he became a soldier, fighting with Andrew Jackson against the Creek people. A politician as well, Houston had served in Congress and as governor of Tennessee.

Houston wanted to prevent other forts from being overrun by the Mexicans. He ordered the troops at **Goliad** to abandon their position. As they retreated, however, they came face to face with Mexican troops led by General Urrea. After a fierce fight, several hundred Texans surrendered. On Santa Anna's orders, the Texans were executed a few days later. This action outraged Texans, who called it the "Goliad Massacre."

The Battle of San Jacinto

Houston moved his small army eastward about 100 miles, watching the movements of Santa Anna and waiting for a chance to strike. Six weeks after the Alamo, he found the opportunity.

After adding some new troops, Houston gathered an army of about 900 at **San Jacinto** (SAN juh•SIHN•toh), near the site of present-day Houston. Santa Anna was camped nearby with an army of more than 1,300. On April 21 the Texans launched a surprise attack on the Mexican camp, shouting, "Remember the Alamo! Remember Goliad!" They killed more than 600 soldiers and captured about 700 more—including Santa Anna. On May 14, 1836, Santa Anna signed a treaty that recognized the independence of Texas.

Reading Check **Identifying** Who was commander in chief of the Texas forces?

The Lone Star Republic

Texans elected Sam Houston as their president in September 1836. Mirabeau Lamar, who had built a fort at Velasco and had fought bravely at the Battle of San Jacinto, served as vice president. Houston sent a delegation to Washington, D.C., asking the United States to annex—take control of—Texas. The nation's president Andrew Jackson refused, however, because the addition of another slave state would upset the balance of slave and free states in Congress. For the moment Texas would remain an independent country.

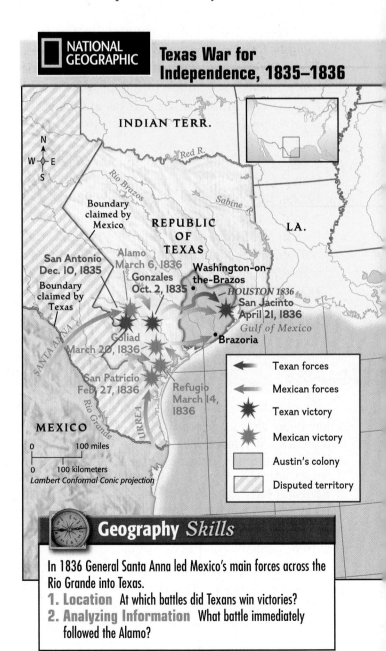

NATIONAL GEOGRAPHIC

Texas War for Independence, 1835–1836

INDIAN TERR.

Red R.

Rio Brazos

Sabine R.

REPUBLIC OF TEXAS

LA.

San Antonio Dec. 10, 1835

Boundary claimed by Mexico

Alamo March 6, 1836

Gonzales Oct. 2, 1835

Washington-on-the-Brazos

HOUSTON 1836

San Jacinto April 21, 1836

Gulf of Mexico

Boundary claimed by Texas

SANTA ANNA

Goliad March 20, 1836

Brazoria

San Patricio Feb. 27, 1836

Refugio March 14, 1836

URREA

MEXICO

Rio Grande

0   100 miles
0   100 kilometers
Lambert Conformal Conic projection

Texan forces
Mexican forces
Texan victory
Mexican victory
Austin's colony
Disputed territory

Geography *Skills*

In 1836 General Santa Anna led Mexico's main forces across the Rio Grande into Texas.

1. **Location** At which battles did Texans win victories?
2. **Analyzing Information** What battle immediately followed the Alamo?

America's Flags

Texas Republic, 1839 For its first six years, this Lone Star flag symbolized the independent nation of the Republic of Texas. Texans kept the Lone Star banner as their official state flag after joining the Union in 1845.

The Question of Annexation

Despite rapid population growth, the new republic faced political and financial difficulties. The Mexican government refused to honor Santa Anna's recognition of independence, and fighting continued between Texas and Mexico. In addition Texas had an enormous debt and no money to repay it.

Many Texans still hoped to join the United States. Southerners favored the annexation of Texas, but Northerners objected that Texas would add another slave state to the Union. President Martin Van Buren, like Jackson, did not want to inflame the slavery issue or risk war with Mexico. He put off the question of annexing Texas.

John Tyler, who became the nation's president in 1841, was the first vice president to become president upon the death of a chief executive. He succeeded William Henry Harrison, who died in April, just one month after taking office. Tyler supported adding Texas to the Union and persuaded Texas to reapply for annexation. However, the Senate was divided over slavery and failed to ratify the annexation treaty.

Texas Becomes a State

The situation changed with the 1844 presidential campaign. The feeling of Manifest Destiny was growing throughout the country. The South favored annexation of Texas. The North demanded that the United States gain control of the Oregon country from Britain. The Democratic candidate, James K. Polk, supported both actions. The Whig candidate, Henry Clay, initially opposed adding Texas to the Union. When he finally came out for annexation, it lost him votes in the North—and the election.

After Polk's victory, supporters of annexation pressed the issue in Congress. They proposed and passed a resolution to annex Texas. On December 29, 1845, Texas officially became a state of the United States.

✓ **Reading Check** **Identifying** Who was president of the Texas Republic?

SECTION 2 ASSESSMENT

Checking for Understanding

1. **Key Terms** Write a short history about events in Texas using the following terms: Tejano, empresario, decree, annex.

2. **Reviewing Facts** Name the four things that American settlers agreed to do in exchange for receiving land in Texas.

Reviewing Themes

3. **Geography and History** Why did Northerners and Southerners disagree on the annexation of Texas?

Critical Thinking

4. **Analyzing Information** How did the fall of the Alamo help the cause of Texas independence, even though it was a defeat for the Texans?

5. **Categorizing Information** Re-create the diagram below. In the boxes, describe two causes of the war between Mexico and Americans in Texas.

Causes

☐ ☐ → War

Analyzing Visuals

6. **Sequencing** Study the map on page 367. Place these battles in order, starting with the earliest: Gonzalez, San Jacinto, the Alamo, Goliad.

Interdisciplinary Activity

Descriptive Writing Look at the painting of the Battle of the Alamo on page 365. Write one paragraph that describes what is happening in the picture.

SECTION 3 War with Mexico

Guide to Reading

Main Idea
American settlement in the Southwest led to conflict with Mexico.

Key Terms
rancho, ranchero, Californios, cede

Reading Strategy
Taking Notes As you read the section, describe the actions and achievements of each of the individuals in the table.

	Actions taken
William Becknell	
Jedediah Smith	
John C. Frémont	

Read to Learn
• why Americans began to settle in the Southwest.
• how the United States acquired New Mexico and California.

Section Theme
Culture and Traditions New Mexico, California, and Texas were Spanish lands with Spanish cultures and traditions.

Preview of Events

♦1820	♦1830	♦1840	♦1850

1821
Mexico gains independence

1833
Mexico abolishes missions

1845
The United States annexes Texas

1846
Congress declares war on Mexico

AN American Story

Long lines of covered wagons stretched as far as the eye could see. "All's set!" a driver called out. "All's set!" everyone shouted in reply.

"Then the 'Heps!' of drivers—the cracking of whips—the trampling of feet—the occasional creak of wheels—the rumbling of wagons—form a new scene of [intense] confusion," reported Josiah Gregg. Gregg was one of the traders who traveled west on the Santa Fe Trail in the 1830s to sell cloth, knives, and other goods in New Mexico.

Wagon wheel

The New Mexico Territory

In the early 1800s, **New Mexico** was the name of a vast region sandwiched between the Texas and California territories. It included all of present-day New Mexico, Arizona, Nevada, and Utah and parts of Colorado and Wyoming.

Native American peoples had lived in the area for thousands of years. Spanish conquistadors began exploring there in the late 1500s and made it part of Spain's colony of Mexico. In 1610 the Spanish founded the settlement of **Santa Fe.** Missionaries followed soon after.

When Mexico won its independence in 1821, it inherited the New Mexico province from Spain. The Mexicans, however, had little control over the distant province. The inhabitants of New Mexico mostly governed themselves.

The Spanish had tried to keep Americans away from Santa Fe, fearing that Americans would want to take over the area. The Mexican government changed this policy, welcoming American traders into New Mexico. It hoped that the trade would boost the economy of the province.

The Santa Fe Trail

William Becknell, the first American trader to reach Santa Fe, arrived in 1821 with a pack of mules loaded with goods. Becknell sold the merchandise he brought for many times what he would have received for it in St. Louis.

Becknell's route came to be known as the **Santa Fe Trail.** The trail left the Missouri River near Independence, Missouri, and crossed the prairies to the Arkansas River. It followed the river west toward the Rocky Mountains before turning south into New Mexico Territory. Because the trail was mostly flat, on later trips Becknell used wagons to carry his merchandise.

Other traders followed Becknell, and the Santa Fe Trail became a busy trade route for hundreds of wagons. Americans brought cloth and firearms, which they exchanged in Santa Fe for silver, furs, and mules. The trail remained in use until the arrival of the railroad in 1880.

As trade with New Mexico increased, Americans began settling in the region. In the United States, the idea of Manifest Destiny captured the popular imagination, and many people saw New Mexico as territory worth acquiring. At the same time, they eyed another prize—the Mexican territory of California, which would provide access to the Pacific.

Reading Check **Describing** Where did the Santa Fe Trail end?

California's Spanish Culture

Spanish explorers and missionaries from Mexico had been the first Europeans to settle in California. In the 1760s Captain Gaspar de Portolá and Father Junípero Serra began building a string of missions that eventually extended from San Diego to Sonoma.

The mission system was a key part of Spain's plan to colonize California. The Spanish used the missions to convert Native Americans to Christianity. By 1820, California had 21 missions, with about 20,000 Native Americans living in them.

In 1820 American mountain man Jedediah Smith visited the San Gabriel Mission east of present-day Los Angeles. Smith reported that the Native Americans farmed thousands of acres and worked at weaving and other crafts. He described the missions as "large farming and grazing establishments." Another American in Smith's party called the Native Americans "slaves in every sense of the word."

History *Through Art*

Vaqueros in a Horse Corral by James Walker
Mexican American cowhands, or vaqueros, work on a ranch in the Southwest. **Why did the number of ranchos grow in the 1820s and 1830s?**

California After 1821

After Mexico gained its independence from Spain in 1821, **California** became a state in the new Mexican nation. At the time only a few hundred Spanish settlers lived in California, but emigrants began arriving from Mexico. The wealthier settlers lived on ranches devoted to raising cattle and horses.

In 1833 the Mexican government passed a law abolishing the missions. The government gave some of the lands to Native Americans and sold the remainder. Mexican settlers bought these lands and built huge properties called ranchos.

The Mexican settlers persuaded Native Americans to work their lands and tend their cattle in return for food and shelter. The California ranchos were similar to the plantations of the South, and the rancheros—ranch owners—treated Native American workers almost like slaves.

Manifest Destiny and California

Americans had been visiting California for years. Most arrived on trading or whaling ships, although a few hardy travelers like Jedediah Smith came overland from the East. Soon more began to arrive.

At first the Mexican authorities welcomed Americans in California. The newcomers included agents for American shipping companies, fur traders from Oregon, and merchants from New Mexico. In the 1840s families began to arrive in California to settle. They made the long journey from Missouri on the Oregon Trail and then turned south after crossing the Rocky Mountains. Still, by 1845 the American population of California numbered only about 700. Most Americans lived in the Sacramento River valley.

Some American travelers wrote glowing reports of California. **John C. Frémont,** an army officer who made several trips through California in the 1840s, wrote of the region's mild climate, scenic beauty, and abundance of natural resources.

Americans began to talk about adding California to the nation. Shippers and manufacturers hoped to build ports on the Pacific coast for trade with China and Japan. Many Americans

John C. Frémont's strong belief in westward expansion advanced the cause of Manifest Destiny.

saw the advantage of extending United States territory to the Pacific. That way the nation would be safely bordered by the sea instead of by a foreign power. In 1845 Secretary of War William Marcy wrote that

❝if the people [of California] should desire to unite their destiny with ours, they would be received as brethren [brothers].❞

President James Polk twice offered to buy California and New Mexico from Mexico, but Mexico refused. Soon, the United States would take over both regions by force.

Reading Check **Examining** What was the purpose of the California missions?

War With Mexico

President James K. Polk was determined to get the California and New Mexico territories from Mexico. Their possession would guarantee that the United States had clear passage to the Pacific Ocean—an important consideration because the British still occupied part of Oregon. Polk's main reason, though, involved fulfilling the nation's Manifest Destiny. Like many Americans, Polk saw California and New Mexico as rightfully belonging to the United States.

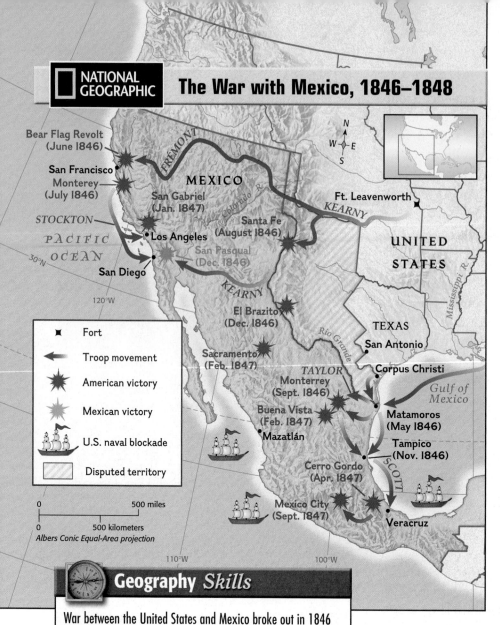

NATIONAL GEOGRAPHIC

The War with Mexico, 1846–1848

Bear Flag Revolt
(June 1846)

San Francisco
Monterey
(July 1846)

MEXICO

STOCKTON

PACIFIC

OCEAN

30°N

San Gabriel
(Jan. 1847)

Los Angeles

Santa Fe
(August 1846)

San Pasqual
(Dec. 1846)

San Diego

120°W

KEARNY

FREMONT

Ft. Leavenworth

KEARNY

UNITED

STATES

El Brazito
(Dec. 1846)

TEXAS

San Antonio

Sacramento
(Feb. 1847)

TAYLOR
Monterrey
(Sept. 1846)

Buena Vista
(Feb. 1847)

Mazatlán

Cerro Gordo
(Apr. 1847)

Mexico City
(Sept. 1847)

Corpus Christi

Gulf of
Mexico

Matamoros
(May 1846)

Tampico
(Nov. 1846)

SCOTT

Veracruz

Rio Grande

Mississippi R.

Legend

- Fort
- Troop movement
- American victory
- Mexican victory
- U.S. naval blockade
- Disputed territory

0   500 miles

0   500 kilometers
Albers Conic Equal-Area projection

110°W   100°W

120°W   30°N

Geography *Skills*

War between the United States and Mexico broke out in 1846
near the Rio Grande.
1. **Location** Which battle occurred farthest north?
2. **Making Inferences** What information on the map
can you use to infer which side won the war?

After Mexico refused to sell California and
New Mexico, President Polk plotted to pull the
Mexican provinces into the Union through war.
He wanted, however, to provoke Mexico into tak-
ing military action first. This way Polk could jus-
tify the war to Congress and the American people.

Relations between Mexico and the United
States had been strained for some years. When
the United States annexed Texas in 1845, the situation worsened. Mexico, which had never recognized the independence of Texas, charged
that the annexation was illegal.

Another dispute con-
cerned the Texas-Mexico
border. The United States
insisted that the **Rio
Grande** formed the border.
Mexico claimed that the
border lay along the **Nueces**
(nu•AY•suhs) **River**, 150
miles farther north. Because
of this dispute, Mexico had
stopped payments to Amer-
ican citizens for losses suffered during Mexico's war
for independence.

Polk sent an agent, John
Slidell, to Mexico to propose a deal. Slidell was
authorized to offer $30 mil-
lion for California and New
Mexico in return for Mex-
ico's acceptance of the Rio
Grande as the Texas boundary. In addition, the United
States would take over payment of Mexico's debts to
American citizens.

Conflict Begins

The Mexican govern-
ment refused to discuss the
offer and announced its intention to reclaim
Texas for Mexico. In response Polk ordered
General Zachary Taylor to march his soldiers
across the disputed borderland between the
Nueces River and the Rio Grande. Taylor
followed the order and built a fort there on
his arrival. On April 24, Mexican soldiers
attacked a small force of Taylor's soldiers.
Taylor sent the report the president wanted to
hear: "Hostilities may now be considered as
commenced."

Polk called an emergency meeting of his cabinet, and the cabinet agreed that the attack was
grounds for war with Mexico. On May 11, 1846,
the president told Congress that Mexico had
"invaded our territory and shed American
blood upon the American soil." Congress
passed a declaration of war against Mexico.

American Attitudes Toward the War

The American people were divided over the war with Mexico. Polk's party, the Democrats, generally supported the war. Many Whigs opposed it, calling Polk's actions aggressive and unjust. Northerners accused Democrats of waging the war to spread slavery.

Illinois congressman Abraham Lincoln demanded to know the exact spot where the first attack against American troops had occurred. Lincoln, like many who opposed the war, claimed that the spot was clearly in Mexico and that Polk therefore had no grounds for blaming the war on Mexico.

Frederick Douglass, an African American leader in the antislavery movement, called the war "disgraceful" and "cruel." Douglass shared the belief that if the United States expanded into the West, the Southern states would carry slavery into the new territories.

Newspapers generally supported the war, and volunteers quickly signed up for military service. As time went on, however, antiwar feeling grew, particularly in the North.

Polk's War Plan

President Polk had a three-part plan for the war with Mexico. First, American troops would drive Mexican forces out of the disputed border region in Texas and make the border secure. Second, the United States would seize New Mexico and California. Finally, American forces would take **Mexico City,** the capital of Mexico.

Zachary Taylor accomplished the first goal. His army captured the town of Matamoros in May 1846 and **Monterrey** in September 1846. The Americans pushed forward and entered the bishop's palace. The Mexican flag was lowered, and a mighty cheer erupted from American forces remaining on the plain below. In February 1847, Taylor defeated the Mexicans again at Buena Vista. The Texas border was secure.

While Taylor made progress in northern Mexico, American forces also advanced farther west. General **Stephen Watts Kearny** led his troops to New Mexico and California. In the summer of 1846, Kearny led about 1,500 cavalry soldiers along the Santa Fe Trail from Fort Leavenworth to New Mexico. The Mexican governor fled, allowing the Americans to capture New Mexico's capital, Santa Fe, on August 18, 1846, without firing a shot. Kearny and his army then headed across the deserts of New Mexico and Arizona to California.

California and the Bear Flag Republic

In June 1846, a small group of Americans had seized the town of Sonoma north of San Francisco and proclaimed the independent Republic of California. They called the new country the **Bear Flag Republic** because their flag showed a bear and a star on a white background. John C. Frémont and mountain man **Kit Carson,** who were already out West on a military expedition in California, joined the Americans in Sonoma.

Though unaware of the outbreak of war with Mexico, Frémont declared that he would conquer California. Frémont's actions outraged many Californios, the Mexicans who lived in California. They might have supported a revolt for local control of government, but they opposed what looked like an attempt by a band of Americans to seize land.

Naval Intervention

In July 1846, a United States Navy squadron under Commodore John Sloat captured the ports of Monterey and San Francisco. Sloat declared California annexed to the United States, and the American flag replaced the Bear Flag in California.

Sloat's fleet sailed for San Diego, carrying Frémont and Carson. The Americans captured San Diego and moved north to Los Angeles. Carson

California Bear Flag

headed east with the news of California's annexation. On his way he met and joined Kearny's force, marching west from Santa Fe.

After Sloat's ships left, many Californios in San Diego rose up in arms against the Americans who had taken over the city. General Kearny and his troops arrived in the midst of the rebellion. They faced a stiff fight but eventually won. By January 1847, California was fully controlled by the United States.

The Capture of Mexico City

With their victories in New Mexico and California, the Americans met their first two goals in the war. President Polk then launched the third part of his war plan—an attack on Mexico City.

Polk gave the task of capturing Mexico City to General **Winfield Scott.** In March 1847, Scott's army landed on the coast of the Gulf of Mexico, near the Mexican port of **Veracruz.** Scott captured Veracruz after a three-week siege and then set out to march the 300 miles to Mexico City.

The Americans had to fight their way toward Mexico City, battling not only the Mexican army but also bands of armed citizens. Scott reached the outskirts of Mexico City with his troops towards the end of August 1847. By mid-September the Americans had taken Mexico City. The Mexican government surrendered.

The United States lost 1,721 men to battle and more than 11,000 to disease in the Mexican War. Mexico's losses were far greater. The war cost the United States nearly $100 million, but here, too, Mexico paid a higher price. The war would cost Mexico half its territory.

The Peace Treaty

Peace talks between the United States and Mexico began in January 1848. The **Treaty of Guadalupe Hidalgo** (GWAH•duhl•OOP hih•DAL•goh) was signed in February 1848.

In the treaty Mexico gave up all claims to Texas and agreed to the Rio Grande as the border between Texas and Mexico. Furthermore, in what was called the **Mexican Cession,** Mexico ceded—gave—its provinces of California and New Mexico to the United States. In return the United States gave Mexico $15 million.

In 1853 the United States paid Mexico an additional $10 million for the **Gadsden Purchase,** a strip of land along the southern edge of the present-day states of Arizona and New Mexico. With the Gadsden Purchase, the United States mainland reached its present size. All that remained was to settle the newly acquired territories.

✓ Reading Check **Describing** What lands did Mexico cede to the United States?

SECTION 3 ASSESSMENT

Checking for Understanding

1. **Key Terms** Write a short paragraph in which you use the following terms: rancho, ranchero, Californios, cede.
2. **Reviewing Facts** According to the Mexican government, where did the border between Texas and Mexico lie?

Reviewing Themes

3. **Culture and Traditions** Why did the Spanish establish missions in the Southwest? What happened to the mission land after Mexico gained its independence?

Critical Thinking

4. **Analyzing Primary Sources** Explain the meaning of this sentence in your own words: "If the people [of California] should desire to unite their destiny with ours, they would be received as brethren [brothers]."
5. **Categorizing Information** Re-create the diagram below and describe the three parts of Polk's strategy and how they were accomplished.

Analyzing Visuals

6. **Geography Skills** List the battles that appear on the map on page 372 in order from first to last. Identify whether each was a Mexican victory or a U.S. victory.

Interdisciplinary Activity

Science Settlers traveling west encountered new wildlife, vegetation, and landforms. Choose one region of the west and investigate as a traveling scientist would. List plants and animals you would see there. Write a report summarizing what you have observed.

New Settlers in California and Utah

Guide to Reading

Main Idea
The lure of gold and the promise of religious freedom drew many settlers westward.

Key Terms
forty-niners, boomtown, vigilante

Reading Strategy
Organizing Information As you read Section 4, re-create the diagram below. In the boxes, describe who these groups and individuals were and what their role was in the settlement of California and Utah.

	What was their role?
Forty-niners	
Mormons	
Brigham Young	

Read to Learn
- how the hopes of getting rich drew thousands of people to California.
- how the search for religious freedom led to the settlement of Utah.

Section Theme
Groups and Institutions In the mid-1800s, people went to California in search of gold, and Mormons settled in Utah in search of religious freedom.

Preview of Events

1846 — — — — — — 1848 — — — — — — 1850

1846
Mormons migrate to the Great Salt Lake area

1848
Gold is discovered at Sutter's Mill

1850
California applies for statehood

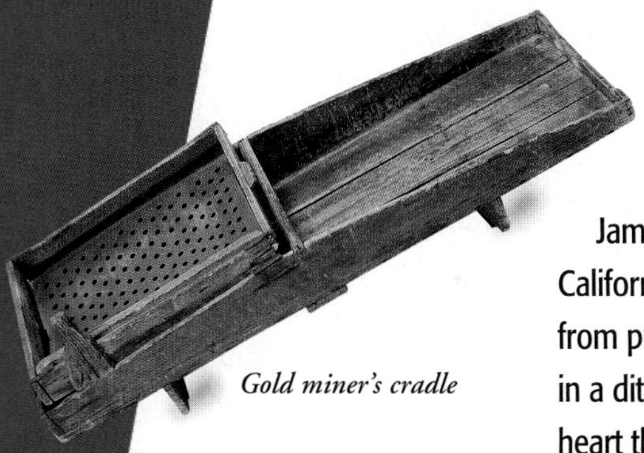

Gold miner's cradle

AN American Story

James Marshall was building a sawmill on the South Fork of the American River in California. He worked for John Sutter, who owned a vast tract of land about 35 miles from present-day Sacramento. On January 24, 1848, Marshall saw something shining in a ditch. "I reached my hand down and picked it up," he wrote later. "It made my heart thump, for I was certain it was gold." Looking around, he found other shiny pieces. Marshall rushed to show the glittering pieces to Sutter, who determined that they were gold. Sutter tried to keep the discovery a secret, but word soon leaked out. The great California Gold Rush was underway!

California Gold Rush

People from all over the world flocked to California in search of quick riches. More than 80,000 people came to California looking for gold in 1849 alone. Those who arrived in 1849 were called forty-niners. An official in Monterey reported that "the farmers have thrown aside their plows, the lawyers their

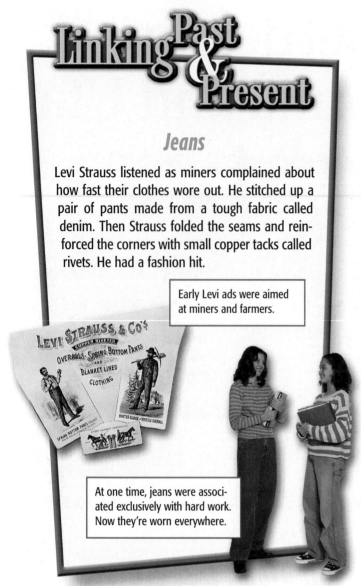

Linking Past & Present

Jeans

Levi Strauss listened as miners complained about how fast their clothes wore out. He stitched up a pair of pants made from a tough fabric called denim. Then Strauss folded the seams and reinforced the corners with small copper tacks called rivets. He had a fashion hit.

Early Levi ads were aimed at miners and farmers.

At one time, jeans were associated exclusively with hard work. Now they're worn everywhere.

briefs, the doctors their pills, the priests their prayer books, and all are now digging gold." By the end of 1848, they had taken $6 million in gold from the American River.

Many of the gold seekers came to California by sea. Others came overland, traveling on the Oregon Trail or the Santa Fe Trail and then pushing westward through California's **Sierra Nevada** mountain range.

Americans made up about 80 percent of the forty-niners. Others came from Mexico, South America, Europe, and Australia. About 300 men arrived from China, the first large group of Asian immigrants to come to America. Although some eventually returned to China, others remained, establishing California's Chinese American community.

The Californios

The Treaty of Guadalupe Hidalgo ending the war with Mexico made **Californios** (Hispanic Californians) citizens of the United States. The treaty also guaranteed them the rights to their lands. But these rights would soon be weakened.

The Land Law of 1851 set up a group of people to review the Californios' land rights. The Californios had to prove what land they owned. When a new settler claimed the rights to a Californio's land, the two parties would go to court. Some Californios were able to prove their claims. Many, however, lost their land.

Life in California

As people rushed to a new area to look for gold, they built new communities, called boomtowns, almost overnight. At one site on the Yuba River where only two houses stood in September 1849, a miner arrived the next year to find a town of 1,000 people "with a large number of hotels, stores, groceries, bakeries, and . . . gambling houses." The miners gave some of the boomtowns colorful names such as Shinbone Peak and You Bet.

Cities also flourished during the Gold Rush. As ships arrived daily with gold seekers and adventurers, San Francisco grew from a tiny village to a city of about 20,000 people.

Most of the hopeful forty-niners had no experience in mining. Rushing furiously from place to place, they attacked hillsides with pickaxes and shovels and spent hours bent over streambeds, "washing" or "panning" the water to seek gold dust and nuggets.

The California Gold Rush more than doubled the world's supply of gold. For all their effort, however, very few of the forty-niners achieved lasting wealth. Most of the miners found little or no gold. Many of those who did lost their riches through gambling or wild spending.

Merchants, however, made huge profits. They could charge whatever they liked because the miners had no place else to go to buy food and other essential items. Eggs sold for $10 a dozen. A Jewish immigrant named **Levi Strauss** sold the miners sturdy pants made of denim. His "Levi's" made him rich.

Gold Rush Society

Very few women lived in the mining camps, which were populated by men of all races and walks of life. Lonely and suffering from the hardships of mining, many men spent their free hours drinking, gambling, and fighting.

Mining towns had no police or prisons, so lawbreakers posed a real threat to business owners and miners. One miner wrote,

> 66Robberies and murders were of daily occurrence. Organized bands of thieves existed in the towns and in the mountains.99

Concerned citizens formed vigilance committees to protect themselves. The vigilantes (VIH•juh•LAN•tees) took the law into their own hands, acting as police, judge, jury, and sometimes executioner.

Economic and Political Progress

The Gold Rush ended within a few years but had lasting effects on California's economy. Agriculture, shipping, and trade expanded to meet the miners' needs for food and other goods. Many people who had come looking for gold stayed to farm or run a business. California's population soared, increasing from about 20,000 in 1848 to more than 220,000 only four years later.

Such rapid growth brought the need for more effective government. Zachary Taylor, the Mexican War hero and now president, urged the people of California to apply for statehood. They did so, choosing representatives in September 1849 to write a constitution. Once their constitution was approved, Californians elected a governor and state legislators.

California applied to Congress for statehood in March 1850. Because California's constitution banned slavery, however, the request caused a crisis in Congress. The Southern states objected to making California a state because it would upset the balance of free and slave states. California did not become a state until Congress worked out a compromise six months later.

☑ **Reading Check** **Explaining** Why did the forty-niners come to California?

A Religious Refuge in Utah

A visitor to the Utah Territory in the 1850s wrote admiringly: "The whole of this small nation occupy themselves as usefully as the working bees of a hive." This account described the **Mormons,** or members of the Church of Jesus Christ of Latter-day Saints. Mormons had come to Utah to fulfill their vision of the godly life.

The First Mormons

Joseph Smith founded the church in 1830 in New York State. He had visions that led him to launch a new Christian church. He hoped to use these visions to build an ideal society.

Smith believed that property should be held in common. He also supported polygamy, the idea that a man could have more than one wife. This angered a large number of people. Mormons eventually gave up this practice.

Smith formed a community in New York, but unsympathetic neighbors disapproved of the

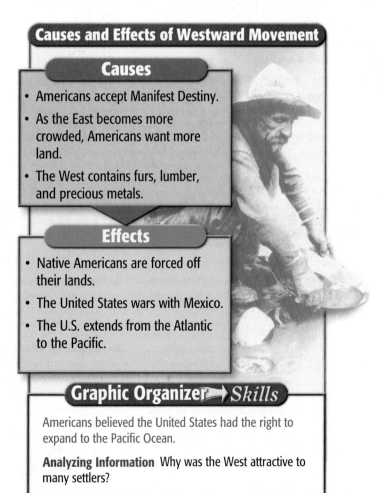

Causes and Effects of Westward Movement

Causes
- Americans accept Manifest Destiny.
- As the East becomes more crowded, Americans want more land.
- The West contains furs, lumber, and precious metals.

Effects
- Native Americans are forced off their lands.
- The United States wars with Mexico.
- The U.S. extends from the Atlantic to the Pacific.

Graphic Organizer ➜ Skills

Americans believed the United States had the right to expand to the Pacific Ocean.

Analyzing Information Why was the West attractive to many settlers?

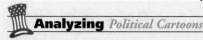
Analyzing *Political Cartoons*

Cartoons of the period often showed Americans rushing to California in hopes of striking it rich. **What idea do you think the cartoonist is presenting?**

Mormons' religion. They forced the Mormons to move on. From New York the Mormons went to Ohio, then to Missouri, and then Illinois.

In 1844 a mob in Illinois killed Smith, and **Brigham Young** took over as head of the Mormons. Young decided the Mormons should move again, this time near the **Great Salt Lake** in present-day Utah. Although part of Mexico at that time, no Mexicans had settled in the region because of its harsh terrain.

A Haven in the Desert

The Mormon migration to the Great Salt Lake area began in 1846. About 12,000 Mormons made the trek—the largest single migration in American history. In the midst of the desert they set up communities in an area they called **Deseret.**

With hard work and determination, the Mormons made Deseret flourish. They planned their towns carefully and built irrigation canals to water their farms. They also founded industries so they could be self-sufficient. Mormon merchants sold supplies to the forty-niners who passed through Utah on their way to California.

In 1848 the United States acquired the Salt Lake area as part of the settlement of the war with Mexico. In 1850 Congress established the Utah Territory, and President Millard Fillmore made Brigham Young its governor.

Utah was not easily incorporated into the United States. The Mormons often had conflicts with federal officials. In 1857 and 1858, war almost broke out between the Mormons and the United States Army. Utah did not become a state until 1896.

Reading Check **Explaining** Why was Deseret able to grow economically?

SECTION 4 ASSESSMENT

Checking for Understanding

1. **Key Terms** Use each of these terms in a complete sentence that will help explain its meaning: forty-niners, boomtown, vigilante.
2. **Reviewing Facts** Why was California's entry into the Union delayed?

Reviewing Themes

3. **Groups and Institutions** What steps did Californians take to apply for statehood? When was California admitted?

Critical Thinking

4. **Predicting Consequences** How might the history of California have been different if the Gold Rush had not happened?
5. **Organizing Information** Re-create the diagram below. In the boxes, describe how the Gold Rush helped California's economy grow.

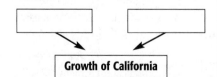

Growth of California

Analyzing Visuals

6. **Graphic Organizer Skills** Study the cause-and-effect chart on page 377. Are each of the effects of the westward movement positive? Explain.

Interdisciplinary Activity

Art Boomtowns sprang up almost overnight as gold seekers flocked to the West. Draw a scene of a boomtown. Include a written description of the activities that took place in the town.

Hamlin Garland (1860–1940)

Hamlin Garland was born in rural Wisconsin and grew up on farms in Iowa and South Dakota. At the age of 24, he moved to Boston to begin his writing career. Although he gave up the life of a prairie farmer, Garland's work—fiction and nonfiction—reflects his background and his concern for the hard, lonely lives of pioneer men and women.

READ TO DISCOVER

A Son of the Middle Border is Garland's autobiography. The following excerpt describes one of the many westward moves that the Garland family made. As you read, pay attention to the emotions that the author expresses when he sees the plains for the first time.

READER'S DICTIONARY

middle border: the advancing frontier across the Mississippi River
habitation: residence
blue-joint: type of prairie grass

A Son of the Middle Border

Late in August my father again loaded our household goods into wagons, and with our small herd of cattle following, set out toward the west, bound once again to overtake the actual line of the **middle border.**

This journey has an unforgettable epic charm as I look back upon it. Each mile took us farther and farther into the unsettled prairie, until in the afternoon of the second day, we came to a meadow so wide that its western rim touched the sky without revealing a sign of man's **habitation** other than the road in which we travelled.

The plain was covered with grass tall as ripe wheat and when my father stopped his team and came back to us and said, "Well, children, here we are on The Big Prairie," we looked about us with awe, so endless seemed this spread of wild oats and waving **blue-joint.**

Far away dim clumps of trees showed, but no chimney was in sight, and no living thing moved save our own cattle and the hawks lazily wheeling in the air. My heart filled with awe as well as wonder. . . .

Sunset came at last, but still he drove steadily on through the sparse settlements. Just at nightfall we came to a beautiful little stream and stopped to let the horses drink.

I heard its rippling, reassuring song on the pebbles. Thereafter all is dim and vague to me until my mother called out sharply, "Wake up, children! Here we are!"

Struggling to my feet I looked about me. Nothing could be seen but the dim form of a small house. On every side the land melted into blackness, silent and without boundary.

Child's doll made of cornhusks

ANALYZING LITERATURE

1. **Recall and Interpret** Give two details that Garland uses to describe "The Big Prairie."
2. **Evaluate and Connect** How does Garland feel about the prairie and the move west? Explain.

Interdisciplinary Activity

Descriptive Writing Write a poem about a vast empty place that you know, or base your poem on a place you have read about.

Chapter Summary

Manifest Destiny

Through war and negotiations, the United States acquires Texas, Oregon, California, Utah, and the remainder of the Southwest. By 1850 thousands and thousands of settlers cross the Great Plains for new homes.

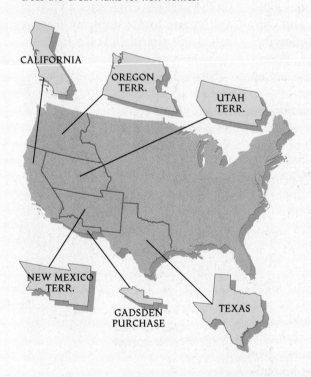

Reviewing Key Terms

Use the vocabulary terms to create a newspaper article in which you describe events in the Southwest during this era.

1. emigrant
2. Tejano
3. empresario
4. ranchero
5. forty-niner

Reviewing Key Facts

6. What agreement did the United States and Great Britain reach about the Oregon Territory?
7. Why did President Jackson refuse to annex Texas?
8. Why did some Americans think that making California part of the United States would strengthen the security of the nation?
9. Explain the two main causes of the United States's war with Mexico.
10. Why did merchants earn such large profits during the Gold Rush?
11. **Analyzing Information** Reread the feature on page 363 about Stephen F. Austin. Why was Austin a good spokesperson for American settlers in Texas?

Critical Thinking

12. **Determining Cause and Effect** How did economic troubles in the East affect settlement in the Oregon area?
13. **Analyzing Themes: Geography and History** How did the war with Mexico change the U.S. border and its land holdings?
14. **Drawing Conclusions** What reactions do you think the governments of Great Britain and Mexico had to the American idea of Manifest Destiny?
15. **Comparing** How did the negotiations between the United States and Britain over the Oregon Territory differ from those between the United States and Mexico over the Southwest?
16. **Determining Cause and Effect** Re-create the diagram below. In the box, explain what led to the need for a more effective government in California.

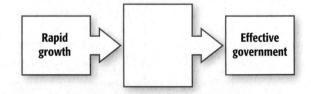

NATIONAL GEOGRAPHIC The Oregon and California Trails

Lambert Equal-Area projection

Geography and History Activity

Study the routes of the western trails shown on the map above. Then answer the questions that follow.

17. Region Which mountains did settlers have to cross to reach Oregon's Pacific coast? California's Pacific coast?

18. Location In what city did the Oregon Trail begin? In what city did it end?

Citizenship Cooperative Activity

19. Analyzing Issues With a partner, read the newspaper to find out what problems your state faces. Perhaps your state has a large budget deficit, or the crime rate has increased sharply. List the problems and describe what you would do if you were governor. List your options and the advantages and disadvantages of each one. Choose a solution and explain why it is the best option.

Practicing Skills

20. Understanding Latitude and Longitude Turn to the map of the world on pages RA12–RA13 of the Reference Atlas. What is the largest land area both west of the Prime Meridian and entirely north of the Equator?

Self-Check Quiz

Visit **taj.glencoe.com** and click on **Chapter 12— Self-Check Quizzes** to prepare for the chapter test.

Technology Activity

21. Using an Electronic Card Catalog Search your library's card catalog for books containing information about Salt Lake City and the state of Utah. Use this information to make an alphabetical directory of historic sites to visit. Your list might include museums, sites of businesses, or other places of interest.

Alternative Assessment

22. Portfolio Writing Activity If you were asked to make a film about one event described in this chapter, what would it be? In your journal describe the event and make a list of at least three people from history who would be in your movie. Then suggest the names of modern movie or TV stars you think would be suitable for these roles.

The Princeton Review
Standardized Test Practice

Directions: Choose the *best* answer to the following question.

The discovery of gold in California led to which of the following?

A Discovery of gold in the Black Hills of the Dakotas

B Increased western expansion and foreign immigration

C Annexation of California as a slave state

D War with Mexico over the independence of California

Test-Taking Tip:

This question is a good example of *cause and effect.* Think about other times in history when people have discovered something of value in an area. What effect did this discovery have on people's behavior?

Let's Move West!

Imagine this: You are a farmer in Missouri in the 1840s. You work hard, but dream of a better life. Often you meet other farmers traveling past your home on their way to the Oregon country or California. These travelers keep speaking of free, fertile land and new opportunities. (In the 1840s, married settlers could claim 640 acres of the Oregon country at no cost.) This year has been the hardest. The crops have failed, and surviving winter will be downright tough. After much thought, you too decide to move your family west.

The Way It Was

You and your family have decided to join a wagon train—a group of other families who have decided to move west. You will be traveling 2,000 miles over rivers and cliffs, finding your way with only the aid of natural landmarks. You will travel to the Oregon country or to California. The trip will take about five months. Your long journey will not end until you stake a claim to your new land somewhere in the vast West. Exciting—and dangerous—events will occur when you cross a high river or encounter a group of Native Americans. You'll have to be careful though. For example, about one of every 10 people making the trip died on the Oregon Trail. You will have to prepare well.

Believe It or Not

Settlers brought new diseases like smallpox and measles to the Native Americans. A single infected sailor on a trading ship killed almost the entire 800-member Multnomah nation. By the mid-1840s, hardly any Native Americans lived in the Willamette Valley. They had all died from plagues!

Materials

✓ pencils or pens and paper
✓ research materials available at your school or local library and/or on the Internet
✓ markers
✓ poster board

What To Do

After your teacher has organized you into groups of four to six, follow the directions below. Decide upon specific tasks for each member of your group.

1 You have just signed on with a wagon train to travel west. You now need to gather provisions for your long journey. You also need to plan the best route to follow and decide when to begin your journey. You will need to plan wisely. Your supplies must fit into your wagon and you must reach your final destination before winter arrives. Your goal is to survive and to make sure your family survives.

2 Work with your team to research the following items:

- your destination and departure date
- the route you should follow
- the supplies you will carry with you

3 As a team, create a list of supplies that you will need to travel. Highlight the essential items, such as staple foods. You will need to research and estimate the weights of these supplies because you may only take with you what you can carry in your wagon. The wagon dimensions are 4 feet by 10 feet, and at least 1,000 pounds of food is needed for a four-person family. Be careful not to overload your wagon—you do not want the wagon to break down or your animals to become exhausted.

4 Each group will submit the following in a class presentation:

- departure and expected arrival dates, and intended destination
- list of provisions to be loaded into the wagon
- a map showing the route the wagon train will take

Project Report

1. What route will you take? What makes this route the best one to follow?

2. What provisions did you want to bring, but could not? What supplies will be most necessary on your trip? Explain.

3. Drawing Conclusions Why do you think families traveled in wagon trains instead of individually?

4. Comparing After listening to reports from other teams, how might you revise your journey plan? Explain.

Go a Step Further

The Oregon Trail is the nation's longest graveyard. It is estimated that about 1 person in 10 died during the trek on the Oregon Trail. Using your experience with this activity, answer this question: What do you think was the major cause for failure for wagon trains traveling west? Answer the question by writing the story of one such possible failure.

CHAPTER 13 North and South

1820–1860

Why It Matters

At the same time that national spirit and pride were growing throughout the country, a strong sectional rivalry was also developing. Both North and South wanted to further their own economic and political interests.

The Impact Today

Differences still exist between the regions of the nation but are no longer as sharp. Mass communication and the migration of people from one region to another have lessened the differences.

The American Journey Video The chapter 13 video, "Young People of the South," describes what life was like for children in the South.

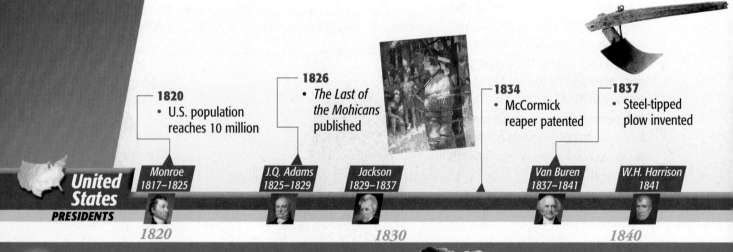

1820
• U.S. population reaches 10 million

1826
• The Last of the Mohicans published

1834
• McCormick reaper patented

1837
• Steel-tipped plow invented

United States PRESIDENTS

Monroe 1817–1825 | J.Q. Adams 1825–1829 | Jackson 1829–1837 | Van Buren 1837–1841 | W.H. Harrison 1841

1820   1830   1840

World

1820
• Antarctica discovered

1825
• World's first public railroad opens in England

Compare-and-Contrast Study Foldable
Make this foldable to help you analyze the similarities and differences between the development of the North and the South.

Step 1 Mark the midpoint of the side edge of a sheet of paper.

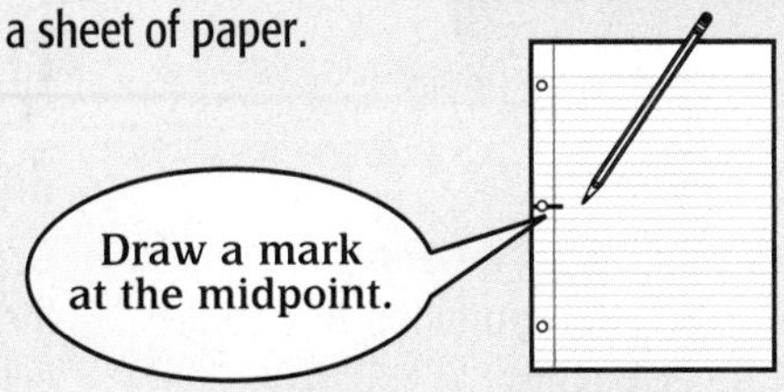

Draw a mark at the midpoint.

Step 2 Turn the paper and fold the outside edges in to touch at the midpoint.

Step 3 Turn and label your foldable as shown.

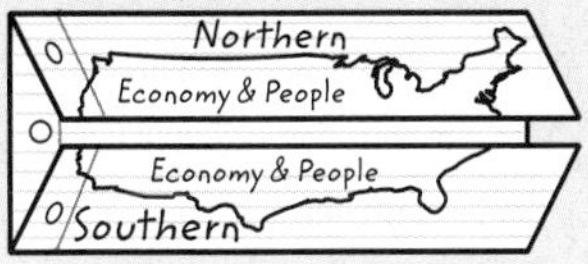

Northern
Economy & People
Economy & People
Southern

Reading and Writing As you read the chapter, collect and write information under the appropriate tab that will help you compare and contrast the people and economics of the Northern and Southern states.

The Oliver Plantation by unknown artist During the mid-1800s, plantations in southern Louisiana were entire communities in themselves.

1845
• Alexander Cartwright sets rules for baseball

1849
• Thoreau writes "Civil Disobedience"

1860
• U.S. population climbs to over 30 million

| Tyler 1841–1845 | Polk 1845–1849 | Taylor 1849–1850 | Fillmore 1850–1853 | Pierce 1853–1857 | Buchanan 1857–1861 |

1850   1860

1845
• Beginning of Irish potato famine

1848
• Revolution in Austrian Empire

1857
• Sepoy Rebellion begins in India

1859
• Darwin's *On the Origin of Species* published

HISTORY
Online

Chapter Overview
Visit taj.glencoe.com and click on **Chapter 13— Chapter Overviews** to preview chapter information.

The North's Economy

Guide to Reading

Main Idea
During the 1800s, advances in technology and transportation shaped the North's economy.

Key Terms
clipper ship, telegraph, Morse code

Reading Strategy
Organizing Information As you read the section, re-create the diagram below and list examples of advances in transportation and technology.

Advances

Read to Learn
• how advances in technology shaped the economy of the North.
• how new kinds of transportation and communication spurred economic growth.

Section Theme
Economic Factors Advances in technology and transportation shaped the North's economy.

Preview of Events

◆1830	◆1840	◆1850	◆1860
1834 Cyrus McCormick patents reaper	**1844** Samuel Morse sends first telegraph message	**1846** Elias Howe patents a sewing machine	**1860** About 3,000 steamboats are operating

Samuel Morse's telegraph key

AN American Story

In the 1840s, telegraph wires and railroads began to cross the nation. But traveling by rail had its discomforts, as writer Charles Dickens describes: "[T]here is a great deal of jolting, a great deal of noise, a great deal of wall, not much window, a locomotive engine, a shriek, and a bell. . . . In the center of the carriage there is usually a stove . . . which is for the most part red-hot. It is insufferably close; and you see the hot air fluttering between yourself and any other object you may happen to look at, like the ghost of smoke. . . ."

Technology and Industry

In 1800 most Americans worked on farms. Items that could not be made at home were manufactured—by hand, one at a time—by local blacksmiths, shoemakers, and tailors. By the early 1800s, changes took place in the Northern states. Power-driven machinery performed many tasks that were once done by hand. Industrialization and technology were changing the way Americans worked, traveled, and communicated.

Industrialization

The industrialization of the North developed in three phases. In the first, manufacturers made products by dividing the tasks involved among the workers. One worker would spin thread all day and another would weave cloth—instead of having one person spin and then weave. During the second phase, manufacturers built factories to bring specialized workers together. This allowed products to be made more quickly than before.

In the third phase, factory workers used machinery to perform some of their work. Many of the new machines ran on waterpower or steam power. For example, power-driven looms took over the task of weaving. The worker's job changed from weaving to tending the machine, which produced more fabric in less time.

Mass production of cotton textiles began in New England in the early 1800s. After **Elias Howe** invented the sewing machine in 1846, machine operators could produce clothing on a large scale from fabrics made by machine. Other types of industries developed during the same period. By 1860 the Northeast's factories produced at least two-thirds of the country's manufactured goods.

Improved Transportation

Improvements in transportation contributed to the success of many of America's new industries. Between 1800 and 1850, construction crews built thousands of miles of roads and canals. The canals opened new shipping routes by connecting many lakes and rivers. The growth of the railroads in the 1840s and 1850s also helped to speed the flow of goods. Inventor **Robert Fulton** demonstrated a reliable steamboat in 1807. Steamboats carried goods and passengers more cheaply and quickly along inland waterways than could flatboats or sail-powered vessels.

In the 1840s canal builders began to widen and deepen canals to accommodate steamboats. By 1860 about 3,000 steamboats traveled the major rivers and canals of the country as well as the Great Lakes. Steamboats spurred the growth of cities such as Cincinnati, Buffalo, and Chicago.

In the 1840s sailing ships were improved. The clipper ships—with sleek hulls and tall sails— were the pride of the open seas. They could sail 300 miles per day, as fast as most steamships of the day. The ships got their name because they "clipped" time from long journeys. Before the clippers, the voyage from New York to Great Britain took about 21 to 28 days. A clipper ship could usually make that trip in half the time.

Picturing **History**

A clipper ship, the *Flying Cloud,* set a new record by sailing from New York to California in less than 90 days. **How did clipper ships get their name?**

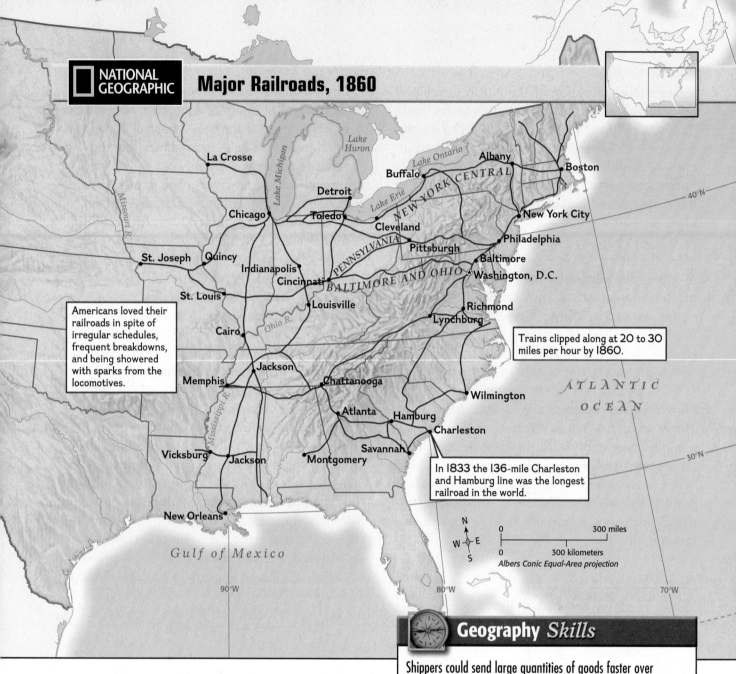

NATIONAL GEOGRAPHIC
Major Railroads, 1860

La Crosse

Lake Huron

Lake Ontario

Albany

Boston

Buffalo

NEW YORK CENTRAL

Detroit

Lake Erie

Chicago

Toledo

New York City

Cleveland

Philadelphia

PENNSYLVANIA

Pittsburgh

St. Joseph

Quincy

Baltimore

Indianapolis

BALTIMORE AND OHIO

Washington, D.C.

Cincinnati

St. Louis

Louisville

Richmond

Cairo

Ohio R.

Lynchburg

Americans loved their railroads in spite of irregular schedules, frequent breakdowns, and being showered with sparks from the locomotives.

Trains clipped along at 20 to 30 miles per hour by 1860.

Jackson

Memphis

Chattanooga

Wilmington

ATLANTIC OCEAN

Atlanta

Hamburg

Charleston

Vicksburg

Savannah

Jackson

Montgomery

In 1833 the 136-mile Charleston and Hamburg line was the longest railroad in the world.

New Orleans

Gulf of Mexico

N
W—E
S

| 0 | | | 300 miles |
| 0 | | | 300 kilometers |

Albers Conic Equal-Area projection

Geography Skills

Shippers could send large quantities of goods faster over railroads than they could over earlier canal, river, and wagon routes.

1. **Location** To what westernmost city did the railroads extend by 1860?
2. **Location** What cities might a train traveler pass through on a trip from Chicago to New Orleans?

Locomotives

The development of railroads in the United States began with short stretches of tracks that connected mines with nearby rivers. Early trains were pulled by horses rather than by locomotives. The first steam-powered passenger locomotive, the *Rocket,* began operating in Britain in 1829.

Peter Cooper designed and built the first American steam locomotive in 1830. Called the *Tom Thumb,* it got off to a bad start. In a race against a horse-drawn train in **Baltimore**, the *Tom Thumb's* engine failed. Engineers soon improved the engine, and within 10 years steam locomotives were pulling trains in the United States.

A Railway Network

In 1840 the United States had almost 3,000 miles of railroad track. By 1860 it had almost 31,000 miles, mostly in the North and the **Midwest.** One railway linked New York City and Buffalo. Another connected Philadelphia and Pittsburgh. Yet another linked Baltimore with Wheeling, Virginia (now West Virginia).

Railway builders connected these eastern lines to lines being built farther west in Ohio, Indiana, and Illinois. By 1860 a network of railroad track united the Midwest and the East.

Moving Goods and People

Along with canals, the railways transformed trade in the nation's interior. The changes began with the opening of the Erie Canal in 1825 and the first railroads of the 1830s. Before this time agricultural goods were carried down the Mississippi River to New Orleans and then shipped to other countries or to the East Coast of the United States.

The development of the east-west canal and the rail network allowed grain, livestock, and dairy products to move directly from the Midwest to the East. Because goods now traveled faster and more cheaply, manufacturers in the East could offer them at lower prices.

The railroads also played an important role in the settlement and industrialization of the Midwest. Fast, affordable train travel brought people into Ohio, Indiana, and Illinois. As the populations of these states grew, new towns and industries developed.

Picturing **History**

The defeat of the train *Tom Thumb* in 1830 did not mean the end of the steam engine. The first successful use of a steam locomotive in the United States took place in South Carolina in 1831. **In 1860 which regions of the United States had the most miles of railroad track?**

Faster Communication

The growth of industry and the new pace of travel created a need for faster methods of communication. The telegraph—an apparatus that used electric signals to transmit messages—filled that need.

Samuel Morse, an American inventor, had been seeking support for a system of telegraph lines. On May 24, 1844, Morse got the chance to demonstrate that he could send messages instantly along wires. As a crowd in the U.S. capital watched, Morse tapped in the words, "What hath God wrought!" A few moments later, the telegraph operator in Baltimore sent the same message back in reply. The telegraph worked! Soon telegraph messages were flashing back and forth between Washington and Baltimore.

Morse transmitted his message in Morse code, a series of dots and dashes representing the letters of the alphabet. A skilled Morse code operator could rapidly tap out words in the dot-and-dash alphabet. Americans adopted the telegraph eagerly. A British visitor marveled at the speed with which Americans formed telegraph companies and erected telegraph lines. Americans, he wrote, were driven to "annihilate [wipe out] distance" in their vast country. By 1852 the United States was operating about 23,000 miles of telegraph lines.

Reading Check **Explaining** How did canals and railways change transportation?

Samuel Morse

Agriculture

The railroads gave farmers access to new markets to sell their products. Advances in technology allowed farmers to greatly increase the size of the harvest they produced.

In the early 1800s, few farmers had ventured into the treeless **Great Plains** west of Missouri, Iowa, and Minnesota. Even areas of mixed forest and prairie west of Ohio and Kentucky seemed too difficult for farming. Settlers worried that their wooden plows could not break the prairie's matted sod and that the soil was not fertile.

Revolution in Agriculture

Three revolutionary inventions of the 1830s changed farming methods and encouraged settlers to cultivate larger areas of the West. One was the steel-tipped plow that **John Deere** invented in 1837. Far sturdier than the wooden plow, Deere's plow easily cut through the hard-packed sod of the prairies. Equally important was the mechanical reaper, which sped up the harvesting of wheat, and the thresher, which quickly separated the grain from the stalk.

McCormick's Reaper

Born on a Virginia farm, **Cyrus McCormick** became interested in machines that would ease the burden of farmwork. After years of tinkering, McCormick designed and constructed the mechanical reaper and made a fortune manufacturing and selling it.

For hundreds of years, farmers had harvested grain with handheld sickles. McCormick's reaper could harvest grain much faster than a hand-operated sickle. Because farmers could harvest wheat so quickly, they began planting more of it. Growing wheat became profitable.

McCormick's reaper ensured that raising wheat would remain the main economic activity in the Midwestern prairies. New machines and railroads helped farmers plant more acres in "cash" crops—crops planted strictly for sale. Midwestern farmers began growing more wheat and shipping it east by train and canal barge. Farmers in the Northeast and Middle Atlantic states increased their production of fruits and vegetables that grew well in Eastern soils.

Despite improvements in agriculture, however, the North turned away from farming and increasingly toward industry. It was difficult making a living farming the rocky soil of New England, but industry flourished in the area. The number of people who worked in factories continued to rise—and so did problems connected with factory labor.

✓ **Reading Check** **Identifying** What innovation sped the harvesting of wheat?

SECTION 1 ASSESSMENT

Checking for Understanding

1. **Key Terms** Use each of these terms in a sentence that will help explain its meaning: clipper ship, telegraph, Morse code.
2. **Reviewing Facts** Identify and describe the three phases of industrialization in the North.

Reviewing Themes

3. **Economic Factors** How did improvements in transportation affect the price of goods?

Critical Thinking

4. **Determining Cause and Effect** How did the steel-tipped plow aid settlers on the Great Plains?
5. **Analyzing Consequences** How might failure to improve transportation have affected the economic and social development of the nation? Re-create the diagram below and list the possible effects.

Effects	
Social	Economic

Analyzing Visuals

6. **Geography Skills** Study the map on page 388, then answer this question: Through what two cities in Mississippi did major rail lines pass?

Interdisciplinary Activity

Math Research the number of acres of wheat harvested in the United States before and after McCormick introduced his reaper. Then create a chart or graph to illustrate your findings.

The North's People

Guide to Reading

Main Idea
Many cities grew tremendously during this period.

Key Terms
trade union, strike, prejudice, discrimination, famine, nativist

Reading Strategy
Determining Cause and Effect As you read the section, re-create the diagram below and list two reasons for the growth of cities.

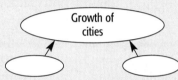

Growth of cities

Read to Learn
- how working conditions in industries changed.
- how immigration affected American economic, political, and cultural life.

Section Theme
Geography and History Growth of industry and an increase in immigration changed the North.

Preview of Events

♦1820   ♦1830   ♦1840   ♦1850   ♦1860

1827	1833	1854	1860
Freedom's Journal, first African American newspaper, is published	The General Trades Union of New York is formed	American Party (Know-Nothings) forms	Population of New York City passes 800,000

AN American Story

"At first the hours seemed very long, but I was so interested in learning that I endured it very well; when I went out at night the sound of the mill was in my ears," a Northern mill worker wrote in 1844. The worker compared the noise of the cotton mill to the ceaseless, deafening roar of Niagara Falls. The roar of machinery was only one feature of factory life workers had to adjust to. Industrialization created new challenges for the men, women, and children who worked in the nation's factories.

12-year-old factory worker

Northern Factories

Between 1820 and 1860, more and more of America's manufacturing shifted to mills and factories. Machines took over many of the production tasks.

In the early 1800s, in the mills established in **Lowell, Massachusetts,** the entire production process was brought together under one roof—setting up the factory system. In addition to textiles and clothing, factories now produced such items as shoes, watches, guns, sewing machines, and agricultural machinery.

Working Conditions

As the factory system developed, working conditions worsened. Factory owners wanted their employees to work longer hours in order to produce more goods. By 1840 factory workers averaged 11.4 hours a day. As the workday grew longer, on-the-job accidents became more and more common.

Factory work involved many dangerous conditions. For example, the long leather belts that connected the machines to the factory's water-powered driveshaft had no protective shields. Workers often suffered injuries such as lost fingers and broken bones from the rapidly spinning belts. Young children working on machines with powerful moving parts were especially at risk.

Workers often labored under unpleasant conditions. In the summer, factories were miserably hot and stifling. The machines gave off heat, and air-conditioning had not yet been invented. In the winter, workers suffered because most factories had no heating.

Factory owners often showed more concern for profits than for the comfort and safety of their employees. Employers knew they could easily replace an unhappy worker with someone else eager for a job. No laws existed to regulate working conditions or to protect workers.

Attempts to Organize

By the 1830s workers began organizing to improve working conditions. Fearing the growth of the factory system, skilled workers had formed trade unions—organizations of workers with the same trade, or skill. Steadily deteriorating working conditions led unskilled workers to organize as well.

In the mid-1830s skilled workers in New York City staged a series of strikes, refusing to work in order to put pressure on employers. Workers wanted higher wages and to limit their workday to 10 hours. Groups of skilled workers formed the General Trades Union of New York.

In the early 1800s going on strike was illegal. Striking workers could be punished by the law, or they could be fired from their jobs. In 1842 a Massachusetts court ruled that workers did have the right to strike. It would be many years, however, before workers received other legal rights.

African American Workers

Slavery had largely disappeared from the North by the 1830s. However, racial prejudice—an unfair opinion not based on facts—and discrimination—unfair treatment of a group—remained in Northern states. For example, in 1821 New York eliminated the requirement that white men had to own property in order to vote—yet few African Americans were allowed to vote. Both Rhode Island and Pennsylvania passed laws prohibiting free African Americans from voting.

Most communities would not allow free African Americans to attend public schools and barred them from public facilities as well. Often African Americans were forced into segregated, or separate, schools and hospitals.

History *Through Art*

Young Man in White Apron by John Mackie Falconer The artist of this painting was known for his watercolors depicting New York City workers such as this African American clerk. **How did prejudice affect the lives of African Americans in the North?**

A few African Americans rose in the business world. Henry Boyd owned a furniture manufacturing company in Cincinnati, Ohio. In 1827 Samuel Cornish and John B. Russwurm founded *Freedom's Journal,* the first African American newspaper, in New York City. In 1845 Macon B. Allen became the first African American licensed to practice law in the United States. The overwhelming majority of African Americans, however, were extremely poor.

Women Workers

Women had played a major role in the developing mill and factory systems. However, employers discriminated against women, paying them less than male workers. When men began to form unions, they excluded women. Male workers wanted women kept out of the workplace so that more jobs would be available for men.

Some female workers attempted to organize in the 1830s and 1840s. In Massachusetts the Lowell Female Labor Reform Organization, founded by a weaver named **Sarah G. Bagley,** petitioned the state legislature for a 10-hour workday in 1845. Because most of the petition's signers were women, the legislature did not consider the petition.

Most of the early efforts by women to achieve equality and justice in the workplace failed. They paved the way, however, for later movements to correct the injustices against female workers.

✔ Reading Check **Describing** How did conditions for workers change as the factory system developed?

The Rise of Cities

The growth of factories went hand in hand with the growth of Northern cities. People looking for work flocked to the cities, where most of the factories were located. The population of New York City, the nation's largest city, passed 800,000, and Philadelphia, more than 500,000 in 1860.

Between 1820 and 1840, communities that had been small villages became major cities, including St. Louis, Pittsburgh, Cincinnati, and Louisville. All of them profited from their location on the

Fact Fiction Folklore

Growth of Cities

Cities grow along fall lines A "fall line" is the boundary between an upland region and a lower region where rivers and streams move down over rapids or waterfalls to the lower region. Cities sprang up along fall lines for a number of reasons. Boats could not travel beyond the fall line, so travelers and merchants had to transfer their goods to other forms of transportation there. Early manufacturers also took advantage of the falls to power their mills. Fall-line cities include Richmond, Virginia; Trenton, New Jersey; and Augusta, Georgia.

Mississippi River or one of the river's branches. These cities became centers of the growing trade that connected the farmers of the Midwest with the cities of the Northeast. After 1830 the Great Lakes became a center for shipping, creating major new urban centers. These centers included Buffalo, Detroit, Milwaukee, and Chicago.

Immigration

Immigration—the movement of people into a country—to the United States increased dramatically between 1840 and 1860. American manufacturers welcomed the tide of immigrants, many of whom were willing to work for long hours and for low pay.

The largest group of immigrants to the United States at this time traveled across the Atlantic from Ireland. Between 1846 and 1860 more than 1.5 million Irish immigrants arrived in the country, settling mostly in the Northeast.

The Irish migration to the United States was brought on by a terrible potato famine. A famine is an extreme shortage of food. Potatoes were the main part of the Irish diet. When a devastating blight, or disease, destroyed Irish potato crops in the 1840s, starvation struck the country. More than one million people died.

Although most of the immigrants had been farmers in Ireland, they were too poor to buy land in the United States. For this reason many Irish immigrants took low-paying factory jobs in

MORE ABOUT...

Immigration

Newcomers came to America from many different countries in the mid-1800s, but the overwhelming majority came from Ireland and Germany.

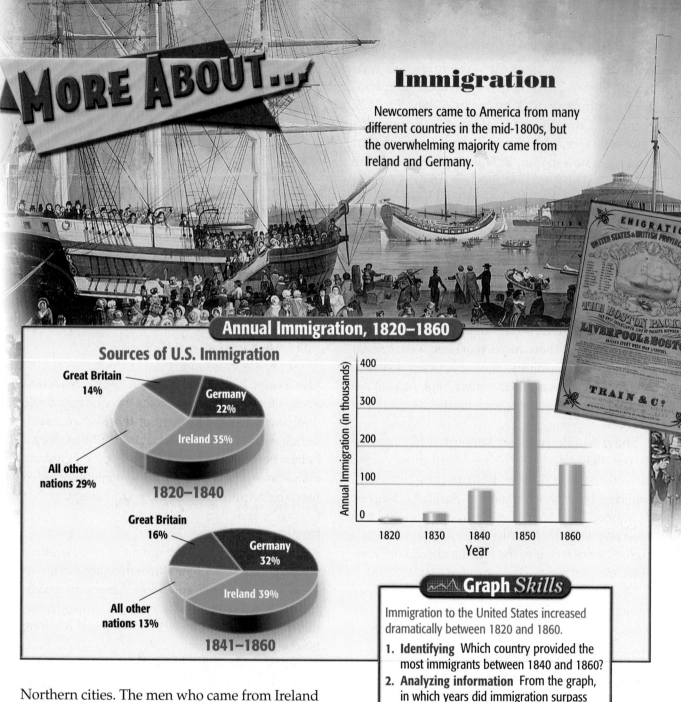

Annual Immigration, 1820–1860

Sources of U.S. Immigration

1820–1840
- Great Britain 14%
- Germany 22%
- Ireland 35%
- All other nations 29%

1841–1860
- Great Britain 16%
- Germany 32%
- Ireland 39%
- All other nations 13%

Graph Skills

Immigration to the United States increased dramatically between 1820 and 1860.

1. **Identifying** Which country provided the most immigrants between 1840 and 1860?
2. **Analyzing information** From the graph, in which years did immigration surpass 100,000?

Northern cities. The men who came from Ireland worked in factories or performed manual labor, such as working on the railroads. The women, who accounted for almost half of the immigrants, became servants and factory workers.

The second-largest group of immigrants in the United States between 1820 and 1860 came from Germany. Some sought work and opportunity. Others had left their homes because of the failure of a democratic revolution in Germany in 1848.

Between 1848 and 1860 more than one million German immigrants—many in family groups—settled in the United States. Many arrived with enough money to buy farms or open their own businesses. They prospered in many parts of the country, founding their own communities and self-help organizations. Some German immigrants settled in New York and Pennsylvania, but many moved to the Midwest and the western territories.

The Impact of Immigration

The immigrants who came to the United States between 1820 and 1860 changed the character of the country. These people brought their languages, customs, religions, and ways of life with them, some of which filtered into American culture.

Before the early 1800s, the majority of immigrants to America had been either Protestants from Great Britain or Africans brought forcibly to America as slaves. At the time, the country had relatively few Catholics, and most of these lived around Baltimore, New Orleans, and St. Augustine. Most of the Irish immigrants and about one-half of the German immigrants were Roman Catholics.

Many Catholic immigrants settled in cities of the Northeast. The Church gave the newcomers more than a source of spiritual guidance. It also provided a center for the community life of the immigrants.

The German immigrants brought their language as well as their religion. When they settled, they lived in their own communities, founded German-language publications, and established musical societies.

Immigrants Face Prejudice

In the 1830s and 1840s, anti-immigrant feelings rose. Some Americans feared that immigrants were changing the character of the United States too much.

People opposed to immigration were known as nativists because they felt that immigration threatened the future of "native"—American-born—citizens. Some nativists accused immigrants of taking jobs from "real" Americans and were angry that immigrants would work for lower wages. Others accused the newcomers of bringing crime and disease to American cities. Immigrants who lived in crowded slums served as likely targets of this kind of prejudice.

The Know-Nothing Party

The nativists formed secret anti-Catholic societies, and in the 1850s they joined to form a new political party: the American Party. Because members of nativist groups often answered questions about their organization with the statement "I know nothing," their party came to be known as the **Know-Nothing Party.**

The Know-Nothings called for stricter citizenship laws—extending the immigrants' waiting period for citizenship from 5 to 21 years—and wanted to ban foreign-born citizens from holding office.

In the mid-1850s the Know-Nothing movement split into a Northern branch and a Southern branch over the question of slavery. At this time the slavery issue was also dividing the Northern and Southern states of the nation.

✓ **Reading Check** **Identifying** What two nations provided the largest number of immigrants to the United States during this era?

SECTION 2 ASSESSMENT

Checking for Understanding

1. **Key Terms** Use each of these terms in a complete sentence that will help explain its meaning: trade union, strike, prejudice, discrimination, famine, nativist.
2. **Reviewing Facts** What was the nation's largest city in 1860?

Reviewing Themes

3. **Geography and History** How did German and Irish immigrants differ in where they settled?

Critical Thinking

4. **Making Inferences** How do you think nativists would have defined a "real" American?
5. **Determining Cause and Effect** Re-create the diagram below and list reasons workers formed labor unions.

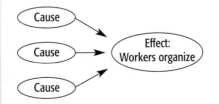

Analyzing Visuals

6. **Graph Skills** Study the graphs on page 394. What country provided about 1 of 4 immigrants to the U.S. between 1820 and 1840?

Interdisciplinary Activity

Geographic Patterns Study the graphs on page 394. Create a quiz for your classmates based on the geographic patterns of immigration to the U.S. as shown on the graphs. Trade quizzes with a classmate and answer those questions.

Social Studies SKILLBUILDER

Reading a Circle Graph

Why Learn This Skill?

Have you ever watched someone dish out pieces of pie? When the pie is cut evenly, everybody gets the same size slice. If one slice is cut a little larger, however, someone else gets a smaller piece. A **circle graph** is like a pie cut in slices. Often, a circle graph is called a *pie chart.*

Learning the Skill

In a circle graph, the complete circle represents a whole group—or 100 percent. The circle is divided into "slices," or wedge-shaped sections representing parts of the whole.

The size of each slice is determined by the percentage it represents.

To read a circle graph, follow these steps:
- Study the labels or key to determine what the parts or "slices" represent.
- Compare the parts of the graph to draw conclusions about the subject.
- When two or more circle graphs appear together, read their titles and labels. Then compare the graphs for similarities and differences.

Practicing the Skill

Read the graphs on this page. Then answer the following questions.

1 What do the four graphs represent?

2 What percentage of workers were in agriculture in 1840? In 1870?

Agricultural and Nonagricultural Workers, 1840–1870

1840: 15%, 16%, 69%
1850: 16%, 20%, 64%
1860: 18%, 23%, 59%
1870: 21%, 26%, 53%

Agricultural · Manufacturing · Other

Source: *Historical Statistics of the United States.*

3 During what decade did the percentage of workers in manufacturing increase the most?

4 What can you conclude from the graphs about the relationship between manufacturing and agricultural workers from 1840 to 1870?

Applying the Skill

Reading a Circle Graph Find a circle graph related to the economy in a newspaper or magazine. Compare its sections. Then draw a conclusion about the economy.

 Glencoe's **Skillbuilder Interactive Workbook CD-ROM, Level 1,** provides instruction and practice in key social studies skills.

Southern Cotton Kingdom

Guide to Reading

Main Idea
Cotton was vital to the economy of the South.

Key Terms
cotton gin, capital

Reading Strategy
Comparing As you read the section, re-create the diagram. In the ovals, give reasons why cotton production grew while industrial growth was slower.

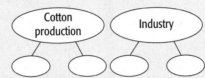

Read to Learn
• how settlement expanded in the South.
• why the economy of the South relied on agriculture.

Section Theme
Science and Technology Technology, a favorable climate, and rising demand led to the cotton boom in the Deep South.

Preview of Events

| ♦1780 | ♦1800 | ♦1820 | ♦1840 | ♦1860 |

1793
Eli Whitney invents cotton gin

1800s
Removal of Native Americans spurs expansion of cotton production

1860
The South remains largely rural and dependent on cotton

★★★★★★★★★★★
AN
American Story

Stem of cotton

Cotton was "king" in the South before 1860. "Look which way you will, you see it; and see it moving," wrote a visitor to Mobile, Alabama. "Keel boats, ships, brigs, schooners, wharves, stores, and press-houses, all appeared to be full." Cotton was also the main topic of conversation: "I believe that in the three days that I was there . . . I must have heard the word *cotton* pronounced more than 3,000 times."

Rise of the Cotton Kingdom

In 1790 the South seemed to be an underdeveloped agricultural region with little prospect for future growth. Most Southerners lived along the Atlantic coast in Maryland, Virginia, and North Carolina in what came to be known as the **Upper South.**

By 1850 the South had changed. Its population had spread inland to the states of the **Deep South**—Georgia, South Carolina, Alabama, Mississippi, Louisiana, and Texas. The economy of the South was thriving. Slavery, which had disappeared from the North, grew stronger than ever in the South.

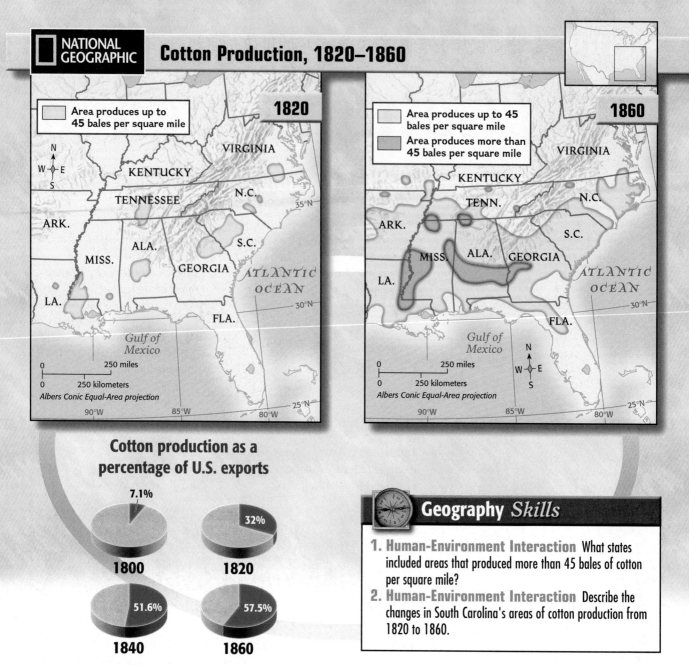

NATIONAL GEOGRAPHIC

Cotton Production, 1820–1860

1820

Area produces up to 45 bales per square mile

VIRGINIA
KENTUCKY
TENNESSEE
N.C.
ARK.
ALA.
S.C.
MISS.
GEORGIA
LA.
FLA.
ATLANTIC OCEAN
Gulf of Mexico

0   250 miles
0   250 kilometers
Albers Conic Equal-Area projection

35°N
30°N
25°N
90°W   85°W   80°W

1860

Area produces up to 45 bales per square mile

Area produces more than 45 bales per square mile

VIRGINIA
KENTUCKY
TENN.
N.C.
ARK.
S.C.
MISS.
ALA.
GEORGIA
LA.
FLA.
ATLANTIC OCEAN
Gulf of Mexico

0   250 miles
0   250 kilometers
Albers Conic Equal-Area projection

30°N
25°N
90°W   85°W   80°W

Cotton production as a percentage of U.S. exports

7.1%
1800

32%
1820

51.6%
1840

57.5%
1860

Source: *Historical Statistics of the United States.*

Geography *Skills*

1. **Human-Environment Interaction** What states included areas that produced more than 45 bales of cotton per square mile?
2. **Human-Environment Interaction** Describe the changes in South Carolina's areas of cotton production from 1820 to 1860.

Cotton Rules the Deep South

In colonial times, rice, indigo, and tobacco made up the South's main crops. After the American Revolution, demand for these crops decreased. European mills, however, wanted Southern cotton. But cotton took time and labor to produce. After harvest, workers had to painstakingly separate the plant's sticky seeds from the cotton fibers.

Cotton production was revolutionized when **Eli Whitney** invented the cotton gin in 1793. The cotton gin was a machine that removed seeds from cotton fibers, dramatically increasing the amount of cotton that could be processed. A worker could clean 50 pounds of cotton a day with the machine—instead of 1 pound by hand. Furthermore the gin was small enough for one person to carry from place to place.

Whitney's invention had important consequences. The cotton gin led to the demand for more workers. Because the cotton gin processed cotton fibers so quickly, farmers wanted to grow more cotton. Many Southern planters relied on slave labor to plant and pick the cotton.

By 1860 the economies of the Deep South and the Upper South had developed in different ways. Both parts of the South were agricultural, but the Upper South still produced tobacco, hemp, wheat, and vegetables. The Deep South was committed to cotton and, in some areas, to rice and sugarcane.

The value of enslaved people increased because of their key role in producing cotton and sugar. The Upper South became a center for the sale and transport of enslaved people throughout the region.

Reading Check **Describing** What effect did the cotton gin have on the South's economy?

Industry in the South

The economy of the South prospered between 1820 and 1860. Unlike the industrial North, however, the South remained overwhelmingly rural, and its economy became increasingly different from the Northern economy. The South accounted for a small percentage of the nation's manufacturing value by 1860. In fact, the entire South had a lower value of manufactured goods than the state of Pennsylvania.

Barriers to Industry

Why was there little industry in the South? One reason was the boom in cotton sales. Because agriculture was so profitable, Southerners remained committed to farming rather than starting new businesses.

Another stumbling block was the lack of capital—money to invest in businesses—in the South. To develop industries required money, but many Southerners had their wealth invested in land and slaves. Planters would have had to sell slaves to raise the money to build factories. Most wealthy Southerners were unwilling to do this. They believed that an economy based on cotton and slavery would continue to prosper.

In addition the market for manufactured goods in the South was smaller than it was in the North. A large portion of the Southern

TECHNOLOGY & History

The Cotton Gin

In 1793 Eli Whitney visited Catherine Greene, a Georgia plantation owner. She asked him to build a device that removed the seeds from cotton pods. Whitney called the machine the cotton gin— "gin" being short for engine. *How did the invention of the cotton gin affect slavery?*

Eli Whitney

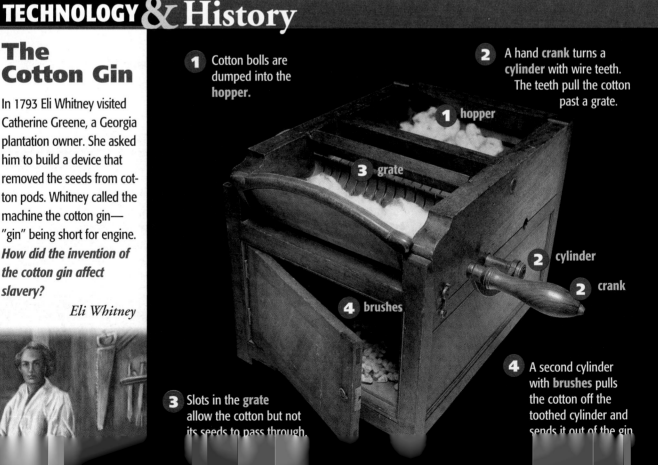

1 Cotton bolls are dumped into the **hopper**.

2 A hand **crank** turns a **cylinder** with wire teeth. The teeth pull the cotton past a grate.

1 hopper

3 grate

2 cylinder

2 crank

4 brushes

4 A second cylinder with **brushes** pulls the cotton off the toothed cylinder and sends it out of the gin

3 Slots in the **grate** allow the cotton but not its seeds to pass through.

population consisted of enslaved people with no money to buy merchandise. So the limited local market discouraged industries from developing.

Yet another reason for the lack of industry is that some Southerners did not want industry to flourish there. One Texas politician summed up the Southerners' point of view this way:

66We want no manufactures; we desire no trading, no mechanical or manufacturing classes. As long as we have our rice, our sugar, our tobacco and our cotton, we can command wealth to purchase all we want.99

Southern Factories

While most Southerners felt confident about the future of the cotton economy, some leaders wanted to develop industry in the region. They argued that, by remaining committed to cotton production, the South was becoming dependent on the North for manufactured goods. These Southerners also argued that factories would revive the economy of the Upper South, which was less prosperous than the cotton states.

One Southerner who shared this view was **William Gregg,** a merchant from Charleston, South Carolina. After touring New England's textile mills in 1844, Gregg opened his own textile factory in South Carolina.

In Richmond, Virginia, **Joseph Reid Anderson** took over the Tredegar Iron Works in the 1840s and made it one of the nation's leading producers of iron. Years later during the Civil War, Tredegar provided artillery and other iron products for the Southern forces.

The industries that Gregg and Anderson built stood as the exception rather than the rule in the South. In 1860 the region remained largely rural and dependent on cotton.

Southern Transportation

Natural waterways provided the chief means for transporting goods in the South. Most towns were located on the seacoast or along rivers. There were few canals, and roads were poor.

Like the North, the South also built railroads, but to a lesser extent. Southern rail lines were short, local, and did not connect all parts of the region in a network. As a result Southern cities grew more slowly than cities in the North and Midwest, where railways provided the major routes of commerce and settlement. By 1860 only about one-third of the nation's rail lines lay within the South. The railway shortage would have devastating consequences for the South during the Civil War.

✓**Reading Check** **Explaining** What is capital? Why is it important for economic growth?

SECTION 3 ASSESSMENT

Checking for Understanding

1. **Key Terms** Use each of these terms in a sentence that will help explain its meaning: cotton gin, capital.
2. **Reviewing Facts** How did the lack of capital affect industrial growth?

Reviewing Themes

3. **Science and Technology** Why did the invention of the cotton gin increase the demand for enslaved Africans?

Critical Thinking

4. **Predicting Consequences** If slavery had been outlawed, how do you think it would have affected the South's economy?
5. **Comparing** How did agriculture in the Upper South differ from agriculture in the Deep South? Re-create the diagram below and describe the differences.

Agriculture	
Upper South	Deep South

Analyzing Visuals

6. **Geography Skills** Look at the maps and the graphs on page 398. What area of Florida specialized in cotton? Did cotton make up more than 50 percent of U.S. exports in 1820?

Interdisciplinary Activity

Informative Writing Research and write a report on a machine mentioned in the chapter—perhaps the steam locomotive, steamboat, or another steam-driven machine. Illustrate your report if you wish. Keep the report in your portfolio.

The South's People

Main Idea

The South's population consisted of wealthy slaveholding planters, small farmers, poor whites, and enslaved African Americans.

Key Terms

yeoman, tenant farmer, fixed cost, credit, overseer, spiritual, slave code

Reading Strategy

Organizing Information As you read the section, re-create the diagram below and describe the work that was done on Southern plantations.

Working on a plantation

Read to Learn

- about the way of life on Southern plantations.
- how enslaved workers maintained strong family and cultural ties.

Section Theme

Culture and Traditions Most of the people in the South worked in agriculture in the first half of the 1800s.

Preview of Events

♦1800	♦1820	♦1840	♦1860

1808
Congress outlaws the slave trade

1831
Nat Turner leads rebellion in Virginia

1859
Arkansas orders free blacks to leave

1860
Population of Baltimore reaches 212,000

AN American Story

Planters gathered in the bright Savannah sunshine. They were asked to bid on a strong slave who could plow their fields. Fear and grief clouded the enslaved man's face because he had been forced to leave his wife and children. Later, he wrote this letter: "My Dear wife I [write] . . . with much regret to inform you that I am Sold to a man by the name of Peterson. . . . Give my love to my father and mother and tell them good Bye for me. And if we Shall not meet in this world, I hope to meet in heaven. My Dear wife for you and my Children my pen cannot express the [grief] I feel to be parted from you all."

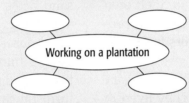

Plow

Small Farms

Popular novels and films often portray the South before 1860 as a land of stately plantations owned by rich white slaveholders. In reality most white Southerners were either small farmers without slaves or planters with a handful of slaves. Only a few planters could afford the many enslaved Africans and the lavish mansions shown in fictional accounts of the Old South. Most white Southerners fit into one of four categories: yeomen, tenant farmers, the rural poor, or plantation owners.

Small Farmers and the Rural Poor

The farmers who did not have slaves—yeomen—made up the largest group of whites in the South. Most yeomen owned land. Although they lived throughout the region, they were most numerous in the Upper South and in the hilly rural areas of the Deep South, where the land was unsuited to large plantations.

A yeoman's farm usually ranged from 50 to 200 acres. Yeomen grew crops both for their own use and to sell, and they often traded their produce to local merchants and workers for goods and services.

Most Southern whites did not live in elegant mansions or on large plantations. They lived in far simpler homes, though the structure of their homes changed over time. In the early 1800s many lived in cottages built of wood and plaster with thatched roofs. Later many lived in one-story frame houses or log cabins.

Not all Southern whites owned land. Some rented land, or worked as tenant farmers, on landlords' estates. Others—the rural poor—lived in crude cabins in wooded areas where they could clear a few trees, plant some corn, and keep a hog or a cow. They also fished and hunted for food.

The poor people of the rural South were stubbornly independent. They refused to take any job that resembled the work of enslaved people. Although looked down on by other whites, the rural poor were proud of being self-sufficient.

Reading Check **Identifying** What group made up the largest number of whites in the South?

Plantations

A large plantation might cover several thousand acres. Well-to-do plantation owners usually lived in comfortable but not luxurious farmhouses. They measured their wealth partly by the number of enslaved people they controlled and partly by such possessions as homes, furnishings, and clothing. A small group of plantation owners—about 4 percent—held 20 or more slaves in 1860. The large majority of slaveholders held fewer than 10 enslaved workers.

A few free African Americans possessed slaves. The Metoyer family of Louisiana owned thousands of acres of land and more than 400 slaves. Most often, these slaveholders were free African Americans who purchased their own family members in order to free them.

Picturing **History**
Wealthy Southerners pose for the camera in front of an elegant plantation home. **What were the duties of the wife of a plantation owner?**

Atlanta, Georgia, business street, c. 1860

$ Economics

Plantation Owners

The main economic goal for large plantation owners was to earn profits. Such plantations had fixed costs—regular expenses such as housing and feeding workers and maintaining cotton gins and other equipment. Fixed costs remained about the same year after year.

Cotton prices, however, varied from season to season, depending on the market. To receive the best prices, planters sold their cotton to agents in cities such as **New Orleans, Charleston, Mobile,** and **Savannah.** The cotton exchanges, or trade centers, in Southern cities were of vital importance to those involved in the cotton economy. The agents of the exchanges extended credit—a form of loan—to the planters and held the cotton for several months until the price rose. Then the agents sold the cotton. This system kept the planters always in debt because they did not receive payment for their cotton until the agents sold it.

Plantation Wives

The wife of a plantation owner generally was in charge of watching over the enslaved workers who toiled in her home and tending to them when they became ill. Her responsibilities also included supervising the plantation's buildings and the fruit and vegetable gardens. Some wives served as accountants, keeping the plantation's financial records.

Women often led a difficult and lonely life on the plantation. When plantation agriculture spread westward into Alabama and Mississippi, many planters' wives felt they were moving into a hostile, uncivilized region. Planters traveled frequently to look at new land or to deal with agents in New Orleans or **Memphis.** Their wives spent long periods alone at the plantation.

Work on the Plantation

Large plantations needed many different kinds of workers. Some enslaved people worked in the house, cleaning, cooking, doing laundry, sewing, and serving meals. They were called domestic slaves. Other African Americans were trained as blacksmiths, carpenters, shoemakers,

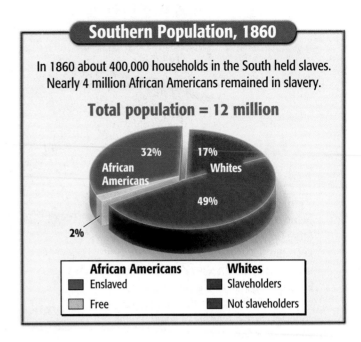

Southern Population, 1860

In 1860 about 400,000 households in the South held slaves. Nearly 4 million African Americans remained in slavery.

Total population = 12 million

32% African Americans
17% Whites
49%
2%

African Americans	Whites
■ Enslaved	■ Slaveholders
▢ Free	■ Not slaveholders

or weavers. Still others worked in the pastures, tending the horses, cows, sheep, and pigs. Most of the enslaved African Americans, however, were field hands. They worked from sunrise to sunset planting, cultivating, and picking cotton and other crops. They were supervised by an overseer—a plantation manager.

✔**Reading Check** **Explaining** Why were many slaves needed on a plantation?

Life Under Slavery

Enslaved African Americans endured hardship and misery. They worked hard, earned no money, and had little hope of freedom. One of their worst fears was being sold to another planter and separated from their loved ones. In the face of these brutal conditions, enslaved African Americans maintained their family life as best they could and developed a culture all their own. They resisted slavery through a variety of ingenious methods, and they looked to the day when they would be liberated.

Life in the Slave Cabins

Enslaved people had few comforts beyond the bare necessities. Josiah Henson, an African American who escaped from slavery, described the quarters where he had lived.

More About...

Living Under Slavery

Enslaved workers reached the fields before the sun came up, and they stayed there until sundown. Planters wanted to keep the slaves busy all the time, which meant long and grueling days in the fields. Enslaved women as well as men were required to do heavy fieldwork. Young children carried buckets of water. By the age of 10, they were considered ready for fieldwork.

Cabins were usually made of small logs, about 10 to 20 feet square. Often, two or three families shared a cabin.

Heavy iron leg shackles were used to punish workers, especially those who tried to run away.

Enslaved people had few personal possessions.

When rented to other masters, enslaved people wore identification tags.

66We lodged in log huts and on the bare ground. Wooden floors were an unknown luxury. In a single room were huddled, like cattle, ten or a dozen persons, men, women and children. . . .

Our beds were collections of straw and old rags, thrown down in the corners and boxed in with boards, a single blanket the only covering. . . . The wind whistled and the rain and snow blew in through the cracks, and the damp earth soaked in the moisture till the floor was miry [muddy] as a pigsty.99

Family Life

Enslaved people faced constant uncertainty and danger. American law in the early 1800s did not protect enslaved families. At any given time a husband or wife could be sold away, or a slaveholder's death could lead to the breakup of an enslaved family. Although marriage between enslaved people was not recognized by law, many couples did marry. Their marriage ceremonies included the phrase "until death or separation do us part"—recognizing the possibility that a marriage might end with the sale of one spouse.

To provide some measure of stability in their lives, enslaved African Americans established a network of relatives and friends, who made up their extended family. If a father or mother were sold away, an aunt, uncle, or close friend could raise the children left behind. Large, close-knit extended families became a vital feature of African American culture.

African American Culture

Enslaved African Americans endured their hardships by extending their own culture, fellowship, and community. They fused African and American elements into a new culture.

The growth of the African American population came mainly from children born in the United States. In 1808 Congress had outlawed the slave trade. Although slavery remained legal in the South, no new slaves could enter the United States. By 1860 almost all the enslaved people in the South had been born there.

These native-born African Americans held on to their African customs. They continued to practice African music and dance. They passed traditional African folk stories to their children. Some wrapped colored cloths around their heads in the African style. Although a large number of enslaved African Americans accepted Christianity, they often followed the religious beliefs and practices of their African ancestors as well.

African American Christianity

For many enslaved African Americans, Christianity became a religion of hope and resistance. They prayed fervently for the day when they would be free from bondage.

The passionate beliefs of the Southern slaves found expression in the spiritual, an African American religious folk song. The song "Didn't My Lord Deliver Daniel," for example, refers to the biblical story of Daniel who was saved from the lions' den.

66Didn't my Lord deliver Daniel,
deliver Daniel, deliver Daniel,
Didn't my Lord deliver Daniel,
An' why not every man?99

Spirituals provided a way for the enslaved African Americans to communicate secretly among themselves. Many spirituals combined Christian faith with laments about earthly suffering.

Slave Codes

Between 1830 and 1860 life under slavery became even more difficult because the slave codes—the laws in the Southern states that controlled enslaved people—became more severe. In existence since the 1700s, slave codes aimed to prevent the event white Southerners dreaded most—the slave rebellion. For this reason slave codes prohibited slaves from assembling in large groups and from leaving their master's property without a written pass.

Slave codes also made it a crime to teach enslaved people to read or write. White Southerners feared that a literate slave might lead other African Americans in rebellion. A slave who did not know how to read and write, whites believed, was less likely to rebel.

Resistance to Slavery

Some enslaved African Americans did rebel openly against their masters. One was **Nat Turner,** a popular religious leader among his fellow slaves. Turner had taught himself to read and write. In 1831 Turner led a group of followers on a brief, violent rampage in Southhampton County, Virginia. Before being captured Turner and his followers killed at least 55 whites. Nat Turner was hanged, but his rebellion frightened white Southerners and led them to pass more severe slave codes.

Armed rebellions were rare, however. African Americans in the South knew that they would only lose in an armed uprising. For the most part enslaved people resisted slavery by working slowly or by pretending to be ill. Occasionally resistance took more active forms, such as setting fire to a plantation building or breaking tools. Resistance helped enslaved African Americans endure their lives by striking back at white masters—and perhaps establishing boundaries that white people would respect.

People In History

Harriet Tubman 1820–1913

Born as a slave in Maryland, Harriet Tubman worked in plantation fields until she was nearly 30 years old. Then she made her break for freedom, escaping to the North with the help of the Underground Railroad.

Realizing the risks of being captured, Tubman courageously made 19 trips back into the South during the 1850s to help other enslaved people escape. Altogether she assisted more than 300 individuals—including her parents—to escape from slavery.

While she did not establish the Underground Railroad, she certainly became its most famous and successful conductor. Tubman was known as the "Moses of her people." Despite huge rewards offered in the South for her capture and arrest, Tubman always managed to elude her enemies.

Escaping Slavery

Some enslaved African Americans tried to run away to the North. A few succeeded. **Harriet Tubman** and **Frederick Douglass,** two African American leaders who were born into slavery, gained their freedom when they fled to the North.

Yet for most enslaved people, getting to the North was almost impossible, especially from the Deep South. Most slaves who succeeded in running away escaped from the Upper South. **The Underground Railroad**—a network of "safe houses" owned by free blacks and whites who opposed slavery—offered assistance to runaway slaves.

Some slaves ran away to find relatives on nearby plantations or to escape punishment. Rarely did they plan to make a run for the North. Moses Grandy, who did escape, spoke about the problems runaways faced:

❝They hide themselves during the day in the woods and swamps; at night they travel. . . . [I]n these dangerous journeys they are guided by the north-star, for they only know that the land of freedom is in the north.❞

Most runaways were captured and returned to their owners. Discipline was severe; the most common punishment was whipping.

✔ **Reading Check** Explaining How did the African American spiritual develop?

City Life and Education

Although the South was primarily agricultural, it was the site of several large cities by the mid-1800s. By 1860 the population of **Baltimore** had reached 212,000 and the population of New Orleans had reached 168,000. The ten largest cities in the South were either seaports or river ports.

With the coming of the railroad, many other cities began to grow as centers of trade. Among the cities located at the crossroads of the railways were Columbia, South Carolina; Chattanooga, Tennessee; Montgomery, Alabama; Jackson, Mississippi; and Atlanta, Georgia. The population of Southern cities included white city dwellers, some enslaved workers, and many of the South's free African Americans.

The cities provided free African Americans with opportunities to form their own communities. African American barbers, carpenters, and small traders offered their services throughout their communities. Free African Americans founded their own churches and institutions. In New Orleans they formed an opera company.

Although some free African Americans prospered in the cities, their lives were far from secure. Between 1830 and 1860 Southern states passed laws that limited the rights of free African Americans. Most states would not allow them to migrate from other states. Although spared the horrors of slavery, free African Americans were denied an equal share in economic and political life.

Education

Plantation owners and those who could afford to do so often sent their children to private schools. One of the best known was the academy operated by Moses Waddel in Willington, South Carolina. Students attended six days a week. The Bible and classical literature were stressed, but the courses also included mathematics, religion, Greek, Latin, and public speaking.

During this era, no statewide public school systems existed. However, cities such as Charleston, Louisville, and Mobile did establish excellent public schools.

By the mid-1800s, education was growing. Hundreds of public schools were operating in North Carolina by 1860. Even before that, the Kentucky legislature set up a funding system for public schools. Many states also had charity schools for students whose parents could not afford to pay.

HISTORY Online

Student Web Activity
Visit taj.glencoe.com and click on **Chapter 13— Student Web Activities** for an activity on family life in the South.

Although the number of schools and teachers in the South grew, the South lagged behind other sections of the country in **literacy,** the number of people who can read and write. One reason for this was the geography of the South. Even in the more heavily populated Southern states there were few people per square mile. Virginia and North Carolina had fewer than 15 white inhabitants per square mile. In contrast, Massachusetts had 124 inhabitants per square mile.

It was too great a hardship for many Southern families to send their children great distances to attend school. In addition, many Southerners believed education was a private matter, not a state function; therefore, the state should not spend money on education.

Reading Check **Describing** What Southern city had surpassed 200,000 in population by the year 1860?

SECTION 4 ASSESSMENT

Checking for Understanding

1. **Key Terms** Use the following terms to create a newspaper article about life in the South during this period of time: yeoman, tenant farmer, overseer, spiritual, slave code.

2. **Reviewing Facts** List two differences between yeomen and plantation owners.

Reviewing Themes

3. **Culture and Traditions** Why were extended families vital to African American culture?

Critical Thinking

4. **Making Generalizations** If you were a plantation owner, what would you tell your son or daughter if he or she asked why you held slaves?

5. **Classifying Information** Re-create the diagram below and in the boxes briefly explain how the slave codes operated.

Slave codes	
Control education	Control assembly

Analyzing Visuals

6. Look at the pictures on pages 402 and 404. Write a paragraph explaining what you think the pictures portray about life in the South.

Interdisciplinary Activity

Geography Research the economic activity of one of the Southern states. Draw a map of the state, and use symbols to represent each resource and show its location in the state.

Chapter Summary
North and South

North	South

Economy

North
- Growth of industrialization.
- Specialization and machinery allow for mass production.

South
- Cotton is leading cash crop.
- Industry limited due to lack of capital and market demand.

Transportation

North
- Roads, canals, and railroads being built.
- Locomotives improve during this era.

South
- Natural waterways chief means of transportation.
- Canals and roads are poor.
- Railroads are limited.

Way of Life

North
- Many people move to cities to find work.
- Cities grow crowded and many live in unhealthy and unsafe conditions.
- African Americans suffer discrimination and have few rights.

South
- Plantation owners farm large tracts of land; plantations are generally self-sufficient.
- Yeomen make up the largest group of whites.
- Tenant farmers farm small tracts of land.
- Enslaved African Americans do most of the work on plantations.

Reviewing Key Terms

On graph paper, create a word search puzzle using the following terms. Crisscross the terms vertically and horizontally, then fill in the remaining squares with extra letters. Use the terms' definitions as clues to find the words in the puzzle.

1. telegraph
2. nativist
3. overseer
4. yeoman
5. credit

Reviewing Key Facts

6. How did the development of the canal and rail network alter the trade route between the Midwest and the East Coast?
7. How did the the telegraph influence long-distance communication?
8. Provide three reasons why cities grew in the early 1800s.
9. What was the goal of workers going on strike?
10. In what ways were women in the workforce discriminated against?
11. Why did immigration from Germany increase after 1848?
12. How did the cotton gin affect cotton production?
13. Why was there little industry in the South?
14. What was the Underground Railroad?
15. What was the purpose of the slave codes?

Critical Thinking

16. **Analyzing Themes: Economic Factors** How did improvements in transportation affect the economy of the North?
17. **Comparing** Discuss one advantage and one disadvantage of city life in the North.
18. **Comparing** Re-create the diagram below and compare the use of railroads in the North and South before 1860.

	North	South
Use of railroads		

19. **Analyzing Information** Describe ways in which enslaved African Americans held on to their African customs.

Practicing Skills

Reading a Circle Graph *Study the circle graphs below; then answer these questions.*

Populations of the North and South in 1860

North

98% white

2% African American

South

66% white

34% African American

Source: *Historical Statistics of the United States.*

20. What does the information in the two graphs represent?

21. In what part of the country did African Americans make up more than one-third of the population?

22. Can you use the graphs to draw a conclusion about the total population of each region? Why or why not?

Geography and History Activity

Study the map on page 388 and answer the questions that follow.

23. **Movement** In which direction would a train travel from Chattanooga, Tennessee, to Lynchburg, Virginia?

24. **Location** What was the easternmost city on the New York Central line?

25. **Movement** What cities would a train passenger pass through taking the most direct Memphis-to-Baltimore route?

Citizenship Cooperative Activity

26. **Community Issues** Working with two other students, contact the office of your local government to find out what is being done to solve local problems and how volunteers can help. Find out when the town board or city council meets. After you obtain the information, interview people in the neighborhood to find out what they think about various problems the community faces. Tell them about the town board or city council meetings, and encourage them to attend or to become involved in community activities. Compare your findings about community issues with the other groups.

HISTORY Online

Self-Check Quiz
Visit taj.glencoe.com and click on **Chapter 13—Self-Check Quizzes** to prepare for the chapter test.

Economics Activity

27. Although railroads helped the economy, why might investors in turnpikes and canals view them as a threat?

Technology Activity

28. **Using Software** Search encyclopedias and other library resources for information about cotton production in the world today. Find out which countries grow cotton, what quantities are grown, and any types of fertilizers used. Create a short report of interesting facts about cotton production in the world today. Share your report with the rest of the class.

Alternative Assessment

29. **Portfolio Writing Activity** Write a conversation between a Southerner and Northerner who meet on a train in the mid-1800s. Have them talk about the differences between their lives. Use the notes from your journal in the script.

Standardized Test Practice

Directions: Choose the *best* answer to the following question.

Labor unions were formed for all of these reasons EXCEPT to

A improve workers' wages.

B protect factory owners from being sued.

C make factories safer.

D prevent children from working long hours.

Test-Taking Tip

When a question uses the word EXCEPT, you need to look for the answer that does *not* fit. Remember that unions were formed to help *workers*. Which answer is least likely to help the workers?

CHAPTER 14

The Age of Reform

1820–1860

Why It Matters

The idea of reform—the drive to improve society and the lives of Americans—grew during the mid-1800s. Reformers set out to improve the lives of the disadvantaged, especially enslaved people and the urban poor.

The Impact Today

The spirit of reform is alive and well in the modern world. Individual freedom became a key goal during the last half of the twentieth century. Civil rights movements have advanced racial equality. In many countries the women's movement has altered traditional female roles and opportunities.

 The American Journey Video The chapter 14 video, "Women and Reform," chronicles the role of women in the reform movements of the 1800s.

1827
• New York bans slavery

1825
• New Harmony, Indiana, established

1830
• *Book of Mormon* published

1836
• Texas gains independence

Monroe
1817–1825

J.Q. Adams
1825–1829

Jackson
1829–1837

Van Buren
1837–1841

W.H. Harris
1841

United States
PRESIDENTS

1820

1830

1840

World

1821
• Mexico becomes independent nation

1837
• Victoria becomes queen of England

The Country School by Winslow Homer By the mid-1800s, the number of public elementary schools was growing.

1848
• Seneca Falls Convention

1851
• Maine bans sale of alcohol

1862
• Mary Jane Patterson is first African American woman to earn a college degree

| Tyler 1841–1845 | Polk 1845–1849 | Taylor 1849–1850 | Fillmore 1850–1853 | Pierce 1853–1857 | | Buchanan 1857–1861 |

1850   *1860*

1847
• Liberia claims independence

1850
• Taiping Rebellion begins in China

1853
• Crimean War begins

1859
• Lenoir builds first practical internal-combustion engine

Guide to Reading

Main Idea
During the early 1800s, many religious and social reformers attempted to improve American life and education and help people with disabilities.

Key Terms
utopia, revival, temperance, normal school, transcendentalist

Reading Strategy
Taking Notes As you read section 1, re-create the diagram below and identify these reformers' contributions.

	Contributions
Lyman Beecher	
Horace Mann	
Thomas Gallaudet	
Dorothea Dix	

Read to Learn
- how religious and philosophical ideas inspired various reform movements.
- why educational reformers thought all citizens should go to school.

Section Theme
Civic Rights and Responsibilities Many reformers worked for change during this era.

Preview of Events

◆1820   ◆1830   ◆1840   ◆1850

1825
Robert Owen establishes New Harmony, Indiana

1835
Oberlin College admits African Americans

1837
Horace Mann initiates education reform

1843
Dorothea Dix reveals abuses of mentally ill

AN
American Story

Henry David Thoreau

According to folklore, Henry David Thoreau sat on the hard, wooden bench in the jail cell, but he did not complain about its stiffness. He felt proud that he had stood up for his beliefs. Thoreau had refused to pay a one-dollar tax to vote, not wanting his money to support the Mexican War. As he looked through the cell bars, he heard a voice. "Why are you here?" asked his friend Ralph Waldo Emerson. Thoreau replied, "Why are you *not* here?" He would later write, "Under a government which imprisons any unjustly, the true place for a just man is also a prison."

The Reforming Spirit

Thoreau represented a new spirit of reform in America. The men and women who led the reform movement wanted to extend the nation's ideals of liberty and equality to all Americans. They believed the nation should live up to the noble goals stated in the Declaration of Independence and the Constitution.

The spirit of reform brought changes to American religion, politics, education, art, and literature. Some reformers sought to improve society by forming utopias, communities based on a vision of a perfect society. In 1825 Robert Owen established New Harmony, Indiana, a village dedicated to cooperation rather than competition among its members.

Founded on high hopes and sometimes impractical ideas, few of the utopian communities lasted more than a few years. The Shakers, the Mormons, and other religious groups also built their own communities. Only the Mormons established a stable, enduring community.

The Religious Influence

In the early 1800s, a wave of religious fervor—known as the **Second Great Awakening**—stirred the nation. The first Great Awakening had spread through the colonies in the mid-1700s.

The new religious movement began with frontier camp meetings called revivals. People came from miles around to hear eloquent preachers, such as Charles Finney, and to pray, sing, weep, and shout. The experience often made men and women eager to reform both their own lives and the world. The Second Great Awakening increased church membership. It also inspired people to become involved in missionary work and social reform movements. *(See page 967 of the Appendix for a primary source account of a revival meeting.)*

War Against Alcohol

Religious leaders stood at the forefront of the war against alcohol. Public drunkenness was common in the early 1800s. Alcohol abuse was widespread, especially in the West and among urban workers. **Lyman Beecher,** a Connecticut minister and crusader against the use of alcohol, wanted to protect society against "rum-selling, tippling folk, infidels, and ruff-scruff."

Reformers blamed alcohol for poverty, the breakup of families, crime, and even insanity. They called for temperance, drinking little or no alcohol. The movement gathered momentum in 1826 when the American Society for the Promotion of Temperance was formed.

Beecher and other temperance crusaders used lectures, pamphlets, and revival-style rallies to warn people of the dangers of liquor. The **temperance movement** gained a major victory in 1851, when Maine passed a law banning the manufacture and sale of alcoholic beverages. Other states passed similar laws. Many Americans resented these laws, however, and most were repealed, or canceled, within several years.

The temperance movement would reemerge in the early 1900s and lead to a constitutional amendment banning alcohol.

Reading Check **Analyzing** What were the effects of the Second Great Awakening?

Reforming Education

In the early 1800s, only New England provided free elementary education. In other areas parents had to pay fees or send their children to schools for the poor—a choice some parents refused out of pride. Some communities had no schools at all.

The leader of educational reform was **Horace Mann,** a lawyer who became the head of the Massachusetts Board of Education in 1837. During his term Mann lengthened the school year to six months, made improvements in the school curriculum, doubled teachers' salaries, and developed better ways of training teachers.

Partly due to Mann's efforts, Massachusetts in 1839 founded the nation's first state-supported normal school, a school for training high-school graduates as teachers. Other states soon adopted the reforms that Mann had pioneered.

Education for Some

By the 1850s most states had accepted three basic principles of public education: that schools should be free and supported by taxes, that teachers should be trained, and that children should be required to attend school.

These principles did not immediately go into effect. Schools were poorly funded, and many teachers lacked training. In addition, some people opposed compulsory, or required, education.

Most females received a limited education. Parents often kept their daughters from school because of the belief that a woman's role was to become a wife and mother and that this role did not require an education. When girls did go to school, they often studied music or needlework rather than science, mathematics, and history, which were considered "men's" subjects.

In the West, where settlers lived far apart, many children had no school to attend. African Americans in all parts of the country had few opportunities to go to school.

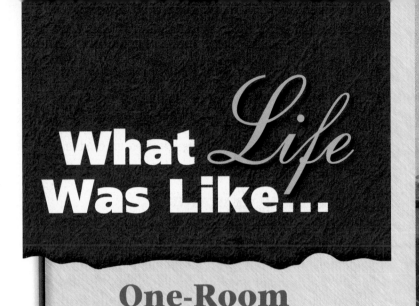

What *Life* Was Like...

One-Room Schoolhouse

Until education became widespread, many children learned to read and write in one-room schoolhouses. Students of all ages learned mostly by rote—one group recited while the rest studied their lessons. The popular McGuffey *Readers* provided moral lessons as well as lessons in reading and grammar.

Lunch pail, left
Hornbook, center
Page from McGuffey's, right

Higher Education

Dozens of new colleges and universities were created during the age of reform. Most admitted only men. Religious groups founded many colleges between 1820 and 1850, including Amherst and Holy Cross in Massachusetts and Trinity and Wesleyan in Connecticut.

Slowly, higher education became available to groups who were previously denied the opportunity. Oberlin College of Ohio, founded in 1833, admitted both women and African Americans to the student body. In 1837 a teacher named Mary Lyon in Massachusetts opened Mount Holyoke, the first permanent women's college in America. The first college for African Americans—Ashmun Institute, which later became Lincoln University—opened in Pennsylvania in 1854.

People With Special Needs

Some reformers focused on the problem of teaching people with disabilities. **Thomas Gallaudet** (ga•luh•DEHT), who developed a method to educate people who were hearing impaired, opened the Hartford School for the Deaf in Connecticut in 1817.

At about the same time, **Dr. Samuel Gridley Howe** advanced the cause of those who were visually impaired. He developed books with large raised letters that people with sight impairments could "read" with their fingers. Howe headed the Perkins Institute, a school for the blind, in Boston.

When schoolteacher **Dorothea Dix** began visiting prisons in 1841, she found the prisoners were often living in inhumane conditions—

chained to the walls with little or no clothing, often in unheated cells. To her further horror, she learned that some of the inmates were guilty of no crime—they were mentally ill persons. Dix made it her life's work to educate the public as to the poor conditions for both the mentally ill and for prisoners.

✓ **Reading Check** **Identifying** How did Dr. Samuel Howe help the visually impaired?

Cultural Trends

The changes in American society influenced art and literature. Earlier generations of American painters and writers looked to Europe for their inspiration and models. Beginning in the 1820s American artists developed their own style and explored American themes.

The American spirit of reform influenced transcendentalists. Transcendentalists stressed the relationship between humans and nature as well as the importance of the individual conscience. Writers such as Margaret Fuller, Ralph Waldo Emerson, and Henry David Thoreau were leading transcendentalists. Through her writings, Fuller supported rights for women. In his poems and essays, Emerson urged people to listen to the inner voice of conscience and to break the bonds of prejudice. Thoreau put his beliefs into practice through **civil disobedience**—refusing to obey laws he thought were unjust. In 1846 Thoreau went to jail rather than pay a tax to support the Mexican War.

The transcendentalists were not the only important writers of the period. Many poets created impresive works during this period. Henry Wadsworth Longfellow wrote narrative, or story, poems, such as the *Song of Hiawatha*. Poet Walt Whitman captured the new American spirit and confidence in his *Leaves of Grass*. Emily Dickinson wrote simple, deeply personal poems. In a poem called "Hope," written in 1861, she compares hope with a bird:

> 66 'Hope' is the thing with feathers—
> That perches in the soul—
> And sings the tune without the words—
> And never stops—at all— 99

Women writers of the period were generally not taken seriously, yet they were the authors of the most popular fiction. Harriet Beecher Stowe wrote the most successful best-seller of the mid-1800s, *Uncle Tom's Cabin*. Stowe's novel explores the injustice of slavery—an issue that took on new urgency during the age of reform.

✓ **Reading Check** **Describing** What was one of the subjects that Margaret Fuller wrote about?

SECTION 1 ASSESSMENT

Checking for Understanding

1. **Key Terms** Use each of these terms in a sentence that helps explain its meaning: utopia, revival, temperance, normal school, transcendentalist.

2. **Reviewing Facts** What were the three accepted principles of public education in the 1850s?

Reviewing Themes

3. **Civic Rights and Responsibilities** How did Thoreau act on his beliefs? What impact might such acts have had on the government?

Critical Thinking

4. **Drawing Conclusions** What did Thomas Jefferson mean when he said that the United States could not survive as a democracy without educated and well-informed citizens?

5. **Determining Cause and Effect** Re-create the diagram below and describe two ways the religious movement influenced reform.

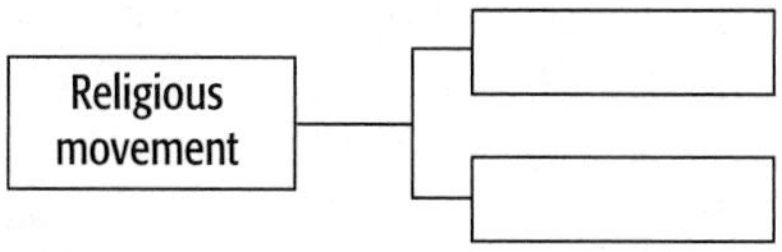

```
┌───────────┐      ┌──────────┐
│ Religious ├──────┤          │
│ movement  │      └──────────┘
│           │      ┌──────────┐
└───────────┴──────┤          │
                   └──────────┘
```

Analyzing Visuals

6. **Picturing History** Study the painting of the school room on page 414. What is pictured that you still use in school today?

Interdisciplinary Activity

Research Interview your grandparents or other adults who are over 50 years old to find out what they remember about their public school days. Before you do the interview, write six questions about the information that interests you.

TIME NOTEBOOK

What were people's lives like in the past?

What—and who—were people talking about? What did they eat? What did they do for fun? These two pages will give you some clues to everyday life in the U.S. as you step back in time with TIME Notebook.

Profile

"My best friends solemnly regard me as a madman." That's what the artist **JOHN JAMES AUDUBON** (left) *writes about himself in his journal. And he does seem to be a bit peculiar. After all, he put a band around a bird's foot so he could tell if it returned from the South in the spring. No one's ever done that before. Audubon is growing more famous thanks to his drawings. His love of the wild and his skill as an artist have awakened a new sense of appreciation for American animal life both here and in Europe. Here is what he wrote recently while on a trip to New Orleans:*

"I TOOK A WALK WITH MY GUN THIS afternoon to see… millions of Golden Plovers [medium-sized shorebirds] coming from the northeast and going nearly south— the destruction… was really astonishing—the Sportsmen here are more numerous and at the same time more expert at shooting on the wing than anywhere in the United States."

PHOTO RESEARCHERS INC., NEW YORK

ACADEMY OF NATURAL SCIENCES OF PHILADELPHIA/CORBIS

SPORTS

Baseball for Beginners

Want to take up the new game of baseball? Keep your eye on the ball—because the rules keep changing!

1845
- canvas bases are set 90 feet apart in a diamond shape
- only nine men play on each side
- pitches are thrown underhanded
- a ball caught on the first bounce is an "out"

1846
- at first base, a fielder can tag the bag before the runner reaches it and so make an out

1847
- players may no longer throw the ball at a runner to put him out

AMERICAN SCENE

Americans Living on Farms

1790: 95% of Americans live on farms

1820: 93% live on farms

1850: 85% live on farms

Personalities Meet Some Concord Residents

YEARS AGO, ONE OF THE FIRST BATTLES OF THE REVOLUTIONARY WAR was fought at Concord, Massachusetts. But now the sparks that fly are of a more intellectual variety. If you want to visit Concord, you should read some of the works of its residents.

Nathaniel Hawthorne
This writer's novel *The Scarlet Letter* moved some readers, and outraged others.

Henry Wadsworth Longfellow
Writes poems about Paul Revere, Hiawatha, and a village blacksmith.

Louisa May Alcott
Author of *Little Women* who published her first book at age16.

Louisa May Alcott

THE SCHLESINGER LIBRARY, RADCLIFFE COLLEGE

MILESTONES

PEOPLE AND EVENTS OF THE TIME

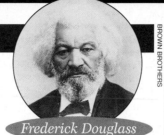
BROWN BROTHERS

Frederick Douglass

EMIGRATED. In 1845, to England, **FREDERICK DOUGLASS**, former slave, author, and abolitionist leader, to escape danger in reaction to his autobiography, *Narrative of the Life of Frederick Douglass.*

MOVED. HENRY DAVID THOREAU, writer, to Walden Pond, Concord, Massachusetts, in 1845. Thoreau intends to build his own house on the shore of the pond and earn his living by the labor of his hands only. "Many of the so-called comforts of life," writes Thoreau, "are not only not indispensable, but positive hindrances to the elevation of mankind."

AILING. EDGAR ALLAN POE, in Baltimore, 1847, following the death of his wife, Virginia. Other than a poem on death, Poe has written little this year, devoting his dwindling energies to lawsuits against other authors he claims copied his work.

INVENTED. Samuel F.B. Morse has revolutionized communications with a series of dots and dashes in 1844.

Edgar Allan Poe

BETTMANN/CORBIS

NUMBERS

U.S. AT THE TIME

9,022 Miles of railways operating in 1850

- - - - - - - - - - - - - - -

3 Number of U.S. Presidents in 1841—Van Buren's term ended, Harrison died, and Tyler took his place

- - - - - - - - - - - - - - -

29 Number of medical schools Elizabeth Blackwell, a woman, applied to before being accepted at one in 1847

- - - - - - - - - - - - - - -

700 Number of New England whaling ships at sea in 1846

- - - - - - - - - - - - - - -

$8 Approximate yearly cost for a newspaper subscription in 1830

- - - - - - - - - - - - - - -

50% Approximate percentage of the American workforce in 1820 under the age of 10

CHILD LABOR

Letter From a Mill Worker

Mary Paul is a worker in her teens at a textile mill in Lowell, Massachusetts. Mary works 12 hours a day, 6 days a week. She sent this letter to her father:

Dear Father,

I am well which is one comfort. My life and health are spared while others are cut off. Last Thursday one girl fell down and broke her neck which caused instant death. Last Tuesday we were paid. In all I had six dollars and sixty cents, paid $4.68 for board [rent and food]....At 5 o'clock in the morning the bell rings for the folks to get up and get breakfast. At half past six it rings for the girls to get up and at seven they are called into the mill. At half past 12 we have dinner, are called back again at one and stay till half past seven. . . . If any girl wants employment, I advise them to come to Lowell.

BETTMANN/CORBIS

The Abolitionists

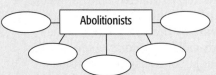

Guide to Reading

Main Idea
Many reformers turned their attention to eliminating slavery.

Key Terms
abolitionist, Underground Railroad

Reading Strategy
Organizing Information As you read Section 2, identify five abolitionists. Below each name, write a sentence describing his or her role in the movement.

Abolitionists

Read to Learn
• how some Americans worked to eliminate slavery.
• why many Americans feared the end of slavery.

Section Theme
Individual Action Leaders such as Harriet Tubman and William Lloyd Garrison strengthened the abolitionist movement.

Preview of Events

◆1815	◆1830	◆1845	◆1860
1816 American Colonization Society is formed	**1822** First African Americans settle in Liberia	**1831** William Lloyd Garrison founds *The Liberator*	**1847** Liberia becomes an independent country

AN American Story

William Lloyd Garrison

William Lloyd Garrison, a dramatic and spirited man, fought strongly for the right of African Americans to be free. On one occasion Garrison was present when Frederick Douglass, an African American who had escaped from slavery, spoke to a white audience about life as a slave. Douglass electrified his listeners with a powerful speech. Suddenly Garrison leaped to his feet. "Is this a man," he demanded of the audience, "or a thing?" Garrison shared Douglass's outrage at the notion that people could be bought and sold like objects.

Early Efforts to End Slavery

The spirit of reform that swept the United States in the early 1800s was not limited to improving education and expanding the arts. It also included the efforts of abolitionists like Garrison and Douglass—members of the growing band of reformers who worked to abolish, or end, slavery.

Even before the American Revolution, some Americans had tried to limit or end slavery. At the Constitutional Convention in 1787, the delegates had reached a compromise on the difficult issue, agreeing to let each state decide whether to allow slavery. By the early 1800s, Northern states had ended slavery, but it continued in the South.

The religious revival and the reform movement of the early and mid-1800s gave new life to the antislavery movement. Many Americans came to believe that slavery was wrong. Yet not all Northerners shared this view. The conflict over slavery continued to build.

Many of the men and women who led the antislavery movement came from the Quaker faith. One Quaker, Benjamin Lundy, wrote:

> ❝I heard the wail of the captive. I felt his pang of distress, and the iron entered my soul.❞

Lundy founded a newspaper in 1821 to spread the abolitionist message.

American Colonization Society

The first large-scale antislavery effort was not aimed at abolishing slavery but at resettling African Americans in Africa or the Caribbean. The **American Colonization Society,** formed in 1816 by a group of white Virginians, worked to free enslaved workers gradually by buying them from slaveholders and sending them abroad to start new lives.

The society raised enough money from private donors, Congress, and a few state legislatures to send several groups of African Americans out of the country. Some went to the west coast of Africa, where the society had acquired land for a colony. In 1822 the first African American settlers arrived in this colony, called **Liberia,** Latin for "place of freedom."

In 1847 Liberia became an independent country. American emigration to Liberia continued until the Civil War. Some 12,000 to 20,000 African Americans settled in the new country between 1822 and 1865.

The American Colonization Society did not halt the growth of slavery. The number of enslaved people continued to increase at a steady pace, and the society could only resettle a small number of African Americans. Furthermore, most African Americans did not want to go to Africa. Many were from families that had lived in America for several generations. They simply wanted to be free in American society. African Americans feared that the society aimed to strengthen slavery.

Reading Check **Explaining** How did the American Colonization Society fight slavery?

The Movement Changes

Reformers realized that the gradual approach to ending slavery had failed. Moreover, the numbers of enslaved persons had sharply increased because the cotton boom in the Deep South made planters increasingly dependent on slave labor. Beginning in about 1830, the American antislavery movement took on new life. Soon it became the most pressing social issue for reformers.

William Lloyd Garrison

Abolitionist **William Lloyd Garrison** stimulated the growth of the antislavery movement. In 1829 Garrison left Massachusetts to work for the country's leading antislavery newspaper in Baltimore. Impatient with the paper's moderate position, Garrison returned to Boston in 1831 to found his own newspaper, *The Liberator.*

"I looked at my hands to see if I was the same person now that I was free . . . I felt like I was in heaven."

—*Harriet Tubman, on her escape from slavery, 1849*

419

TWO VIEWPOINTS

Is American Slavery Compassionate or Cruel?

More than any other factor, slavery isolated the South from the rest of the United States. While abolitionists cried out to bring the cruel practice to an end, Southern slaveholders defended the only way of life they knew.

Sojourner Truth, former slave, 1851

Look at me! Look at my arm! I have ploughed, and planted, and gathered into barns, and no man could head me! . . . I could work as much and eat as much as a man—when I could get it—and bear the lash as well! And ain't I a woman?

I have borne thirteen children, and seen them most all sold off to slavery, and when I cried out with my mother's grief, none but Jesus heard me! And ain't I a woman?

Sojourner Truth

Jeremiah Jeter, Southern slaveholder, c. 1820

I could not free them, for the laws of the State forbade it. Yet even if they had not forbidden it, the slaves in my possession were in no condition to support themselves. It was simple cruelty to free a mother with dependent children. Observation, too, had satisfied me that the free negroes were, in general, in a worse condition than the slaves. The manumission [setting free] of my slaves to remain in the State was not to be thought of. Should I send them to Liberia? Some of them were in a condition to go, but none of them desired to. If sent, they [would] be forced to leave wives and children belonging to other masters [on nearby plantations], to dwell in a strange land.

Learning From History

1. Why do you think Sojourner Truth was an effective speaker?
2. Why didn't Jeremiah Jeter just free his slaves?
3. Do the two excerpts contradict each other? In what way?

Garrison was one of the first white abolitionists to call for the "immediate and complete emancipation [freeing]" of enslaved people. Promising to be "as harsh as truth, and as uncompromising as justice," he denounced the slow, gradual approach of other reformers. In the first issue of his paper he wrote: "I will not retreat a single inch—AND I WILL BE HEARD."

Garrison *was* heard. He attracted enough followers to start the New England Antislavery Society in 1832 and the American Antislavery Society the next year. The **abolitionist movement** grew rapidly. By 1838 the antislavery societies Garrison started had more than 1,000 chapters, or local branches.

The Grimké Sisters

Among the first women who spoke out publicly against slavery were **Sarah** and **Angelina Grimké.** Born in South Carolina to a wealthy slaveholding family, the sisters moved to Philadelphia in 1832.

In the North the Grimké sisters lectured and wrote against slavery. At one antislavery meeting, Angelina Grimké exclaimed,

> 66As a Southerner, I feel that it is my duty to stand up . . . against slavery. I have seen it! I have seen it!99

The Grimkés persuaded their mother to give them their share of the family inheritance. Instead of money or land, the sisters asked for several of the enslaved workers, whom they immediately freed.

Angelina Grimké and her husband, abolitionist Theodore Weld, wrote *American Slavery As It Is* in 1839. This collection of firsthand accounts of life under slavery was one of the most influential abolitionist publications of its time.

African American Abolitionists

Although white abolitionists drew public attention to the cause, African Americans themselves played a major role in the abolitionist movement from the start. The abolition of slavery was an especially important goal to the free African Americans of the North.

Most African Americans in the North lived in poverty in cities. Although they were excluded from most jobs and were often attacked by white mobs, a great many of these African Americans were intensely proud of their freedom and wanted to help those who were still enslaved.

African Americans took an active part in organizing and directing the American Antislavery Society, and they subscribed in large numbers to William Lloyd Garrison's *The Liberator*. In 1827 Samuel Cornish and John Russwurm started the country's first African American newspaper, *Freedom's Journal*. Most of the other newspapers that African Americans founded before the Civil War also promoted abolition.

Born a free man in North Carolina, writer **David Walker** of Boston published an impassioned argument against slavery, challenging African Americans to rebel and overthrow slavery by force. "America is more our country than it is the whites'—we have enriched it with our blood and tears," he wrote.

In 1830 free African American leaders held their first convention in Philadelphia. Delegates met "to devise ways and means for the bettering of our condition." They discussed starting an African American college and encouraging free African Americans to emigrate to Canada.

Frederick Douglass

Frederick Douglass, the most widely known African American abolitionist, was born enslaved in Maryland. After teaching himself to read and write, he escaped from slavery in Maryland in 1838 and settled first in Massachusetts and then in New York.

As a runaway, Douglass could have been captured and returned to slavery. Still, he joined the Massachusetts Antislavery Society and traveled widely to address abolitionist meetings. A powerful speaker, Douglass often moved listeners to tears with his message. At an Independence Day gathering he told the audience:

> 66 What, to the American slave, is your Fourth of July? I answer: a day that reveals to him, more than all other days in the year, the gross injustice and cruelty to which he is the constant victim. To him, your celebration is a sham . . . your national greatness, swelling vanity; your sounds of rejoicing are empty and heartless . . . your shouts of liberty and equality, hollow mockery. 99

For 16 years, Douglass edited an antislavery newspaper called the *North Star*. Douglass won admiration as a powerful and influential speaker and writer. He traveled abroad, speaking to huge antislavery audiences in London and the West Indies.

Douglass returned to the United States because he believed abolitionists must fight slavery at its source. He insisted that African Americans receive not just their freedom but full equality with whites as well. In 1847 friends helped Douglass purchase his freedom from the slaveholder from whom he had fled in Maryland.

Sojourner Truth

"I was born a slave in Ulster County, New York," Isabella Baumfree began when she told her story to audiences. Called "Belle," she lived in the cellar of a slaveholder's house. She escaped in 1826 and gained official freedom in 1827 when New York banned slavery. She eventually settled in New York City.

In 1843 Belle chose a new name. "**Sojourner Truth** is my name," she said, "because from this day I will walk in the light of [God's] truth." She began to work in the movements for abolitionism and for women's rights.

✓ **Reading Check** **Explaining** Why did Frederick Douglass return to the United States?

HISTORY Online

Student Web Activity
Visit taj.glencoe.com and click on **Chapter 14— Student Web Activities** for an activity on the abolitionist movement.

MORE ABOUT...

The Underground Railroad

The Underground Railroad was neither "underground" nor a "railroad." It was a secret organization to help African Americans escape from slavery. The escape of Henry Brown is one of the most remarkable stories in the history of the Underground Railroad.

Henry Brown Henry "Box" Brown escaped slavery by having himself sealed into a small box and shipped from Richmond to Philadelphia. Although "this side up" was marked on the crate, he spent a good part of the trip upside down. When news of his escape spread, he wrote an autobiography and spoke to many anti-slavery groups.

RESURRECTION OF HENRY BOX BROWN, AT PHILADELPHIA.

"It all seemed a comparatively light price to pay for liberty."

—*Henry "Box" Brown*

After his wife and children were sold to a slaveholder in another state, Brown was determined to escape.

Another man transported the crate, with Brown in it, to a shipping company in Richmond, Virginia.

From there, the crate was sent to the Philadelphia Anti-Slavery Office.

Twenty-six hours later, the top of the crate was pried off and Brown emerged, a free man.

Philadelphia, PA

Richmond, VA

The Underground Railroad

Some abolitionists risked prison—even death —by secretly helping African Americans escape from slavery. The network of escape routes from the South to the North came to be called the Underground Railroad.

The Underground Railroad had no trains or tracks. Instead, passengers on this "railroad" traveled through the night, often on foot, and went north—guided by the North Star. The runaway slaves followed rivers and mountain chains, or felt for moss growing on the north side of trees.

Songs such as "Follow the Drinkin' Gourd" encouraged runaways on their way to freedom. A hollowed-out gourd was used to dip water for drinking. Its shape resembled the Big Dipper, which pointed to the North Star.

❝When the river ends in between two hills,
Follow the drinkin' gourd,
For the Ole Man's waitin' for to carry you
to freedom.
Follow the drinkin' gourd.❞

During the day passengers rested at "stations"—barns, attics, church basements, or other places where fugitives could rest, eat, and hide until the next night's journey. The railroad's "conductors" were whites and African Americans who helped guide the escaping slaves to freedom in the North.

In the early days, many people made the journey north on foot. Later they traveled in wagons, sometimes equipped with secret compartments. African Americans on the Underground Railroad hoped to settle in a free state in the North or to move on to Canada. Once in the North, however, fugitives still feared capture. Henry Bibb, a runaway who reached Ohio, arrived at "the place where I was directed to call on an Abolitionist, but I made no stop: so great were my fears of being pursued."

After her escape from slavery, Harriet Tubman became the most famous conductor on the Underground Railroad. Slaveholders offered a large reward for Tubman's capture or death.

The Underground Railroad helped only a tiny fraction of the enslaved population. Most who used it as a route to freedom came from the states located between the northern states

and the Deep South. Still, the Underground Railroad gave hope to those who suffered in slavery. It also provided abolitionists with a way to help some enslaved people to freedom.

Clashes Over Abolitionism

The antislavery movement led to an intense reaction against abolitionism. Southern slaveholders—and many Southerners who did not have slaves—opposed abolitionism because they believed it threatened the South's way of life, which depended on enslaved labor. Many people in the North also opposed the abolitionist movement.

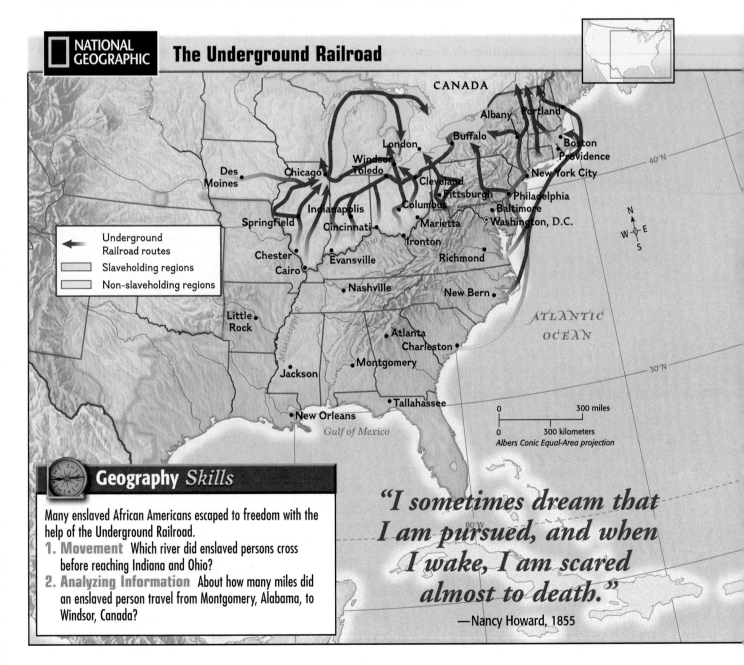

NATIONAL GEOGRAPHIC

The Underground Railroad

Underground Railroad routes
Slaveholding regions
Non-slaveholding regions

CANADA

Albany Portland
Buffalo Boston
London Providence
Windsor New York City
Toledo
Cleveland Pittsburgh Philadelphia
Des Moines Chicago Columbus Baltimore
Indianapolis Marietta Washington, D.C.
Springfield Cincinnati
Ohio R. Ironton
Chester Evansville Richmond
Cairo
Nashville New Bern
Little Rock
ATLANTIC OCEAN
Mississippi R. Atlanta
Charleston
Jackson Montgomery
Tallahassee
New Orleans
Gulf of Mexico

N W E S

40°N
30°N

0 300 miles
0 300 kilometers
Albers Conic Equal-Area projection

Geography *Skills*

Many enslaved African Americans escaped to freedom with the help of the Underground Railroad.
1. **Movement** Which river did enslaved persons cross before reaching Indiana and Ohio?
2. **Analyzing Information** About how many miles did an enslaved person travel from Montgomery, Alabama, to Windsor, Canada?

"I sometimes dream that I am pursued, and when I wake, I am scared almost to death."
—Nancy Howard, 1855

Opposition in the North

Even in the North, abolitionists never numbered more than a small fraction of the population. Many Northerners saw the antislavery movement as a threat to the nation's social order. They feared the abolitionists could bring on a destructive war between the North and the South. They also claimed that, if the enslaved African Americans were freed, they could never blend into American society.

Economic fears further fed the backlash against abolitionism. Northern workers worried that freed slaves would flood the North and take jobs away from whites by agreeing to work for lower pay.

Opposition to abolitionism sometimes erupted into violence against the abolitionists themselves. In the 1830s a Philadelphia mob burned the city's antislavery headquarters to the ground and set off a bloody race riot. In Boston a mob attacked abolitionist William Lloyd Garrison and threatened to hang him. Authorities saved his life by locking him in jail.

Elijah Lovejoy was not so lucky. Lovejoy edited an abolitionist newspaper in Illinois. Three times angry whites invaded his offices and wrecked his presses. Each time Lovejoy installed new presses and resumed publication. The fourth time the mob set fire to the building. When Lovejoy came out of the blazing building, he was shot and killed.

The South Reacts

Southerners fought abolitionism by mounting arguments in defense of slavery. They claimed that slavery was essential to the South. Slave labor, they said, had allowed Southern whites to reach a high level of culture.

Southerners also argued that they treated enslaved people well. Some Southerners argued that Northern workers were worse off than slaves. The industrial economy of the North employed factory workers for long hours at low wages. These jobs were repetitious and often dangerous, and Northern workers had to pay for their goods from their small earnings. Unlike the "wage slavery" of the North, Southerners said that the system of slavery provided food, clothing, and medical care to the workers.

Other defenses of slavery were based on racism. Many whites believed that African Americans were better off under white care than on their own. "Providence has placed [the slave] in our hands for his own good," declared one Southern governor.

The conflict between proslavery and antislavery groups continued to mount. At the same time, a new women's rights movement was growing, and many leading abolitionists were involved in that movement as well.

✓ **Reading Check** **Explaining** Why did many Northerners oppose the abolition of slavery?

SECTION 2 ASSESSMENT

Checking for Understanding

1. **Key Terms** Write a short paragraph in which you use these key terms: abolitionist, Underground Railroad.
2. **Reviewing Facts** Describe the American Colonization Society's solution to slavery.

Reviewing Themes

3. **Individual Action** What role did Harriet Tubman play in the antislavery movement?

Critical Thinking

4. **Comparing** Compare the arguments of Northerners with Southerners who opposed abolitionism.
5. **Organizing Information** Use a diagram like the one below to identify actions that abolitionists took to free enslaved people.

Freeing of enslaved people

Analyzing Visuals

6. **Geography Skills** Study the map of the Underground Railroad on page 423. Why do you think more enslaved people escaped from the border states than from the Deep South?

Interdisciplinary Activity

Informative Writing Research the life of an abolitionist. Write a one-page biography that describes important events in his or her life.

The Women's Movement

Guide to Reading

Main Idea
Women reformers campaigned for their own rights.

Key Terms
suffrage, coeducation

Reading Strategy
Taking Notes As you read the section, use a chart like the one below to identify the contributions these individuals made to women's rights.

	Contributions
Lucretia Mott	
Elizabeth Cady Stanton	
Susan B. Anthony	
Elizabeth Blackwell	

Read to Learn
- how the antislavery and the women's rights movements were related.
- what progress women made toward equality during the 1800s.

Section Theme
Groups and Institutions Women in the 1800s made some progress toward equality.

Preview of Events

♦1830	♦1860	♦1890

1837
Mary Lyon establishes Mount Holyoke Female Seminary

1848
First women's rights convention held in Seneca Falls, New York

1857
Elizabeth Blackwell founds the New York Infirmary for Women and Children

1869
Wyoming Territory grants women the right to vote

Mary Lyon, pioneer in higher education for women

AN American Story

Women who fought to end slavery began to recognize their own bondage. On April 19, 1850, about 400 women met at a Quaker meetinghouse in the small town of Salem, Ohio. They came together "to assert their rights as independent human beings." One speaker stated: "I use the term *Woman's Rights,* because it is a technical phrase. I like not the expression. It is not Woman's *Rights* of which I design to speak, but of Woman's *Wrongs.* I shall claim nothing for ourselves because of our sex. . . . [W]e should demand *our* recognition as equal members of the human family. . . ."

Women and Reform

Many women abolitionists also worked for women's rights. They launched a struggle to improve women's lives and win equal rights. Like many of the women reformers, **Lucretia Mott** was a Quaker. Quaker women enjoyed a certain amount of equality in their own communities. Mott gave lectures in Philadelphia calling for temperance, peace, workers' rights, and abolition. Mott

The Seneca Falls Convention

Throughout the nation's history, women had fought side by side with the men to build a new nation and to ensure freedom. Even though the Declaration of Independence promised equality for all, the promise rang hollow for women.

Female reformers began a campaign for their own rights. In 1848 Lucretia Mott and Elizabeth Cady Stanton organized the Seneca Falls Convention. One of the resolutions demanded suffrage, or the right to vote, for women. This marked the beginning of a long, hard road to gain equal rights.

Gaining the Right to Vote, 1848–1920

The Seneca Falls Convention led to the growth of the woman suffrage movement.

1848 →	1850 →	1866 →	1869 →	1878 →	1884 →
Seneca Falls Convention	First national women's rights convention held in Worcester, Massachusetts	Susan B. Anthony forms Equal Rights Association	Women granted voting rights in Wyoming Territory	Woman suffrage amendment first introduced in U.S. Congress	Belva Lockwood runs for president

Lucretia Mott (below) and Susan B. Anthony were leaders in the effort to allow women a greater role in American society.

"We hold these truths to be self-evident: that all men and women are created equal."
— *Declaration of the Seneca Falls Convention, 1848*

also helped fugitive slaves and organized the Philadelphia Female Anti-Slavery Society. At the world antislavery convention in London, Mott met **Elizabeth Cady Stanton.** There the two female abolitionists joined forces to work for women's rights.

The Seneca Falls Convention

In July 1848, Elizabeth Cady Stanton, Lucretia Mott, and a few other women organized the first women's rights convention in **Seneca Falls, New York.** About 200 women and 40 men attended.

The convention issued a Declaration of Sentiments and Resolutions modeled on the Declaration of Independence. The women's document declared: "We hold these truths to be self-evident: that all men and women are created equal."

The women's declaration called for an end to all laws that discriminated against women. It demanded that women be allowed to enter the all-male world of trades, professions, and businesses. The most controversial issue at the Seneca Falls Convention concerned suffrage, or the right to vote.

Elizabeth Stanton insisted that the declaration include a demand for woman suffrage, but delegates thought the idea of women voting was too radical. Lucretia Mott told her friend, "Lizzie, thee will make us ridiculous." Frederick Douglass stood with Stanton and argued powerfully for women's right to vote. After a heated debate, the convention voted to include the demand for woman suffrage in the United States. *(See page 989 of the Appendix for excerpts of the Seneca Falls Declaration.)*

Maria Mitchell gained world renown when she discovered a comet in 1847. She became a professor of astronomy and the first woman elected to the American Academy of Arts and Sciences.

Mary Ann Shadd Cary was the first African American woman in the nation to earn a law degree.

Elizabeth Blackwell was the first woman to receive a medical degree in the United States.

Helen Keller overcame the challenges of an illness that left her deaf, blind, and mute to help others with similar disabilities.

Susette La Flesche was a member of the Omaha tribe and campaigned for Native American rights.

1893 → Colorado adopts woman suffrage

1896 → Utah joins the Union, granting women full suffrage

1910–1918 → States including Washington, Kansas, and Michigan adopt woman suffrage

1919 → House and Senate pass the federal woman suffrage amendment

1920 → Tennessee ratifies the Nineteenth Amendment, called the Susan B. Anthony Amendment. It becomes law on August 26, 1920.

The Movement Grows

The Seneca Falls Convention paved the way for the growth of the **women's rights movement.** During the 1800s women held several national conventions. Many reformers—male and female—joined the movement.

Susan B. Anthony, the daughter of a Quaker abolitionist in rural New York, worked for women's rights and temperance. She called for equal pay for women, college training for girls, and coeducation—the teaching of boys and girls together. Anthony organized the country's first women's temperance association, the Daughters of Temperance.

Susan B. Anthony met Elizabeth Cady Stanton at a temperance meeting in 1851. They became lifelong friends and partners in the struggle for women's rights. For the rest of the century, Anthony and Stanton led the women's movement. They worked with other women to win the right to vote. Beginning with Wyoming in 1890, several states granted women the right to vote. It was not until 1920, however, that woman suffrage became a reality everywhere in the United States.

 Reading Check Explaining What is suffrage?

Progress by American Women

Pioneers in women's education began to call for more opportunity. Early pioneers such as Catherine Beecher and Emma Hart Willard believed that women should be educated for their traditional roles in life. They also thought that women could be capable teachers. The Milwaukee College for Women set up courses based on Beecher's ideas "to train women to be healthful, intelligent, and successful wives, mothers, and housekeepers."

Education

After her marriage Emma Willard educated herself in subjects considered suitable only for boys, such as science and mathematics. In 1821 Willard established the Troy Female Seminary in upstate New York. Willard's Troy Female Seminary taught mathematics, history, geography, and physics, as well as the usual homemaking subjects.

Mary Lyon established Mount Holyoke Female Seminary in Massachusetts in 1837. She modeled its curriculum on that of nearby Amherst College. Some young women began to make their own opportunities. They broke the barriers to female education and helped other women do the same.

Marriage and Family Laws

During the 1800s women made some gains in the area of marriage and property laws. New York, Pennsylvania, Indiana, Wisconsin, Mississippi, and the new state of California recognized the right of women to own property after their marriage.

Some states passed laws permitting women to share the guardianship of their children jointly with their husbands. Indiana was the first of several states that allowed women to seek divorce if their husbands were chronic abusers of alcohol.

Breaking Barriers

In the 1800s women had few career choices. They could become elementary teachers—although school boards often paid lower salaries to women than to men. Breaking into fields such as medicine and the ministry was more difficult. Some strong-minded women, however, succeeded in entering these all-male professions.

Hoping to study medicine, **Elizabeth Blackwell** was turned down by more than 20 schools. Finally accepted by Geneva College in New York, Blackwell graduated at the head of her class. She went on to win acceptance and fame as a doctor.

Despite the accomplishments of notable women, gains in education, and changes in state laws, women in the 1800s remained limited by social customs and expectations. The early feminists—like the abolitionists, temperance workers, and other activists of the age of reform—had just begun the long struggle to achieve their goals.

✓ Reading Check **Identifying** Who established the Troy Female Seminary?

SECTION 3 ASSESSMENT

Checking for Understanding

1. **Key Terms** Define the following terms: suffrage, coeducation.
2. **Reviewing Facts** How did the fight to end slavery help spark the women's movement?

Reviewing Themes

3. **Groups and Institutions** Discuss three specific goals of the women's rights movement.

Critical Thinking

4. **Making Generalizations** What qualities do you think women such as Sojourner Truth, Susan B. Anthony, Elizabeth Cady Stanton, and Elizabeth Blackwell shared?
5. **Organizing Information** Re-create the diagram below and list the areas where women gained rights.

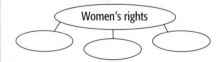

Analyzing Visuals

6. **Sequencing Information** Study the information on the feature on the Seneca Falls Convention on pages 426–427. When did Wyoming women gain the right to vote? What "first" did Elizabeth Blackwell accomplish?

Interdisciplinary Activity

Music Write and record a song designed to win supporters for the women's rights movement. Include lyrics that will draw both men and women supporters.

Technology SKILLBUILDER

Evaluating a Web Site

Why Learn This Skill?

The Internet has become a valuable research tool. It is convenient to use, and the information contained on the Internet is plentiful. However, some Web site information is not necessarily accurate or reliable. When using the Internet as a research tool, the user must distinguish between quality information and inaccurate or incomplete information.

Learning the Skill

There are a number of things to consider when evaluating a Web site. Most important is to check the accuracy of the source and content. The author and publisher or sponsor of the site should be clearly indicated. The user must also determine the usefulness of the site. The information on the site should be current, and the design and organization of the site should be appealing and easy to navigate.

To evaluate a Web site, ask yourself the following questions:

- Are the facts on the site documented?
- Is more than one source used for background information within the site?
- Does the site contain a bibliography?
- Are the links within the site appropriate and up-to-date?
- Is the author clearly identified?
- Does the site explore the topic in-depth?
- Does the site contain links to other useful resources?
- Is the information easy to access? Is it properly labeled?
- Is the design appealing?

Practicing the Skill

Visit the Web site featured on this page at www. nationalgeographic.com/features/99/railroad/ and answer the following questions.

1. Who is the author or sponsor of the Web site?

2. What links does the site contain? Are they appropriate to the topic?

3. Does the site explore the topic in-depth? Why or why not?

4. Is the design of the site appealing? Why or why not?

5. What role did William Still play on the Underground Railroad? How easy or difficult was it to locate this information?

Applying the Skill

Comparing Web Sites Locate two other Web sites about the Underground Railroad. Evaluate them for accuracy and usefulness. Then compare them to the site featured above.

Chapter Summary

The Age of Reform

Utopian communities

- Groups start small voluntary communities to put their idealistic ideas into practice.

Religion

- Great revival meetings, the building of new churches, and the founding of scores of colleges and universities mark the Second Great Awakening.

Temperance

- Reformers work to control consumption of alcohol.

Education

- A movement grows to improve education, make school attendance compulsory, and help students with special needs.

Abolition

- Reformers work to help enslaved people escape to freedom and to ban slavery.

Women's rights

- Reformers call for equal rights, including the right to vote.

The Arts

- Writers and painters turn their attention to the American scene.

Reviewing Key Terms

On graph paper, create a word search puzzle using the following terms. Crisscross the terms vertically and horizontally, then fill in the remaining squares with extra letters. Use the terms' definitions as clues to find the words in the puzzle. Share your puzzle with a classmate.

1. utopia
2. revival
3. temperance
4. normal school
5. transcendentalist
6. civil disobedience
7. abolitionist
8. Underground Railroad
9. suffrage
10. women's rights movement
11. coeducation

Reviewing Key Facts

12. What were the founders of utopias hoping to achieve?
13. What problems in society did reformers in the temperance movement blame on the manufacture and sale of alcoholic beverages?
14. What were the basic principles of public education?
15. What was unique about the subject matter that American artists and writers of the mid-1800s used?
16. How did William Lloyd Garrison's demands make him effective in the anti-slavery movement?
17. What was the purpose of the Underground Railroad?
18. What role did Catherine Beecher play in education for women?

Critical Thinking

19. **Analyzing Information** What role did Dorothea Dix play regarding prison inmates and people with mental illness?
20. **Making Generalizations** What was the significance of the Seneca Falls Convention?
21. **Organizing Information** Re-create the diagram below and describe the contributions Frederick Douglass made to the abolitionist movement.

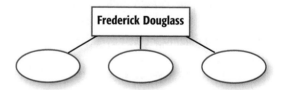

Frederick Douglass

Practicing Skills

Evaluating a Web Site *Review the information about evaluating a Web site on page 429. Visit the Web site www.greatwomen.org/index.php and answer the following questions.*

22. What information is presented on this Web site?

23. What categories are used to organize the information?

24. What links does the site contain? Are they appropriate to the topic?

25. Do you think the site explores the topic in depth? Explain.

 Geography and History Activity

Use the map on page 423 to answer the following questions.

26. **Region** What other country did passengers on the Underground Railroad travel to?

27. **Location** From what Southern ports did African Americans flee by ship?

28. **Location** What kinds of places were used as "stations" of the Underground Railroad?

29. **Human-Environment Interaction** Why do you think the routes of the Underground Railroad included many coastal cities?

 Technology Activity

30. **Using the Internet** Search the Internet for a modern organization founded to support women's rights. Write a brief description of the organization, including its name, location, and a description of its purpose or activities.

Citizenship Cooperative Activity

31. **The Importance of Voting** Work with a partner to complete this activity. You know that the right to vote belongs to every United States citizen. In your opinion, what do citizens forfeit if they do not exercise their right to vote? Write a one-page paper that answers this question and share your paper with the other students.

Economics Activity

32. Goods are the items people buy. Services are activities done for others for a fee. List five goods you have purchased in the past month. List five services you purchased.

Self-Check Quiz
Visit taj.glencoe.com and click on **Chapter 14—Self-Check Quizzes** to prepare for the chapter test.

 Alternative Assessment

33. **Portfolio Writing Activity** Write a poem designed to win supporters for one of the reform movements discussed in Chapter 14.

 Standardized Test Practice

Directions: Choose the *best* answer to the following question.

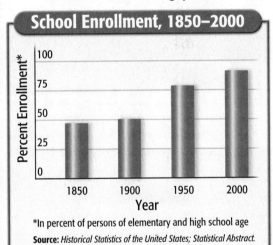

School Enrollment, 1850–2000

In percent of persons of elementary and high school age

Source: *Historical Statistics of the United States; Statistical Abstract.*

According to the graph above, the greatest increase in the percentage of school enrollment occurred between

F 1850 and 1880. **H** 1900 and 1950.

G 1850 and 1900. **J** 1950 and 2000.

Test-Taking Tip

Use the information on the *graph* to help you answer this question. Look carefully at the information on the bottom and the side of a bar graph to understand what the bars represent. Process of elimination is helpful here. For example, answer F cannot be correct because this time period is not shown on the graph.

UNIT 6 Civil War and Reconstruction

1846–1896

Why It Matters

As you study Unit 6, *you will learn how social, economic, and political differences between the North and South grew. As compromises failed, the country plunged into civil war. The following resources offer more information about this period in American history.*

Primary Sources Library

See pages 968–969 for primary source readings to accompany Unit 6.

*Use the **American History Primary Source Document Library** **CD-ROM** to find additional primary sources about the Civil War and Reconstruction.*

Confederate soldier's cap (upper left) and Union soldier's cap (lower right)

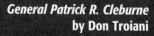

General Patrick R. Cleburne by **Don Troiani**

"A house divided
against itself
cannot stand."

—*Abraham Lincoln, 1858*

CHAPTER 15 Road to Civil War
1820–1861

Why It Matters

Slavery was a major cause of the worsening division between the North and South in the period before the Civil War. The struggle between the North and South turned more hostile, and talk grew of separation and civil war.

The Impact Today

"If slavery is not wrong, nothing is wrong," Abraham Lincoln wrote in a letter to A.G. Hodges in 1864. By studying this era of our history, we can better understand the state of racial relations today and develop ways for improving them.

The American Journey *Video* The chapter 15 video, "Secrets of the Underground Railroad," tells how enslaved African Americans escaped to freedom.

1850
- Compromise of 1850 passed

1845
- Texas becomes a state

1852
- *Uncle Tom's Cabin* published

United States
PRESIDENTS

| W.H. Harrison 1841 | Tyler 1841–1845 | Polk 1845–1849 | Taylor 1849–1850 | Fillmore 1850–1853 |

1840   1845   1850

World

1845
- Many people begin emigrating to escape potato famine in Ireland

1848
- Marx publishes *The Communist Manifesto*

African Americans in 1850 About 425,000 African Americans in the United States were free while 3.2 million lived in slavery.

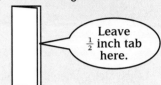

1854
• Kansas-Nebraska Act passed

1857
• *Dred Scott* decision

1860
• Lincoln elected president

1859
• Raid on Harpers Ferry

1861
• Civil War begins

Pierce 1853–1857

Buchanan 1857–1861

1855

1860

1856
• Bessemer patents steel process

1861
• Alexander II frees serfs in Russia

1863
• French troops occupy Mexico City

HISTORY
Online

Chapter Overview
Visit taj.glencoe.com and click on **Chapter 15— Chapter Overviews** to preview chapter information.

Slavery and the West

Preview of Events

◆1820	◆1830	◆1840	◆1850

1820
Missouri Compromise is passed

1845
Texas becomes a state

1848
Free-Soil Party nominates Martin Van Buren

1850
Compromise of 1850 diverts war

CAUTION!!
COLORED PEOPLE
OF BOSTON, ONE & ALL,
You are hereby respectfully CAUTIONED and advised, to avoid conversing with the
Watchmen and Police Officers of Boston,
For since the recent ORDER OF THE MAYOR & ALDERMEN, they are empowered to act as
KIDNAPPERS
AND
Slave Catchers,
And they have already been actually employed in KIDNAPPING, CATCHING, AND KEEPING SLAVES. Therefore, if you value your LIBERTY, and the Welfare of the Fugitives among you, Shun them in every possible manner, as so many HOUNDS on the track of the most unfortunate of your race.
Keep a Sharp Look Out for KIDNAPPERS, and have TOP EYE open.
APRIL 24, 1851.

Poster warning African Americans

AN American Story

"The deed is done. The . . . chains of slavery are forged for [many] yet unborn. Humble yourselves in the dust, ye high-minded citizens of Connecticut. Let your cheeks be red as crimson. On *your* representatives rests the stigma of this foul disgrace." These biting, fiery words were published in a Connecticut newspaper in 1820. They were in response to members of Congress who had helped pave the way for the admission of Missouri as a slaveholding state.

The Missouri Compromise

The request by slaveholding **Missouri** to join the Union in 1819 caused an angry debate that worried former president Thomas Jefferson and Secretary of State John Quincy Adams. Jefferson called the dispute "a fire-bell in the night" that "awakened and filled me with terror." Adams accurately predicted that the bitter debate was "a mere preamble—a title-page to a great tragic volume."

Many Missouri settlers had brought enslaved African Americans into the territory with them. By 1819 the Missouri Territory included about 50,000 whites and 10,000 slaves. When Missouri applied to Congress for admission as a state, its constitution allowed slavery.

In 1819, 11 states permitted slavery and 11 did not. The Senate—with two members from each state—was therefore evenly balanced between slave and free states. The admission of a new state would upset that balance.

In addition, the North and the South, with their different economic systems, were competing for new lands in the western territories. At the same time, a growing number of Northerners wanted to restrict or ban slavery. Southerners, even those who disliked slavery, opposed these antislavery efforts. They resented the interference by outsiders in Southerners' affairs. These differences between the North and the South grew into sectionalism—an exaggerated loyalty to a particular region of the country.

Clay's Proposal

The Senate suggested a way to resolve the crisis by allowing Missouri's admittance as a slave state while simultaneously admitting Maine as a free state. Maine, formerly part of Massachusetts, had also applied for admission to the Union. The Senate also sought to settle the issue of slavery in the territories for good. It proposed prohibiting slavery in the remainder of the Louisiana Purchase north of 36°30′N latitude.

Speaker of the House **Henry Clay** of Kentucky skillfully maneuvered the Senate bill to passage in 1820 by dividing it into three proposals. The **Missouri Compromise** preserved the balance between slave and free states in the Senate and brought about a lull in the bitter debate in Congress over slavery.

Reading Check **Explaining** What is sectionalism?

New Western Lands

For the next 25 years, Congress managed to keep the slavery issue in the background. In the 1840s, however, this heated debate moved back into Congress. Once again the cause of the dispute was the issue of slavery in new territories. The territories involved were **Texas,** which had won its independence from Mexico in 1836, and **New Mexico** and **California,** which were still part of Mexico.

Many Southerners hoped to see Texas, where slavery already existed, join the Union. As a result, the annexation of Texas became the main issue in the presidential election of 1844. Democrat **James Polk** of Tennessee won the election and pressed forward on acquiring Texas, and Texas became a state in 1845. At the same time, support for taking over New Mexico and California also grew in the South. The federal government's actions on these lands led to war with Mexico.

Conflicting Views

Just months after the Mexican War began, Representative David Wilmot of Pennsylvania introduced a proposal in Congress. Called the **Wilmot Proviso,** it specified that slavery should be prohibited in any lands that might be acquired from Mexico. Southerners protested furiously. They wanted to keep open the possibility of introducing slavery to California and New Mexico.

Senator **John C. Calhoun** of South Carolina countered with another proposal. It stated that neither Congress nor any territorial government had the authority to ban slavery from a territory or regulate it in any way.

Polk campaign banner

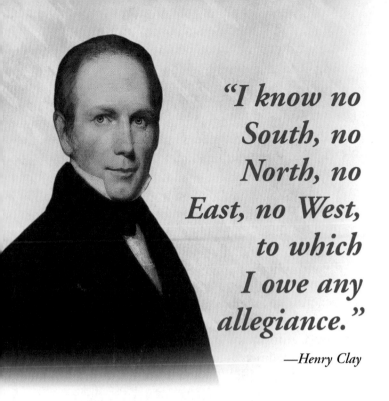

"I know no South, no North, no East, no West, to which I owe any allegiance."

—Henry Clay

Neither Wilmot's nor Calhoun's proposal passed, but both caused bitter debate. By the time of the 1848 presidential election, the United States had gained the territories of California and New Mexico from Mexico but had taken no action on the issue of slavery in those areas.

The Free-Soil Party

The debate over slavery led to the formation of a new political party. In 1848 the Whigs chose **Zachary Taylor,** a Southerner and a hero of the Mexican War, as their presidential candidate. The Democrats selected Senator Lewis Cass of Michigan. Neither candidate took a stand on slavery in the territories.

This failure to take a position angered voters. Many antislavery Democrats and Whigs left their parties and joined with members of the old Liberty Party to form the **Free-Soil Party.** The new party proclaimed "Free Soil, Free Speech, Free Labor, and Free Men," and endorsed the Wilmot Proviso. The party nominated former president **Martin Van Buren** as its presidential candidate.

Whig candidate Zachary Taylor won the election by successfully appealing to both slave and free states. Taylor defeated Cass 163 to 127 in electoral votes. Van Buren captured only 14 percent of the popular vote in the North, but several candidates of the Free-Soil Party won seats in Congress.

California

Once in office President Taylor urged leaders in the two territories of California and New Mexico to apply for statehood immediately. Once these lands had become states, he reasoned, their citizens could decide whether to allow slavery. New Mexico did not apply for statehood, but California did in 1850.

Taylor's plan ran into trouble when California's statehood became tangled up with other issues before Congress. Antislavery forces wanted to abolish slavery in the District of Columbia, the nation's capital. Southerners wanted a strong national law requiring states to return fugitive, or runaway, slaves to their masters. Another dispute involved the New Mexico–Texas border.

The greatest obstacle to Taylor's plan was concern over the balance of power in the Senate. In 1849 the nation included 15 slave states and 15 free states. If California entered as a free state—and New Mexico, Oregon, and Utah followed as free states, which seemed likely—the South would be hopelessly outvoted in the Senate. As tension grew, some Southerners began talking about having their states secede from, or leave, the United States.

Reading Check **Explaining** How was John C. Calhoun's proposal different from the Wilmot Proviso?

A New Compromise

In January 1850, Henry Clay, now a senator, presented a multi-part plan to settle all the issues dividing Congress. First, California would be admitted as a free state. Second, the New Mexico Territory would have no restrictions on slavery. Third, the New Mexico–Texas border dispute would be settled in favor of New Mexico. Fourth, the slave trade, but not slavery itself, would be abolished in the District of Columbia. Finally, Clay pushed for a stronger fugitive slave law.

Clay's proposal launched an emotional debate in Congress that raged for seven months. Opening that debate were Clay and two other distinguished senators—John C. Calhoun of South Carolina and **Daniel Webster** of Massachusetts.

Calhoun opposed Clay's plan. He believed that the only way to save the Union was to protect slavery. If Congress admitted California as a free state, Calhoun warned, the Southern states had to leave the Union.

Three days later Webster gave an eloquent speech in support of Clay's plan. He argued that antislavery forces lost little in agreeing to the compromise:

❝I would rather hear of natural blasts and mildews, war, pestilence, and famine, than to hear gentlemen talk of secession.❞

Webster reasoned that geography would prevent slavery from taking root in the new territories, since most of the land was not suited for plantations. What was most important was to preserve the Union.

The Compromise of 1850

Clay's plan could not pass as a complete package. Too many members of Congress objected to one part of it or another. President Taylor also opposed the plan and threatened to use force against the South if states tried to secede.

Then in July President Taylor suddenly died. The new president, **Millard Fillmore,** supported some form of compromise. At the same time, **Stephen A. Douglas,** a young senator from Illinois, took charge of efforts to resolve the crisis. Douglas divided Clay's plan into a series of

Before They Were Presidents

Like Zachary Taylor, did most presidents make the military their profession? Some presidents *did* make the military their principal profession. Washington, William Henry Harrison, Grant, and Eisenhower, as well as Taylor, all made a career in the military. However, more presidents came from the ranks of attorneys than from any other profession. More than half of all presidents, including Jefferson and Lincoln, made their living in the practice of law.

measures that Congress could vote on separately. In this way members of Congress would not have to support proposals they opposed.

President Fillmore persuaded several Whig representatives to abstain—not to cast votes—on measures they opposed. Congress finally passed a series of five separate bills in August and September of 1850. Taken together these laws, known as the **Compromise of 1850,** contained the five main points of Clay's original plan. Fillmore called the compromise a "final settlement" of the conflict between North and South. The president would soon be proved wrong.

✓ **Reading Check** **Explaining** How did the Compromise of 1850 affect the New Mexico Territory?

SECTION 1 ASSESSMENT

Checking for Understanding

1. **Key Terms** Use each of these social studies terms in a sentence that will help explain its meaning: sectionalism, fugitive, secede, abstain.
2. **Reviewing Facts** List the provisions of the Missouri Compromise.

Reviewing Themes

3. **Government and Democracy** Why was the Free-Soil Party created?

Critical Thinking

4. **Analyzing Information** What was the Wilmot Proviso? Why was it controversial?
5. **Comparing** Re-create the table below and describe what the North and South each gained from the Compromise of 1850.

Compromise of 1850	
Northern gains	Southern gains

Analyzing Visuals

6. **Examining Artifacts** Look at the campaign banner on page 437. Compare it to a modern political button or advertisement you have seen. In what ways are they similar? In what ways are they different?

Interdisciplinary Activity

Government Create a poster for the Free-Soil Party presidential candidate. Include slogans or symbols to gain popular support.

Critical Thinking
SKILLBUILDER

Recognizing Bias

Why Learn This Skill?

Cats make better pets than dogs. If you say this, then you are stating a bias. A bias is a prejudice. It can prevent you from looking at a situation in a reasonable or truthful way.

Learning the Skill

Most people have feelings and ideas that affect their point of view. This viewpoint, or *bias,* influences the way they interpret events. For this reason, an idea that is stated as a fact may really be only an opinion. Recognizing bias will help you judge the accuracy of what you read. There are several things you should look for that will help you recognize bias. Identify the author of the statement and examine his or her views and possible reasons for writing the material. Look for language that reflects an emotion or opinion—words such as *all, never, best, worst, might,* or *should.* Examine the writing for imbalances—leaning only to one viewpoint and failing to provide equal coverage of other possible viewpoints.

Practicing the Skill

Read the excerpts on this page. The first excerpt is from an 1858 newspaper editorial. The second is from a speech by Senator John C. Calhoun of South Carolina. Then answer the four questions that follow.

> 66Popular sovereignty for the territories will never work. Under this system, each territory would decide whether or not to legalize slavery. This method was tried in the territory of Kansas and all it produced was bloodshed and violence.99
>
> —*The Republican Leader,* 1858

> 66... [T]he two great divisions of society are not rich and poor, but white and black; and all the former, the poor as well as the rich, belong to the upper classes, and are respected and treated as such.99
>
> —Senator Calhoun

1 Is Senator Calhoun expressing a proslavery or antislavery bias?

2 What statements indicate the racism in Calhoun's bias?

3 What political party's view does the editorial represent?

4 What biases or beliefs are expressed in the editorial?

Applying the Skill

Recognizing Bias Look through the letters to the editor in your local newspaper. Write a short report analyzing one of the letters for evidence of bias.

 Glencoe's **Skillbuilder Interactive Workbook CD-ROM, Level 1,** provides instruction and practice in key social studies skills.

A Nation Dividing

Guide to Reading

Main Idea

Growing tensions led to differences that could not be solved by compromise.

Key Terms

popular sovereignty, border ruffians, civil war

Reading Strategy

As you read the section, re-create the table below and describe how Southerners and Northerners reacted to the Kansas-Nebraska Act.

Kansas-Nebraska Act	
Southern reaction	Northern reaction

Read to Learn

• how the Fugitive Slave Act and the Kansas-Nebraska Act further divided the North and South.
• how popular sovereignty led to violence.

Section Theme

Continuity and Change As they grew farther apart, Northerners and Southerners sought compromise.

Preview of Events

♦1850	♦1853	♦1856
1850 Fugitive Slave Act is passed	**1852** *Uncle Tom's Cabin* is published	**1854** Kansas-Nebraska Act is passed	**1856** Charles Sumner attacked in Senate

AN American Story

On May 24, 1854, the people of Boston erupted in outrage. Federal officers had seized Anthony Burns, a runaway slave who lived in Boston, to send him back to slavery. Abolitionists tried to rescue Burns from the federal courthouse, and city leaders attempted to buy his freedom. All efforts failed. Local militia units joined the marines and cavalry in Boston to keep order. Federal troops escorted Burns to a ship that would carry him back to Virginia and slavery. In a gesture of bitter protest, Bostonians draped buildings in black and hung the American flag upside down.

Anthony Burns

The Fugitive Slave Act

The **Fugitive Slave Act** of 1850 required all citizens to help catch runaways. Anyone who aided a fugitive could be fined or imprisoned. People in the South believed the law would force Northerners to recognize the rights of Southerners. Instead, enforcement of the law led to mounting anger in the North, convincing more people of the evils of slavery.

After passage of the Fugitive Slave Act, slaveholders stepped up their efforts to catch runaway slaves. They even tried to capture runaways who had lived in freedom in the North for years. Sometimes they seized African Americans who were not escaped slaves and forced them into slavery.

People In History

Harriet Beecher Stowe 1811–1896

Writer Harriet Beecher Stowe called the Fugitive Slave Act a "nightmare abomination." Stowe, the daughter of a New England minister, spent part of her childhood in Cincinnati. There, on the banks of the Ohio River, she saw enslaved people being loaded onto ships to be taken to slave markets. As an adult and the wife of a religion professor, she wrote many books and stories about social reform. Her most famous work was a novel about the evils of slavery. *Uncle Tom's Cabin* was published in 1852. Packed with dramatic incidents and vivid characters, the novel shows slavery as a cruel and brutal system.

Uncle Tom's Cabin quickly became a sensation, selling over 300,000 copies in the first year of publication. The book had such an impact on public feelings about slavery that when Abraham Lincoln was introduced to Stowe during the Civil War, he said, so, you "wrote the book that started this great war."

Resistance to the Law

In spite of the penalties, many Northerners refused to cooperate with the law's enforcement. The Underground Railroad, a network of free African Americans and whites, helped runaways make their way to freedom. Antislavery groups tried to rescue African Americans who were being pursued or to free those who were captured. In Boston, members of one such group followed federal agents shouting, "Slave hunters—there go the slave hunters." People contributed funds to buy the freedom of African Americans. Northern juries refused to convict those accused of breaking the Fugitive Slave Law.

Reading Check **Explaining** What was the purpose of the Underground Railroad?

The Kansas–Nebraska Act

Franklin Pierce, a New Hampshire Democrat who supported the Fugitive Slave Act, became president in 1853. Pierce intended to enforce the Fugitive Slave Act, and his actions hardened the opposition.

In 1854 the dispute over slavery erupted in Congress again. The cause was a bill introduced by Stephen A. Douglas, the Illinois senator who had forged the Compromise of 1850.

Hoping to encourage settlement of the West and open the way for a transcontinental railroad, Douglas proposed organizing the region west of Missouri and Iowa as the territories of **Kansas** and **Nebraska.** Douglas was trying to work out a plan for the nation to expand that both the North and the South would accept. Instead his bill reopened the conflict about slavery in the territories.

Because of their location, Kansas and Nebraska seemed likely to become free states. Both lay north of 36°30'N latitude, the line established in the Missouri Compromise as the boundary of slavery. Douglas knew that Southerners would object to having Kansas and Nebraska become free states because it would give the North an advantage in the Senate. As a result Douglas proposed abandoning the Missouri Compromise and letting the settlers in each territory vote on whether to allow slavery. He called this popular sovereignty—allowing the people to decide.

Passage of the Act

Many Northerners protested strongly. Douglas's plan to repeal the Missouri Compromise would allow slavery into areas that had been free for more than 30 years. Opponents of the bill demanded that Congress vote down the bill.

Southerners in Congress, however, provided solid support for the bill. They expected that Kansas would be settled in large part by slaveholders from Missouri who would vote to keep slavery legal. With some support from Northern Democrats and the backing of President Pierce, Congress passed the **Kansas–Nebraska Act** in May 1854.

Division Grows

Northern Democrats in the House split almost evenly on the vote, revealing deep divisions in the party. Many Northerners became convinced that compromise with the South was no longer possible. Sam Houston, senator from Texas, predicted that the bill "will convulse [upset] the country from Maine to the Rio Grande."

 **Describing** Write a definition of "popular sovereignty" in your own words.

Conflict in Kansas

Right after passage of the Kansas–Nebraska Act, proslavery and antislavery groups rushed supporters into Kansas. In the spring of 1855, when elections took place in Kansas, a proslavery legislature was elected.

Although only about 1,500 voters lived in Kansas at the time, more than 6,000 people cast ballots in the elections. Thousands of proslavery supporters from Missouri had crossed the border just to vote in the election. These Missourians traveled in armed groups and became known as border ruffians. Soon after the election, the new Kansas legislature passed laws supporting slavery. One law even restricted political office to proslavery candidates.

The antislavery people refused to accept these laws. Instead they armed themselves, held their own elections, and adopted a constitution that banned slavery. By January 1856, rival governments existed in Kansas, one for and one against slavery. Each asked Congress for recognition. To confuse matters further, President Pierce and the Senate favored the proslavery government, while the House backed the forces opposed to slavery.

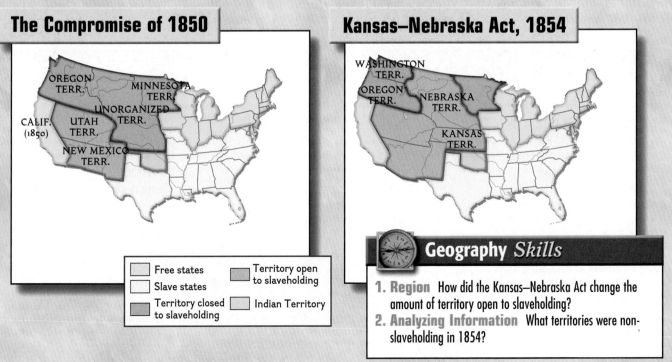

NATIONAL GEOGRAPHIC

Slavery and Sectionalism

The Compromise of 1850

Kansas–Nebraska Act, 1854

Free states
Slave states
Territory closed to slaveholding
Territory open to slaveholding
Indian Territory

Geography *Skills*

1. **Region** How did the Kansas–Nebraska Act change the amount of territory open to slaveholding?
2. **Analyzing Information** What territories were non-slaveholding in 1854?

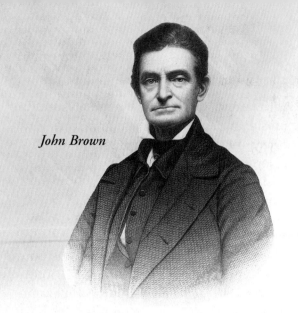

John Brown

"Bleeding Kansas"

With proslavery and antislavery forces in Kansas arming themselves, the outbreak of violence became inevitable. In May 1856, 800 slavery supporters attacked the town of Lawrence, the antislavery capital. They sacked the town, burned the hotel and the home of the governor, and destroyed two newspaper offices. Soon after, forces opposed to slavery retaliated.

John Brown, a fervent abolitionist, believed God had chosen him to end slavery. When he heard of the attack on Lawrence, Brown went into a rage. He vowed to "strike terror in the hearts of the proslavery people." One night Brown led four of his sons and two other men along Pottawatomie Creek, where they seized and killed five supporters of slavery.

More violence followed as armed bands roamed the territory. Newspapers began referring to "Bleeding Kansas" and "the Civil War in Kansas." A civil war is a conflict between citizens of the same country. Not until October of 1856 did John Geary, the newly appointed territorial governor, stop the bloodshed in Kansas. He suppressed guerrilla forces and used 1,300 federal troops.

Violence in Congress

The violence that erupted in Kansas spilled over to the halls of Congress as well. Abolitionist senator **Charles Sumner** of Massachusetts delivered a speech entitled "The Crime Against Kansas." Sumner lashed out against proslavery forces in Kansas. He also criticized proslavery senators, repeatedly attacking Andrew P. Butler of South Carolina.

Two days after the speech, Butler's distant cousin, Representative **Preston Brooks,** walked into the Senate chamber. He hit Sumner again and again over the head and shoulders with a cane. Sumner fell to the floor, unconscious and bleeding. He suffered injuries so severe that he did not return to the Senate for several years. The Brooks-Sumner incident and the fighting in "Bleeding Kansas" revealed the rising level of hostility between North and South.

Reading Check **Explaining** What is a civil war?

SECTION 2 ASSESSMENT

Checking for Understanding

1. **Key Terms** Use each of these terms in a sentence that will help explain its meaning: popular sovereignty, border ruffians, civil war.
2. **Reviewing Facts** Describe how Northern abolitionists reacted to the Fugitive Slave Act.

Reviewing Themes

3. **Continuity and Change** How did popular sovereignty lead to violence in Kansas?

Critical Thinking

4. **Predicting Consequences** Could the violence in Kansas have been prevented if Congress had not abandoned the Missouri Compromise? Explain.
5. **Organizing Information** Re-create the diagram below and list the steps that led to bloodshed in Kansas.

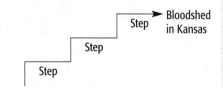

Analyzing Visuals

6. **Geography Skills** Study the maps on page 443. From which territory or territories were the Nebraska and Kansas Territories formed? Was the Utah territory closed to slaveholding?

Interdisciplinary Activity

Descriptive Writing With members of your class, choose a scene from *Uncle Tom's Cabin* to portray in a one-act play. Write a short script, assign roles, and present it to the class.

Challenges to Slavery

Main Idea

Social, economic, and political differences divided the North and South.

Key Terms

arsenal, martyr

Reading Strategy

Sequencing Information As you read the section, re-create the diagram below and list major events for each year.

1846	1854	1856	1858

Read to Learn

• why the Republican Party was formed.

• how the *Dred Scott* decision, the Lincoln-Douglas debates, and John Brown's raid affected Americans.

Section Theme

Continuity and Change The slavery issues continued to drive the North and South further apart.

Preview of Events

◆*1854*   ◆*1856*   ◆*1858*   ◆*1860*

1854
Republican Party is formed

1856
James Buchanan is elected president

1857
Dred Scott decision states that all slaves are property

1859
John Brown raids Harpers Ferry, Virginia

Kansas Free-Soil poster

★★★★★★★

AN

American Story

Many people considered John Brown to be a radical murderer, while others viewed him as a fighter for the cause of freedom. When he was executed in 1859, the *Anglo-African Magazine* wrote that, as John Brown left the jail, "a black woman, with a little child in her arms, stood near his way. . . . He stopped for a moment in his course, stooped over, and with the tenderness of one whose love is as broad as the brotherhood of man, kissed the child affectionately."

A New Political Party

Even before Brown's raid, other events had driven the North and South further apart. After the Kansas–Nebraska Act, the Democratic Party began to divide along sectional lines, with Northern Democrats leaving the party. Differing views over the slavery issue destroyed the Whig Party.

In 1854 antislavery Whigs and Democrats joined forces with Free-Soilers to form the **Republican Party.** The new party was determined to rally "for the establishment of liberty and the overthrow of the Slave Power."

The Republicans challenged the proslavery Whigs and Democrats, choosing candidates to run in the state and congressional elections of 1854. Their main message was that the government should ban slavery from new territories.

The Republican Party quickly showed its strength in the North. In the election, the Republicans won control of the House of Representatives and of several state governments. In the South the Republicans had almost no support.

Northern Democrats suffered a beating. Almost three-fourths of the Democratic candidates from free states lost in 1854. The party was increasingly becoming a Southern party.

The Election of 1856

Democrats and Republicans met again in the presidential election of 1856. The Whig Party, disintegrating over the slavery issue, did not offer a candidate of its own.

The Republicans chose **John C. Frémont** of California as their candidate for president. Frémont had gained fame as an explorer in the West. The party platform called for free territories and its campaign slogan became "Free soil, free speech, and Frémont."

The Democratic Party nominated **James Buchanan** of Pennsylvania, an experienced diplomat and former member of Congress. The party endorsed the idea of popular sovereignty.

The American Party, or Know Nothings, had grown quickly between 1853 and 1856 by attacking immigrants. The Know Nothings nominated former president Millard Fillmore.

The presidential vote divided along rigid sectional lines. Buchanan won the election, winning all of the Southern states except Maryland and received 174 electoral votes compared to 114 for Frémont and 8 for Fillmore. Frémont did not receive a single electoral vote south of the Mason-Dixon line, but he carried 11 of the 16 free states.

Reading Check **Explaining** What stand did the new Republican party take on the issue of slavery?

The *Dred Scott* Decision

President Buchanan took office on March 4, 1857. Two days later the Supreme Court announced a decision about slavery and the territories that shook the nation.

Dred Scott was an enslaved African American bought by an army doctor in Missouri, a slave state. In the 1830s the doctor moved his household to Illinois, a free state, and then to the Wisconsin Territory, where slavery was banned by the Northwest Ordinance of 1787. Later the family returned to Missouri, where the doctor died. In 1846, with the help of antislavery lawyers, Scott sued for his freedom. He claimed he should be free because he had once lived on free soil. Eleven years later, in the midst of growing anger over the slavery issue, the case reached the Supreme Court.

The case attracted enormous attention. While the immediate issue was Dred Scott's status, the

Picturing **History**

Family members (left) honor the memory of Dred Scott. Scott (above), who lived in slavery, had appealed to the Supreme Court in hopes of being granted his freedom. **How did the Court rule?**

"This Union can exist forever divided into free and slave states, as our fathers made it."
—Stephen Douglas

"I believe that this government cannot endure permanently half slave and half free."
—Abraham Lincoln

Court also had the opportunity to rule on the question of slavery in territories. Many Americans hoped that the Court would resolve the issue for good.

The Court's Decision

The Court's decision electrified the nation. Chief Justice **Roger B. Taney** (TAW•nee) said that Dred Scott was still a slave. As a slave, Scott was not a citizen and had no right to bring a lawsuit. Taney could have stopped there, but he decided to address the broader issues.

Taney wrote that Scott's residence on free soil did not make him free. An enslaved person was property, and the Fifth Amendment prohibits Congress from taking away property without "due process of law."

Finally, Taney wrote that Congress had no power to prohibit slavery in any territory. The Missouri Compromise—which had banned slavery north of 36°30'N latitude—was unconstitutional. For that matter, so was popular sovereignty. Not even the voters in a territory could prohibit slavery because that would amount to taking away a person's property. In effect, the decision meant that the Constitution protected slavery. 📖 *(See page 997 of the Appendix for a summary of the* Dred Scott *decision.)*

Reaction to the Decision

Rather than settling the issue, the Supreme Court's decision divided the country even more. Many Southerners were elated. The Court had reaffirmed what many in the South had always maintained: Nothing could legally prevent the spread of slavery. Northern Democrats were pleased that the Republicans' main issue—restricting the spread of slavery—had been ruled unconstitutional.

Republicans and other antislavery groups were outraged, calling the *Dred Scott* decision "a wicked and false judgment" and "the greatest crime" ever committed in the nation's courts.

Lincoln and Douglas

In the congressional election of 1858, the Senate race in Illinois was the center of national attention. The contest pitted the current senator, Democrat Stephen A. Douglas, against Republican challenger **Abraham Lincoln.** People considered Douglas a likely candidate for president in 1860. Lincoln was nearly an unknown.

Douglas, a successful lawyer, had joined the Democratic Party and won election to the House in 1842 and to the Senate in 1846. Short, stocky, and powerful, Douglas was called "the Little Giant." He disliked slavery but thought that the controversy over it would interfere with the nation's growth. He believed the issue could be resolved through popular sovereignty.

Born in the poor backcountry of Kentucky, Abraham Lincoln moved to Indiana as a child, and later to Illinois. Like Douglas, Lincoln was intelligent, ambitious, and a successful lawyer. He had little formal education—but excellent political instincts. Although Lincoln saw slavery as morally wrong, he admitted there was no easy way to eliminate slavery where it already existed. He was certain, though, that slavery should not be allowed to spread.

The Lincoln–Douglas Debates

Not as well known as Douglas, Lincoln challenged the senator to a series of debates. Douglas reluctantly agreed. The two met seven times in August, September, and October of 1858 in cities and villages throughout Illinois. Thousands came to these debates. The main topic, of course, was slavery.

During the debate at Freeport, Lincoln pressed Douglas about his views on popular sovereignty. Could the people of a territory legally exclude slavery before achieving statehood? Douglas replied that the people could exclude slavery by refusing to pass laws protecting slaveholders' rights. Douglas's response, which satisfied antislavery followers but lost him support in the South, became known as the **Freeport Doctrine.**

Douglas claimed that Lincoln wanted African Americans to be fully equal to whites. Lincoln denied this. Still, Lincoln said, "in the right to eat the bread . . . which his own hand earns, [an African American] is my equal and the equal of [Senator] Douglas, and the equal of every living man." The real issue, Lincoln said, is "between the men who think slavery a wrong and those who do not think it wrong. The Republican Party thinks it wrong."

Following the debates, Douglas won a narrow victory in the election. Lincoln lost the election but gained a national reputation.

The Raid on Harpers Ferry

After the 1858 elections, Southerners began to feel threatened by growing Republican power. In late 1859, an act of violence greatly increased their fears. On October 16 the abolitionist John Brown led 18 men, both whites and African Americans, on a raid on Harpers Ferry, Virginia. His target was an arsenal, a storage place for weapons and ammunition. Brown—who had killed five proslavery Kansans in 1856—hoped to start a rebellion against slaveholders by arming enslaved African Americans. His raid had been financed by a group of abolitionists.

Brown and his men were quickly defeated by local citizens and federal troops. Brown was convicted of treason and murder and was sentenced to hang. His execution caused an uproar in the North. Some antislavery Northerners, including Republican leaders, denounced Brown's use of violence. Others viewed Brown as a hero. Writer Ralph Waldo Emerson called Brown a martyr—a person who dies for a great cause.

John Brown's death became a rallying point for abolitionists. When Southerners learned of Brown's connection to abolitionists, their fears of a great Northern conspiracy against them seemed to be confirmed. The nation was on the brink of disaster.

Reading Check **Explaining** How did the *Dred Scott* decision regulate the spread of slavery?

SECTION 3 ASSESSMENT

Checking for Understanding

1. **Key Terms** Use the terms arsenal and martyr in a paragraph about John Brown's raid on Harpers Ferry.
2. **Reviewing Facts** Discuss the stages in the development of the Republican Party.

Reviewing Themes

3. **Continuity and Change** How did the *Dred Scott* decision reverse a previous decision made by Congress?

Critical Thinking

4. **Making Inferences** Why did Lincoln emerge as a leader after the Lincoln-Douglas debates?
5. **Organizing Information** Re-create the table shown here, and describe the positions taken by Lincoln and Douglas in their debates.

Lincoln–Douglas Debates	
Lincoln's position	Douglas's position

Analyzing Visuals

6. **Examining Artifacts** Examine the poster on page 445. What is the poster advertising? Explain why some of the phrases are in larger type.

Interdisciplinary Activity

Government Draw a political cartoon that illustrates Lincoln's statement "A house divided against itself cannot stand."

Secession and War

Guide to Reading

Main Idea
In 1860 Abraham Lincoln's election as president of the United States was followed by Southern states leaving the Union.

Key Terms
secession, states' rights

Reading Strategy
Sequencing Information As you read the section, re-create the time line below and list the major events at each time.

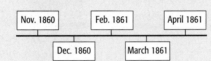

| Nov. 1860 | | Feb. 1861 | | April 1861 |

| | Dec. 1860 | | March 1861 | |

Read to Learn
- how the 1860 election led to the breakup of the Union.
- why secession led to the Civil War.

Section Theme
Geography and History The election of 1860 clearly divided the nation along sectional lines.

Preview of Events

♦1860   ♦1861   ♦1862

Nov. 1860
Abraham Lincoln is elected president

Dec. 1860
South Carolina secedes

February 1861
Southern states form the Confederate States of America

April 1861
Confederate forces attack Fort Sumter; the Civil War begins

Secessionist ribbon

AN American Story

After John Brown's raid on Harpers Ferry, calls for secession grew. South Carolina's *Charleston Mercury* declared "The day of compromise is passed . . . [T]here is no peace for the South in the Union." The *Nashville Union and American* said, "The South will hold the whole party of Republicans responsible for the bloodshed at Harpers Ferry." Republicans refused to take the threat of secession seriously. Secession is only a scare tactic, they argued, aimed at frightening voters from casting their ballot for Abraham Lincoln. To many Southerners, however, the election of Lincoln would be a final signal that their position in the Union was hopeless.

The Election of 1860

Would the Union break up? That was the burning question in the months before the presidential election of 1860. The issue of slavery was seriously discussed and eventually caused a break in the Democratic Party. As the election approached, a northern wing of the Democratic Party nominated Stephen

TWO VIEWPOINTS

Union or Secession?

President Abraham Lincoln and Jefferson Davis, president of the Confederacy, were inaugurated just several weeks apart. These excerpts from their Inaugural Addresses will help you understand differing points of view about secession from the United States in 1861.

Abraham Lincoln's Inaugural Address, March 4, 1861

One section of our country believes slavery is *right* and ought to be extended, while the other believes it is *wrong* and ought not to be extended. This is the only substantial dispute . . . .

Physically speaking, we can not separate. We can not remove our respective sections from each other nor build an impassable wall between them. A husband and wife may be divorced and go out of the presence and beyond the reach of each other; but the different parts of our country can not do this. . . .

In *your* hands, my dissatisfied fellow countrymen, and not in *mine,* is the momentous issue of civil war.

Abraham Lincoln

Jefferson Davis's Inaugural Address, February 18, 1861

As a necessity, not a choice, we have resorted to the remedy of separation, and henceforth our energies must be directed to the conduct of our own affairs, and the [continuation] of the Confederacy which we have formed. If a just perception of mutual interest shall permit us peaceably to pursue our separate political career, my most earnest desire will have been fulfilled. But if this be denied to us . . . [we will be forced] to appeal to arms. . . .

Jefferson Davis

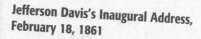

Learning From History

1. According to Lincoln, what was the only substantial disagreement between the North and the South?
2. What did Lincoln compare the United States to?
3. Did Lincoln and Davis say anything in their inaugural addresses that was similar?

Douglas for the presidency and supported popular sovereignty. Southern Democrats—vowing to uphold slavery—nominated John C. Breckinridge of Kentucky and supported the *Dred Scott* decision. Moderates from both the North and South who had formed the Constitutional Union Party nominated John Bell of Tennessee. This party took no position on slavery.

Lincoln Nominated

The Republicans nominated Abraham Lincoln. Their platform, designed to attract voters from many quarters, was that slavery should be left undisturbed where it existed, but that it should be excluded from the territories. Many Southerners feared, however, that a Republican victory would encourage slave revolts.

Lincoln Elected

With the Democrats divided, Lincoln won a clear majority of the electoral votes—180 out of 303. He received only 40 percent of the popular vote, but this was more than any other candidate. Douglas was second with 30 percent of the vote.

The vote was along purely sectional lines. Lincoln's name did not even appear on the ballot in most Southern states, but he won every Northern state. Breckinridge swept the South, and Bell took most border states. Douglas won only the state of Missouri and three of New Jersey's seven electoral votes.

In effect, the more populous North had outvoted the South. The victory for Lincoln was a short-lived one, however, for the nation Lincoln was to lead would soon disintegrate.

✓**Reading Check** **Examining** What caused the split in the Democratic Party in 1860?

The South Secedes

Lincoln and the Republicans had promised not to disturb slavery where it already existed. Many people in the South, however, did not trust the party, fearing that the Republican administration would not protect Southern rights. On December 20, 1860, the South's long-standing threat to leave the Union became a reality when South Carolina held a special convention and voted to secede.

Attempt at Compromise

Even after South Carolina's action, many people still wished to preserve the Union. The question was *how.* As other Southern states debated secession—withdrawal from the Union—leaders in Washington, D.C., worked frantically to fashion a last-minute compromise. On December 18, 1860, Senator **John Crittenden** of Kentucky proposed a series of amendments to the Constitution. Central to Crittenden's plan was a provision to protect slavery south of 36°30'N latitude—the line set by the Missouri Compromise—in all territories "now held or hereafter acquired."

Republicans considered this unacceptable. They had just won an election on the principle that slavery would not be extended in any territories. "Now we are told," Lincoln said,

> **66**the government shall be broken up, unless we surrender to those we have beaten.**99**

Leaders in the South also rejected the plan. "We spit upon every plan to compromise," exclaimed one Southern leader. "No human power can save the Union," wrote another.

The Confederacy

By February 1861, Texas, Louisiana, Mississippi, Alabama, Florida, and Georgia had joined South Carolina and also seceded. Delegates from these states and South Carolina met in Montgomery, Alabama, on February 4 to form a new nation and government. Calling themselves the **Confederate States of America,** they chose **Jefferson Davis,** a senator from Mississippi, as their president.

Southerners justified secession with the theory of states' rights. The states, they argued, had voluntarily chosen to enter the Union. They defined the Constitution as a contract among the independent states. Now because the national government had violated that contract—by refusing to enforce the Fugitive Slave Act and by denying the Southern states equal rights in the territories—the states were justified in leaving the Union.

Reactions to Secession

Many Southerners welcomed secession. In Charleston, South Carolina, people rang church bells, fired cannons, and celebrated in the streets. A newspaper in Atlanta, Georgia, said the South "will never submit" and would defend its liberties no matter what the cost.

Other Southerners, however, were alarmed. A South Carolinian wrote,

> **66**My heart has been rent [torn] by . . . the destruction of my country—the dismemberment of that great and glorious Union.**99**

Virginian Robert E. Lee expressed concern about the future. "I see only that a fearful calamity is upon us," he wrote.

In the North some abolitionists preferred to allow the Southern states to leave. If the Union could be kept together only by compromising on slavery, they declared, then let the Union be destroyed. Most Northerners, however, believed that the Union must be preserved. For Lincoln the issue was "whether in a free government the minority have the right to break up the government whenever they choose."

Presidential Responses

Lincoln had won the election, but he was not yet president. James Buchanan's term ran until March 4, 1861. In December 1860, Buchanan sent a message to Congress saying that the Southern states had no right to secede. Then he added that he had no power to stop them from doing so.

As Lincoln prepared for his inauguration on March 4, 1861, people in both the North and the South wondered what he would say and do. They wondered, too, what would happen in Vir-

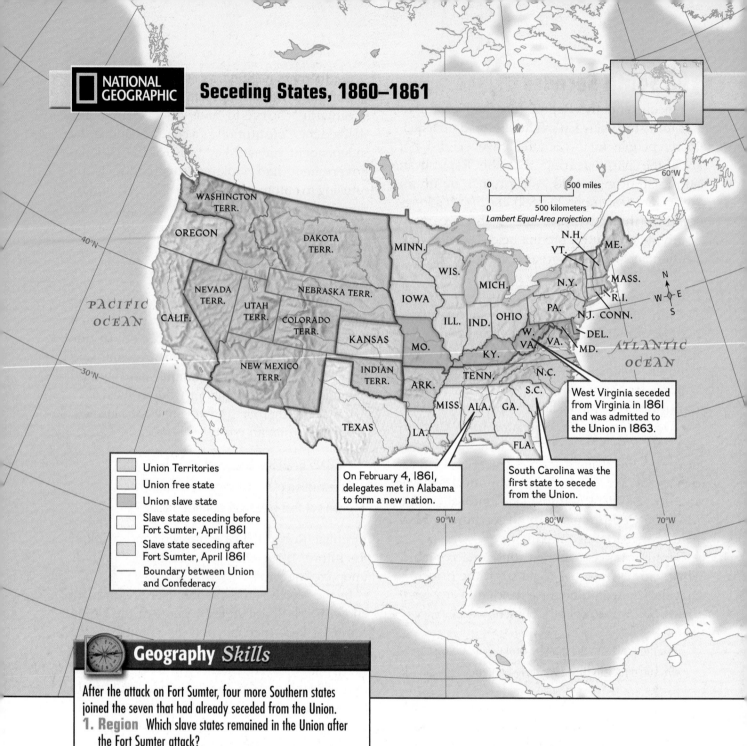

Seceding States, 1860–1861

0 — 500 miles

0 — 500 kilometers
Lambert Equal-Area projection

WASHINGTON TERR.

OREGON

40°N

PACIFIC OCEAN

NEVADA TERR.

CALIF.

UTAH TERR.

NEW MEXICO TERR.

30°N

DAKOTA TERR.

MINN.

WIS.

NEBRASKA TERR.

IOWA

COLORADO TERR.

KANSAS

MICH.

ILL. IND. OHIO

MO.

INDIAN TERR.

ARK.

TENN.

MISS. ALA. GA.

TEXAS

LA.

FLA.

N.H.

VT. ME.

N.Y. MASS.

R.I.

PA. N.J. CONN.

W. VA. VA. DEL.

KY. MD.

N.C.

S.C.

ATLANTIC OCEAN

60°W

90°W 80°W 70°W

West Virginia seceded from Virginia in 1861 and was admitted to the Union in 1863.

On February 4, 1861, delegates met in Alabama to form a new nation.

South Carolina was the first state to secede from the Union.

N
W E
S

Union Territories

Union free state

Union slave state

Slave state seceding before Fort Sumter, April 1861

Slave state seceding after Fort Sumter, April 1861

— Boundary between Union and Confederacy

Geography *Skills*

After the attack on Fort Sumter, four more Southern states joined the seven that had already seceded from the Union.

1. Region Which slave states remained in the Union after the Fort Sumter attack?

2. Analyzing Information Which states did not secede until after the Fort Sumter attack?

ginia, North Carolina, Kentucky, Tennessee, Missouri, and Arkansas. These slave states had chosen to remain in the Union, but the decision was not final. If the United States used force against the Confederate States of America, the remaining slave states also might secede. In his Inaugural Address, the new president mixed toughness and words of peace. He said that

secession would not be permitted, vowing to hold federal property in the South and to enforce the laws of the United States. At the same time, Lincoln pleaded with the people of the South for reconciliation:

❝We are not enemies, but friends. We must not be enemies. Though passion may have strained, it must not break our bonds of affection.❞

Reading Check **Explaining** How did the seceding states justify their right to leave the Union?

Fort Sumter

The South soon tested President Lincoln's vow to hold federal property. Confederate forces had already seized some United States forts within their states. Although Lincoln did not want to start a war by trying to take the forts back, allowing the Confederates to keep them would amount to admitting their right to secede.

On the day after his inauguration, Lincoln received a dispatch from the commander of **Fort Sumter,** a United States fort on an island guarding Charleston Harbor. The message warned that the fort was low on supplies and that the Confederates demanded its surrender.

The War Begins

Lincoln responded by sending a message to Governor Francis Pickens of South Carolina. He informed Pickens that he was sending an unarmed expedition with supplies to Fort Sumter. Lincoln promised that Union forces would not "throw in men, arms, or ammunition" unless they were fired upon. The president thus left the decision to start shooting up to the Confederates.

Confederate president Jefferson Davis and his advisers made a fateful choice. They ordered their forces to attack Fort Sumter before the Union supplies could arrive. Confederate guns opened fire on the fort early on April 12, 1861. Union captain Abner Doubleday witnessed the attack from inside the fort:

> 66 Showers of balls . . . and shells . . . poured into the fort in one incessant stream, causing great flakes of masonry to fall in all directions. 99

High seas had prevented Union relief ships from reaching the besieged fort. The Union garrison held out for 33 hours before surrendering on April 14. Thousands of shots were exchanged during the siege, but there was no loss of life on either side. The Confederates hoisted their flag over the fort, and all the guns in the harbor sounded a triumphant salute.

News of the attack galvanized the North. President Lincoln issued a call for 75,000 troops to fight to save the Union, and volunteers quickly signed up. Meanwhile, Virginia, North Carolina, Tennessee, and Arkansas voted to join the Confederacy. The Civil War had begun.

Reading Check **Explaining** What action did Lincoln take after the attack on Fort Sumter?

HISTORY Online

Student Web Activity
Visit taj.glencoe.com and click on **Chapter 15— Student Web Activities** for an activity on the period leading up to the Civil War.

SECTION 4 ASSESSMENT

Checking for Understanding

1. **Key Terms** Write a newspaper article about the election of 1860, using the terms states' rights and secession.

2. **Reviewing Facts** Who served as the president of the Confederate States of America?

Reviewing Themes

3. **Geography and History** What role did sectionalism play in Lincoln's winning the 1860 election?

Critical Thinking

4. **Drawing Conclusions** Do you think either Northerners or Southerners believed that secession would *not* lead to war? Explain.

5. **Organizing Information** Re-create the diagram below. In the ovals, describe the events leading to the firing on Fort Sumter.

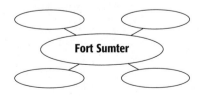

Fort Sumter

Analyzing Visuals

6. **Geography Skills** Examine the map on page 452. How many states made up the Confederacy? Which state seceded earlier—Mississippi or Arkansas?

Interdisciplinary Activity

Citizenship Make up a campaign slogan or song for Abraham Lincoln, Stephen A. Douglas, John C. Breckinridge, or John Bell in the 1860 presidential election.

What were people's lives like in the past?

What—and who—were people talking about? What did they eat? What did they do for fun? These two pages will give you some clues to everyday life in the U.S. as you step back in time with TIME Notebook.

Profile

It's 1853, and **AMELIA STEWART** *is heading west to Oregon with her husband and seven children in a covered wagon. How hard can the five-month trip be? Here are two entries from her diary:*

MONDAY, AUGUST 8 We have to make a drive of 22 miles without water today. Have our cans filled to drink. Here we left, unknowingly, our [daughter] Lucy behind, not a soul had missed her until we had gone some miles, when we stopped a while to rest the cattle; just then another train drove up behind us, with Lucy. She was terribly frightened and said she was sitting under the bank of the river when we started, busy watching some wagons cross, and did not know that we were ready....It was a lesson for all of us.

FRIDAY, AUGUST 12 Lost one of our oxen. We were traveling slowly along, when he dropped dead in the yoke....I could hardly help shedding tears, when we drove round this poor ox who had helped us along thus far, and had given us his very last step.

EVENTS OF THE TIME

CLOTHED. Hundreds of miners in 1850 by **LEVI STRAUSS**. Using canvas he originally intended to make into tents, Levi made sturdy, tough pants with lots of pockets—perfect clothing for the rough work of mining. Can you imagine anyone in the city ever wearing them?

MARCHED. Just under 100 camels in 1857, from San Antonio to Los Angeles, led by hired Turkish, Greek, and Armenian camel drivers. It is hoped the desert beasts will help the U.S. Army open the West.

MAILED. Thousands of letters carried by **PONY EXPRESS** in 1860 from Missouri to California in an extremely short time—only 10 days! Riders switch to fresh horses every 10 or 15 miles and continue through the night, blizzards, and attacks by outlaws.

FRONTIER FOOD

Trail Mix

Hard Tack for a Hard Trip

INGREDIENTS: 3 cups flour • 3 tsp. salt • 1 cup water

Mix all ingredients and stir until it becomes too difficult. Knead the dough; add more flour until mixture is very dry. Roll to 1/2-inch thickness and cut into 3" squares, poke with a skewer [pin] to make several holes in each piece (for easy breaking). Bake 30 minutes in a hot oven until hard. Store for up to 10 years.

Word Watch

Can you talk "Western"? Match the words below to their meaning.

1. maverick
2. Hangtown fry
3. grubstake
4. bonanza
5. palo alto
6. pard or rawwheel

a. gold rush favorite, made of eggs, bacon, and oysters

b. inexperienced '49er; eastern type not used to wearing boots

c. a lucky discovery of gold; a source of sudden wealth

d. a style of hat worn by gold rush miners

e. an individual who takes an independent stand, from the name of a Texas cattleman who left his herd unbranded

f. food provided by an investor to a gold prospector in exchange for a share of whatever gold the prospector finds

answers: 1. e; 2. a; 3. f; 4. c; 5. d; 6. b

The Price of a Life

This notice appeared in 1852.

CREDIT SALE OF A CHOICE GANG OF 41 SLAVES!

COMPRISING MECHANICS, LABORERS, ETC.,
FOR THE SETTLEMENT OF A CO-PARTNERSHIP OF RAILROAD CONTRACTORS.

BY J. A. BEARD & MAY, J. A. BEARD, AUCT'R.

WILL BE SOLD AT AUCTION, AT BANKS' ARCADE, MAGAZINE STREET.

SALE OF SLAVES AND STOCK

The Negroes and Stock listed below are a Prime Lot, and belong to the ESTATE OF THE LATE LUTHER McGOWAN, and will be sold on Monday, Sept. 22nd, 1852, at the Fair Grounds, in Savannah, Georgia, at 1:00 P.M. The Negroes will be taken to the grounds two days previous to the Sale, so that they may be inspected by prospective buyers.

On account of the low prices listed below, they will be sold for cash only, and must be taken into custody within two hours after sale.

No.	Name	Age	Remarks	Price
1	Lunesta	27	Prime Rice Planter	$1,275.00
2	Violet	16	Housework and Nursemaid	900.00
3	Lizzie	30	Rice, Unsound	300.00
4	Minda	27	Cotton, Prime Woman	1,200.00
5	Adam	28	Cotton, Prime Young Man	1,100.00
6	Abel	41	Rice Hand, Eyesight Poor	675.00
7	Tanney	22	Prime Cotton Hand	
8	Flementina	39		950.00

NUMBERS

U.S. AT THE TIME

$81,249,700
Estimated value of gold mined in 1852

89 Days it takes the American clipper ship, the *Flying Cloud*, to go from Boston around Cape Horn to San Francisco in 1851—a trip that normally takes eight or nine months

12 Poems included in Walt Whitman's new collection, called *Leaves of Grass* (1855)

33 Number of states in 1859 after Oregon enters the union

100 Seats in Congress won by the Republicans in 1854, the year the party was created

300,000 Copies of Harriet Beecher Stowe's novel, *Uncle Tom's Cabin*, sold in 1852

UNCLE TOM'S CABIN;

OR,

LIFE AMONG THE LOWLY.

BY

HARRIET BEECHER STOWE.

FIFTEENTH THOUSAND.

BOSTON:
JOHN P. JEWETT & COMPANY.
CLEVELAND, OHIO:
JEWETT, PROCTOR & WORTHINGTON.
1852.

VOL. I.

Chapter Summary

Road to Civil War

1820
- Missouri Compromise passed

1844
- Polk elected president

1845
- Texas becomes a state

1848
- Free-Soil Party nominates Van Buren

1850
- Compromise of 1850 passed

1852
- *Uncle Tom's Cabin* published

1854
- Kansas-Nebraska Act passed
- Republican Party formed

1856
- Violence erupts in Kansas
- Buchanan elected president

1857
- *Dred Scott* decision handed down

1858
- Lincoln-Douglas debates held

1859
- John Brown attacks Harpers Ferry

1860
- Lincoln is elected president
- South Carolina becomes first state to secede

1861
- Confederate States of America formed
- Fort Sumter attacked

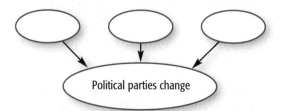

Reviewing Key Terms

Write five true *and five* false *statements using the terms below. Use only one term in each statement. Indicate which statements are true and which are false. Below each false statement explain why it is false.*

1. sectionalism
2. secede
3. border ruffians
4. arsenal
5. secession
6. fugitive
7. popular sovereignty
8. civil war
9. martyr
10. states' rights

Reviewing Key Facts

11. What was the purpose of the Missouri Compromise?
12. List the five parts of the Compromise of 1850.
13. What was Stephen Douglas's solution to the slavery issue in the Kansas and Nebraska territories?
14. How did Abraham Lincoln become a national figure in politics?
15. What was the *Dred Scott* decision? What did it mean for those opposed to slavery?
16. Why were there four parties and candidates in the presidential election of 1860?
17. How did Lincoln plan to prevent secession?

Critical Thinking

18. **Finding the Main Idea** Why was the balance of free and slave states in the Senate such an important issue?
19. **Drawing Conclusions** Why did Northerners protest Douglas's plan to repeal the Missouri Compromise?
20. **Determining Cause and Effect** Re-create the diagram below. List three ways pro- or antislavery groups changed the structure of political parties in the 1850s.

Political parties change

21. **Analyzing Themes: Geography and History** How did the North's larger population give it an edge over the South in the 1860 election?

Geography and History Activity

The election of 1860 divided the nation along sectional lines. Study the map below; then answer the questions that follow.

Self-Check Quiz

Visit **taj.glencoe.com** and click on **Chapter 15—Self-Check Quizzes** to prepare for the chapter test.

NATIONAL GEOGRAPHIC	**Election of 1860**

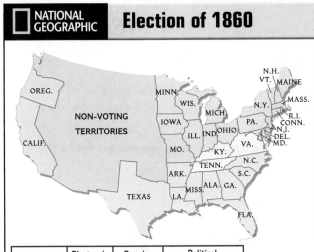

Candidate	Electoral Vote	Popular Vote	Political Party
Lincoln	180	1,865,593	Republican
Breckinridge	72	848,356	Southern Democrat
Bell	39	592,906	Constitutional Union
Douglas	12	1,382,713	Northern Democrat

22. **Location** Which states supported Douglas?

23. **Region** In what region(s) was the Republican Party strongest?

24. **Region** In what region did Breckinridge find support?

Practicing Skills

25. **Recognizing Bias** Find written material about a topic of interest in your community. Possible sources include editorials, letters to the editor, and pamphlets from political candidates and interest groups. Write a short report analyzing the material for evidence of bias.

Technology Activity

26. **Using the Internet** Search the Internet for a list of political parties in existence today. Make a table that briefly summarizes each party's current goals. Then research to find the date that the party was founded. Include this information on your table, too. Then compare your table to the political parties discussed in Chapter 15.

Citizenship Cooperative Activity

27. **Making Compromises** With a partner, think of a controversial issue that is a source of disagreement today. Take opposite sides on the issue; then work together to come up with a list of three compromises that would make the solution to this problem acceptable to both sides. Share the issue and your compromises with the class.

Alternative Assessment

28. **Portfolio Writing Activity** Make a list of 10 important events that you read about in Chapter 15. Next select the two events that you think did the most to create conflict between the North and South. Write a one-page essay in which you explain how these events led to conflict.

Standardized Test Practice

The Princeton Review

Directions: Use the map of the Compromise of 1850 on page 443 to choose the *best* answer to the following question.

Which of the following statements is true?

A The Compromise of 1850 allowed the Oregon Territory to be open to slaveholding.

B The Compromise of 1850 did not make any land on the Pacific Ocean open to slaveholding.

C The Compromise of 1850 made every state touching the southern border of the United States open to slaveholding.

D The Compromise of 1850 gave the Minnesota Territory the authority to choose whether it would allow slaveholding.

Test-Taking Tip

Remember to use the information on the map to support your answer. Don't rely only on your memory. Check each answer choice against the map. Only one choice is correct.

CHAPTER 16 The Civil War

1861–1865

Why It Matters

The Civil War—a war in which Americans fought other Americans—transformed the United States. It shattered the economy of the South while contributing to the rapid economic growth of the North and the West. African Americans gained freedom when slavery was abolished, but the war left a legacy of bitterness between North and South that lasted for generations.

The Impact Today

Key events during this era still shape our lives today. For example:
- The institution of slavery was abolished.
- The war established the power of the federal government over the states.

The American Journey *Video* The chapter 16 video, "The Face of War," gives insight into the realities of the Civil War.

1861
- Confederate States of America formed
- Conflict at Fort Sumter, South Carolina, begins Civil War

1863
- Emancipation Proclamation issued
- Battle of Gettysburg

1862
- Robert E. Lee named commander of Confederate armies

United States
PRESIDENTS

Lincoln
1861–1865

1861

1862

1863

World

1861
- Charles Dickens's *Great Expectations* published
- Victor Emmanuel II recognized as king of unified Italy

1862
- Otto von Bismarck named premier of Prussia

1863
- Discovery of Lake Victoria as source of Nile River
- International Red Cross established

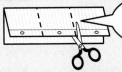

Fight for the Colors by Don Troiani Troiani has painted many dramatic war scenes, such as this one of the Battle of Gettysburg.

1864
- Sherman's "march to the sea" begins
- Lincoln reelected president

1865
- Civil War ends
- Lincoln assassinated

1864 *1865*

1864
- Maximilian installed as emperor of Mexico

1865
- Lewis Carroll publishes *Alice's Adventures in Wonderland*

HISTORY
Online

Chapter Overview
Visit taj.glencoe.com and click on **Chapter 16— Chapter Overviews** to preview chapter information.

Guide to Reading

Main Idea
Both the North and the South had strengths and weaknesses that helped determine their military strategies.

Key Terms
border state, blockade, offensive, Rebel, Yankee

Reading Strategy
Classifying Information As you read the section, complete a chart like the one shown here by listing the strengths and weaknesses of the Union and the Confederacy.

	Union	Confederacy
Strengths		
Weaknesses		

Read to Learn
• why the border states played an important part in the war.
• how the North and South compared in terms of population, industry, resources, and war aims.

Section Theme
Government and Democracy The Southern states seceded from the Union to protect states' rights.

Preview of Events

♦1861   ♦1862   ♦1863

February 1861
The Confederacy forms

April 1861
Four more states join the Confederacy

Summer 1861
Confederate forces total 112,000; Union 187,000

June 1863
West Virginia joins Union

Confederate soldier, 1861

AN
American Story

Union sergeant Driscoll directed his troops at Malvern Hill on July 1, 1862. The enemy fought fiercely, especially one young Confederate soldier. Driscoll raised his rifle, took aim, and shot the boy. As he passed the spot where the boy had fallen, Driscoll turned the daring soldier over to see what he looked like. The boy opened his eyes and faintly murmured, "Father," then his eyes fluttered shut, never to open again. A Union captain later wrote, "I will forever recollect the frantic grief of Driscoll; it was harrowing to witness. He [had killed] his son, who had gone South before the war."

Like the Driscolls, many families were divided by the war. Neither side imagined, however, that the war would cost such a terrible price in human life. During the four years of fighting, hundreds of thousands of Americans were killed in battle.

Choosing Sides

By February 1861, seven states had left the Union and formed the Confederacy. After the Confederate bombardment of Fort Sumter, President Abraham Lincoln issued a call for troops to save the Union. His action caused Virginia, North Carolina, Tennessee, and Arkansas to join the Confederacy. These four states brought needed soldiers and supplies to the Confederacy. For its capital, the Confederacy chose **Richmond,** Virginia, a city only about 100 miles from the Union capital of Washington, D.C.

Four states that allowed slavery—Missouri, Kentucky, Maryland, and Delaware—remained in the Union. The people of these border states were divided over which side to support. Missouri, Kentucky, and Maryland had such strong support for the South that the three states teetered on the brink of secession.

Losing the border states would seriously damage the North. All had strategic locations. Missouri could control parts of the Mississippi River and major routes to the West. Kentucky controlled the Ohio River. Delaware was close to the important Northern city of Philadelphia.

Maryland, perhaps the most important of the border states, was close to Richmond. Vital railroad lines passed through Maryland. Most significantly, Washington, D.C., lay within the state. If Maryland seceded, the North's government would be surrounded.

Maryland's key role became clear in April 1861. A mob in Baltimore attacked Northern troops; Confederate sympathizers burned railroad bridges and cut the telegraph line to Washington, isolating the capital from the rest of the North. Northern troops soon arrived, but the nation's capital had suffered some anxious days.

Remaining With the Union

Lincoln had to move cautiously to avoid upsetting people in the border states. If he announced that he aimed to end slavery, for instance, groups supporting the Confederacy might take their states out of the Union. If he ordered Northern troops into Kentucky, Confederate sympathizers there would claim the state had been invaded and swing it to the South.

In some ways Lincoln acted boldly. He suspended some constitutional rights and used his power to arrest people who supported secession. In the end Lincoln's approach worked. The border states stayed in the Union, but many of their citizens joined armies of the South.

A Secession From the South

Most white Southerners favored secession. Still, pockets of Union support existed in parts of Tennessee and Virginia. People in the

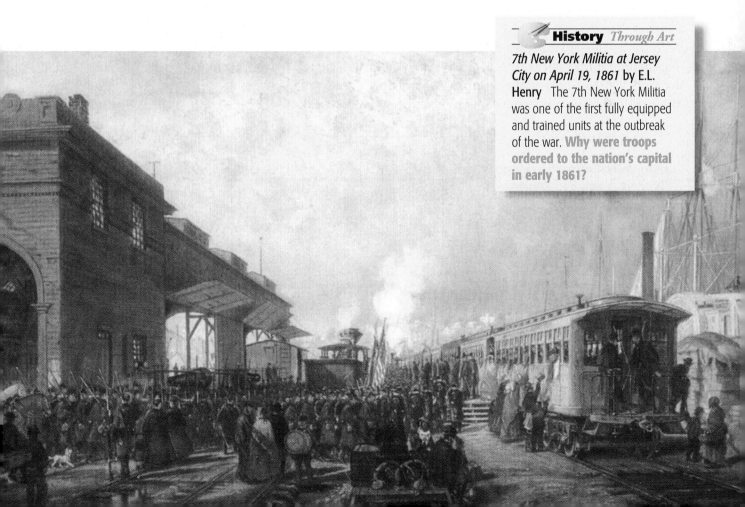

History *Through Art*

7th New York Militia at Jersey City on April 19, 1861 by E.L. Henry The 7th New York Militia was one of the first fully equipped and trained units at the outbreak of the war. **Why were troops ordered to the nation's capital in early 1861?**

Appalachian region generally opposed secession. In western Virginia a movement to secede from the state and rejoin the Union grew. In 1861, 48 Virginia counties organized themselves as a separate state called **West Virginia.** Congress admitted this state to the Union in 1863.

✓ **Reading Check** **Explaining** Why was Maryland strategically important?

Comparing North and South

When the war began, both sides had advantages and disadvantages. How they would use those strengths and weaknesses would determine the war's outcome.

The North enjoyed the advantages of a larger population, more industry, and more abundant resources than the South. It had a better banking system, which helped to raise money for the war. The North also possessed more ships, and almost all the members of the regular navy remained loyal to the Union. Finally, the North had a larger and more efficient railway network.

The North also faced disadvantages. Bringing the Southern states back into the Union would be difficult. The North would have to invade and hold the South—a large area filled with a hostile population. Furthermore, the Southern people's support for the war remained strong. Recalling the example of the American Revolution, when

the smaller, weaker colonies had won independence from wealthy Great Britain, many believed the South had a good chance of winning.

One Northern advantage was not obvious until later. Both sides greatly underestimated Abraham Lincoln. His dedication, intelligence, and humanity would lead the North to victory.

One of the main advantages of the South was the strong support its white population gave the war. Southerners also had the advantage of fighting in familiar territory—defending their land, their homes, and their way of life.

The military leadership of the South, at least at first, was superior to the North's. Southern families had a strong tradition of military training and service, and military college graduates provided the South with a large pool of officers. Overseeing the Southern effort was Confederate president **Jefferson Davis,** a West Point graduate and an experienced soldier.

The South faced material disadvantages. It had a smaller population of free men to draw upon in building an army. It also possessed very few factories to manufacture weapons and other supplies, and it produced less than half as much food as the North. With less than half the miles of railroad tracks and vastly fewer trains than the North, the Confederate government had difficulty delivering food, weapons, and other supplies to its troops.

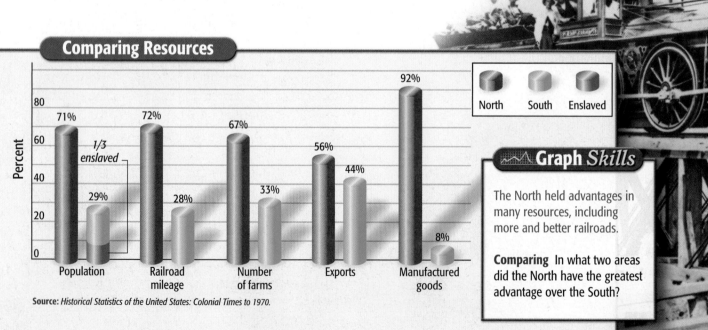

Comparing Resources

Percent

North   South   Enslaved

Population: 71%, 29% (1/3 enslaved)
Railroad mileage: 72%, 28%
Number of farms: 67%, 33%
Exports: 56%, 44%
Manufactured goods: 92%, 8%

Source: *Historical Statistics of the United States: Colonial Times to 1970.*

📈 **Graph Skills**

The North held advantages in many resources, including more and better railroads.

Comparing In what two areas did the North have the greatest advantage over the South?

The belief in **states' rights**—a founding principle of the Confederacy—also hampered the South's efforts. The individual states refused to give the Confederate government sufficient power. As a result, the government found it difficult to fight the war effectively.

War Aims and Strategy

The North and the South entered the Civil War with different aims. The main goal of the North at the outset was to bring the Southern states back into the Union. Ending slavery was not a major Northern goal at first, but this changed as the war continued.

The Union's plan for winning the war included three main strategies. First the North would blockade, or close, Southern ports to prevent supplies from reaching the South—and to prevent the South from earning money by exporting cotton. Second, the Union intended to gain control of the Mississippi River to cut Southern supply lines and to split the Confederacy. Third, the North planned to capture Richmond, Virginia, the Confederate capital.

For the South, the primary aim of the war was to win recognition as an independent nation. Independence would allow Southerners to preserve their traditional way of life— a way of life that included slavery.

To achieve this goal, the South worked out a defensive strategy. It planned to defend its homeland, holding on to as much territory as possible until the North tired of fighting. The South expected that Britain and France, which imported large quantities of Southern cotton, would pressure the North to end the war to restore their cotton supply.

During the war Southern leaders sometimes changed strategy and took the offensive—went on the attack. They moved their armies northward to threaten Washington, D.C., and other Northern cities, hoping to persuade the North it could not win the war.

✓Reading Check **Explaining** What role did Jefferson Davis play in the war?

American People at War

The Civil War was more than a war between the states. It often pitted brother against brother, parents against their children, and neighbor against neighbor.

American Against American

The leaders from both North and South—and their families—felt these divisions. President Lincoln's wife, Mary Todd Lincoln, had several relatives who fought in the Confederate army. John Crittenden, a senator from Kentucky, had two sons who became generals in the war—one for the Confederacy and one for the Union. Officers on both sides—including Confederate general Robert E. Lee, and Union generals George McClellan and William Tecumseh Sherman— had attended the United States Military Academy at West Point, never dreaming that they would one day command forces against each other.

Who Were the Soldiers?

Most of the soldiers were young. The average age of a recruit was 25 years old, but about 40 percent were 21 or younger. Ted Upson of Indiana was only 16 when he begged his father to let him join the Union army. His father replied, "This Union your ancestors and mine helped to make must be saved from destruction." 📖 *(See page 969 for an additional primary source reading about Civil War soldiers.)*

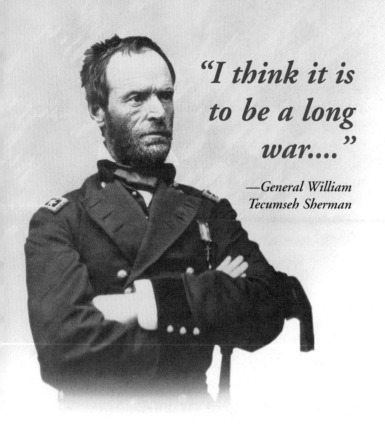

"I think it is to be a long war...."

—General William Tecumseh Sherman

William Stone from Louisiana rushed to join the Confederate army after the attack on Fort Sumter. His sister Kate wrote that he was

66 . . . wild to be off to Virginia. He so fears that the fighting will be over before he can get there. 99

Soldiers came from every region and all walks of life. Most, though, came from farms. Almost half of the North's troops and more than 60 percent of the South's had owned or worked on farms. The Union army did not permit African Americans to join at first, but they did serve later. Lincoln's early terms of enlistment asked governors to supply soldiers for 90 days. When the conflict did not end quickly, soldiers' terms became longer.

By the summer of 1861 the Confederate army had about 112,000 soldiers, who were sometimes called Rebels. The Union had about 187,000 soldiers, or Yankees, as they were also known. By the end of war, about 850,000 men fought for the Confederacy and about 2.1 million men fought for the Union. The Union number included just under 200,000 African Americans. About 10,000 Hispanic soldiers fought in the conflict.

False Hopes

When the war began, each side expected an early victory. A Confederate soldier from a town in Alabama expected the war to be over well within a year because "we are going to kill the last Yankee before that time if there is any fight in them still." Northerners were just as confident that they would beat the South quickly.

Some leaders saw the situation more clearly. Northern general William Tecumseh Sherman wrote, "I think it is to be a long war—very long—much longer than any politician thinks." The first spring of the war proved that Sherman's prediction was accurate.

✓ **Reading Check** **Comparing** Which side had the larger fighting force?

SECTION 1 ASSESSMENT

Checking for Understanding

1. **Key Terms** Write a short paragraph in which you use all of the following key terms: border state, blockade, offensive, Rebel, Yankee.
2. **Reviewing Facts** Why were the border states important to the North?

Reviewing Themes

3. **Government and Democracy** How did a strong belief in states' rights affect the South during the war?

Critical Thinking

4. **Predict** What do you think would be the South's greatest advantage in the war?
5. **Comparing** Create a diagram like the one shown here. Then compare Northern and Southern aims and strategies.

	North	South
Aims		
Strategies		

Analyzing Visuals

6. **Making Generalizations** Review the graph on page 462 and write a general conclusion based on the data presented in the graph.

Interdisciplinary Activity

Expository Writing You are a Southerner (or a Northerner) in 1861. Write a journal entry that explains your reasons for joining the Confederate (or Union) army.

Stephen Crane (1871–1900)

Stephen Crane began his career in journalism while still in his teens. Later, as a reporter, Crane covered several wars in the late 1890s. He had not yet seen a battlefield, however, when he wrote *The Red Badge of Courage.* Even so, he described the experience of war so realistically that even combat veterans admired his work.

READ TO DISCOVER

What is it like to be a soldier facing battle for the first time? Henry Fleming, the young recruit in *The Red Badge of Courage,* offers some answers as he thinks about his role in the war. What battle does Henry fight with himself before he fights in an actual Civil War battle?

READER'S DICTIONARY

Huns: soldiers known for their fierce fighting

haversack: bag soldiers used to carry personal items

obliged: felt it necessary to do something

confronted: faced

lurking: lying in wait

tumult: uproar

The Red Badge of Courage

Various veterans had told him tales. Some talked of . . . tremendous bodies of fierce soldiery who were sweeping along like the **Huns.** Others spoke of tattered and eternally hungry men. . . . "They'll charge through hell's fire an' brimstone t' git a holt on a **haversack . . .**" he was told. From the stories, the youth imagined the red, live bones sticking out through slits in the faded uniforms.

Still, he could not put a whole faith in veterans' tales, for recruits were their prey. They talked much of smoke, fire, and blood, but he could not tell how much might be lies. They persistently yelled "Fresh fish!" at him, and were in no wise to be trusted.

However, he perceived now that it did not greatly matter what kind of soldiers he was going to fight. . . . There was a more serious problem. He lay in his bunk pondering upon it. He tried to mathematically prove to himself that he would not run from a battle.

Previously he had never felt **obliged** to wrestle too seriously with this question. In his life he had taken certain things for granted, never challenging his belief in ultimate success. . . . But here he was **confronted** with a thing of moment. It had suddenly appeared to him that perhaps in a battle he might run.

He was forced to admit that as far as war was concerned he knew nothing of himself. . . .

A little panic-fear grew in his mind. As his imagination went forward to a fight, he saw hideous possibilities. He contemplated the **lurking** menaces of the future, and failed in an effort to see himself standing stoutly in the midst of them. He recalled his visions of broken-bladed glory, but in the shadow of the impending **tumult** he suspected them to be impossible pictures.

Medal of Honor

ANALYZING LITERATURE

1. **Recall and Interpret** How did Henry view the veterans and their war tales?
2. **Evaluate and Connect** What feelings do you think you might have just before going into battle?

Interdisciplinary Activity

Descriptive Writing Write a conversation between two young soldiers before their first battle. Save your work for your portfolio.

Early Years of the War

Guide to Reading

Main Idea

Neither the Union nor the Confederate forces gained a strong advantage during the early years of the war.

Key Terms

blockade runner, ironclad, casualty

Reading Strategy

Classifying Information As you read, describe the outcome of each of these battles on a chart like the one shown.

Battle	Outcome
First Battle of Bull Run (Manassas)	
Monitor v. *Merrimack*	
Antietam	

Read to Learn

- what successes and failures the North and the South had in the early years of the war.
- how the North's naval blockade hurt the South.

Section Theme

Geography and History The North and the South fought the war differently in different geographic regions.

Preview of Events

♦1861   ♦1862   ♦1863

July 1861
First Battle of Bull Run (Manassas)

February 1862
Grant captures Fort Henry and Fort Donelson

April 1862
Battle of Shiloh

September 1862
Battle of Antietam

AN American Story

Sunday, July 21, 1861, was a pleasant, sunny day in Washington, D.C. Hundreds of cheerful residents, food baskets in hand, left the city and crossed the Potomac River to spend the day in Virginia. They planned to picnic while watching the first battle between the Union and the Confederate armies. Expecting to see Union troops crush the Rebels, they looked forward to a quick victory. The Confederate soldiers also expected a quick victory. They "carried dress suits with them, and any quantity of fine linen. Every soldier, nearly, had a servant with him, and a whole lot of spoons and forks, so as to live comfortably and elegantly in camp...."

Civil War cannon

First Battle of Bull Run

This first major battle of the Civil War was fought in northern Virginia, about five miles from a town called Manassas Junction near Bull Run—a small river in the area. Usually called the **First Battle of Bull Run,** it began when about 30,000 inexperienced Union troops commanded by General Irvin McDowell attacked a smaller, equally inexperienced Confederate force led by General P.G.T. Beauregard.

President Lincoln meets General McClellan and other Union officers.

The Yankees drove the Confederates back at first. Then the Rebels rallied, inspired by reinforcements under General Thomas Jackson. Jackson, who was seen holding out heroically "like a stone wall," became known thereafter as **"Stonewall" Jackson.** The Confederates unleashed a savage counterattack that forced the Union lines to break.

The Confederates surged forward with a strange, unearthly scream that came to be known as the Rebel yell. Terrified, the Northern soldiers began to drop their guns and packs and run. One observer, Representative Albert Riddle, reported:

> ❝ A cruel, crazy, mad, hopeless panic possessed them. . . . The heat was awful . . . the men were exhausted—their mouths gaped, their lips cracked and blackened with the powder of the cartridges they had bitten off in the battle, their eyes staring in frenzy. ❞

The Union army began an orderly retreat that quickly became a mad stampede when the retreating Union troops collided with the civilians, fleeing in panic back to Washington, D.C. The Confederates, though victorious, were too disorganized and weakened to pursue the retreating Yankees. Regardless, the South rejoiced. Edmund Ruffin of Virginia thought it meant "the close of the war."

A Shock for the North

The outcome of the battle shocked the North. Northerners began to understand that the war could be a long, difficult, and costly struggle. Although discouraged by the results, President Abraham Lincoln was also determined. Within days he issued a call for more volunteers for the army. He signed two bills requesting a total of one million soldiers, who would serve for three years. Volunteers soon crowded into recruiting offices. Lincoln also appointed a new general, **George B. McClellan,** to head the Union army of the East—called the **Army of the Potomac—**and to organize the troops.

✔️ **Reading Check** **Explaining** How did the First Battle of Bull Run change people's views about the war?

War at Sea

Even before Bull Run, Lincoln had ordered a naval blockade of Southern ports. An effective blockade would prevent the South from exporting its cotton and from importing the supplies necessary to continue the war.

Enforcing the Blockade

When the war began, the North did not have enough ships to blockade the South's entire 3,500-mile coastline. Many Confederate ships, called blockade runners, could sail in and out of Southern ports. In time, the North built more ships and became better able to enforce the blockade.

The blockade caused serious problems for the South. Although the blockade could never close off all Southern trade, it did reduce the trade by more than two-thirds. Goods such as coffee, shoes, nails, and salt—as well as guns and ammunition—were in short supply throughout the war.

The *Monitor* Versus the *Merrimack*

The South did not intend to let the blockade go unchallenged. Southerners salvaged the *Merrimack,* a Union warship that Northern forces had abandoned when Confederate forces seized the naval shipyard in **Norfolk, Virginia.** The Confederates rebuilt the wooden ship, covered it with thick iron plates, and renamed it the *Virginia.*

On March 8, 1862, this ironclad warship attacked a group of Union ships off the coast of Virginia. The North's wooden warships could not damage the Confederate ship—shells simply bounced off its sides.

Some Northern leaders feared the South would use the ironclad warship to destroy much of the Union navy, steam up the Potomac River, and bombard Washington, D.C. However, the North had already built an ironclad ship of its own, the *Monitor.* Described as looking like a "tin can on a shingle," the *Monitor* rushed south to engage the Confederate ship in battle.

On March 9, the two ironclads exchanged fire, but neither ship could sink the other. The Union succeeded in keeping the *Merrimack* in the harbor, so it never again threatened Northern ships. The battle marked a new age in naval warfare— the first battle between two metal-covered ships.

Reading Check **Explaining** What was significant about the battle between the *Merrimack* and the *Monitor*?

War in the West

After the First Battle of Bull Run in July 1861, the war in the East settled into a stalemate as each side built its strength. Generals focused on training raw recruits, turning civilians into soldiers. For a while the action shifted to the West.

Early Victories for the North

One of the North's primary goals in the West was to gain control of the Mississippi and Tennessee Rivers. This would split the Confederacy and hinder Southern efforts to transport goods.

The Union launched its operations in the West from Cairo, Illinois. The city was strategically located where the Ohio and Mississippi Rivers meet. In addition, Cairo was only a short distance from the Cumberland and Tennessee Rivers. The Union commander at Cairo was **Ulysses S. Grant.**

Ironclads marked the beginning of the modern, armored, self-propelled warship.

Early in 1862, Grant was ordered to move against Confederate forces under General Albert Sidney Johnson in Kentucky and Tennessee. On February 6, with the aid of a fleet of newly made ironclads under Andrew Foote, Grant captured Fort Henry on the Tennessee River. Ten days later Grant captured Fort Donelson on the Cumberland. When the Confederate commander at Fort Donelson realized he was trapped, he asked Grant for his terms. Grant's reply was,

❝No terms except unconditional and immediate surrender can be accepted.❞

"Unconditional Surrender" Grant became the North's new hero.

Grant's victories helped secure the lower Tennessee River. They also opened a path for Union troops to march into Tennessee, Mississippi, and Alabama. The victories drove the Confederates out of Kentucky, where the South had been attempting to persuade Kentuckians to secede from the Union.

✦Geography
The Battle of Shiloh

General Grant and about 40,000 troops then headed south along the Tennessee River toward Corinth, Mississippi, an important railroad junction. In early April 1862, the Union army camped at Pittsburg Landing, 20 miles from Corinth. Nearby was a church named Shiloh. Additional Union forces came from Nashville to join Grant.

Confederate leaders decided to strike first, before the reinforcements arrived. Early in the morning of April 6, Confederate forces led by Albert Sidney Johnston and P.G.T. Beauregard launched a surprise attack on the Union troops. The **Battle of Shiloh** lasted two days, with some of the most bitter, bloody fighting of the war. The first day, the Confederates drove Grant and his troops back to the Tennessee River. The second day, the Union forces recovered. Aided by the 25,000 troops from Nashville and shelling by gunboats on the river, they defeated the Confederates, who withdrew to Corinth.

Names of Battles

Many Civil War battles have two names. The Union named battles after the nearest body of water. The Confederacy named them after the nearest settlement. Therefore, the battle called the Battle of Bull Run (a river) in the North was known as the Battle of Manassas (a settlement) in the South.

The losses in the Battle of Shiloh were enormous. Together the two armies suffered more than 20,000 casualties—people killed or wounded. Confederate general Johnston also died in the bloodbath. One Confederate soldier lamented that the battle "was too shocking [and] too horrible."

After their narrow victory at Shiloh, Union forces gained control of Corinth on May 30. Memphis, Tennessee, fell to Union armies on June 6. The North seemed well on its way to controlling the Mississippi River.

New Orleans Falls

A few weeks after Shiloh, the North won another important victory. On April 25, 1862, Union naval forces under **David Farragut** captured New Orleans, Louisiana, the largest city in the South. Farragut, who was of Spanish descent, had grown up in the South but remained loyal to the Union. His capture of New Orleans, near the mouth of the Mississippi River, meant that the Confederacy could no longer use the river to carry its goods to sea. Together with Grant's victories to the north, Farragut's capture of New Orleans gave Union forces control of almost all the Mississippi River.

✓Reading Check **Analyzing** Why was control of the Mississippi River important to the Union?

War in the East

In the East, General McClellan was training the Army of the Potomac to be an effective fighting force. An expert at training soldiers,

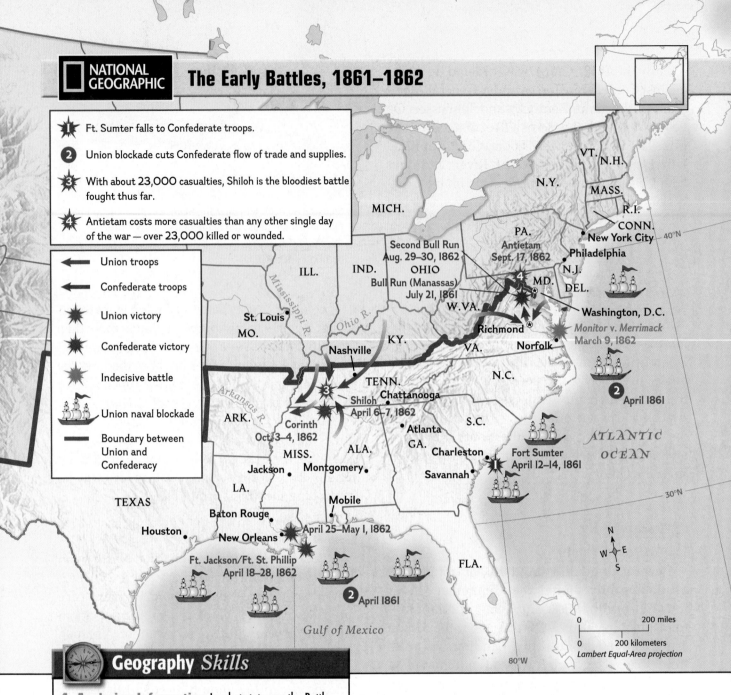

The Early Battles, 1861–1862

NATIONAL GEOGRAPHIC

1. Ft. Sumter falls to Confederate troops.

2. Union blockade cuts Confederate flow of trade and supplies.

3. With about 23,000 casualties, Shiloh is the bloodiest battle fought thus far.

4. Antietam costs more casualties than any other single day of the war — over 23,000 killed or wounded.

Union troops
Confederate troops
Union victory
Confederate victory
Indecisive battle
Union naval blockade
Boundary between Union and Confederacy

MICH.
ILL.
IND.
OHIO
Mississippi R.
Ohio R.
St. Louis
MO.
Nashville
KY.
TENN.
Chattanooga
Shiloh
April 6–7, 1862
Corinth
Oct 3–4, 1862
ARK.
Arkansas R.
MISS.
ALA.
Jackson
Montgomery
LA.
Mobile
Baton Rouge
Houston
New Orleans
Ft. Jackson/Ft. St. Phillip
April 18–28, 1862
April 25–May 1, 1862
TEXAS
Gulf of Mexico
2 April 1861
FLA.
GA.
Atlanta
S.C.
Charleston
Savannah
Fort Sumter
April 12–14, 1861
1
N.C.
Richmond
VA.
W. VA.
Norfolk
Monitor v. Merrimack
March 9, 1862
2 April 1861
ATLANTIC OCEAN
Second Bull Run
Aug. 29–30, 1862
Bull Run (Manassas)
July 21, 1861
Antietam
Sept. 17, 1862
4
MD.
Washington, D.C.
DEL.
N.J.
PA.
Philadelphia
New York City
CONN.
R.I.
MASS.
N.H.
VT.
N.Y.

40°N
30°N
80°W

0   200 miles
0   200 kilometers
Lambert Equal-Area projection

Geography *Skills*

1. **Analyzing Information** In what state was the Battle of Shiloh fought?
2. **Summarizing** In what battles were Confederate forces victorious?

McClellan thoroughly reorganized and drilled the Army of the Potomac. However, when faced with the prospect of battle, McClellan was cautious and worried that his troops were not ready. He hesitated to fight because of reports that overestimated the size of the Rebel forces. Finally, in March 1862, the Army of the Potomac was ready for action. Its goal was to capture Richmond, the Confederate capital.

Union Defeat at Richmond

Instead of advancing directly overland to Richmond as Lincoln wished, McClellan moved his huge army by ship to a peninsula between the York and the James Rivers southeast of the city. From there he began a major offensive known as the **Peninsular Campaign.** The operation took many weeks. Time passed and opportunities to attack slipped away as General McClellan readied his troops and tried to evaluate the enemy's strength. Lincoln, constantly prodding McClellan to fight, ended one message with an urgent plea: "You must act." Complaining of his difficult situation, McClellan did not act. His delays allowed the Confederates to prepare their defense of Richmond.

McClellan and his army inched slowly toward Richmond, getting so close that the troops could hear the city's church bells. At the end of June, the Union forces finally met the Confederates in a series of encounters known as the Seven Days' Battles. In these battles Confederate general **Robert E. Lee** took command of the army opposing McClellan. Before the battles began, Lee's cavalry leader, **James E.B. (J.E.B.) Stuart,** performed a daring tactic. He led his 1,200 troops in a circle around the Union army, gathering vital information about Union positions and boosting Southern morale. Stuart lost only one man in the action. General Lee then boldly countered Union advances and eventually drove the Yankees back to the James River. The Union troops had failed to capture Richmond.

Gloom in the North

Reports from Richmond disheartened the North. Despite the good news of Union victories in the West, failure to take the Confederate capital left Northerners with little hope. There was another call for volunteers—300,000 this time—

but the response was slow. The Southern strategy of making the North weary of war seemed to be working.

The defeat had not been complete, however. McClellan's army had been pushed back, but it was larger than Lee's and still only 25 miles from Richmond. When McClellan failed to renew the attack, President Lincoln ordered him to move his army back to northern Virginia and join the troops led by Major General John Pope.

Stonewall Jackson's forces moved north to attack Pope's supply base at Manassas. Jackson's troops marched 50 miles in two days and were then joined by the rest of Lee's army. On August 29, 1862, Pope attacked the approaching Confederates and started the Second Battle of Bull Run. The battle ended in a Confederate victory. Richmond was no longer threatened. Indeed, the situation of the two sides was completely reversed. Lee and the Confederates now stood only 20 miles from Washington, D.C.

The Battle of Antietam

Following these Southern victories, Confederate president **Jefferson Davis** ordered Lee to launch an offensive into Maryland, northwest of

Wounded soldiers at a military hospital at Alexandria, Virginia.

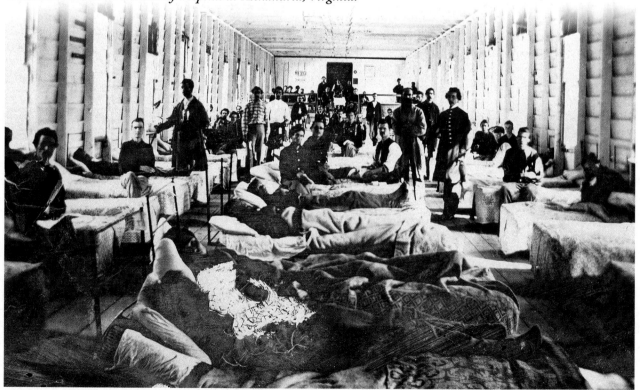

Washington. He hoped another victory would win aid from Great Britain and France. Lee also issued a proclamation urging the people of Maryland to join the Confederacy, but he received no response.

As Lee's army marched into Maryland in September 1862, McClellan and 80,000 Union troops moved slowly after them. On September 13 the North had an extraordinary piece of good luck. In a field near Frederick, Maryland, two Union soldiers found a copy of Lee's orders for his army wrapped around three cigars. The bundle had probably been dropped by a Southern officer.

Now McClellan knew exactly what Lee planned to do. He also learned that Lee's army was divided into four parts. This provided McClellan with an opportunity to overwhelm Lee's army one piece at a time.

Once again, McClellan was overly cautious. He waited four days before he decided to attack the Confederates. This enabled Lee to gather most of his forces together near Sharpsburg, Maryland, along the Antietam Creek.

The Union and the Confederate armies clashed on September 17 in the **Battle of Antietam.** It was the single bloodiest day of the entire war. A Union officer wrote that

66In the time that I am writing, every stalk of corn in [cornfields to the north] was cut as closely as could have been with a knife, and the slain lay in rows precisely as they had stood in their ranks a few minutes before.99

By the time the fighting ended, close to 6,000 Union and Confederate soldiers lay dead or dying, and another 17,000 were seriously wounded. Although both armies suffered heavy losses, neither was destroyed.

The day after the battle, Lee withdrew to Virginia. The Confederate retreat allowed the Union troops to claim victory. However, McClellan, who had been ordered by President Lincoln to "destroy the rebel army," did not pursue the Confederate troops. The president, disgusted with McClellan's failure to follow up his victory, removed McClellan from his command in November. Lincoln placed General **Ambrose Burnside** in command.

Antietam had a profound impact on the war. The Army of the Potomac finally gained some confidence, having forced Lee and his soldiers back south. More important, the battle marked a major change in Northern war aims. President Lincoln used the battle to take action against slavery.

Reading Check **Summarizing** What was the outcome of the Seven Days' Battles?

SECTION 2 ASSESSMENT

Checking for Understanding

1. **Key Terms** Use each of these terms in a sentence that will help explain its meaning: blockade runner, ironclad, casualty.
2. **Reviewing Facts** Explain why the North wanted to blockade the South.

Reviewing Themes

3. **Geography and History** What was the North's main goal in the western campaign?

Critical Thinking

4. **Analyzing Information** Why was Union general McClellan not effective as a military commander?
5. **Drawing Conclusions** Why was control of the Mississippi River important? Use a web like the one shown here.

Control of the Mississippi River

Analyzing Visuals

6. **Geography Skills** Study the map on page 470. Who claimed victory at the First Battle of Bull Run? When was the Battle of Shiloh fought?

Interdisciplinary Activity

Art Draw a cartoon that would accompany a front-page newspaper story describing the battle between the *Merrimack* and the *Monitor.*

SECTION 3 A Call for Freedom

Guide to Reading

Main Idea
The Civil War provided opportunities for African Americans to contribute to the war effort.

Key Terms
emancipate, ratify

Reading Strategy
Classifying Information As you read the section, complete a table like the one shown describing what the Emancipation Proclamation and the Thirteenth Amendment to the Constitution were meant to accomplish.

	Goal
Emancipation Proclamation	
Thirteenth Amendment	

Read to Learn
• why Lincoln issued the Emancipation Proclamation.
• what role African Americans played in the Civil War.

Section Theme
Groups and Institutions The North's main goal from the start of the war was to preserve the Union, not to abolish slavery.

Preview of Events

◆1862   ◆1863   ◆1864   ◆1865

1862
African Americans allowed to serve in the Union army

January 1863
Lincoln signs the Emancipation Proclamation

July 1863
Nearly half of the 54th Massachusetts Regiment is wiped out

1865
Thirteenth Amendment is ratified

Lincoln portrait, by artist Peter Baumgras

AN American Story

President Lincoln shook many hands on New Year's Day of 1863, as a reception was held to commemorate the official signing of the Emancipation Proclamation. Diplomats, cabinet members, and army officers filed past the president, and when he finally left the reception he noted that his arm was very stiff. As the document was presented, Lincoln remarked, "Now, this signature is one that will be closely examined and if they find my hand trembled, they will say 'he had some compunctions [second thoughts].' But, any way, it is going to be done!"

Emancipation

From the start of the war through the brutal Battle of Antietam, the Northerners' main goal was to preserve the Union rather than to destroy slavery. Abolitionists did not control the North, or even the Republican Party. Abraham Lincoln and other Republican leaders insisted on many occasions that they would act only to prevent the expansion of slavery.

CHAPTER 16   The Civil War   **473**

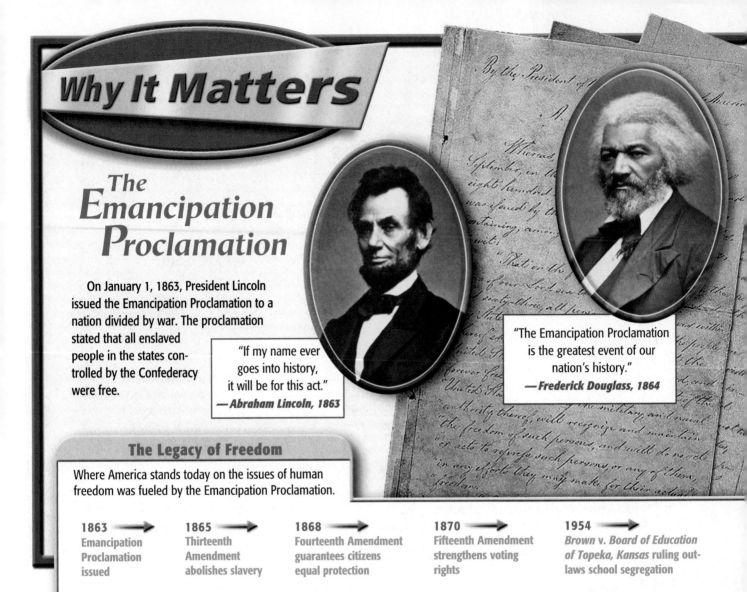

Why It Matters

The Emancipation Proclamation

On January 1, 1863, President Lincoln issued the Emancipation Proclamation to a nation divided by war. The proclamation stated that all enslaved people in the states controlled by the Confederacy were free.

> "If my name ever goes into history, it will be for this act."
> — *Abraham Lincoln, 1863*

> "The Emancipation Proclamation is the greatest event of our nation's history."
> — *Frederick Douglass, 1864*

The Legacy of Freedom

Where America stands today on the issues of human freedom was fueled by the Emancipation Proclamation.

1863	1865	1868	1870	1954
Emancipation Proclamation issued	Thirteenth Amendment abolishes slavery	Fourteenth Amendment guarantees citizens equal protection	Fifteenth Amendment strengthens voting rights	*Brown* v. *Board of Education of Topeka, Kansas* ruling outlaws school segregation

Although Lincoln considered slavery immoral, he hesitated to move against slavery because of the border states. Lincoln knew that making an issue of slavery would divide the people and make the war less popular. In August 1862, Abraham Lincoln responded to pressure to declare an end to slavery.

> 66 If I could save the Union without freeing *any* slave, I would do it; and if I could save it by freeing *all* the slaves, I would do it; and if I could save it by freeing some and leaving others alone, I would also do that. 99

That was his official position. His personal wish was "that all men everywhere could be free."

As the war went on, attitudes toward slavery began to change. More Northerners believed that slavery was helping the war effort in the South. Enslaved people in the Confederacy raised crops used to feed the armies and did the heavy work in the trenches at the army camps. In the North's view, anything that weakened slavery struck a blow against the Confederacy.

As early as May 1861, some African Americans in the South escaped slavery by going into territory held by the Union army. In 1861 and 1862, Congress passed laws that freed enslaved people who were held by those active in the rebellion against the Union.

Citizenship

The Emancipation Proclamation

Lincoln was keenly aware of the shift in public opinion. He also knew that striking a blow against slavery would make Britain and France

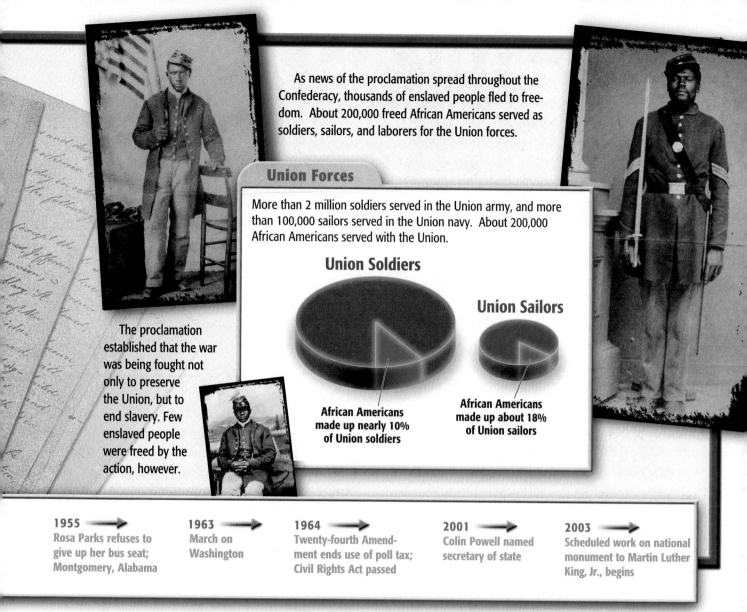

As news of the proclamation spread throughout the Confederacy, thousands of enslaved people fled to freedom. About 200,000 freed African Americans served as soldiers, sailors, and laborers for the Union forces.

The proclamation established that the war was being fought not only to preserve the Union, but to end slavery. Few enslaved people were freed by the action, however.

Union Forces

More than 2 million soldiers served in the Union army, and more than 100,000 sailors served in the Union navy. About 200,000 African Americans served with the Union.

Union Soldiers

Union Sailors

African Americans made up nearly 10% of Union soldiers

African Americans made up about 18% of Union sailors

1955 Rosa Parks refuses to give up her bus seat; Montgomery, Alabama

1963 March on Washington

1964 Twenty-fourth Amendment ends use of poll tax; Civil Rights Act passed

2001 Colin Powell named secretary of state

2003 Scheduled work on national monument to Martin Luther King, Jr., begins

less likely to aid the South. Moreover, Lincoln became convinced that slavery helped the South continue fighting. Every enslaved person who worked enabled a white Southerner to fight in the Confederate army.

Lincoln also had political reasons for taking action on slavery. He believed it was important that the president rather than the antislavery Republicans in Congress make the decision on ending slavery. Lincoln told the members of his cabinet, "I must do the best I can, and bear the responsibility."

By the summer of 1862, Lincoln had decided to emancipate—or free—all enslaved African Americans in the South. He waited for the right moment so that he would not appear to be acting in desperation when the North seemed to be losing the war. On September 22, 1862, five days

after the Union forces turned back the Confederate troops at the Battle of Antietam, Lincoln announced his plan to issue an order freeing all enslaved people in the Confederacy. On January 1, 1863, Lincoln signed the **Emancipation Proclamation,** which said that

66...all persons held as slaves within any state...in rebellion against the United States, shall be then, thenceforward, and forever free. 99

Effects of the Proclamation

Because the Emancipation Proclamation applied only to areas that the Confederacy controlled, it did not actually free anyone. Lincoln knew, however, that many enslaved people would hear about the proclamation. He hoped

Nearly 200,000 African Americans joined Union forces.

that knowledge of it would encourage them to run away from their slaveholders. Even before the Emancipation Proclamation, some 100,000 African Americans had left slavery for the safety of Union lines. 📖 *(See page 990 of the Appendix for the text of the Emancipation Proclamation.)*

Despite the limitations of the Emancipation Proclamation, African Americans in the North greeted it joyfully. On the day it was signed, a crowd of African Americans gathered at the White House to cheer the president. Frederick Douglass wrote, "We shout for joy that we live to record this righteous decree."

The proclamation had the desired effect in Europe as well. The Confederacy had been seeking support from its trading partners, Britain and France. However, the British took a strong position against slavery. Once Lincoln proclaimed emancipation, Britain and France decided to withhold recognition of the Confederacy.

In 1864 Republican leaders in Congress prepared a constitutional amendment to abolish slavery in the United States. In 1865 Congress passed the **Thirteenth Amendment,** which was ratified, or approved, the same year by states loyal to the Union. It was this amendment that truly freed enslaved Americans. 📖 *(See page 246 for the complete text of the Thirteenth Amendment.)*

✓**Reading Check** **Explaining** What did the Thirteenth Amendment do?

African Americans in the War

Early in the war, Lincoln opposed enlisting African Americans as soldiers. The Emancipation Proclamation announced Lincoln's decision to permit African Americans to join the Union army. In the South, as well as in the North, the Civil War was changing the lives of all African Americans.

In the South

When the war began, over 3.5 million enslaved people lived in the Confederacy. Making up more than 30 percent of the region's population and the bulk of its workforce, enslaved workers labored on plantations and in vital iron, salt, and lead mines. Some worked as nurses in military hospitals and cooks in the army. By the end of the war, about one-sixth of the enslaved population had fled to areas controlled by Union armies.

The possibility of a slave rebellion terrified white Southerners. For this reason most Southerners refused to use African Americans as soldiers—for then they would be given weapons.

Near the end of the war, however, the Confederate military became desperate. Robert E. Lee and some others supported using African Americans as soldiers and believed that those who fought should be freed. The Confederate Congress passed a law in 1865 to enlist enslaved people, although the law did not include automatic freedom. The war ended before any regiments could be organized.

Helping the North

The story was different in the North. At the start of the war, African Americans were not permitted to serve as soldiers in the Union army. This disappointed many free African Americans who had volunteered to fight for the Union.

Yet African Americans who wished to help the war effort found ways to do so. Although the army would not accept them, the Union navy did. African Americans who had escaped slavery often proved to be especially useful as guides and spies because of their knowledge of the South. Some women, such as **Harriet Tubman,** who had helped hundreds escape slavery by way of the Underground Railroad, repeatedly spied behind Confederate lines.

In 1862 Congress passed a law allowing African Americans to serve in the Union army. As a result both free African Americans and those who had escaped slavery began enlisting. In the Emancipation Proclamation, Lincoln supported the use of African American soldiers, and more African Americans began enlisting.

By the end of the war, African American volunteers made up nearly 10 percent of the Union army and about 18 percent of the navy. In all, nearly 200,000 African Americans served. About 37,000 lost their lives defending the Union. By becoming soldiers, African Americans were taking an important step toward securing civil rights.

African American Soldiers

African American soldiers were organized into regiments separate from the rest of the Union army. Most commanding officers of these regiments were white. African Americans received lower pay than white soldiers at first, but protests led to equal pay in 1864.

One of the most famous African American regiments was the **54th Massachusetts,** led by white abolitionists. On July 18, 1863, the 54th spearheaded an attack on a Confederate fortification near Charleston, South Carolina. Under heavy fire, the troops battled their way to the top of the fort. The Confederates drove them back with heavy fire. Nearly half of the 54th were wounded, captured, or killed. Their bravery won respect for African American troops.

Lincoln's political opponents criticized the use of African American soldiers. Lincoln replied by quoting General Grant, who had written to Lincoln that "[they] will make good soldiers and taking them from the enemy weakens him in the same proportion they strengthen us."

Many white Southerners, outraged by African American soldiers, threatened to execute any they captured. In a few instances, this threat was carried out. However, enslaved workers were overjoyed when they saw that the Union army included African American soldiers. As one African American regiment entered Wilmington, North Carolina, a soldier wrote, "Men and women, old and young, were running throughout the streets, shouting and praising God. We could then truly see what we have been fighting for."

✓ **Reading Check** **Comparing** How were African American soldiers treated differently than white soldiers?

SECTION 3 ASSESSMENT

Checking for Understanding

1. **Key Terms** Use the vocabulary terms that follow to write a paragraph about the Thirteenth Amendment: emancipate, ratify.
2. **Reviewing Facts** Summarize President Lincoln's reasons for issuing the Emancipation Proclamation.

Reviewing Themes

3. **Groups and Institutions** How did African Americans help the war effort in the North? What roles did they play in the South?

Critical Thinking

4. **Comparing** How did President Lincoln's political stand on slavery differ from his personal stand during the war?
5. **Determining Cause and Effect** Re-create the diagram below and list the factors that caused Lincoln to change his war goals to include freeing enslaved persons.

The Emancipation Proclamation

Analyzing Visuals

6. **Picturing History** Study the pictures of the African American soldiers on pages 475 and 476. Do you think that these soldiers have fought in battle? Explain your reasoning.

Interdisciplinary Activity

Citizenship It is 1865 and you have heard about the passage of the Thirteenth Amendment. Using material, thread, beads, and/or felt letters, create a banner that you anticipate carrying in a parade after the Civil War is over.

Life During the Civil War

Main Idea
Civilians as well as soldiers had an impact on the war effort.

Key Terms
habeas corpus, draft, bounty, greenback, inflation

Reading Strategy
Classifying Information As you read the section, complete a table like the one shown by describing the roles of these individuals during the war.

	Role
Loretta Janeta Velázquez	
Dorothea Dix	
Clara Barton	

Read to Learn
• what life was like for the soldiers.
• what role women played in the war.
• how the war affected the economies of the North and the South.

Section Themes
Economic Factors The Civil War strained the Northern and Southern economies.

Preview of Events

♦1861	♦1862	♦1863	♦1864

1861
Union Congress passes income tax

April 1862
Confederate Congress passes draft law

March 1863
The Union passes draft law

July 1863
Angry mobs oppose the draft in New York City

AN American Story

A soldier's life was not easy—whether in battle or in the mess tent! A Louisiana soldier wrote, "No soldier will forget his first horse-meat breakfast. It was comical to see the facial expression as they viewed the platters of hot steak fried in its own grease or the "chunk" of boiled mule as it floated in a bucket of "stew." However, there seemed to be perfect good humor as they one after the other 'tackled the job.'. . .Occasionally would some stalwart fellow throw back his head and utter a long and loud 'Ye-ha, ye-ha, yehaw!' in imitation of a . . . mule."

Union soldier and family, 1861

The Lives of Soldiers

In both the North and the South, civilians and soldiers suffered terrible hardships and faced new challenges. In touching letters to their families and friends at home, soldiers described what they saw and how they felt—their boredom, discomfort, sickness, fear, and horror.

At the start of the war, men in both the North and the South rushed to volunteer for the armies. Their enthusiasm did not last.

Most of the time the soldiers lived in camps. Camp life had its pleasant moments of songs, stories, letters from home, and baseball games. Often, however, a soldier's life was dull, a routine of drills, bad food, marches, and rain.

During lulls between battles, Confederate and Union soldiers sometimes forgot that they were enemies. A Southern private described a Fourth of July on the front lines in 1862:

66 Our boys and Yanks made a bargain not to fire at each other . . . and talked over the fight, and traded tobacco and coffee and newspaper as peacefully and kindly as if they had not been engaged . . . in butchering one another. 99

The Reality of War

In spite of fleeting moments of calm, the reality of war was never far away. Both sides suffered terrible losses. The new rifles used during the Civil War fired with greater accuracy than the muskets of earlier wars.

Medical facilities were overwhelmed by the thousands of casualties in each battle. After the Battle of Shiloh, many wounded soldiers lay in the rain for more than 24 hours waiting for medical treatment. A Union soldier recalled, "Many had died there, and others were in the last agonies as we passed. Their groans and cries were heart-rending."

Faced with such horrors, many men deserted. About one of every 11 Union soldiers and one of every 8 Confederates ran away because of fear, hunger, or sickness.

Rebel soldiers suffered from a lack of food and supplies. One reason for Lee's invasion of Maryland in 1862 was to allow his army to feed off Maryland crops. A woman who saw the Confederates march to Antietam recalled the "gaunt starvation that looked from their cavernous eyes."

✓ **Reading Check** **Explaining** Why did many soldiers desert from the armies?

Women and the War

Many Northern and Southern women took on new responsibilities during the war. They became teachers, office workers, salesclerks, and government workers. They worked in factories

Picturing **History**

Some paintings offered an idealized picture of the Civil War. Photographs provided a chilling account of life—and death—at the front lines. **In what ways might photographs have affected Americans' view of the war in a way that paintings did not?**

People In History

Clara Barton 1821–1921

When the Civil War began, Clara Barton, a U.S. Patent Office clerk, began collecting provisions for the Union army. In 1862 she began to deliver supplies directly to the front and to tend to the wounded and dying during battle.

Arriving at Antietam, Barton watched as surgeons dressed the soldiers' wounds with cornhusks because they did not have bandages. Barton was able to give the doctors a wagonload of bandages and other medical supplies. As the battle raged around her, Barton comforted the wounded and helped the doctors with their work.

As night neared, the medical staff had trouble working. From her supply wagon, Barton fetched lanterns and the doctors went back to work.

At Antietam and many other battles, Barton showed courage on the battlefield and gave aid to many. In 1881 Barton organized the American Red Cross and served as its first president for more than 20 years.

---

and managed farms. They also suffered the loss of husbands, fathers, sons, and brothers. As **Mary Chesnut** of South Carolina wrote:

> 66 Does anyone wonder [why] so many women die? Grief and constant anxiety kill nearly as many women at home as men are killed on the battle-field. 99

Women performed many jobs that helped the soldiers and the armies. They rolled bandages, wove blankets, and made ammunition. Many women collected food, clothing, and medicine to distribute to the troops. They also raised money for supplies.

Life at Home

For the most part, Northerners saw the war from a distance, since most of the battles took place in the South. News from the battlefront and letters home from the soldiers kept the war in people's minds.

Almost every woman who stayed at home was touched in some way by the war. But while everyday life in the North suffered little disruption, life in the South was dramatically changed. The fighting and the ever-tightening blockade disrupted everyday life. Those who lived in the paths of marching armies lost crops and homes. As one Southerner noted: the South had depended upon the outside world "for everything from a hairpin to a toothpick, and from a cradle to a coffin." As the war dragged on, shortages became more commonplace.

The South ran out of almost everything. Shortages in feed for animals and salt for curing meant that little meat was available. Shortages in meat were matched by shortages in clothing, medicine, and even shelter.

Spies

Some women were spies. While Harriet Tubman spied for the North, **Rose O'Neal Greenhow** entertained Union leaders in Washington, D.C., picking up information about Union plans that she passed to the South. Greenhow was caught, convicted of treason, and exiled.

Belle Boyd, of Front Royal, Virginia, informed Confederate generals of Union army movements in the Shenandoah Valley. Some women disguised themselves as men and became soldiers. **Loretta Janeta Velázquez** fought for the South at the First Battle of Bull Run and at Shiloh. Later she became a Confederate spy.

Treating the Sick and Wounded

In the Civil War, for the first time, thousands of women served as nurses. At first many doctors did not want women nurses on the grounds that women were too delicate for such work. Men also disapproved of women doing what was considered male work, and felt it was improper for women to tend the bodies of unknown men.

Strong-minded women disregarded these objections. In the North **Dorothea Dix** organized large numbers of women to serve as military nurses. Another Northerner, **Clara Barton,** became famous for her work with wounded soldiers. In the South **Sally Tompkins** established a hospital for soldiers in Richmond, Virginia.

Nursing was hard work. Kate Cummings of Alabama, who nursed the wounded in Corinth after the Battle of Shiloh, wrote, "Nothing that I had ever heard or read had given me the faintest idea of the horrors witnessed here." Yet women did a remarkable job in the war.

✓ Reading Check **Describing** What role did Sally Tompkins play in the war effort?

Opposition to the War

The war efforts of the Union and the Confederate governments faced opposition. Politicians objected to wartime policies, and ordinary citizens protested the way the war affected their lives.

When the war began, Northern Democrats split into two groups. One group supported most of Lincoln's wartime policies. The other, the "Peace Democrats," favored negotiating with the Confederacy. The Peace Democrats warned that continuing the war would lead to "terrible social change and revolution." They also appealed to racist feelings among Northern whites. Republican newspapers called the Peace Democrats "Copperheads." When Union armies fared poorly, support for the Copperheads rose.

Some Republicans suspected Copperheads of aiding the Confederates. The president ordered the arrest of anyone interfering with the war effort, such as discouraging men from enlisting in the army. Several times Lincoln suspended the right of habeas corpus, which guarantees accused individuals the right to a hearing before being jailed. Lincoln defended his actions, asking "Must I shoot a simple-minded soldier boy who deserts while I must not touch a hair of a wily agitator who induces him to desert?"

Enlistments Decline

As the war dragged on, the number of volunteers declined. Enlisting enough soldiers became a problem, and both the Confederacy and the Union tried new measures.

In April 1862, the Confederate Congress passed a draft law that required men between ages 18 and 35 to serve in the army for three years. A person could avoid the draft by hiring a

Picturing **History**

This 1862 photo shows a Union soldier with his family at the front near Washington, D.C. Most soldiers on both sides, however, faced long separations from their families. **What other hardships did Civil War soldiers face?**

substitute. Later, Congress exempted one white man on every plantation with 20 or more enslaved people. This led ordinary people to complain of "a rich man's war but a poor man's fight." In reality people from all levels of society served in both armies.

Union states encouraged enlistment by offering bounties—payments to encourage volunteers. In March 1863, when this system failed, the North turned to a draft. All men from age 20 to 45 had to register, and the army drew the soldiers it needed from this pool of names. A person could avoid the draft by hiring a substitute or by paying the government $300.

Draft laws aroused opposition, with protests erupting into riots in several Northern cities. The worst disturbance took place in New York City in July 1863. Angry mobs, opposed to the draft and to fighting to free African Americans, went on a rampage of burning, looting, and killing. After four days of terror, more than 100 people were dead. Troops from the Army of the Potomac had to be rushed in to end the rioting.

No disturbance as severe took place in the South, but many opposed the draft. The strong opposition led Jefferson Davis, the president of the Confederacy, to proclaim military law and suspend habeas corpus as Lincoln had done early in the war. Davis's action outraged Southerners who feared that they would lose the liberties for which they had gone to war.

✓ Reading Check **Examining** Why did the governments institute a draft?

$ Economics

War and the Economy

The Civil War strained the Northern and the Southern economies. The North, with its greater resources, was better able to cope with wartime demands than the South was.

TECHNOLOGY & History

Civil War Camera

Photographer Mathew Brady and his many assistants recorded the camps, lives, and deaths of soldiers in more than 10,000 photos. *What is the biggest difference between this camera and a more modern one?*

1 The photographer looks at the subject through a **glass plate.**

2 A **plate holder** is inserted into the back panel.

3 The photographer opens the **lens.** The lens creates a reversed, upside-down image on the "wet" plate.

4 The **body** of the camera protects the wet plate.

The plate holder and the exposed wet plate are removed from the back panel, then developed into a negative in the photographer's "traveling" **darkroom.**

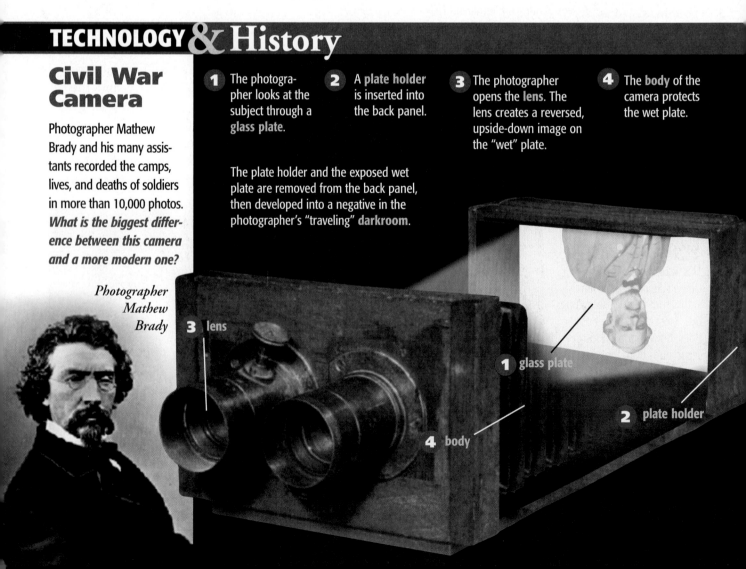

Photographer Mathew Brady

3 lens

1 glass plate

4 body

2 plate holder

Both the Union and the Confederacy financed the war by borrowing money, increasing taxes, and printing paper money. The North borrowed more than $2 billion, mainly by selling war bonds that promised high interest. The South borrowed more than $700 million. It issued so many bonds that people stopped buying them.

Both sides imposed new taxes as well. The Union passed an income tax in 1861. When Southern states did not provide sufficient funds, the Confederacy also imposed an income tax.

Because neither borrowing nor taxes raised enough money, both sides began printing paper money. Northern money was called greenbacks because of its color. The Confederacy also issued paper money—several times the amount printed in the North.

The North Prospers

During the war prices rose faster than wages in the North. This inflation—a general increase in prices—caused great hardship for working people. Overall, however, the Northern economy boomed. The need for a steady supply of food for Union troops helped farmers prosper.

Factory production grew as manufacturers responded to the demands of war. The army needed many items, from guns and ammunition to shoes and uniforms. Greater use of machinery and the standardization of parts made it possible for the North to produce what it needed.

Economic Troubles in the South

The Civil War is often called the first "modern" war because it required the total commitment of resources. Such a war has an impact on every part of life. However, the impact was more devastating on the South than on the North.

The South struggled to carry out its war effort. Its government encouraged factories to supply arms and ammunition, but the South lacked the industry to provide other necessities.

The economy of the South suffered far more than that of the North. Because most fighting occurred in the South, Southern farmland was overrun and rail lines were torn up. By the end of the war, large portions of the South lay in ruins and thousands of people were homeless.

The North's blockade of Southern ports caused severe shortages of essential goods. A scarcity of food led to riots in Atlanta, Richmond, and other cities. Inflation, too, was much worse in the South. During the course of the war, prices rose 9,000 percent—compared to a rise of 80 percent in the North.

These conditions affected soldiers. Worries about their families caused many men to desert. A Mississippi soldier who overstayed his leave to help his family wrote the governor: "We are poor men and are willing to defend our country but our families [come] first."

 **Reading Check** **Explaining** What is inflation?

SECTION 4 ASSESSMENT

Checking for Understanding

1. **Key Terms** Use each of these terms in a complete sentence that will help explain its meaning: habeas corpus, draft, bounty, greenback, inflation.
2. **Reviewing Facts** Why was life on the home front more difficult for Southerners?

Reviewing Themes

3. **Economic Factors** How did the war affect the economy of the South?

Critical Thinking

4. **Making Inferences** Why do you think President Lincoln believed the Copperheads were a threat to the Union war effort?
5. **Analyzing Information** Describe three ways that both the North and South raised money for the war. Use a chart like the one shown below.

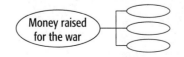
Money raised for the war

Analyzing Visuals

6. **Picturing History** Study the photograph of the family on page 481. Why do you think some families accompanied the armies in the field?

Interdisciplinary Activity

Economics List three sectors of the economy that welcomed women during the Civil War. Describe the jobs women held and the contributions they made.

Study & Writing
SKILLBUILDER

Taking Notes

Why Learn This Skill?

One of the best ways to remember something is to write it down. Taking notes—writing down information in a brief and orderly form—not only helps you remember, but it also makes your studying easier.

Learning the Skill

There are several styles of note taking, but all explain and put information in a logical order. When you are taking notes, it will help to keep in mind these guidelines:

Identify the subject and write it at the top of the page. In your text, for example, look at the chapter title, section title, and other headings.

Select specific information for your notes. For example, anything your teacher writes on the chalkboard or shows you from a transparency should be included. If your teacher emphasizes a point or spends a large amount of time on a topic, this is also a clue to its importance.

Paraphrase the information. That means putting the information in your own words rather than trying to take it down word for word. Doing so helps you think about what the speaker or writer means.

To save time, you might want to develop different strategies. One way is to create a personal "shorthand." For example, use symbols, arrows, or rough drawings: "+" for "and." Practice your shorthand in all of your classes.

Write legible and neat notes so that you will be able to understand them when you read them again.

Practicing the Skill

Review the guidelines for taking notes. Then read Section 5, entitled "The Way to Victory." After you have carefully read the section, follow the guidelines and create shorthand notes for the subsection entitled "The Tide of War Turns," which begins on page 486.

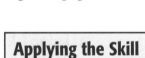

Applying the Skill

Taking Notes Scan a local newspaper for a short editorial or article about your local government. Take notes by using shorthand or by creating an outline. Summarize the article, using only your notes.

 Glencoe's **Skillbuilder Interactive Workbook CD-ROM, Level 1,** provides instruction and practice in key social studies skills.

SECTION 5 The Way to Victory

Guide to Reading

Main Idea
After four years of war that claimed the lives of more than 600,000 Americans, the Northern forces defeated the Southern forces.

Key Terms
entrenched, total war

Reading Strategy
Organizing Information Use a web like the one shown to describe the strategy Grant adopted to defeat the Confederacy.

Grant's strategy

Read to Learn
• what battles turned the tide of the war in 1863.
• what events led the South to surrender in 1865.

Section Theme
Individual Action Brave soldiers from both the North and the South fought gallantly during the Civil War.

Preview of Events

♦1862 ———— ♦1863 ———— ♦1864 ———— ♦1865

December 1862
Lee wins the Battle of Fredericksburg

July 1863
Battle of Gettysburg

March 1864
Grant takes over Union command

April 1865
Lee surrenders to Grant

Confederate soldier

AN American Story

"My shoes are gone; my clothes are almost gone. I'm weary, I'm sick, I'm hungry. My family have been killed or scattered, and may be now wandering helpless and unprotected in a strange country. And I have suffered all this for my country. I love my country. I would die—yes, I would die willingly because I love my country. But if this war is ever over, I'll…[n]ever love another country!" A Confederate soldier expressed these thoughts during difficult times in 1863.

Southern Victories

Gone were the parades and masses of volunteers, the fancy uniforms and optimism of the first years of the war. From 1862 until 1865, the soldiers and civilians faced a grim conflict marked by death, destruction, and wrenching change. What endured on each side was a fierce dedication to its own cause.

The winter of 1862–1863 saw gloom in the North and hope in the South. Robert E. Lee's **Army of Northern Virginia** seemed unbeatable. Lee's grasp of strategy made him more than a match for weak Union generals.

Fredericksburg and Chancellorsville

Lee needed little skill to win the **Battle of Fredericksburg.** On December 13, 1862, Union general **Ambrose Burnside** clashed with Lee near the Virginia town. Burnside had the larger army, but the Confederates were entrenched, or set up in a strong position, on a number of hills south of the town. Repeated attacks failed to overcome Lee's troops as thousands of Union soldiers fell on the hillside. Devastated by his failure, Burnside resigned his command and was replaced by General **Joseph Hooker.**

Hooker rebuilt the army and in early May 1863, launched a campaign against Lee. Before Hooker could mount a major attack, Lee struck at **Chancellorsville,** Virginia, a few miles west of Fredericksburg. Boldly dividing his troops for an assault on the Union forces, Lee won another victory—but it proved costly. The battle's heavy casualties included General Stonewall Jackson.

On May 2, Jackson and his troops attacked Union troops at dusk. One of the Confederate companies fired on Jackson's party by mistake, wounding the general in the left arm. Jackson's arm had to be amputated and he died a week later.

✓ **Reading Check** **Describing** At what Virginia town did Lee defeat Burnside's forces?

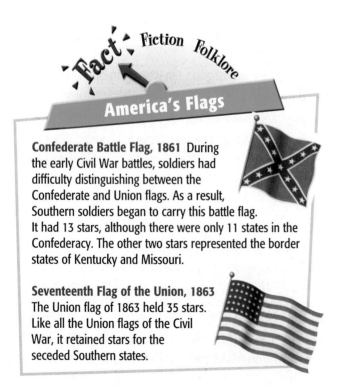

America's Flags

Confederate Battle Flag, 1861 During the early Civil War battles, soldiers had difficulty distinguishing between the Confederate and Union flags. As a result, Southern soldiers began to carry this battle flag. It had 13 stars, although there were only 11 states in the Confederacy. The other two stars represented the border states of Kentucky and Missouri.

Seventeenth Flag of the Union, 1863 The Union flag of 1863 held 35 stars. Like all the Union flags of the Civil War, it retained stars for the seceded Southern states.

The Tide of War Turns

Despite his own heavy losses, Lee decided to invade the North. Another victory—one on Northern soil—might persuade Britain and France to aid the Confederacy.

The Battle of Gettysburg

In June, Lee began moving north with an army of 75,000. Union general Hooker wanted to advance against Richmond, but Lincoln told him to attack Lee's army. When Hooker failed to do this, Lincoln replaced him with General **George Meade.** Meade's mission was to find and fight Lee's forces and to protect Washington and Baltimore from Confederate attack.

The two armies met by accident on July 1, 1863, near the small town of Gettysburg, Pennsylvania. The three-day **Battle of Gettysburg** began when Union cavalry surprised Rebel infantry raiding the town for shoes. Outnumbered, the Northerners fought desperately to hold the town before retreating to Cemetery Ridge, a line of hills south of Gettysburg. The next day the Rebels launched another assault, but a counterattack saved the Union position.

On the third and final day of battle, Lee decided to launch an attack, determined to "create a panic and virtually destroy the [Union] army."

This last attack, led by General George Pickett, is remembered as **Pickett's Charge.** About 14,000 Confederate soldiers advanced across about one-half mile of open ground toward the Union lines. They made easy targets for Union fire as they marched. Barely half of the Rebels returned from the charge. Lee knew the battle was lost. "It's all my fault," he told his troops as they retreated to Virginia.

Victory at Vicksburg

Meanwhile, a great battle was taking place at **Vicksburg, Mississippi.** Vicksburg stood on a high bluff above the Mississippi River. To gain control of the river, one of the North's major war goals, the Union needed to seize Vicksburg. For several months, Union forces under **Ulysses S. Grant** had laid siege to the town. Finally, on July 4, 1863, Vicksburg surrendered.

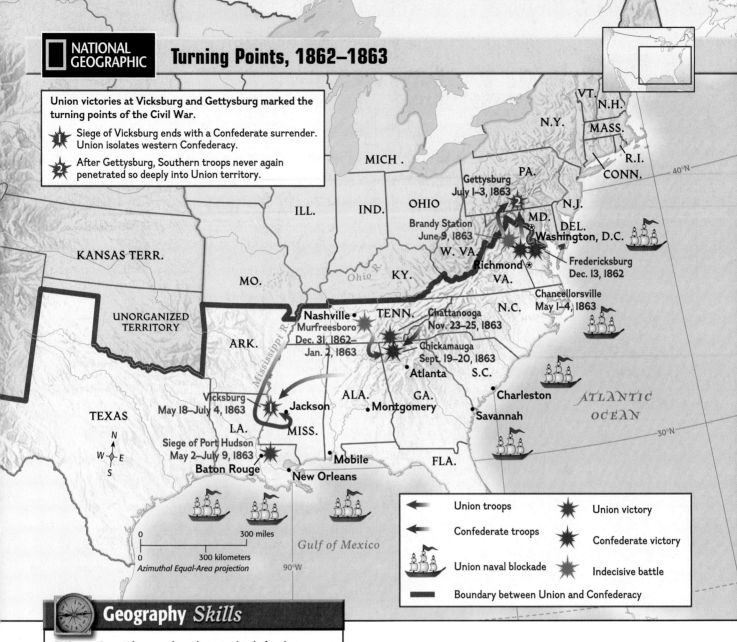

NATIONAL GEOGRAPHIC

Turning Points, 1862–1863

Union victories at Vicksburg and Gettysburg marked the turning points of the Civil War.

1. Siege of Vicksburg ends with a Confederate surrender. Union isolates western Confederacy.

2. After Gettysburg, Southern troops never again penetrated so deeply into Union territory.

Gettysburg July 1–3, 1863

Brandy Station June 9, 1863

Fredericksburg Dec. 13, 1862

Chancellorsville May 1–4, 1863

Nashville • **Murfreesboro** Dec. 31, 1862– Jan. 2, 1863

Chattanooga Nov. 23–25, 1863

Chickamauga Sept. 19–20, 1863

Atlanta

Vicksburg May 18–July 4, 1863

Jackson

Montgomery

Charleston

Savannah

Siege of Port Hudson May 2–July 9, 1863

Baton Rouge

Mobile

New Orleans

KANSAS TERR. • UNORGANIZED TERRITORY • TEXAS • MO. • ARK. • LA. • MISS. • ALA. • GA. • FLA. • ILL. • IND. • OHIO • KY. • TENN. • W. VA. • VA. • N.C. • S.C. • PA. • MD. • DEL. • N.J. • N.Y. • VT. • N.H. • MASS. • R.I. • CONN. • MICH. • Richmond • Washington, D.C.

Ohio R. • Mississippi R.

ATLANTIC OCEAN

Gulf of Mexico

0 — 300 miles
0 — 300 kilometers
Azimuthal Equal-Area projection

40°N · 30°N · 90°W

← Union troops
← Confederate troops
⚓ Union naval blockade
━ Boundary between Union and Confederacy
✦ Union victory
✦ Confederate victory
✦ Indecisive battle

Geography Skills

1. **Location** What was the only major battle fought on Union soil?

2. **Analyzing Information** Why was success at Vicksburg so important to the Union?

With the surrender of Vicksburg and then Port Hudson—a Confederate fort in Louisiana—the Union now held the entire Mississippi River. Texas, Louisiana, and Arkansas were sealed off from the Confederacy.

The Union victories at Gettysburg and Vicksburg marked a turning point in the war. They drove Lee's army out of Pennsylvania, secured the Mississippi as a Union highway, and cut the South in two. Nevertheless, the South still had troops and a will to fight. The war would continue for two more terrible years.

Lincoln at Gettysburg

On November 19, 1863, at a ceremony dedicating a cemetery at Gettysburg, scholar Edward Everett spoke for two hours. Then in a two-minute speech, called the **Gettysburg Address,** President Lincoln beautifully expressed what the war had come to mean:

66 It is for us the living . . . to be here dedicated to the great task remaining before us . . . that these dead shall not have died in vain— that this nation, under God, shall have a new birth of freedom—and that government of the people, by the people, for the people shall not perish from the earth. 99

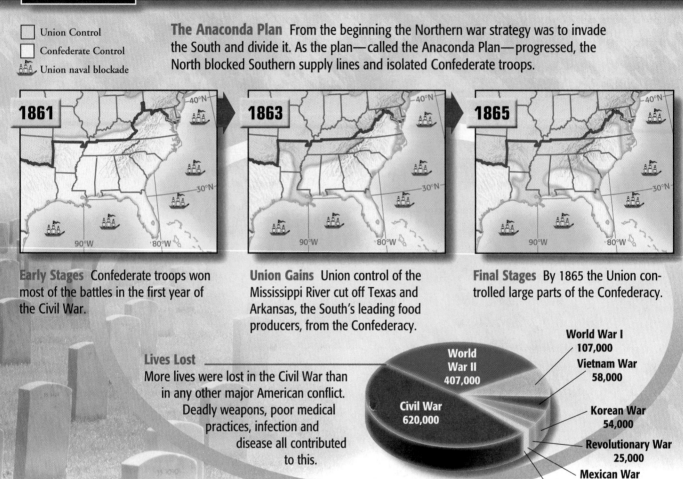

☐ Union Control
☐ Confederate Control
🚢 Union naval blockade

The Anaconda Plan From the beginning the Northern war strategy was to invade the South and divide it. As the plan—called the Anaconda Plan—progressed, the North blocked Southern supply lines and isolated Confederate troops.

1861

1863

1865

Early Stages Confederate troops won most of the battles in the first year of the Civil War.

Union Gains Union control of the Mississippi River cut off Texas and Arkansas, the South's leading food producers, from the Confederacy.

Final Stages By 1865 the Union controlled large parts of the Confederacy.

Lives Lost
More lives were lost in the Civil War than in any other major American conflict. Deadly weapons, poor medical practices, infection and disease all contributed to this.

World War II 407,000
Civil War 620,000
World War I 107,000
Vietnam War 58,000
Korean War 54,000
Revolutionary War 25,000
Mexican War 13,000
Other major wars 5,000

The speech helped war-weary Americans look beyond the images of the battlefield and focus on their shared ideals. 📖 *(See page 991 of the Appendix for the entire text of the Gettysburg Address.)*

✓ **Reading Check** **Identifying** What battle victories gave the Union control of the Mississippi River?

Final Phases of the War

In November 1863, Grant and General **William Tecumseh Sherman** won an important victory at Chattanooga, Tennessee. Following the Northern triumphs at Vicksburg and Gettysburg, Chattanooga further weakened the Confederates. The following March, President Lincoln turned to Grant for help.

Ulysses S. Grant was small and unimpressive in appearance. His early army career was not impressive either, and in 1854 he had been forced to resign because of a drinking problem. When the war began, he rejoined the army. His victories in the West and his willingness to attack hard impressed President Lincoln. "I can't spare this man," the president said. "He fights." After the victory at Chattanooga, Lincoln named Grant commander of all the Union armies.

Grant devised a plan to attack the Confederacy on all fronts. The Army of the Potomac would try to crush Lee's army in Virginia. The western army, under Sherman, would advance to Atlanta, Georgia, and crush the Confederate forces in the Deep South. If the plan succeeded, they would destroy the Confederacy.

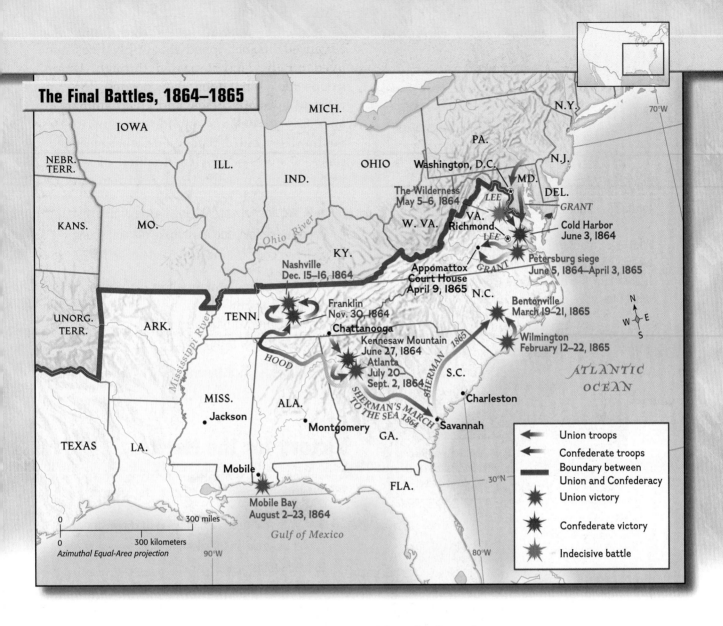

The Final Battles, 1864–1865

The Wilderness May 5–6, 1864

Cold Harbor June 3, 1864

Petersburg siege June 5, 1864–April 3, 1865

Appomattox Court House April 9, 1865

Nashville Dec. 15–16, 1864

Franklin Nov. 30, 1864

Bentonville March 19–21, 1865

Wilmington February 12–22, 1865

Kennesaw Mountain June 27, 1864

Atlanta July 20–Sept. 2, 1864

Mobile Bay August 2–23, 1864

SHERMAN'S MARCH TO THE SEA 1864

0 — 300 miles
0 — 300 kilometers
Azimuthal Equal-Area projection

←	Union troops
←	Confederate troops
▬	Boundary between Union and Confederacy
✦	Union victory
✦	Confederate victory
✦	Indecisive battle

Grant soon put his strategy into effect. In May and June of 1864, Grant's army of 115,000 men smashed into Lee's 64,000 troops in a series of three battles near Richmond, Virginia—the Battles of the Wilderness, Spotsylvania Courthouse, and Cold Harbor. Each time, Confederate lines held, but each time Grant quickly resumed the attack.

The battles cost the North thousands of men. Critics called Grant a butcher, but he said, "I propose to fight it out on this line if it takes all summer." Lincoln supported Grant.

After Cold Harbor, Grant swung south of Richmond to attack **Petersburg,** an important railroad center. If it fell, Richmond would be cut off from the rest of the Confederacy. Grant's assault turned into a nine-month siege.

The Election of 1864

To the war-weary North, the events of the first half of 1864 were discouraging. Grant was stuck outside Richmond and Petersburg, and Sherman was stuck outside Atlanta. Sentiment for a negotiated peace grew. The Democrats wanted to make peace with the South, even though that might result in Confederate independence. Lincoln was determined to push for restoring the Union.

In the summer of 1864, Lincoln's chances for reelection did not look good. "I am going to be beaten and unless some great change takes place, badly beaten," he said.

Great changes did take place. In August, David Farragut led a Union fleet into **Mobile Bay**. The Union now controlled the Gulf of Mexico. In September, news arrived that Sherman

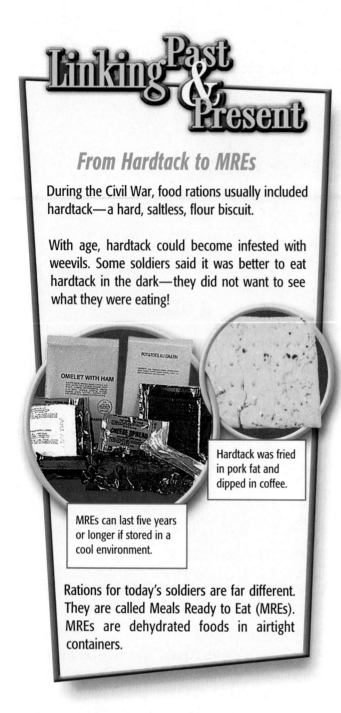

advanced, it abandoned its supply lines and lived off the land it passed through. Union troops took what food they needed, tore up railroad lines and fields, and killed animals in an effort to destroy anything useful to the South. They cut a path of destruction sometimes 50 miles wide. This method of waging war was known as total war. Sherman said:

> 66 We are not only fighting hostile armies, but a hostile people, and must make old and young, rich and poor, feel the hard hand of war. 99

After capturing Savannah in December, Sherman turned north. The army marched through South Carolina, devastating the state. Sherman planned to join Grant's forces in Virginia.

✓ **Reading Check** **Describing** What was the "march to the sea"?

Victory for the North

In his second Inaugural Address on March 4, 1865, Lincoln spoke of the coming peace:

> 66 With malice toward none, with charity for all . . . let us strive on to finish the work we are in, to bind up the nation's wounds . . . to do all which may achieve and cherish a just and lasting peace among ourselves and with all nations. 99

Throughout the fall and winter of 1864, Grant continued the siege of Petersburg. Lee and his troops defended the town, but sickness, hunger, casualties, and desertion weakened them. Finally, on April 2, 1865, the Confederate lines broke and Lee withdrew his troops.

Richmond fell the same day. Rebel troops, government officials, and many residents fled the Confederate capital. As they left, they set fire to much of the city to keep it from falling into Union hands.

On April 4 Lincoln visited Richmond and walked its streets. One elderly African American man approached the president, took off his hat, and bowed. Tearfully, he said, "May God bless you." Lincoln removed his own hat and bowed in return.

had captured Atlanta. Then in October, General Sheridan's Union forces completed a campaign that drove the Rebels out of the Shenandoah Valley in Virginia. With these victories the end of the war was in sight. Lincoln easily won reelection, taking 55 percent of the popular vote.

Total War

Leaving Atlanta in ruins, Sherman convinced Grant to let him try a bold plan. Sherman's army began the historic "march to the sea" to **Savannah, Georgia.** As the army

Surrender at Appomattox

Lee moved his army west of Richmond, hoping to link up with the small Confederate force that was trying to stop Sherman's advance. But the Union army blocked his escape route. Realizing the situation was hopeless, Lee said:

❝ There is nothing left for me to do but go and see General Grant, and I would rather die a thousand deaths. ❞

On April 9, 1865, Lee and his troops surrendered to Grant in a small Virginia village called **Appomattox Court House.** Grant's terms were generous. The Confederate soldiers had to lay down their arms, but then were free to go home. Grant allowed them to keep their horses so that they could, as he said, "put in a crop to carry themselves and their families through the next winter." Grant also ordered three days' worth of food sent to Lee's hungry troops.

Several days after Lee's surrender, the Confederate forces in North Carolina surrendered to General Sherman. Jefferson Davis, the president of the Confederacy, was captured in Georgia on May 10. The Civil War was over at last.

Results of the War

The Civil War was the most devastating conflict in American history. More than 600,000 soldiers died, and the war caused billions of dollars of damage, most of it in the South. The war also created bitter feelings among defeated Southerners that lasted for generations.

The war had other consequences as well. The North's victory saved the Union. The federal government was strengthened and was now clearly more powerful than the states. Finally, the war freed millions of African Americans. How the nation would treat these new citizens remained to be seen.

☑ **Reading Check** **Identifying** Where did General Lee surrender?

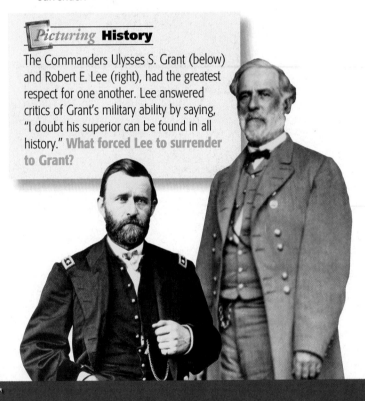

Picturing **History**
The Commanders Ulysses S. Grant (below) and Robert E. Lee (right), had the greatest respect for one another. Lee answered critics of Grant's military ability by saying, "I doubt his superior can be found in all history." **What forced Lee to surrender to Grant?**

SECTION 5 ASSESSMENT

Checking for Understanding

1. **Key Terms** Use the following terms in complete sentences that will help explain their meaning: entrenched, total war.
2. **Reviewing Facts** Identify the reasons that Gettysburg and Vicksburg were important battles.

Reviewing Themes

3. **Individual Action** What thoughts about peace did Lincoln express in his second Inaugural Address?

Critical Thinking

4. **Drawing Conclusions** How did the Union's victory strengthen the federal government?
5. **Analyzing Information** Use a chart like the one shown to explain the significance of each battle listed.

Battle	Importance
Gettysburg	
Vicksburg	
Mobile Bay	
Richmond	

Analyzing Visuals

6. **Geography Skills** Study the map of the final battles on page 489. In which directions did Sherman's army travel from Atlanta to Savannah and then to Bentonville?

Interdisciplinary Activity

Expository Writing Refer to Lincoln's Gettysburg Address on page 991. Write three paragraphs discussing Lincoln's ideas on freedom and the importance of saving the Union.

West Woods

Hagerstown Pike

Dunker Church

This is the area that is shown above.

Potomac River

Hagerstown Pike

Dunker Church

Bloody Lane

Union Headquarters

SHARPSBURG

Confederate Headquarters

Antietam Creek

0   1/2 mile

0   1/2 kilometer

Miller Cornfield

East Woods

ANTIETAM: THE BLOODIEST DAY

FOUGHT ON SEPTEMBER 17, 1862, the Battle of Antietam, or Sharpsburg, was the bloodiest day in American history, with over 23,000 soldiers killed or wounded. Antietam changed the course of the Civil War. McClellan's Union forces stopped Lee's invasion of the North and forced him on the defensive. This strategic victory encouraged Lincoln to issue the Emancipation Proclamation.

MORNING

The battle began at dawn when Union artillery fired on Stonewall Jackson's forces in Miller Cornfield north of town. Union troops attacked the Confederates north of Dunker Church. For three hours, the battle lines swept back and forth along the West and East Woods, the Cornfield, and along Hagerstown Pike.

MIDDAY

Union soldiers emerged from the East Woods and were turned back by the Confederates in the West Woods. Later, the Yankees advanced toward "Bloody Lane," a sunken farm road held by the Confederates just south of Dunker Church. The Confederates held their line until midday, when the fighting stopped briefly.

AFTERNOON

After much fighting, the Union troops crossed Antietam Creek and slowly drove the Confederate forces back toward Sharpsburg. Just when all hope seemed lost, Confederate forces arrived from Harpers Ferry and stopped the Union advance. The day ended in a standoff that halted Lee's march northward. The next day, Lee began his retreat along the Potomac River.

LEARNING *from* GEOGRAPHY

1. **How do you think Bloody Lane got its name?**
2. **Why do you think Lee retreated after the Battle of Antietam?**

493

Chapter Summary

The Civil War

Secession

1860
- South Carolina secedes from Union

1861
- Lincoln inaugurated
- Confederate States of America formed
- Fort Sumter falls—Civil War begins
- Confederate forces win at Bull Run

1862
- Union victorious at Shiloh
- Union captures New Orleans
- Union wins at Antietam
- Lee named commander of Confederate armies

1863
- Lincoln issues Emancipation Proclamation
- Lee's forces turn back at Gettysburg
- Vicksburg surrenders

1864
- Petersburg, Virginia, under siege
- Sherman captures Atlanta
- March to the sea begins
- Lincoln reelected president

1865
- Lee surrenders to Grant at Appomattox
- Lincoln assassinated
- Thirteenth Amendment abolishing slavery is ratified

Reconstruction

494

Reviewing Key Terms

Examine the pairs of words below. Then write a sentence explaining what each of the pairs has in common.

1. blockade, offensive
2. ironclad, blockade runner
3. border state, Union
4. draft, habeas corpus

Reviewing Key Facts

5. During what years was the Civil War fought?
6. What three advantages did the Confederate states have in the war?
7. Who were the presidents of the United States and of the Confederate States of America?
8. What role did Clara Barton play in the Civil War?
9. Why did the Union blockade Southern ports?
10. What was the outcome of the Battle of Gettysburg?
11. What did the Emancipation Proclamation state?
12. In what ways did African Americans contribute to the war efforts?
13. How did the Civil War hurt the South's economy?
14. What terms of surrender did Grant offer to Lee?

Critical Thinking

15. **Analyzing Themes: Government and Democracy** How did the people of western Virginia respond to Virginia's secession from the Union?
16. **Determining Cause and Effect** Why was controlling the Mississippi River vital to the North and the South?
17. **Analyzing Themes: Groups and Institutions** Why do you think many leaders called for African Americans to be allowed to fight in the Civil War?
18. **Making Inferences** Why do you think General Lee was such an effective military leader?
19. **Analyzing Information** Re-create the diagram below. Fill in the year for each event. Then explain the significance of each event.

Event	Year	Significance
Attack on Fort Sumter		
Monitor v. *Merrimack*		
Emancipation Proclamation issued		
Lincoln is reelected		
Appomattox Court House		

Geography and History Activity

Study the map below and answer the questions.

20. Along what ridge were the Union troops positioned?

21. Who led forces across Rock Creek?

22. What five Confederate commanders are shown?

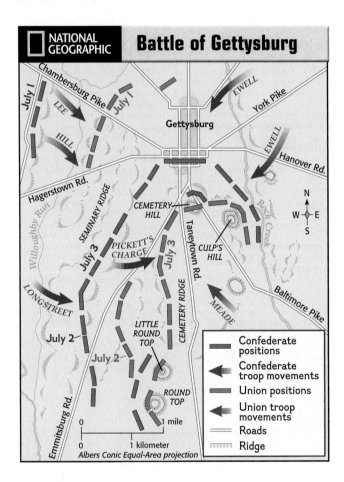

NATIONAL GEOGRAPHIC

Battle of Gettysburg

Chambersburg Pike

July 1

LEE

HILL

July 1

EWELL

York Pike

Gettysburg

EWELL

Hanover Rd.

Hagerstown Rd.

Willoughby Run

SEMINARY RIDGE

CEMETERY HILL

Taneytown Rd.

CULP'S HILL

Rock Creek

N
W—E
S

July 3

PICKETT'S CHARGE

July 3

LONGSTREET

CEMETERY RIDGE

MEADE

Baltimore Pike

LITTLE ROUND TOP

July 2

July 2

Emmitsburg Rd.

ROUND TOP

	Confederate positions
←	Confederate troop movements
	Union positions
←	Union troop movements
⟋⟋	Roads
⟋⟋	Ridge

0   1 mile
0   1 kilometer
Albers Conic Equal-Area projection

Practicing Skills

23. **Taking Notes** Review the guidelines for taking notes on page 484. Then reread Section 5 about the last years of the Civil War. Create a time line showing the dates of battles and other important events discussed in the section.

Technology Activity

24. **Using the Internet** Search the Internet for museums that specialize in Civil War artifacts and photo collections. Make a map showing the names and locations of these museums.

Self-Check Quiz
Visit taj.glencoe.com and click on **Chapter 16—Self-Check Quizzes** to prepare for the chapter test.

Citizenship Cooperative Activity

25. **Debating Issues** A writ of habeas corpus is a court order that guarantees a person who is arrested the right to appear before a judge in a court of law. During the Civil War, President Lincoln suspended habeas corpus. Do you think that action was justified? Debate the issue as a group, with one side supporting and one side criticizing Lincoln's actions.

Economics Activity

26. Economic differences had always existed between the North and the South. From your reading of Chapter 16, would you say that the North or the South was better equipped economically for war? Explain your reasoning.

Alternative Assessment

27. **Portfolio Writing Activity** To explain his reelection, Lincoln stated, "it is not best to swap horses while crossing the river." Write a paragraph that explains Lincoln's quotation and how it applied to him. Save your work for your portfolio.

The Princeton Review

Standardized Test Practice

Directions: Choose the *best* answer to the following question.

By gaining control of the Mississippi and Tennessee rivers, the Union was able to

A   capture Fort Sumter.

B   force the Confederacy to surrender.

C   split the Confederacy.

D   defeat the Confederate forces at Gettysburg.

Test-Taking Tip:

Eliminate answers that don't make sense. For example, Confederate forces, not Union forces, captured Fort Sumter. Therefore, choice **A** is incorrect.

Making a Civil War Quilt

Quilts were not just used for soldiers during the Civil War. They also served as patriotic symbols, and they helped raise money for war materials. In this activity, your group will be making a quilt about the Civil War.

The Way It Was

Quilts created during the Civil War were as different as the regions from which they came. Northern quilts often reflected abolition themes. Patterns were created that were named "North Star" and "Underground Railroad." In the South, slaves made most of the quilts and designed them using colors and patterns inspired by African traditions. As a class, make a quilt that reflects what you have learned about the Civil War.

Civil War Quilt

Believe It or Not

When the Civil War was over, fabric was hard to find, especially in the South. Quilts were made from uniforms of dead or returning soldiers. Family members inscribed on the quilts the dates and names of the battles fought by the soldiers.

Materials

✓ pencil
✓ notebook paper
✓ colored pencils/markers
✓ construction paper
✓ laminating machine (if available)
✓ paper punch
✓ yarn

What To Do

After your teacher has organized you into groups of three or four, follow the directions below. Decide upon specific tasks for each member of the group.

1 As a group, select something that you learned about or that interested you while studying the Civil War. Sketch your selection, using a pencil and a piece of notebook paper. Your picture may include a person, a battle scene, or an event that took place during the war.

2 Use colored pencils or markers to draw your picture on a piece of construction paper. If possible, and with teacher supervision, laminate your drawings using a laminating machine.

3 Lay the pictures out on the floor to form a large square. Depending upon the desired size of the quilt, each group may need to produce more than one picture.

4 Take the paper puncher and place holes along the tops, bottoms, and sides of the drawings for those pictures inside the square. Do not punch holes along the sides of the drawings that border the outside edges of the quilt.

5 String the yarn loosely through the holes so that each drawing is connected to the ones around it. Pull any yarn slack after the drawings are connected and tie the loose ends.

6 Hang your quilt on the classroom wall.

Project Report

1. Describe various themes that you see in the class's Civil War quilt.

2. How did you decide where to position each drawing in the quilt? Is there a pattern to your quilt? Explain.

3. What problems did you encounter in creating your quilt? How did you solve them?

4. **Drawing Conclusions** How did quilts serve as political symbols during the Civil War?

Go a Step Further

Find out more about the art of quilting. Research how and why communities such as the Amish continue to make quilts.

CHAPTER 17

Reconstruction and Its Aftermath

1865–1896

Why It Matters

We had survived our worst war, but the end of the Civil War left Americans to deal with a set of pressing issues. The status of some 3.5 million former enslaved people had yet to be decided. Nor had the terms by which the former Confederate states would rejoin the union been decided. How Americans would handle these issues would shape the future of our country.

The Impact Today

Debate over the rightful power of the federal government and the states continues to this day. Americans continue to wrestle with the problem of providing civil rights and equal opportunity to all citizens.

 The American Journey *Video* *The chapter 17 video, "Life After the War," tells the story of Reconstruction through the eyes of writers and artists of the period.*

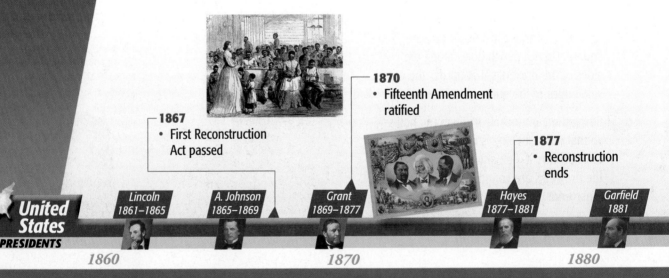

1867
• First Reconstruction Act passed

1870
• Fifteenth Amendment ratified

1877
• Reconstruction ends

United States PRESIDENTS

| Lincoln 1861–1865 | A. Johnson 1865–1869 | Grant 1869–1877 | Hayes 1877–1881 | Garfield 1881 |

1860   1870   1880

World

1868
• Meiji era begins in Japan

1871
• Bismarck unifies Germany

1874
• First major exhibit of impressionist art in Paris

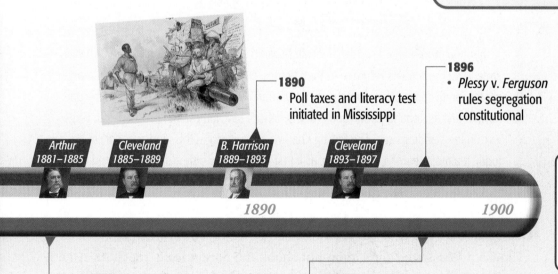

Ruins of the North Eastern Depot, Charleston, South Carolina Southerners faced the task of rebuilding cities, industries, and farms devastated by war.

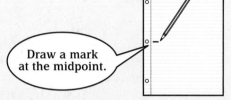
Comparison Study Foldable Make this foldable to help you compare and contrast Reconstruction in the Northern and Southern states.

Step 1 Mark the midpoint of the side edge of a sheet of paper.

> Draw a mark at the midpoint.

Step 2 Turn the paper and fold the edges in to touch at the midpoint.

Step 3 Turn and label your foldable as shown.

North Reconstruction
South

Reading and Writing As you read the chapter, write facts that show how Reconstruction differed and was the same in the Northern states and Southern states. Write the facts in the appropriate places inside your foldable.

1890
• Poll taxes and literacy test initiated in Mississippi

1896
• *Plessy* v. *Ferguson* rules segregation constitutional

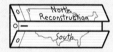

| Arthur 1881–1885 | Cleveland 1885–1889 | B. Harrison 1889–1893 | Cleveland 1893–1897 |

1890   *1900*

1882
• Beginning of British occupation of Egypt

1896
• Ethiopia defeats invading Italians

HISTORY
Online

Chapter Overview
Visit taj.glencoe.com and click on **Chapter 17— Chapter Overviews** to preview chapter information.

Reconstruction Plans

Guide to Reading

Main Idea
Differences over how Reconstruction should be carried out divided the government.

Key Terms
Reconstruction, amnesty, radical, freedmen

Reading Strategy
Taking Notes As you read the section, re-create the diagram below and describe each of the Reconstruction plans.

Plan	Description
Ten Percent Plan	
Wade-Davis Plan	
Restoration	

Read to Learn
- how the Reconstruction plans of Lincoln and the Radical Republicans differed.
- what President Johnson's Reconstruction plans were.

Section Theme
Groups and Institutions The South worked to rebuild its economy and its institutions.

Preview of Events

1864	1865	1866

July 1864
Congress passes Wade-Davis Bill

March 1865
Freedmen's Bureau is established

April 9, 1865
Lee surrenders

April 14, 1865
President Lincoln is assassinated

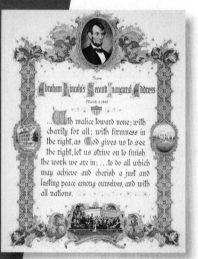

Lincoln's second Inaugural Address

AN American Story

About a month after President Lincoln began his second term of office, the Civil War ended and the soldiers returned to their homes. One Illinois veteran wrote upon reaching the family farm, "The morning after my arrival, September 29th, I [took off] my uniform of first lieutenant, put on some of my father's old clothes, and proceeded to wage war on the standing corn. The feeling I had while engaged in this work was sort of [odd]. It almost seemed, sometimes, as if I had been away only a day or two, and had just taken up the farm work where I had left off."

Reconstruction Debate

The Civil War saved the Union but shook the nation to its roots. As Americans attempted to reunite their shattered nation, they faced many difficult questions. For example, should the slaveholding Southerners be punished or forgiven? What rights should be granted to the freed African Americans? How could the war-torn nation be brought back together?

The war had left the South with enormous problems. Most of the major fighting had taken place in the South. Towns and cities were in ruin, plantations had been burned, and roads, bridges, and railroads destroyed.

More than 258,000 Confederate soldiers had died in the war, and illness and wounds weakened thousands more. Many Southern families faced the task of rebuilding their lives with few resources and without the help of adult males.

People in all parts of the nation agreed that the devastated Southern economy and society needed rebuilding. They disagreed bitterly, however, over how to accomplish this. This period of rebuilding is called Reconstruction. This term also refers to the various plans for accomplishing the rebuilding.

Lincoln's Plan

President Lincoln offered the first plan for accepting the Southern states back into the Union. In December 1863, during the Civil War, the president announced what came to be known as the **Ten Percent Plan.** When 10 percent of the voters of a state took an oath of loyalty to the Union, the state could form a new government and adopt a new constitution—a constitution banning slavery.

Lincoln wanted to encourage Southerners who supported the Union to take charge of the state governments. He believed that punishing the South would serve no useful purpose and would only delay healing the torn nation.

The president offered amnesty—a pardon—to all white Southerners, except Confederate leaders, who were willing to swear loyalty to the Union. Lincoln also supported granting the right to vote to African Americans who were educated or had served in the Union army. However, he would not force the Southern states to give rights held by white Americans to African Americans.

In 1864 three states that the Union army occupied—Louisiana, Arkansas, and Tennessee—established governments under Lincoln's plan. These states then became caught in a struggle between the president and Congress when Congress refused to seat the states' representatives.

A Rival Plan

A group of Republicans in Congress considered Lincoln's plan too mild. They argued that Congress, not the president, should control Reconstruction policy. Because these Republicans favored a tougher and more radical, or extreme, approach to Reconstruction, they were called **Radical Republicans.** A leading Radical Republican, **Thaddeus Stevens,** declared that Southern institutions "must be broken up and relaid, or all our blood and treasure have been spent in vain."

Controlled by the Radical Republicans, Congress voted to deny seats to representatives from any state reconstructed under Lincoln's plan. Then Congress began to create its own plan.

The Wade-Davis Bill

In July 1864, Congress passed the **Wade-Davis Bill.** The bill offered a plan much harsher than Lincoln's. First, a majority of white males in a state had to swear loyalty to the Union. Second, a state constitutional convention could be held,

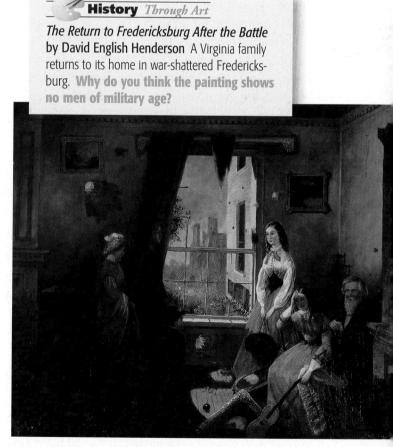

History *Through Art*

The Return to Fredericksburg After the Battle by David English Henderson A Virginia family returns to its home in war-shattered Fredericksburg. **Why do you think the painting shows no men of military age?**

but only white males who swore they had never taken up arms against the Union could vote for delegates to this convention. Former Confederates were also denied the right to hold public office. Finally, the convention had to adopt a new state constitution that abolished slavery. Only then could a state be readmitted to the Union.

Lincoln refused to sign the bill into law. He wanted to encourage the formation of new state governments so that order could be restored quickly. Lincoln realized that he would have to compromise with the Radical Republicans.

The Freedmen's Bureau

More progress was made on the other great issue of Reconstruction—helping African Americans freed from slavery. In March 1865, during the final weeks of the war, Congress and the president established a new government agency to help former enslaved persons, or freedmen. Called the **Freedmen's Bureau,** this agency was actually part of the war department.

In the years following the war, the Freedmen's Bureau played an important role in helping African Americans make the transition to freedom. The agency distributed food and clothing, and also provided medical services that lowered the death rate among freed men and women.

The Freedmen's Bureau achieved one of its greatest successes in the area of education. The bureau established schools, staffed mostly by teachers from the North. It also gave aid to new African American institutions of higher learning, such as Atlanta University, Howard University, and Fisk University.

The bureau helped freed people acquire land that had been abandoned by owners or seized by Union armies. It offered African Americans free transportation to the countryside where laborers were needed, and it helped them obtain fair wages. Although its main goal was to aid African Americans, the bureau also helped Southerners who had supported the Union.

✓ **Reading Check** **Examining** Why did Lincoln offer his plan for Reconstruction before the Civil War was over?

Picturing **History**

Actor John Wilkes Booth used this pistol to shoot Lincoln at Ford's Theater. The "wanted" poster promises a large reward for help in capturing Booth. **How was Booth finally captured?**

Lincoln Assassinated!

A terrible event soon threw the debates over Reconstruction into confusion. On the evening of April 14, 1865, President and Mrs. Lincoln attended the play *Our American Cousin* at Ford's Theater in **Washington, D.C.** It was just five days after the surrender of Lee's army and four years to the day after the fall of Fort Sumter.

As the Lincolns watched the play from a private box in the balcony, **John Wilkes Booth,** an actor and Confederate sympathizer, entered the box without anyone seeing him. Booth shot the president in the back of the head, then leaped to the stage and escaped during the chaos that followed the shooting. Aides carried the wounded president to the nearby house of William Petersen, a tailor. Lincoln died there a few hours later, without ever regaining consciousness.

After escaping from Ford's Theater, Booth fled on horseback to Virginia. Union troops tracked him down and on April 26 cornered him in a barn near Port Royal, Virginia. When Booth refused to surrender, he was shot to death.

Booth was part of a small group that plotted to kill high officials of the United States government. A military court convicted eight people of taking part in the plot. Four were hanged and the others imprisoned for life.

News of Lincoln's assassination shocked the nation. African Americans mourned the death of the man who had helped them win their freedom. Northern whites grieved for the leader who had saved the Union.

A New President

When Lincoln died, Vice President **Andrew Johnson** became president. Formerly a Democratic senator from Tennessee, Johnson had been the only Southern senator to support the Union during the Civil War.

Soon after taking office, President Johnson revealed his plan for Reconstruction. He resented the slaveholders who had dominated the South and wished to punish them. As a result Radicals thought Johnson would create a harsh plan they could accept. Johnson, however, believed in giving the states control over many decisions, and he had no desire to help African Americans.

"Restoration"

Johnson announced his plan, which he preferred to call "Restoration," in May of 1865. Under his plan, most Southerners would be granted amnesty once they swore an oath of loyalty to the Union. High-ranking Confederate officials and wealthy landowners, however, could be pardoned only by applying personally to the president. This provision was Johnson's attack on the wealthy leaders who he believed had tricked the people of the South into seceding.

Johnson also appointed governors to Southern states and required them to hold elections for state constitutional conventions. Only whites who had sworn their loyalty and been pardoned would be allowed to vote. Johnson opposed granting all freed African Americans equal rights or letting them vote. He believed that each Southern state should decide what to do about freed people, saying, "White men alone must manage the South."

Before a state could reenter the Union, its constitutional convention had to denounce secession and abolish slavery. States also had to ratify the **Thirteenth Amendment** to the Constitution, which Congress had passed in January 1865. This amendment abolished slavery in all parts of the United States. By the end of 1865, all the former Confederate states except Texas had formed new governments and were ready to rejoin the Union. President Johnson declared that "Restoration" was almost complete.

✓ **Reading Check** **Comparing** How did President Johnson's plan for Reconstruction differ from that of the Radical Republicans?

SECTION 1 ASSESSMENT

Check for Understanding

1. **Key Terms** Use each of these terms in a sentence that will help explain its meaning: Reconstruction, amnesty, radical, freedmen.
2. **Reviewing Facts** What did the Thirteenth Amendment provide?

Reviewing Themes

3. **Groups and Institutions** Why do you think both Lincoln and the Radical Republicans excluded former Confederate officers from their Reconstruction plans?

Critical Thinking

4. **Drawing Conclusions** Do you think President Johnson's early ties to the South influenced his treatment of African Americans in his Reconstruction plans? Explain your answer.
5. **Comparing** Re-create the diagram below and compare Lincoln's Ten Percent Plan to the Radical Republicans' Wade-Davis Bill.

Reconstruction Plans	
Ten Percent Plan	Wade-Davis Bill

Analyzing Visuals

6. **Picturing History** Study the painting on page 501. What words would you use to describe the mood of the people?

Interdisciplinary Activity

Math Use the *Statistical Abstract of the United States* or another reference book to find information on the percentages of African American students enrolled in schools in 1860, 1870, and 1880. Use this information to create a bar graph.

Radicals in Control

Guide to Reading

Main Idea
Radical Republicans were able to put their version of Reconstruction into action.

Key Terms
black codes, override, impeach

Reading Strategy
Organizing Information As you read the section, re-create the diagram below and provide information about impeachment.

Impeachment	
What is it?	
Who was impeached?	
Outcome of the trial?	

Read to Learn
• what some Southerners did to deprive freed people of their rights, and how Congress responded.
• what the main features of Radical Reconstruction were.

Section Theme
Civic Rights and Responsibilities Southern states created new governments and elected new representatives.

Preview of Events

♦1865	♦1867	♦1869	♦1871

1865
First black codes passed

March 1867
Radical Reconstruction begins

November 1868
Ulysses S. Grant elected president

February 1870
Fifteenth Amendment extends voting rights

Ku Klux Klan flag

AN American Story

For three days in May 1866, white mobs in Memphis, Tennessee, burned African American churches, schools, and homes. Close to fifty people, nearly all of them African American, were killed in the rioting. Many Northerners saw the rampage as an attempt by whites to terrorize African Americans and keep them from exercising their new freedoms. This incident and similar riots in other Southern cities helped convince Radical Republicans that President Johnson's Reconstruction plans were not strong enough.

African Americans' Rights

During the fall of 1865, the Southern states created new governments that met the rules President Johnson laid down, and Southern voters elected new representatives to Congress. More than one dozen of these representatives had been high-ranking officials in the Confederacy—including the Confederacy's vice president, Alexander H. Stephens. When the newly elected Southern representatives arrived in Washington, D.C., Congress refused to seat them. Many Republicans refused to readmit the Southern states on such easy terms and rejected Johnson's claim that Reconstruction was complete.

To many in the North, it seemed that Johnson's plan for Reconstruction was robbing the Union of its hard-won victory. In addition Northerners realized that the treatment of African Americans in Southern states was not improving.

Black Codes

In 1865 and early 1866, the new Southern state legislatures passed a series of laws called black codes. Key parts of these laws aimed to control freed men and women and to enable plantation owners to exploit African American workers.

Modeled on laws that had regulated free African Americans before the Civil War, the black codes of each Southern state trampled the rights of African Americans. Some laws allowed local officials to arrest and fine unemployed African Americans and make them work for white employers to pay off their fines. Other laws banned African Americans from owning or renting farms. One law allowed whites to take orphaned African American children as unpaid apprentices. To freed men and women and many Northerners, the black codes reestablished slavery in disguise.

Challenging the Black Codes

In early 1866 Congress extended the life of the Freedmen's Bureau and granted it new powers. The Freedmen's Bureau now had authority to set up special courts to prosecute individuals charged with violating the rights of African Americans. These courts provided African Americans with a form of justice where they could serve on juries.

Congress also passed the **Civil Rights Act of 1866.** This act granted full citizenship to African Americans and gave the federal government the power to intervene in state affairs to protect their rights. The law overturned the black codes. It also contradicted the 1857 *Dred Scott* decision of the Supreme Court, which had ruled that African Americans were not citizens.

President Johnson vetoed both the Freedmen's Bureau bill and the Civil Rights Act, arguing that the federal government was overstepping its proper authority. He also said that the laws were unconstitutional because they were passed by a Congress that did not include representatives from all the states. By raising the issue of representation, Johnson indirectly threatened to veto any law passed by this Congress.

Republicans in Congress had enough votes to override, or defeat, both vetoes, and the bills became law. As the split between Congress and the president grew, the possibility of their working together faded. The Radical Republicans abandoned the idea of compromise and drafted a new Reconstruction plan—one led by Congress.

⬛Citizenship
The Fourteenth Amendment

Congress wanted to ensure that African Americans would not lose the rights that the Civil Rights Act granted. Fearing it might be

🖌 **History** *Through Art*

His First Vote by Thomas Waterman Wood
Wood's oil painting emphasized the importance of the ballot to African American voters. **How did African American males gain the right to vote?**

challenged and overturned in court, Congress in June 1866 passed a new amendment to the Constitution.

The **Fourteenth Amendment** granted full citizenship to all individuals born in the United States. Because most African Americans in the United States had been born there, they became full citizens. The amendment also stated that no state could take away a citizen's life, liberty, and property "without due process of law," and that every citizen was entitled to "equal protection of the laws." States that prevented any adult male citizen from voting could lose part of their representation in Congress. 📖 *(See pages 247–248 for the entire text of the Fourteenth Amendment.)*

The amendment barred prominent former Confederates from holding national or state office unless pardoned by a vote of two-thirds of Congress. The Fourteenth Amendment was interpreted as not including members of the Native American tribes. Not until 1924 did Congress make all Native Americans citizens of the United States.

Congress declared that Southern states had to ratify the amendment to be readmitted to the Union. Of the 11 Southern states, only Tennessee ratified the Fourteenth Amendment. The refusal of the other states to ratify the amendment delayed its adoption until 1868.

Republican Victory

The Fourteenth Amendment became a major issue in the congressional elections of 1866. Johnson urged Northern and Southern state legislatures to reject it. He also campaigned vigorously against Republican candidates. Many Northerners were disturbed by the nastiness of Johnson's campaign. They also worried about violent clashes between whites and African Americans, such as the riots that erupted in Memphis, Tennessee, and New Orleans, Louisiana.

The Republicans won a decisive victory, increasing their majorities in both houses of Congress. The Republicans also gained control of the governments in every Northern state. The election gave Congress the signal to take Reconstruction into its own hands.

✓ **Reading Check** **Describing** What does the Fourteenth Amendment provide?

Radical Reconstruction

The Republicans in Congress quickly took charge of Reconstruction. Most Radicals agreed with Congressman James Garfield of Ohio that

❝we must compel obedience to the Union, and demand protection for its humblest citizen.❞

President Johnson could do little to stop them because Congress could easily override his vetoes. Thus began a period known as Radical Reconstruction.

Reconstruction Act of 1867

On March 2, 1867, Congress passed the **First Reconstruction Act.** The act called for the creation of new governments in the 10 Southern states that had not ratified the Fourteenth Amendment. Tennessee, which had ratified the amendment, kept its government, and the state was quickly readmitted to the Union.

The act divided the 10 Southern states into five military districts and placed each under the authority of a military commander until new governments were formed. The act also guaranteed African American males the right to vote in state elections, and it prevented former Confederate leaders from holding political office.

To gain readmission to the Union, the states had to ratify the Fourteenth Amendment and submit their new state constitutions to Congress for approval. A **Second Reconstruction Act,** passed a few weeks later, required the military commanders to begin registering voters and to prepare for new state constitutional conventions.

Readmission of States

Many white Southerners refused to take part in the elections for constitutional conventions and state governments. Thousands of newly registered African American voters did use their right to vote. In the elections, Republicans gained control of Southern state governments. By 1868, seven Southern states—Alabama, Arkansas, Florida, Georgia, Louisiana, North Carolina, and South Carolina—had established new governments and met the conditions for readmission to the Union. By 1870, Mississippi, Virginia, and Texas were restored to the Union.

Military Reconstruction Districts, 1867

NATIONAL GEOGRAPHIC

1st District
⭐ John Schofield

VA.

Tennessee rejoined the Union in 1866.

TENN.

N.C.

4th District
⭐ Edward Ord

ARK.

S.C.

2nd District
⭐ Daniel Sickles

MISS.   ALA.   GA.

TEXAS   LA.

3rd District
⭐ John Pope

MEXICO

FLA.

ATLANTIC OCEAN

30°N

Military district boundary
⭐ Union general in command

5th District
⭐ Philip Sheridan

Gulf of Mexico

0   250 miles
0   250 kilometers
Lambert Equal-Area projection

Geography Skills

After taking control of Reconstruction, Congress divided the South into five districts under the command of military officers.
1. **Region** Which two states made up the largest district?
2. **Analyzing Information** Why did no Union troops occupy Tennessee?

Challenge to Johnson

Strongly opposed to Radical Reconstruction, President Johnson had the power as commander in chief of the army to direct the actions of the military governors. For this reason Congress passed several laws to limit the president's power.

One of these laws, the **Tenure of Office Act** of March 1867, was a deliberate challenge. It prohibited the president from removing government officials, including members of his own cabinet, without the Senate's approval. The act violated the tradition that presidents controlled their cabinets, and it threatened presidential power.

Impeaching the President

The conflict between Johnson and the Radicals grew more intense. In August 1867—when Congress was not in session—Johnson suspended Secretary of War **Edwin Stanton** without the Senate's approval. When the Senate met

again and refused to approve the suspension, Johnson removed Stanton from office—a deliberate violation of the Tenure of Office Act. Johnson angered the Republicans further by appointing some generals the Radicals opposed as commanders of Southern military districts.

Outraged by Johnson's actions, the House of Representatives voted to impeach—formally charge with wrongdoing—the president. The House accused Johnson of misconduct and sent the case to the Senate for trial.

The trial began in March 1868 and lasted almost three months. Johnson's defenders claimed that the president was exercising his right to challenge laws he considered unconstitutional. The impeachment, they argued, was politically motivated and thus contrary to the spirit of the Constitution. Samuel J. Tilden, a Democrat from New York, claimed that Congress was trying to remove the president from office without accusing him of a crime "or anything more than a mere difference of opinion."

Johnson's accusers argued that Congress should retain the supreme power to make the laws. Senator Charles Sumner of Massachusetts declared that Johnson had turned

> 66the veto power conferred by the Constitution as a remedy for ill-considered legislation . . . into a weapon of offense against Congress.99

In May the senators cast two votes. In both instances the result was 35 to 19 votes to convict the president—one vote short of the two-thirds majority required by the Constitution for conviction. Several moderate Republicans voted for a verdict of not guilty because they did not believe a president should be removed from office for political differences. As a result, Johnson stayed in office until the end of his term in March 1869.

Election of 1868

By the presidential election of 1868, most Southern states had rejoined the Union. Many Americans hoped that conflicts over Reconstruction and sectional divisions were behind them.

Abandoning Johnson, the Republicans chose General **Ulysses S. Grant,** the Civil War hero, as their presidential candidate. The Democrats nominated Horatio Seymour, a former governor of New York.

Grant won the election, gaining 214 of 294 electoral votes. He also received most of the votes of African Americans in the South. The 1868 election was a vote on Reconstruction, and the voters supported the Republican approach to the issue.

The Fifteenth Amendment

After the election Republicans developed their last major piece of Reconstruction legislation. In February 1869, Congress passed the **Fifteenth Amendment.** It prohibited the state and federal governments from denying the right to vote to any male citizen because of "race, color, or previous condition of servitude."

African American men won the right to vote when the Fifteenth Amendment was ratified and became law in February 1870. Republicans thought that the power of the ballot would enable African Americans to protect themselves. That belief, it turned out, was too optimistic.

📖 *(See page 248 for the entire text of the Fifteenth Amendment.)*

✓ **Reading Check** **Explaining** What was the outcome of the impeachment trial of President Johnson?

SECTION 2 ASSESSMENT

Checking for Understanding

1. **Key Terms** Write a short paragraph in which you use these key terms: black codes, override, impeach.
2. **Reviewing Facts** Discuss two ways Southerners violated Lincoln's plan for Reconstruction.

Reviewing Themes

3. **Civic Rights and Responsibilities** How did Congress challenge the black codes set up by Southern states?

Critical Thinking

4. **Drawing Conclusions** If you had been a member of the Senate, would you have voted for or against convicting President Johnson? Why?
5. **Summarizing Information** Re-create the diagram below and answer the questions about these amendments.

	Date ratified	Impact on life
Fourteenth Amendment		
Fifteenth Amendment		

Analyzing Visuals

6. **Geography Skills** Examine the map that appears on page 507; then answer these questions. What are the geographic divisions of the South shown on the map? Which military district was composed of only one state? Which states made up the Third District?

Interdisciplinary Activity

Expository Writing Write a one-page essay in which you argue for or argue against the Radical Republicans' plan for Reconstruction.

The South During Reconstruction

Guide to Reading

Main Idea
After the Civil War the South had to rebuild not only its farms and roads, but its social and political structures as well.

Key Terms
scalawag, carpetbagger, corruption, integrate, sharecropping

Reading Strategy
Organizing Information As you read the section, re-create the diagram below and describe improvements in the South in the field of education.

Read to Learn
• what groups participated in Reconstruction in the South.
• how Southern life changed during Reconstruction.

Section Theme
Continuity and Change The Republican Party dominated Southern politics during Reconstruction.

Preview of Events

♦1865   ♦1867   ♦1869   ♦1871

1865
Freedmen's Bank is established

1866
Ku Klux Klan is formed

1869
African Americans serve in House of Representatives

1870
First African American is elected to the Senate

AN American Story

Mississippi Senator Hiram Revels

"The dust of our fathers mingles with yours in the same graveyards. . . . This is your country, but it is ours too." So spoke an emancipated African American after the Civil War. Most formerly enslaved people did not seek revenge or power over whites, only respect and equality. The petition of an African American convention in 1865 stated: "We simply ask that we shall be recognized as *men;* . . . that the same laws which govern *white men* shall govern *black men;* . . . that, in short, we be dealt with as others are—in equity and justice."

New Groups Take Charge

During Reconstruction the Republican Party came to dominate Southern politics. Support for the Republican Party came mainly from three groups. One group was African Americans who were overwhelmingly Republican. Support also came from white Southerners who supported Republican policies, and white settlers from the North. These groups dominated the state constitutional conventions and state governments.

African Americans in Government

African Americans played an important role in Reconstruction politics both as voters and as elected officials. In states where African American voters were the majority, they contributed heavily to Republican victories.

African Americans did not control the government of any state, although they briefly held a majority in the lower house of the South Carolina legislature. In other Southern states they held important positions, but never in proportion to their numbers.

At the national level, 16 African Americans served in the House of Representatives and 2 in the Senate between 1869 and 1880. **Hiram Revels,** one of the African American senators, was an ordained minister. During the Civil War he had recruited African Americans for the Union army, started a school for freed African Americans in St. Louis, Missouri, and served as chaplain of an African American regiment in Mississippi. Revels remained in Mississippi after the war and was elected to the Senate in 1870. He served a year in the Senate, where he declared he received "fair treatment."

Blanche K. Bruce, the other African American senator, also came from Mississippi. A former runaway slave, Bruce had taught in a school for African Americans in Missouri when the war began. In 1869 he went to Mississippi, entered politics, and became a superintendent of schools. He was elected to the Senate in 1874, serving there for six years.

Scalawags and Carpetbaggers

Some Southern whites supported Republican policy throughout Reconstruction. Many were nonslaveholding farmers or business leaders who had opposed secession in the first place. Former Confederates despised them for siding with the Republicans and called them scalawags, a term meaning "scoundrel" or "worthless rascal."

Many Northern whites who moved to the South after the war also supported the Republicans and served as Republican leaders during Reconstruction. Critics called these Northerners carpetbaggers because they arrived with all their belongings in cheap suitcases made of carpet fabric. Although some of the carpetbaggers were greedy and took advantage of the situation in the South, most did not. Many carpetbaggers were former Union army soldiers or members of the Freedmen's Bureau who liked the South and wanted to settle there. Others were reformers from the North—including lawyers, doctors, and teachers—who wanted to help reshape Southern society.

Many Southerners ridiculed the Reconstruction governments and accused them of corruption—dishonest or illegal actions—and financial mismanagement. While some officials made money illegally, the practice was hardly widespread. Indeed, there was probably less corruption in the South than in the North.

Resistance to Reconstruction

Most white Southerners opposed efforts to expand African Americans' rights. Carl Schurz, a Republican from Missouri who toured the South right after the war, reported:

> 66Wherever I go—the street, the shop, the house, the hotel, or the steamboat—I hear the people talk in such a way as to indicate that they are yet unable to conceive of the Negro as possessing any rights at all.99

Plantation owners tried to maintain control over freed people in any way they could. Many told African Americans they could not leave the plantations. Most white land owners refused to rent land to freedmen.

Other white Southerners also made life difficult for African Americans. Store owners refused them credit, and employers refused to give them work. Some whites also used fear and force to keep freedmen in line.

The Ku Klux Klan

Violence against African Americans and their white supporters became commonplace during Reconstruction. Much of this violence

People In History

Frederick Douglass 1817–1895

Frederick Douglass escaped slavery in 1838 and quickly emerged as a leader of the movement for liberty for African Americans. During the Civil War, he urged President Lincoln to free the enslaved people, and he helped organize African American troops to fight for freedom.

After Lincoln was assassinated, Douglass opposed President Johnson's Reconstruction program. Instead he supported the Radical Republican plan. A skilled and powerful speaker, Douglass traveled throughout the nation insisting on full equality for African

Americans. He was particularly outspoken in support of the Fifteenth Amendment, guaranteeing African American men the right to vote. To Douglass, the vote meant that African Americans would not only be full citizens but would also have a weapon to protect their rights.

---

was committed by secret societies organized to prevent freed men and women from exercising their rights and to help whites regain power.

The most terrifying of these societies, the **Ku Klux Klan,** was formed in 1866. Wearing white sheets and hoods, members of the Klan launched "midnight rides" against African Americans, burning their homes, churches, and schools. The Klan killed as well. In Jackson County, Florida, the Klan murdered more than 150 people over a three-year period. Klan violence often increased before elections, as the group tried to scare African Americans to keep them from voting. The Klan also attacked white supporters of Reconstruction.

The tactics of the Klan and other violent groups had the support of many Southerners, especially planters and Democrats. These Southerners, who had the most to gain from the reestablishment of white supremacy, saw violence as a defense against Republican rule.

Taking Action Against Violence

Southerners opposed to terrorism appealed to the federal government to do something. In 1870 and 1871, Congress passed several laws to try to

stop the growing violence of the Klan. These laws had limited success. Most white Southerners refused to testify against those who attacked African Americans and their white supporters. Still, enough arrests were made to restore order for the 1872 presidential election.

✓ **Reading Check** **Explaining** Why did laws to control the Ku Klux Klan have little effect?

Some Improvements

Despite the violence, Reconstruction brought important changes throughout the South. This was especially true in education.

Education improved for both African Americans and whites. African Americans saw education as an important step to a better life. In many regions they created their own schools, contributing both labor and money to build the schools.

The Freedmen's Bureau and private charities played a major role in spreading education. Northern women and free African Americans came South to teach in these schools. By 1870 about 4,000 schools had been established, with 200,000 students. More than half the teachers in these schools were African American.

Mother and daughter reading

advanced education for African Americans. Some academies developed into colleges and universities, such as Morehouse College and Atlanta University.

Generally, African American and white students attended different schools. Only Louisiana, South Carolina, and Florida required that schools be integrated—include both whites and African Americans—but the laws were not enforced.

Farming the Land

Along with education, most freed people wanted land. Some African Americans were able to buy land with the assistance of the Freedmen's Bank, established in 1865. Most, however, failed to get their own land.

The most common form of farmwork for freed individuals was sharecropping. In this system a landowner rented a plot of land to a sharecropper, or farmer, along with a crude shack, some seeds and tools, and perhaps a mule. In return sharecroppers shared a percentage of their crop with the landowner.

After paying the landowners, sharecroppers often had little left to sell. Sometimes there was barely enough to feed their families. For many, sharecropping was little better than slavery.

✓ **Reading Check** **Explaining** How did sharecroppers get land to farm?

Public Schools

In the 1870s Reconstruction governments began creating public school systems for both races, which had not existed in the South before the war. Within a few years, more than 50 percent of the white children and about 40 percent of African American children in the South were enrolled in public schools. Northern missionary societies also established academies offering

SECTION 3 ASSESSMENT

Checking for Understanding

1. **Key Terms** Define each term using a complete sentence: scalawag, carpetbagger, corruption, integrate, sharecropping.
2. **Reviewing Facts** How did some Southerners try to maintain control over freed people?

Reviewing Themes

3. **Continuity and Change** How did the state governments under Reconstruction reform education?

Critical Thinking

4. **Drawing Conclusions** Why was voting and owning land so important to newly freed African Americans?
5. **Organizing Information** Re-create the diagram below and identify the three groups that made up the Southern Republican Party.

Southern Republican Party

Analyzing Visuals

6. **Picturing History** Study the picture above. Write a paragraph that explains who the people are and why reading is important to them.

Interdisciplinary Activity

Reading Bring newspapers to class and search for stories that show groups of people struggling for their rights throughout the world. After reading the articles aloud in class, post the items on the bulletin board with the heading "Let Freedom Ring."

Change in the South

Guide to Reading

Main Idea

Democrats steadily regained control of Southern governments as support for Radical Reconstruction policies decreased.

Key Terms

reconciliation, commission, cash crop, poll tax, literacy test, grand-father clause, segregation, lynching

Reading Strategy

Comparing As you read the section, re-create the diagram below and list the advantages and disadvantages of an agricultural economy.

Agricultural Economy

Advantages	Disadvantages

Read to Learn

• what changes occurred in the South during the last years of Reconstruction.

• how African Americans were denied their rights.

Section Theme

Continuity and Change The Democratic Party began to regain control of Southern politics.

Preview of Events

♦1870   ♦1885   ♦1900

1877
Hayes wins presidency; Reconstruction ends

1890
Poll taxes and literacy tests begin in Mississippi

1896
Plessy v. *Ferguson* rules segregation constitutional

Struggle for the Speaker's chair in a Southern statehouse, 1875

★★★★★★★★★ AN American Story

In 1875 the carpetbag governor of Mississippi faced growing violence between whites and African Americans in his state. He appealed to President Grant for troops to restore order. The president's attorney general responded: "The whole public are tired out with these . . . outbreaks in the South, and the great majority are now ready to condemn any interference on the part of the government. . . . Preserve the peace by the forces in your own state. . . ." Sharp in tone, the attorney general's letter reflected the government's desire to end Reconstruction.

Reconstruction Declines

During the Grant administration, Northerners began losing interest in Reconstruction. Many believed it was time for the South to solve its own problems. By 1876 Southern Democrats were regaining political and economic control in the South. Some freed men and women went back to work for landholders because they had no other way to make a living.

Reconstruction declined for other reasons. The old Radical leaders began to disappear from the political scene. Thaddeus Stevens died in 1868, and others retired or lost elections.

Another factor that weakened enthusiasm for Reconstruction was racial prejudice in the North. This prejudice was exploited by opponents of Reconstruction. They argued that only Southerners really knew how to deal with African Americans and that the fate of the freed people should be left to the South.

Southerners protested what they called "bayonet rule"—the use of federal troops to support Reconstruction governments. President Grant had sent federal troops to the South to stop violence or to enforce the law only when absolutely necessary. Generally, though, he tried to avoid any clashes with the South.

Republican Revolt

In the early 1870s, reports of corruption in Grant's administration and in Reconstruction governments spread throughout the nation. Some Republicans split with the party over the issue of corruption. Another group of Republicans broke with the party over Reconstruction, proposing peaceful reconciliation—coming together again—with Southern whites. Calling themselves Liberal Republicans, these two groups nominated **Horace Greeley,** a newspaper editor from New York, to run against Grant in the 1872 presidential election.

The Democrats also supported Greeley for president because he offered a chance to defeat the Republicans. Despite the division in the Republican ranks, however, Grant was reelected.

The Amnesty Act

During the 1872 election campaign, Liberal Republicans called for expanded amnesty for white Southerners. In May 1872, Congress passed the **Amnesty Act,** which pardoned most former Confederates. Nearly all white Southerners could vote and hold office again. The amnesty changed the political balance in the South by restoring full rights to people who supported the Democratic Party.

Democrats Regain Power

In Southern states such as Virginia and North Carolina, where a majority of voters were white, Democrats soon regained control of state governments. In states where African Americans held a majority or where white and African American populations were nearly equal, the Ku Klux Klan and other violent groups helped the Democrats take power by terrorizing Republican voters.

In an election in Mississippi in 1875, Democrats won by a 30,000 majority, although the Republicans had held a 30,000 majority in the previous election. The Democrats used threats to pressure white Republicans to become Democrats. As one Republican put it:

> 66No white man can live in the South in the future and act with any other than the Democratic Party unless he is willing and prepared to live a life of social isolation.99

Analyzing *Political Cartoons*

Problems in the Grant administration hurt the Republican Party. Who does the woman at the far right represent? Why is she turning away?

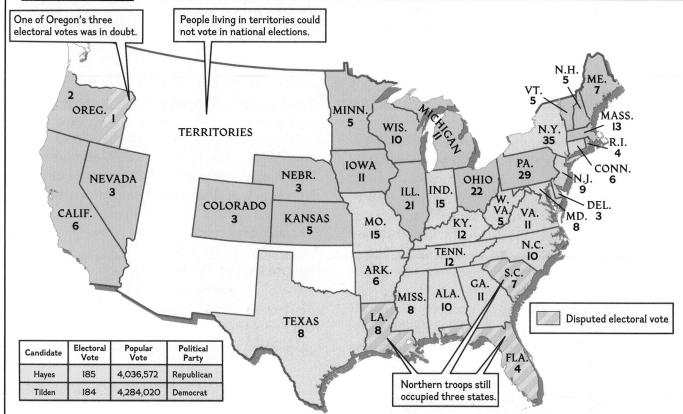

One of Oregon's three electoral votes was in doubt.

People living in territories could not vote in national elections.

Northern troops still occupied three states.

Disputed electoral vote

Candidate	Electoral Vote	Popular Vote	Political Party
Hayes	185	4,036,572	Republican
Tilden	184	4,284,020	Democrat

The Democrats also used violence to persuade African Americans not to vote. By 1876 Republicans held a majority in Congress in only three Southern states—Florida, South Carolina, and Louisiana.

During these years the Republicans had other problems they could not blame on the Democrats. In 1873 a series of political scandals came to light. Investigations uncovered top government officials making unfair business deals, scheming to withhold public tax money, and accepting bribes. One scandal involved the vice president, and another the secretary of war. These scandals further damaged the Grant administration and the Republicans. At the same time, the nation suffered an economic depression. Blame for the hard times fell on the Republicans.

By the time of the congressional elections in 1874, charges of corruption and economic mismanagement had badly weakened the Republican Party. Democrats gained seats in the Senate and won control of the House. For the first time since the Civil War, the Democratic Party controlled

Geography *Skills*

Because of some conflicting results, a committee of 15 members from Congress and the Supreme Court decided the final count in the 1876 election.

1. **Location** Which Southern states sent in election returns that were disputed?
2. **Analyzing Information** By how many electoral votes did Hayes finally win?

a part of the federal government. This situation further weakened Congress's commitment to Reconstruction and protecting the rights of newly freed African Americans.

Reading Check **Identifying** Who was reelected president in 1872?

The End of Reconstruction

President Grant considered running for a third term in 1876. Most Republican leaders preferred a new candidate—one who could win back the Liberal Republicans and unite the party.

The Election of 1876

The Republicans nominated **Rutherford B. Hayes,** governor of Ohio, for president. A champion of political reform, Hayes had a reputation for honesty, and he held moderate views on Reconstruction. The Democrats nominated New York governor **Samuel Tilden.** Tilden had gained national fame for fighting political corruption in New York City.

After the election, Tilden appeared to be the winner, receiving almost 250,000 more votes than Hayes. However, disputed returns from Florida, Louisiana, South Carolina, and Oregon—representing 20 electoral votes—kept the outcome in doubt. Tilden had 184 electoral votes, only one short of what he needed to win. Yet if Hayes received all 20 of the disputed votes, he would have the 185 electoral votes required for victory.

In January Congress created a special commission, or group, of seven Republicans, seven Democrats, and one independent to review the election results. But the independent resigned, and a Republican took his place. After examining the reports of state review boards, the commission voted 8 to 7 to award all 20 disputed votes, and the election, to Hayes. The vote followed party lines.

Democrats in Congress threatened to fight the verdict. Republican and Southern Democratic leaders met secretly to work out an agreement that would allow the Democrats to accept Hayes as president. On March 2, 1877—almost four months after the election—Congress confirmed the verdict of the commission and declared Hayes the winner. He was inaugurated president two days later.

Compromise of 1877

The deal congressional leaders made to settle the election dispute, the **Compromise of 1877,** included various favors to the South. The new government would give more aid to the region

What If...

Lincoln Had Survived?

Lincoln's main goal had been to preserve the Union. In his second Inaugural Address, he indicated that he would deal compassionately with the South after the war ended:

❝With malice toward none; with charity for all, with firmness in the right as God gives us to see the right, let us strive on to finish the work we are in, to bind up the nation's wounds, to care for him who shall have borne the battle and for his widow and his orphan. . . .❞

—Abraham Lincoln, Second Inaugural Address, March 1865

President Lincoln did not live to carry out his plan. On April 14, 1865, just five days after Lee's surrender, he was assassinated.

Andrew Johnson, who succeeded to the presidency, attempted to carry out Lincoln's Reconstruction policies. He was hampered in this effort because as an unelected president he had little popular following. In addition, as a former Democrat, he could not command the support of the Republican majority in Congress. As a Tennessean and former slaveholder, he offended the Radicals. If these handicaps were not enough, his critics viewed Johnson as self-righteous, hot-tempered, stubborn, and crude.

Ticket to Johnson's impeachment trial

In March 1868 the House adopted 11 articles of impeachment against Johnson. Although Johnson was acquitted and served out his term, any influence he might have had on Reconstruction was lost.

and withdraw all remaining troops from Southern states. The Democrats, in turn, promised to maintain African Americans' rights.

In his Inaugural Address, Hayes declared that what the South needed most was the restoration of "wise, honest, and peaceful local self-government." During a goodwill trip to the South, Hayes announced his intention of letting Southerners handle racial issues. In Atlanta he told an African American audience:

> 66 . . . your rights and interests would be safer if this great mass of intelligent white men were left alone by the general government. 99

Hayes's message was clear. The federal government would no longer attempt to reshape Southern society or help Southern African Americans. Reconstruction was over.

Reading Check **Summarizing** What effect did the Compromise of 1877 have on Reconstruction?

Lincoln's funeral carriage

What might have happened?

1. How did Lincoln and Johnson differ in qualities of leadership? In personality? Do you think these qualities made a difference in the way political leaders responded to the two presidents?

2. Would Reconstruction have taken a different course if Lincoln had not been assassinated? Explain.

Change in the South

> 66 I am treated not as an American citizen, but as a brute. . . . [A]nd for what? Not that I am unable to or unwilling to pay my way; not that I am obnoxious in my personal appearance or disrespectful in my conduct; but simply because I happen to be of a darker complexion. 99

John Lynch, a member of Congress who had once been enslaved, spoke these words. At the end of Reconstruction, many African Americans faced lives of poverty, indignity, and despair.

A New Ruling Party

Many Southern whites hated Republicans because of their role in the Civil War and in Reconstruction. When Reconstruction ended, political power in the South shifted from the Republicans to the Democrats.

In some regions, the ruling Democrats were the large landowners and other groups that had held power before the Civil War. In most areas, however, a new ruling class took charge. Among their ranks were merchants, bankers, industrialists, and other business leaders who supported economic development and opposed Northern interference. These Democrats called themselves **"Redeemers"** because they had "redeemed," or saved, the South from Republican rule.

The Redeemers adopted conservative policies such as lower taxes, less public spending, and reduced government services. They drastically cut, or even eliminated, many social services started during Reconstruction, including public education. Their one-party rule and conservative policies dominated Southern politics well into the 1900s.

Rise of the "New South"

By the 1880s forward-looking Southerners were convinced that their region must develop a strong industrial economy. They argued that the South had lost the Civil War because its industry and manufacturing did not match the North's. **Henry Grady,** editor of the *Atlanta Constitution,* headed a group that urged Southerners to "out-

Yankee the Yankees" and build a "New South." This New South would have industries based on coal, iron, tobacco, cotton, lumber, and the region's other abundant resources. Southerners would create this new economy by embracing a spirit of hard work and regional pride. In 1886 Grady told a Boston audience that industrial development would allow the New South to match the North in a peaceful competition.

Southern Industries

Industry in the South made dramatic gains after Reconstruction. Some of the strongest advances were in the textile industry. Before the Civil War, Southern planters had shipped cotton to textile mills in the North or in Europe. In the 1880s textile mills sprang up throughout the South. Many Northern mills would later close as companies built new plants in the South.

Other important industries were lumbering and tobacco processing. The tobacco industry was developed largely through the efforts of **James Duke** of North Carolina. Duke's American Tobacco Company eventually controlled almost all tobacco manufacturing in the nation.

The iron and steel industry also grew rapidly. In the mid-1800s William Kelly, an American ironworker, and Henry Bessemer, a British engineer, had developed methods—called the **Bessemer process**—to inexpensively produce steel from iron. Steel answered industry's need for a sturdy, workable metal. By 1890 Southern mills produced nearly 20 percent of the nation's iron and steel. Much of the industry was in Alabama near deposits of iron ore.

Presidential Elections

Hayes was the only president to win the electoral vote, but lose the popular vote. Actually, three other times in American history—in the elections of John Quincy Adams in 1824, Benjamin Harrison in 1888, and George W. Bush in 2000—the candidate who lost the popular vote won the election.

Factors in Growth

A cheap and reliable workforce helped Southern industry grow. Most factory workers put in long hours for low wages. Sometimes whole families, including children, worked in factories. African Americans got few opportunities in industry except in the lowest-paying jobs.

A railroad-building boom also aided industrial development. By 1870 the Southern railroad system, which had been destroyed during the war, was largely rebuilt. The miles of track more than doubled between 1880 and 1890.

Still, the South did not develop an industrial economy as strong as the North's. The North was still industrializing more rapidly. The South remained primarily agricultural.

⑤ Economics
Rural Economy

Supporters of the New South hoped to change Southern agriculture as well as industry. They pictured small, profitable farms raising a variety of crops rather than large plantations devoted to growing cotton.

A different economy emerged, however. Some plantations were broken up, but many large landowners kept control of their property. When estates were divided, much of the land went to sharecropping and tenant farming, neither of which was profitable.

Debt caused problems as well. Poor farmers had to buy on credit to get the food and supplies they needed. The merchants who sold on credit charged high prices for their goods, increasing the farmers' debt. The quickest way for farmers to repay that debt, they thought, was to grow cash crops—crops that could be sold for money. As in the past, the biggest cash crop was cotton. An oversupply of cotton forced prices down, however. The farmers then had to grow even more cotton to try to recover their losses.

Sharecropping and reliance on a single cash crop hampered the development of a more modern agricultural economy. Instead, the rural South sank deeper into poverty and debt.

✓ **Reading Check** Describing What happened to prices when more cotton was produced than could be sold?

A Divided Society

As Reconstruction ended, African Americans' dreams for justice faded. In the last 20 years of the 1800s, racism became firmly entrenched, and individuals took steps to keep African Americans separated from whites and to deny them basic rights.

Voting Restrictions

The Fifteenth Amendment prohibited any state from denying an individual the right to vote because of race. Southern leaders, however, found ways to get around the amendment and prevent African Americans from voting.

Many Southern states required a poll tax, a fee that people had to pay before voting. Because many African Americans could not afford the tax, they could not vote. The tax also prevented many poor whites from voting. Another approach was to make prospective voters take a literacy test in which they had to read and explain difficult parts of state constitutions or the federal Constitution. Because most African Americans had little education, literacy tests prevented many from voting.

Literacy tests could also keep some whites from voting. For this reason some states passed grandfather clauses. These laws allowed individuals who did not pass the literacy test to vote if their fathers or grandfathers had voted before Reconstruction. Because African Americans could not vote until 1867, they were excluded. Georgia enacted a poll tax and other limits as early as 1870. Such laws, however, did not become widespread until after 1889. African Americans continued to vote in some states until the end of the 1800s. Then, voting laws and the constant threat of violence caused African American voting to drastically decline.

Jim Crow Laws

Another set of laws hurt African Americans. By the 1890s segregation, or the separation of the races, was a prominent feature of life in the South.

The Southern states formed a segregated society by passing so-called **Jim Crow laws.** Taking their name from a character in a song, Jim Crow

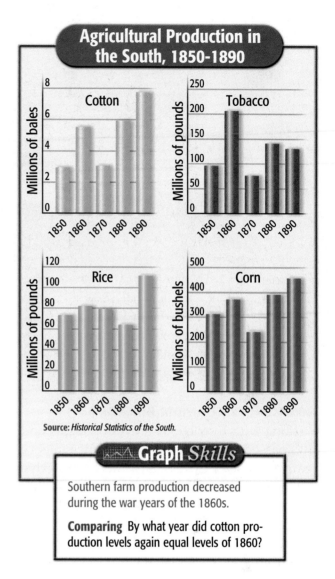

Agricultural Production in the South, 1850-1890

Source: *Historical Statistics of the South.*

Graph *Skills*

Southern farm production decreased during the war years of the 1860s.

Comparing By what year did cotton production levels again equal levels of 1860?

laws required African Americans and whites to be separated in almost every public place where they might come in contact with each other.

In 1896 the Supreme Court upheld Jim Crow laws and segregation in *Plessy v. Ferguson.* The case involved a Louisiana law requiring separate sections on trains for African Americans. The Court ruled that segregation was legal as long as African Americans had access to public facilities or accommodations equal to those of whites.
(See page 999 of the Appendix for a summary of Plessy v. Ferguson.*)*

The problem, however, was that the facilities were separate but in no way equal. Southern states spent much more money on schools and other facilities for whites than on those for African Americans. This "separate but equal" doctrine provided a legal foundation for segregation in the South that lasted for more than 50 years.

Analyzing *Political Cartoons*

African Americans were often barred from voting. **What do the people in the cartoon represent?**

Violence Against African Americans

Along with restrictions on voting rights and laws passed to segregate society, white violence against African Americans increased. This violence took many terrible forms, including lynching, in which an angry mob killed a person by hanging. African Americans were lynched because they were suspected of committing crimes—or because they did not behave as whites thought they should.

Reconstruction's Impact

Reconstruction was both a success and a failure. It helped the South recover from the war and begin rebuilding its economy. Yet economic recovery was far from complete. Although Southern agriculture took a new form, the South was still a rural economy, and that economy was still very poor.

Under Reconstruction African Americans gained greater equality and began creating their own institutions. They joined with whites in new governments, fairer and more democratic than the South had ever seen. This improvement for African Americans did not last long, however. In the words of African American writer and civil rights leader **W.E.B. Du Bois,**

❝The slave went free; stood a brief moment in the sun; then moved back again toward slavery.❞

The biggest disappointment of Reconstruction was that it did not make good on the promise of true freedom for freed African Americans. The South soon created a segregated society.

✓Reading Check **Describing** What is segregation?

SECTION 4 ASSESSMENT

Checking for Understanding

1. **Key Terms** Define the following terms: reconciliation, commission, cash crop, poll tax, literacy test, grandfather clause, segregation, lynching.
2. **Reviewing Facts** Why was the presidential election of 1876 controversial?

Reviewing Themes

3. **Continuity and Change** In what industries did the South make great gains after Reconstruction?

Critical Thinking

4. **Determining Cause and Effect** Explain how the Amnesty Act helped the Democratic Party regain its strength.
5. **Organizing Information** Re-create the diagram below and describe how the poll tax and literacy tests restricted voting rights.

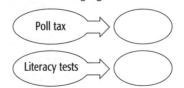

Analyzing Visuals

6. Study the election map on page 515. Which candidate received the greater number of popular votes? Who won the election?

Interdisciplinary Activity

Government Research to find out how many African Americans hold seats in Congress today. Make a list of their names and states of residence. Be sure to include members of both the House of Representatives and the Senate.

Critical Thinking
SKILLBUILDER

Identifying the Main Idea

Why Learn This Skill?

Historical details, such as names, dates, and events, are easier to remember when they are connected to a main idea. Understanding the main idea allows you to grasp the whole picture or story.

Learning the Skill

Follow these steps to identify a main idea:
• Before you read the material, find out the setting of the article or document: the time, the place, and who the writer is.
• Read the material and ask, "What is the purpose of this information?"
• Identify supporting details.
• Identify the main idea or central issue.

Practicing the Skill

In the passage below, W.E.B. Du Bois, an African American scholar, describes the attitudes of people in Charleston, South Carolina, just after the Civil War. Read the passage and answer the questions that follow.

66The economic loss which came through war was great, but not nearly as influential as the psychological change, the change in habit and thought….

The hatred of the Yankees was increased. The defeated Southern leaders were popular heroes. Numbers of Southerners planned to leave the country and go to South America or Mexico….

The labor situation, the prospect of free Negroes, caused great apprehension. It was accepted as absolutely true by most planters that the Negro could not work without a white master.99

A plantation owner meets her former slaves following emancipation.

❶ Du Bois begins by naming two kinds of losses from the war. What are they? Which does he say was greater?

❷ What is the main idea of the passage?

❸ What details support the main idea?

❹ Does the painting support or negate Du Bois's main idea?

Applying the Skill

Identifying the Main Idea Bring a news article about a current event to class. Identify the main idea and supporting details in the article.

Glencoe's **Skillbuilder Interactive Workbook CD-ROM, Level 1,** provides instruction and practice in key social studies skills.

Chapter Summary

Reconstruction and Its Aftermath

Reconstruction Plans
- Ten Percent Plan
- Wade-Davis Bill
- "Restoration"

Radicals in Control
- Civil Rights Act of 1866
- The Fourteenth Amendment
- President Johnson is impeached
- The Fifteenth Amendment

End of Reconstruction
- Interest in Reconstruction declines
- Amnesty Act
- Election of 1876
- Compromise of 1877

Change in the South
- Southern industry grows
- Economy remains agricultural
- Many white and African American farmers turn to sharecropping
- Jim Crow laws promote segregation

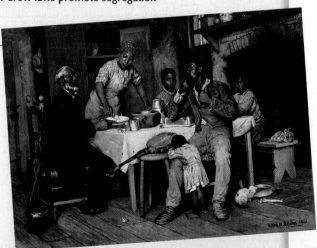

Reviewing Key Terms

Explain why each of these terms is used in a chapter about Reconstruction.

1. amnesty
2. black codes
3. poll tax
4. freedmen
5. impeach
6. segregation

Reviewing Key Facts

7. What services did the Freedmen's Bureau provide?
8. Who succeeded Lincoln as president?
9. How was the Fourteenth Amendment supposed to help African Americans?
10. What verdict did the Senate reach in the trial of President Johnson?
11. What right does the Fifteenth Amendment protect?
12. What role did African Americans play in early Reconstruction politics in the South?
13. What tactic did the Ku Klux Klan use to influence elections in the South?
14. Why was a special commission needed to decide the presidential election of 1876?
15. What Supreme Court decision upheld the legality of segregation so long as "separate but equal" facilities were provided?

Critical Thinking

16. **Analyzing Themes: Civic Rights and Responsibilities** How did the black codes deny rights?
17. **Analyzing Primary Sources** Explain the following quote as it applies to Reconstruction: "The slave went free; stood a brief moment in the sun; then moved back again toward slavery."
18. **Analyzing Themes: Economic Factors** Why did growing cotton after the Civil War send many Southern farmers into debt?
19. **Organizing Information** Re-create the diagram below and explain two important concessions that were made in the Compromise of 1877.

Compromise of 1877

HISTORY Online

Self-Check Quiz

Visit taj.glencoe.com and click on **Chapter 17—Self-Check Quizzes** to prepare for the chapter test.

Practicing Skills

The excerpt below was written by Charlotte Forten, one of many African American teachers who went South to teach freed individuals during the period of Reconstruction. Read the excerpt, which describes her first days of teaching school. Then answer the questions that follow.

66. . . I never before saw children so eager to learn, although I had had several years' experience in New England schools. Coming to school is a constant delight and recreation to them. They come here as other children go to play. The older ones, during the summer, work in the fields from early morning until eleven or twelve o'clock, and then come to school, after their hard toil in the hot sun, as bright and as anxious to learn as ever.99

20. What is the main idea of this passage?

21. What details support the main idea of this passage?

Citizenship Cooperative Activity

22. Registering to Vote Laws about voter registration vary from place to place. Working with a partner, contact your local election board to find out what the requirements for voter registration are in your community. Then design a brochure that encourages citizens to register to vote.

Economics Activity

23. What happened to the price of cotton when an oversupply of cotton was on the market? How do you think prices would change if the demand for cotton were greater than the supply? Explain.

 Geography and History Activity

Turn to the map on page 515 to answer the following questions.

24. Location Electoral votes are based on population. What were the six most populous states in 1876?

25. Region Which political party gained the most votes in the western states?

26. Place How many electoral votes were in dispute?

 Alternative Assessment

27. Portfolio Writing Activity Review the chapter to make a list of specific ways that Southern states tried to deny equal rights to African Americans after the war. Then decide which amendment(s)—Thirteenth, Fourteenth, or Fifteenth—should have prevented each action. Put this information in an essay using standard grammar and spelling.

 The Princeton Review

Standardized Test Practice

Directions: Read the passage below. It is an excerpt from the Fifteenth Amendment to the Constitution. Then answer the question that follows.

The right of citizens of the United States to vote shall not be denied or abridged by the United States or any State on account of race, color, or previous condition of servitude.

The Congress shall have power to enforce this article by appropriate legislation.

The main idea of the Fifteenth Amendment is that

A enslaved people convicted of crimes had the right to a fair trial.

B slavery was made illegal in every state of the Union.

C the government was not allowed to deny a person's right to vote on the basis of race.

D Congress had the right to set voting restrictions in whatever state it chose.

Test-Taking Tip

This question asks for the *main idea* of the passage—in this case, of the Fifteenth Amendment. Read through all the answer choices before choosing the best one. Make sure you look for information in the passage to support your answer.

7 Reshaping the Nation

1858–1914

Traveler's trunk

Why It Matters

As you study Unit 7, you will learn that pioneers continued to spread across the continent, and immigrants flocked to industrial centers. The following resources offer more information about this period in American history.

Primary Sources Library

See pages 970–971 for primary source readings to accompany Unit 7.

Use the **American History Primary Source Document Library CD-ROM** to find additional primary sources about the western frontier and the growth of industry.

Hudson River by Gari Melchers

The Western Frontier

1858–1896

Why It Matters

Many Native American nations lived on the Great Plains, along with the buffalo herds that were their primary source of food. Then, beginning in 1869, transcontinental railroad lines opened the West for white settlers, forever changing the Native American way of life.

The Impact Today

Settlement of the Great Plains came along with the development of machines for plowing, planting, and harvesting. This combination still makes the Midwest a leader in supplying meat and grain to the world.

 The American Journey Video *The chapter 18 video, "Life on the Western Frontier," explores what life in the West was like for cowhands and Native Americans.*

1862
• Homestead Act passed

1876
• Battle of Little Bighorn

United States PRESIDENTS	Buchanan 1857–1861	Lincoln 1861–1865	A. Johnson 1865–1869	Grant 1869–1877	Hayes 1877–1881

1860   1870   1880

World

1861
• Italians establish a united kingdom

1869
• Suez Canal opens

1871
• Stanley and Livingstone meet in Africa

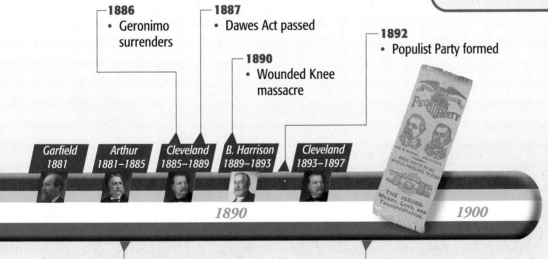

The Race by Mort Künstler The artist is well known for realistic portrayals of dramatic events in American history.

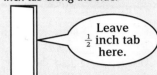
1886
• Geronimo surrenders

1887
• Dawes Act passed

1890
• Wounded Knee massacre

1892
• Populist Party formed

| Garfield 1881 | Arthur 1881–1885 | Cleveland 1885–1889 | B. Harrison 1889–1893 | Cleveland 1893–1897 |

1890

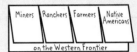

1900

1885
• European powers partition Africa

1895
• X rays discovered by Wilhelm Roentgen

HISTORY Online

Chapter Overview
Visit taj.glencoe.com and click on **Chapter 18— Chapter Overviews** to preview chapter information.

The Mining Booms

Guide to Reading

Main Idea
Discoveries of gold and silver drew thousands of fortune seekers to the West.

Key Terms
lode, ore, vigilante, ghost town, subsidy, transcontinental

Reading Strategy
Analyzing Information As you read the section, re-create the diagram below and explain why these places were significant to the mining boom.

	Significance
Pikes Peak	
Comstock Lode	
Promontory Point	

Read to Learn
• how the rush to find gold and silver led to the growth of new communities in the West.
• how development of the railroads affected the nation.

Section Theme
Geography and History Rail lines and mining speeded the flow of settlers to the West.

Preview of Events

♦1855	♦1865	♦1875	♦1885

1858
Gold is discovered at Pikes Peak

1869
Transcontinental railroad links East and West

1876
Colorado joins the Union

1883
Nation is divided into four time zones

AN American Story

"We'll cross the bold Missouri, and we'll steer for the West,
And we'll take the road we think is the shortest and the best,
We'll travel over plains where the wind is blowing bleak,
And the sandy wastes shall echo with—Hurrah for Pikes Peak."
— *"The Gold Seeker's Song"*

Miners sang this hopeful song in 1859 as they headed for Pikes Peak, Colorado, where gold had been discovered.

Gold nuggets

Mining Is Big Business

By the mid-1850s the California Gold Rush had ended. Disappointed miners, still hoping to strike it rich, began prospecting in other parts of the West.

In 1858 a mining expedition found gold on the slopes of **Pikes Peak** in the Colorado Rockies. Newspapers claimed that miners were making $20 a day panning for gold—a large sum at a time when servants made less than a dollar a day. By the spring of 1859, about 50,000 prospectors had flocked to Colorado. Their slogan was "Pikes Peak or Bust."

Prospectors skimmed gold dust from streams or scratched particles of gold from the surface of the land. Most of the gold, however, was deep in underground lodes, rich streaks of ore sandwiched between layers of rock. Mining this rock, or ore, and then extracting the gold required expensive machinery, many workers, and an organized business. Companies made up of several investors had a better chance of getting rich in the goldfields than individual miners did. At most gold rush sites, mining companies soon replaced the lone miner.

Gold and silver mining attracted foreign as well as American investors. The British, for example, invested heavily in the American mining industry.

The Comstock Lode

In 1859 several prospectors found a rich lode of silver-bearing ore on the banks of the Carson River in Nevada. The discovery was called the **Comstock Lode** after Henry Comstock, who owned a share of the claim.

Thousands of mines opened near the site, but only a few were profitable. Mining companies reaped the largest share of the profits. When Comstock sold his share of the claim, he received $11,000 and two mules—a huge sum at the time. It was, however, just a tiny fraction of the hundreds of millions of dollars worth of gold and silver pulled from the Comstock Lode strike.

✓ **Reading Check** **Describing** What was the Comstock Lode?

America's Flags

Twentieth Flag of the Union, 1876
Statehood for Colorado in 1876 brought the number of stars in the flag to 38. This was the twentieth flag.

The Mining Frontier

The gold strikes created **boomtowns**—towns that grew up almost overnight around mining sites. The Comstock boomtown was **Virginia City, Nevada.** In 1859 the town was a mining camp. Two years later it had a stock exchange, hotels, banks, an opera company, and five newspapers.

Boomtowns were lively, and often lawless, places filled with people from far-off regions. Gold and silver strikes attracted eager prospectors from Mexico, China, and other countries.

Money came quickly—and was often lost just as quickly through extravagant living and gambling. A fortunate miner could earn as much as $2,000 a year, about four times the annual salary of a teacher at that time. Still food, lodging, clothing, and other goods cost dearly in the boomtowns, draining the miners' earnings.

Violence was part of everyday life in boomtowns, where many people carried large amounts of cash and guns. Cheating and stealing were common. Few boomtowns had police or prisons, so citizens sometimes took the law into their own hands. These vigilantes dealt out their own brand of justice without benefit of judge or jury, often hanging the accused person from the nearest tree.

Women in the Boomtowns

Boomtowns were largely men's towns in the early days. Men outnumbered women by two to one in Virginia City, and children made up less than 10 percent of the population.

Eager to share in the riches of the boomtowns, some women opened businesses. Others worked as laundresses, cooks, or dance-hall entertainers. Women often added stability to the boomtowns, founding schools and churches and working to make the communities safer and more orderly.

Boom and Bust

Many mining "booms" were followed by "busts." When the mines no longer yielded ore, people left the towns. At its peak in the 1870s, Virginia City had about 30,000 inhabitants. By 1900 its population had dropped below 4,000.

The boomtown of Leadville, Colorado, surrounds a settler's cabin that sits in the middle of the main street.

Many boomtowns turned into ghost towns—deserted as prospectors moved on to more promising sites or returned home. Some ghost towns still exist in the West today, as reminders of the glory days of the mining frontier.

Mining Expands

Toward the end of the rush, gold and silver mining in some places gave way to the mining of other metals. Copper became the key metal found in Montana, New Mexico, and Arizona in the 1870s.

In the 1890s people began mining lead and zinc in some of the former silver-mining towns of Colorado. Finally, the mining frontier became part of American industry, providing raw materials for manufacturers.

New States Enter the Union

Many people who went west to seek their fortunes in gold or silver settled there permanently. Frontier areas around the boomtowns eventually became states. Colorado joined the United States in 1876. North Dakota, South Dakota, Washington, and Montana became states in 1889. Wyoming and Idaho were admitted to the Union in 1890.

Reading Check **Explaining** Why did many boomtowns turn into ghost towns?

Railroads Connect East and West

The western mines operated far from the industrial centers of the East and Midwest. For this reason transportation played a vital role in the survival of mining communities. Gold and silver had little value unless they could reach factories, ports, and markets. At the same time, the miners and others in the boomtowns needed shipments of food and other supplies.

Wagon trains and stagecoach lines could not move people and goods fast enough to meet these demands. Railroads could—and did. The nation's railroad network expanded rapidly between 1865 and 1890. During that period the miles of track in the United States soared from about 35,000 to more than 150,000.

Government and the Railroads

Railroad construction was often supported by large government subsidies—financial aid and land grants from the government. Railroad executives made the argument that their companies should receive free public land on which to lay track because a rail network would benefit the entire nation.

The national government and states agreed. In all, the federal government granted more than 130 million acres of land to the railroad companies. Much of the land was purchased or obtained by treaties from Native Americans. The government grants included the land for the tracks plus strips of land along the railway, 20 to 80 miles wide. Railroad companies sold those strips of land to raise additional money for construction costs.

States and local communities also helped the railroads. Towns offered cash subsidies to make sure that the railroads came to their communities. For example, Los Angeles gave the Southern Pacific Railroad money and paid for a passenger terminal to ensure that the railroad would come to the town.

Spanning the Continent

The search for a route for a transcontinental rail line—one that would span the continent and connect the Atlantic and Pacific coasts—began in the 1850s. Southerners wanted the route to run through the South, and Northerners through the North. During the Civil War, the Union government chose a northerly route. The government offered land grants to railroad companies willing to build the transcontinental line.

The challenge was enormous—laying track for more than 1,700 miles across hot plains and through rugged mountains. Two companies accepted the challenge. The Union Pacific Company began laying track westward from Omaha, Nebraska, while the Central Pacific Company worked eastward from Sacramento, California.

The two companies competed fiercely. Each wanted to cover a greater distance in order to receive more of the government subsidies.

The Central Pacific hired about 10,000 Chinese laborers to work on its tracks. The first Chinese were hired in 1865 at about $28 per month. The Union Pacific relied on Irish and African American workers. All workers toiled

TECHNOLOGY & History

Steam Locomotive

Since 1825, when the first steam locomotive was built in the United States, trains have crisscrossed the country. As America's transportation needs increased, so did the miles of railroad track linking its people. *Why do you think steam power was the first power source for locomotives?*

1 The **firebox** burns coal, wood, or sometimes oil.

2 Water in the **boiler**, heated by gases from the firebox, creates steam.

3 The **smokebox** draws hot gases from the firebox, and keeps an even fire burning.

4 In the **steam header tank**, the heated steam expands and creates great pressure.

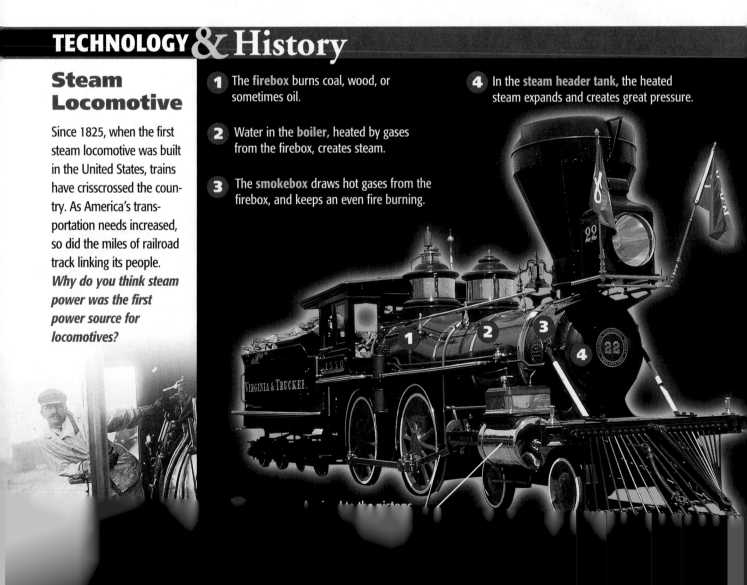

for low wages in harsh conditions. In the choking heat of summer and the icy winds of winter, they cleared forests, blasted tunnels through mountains, and laid hundreds of miles of track. In the end the Union Pacific workers laid 1,038 miles of track, and the Central Pacific workers laid 742 miles. However, the Central Pacific covered a much harsher terrain.

The Transcontinental Railway

On May 10, 1869, construction was completed. A Chinese crew was chosen to lay the final ten miles of track, which was completed in only twelve hours. The two sets of track met at **Promontory Point** in Utah Territory. **Leland Stanford,** governor of California, drove a final golden spike into a tie to join the two railroads. Almost as the event occurred, telegraph lines flashed the news across the country:

> 66 The last rail is laid . . . the last spike driven.
> . . . The Pacific Railroad is completed. 99

$ Economics

Effects of the Railroads

By 1883 two more transcontinental lines and dozens of shorter lines connected cities in the West with the rest of the nation. The economic consequences were enormous. The railroads brought thousands of workers to the West. Trains carried metals and produce east and manufactured goods west. As more tracks were laid, more steel was needed, and the demand boosted the nation's steel industry. Coal producers, railroad car manufacturers, and construction companies also flourished as the railroads spread across the West.

Towns sprang up along the rail lines that carried the settlers' agricultural goods to market. Some of these towns eventually grew into large cities such as Denver, Colorado. The railroads also brought the next wave of new settlers to the West—cattle ranchers and farmers.

Railroads even changed how people measured time. Before railroads, each community kept its own time. Clocks in Boston, for example, were 11 minutes ahead of clocks in New York. The demand for sensible train schedules, however, changed that. In 1883 the railroad companies divided the country into four **time zones.** All communities in each zone would share the same time, and each zone was exactly one hour apart from the zones on either side of it. Congress passed a law making this practice official in 1918.

✓ **Reading Check** **Identifying** To what California city did the transcontinental railroad extend?

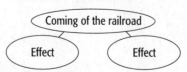

SECTION 1 ASSESSMENT

Checking for Understanding

1. **Key Terms** Explain why each of these terms is used in a section about mining and the railroads: lode, ore, vigilante, ghost town, subsidy, transcontinental.

2. **Reviewing Facts** Describe life in a typical boomtown.

Reviewing Themes

3. **Geography and History** What physical features and climates made building the transcontinental railroad difficult?

Critical Thinking

4. **Drawing Conclusions** Some boomtowns thrived after the mining boom, while others became ghost towns. Why do you think some towns survived while others did not?

5. **Determining Cause and Effect** Re-create the diagram below and explain how railroads helped open the West to settlement.

> Coming of the railroad
>
> Effect   Effect

Analyzing Visuals

6. **Picturing History** Look at the diagram of the steam locomotive on page 531. What is the purpose of the firebox? How were the drive wheels set in operation?

Interdisciplinary Activity

Geography Draw a freehand outline map of the United States today. Shade in the area covered by the states that came into being during the period of the mining boom.

Social Studies
SKILLBUILDER

Reading a Special-Purpose Map

Why Learn This Skill?

Maps that show information on specialized subjects, or themes, are called special-purpose maps. They differ from general-purpose maps in that they show more than basic physical features or political boundaries. Special-purpose maps can contain physical, economic, climatic, historic, or cultural information—almost anything that can be expressed geographically.

Learning the Skill

Begin by reading the map title and labels to determine the subject and purpose of the map. Then study the map key. Identify each symbol and color shown in the key and locate these on the map. Use this information to look for similarities and differences in the region shown on the map.

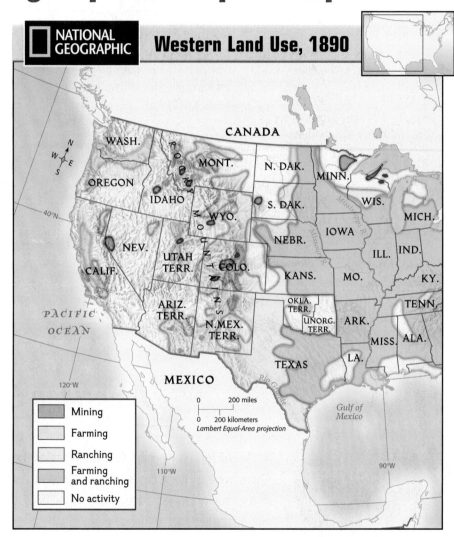

NATIONAL GEOGRAPHIC | **Western Land Use, 1890**

Key:
- Mining
- Farming
- Ranching
- Farming and ranching
- No activity

0 — 200 miles
0 — 200 kilometers
Lambert Equal-Area projection

Practicing the Skill

Look at the map of Western Land Use, 1890. Then answer the following questions.

1. What is the subject of the map?

2. What do the colors represent?

3. What are the most common uses of land in Texas?

4. What were the uses of land in Montana? In Nebraska?

Applying the Skill

Reading a Special-Purpose Map Look at the map on page 544. Where were Native American reservations placed in relation to productive ranching and farming land in 1890?

Glencoe's **Skillbuilder Interactive Workbook CD-ROM, Level 1,** provides instruction and practice in key social studies skills.

Ranchers and Farmers

Guide to Reading

Main Idea
Following the Civil War, settlers began to move west in great number.

Key Terms
open range, brand, vaquero, homestead, sodbuster, dry farming

Reading Strategy
Taking Notes As you read the section, re-create the diagram below and list the challenges settlers faced on the Great Plains.

Challenges

Read to Learn
• how the railroads helped create a "Cattle Kingdom" in the Southwest.
• how women contributed to the settling of the Great Plains.

Section Theme
Economic Factors Ranchers and farmers had to overcome many difficulties to make a profit.

Preview of Events

♦1860	♦1870	♦1880	♦1890

1862
Homestead Act gives free land to settlers

1865
Missouri Pacific Railroad reaches Missouri

1880
Railroad extends from Kansas to Santa Fe

1889
Oklahoma land rush occurs

AN
American Story

Cattle-branding iron

An old Texas cowhand, E.C. Abbott, recalled the early days of riding the trail: "Here [were] all these cheap long-horned steers overrunning Texas; here was the rest of the country crying for beef—and no railroads to get them out. So we trailed them out, across hundreds of miles of wild country that was thick with Indians. . . . In 1867 the town of Abilene was founded at the end of the Kansas Pacific Railroad and that was when the trail really started."

Cattle on the Plains

When the Spanish settled Mexico and Texas, they brought a tough breed of cattle with them. Called **longhorns** because of their prominent horns, these cattle gradually spread across Texas.

At this time much of Texas was open range—not fenced or divided into lots. Huge ranches covered other areas of the state. Ranchers added to their own herds by rounding up wild cattle. The ranchers burned a brand, or symbol, into the animals' hides to show who owned the cattle.

Railroads and Cow Towns

Although Texas ranchers had plenty of cattle, the markets for beef were in the North and the East. In 1866 the Missouri Pacific Railroad reached Missouri, and Texas cattle suddenly increased in value. The cattle could be loaded onto trains in Missouri for shipment north and east. Some Texans drove their combined herds—sometimes 260,000 head of cattle—north to **Sedalia, Missouri,** the nearest rail point. Longhorns that had formerly been worth $3 each quickly rose in value to $40.

Cattle drives to **cow towns**—towns located near railroads to market and ship cattle—turned into a yearly event. Over the next decade, cow towns such as **Abilene** and **Dodge City, Kansas,** and **Cheyenne, Wyoming,** became important rail stations.

★ Geography
The Long Drive

The sudden increase in the longhorns' value set off what became known as the **Long Drive**—the herding of cattle 1,000 miles or more to meet the railroads. The drives left Texas in the spring, when there was enough grass along the way to feed the cattle. The longhorns had to remain well fed because underweight cattle could not be sold.

Some of the largest Long Drives led from central Texas to Abilene, Kansas, on the **Chisholm Trail.** The **Goodnight-Loving Trail,** named for ranchers Charlie Goodnight and Oliver Loving, swung west through the New Mexico Territory and then turned north. During the heyday of the "Cattle Kingdom," from the late 1860s to the mid-1880s, the trails carried more than five million cattle north.

✓ **Reading Check** **Explaining** Why did the value of cattle increase in the mid-1860s?

Life on the Trail

The cattle drives and the cowhands who worked on them captured the imagination of the nation. Cattle driving, however, was hard work. Cowhands rode in the saddle up to 15 hours every day, in driving rain, dust storms, and blazing sun. Life on the trial was lonely too. Cowhands saw few outsiders.

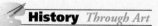

History *Through Art*

Jerked Down **by Charles Russell** Celebrated for his detailed and dramatic scenes of Western life, Charles Russell depicts cowhands on their surefooted horses lassoing cattle. **Where did the traditions of cattle herding begin?**

Spanish Influence

Many cowhands were veterans of the Confederate army. Some were African Americans who moved west in search of a better life after the Civil War. Others were Hispanics. In fact, the traditions of cattle herding began with Hispanic ranch hands in the Spanish Southwest. These *vaqueros* developed many of the skills—riding, roping, and branding—that cowhands used on the drives. Much of the language of the rancher today is derived from Spanish words used by vaqueros for centuries. Even the word *ranch* comes from the Spanish word *rancho.*

The cowhand's equipment was based on the vaquero's equipment too. Cowhands wore wide-brimmed hats to protect themselves from the sun and leather leggings, called **chaps,** to shield their legs from brush and mishaps with cattle. They used ropes called **lariats** to lasso cattle that strayed from the herd.

Hazards on the Trail

During the months on the trail the cowhands faced violent storms, "rustlers" who tried to steal cattle, and many other dangers. They had to drive the herds across swift-flowing rivers, where cattle could be lost.

One of the greatest dangers on the trail was the **stampede,** when thousands of cattle ran in panic. Any sudden sound—a roar of thunder or the crack of a gunshot—could set off the cattle. The cowhands had to race on horseback with the stampeding cattle and bring them under control.

Nat Love was one of many African Americans who rode the cattle trails.

The "Wild West"

African American, Native American, Hispanic, and Anglo cowhands all met and worked together. Yet discrimination existed in the West just as it did elsewhere in the nation. Members of minorities rarely became trail bosses and often received less pay for their work. Some towns discriminated against Hispanics, segregated African Americans, and excluded Chinese cowhands altogether.

After many tiring weeks on the trail, the cowhands delivered their cattle and enjoyed some time off in cow towns. Cowhands drank and gambled, and got involved in fistfights and gunplay. Some towns, such as Dodge City and Abilene, were rowdy, lawless, and often violent. Eventually, though, they grew into settled, businesslike communities.

The Cattle Kingdom Ends

As profits from cattle increased, cattle ranching spread north from Texas. On the northern Plains, ranchers crossbred the longhorns with fatter Hereford and Angus cattle to produce hardy and plumper new breeds.

On the northern Plains, ranching began to replace the Long Drive. The sturdy crossbred cattle multiplied on open-range ranches. When cattle prices "boomed" in the early 1880s, ranchers became rich. The boom, however, was soon followed by a bust. Overgrazing depleted the grasslands. In addition, too many cattle glutted the beef market and prices fell. The bitterly cold winters of 1885 and 1886 killed large numbers of cattle.

The price collapse of the mid-1880s marked the end of the "Cattle Kingdom." Ranchers built fences and grew hay to feed their cattle during the harsh winters. Another type of life would rise on the Plains—farming.

✔ Reading Check **Describing**
Who were the vaqueros?

On the Great Plains *To survive on the Plains, settlers had to build houses that did not require lumber on this treeless land. A Plains family's first home was usually made of sod, rectangular pieces of soil and grass.*

Farmers Settle the Plains

The early pioneers who reached the Great Plains did not believe they could farm the dry, treeless area. In the late 1860s, however, farmers began settling there and planting crops. In a surprisingly short time, much of the Plains changed from "wilderness" to farmland. In 1872 a Nebraska settler wrote,

> ❝One year ago this was a vast houseless, uninhabited prairie. . . . Today I can see more than thirty dwellings from my door.❞

Several factors brought settlers to the Plains. The railroads made the journey west easier and cheaper. New laws offered free land. Finally, above-average rainfall in the late 1870s made the Plains better suited to farming.

The Homestead Act

In 1862 Congress passed the **Homestead Act,** which gave 160 free acres of land to a settler who paid a filing fee and lived on the land for five years. This federal land policy brought farmers to the Plains to homestead—earn ownership of land by settling on it.

Homesteading lured thousands of new settlers. Some were immigrants who had begun the process of becoming American citizens and were eligible to file for land. Others were women. Although married women could not claim land, single women and widows had the same rights as men—and they used the Homestead Act to acquire property. In Colorado and Wyoming, 12 percent of all those who filed homestead claims were women.

Promoting the Plains

Homesteaders came to the Plains to own land and be independent. They were also swayed by advertising paid for by railroads, steamship companies, land speculators, and western states and territories.

Railroad companies wanted to sell the strips of land alongside the rail lines to raise cash. Steamship companies went to great lengths to advertise the American Plains in Scandinavia. By 1880 more than 100,000 Swedes and Norwe-

European immigrants on a railroad flatcar view land open for settlement on the Great Plains.

gians had settled in the northern Plains—Minnesota and the Dakotas. The Scandinavian influence remains strong in this region today.

African American Settlers

Thousands of African Americans also migrated from the Southern states into Kansas in the late 1870s. They called themselves **"Exodusters,"** from the biblical book of Exodus, which describes the Jews' escape from slavery in Egypt.

The end of Reconstruction in 1877 had meant the end of federal protection for African Americans. Fearing for their safety in former slave regions, freed people sought land farther west. By 1881 more than 40,000 African Americans had migrated to Kansas. Some, however, had to return to the South because they lacked the money to start new farms or businesses.

★ Geography

The Farmers' Frontier

The climate of the Plains presented farmers with their greatest challenge. Generally there was little rainfall, but in some years rain came down in torrents, destroying crops and flooding homesteads. The other extreme—drought—also threatened crops and lives. Fire was another enemy. In times of drought, brushfires swept rapidly through a region, destroying crops, livestock, and homes.

Summer might bring plagues of grasshoppers. Several times during the 1870s, swarms of the insects swept over the Plains. Thousands of grasshoppers would land on a field of corn. When they left, not a stalk would remain.

Winters presented even greater dangers. Winds howled across the open Plains, and deep snow could bury animals and trap families in their homes. Farm families had to plan ahead and store food for the winter.

Farm Families

Farming on the Great Plains was a family affair. Men labored hard in the fields. Women often did the same work, but they also cared for the children. A farm wife sewed clothing, made candles, and cooked and preserved food. In the absence of doctors and teachers, she also tended to the children's health and education. When her husband was away—taking the harvest to town or buying supplies—she bore all responsibility for keeping the farm running.

When children grew old enough, they too worked the farm. Children helped in the fields, tended animals, and did chores around the house. Farmwork often kept children from attending school.

Although separated by great distances, farm families socialized whenever they could. People took great pleasure in getting together for weddings, church services, picnics, and other occasions. As communities grew, schools and churches began to dot the rural landscape.

New Farming Methods

The Plains could not be farmed by the usual methods of the 1860s. Most parts of the region had little rainfall and too few streams for irrigation. The Plains farmers, known as sodbusters, needed new methods and tools.

One approach, called dry farming, was to plant seeds deep in the ground where there was some moisture. Wooden plows could not penetrate the tough layer of sod, but in the late 1870s farmers could use the newly invented lightweight steel plows to do the job.

The sodbusters had other tools to help them conquer the Plains—windmills to pump water from deep in the ground and a new fencing called **barbed wire.** With no wood to build fences, farmers used these wire fences to protect their land.

Dry farming, however, did not produce large crop yields, and the 160-acre grants were too small to make a living. Most farmers needed at least 300 acres, as well as advanced machinery, to make a Plains farm profitable. Many farmers went into debt. Others lost ownership of their farms and then had to rent the land.

The Oklahoma Land Rush

The last part of the Plains to be settled was the Oklahoma Territory, which Congress had designated as "Indian Territory" in the 1830s. In 1889, after years of pressure from land dealers and settlers' groups, the federal government opened Oklahoma to homesteaders.

On the morning of April 22, 1889—the official opening day—more than 10,000 people lined up on the edge of this land. At the sound of a bugle, the homesteaders charged across the border to stake their claims. The eager **boomers,** as the homesteaders were called, discovered to their dismay that some settlers had already slipped into Oklahoma. These so-called **sooners** had already claimed most of the best land. Within a few years, all of Oklahoma was opened to settlement.

Closing the Frontier

Not long after the Oklahoma land rush, the government announced in the 1890 census that the frontier no longer existed. Settlement had changed the Plains dramatically. No one felt these changes more keenly than the Native Americans who had lived on the Plains for centuries.

Reading Check **Explaining** Why was the Homestead Act important to settlers?

SECTION 2 ASSESSMENT

Checking for Understanding

1. **Key Terms** Use each of these terms in a sentence that will help explain its meaning: open range, brand, vaquero, homestead, sodbuster, dry farming.
2. **Reviewing Facts** Explain why cow towns developed.

Reviewing Themes

3. **Economic Factors** Discuss two developments that contributed to the collapse of the cattle industry during the mid-1880s.

Critical Thinking

4. **Analyzing Information** What opportunities did settlement on the Plains provide for women and African Americans?
5. **Determining Cause and Effect** Re-create the diagram below and explain how the Homestead Act encouraged settlement of the Great Plains.

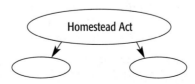

Homestead Act

Analyzing Visuals

6. **Picturing History** Study the photographs that appear on page 537. What image of life on the Plains do the photographs depict? How would you describe the mood of the people?

What were people's lives like in the past?

What—and whom—were people talking about? What did they eat? What did they do for fun? These two pages will give you some clues to everyday life in the U.S. as you step back in time with TIME Notebook.

Profile

WYATT EARP *has been a buffalo hunter, a gambler, a con man, a bartender, and a legendary lawman. In Tombstone, Arizona, where his brother Virgil was sheriff, Wyatt served as a deputy U.S. marshal.*

IN OCTOBER 1881, A FEUD BETWEEN THE EARP FAMILY AND A GANG LED BY Ike Clanton led to one of the most famous gunfights of all time—the showdown at the O.K. Corral. The Earps and their friend Doc Holliday shot and killed three of Clanton's gang members (Billy Clanton, Frank McLaury and Tom McLaury). Wyatt claims they were simply trying to arrest the three. Others say the Earps used murder to settle the feud with the Clantons—and that Wyatt fired the first shot. Judge Spicer called a hearing to investigate the matter. Here's what Wyatt told him about the gunfight.

"Billy Clanton and Frank McLaury commenced to draw their pistols. The first two shots were fired by Billy Clanton and myself. . . . We fired almost together. I don't know which [gun] was fired first. . . ."

Wyatt Earp

BROWN BROTHERS

WHAT PEOPLE ARE SAYING

"We sat and looked as the lamp continued to burn, and the longer it burned, the more fascinated we were. None of us could go to bed. There was no sleep for any of us for 40 hours."

THOMAS EDISON
on inventing the light bulb, which he patented in 1883

TIME PIX

"'We the people' does not mean 'We the male citizens'."

SUSAN B. ANTHONY,
crusader for women's rights in 1872

"Every time you stop a school, you will have to build a jail. What you gain at one end you lose at the other. It's like feeding a dog on his own tail. It won't fatten the dog."

SAMUEL CLEMENS
(also known as Mark Twain)

"I asked a man in prison once how he happened to be there and he said he had stolen a pair of shoes. I told him if he had stolen a railroad, he would be a United States senator."

"MOTHER" MARY JONES,
labor activist

The Eighth Wonder of the World

Sixteen years after the project began, the **Brooklyn Bridge**—the largest suspension bridge in the world—opens in 1883. Schools and shops in Brooklyn are closed so everyone can celebrate. President Chester Arthur is the first to walk across.

Hung from great steel cables, with a span half again as long as that of any previous bridge, it was designed and built by John Roebling. During the project, John was killed on the job. His son, Washington, continued directing the work until he himself was injured. Then Washington's wife Emily completed the job, making her possibly the first woman field engineer.

NORTH WIND PICTURES

MILESTONES

PEOPLE AND EVENTS OF THE TIME

1870 LOUISA SWAIN, age 70, casts a ballot in Wyoming and thus becomes the first woman in the U.S. to vote in a public election.

1871 Fire breaks out on October 8—by most accounts in Mrs. Patrick O'Leary's barn—on Chicago's West Side. Because of the city's 651 miles of wooden sidewalks and 60,000 mostly wooden buildings, Chicago's 200 firemen are unable to bring the blaze under control for 30 hours. In a city of about 300,000, some 100,000 are left homeless.

BROWN BROTHERS

Alexander Graham Bell

NORTH WIND PICTURES

1876 In a building in Boston, **ALEXANDER GRAHAM BELL** makes the first phone call—to Mr. Watson, his assistant upstairs. Bell's message is simple: "Mr. Watson, come here. I want you!" Bell starts his own company because others dismiss the idea of the telephone as foolish. They see the telephone as just a toy.

1878 The first commercial telephone switchboard opens for business in New Haven, Connecticut. There are 21 subscribers.

NUMBERS

U.S. AT THE TIME

10,000 Number of people who watched the first Kentucky Derby in 1875

4 Number of time zones for the United States under 1883 system

5¢ Price for all the goods in F.W. Woolworth's "Great Five-Cent Store" in Utica, New York (1879)

11 Number of days the stock exchange closes as a result of a panic on Wall Street in 1873

14,000 Number of deaths in southern states because of a yellow fever epidemic that raged in 1878

Western Words

Settlers of the western United States are learning some "new" words that come from Spanish.

mesa: an elevated, flat-topped piece of land

stampede: a wild rush of frightened animals

mesquite: wood of a spiny, southwestern tree or shrub sometimes used in cooking

pinto: a horse or pony that's spotted with white and another color

lariat: lasso; a long rope with a noose used to catch livestock

corral: a pen or enclosure for holding livestock

The Well-Dressed Cowhand

These are prices from the Montgomery Ward catalogs of the 1880s.

Stetson hat	$10.00
Leather vest	$3.00
Cotton shirt (no collar)	$1.25
Chaps and pants	$8.00
Leather boots	$20.00
Spurs	$0.70
Raincoat	$2.75
Winchester rifle	$20.50
Colt pistol	$12.20
Holster, cartridge belt	$2.00
Horse (usually provided by ranch)	$35.00
Saddle	$40.00
Single-ear bridle	$2.30
Lariat	$7.75
Saddlebags	$5.00

Native American Struggles

Main Idea
During the late 1800s, whites and Native Americans fought while Native Americans tried to preserve their civilizations.

Key Terms
nomadic, reservation

Reading Strategy
Determining Cause and Effect As you read the section, re-create the diagram below and describe how Western settlement affected Native Americans.

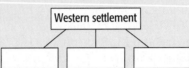

Read to Learn
• why the government forced Native Americans to move to reservations.
• how conflict between Native Americans and whites grew.

Section Theme
Culture and Traditions The settlement of white people in the West forced change on the Native Americans of the Plains.

Preview of Events

1860	1870	1880	1890
1864 Sand Creek massacre occurs	**1876** Sioux victorious at Little Bighorn	**1886** Geronimo surrenders to the army	**1890** Battle at Wounded Knee

Native American buffalo shield

AN American Story

In May 1876, George Crook led an army from the North Platte River to round up Native American bands. Sioux chief Crazy Horse urged on his warriors with the cry, "Come on Dakotas, it's a good day to die." The two sides fought until midafternoon. Then the Native Americans began to drift away. "They were tired and hungry, so they went home," one warrior later explained. The Native Americans retired to a large camp on the Little Bighorn River. Great leaders were there—Sitting Bull, Gall, Crazy Horse. A vast pony herd grazed nearby; the grass was green; there was dancing at night. . . .

Following the Buffalo

Starting in the mid-1850s, miners, railroads, cattle drives, and farmers came to the Plains. Each new group dealt another blow to Native Americans living there. The Sioux chief Red Cloud lamented,

66The white children [settlers] have surrounded me and left me nothing but an island.99

For centuries the Great Plains was home to many Native American nations. Some, like the Omaha and the Osage nations, lived in communities as farmers and hunters. Most of the Plains Indians, however, including the Sioux, the Comanche, and the Blackfeet, lived a nomadic life. They traveled vast distances following their main source of food—the great herds of buffalo that lived on the Great Plains.

Despite their differences, the people of the Plains were similar in many ways. Plains Indian nations, sometimes numbering several thousand people, were divided into bands consisting of up to 500 people each. A governing council headed each band, but most members participated in making decisions.

The women reared the children, cooked, and prepared hides. The men hunted, traded, and supervised the military life of the band. Most Plains Indians practiced a religion based on a belief in the spiritual power of the natural world.

Threats to the Buffalo

The Plains Indians had millions of buffalo to supply their needs. After the Civil War, though, American hunters hired by the railroads began slaughtering the animals to feed the crews building the railroad. The railroad companies also wanted to prevent huge herds of buffalo from blocking the trains. William Cody, hired by the Kansas Pacific Railroad, once claimed that he had killed more than 4,000 buffalo in less than 18 months. He became known as Buffalo Bill. Starting in 1872 hunters targeted buffalo to sell the hides to the East, where tanneries made them into leather goods.

Reading Check **Describing** What is a nomadic way of life?

Conflict

As long as white people regarded the Plains as the "Great American Desert," they left the Native Americans who lived there more or less alone. When whites began settling the Plains, the situation changed. In the late 1860s, the government tried a new Indian policy.

Reservation Policy

In 1867 the federal government appointed the Indian Peace Commission to develop a policy toward Native Americans. The commission recommended moving the Native Americans to a few large reservations—tracts of land set aside for them. Moving Native Americans to reservations was not a new policy, and the government now increased its efforts in that direction.

Native Americans of the Great Plains settled in one place for only part of the year.

Native American Population

Source: Paul Stuart, *Nations within a Nation.*

Graph *Skills*

Census figures show a declining Native American population before 1900.

Analyzing Information During what 10-year period did the Native American population decline the least?

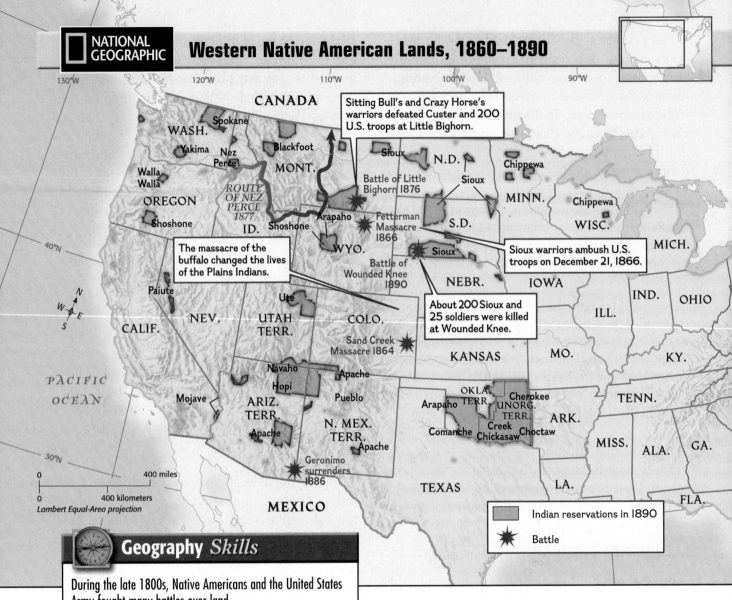

Sitting Bull's and Crazy Horse's warriors defeated Custer and 200 U.S. troops at Little Bighorn.

The massacre of the buffalo changed the lives of the Plains Indians.

Sioux warriors ambush U.S. troops on December 21, 1866.

About 200 Sioux and 25 soldiers were killed at Wounded Knee.

ROUTE OF NEZ PERCE 1877

Battle of Little Bighorn 1876

Fetterman Massacre 1866

Battle of Wounded Knee 1890

Sand Creek Massacre 1864

Geronimo surrenders 1886

Indian reservations in 1890

Battle

400 miles

400 kilometers

Lambert Equal-Area projection

PACIFIC OCEAN

CANADA

MEXICO

Geography Skills

During the late 1800s, Native Americans and the United States Army fought many battles over land.

1. Location In what state did the Battle of Little Bighorn take place?

2. Analyzing Information Which Native American nations resettled in present-day Oklahoma?

One large reservation was in **Oklahoma,** the "Indian Territory" that Congress had created in the 1830s for Native Americans relocated from the Southeast. Another one, meant for the Sioux people, was in the **Dakota Territory.** Managing the reservations would be the job of the federal Bureau of Indian Affairs.

Government agents often used trickery to persuade Native American nations to move to the reservations. Many reservations were located on poor land. In addition the government often failed to deliver promised food and

supplies, and the goods that were delivered were of poor quality.

A great many Native Americans accepted the reservation policy at first. Many southern Kiowa, Comanche, Cheyenne, and Arapaho agreed to stay on the Oklahoma reservation. Thousands of Sioux agreed to move onto the Dakota reservation in the North.

Pockets of resistance remained, however. Some Native Americans refused to make the move, and some who tried reservation life abandoned it. The stage was set for conflict.

Conflict on the Plains

During the 1860s, many armed clashes between Native Americans and whites took place. Minnesota Territory was the site of one especially bloody confrontation. Resentful of the settlers, Sioux warriors, led by **Red Cloud,** burned and looted white settlers' homes in the summer of 1862. Hundreds died before troops arrived from St. Paul and put down the uprising.

Following the Minnesota uprising, the army sent patrols far out onto the northern Great Plains. This action brought troops into contact with another branch of the Sioux—the nomadic **Lakota.** The Lakota fought hard to keep control of their hunting grounds, which extended from the Black Hills and the surrounding Badlands—rocky and barren terrain in the western parts of the Dakotas and northwestern Nebraska—westward to the Bighorn Mountains.

The Sioux, along with Cheyenne and Arapaho warriors, staged a series of attacks from 1865 to 1867. The bloodiest incident occurred on December 21, 1866. Army troops were manning a fort on the Bozeman Trail, used by prospectors to reach gold mines in Montana. A Sioux military leader, **Crazy Horse,** acted as a decoy and lured the troops into a deadly trap. He tricked the fort's commander into sending a detachment of about 80 soldiers in pursuit. Hundreds of warriors were waiting in ambush and wiped out the entire detachment. This incident was known as the **Fetterman Massacre.**

Colorado was another site of conflict. The number of miners who had flocked to Colorado in search of gold and silver grew. Bands of Cheyenne and Arapaho began raiding wagon trains and stealing cattle and horses from ranches. By the summer of 1864, travelers heading to Denver or the mining camps were no longer safe. Dozens of ranches had been burned and an estimated 200 settlers had been killed. The territorial governor of Colorado ordered the Native Americans to surrender at Fort Lyon, where he said they would be given food and protection.

Although several hundred Native Americans surrendered at the fort, many others did not. In November 1864, Chief **Black Kettle** brought several hundred Cheyenne to negotiate a peace deal. They camped at Sand Creek. Shortly after, Colonel John Chivington led the Colorado Volunteers on an attack on the unsuspecting Cheyenne. Fourteen volunteers and hundreds of

Cheyenne died. Retaliation by the Cheyenne was swift, provoking widespread uprisings before some of the Cheyenne and Arapaho leaders agreed to stop the fighting in October 1865.

Little Bighorn

An 1868 treaty was supposed to bring peace, but tensions remained and erupted in more fighting a few years later.

This time the conflict arose over the **Black Hills** of the Dakotas. The government had promised that "No white person or persons shall be permitted to settle upon or occupy" or even "to pass through" these hills. However, the hills were rumored to contain gold. In 1874 Custer led an army expedition to check on the rumors and confirmed that there was gold, "from the grass roots down." Prospectors swarmed into the area.

The Sioux protested against the trespassers. Instead of protecting the Sioux's rights, the government tried to buy the hills. **Sitting Bull,** an important leader of the Lakota Sioux, refused. "I do not want to sell any land. Not even this much," he said, holding a pinch of dust.

Sitting Bull gathered Sioux and Cheyenne warriors along the **Little Bighorn River** in present-day Montana. They were joined by **Crazy Horse,** another Sioux chief, and his

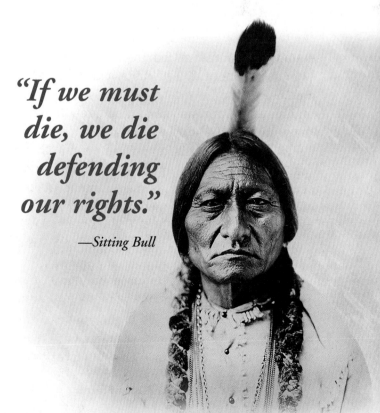

"If we must die, we die defending our rights."

—*Sitting Bull*

Chief Joseph 1840—1904

In 1877 the United States government demanded the Nez Perce give up their lands and move onto a reservation in Idaho. Chief Joseph was preparing his people for the move when he learned that several young braves had attacked a group of white settlers. Fearing revenge, Chief Joseph led his followers over 1,000 miles across Oregon, Washington, Idaho, and Montana.

For more than three months he managed to evade a U.S. force ten times larger than his group. Along the way, he won the admiration of many whites for his humane treatment of prisoners, and for his concern for women, children, and the elderly.

Just 40 miles from the Canadian border the Nez Perce were surrounded. Chief Joseph's words of surrender reflect the tragedy of his people:

"The little children are freezing to death. My people . . . have no blankets, no food . . . . I am tired; my heart is sick and sad. From where the sun now stands I will fight no more forever."

---

forces. The United States Army was ordered to round up the warriors and move them to reservations. The Seventh Cavalry, led by Lieutenant Colonel **George Custer,** was ordered to scout the Native American encampment.

Custer wanted the glory of leading a major victory. He divided his regiment and attacked the Native Americans on June 25, 1876. He had seriously underestimated their strength, however. With about 250 soldiers, Custer faced a Sioux and Cheyenne force of thousands. Custer and his entire command lost their lives. News of the army's defeat shocked the nation.

The Native American triumph at Little Bighorn was short-lived. The army soon crushed the uprising, sending most of the Native Americans to reservations. Sitting Bull and his followers fled north to Canada. By 1881, exhausted and starving, the Lakota and Cheyenne agreed to live on a reservation.

The Apache Wars

Trouble also broke out in the Southwest. The Chiracahua Apache had been moved from their homeland to the San Carlos reservation in Arizona in the mid-1870s. Many Apache resented confinement to this reservation. The Apache leader, **Geronimo,** escaped from San Carlos and fled to Mexico with a small band of followers. During the 1880s he led raids against settlers and the army in Arizona.

Thousands of troops pursued Geronimo and his warriors. Several times he went back to the reservation. Geronimo said,

❝Once I moved about like the wind. Now I surrender to you.❞

But again he left the reservation. In 1886 Geronimo finally gave up—the last Native American to surrender formally to the United States.

A Changing Culture

Many things contributed to changing the traditional way of life of Native Americans—the movement of whites onto their lands, the slaughter of the buffalo, United States Army attacks, and the reservation policy. More change came from well-meaning reformers who wanted to abolish reservations and absorb the Native Americans into white American culture.

American reformers such as **Helen Hunt Jackson** were horrified by the massacres of Native Americans and by the cruelty of the reservation system. Describing the whites' treatment of Native Americans in her 1881 book, *A Century of Dishonor,* Jackson wrote:

❝It makes little difference . . . where one opens the record of the history of the Indians; every page and every year has its dark stain.❞

Congress changed government policy with the **Dawes Act** in 1887. The law aimed to eliminate what Americans regarded as the two weaknesses of Native American life: the lack of private property and the nomadic tradition.

The Dawes Act proposed to break up the reservations and to end identification with a tribal group. Each Native American would receive a plot of reservation land. The goal was to encourage native peoples to become farmers and, eventually, American citizens. Native American children would be sent to white-run boarding schools. Some of the reservation lands would be sold to support this schooling.

Over the next 50 years, the government divided up the reservations. Speculators acquired most of the valuable land. Native Americans often received dry, gravelly plots that were not suited to farming.

Wounded Knee

The Dawes Act changed forever the Native American way of life and weakened their cultural traditions. In their despair the Sioux turned in 1890 to Wovoka, a prophet. Wovoka claimed that the Sioux could regain their former greatness if they performed a ritual known as the **Ghost Dance.**

The Ghost Dance was a way for the Sioux to express their culture that was being destroyed. As the ritual spread, reservation officials became alarmed and decided to ban the dance. Believing that their chief, Sitting Bull, was the leader of the movement, police went to his camp to arrest him. During a scuffle, they shot Sitting Bull.

Several hundred Lakota Sioux fled in fear after Sitting Bull's death. They gathered at a creek called **Wounded Knee** in southwestern South Dakota. On December 29, 1890, the army went there to collect the Sioux's weapons. No one knows how the fighting started, but when a pistol shot rang out, the army responded with fire. More than 200 Sioux and 25 soldiers were killed.

Wounded Knee marked the end of armed conflict between whites and Native Americans. The Native Americans had lost their long struggle.

✓ **Reading Check** **Describing** What was the purpose of the Dawes Act?

SECTION 3 ASSESSMENT

Checking for Understanding

1. **Key Terms** Use each of these terms in a sentence that will help explain its meaning: nomadic, reservation.
2. **Reviewing Facts** Who were Geronimo and Chief Joseph?

Reviewing Themes

3. **Culture and Traditions** What two aspects of Native American life was the Dawes Act supposed to eliminate?

Critical Thinking

4. **Identifying Central Issues** Re-create the diagram below and identify ways the government reservation policy ignored the needs of Native Americans.

Government policy

5. **Drawing Conclusions** Did the Dawes Act reflect an effort by the United States government to change Native American life? If so, how?

Analyzing Visuals

6. **Geography Skills** Study the map of Western Native American Lands on page 544. When did the Battle of Wounded Knee occur? Where were the Shoshone reservations located?

Interdisciplinary Activity

Science Research to find out more about the buffalo. With the buffalo at the center, create a diagram that shows the importance of this animal in the everyday life and culture of Plains Native Americans.

SECTION 4 Farmers in Protest

Guide to Reading

Main Idea
In the late 1800s, farmers began to band together in groups and associations to fight their problems.

Key Terms
National Grange, cooperative, Populist Party, free silver

Reading Strategy
Identifying Central Issues As you read the section, re-create the diagram below and identify the problems farmers faced in the late 1800s.

Farmers' problems

Read to Learn
• why farmers faced hard times in the late 1800s.
• how farmers tried to solve their problems.

Section Theme
Groups and Institutions During the late 1800s, farmers worked together to try to improve their lives.

Preview of Events

1870	1880	1890	1900

1870s
The Grange works to reduce shipping costs

1880s
Farmers' Alliances seek federal support

1890
Alliance members form the Populist Party

1896
William McKinley is elected president

AN American Story

In the last decades of the 1800s, farmers suffered from falling prices and rising costs. They expressed their frustration in a popular song:

> "When the banker says he's broke
> And the merchant's up in smoke
> They forget that it's the farmer feeds them all. . . .
> The farmer is the man,
> Lives on credit till the fall;
> With the interest rates so high,
> It's a wonder he don't die,
> For the mortgage man's the one who gets it all."

Poster celebrating the farmer, 1876

The Farmers Organize

After the Civil War, farming expanded in the West and the South, and more land came under cultivation. The supply of crops grew faster than the demand for them, however, and prices fell steadily. In 1866 a bushel of wheat sold for $1.45. By the mid-1880s the price had dropped to 80 cents and by the mid-1890s to 49 cents. At the same time, farmers' expenses—for transporting their goods to market, for seed, and for equipment and other manufactured goods—remained high. The farmers' plight gave rise to bitter feelings.

Farmers blamed their troubles on three groups in particular. They resented the railroad companies, which charged farmers more to ship crops than they charged manufacturers to ship goods. They were angry at the Eastern manufacturers, who charged high prices for their products. They also had problems with bankers.

Farmers needed to borrow money to buy seed, equipment, and other goods. After they sold their crops, they had to pay the high interest rates set by bankers. If crops failed and farmers could not repay the loans, they were in danger of losing their farms.

Farmers with small and middle-sized holdings struggled to survive. Senator William A. Peffer of Kansas summed up the farmers' plight when he noted that the railroad companies "took possession of the land" and the bankers "took possession of the farmer."

The Grange

Farmers began to organize in an effort to solve their problems. Within a short time, they had created a mass political movement.

The first farmers' organization of this period was a network of local self-help organizations that eventually came to be called the National Grange. The Grange offered farmers education, fellowship, and support. For inexperienced farmers, the Grange provided a library with books on planting and livestock raising. For lonely farm families, it organized social gatherings. In an 1874 declaration of purposes, the Grange said,

> ❝We propose meeting together, talking together, working together, buying together, selling together....❞

Above all, the Grange tried to encourage economic self-sufficiency. It set up "cash-only" cooperatives, stores where farmers bought products from each other. The cooperatives charged lower prices than regular stores and provided an outlet for farmers' crops. The purpose of the "cash-only" policy was to remove the burden of credit buying that threatened farmers.

HISTORY Online

Student Web Activity
Visit taj.glencoe.com and click on **Chapter 18— Student Web Activities** for an activity on the life of a farmer in the late 1800s.

In the 1870s the Grange tried to cut farmers' costs by getting state legislatures to limit railroad shipping rates. Many Midwestern states did pass such laws. By 1878, however, the railroads had put so much pressure on state legislatures that these states repealed the rate regulations.

The Grange cooperatives also failed. Farmers were always short of cash and had to borrow money until their next crop was sold. The cash-only cooperative could not work if borrowing was necessary. By the late 1870s, the Grange had declined. Rural reformers then tried to help farmers through the Farmers' Alliances.

The Farmers' Alliances

The **Farmers' Alliances** were networks of organizations that sprang up in the West and the South in the 1880s. The Southern Alliance was founded in Texas when farmers rallied against the railroads and against "money power."

Alliance leaders extended the movement to other states. By 1890 the Southern Alliance had more than three million members, and the Colored Farmers' National Alliance, a separate organization of African American farmers, had one million members. An Alliance movement developed in the Plains states as well.

Like the Grange, the Farmers' Alliances sponsored education and cooperative buying and selling. The Alliances also proposed a plan in which the federal government would store farmers' crops in warehouses and lend money to the farmers. When the stored crops were sold, the farmers would pay back the government loans. Such a plan would reduce the power that railroads, banks, and merchants had over farmers and would offer farmers some federal protection.

If the Alliances had remained united, they would have been a powerful political force. Regional differences and personality clashes kept the groups apart, however.

✓ **Reading Check** **Describing** What is the purpose of a cooperative?

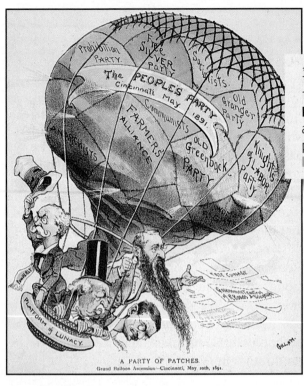

A PARTY OF PATCHES.
Grand Balloon Ascension—Cincinnati, May 20th, 1891.

Analyzing *Political Cartoons*

Party of Patches The cartoonist shows the Populist Party as a collection of special interest groups and minor political parties. **Does the cartoon support or ridicule the Populist Party? Explain.**

A Party of the People

In the 1890 election, the Alliances became active in political campaigns. Candidates they supported won 6 governorships, 3 seats in the United States Senate, and 50 seats in the House of Representatives.

The Populist Party

Pleased with such successes, Alliance leaders worked to turn the movement into a national political party. In February 1890, Alliance members formed the People's Party of the U.S.A., also known as the Populist Party. The goals of this new party were rooted in **populism,** or appeal to the common people.

The new party claimed that the government, not private companies, should own the railroads and telegraph lines. The Populists also wanted to replace the country's gold-based currency system with a flexible currency system that was based on free silver—the unlimited production of silver coins. They believed that putting more silver coins into the economy would give farmers more money to pay their debts.

The Populist Party supported a number of political and labor reforms. They wanted election reforms such as limiting the president and vice president to a single term, electing senators

directly, and introducing the use of secret ballots. They also called for shorter hours for workers and the creation of a national income tax.

Populist Gains and Problems

At a convention in **Omaha, Nebraska,** in July 1892, the Populist Party nominated **James B. Weaver** of Iowa to run for president. In the election Weaver received more than 1 million votes—8.5 percent of the total—and 22 electoral votes. **Grover Cleveland,** the Democratic candidate, won the election, but the Populists had done well for a third party.

The Populists made a strong showing in the state and local elections of 1894 and had high hopes for the presidential election of 1896. The party nominated a number of energetic candidates, but it lacked money and organization.

Economics
Free Silver

To make matters worse, antagonism between the North and the South plagued the Populist Party. In addition many white Southerners could not bring themselves to join forces with African American Populists.

Another blow against populism was struck by the Democratic Party in the South. In the 1890s Democrat-controlled Southern state legislatures placed strict limits on the rights of African Americans to vote. Many freedmen—who might have supported the Populists—were unable to vote.

The Populist crusade for free silver and against the "money power" continued, however. Banking and business interests warned that coining unlimited amounts of new currency would lead to inflation and ruin the economy.

Farmers were joined by debtors in supporting free silver, hoping that loans could be repaid more cheaply. Silver-mining companies in the West also supported the cause. If the government coined large quantities of silver, they had a place to sell their metal.

In the mid-1890s Democrats from farm and silver-producing states took up the free silver issue. This created a problem for Populists. Should they ally themselves with these Democrats? Or should they remain a separate party and risk dividing the free-silver vote?

The Election of 1896

President Grover Cleveland, a Democrat, opposed free silver. At their 1896 convention, however, the Democrats chose a candidate for president who supported free silver and other Populist goals. He was 36-year-old **William Jennings Bryan,** known as the Great Commoner because of his appeal to average Americans. Bryan passionately believed in the farmers' causes.

The Populists decided to endorse Bryan as their candidate for president and to nominate their own candidate, Tom Watson of Georgia, for vice president. The Republicans nominated **William McKinley** of Ohio for president. A former representative and governor of Ohio, McKinley was a shrewd politician who opposed free silver.

A fiery speaker, Bryan proved to be an outstanding campaigner. He crossed the nation giving one dynamic speech after another, attacking bankers and other money interests.

Bryan's strenuous campaigning was in vain. By the time of the election, an economic depression that had slowed business in the early 1890s was nearly over. Voters believed that good times were returning, and they put their trust in the Republican candidate McKinley, who represented stability. Even the economic situation of the farmers was improving. The Populists' message no longer seemed urgent. McKinley won 271 electoral votes to Bryan's 176. McKinley received 7.1 million popular votes to 6.5 million for Bryan. The Populist ticket received only 222,600 popular votes and won no electoral votes.

The Populist Legacy

In one sense, however, the Populists were victorious. Reformers adopted many Populist ideas and succeeded in getting many new laws passed. In the 1900s, the United States abandoned the gold standard, adopted an eight-hour workday, and introduced an income tax. Election reforms brought in the secret ballot and direct election of senators. These were Populist goals.

Reading Check **Examining** Which of the Populists' political reforms are a part of our political system today?

SECTION 4 ASSESSMENT

Checking for Understanding

1. **Key Terms** Write a one-page newsletter for the Populist Party that uses these terms: National Grange, cooperative, Populist Party, free silver.

2. **Reviewing Facts** Who were the presidential candidates in the election of 1896?

Reviewing Themes

3. **Groups and Institutions** Why were granges and alliances formed?

Critical Thinking

4. **Making Inferences** Why do you think the Populists considered themselves to be a party of the people?

5. **Analyzing Information** Re-create the diagram below and explain what actions farmers took to address their problems.

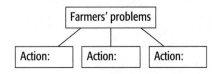

Farmers' problems

Action: | Action: | Action:

Analyzing Visuals

6. **Analyzing Political Cartoons** Look at the cartoon on page 550. Why are the names of many groups shown on the balloon?

Interdisciplinary Activity

Citizenship Write a campaign slogan for a Populist candidate who is running for office, and make a bumper sticker displaying your slogan.

Chapter Summary

The Western Frontier

Mining

- Gold is discovered on Pikes Peak
- Comstock Lode discovered
- Mining companies form
- Boomtowns appear
- Many boomtowns turn into ghost towns

Railroads

- Railroads expand to meet needs of Western mines
- Railroads receive government grants
- Transcontinental rail line completed
- More settlers move west
- Raw materials shipped east; manufactured goods shipped west

Western Frontier

Ranchers and Farmers

- Long drives move cattle to railroad towns
- Cow towns become important stations
- Homestead Act increases settlement of Great Plains
- Oklahoma opened to homesteaders

Native Americans

- Plains Native Americans depend on the buffalo
- Whites massacre the buffalo
- Government moves Native Americans to reservations
- Native American resistance leads to war
- Conflict with Native Americans ends with massacre at Wounded Knee

Reviewing Key Terms

On a sheet of paper, create a crossword puzzle using the following terms. Use the terms' definitions as your crossword clues.

1. lode
2. ore
3. vigilante
4. cooperative
5. nomadic
6. reservation

Reviewing Key Facts

7. In what ways did the transcontinental railroad help to boost the American economy?
8. Where did the Chisholm Trail begin?
9. What attracted farmers to the Great Plains?
10. Who were the Exodusters?
11. What problem did dry farming address?
12. What actions by whites destroyed the buffalo population?
13. In what present-day state was the Indian Territory located?
14. Who was Geronimo?
15. How did the Grange help farmers?
16. What political reforms did the Populists support?

Critical Thinking

17. **Geography and History** How did the rush to find gold and silver spark the creation of new communities in the West?
18. **Analyzing Themes: Economic Factors** Why was the Cattle Kingdom dependent on the railroads?
19. **Analyzing Themes: Groups and Institutions** Describe the problems that led farmers to organize granges and alliances.
20. **Analyzing Themes: Culture and Traditions** Re-create the diagram below and describe what actions by the United States government and white settlers brought an end to the traditional Native American way of life.

Actions

Geography and History Activity

Study the map on page 544 and answer these questions.

21. Location In what state did the Battle of Little Bighorn take place?

22. Movement In which direction from Wyoming did the Nez Perce people travel?

23. Region In what area did the Hopi people live?

Practicing Skills

Reading a Special-Purpose Map

Study the special-purpose map below; then answer the questions that follow.

24. What geographic region is shown?

25. In what part of Texas were most of the large cattle ranches located?

26. Where did the Western Trail end?

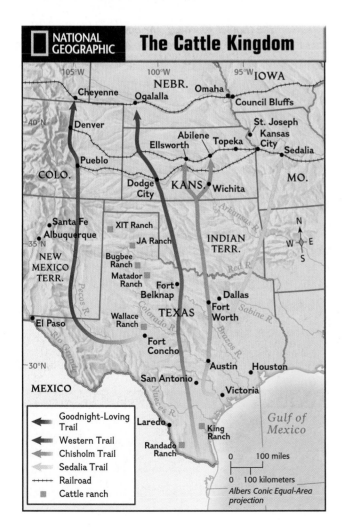

Self-Check Quiz
Visit **taj.glencoe.com** and click on **Chapter 18—Self-Check Quizzes** to prepare for the chapter test.

Citizenship Cooperative Activity

27. Constitutional Interpretations With a partner, find information about the Civil Rights Act of 1964, the Voting Rights Act of 1975, and Americans with Disabilities Act of 1990. Prepare an informational brochure that describes these acts.

Economics Activity

28. History and Economics Today many Native Americans still live on reservations. Some reservations have developed their own businesses and industries to help make them more self-sufficient. With a partner, research to find information about a reservation in the United States today. Write a report describing one of the major businesses on that reservation.

Alternative Assessment

29. Portfolio Writing Activity Reread and take notes on the section of the chapter that discusses the chores of a farm woman. Use your notes to create an hour-by-hour schedule to show one day's typical activities for a farm wife living on the Great Plains.

The Princeton Review
Standardized Test Practice

Directions: Choose the *best* answer to the following question.

People in the late 1800s took advantage of the open grasslands of the West to develop which of these industries?

A Banking   **C** Ranching

B Manufacturing   **D** Mining

Test-Taking Tip

The important words in this question are *open grasslands.* Banking and manufacturing do not need open grasslands, so you can easily eliminate answers **A** and **B.**

CHAPTER 19

The Growth of Industry

1865–1914

Why It Matters

Innovations in technology and new business combinations helped the United States develop into a great industrial power. By the year 1900, United States industrial production was the greatest in the world.

The Impact Today

Innovations in technology and economics have transformed national and regional economies into a global economy. Developments in transportation and communications have made international trade an economic driving force in today's world.

The American Journey Video *The chapter 19 video, "The Builders of Our Railroads," examines the life and hardships that immigrants faced as workers on the railroads.*

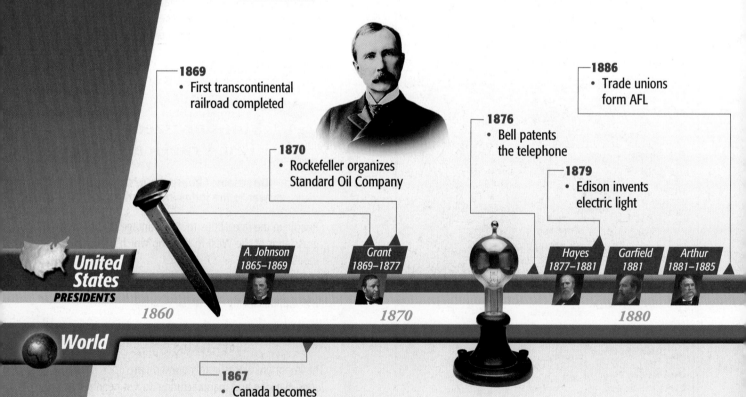

1869
• First transcontinental railroad completed

1870
• Rockefeller organizes Standard Oil Company

1876
• Bell patents the telephone

1879
• Edison invents electric light

1886
• Trade unions form AFL

United States
PRESIDENTS

A. Johnson 1865–1869

Grant 1869–1877

Hayes 1877–1881

Garfield 1881

Arthur 1881–1885

1860

1870

1880

World

1867
• Canada becomes self-governing dominion

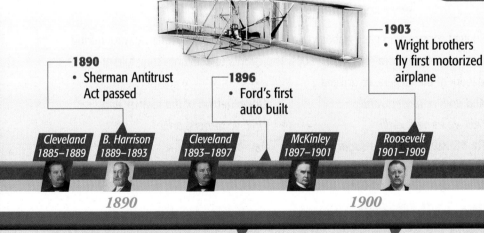

The Ironworkers' Noontime by **Thomas Pollock Anshutz** Factory workers in Wheeling, West Virginia, take their noontime break.

1890
- Sherman Antitrust Act passed

1896
- Ford's first auto built

1903
- Wright brothers fly first motorized airplane

1908
- Ford introduces Model T

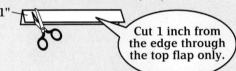

Cleveland 1885–1889 | *B. Harrison 1889–1893* | *Cleveland 1893–1897* | *McKinley 1897–1901* | *Roosevelt 1901–1909*

1890   *1900*

1895
- Marconi sends first radio signals
- Lumière brothers introduce motion pictures

1901
- Australia becomes self-governing dominion

1907
- New Zealand becomes self-governing dominion

HISTORY
Online

Chapter Overview
Visit taj.glencoe.com and click on **Chapter 19— Chapter Overviews** to preview chapter information.

SECTION 1 Railroads Lead the Way

Guide to Reading

Main Idea

A growing transportation network spread people, products, and information across the nation.

Key Terms

consolidation, standard gauge, rebate, pool

Reading Strategy

Analyzing Information As you read the section, complete a diagram like the one shown by describing the contributions of the railroad to the growth of industry.

The role of the railroad

Read to Learn

- how the railroad barons made huge fortunes.
- how the national railroad system changed the American economy.

Section Theme

Geography and History As the railroads expanded, the centers of some industries shifted.

Preview of Events

♦1860	♦1870	♦1880	♦1890

1869
First transcontinental railroad completed

1880s
Standard width for railroad tracks adopted

1883
Northern Pacific Railroad opens

1890s
Five railway lines cross the country

Train song sheet

AN American Story

Rugged construction gangs labored on the Union Pacific and other railways during the transportation boom of the late 1800s. The chorus of a favorite song told of the hard work of the tarriers, or drillers:

And drill, ye tarriers, drill!
Drill, ye tarriers, drill!
For it's work all day for sugar in
your tay,

Down behind of the railway and,
Drill, ye tarriers, drill!
And blast!
And fire!

Railroad Expansion

During the Civil War, trains carried troops, weapons, and supplies to the front. The superior railroad system of the North played an important role in its victory over the South. In the decades after the war, railroads became a driving force behind America's economic growth. The first transcontinental railroad, completed in 1869, was soon followed by others. By the 1890s five railway lines crossed the country, and hundreds of smaller lines branched off from them. The railroad system grew rapidly. In 1860 the United States had about 30,000 miles (48,270 km) of railroad track. By 1900, the nation had nearly 250,000 miles (402,250 km) of track.

Work songs such as "John Henry" and "I've Been Working on the Railroad" were popular among those who labored to build these miles of track. They sang:

> 66I've been working on the railroad,
> All the live-long day,
> I've been working on the railroad,
> Just to pass the time away.99

The expansion of the railroad system was accompanied by consolidation—the practice of combining separate companies—in the industry. Large railroad companies expanded by buying smaller companies or by driving them out of business. Consolidation made the large companies more efficient. After consolidation, a few powerful individuals known as **railroad barons** controlled the nation's rail traffic.

Railroad Barons

New Yorker Cornelius Vanderbilt, one of the first railroad barons, gained control of the New York Central line and then made a fortune by consolidating several companies. His railroad empire stretched from New York City to the Great Lakes.

Another railroad baron, James J. Hill, built the Great Northern line between Minnesota and Washington State. Until his death in 1916, Hill continued building and directing his ever-growing business empire. Collis P. Huntington, Leland Stanford, and two other partners founded the Central Pacific, which connected California and Utah.

The railroad barons were aggressive and competitive. They lived in an age when few laws had been passed to regulate business, and some of their methods were highly questionable. Nevertheless, the railroad barons played an important part in building the nation's transportation system.

Reading Check **Analyzing** What did consolidation mean for many small companies?

Economics

Railroads Stimulate the Economy

The fast-growing national rail system created new economic links in the country. The railroads carried raw materials such as iron ore, coal, and timber to factories. They also carried manufactured goods from factories to markets and transported produce from farming areas to the cities.

The national railroad system encouraged the expanding economy in many other ways. At first the demand for iron tracks and locomotives helped the iron mining and processing industries grow. Around 1880 railroad companies began using tracks of steel—a metal made stronger by adding carbon and other elements to refined iron. The use of steel in railroad tracks stimulated America's steel industry.

The railroads also helped other industries to thrive. The lumber industry, which supplied wood for railway ties, and the coal industry, which provided fuel for locomotives, saw extraordinary growth. In addition railroad companies provided work for thousands of people who laid tracks and built stations and for those who manufactured railway cars and equipment.

Improving the Railroads

Increased use made it necessary for railroads to expand and unify their systems. While railroads were being built across the country, different lines used rails of different gauges, or widths. As a result trains of one line could not use another line's tracks. Many early local lines carried goods for short distances and did not even

Fact · Fiction · Folklore

Labor

Railroads employed more workers in the late 1800s than any other industry. In the late 1800s, railroads became the nation's largest industry. It surpassed all others as a buyer of iron, steel, and coal, and became the nation's largest employer.

Major Western Railroads before 1900

NATIONAL GEOGRAPHIC

By 1883 several railroads crossed the West. The transcontinentals shipped settlers and goods there and hauled out raw resources.

Trains could carry passengers from New York City to San Francisco in less than 10 days.

The refrigerated railroad car in the 1870s allowed fresh meat and produce to be transported all over the nation.

Railroads
Mining centers

0 — 300 miles
0 — 300 kilometers
Lambert Equal-Area projection

Geography *Skills*

By the 1890s more than 150,000 miles (241,350 km) of tracks had been laid.

1. **Identifying** Which railroad connected Los Angeles to New Orleans?
2. **Analyzing Information** Which railroads would a traveler use from St. Louis to Virginia City?

connect with other lines. The gaps in service between the various lines made long-distance railroad travel slow and inefficient.

As the railroad companies consolidated, railroad barons saw the advantages of being part of a national railroad network. During the late 1880s, almost all companies adopted a standard gauge of 4 feet, 8.5 inches as the width of the railroad track. A standard gauge allowed faster shipment of goods at a reduced cost. It was no longer necessary to load and unload goods from one train to another. One train could make the entire journey.

Railroad Technology

Railway transportation also improved with the introduction of new technology. Four developments were particularly important. Inventor **George Westinghouse** devised air brakes that improved the system for stopping trains, making train travel safer. Janney car couplers, named after inventor **Eli H. Janney,** made it easier for railroad workers to link cars. Refrigerated cars, developed by **Gustavus Swift,** enabled the railroads to ship meat and other perishable goods over long distances. Finally, **George M. Pullman** developed the Pullman sleeping car—

a luxury railway car with seats that converted into beds for overnight journeys. Pullman also introduced improved dining cars, raising train travel to a new level of comfort.

Competing for Customers

As the railroad network expanded, the railroad companies competed fiercely with one another to keep old customers and to win new ones. Large railroads offered secret discounts called rebates to their biggest customers. Smaller railroads that could not match these rebates were often forced out of business. Giving discounts to big customers raised freight rates for farmers and other customers who shipped small amounts of goods.

The railroad barons also made secret agreements among themselves, known as pools. They divided the railway business among their companies and set rates for a region. With no other competition in its region, a railroad could charge higher rates and earn greater profits. Although Congress and some states passed laws to regulate the railroads, these laws did little to curb the railroad barons.

Railroads Change America

The growing railroad network paved the way for American industry to expand into the West. The center of the flour milling industry, for example, shifted westward in the 1800s, moving from the East Coast to Ohio, to Minneapolis, and finally to Kansas City. Other industries followed the same pattern. As farmers settled the Great Plains, the manufacturing center for agricultural equipment moved from central New York State to Illinois and Wisconsin.

Railroads also touched the lives of thousands of Americans. Trains redistributed the population. They carried homesteaders into the Great Plains and the West. Trains also made it easy for people to move from rural areas to the cities.

Time Zones

Railroads affected the way Americans thought about time as well. As train travel became more common, people began measuring distances by how many hours the trip would take rather than by the number of miles traveled. The spread of the railroad system led to a national system of time with four time zones.

The railroads opened the entire United States to settlement and economic growth and united the different regions of the country into a single network. At the same time, inventions that revolutionized transportation and communication brought Americans together in new ways.

Reading Check **Explaining** Why was adopting standard-gauge tracks important for the railroad industry?

SECTION 1 ASSESSMENT

Checking for Understanding

1. **Key Terms** Use each of these terms in a sentence that will help explain its meaning: consolidation, standard gauge, rebate, pool.
2. **Reviewing Facts** Describe the methods used by railroad barons to drive smaller companies out of business.

Reviewing Themes

3. **Geography and History** How did the railroads pave the way for the expansion of industry in the West?

Critical Thinking

4. **Making Inferences** Do you think the federal government should have intervened to regulate the unfair practices of the railroad barons? Why or why not?
5. **Organizing Information** Re-create the diagram below and identify the developments in technology that improved railroad transportation.

Railroad technology

Analyzing Visuals

6. **Geography Skills** Study the map of the major western railroads that appears on page 558. Through what states did the Great Northern Railroad pass? Through what cities in Montana did railroads pass?

Interdisciplinary Activity

Art Create an ad with words and pictures to announce the development of the new Pullman sleeping car.

Social Studies
SKILLBUILDER

Reading a Time Zone Map

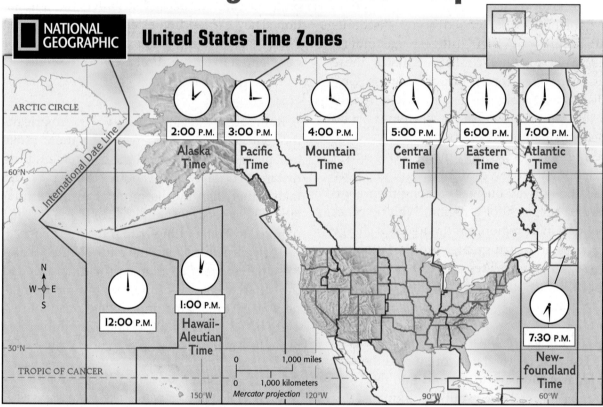

NATIONAL GEOGRAPHIC

United States Time Zones

ARCTIC CIRCLE

International Date Line

60°N

N
W—E
S

2:00 P.M. Alaska Time

3:00 P.M. Pacific Time

4:00 P.M. Mountain Time

5:00 P.M. Central Time

6:00 P.M. Eastern Time

7:00 P.M. Atlantic Time

12:00 P.M.

1:00 P.M. Hawaii-Aleutian Time

7:30 P.M. New-foundland Time

30°N

TROPIC OF CANCER

0   1,000 miles
0   1,000 kilometers
Mercator projection 120°W

150°W   90°W   60°W

Earth's surface is divided into 24 time zones. Each zone represents 15° longitude, or the distance the earth rotates in one hour. The 0° line of longitude—the Prime Meridian—is the starting point for figuring time around the world. Traveling west from the Prime Meridian, it becomes one hour earlier; traveling east, it becomes one hour later. To read a time zone map, follow these steps:

- Locate a place where you know what time it is and select another place where you wish to know the time.
- Notice the time zones you cross between these two places.
- If the second place lies east of the first, add an hour for each time zone. If it lies west, subtract an hour for each zone.

Practicing the Skill

❶ Describe how U.S. time changes as you move from east to west.

❷ What U.S. time zone lies farthest west?

❸ If it is 6:00 P.M. in Washington, D.C., what time is it in San Diego, California?

Applying the Skill

Reading a Time Zone Map It takes two hours to fly from Denver, Colorado, to Chicago, Illinois. If you leave Denver at 2:00 A.M., what time will it be in Chicago when you arrive?

GO TO

Glencoe's **Skillbuilder Interactive Workbook CD-ROM, Level 1,** provides instruction and practice in key social studies skills.

Inventions

Main Idea

Inventions improved the transportation and communication networks that were vital to the nation's industrial growth.

Key Terms

assembly line, mass production

Reading Strategy

Organizing Information As you read the section, re-create the diagram below to list each person's invention and to explain the significance of each invention to industrial growth.

	Invention	Significance
Samuel Morse		
Alexander Bell		
Thomas Edison		

Read to Learn

- what changes in transportation and communication transformed America.
- how labor-saving inventions affected life.

Section Theme

Science and Technology New inventions promoted economic growth.

Preview of Events

◆1870   ◆1890   ◆1910

1868
Christopher Sholes invents the typewriter

1876
Alexander Bell develops the telephone

1879
Edison develops first practical lightbulb

1903
The Wright brothers fly at Kitty Hawk

1908
Henry Ford introduces the Model T

Auto hood ornament

★★★★★★★
AN
American Story

In the early 1900s, American songwriters were caught up in the public fascination with new inventions. One of the most popular songs of 1905, "In My Merry Oldsmobile," celebrated the automobile:

> *"Come away with me Lucile,*
> *In my merry Oldsmobile.*
> *Down the road of life we'll fly,*
> *Automobubbling you and I.*

> *To the church we'll swiftly steal,*
> *Then our wedding bells will peal;*
> *You can go as far as you like, . . .*
> *In my merry Oldsmobile."*

Communication Changes

By 1910 Americans in cities drove cars through streets lit with electric lights. They went to department stores where they bought everything from kitchen sinks to shoes. Americans could also do their shopping by mail—or pick up the telephone and order groceries from the local store. The automobile, the electric light, and the telephone were all invented after 1870. Within a generation they had become part of everyday life for millions of people. New inventions helped people communicate more quickly over long distances. Improvements in communication helped unify the regions of the country and promoted economic growth.

The First Flight at Kitty Hawk

A small crowd of people assembled on the sand dunes at Kitty Hawk, North Carolina, to test the Wrights' Flyer. Covering a few hundred feet in 12 seconds, the flight came to a halt when the Flyer's wing caught on one of the dunes. It was enough to encourage the Wrights to try further flights. They would soon have a practical aircraft and the world would have a new form of transportation.

Space shuttle Discovery, 1990

The Beginning of Controlled, Powered Flight

Inventors experimented with engine-powered aircraft in the 1800s, but the age of air travel did not begin until 1903 at Kitty Hawk, North Carolina. Orville and Wilbur Wright, brothers and bicycle mechanics, built a wood-and-canvas plane with a 12-horsepower engine. On the morning of December 17, Orville Wright took off in their plane and flew a distance of 120 feet.

Firsts in Aviation History

In less than 100 years, aviators advanced from making the first flight in a glider to breaking the speed of sound.

1853 → Human-carrying flight in a glider built by Sir George Cayley takes place

1874 → Steam-powered monoplane is briefly airborne

1903 → Wright brothers take flight at Kitty Hawk

1909 → Louis Blériot flies across the English Channel

1914 → Scheduled airline service opens between St. Petersburg and Tampa, Florida

The Telegraph

Samuel Morse had introduced the telegraph in 1844. By 1860 the United States had thousands of miles of telegraph lines, which were controlled for the most part by the Western Union Telegraph Company. At telegraph offices, trained operators transmitted messages in Morse code. Telegrams offered almost instant communication and had many uses. Shopkeepers relied on telegrams to order goods, and reporters used them to transmit stories to their newspapers. Americans also began sending personal messages by telegram.

The telegraph soon linked the United States and Europe. In the 1860s news from Europe traveled to this country by ship and took several weeks. **Cyrus Field** wanted to speed up the process. After several unsuccessful attempts, in 1866 Field managed to lay a telegraph cable across the Atlantic Ocean. The new transatlantic telegraph carried messages in a matter of seconds, bringing the United States and Europe closer together.

The Telephone Rings In

Alexander Graham Bell invented a device that revolutionized communications even more than Morse's telegraph. Born and educated in Scotland, Bell moved to the United States, where he studied ways of teaching hearing-impaired people to speak. At the same time, he experimented with sending voices through electrical wires.

Bi-wing plane, early 1900s

Taking to the Air

- The Flyer was a biplane with a light and powerful gas engine.

- The Wrights used adjustable rudders to control the aircraft as it turned.

- The two propellers were each $8\frac{1}{2}$ feet in diameter.

- The wingspan reached 40 feet, 4 inches.

- The distance from the nose to the tail was 21 feet, 1 inch.

- The weight of the craft was 605 pounds.

Chuck Yeager and the Bell X-1

1914 → Aerial combat between German and French World War I pilots

1919 → First nonstop flight across the Atlantic Ocean

1927 → Lindbergh completes first nonstop solo transatlantic flight

1939 → German Heinkel is first jet-powered aircraft to fly

1947 → Chuck Yeager is first to fly faster than the speed of sound

By 1876 Bell developed a device that transmitted speech—the telephone. While Bell was preparing to test the device, he accidentally spilled some battery acid on his clothes. In panic Bell called out to his assistant in another room: "Mr. Watson, come here. I want you!" Watson heard Bell's voice coming through the telephone. The invention was a success.

Bell formed the Bell Telephone Company in 1877. By the 1890s he had sold hundreds of thousands of phones. Most early telephone customers were businesses. Before long, though, telephones became common in homes.

✓ Reading Check **Explaining** How did the telegraph affect communication?

The Genius of Invention

The late 1800s saw a burst of inventiveness in the United States. Between 1860 and 1890, the United States government granted more than 400,000 patents for new inventions.

Many of the inventions helped businesses operate more efficiently. Among these were Christopher Sholes's typewriter (1868) and William Burroughs's adding machine (1888).

Other inventions affected everyday life. In 1888 **George Eastman** invented a small box camera—the Kodak—that made it easier and less costly to take photographs. **John Thurman** developed a vacuum cleaner in 1899 that simplified housework.

Thomas Edison

The Wizard of Menlo Park

Thomas Edison was called "dull" by his teachers. Because of poor hearing he had trouble in school and often didn't attend. His mother finally removed him from school and taught him at home. He loved anything related to science, and she allowed him to set up a chemistry lab in the family's basement. When he was 12, he got a job working for the railroad, where he set up a new lab in an empty freight car. One day, Edison saved the life of a child who had fallen onto the tracks of an oncoming train. The child's father took an interest in Edison and taught him to use the telegraph. Edison's first invention was a gadget that sent automatic telegraph signals—which he invented so he could sleep on the job.

While still in his 20s, Edison decided to go into the "invention business." In 1876 Edison set up a workshop in Menlo Park, New Jersey. Out of this famous laboratory came the phonograph, the motion picture projector, the telephone transmitter, and the storage battery. But Edison's most important invention was the electric lightbulb.

Edison developed the first workable lightbulb in 1879. He then designed power plants that could produce electric power and distribute it to lightbulbs. For Christmas in 1880, Edison used 40 bulbs to light up Menlo Park. Visitors flocked to see the "light of the future." He built the first central electric power plant in 1882 in New York City—illuminating 85 buildings!

Inventor **George Westinghouse** took Thomas Edison's work with electricity even further. In 1885 Westinghouse developed and built transformers that could send electric power more cheaply over longer distances. Soon electricity powered factories, trolleys, streetlights, and lamps all over America. Westinghouse also developed a system for transporting natural gas and invented many safety devices.

African American Inventors

A number of African Americans contributed to the era of invention. **Lewis Howard Latimer,** an engineer, developed an improved filament for the lightbulb and joined Thomas Edison's company. **Granville Woods,** an electrical and mechanical engineer from Ohio, patented dozens of inventions. Among them were an electric incubator and railroad improvements such as an electromagnetic brake and an automatic circuit breaker. **Elijah McCoy** invented a mechanism for oiling machinery.

Jan E. Matzeliger, another African American inventor, developed a shoe-making machine that performed many steps previously done by hand. His device, which revolutionized the shoe industry, was adopted in shoe factories in the United States and overseas.

> ✓ Reading Check **Evaluating** Which of Edison's inventions do you think is the most valuable to our world? Explain your reasoning.

A Changing Society

In the 1900s improvements ushered in a new era of transportation. After a period of experimentation, the automobile became a practical method of getting from place to place.

Henry Ford's Automobiles

Henry Ford wanted to build an inexpensive car that would last a lifetime. While working as an engineer in **Detroit, Michigan,** in the 1890s, Ford had experimented with an automobile engine powered by gasoline. In 1903 he established an automaking company and began designing cars.

In 1906 Ford had an idea for a new type of car. He told Charles Sorenson, later Ford's general superintendent, "We're going to get a car now that we can make in great volume and get the prices way down." For the next year, Ford and Sorenson worked on the **Model T,** building the car and testing it on rough roads. In 1908 Ford introduced the Model T to the public. Sorenson described the sturdy black vehicle as

66. . . a car which anyone could afford to buy, which anyone could drive anywhere, and which almost anyone could keep in repair.**99**

These qualities made the Model T immensely popular. During the next 18 years, Ford's company sold 15 million Model T's. Henry Ford also pioneered a new, less expensive way to manufacture cars—the assembly line. On the assembly line, each worker performed an assigned task again and again at a certain stage in the production of the automobile. The assembly line

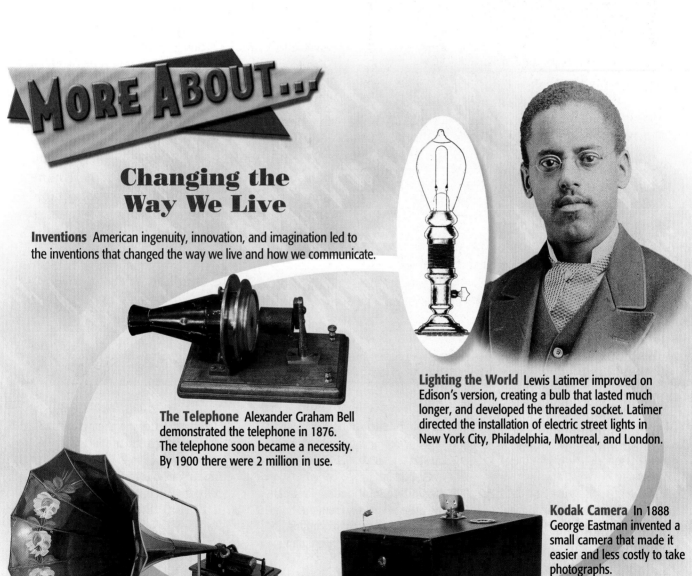

MORE ABOUT...

Changing the Way We Live

Inventions American ingenuity, innovation, and imagination led to the inventions that changed the way we live and how we communicate.

The Telephone Alexander Graham Bell demonstrated the telephone in 1876. The telephone soon became a necessity. By 1900 there were 2 million in use.

Lighting the World Lewis Latimer improved on Edison's version, creating a bulb that lasted much longer, and developed the threaded socket. Latimer directed the installation of electric street lights in New York City, Philadelphia, Montreal, and London.

Kodak Camera In 1888 George Eastman invented a small camera that made it easier and less costly to take photographs.

Phonograph The first practical phonograph was built by Thomas Edison in 1877.

1912 Model T Ford

revolutionized industry, enabling manufacturers to produce large quantities of goods more quickly. This mass production of goods decreased manufacturing costs, so products could be sold more cheaply.

Selling Goods

With factories churning out more and more products, merchants looked for better ways to sell their goods. One way was through the mail. In 1863 mail delivery to homes began— up to then, service was only to post offices. By the 1890s, the U.S. Post Office had expanded its delivery service in rural areas.

Merchants could now send goods across the country nearly as easily as across town. Some firms developed mail order businesses, receiving and shipping orders by mail. Companies such as Montgomery Ward and Sears Roebuck published catalogs that offered a wide range of goods from shoes to farm equipment. Catalogs introduced rural families to a wide assortment of goods not found in country stores.

Chain stores—stores with identical branches in many places—grew rapidly. F.W. Woolworth's chain of "five-and-ten-cent stores" specialized in the sale of everyday household and personal items at bargain prices. By 1911 more than a thousand Woolworth's were in operation. The Woolworth Building, erected in New York City in 1913, stood 792 feet (241 meters) tall—the tallest building in the world at that time.

HISTORY Online
Student Web Activity
Visit taj.glencoe.com and click on **Chapter 19— Student Web Activities** for an activity on inventions.

✓ Reading Check **Describing** What qualities made the Model T popular?

SECTION 2 ASSESSMENT

Checking for Understanding

1. **Key Terms** Use the terms assembly line and mass production in a complete sentence that explains their meaning.
2. **Reviewing Facts** Name and describe two inventions that changed the way Americans communicated in the 1800s.

Reviewing Themes

3. **Science and Technology** How was transportation improved during the early 1900s?

Critical Thinking

4. **Drawing Conclusions** Which invention do you think brought about the most dramatic change in people's lives? Explain.
5. **Organizing Information** Re-create the diagram below. From the description of inventions in this section, classify each invention in one of the categories.

Mostly rural use	Mostly urban use	Both urban and rural	Mostly used by business and industry

Analyzing Visuals

6. **Artifacts** Study the photographs of the inventions and products that appear in Section 2. Which have undergone the greatest change? Why do you think this is so?

Interdisciplinary Activity

Economics Which of the inventions discussed in the section do you think had the greatest impact on the economy of the United States? Draw a picture of the invention and write captions that point out its significance.

An Age of Big Business

Main Idea

Business growth was driven by the formation of corporations and the ambition of their owners.

Key Terms

corporation, stock, shareholder, dividend, horizontal integration, trust, monopoly, vertical integration, philanthropy, merger

Reading Strategy

Analyzing Information As you read the section, re-create the diagram below and explain the significance of each term to business in the late 1800s.

	Significance
Shareholders	
Stock exchanges	
Mergers	

Read to Learn

- how new discoveries and inventions helped industries grow.
- why the development of large corporations brought both benefits and problems.

Section Theme

Economic Factors Corporations changed the American economy of the late 1800s.

Preview of Events

♦1850		♦1875		♦1900

1859
Oil discovered in Titusville, Pennsylvania

1870
Rockefeller organizes the Standard Oil Company

1890
Sherman Antitrust Act prohibits monopolies

1900
Andrew Carnegie rules the steel industry

AN American Story

John D. Rockefeller, a young oil man, never tired until he got what he wanted. One person commented: "The only time I ever saw John Rockefeller enthusiastic was when a report came in . . . that his buyer had secured a cargo of oil at a figure much below the market price. He bounded from his chair with a shout of joy, danced up and down, hugged me, threw up his hat, acted so like a madman that I have never forgotten it. . . . "

Foundations for Growth

In the hills of western Pennsylvania, a sticky black substance—petroleum—seeped from the ground. For a while promoters sold the oil as medicine. Then in the 1850s researchers found they could burn petroleum to produce heat and smoke-free light. It could also be used to lubricate machinery. Suddenly oil became valuable. A former railroad conductor named Edwin L. Drake believed that he could find petroleum by digging a well. People thought Drake was wrong. Few people knew that pools of oil did indeed exist underground.

John D. Rockefeller

In 1859 Drake decided to test his belief. He drilled a well in **Titusville, Pennsylvania,** and struck oil. This led to the creation of a multimillion-dollar petroleum industry.

Factors of Production

The period from the end of the Civil War to 1900 was an era of unmatched economic growth in the United States. New methods in technology and business allowed the country to tap its rich supply of natural resources, increase its production, and raise the money needed for growth. The growing transportation system made it easier for merchants to reach distant markets.

The change from an agricultural economy to an industrial one was possible because the United States had the resources needed for a growing economy. Among these resources were what economists call the **factors of production**: land, labor, and capital.

The first factor of production, **land,** means not just the land itself but all natural resources. The United States held a variety of natural resources that were useful for industrial production.

The second production factor is **labor.** Large numbers of workers were needed to turn raw materials into goods. This need was met by the rapid growth of population. Between 1860 and 1900, the population of the country more than doubled.

The third production factor, **capital,** is the equipment—buildings, machinery, and tools—used in production. Land and labor are needed to produce capital goods. These goods, in turn, are essential for the production of consumer goods.

The term "capital" is also used to mean money for investment. Huge amounts of money were needed to finance industrial growth. One source of money was the selling of stock by corporations. Another was corporate savings, or businesses investing a portion of their earnings in better equipment.

Raising Capital

With the economy growing after the Civil War, many railroads and other businesses looked for ways to expand. To do so they had to raise capital. They needed capital to buy raw materials and equipment, to pay workers, and to cover shipping and advertising costs.

One way a company could raise capital was by becoming a corporation. A corporation is a company that sells shares, or stock, of its business to the public. The people who invest in the corporation by buying stock are its shareholders, or partial owners.

In good times shareholders earn dividends—cash payments from the corporation's profits—on the stock they own. If the company prospers, its stock rises in value, and the shareholders can sell it for a profit. If the company fails, however, the shareholders lose their investment. In the late 1800s hundreds of thousands of people shared in corporate profits by buying and selling stocks in special markets known as **stock exchanges.**

Growth of Corporations

Railroads were the first businesses to form corporations, or "incorporate." Soon manufacturing firms and other businesses were incorporating as well. The growth of corporations helped fuel America's industrial expansion in the years following the Civil War.

Banks played a major role in this period of economic growth. Businesses borrowed money from banks to start or expand their operations. The banks, in turn, made profits on the loans.

✔**Reading Check**
Explaining What are dividends?

Sign advertising oil

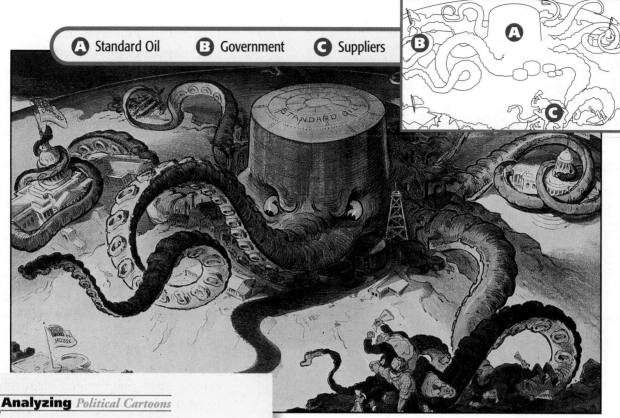

Ⓐ Standard Oil　　Ⓑ Government　　Ⓒ Suppliers

Analyzing *Political Cartoons*

Standard Oil was often portrayed as a "monopoly monster," with its arms reaching out to control government and suppliers. **Why do you think the cartoonist chose an octopus to represent Standard Oil?**

The Oil Business

The oil industry grew rapidly in the late 1800s. Edwin Drake's Titusville well produced 15 barrels of petroleum a day. As word of his success spread, prospectors and investors hurried to western Pennsylvania. "Oil rush" towns with names such as Oil City and Petroleum Center sprang up overnight. The oil boom expanded as prospectors struck oil in Ohio and West Virginia.

John D. Rockefeller

Born in Richford, New York, in 1839, **John D. Rockefeller** made his fortune from oil. When Rockefeller was 26 years old, he and four partners set up an oil refinery—a plant to process oil—in **Cleveland, Ohio.**

In 1870 Rockefeller organized the Standard Oil Company of Ohio and set out to dominate the oil industry. He acquired most of the oil refineries in Cleveland and other cities.

One method Rockefeller used to build his empire was horizontal integration—combining competing firms into one corporation. The corporation produced and used its own tank cars, pipelines, and even its own wooden barrels—made from forests owned by Standard Oil. Standard Oil grew in wealth and power, becoming the most famous corporate empire of the day.

The Standard Oil Trust

To strengthen Standard Oil's position in the oil industry, Rockefeller lowered his prices to drive his competitors out of business. In addition he pressured customers not to deal with rival oil companies, and he persuaded the railroads to grant him rebates in exchange for his business.

Rockefeller increased his control of the oil industry in 1882 by forming a trust, a group of companies managed by the same board of directors. First he acquired stock in many different oil companies. Then the shareholders of these companies traded their stock for Standard Oil stock, which paid higher dividends. This gave Standard Oil's board of directors ownership of the

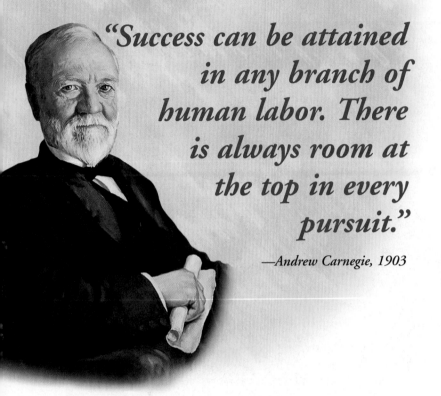

"Success can be attained in any branch of human labor. There is always room at the top in every pursuit."

—Andrew Carnegie, 1903

other companies' stock and the right to manage those companies. Rockefeller had created a monopoly—almost total control by a single producer—of the oil industry.

Reading Check **Explaining** What method did Rockefeller use to build his oil empire?

The Steel Business

Steel also became a huge business in the late 1800s. Steel is a strong and long-lasting form of iron treated with carbon—the ideal material for railroad tracks, bridges, and many other products. Before the 1860s, however, steel was not widely used because it was expensive to manufacture. The development of new manufacturing techniques helped to overcome this problem.

Steel Industry Growth

Two new methods of making steel—the Bessemer process, developed by Henry Bessemer of England, and the open-hearth process—changed the industry. With the new methods, mills could produce steel at affordable prices and in large quantities. In the 1870s large steel mills emerged close to sources of iron ore in western Pennsylvania and eastern Ohio.

Pittsburgh, Pennsylvania, became the steel capital of the United States. Cities located near the mines and close to waterways like Cleveland, Chicago, Detroit, and Birmingham, Alabama, also became centers of steel production.

Andrew Carnegie

The leading figure in the early years of the American steel industry was **Andrew Carnegie,** son of a Scottish immigrant. Starting as a telegraph operator, Carnegie worked his way up to become manager of the Pennsylvania Railroad. In 1865 he left that job to invest in the growing iron industry.

Carnegie soon realized that steel would have an enormous market. After learning about the Bessemer process, he built a steel plant near Pittsburgh that used the new process. Carnegie named the plant the J. Edgar Thompson Steel Works, after the president of the Pennsylvania Railroad—his biggest customer.

Vertical Integration

By 1890 Andrew Carnegie dominated the steel industry. His company became powerful through vertical integration, acquiring companies that provided the equipment and services he needed. Carnegie bought iron and coal mines, warehouses, ore ships, and railroads to gain control of all parts of the business of making and selling steel. When Carnegie combined all his holdings into the Carnegie Steel Company in 1900, he was producing one-third of the nation's steel.

In 1901 Carnegie sold his steel company to banker **J. Pierpont Morgan.** Morgan combined the Carnegie company with other businesses to form the United States Steel Corporation, the world's first billion-dollar corporation.

Philanthropists

Andrew Carnegie, John D. Rockefeller, and other industrial millionaires of the time grew interested in philanthropy—the use of money to benefit the community. The philanthropists founded schools, universities, and other civic institutions across the United States.

Carnegie donated $350 million to various organizations. He built Carnegie Hall in New York City, one of the world's most famous concert halls; the Carnegie Foundation for the Advancement of Teaching; and more than 2,000 libraries worldwide. Rockefeller used his fortune to establish the University of Chicago in 1890 and New York's Rockefeller Institute for Medical Research.

Corporations Grow Larger

In 1889 New Jersey encouraged the trend toward business monopolies by allowing holding companies to obtain charters, a practice that some states prohibited. A holding company would buy controlling interests in the stock of other companies instead of purchasing the companies outright. Rockefeller formed Standard Oil of New Jersey so that the corporation could expand its holdings. Other states also passed laws that made corporate mergers—the combining of companies—easier.

Mergers concentrated economic power in a few giant corporations and a few powerful individuals, such as Rockefeller and banker J. Pierpont Morgan. By 1900 one-third of all American manufacturing was controlled by just 1 percent of the country's corporations. These giant corporations were the driving force behind the great economic growth of the period, but they also posed problems. On the one hand, many Americans admired the efficiencies that large businesses provided. On the other hand, some argued that a lack of competition hurt consumers. Without competition, corporations had no reason to keep their prices low or to improve their goods and services.

Government Regulation

State governments responded to the growing opposition to trusts and monopolies. During the 1880s, several states passed laws restricting business combinations. Corporations, however, avoided these laws by doing business in states that had no such laws.

Public pressure for a federal law to prohibit trusts and monopolies led Congress to pass the **Sherman Antitrust Act** in 1890. The law sought "to protect trade and commerce against unlawful restraint and monopoly." The act did not clearly define either "trusts" or "monopolies," however.

In its early years, the Sherman Antitrust Act did little to curb the power of big business. By contrast, in the 1890s the government did use the act to stop a strike by railroad workers that threatened to "restrain" the nation's mail delivery.

✓ **Reading Check** **Comparing** How does vertical integration differ from horizontal integration?

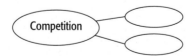

SECTION 3 ASSESSMENT

Checking for Understanding

1. **Key Terms** Use the key terms that follow to write a newspaper article about Andrew Carnegie: corporation, monopoly, vertical integration, philanthropy.

2. **Reviewing Facts** What cities became centers of steel production in the late 1800s?

Reviewing Themes

3. **Economic Factors** Summarize the steps that John D. Rockefeller took to gain control of the oil industry.

Critical Thinking

4. **Determining Cause and Effect** Recreate the diagram below and list the benefits of competition to consumers.

```
Competition ──⬭
            ──⬭
```

5. **Comparing** Compare the methods used by Rockefeller and Carnegie to build their industrial empires. Describe any differences between the two.

Analyzing Visuals

6. **Analyzing Political Cartoons** Study the cartoon on page 569. Whom do the figures represent? What is the cartoon saying about the Standard Oil Company?

Interdisciplinary Activity

Citizenship Research to find a philanthropist who has provided benefits to the community in which you live—in the past or present. Share your findings with the class.

SECTION 4 Industrial Workers

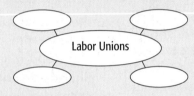

Guide to Reading

Main Idea
Workers organized to demand better pay and working conditions.

Key Terms
sweatshop, trade union, collective bargaining, strikebreaker, injunction

Reading Strategy
Organizing Information As you read the section, re-create the diagram below and list actions labor unions took to improve working conditions.

Labor Unions

Read to Learn
• why workers demanded changes in their working conditions and wages.
• how labor unions helped workers gain economic and political power.

Section Theme
Groups and Institutions Industrial workers labored long hours for low pay.

Preview of Events

♦1870   ♦1880   ♦1890

1869
Knights of Labor organized

1877
Railroad workers on strike

1886
Riots erupt in Haymarket Square

Haymarket Riot news report

AN American Story

On a spring day in 1886, about 12,000 workers in Chicago's Haymarket Square manufacturing district were on strike. Nearly all were immigrants, and many wore small red ribbons on their jackets. At 2 o'clock a man climbed up on an empty freight car near the crowd. He moved to the edge of the roof and waved frantically at the crowd below. "Stand firm," he yelled. "Let every man stand shoulder to shoulder and we will win this fight. We must have our rights. Strike while the iron is hot. . . ."

Working Conditions

The industrial growth of the late 1800s created new jobs. Growth also raised the standard of living for many American workers. That is, necessities and luxuries were more available and affordable. Yet workers paid a price for economic progress. Factories had once been small workplaces where employers and employees knew one another and often worked side by side. As mass production spread, however, factories became larger and less personal.

Industrial laborers worked for 10 or 12 hours a day, six days a week. They could be fired at any time for any reason. Many lost their jobs during business downturns or were replaced by immigrants who were willing to work for lower pay.

Factories and mines were noisy, unhealthy, and unsafe. Accidents were common. Steel workers suffered burns from spills of hot steel. Coal miners died in cave-ins and from the effects of gas and coal dust. Textile workers' lungs were damaged by airborne lint. Garment workers toiled in crowded urban factories called sweatshops, where their eyesight was ruined by sewing for hours in poor light. Filled with flammable materials, the sweatshops were also terrible firetraps.

(See page 971 for a first-person account of sweatshop conditions.)

Women Workers

Although the majority of working women in the late 1800s had jobs as domestic servants, women also joined the industrial workforce, especially the textile industry. By 1900 more than one million women worked in industry. However, because no laws regulated workers' salaries, women generally received about half of what men earned for the same work.

Child Labor

Industries also hired children. In 1900, hundreds of thousands of children under 16 years of age worked in factories. Concerned groups brought child labor to the attention of their state legislatures. As a result many states passed child-labor laws. These laws stated that children working in factories had to be at least 12 years old and should not work more than 10 hours a day. Employers widely ignored child-labor laws, however. Also, the laws did not apply to agriculture, which employed about one million children.

Reading Check **Examining** How did mass production change the size of factories?

Labor Unions Form

Dissatisfied workers organized into groups—labor unions—to demand better pay and working conditions from their employers. Earlier in the 1800s, skilled workers had formed unions to represent workers in certain crafts or trades, such as carpentry. These trade unions had little influence because each represented only one trade. By the mid-1800s labor leaders looked to expand their unions.

In 1869 garment cutters in Philadelphia founded the Noble and Holy Order of the **Knights of Labor.** Employers fired workers who joined labor organizations, so the Knights met secretly and used special handshakes to identify each other. Under the leadership of **Terence V. Powderly,** the Knights of Labor became a national labor organization in the 1880s. Unlike most unions, the Knights recruited people who had been kept out of trade unions, including women, African Americans, immigrants, and unskilled laborers.

The Knights of Labor grew rapidly to more than 700,000 members by 1886. However, a wave of strikes turned public opinion against the union, and it lost members and power in the 1890s.

In 1881 a group of national trade unions formed a federation that five years later became known as the **American Federation of Labor** (AFL). The AFL represented skilled workers in various crafts.

Young coal miners in Kingston, Pennsylvania, c. 1900

NATIONAL GEOGRAPHIC — Labor's Struggle for Justice, 1877–1914

Labor Unrest

1. **1877 Great Railway Strike**
   Workers protest pay cuts

2. **1886 Haymarket Affair**
   Labor rally ends in violence

3. **1892 New Orleans**
   Workers from 42 unions demand shorter hours and better pay

4. **1892 Homestead Strike**
   Steelworkers protest wage cut

5. **1892 Silver Mines Unrest**
   State jails hundreds of striking workers

6. **1894 Pullman Strike**
   Federal troops quell riots

7. **1902 Anthracite Coal Strike**
   Miners strike to win union recognition

8. **1914 Ludlow Massacre**
   State militia burns striking miners' tent colony

Geography Skills

The strike was the major weapon for workers against the management for whom they worked.

1. **Location** Which strikes involved miners?
2. **Analyzing Information** Which strike occurred in Martinsburg?

The AFL was led by **Samuel Gompers,** the tough, practical-minded president of the Cigar Makers' Union. The organization pressed for higher wages, shorter hours, better working conditions, and the right to bargain collectively with employers. In collective bargaining, unions represent workers in bargaining with management.

Although violent strikes turned public feeling against workers and unions in the late 1880s, the AFL survived and grew. By 1904 the AFL claimed more than 1.6 million members.

Women and the Unions

Many unions would not admit women workers, so some women formed their own unions. **Mary Harris Jones,** better known as Mother Jones, spent 50 years fighting for workers' rights.

In 1911 a fire broke out at the **Triangle Shirtwaist Company** factory, a crowded sweatshop in New York City. The workers, mostly young immigrant women, could not escape from the building because the company had locked the doors to prevent employees from leaving early. Nearly 150 workers died in the fire. The disaster led the **International Ladies' Garment Workers Union** (ILGWU) to push for a safer working environment.

Reading Check **Comparing** Who was eligible for membership in the AFL? In the Knights of Labor?

The Unions Act

Economic depressions in the 1870s and the 1890s led companies to fire workers and lower wages. Unions responded with large strikes that sometimes sparked violence.

Economic depression hit the nation following a financial panic in 1873. To cut costs, companies forced their workers to take pay cuts. In July 1877 angry strikers burned rail yards, ripped up track, and destroyed railroad property. The companies hired strikebreakers to replace the striking workers, and federal troops restored order.

Antilabor feeling grew stronger after a bloody clash between police and strikers in Chicago's Haymarket Square in May 1886. Striking workers from the McCormick Harvester Company gathered to protest the killings of four strikers the previous day. When police ordered the crowd to break up, an unidentified person threw a bomb that killed a police officer. Several more were killed in a riot that followed. Following the **Haymarket Riot,** many Americans associated the labor movement with terrorism and disorder.

In 1892 workers went on strike at Andrew Carnegie's steel plant in Homestead, Pennsylvania. Plant managers had cut workers' wages, hoping to weaken the steelworkers' union. When the union called a strike, Homestead managers hired nonunion workers and brought in 300 armed guards to protect them. A fierce battle left at least 10 people dead. Pennsylvania's governor sent the state's militia to Homestead to restore order. The plant reopened with nonunion workers, protected by the troops. After the failure of the **Homestead Strike,** the steelworkers' union dwindled.

The employees of George Pullman's railway-car plant near Chicago went on strike in May 1894, when the company cut wages. Pullman responded by closing the plant. One month later, workers in the American Railway Union supported the strikers by refusing to handle Pullman cars, paralyzing rail traffic.

Pullman and the railroad owners fought back. They persuaded U.S. Attorney General Richard Olney to obtain an injunction, or court order, to stop the union from "obstructing the railways and holding up the mails." The workers and their leader, **Eugene V. Debs,** refused to end the strike. Debs was sent to jail.

President **Grover Cleveland** sent federal troops to Chicago, and soon the strike was over. The failure of the **Pullman Strike** dealt another blow to the union movement. Despite these setbacks, workers continued to organize to work for better wages and working conditions.

✓ **Reading Check** **Describing** Why did the Pullman workers go on strike?

SECTION 4 ASSESSMENT

Checking for Understanding

1. **Key Terms** Write a paragraph about the American Federation of Labor. Use the following terms: sweatshop, trade union, collective bargaining, strikebreaker, injunction.
2. **Reviewing Facts** What role did Samuel Gompers play in union growth?

Reviewing Themes

3. **Groups and Institutions** What were the goals of the American Federation of Labor when it was founded?

Critical Thinking

4. **Drawing Conclusions** Why do you think many Americans did not immediately support the labor unions?
5. **Organizing Information** Re-create the diagram below and describe the roles each played in labor-management issues.

Individual	Role
Terence Powderly	
Mary Harris Jones	
George Pullman	
Grover Cleveland	

Analyzing Visuals

6. **Geography Skills** Study the map on page 574. Which of the incidents shown on the map occurred in the 1890s? What events took place in Illinois? When did they occur?

Interdisciplinary Activity

Art Design a board game in which players can experience the ups and downs of factory work in the late 1800s. Include spaces such as "Workday extended to 12 hours. Miss a turn." and "Your union wins a pay hike. Collect $5."

Chapter Summary

The Growth of Industry

Railroads

- Settlers are transported west.
- Railroads deliver raw materials and finished goods.
- Thousands of jobs are provided.
- Large railroads offer secret rebates to customers and make secret agreements that raise rates.

Inventions

- The telegraph links the United States and Europe.
- Alexander Graham Bell invents the telephone.
- Thomas Alva Edison invents the electric lightbulb.
- Henry Ford uses assembly lines to mass-produce the automobile.
- Wright brothers fly airplane at Kitty Hawk.
- New processes improve steel production.

Companies

- Railroads are the first businesses to incorporate.
- John D. Rockefeller organizes Standard Oil, forms a trust, and creates a monopoly.
- Andrew Carnegie forms Carnegie Steel Company.
- Congress passes the Sherman Antitrust Act.

Labor Movement

- Working conditions in factories and mines are unhealthy.
- Women workers paid half of men's wages for same work.
- Child workers are exploited.
- Labor unions form to improve wages and working conditions.
- Labor union strikes sometimes result in violence.

Reviewing Key Terms

Use each of the following terms in a statement that might have been made by the person indicated.

1. **Railroad owner:** rebate, pool, standard gauge
2. **Union member:** trade union, collective bargaining
3. **Factory owner:** mass production, assembly line
4. **Shareholder:** stock, dividend

Reviewing Key Facts

5. What improvements in railway transportation were brought about by new technology?
6. What were four of Thomas Edison's inventions?
7. What inventions improved communications in the late 1800s?
8. What manufacturing methods did Henry Ford use to make his new automobile affordable?
9. What is vertical integration?
10. What action did Congress take to control trusts and monopolies in response to pressure from the American people?
11. What is collective bargaining?
12. How did the Haymarket Riot of 1886 affect public opinion about the labor movement?

Critical Thinking

13. **Analyzing Information** Describe the contributions of African American inventors in the late 1800s.
14. **Analyzing Themes: Economic Factors** How did horizontal integration differ from vertical integration?
15. **Drawing Conclusions** Why did workers think that forming organized labor unions would help them get what they wanted from employers?
16. **Analyzing Themes: Geography and History** Re-create the diagram below and describe two ways in which the growing railroad network helped American industry.

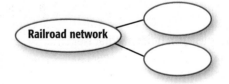

Railroad network

Self-Check Quiz
Visit taj.glencoe.com and click on **Chapter 19—Self-Check Quizzes** to prepare for the chapter test.

Geography and History Activity

Study the map below and answer the questions that follow.

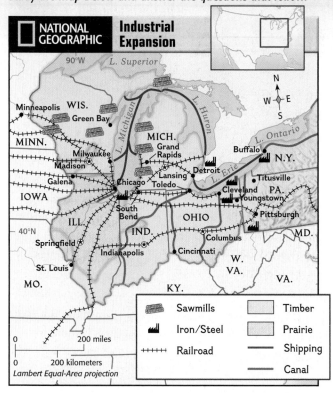

NATIONAL GEOGRAPHIC **Industrial Expansion**

Legend:
- Sawmills
- Iron/Steel
- Railroad
- Timber
- Prairie
- Shipping
- Canal

0 — 200 miles
0 — 200 kilometers
Lambert Equal-Area projection

17. Movement What forms of transportation moved goods into and out of this region?

18. Human/Environment Interaction What industry grew in the timbered regions of Wisconsin and Michigan?

19. Location Identify the major iron/steel manufacturing centers shown on the map.

Practicing Skills

Reading a Time Zone Map *Study the time zone map on page 560. Use the map to answer the following questions.*

20. If you traveled from Florida to California, what time zones would you cross?

21. If it is 6:00 a.m. in Maine, what time is it in Hawaii?

22. If it is 3:00 p.m. in Texas, what time is it in Alaska?

Citizenship Cooperative Activity

23. Labor Unions With another student, write a short essay in which you support or criticize labor unions from the point of view of a young person who has just entered the workforce. Note how you think a union could or could not improve your life. Share your essay with the class.

Economics Activity

24. Using a product that is familiar to you, explain how each of the factors of production was used in its creation.

Technology Activity

25. Using a Spreadsheet Become an imaginary shareholder in a corporation. Search for stock market data in a daily newspaper. Choose one stock to follow for a two-week period. Track the performance of the stock on a spreadsheet by marking its daily increases and decreases. Compare your spreadsheet with classmates' results and decide if you made a good investment.

Alternative Assessment

26. Portfolio Writing Activity Review the chapter for information about the four major union strikes between 1877 and 1894. Write a headline for each that might have appeared in newspapers following the strike.

Standardized Test Practice

Directions: Choose the *best* answer to the following question.

The development of the transformers that Westinghouse built led to an increase in

F the price of electricity.

G the use of gas to heat homes.

H the use of electricity to power factories.

J imported goods.

Test-Taking Tip

The phrase *led to* indicates that this question is looking for a *cause-and-effect* relationship. Remember that a *cause* is any person, event, or condition that makes something happen. What happens as a result is known as an *effect*.

Building a Conductivity Tester

What role does electricity play in your life? Can you imagine your life without electricity? Electricity powers lights, TVs, radios, ovens, microwaves, and computers, along with countless other objects you use every day.

The Way It Was

The Civil War had ended. No longer divided by war, Americans set about improving their lives. Inventors led the way. Inventors such as George Westinghouse, Lewis Howard Latimer, and Thomas Edison learned from one another, and together pushed the United States to become an industrial nation. To create the lightbulb, Edison first had to understand how electricity works. Now, conduct your own investigation of electrical currents, much as Edison did, and experience the life of an inventor. Find out which common objects are conductors and which are insulators by building and testing a battery-powered conductivity tester.

Believe It or Not

Thomas Edison suffered from hearing problems throughout his life. Although an operation could have saved his hearing, Edison refused it. He claimed he preferred deafness because it helped him concentrate.

Materials

✓ flashlight with one fresh D cell (battery)
✓ 3 pieces of insulated wire (each about 6 inches (15 cm) long, with the ends stripped)
✓ roll of masking or duct tape
✓ a penny
✓ a plastic comb
✓ several pieces of fabric
✓ a metal fork or spoon
✓ several different rocks
✓ various other objects to test

What To Do

Build your conductivity tester by unscrewing the top of the flashlight. You will find that the flashlight contains a bulb assembly.

1 Take one wire and tape it to the metal tip of the flashlight lightbulb. Tape a second wire to the metal ring that touches the side of the bulb.

2 Tape the other end of the wire that is connected to the tip of the lightbulb to the positive (+) end of a D cell (battery) and touch the free end of the second wire to the negative (–) end of the cell. The light should go on because you have made an electrical current. (If the light does not go on, make sure all the connections are taped tightly and make good contact.)

3 Tape one end of a third wire to the negative (–) end of the cell and touch the free end of that wire to the wire coming from the bulb holder. Again, the light should go on. Try touching the two free ends of the wires to the penny at the same time. The bulb should light because the penny is a good conductor.

Test your other objects in the same way that you tested the penny. Record whether they are conductors or insulators.

Project Report

1. In general, what types of materials make the best conductors?

2. From your experiment, how would you define an electrical current?

3. **Drawing Conclusions** What are some of the risks inventors take when experimenting with unfamiliar materials?

Go a Step Further

How was Edison able to invent such useful things? How would you go about inventing something? Research and learn about some of the inventors from the late 1800s and early 1900s. Note how these inventors got started. Then create a diagram that explains how you would go about creating a new invention.

CHAPTER 20

Toward an Urban America

1865–1914

Why It Matters

By 1914 as many Americans lived in cities as in rural areas. Between 1860 and 1910, the urban population of the nation grew from a little over 6 million people to more than 40 million.

The Impact Today

During these years of urban growth, many aspects of modern city life emerged. Problems arose, such as poverty, crime, and inadequate housing, but benefits such as daily newspapers, libraries, and public parks appeared as well.

 The American Journey Video *The chapter 20 video, "Ellis Island: In the Shadow of Lady Liberty," details the hardships immigrants faced when arriving in America.*

1882
• Chinese Exclusion Act passed

1884
• First skyscraper built in Chicago

1871
• Great Chicago fire

1886
• Statue of Liberty dedicated

United States PRESIDENTS

| A. Johnson 1865–1869 | Grant 1869–1877 | Hayes 1877–1881 | Garfield 1881 | Arthur 1881–1885 | Cleveland 1885–1889 | B. Harrison 1889–1893 |

1865   1875   1885

World

1866
• Transatlantic telegraph line successfully completed

1889
• Eiffel Tower erected

1900
• Freud's *Interpretation of Dreams* published

New York City, East Side, 1900 New arrivals crowded into America's cities and brought with them the cultural heritage of their homelands.

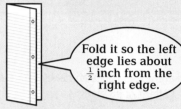
Study Organizer

Sequencing Events Study Foldable Analyze and sequence key influences that led to the urbanization of the United States by making this foldable.

Step 1 Fold a sheet of paper in half from side to side.

Fold it so the left edge lies about $\frac{1}{2}$ inch from the right edge.

Step 2 Turn the paper and fold it into thirds.

Step 3 Unfold and cut the top layer only along both folds.

This will make three tabs.

Step 4 Label as shown.

The New Immigrants · Moving to the City · A Changing Culture

Reading and Writing As you read the chapter, write information about these influences under the appropriate tabs. Think about how these influences followed and affected one another.

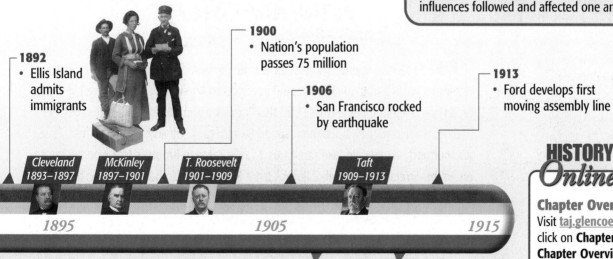

1892
• Ellis Island admits immigrants

1900
• Nation's population passes 75 million

1906
• San Francisco rocked by earthquake

1913
• Ford develops first moving assembly line

Cleveland 1893–1897

McKinley 1897–1901

T. Roosevelt 1901–1909

Taft 1909–1913

1895

1905

1915

c. 1907
• Cubism arises in art

1911
• Italy seizes Libya

HISTORY Online

Chapter Overview
Visit taj.glencoe.com and click on **Chapter 20— Chapter Overviews** to preview chapter information.

SECTION 1 The New Immigrants

Guide to Reading

Main Idea
In the late 1800s and early 1900s, the pattern of immigration was changing.

Key Terms
emigrate, ethnic group, steerage, sweatshop, assimilate

Reading Strategy
Analyzing Information As you study Section 1, re-create the diagram below and write the reasons immigrants came to America.

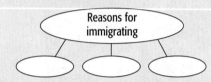

Reasons for immigrating

Read to Learn
• what opportunities and difficulties immigrants found in the United States.
• how the arrival of new immigrants changed American society.

Section Theme
Culture and Traditions The number of immigrants from southern and eastern Europe increased dramatically.

Preview of Events

♦1880	♦1900	♦1920

1882
Chinese Exclusion Act is passed

1886
Statue of Liberty is erected

1892
Ellis Island starts processing immigrants

1917
Immigration Act of 1917 requires literacy

Immigrant's ticket

AN American Story

In the 1870s two young brothers left Italy for America. "We were so long on the water that we began to think we should never get to America. . . . We were all landed on an island and the bosses there said that Francisco and I must go back because we had not enough money, but a man named Bartolo came up and told them that . . . he was our uncle and would take care of us. . . . We came to Brooklyn to a wooden house on Adams Street that was full of Italians from Naples. Bartolo had a room on the third floor and there were fifteen men in the room, all boarding with Bartolo. . . . It was very hot in the room, but we were soon asleep, for we were very tired."

A Flood of Immigrants

Before 1865 most immigrants to the United States—except for the enslaved —came from northern and western Europe. The greater part of these "old" immigrants were Protestant, spoke English, and blended easily into American society. After the Civil War, even greater numbers of immigrants made the journey to the United States. The tide of newcomers reached a peak in 1907 when nearly 1.3 million people came to America.

★ Geography

New Immigration

In the mid-1880s the pattern of immigration started to change. Large groups of "new" immigrants arrived from eastern and southern Europe. Greeks, Russians, Hungarians, Italians, Turks, and Poles were among the newcomers. At the same time, the number of "old" immigrants started to decrease. By 1907 only about 20 percent of the immigrants came from northern and western Europe, while 80 percent came from southern and eastern Europe.

Many of the newcomers from eastern and southern Europe were Catholics or Jews. Few spoke English. Because of this, they did not blend into American society as easily as the "old" immigrants had. Many felt like outsiders, and they clustered together in urban neighborhoods made up of people of the same nationality.

After 1900 immigration from Mexico also increased. In addition many people came to the United States from China and Japan. They, too, brought unfamiliar languages and religious beliefs and had difficulty blending into American society.

Leaving Troubles Behind

Why did so many people leave their homelands for the United States in the late 1800s and early 1900s? They were "pushed" away by difficult conditions at home and "pulled" to the United States by new opportunities.

Many people emigrated, or left their homelands, because of economic troubles. In Italy and Hungary, overcrowding and poverty made jobs scarce. Farmers in Croatia and Serbia could not own enough land to support their families. Sweden suffered major crop failures. New machines such as looms put many craft workers out of work.

Persecution also drove people from their homelands. In some countries the government passed laws or followed policies against certain ethnic groups—minorities that spoke different languages or followed different customs from those of most people in a country. Members of these ethnic groups often emigrated to escape discrimination or unfair laws. Many Jews fled persecution in Russia in the 1880s and came to the United States.

Seeking Opportunity

Immigrants saw the United States as a land of jobs, plentiful and affordable land, and opportunities for a better life. Although some immigrants returned to their homelands after a few years, most came to America to stay.

✓ **Reading Check** **Describing** Who were the "new" immigrants?

Picturing **History**

Immigrants arrive in New York Harbor from Hamburg, Germany, in 1906. **Where did most immigrants to America come from after 1880?**

The first stop for millions of immigrants was Ellis Island. About 12 million people passed through the Ellis Island immigration center between 1892 and 1954. The main building was reopened in 1990 as the Ellis Island Museum of Immigration. Located a short distance north of the Statue of Liberty in New York Harbor, Ellis Island stands as a memorial to the traditions of freedom and opportunity in America.

The Journey to America

Immigrants often had a difficult journey to America. Many had to first travel to a seaport to board a ship. Often they traveled for hundreds of miles on foot or on horseback and through foreign countries to get to the port cities.

Then came the long ocean voyage to America—12 days across the Atlantic or several weeks across the Pacific. Immigrants usually could afford only the cheapest tickets, and they traveled in steerage—cramped, noisy quarters on the lower decks.

The Statue of Liberty

Most European immigrants landed at New York City. After 1886 the magnificent sight of the **Statue of Liberty** greeted the immigrants as they sailed into **New York Harbor.** The statue, a gift from France, seemed to promise hope for a better life in the new country. On the base of the statue, the stirring words of **Emma Lazarus,** an American poet, welcomed immigrants from Europe:

❝Give me your tired, your poor,
Your huddled masses yearning to breathe free,
The wretched refuse of your teeming shore.
Send these, the homeless, tempest-tossed to me,
I lift my lamp beside the golden door!❞

Entering America

Bianca De Carli arrived from Italy in 1913 as a young girl. Many years later she remembered how she felt as her ship reached New York City:

❝We all trembled because of the strangeness and the confusion. . . . Some were weak from no movement and exercise, and some were sick because of the smells and the unfresh air. But somehow this did not matter because we now knew it was almost over.❞

Before the new arrivals could actually pass through the "golden door" to America, they had to register at government reception centers. In the East immigrants were processed at Castle Garden, a former fort on Manhattan Island, and after 1892 at **Ellis Island** in New York Harbor. Most Asian immigrants arrived in America on the West Coast and went through the processing center on **Angel Island** in **San Francisco Bay.**

Examiners at the centers recorded the immigrants' names—sometimes shortening or simplifying a name they found too difficult to write. The examiners asked the immigrants where they came from, their occupation, and whether they had relatives in the United States. The examiners also gave health examinations. Immigrants with contagious illnesses could be refused permission to enter the United States.

✓ **Reading Check** **Describing** How long did the ocean voyage across the Atlantic take?

The Immigrant Experience

After passing through the reception centers, most immigrants entered the United States. Where would they go? How would they live? Some had relatives or friends to stay with and to help them find jobs. Others knew no one and would have to strike out on their own.

Finding Work

An immigrant's greatest challenge was finding work. Sometimes organizations in his or her homeland recruited workers for jobs in the United States. The organization supplied American employers with unskilled workers who worked unloading cargo or digging ditches.

Some of America's fastest-growing industries hired immigrant workers. In the steel mills of Pittsburgh, for example, most of the common laborers in the early 1900s were immigrant men. They might work 12 hours a day, seven days a week.

Many immigrants, including women and children, worked in sweatshops in the garment industry. These were dark, crowded workshops where workers made clothing. The work was repetitious and hazardous, the pay low, and the hours long.

Pauline Newman, who later became an official in the International Ladies' Garment Workers Union, worked in a New York sweatshop as a child. She recalled:

> 66We started work at seven-thirty in the morning, and during the busy season we worked until nine in the evening. They didn't pay you any overtime and they didn't give you anything for supper money. Sometimes they'd give you a little apple pie if you had to work very late.99

Adjusting to America

In their new homes, immigrants tried to preserve some aspects of their own cultures. At the same time, most wanted to assimilate, or become part of the American culture. These two desires sometimes came into conflict.

Language highlighted the differences between generations. Many immigrant parents continued to speak their native languages. Their children spoke English at school and with friends, but they also spoke their native language at home. On the other hand, the grandchildren of many immigrants spoke only English.

The role of immigrant women also changed in the United States, where women generally had more freedom than women in European and Asian countries. New lifestyles conflicted with traditional ways and sometimes caused family friction. 📖 *(See page 971 of the Primary Sources Library for one woman's account of leaving her native country.)*

Building Communities

Most of the new immigrants were from rural areas. Because they lacked the money to buy farmland in America, however, they often settled in industrial cities. With little or no education, they usually worked as unskilled laborers.

Relatives who had immigrated earlier helped new arrivals get settled, and people of the same ethnic group naturally tended to form

HISTORY Online

Student Web Activity
Visit taj.glencoe.com and click on **Chapter 20— Student Web Activities** for an activity on immigration.

Immigrant children learn American ways in the classroom.

TWO VIEWPOINTS

Should We Welcome or Prevent Immigration to Our Country?

Immigrants struggled to find their place in American society. They changed American society with customs from their cultures. Many Americans resisted these changes and warned against further immigration.

San Francisco Real Estate Circular, September 1874

The Chinese come for a season only; and, while they give their labor, they do not [spend the money they earn] in the country. They do not come to settle or make homes . . . To compare the Chinese with even the lowest white laborers is, therefore, absurd.

Our best interests are suffering of these Asiatic slaves; we are trying to make them live decently while here, and to discourage their arrival in such numbers as to drive white laborers out of the country. . . .

Chinese immigrants

Attorney Louis Marshall Speaks Out Against Limiting Immigration, 1924

In common with all other immigrants, those who have come from the countries sought to be tabooed [forbidden] have been industrious, and law-abiding and have made valuable contributions to our industrial, commercial and social development. . . .

To say that they are not assimilable argues ignorance. The facts show that they adopt American standards of living and that they are permeated [filled] with the spirit of our institutions. It is said that they speak foreign languages, but in those foreign languages they are taught to love our Government. . . .

Louis Marshall

Learning From History

1. What did the writer from San Francisco seem to fear?
2. What did Louis Marshall claim about the immigrants' contributions?
3. What facts does Marshall use to support his view that the newcomers are "assimilable"?

---

communities. As a result neighborhoods of Jewish, Italian, Polish, Chinese, and other groups quickly developed in New York, Chicago, San Francisco, and other large cities.

The immigrants sought to re-create some of the life they had left behind. The communities they established revolved around a number of traditional institutions. Most important were the houses of worship—the churches and synagogues—where worship was conducted and holidays were celebrated as they had been in their homelands. Priests and rabbis often acted as community leaders.

The immigrants published newspapers in their native languages, opened stores and theaters, and organized social clubs. Ethnic communities and institutions helped the immigrants preserve their cultural heritage.

✓ **Reading Check** **Describing** What is assimilation?

Nativist Movement

Assimilation was also slowed by the attitudes of many native-born Americans. Although employers were happy to hire immigrant workers at low wages, some American-born workers resented the immigrants. These Americans feared that the immigrants would take away their jobs or drive down everyone's wages by accepting lower pay.

Ethnic, religious, and racial differences contributed to tensions between Americans and the new immigrants. Some Americans argued that the new immigrants—with their foreign languages, unfamiliar religions, and distinctive customs—did not fit into American society.

People found it easy to blame immigrants for increasing crime, unemployment, and other problems. The nativist movement, for example, had opposed immigration since the 1830s. Nativism gained strength in the late 1800s. Calls for restrictions on immigration mounted.

New Immigration Laws

Lawmakers responded quickly to the tide of anti-immigrant feeling. In 1882 Congress passed the first law to limit immigration—the **Chinese Exclusion Act.** This law prohibited Chinese workers from entering the United States for 10 years. Congress extended the law in 1892 and again in 1902.

In 1907 the federal government and Japan came to a "gentleman's agreement." The Japanese agreed to limit the number of immigrants to the United States, while the Americans pledged fair treatment for Japanese Americans already in the United States.

Other legislation affected immigrants from all nations. An 1882 law made each immigrant pay a tax and also barred criminals from entering the country. In 1897 Congress passed a bill requiring immigrants to be able to read and write in some language. Although President Cleveland vetoed the bill as unfair, Congress later passed the **Immigration Act of 1917,** which included a similar literacy requirement.

Support for Immigrants

Despite some anti-immigrant sentiment, many Americans—including **Grace Abbott** and **Julia Clifford Lathrop,** who helped found the Immigrants' Protective League—spoke out in support of immigration. These Americans recognized that the United States was a nation of immigrants and that the newcomers made lasting contributions to their new society.

Immigrants' Contributions

The new immigrants supplied the country's growing industries with the workers that were necessary for economic growth. At the same time, the new immigrants and their children—like the old immigrants before them—helped shape American life. They gave the nation its major religious groups—Protestants, Catholics, and Jews. As they became part of the society around them, they enriched that society with the customs and cultures and the language and literature of their homelands.

The effects of immigration were most visible in the cities, with their fast-growing ethnic neighborhoods. The flow of immigrants was one of the factors that transformed America's cities in the late 1800s and the early 1900s.

Reading Check **Explaining** What was the nativist movement?

SECTION 1 ASSESSMENT

Checking for Understanding

1. **Key Terms** Use each of these terms in a sentence that will help explain its meaning: emigrate, ethnic group, steerage, sweatshop, assimilate.
2. **Reviewing Facts** Explain the difference between "old immigration" and "new immigration."

Reviewing Themes

3. **Culture and Traditions** What were some of the cultural differences that immigrants had to adjust to in the United States?

Critical Thinking

4. **Drawing Conclusions** Why do you think some Americans blamed the "new" immigrants for many of society's problems?
5. **Organizing Information** Re-create the diagram below and give three reasons why some Americans did not accept the new immigrants.

```
[ ]    [ ]    [ ]
  ↓      ↓      ↓
  Anti-immigrant feelings
```

Analyzing Visuals

6. **Picturing History** Select one of the photographs that appear in Section 1 and write a paragraph in which you describe the scene. Include a title for the photograph.

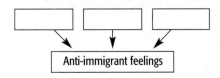

Interdisciplinary Activity

Art Create a collage illustrating the origins of immigrants who came to the United States after 1880. Clip photographs from advertisements and newsmagazines to make your collage.

NEW AMERICANS

BETWEEN 1890 AND 1930 people viewed the United States as a land of opportunity because growing American industries were searching for workers. More than 20 million immigrants poured into the country. The largest groups came from southern, central, and eastern Europe. Immigrants came seeking jobs and freedom. They fled from crop failures, political repression, and military service.

LIFE IN AMERICA

Most newcomers settled near other immigrants from their own country. The largest group, Italians, settled primarily in the Midwest and Northeast. They were escaping from a disastrous cholera epidemic and repeated crop failures. Although they had been farm workers in southern Italy, they settled in cities and found jobs building railroads, streets, and buildings, or selling produce. Many of the women went to work for the garment industry.

Poles, Czechs, Serbs, Croats, and Russians came seeking more freedom. Poles tended to form close-knit communities in the industrial cities of the Midwest and Northeast. For many of them life centered on the Catholic Church, and they sent their children to parochial schools. Women tended to establish boardinghouses or laundries. The men worked in steel mills and slaughterhouses.

Japanese immigrants settled in Hawaii, California, and the Pacific Northwest. They found work in agriculture, forestry, and fisheries. Soon Japanese immigrants were growing 10 percent of California's produce.

The tide of immigration slowed in the early 1920s, when the government imposed new restrictions. Nevertheless, immigrants still continued to play an important role shaping American culture.

LEARNING from GEOGRAPHY

1. **Why do you think Italian, Polish, and Japanese immigrants settled where they did?**

2. **In what regions of the world did the number of emigrants change the most from 1890 to 1930?**

Canada
1,849,000

United States

1,215,000

LATIN AMERICA

U.S. Immigration 1890–1930

3,323,000   Number of immigrants per region

0   1500 miles

0   1500 kilometers

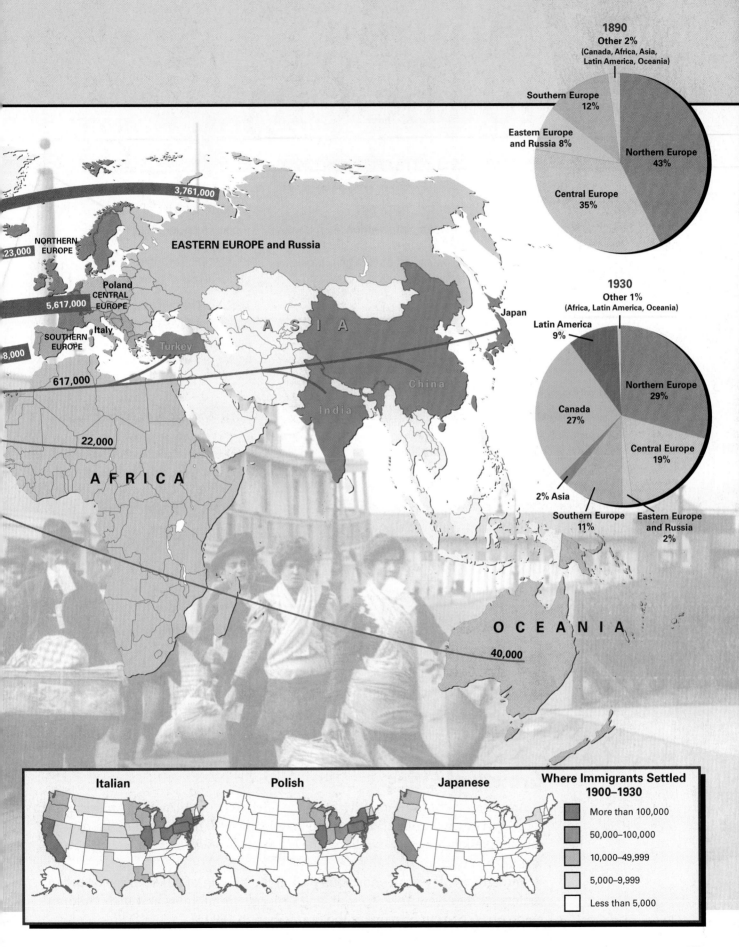

1890

Other 2%
(Canada, Africa, Asia,
Latin America, Oceania)

Southern Europe
12%

Eastern Europe
and Russia 8%

Central Europe
35%

Northern Europe
43%

1930

Other 1%
(Africa, Latin America, Oceania)

Latin America
9%

Canada
27%

2% Asia

Southern Europe
11%

Eastern Europe
and Russia
2%

Central Europe
19%

Northern Europe
29%

3,761,000

NORTHERN
EUROPE

23,000

Poland
CENTRAL
EUROPE

5,617,000

Italy

SOUTHERN
EUROPE

8,000

617,000

22,000

40,000

EASTERN EUROPE and Russia

A S I A

Turkey

China

India

Japan

A F R I C A

O C E A N I A

Italian	Polish	Japanese	**Where Immigrants Settled 1900–1930**
			More than 100,000
			50,000–100,000
			10,000–49,999
			5,000–9,999
			Less than 5,000

Moving to the City

Guide to Reading

Main Idea

Cities in the United States expanded rapidly in the late 1800s.

Key Terms

tenement, slum, suburb, The Gilded Age, settlement house

Reading Strategy

Analyzing Information As you study Section 2, re-create the diagram below and list three serious problems facing American cities in the late 1800s.

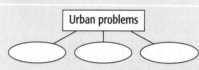

Urban problems

Read to Learn

• how American cities grew and changed.
• what problems cities faced and how people tried to solve them.

Section Theme

Science and Technology Many Americans left the nation's farms, hoping to make their fortunes in the cities.

Preview of Events

♦1870	♦1880	♦1890

1873
The Gilded Age is published

1883
The Brooklyn Bridge opens

1884
First skyscraper constructed in Chicago

1889
Jane Addams founds Hull House

AN American Story

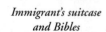

Immigrant's suitcase and Bibles

A train pulling into Chicago in 1884 carried a young passenger named Hamlin Garland. For Garland, who had grown up on a farm, the big city was a bewildering sight. Garland later became famous for his stories about the Midwest. In one novel he described his feeling of dismay when he first saw Chicago. "The mere thought of a million people stunned my imagination." Garland wondered, "How can so many people find a living in one place?"

Growth of Cities

American cities grew rapidly after the Civil War. In 1870, one American in four lived in cities with 2,500 or more people. By 1910 nearly half of the American population were city dwellers. The United States was changing from a rural to an urban nation.

Immigrants played an enormous part in the growth of cities. In major urban centers such as New York, Detroit, and Chicago, immigrants and their children made up 80 percent or more of the population in 1890.

Native-born Americans also contributed to urban growth. Americans moved in huge numbers from farming areas to cities, looking for jobs.

The industrialization of America had changed work on farms. New farm machinery made it possible to produce crops, using fewer farmworkers. In addition women in rural areas no longer had to make clothing and household goods. These items, made by machine, could now be bought in stores or from catalogs. Freed from such chores, many women left farms to look for jobs in the cities.

African Americans also migrated to cities in large numbers. The vast majority of the country's African American population lived in the rural South in great poverty. Many African Americans began moving to Southern cities in search of jobs and to escape debt, injustice, or discrimination. After 1914 a large number of African Americans moved to Northern cities, which offered more jobs in industry and manufacturing than Southern cities did. Many African Americans also hoped to find less discrimination and violence in the North.

Transportation and Resources

America's expanding railroad network fed the growth of the cities. Railroads helped people move to the cities, and they transported the raw materials for industry. Trains carried cattle to Chicago and **Kansas City,** making these cities great meatpacking centers.

Some cities flourished because of nearby resources. **Pittsburgh** developed rapidly as a center for iron and steel manufacturing because both iron ore and coal—to fuel the industry's huge furnaces—were found in the area.

Seaports such as **New York** and **San Francisco** developed as American trade with the rest of the world increased. In addition the immigrant population of these cities provided a large pool of workers who were available for low wages.

Tenement Living

Cities were exciting places that offered jobs, stores, and entertainment. But there was also substandard housing and desperate poverty. People poured into the cities faster than housing could be built to accommodate them. In the biggest, most crowded cities, the poorest residents—including most immigrants—lived in tenements. Originally a tenement was simply a building in which several families rented rooms. By the late 1800s, however, a tenement had come to mean an apartment building in the slums—poor, run-down urban neighborhoods.

Tenements had many small, dark rooms. One young immigrant from Poland spoke of living in the dimly lit rooms in the back of a New York City tenement:

66 We would so like to live in the front, but we can't pay the rent. . . . Why, they have the sun in there. When the door is opened the light comes right in your face. 99

Three, four, or more people lived in each room. Usually several families had to share a cold-water tap and a toilet. Few tenement houses had hot water or bathtubs. A government inspector wrote of the "filthy and rotten tenements" of the Chicago slums in 1896, where children filled "every nook, eating and sleeping in every windowsill, pouring in and out of every door."

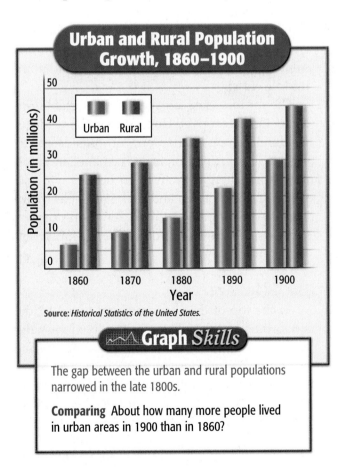

Urban and Rural Population Growth, 1860–1900

Population (in millions)

Urban   Rural

Year

Source: *Historical Statistics of the United States.*

Graph Skills

The gap between the urban and rural populations narrowed in the late 1800s.

Comparing About how many more people lived in urban areas in 1900 than in 1860?

People In History

Jacob Riis 1849–1914

Jacob Riis came to the United States from Denmark when he was 21. Riis worked as a reporter and photographer for New York City newspapers for 20 years. Many of his stories and pictures called attention to the living conditions in the poorer sections of the city. In 1890 Riis wrote *How the Other Half Lives.*

By taking pictures of the tenements, Riis was able to bring the terrible conditions of the slums to the attention of readers. His book helped establish housing codes to prevent the worst abuses.

When Theodore Roosevelt became the city's police commissioner, he asked Riis to present a reform program. Through Riis's efforts, many playgrounds and parks were established in the city. Riis helped make others aware of the problems many urban Americans faced in their daily lives. In addition, he served as an example of what individuals could do to lessen these problems.

Middle-Class Comfort

The cities also had a growing middle class. The middle class included the families of professional people such as doctors, lawyers, and ministers. An increasing number of managers and salaried office clerks also became part of the middle class.

The middle class enjoyed a comfortable life. Many families moved from cities to the suburbs, residential areas that sprang up outside of city centers as a result of improvements in transportation. There they lived in houses with hot water, indoor toilets, and—by 1900—electricity. Middle-class families might have one or two servants and the leisure time to enjoy music, art, and literature.

The Gilded Age

At the top of the economic and social ladder stood the very rich. The wealthy lived very different lives from most Americans. They built enormous mansions in the cities and huge estates in the country. Some homes, such as those of J.P. Morgan and Henry Clay Frick in New York City, are now museums.

In these mansions, the rich lived lives of extreme luxury, throwing enormous parties and dinners. In 1883 Alva and William Kissam Vanderbilt gave a party for more than 1,000 guests at their New York mansion. The party was estimated to have cost $75,000 for food and entertainment, which is equal to about $1.3 million today.

Mark Twain and Charles Dudley Warner published a novel in 1873 called *The Gilded Age.* The name—which refers to something covered with a thin layer of gold—became associated with America of the late 1800s. The Gilded Age suggested both the extravagant wealth of the time and the terrible poverty that lay underneath.

✓ **Reading Check** **Describing** Why was tenement living difficult?

Cities in Crisis

The rapid growth of the cities produced serious problems. The terrible overcrowding in tenement districts created sanitation and health problems. Garbage and horse manure accumulated in city streets, and the sewers could not handle the flow of human waste. Filth created a breeding ground for diseases, which spread rapidly through the crowded districts.

Fires were an ever-present threat. About 18,000 buildings were destroyed and 100,000 Chicagoans lost their homes in the Chicago fire of 1871. Two years later, Boston experienced a devastating fire.

Health and Crime Problems

In a poor Chicago neighborhood in 1900, babies often died of whooping cough, diphtheria, or measles before their first birthday. A section of New York was called the "lung block" because so many residents had tuberculosis.

In an effort to control disease, New York City began to screen schoolchildren for contagious diseases and to provide visiting nurses to mothers with young children. The city also established public health clinics for those who could not pay for medical care.

The poverty in the cities inevitably led to crime. Orphaned and homeless children sometimes resorted to picking pockets and other minor crimes to survive. Gangs roaming the poor neighborhoods committed more serious crimes. **Jacob Riis** reported:

> ❝The gang is an institution in New York. The police deny its existence while nursing the bruises received in nightly battles with it. . . . The gang is the ripe fruit of tenement-house growth. It was born there.❞

Seeking Solutions

The problems of the cities did not go unnoticed. Many dedicated people worked to improve urban life and help the poor.

Religious groups aided the poor. Some religious orders helped the poor in orphanages, prisons, and hospitals. Organizations such as the **YMCA** (Young Men's Christian Association) and **YWCA** (Young Women's Christian Association) offered recreation centers where city youngsters could meet and play.

The poor also received assistance from establishments called settlement houses. The settlement house movement had spread to the

United States from Britain. Located in poor neighborhoods, settlement houses provided medical care, playgrounds, nurseries, and libraries as well as classes in English, music, and arts and crafts. Settlement workers—mostly women—also tried to get better police protection, garbage removal, and public parks for poor districts.

One of the most famous settlement houses was Chicago's **Hull House,** founded by **Jane Addams** in 1889. Addams explained:

> ❝We were ready to perform the humblest neighborhood services. We were asked to wash the new-born babies, and to prepare the dead for burial, to nurse the sick, and to 'mind the children.'❞

Jane Addams

✓ **Reading Check** **Explaining** What purpose did settlement houses serve?

The Changing City

Urban growth led to important new developments. In the late 1800s, cities saw the introduction of a new type of building, new kinds of public transportation, and public parks.

Building Up—Not Out

Because of the limited space in cities, imaginative architects began building upward rather than outward. In the 1860s architects started to use iron frames to strengthen the walls of buildings. Iron supports—together with the safety elevator that **Elisha Otis** invented in 1852—made taller buildings possible.

In 1884 **William LeBaron Jenney** constructed a 10-story office building in Chicago. Supported by an iron-and-steel frame, it was the world's first **skyscraper.** Architect **Louis Sullivan** gave style to the skyscraper. "It must be every inch a proud and soaring thing, rising

The Woolworth building was designed and built to be the tallest building in the world.

in sheer exultation," he said. Sullivan and his colleagues changed the face of America's cities. Soon people built even higher structures. New York's **Woolworth Building,** completed in 1913, soared an incredible 55 stories—792 feet (241 m) high. People called the building the Cathedral of Commerce.

New Designs

Some people looked to reshape the urban landscape. A group known as the "City Beautiful" movement believed city dwellers should be able to enjoy the beauties of nature. **Frederick Law Olmsted,** a leader in this movement, designed New York's Central Park as well as several parks in Boston.

In 1892 and 1893, Chicago hosted a World's Fair on fairgrounds designed by Olmsted. The Fair revealed that American architecture was dynamic and original. The best architects thoroughly understood European styles and adapted them for modern use. The firm of

McKim, Mead, and White used the Italian Renaissance style in its design for the Boston Public Library. Henry Richardson adapted styles from ancient Rome in his design for churches, libraries, and even department stores.

New Forms of Transportation

As cities grew, people needed new means of transportation. Mark Twain complained in 1867 that

> 66New York is too large. You cannot accomplish anything . . . without devoting a whole day to it. . . . The distances are too great.99

Streetcars, which horses pulled on tracks, provided public transportation at the time. Horses were slow, however, and left piles of manure. In 1873 San Francisco began construction of cable-car lines. A large underground cable powered by a motor at one end of the rail line moved passengers along. In 1888 Richmond,

Virginia, pioneered the use of the trolley car, a motorized train that was powered by electricity supplied through overhead cables. By the turn of the century, the trolley was everywhere. In 1897, Boston opened the nation's first subway, or underground railway. In 1904, New York City opened the first section of what was to become the largest subway system in the world.

Another improvement that helped transportation was the paving of streets. During most of the 1800s, city streets remained poorly paved. For example, although the rapid growth of Cleveland, Ohio, made that city an important urban center, most of its streets were nothing more than sand and gravel. Other cities used wood blocks, brick, or cobblestone, all of which were bumpy, noisy, and hard to repair. The growing use of asphalt—a by-product of petroleum refining—beginning in the 1890s made city streets smoother and quieter.

Building Bridges

Bridge construction provided another improvement in urban transportation. Many American cities were divided or bounded by rivers. Using new construction technology, architects and engineers designed huge steel bridges to link sections of cities. The 520-foot (156-m) **Eads Bridge** across the Mississippi River in St. Louis opened in 1874. Ten years later

Skyscrapers

The Empire State Building is the world's tallest building. That was once true, but no longer. By 1931 the Empire State Building dwarfed all other buildings in the world at 102 stories. Today the nation's tallest building is the Sears Tower in Chicago. It is 1,450 feet (442 m) high and has 110 stories.

New York's majestic **Brooklyn Bridge,** 1,600 feet (488 m) long, connected Manhattan and Brooklyn. Both bridges remain in use today.

The new forms of transportation not only helped people travel within the cities, but they also helped the cities grow. Middle-class suburbs developed along train or trolley lines stretching away from city centers. People who moved out of the city centers could easily travel downtown to work or shop.

The increase in immigration and the growth of the cities went hand in hand with other changes in American life. Education, culture, and recreation were changing too.

Reading Check **Summarizing** What new forms of urban transportation were developed?

SECTION 2 ASSESSMENT

Checking for Understanding

1. **Key Terms** Use the vocabulary terms that follow to write a paragraph about life in the cities: tenement, slum, suburb, settlement house.
2. **Reviewing Facts** Who founded Hull House?

Reviewing Themes

3. **Science and Technology** What improvements in transportation helped cities and suburbs grow?

Critical Thinking

4. **Analyzing Information** How did the efforts of religious groups help those living in poverty?
5. **Summarizing Information** Re-create the diagram below and describe three efforts made to improve living conditions in the cities.

Analyzing Visuals

6. **Graph Skills** According to the graph on page 591, what was the range of urban population between 1890 and 1900? About how many more people lived in rural than in urban areas in 1860?

Interdisciplinary Activity

Art Draw the front of a postcard that shows a scene of an American city in 1900. On the reverse side, write a note that an immigrant may have sent home to relatives.

Social Studies
SKILLBUILDER

Reading a Line Graph

Why Learn This Skill?

Graphs are a way of showing numbers visually, making them easier to read and understand. Graphs are often used to compare changes over time or differences between places, groups of people, or related events.

Learning the Skill

On a line graph, numbers usually appear along the left side of the graph, or the vertical axis. Time is usually shown along the bottom of the graph, or the horizontal axis. A line on the graph shows whether the numbers go up or down over time. Sometimes a graph contains more than one line to record two or more related quantities.

To read a line graph, follow these steps:
• Read the title of the graph.
• Read the information on the horizontal axis and the vertical axis.
• Study the points where the line intersects the grid on the line graph. This step tells you what amount existed at a given time.
• Study the changes over time that the line on the graph illustrates. Look for increases, decreases, and sudden shifts.
• Draw conclusions from the statistics presented. What trends or patterns appear?

Practicing the Skill

Study the line graph on this page and answer the following questions.

1 What is the subject of this line graph?

2 What information is presented on the horizontal axis? On the vertical axis?

3 In about what year did immigration from northern and western Europe peak?

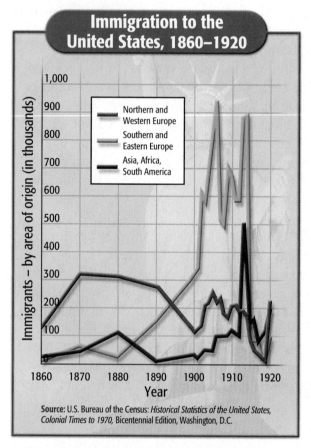

Immigration to the United States, 1860–1920

Northern and Western Europe
Southern and Eastern Europe
Asia, Africa, South America

Immigrants – by area of origin (in thousands)

Year

Source: U.S. Bureau of the Census: *Historical Statistics of the United States, Colonial Times to 1970,* Bicentennial Edition, Washington, D.C.

4 In about what year was immigration from Asia, Africa, and South America the lowest?

5 During what two decades did immigration from southern and eastern Europe peak?

Applying the Skill

Making a Line Graph Keep track of the number of hours you spend on homework each day for a one-week period. Chart the information on a line graph.

Glencoe's **Skillbuilder Interactive Workbook CD-ROM, Level 1,** provides instruction and practice in key social studies skills.

596   CHAPTER 20   Toward an Urban America

A Changing Culture

★★★★★★★★
AN
American Story

A student's award

Mary Antin, a young girl who came to the United States from Russia in 1894, never forgot her first day of school. "Father himself conducted us to school. He would not have delegated that mission to the president of the United States." For her father, Mary explained, education was "the essence of American opportunity, the treasure no thief could touch, not even misfortune or poverty. . . . The door stood open for every one of us."

Expanding Education

Most Americans in 1865 had attended school for an average of only four years. Government and business leaders and reformers believed that for the nation to progress, the people needed more schooling. Toward the end of the 1800s, the "treasure" of education became more widely available to Americans.

By 1914 most states required children to have at least some schooling. More than 80 percent of all children between the ages of 5 and 17 were enrolled in elementary and secondary schools.

Public Schools

The expansion of public education was particularly notable in high schools. The number of public high schools increased from 100 in 1860 to 6,000 in 1900, and increased to 12,000 in 1914. Despite this huge increase, however, many teenagers did not attend high school. Boys often went to work to help their families instead of attending school. The majority of high school students were girls.

The benefits of a public school education were not shared equally by everyone. In the South many African Americans received little or no education. In many parts of the country, African American children had no choice but to attend segregated elementary and secondary schools.

Progressive Education

Around 1900 a new philosophy of education emerged in the United States. Supporters of this "progressive education" wanted to shape students' characters and teach them good citizenship as well as facts. They also believed children should learn through the use of "hands-on" activities. These ideas had the greatest effect in elementary schools.

John Dewey, the leading spokesperson for progressive education, criticized schools for overemphasizing memorization of information. Instead, Dewey argued, schools should relate learning to the interests, problems, and concerns of students.

Higher Education

Colleges and universities also changed and expanded. An 1862 law called the **Morrill Act** gave the states large amounts of federal land that could be sold to raise money for education. The states used these funds to start dozens of schools called land-grant colleges. Wealthy individuals also established and supported colleges and universities. Some schools were named for the donors—for example, Cornell University for Ezra Cornell and Stanford University for Leland Stanford.

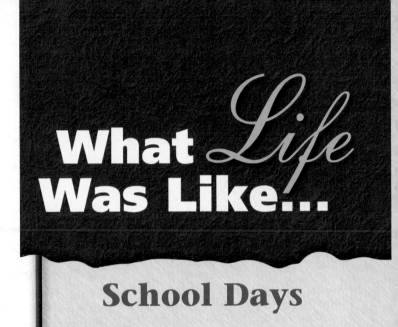

What Life Was Like...

School Days

◀ On the Bus

Students line up for a ride to school in Fresno, California. Few schools were lucky enough to have their own buses in the early 1900s. Not until 1939 were national standards for school buses adopted, including the color "school-bus yellow" to promote visibility and safety.

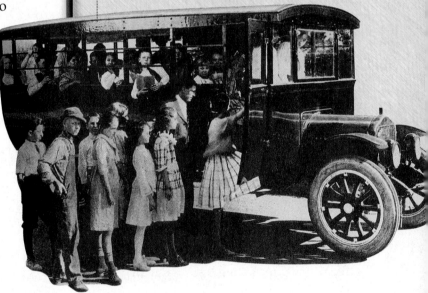

Women and Higher Education

In 1865 only a handful of American colleges admitted women. The new land-grant schools admitted women students, as did new women's colleges—Vassar, Smith, Wellesley, and Bryn Mawr—founded in the late 1800s. By 1890 women could attend a wide range of schools, and by 1910 almost 40 percent of all American college students were women.

Writing

By 1900, the Palmer method of penmanship was taught everywhere. In the Palmer method, some capital letters were no longer written separately, and entire words could be completed before the pen was lifted to cross a "t" or dot an "i." Writing sets included ink bottles like this one. Its double covers prevented evaporation and protected against leakage.

Crossing Guard

A New York City police officer guides students on their way to school in 1899. By the early 1900s, the police provided this service in many communities.

Bookmobile

Librarians attempted to provide reading material to rural communities. Here, a traveling library makes book deliveries in Washington County, Maryland.

The Classroom

Students observe an experiment and take notes during science class in 1900.

Elementary Students

The classroom was the major place where immigrant children learned American ways.

Minorities and Higher Education

Some new colleges, such as Hampton Institute in Virginia, provided higher education for African Americans and Native Americans. Howard University in Washington, D.C., founded shortly after the Civil War, had a largely African American student body. By the early 1870s, Howard offered degrees in theology, medicine, law, and agriculture. Prominent graduates of Howard include Thurgood Marshall, who later became a justice of the Supreme Court, writer Toni Morrison, and political scientist Ralph Bunche, the first African American to win the Nobel Peace Prize.

One Hampton Institute student, **Booker T. Washington,** became an educator. In 1881 Washington founded the **Tuskegee Institute** in Alabama to train teachers and to provide practical education for African Americans. As a result of his work as an educator and public speaker, Washington became influential in business and politics.

In 1896, scientist **George Washington Carver** joined the Tuskegee faculty. His research transformed agricultural development in the South. From the peanut, which was formerly of little use, Carver developed hundreds of products, including plastics, synthetic rubber, shaving cream, and paper.

These two photographs of a young Navajo, Tom Torlino, show how his appearance changed a short time after he entered the Carlisle Indian School.

Schools for Native Americans

Reservation schools and boarding schools also opened to train Native Americans for jobs. The Carlisle Indian Industrial School in Pennsylvania was founded in 1879, and similar schools opened in the West. Although these schools provided Native Americans with training for jobs in industry, they also isolated Native Americans from their tribal traditions. Sometimes, boarding schools were located hundreds of miles away from a student's family.

✓ **Reading Check** **Comparing** What did the colleges Bryn Mawr, Vassar, and Smith have in common?

A Nation of Readers

As opportunities for education grew, a growing number of Americans became interested in reading. Public libraries opened across the nation, and new magazines and newspapers were created for the reading public.

Public Libraries

In 1881 **Andrew Carnegie,** the wealthy steel industrialist, made an extraordinary announcement. He pledged to build a public library in any city that would agree to pay its operating costs. In the next 30 years, Carnegie donated more than $30 million to found more than 2,000 libraries throughout the world. With gifts from Carnegie and others, and the efforts of state and local governments, every state in the Union established free public libraries.

Spreading the News

Technological advances in printing, paper making, and communications made it possible to publish a daily paper for a large number of readers. The growing cities provided readers for the newspapers.

In 1883 **Joseph Pulitzer** purchased the New York *World* and created a new kind of newspaper. The paper grabbed the reader's attention with illustrations, cartoons, and sensational stories with huge, scary headlines—such as "ANOTHER MURDERER TO HANG." Under Pulitzer's management, the *World* built up its circulation to more than one million readers every day.

Other newspapers soon imitated Pulitzer's style. **William Randolph Hearst's** New York *Morning Journal* became even more successful than the *World*, attracting readers by exaggerating the dramatic or gruesome aspects of stories. This style of sensational writing became known as yellow journalism—a name that came from the paper's popular comic strip, "The Yellow Kid."

Ethnic and minority newspapers thrived as well. By 1900 there were six daily Jewish-language newspapers operating in New York City. African Americans started more than 1,000 newspapers between 1865 and 1900.

More magazines took advantage of printing improvements and mass circulation techniques to reach a national market. Between 1865 and 1900, the number of magazines in the United States rose from about 700 to 5,000. Some magazines of that era—the *Atlantic Monthly, Harper's Magazine,* and *Ladies' Home Journal*—are still published today.

Changes in Literature

Many writers of the era explored new themes and subjects. Their approach to literature was called realism because they sought to describe the lives of people. Related to realism was regionalism, writing that focused on a particular region of the country.

Mark Twain was a realist and a regionalist. Many of his books, including *Adventures of Huckleberry Finn* and *The Adventures of Tom Sawyer,* are set along the Mississippi River, where Twain grew up.

Stephen Crane wrote about city slums in *Maggie* and about the Civil War in *The Red Badge of Courage.* In books such as *The Call of the Wild* and *The Sea Wolf,* **Jack London** portrayed the lives of miners and hunters in the far Northwest. **Edith Wharton** described the joys and sorrows of the upper-class Easterners in *The House of Mirth* and *The Age of Innocence.*

Paul Laurence Dunbar, the son of former slaves, wrote poetry and novels that used the dialects and folktales of Southern African Americans. Dunbar was one of the first African American writers to gain fame worldwide.

Paperback books appeared for the first time in the late 1800s, and these inexpensive books helped expand the reading public. Many paperbacks featured lively adventure tales or stories of athletic boys and girls.

Horatio Alger wrote a successful series of young adult books with such titles as *Work and Win* and *Luck and Pluck.* Based on the idea that hard work and honesty brought success, Alger's books sold millions of copies.

✓ **Reading Check** **Explaining** What is regionalism?

Art, Music, and Leisure

For most of the 1800s, the work of American artists and musicians reflected a European influence. After the Civil War, Americans began to develop a distinctively American style.

American Artists

Some American painters pursued realist themes. **Thomas Eakins** painted the human anatomy and surgical operations. One of Eakins's students, **Henry Tanner,** depicted warm family scenes of African Americans in the South. **Frederic Remington** portrayed the American West, focusing on subjects such as cowhands and Native Americans. **Winslow Homer** painted Southern farmers, Adirondack campers, and stormy sea scenes. **James Whistler's** *Arrangement in Grey and Black,* commonly known as *"Whistler's Mother,"* is one of the best-known American paintings. **Mary Cassatt** was influential in the French Impressionist school of

painting. Impressionists tried to capture the play of light, color, and patterns as they made immediate impressions on the senses.

Music in America

More distinctively American kinds of music were also becoming popular. Bandleader **John Philip Sousa** composed many rousing marches, including "The Stars and Stripes Forever." African American musicians in New Orleans in the late 1800s developed an entirely new kind of music—jazz. **Jazz** combined elements of work songs, gospel music, spirituals, and African rhythms. Related to jazz was ragtime music. For about 20 years, beginning around the turn of the century, ragtime—with its complex rhythms—was the dominant force in popular music. One of the best-known ragtime composers is **Scott Joplin.** He wrote "Maple Leaf Rag" and many other well-known works.

The symphony orchestras of New York, Boston, and Philadelphia—all founded before 1900—were among the world's finest. Great singers and conductors came from all over the world to perform at New York's Metropolitan Opera House.

Leisure Time

Although sweatshop workers labored long hours for six or even seven days a week, middle-class people and even some factory workers enjoyed increasing amounts of leisure time.

History *Through Art*

Girls with Lobster by **Winslow Homer** Homer painted scenes of people enjoying the New Jersey and New England seashores. **What themes did many American painters represent in their works?**

Unlike round-the-clock farmwork, professional and industrial jobs gave people hours and even days of free time. Americans developed new forms of recreation.

A favorite leisure-time activity for many people was watching and following sports. Baseball became the most popular **spectator sport** in America. By the turn of the century, both the National and American Leagues had been founded—each made up of teams from major cities. Their games drew large crowds of enthusiastic fans, and in 1903 the first World Series was held.

Another popular spectator sport was football, which developed from the English game of rugby. By the 1890s college games were drawing huge crowds.

Basketball, invented by Dr. James Naismith of Springfield, Massachusetts, also became popular. Naismith developed the game in the 1890s as an indoor winter sport for the boys in his YMCA physical education classes. Considered the only major sport that is completely American in origin, basketball soon spread to other countries.

Americans not only watched but also participated in sports. Tennis and golf were enjoyed by the wealthy, usually in exclusive private clubs. Bicycling grew in popularity after the "safety" bicycle was developed. Older bicycles had metal-rimmed wheels—a large one in front and a small one in back—while the new ones had two air-filled rubber tires of the same size.

These improvements helped bicycle riding take the country by storm. One romantic song celebrated the bicycle:

> ❝It won't be a stylish marriage,
> I can't afford a carriage,
> But you'll look sweet on the seat of a
> bicycle built for two.❞

Large cities had many theaters. Plays performed ranged from serious dramas by Shakespeare to vaudeville shows, which were variety shows with dancing, singing, comedy, and magic acts. Many people could afford the price of a ticket, and in the early 1900s, vaudeville offered the most popular shows in town. The circus also attracted large crowds. In 1910 the United States had about 80 traveling circuses.

Thomas Edison invented "moving pictures" in the 1880s. The "movies" soon became enormously popular. Some theaters, called nickelodeons, charged five cents to see short films. The nickelodeons were the beginning of today's film industry.

✓ **Reading Check** **Describing** What elements made up jazz music?

SECTION 3 ASSESSMENT

Checking for Understanding

1. **Key Terms** Use each of these terms in a complete sentence that will help explain its meaning: land-grant college, yellow journalism, realism, regionalism, ragtime, vaudeville.
2. **Reviewing Facts** Summarize the new philosophy of education that emerged around 1900.

Reviewing Themes

3. **Continuity and Change** What sparked an increase in the number of newspapers, magazines, and books in the late 1800s?

Critical Thinking

4. **Determining Cause and Effect** Explain the connection between leisure time and the development of the arts.
5. **Analyzing Information** Re-create the diagram below and describe the work of each of these writers.

Writer	Description of work
Horatio Alger	
Stephen Crane	
Edith Wharton	

Analyzing Visuals

6. **Picturing History** Look at the pictures of classrooms that appear in the section. In what ways are they similar to and in what ways are they different from classrooms today?

Interdisciplinary Activity

Art Create your own moving pictures by making a series of drawings (that build on one another) on 2-inch by 4-inch slips of paper. Staple the slips of paper together on one side, then flip through them slowly to view your motion picture.

America's LITERATURE

Mark Twain (1835–1910)

Mark Twain, who was born Samuel Langhorne Clemens in 1835, spent his early life in Hannibal, Missouri. There he became a printer and later a riverboat pilot. So much did he love life on the Mississippi River that he later chose a pen name that would link him with the river forever. "Mark twain!" was a river call meaning "two fathoms," or that the water was deep enough for safe passage.

READ TO DISCOVER

Mark Twain's boyhood dreams and memories are the sources of *Life on the Mississippi.* As you read this excerpt, think about the importance of the riverboat's arrival to the town and to young Twain.

READER'S DICTIONARY

packet: boat that carries mail, passengers, and freight at fixed times over a fixed route

Keokuk: town at the southeastern tip of Iowa

drayman: driver of a dray—a low sturdy cart with removable sides

Life on the Mississippi

When I was a boy, there was but one permanent ambition among my comrades in our village on the west bank of the Mississippi River. That was, to be a steamboatman. . . .

Once a day a cheap, gaudy **packet** arrived upward from St. Louis, and another downward from **Keokuk.** Before these events, the day was glorious with expectancy; after them, the day was a dead and empty thing. Not only the boys, but the whole village, felt this. After all these years I can picture that old time to myself now, just as it was then: the white town drowsing in the sunshine of a summer's morning; the streets empty, . . . the magnificent Mississippi, rolling its mile-wide tide along, shining in the sun; . . . Presently a film of dark smoke appears . . . ; instantly a . . . **drayman,** famous for his quick eye and prodigious voice, lifts up the cry, "S-t-e-a-m-boat a-comin'!" and the scene changes! . . . [A]ll in a twinkling the dead town is alive and moving. Drays, carts, men, boys, all go hurrying from many quarters to a common center, the wharf. Assembled there, the people fasten their eyes upon the coming boat as upon a wonder they are seeing for the first time. And the boat *is* rather a handsome sight, too. . . . [T]he captain stands by the big bell, calm, imposing, the envy of all; great volumes of the blackest smoke are rolling and tumbling out of the chimneys; . . . the captain lifts his hand, a bell rings, the wheels stop; then they turn back, churning the water to foam, and the steamer is at rest. Then such a scramble as there is to get aboard, and to get ashore, and to take in freight and to discharge freight, all at one and the same time; . . . Ten minutes later the steamer is under way again, with no flag on the jack-staff and no black smoke issuing from the chimneys. After ten more minutes the town is dead again. . . .

ANALYZING LITERATURE

1. **Recall and Interpret** What major event takes place once a day?
2. **Evaluate and Connect** Why is the event so important?

Interdisciplinary Activity

Art Read again Twain's descriptions. Then draw a picture of one of these scenes. Be sure to add details that reflect Twain's words.

Chapter Summary
Toward an Urban America

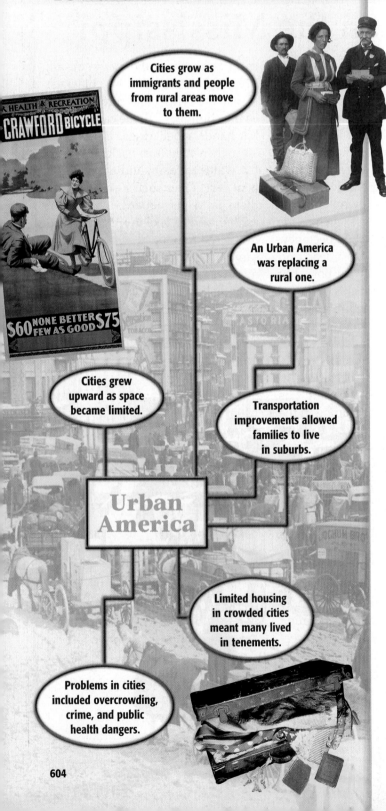

Cities grow as immigrants and people from rural areas move to them.

An Urban America was replacing a rural one.

Cities grew upward as space became limited.

Transportation improvements allowed families to live in suburbs.

Urban America

Limited housing in crowded cities meant many lived in tenements.

Problems in cities included overcrowding, crime, and public health dangers.

Reviewing Key Terms

On a sheet of paper, define the following terms.

1. ethnic group
2. tenement
3. settlement house
4. yellow journalism
5. ragtime
6. assimilate

Reviewing Key Facts

7. What did nativist groups try to do?
8. What was the purpose of the Morrill Act?
9. What project did Andrew Carnegie fund?

Critical Thinking

10. **Analyzing Information** What new styles of writing did American authors adopt during this period?

11. **Drawing Conclusions** Re-create the diagram below and describe three ways newcomers to America tried to preserve their culture.

Preserving cultural heritage

Practicing Skills

Reading a Line Graph *Study the line graph below and answer the questions that follow.*

12. What was the average number of school days in 1920?
13. What trend is shown in this line graph?

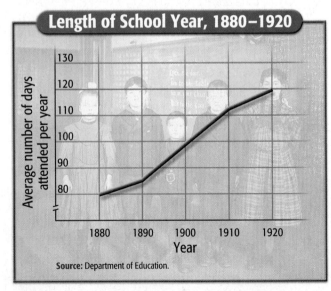

Length of School Year, 1880–1920

Average number of days attended per year

130
120
110
100
90
80

1880 1890 1900 1910 1920
Year

Source: Department of Education.

Geography and History Activity

Study this map and answer the questions below.

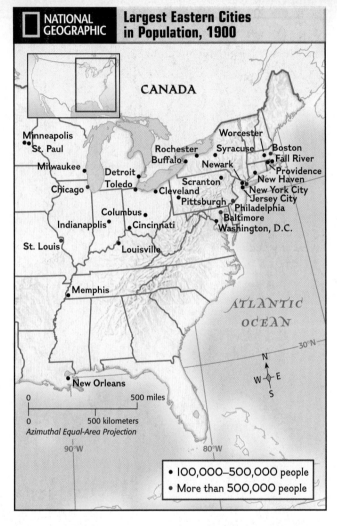

NATIONAL GEOGRAPHIC

Largest Eastern Cities in Population, 1900

CANADA

Minneapolis
St. Paul
Milwaukee
Detroit
Toledo
Chicago
Columbus
Indianapolis
St. Louis
Memphis

Rochester
Buffalo
Newark
Scranton
Cleveland
Pittsburgh
Cincinnati
Louisville

Worcester
Syracuse
Boston
Fall River
Providence
New Haven
New York City
Jersey City
Philadelphia
Baltimore
Washington, D.C.

ATLANTIC OCEAN

30°N

New Orleans

0   500 miles
0   500 kilometers
Azimuthal Equal-Area Projection

90°W   80°W

N W E S

- 100,000–500,000 people
- More than 500,000 people

14. **Location** Which cities had more than 500,000 people?

15. **Place** About how many people lived in Louisville?

16. **Location** What do the cities with more than 500,000 people have in common?

Citizenship Cooperative Activity

17. **Citizenship Test** Immigrants who want to become United States citizens today must pass a written test to qualify. Many of the questions on the test deal with United States history and customs. Work with members of your group to design a 15-question test that you think prospective citizens should be required to pass.

HISTORY Online

Self-Check Quiz
Visit taj.glencoe.com and click on **Chapter 20— Self-Check Quizzes** to prepare for the chapter test.

Economics Activity

18. Research for information, and then summarize your findings in a short report that answers these questions. What field or career area interests you? What education and skills are required to enter it? What attitudes, work habits, and other qualities does it take to succeed on the job?

Alternative Assessment

19. **Portfolio Writing Activity** Choose one problem of the early 1900s and describe what you would do to help correct it.

The Princeton Review

Standardized Test Practice

Read the passage about American life and choose the *best* answer to the question that follows.

"Between 1860 and 1900 American urban areas grew twice as fast as the total population. Chicago, which in the 1830s had been a frontier town with a few hundred residents, became a vast metropolis. New York became the second-largest city in the world. During the same span of years, the populations of Boston, Baltimore, and Philadelphia also grew rapidly."

The main idea of the passage is best expressed by

A New York City grew rapidly.

B Only cities in the northeastern United States grew rapidly.

C Population of urban America grew at a very fast rate during this era.

D Rural growth continued, but not as quickly as urban growth.

Test-Taking Tip

Make sure that your answer is supported by information in the quotation. Do not rely only on your memory. Keep in mind that a *metropolis* is a "large city."

UNIT 8

Reform, Expansion, and War

1865–1920

Why It Matters

As you study Unit 8, you will learn that progressive reforms affected many areas of American life during this era. You will also learn why the United States took a more active role in international affairs. The following resources offer more information about this period in American history.

Primary Sources Library

See pages 972–973 for primary source readings to accompany Unit 8.

Use the American history **Primary Source Document Library CD-ROM** *to find additional primary sources about reform, expansion, and World War I.*

I WANT YOU for the **U.S. ARMY ENLIST NOW**

World War I enlistment poster

Yosemite Valley by Ansel Adams

"Suffrage is the pivotal right."

—Susan B. Anthony, 1897

Progressive Reforms

1877–1920

Why It Matters

The spirit of reform gained strength in the late 1800s and thrived during the early 1900s. The reformers, called progressives, were confident in their ability to improve government and the quality of life.

The Impact Today

Progressive reforms affected many areas of American life. Among these are government, consumers' rights, and education.

 The American Journey *Video* *The chapter 21 video "The Progressive Movement," studies the movement and how it gained strength over time.*

1887
• Interstate Commerce Commission formed

1901
• President McKinley assassinated

United States PRESIDENTS

| Hayes 1877–1881 | Garfield 1881 | Arthur 1881–1885 | Cleveland 1885–1889 | B. Harrison 1889–1893 | Cleveland 1893–1897 | McKinley 1897–1901 |

1880   1890   1900

World

1879
• British win Zulu War

1889
• Brazil becomes a republic

1893
• New Zealand grants women suffrage

1897
• First World Zionist Congress convenes

The Lone Tenement by George Bellows, 1909 Bellows's favorite themes, which include city scenes and athletic events, mark him as a uniquely American painter.

1906
• Sinclair's *The Jungle* published

1909
• The NAACP is formed

1919
• Eighteenth Amendment prohibits alcohol

1920
• Nineteenth Amendment grants woman suffrage

Roosevelt 1901–1909

Taft 1909–1913

Wilson 1913–1921

1910   *1920*

1905
• Einstein announces theory of relativity

1911
• Rutherford discovers structure of atom

HISTORY Online

Chapter Overview
Visit taj.glencoe.com and click on **Chapter 21— Chapter Overviews** to preview chapter information.

The Progressive Movement

Guide to Reading

Main Idea

Many men and women became part of a widespread movement to bring about reform.

Key Terms

political machine, patronage, civil service, trust, muckraker, primary, initiative, referendum, recall

Reading Strategy

Organizing Information As you read Section 1, re-create the diagram below and list two or more reforms for each category.

Reforms		
Government	Business	Voting

Read to Learn

- how journalists helped shape the reform movement.
- how cities, states, and Congress answered the call for reform of the government.

Section Theme

Government and Democracy Americans took action against corruption in business and government.

Preview of Events

♦1885   ♦1895   ♦1905   ♦1915

1887
Interstate Commerce Commission is established

1890
Congress passes Sherman Antitrust Act

1906
Upton Sinclair writes *The Jungle*

1912
Congress passes the Seventeenth Amendment

AN American Story

Newspaper reporter Jacob Riis shocked Americans in 1890 with his book *How the Other Half Lives.* With words and powerful photographs, Riis vividly portrayed immigrant life in New York City's crowded tenements. Said Riis: "We used to go in the small hours of the morning into the worst tenements to count noses and see if the law against overcrowding was violated and the sights I saw there gripped my heart until I felt that I must tell of them, or burst."

How the Other Half Lives *by Jacob Riis*

Fighting Corruption

Many Americans called for reform in the late 1800s. The reformers had many different goals. Progressive reformers focused on urban problems, government, and business. They claimed that government and big business were taking advantage of the American people rather than serving them.

Political machines—powerful organizations linked to political parties—controlled local government in many cities. In each ward, or political district within a city, a machine representative controlled jobs and services. This representative was the **political boss.** The bosses gained votes for their parties by doing favors for people, such as offering turkey dinners and summer boat rides, providing jobs for immigrants, and helping needy families. A political boss was often a citizen's closest link to local government. Although they did help people, many bosses were dishonest.

Corrupt politicians found numerous ways to make money. They accepted bribes from tenement landlords in return for overlooking violations of city housing codes. They received campaign contributions from contractors hoping to do business with the city. They also accepted kickbacks. A **kickback** is an arrangement in which contractors padded the amount of their bill for city work and paid, or "kicked back," a percentage of that amount to the bosses.

Some politicians used their knowledge of city business for personal profit. A person who knew where the city planned to build a road could buy land there before the route became public knowledge. Later the land could be sold for a huge profit.

One of the most corrupt city bosses, William M. Tweed, known as **Boss Tweed,** headed New York City's Democratic political machine in the 1860s and 1870s. Tweed and a network of city officials—the Tweed ring—controlled the police, the courts, and some newspapers. They collected millions of dollars in illegal payments from companies doing business with the city. Political cartoonist Thomas Nast exposed the Tweed ring's operations in his cartoons for *Harper's Weekly.* Tweed was convicted and sentenced to prison.

Citizenship
New Ways to Govern Cities

To break the power of political bosses, reformers founded organizations such as the National Municipal League in Philadelphia. These groups worked to make city governments more honest and efficient.

Cities troubled by poor management or corruption tried new forms of government. After a tidal wave devastated **Galveston, Texas,** in 1900, the task of rebuilding the city overwhelmed the mayor and city council. Galveston's citizens persuaded the Texas state legislature to approve a new charter that placed the city government in the hands of five commissioners. The new commission efficiently rebuilt the city. By 1917

Analyzing *Political Cartoons*

The Tweed Ring Boss Tweed and New York City officials are shown pointing to one another in response to the question "Who stole the people's money?" On Tweed's right a man holds a hat labeled "Chairs," a reference to the $179,000 New York City paid for 40 chairs and three tables. Other contractors and cheats—their names on their coats—complete the "ring." **How did political bosses gain votes for their parties?**

"WHO STOLE THE PEOPLE'S MONEY?" — DO TELL . N.Y.TIMES   'TWAS HIM.

A Boss Tweed   **B** Peter Sweeny   **C** Richard Connelly   **D** Mayor A. Oakey Hall

commissions governed nearly 400 cities. Many other cities, mostly small ones, hired professional city managers.

One successful civic reformer was **Tom Johnson,** mayor of Cleveland, Ohio, from 1901 to 1909. He battled corporations and party bosses to lower streetcar fares, improve food inspections, and build parks. Because of Johnson's reforms, Cleveland became known as the best-governed city in the United States.

Fighting the Spoils System

The spoils system—rewarding political supporters with jobs and favors—had been common practice since the time of Andrew Jackson. Whenever a new president came to power, job seekers flooded the nation's capital.

The spoils system—also called patronage—existed at all levels of government and led to numerous abuses. Many who received government jobs were not qualified. Some were dishonest.

Presidents **Rutherford B. Hayes** (1877–1881) and **James Garfield** (1881) wanted to change the spoils system. Hayes tried to do this by reforming the civil service—the body of nonelected government workers—but neither the Democratic nor the Republican Party supported his efforts.

Garfield also hoped to reform the civil service. He believed that people should be appointed to government jobs not as a reward for political support but because of their qualifications. Garfield took office in 1881 but was assassinated by an unsuccessful office seeker before he could launch his reforms.

When Vice President **Chester A. Arthur** succeeded Garfield, he tried to end the spoils system. In 1883 Congress passed the **Pendleton Act,** which established the **Civil Service Commission** to set up competitive examinations for federal jobs. Applicants had to demonstrate their abilities in this examination. By 1900 the commission controlled the hiring of many federal employees.

✓ Reading Check **Explaining** Whom did the spoils system reward?

$ Economics

Controlling Business

During the late 1800s, many Americans came to believe that trusts, or combinations of companies, were becoming too large. They believed these trusts had too much control over the economy and the government. This public concern led to new laws regulating big business.

In 1890 Congress passed the **Sherman Antitrust Act,** the first federal law to control trusts and monopolies. Supporters of the law hoped it would keep trusts from limiting competition. During the 1890s, however, the government rarely used the Sherman Act to curb business. Instead, it applied the act against labor unions, claiming that union strikes interfered with trade. Not until the early 1900s did the government win cases against trusts by using the Sherman Act.

Reining in the Railroads

The railroads functioned as an **oligopoly**—a market structure in which a few large companies control the prices of the industry. Reformers called for regulations on railroad rates, but the Supreme Court ruled that only Congress could enact legislation to regulate commerce that crossed state lines.

So in 1887 Congress passed the **Interstate Commerce Act,** which required railroads to charge "reasonable and just" rates and to publish those rates. The act also created the **Interstate Commerce Commission** (ICC) to supervise the railroad industry and, later, the trucking industry.

Lowering Tariffs

Reformers also wanted to lower tariffs. Many people believed that high tariffs led to higher prices for goods. In 1890 the Republicans raised tariffs sharply to protect American businesses from international competition. Voters showed their opposition to high tariffs by sending many Democrats to Congress. **Grover Cleveland,** who became president in 1893, also supported lower tariffs.

✓ Reading Check **Explaining** Why did many people want lower tariffs?

The New Reformers

In the early 1900s, new ideas for correcting injustice and solving social problems emerged among American reformers. Socialism and progressivism were two such ideas.

Socialists believed a nation's resources and major industries should be owned and operated by the government on behalf of all the people—not by individuals and private companies for their own profit. **Eugene V. Debs** helped found the American Socialist Party in 1898. Under Debs's leadership the party won some support in the early 1900s. Debs ran for president five times but never received more than 6 percent of the popular vote.

During the same period, progressives brought new energy to the reform movement. Like the socialists, many progressives were alarmed by the concentration of wealth and power in the hands of a few. Progressives rejected the socialist idea of government ownership of industries. Instead, they supported government efforts to regulate industry.

They also sought to reform government, to make it more efficient and better able to resist the influence of powerful business interests. Progressives also believed that society had an obligation to protect and help all its members. Many progressive reforms aimed to help those who lacked wealth and influence.

Muckrakers Expose Problems

Journalists aided the reformers by exposing injustices and corruption. Investigative reporters wrote newspaper and magazine stories that brought problems to the attention of the public—and gained readers. These journalists were called muckrakers because they "raked" (brought to light) the "muck" (dirt and corruption) underlying society.

One of the most effective muckrakers, **Lincoln Steffens,** reported for *McClure's Magazine.* Steffens exposed corrupt machine politics in New York, Chicago, and other cities. His articles, collected in a book called *The Shame of the Cities* (1904), strengthened the demand for urban reform.

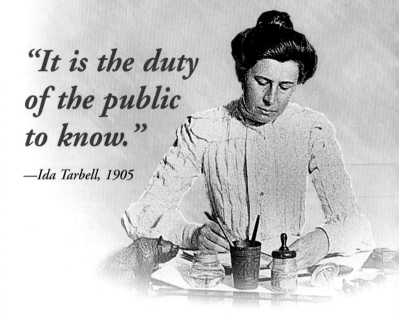

"It is the duty of the public to know."

—*Ida Tarbell, 1905*

Ida Tarbell, also writing for *McClure's,* described the unfair practices of the oil trust. Her articles led to public pressure for more government control over big business. In her 1904 book, *The History of the Standard Oil Company,* she warned of the giant corporation's power.

In his novel *The Jungle* (1906), **Upton Sinclair** described the horrors of the meatpacking industry in Chicago. Although Sinclair's aim was to arouse sympathy for the workers, his vivid descriptions shocked Americans. The uproar caused by Sinclair's book helped persuade Congress to pass the **Meat Inspection Act** in 1906. That same year Congress also passed the **Pure Food and Drug Act,** requiring accurate labeling of food and medicine and banning the sale of harmful food.

Reading Check **Identifying** Who wrote about unfair practices in the oil industry?

Citizenship

Expanding Democracy

In the early 1900s, progressives backed a number of reforms designed to increase the people's direct control of the government. **Robert La Follette** led Wisconsin's reform-minded Republicans. "Fighting Bob," as he was called, won the support of farmers and workers with his fiery attacks on big business and the railroads. While governor, La Follette brought

Presidential Elections

Debs ran for president while in prison. Eugene Debs was the candidate of the Socialist Party for president in 1904, 1908, and 1912. For his opposition to the entry of the United States into World War I, Debs was convicted in 1918 and sentenced to 10 years in prison. While in prison in 1920 he ran again for president on the Socialist ticket and received almost 1 million votes—about 3.5 percent of the total. His sentence was commuted in 1921.

about reforms such as improving the civil service. His greatest achievement, however, was reforming the state electoral system. Candidates for general elections in Wisconsin had been chosen at state conventions run by party bosses. La Follette introduced a direct primary election, allowing the state's voters to choose their party's candidates. Reformers in other states copied this "Wisconsin idea."

The Oregon System

The state of Oregon also made important changes in the political process to give voters more power and to limit the influence of political parties. The reforms in Oregon included a direct primary election and the initiative, the referendum, and the recall.

The initiative allowed citizens to place a measure or issue on the ballot in a state election. The referendum gave voters the opportunity to accept or reject measures that the state legislature enacted. The recall enabled voters to remove unsatisfactory elected officials from their jobs. These reforms were called the **Oregon System.** Other western states soon adopted the reforms.

The Seventeenth Amendment

Progressives also changed the way United States senators are elected. The Constitution had given state legislatures the responsibility for choosing senators, but party bosses and business interests often controlled the selection process. Progressives wanted to give the people an opportunity to vote for their senators directly. Support for this idea grew. In 1912 Congress passed the **Seventeenth Amendment** to the Constitution to provide for the direct election of senators. Ratified in 1913, the amendment gave the people a voice in selecting their representatives. 📖 *(See page 248 for the text of the Seventeenth Amendment.)*

✓ **Reading Check** **Identifying** What reform allowed voters to place a measure on the ballot?

SECTION 1 ASSESSMENT

Checking for Understanding

1. **Key Terms** Use each of these terms in a complete sentence that will help explain its meaning: political machine, patronage, civil service, trust, muckraker, primary, initiative, referendum, recall.

2. **Reviewing Facts** Explain how the Civil Service Commission helped to eliminate the spoils system.

Reviewing Themes

3. **Government and Democracy** Identify and describe three reforms that gave the American people more direct control of the government.

Critical Thinking

4. **Comparing** Compare socialist and progressive views on industry.

5. **Organizing Information** Re-create the diagram below and show how the Seventeenth Amendment reformed the political process.

Seventh Amendment	
Policy before	Policy after

Analyzing Visuals

6. **Analyzing Political Cartoons** Examine the political cartoon on page 611. Why are the individuals pointing to someone else? What statement is cartoonist Thomas Nast making about the extent of political corruption in New York City?

Interdisciplinary Activity

Civics Citizens must prepare to vote. Create a pamphlet describing the kinds of things voters should know in order to make their ballots meaningful.

Women and Progressives

Guide to Reading

Main Idea
Women worked for the right to vote, for improved working conditions, and for temperance.

Key Terms
suffragist, prohibition

Reading Strategy
Organizing Information As you read the section, re-create the diagram below and describe the role of each individual.

Individual	Role in Progressive movement
Mary Church Terrell	
Susan B. Anthony	
Frances Willard	

Read to Learn
• how the role of American women changed during the Progressive Era.
• how women fought for the right to vote.

Section Theme
Groups and Institutions Many women worked for a constitutional amendment to gain suffrage.

Preview of Events

♦1890	♦1900	♦1910	♦1920

1890
National American Woman Suffrage Association emerges

1896
National Association of Colored Women is formed

1919
The Eighteenth Amendment is ratified

1920
The Nineteenth Amendment is ratified

Lillian D. Wald

AN American Story

Nurse Lillian Wald followed a young girl up a rickety staircase in a filthy tenement house on New York City's Lower East Side. The girl had begged Wald to help her mother who had just given birth to a baby. A doctor had refused to treat the girl's mother because she could not pay his fee. The sight of the desperate mother and her baby was a turning point in Wald's life. Wald dedicated herself to helping poor people and educating them about health care. Eventually Wald became a national reform leader who was known to say, "The whole world is my neighborhood."

Women's Roles Change

Many leaders of the urban reform movement, including Lillian Wald, were middle-class women. The situation of middle-class women changed during the late 1800s. Their responsibilities at home lessened as families became smaller, more children spent the day at school, and men worked away from home. Women also gained more free time as technology made housework easier.

Many more middle-class women were gaining higher education. About 40 percent of all college students in 1910 were women. Women were also starting professional careers—mostly in teaching but also in nursing, medicine, and other fields. Between 1890 and 1910, the number of women working outside the home increased from 4 million to nearly 7.5 million.

These changes created the "new woman"—a popular term for educated, up-to-date women who pursued interests outside their homes. Many such women became role models.

As you read in Chapter 20, **Jane Addams** established Hull House, a settlement house, in **Chicago.** Working there gave Addams an outlet for her energy and intelligence, as well as a sense of satisfaction with helping poor people.

📖 *(See page 972 for an account of settlement houses.)*

Settlement workers such as Addams gained notice as writers, public speakers, fund-raisers, and reformers. Many young women followed the example of these talented public figures. Others found inspiration in the life of **Mother Cabrini,** an Italian nun who came to the United States to work with the poor.

Women's Clubs

Women found another outlet for their talent and energy in women's clubs, which rapidly increased in number. At first the clubs focused on such cultural activities as music and painting. Many clubs gradually became more concerned with social problems.

When some clubs refused to admit African Americans, African American women established their own network of clubs. Clubs such as the Phyllis Wheatley Club of New Orleans organized classes, recreational activities, and social services. In 1896 women from these clubs formed the **National Association of Colored Women.** Its first president, **Mary Church Terrell,** was an active

Mary Church Terrell

leader for women's rights. The association established homes for orphans, founded hospitals, and worked for woman suffrage, fulfilling its motto "Lifting As We Climb."

✅ **Reading Check** **Identifying** Who was Mary Church Terrell?

The Fight for Suffrage

At the Seneca Falls Convention in 1848, women had called for the right to vote. After the Civil War, Congress passed the Fifteenth Amendment, giving voting rights to freed men—but not to women. Some leading abolitionists became suffragists, men and women who fought for woman suffrage, or women's right to vote.

Like other reformers, the suffragists formed organizations to promote their cause. **Elizabeth Cady Stanton** and **Susan B. Anthony** founded the **National Woman Suffrage Association,** which called for a constitutional amendment allowing women to vote in national elections. A second organization, the American Woman Suffrage Association, focused on winning woman suffrage in state elections.

In 1890 the two groups merged to form the National American Woman Suffrage Association. Led by **Anna Howard Shaw,** a minister and doctor, and **Carrie Chapman Catt,** an educator and newspaper editor, this organization grew to more than two million members by 1917. In a speech to the association in 1902, Catt declared:

> ❝The whole aim of the [women's] movement has been to destroy the idea that obedience is necessary to women; to train women to such self-respect that they would not grant obedience and to train men to such comprehension of equity [fairness] they would not exact [demand] it.❞

Opposition to Woman Suffrage

Groups formed to protest the idea of giving women the vote. These organizations—supported by some women as well as by men—claimed that woman suffrage would upset society's "natural" balance and lead to divorce and neglected children.

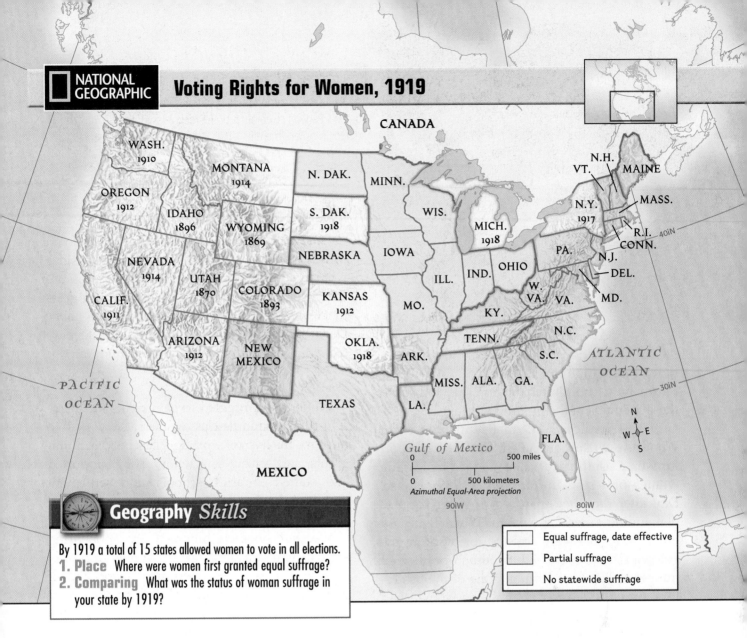

NATIONAL GEOGRAPHIC
Voting Rights for Women, 1919

CANADA

WASH.
1910

MONTANA
1914

N. DAK.

MINN.

OREGON
1912

IDAHO
1896

WYOMING
1869

S. DAK.
1918

WIS.

MICH.
1918

N.H.
VT.   MAINE

N.Y.
1917   MASS.

R.I.
CONN.

NEVADA
1914

UTAH
1870

COLORADO
1893

NEBRASKA

IOWA

ILL.

IND.

OHIO

PA.

N.J.

DEL.

CALIF.
1911

KANSAS
1912

MO.

W.
VA.

VA.

MD.

KY.

ARIZONA
1912

NEW
MEXICO

OKLA.
1918

ARK.

TENN.

N.C.

S.C.

ATLANTIC
OCEAN

PACIFIC
OCEAN

MISS.

ALA.

GA.

TEXAS

LA.

40iN

30iN

FLA.

MEXICO

Gulf of Mexico

0   500 miles

0   500 kilometers
Azimuthal Equal-Area projection

N
W   E
S

90iW   80iW

Equal suffrage, date effective

Partial suffrage

No statewide suffrage

Geography *Skills*

By 1919 a total of 15 states allowed women to vote in all elections.
1. **Place** Where were women first granted equal suffrage?
2. **Comparing** What was the status of woman suffrage in your state by 1919?

The suffrage movement gained strength, however, when respected public figures such as Jane Addams spoke out in support of the vote for women. Alice Duer Miller brought humor to the struggle for the right to vote:

"Said Mr. Jones in 1910:
'Women, subject yourselves to men.'
Nineteen-Eleven heard him quote:
'They rule the world without the vote.'

. . . .

By Nineteen-Thirteen, looking glum,
He said that it was bound to come.

. . . .

By Nineteen-Fifteen, he'll insist
He's always been a suffragist."

The suffragists won their early victories in the West. First as a territory in 1869 and then as a state in 1890, **Wyoming** led the nation in giving women the vote. Between 1910 and 1913, five other states adopted woman suffrage. By 1919 women could vote in at least some elections in most of the 48 states.

Continuing the Fight

In the meantime suffragists continued their struggle to win the vote everywhere. **Alice Paul,** a Quaker who founded the National Woman's Party in 1916, was a forceful leader of the suffragist movement. She sought greater economic and legal equality as well as suffrage for women.

During a visit to Great Britain, Paul saw suffragists use protest marches and hunger strikes

to call attention to their cause. When she returned to the United States, she, too, used these methods in the fight for suffrage.

In 1917 Alice Paul met with President **Woodrow Wilson** but failed to win his support for woman suffrage. Paul responded by leading women protestors in front of the White House. Day after day they marched carrying banners demanding votes for women. When Paul and other protestors were arrested for blocking the sidewalk, they started a much-publicized hunger strike. Alva Belmont, one of the protestors, proudly declared that all the women had done was to stand there "quietly, peacefully, lawfully, and gloriously."

Women Vote Nationally

By 1917 the national tide was turning in favor of woman suffrage. New York and, a year later, South Dakota and Oklahoma granted equal suffrage. Meanwhile Congress began debating the issue, and President Wilson agreed to support an amendment to the Constitution.

In 1919 the Senate voted in favor of the **Nineteenth Amendment,** which allowed woman suffrage. The amendment was ratified in 1920, in time for women to vote in that year's presidential election. For the first time, American women were able to participate in the election of their national leaders.

Reading Check **Identifying** What state was the first to give women the right to vote?

Women and Social Reform

During the Progressive Era, women involved themselves in many reform movements besides woman suffrage. In 1912, for example, pressure from women's clubs helped persuade Congress to create the Children's Bureau in the Labor Department. The bureau's task was to develop federal policies that would protect children.

Working for a Better Life

While they struggled to gain rights for themselves, many middle-class women also worked to improve the lives of working-class people, immigrants, and society as a whole. They supported and staffed libraries, schools, and settlement houses and raised money for charities.

Some women promoted other causes. They challenged business interests by sponsoring laws to regulate the labor of women and children and to require government inspection of workplaces. Women also played an important role in the movement to reform and regulate the food and medicine industries.

In many states across the country, women pressured state legislatures to provide pensions for widows and abandoned mothers with children. These pensions later became part of the Social Security system.

Labor Movement

Reform efforts brought upper-class women reformers into alliance with working women. In 1903 women's groups joined with working-class union women to form the **Women's Trade Union League** (WTUL).

The WTUL encouraged working women to form women's labor unions. It also supported laws to protect the rights of women factory workers. WTUL members raised money to help striking workers and to pay bail for women who were arrested for participating in strikes.

The Temperance Crusade

A crusade against the use of alcohol had begun in New England and the Midwest in the early 1800s. The movement continued throughout the late 1800s. Protestant churches strongly supported the anti-alcohol movement.

Two driving forces in the crusade were the **Woman's Christian Temperance Union** (WCTU), established in 1874, and the **Anti-Saloon League,** founded 20 years later. They called for temperance, urging individuals to stop drinking, and prohibition, the passing of laws to prohibit the making or selling of alcohol.

In 1879 **Frances Willard** became head of the WCTU. Willard led a campaign to educate the public about the links between alcohol abuse and violence, poverty, and unemployment. She turned the WCTU into a powerful organization with chapters in every state.

The WCTU's main goal was prohibition. However, the WCTU also supported other causes, including prison reform, woman suffrage, improved working conditions, and world peace. Through WCTU chapters, thousands of women combined their traditional role as guardians of the family and home with social activism.

Carry Nation was an especially colorful crusader for temperance. Her most dramatic protests occurred when she pushed her way into saloons and broke bottles and kegs with an ax.

Carry Nation went from praying outside taverns to destroying them with a hatchet.

Temperance poster

The Prohibition Amendment

The anti-alcohol movement grew during the early 1900s. Progressive reformers who wanted to ban alcohol for social reasons were joined by Americans who opposed alcohol for religious or moral reasons. In 1917 they persuaded Congress to pass a constitutional amendment making it illegal to make, transport, or sell alcohol in the United States. The **Eighteenth Amendment,** known as the Prohibition Law, was ratified in 1919. 📖 *(See page 249 for the text of the Eighteenth Amendment.)*

✓ **Reading Check** **Describing** What was the goal of the temperance movement?

SECTION 2 ASSESSMENT

Checking for Understanding

1. **Key Terms** Use each of these terms in a complete sentence that will help explain its meaning: suffragist, prohibition.

2. **Reviewing Facts** What did the Nineteenth Amendment provide?

Reviewing Themes

3. **Groups and Institutions** How did women's clubs help to change the role of women?

Critical Thinking

4. **Drawing Conclusions** Why do you think the right to vote was important to women?

5. **Sequencing Information** Re-create the time line below and identify the events regarding woman suffrage that happened in these years.

1848   1869   1896   1920

Analyzing Visuals

6. **Geography Skills** Examine the map on page 617. Which regions of the country provided no statewide suffrage?

Interdisciplinary Activity

Expository Writing Find a newspaper article that deals with the role of women today. Rewrite the article to reflect how this information might have been presented in the late 1800s and early 1900s.

Progressive Presidents

Guide to Reading

Main Idea
Presidents during the Progressive Era worked to control big business and to deal with labor problems.

Key Terms
trustbuster, arbitration, square deal, laissez-faire, conservation

Reading Strategy
Taking Notes As you read Section 3, re-create the diagram below and explain why each of these acts of legislation is important.

Legislation	Importance
Sixteenth Amendment	
Pure Food and Drug Act	
Federal Reserve Act	

Read to Learn
• how President Theodore Roosevelt took on big business.
• why the progressives formed their own political party.

Section Theme
Economic Factors Government tried various means to regulate big business.

Preview of Events

♦1900   ♦1910   ♦1920

1901
President McKinley is assassinated

1905
Roosevelt proposes the U.S. Forest Service

1913
Federal Reserve Act creates 12 regional banks

1914
Congress establishes the Federal Trade Commission

Theodore Roosevelt board game

AN American Story

"We were still under a heavy fire and I got together a mixed lot of men and pushed on from the trenches and ranch houses which we had just taken, driving the Spaniards through a line of palm-trees, and over the crest of a chain of hills. . . ." With these words, a young lieutenant colonel named Theodore Roosevelt described his military adventures in Cuba during the Spanish-American War. Known for his vigor, enthusiasm, and a colorful personality, Roosevelt became president in 1901 upon the assassination of President William McKinley.

Theodore Roosevelt

When **Theodore Roosevelt** received the Republican vice-presidential nomination in 1900, the powerful Republican leader Mark Hanna warned that there would be only one life between "that cowboy" and the White House. When the election resulted in a Republican victory, Hanna turned to McKinley and said, "Now it is up to you to live." Less than a year later, President McKinley was assassinated. Suddenly, 42-year-old Theodore Roosevelt became president—the youngest president in the nation's history. When Roosevelt moved into the White House in 1901, he brought progressivism with him.

The "Trustbuster"

President McKinley had favored big business, but President Roosevelt was known to support business regulation and other progressive reforms. In 1902 Roosevelt ordered the Justice Department to take legal action against certain trusts that had violated the Sherman Antitrust Act. His first target was the **Northern Securities Company,** a railroad monopoly formed by financiers J.P. Morgan and James J. Hill to control transportation in the Northwest. Northern Securities fought the government's accusations of illegal activity all the way to the Supreme Court. Finally, in 1904 the Justice Department won its case. The Supreme Court decided that Northern Securities had illegally limited trade and ordered the trust to be taken apart.

During the rest of Roosevelt's term as president, he obtained a total of 25 indictments (legal charges) against trusts in the beef, oil, and tobacco industries. Although hailed as a trustbuster, Roosevelt did not want to break up all trusts. As he saw it, trusts should be regulated, not destroyed. He distinguished between "good trusts," which were concerned with public welfare, and "bad trusts," which were not.

Labor Crisis

In 1902 Roosevelt faced a major labor crisis. More than 100,000 Pennsylvania coal miners, members of the **United Mine Workers,** went on strike. They demanded better pay, an eight-hour workday, and recognition of the union's right to represent its members in discussions with mine owners.

The mine owners refused to negotiate with the workers. The **coal strike** dragged on for months. As winter approached, coal supplies dwindled. Public opinion began to turn against the owners. As public pressure mounted, Roosevelt invited representatives of the owners and miners to a meeting at the White House. Roosevelt was outraged when the owners refused to negotiate. He threatened to send federal troops to work in the mines and produce the coal. The owners finally agreed to arbitration—settling the dispute by agreeing to accept the decision of an impartial outsider. Mine workers won a pay increase and a reduction in hours, but they did not gain recognition for the union.

Roosevelt's action marked a departure from normal patterns of labor relations at the time. Earlier presidents had used troops against strikers, but Roosevelt had used the power of the federal government to force the company owners to negotiate. In other labor actions, however, Roosevelt supported employers in disputes with workers.

Square Deal

Roosevelt ran for the presidency in 1904, promising the people a square deal—fair and equal treatment for all. He was elected with more than 57 percent of the popular vote.

Roosevelt's "square deal" called for a considerable amount of government regulation of business. This contrasted with an attitude toward business that dated back to the presidency of Thomas Jefferson, which was summed up in the phrase laissez-faire (LEH•say FEHR). This French term generally means, "let people do as they choose."

McKinley/Roosevelt glass canteen, 1900

Roosevelt introduced a new era of government regulation. He supported the **Meat Inspection** and **Pure Food and Drug Acts;** these acts gave the Department of Agriculture and the Food and Drug Administration the power to visit businesses and inspect their products.

Conserving the Wilderness

Roosevelt held a lifelong enthusiasm for the great outdoors and the wilderness. He believed in the need for conservation, the protection and preservation of natural resources.

As president, Roosevelt took steps to conserve the country's forests, mineral deposits, and water resources. In 1905 he proposed the **U.S. Forest Service.** He pressured Congress to set aside millions of acres of national forests and created the nation's first wildlife sanctuaries. Roosevelt also formed the National Conservation Commission, which produced the first survey of the country's natural resources.

Roosevelt has been called America's first environmental president. While he made conservation an important public issue, Roosevelt also recognized the need for economic growth and development. He tried to strike a balance between business interests and conservation.

Reading Check **Describing** What is conservation?

William Howard Taft

No president before had ever served more than two terms. In keeping with that tradition, Roosevelt decided not to run for reelection in 1908. Instead Roosevelt chose William Howard Taft, an experienced diplomat, to run for president. In the election of 1908, Taft easily defeated Democrat William Jennings Bryan.

Although he had none of Roosevelt's flair, Taft carried out—and went beyond—many of Roosevelt's policies. The Taft administration won more antitrust cases in four years than Roosevelt had won in seven. Taft also favored the introduction of safety standards for mines and railroads.

Taft supported the **Sixteenth Amendment,** which gave Congress the power to tax people's incomes to generate revenue for the federal

Why It Matters

The Influence of
Minor Political Parties

Minor Political Parties The Republican and Democratic parties dominate the nation's two-party system. Yet the United States has a long history of other political parties that have risen to challenge the major parties. Minor parties pushed for an end to slavery, and supported voting rights for women, and child and labor regulation long before the major parties did.

Populist proposals that are in effect today include the federal income tax, the secret ballot, and the initiative and referendum.

government. Progressives hoped the income tax would enable the government to lower tariffs. In their view high tariffs led to higher prices for goods, which caused hardship for the poor. Progressives believed that taxes based on income were fairer. The Sixteenth Amendment, added to the Constitution in 1913, did not specify how income would be taxed. Congress passed additional laws so that higher incomes were taxed at a higher rate than lower incomes.

Despite his progressive reforms, President Taft disappointed progressives in two important areas—tariffs and conservation. He failed to fight for a lower tariff, and he modified some conservation policies so that they favored businesses.

Some third parties have presented a strong challenge to the major parties. The Republican Party was itself a third party in 1856. Four years later it captured the White House.

Third-Party Results

Presidential Election Year	Candidate/party	Results: % of popular vote	Electoral votes
1848	Martin Van Buren, Free Soil	10.1	0
1856	John C. Fremont, Republican	33.1	114
1892	James Weaver, Populist	8.5	22
1912	Theodore Roosevelt, Progressive	27.4	88
1924	Robert La Follette, Progressive	16.6	13
1948	Strom Thurmond, States Rights	2.4	39
1968	George Wallace, Am. Independent	13.5	46
1992	Ross Perot, Reform	19.0	0
2000	Ralph Nader, Green	2.7	0

For the People PER★T By the People

"Look up, not down— Look out, not in— Look forward, not backward— And lend a hand."

Founders' Day October 27, 1912 THE Progressive Party

A SQUARE DEAL NATIONAL PRESIDENTIAL CLUB 1912

Former President Theodore Roosevelt left the Republican Party to form the Progressive, or "Bull Moose," Party.

Roosevelt Challenges Taft

By 1912 Roosevelt had become completely disappointed in Taft. With a new presidential election on the horizon, Roosevelt decided to challenge Taft for the Republican presidential nomination. Roosevelt claimed that Taft had "completely twisted around" his own policies.

The showdown between Roosevelt and Taft came at the Republican national convention in Chicago in June. Although Roosevelt won every primary and had many supporters, Taft had the backing of Republican Party leaders and influential business interests who controlled the party machinery. When Taft received the nomination on the first ballot, Roosevelt charged the Republican party leaders with stealing the presidential nomination from him.

A fiery Roosevelt led his supporters out of the convention hall. He and his followers formed a new party, the **Progressive Party.** In August the Progressives held their own convention in Chicago and nominated Roosevelt for president.

When a reporter asked Roosevelt about his health, the candidate thumped himself on the chest and declared, "I feel as strong as a bull moose!" From then on, the Progressive Party was known as the **Bull Moose Party.**

The Election of 1912

The split in the Republican Party hurt both Taft and Roosevelt. While Republicans and Progressives battled each other at the polls, Democrat **Woodrow Wilson** gathered enough support to defeat them in the election. Wilson had

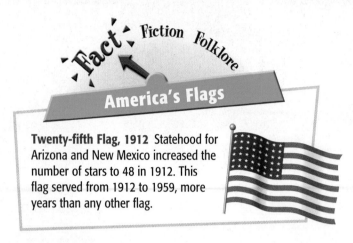

Twenty-fifth Flag, 1912 Statehood for Arizona and New Mexico increased the number of stars to 48 in 1912. This flag served from 1912 to 1959, more years than any other flag.

acquired a reputation as a progressive reformer while serving as president of Princeton University and governor of New Jersey.

Wilson gained only 42 percent of the popular vote, with Roosevelt receiving 27 percent and Taft 23 percent. However, Wilson won the presidency by the largest electoral majority up to that time, sweeping 435 of the 531 electoral votes.

Wilson in the White House

During his campaign Woodrow Wilson had criticized big government as well as big business. Wilson called his program the "New Freedom."

In 1913 Wilson achieved a long-awaited progressive goal—tariff reform. He persuaded the Democrat-controlled Congress to adopt a lower tariff on imported goods such as sugar, wool, steel, and farm equipment. Wilson believed that the pressure of foreign competition would lead American manufacturers to improve their

products and lower their prices. The government income lost by lowering tariffs would be replaced by the new income tax.

That same year Congress also passed the **Federal Reserve Act** to regulate banking. By creating 12 regional banks supervised by a central board in Washington, D.C., the act gave the government more control over banking activities. Banks that operated nationally were required to join the Federal Reserve System and abide by its regulations.

Wilson also worked to strengthen government control over business. In 1914 Congress established the **Federal Trade Commission (FTC)** to investigate corporations for unfair trade practices. Wilson also supported the **Clayton Antitrust Act** of 1914, which joined the Sherman Antitrust Act as one of the government's chief weapons against trusts. The government also tried to regulate child labor. The Keating-Owen Act of 1916 banned goods produced by child labor from being sold in interstate commerce. The act was struck down as unconstitutional just two years later.

By the end of Wilson's first term, progressives had won many victories. The Progressive movement lost some of its momentum as Americans turned their attention to world affairs—especially the war that had broken out in Europe in 1914.

Reading Check **Analyzing** How did Roosevelt's run for the presidency affect the election of 1912?

SECTION 3 ASSESSMENT

Checking for Understanding

1. **Key Terms** Write a paragraph in which you use all of the following key terms: trustbuster, arbitration, laissez-faire.
2. **Reviewing Facts** What candidate won the presidential election of 1912?

Reviewing Themes

3. **Economic Factors** Why did progressives support an income tax?

Critical Thinking

4. **Analyzing Information** Explain why Roosevelt preferred regulation to trustbusting.
5. **Determining Cause and Effect** Re-create the diagram below and explain the reasons for, and the outcome of, the 1902 coal strike.

```
┌────────┐     ┌────────┐     ┌────────┐
│        │ ──▶ │  1902  │ ──▶ │        │
│        │     │  Coal  │     │        │
└────────┘     │ Strike │     └────────┘
               └────────┘
```

Analyzing Visuals

6. **Chart Skills** Study the chart on page 623 that shows third-party results. What party did James Weaver represent? What third party received the largest percentage of the popular vote? The largest number of electoral votes?

Interdisciplinary Activity

Art Draw a political cartoon that supports Theodore Roosevelt's actions as a "trustbuster."

Interpreting a Political Cartoon

Why Learn This Skill?

You've probably heard the saying, "A picture is worth a thousand words." For more than 200 years, political cartoonists have drawn pictures to present their opinions about a person or event. Learning to interpret political cartoons can help you understand issues of both the past and present.

Learning the Skill

Political cartoons state opinions about particular subjects. To illustrate those opinions, cartoonists provide clues, using several different techniques. They often exaggerate a person's physical features or appearance in a special effect called "caricature." A caricature can be positive or negative, depending on the artist's point of view.

Cartoonists also use symbols to represent something else. The bald eagle is often shown in political cartoons as a symbol of the United States. Sometimes cartoonists help readers interpret their message by adding labels or captions.

To interpret a political cartoon, follow these steps:

• Read the caption and any other words printed in the cartoon.

• Analyze each element in the cartoon.

• Identify the clues: What is happening in the cartoon? Who or what is represented by each part of the drawing? What or whom do the figures represent? To what do the symbols refer?

• Study all these elements to decide the point the cartoonist is making.

Practicing the Skill

The cartoon on this page shows Theodore Roosevelt looking in a window at President Taft. Analyze the cartoon, and then answer the following questions.

1 What is going on in this picture?

2 What caricatures are included in this cartoon?

3 What symbols are shown in the cartoon? What do these symbols represent?

4 What point is the cartoonist making?

Applying the Skill

Interpreting a Political Cartoon Bring to class a copy of a political cartoon from a recent newspaper or magazine. Explain the cartoonist's point of view and the tools used to express it.

 Glencoe's **Skillbuilder Interactive Workbook CD-ROM, Level 1,** provides instruction and practice in key social studies skills.

WILD WONDERS

GRIZZLY BEARS, WOLVES, MOOSE, CARIBOU, DALL'S SHEEP and many other animals roam Alaska's Denali National Park and Preserve. Larger than Massachusetts, the six-million-acre park includes the highest mountain in North America.

The Alaskan wilderness area set aside as Mount McKinley National Park in 1917 was renamed Denali in 1980 when Congress tripled the size of the park. Denali was the peak's Native American name, meaning "the High One."

The idea of setting aside areas of natural beauty and historic importance for the benefit of the people dates back to the mid-1800s. Before then Americans had viewed wild places either as obstacles or as a source of natural resources for people to use.

The conservation movement gained popularity in the early 1900s when President Theodore Roosevelt and other conservationists urged Americans to protect natural resources.

Today conservation continues to be an important issue. Although many of us enjoy visiting national parks such as Denali, the parks also serve as refuges for wildlife. Scientists study the plants and animals so that they can protect them. With 430 species of flowering plants, 37 species of mammals, and 156 species of birds, Denali stands as one of America's great areas of unspoiled wilderness.

Mt. Foraker
17,400 ft. (5,303 m)

Avalanche Spire
10,105 ft. (3,080 m)

Kahiltna Glacier

ALASKA

CANADA

U.S.

Yukon River

Denali National Park and Preserve

0   500 miles

0   500 kilometers

LEARNING from GEOGRAPHY

1. **Which peaks are higher than 15,000 feet?**

2. **How do you think attitudes toward wilderness areas have changed during the last century?**

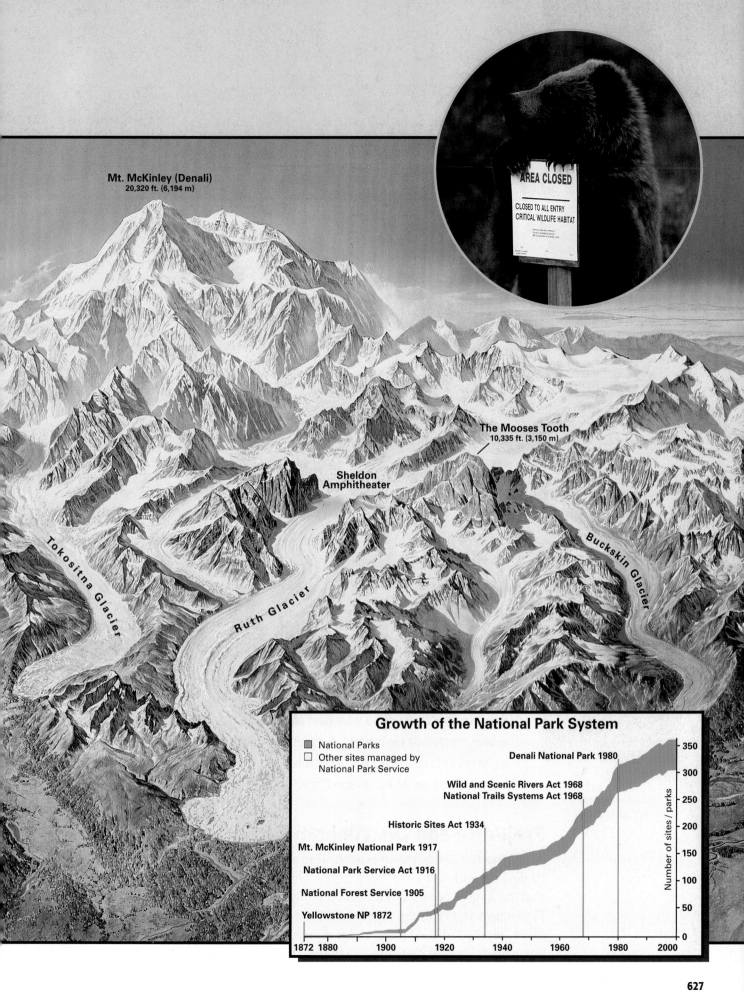

Mt. McKinley (Denali)
20,320 ft. (6,194 m)

AREA CLOSED

CLOSED TO ALL ENTRY
CRITICAL WILDLIFE HABITAT

The Mooses Tooth
10,335 ft. (3,150 m)

Sheldon
Amphitheater

Tokositna Glacier

Ruth Glacier

Buckskin Glacier

Growth of the National Park System

■ National Parks
□ Other sites managed by
National Park Service

Denali National Park 1980

Wild and Scenic Rivers Act 1968
National Trails Systems Act 1968

Historic Sites Act 1934

Mt. McKinley National Park 1917

National Park Service Act 1916

National Forest Service 1905

Yellowstone NP 1872

Number of sites / parks

350
300
250
200
150
100
50
0

1872 1880   1900   1920   1940   1960   1980   2000

Excluded from Reform

Main Idea

Progressive reform did little to expand the rights and opportunities for minorities.

Key Terms

discrimination, barrio

Reading Strategy

Taking Notes As you read Section 4, re-create the diagram below and describe each person's accomplishments.

Individual	Accomplishments
Booker T. Washington	
Ida Wells	
W.E.B. Du Bois	
Carlos Montezuma	

Read to Learn

• why progressive reforms did not include all Americans.
• how minorities worked to move toward greater equality.

Section Theme

Civic Rights and Responsibilities Minorities discovered that progressive reforms often did not advance their own rights and responsibilities.

Preview of Events

◆1880   ◆1900   ◆1920

1887
American Protective Association targets Catholics

1907
Gentlemen's Agreement restricts Japanese immigration

1909
W.E.B. Du Bois helps form the NAACP

1915
Ku Klux Klan reappears

Chinese shopkeeper in California

AN American Story

Like many seeking their fortunes, 16-year-old Lee Chew left his farm in China and booked passage on a steamer. When he and other Chinese immigrants arrived in San Francisco, they confronted a great wave of anti-Asian feeling. In the city's Chinese quarter, immigrants ran markets, laundries, and other small shops. Chew worked for an American family. "Chinese laundrymen [like me] were taught by American women," he said. "There are no laundries in China."

Prejudice and Discrimination

During the 1800s the overwhelming majority of Americans were white and Protestant and had been born in the United States. Many Americans believed that the United States should remain a white, Protestant nation. Nonwhite, non-Protestant, and non-native residents often faced discrimination—unequal treatment because of their race, religion, ethnic background, or place of birth. The government rarely interfered with this discrimination.

In 1908 violence erupted in **Springfield, Illinois,** when a white woman claimed to have been attacked by an African American man. Authorities jailed the man, but by that time, white townspeople had formed an angry mob.

Armed with axes and guns, the mob stormed through African American neighborhoods, destroying businesses and driving people from their homes. Rioters lynched two African American men and injured dozens more. Yet no one was ever punished for these violent crimes. Later, the woman who claimed she was attacked admitted that her accusation was untrue.

The Springfield riot shocked the nation and highlighted the deep racial divisions in American life. The riot took place in the hometown of Abraham Lincoln, the president who signed the Emancipation Proclamation. African Americans were no longer enslaved—but they were still pursued by prejudice and racial hatred.

Anti-Catholicism

Some Americans faced discrimination because of their religion. America's largely Protestant population feared that Catholic immigrants threatened the "American" way of life. Anti-Catholic Iowans formed the American Protective Association (APA) in 1887. By the mid-1890s, the APA claimed a membership of two million across the nation. Among other activities, the APA spread rumors that Catholics were preparing to take over the country.

Anti-Semitism

Many Jewish immigrants came to the United States to escape prejudice in their homelands. Some of them found the same anti-Semitic attitudes in America. Landlords, employers, and schools discriminated against Jews. Eastern European Jews faced prejudice both as Jews and as eastern Europeans, whom many Americans regarded as more "foreign" than western Europeans.

MORE ABOUT...

Immigration

Immigration rose during the period of rapid industrialization at the turn of the century. Then, immigration decreased when Congress imposed immigration restrictions. Towards the end of the century, a dramatic increase took place after the restrictions were relaxed.

Percentage of U.S. Population That Is Foreign Born

Population Percentage by Year:
- 1900: 13.6
- 1910: 14.7
- 1920: 13.2
- 1930: 11.6
- 1940: 8.8
- 1950: 6.9
- 1960: 5.4
- 1970: 4.7
- 1980: 6.2
- 1990: 8.0
- 2000: 10.4

Source: U.S. Bureau of the Census.

Percent Foreign Born by Region of Birth: 1900

- 84.9
- 1.3
- 1.2
- 12.6

Europe
All other
Latin America
Asia

Percent Foreign Born by Region of Birth: 2000

- 51.0
- 25.5
- 15.3
- 8.2

Latin America
Asia
Europe
All other

Anti-Asian Policies

Discrimination was also based on race. In California and other western states, Asians struggled against prejudice and resentment. White Americans claimed that Chinese immigrants, who worked for lower wages, took away jobs. Congress passed the Chinese Exclusion Act in 1882 to prevent Chinese immigrants from entering the United States.

America's westward expansion created opportunities for thousands of Japanese immigrants who came to the United States to work as railroad or farm laborers. Like the Chinese before them, Japanese immigrants encountered prejudice. California would not allow them to become citizens. In 1906 in San Francisco, the school board tried to make Japanese children attend a separate school for Asians until President Roosevelt stepped in to prevent such segregation.

Roosevelt yielded to a rising tide of anti-Japanese feeling, however, and authorized the **Gentlemen's Agreement** with Japan in 1907. This accord restricted Japanese immigration to the United States, but it did not bring an end to anti-Japanese feeling. In 1913 California made it illegal for Japanese immigrants to buy land. Other Western states passed similar laws.

Discrimination Against African Americans

African Americans faced discrimination in both the North and the South. Although officially free, African Americans were systematically denied basic rights and restricted to second-class citizenship.

Four-fifths of the nation's African Americans lived in the South. Most worked as rural sharecroppers or in low-paying jobs in the cities. They were separated from white society in their own neighborhoods, schools, parks, restaurants, theaters, and even cemeteries. In 1896 the Supreme Court legalized segregation in the case of *Plessy* v. *Ferguson,* which recognized "separate but equal" facilities.

The **Ku Klux Klan,** which had terrorized African Americans during Reconstruction, was reborn in Georgia in 1915. The new Klan wanted to restore white, Protestant America. The Klan lashed out against minorities—Catholics, Jews, and immigrants, as well as African Americans. Calling for "100 percent Americanism," the Klan kept growing and claimed more than two million members by 1924, many of them in Northern cities and towns.

Picturing **History**

A Ku Klux Klan pamphlet (right) promotes the Klan's hate campaign. Meanwhile, opponents of lynching called for an end to racial murders. **What two groups experienced the terror of lynching?**

Racial Violence

People who lost their jobs during the economic depressions of 1893 and 1907 sometimes unleashed their anger against African Americans and other minorities. More than 2,600 African Americans were lynched between 1886 and 1916, mostly in the South. Lynchings were also used to terrorize Chinese immigrants in the West.

Progressivism and Prejudice

In the late 1800s and the early 1900s, many Americans held biased views. They believed that white, male, native-born Americans had the right to make decisions for all of society.

Most of the progressive reformers came from the middle and upper classes. They saw themselves as moral leaders working to improve the lives of people less fortunate than themselves. Nevertheless, the reforms they supported often discriminated against one group as they tried to help another group.

Trade unions often prohibited African Americans, women, and immigrants from joining. Skilled laborers, these unions argued, could obtain better working conditions for themselves if they did not demand improved conditions for all workers.

Sometimes reforms instituted by the progressives were efforts to control a particular group. The temperance movement, for example, was partly an attempt to control the behavior of Irish Catholic immigrants. Civil service reforms required job applicants to be educated—this reduced the political influence that immigrants had begun to have in some cities. In spite of their contradictions, progressive reforms did succeed in improving conditions for many Americans.

Reading Check **Identifying** What Supreme Court decision legalized segregation?

Struggle for Equal Opportunity

Often excluded from progressive organizations because of prejudice, minorities battled for justice and opportunity on their own. African Americans, Hispanics, and Native Americans took steps to improve their lives.

African Americans rose to the challenge of achieving equality. **Booker T. Washington,** who had been born enslaved and taught himself to read, founded the Tuskegee Institute in 1881. The institute taught African Americans farming and industrial skills.

People In History

W.E.B. Du Bois 1868–1963

W.E.B. Du Bois was the first African American to receive a doctorate degree from Harvard. As an educator he refused to accept racial inequality. Du Bois helped start the Niagara Movement in 1905 to fight against racial discrimination and demand full political rights and responsibilities for African Americans. Later, Du Bois joined others to form the National Association for the Advancement of Colored People (NAACP). This group today remains a force in the efforts to gain legal and economic equality for African Americans.

Du Bois rejected Booker T. Washington's emphasis on job skills and argued that the right to vote was the way to end racial inequality, stop lynching, and gain better schools. "The power of the ballot we need in sheer self-defense," he said, "else what shall save us from a second slavery?"

Washington believed that if African Americans had more economic power they would be in a better position to demand social equality and civil rights. Washington founded the **National Negro Business League** to promote business development among African Americans. In Washington's autobiography, *Up from Slavery,* he counseled African Americans to work patiently toward equality. Washington argued that equality would be achieved when African Americans gained the education and skills to become valuable members of their community.

Some African Americans thought that they would be better off in separate societies, either in the United States or in Africa. They founded organizations to establish African American towns and promoted a back-to-Africa movement. These movements were not popular, however, and their goals gained few supporters.

African American Women Take Action

African American women worked together through groups such as the National Association of Colored Women to fight the practice of lynching and other forms of racial violence. **Ida B. Wells,** the editor of an African American newspaper in Memphis, Tennessee, was forced to leave town after publishing the names of people involved in a lynching. The incident started Wells on a national crusade against the terrible practice of lynching.

In her 1895 book, *A Red Record,* Wells showed that lynching was used primarily against African Americans who had become prosperous or who competed with white businesses. "Can you remain silent and inactive when such things are done in your own community and country?" she asked.

Other Successes

During the early 1900s African Americans achieved success in a variety of professions. Chemist **George Washington Carver,** director of agricultural research at Tuskegee Institute, helped improve the economy of the South through his discoveries of plant products. **Maggie Lena** founded the St. Luke Penny Savings Bank in Richmond, Virginia. She was the first American woman to serve as a bank president.

Native Americans Seek Justice

The federal government's efforts to assimilate Native Americans into white society threatened to break down traditional native cultures. In 1911 Native American leaders from around the country formed the **Society of American Indians** to seek justice for Native Americans, to improve their living conditions, and to educate white Americans about different Native American cultures.

One of the society's founding members was **Dr. Carlos Montezuma,** an Apache who had been raised by whites. Convinced that federal policies were hurting Native Americans, Montezuma became an activist, exposing government abuse of Native American rights. Montezuma believed that Native Americans should leave the reservations and make their own way in white society.

Mexican Americans Work Together

Immigrants from Mexico had long come to the United States as laborers, especially in the West and Southwest. Between 1900 and 1914, the Mexican American population grew dramatically as people crossed the border to escape revolution and economic troubles in Mexico.

Like the Japanese and other immigrant groups, Mexican Americans encountered discrimination and violence. Relying on themselves to solve their problems, they formed *mutualistas*—self-defense associations—to raise money for insurance and legal help. One of the first *mutualistas* was the *Alianza Hispano Americo* (Hispanic American Alliance), formed in Tucson, Arizona, in 1894. Another *mutualista*, the

"Is there no redress, no peace, no justice in this land for us? Tell the world the facts."

—*Ida B. Wells*

Orden Hijos de America (Order of Sons of America), formed in San Antonio, Texas, in 1921 to work for equality and raise awareness of Mexican Americans' rights as U.S. citizens. In labor camps and Mexican neighborhoods called barrios, *mutualistas* organized self-help groups to deal with overcrowding, poor sanitation, and inadequate public services.

Widespread prejudice excluded Mexican Americans from many reform groups. Yet Mexican Americans produced dynamic leaders and created organizations to improve their circumstances and fight for justice.

✓ **Reading Check** **Describing** Against what type of violence did Ida B. Wells speak out?

SECTION 4 ASSESSMENT

Checking for Understanding

1. **Key Terms** Define discrimination and barrio.
2. **Reviewing Facts** What were the results of the Gentlemen's Agreement with Japan, authorized by Theodore Roosevelt?

Reviewing Themes

3. **Civic Rights and Responsibilities** Give an example of a progressive reform that resulted in discrimination.

Critical Thinking

4. **Comparing** How did the views of Booker T. Washington differ from those of W.E.B. Du Bois?
5. **Analyzing Information** Re-create the diagram below and list the actions these groups took to battle prejudice and discrimination.

Groups	Actions taken
Native Americans	
Mexican Americans	
African Americans	

Analyzing Visuals

6. **Graph Skills** Examine the graphs on page 629. What was the percentage of foreign-born people in 1900? In 2000? Did Latin American people make up a larger or smaller percentage of the foreign-born population in 2000 or in 1900? Explain.

Interdisciplinary Activity

Art Create a title and cover design for a book about discrimination that might have been written during this time.

Chapter Summary
Progressive Reforms

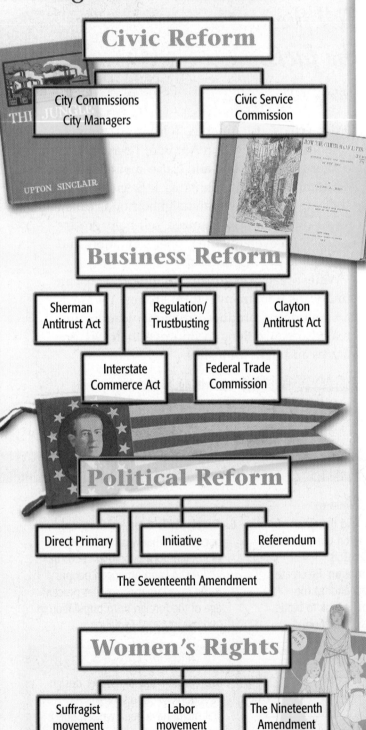

Civic Reform

- City Commissions / City Managers
- Civic Service Commission

Business Reform

- Sherman Antitrust Act
- Regulation/ Trustbusting
- Clayton Antitrust Act
- Interstate Commerce Act
- Federal Trade Commission

Political Reform

- Direct Primary
- Initiative
- Referendum
- The Seventeenth Amendment

Women's Rights

- Suffragist movement
- Labor movement
- The Nineteenth Amendment

Reviewing Key Terms

You are a journalist writing about the impact of progressive reforms. Write an article in which you use at least three of the following key terms.

1. political machine
2. civil service
3. primary
4. referendum
5. initiative
6. recall

Reviewing Key Facts

7. How did corrupt political bosses get voters for their parties?
8. Why were journalists important to the reform movement?
9. What amendment provided for the direct election of senators?
10. What amendment provided for woman suffrage?
11. What is arbitration?
12. Why did progressives form their own political party?
13. What was the purpose of the Federal Reserve Act?
14. What is discrimination?
15. What did Dr. Carlos Montezuma think about Native American reservations?
16. Why did Mexican Americans organize *mutualistas*?

Critical Thinking

17. **Analyzing Themes: Government and Democracy** How did the Seventeenth Amendment give people a greater voice in government?
18. **Determining Cause and Effect** Why was the railroad industry subject to so many government regulations?
19. **Analyzing Themes: Civic Rights and Responsibilities** Re-create the diagram below and identify how these laws promote justice and insure citizens' rights.

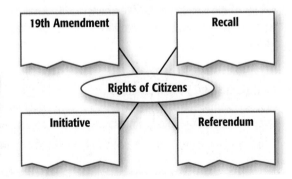

19th Amendment — Recall — Rights of Citizens — Initiative — Referendum

Practicing Skills

Interpreting a Political Cartoon *Study the cartoon on this page; then answer the following questions.*

20. Who are the people grouped on the left of the cartoon?
21. What is the meaning of the comment made by the person on the right?
22. How does the cartoonist define "illegal immigrants?"

 Geography and History Activity

Examine the map on voting rights for women on page 617 and answer the questions that follow.

23. Which state was the first to provide equal suffrage?
24. By 1919 how many states allowed equal suffrage?
25. **Making Generalizations** Why do you think the percentage of states allowing woman suffrage was much higher in the West than in the East?

 Technology Activity

26. **Using E-Mail** Research the names of five modern organizations that have some of the same goals as the progressive reformers of the late 1800s and early 1900s. Choose one organization that interests you and make contact through E-mail to get more information about the group.

Self-Check Quiz
Visit taj.glencoe.com and click on **Chapter 21—Self-Check Quizzes** to prepare for the chapter test.

Citizenship Cooperative Activity

27. **Consumer Rights** Working with a partner, contact a local consumer league to learn about consumer rights. Then prepare a pamphlet on consumer rights. List the various rights consumers have and provide the names, addresses, and phone numbers of consumer groups to contact with problems. Distribute this pamphlet to people in your neighborhood.

 Alternative Assessment

28. **Portfolio Activity** Scan the chapter and make a list of the constitutional amendments that were passed during the Progressive Era. Make a cause-and-effect chart to show what needs, actions, or abuses led to the passage of each. Save your work for your portfolio.

The Princeton Review

Standardized Test Practice

Directions: Choose the *best* answer to the following question.

The main goal of the Woman's Christian Temperance Union was to pass laws to ban the making or selling of alcohol. Which of the following was a secondary goal?

A prison reform

B limit immigration

C promote the Square Deal

D pass the Gentlemen's Agreement

Test-Taking Tip

This question requires you to remember a *fact* about the WCTU. By reading the question carefully, you can find clues about the organization. It worked for *reform*. Which answer fits best with this information?

CHAPTER 22

Overseas Expansion

1865–1917

Why It Matters

International power came to the United States with political strength and industrial growth. As its power increased, the United States moved beyond its territorial limits in search of new markets and colonies.

The Impact Today

The United States began to compete with other nations for more trade and more land. From this rivalry, the United States rose to take a major role in shaping world affairs.

 The American Journey Video The chapter 22 video, "Bring Me the Pictures and I'll Bring You the War," discusses the rise of yellow journalism and its role in the Spanish-American War.

1889
• Pan-American Union established

1887
• U.S. establishes naval base at Pearl Harbor

1867
• Alaska purchased from Russia

United States PRESIDENTS

| Johnson 1865–1869 | Grant 1869–1877 | | Hayes 1877–1881 | Garfield 1881 | Arthur 1881–1885 | Cleveland 1885–1889 | B. Harrison 1889–1893 |

1865   1875   1885

World

1867
• Japan ends 675-year shogun rule

1875
• Suez Canal comes under British control

1883
• Vietnam becomes French protectorate

San Juan Hill Theodore Roosevelt, who later became the twenty-sixth president of the United States, leads the Rough Riders cavalry regiment during the Spanish-American War, July 1898.

FOLDABLES™
Study Organizer

Drawing Conclusions Study Foldable
Investigate the pros, or positive outcomes, and the cons, or negative outcomes, of overseas expansion by making this foldable.

Step 1 Fold one sheet of paper in half from top to bottom.

Step 2 Fold it in half again, from side to side.

Step 3 Unfold the paper once. Cut up the fold of the top flap only.

> This cut will make two tabs.

Step 4 Label the foldable as shown.

PROS of Overseas Expansion | CONS of Overseas Expansion

Reading and Writing As you read, write what you learn about the positive and negative effects of United States overseas expansion under the appropriate tabs of your foldable.

1900
• Hawaii becomes U.S. territory

1898
• Spanish-American War

1901
• Cuba granted independence

1904
• Roosevelt Corollary issued

1914
• Panama Canal opens

Cleveland 1893–1897 | McKinley 1897–1901 | Roosevelt 1901–1909 | Taft 1909–1913 | Wilson 1913–1921

1895   1905   1915

1895
• José Martí leads revolt in Cuba

1910
• British form Union of South Africa

1911
• Qing dynasty overthrown in China

HISTORY Online

Chapter Overview
Visit <u>taj.glencoe.com</u> and click on **Chapter 22— Chapter Overviews** to preview chapter information.

Expanding Horizons

Main Idea
In the late 1800s the United States acquired lands overseas.

Key Terms
isolationism, expansionism, imperialism

Reading Strategy
Analyzing Information As you read the section, re-create the diagram below and explain how the United States made its presence felt in each country or region.

	U.S. role
Japan	
Latin America	
Russia	

Read to Learn
- what factors contributed to the growth of American imperialism.
- how the United States expanded its economic and political influence in the late 1800s.

Section Theme
Economic Factors Americans expanded trade with other countries and competed for political influence.

Preview of Events

♦1850   ♦1870   ♦1890

1853
Matthew Perry sails into Tokyo Bay

1854
Japan signs Treaty of Kanagawa

1867
William Seward signs treaty to buy Alaska

1889
Pan-American Union established

Patriotic song sheet, 1898

AN American Story

In the late 1800s and early 1900s, Americans looked beyond their borders and yearned for an empire. Merchants desired overseas markets, and adventurers wanted another frontier to conquer. Senator Albert Beveridge voiced the feelings of many when he proclaimed in 1900: "The Philippines are ours forever. . . . And just beyond the Philippines are China's illimitable markets. We will not retreat from either. . . . The Pacific is our ocean."

American Foreign Policy

When President George Washington published his Farewell Address in 1796, he advised Americans to increase trade with other countries but to have "as little political connection as possible." Above all else, he warned Americans to "steer clear of permanent alliances with any portion of the foreign world." These principles guided American foreign policy for about 100 years. However, various people interpreted Washington's words in different ways. Some believed he meant that the United States should follow a policy of isolationism, or noninvolvement, in world affairs. Others pointed out that Washington supported trade with other countries and was not calling for complete isolation from the world.

American Expansionism

For many years some Americans dreamed of expanding their territory from ocean to ocean. Seeking land and better opportunities, many Americans moved to territories in the West and the South. This expansionism was a driving force in American history. During the Civil War, while the nation was torn apart, expansion came to a halt. After the war the United States began rebuilding and expanding again.

Americans settled the vast Great Plains, built railroads, and created large cities booming with people and busy factories. In 1890, when the nation spanned the North American continent from the Atlantic Ocean to the Pacific Ocean, the government issued a report announcing the end of the "frontier." Although areas of unsettled land remained, settlements could now be found from coast to coast.

To many Americans the frontier meant growth and opportunity. The idea that the frontier no longer existed was alarming. Americans began to look beyond the nation's borders to frontiers overseas where they could expand trade and compete for political influence.

Foreign Trade

In the mid-1800s, American merchants carried on a profitable trade with China and hoped to expand trade in other areas of the world. Many wanted to open trading relations with Japan, which had long been isolated from the West.

In 1853 President Millard Fillmore sent Commodore **Matthew Perry** on a mission to Japan. After steaming into Tokyo Bay with four warships, Perry asked the Japanese to open up their ports to U.S. ships. He told them he would return in several months for their answer.

The American show of force alarmed the Japanese. When Perry returned in 1854, the Japanese signed the **Treaty of Kanagawa** and opened two ports to American ships. Perry's successful mission began a period of trade between Japan and the United States. It also marked the start of greater American involvement in Asia.

Reading Check **Explaining** What did Washington say about alliances in his Farewell Address?

An Age of Imperialism

The United States was not the only Western nation expanding its trade and influence in Asia and other parts of the world. The late 1800s and

History *Through Art*

Perry's First Landing in Japan at Kurihama by **Gessan Ogata** A Japanese artist depicts Commodore Matthew Perry's 1853 arrival in Japan. **Why was Perry sent on a mission to Japan?**

the early 1900s were called an age of imperialism, a time when powerful European nations created large empires by exercising economic and political control over weaker regions.

The search for materials and markets drove imperialism. The industrial nations of Europe needed raw materials from Asia and Africa. The Europeans also sought new markets for the goods they manufactured. In their drive for raw materials and new markets, European powers competed with one another for power and influence in Asia and Africa.

Toward an Empire

American interest in political as well as economic expansion developed after the Civil War. Some Americans wanted the nation to build an empire. By annexing new lands, they argued, the United States would join the ranks of the world's great powers and take its rightful place at the center of power.

Secretary of State **William H. Seward,** appointed by Abraham Lincoln, supported this view. Seward pictured an American empire that dominated the Caribbean, Central America, and the Pacific. Holding this empire together would be a canal across Central America linking the Atlantic and Pacific Oceans, a thriving transcontinental railroad system, and rapid communication by means of the telegraph.

The Purchase of Alaska

Seward took a major step toward making his vision a reality with the purchase of **Alaska.** In 1867 Seward signed a treaty with Russia to buy the Russian colony for $7.2 million—an extraordinary bargain for a territory that was twice the size of Texas.

At the time many people ridiculed Seward's purchase. They regarded Alaska as a barren, icebound land. Newspapers mocked the purchase as "Seward's Ice Box" and a "polar bear garden." After gold was discovered in Alaska in the 1890s, however, Seward's "folly" began to seem more like a wise purchase. In 1912 Alaska became a territory of the United States.

A Sense of Mission

Some Americans had another reason for imperialist expansion. They had a sense of mission— a belief that they could "lift up" people they considered "uncivilized" by sharing Christianity and Western civilization with the rest of the world. **Josiah Strong,** a Congregational minister, proposed an "imperialism of righteousness," with Americans bringing their religion and their culture to the peoples of Africa, Asia, and the United States's closest neighbor, Latin America.

American Interest in Latin America

Since colonial times, the United States had carried on a flourishing trade with Latin America, including the Caribbean region. Fear of European influence in the region was a factor that led to the Monroe Doctrine in 1823, when President James Monroe warned European nations not to attempt to establish new colonies in North or South America.

United States merchants used the Monroe Doctrine to their advantage. In 1884 **James G. Blaine,** then the Republican nominee for president, declared:

> ❝While the great powers of Europe are steadily enlarging their colonial domination in Asia and Africa, it is the [particular] province of this country to improve and expand its trade with the nations of America.❞

Meanwhile, the United States signed treaties with a number of Latin American countries, allowing American businesses to influence those nations' economies.

As secretary of state in 1889, Blaine invited Latin American countries to attend a Pan-American Conference held in Washington, D.C. Blaine hoped to develop economic and political ties among the nations of the region. Although many Latin American countries worried about American domination, they decided to attend the meeting. The conference established the **Pan-American Union** to share information among member nations.

Building Sea Power

As the United States looked to expand its horizons, Captain **Alfred Thayer Mahan,** president of the Naval War College, called for improving and enlarging the navy. Mahan argued that sea power would protect shipping and provide access to world markets:

> ❝Sea power is essential to the greatness of every splendid people.❞

To maintain a powerful navy, the United States would need overseas colonies where ships could be refueled.

Transforming and expanding the navy began in 1883, when Congress authorized construction of the first steel-hulled warships. In the following years, the navy gradually shifted from sails to steam power and from wood to steel hulls. By the early 1900s, the United States had the naval power it needed to back up an expanded role in foreign affairs.

✓ **Reading Check** **Explaining** Why did many people criticize the purchase of Alaska?

SECTION 1 ASSESSMENT

Checking for Understanding

1. **Key Terms** Use the following terms to create a newspaper article about United States expansion during the late 1800s: isolationism, expansionism, imperialism.
2. **Reviewing Facts** Discuss the main points of the Monroe Doctrine.

Reviewing Themes

3. **Economic Factors** What price did the United States pay for Alaska? Why was the purchase of this territory ridiculed?

Critical Thinking

4. **Determining Cause and Effect** What did Alfred Thayer Mahan say would result from American sea power?
5. **Organizing Information** Re-create the diagram below and list two economic reasons for United States expansion.

Reasons for expansion

Analyzing Visuals

6. **Picturing History** Study the painting on the chapter opening page on page 637. What does it show? What idea do you think the artist is expressing?

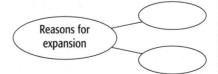
Interdisciplinary Activity

Geography Research the natural resources of Alaska. Draw a map of the state and use symbols to represent each resource and show its location in the state.

TIME NOTEBOOK

STEP BACK IN TIME

What—and who—were people talking about? What did they eat? What did they do for fun? These two pages will give you some clues to everyday life in the U.S. as you step back in time with TIME Notebook.

Profile

BOOKER T. WASHINGTON *Teaching industrial training as a means to success, in 1881 Washington founded the Tuskegee Institute in Alabama. Here is an excerpt from his autobiography,* Up From Slavery.

FROM THE VERY BEGINNING, AT TUSKEGEE, I was determined to have the students do not only the agricultural and domestic work, but to have them erect their own buildings. My plan was to have them, while performing this service, taught the latest and best methods of labour, so that the school would not only get the benefit of their efforts, but the students themselves would be taught to see not only utility in labour, but beauty and dignity. ... My plan was not to teach them to work in the old way, but to show them how to make the forces of nature—air, water, steam, electricity, horse-power— assist them in their labour.

Booker T. Washington

VERBATIM

WHAT PEOPLE ARE SAYING

If you pick up a starving dog and make him prosperous, he will not bite you. This is the principal difference between a dog and a man.
MARK TWAIN,
author of
The Adventures of Tom Sawyer

Speak softly and carry a big stick; you will go far.
PRESIDENT TEDDY ROOSEVELT,
proposing action when asked how the United States will deal with its new far-flung colonies in 1901

Give me your tired, your poor, your huddled masses yearning to breathe free.
WORDS BY EMMA LAZARUS,
engraved on the Statue of Liberty in 1903

Mountains! Look at them!
EDWARD CORSI,
10-year-old Italian immigrant on spotting the high-rise buildings in New York City for the first time in 1907

It's The Law

Two laws were passed in 1902 to deal with the automobile.

1 Tennessee demands all drivers give the public a week's notice before they start any trip.

2 Vermont states an adult waving a red flag has to walk in front of any moving automobile.

MILESTONES

EVENTS AND PEOPLE OF THE TIME

SIGNED UP. Sharpshooter **ANNIE OAKLEY** to Buffalo Bill's Wild West Show in 1885.

FLEW. 19-year-old Cromwell Dixon over the Continental Divide in 1911 in a biplane. At age 14, Dixon was building **DIRIGIBLES** (sausage-shaped balloons), including a model that could be pedaled through the air like a bicycle. Dixon later traveled around the country, flying at state fairs.

Annie Oakley

BETTMANN/CORBIS

AMERICAN SCENE

Average Lifespans in 1900

Average life expectancy: **47.3 years**

Male life expectancy: **46.3 years**

Female life expectancy: **48.3 years**

White life expectancy: **47.6 years**

Nonwhite life expectancy: **33.0 years**

| 0 | 10 | 20 | 30 | 40 | 50 years |

TRANSPORTATION

Take a Ride in My Car!

Here's what one magazine from the early 1900s recommends you carry in your car at all times:

1 Efficient tire pump

1 Strong two-gallon can extra gasoline

1 Sheet fine sandpaper

1 Small, short-handled axe

1 Ball asbestos cord

4 Half-pound cans of meat or fish

2 Pounds sweet chocolate

BETTMANN/CORBIS

NUMBERS

U.S. AT THE TIME

12¢ Price of a dozen eggs in 1910

$12 Price of a sewing machine in 1900

SCHENECTADY MUSEUM/HALL OF ELECTRICAL HISTORY FOUNDATION/CORBIS

$12 Lowest price for a steamship ticket from Italy to America in 1905

$12 Average weekly salary (seven-day weeks/12-hour days) for arriving immigrants in 1907

Wright brothers

BETTMANN/CORBIS

12 seconds Air time of Wright brothers' first flight in 1903

1.2 million Approximate number of immigrants who entered the U.S. in 1907

395,000 Approximate number of immigrants in 1908 who gave up on America and returned home

50¢ Price of cheapest seat at baseball's first World Series in 1903

Imperialism in the Pacific

Guide to Reading

Main Idea

The United States expanded into the Pacific Ocean region to set up trading bases.

Key Terms

annexation, spheres of influence, Open Door policy

Reading Strategy

Sequencing Information As you read the section, complete a time line like the one shown with important events in Hawaii's history.

1820 1842 1875 1887 1891 1898 1900

Read to Learn

• how the United States gained control of Hawaii and Samoa.

• how competition for influence in China and the Pacific region led to new foreign policies.

Section Theme

Geography and History The United States exercised its influence in China and the Pacific region.

Preview of Events

♦1890   ♦1900   ♦1910

1893
American planters overthrow Queen Liliuokalani

1899
U.S., Britain, and Germany divide Samoa

1900
Hawaii becomes a U.S. territory

1907
The Great White Fleet begins its voyage

★★★★★★★★
AN
American Story

Hawaiian stamp

As more Americans arrived in Honolulu, many Hawaiians feared that time was running out for their people. Kaona, a local judge in Honolulu, had visions that the end of the world was near. When volcanoes erupted and earth tremors plagued the island, his visions seemed to be coming true. Kaona and his followers prepared for the end. They dressed in flowing white robes and prayed loudly. Kaona had indeed been correct. The world that he and native Hawaiians had known would soon end.

✦Geography

Hawaii

Secretary of State William H. Seward believed the United States could build its empire in Hawaii and other regions through trade. The Pacific region played a key part in Seward's plan. In 1867 Seward acquired the two small Pacific islands of **Midway.** He thought that these islands, more than 3,000 miles (4,800 km) west of California, would serve as an important stopping place for American ships en route to China. American merchants and the United States Navy would need more than two small islands, however, to establish a secure foothold in the vast stretches of the Pacific.

The lush Hawaiian Islands, a chain of 8 large and 100 or so smaller islands, lay about 2,000 miles (3,200 km) west of California. The Hawaiian people dwelled in independent communities, each with its own chieftain, and lived by farming and fishing. American trading ships and whalers often stopped at the islands to take on supplies and fresh water.

In the 1790s Americans began trading with the Hawaiians for local resources. About that same time, King Kamehameha I unified the islands. Villages with good ports such as **Honolulu** and **Lahaina** (luh•HY•nuh) began to grow in importance, and trade increased. However, American and European ships also brought infectious diseases to the islands. These diseases devastated the island population just as they had once devastated the Native Americans.

Missionaries and Sugar Growers

In 1820 Christian missionaries from the United States began arriving in Hawaii. They established schools, created a written Hawaiian alphabet, and translated the Bible into Hawaiian. Increasing numbers of American merchants in the whaling trade came to settle there, too.

An American firm introduced sugarcane in Hawaii in the 1830s, and the missionaries and traders began buying land and establishing sugar plantations. The sugar industry grew quickly, and plantation owners brought in thousands of immigrants from Japan, China, and other Pacific lands to work in the fields. Gradually the Americans took control of most of the land and businesses. They also influenced Hawaiian politics, serving as advisers to the Hawaiian ruling family. Although the United States recognized Hawaiian independence in 1842, the islands came increasingly under American influence.

In 1875 the United States agreed to allow Hawaiian sugar to enter the country without tariffs. As sugar exports to the United States soared, American planters in Hawaii reaped enormous profits. In 1887, in return for renewal of the trade agreement, the United States pressured King Kalakaua (kah•LAH•KAH•u•ah) to allow it to establish a naval base at **Pearl Harbor,** the best seaport in the islands.

In the early 1890s, under pressure from American sugar producers, Congress revised the tariff laws and eliminated the exemption for Hawaiian sugar. As a result, Hawaiian sugar planters had to drop their prices drastically in order to sell any sugar. Sugar exports to the United States dropped sharply. Facing ruin, the planters plotted a way to avoid the new tariff. They decided to make Hawaii a territory of the United States.

American Planters' Revolt

The Hawaiians, meanwhile, had begun to resist the growing influence of Americans. In 1891 Queen **Liliuokalani** (lih•LEE•uh•woh•kuh•LAH•nee) came to the throne. The new ruler wanted Hawaiians to regain economic control of their islands, and she took away powers that the American sugar planters had held. In response, the white planters overthrew Liliuokalani and set up their own **provisional,** or temporary, government in 1893. The queen left under protest:

66 Now, to avoid any collision of armed forces and perhaps the loss of life, I . . . yield my authority. 99

Queen Liliuokalani

Annexation

The success of the planters' revolt stemmed in part from the support of the chief American diplomat in Hawaii, **John Stevens,** who arranged for marines from the warship *Boston* to assist in the uprising. Stevens immediately recognized the new government, which sent a delegation to Washington to seek a treaty of annexation that would add Hawaii to the United States. President Benjamin Harrison signed the treaty during the final days of his administration and forwarded it to the Senate for approval.

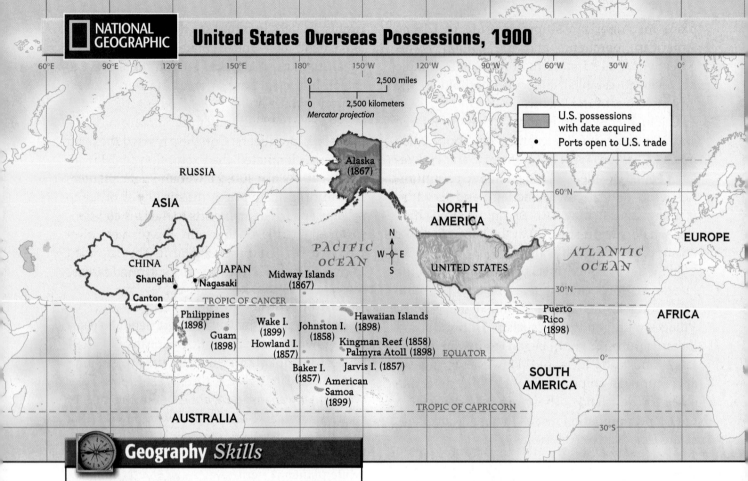

NATIONAL GEOGRAPHIC

United States Overseas Possessions, 1900

0 — 2,500 miles
0 — 2,500 kilometers
Mercator projection

U.S. possessions with date acquired
• Ports open to U.S. trade

RUSSIA

ASIA

Alaska (1867)

NORTH AMERICA

EUROPE

CHINA

JAPAN

Shanghai • Nagasaki

Midway Islands (1867)

PACIFIC OCEAN

UNITED STATES

ATLANTIC OCEAN

AFRICA

Canton

TROPIC OF CANCER

Philippines (1898)

Wake I. (1899)

Johnston I. (1858)

Hawaiian Islands (1898)

Puerto Rico (1898)

Guam (1898)

Howland I. (1857)

Kingman Reef (1858)

Palmyra Atoll (1898)

EQUATOR

Baker I. (1857)

Jarvis I. (1857)

SOUTH AMERICA

American Samoa (1899)

TROPIC OF CAPRICORN

AUSTRALIA

Geography Skills

1. **Location** Locate Puerto Rico, Guam, and the Philippines. Which of these is the farthest from the continental United States?
2. **Analyzing Information** When were the Hawaiian Islands acquired?

However, the Senate did not act quickly enough. It failed to ratify the treaty before Harrison left office. The new president, **Grover Cleveland,** opposed annexation and withdrew the treaty from the Senate after discovering that Hawaiians did not support the revolt. Cleveland called American interference in the Hawaiian revolution "disgraceful."

Although most of the Hawaiians and the Asian immigrants in Hawaii opposed annexation, their opposition made no difference. A small, powerful group of American sugar growers, traders, and missionaries—and their Hawaiian allies, along with influential people in the United States—had the final word. Congress approved the annexation of Hawaii in 1898, after William McKinley became president. In 1900 Hawaii became a territory of the United States.

The Islands of Samoa

About 3,000 miles (4,800 km) south of Hawaii lay the **Samoa Islands,** directly on the trade route linking Australia and the United States. As early as the 1830s, missionaries from the United States landed in Samoa and began converting the people to Christianity.

In 1878 Samoa agreed to give Americans special trading rights and permission to build a naval station at the port of Pago Pago. Great Britain and Germany also secured trading rights. During the 1880s, tensions mounted as the three rivals competed for power in Samoa.

In 1899 the United States, Great Britain, and Germany met in Berlin and—without consulting the Samoans—decided to divide up the islands. The United States and Germany split Samoa between them, while Great Britain agreed to withdraw from the area in return for rights on other Pacific islands. The Americans annexed their portion of Samoa the same year.

Reading Check **Explaining** Why did some American planters want to make Hawaii a territory of the United States?

China and the Open Door

For Americans the island territories in the Pacific, while important in themselves, represented stepping-stones to a larger prize—China. Torn apart by warring factions and lacking industry, China was too weak to resist the efforts of foreign powers that wanted to exploit its vast resources and markets.

Rivalries in China

By the late 1890s, Japan and the leading European powers had carved out spheres of influence in China—sections of the country where each of the foreign nations enjoyed special rights and powers. Japan held the island of Formosa and parts of the Chinese mainland. Germany controlled the Shandong area in east-central China. Great Britain and France held a number of Chinese provinces, and Russia moved into Manchuria and other areas in northern China.

An Open Door to China

In the United States, some government and business leaders worried about being squeezed out of the profitable China trade. Although the United States could not force the other foreign powers out of China, Secretary of State **John Hay** wanted to protect and expand American trading interests in the country. Hay proposed an Open Door policy under which each foreign nation in China could trade freely in the other nations' spheres of influence.

The Boxer Rebellion

The other major powers were reluctant to accept a policy that would benefit the United States most of all. The situation soon changed, however. Beginning in late 1899 a secret Chinese martial arts society, known as the Boxers, led a violent uprising against the "foreign devils" in China. Many died and for nearly two months, hundreds more were trapped in the besieged capital city of **Beijing.** Finally, in August 1900, foreign troops broke the siege and defeated the Boxers.

Out of the Boxer Rebellion came a second Open Door proposal, which stressed the importance of maintaining China's independence and respecting its borders. Alarmed by the rebellion, the other foreign powers accepted Hay's policy.

✓ **Reading Check** **Analyzing** What was the purpose of the Open Door policy?

History *Through Art*

View of Peking After the Boxer Rebellion by Yoshikazu Ichikawa American soldiers march through the Chinese capital after the Boxer Rebellion. **What policy did the United States want for China?**

Japan

Eager to expand its power in Asia, Japan began to ignore the Open Door policy. Japan's actions led to war with Russia and conflict with the United States.

In the early 1900s, Japan and Russia clashed over Manchuria, a Chinese province rich in natural resources. On February 8, 1904, Japan launched an attack on the Russian fleet at Port Arthur in southern Manchuria, starting the **Russo-Japanese War.** By the spring of 1905, both Japan's and Russia's resources were nearly exhausted, and both countries were eager to make peace.

Treaty of Portsmouth

President Theodore Roosevelt offered to meet with their leaders in Portsmouth, New Hampshire, to help settle the conflict. In September 1905, Japan and Russia signed the **Treaty of Portsmouth,** which recognized Japan's control of Korea in return for a pledge by Japan to halt its expansion.

Roosevelt hoped the treaty would preserve a balance of power in Asia, but it failed to do so. Japan emerged as the strongest naval power in the Pacific, and it challenged the United States for influence in the region. Relations between the two nations deteriorated steadily.

Strained Relations

During the Russo-Japanese War, Japanese immigration to the United States—especially to California—increased. Many Americans resented the Japanese newcomers, claiming that they took jobs from Americans.

As you read in Chapter 21, in 1906 the San Francisco Board of Education ordered that all Asian students attend separate schools. The Japanese government protested. An 1894 treaty had guaranteed that Japanese living in the United States would be treated well. The Japanese felt that the treaty had been broken.

President Roosevelt forced the San Francisco school board to change its policies. In return, he persuaded Japan to consent to an agreement, promising to restrict emigration. The Japanese resented the agreement and relations between the two nations worsened. Some Americans called for war.

Although President Roosevelt had no plan for war, in 1907 he sent 16 gleaming white battleships on a cruise around the world to display the nation's naval power. The **"Great White Fleet"** greatly impressed the Japanese. By 1909 the United States and Japan had resolved many of their differences.

Reading Check **Identifying** Who offered to help settle the Russo-Japanese War?

SECTION 2 ASSESSMENT

Checking for Understanding

1. **Key Terms** Use each of these terms in a complete sentence that will help explain its meaning: annexation, spheres of influence, Open Door policy.

2. **Reviewing Facts** Name three Pacific Islands that the United States acquired in the late 1800s and early 1900s.

Reviewing Themes

3. **Geography and History** Why were American political leaders interested in the Pacific islands in the 1800s?

Critical Thinking

4. **Making Inferences** Why do you think Roosevelt considered the cruise of the Great White Fleet to be "the most important service [he] rendered for peace"?

5. **Determining Cause and Effect** Re-create the diagram below and list the cause and effects of the Boxer Rebellion.

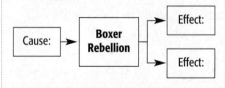

Cause: → Boxer Rebellion → Effect: / Effect:

Analyzing Visuals

6. **Geography Skills** Study the map on page 646. What particular geographic region of the world is the focus of the map? Which location is farthest west—Hawaii, Baker Island, or Wake Island?

Interdisciplinary Activity

Science Research the process of turning sugarcane into the refined sugar available in supermarkets. Draw a diagram showing the steps involved.

Spanish-American War

Guide to Reading

Main Idea
The Spanish-American War emerged out of events in Cuba, where the Cuban people were resisting Spanish rule.

Key Terms
yellow journalism, armistice, protectorate

Reading Strategy
Analyzing Information As you read the section, complete a diagram like the one shown by listing two reasons the United States went to war over Cuba.

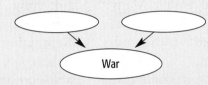

War

Read to Learn
- why the Spanish-American War began.
- how the United States's role in global affairs grew after the war.

Section Theme
Continuity and Change Through the Spanish-American War, the United States took control of new territory.

Preview of Events

◆1894	◆1896	◆1898	◆1900

1895
José Martí leads revolt in Cuba

1897
William McKinley becomes president

1898
The *Maine* explodes; the Spanish-American War takes place

1900
Foraker Act sets up new government in Puerto Rico

Charles M. Young

AN American Story

African Americans had fought in military conflicts since colonial times. The Buffalo Soldiers—named for their bravery and fighting ability by their Apache and Cheyenne foes—also answered the nation's call to arms during the Spanish-American War. On the front lines of the Spanish-American War, the 9th and 10th Cavalry, with valiant soldiers like Charles Young, led the charge up San Juan Hill with Colonel Teddy Roosevelt and his Rough Riders.

The Cuban Rebellion

The people of Cuba had lived under Spanish rule for centuries. The Cubans rebelled several times in the late 1800s, but each time the Spanish overpowered them and smashed their dreams of independence. **José Martí,** one of the heroes of the Cuban independence movement, fled to the United States to gather money, arms, and troops. In 1895, as economic conditions in Cuba worsened, Martí returned to Cuba to lead his people in a new revolt.

Martí's revolution led to terrible losses in human life and property. The rebels burned sugarcane fields and destroyed buildings in hopes of forcing the Spaniards to leave. In retaliation Spanish troops herded Cuban people into camps to separate them from the rebels and to break their morale. Thousands of Cubans died of starvation and disease.

War Fever

The Cuban people's struggle against Spain attracted much sympathy in the United States. Businesspeople worried about the destruction of trade and their loss of investments in Cuba. Government leaders were concerned about a rebellion so close to the United States. Many Americans were horrified by the atrocities against Cuban citizens and called for the government to do something about it.

President Grover Cleveland opposed any American involvement in Cuba. In March 1897, **William McKinley** became president. He, too, hoped the conflict could be settled peacefully.

The American press reported the unfolding tragedy in Cuba in graphic detail, and its coverage intensified the debate over America's role in the crisis. Newspapers, including **Joseph Pulitzer's** *World* and **William Randolph Hearst's** *Journal,* tried to outdo each other with shocking reports on the revolution. Hearst supposedly told an artist who was illustrating a story on Cuba, "You furnish the pictures, and I'll furnish the war." This type of sensational, biased, and often false reporting—known as yellow journalism—played a major role in fanning the flames of pro-war sentiment in the United States. 📖 *(See page 973 for one newspaper's account of Cuba's struggle.)*

"Remember the *Maine*"

The pressure on President McKinley to take action seemed to grow by the hour. After rioting broke out in the Cuban capital of Havana in January 1898, McKinley sent the battleship *Maine* to protect American citizens and property.

The ship remained quietly at anchor in Havana Harbor for three weeks. Then, on the night of February 15, 1898, an enormous explosion shattered the *Maine,* killing 260 officers and crew members. American newspapers immediately blamed the Spanish, and the slogan **"Remember the *Maine*"** became a rallying cry for revenge. Spain denied responsibility for the explosion. Much later, evidence indicated that the explosion may have been accidental, but at the time, Americans clamored for war with Spain.

After the *Maine* incident, President McKinley sent the Spanish a strong note demanding a truce and an end to brutality against the Cubans. The Spanish agreed to some American demands, but not enough to satisfy McKinley or Congress. On April 19 Congress recognized Cuban independence. It also demanded the withdrawal of Spanish forces and authorized the president to use the army and navy to enforce American aims. On April 25, 1898, Congress declared war on Spain.

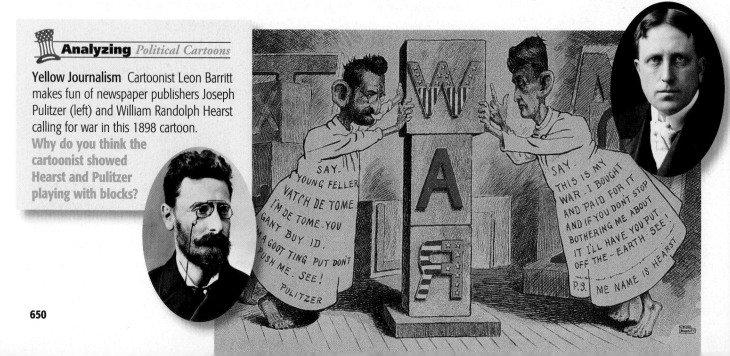

Analyzing *Political Cartoons*

Yellow Journalism Cartoonist Leon Barritt makes fun of newspaper publishers Joseph Pulitzer (left) and William Randolph Hearst calling for war in this 1898 cartoon. **Why do you think the cartoonist showed Hearst and Pulitzer playing with blocks?**

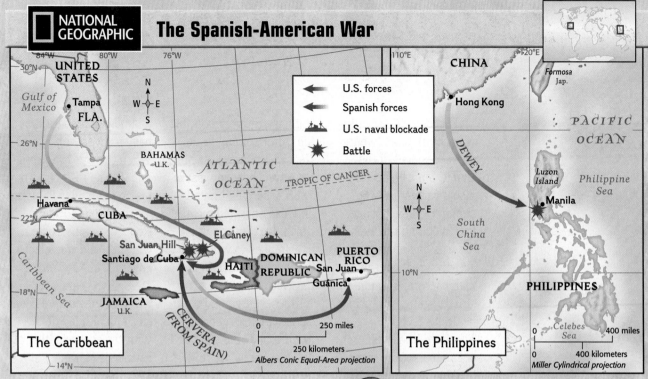

NATIONAL GEOGRAPHIC — The Spanish-American War

Legend:
- U.S. forces
- Spanish forces
- U.S. naval blockade
- Battle

The Caribbean

The Philippines

Albers Conic Equal-Area projection

Miller Cylindrical projection

Geography Skills

American troops sailed from Tampa, Florida, to the south coast of Cuba in June 1898. Admiral Dewey had already sailed from Hong Kong to Manila.

1. **Movement** According to the two maps, in which area did more of the fighting take place?
2. **Analyzing Information** On what two Caribbean islands did United States forces land?

War in the Philippines

Although events in Cuba triggered the Spanish-American War, the war's first military actions happened thousands of miles away in the Spanish colony of the **Philippines.** These islands served as a base for part of the Spanish fleet. In late February 1898, Assistant Secretary of the Navy **Theodore Roosevelt** had wired Commodore **George Dewey** and his squadron of navy vessels to prepare for action in the Philippines "in the event of declaration of war." In the early morning hours of May 1, Dewey launched a surprise attack on the Spanish fleet in Manila Bay, destroying most of the ships.

American troops arrived in July. With the help of Filipino rebels led by **Emilio Aguinaldo** (AH•gee•NAHL•doh), the Americans captured the city of Manila. As in Cuba, the Filipino rebels had struggled for years to win independence from Spain. Using American-supplied arms, they seized the main island of **Luzon,** declared independence, and created a democratic republic. The rebels expected the United States to support their independence. However, the United States debated what to do with the islands.

Fighting in Cuba

Meanwhile in the Caribbean, a Spanish fleet entered the harbor of **Santiago** on the southeastern shore of Cuba on May 19. Several days later, an American naval force blockaded the coast, trapping the Spanish in the harbor.

An American land force of about 17,000—nearly a quarter of them African American—landed near the city of Santiago. The inexperienced, ill-equipped Americans disembarked while forces under Cuban general Calixto García drove off the Spanish soldiers. When the Cuban and American forces advanced, Sergeant Major Frank W. Pullen, Jr., wrote that they faced "a perfect hailstorm of bullets, which, thanks to the poor marksmanship of the Spaniards, 'went high.'" Heavy fighting followed.

People In History

Theodore Roosevelt 1858–1919

Theodore Roosevelt was not only the twenty-sixth president of the United States—he was also a writer, historian, explorer, soldier, conservationist, and rancher. His life was one of constant activity, great energy, and many accomplishments.

Struggling with poor health as a child, Theodore Roosevelt began to exercise vigorously, gaining strength and a love of the outdoors that lasted throughout his life. After serving in the New York State Assembly, Roosevelt headed west in 1883, where he hunted and also operated a cattle ranch. He drew on these experiences to write several books about life in the West.

Roosevelt gained political experience working for reform at the local and national levels. In 1897 he was appointed assistant secretary of the navy and helped prepare the navy for war with Spain. When the war broke out in 1898, he resigned from his post and helped organize the "Rough Riders." Roosevelt came home a war hero and was elected governor of New York in 1898. Two years later he was elected vice president on the McKinley ticket. With the assassination of President McKinley in 1901, Roosevelt became president.

The Rough Riders

Theodore Roosevelt resigned his position as assistant secretary of the navy to join the fighting in Cuba. He led the First Regiment of U.S. Cavalry Volunteers, an assorted group of former cowhands and college students, popularly known as the **Rough Riders.** On July 1 the Rough Riders, with African American soldiers of the Ninth and Tenth Cavalries, joined the **Battle of San Juan Hill.** "I waved my hat and we went up the hill with a rush," Roosevelt wrote later.

The Americans captured San Juan Hill after intense fighting. Two days later the Spanish fleet attempted to break out of Santiago. In a battle that lasted about four hours, the Spanish fleet was completely destroyed. This defeat ended Spanish resistance in Cuba.

The United States then turned its attention to the Spanish colony of **Puerto Rico,** east of Cuba. American troops landed on Puerto Rico in late July and quickly took control of the island. On August 12 the Spanish signed an armistice—a peace agreement—ending the war.

"A Splendid Little War"

Secretary of State John Hay called the Spanish-American War "a splendid little war." The war lasted fewer than four months, and about 400 Americans were killed in battle or died from wounds received in the fighting.

Yet the war had other aspects that were not at all "splendid." More than 2,000 Americans died of diseases such as yellow fever, malaria, and other diseases contracted in the tropical climate. The African Americans who served faced the additional burden of discrimination. Serving in segregated units, African Americans battled alongside the Cuban rebel army, in which black and white troops fought as equals.

Reading Check **Explaining** Why did Filipino rebels help the United States fight against Spain?

Acquisitions

The United States and Spain signed the Treaty of Paris on December 10, 1898, marking the official end of the war. The treaty dissolved most of the Spanish empire. Cuba became an American protectorate, a country that is technically independent but actually under the control of another country. Puerto Rico and the Pacific island of **Guam** became territories of the United States. Spain also surrendered the Philippines to the United States in exchange for $20 million. The American empire had become a reality, and with the empire came new responsibilities.

Cuban Protectorate

Americans debated what to do about Cuba. Many congressional leaders believed that the Cubans were not ready for complete self-government. American business leaders feared that leaving Cuba might weaken the political stability of Cuba and jeopardize American interests there.

While Congress considered the matter, American troops remained in Cuba. Finally, in 1901, the United States agreed to grant Cubans full independence, but only if their new constitution included clauses giving the United States certain rights. Known as the **Platt Amendment,** these clauses prohibited Cuba from making treaties with other nations and gave America control of a naval base at Guantanamo Bay. The Platt Amendment also gave the United States the right to intervene in Cuban affairs if the country's independence was threatened.

New Government for Puerto Rico

After the war, Puerto Rico remained under direct military rule. In 1900 the United States set up a new Puerto Rican government under the **Foraker Act.** The American government controlled the new administration. In 1917 the Jones Act made Puerto Rico a territory of the United

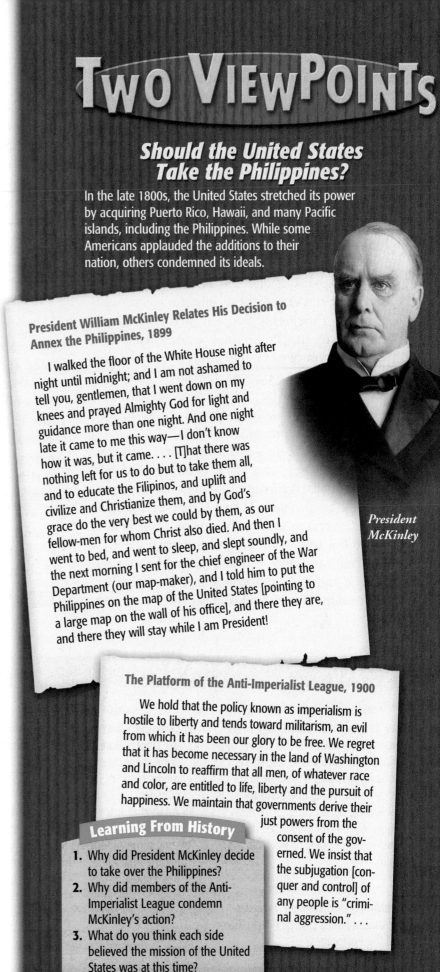

TWO VIEWPOINTS

Should the United States Take the Philippines?

In the late 1800s, the United States stretched its power by acquiring Puerto Rico, Hawaii, and many Pacific islands, including the Philippines. While some Americans applauded the additions to their nation, others condemned its ideals.

President William McKinley Relates His Decision to Annex the Philippines, 1899

I walked the floor of the White House night after night until midnight; and I am not ashamed to tell you, gentlemen, that I went down on my knees and prayed Almighty God for light and guidance more than one night. And one night late it came to me this way—I don't know how it was, but it came. . . . [T]hat there was nothing left for us to do but to take them all, and to educate the Filipinos, and uplift and civilize and Christianize them, and by God's grace do the very best we could by them, as our fellow-men for whom Christ also died. And then I went to bed, and went to sleep, and slept soundly, and the next morning I sent for the chief engineer of the War Department (our map-maker), and I told him to put the Philippines on the map of the United States [pointing to a large map on the wall of his office], and there they are, and there they will stay while I am President!

President McKinley

The Platform of the Anti-Imperialist League, 1900

We hold that the policy known as imperialism is hostile to liberty and tends toward militarism, an evil from which it has been our glory to be free. We regret that it has become necessary in the land of Washington and Lincoln to reaffirm that all men, of whatever race and color, are entitled to life, liberty and the pursuit of happiness. We maintain that governments derive their just powers from the consent of the governed. We insist that the subjugation [conquer and control] of any people is "criminal aggression." . . .

Learning From History

1. Why did President McKinley decide to take over the Philippines?
2. Why did members of the Anti-Imperialist League condemn McKinley's action?
3. What do you think each side believed the mission of the United States was at this time?

States and granted American citizenship to all Puerto Ricans. However, many Puerto Ricans still wanted independence.

Acquiring the Philippines

The United States had gained possession of the Philippines in the treaty that ended the Spanish-American War. But acquisition of the Philippines aroused fierce debate.

During the 1890s some people—**anti-imperialists**—opposed the American enthusiasm for foreign expansion and the Spanish-American War. After the war the anti-imperialists fought approval of the treaty. Some argued that American rule of the Philippines contradicted the principles on which the United States was founded. Others opposed the large standing army that would be necessary to control the Philippines. Still others feared competition from Filipino laborers.

Many Americans—including Carl Schurz, Andrew Carnegie, and Mark Twain—joined the anti-imperialist campaign. The imperialists, however, led by Senators Henry Cabot Lodge and Albert Beveridge, eventually won out. The Senate ratified the Treaty of Paris on February 6, 1899.

In February 1899, Emilio Aguinaldo's forces began a fight for independence. This conflict became a mammoth undertaking for the United

Puerto Rico

Puerto Rico has its own constitution. Puerto Rico was granted status as a commonwealth in 1952. This means that it is a territory of the United States but governs itself under its own constitution. Even though they are citizens, Puerto Ricans pay no federal income tax and they cannot vote for president. Many Puerto Ricans have immigrated to the United States mainland, which as citizens they can do freely.

States. More than 4,000 Americans died. Filipinos suffered far greater casualties—at least 200,000 soldiers and civilians died.

When Aguinaldo was captured in March 1901, many Filipino military officers and soldiers surrendered. Others refused to give up even after Aguinaldo urged them to stop fighting.

In the summer of 1901, the United States transferred authority in the Philippines from the military to a civilian government headed by **William Howard Taft.** Taft set out to prepare the islands for eventual self-rule. However, the Philippines did not gain full independence until 1946.

✓ **Reading Check** **Describing** What is a protectorate?

SECTION 3 ASSESSMENT

Checking for Understanding

1. **Key Terms** Write a one-page newspaper article about events during the Spanish-American War. Use these terms in your article: yellow journalism, armistice, protectorate.
2. **Reviewing Facts** Summarize how yellow journalism influenced Americans' views of going to war with Spain.

Reviewing Themes

3. **Continuity and Change** How did the United States govern Puerto Rico and the Philippines?

Critical Thinking

4. **Drawing Conclusions** Do you think the United States should have taken permanent control of Cuba and made it part of its empire? Why or why not?
5. **Analyzing Information** Re-create the diagram below and list the reasons some Americans opposed making the Philippines a United States possession.

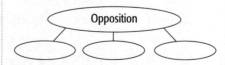

Opposition

Analyzing Visuals

6. **Geography Skills** Study the maps of the war on page 651. Near what Cuban city was the Battle of San Juan Hill fought?

Interdisciplinary Activity

Expository Writing Write a 45-second news report to convince viewers that they should pressure the United States to get involved in a war with Spain over Cuba. Be as persuasive as possible. Present your report to the class.

Technology
SKILLBUILDER

Developing Multimedia Presentations

Why Learn This Skill?

You want to present a research report to the rest of your class, and you want to really hold their attention. How do you do it? Your presentation can be exciting if you use various media.

Learning the Skill

At its most basic, a multimedia presentation involves using several types of media. To discuss life in the Philippines, for example, you might show photographs of the country. You could also play a recording of the country's language and music, or present a video showing the Filipino people at work and at play.

You can also develop a multimedia presentation on a computer. Multimedia, as it relates to computer technology, is the combination of text, video, audio, and animation in a computer program.

In order to create multimedia productions or presentations on a computer, you need to have certain tools. These may include traditional computer graphic tools and drawing programs, animation programs that make still images move, and authoring systems that tie everything together. Your computer manual will tell you which tools your computer can use.

Practicing the Skill

This chapter focuses on the overseas expansion of the United States in the late 1800s and early 1900s. Ask yourself questions like the following to develop a multimedia presentation on the people, politics, and industries of that era:

- Which forms of media do I want to include? Video? Sound? Animation? Photographs? Graphics? Other?

- Which of these media forms does my computer support?
- What kind of software programs or systems do I need? A paint program? A drawing program? An animation program? A program to create interactive, or two-way, communication? An authoring system that will allow me to change images, sound, and motion?
- Is there a "do-it-all" program I can use to develop the kind of presentation I want?

Developing Multimedia Presentations

Keeping in mind the four guidelines given above, write a plan describing a multimedia presentation you would like to develop. Indicate what tools you will need and what steps you must take to make the presentation a reality.

Latin American Policies

Main Idea

After the Spanish-American War, the United States attempted to extend its political and economic influence in Latin America.

Key Terms

isthmus, anarchy, dollar diplomacy

Reading Strategy

Analyzing Information As you read the section, re-create the diagram below and describe these policies.

	Description
Roosevelt Corollary	
Dollar Diplomacy	
Moral Diplomacy	

Read to Learn

- what shaped the policies the United States followed in Latin America.
- where and how the United States intervened in Latin America.

Section Theme

Global Connections American investments in Latin America grew in the early 1900s.

Preview of Events

| ♦1900 | ♦1910 | ♦1920 |

1904
Roosevelt Corollary is issued

1911
Revolution occurs in Mexico

1914
Panama Canal opens

1916
Francisco "Pancho" Villa launches uprising in Mexico

Canal brochure

***

AN American Story

On August 15, 1914, something described as the "greatest liberty that Man has taken with Nature" occurred. On that day, the first ship, the *Ancon,* traveled through the newly built Panama Canal. The world barely noticed, however. Most eyes were watching Europe, where World War I was beginning. As the ship passed the words on the great seal of the Panama Canal Zone—THE LAND DIVIDED, THE WORLD UNITED—the world was setting out to tear itself to pieces.

Panama

Americans and Europeans had dreamed of building a canal across Central America to connect the Atlantic and Pacific Oceans and to eliminate the long and dangerous sea voyage around South America. Now that the United States controlled territory in both oceans, a canal that would allow easier access to American overseas territory became increasingly important.

In 1879 a French company had acquired a lease from the government of Colombia to construct a canal across its province of **Panama.** Panama was an isthmus—a narrow strip of land connecting two larger bodies of land—about 50 miles (80 km) wide. Wedged between the Caribbean Sea and the Pacific Ocean, Panama seemed like the perfect site for the canal.

French efforts to build a canal failed, and in 1901 the United States bought the lease from the French for $40 million. In 1903 Secretary of State John Hay negotiated a treaty with Colombia that granted the United States a 99-year lease on a strip of land across Panama in return for a payment of $10 million and an annual rent of $250,000.

In Colombia, opposition to the low price offered by the Americans led the Colombian senate to reject the treaty. In a fit of anger, President Roosevelt referred to the Colombians who rejected the treaty as "bandits." He believed the canal was vital to America's national defense.

Revolution in Panama

Roosevelt began looking for other ways to get land for the canal, and he wrote that he would "be delighted if Panama were an independent state." The Panamanians had staged revolts against Colombia in the past, but never with success. This time, however, the Panamanians had reason to believe that the Americans would support them in a revolt against Colombia.

On November 2, 1903, the American warship *Nashville* steamed into the port of Colón on the Caribbean coast of Panama. Encouraged by this show of support, the Panamanians revolted the next day and declared their independence. When Colombia sent forces to stop the revolt, the United States intervened and turned them back.

The Panama Canal

On November 6, the United States recognized Panama's independence. Less than two weeks later, Hay signed a treaty with the new nation of Panama. It gave the United States a 10-mile (16-km) strip of land across the country for the same amount offered earlier to Colombia. The United States now had land to build a canal. Roosevelt's actions in Panama angered many Latin Americans and some members of Congress and other Americans. The president, however, took great pride in his accomplishment. "I took the canal zone and let Congress debate," he said later, "and while the debate goes on, the canal does also."

The United States could now start work on the canal—not an easy undertaking. Disease struck the workers. An English writer described Panama as "a damp, tropical jungle, intensely hot, swarming with mosquitoes." These mosquitoes carried two deadly diseases—yellow fever and malaria.

History *Through Art*

***Work Trains, Miraflores* by Alson Skinner Clark** The building of the Panama Canal was a tribute to the skill of American engineers. The stamp commemorates the canal's 25th anniversary. **What challenges did American engineers face in building the canal?**

Analyzing *Political Cartoons*

This cartoon shows President Theodore Roosevelt in the role of the world's policeman. Roosevelt was given the title because of his "big stick" diplomacy. Do you think the cartoonist agrees with Roosevelt acting as an international policeman? Why or why not?

Colonel **William Gorgas,** an army doctor who had helped eliminate yellow fever in Cuba, went to Panama to fight the diseases. Gorgas instructed workers to drain swamps, spray insecticides, spread oil on stagnant pools of water, and cut grassy marshes in order to destroy mosquito breeding places. By 1906 these measures had eliminated yellow fever and greatly reduced the number of malaria cases. Without controlling disease, the United States could not have built the canal.

The Panama Canal was regarded as one of the great engineering feats of the time. Thousands of workers struggled to carve a path through the dense jungle and over mountains. They dug out huge amounts of earth and rock and used them to build a dam. They created a large lake and constructed giant locks to raise and lower ships from sea level over the mountains and then back to sea level again on the other side of the isthmus.

The Grand Opening

The Panama Canal opened on August 15, 1914, and a cargo ship, the *Ancon,* made the first trip through the canal. A great success from the start, the canal reduced shipping costs by cutting more than 7,000 miles off the voyage from New York City to San Francisco. The canal also helped extend American naval power by allowing the United States fleet to move freely between the Atlantic and Pacific Oceans.

In the long run, the canal guaranteed a strong American presence in Latin America, where the United States now had a valuable

property it intended to protect. Yet many Latin Americans remained bitter over how the Canal Zone was acquired. This resentment soured relations between the United States and Latin America for years.

Reading Check **Analyzing** Why was Panama chosen as the site for a canal connecting the Atlantic and Pacific Oceans?

Policing the Western Hemisphere

President Roosevelt often quoted an African proverb, "Speak softly and carry a big stick." He believed the United States should respond to foreign crises not by threats but by military action. Roosevelt became known for his "big stick" approach to foreign affairs. America must exercise "an international police power," he maintained, to preserve order and prevent the world from falling into anarchy—disorder and lawlessness.

Roosevelt Corollary

Roosevelt worried that instability in the Caribbean region would lead European powers to intervene. Two incidents confirmed his fears. In 1902, when Venezuela failed to meet payments on its loans, European nations imposed a blockade. The following year a revolution in the Dominican Republic toppled the government, causing concern that European powers would step in to protect their financial interests there.

The president responded to these incidents in 1904 by asserting America's right to act as a "policeman" in Latin America, intervening "however reluctantly . . . in cases of wrongdoing." This policy, known as the **Roosevelt Corollary,** was an addition to the Monroe Doctrine. Up to that time, the United States had used the Monroe Doctrine only to prevent European intervention in Latin America. Under the Roosevelt Corollary, the United States now claimed the right to intervene in the affairs of Latin American nations whenever those nations seemed unstable.

The United States first applied the Roosevelt Corollary in 1905, when it took control of the Dominican Republic's finances. This arrangement continued for more than 30 years. The United States used the policy again in 1906, when troops were sent to Cuba to stop a revolution there.

Dollar Diplomacy

Theodore Roosevelt thought of American power mostly in military terms. His successor in the White House, William Howard Taft, took a different view. Taft hoped to modify American foreign policy by "substituting dollars for bullets."

President Taft was willing to intervene in other nations whenever American business interests were threatened. He believed that American investments would bring stability to troubled areas of the world, as well as profit and power to the United States, without the need for force. Taft's policy of linking American business interests to diplomatic interests abroad was known as dollar diplomacy. This policy set in motion some positive effects.

Encouraged by dollar diplomacy, American investments in Latin America grew in the early 1900s. American investments helped build roads, railroads, and harbors, which stimulated trade and brought benefits to both Latin American countries and the United States.

Analyzing *Political Cartoons*

Uncle Sam is the nickname of the character often used to represent the United States in political cartoons. In this cartoon, Uncle Sam uses the Monroe Doctrine to warn the leaders of Europe not to interfere in the affairs of Latin America. **How are the European leaders reacting to Uncle Sam?**

Ⓐ European Leaders   Ⓑ Uncle Sam   Ⓒ Latin America

People In History

Jovita Idar 1885-1946

Through her work as a teacher and newspaper writer, Jovita Idar championed the cause of equal rights for Mexican Americans. Born in Laredo, Texas, Jovita Idar grew up in a family that devoted its skills to the cause. Her father, Clemente Idar, formed unions and spoke out against injustice in his newspaper, *La Crónica*.

In 1910 and 1911, Jovita, along with her father, wrote a series of articles about the discrimination and violence against Mexican Americans in South Texas. Calling on both the U.S. and Mexican governments for help, the Idar newspaper demanded equal treatment for Mexican American students and for Mexican Americans in the justice system.

During the Mexican Revolution of 1910, Jovita helped organize the White Cross to care for the wounded on both sides of the battle.

She was also instrumental in forming the League of Mexican Women. Jovita became its first president and worked hard to provide education for Mexican American students. The organization also provided free food and clothing for the needy in the community.

Dollar diplomacy also resulted in a stronger role for the United States overseas. Large American companies gained great power in Latin America and controlled the politics of some nations in the region. Furthermore, when American business interests were endangered, military intervention often followed. In 1912, when a revolution in Nicaragua threatened American business interests, the United States quickly sent marines to restore peace. Such interference led to increased anti-U.S. feelings throughout Latin America.

Relations with Mexico

In the early 1900s, Mexico was a poor country controlled by a tiny group of rich landholders. Investors in the United States poured millions of dollars into Mexican oil wells and other businesses. Then, in 1910, Mexico entered a turbulent period in its history—one that threatened American investments, revealed the weaknesses of dollar diplomacy, and led to military intervention by the United States.

In 1911 a popular Mexican reformer named **Francisco Madero** (muh•DEHR•oh) led a revolution to overthrow Mexico's brutal dictator **Porfirio Díaz** (DEE•ahs). Although foreign business and some Mexican politicians and landowners had prospered under the rule of Díaz, the lives of most Mexicans had grown worse.

Two years after taking power, Madero was overthrown and killed by General **Victoriano Huerta** (WEHR•tuh), who—like Díaz—favored the wealthy and foreign interests. President **Woodrow Wilson,** who had just taken office, refused to recognize Huerta's "government of butchers."

Wilson's "Moral Diplomacy"

A sincere believer in the ideals of democracy, Wilson thought the United States had a duty "to teach the South American republics to elect good men." Like Roosevelt and Taft, Wilson recognized the importance of military power and economic interests. Yet Wilson also attempted to follow a foreign policy based on moral principles.

Wilson's "moral diplomacy" faced a serious challenge in Mexico. After Huerta took power, a civil war broke out in Mexico. Wilson hoped that the Huerta government, without American support, would fall. When that did not happen, Wilson authorized arms sales to Huerta's rival, **Venustiano Carranza** (kuh•RAN•ZUH).

In April 1914, after Huerta's troops arrested some American sailors, Wilson ordered United States troops to seize the port of **Veracruz.** This show of force strengthened Carranza's position and forced Huerta to flee in August. Carranza took power, and American troops withdrew.

Francisco "Pancho" Villa

Huerta's resignation did not end civil war in Mexico. Rebel leader **Francisco "Pancho" Villa** launched an uprising against Carranza. In January 1916, Villa seized and shot 16 Americans because of United States support for the Carranza government. Villa hoped his action would damage relations between the United States and the Carranza government, but the United States did not take steps

against Mexico. Then Villa and his rebels crossed the border into New Mexico and burned the town of Columbus, killing 18 Americans there.

Villa's actions outraged the American public. The president sent General **John J. Pershing** with a large force of troops across the border into Mexico to capture Pancho Villa. For almost a year, Pershing's troops pursued Villa across Mexico, but the Mexican people protected Villa.

In 1917, when America's attention turned to the war raging in Europe, President Wilson withdrew the troops from Mexico. Mexico and the United States had come close to war, and American actions had caused great resentment in Mexico. America's experience in Mexico, like its policies in the Caribbean, showed that it would willingly use its power when it believed its interests or honor was threatened.

Pancho Villa

✓ **Reading Check**
Explaining On what principles did Wilson base his foreign policy?

SECTION 4 ASSESSMENT

Checking for Understanding

1. **Key Terms** Use each of these terms in a sentence that helps explain its meaning: isthmus, anarchy, dollar diplomacy.

2. **Reviewing Facts** Describe how the United States used Panama's desire for independence to its advantage.

Reviewing Themes

3. **Global Connections** Compare the different diplomacy styles of Presidents Roosevelt, Taft, and Wilson.

Critical Thinking

4. **Making Generalizations** Do you think our government today follows Roosevelt's, Taft's, or Wilson's diplomatic ideas in setting foreign policy? Explain.

5. **Compare and Contrast** Re-create the diagram below and list the differences between the Roosevelt Corollary and the Monroe Doctrine.

Monroe Doctrine	Roosevelt Corollary

Analyzing Visuals

6. **Analyzing Political Cartoons** Examine the cartoon on page 659. Whom do the figures on the left represent? Who is stopping them from crossing to the other side?

Interdisciplinary Activity

Economics Use a reference such as *Historical Abstract of the United States* to find the value of the United States's imports and exports to a Latin American country from 1890 to 1910. Create a double-line graph showing this information.

Chapter Summary

Overseas Expansion

Expansion

- Acquisition of Alaska, new trading ties with Hawaii and Latin America, and a strong stand against European intervention in the Americas raise the stature of the United States.

Spanish-American War

- In fighting the Spanish-American War, the United States establishes its willingness to become involved in conflict to help oppressed people and to protect its own interests.

Building an Empire

- As a result of the war, the United States gains a colonial empire and with it the challenge of governing overseas possessions.

Diplomacy

- United States intervention in foreign countries is accomplished with the use or show of force—sanctioned by Roosevelt's Big Stick diplomacy. Later, in the Pacific and East Asia, a combination of diplomacy and dollars helps the United States engage in trade and spread its influence.

Reviewing Key Terms

For each of the pairs of terms below, write a sentence or short paragraph showing how the two are related.

1. expansionism, imperialism
2. spheres of influence, dollar diplomacy
3. annexation, protectorate

Reviewing Key Facts

4. Why did many Americans oppose the purchase of Alaska?
5. How did the United States gain access to trade in China?
6. Who were the Rough Riders?
7. Why did the United States encounter difficult problems in trying to govern the Philippines?
8. What was the purpose of the Roosevelt Corollary?

Critical Thinking

9. **Analyzing Themes: Economic Factors** What economic reasons did the United States have for expanding its foreign interests?
10. **Drawing Conclusions** Re-create the diagram below and list the three types of diplomacy. Underline which type was the most effective during this period. Explain why you think so.

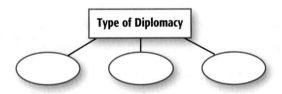

Practicing Skills

11. **Developing Multimedia Presentations** Study the list of topics below. Choose one of the topics and explain how you would use at least three types of media in a presentation to best teach the topic to your class.
    - Matthew Perry's mission to Japan
    - The development of the American navy
    - How the United States changed Hawaii forever
    - The Battle of San Juan Hill
    - Building the Panama Canal

Geography and History Activity

The building of the Panama Canal was regarded as a great engineering feat. Study the map of the canal below; then answer the questions that follow.

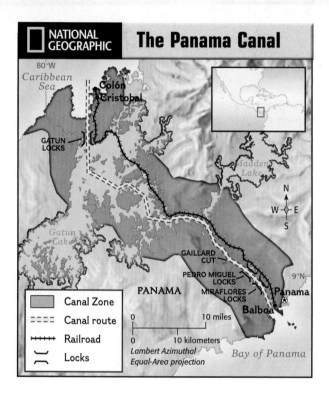

NATIONAL GEOGRAPHIC — The Panama Canal

80°W
Caribbean Sea
Colón
Cristobal
GATUN LOCKS
Madden Lake
Gatun Lake
GAILLARD CUT
PEDRO MIGUEL LOCKS
PANAMA
MIRAFLORES LOCKS
9°N
Panama
Balboa
Bay of Panama
Lambert Azimuthal Equal-Area projection

Legend:
- Canal Zone
- Canal route
- Railroad
- Locks

0 — 10 miles
0 — 10 kilometers

12. **Location** What bodies of water are shown on the map of the Panama Canal?

13. **Human-Environment Interaction** What is the approximate length of the Panama Canal? How did you determine your answer?

14. **Location** What cities are located near the path of the canal?

15. **Movement** In which direction would a ship en route to Cristobal from Balboa travel?

16. **Human-Environment Interaction** What does the location of Panama tell you about the climatic conditions the canal workers faced?

Citizenship Cooperative Activity

17. **Community Service** Working in groups of three, interview one of your community's officials to learn how you can begin taking an active role in the community. Members of your group may wish to volunteer for some sort of community service, then perform the service and report your experiences to your classmates.

Self-Check Quiz
Visit taj.glencoe.com and click on **Chapter 22— Self-Check Quizzes** to prepare for the chapter test.

Economics Activity

18. Work with a partner to create a map showing all of the areas acquired by the United States during the late 1800s and early 1900s. Research to find out about the natural resources that existed in each area and the importance of the area's location in world trade. Then, starting with these two factors, rank each of the areas on your map as to its economic value to the United States. The area ranked number "1" should be the most valuable. Compare your maps and rankings with other members of the class and create a chart of the overall ratings.

Alternative Assessment

19. **Portfolio Writing Activity** Review the chapter for information about treaties and agreements between various nations during this period. Make a list of the agreements and draw a picture or symbol next to each that will help you recall its terms.

The Princeton Review — Standardized Test Practice

Directions: Choose the *best* answer to the following question.

The manner in which President Roosevelt acquired the Panama Canal Zone

A angered some members of Congress.

B led to better relations with Latin America.

C ended the Spanish-American War.

D led to McKinley's election.

Test-Taking Tip.

Be aware of the order of events asked about in a question. This question specifically asks about the takeover of the Panama Canal Zone. Both choices **C** and **D** are events that occurred before the events in Panama. Therefore, answers **C** and **D** are incorrect.

World War I

1914–1919

Why It Matters

World War I changed the world. The people of the time called the conflict the Great War, and they believed that there could never again be another like it. Although the United States tried to remain neutral, it was drawn into the conflict.

The Impact Today

The war touched all aspects of life. When the fighting was over, the United States emerged as one of the great powers in the world.

The American Journey *Video* *The chapter 23 video, "Over There," examines the impact of technology in World War I.*

1917
- Zimmermann telegram angers U.S.
- United States enters WW I
- Selective Service Act passed

1914
- Beginning of Great Migration

1915
- Germany torpedoes the *Lusitania*

United States
PRESIDENTS

Wilson
1913–1921

1914

1916

World

1914
- Franz Ferdinand assassinated
- World War I begins

1917
- Lenin leads Bolshevik Revolution

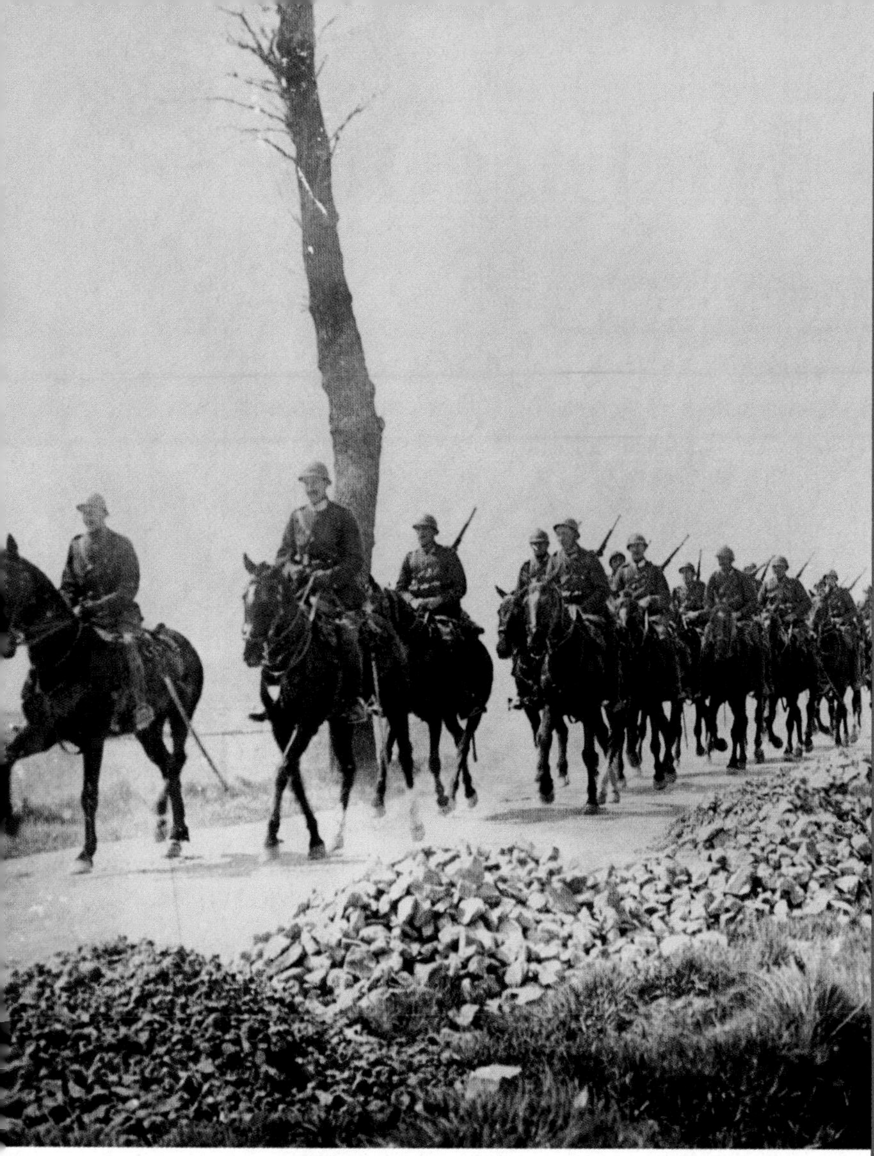

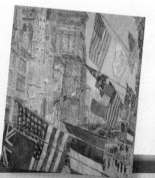

To the Front World War I combined traditional means of warfare, such as the cavalry, with modern means, such as the tank and the airplane.

FOLDABLES™ Study Organizer

Time Line Study Foldable Time lines are used to list important dates in chronological order. Use this foldable to sequence key events of World War I.

Step 1 Fold two sheets of paper in half from top to bottom.

Step 2 Turn the papers and cut each in half.

Step 3 Fold the four pieces in half from top to bottom.

Step 4 Tape the ends of the pieces together (overlapping the edges very slightly) to make an accordion time line and label it as shown.

Reading and Writing As you read the chapter, record key events that occurred during each year of World War I.

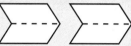

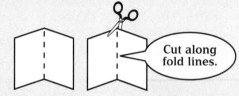

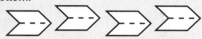

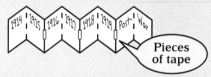

1918
- National War Labor Board is set up

1920
- Senate rejects League of Nations

1918 *1920*

1918
- World War I ends
- Flu epidemic kills more than 20 million worldwide

1919
- Treaty of Versailles signed

HISTORY Online

Chapter Overview
Visit taj.glencoe.com and click on **Chapter 23—Chapter Overviews** to preview chapter information.

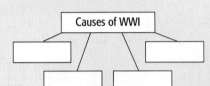

Guide to Reading

Main Idea
When Europe went to war in 1914, the United States tried to stay out of the conflict.

Key Terms
nationalism, ethnic groups, militarism, alliance system, entente, balance of power

Reading Strategy
Organizing Information As you read the section, re-create the diagram below, and identify four causes of World War I.

Causes of WWI

Read to Learn
• what factors led to World War I.
• how the early fighting progressed in Europe.

Section Theme
Science and Technology New weapons and other technology were used in fighting the war.

Preview of Events

♦1914 ♦1915 ♦1916

June 1914
Franz Ferdinand is assassinated

July 1914
Austria-Hungary declares war on Serbia

August 1914
Germany declares war on Russia and France

1916
France and Germany fight the Battle of Verdun

Jeannette Rankin

★★★★★★★★★
AN
American Story

The swift chain of events that led to war in Europe in 1914 stunned Americans. Most agreed with Jeannette Rankin—the first woman to serve in the U.S. Congress at a time when women could not even vote in most states—that "You can no more win a war than you can win an earthquake." Most Americans wanted the country to stay out of other countries' affairs. They saw no good reason to get involved in a conflict that they believed grew out of national pride and greed. As time went on, the United States found it more and more difficult to remain neutral.

Troubles in Europe

The people of Sarajevo crowded the streets of their city on the morning of June 28, 1914. They wanted to see **Archduke Franz Ferdinand,** the heir to the throne of the Austro-Hungarian Empire. The royal couple had come on a state visit to **Bosnia,** an Austrian province. Suddenly shots rang out. The archduke and his wife were hit and died soon after. The assassination destroyed the delicate balance of European stability. Within weeks Europe was at war. The tensions that led to World War I had roots that went back many years. The conflicts grew as European nations pursued dreams of empires, built up their armies, and formed alliances.

Nationalism

Nationalism, a feeling of intense loyalty to one's country or group, caused much of the tension in Europe. On the one hand, nationalism encouraged new nations, such as Italy and Germany, to unify and to establish their power in the world. Italy had become a kingdom in the 1860s, and the German states had united in the 1870s. Their actions challenged the position of older nations such as Great Britain and France.

On the other hand, nationalism inspired certain groups of people to break away from existing nations. Some of these ethnic groups—people who share a common language and traditions—demanded independent nations of their own.

Imperial Expansion

Tension in Europe also grew out of the desire of nations to expand their empires. Nations competed for colonies in Africa, Asia, and other parts of the world. These colonies not only brought new markets and raw materials, they also added to a nation's prestige.

Great Britain and France already possessed large overseas empires, but they wanted to expand them even more. Germany, Italy, and Russia wanted to increase their colonial holdings as well. Because few areas were left to colonize, however, expansion by one European nation often brought it into conflict with another power.

Military Buildup

As European nations competed for colonies, they strengthened their armies and navies to protect their interests. If one nation increased its military strength, its rivals felt threatened and built up their own military in response. In this atmosphere of militarism, Germany, France, and Russia developed huge armies in the early 1900s.

Great Britain, an island nation, had the world's largest and strongest navy. When Germany began to challenge Britain's naval power in the early 1900s, a bitter rivalry grew between the two nations. The rivalry led to an arms race that threatened peace in Europe.

Forming Alliances

Along with militarism came a strengthening of the alliance system, or the defense agreements among nations. By 1914 two major alliances had been established. Germany, Austria-Hungary, and Italy banded together in the **Triple Alliance,** while Great Britain, France, and Russia joined in the **Triple Entente.** An entente is an understanding among nations.

The alliances aimed to keep peace by creating a balance of power—a system that prevents any one country from dominating the others. Yet the alliance system actually posed a great danger. An attack on one nation was all that was needed to trigger a war involving many countries.

Europe was like a powder keg. One American diplomat noted that it would take "only a spark to set the whole thing off." That spark was ignited in the **Balkans.**

Reading Check **Describing** What was the purpose of the alliance system?

Crisis in the Balkans

The Balkan Peninsula in southeastern Europe was a hotbed of nationalist and ethnic rivalries in the early 1900s. The nations of Greece, Albania, Romania, and Bulgaria argued over territory, while Slavic nationalists hoped to unite all the Slavic peoples in the region. Especially bitter was the dispute between Austria-Hungary, whose Slavic people desired independence, and the neighboring nation of Serbia, which supported the Slavs and opposed the empire.

An Assassination Leads to War

Franz Ferdinand's assassin, Gavrilo Princip, was a member of a Serbian nationalist group. Princip and other terrorists had plotted the murder to advance the cause of the unification of Slavic peoples.

Archduke Franz Ferdinand

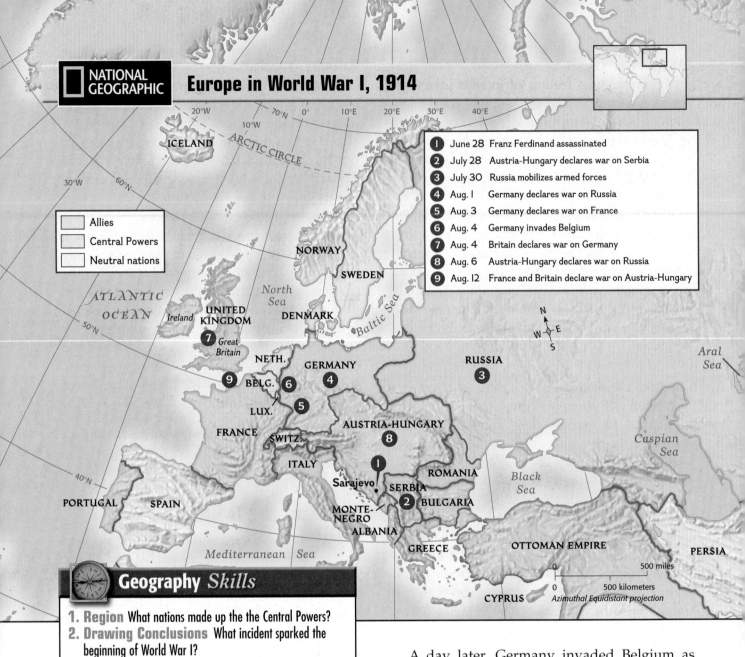

Europe in World War I, 1914

Allies
Central Powers
Neutral nations

1	June 28	Franz Ferdinand assassinated
2	July 28	Austria-Hungary declares war on Serbia
3	July 30	Russia mobilizes armed forces
4	Aug. 1	Germany declares war on Russia
5	Aug. 3	Germany declares war on France
6	Aug. 4	Germany invades Belgium
7	Aug. 4	Britain declares war on Germany
8	Aug. 6	Austria-Hungary declares war on Russia
9	Aug. 12	France and Britain declare war on Austria-Hungary

ICELAND
ARCTIC CIRCLE
NORWAY
SWEDEN
ATLANTIC OCEAN
Ireland
UNITED KINGDOM
Great Britain
North Sea
DENMARK
Baltic Sea
NETH.
BELG.
LUX.
GERMANY
RUSSIA
FRANCE
SWITZ.
ITALY
AUSTRIA-HUNGARY
Sarajevo
SERBIA
MONTE-NEGRO
ALBANIA
ROMANIA
BULGARIA
GREECE
Black Sea
Caspian Sea
Aral Sea
OTTOMAN EMPIRE
PERSIA
CYPRUS
PORTUGAL
SPAIN
Mediterranean Sea

500 miles
500 kilometers
Azimuthal Equidistant projection

Geography Skills

1. **Region** What nations made up the the Central Powers?
2. **Drawing Conclusions** What incident sparked the beginning of World War I?

The rulers of Austria-Hungary blamed the Serbian government for the assassination and moved to crush the Serbian nationalist movement. After making sure its ally, Germany, supported its decision, Austria-Hungary sent a letter to Serbia listing harsh demands. When Serbia refused the conditions, Austria-Hungary declared war on Serbia on July 28, 1914.

Europe's system of alliances caused the war to spread. Russia, which had agreed to protect Serbia, prepared for war. This brought Germany to the side of its ally, Austria-Hungary. Germany declared war on Russia on August 1, 1914. Knowing France was an ally of Russia, Germany declared war on France on August 3.

A day later, Germany invaded Belgium as part of a plan to sweep across eastern and northern France. In doing so, Germany violated a treaty signed in 1839 guaranteeing Belgium's neutrality. The invasion of Belgium prompted Great Britain to honor its pledge to protect Belgium, and Britain declared war on Germany.

Reading Check **Describing** What actions did Austria-Hungary take after the assassination of Franz Ferdinand?

A World War Begins

The "Great War" had begun. On one side were the **Allied Powers,** or the Allies—Great Britain, France, and Russia. On the other were the **Central**

Powers—Germany, Austria-Hungary, and the Ottoman (Turkish) Empire, which joined the war in October 1914. **Japan,** a rival of Germany in Asia, joined the Allies in late August 1914. Italy refused to honor its alliance with Germany and Austria-Hungary. Instead, it joined the Allies in 1915 after being promised territory in Austria after the war.

Fighting on the Western Front

In launching an offensive through Belgium, Germany hoped to defeat France quickly and destroy the French armies. This would allow Germany to move troops east against Russia.

The plan almost succeeded. The Belgians, however, held out heroically for nearly three weeks against the powerful German army. This delay gave the French and British time to mobilize their forces.

After defeating the Belgians, the Germans marched into France and advanced to within 15 miles of Paris. The British and French finally managed to stop the German advance at the Marne River just a few miles east of the city. The **Battle of the Marne,** fought between September 5 and 12, 1914, saved Paris from invasion by the Germans and boosted French morale. It also made it clear that neither side was capable of winning the war quickly or easily.

After the Battle of the Marne, the fighting in western Europe reached a stalemate. For the next three years, the opposing armies faced each other across an elaborate network of deep **trenches.** Trenches along the front lines provided some protection from flying bullets and artillery shells. Support trenches behind the lines served as headquarters, first-aid stations, and storage areas.

In 1916 both sides attempted to break the deadlock of trench warfare by launching major offensives. The German offensive, the **Battle of Verdun** in northeastern France, began in February and continued on and off until December. At first the Germans made small gains, but these were lost after the French counterattacked. Verdun

was one of the longest and bloodiest battles of the war. When it was over, more than 750,000 French and German soldiers had lost their lives.

While the Battle of Verdun raged, the British and French launched their own offensive in northern France in July—the **Battle of the Somme.** Again the number of casualties was extremely high. The Allies gained only about 7 miles (11.2 km) in the offensive.

Deadly Technology

New and more deadly weapons accounted for the terrible slaughter during these battles. Improved cannons and other artillery fired larger shells greater distances than ever before. Better rifles enabled soldiers to hit targets with greater accuracy.

Poison gas, another new and devastating weapon, was first used by the Germans over Allied lines in April 1915. The gas could kill or seriously injure anyone who breathed it. A British officer said,

> 66 They fought with terror, running blindly in the gas cloud, and dropping . . . in agony. 99

Airplanes were first used in combat during World War I.

United States neutrality was put to a test when German U-boats (shown here) attacked American ships.

The Allies began to use poison gas also, and gas masks became necessary equipment for soldiers in the trenches.

The armored tank, first used in World War I in January 1916, proved effective for crossing battle lines to fire on the enemy at close range. Tanks also could crush barbed wire, providing an easier route for advancing troops. After the Germans saw the effectiveness of tanks, they produced them too.

The most dramatic new weapon—the airplane—added a new dimension to fighting in World War I. Both sides used airplanes for watching troop movements and bombing enemy targets. Daring pilots waged duels in the skies called "dogfights." The first fighter planes were only equipped with machine guns, which were fastened to the top wing. The most famous pilots included Germany's "Red Baron," **Baron von Richthofen,** and America's **Eddie Rickenbacker,** who served in the French air force. The Germans used the zeppelin, or blimp, to bomb Allied cities.

On the Seas

With their land armies deadlocked in western Europe, both sides looked to the sea to gain an advantage in the war. Great Britain blockaded all ports under German control, eventually causing serious shortages. Many Germans suffered from malnutrition and illness because of lack of food and other supplies.

Germany had an effective naval weapon of its own: the submarine. Known as **U-boats**—from the German word for submarine, *Unterseeboot*—submarines prevented supplies, including food, from reaching Great Britain. U-boat attacks on ships at sea eventually affected the United States and changed the course of the war.

Reading Check **Explaining** What did both sides realize after the Battle of the Marne?

SECTION 1 ASSESSMENT

Checking for Understanding

1. **Key Terms** Write headlines for events during the World War I era; use each of the following terms: nationalism, militarism, alliance system, entente.
2. **Reviewing Facts** What nations made up the Triple Alliance? The Triple Entente?

Reviewing Themes

3. **Science and Technology** Why were casualties so high in World War I?

Critical Thinking

4. **Determining Cause and Effect** How did forming alliances increase the likelihood of war in Europe?
5. **Determining Cause and Effect** Re-create the diagram below and describe two effects that militarism had on rival nations.

```
┌───────────┐     ┌──────────┐
│ Militarism │────▶│          │
└───────────┘     └──────────┘
                  ┌──────────┐
              ───▶│          │
                  └──────────┘
```

Analyzing Visuals

6. **Geography Skills** Examine the map on page 668. When did Germany declare war on France? On what side did Belgium fight?

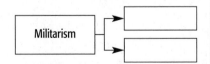
Interdisciplinary Activity

Science Research the inventions that were developed in World War I. Make a chart in which you describe each invention and a possible peacetime use of the invention.

America's Road to War

Guide to Reading

Main Idea
The United States entered the conflict on the side of the Allies.

Key Terms
propaganda, autocracy

Reading Strategy
Analyzing Information As you read the section, re-create the diagram below and list two reasons the United States found it difficult to maintain neutrality.

Maintaining neutrality

Read to Learn
• how Americans responded to the war in Europe.
• what led to American involvement in the war.

Section Theme
Government and Democracy The United States, officially neutral at first, entered the conflict.

Preview of Events

♦1914   ♦1916   ♦1918

August 1914
Europe goes to war

May 1915
Germany torpedoes the *Lusitania*

March 1917
Zimmermann telegram angers U.S.

April 1917
U.S. declares war on Germany

Magazine cover, 1914

AN American Story

President Wilson struggled to remain neutral, even after Americans had been killed at the outbreak of World War I. Others felt differently. An American businessman cabled the president after the *Laconia* was sunk by Germans: "My beloved mother and sister . . . have been foully murdered on the high seas. . . . I call upon my government to preserve its citizens' self-respect and save others of my countrymen from such deep grief as I now feel. I am of military age, able to fight. If my country can use me against these brutal assassins, I am at its call." Remaining neutral grew more and more difficult.

American Neutrality

President Wilson had to make some difficult decisions. He declared that the United States would be neutral in the war and called on Americans to be "neutral in fact as well as in name, impartial in thought as well as in action." Other influential political leaders also argued strongly in favor of neutrality.

When Europe went to war in August 1914, most Americans believed that the war did not concern them. Many shared the view expressed in an editorial in the *New York Sun:*

> ❝There is nothing reasonable in such a war, and it would be [foolish] for the country to sacrifice itself to the . . . policies and the clash of ancient hatreds which is urging the Old World to destruction.❞

Despite Wilson's plea to remain neutral, Americans soon began to take sides. More than one-third of the nation's 92 million people were either foreign-born or the children of immigrants. Many of these people naturally sympathized with their countries of origin. Some of the 8 million Americans of German or Austrian descent and the 4.5 million Irish Americans—who hated the British because they ruled Ireland—favored the Central Powers.

Even more Americans, however, including President Wilson, felt sympathetic to the Allies. Ties of language, customs, and traditions linked the United States to Great Britain, and many Americans were of British descent. President Wilson told the British ambassador: "Everything

I love most in the world is at stake." A German victory "would be fatal to our form of government and American ideals."

Using Propaganda

To gain the support of Americans, both sides in the war used propaganda—information designed to influence opinion. Allied propaganda emphasized the German invasion of neutral Belgium and included horror stories of German atrocities. It called the Germans "Huns" and pictured them as savage barbarians.

The propaganda from the Central Powers was equally horrible, but because of British sympathies, the Allied propaganda was more effective in influencing Americans.

America's Early Involvement

Trade between the United States and the Allies helped build support for the Allied cause. As a neutral nation, America sought to trade with both sides, but Britain's blockade of Germany made this difficult.

The British navy stopped and searched American ships headed for German ports, often seizing the ships' goods. The United States protested that its ships should be able to pass without interference. The British responded with the defense that they were fighting for their survival. "If the American shipper grumbles," wrote a London paper, "our reply is that this war is not being conducted for his pleasure or profit." The United States government could do nothing about the blockade. Barred from trading with Germany, it continued trading with Britain.

Indeed, American trade with the Allies soared. In addition, Great Britain and France borrowed billions of dollars from American banks to help pay for their war efforts. All this business caused an economic boom in the United States. It also upset the Germans, who watched the United States—supposedly a neutral nation—helping the Allies.

Submarine Warfare

To stop American aid to Britain, Germany announced in February 1915 that it would use its U-boats to sink any vessels that entered or left British ports. President Wilson warned that America would hold Germany responsible for any American lives lost in submarine attacks. Determined to cut off supplies to Great Britain, the Germans ignored this threat.

On May 7, 1915, a German U-boat torpedoed the British passenger liner *Lusitania* off the coast of Ireland. W.T. Turner, the captain, reported:

> ❝I saw the torpedo speeding towards us. Immediately I tried to change our course, but was unable to maneuver out of its way. There was a terrible impact as the torpedo struck the starboard side of the vessel. . . . It was cold-blooded murder.❞

The *Lusitania* sank in about 15 minutes. More than 1,000 people died, including 128 United States citizens. Americans were outraged, and President Wilson denounced the attack. Later it was learned that the ship carried war materials.

📖 *(See page 973 for a passenger's account of the sinking.)*

TECHNOLOGY & History

Submarine

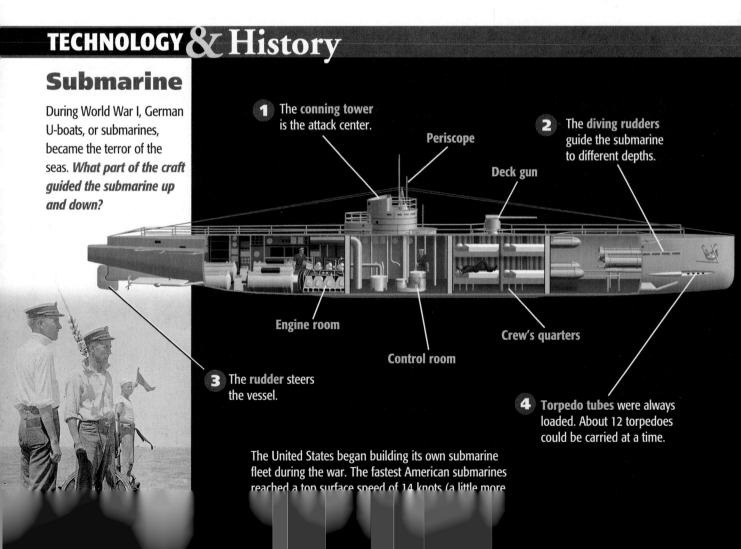

During World War I, German U-boats, or submarines, became the terror of the seas. *What part of the craft guided the submarine up and down?*

1 The **conning tower** is the attack center.

Periscope

2 The **diving rudders** guide the submarine to different depths.

Deck gun

Engine room

Control room

Crew's quarters

3 The **rudder** steers the vessel.

4 **Torpedo tubes** were always loaded. About 12 torpedoes could be carried at a time.

The United States began building its own submarine fleet during the war. The fastest American submarines reached a top surface speed of 14 knots (a little more

Several months later a German U-boat torpedoed the unarmed French passenger ship *Sussex*, injuring several Americans. Fearing that the Americans might enter the war, Germany offered to compensate Americans injured on the *Sussex* and promised to warn neutral ships and passenger vessels before attacking. The Sussex Pledge, as it was called, seemed to resolve the issue.

✓ **Reading Check** **Describing** What is the aim of propaganda?

The End of Neutrality

The crisis over submarine warfare led the United States to take steps to strengthen its military. In the summer of 1916, Congress passed legislation that doubled the size of the army and provided funds to build new warships. President Wilson still hoped, however, to stay out of the war.

Antiwar sentiment remained very strong. Some Americans criticized the nation's military buildup, seeing it as a step toward entering the war. A popular song in 1915 expressed this opposition:

    ❝I didn't raise my boy to be a soldier,
    I brought him up to be my pride and joy.
    Who dares place a musket on his shoulder,
    To shoot some other mother's darling boy?❞

Antiwar sentiment was strong at the 1916 Democratic national convention, where all references to the president's efforts to keep the country out of war brought wild applause. After Wilson was nominated for a second term, the phrase "He Kept Us Out of War" became the Democrats' slogan. The question of neutrality divided the Republicans, and Republican presidential candidate Charles Evans Hughes avoided discussing the issue. Wilson narrowly defeated Hughes.

What If...

The British Had Not Intercepted the Zimmermann Note?

In January 1917 German foreign minister Arthur Zimmermann cabled the German ambassador in Mexico instructing him to make an offer to the Mexican government. Zimmermann proposed that Mexico help Germany in the event that the United States entered the war. To encourage Mexico's cooperation, Germany promised that Mexico would regain some of the region that it lost to the United States in 1848. A British official intercepted Zimmermann's telegram. The telegram read:

❝On the first of February we intend to begin submarine warfare unrestricted. In spite of this, it is our intention to endeavor to keep neutral the United States of America.

If this attempt is not successful, we propose an alliance on the following basis with Mexico: That we shall make war together and together make peace. We shall give generous financial support, and it is understood that Mexico is to reconquer the lost territory in New Mexico, Texas, and Arizona. The details are left to you for settlement....

You are instructed to inform the President of Mexico of the above in the greatest confidence as soon as it is certain that there will be an outbreak of war with the United States and suggest that the President of Mexico, on his own initiative, should communicate with Japan suggesting adherence at once to this plan; at the same time, offer to mediate between Germany and Japan.

Please call to the attention of the President of Mexico that the employment of ruthless submarine warfare now promises to compel England to make peace in a few months.❞

Widely publicized by British and in the American press, the Zimmermann telegram angered Americans and helped build popular sentiment for the war. Then, between March 12 and March 19, four American merchant ships were sunk without warning. On April 2, 1917, President Wilson asked the members of Congress to declare war on Germany.

—adapted from *Almost History*, Roger Bruns ©2000

On the Brink of War

In January 1917, Germany reversed its policy on submarine warfare. It announced that it would sink on sight all merchant vessels, armed or unarmed, sailing to Allied ports. While realizing that their policy might bring the Americans into the war, the Germans believed they could defeat the Allies before the United States became heavily involved. An angry President Wilson broke off diplomatic relations with Germany.

A few weeks later, a secret telegram—intercepted by the British government—set off a new wave of anti-German feeling. In late February the German foreign minister, Arthur Zimmermann, sent a telegram to Mexico with an offer to the Mexican government:

> 66[W]e shall make war together and together make peace. . . . [A]nd it is understood that Mexico is to reconquer the lost territory in New Mexico, Texas, and Arizona.99

> TELEGRAM RECEIVED.
> FROM 2nd from London # 5747.
>
> "We intend to begin on the first of February unrestricted submarine warfare. We shall endeavor in spite of this to keep the United States of America neutral. In the event of this not succeeding, we make Mexico a proposal of alliance on the following basis: make war together, make peace together, generous financial support and an understanding on our part that Mexico is to reconquer the lost territory in Texas, New Mexico, and Arizona. The settlement in detail is left to you. You will inform the President of the above most secretly as soon as the outbreak of war with the United States of America is certain and add the suggestion that he should, on his own initiative, invite Japan to immediate adherence and at the same time mediate between Japan and ourselves. Please call the President's attention to the fact that the ruthless employment of our submarines now offers the prospect of compelling England in a few months to make peace." Signed, ZIMMERMANN.
>
> The receipt of this information has so greatly exercised the British Government that they have lost no time in communicating it to me to transmit to you, in order that our Government may be able without delay to make such disposition as may

What might have happened?

1. Why was the British government eager to inform the United States of Germany's offer to Mexico? What did it hope to gain?

2. If there were no Zimmermann note, do you think the United States would have: a) entered the war when it did in April; b) entered the war at a later time; or c) not been drawn into the war at all?

Newspapers published the secret **Zimmermann telegram** on March 1, and Americans reacted angrily to the German action.

Revolution in Russia

In the weeks following publication of the Zimmermann telegram, dramatic events pushed the United States to the brink of war. First, a revolution took place in Russia. Following a period of rioting and strikes, the Russian people overthrew the monarchy. In its place they established a temporary government that promised free elections.

Many Americans believed that the new Russian government, which vowed to defeat Germany, would help the Allies. With Russia's change to a democratic form of government, Wilson could now claim that the Allies were fighting a war of democracy against autocracy—rule by one person with unlimited power.

Other critical events took place at sea. In March 1917, within a few days time, the Germans attacked and sank four American ships—the *Algonquin*, the *City of Memphis*, the *Illinois*, and the *Vigilancia*. Thirty-six lives were lost.

President Wilson continued to struggle with his conscience. He was convinced that war would destroy much of the optimism and sympathy to human needs that had allowed America to make the social progress it had. His cabinet, on the other hand, strongly favored war. One government official later explained:

> 66If we had stayed out of the war, and Germany had won, there would no longer have been a balance of power in Europe, or a British fleet to support the Monroe Doctrine and to protect America.99

President Wilson decided that the United States could no longer remain neutral.

America Enters the War

On the cold, rainy evening of April 2, 1917, President Wilson stood before a special session of Congress to ask for a declaration of war against Germany.

> 66The world must be made safe for democracy. . . . It is a fearful thing to lead this great peaceful people into war, into the most terrible and disastrous of all wars. . . . But the right is more precious than peace. . . .99

Congress did not agree at once to a formal resolution of war. Some members of Congress agreed with Senator George Norris of Nebraska. He held that America's involvement in the war was the fault of American financiers and arms manufacturers who were determined to profit from the war no matter what it cost the rest of the country.

In the end, however, most members of Congress agreed that if the United States wished to remain a great world power it must defend its rights. As a result, Congress passed a declaration of war, and Wilson signed it on April 6. Fifty-six members of the House and Senate voted against war, including Representative Jeannette Rankin of Montana—the first woman to serve in Congress.

The United States had to raise an army quickly. On May 18, Congress passed the **Selective Service Act,** establishing a military draft. Unlike the draft during the Civil War that led to riots, this draft had the support of most of the American public.

Men aged 21 to 30 (later the draft age was extended from 18 to 45) registered by the millions. By the end of the war, some 24 million men had registered. Of those, about 3 million were called to serve; another 2 million joined the armed forces voluntarily.

In addition thousands of women enlisted in the armed forces—the first time they were allowed to do so. Women did noncombat work, serving as radio operators, clerks, and nurses.

Many African Americans also wanted to serve their country. More than 300,000 joined the army and navy—the marines would not accept them. African Americans faced discrimination and racism in the armed forces just as they did in civilian life. Most held low-level jobs on military bases in the United States. Among the 140,000 African American soldiers sent to Europe, 40,000 saw actual combat. Many served with distinction. An African American regiment received medals for bravery from the French government. One of its members, Henry Johnson, was the first American to receive the French Croix de Guerre [Cross of War] for bravery.

✓ Reading Check **Describing** What was the purpose of the Selective Service Act?

HISTORY Online
Student Web Activity
Visit taj.glencoe.com and click on **Chapter 23— Student Web Activities** for an activity on World War I.

SECTION 2 ASSESSMENT

Critical Thinking

1. **Key Terms** Define propaganda and autocracy.
2. **Reviewing Facts** What did the Zimmermann telegram promise to Mexico?

Reviewing Themes

3. **Government and Democracy** What steps did President Wilson have to take to make an official declaration of war?

4. **Determining Cause and Effect** Explain how the war in Europe brought about an economic boom in the United States.
5. **Sequencing Information** Re-create the diagram below and explain how these events led the United States into the war.

Event	
Sinking of *Lusitania*	
Zimmermann note	

Analyzing Visuals

6. **Picturing History** Examine the submarine on page 673. What was the top speed of American submarines? What was the purpose of the diving rudders?

Interdisciplinary Activity

Expository Writing Create headlines announcing major events described in Section 2. Keep in mind that headlines condense much information into a few words.

SECTION 3 Americans Join the Allies

Guide to Reading

Main Idea
With the help of American troops and supplies, the Allies turned the tide against Germany.

Key Terms
convoy, front, armistice

Reading Strategy
Sequencing Information As you read the section, re-create the time line below and identify the events that took place.

Nov. 1917	June 1918	Oct. 4, 1918	Nov. 11, 1918

Read to Learn
• what was happening in Europe when the United States entered the war.
• what role American troops played in the fighting.

Section Theme
Global Connections The entry of the United States into the war made an immediate difference, eventually leading to Germany's surrender.

Preview of Events

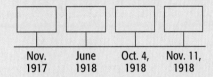

◆1917 ◆1918 ◆1919

June 1917
American troops land in France

March 1918
Russia withdraws from the war

June 1918
American Expeditionary Force begins to fight

November 1918
Armistice ends World War I

Medal of Honor

AN American Story

Drafted into the United States Army in 1917, Alvin York was reluctant to serve. "I was worried clean through," he said. "I didn't want to go and kill." York had grown up in the mountains of Tennessee, where he learned to shoot while hunting wild turkeys. Applying his sharpshooting skills in World War I, York killed 17 German soldiers with 17 shots. He also took 132 Germans prisoner and captured 35 enemy machine guns. For his actions and bravery in combat, Sergeant York received the Medal of Honor.

Supplying the Allies

In 1917 the Allies desperately needed the help of American soldiers. Years of trench warfare had exhausted the Allied armies, and some French troops refused to continue fighting after a failed offensive in 1917. The British had started to run out of war supplies and food; their people were starving. Furthermore, German submarines were taking a deadly toll on Allied shipping—sinking one of every four ships that left British ports.

The American entry into the war made an immediate difference. To ensure that needed supplies reached Great Britain, the United States Navy took two steps. First, it helped the British find and destroy German submarines. Then convoys—teams—of navy destroyers escorted groups of merchant ships across the Atlantic. The convoy system worked well. In one year it reduced Allied shipping losses from 900,000 to 300,000 tons a month. With the convoy system, not one American soldier bound for Europe was lost to submarine attack.

Russian Withdrawal

The Allies needed more troops because of a second revolution in Russia. In November 1917, the **Bolsheviks,** a group of communists, overthrew the democratic Russian government established in March 1917.

Led by **Vladimir Lenin,** the Bolsheviks wanted to end Russia's participation in the war so they could focus their energies and resources on setting up a new Communist state. Lenin took Russia out of the war in December. In March 1918, he signed the **Treaty of Brest-Litovsk** with

NATIONAL GEOGRAPHIC
Europe During World War I, 1914–1918

Allies
Central Powers
Neutral nations

250 miles
250 kilometers
Lambert Azimuthal Equal-Area projection

NORWAY
SWEDEN
North Sea
DENMARK
Baltic Sea
UNITED KINGDOM
May, 1915 Germany sinks *Lusitania*
Western Front
GERMANY
BELGIUM
LUX.
ATLANTIC OCEAN
RUSSIA
Eastern Front
FRANCE
Western Front
AUSTRIA-HUNGARY
PORTUGAL
SPAIN
Mediterranean Sea
ITALY
SERBIA
ROMANIA
BULGARIA
Black Sea
GREECE
OTTOMAN EMPIRE

Major Battles
1. Tannenberg, Aug. 1914
2. 1st Marne, Sept. 1914
3. Gallipoli, Apr. 1915 – Jan. 1916
4. Verdun, Feb.–Dec. 1916
5. Somme, July–Nov. 1916
6. Château-Thierry and Belleau Wood, June 1918
7. 2nd Marne, July 1918
8. St. Mihiel, Sept. 1918
9. Meuse-Argonne, Sept.–Nov. 1918

Geography *Skills*

1. **Location** What country was the site of most Western Front battles?
2. **Location** Nearest to what front was the battle of Tannenberg fought?

Life in the trenches was miserable. Soldiers lived in dirt and mud for months at a time. Between the enemy lines lay a "no-man's land" of barbed wire and land mines. Endless days of shelling the enemy might sometimes be interrupted by an attempt to "break out" of the trenches and advance into enemy territory.

Germany, surrendering Poland, the Ukraine, and other territory to the Germans. Russia's withdrawal from the war allowed the Germans to move hundreds of thousands of troops from the Eastern Front—line of battle—to the Western Front in France.

New German Offensive

Reinforced by the transfer of troops, the Germans now launched a powerful offensive against the Allies. German military leaders hoped to drive a wedge in the Allied lines and to capture the city of Amiens before proceeding to Paris. Between March and June 1918, they hammered at Allied lines, pushing them back to within 40 miles (64 km) of Paris. After years of stalemate along the Western Front—the area along the French-German border—it suddenly looked as if Germany might win the war.

American Troops in the War

Although the first American soldiers had reached France in June 1917, many months passed before they were ready for battle. When they finally began to fight, the Americans helped turn the war around.

General **John J. Pershing** led the **American Expeditionary Force** (AEF), the American troops in Europe. American correspondent Floyd Gibbons described the tremendous welcome the French gave Pershing and his troops in Paris:

66The sooty girders of the Gare du Nord [railroad station] shook with cheers when the special train pulled in. . . . A minute later, there was a terrific roar from beyond the walls of the station. The crowds outside had heard the cheering within. . . . Pershing took Paris by storm.99

The AEF reached full strength in Europe in the spring of 1918. The French and British wanted to use the American soldiers to build up their own troops, but General Pershing refused. He preferred to keep the AEF a separate force.

The American Expeditionary Force saw its first serious fighting in early June 1918. It helped turn back a German offensive at **Château-Thierry** on the **Marne River** east of Paris. The American troops then advanced to nearby **Belleau Wood.** For 24 hours a day for the next three weeks, American forces fought their way through the forest against a solid wall of German machine-gun fire. In July the Americans and the French fought back German attacks on Allied forces along the Marne and the Somme Rivers.

By the middle of July, the Allies had stopped the German offensive. General Pershing wrote that the battles had "turned the tide of war." The Allies now began an offensive of their own. In mid-September about 500,000 "doughboys"—the nickname given to American soldiers—fighting alone, defeated the Germans at Saint Mihiel, east of **Verdun.** Later in the month, more than one million American troops joined the Allies in the **Battle of the Argonne Forest,** west of Verdun.

The Battle of the Argonne Forest raged for nearly seven weeks, with soldiers struggling over the rugged, heavily forested ground. Rain, mud, barbed wire, and withering fire from German machine guns hindered the Allies' advance, and many lives were lost.

American lieutenant Elden Betts wondered if he would survive the battle and wrote home—in case "I get mine tomorrow." He said he hoped his family would be proud of him, ending with "Now good-bye, and thank you Pop, Edie and Margie." Four days later Betts was killed.

The Battle of the Argonne Forest ended in early November, when the Allies finally pushed back the Germans and broke through the enemy lines. The Germans now were faced with an invasion of their own country.

✔ **Reading Check** **Identifying** What was the first major battle to involve Americans?

The End of the War

With their troops in retreat, German military leaders realized they had little chance of winning the war. The Allied forces were now fortified by the Americans. In addition, the Germans suffered from severe shortages of food and other essential supplies.

Request for an Armistice

On October 4, 1918, the German government appealed to President Wilson for an armistice. An armistice is an agreement to end the fighting. Wilson consented under certain conditions. Germany must accept his plan for peace and

In 1915 the Germans introduced a new weapon—poison gas. In time, all of the combatants would use gas warfare. Artillery shells containing gas were fired at the enemy, and wind carried the gas into trenches, causing blindness, choking, damaged lungs, and death.

promise not to renew hostilities. All German troops must leave Belgium and France. Finally, Wilson would deal only with civilian leaders, not with the military.

While German leaders considered Wilson's demands, political unrest erupted in Germany. On November 9, the German **kaiser,** or emperor, **Wilhelm II,** was forced to give up his throne. Germany became a republic, and its new leaders quickly agreed to Wilson's terms for the armistice.

Peace Begins

The armistice began on November 11, 1918. Germany agreed to withdraw all land forces west of the **Rhine River,** withdraw its fleet to the Baltic Sea, and surrender huge amounts of equipment.

With the signing of the armistice, the Great War ended. President Wilson announced:

> ❝Everything for which America fought has been accomplished. It will now be our duty to assist by example, by sober, friendly counsel, and by material aid in the establishment of just democracy throughout the world.❞

✓ Reading Check **Describing** What conditions did Germany accept to end the fighting?

Honoring the Veterans

Armistice Day, first observed on November 11, 1919, honored the Allied soldiers who died in World War I. In 1954 Armistice Day was renamed Veterans' Day in honor of all those, living and dead, who had served with U.S. armed forces in wartime. Similar commemorations take place in Canada on Remembrance Day and the United Kingdom on Remembrance Sunday.

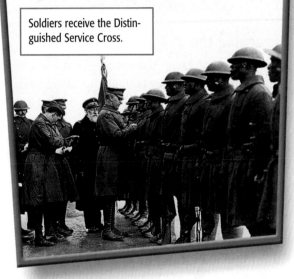

Soldiers receive the Distinguished Service Cross.

SECTION 3 ASSESSMENT

Checking for Understanding

1. **Key Terms** Write headlines for three news stories about World War I; use each of the following terms: convoy, front, armistice.

2. **Reviewing Facts** Who led the American forces in Europe?

Reviewing Themes

3. **Global Connections** According to the armistice, from where did Germany agree to withdraw its land forces?

Critical Thinking

4. **Predicting Consequences** Do you think the Allies would have won the war if the United States had not intervened? Why or why not?

5. **Determining Cause and Effect** Re-create the diagram below and list three reasons the Allies needed the help of American forces.

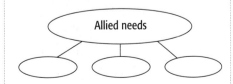

Allied needs

Analyzing Visuals

6. **Geography Skills** Examine the map on page 678. When was the battle at St. Mihiel fought? When was the Battle of Gallipoli fought? Do you think it was easier for Norway, Spain, and Sweden to remain neutral than it was for Switzerland? Why?

Interdisciplinary Activity

Descriptive Writing Write the text for a radio broadcast announcing the arrival of American soldiers in Paris in 1917.

Study & Writing
SKILLBUILDER

Outlining

Why Learn This Skill?

To sketch a scene, you first draw the rough shape, or outline, of the picture. Then you fill in this rough shape with details. Outlining written material is a similar process. You begin with the rough shape of the material and gradually fill in the details.

Learning the Skill

There are two kinds of outlines—formal and informal. An informal outline is similar to taking notes. You write only the words and phrases needed to remember main ideas.

A formal outline has a standard format. In a formal outline, label main heads with Roman numbers, subheads with capital letters, and details with Arabic numerals and lowercase letters. Each level should have at least two entries and should be indented from the level above.

When outlining written material, first read the material to identify the main ideas. In textbooks, section heads provide clues to main topics. Then identify the subheads. Place supporting details under the appropriate head.

Practicing the Skill

Study the partial outline of Section 3 on this page. Then answer the following questions.

❶ Is this a formal or an informal outline?

❷ What are the three main topics?

❸ If you wanted to add two facts about the AEF, where would you put them in the outline? Would you use numbers or letters to label the facts?

Outline of Chapter 23, Section 3

I. European Allies need help.
    A. Allied armies are exhausted.
        1. Trench warfare depletes supplies.
        2. Russia leaves war.
    B. Civilians are in trouble.
        1. People are starving.
        2. Supply ships are sunk by Germans.
II. Americans enter the war.
    A. United States Navy patrols seas.
        1. German U-boats are destroyed.
        2. Convoys protect Allied ships.
            a. Losses are reduced by two-thirds.
            b. No American soldiers are killed.
    B. American Expeditionary Force (AEF) lands in Europe.
        1. Germans lose at Château-Thierry.
        2. Germans are defeated at Belleau Wood.
III. Allies take the offensive.
    A. Battle of Argonne Forest is fought.
    B. President Wilson lists conditions for armistice.

Applying the Skill

Outlining Following the guidelines above, prepare an outline for Section 2 of Chapter 23.

 Glencoe's **Skillbuilder Interactive Workbook CD-ROM, Level 1,** provides instruction and practice in key social studies skills.

SECTION 4 The War at Home

Guide to Reading

Main Idea
World War I drastically changed life in the United States.

Key Terms
mobilization, dissent, socialist, pacifist, espionage, sabotage

Reading Strategy
Analyzing Information As you read the section, re-create the diagram below and describe the goals of these agencies.

Agency	Goals
Food Administration	
War Industries Board	
Committee on Public Information	

Read to Learn
- what steps the United States took to organize and prepare for World War I.
- how the war affected Americans.

Section Theme
Economic Factors America's involvement in the war in Europe led to economic challenges and opportunities at home.

Preview of Events

♦1917   ♦1918   ♦1919

July 1917
Race riots occur in East St. Louis

April 1918
National War Labor Board is set up

June 1918
Congress passes Sabotage and Sedition acts

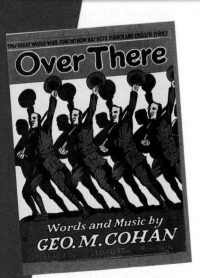

"Over There" sheet music

AN American Story

"Over there, over there,
Send the word, send the word
over there
That the Yanks are coming, the Yanks
are coming,
The drums rum-tumming ev'rywhere

So prepare, say a pray'r,
Send the word, send the word to
beware,
We'll be over, we're coming over,
And we won't come back till it's over
over there."

George M. Cohan wrote this rousing song to help create enthusiasm for America's participation in World War I. "Over There" was performed at rallies to raise money for the war.

Mobilizing the Nation

After declaring war on Germany in 1917, Americans immediately focused their energies on getting ready to fight a war. Mobilization—the gathering of resources and the preparation for war—affected almost every part of American life.

To ensure production of vital war materials, the government created the **National War Labor Board** in April 1918. The board pressured businesses to grant some of the workers' pressing demands. As a result workers won an eight-hour working day, extra pay for overtime, equal pay for women, and the right to form unions. In return workers agreed not to go on strike.

Workers During the War

To meet the need for supplies and weapons, the nation's industries had to expand. At the same time, however, millions of men left their jobs in industry to serve in the armed forces, and few European immigrants—who might have taken these jobs—came to the United States during the war.

The labor shortage provided new job opportunities for women and minorities. Many women joined the workforce for the first time. Women were hired for jobs previously held by men.

Causes and Effects of World War I

Causes

- Nationalistic pride
- Competition for colonies
- Military buildup
- Tangled web of alliances
- Assassination of Franz Ferdinand

Effects

- Destruction in Europe
- Boom in the American economy
- Suppression of dissent in U.S.
- Allied victory
- Defeated empires lose their colonies

Graphic Organizer → Skills

After World War I, the United States was established as a world leader and an economic giant.

Analyzing Information How did World War I affect the economy of the United States?

The prospect of finding good jobs also brought hundreds of thousands of African Americans to Northern cities from the rural South. In addition, thousands of Mexicans migrated to the United States in search of jobs.

Paying for the War

War is costly. World War I cost the United States an enormous amount of money—about $32 billion. Two-thirds of this money was raised by selling the American people war bonds, or **Liberty Bonds.**

The federal government also raised money for the war by increasing taxes and requiring a greater number of Americans to pay income taxes. It taxed wealthy Americans at rates as high as 70 percent of their income. The government also imposed steep taxes on business profits.

$ Economics
Producing Supplies

The United States had to produce food not only for its own needs but also for the Allies. President Wilson appointed **Herbert Hoover,** who had helped organize food for war refugees in Europe, to head a new **Food Administration.** This agency launched a campaign to encourage American farmers to produce more and to persuade the public to eat less. The agency urged people to observe "Wheatless Mondays," "Meatless Tuesdays," and "Porkless Thursdays," and to add to their own store of food by planting "victory gardens." Slogans such as "Serve Just Enough" and "Use All Leftovers" reminded Americans to conserve food.

The Food Administration also imposed price controls on various agricultural products to encourage voluntary **rationing**—limitation of use. As a result of such efforts, Americans consumed less food, expanded food production, and increased food exports.

Another government agency, the **War Industries Board,** supervised the nation's industrial production. The board's responsibilities included converting factories to the production of war-related goods and setting prices for key consumer products.

People In History

Edward Rickenbacker 1890-1973

The son of Swiss immigrants who settled in Ohio, Edward Rickenbacker was the leading American combat pilot of World War I. "Captain Eddie" recorded 26 official victories against German aircraft during World War I and was awarded the Medal of Honor.

From his youngest days, Rickenbacker was fascinated by technology and speed. He worked on automobile engines, then struck out on his own as a race car driver; he won many championships and set a world record for speed driving.

When the United States entered the war, Rickenbacker volunteered. After less than three weeks of training he was assigned to the 94th Aero Squadron. The 94th was the first patrol flown in France by an all-American squadron and won more victories than any other squadron.

After the war, Rickenbacker was associated with several automotive and aviation companies. He purchased and managed the Indianapolis Motor Speedway. He also built Eastern Airlines into one of the nation's largest airlines.

Mobilizing Support

The federal government also needed to mobilize public support for the war because antiwar sentiment remained strong even after the United States entered the war. President Wilson appointed journalist George Creel to head the **Committee on Public Information.** The mission of the committee was to persuade Americans that the war represented a battle for democracy and freedom.

The Committee on Public Information distributed millions of pro-war pamphlets, posters, articles, and books. It provided newspapers with government accounts of the war and advertisements. It arranged for short patriotic talks, called Four-Minute Speeches, to be presented before plays and movies. The committee hired speakers, writers, artists, and actors to build support for the war. It was the greatest propaganda campaign the nation had ever seen.

✓ **Reading Check** **Explaining** Why did the United States face a labor shortage during the early days of World War I?

Americans and the War

World War I provided a boost for the American economy. Yet the war had harmful effects on American society as well. In the interest of national unity, the government stifled voices of dissent, or opposition. Racial and other tensions remained, and many Americans became intolerant of those who were "different."

African American Migration

From 1914 to 1920, between 300,000 and 500,000 African Americans left their homes in the rural South to seek jobs and settle in Northern cities. Known as the **Great Migration,** this tremendous population movement continued the northward migration that had begun in the late 1800s.

Many African American workers who traveled north did find jobs. But their new lives were not easy. Often they lived in tiny, crowded apartments in segregated neighborhoods, and they found that racial prejudice continued to haunt their lives in the North.

Terrible race riots took place in several Northern cities during the war years. One of the worst occurred in **East St. Louis, Illinois.** In July 1917, a white mob attacked an African American neighborhood, burning houses and firing on residents as they tried to escape. During the riot, as many as 40 African Americans died and thousands lost their homes.

Controlling Public Opinion

Even after America entered the war, opposition to it remained strong. Some German Americans and Irish Americans sympathized with the Central Powers. Many socialists—people who believe industries should be publicly owned—opposed the war because they thought it would only help rich business owners and hurt working people. Also against the war were pacifists—people opposed to the use of violence.

During the war, the Committee on Public Information began trying to silence dissent and portrayed people who were against the war as unpatriotic. **The Espionage Act** that Congress passed in 1917 gave the government a new weapon to combat dissent to the war. The law provided stiff penalties for espionage, or spying, as well as for aiding the enemy or interfering with army recruiting. Congress passed even harsher measures in 1918—the **Sabotage Act** and

the **Sedition Act.** These laws made it a crime to say, print, or write almost anything perceived as negative about the government. Such acts would be considered sabotage—secret action to damage the war effort. Thousands of people—especially immigrants, socialists, pacifists, and labor activists—were convicted under the laws.

People became suspicious of German Americans. A few communities prohibited such activities as performing German music and teaching the German language in schools. As a result some German Americans concealed their ancestry. They even gave patriotic names—such as "liberty cabbage" and "liberty sausage"—to German-sounding words such as *sauerkraut* and *frankfurter.*

Some people spoke out against these laws and the intolerance they produced. Most Americans, however, believed that in wartime no measure could be "too drastic" toward traitors and disloyal Americans.

✓ **Reading Check** **Identifying** What act provided stiff penalties for spies?

SECTION 4 ASSESSMENT

Checking for Understanding

1. **Key Terms** Use each of these terms in a sentence that will help explain its meaning: mobilization, dissent, socialist, pacifist, espionage, sabotage.

2. **Reviewing Facts** Describe the role of the Committee on Public Information.

Reviewing Themes

3. **Economic Factors** Where did the United States get most of the money to finance the war?

Critical Thinking

4. **Predicting Consequences** Do you think it was necessary for the government to take strong measures against people who opposed the war? Explain.

5. **Organizing Information** Re-create the diagram below and describe three ways that Americans supported the war effort at home.

```
        Aiding the war effort
    ┌──────────┼──────────┐
  [   ]      [   ]      [   ]
```

Analyzing Visuals

6. **Graphic Organizer Skills** Examine the cause-and-effect chart on page 684. What happened to the colonies of the defeated nations after World War I ended in 1918?

Interdisciplinary Activity

Citizenship Suppose that the United States was at war today. Write a law that states who is eligible to be drafted and what to do about people who refuse to serve.

America's LITERATURE

George M. Cohan (1878–1942)

As the United States entered World War I, rousing songs helped bolster the spirits of soldiers and civilians alike. Composer George M. Cohan was awarded the Medal of Honor for writing "Over There," the most popular patriotic song of the war, and for writing "You're a Grand Old Flag."

READ TO DISCOVER

As you read the lyrics for the following song, think about its purpose. How might it have helped the country's war effort? What words used by the composer are especially patriotic?

READER'S DICTIONARY

Jubilee: celebration
emblem: symbol
auld: old

You're a Grand Old Flag

There's a feeling comes a-stealing,
And it sets my brain a-reeling,
When I'm listening to the music
of a military band.

Any tune like "Yankee Doodle"
Simply sets me off my noodle,
It's that patriotic something that
no one can understand.

"Way down South, in the
land of cotton,"
Melody untiring,
Ain't that inspiring?
Hurrah! Hurrah! We'll join the
Jubilee And that's going some,
For the Yankees, by gum!

Red, white and blue, I am for you!
Honest, you're a grand old flag!

You're a grand old flag
You're a high flying flag
And forever in peace may
you wave.
You're the **emblem** of
The land I love,
The home of the free and
the brave.
Ev'ry heart beats true
'neath the Red, White, and Blue,
Where there's never a boast
or brag.
But should **auld** acquaintance
be forgot
Keep your eye on the grand
old flag.

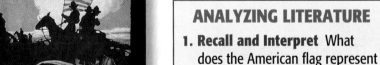

SPIRIT *of* 1917

JOIN THE UNITED STATES MARINES
AND BE
FIRST IN DEFENSE ON LAND OR SEA
APPLY AT   New York, N. Y.
24 East 23rd Street

Food is Ammunition—
Don't waste it.

ANALYZING LITERATURE

1. **Recall and Interpret** What does the American flag represent to Cohan?
2. **Evaluate and Connect** How does Cohan include the South in the song?

Interdisciplinary Activity

Science World War I caused a horrifying number of casualties, partly because of new technology. Research some medical practices and equipment used on the battlefield at the time. Describe these in a report. Photocopy pictures from books and encyclopedias to illustrate your report.

Searching for Peace

Guide to Reading

Main Idea
Strong opposition greeted President Wilson's plans for peace.

Key Terms
Fourteen Points, League of Nations, reparations

Reading Strategy
Analyzing Information As you read the section, re-create the diagram below and identify these individuals and the role each played in the post-war era.

Individual	Identity and Role
Woodrow Wilson	
David Lloyd George	
Henry Cabot Lodge	

Read to Learn
- what principles Woodrow Wilson proposed as the basis for peace.
- why many Americans opposed the Treaty of Versailles.

Section Theme
Global Connections The end of the war brought changes to many parts of the world and an attempt to establish world peace.

Preview of Events

♦1919	♦1920	♦1921
1919 Paris Peace Conference begins; Treaty of Versailles is signed	**1920** Senate rejects the League of Nations	**1921** U.S. signs separate peace treaty with Central Powers

THE GREAT AMERICAN PEACE SONG
WE TAKE OUR HATS OFF TO YOU—MR. WILSON

Words and Music by BLANCHE MERRILL.

Peace song honoring Wilson

AN American Story

"We want Wilson," the war-weary crowd roared. "Long live Dr. Wilson!" British students with American flags smiled, tossing flowers in the President's path. Everywhere in Europe the Wilsons visited—Paris, Rome, Milan—the reception was jubilant. Boosted by the cheers of the European crowds, Wilson walked into the Paris Peace Conference at the Palace of Versailles with confidence. He was sure that his plan for a just and lasting peace would win swift approval both in Europe and in America.

After the War

In January 1919, world leaders from 27 nations gathered in Paris, France, for the peace conference following World War I. President Woodrow Wilson led the American delegation. When Wilson arrived in the city, enormous crowds cheered him. Well-wishers threw flowers in his path and unfurled banners that read "Long Live Wilson!" With great hope, Europeans looked to Wilson to help build a better postwar world. Yet enormous problems lay ahead.

Europe lay in ruins. Much of its landscape was devastated, its farms and towns destroyed. The human losses were terrible. France, Russia, Germany, and Austria-Hungary each lost between one and two million people in the fighting. Millions more were wounded. More than 50,000 Americans were killed in battle, while another 60,000 soldiers died from disease. Estimates for the whole war placed the number of soldiers killed worldwide at nearly 9 million. Millions of civilians also lost their lives.

Europe also faced social and political turmoil. Millions of people found themselves homeless and hungry. Civil war raged in Russia. Poles, Czechs, and other peoples struggled to form independent nations out of the collapsed empires of Turkey, Russia, and Austria-Hungary. These problems complicated the search for peace and stability.

Wilson's Fourteen Points

Woodrow Wilson had a vision of a just and lasting peace. Wilson outlined his peace plan in a proposal known as the Fourteen Points. Several of the points concerned the adjustment of boundaries in Europe and the creation of new nations. These points reflected Wilson's belief in **"national self-determination"**—the right of the people to decide how they should be governed.

Wilson also proposed a number of principles for conducting international relations. These included calls for free trade, freedom of the seas, an end to secret treaties or agreements, reductions and limits on arms, and the peaceful settlement of disputes over colonies. 📖 *(See page 993 of the Appendix for an excerpt of Wilson's Fourteen Points.)*

League of Nations

Wilson's final point concerned the creation of a League of Nations. The League's member nations would help preserve peace and prevent future wars by pledging to respect and protect one another's territory and political independence.

Wilson's Fourteen Points reflected his strong faith in the ability of governments to resolve their problems fairly. At first many Europeans welcomed Wilson's ideas. Then problems arose when the plan interfered with the competing

Total Mobilized Forces
- Allies 42 million
- Central Powers 23 million

Military Deaths
- Allies 5.1 million
- Central Powers 3.4 million

Graph *Skills*

Analyzing Information Which side had the larger fighting force? More casualties?

interests of the individual nations. Also, some of Wilson's points were vague. They did not propose concrete solutions to difficult questions—such as how to achieve self-determination in regions where many different ethnic groups lived closely together.

✓**Reading Check** **Explaining** What is "national self-determination"?

The Peace Conference

The victorious Allies dominated the talks at the Paris Peace Conference. The Allies did not invite either Germany or Russia—now ruled by the Bolsheviks—to participate. The major figures in the negotiations were the Big Four—President Wilson, Prime Minister David Lloyd George of Great Britain, Premier Georges Clemenceau of France, and Prime Minister Vittorio Orlando of Italy.

The Allies Disagree

Wilson faced a difficult task. Although Europeans cheered him, their leaders showed little enthusiasm for the Fourteen Points.

While Wilson opposed punishing the defeated nations, the European Allies sought revenge. Clemenceau wanted to make sure that Germany, which had invaded France twice in

NATIONAL GEOGRAPHIC   Europe After World War I

New Nations

300 miles
300 kilometers
Azimuthal Equidistant projection

ICELAND

ARCTIC CIRCLE

SWEDEN
FINLAND
NORWAY
ESTONIA
North
Sea
LATVIA
LITHUANIA
UNITED
KINGDOM
DENMARK
GER.
RUSSIA
NETH.
GERMANY
BELG.
POLAND
ATLANTIC
OCEAN
LUX.
FRANCE
SWITZ.
CZECHOSLOVAKIA
AUSTRIA
HUNGARY
ITALY
ROMANIA
YUGOSLAVIA
Black
Sea
PORTUGAL
SPAIN
BULGARIA
Mediterranean Sea
GREECE
TURKEY
SPANISH
MOROCCO
ALBANIA
MOROCCO
ALGERIA
TUNISIA

Geography *Skills*

1. **Region** What new nations bordered on Germany?
2. **Analyzing Information** Which new nations did not have any coastline along a sea or ocean?

his lifetime, could never invade his country again. He believed that Germany should be broken up into smaller countries. Both he and Lloyd George demanded that Germany make large reparations, or payments, for the damage Germans caused in the war. Although Wilson struggled to uphold the principles of his Fourteen Points at the Paris meeting, he was forced again and again to compromise or give in to the demands of the other Allies.

At the same time, the Allies had to decide how to deal with the new Bolshevik government of Russia. Fearing the spread of communism, France,

Britain, and the United States supported anti-Bolshevik forces fighting for control of Russia. All three countries sent troops to Russia.

The Treaty of Versailles

On June 28, 1919, after months of difficult negotiations, the Allies and Germany signed a treaty at the Palace of Versailles outside of Paris. The harsh terms of the treaty shocked the Germans. In defeat, however, they had no choice but to sign.

Under the terms of the **Treaty of Versailles,** Germany had to accept full responsibility for the war and to pay billions of dollars in reparations to the Allies. Germany also had to disarm completely and give up all its overseas colonies and some territory in Europe.

The treaty carved up the Austro-Hungarian and Russian Empires to create new nations or restore old ones. The emergence of these nations fulfilled part of Wilson's vision of "national self-determination." Many of the borders of the new countries were disputed, however, and this led to future conflicts.

Though disappointed by the rejection of much of his Fourteen Points, Wilson succeeded in having the League of Nations included in the treaty. He believed that the League would correct any mistakes in the rest of the treaty.

Reading Check **Explaining** What provisions about reparations were included in the Treaty of Versailles?

Opposition at Home

Wilson presented the Treaty of Versailles to the United States Senate for ratification in July 1919. "Dare we reject it and break the heart of the world?" he asked. In spite of his plea, a difficult struggle lay ahead.

Many Americans had doubts about the treaty. Some thought the treaty dealt too harshly with Germany. A great many Americans worried about participation in the League of Nations, which marked a permanent American commitment to international affairs.

In 1919 the Republicans controlled the Senate, which had to ratify the treaty. Some Republican senators saw the ratification issue as a chance to embarrass President Wilson, a Democrat, and to weaken the Democratic Party before the upcoming elections of 1920. Other senators had sincere concerns about the treaty, particularly the League of Nations. A few senators opposed signing any treaty.

The most powerful opponent of the treaty was **Henry Cabot Lodge** of Massachusetts, head of the Senate Foreign Relations Committee. Lodge, a longtime foe of President Wilson, claimed that membership in the League would mean that

❝American troops and American ships may be ordered to any part of the world by nations other than the United States, and that is a proposition to which I, for one, can never assent.❞

Lodge delayed a vote on the treaty so that opponents could present their cases. He then proposed a number of reservations that would limit America's obligations under the treaty.

In September, Wilson went on a national speaking tour to rally support for the treaty and the League of Nations. On September 25, Wilson collapsed. The rest of his tour was canceled. Back in Washington Wilson suffered a stroke that left him partially paralyzed. During the president's illness, his wife, Edith Wilson, tried to shield him from the pressures of responsibility and took a leading role in deciding which issues were important enough to raise with him.

The Treaty Is Rejected

In the months following Wilson's stroke, opposition to the treaty grew. In March 1920, when the Senate voted on the treaty with Lodge's changes, Wilson ordered loyal Democrats to vote against it.

Opposed by most Republicans and deserted by former supporters, the Treaty of Versailles—along with the League of Nations—was rejected in the Senate. Wilson hoped the 1920 election would be a "great and solemn referendum" on the League. He even considered running for a third term. In the end, however, Wilson did not run. In 1921 the United States signed a separate peace treaty with each of the Central Powers, and it never joined the League of Nations.

✓ Reading Check **Explaining** How did the Senate vote on the treaty?

SECTION 5 ASSESSMENT

Checking for Understanding

1. **Key Terms** Write a short article about the plans for peace after World War I; use each of these key terms: Fourteen Points, League of Nations, reparations.
2. **Reviewing Facts** What nations were created or restored through the Treaty of Versailles?

Reviewing Themes

3. **Global Connections** How did President Wilson think the League of Nations would help maintain world peace?

Critical Thinking

4. **Analyzing Information** Some Americans thought the Treaty of Versailles was too hard on Germany. What terms would you have proposed for Germany?
5. **Organizing Information** Re-create the diagram below and describe the provisions of the treaty ending World War I.

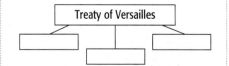

Analyzing Visuals

6. **Geography Skills** Examine the map on page 690 showing European borders following World War I. Which of the following was not a new nation—Poland, Latvia, or Bulgaria? Was Portugal a new nation?

Interdisciplinary Activity

Geography Compare the map of Europe after World War I to a map of Europe today. Make a list of the significant border changes that have occurred since that time.

Chapter Summary
World War I

1914
- Archduke Franz Ferdinand assassinated
- Austria-Hungary declares war on Serbia
- Germany declares war on Russia and France
- Germany invades Belgium
- Great Britain joins Allies
- Allies turn back German forces at Marne

1915
- Poison gas used for first time in battle
- Submarine warfare begins
- President Wilson declares he will keep America out of war
- *Lusitania* is sunk

1916
- French suffer heavy losses at Battle of Verdun
- President Wilson calls for Germany to stop submarine warfare

1917
- U.S. severs diplomatic relations with Germany
- U.S. declares war on Germany in April
- First American troops reach France in June

1918
- General Pershing leads the American Expeditionary Force in Europe
- Allies turn back Central Powers at Château-Thierry
- U.S. troops drive Germans out of Belleau Wood
- Allies defeat German forces at Second Battle of Marne

1919
- Treaty of Versailles signed, officially ending the Great War

Reviewing Key Terms

Examine the pairs of words below. Then write a sentence explaining what each of the pairs has in common.

1. nationalism, militarism
2. mobilization, convoy
3. Fourteen Points, League of Nations
4. espionage, sabotage

Reviewing Key Facts

5. Why did European nations form alliances?
6. Why did the Zimmermann telegram push the United States toward war?
7. What was the Sussex Pledge?
8. Who won the presidency in the election of 1916?
9. How did Russia's withdrawal affect World War I?
10. In what ways did the war help improve conditions for American workers?
11. Who were the leaders at the Paris Peace Conference?
12. What was Henry Cabot Lodge's greatest concern about the League of Nations?

Critical Thinking

13. **Science and Technology** What advantages did airplanes provide in the war?
14. **Government and Democracy** How did President Wilson use Russia's revolution in March of 1917 to gain support for the war?
15. **Analyzing Information** What four nations dominated the Paris Peace Conference?
16. **Determining Cause and Effect** Re-create the diagram below and explain the causes of the labor shortage in the United States during the war.

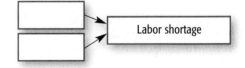

Labor shortage

Practicing Skills

17. **Outlining** On a separate sheet of paper, prepare an outline of Section 5 of the text.

Geography and History Activity

Study the map below; then answer the questions that follow.

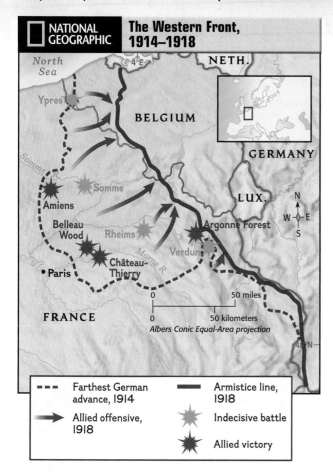

The Western Front, 1914–1918

NATIONAL GEOGRAPHIC

- - - Farthest German advance, 1914

→ Allied offensive, 1918

✷ Indecisive battle

✷ Allied victory

━━ Armistice line, 1918

18. Location About how far from Paris was the Battle of Amiens?

19. Movement In which direction did Allied forces move after the battle of Ypres?

20. Location In what country were the battles of Amiens and Verdun fought?

Technology Activity

21. Using the Internet Search the Internet to find out more details about the time of the "Great War"—World War I. Use the information you find to create a chart titled "World War I—A Closer Look." Focus on causes of the war, methods of warfare, and the outcome of the war for various countries. Include numbers of casualties and costs of rebuilding.

Self-Check Quiz
Visit at taj.glencoe.com and click on **Chapter 23— Self-Check Quizzes** to prepare for the chapter test.

Citizenship Cooperative Activity

22. Drawing Conclusions With a partner, research primary and secondary sources about the Espionage Act of 1917. Write a one-page paper to answer these questions: Are restrictive laws necessary during wartime? Why or why not? Share your paper with your classmates.

Economics Activity

23. What effects does war have on a nation's economy? Describe at least one positive and one negative effect.

Alternative Assessment

24. Expository Writing Write a paragraph to explain why the League of Nations was so important to President Wilson.

The Princeton Review

Standardized Test Practice

Directions: Choose the *best* answer to the following question.

The United States did not enter World War I until 1917. Which of the following was the most important factor in convincing the American public to support the war?

A German submarine attacks against American merchant ships

B Continued loss of troops and land by the Russian army

C Failure of the British and French to defeat Germany

D The threat of a German invasion

Test-Taking Tip

This question asks you to remember a *fact* about World War I. Since most Americans favored a policy of isolation, answer **C** is not a strong enough reason to change public opinion.

HANDS-ON HISTORY

Creating a Special-Edition Newspaper

How did you learn about the latest exciting national or international event? You probably heard or read about it in the mass media—newspapers, magazines, radio, and television. Throughout history the media have played a major part in shaping the opinions of Americans about national and international events. Imagine you are a news reporter. Create a newspaper that reports the events of World War I to the American public.

The Way It Was

Today almost every American receives information from the mass media. The media did not always grab the public's attention so easily though. Before the late 1800s, newspapers simply reported the news. In the late 1800s, however, newspapers started using sensational headlines. When many Americans picked up their papers and read "LUSITANIA SUNK BY A SUBMARINE, PROBABLY 1,260 DEAD," they felt angry. Many called for revenge and war against the aggressor, which many newspapers claimed was Germany. Eventually this outrage led to America's involvement in World War I. Throughout the war, while American soldiers fought with the Allies in Europe, their friends and family eagerly scanned the newspapers to learn what was happening on the war front. Americans relied on the newspapers to keep them up to date on the latest happenings. Now, create a special edition newspaper to inform Americans of an event or battle of World War I.

Materials

✓ paper and pen or pencil
✓ access to library and/or Internet resources
✓ newspapers or magazines
✓ tape or paste
✓ a typewriter or PC (optional)

THE LUSITANIA IS SUNK; 1,000 PROBABLY ARE LOST

GERMANS TORPEDO THE GIANT STEAMSHIP AND SHE FOUNDERS EIGHT MILES FROM IRISH COAST

RESCUE VESSELS SPEED TO THE SCENE TO PICK UP SURVIVORS

What To Do

After you have organized into groups of three or four, follow the directions below. Decide upon specific tasks for each member.

1 As a group, use your textbook or other sources to research and decide what event, situation, or person(s) will be the focus of your special-edition World War I newspaper.

2 As a group, assign the following roles to group members: historian, journalist, illustrator/cartographer, and biographer.

3 Individually, complete the research that relates to the role you have been assigned. Keep in mind that newspaper reporters focus on answering the "five W" questions when researching their stories: *Who* was involved, *What* happened, *When* it happened, *Where* it happened, and *Why* it happened.

4 After you complete your research, write one feature story from the viewpoint of your role. (Remember to include the five W's!) Don't forget to include a headline that will catch readers' attention.

5 Provide one another with constructive advice and revise the stories as needed.

6 Combine your final articles into a group newspaper. Work together to choose the best layout for the newspaper. Together, decide if the special-edition newspaper is complete. Is it missing some graphics? Would it look better with a cartoon or photograph? Are some of the stories too long or too short? Revise your newspaper if needed.

7 Distribute your special-edition newspaper to the class.

Project Report

1. What is the subject of your special-edition newspaper? Why did your group select this topic?

2. How did working with a group help you create a better newspaper? How might your newspaper be different if you had worked on it alone?

3. **Analyzing Information** What advice would you give to a younger student who wants to become a newspaper reporter?

Go a Step Further

Turn one of the feature stories in your newspaper into a late-breaking radio broadcast. Before writing your broadcast, consider how an audio story would be different from a written story. Read your broadcast to the class.

UNIT
9

Turbulent Decades

1919–1945

Why It Matters

*As you study Unit 9, you will exam-
ine how the Great Depression affected
people's lives and the nation as a
whole. You will also learn about the
causes of World War II. The following
resources offer more information
about this period in American history.*

General George A. Patton's helmet

Primary Sources Library

*See pages 974–975 for primary source
readings to accompany Unit 9.*

*Use the **American History
Primary Source Document Library
CD-ROM** to find additional primary
sources about the Great Depression
and World War II.*

People of Palermo, Sicily,
welcome American forces,
July 1943

"*The only thing we have to fear is fear itself.*"

—*Franklin Delano Roosevelt, 1933*

CHAPTER 24

The Jazz Age

1919–1929

Why It Matters

People called the 1920s the Jazz Age—in part because of the popular new music—but also because of the restless, carefree spirit of the time. The economy boomed and many Americans prospered. Many Americans, however, did not share in the economic gains of this era.

The Impact Today

The 1920s produced striking new changes in American society. New forms of entertainment such as radio and film remain popular today. The automobile forever changed the American way of life. It helped shift homes, shops, and factories from the inner cities to the suburbs.

 The American Journey Video *The chapter 24 video, "The Jazz Age," explores the development of jazz music in American culture.*

1920
- Prohibition begins
- Nineteenth Amendment grants woman suffrage

MOOD INDIGO

1923
- Duke Ellington forms Washingtonians

1924
- National Origins Act passed

1925
- Scopes Trial

 United States **PRESIDENTS**

Harding
1921–1923

Coolidge
1923–1929

1921

1923

1925

World

1922
- Joyce's *Ulysses* published
- Mussolini becomes prime minister of Italy

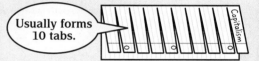

Explaining Vocabulary Study Foldable
To fully understand what you read you must be able to identify and explain key vocabulary terms. Use this foldable to identify, define, and use important terms in Chapter 24.

Step 1 Fold a sheet of notebook paper in half from side to side.

Step 2 On one side, cut along every third line.

Tabs will form as you cut.

Step 3 Label your foldable as you read the chapter. The first vocabulary term is labeled in the model below.

Usually forms 10 tabs.

Capitalism

Reading and Writing As you read the chapter, write key vocabulary terms on the front tabs of your foldable. Then write the definition of each term under the tab and write a sentence using each term correctly.

Safety Last Actor Harold Lloyd's movie adventures symbolized the thrills and excitement of the Jazz Age.

1927
- Lindbergh flies across Atlantic
- Babe Ruth hits 60 home runs
- *The Jazz Singer,* the first movie with sound, premiers

1927

1929

HISTORY
Online

Chapter Overview
Visit taj.glencoe.com and click on **Chapter 24— Chapter Overviews** to preview chapter information.

1927
- Working model of television demonstrated
- Lemaitre proposes big bang theory

1928
- Kellogg-Briand Pact signed by 15 nations
- Fleming discovers penicillin

1929
- Hubble proposes theory of expanding universe
- U.S. stock market crash triggers global depression

Time Of Turmoil

Guide to Reading

Main Idea
World War I made some Americans intolerant—not willing to respect the beliefs or practices of others.

Key Terms
capitalism, anarchist, deport

Reading Strategy
Analyzing Information As you read the section, re-create the diagram below and answer the question for each blank.

	What was it?
The Red Scare	
Sacco-Vanzetti trial	
UNIA	

Read to Learn
- what factors contributed to prejudice toward foreigners.
- how the labor and racial unrest of the 1920s affected the nation.

Section Theme
Continuity and Change After World War I, conflicts came to the surface, especially among workers and different races.

Preview of Events

1910	1915	1920	1925

1914
Marcus Garvey founds Universal Negro Improvement Association

1917
Bolsheviks seize control of Russia

1920
Thousands arrested during Palmer raids

1921
Sacco and Vanzetti declared guilty

Marcus Garvey

AN American Story

On a hot summer day in 1920, about 50,000 African Americans marched through the streets of Harlem in New York City. Thousands more lined the sidewalks, cheering the marchers. Their leader, Marcus Garvey, stirred new hope in African Americans, saying: "We are descendants of a people determined to suffer no longer." A participant at the march later recalled, "It was the greatest demonstration of [African American unity] in American history. . . ."

Fear of Radicalism

Most of the 1920s was anything but unified. During World War I, the United States government had taken away some of the liberties of American citizens. Many people who opposed the nation's role in the war were arrested. After the war an atmosphere of distrust remained. Tired of war and world responsibilities, Americans were eager to return to normal life. They grew more and more suspicious of foreigners, foreign ideas, and those who held views different from their own.

In 1919 Wilson and the world leaders attending the peace conference signed the **Treaty of Versailles.** Despite Wilson's efforts, however, the Senate refused to ratify the treaty.

At about the same time, the Russian Revolution deeply disturbed some Americans. As you read in Chapter 23, the Bolsheviks took control of Russia in November 1917 and began establishing a Communist state. They encouraged workers around the world to overthrow capitalism—an economic system based on private property and free enterprise—anywhere it existed. Many Americans feared that "bolshevism" threatened American government and institutions.

Fanning those fears were the actions of anarchists—people who believe there should be no government. A series of anarchist bombings in 1919 frightened Americans. A number of public officials—mayors, judges, and the attorney general of the United States—received packages containing bombs. One bomb blew off the hands of the maid of a United States senator. Many of the anarchists were foreign-born, which contributed to the fear of foreigners that was sweeping the country.

The Red Scare

This wave of fear led to the **Red Scare,** a period when the government went after "Reds"—as Communists were known—and others with radical views. In late 1919 and early 1920, Attorney General **A. Mitchell Palmer** and his deputy, J. Edgar Hoover, ordered the arrest of people suspected of being Communists and anarchists. Palmer and Hoover also staged raids on the headquarters of various "suspicious" groups. In the raids, the government arrested a few thousand people, ransacked homes and offices, and seized records. They did not find the large stockpiles of weapons and dynamite they claimed they were seeking.

Palmer said the raids were justified. "The blaze of revolution was sweeping over every American institution of law and order," he declared, "burning up the foundations of society." The government deported—expelled from the United States—a few hundred of the aliens it had arrested but quickly released many others for lack of evidence. In time people realized that the danger of revolution was greatly exaggerated. The Red Scare passed—but the fear underlying it remained.

Sacco and Vanzetti

Fear of immigrants and radical ideas surfaced in a criminal case in Massachusetts in 1920. Two men robbed a shoe factory in South Braintree, Massachusetts, shooting and killing a guard and

Strikes, such as the 1919 steel strike, lessened public support for labor unions.

paymaster. Soon afterward the police arrested Italian immigrants **Nicola Sacco** and **Bartolomeo Vanzetti** for the crime. The two men were tried and convicted in July 1921 and were sentenced to death.

The Sacco and Vanzetti case created a furor. Neither man had a criminal record. Both men were anarchists, and Sacco owned a pistol similar to the murder weapon. Future Supreme Court justice Felix Frankfurter wrote a defense of the two men. Chief Justice William Howard Taft attacked Frankfurter for "vicious propaganda."

Many Americans demanded that the death sentence be carried out. In 1927 a special commission appointed by the governor of Massachusetts upheld the verdict. Sacco and Vanzetti—proclaiming their innocence—were executed. While historians continue to debate the verdict, the case suggested the depth of feelings against foreigners and radicals in the United States in the 1920s.

✓**Reading Check** **Explaining** What is capitalism based on?

Labor Unrest

During the war years, labor and management had put aside their differences. A sense of patriotism, high wages, and wartime laws kept conflict to a minimum. When the war ended, conflict flared anew. American workers demanded

increases in wages to keep up with rapidly rising prices. They launched more than 2,500 strikes in 1919. The wave of strikes fueled American fears of Bolsheviks and radicals, whom many considered to be the cause of the labor unrest.

Strikes Sweep Country

A long and bitter strike—the largest in American history to that point—occurred in the steel industry. Demanding higher wages and an eight-hour workday, about 350,000 steelworkers went on strike in September 1919. Using propaganda techniques learned during the war, the steel companies started a campaign against the strikers. In newspaper ads they accused the strikers of being "Red agitators." Charges of communism cost the strikers much needed public support and helped force them to end the strike—but not before violence had occurred on both sides. Eighteen strikers had died in a riot in Gary, Indiana.

In September 1919, police officers in **Boston** went on strike, demanding the right to form a union. This strike by public employees angered many Americans, and they applauded the strong stand Massachusetts governor **Calvin Coolidge** took against the strikers. Coolidge said,

❝There is no right to strike against the public safety by anybody, anywhere, any time.❞

When the strike collapsed, officials fired the entire Boston police force. Most Americans approved of the decision.

Workers found themselves deeper in debt because of rising prices and unchanged wages. Still labor unions failed to win wide support among working families. Many Americans connected unions with radicalism and bolshevism. A growing feeling against unions, together with strong pressure from employers and the government not to join unions, led to a sharp drop in union membership in the 1920s.

During this period of union decline, a dynamic African American, **A. Philip Randolph,** started the Brotherhood of Sleeping Car Porters. Made up mostly of African Americans, this union of railroad workers struggled during its early years but began to grow in the 1930s, when government policy encouraged unions. In the 1950s and the 1960s, Randolph would emerge as a leader of the civil rights movement.

Reading Check **Summarizing** What was the outcome of the Boston police strike?

Racial Unrest

During World War I, more than 500,000 African Americans had left the South for new jobs in the North. Many Northern whites resented African American competition for jobs.

In 1919 rising racial tensions led to violence. In the South more than 70 African Americans were lynched. In Chicago a violent riot broke out after a group of whites stoned an African American youth who was swimming in Lake Michigan. The youth drowned, and the incident set off rioting. For two weeks African American and white gangs roamed city streets, attacking each other and burning buildings. The riot left 15 whites and 23 African Americans dead and more than 500 people injured.

Many African Americans turned to **Marcus Garvey** for answers. Marcus Garvey was born to a poor family in Jamaica, the youngest of 11 children. Educated as a journalist and filled with ambition, Garvey arrived in New York City at the age of 28. A powerful leader with a magnetic personality, Garvey opposed integration. Instead he supported a "back-to-Africa" movement, urging African Americans to establish their own country in Africa. Garvey founded the **Universal Negro Improvement Association** (UNIA) in 1914 to promote racial unity and pride.

During the 1920s Garvey gained an enormous following and great influence, especially among the urban poor. Garvey told audiences that "to be a Negro is no disgrace, but an honor." With branches in many states, the UNIA organized rallies and parades to build pride and confidence among African Americans. It helped African Americans start businesses. One African American newspaper summed up Garvey's achievements: "He taught [African Americans] to admire and praise black things and black people."

Reading Check **Explaining** Did Marcus Garvey support or oppose integration? Explain.

SECTION 1 ASSESSMENT

Checking for Understanding

1. **Key Terms** Define each of the following terms: capitalism, anarchist, deport.
2. **Reviewing Facts** Who were Sacco and Vanzetti? Explain how the fear of radicals and foreigners affected the outcome of the Sacco and Vanzetti trial.

Reviewing Themes

3. **Continuity and Change** Why was there a sharp drop in union membership during the 1920s?

Critical Thinking

4. **Drawing Conclusions** Suppose you are making a video about the life of Marcus Garvey. If he could speak to American youth today, what statement might he make?
5. **Making Generalizations** Re-create the diagram below and list the reasons organized labor had for demanding better wages after the war.

Reasons for demanding better wages

Analyzing Visuals

6. **Picturing History** Compare the photographs of the demonstrators on pages 701 and 702. What are the purposes of the demonstrations? In what ways are the photos similar? Different?

Interdisciplinary Activity

Descriptive Writing Make a list of three to five adjectives that you think describe the mood of the country during this era. Draw or paint these adjectives on poster board in a way that expresses the words' meanings.

SECTION 2 Desire for Normalcy

Guide to Reading

Main Idea
The Harding and Coolidge administrations stressed a return to government as it had been before progressivism and World War I.

Key Terms
lease, isolationism

Reading Strategy
Organizing Information As you read the section, re-create the diagram below and describe the policies the Harding and Coolidge administrations followed.

Administration policies	
Domestic affairs	Foreign affairs

Read to Learn
• what problems faced the Harding presidency.
• what policies Presidents Harding and Coolidge followed in business and foreign affairs.

Section Theme
Continuity and Change Presidents Harding and Coolidge promised to return America to normalcy after the war.

Preview of Events

♦1920   ♦1925   ♦1930

1920
Warren G. Harding is elected president

1922
Senate investigates Teapot Dome lease

1923
Calvin Coolidge becomes president

1928
Kellogg-Briand Pact aims to outlaw war

Harding/Coolidge decal, 1920

AN American Story

Warren G. Harding attracted attention with his friendly personality, fine voice, and handsome appearance. These glowing assets could easily make Harding president, thought political strategist Harry Daugherty. As Harding's campaign manager, Daugherty took credit for prodding Harding into the 1920 presidential race: "I found him sunning himself, like a turtle on a log, and I pushed him into the water."

The Harding Presidency

In the summer of 1920, the Republicans gathered in Chicago to nominate a candidate for president. Although confident of victory in the upcoming election, they had no outstanding leaders to head the party ticket. As one Republican noted, "There ain't any first raters this year." So party bosses chose "the best of the second raters" as their presidential candidate—Senator **Warren G. Harding** of Ohio. Harding had earned a reputation as a loyal Republican, and Ohio political boss Harry Daugherty pushed through his nomination.

Sensing Americans' longing for calm and stability after decades of progressive reform and world war, Harding declared in his campaign that "America's present need is not heroics, but healing." He promised a return to "normalcy." What Harding meant by "normalcy" was not really clear, but the word sounded reassuring to those Americans who wanted an end to foreign involvement and domestic turmoil.

As Harding's running mate, the Republicans nominated Massachusetts governor **Calvin Coolidge,** who was recognized for his firm stand in the Boston police strike. The Harding-Coolidge ticket won a landslide victory in November 1920—the first presidential election in which women could vote. The Republicans defeated the Democratic candidate, Governor **James Cox** of Ohio, and his young running mate, **Franklin Delano Roosevelt** of New York. The Republicans also made large gains in Congress.

Harding admitted having doubts about his qualifications for the presidency. He reportedly told a friend, "I knew that this job would be too much for me." He tried to compensate by appointing several talented people to the cabinet—**Charles Evans Hughes,** a former Supreme Court justice, as secretary of state; **Andrew Mellon,** a prominent Pittsburgh banker and financier, to head the Treasury Department; and **Herbert Hoover,** a talented organizer, as secretary of commerce.

The "Ohio Gang"

President Harding also gave jobs in government to many of his friends and political supporters—the so-called **Ohio Gang.** He appointed **Harry Daugherty** attorney general. He named Senator **Albert Fall** of New Mexico, a close friend, secretary of the interior. **Charles Forbes,** another friend, became head of the Veterans Bureau. Other friends of Harding filled offices throughout the administration.

Many of these appointees were unqualified; some turned out to be corrupt. By 1922 Washington buzzed with rumors of scandals within the Harding administration. Forbes, convicted of stealing funds from the Veterans Bureau, fled to avoid imprisonment. Daugherty was accused of receiving bribes but refused to resign.

Teapot Dome Scandal

The biggest scandal of the Harding administration involved Albert Fall. In 1922 Fall secretly leased, or rented, government oil reserves in Elk Hills, California, and Teapot Dome, Wyoming, to the owners of two oil companies. In exchange Fall received more than $400,000. After the scandal became public, Fall was convicted of bribery and sent to prison, becoming the first cabinet officer ever to go to jail. **Teapot Dome** became a symbol of the corruption in the Harding administration and of government corruption and scandal in general.

Harding himself was not directly involved in any scandals, but as the rumors spread, he grew increasingly distressed. "I have no trouble with my enemies," he said. "But my friends . . . they're the ones that keep me walking the floor nights!"

Warren G. Harding conducted a successful "front porch" campaign for the presidency in 1920.

Analyzing *Political Cartoons*

The cartoonist uses familiar images of the 1920s. "Big Business", portrayed as a carefree "flapper" girl, dances to jazz music played by President Coolidge. **What was the relationship between government and business during Coolidge's presidency?**

Although Coolidge and Harding differed in style, they held similar political views. Coolidge believed that the best government was the least government and that government should not interfere in the life of the nation. He once said approvingly, "If the federal government should go out of existence, the common run of the people would not detect the difference for a considerable length of time."

In the summer of 1923, before the full story of the scandals came out, Harding escaped the stresses of Washington, D.C., by taking a trip west. During the trip he became ill, suffered a heart attack, and died.

Vice President Calvin Coolidge was visiting his father in Vermont when he was awakened in the early morning hours of August 3, 1923, with the news of President Harding's death. Coolidge's father, a justice of the peace, administered the presidential oath of office. Then the new president—in characteristic Coolidge fashion—calmly turned off the lights and went back to bed.

Honesty Returns to the White House

Calvin Coolidge was in many ways the complete opposite of Harding. While Harding loved to talk and meet people, Coolidge said very little and earned the name "Silent Cal." In addition, Coolidge had a reputation for honesty. After becoming president, he allowed the investigations into the Harding scandals to proceed without interference. He fired Daugherty and replaced the remaining members of the Ohio Gang with honest officials.

A Friend to Business

Under President Coolidge the government took an active role in supporting business. As the president explained, "The chief business of the American people is business. . . . The man who builds a factory builds a temple."

Coolidge and the Republican-dominated Congress aimed to create a favorable climate for business to promote the nation's economic prosperity. The government lowered income tax rates on the wealthiest Americans and on corporate profits and cut government spending. It also raised tariffs to protect American business and overturned laws regulating child labor and wages for women.

A New Term

Coolidge seemed to be exactly what the country wanted. At the Republican national convention in 1924, the president was nominated without opposition. The Democrats took more than 100 ballots to nominate a little-known lawyer, John W. Davis of West Virginia, as their presidential candidate. Wisconsin senator Robert La Follette led a third party, the Progressives, in the race. Coolidge swept the 1924 presidential election with 54 percent of the popular vote. For the first time in America's history, women won governors' races—**Nellie Tayloe Ross** in Wyoming and **Miriam Ferguson** in Texas.

✓ **Reading Check** **Comparing** Do you think Coolidge followed Harding's policies about business? Explain.

Foreign Policy

Harding and Coolidge both favored a limited role for the nation in world affairs. They desired world peace but did not want the nation to join the League of Nations or become involved in international disagreements. Harding had promised the American people that he would not lead them into the League "by the side door, back door, or cellar door." Many Americans supported this policy of isolationism.

Promoting Peace

The Harding administration made serious efforts to promote peace. After the war the United States, Great Britain, and Japan began a naval arms race. In 1921 Secretary of State Hughes invited Japan and Britain to Washington, D.C., to discuss the problem. In February 1922 the three nations, along with France and Italy, signed the **Five-Power Treaty** to limit the size of the nations' navies. The treaty marked the first time in modern history that world powers agreed to disarm.

The United States continued working for peace. In August 1928, it joined 14 other nations in signing the **Kellogg-Briand Pact,** which called for outlawing war. Within a few years, 48 other nations had signed the pact, but it lacked any means of enforcing peace.

A More Friendly Neighbor

The United States had intervened in Latin American countries several times in the early 1900s to support American business interests. When Harding took office, American troops were stationed in Haiti, the **Dominican Republic,** and **Nicaragua,** and relations with Mexico were tense.

After the Dominican Republic and Nicaragua held elections in the mid-1920s, the United States withdrew its troops from those countries.

At about the same time, American investors asked President Coolidge to send troops into Mexico when its government threatened to take over foreign-owned oil and mining companies. Coolidge chose to negotiate instead, and the United States reached a settlement with Mexico.

✓ **Reading Check** **Explaining** Why would the Kellogg-Briand Pact prove to be ineffective?

SECTION 2 ASSESSMENT

Checking for Understanding

1. **Key Terms** Use the terms lease and isolationism in separate sentences that will help explain their meanings.
2. **Reviewing Facts** Where was Teapot Dome? What did Teapot Dome come to symbolize?

Reviewing Themes

3. **Continuity and Change** What actions did the United States take to promote world peace in the 1920s?

Critical Thinking

4. **Comparing** What role did Harding and Coolidge think the government should play in people's lives?
5. **Making Generalizations** Re-create the diagram below and list two ways the United States government worked to promote American business.

Promoting business

Analyzing Visuals

6. **Political Cartoons** Study the cartoon on page 706. Who do the figures represent? What image of the Federal government does the cartoon portray?

Interdisciplinary Activity

Art Draw a political cartoon that illustrates an example of an event that took place during the Harding presidency. Make sure to include a caption with your cartoon.

Critical Thinking SKILLBUILDER

Making Generalizations

Why Learn This Skill?

If you say "We have a great football team," you are making a generalization, or general statement, about your team. If you go on to say that your team has not lost a game this season and is the top-ranked team, you are providing evidence to support your generalization. When you are studying history, it is often necessary to put together pieces of information, called supporting statements, to arrive at a full picture.

Learning the Skill

In some cases, authors provide only supporting statements, and you need to make the generalizations on your own.

To make generalizations, follow these steps:

- Identify the subject matter.
- Gather facts and examples related to it.
- Identify similarities or patterns among these facts.
- Use these similarities or patterns to form some general ideas about the subject.

Practicing the Skill

Read the passage and the generalizations. Then answer the questions that follow.

By 1927, 4 out of 5 cars had closed tops, compared with only 1 in 10 in 1919. Now protected from the weather, many families hopped into their cars for short day trips. Many city workers moved to houses in the new suburbs. Car owners now traveled easily to once-distant places, bringing far-flung Americans together for the first time.

Generalizations About the Automobile

a. Automobiles were too expensive to buy.
b. The automobile changed American culture in many ways.
c. Many businesses arose from the need to service the newly mobile nation.
d. Suburbs grew as a result of the automobile.

1 Which of the generalizations above are supported by the details in this passage?

2 Write one or two statements that support each of these generalizations.

3 Which of the generalizations are not supported by the passage? Explain.

Traffic jam, 1920s

Applying the Skill

Making Generalizations Make a general statement about your class that describes it. Then write three or four supporting details for that generalization.

 Glencoe's **Skillbuilder Interactive Workbook CD-ROM, Level 1,** provides instruction and practice in key social studies skills.

A Booming Economy

Guide to Reading

Main Idea

The United States experienced periods of prosperity and economic expansion during the 1920s.

Key Terms

recession, gross national product, productivity, installment buying

Reading Strategy

Analyzing Information As you read the section, re-create the diagram below and describe how these ideas affected the American economy.

	Effect on economy
Scientific management	
Assembly line	
Installment buying	

Read to Learn

- how the prosperity of the 1920s affected the nation and the American people.
- what impact the automobile had on American life.

Section Theme

Economic Factors After a brief postwar recession, the American economy began a steady growth that lasted for most of the 1920s.

Preview of Events

♦1920	♦1925	♦1930

1920s
Stock market booms

1922
GNP reaches $70 billion

1924
Model T sells for less than $300

1929
Electricity runs 70 percent of factories

AN
American Story

During the "golden age of the automobile" in the 1920s, the car became a vital part of many Americans' lives. A mother of nine children said that her family "would rather do without clothes than give up the car." In the past, they had wanted to visit her sister-in-law, but by the time the children were "shoed and dressed" there wasn't any money left to pay for trolley fare. "Now no matter how [the children] look, we just poke 'em in the car and take 'em along."

Growth in the 1920s

After World War I, the American economy experienced problems readjusting to peacetime. Millions of soldiers returned, entering the labor force and competing for jobs. Government orders for wartime goods came to a halt, forcing many companies to lay off workers. Other companies went bankrupt. Prices rose, making it hard for workers to make ends meet. This economic downturn, or recession, lasted about two years. The economy then began a steady growth that lasted most of the decade. In 1922 the nation's gross national product

1920s gas pump

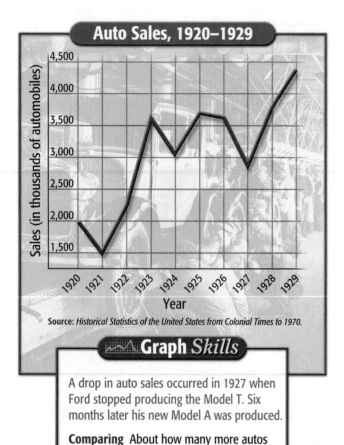

Auto Sales, 1920–1929

Sales (in thousands of automobiles)

4,500
4,000
3,500
3,000
2,500
2,000
1,500

1920 1921 1922 1923 1924 1925 1926 1927 1928 1929

Year

Source: *Historical Statistics of the United States from Colonial Times to 1970.*

Graph *Skills*

A drop in auto sales occurred in 1927 when Ford stopped producing the Model T. Six months later his new Model A was produced.

Comparing About how many more autos were sold in 1928 than in 1924?

(GNP)—the total value of all goods and services produced—was $70 billion. By 1929 it had risen to $100 billion!

Technology made rapid industrial growth possible, and electricity powered American industry. Before World War I, only 30 percent of factories were run by electricity. By 1929 this figure had risen to 70 percent. Electricity was cheaper than steam power. By cutting costs, businesses could lower prices and increase profits.

Scientific Management

New ways of managing operations contributed to economic growth as well. Many employers used **scientific management**—hiring experts to study how goods could be produced more quickly. By adopting new work methods, businesses tried to lower costs and increase productivity—the amount of work each worker could do.

Many businesses adopted mass production techniques using the **assembly line,** which was first introduced in Henry Ford's automobile factories. Assembly line methods increased productivity and cut production costs.

Worker Relations

Businesses tried to build better relations with workers. Many companies set up safety programs that lowered the risk of death or injury on the job. Some began to provide health and accident insurance. Many companies encouraged workers to buy stock in the company. These steps—known as **welfare capitalism**—were designed to link workers more closely to the company they worked for. Business also adopted these steps to discourage workers from joining independent unions.

The Consumer Economy

American industry changed in another way as well. As electricity became more available, demand grew for appliances using electric power. By the 1920s, more than 60 percent of American households had electricity. Consumers eagerly acquired refrigerators, stoves, vacuum cleaners, fans, and radios. As demand for these items grew, more and more of them were produced, leading to reduced production costs and lower prices. Between 1920 and 1929, for example, the cost of a refrigerator dropped from $600 to $300.

These appliances transformed daily life. People did not have to spend as much time on household chores. Now they had more leisure time.

In the 1920s successful companies joined with or purchased competitors. Three companies—Ford, General Motors, and Chrysler—dominated the auto industry. One grocery chain—the Great Atlantic and Pacific Tea Company (A&P)—had more than 15,000 stores across the country. Businesses became national as the products of many local companies were replaced by national brands.

To market those national brands, businesses spent more and more money on advertising. Propaganda techniques learned during World War I were now used to persuade consumers to buy a particular brand of toothpaste, clothing, or soap. Newspapers and magazines were filled with ads, and with the spread of radio a new advertising form—the commercial announcement—was born.

Spurred by ads to buy more and more, consumers found a new way to make those purchases—installment buying. Consumers could now buy products by promising to pay small, regular amounts over a period of time. One critic of installment buying called the system "a dollar down and a dollar a week forever." The installment method of buying boosted consumer spending.

✓ **Reading Check** **Explaining** Why did the price of some consumer goods decrease?

The Automobile Age

More often than not, people used the installment plan to buy a new car. During the 1920s, automobile registrations jumped from 8 million to 23 million. America quickly became a "car culture," in which people's lives revolved around the automobile. The nation's economy, too, revolved around the automobile. Almost four million Americans worked for auto companies or in related jobs. **Detroit, Michigan,** became the automobile manufacturing center of the world.

Henry Ford was a pioneer in the manufacture of affordable automobiles with his **Model T,** which was built using assembly line methods. The car was sturdy, reliable, inexpensive, and available only in black. In 1914 Ford stunned the auto industry—and all corporate leaders, for that matter—by announcing that he would pay his workers the high wage of $5 per day. Workers were happy, and Ford had more potential customers as he steadily dropped the price of his Model T. By 1924 the car sold for less than $300. With the average industrial worker earning about $1,300 a year, many families could afford to buy a Model T.

TECHNOLOGY & History

Henry Ford's Assembly Line

The industrial boom of the 1920s owed much to the assembly line Henry Ford first used in 1913–1914. Parts moved on a conveyor belt. Workers attached the parts to cars moving past them at a steady speed of six feet per minute.
How large was Ford's plant?

Henry Ford

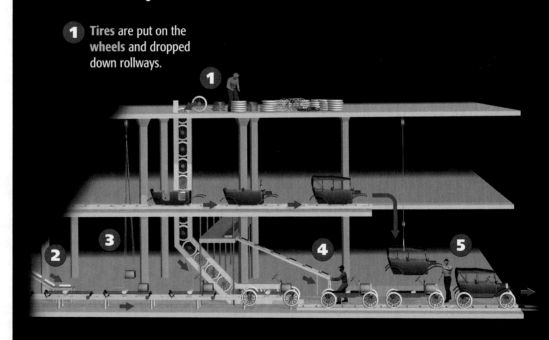

1 **Tires** are put on the **wheels** and dropped down rollways.

2 **Tanks** filled with one gallon of gas slide from the "Tank Bridge."

3 **Engines** built on the third floor are lowered onto the chassis.

4 **Radiators** arrive from the far end of the 60-acre

5 **Auto bodies** are assembled on the second floor, then lowered through

By the mid-1920s, other automobile models challenged the Model T. General Motors cut into Ford's sales by offering a line of cars in a range of colors and with features to improve passenger comfort. In 1927 Ford responded with the **Model A,** which had better engineering and came in several colors. Out of this competition came the practice of introducing new car models each year.

Effect on Other Industries

The automobile had a tremendous impact on other American industries. Americans' love of driving called for new roads and highways. Highways, in turn, needed gas stations and rest stops. Businesses along major roads profited from the millions of people now traveling around the country by car. Tourism grew dramatically.

The car boom affected industries that made products used in cars. The steel, rubber, and glass industries grew. During the 1920s the oil industry shifted from producing lubricants to refining gasoline for automobiles.

The automobile dramatically changed the lives of many Americans. Travel for pleasure became a regular part of American life. People could now go wherever they wished. Cars also contributed to the spread of suburbs. Because people could now drive to work, they could live in a suburb and still hold a job in the city.

Those Left Behind

Despite all the signs of prosperity, many Americans did not share in the boom of the 1920s. Farmers had an especially difficult time. During the war, the federal government had purchased wheat, corn, and other products, and farmers had prospered from higher prices. When the war ended, farmers had to compete with European agriculture again. Food prices fell, and farm income plummeted. Unable to pay their debts, many farmers lost their farms.

Farmers were not the only ones feeling the pinch. Those who worked in the railroad and coal mining industries had a difficult time as trucks took business from railroads and electricity replaced coal as a power source. Americans now were buying less cotton and more clothes made of synthetic fibers. As cotton prices plunged, many textile factories were forced to shut down. Wages rose slightly for most workers, but the cost of living rose more. By 1929 nearly three-fourths of families had incomes below $2,500, the accepted level necessary for a comfortable life.

Reading Check **Explaining** What action did Henry Ford take when other auto manufacturers offered new lines of cars?

SECTION 3 ASSESSMENT

Checking for Understanding

1. **Key Terms** Define each of the following terms: recession, gross national product, productivity, installment buying.
2. **Reviewing Facts** Describe the economic problems that existed in America after World War I.

Reviewing Themes

3. **Economic Factors** How did the auto industry help boost other industries?

Critical Thinking

4. **Drawing Conclusions** How did welfare capitalism discourage people from joining unions?
5. **Organizing Information** Re-create the diagram below and identify three factors that helped to bring about a strong economy.

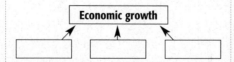

Analyzing Visuals

6. **Graph Skills** Study the graph on page 710. In which year did auto sales first pass three million?

Interdisciplinary Activity

Math Research to find the total auto sales for a recent 10-year period. Compare your findings with the auto sales figures on page 710. Write a short paragraph comparing the two sets of figures. Include any conclusions you reach.

The Roaring Twenties

Guide to Reading

Main Idea
Many Americans favored traditional values, while others favored change.

Key Terms
flapper, mass media, expatriate, Prohibition, nativism, quota system, evolution

Reading Strategy
Organizing Information As you read the section, re-create the diagram below and describe the accomplishments of these individuals.

	Accomplishments
Charles Lindbergh	
Bessie Smith	
Langston Hughes	
Ernest Hemingway	

Read to Learn
• how lifestyles in America changed in the 1920s.
• what cultural clashes occurred in the United States in the 1920s.

Section Theme
Continuity and Change The Roaring Twenties were a time of changing attitudes and clashing cultures.

Preview of Events

1920	1925	1930

1920
Nineteenth Amendment grants woman suffrage

1924
Congress passes National Origins Act

1927
Lindbergh flies solo across the Atlantic

1928
Herbert Hoover is elected president

Song sheet honoring Lindbergh

AN
American Story

On the evening of May 19, 1927, a young pilot named Charles Lindbergh learned that, although it was drizzling on Long Island, the weather reports predicted fair skies for his miraculous trip. He decided to get ready. Throughout a sleepless night, Lindbergh made the final preparations for takeoff. Shortly before 8:00 A.M., Lindbergh climbed into his aircraft and took off for Paris. With the news of his departure "flashing along the wires," the American people were united in "the exaltation of a common emotion." All minds and hearts were focused on the brave pilot who was crossing the vast Atlantic Ocean.

New Directions

In May 1927, aviator **Charles Lindbergh** became the first person to fly alone across the Atlantic Ocean. He did so in a tiny, single-engine plane named the *Spirit of St. Louis*. Americans went wild and hailed a new hero. Cities across the nation held parades to honor Lindbergh—in New York City well-wishers threw

Flappers reflected the
modern spirit of the
Jazz Age.

Movie poster, 1926

1,800 tons of paper
streamers—and
newspapers reported
on his every move. The national
embrace of Lindbergh showed what one historian called a "delighted concern over things that
were exciting but didn't matter profoundly."

Changes for Women

The 1920s did bring profound changes for
women. One important change took place with
the ratification of the **Nineteenth Amendment**
in 1920. The amendment guaranteed women in
all states the right to vote. Women also ran for
election to political offices. 📖 *(See page 249 for the text
of the Nineteenth Amendment.)*

Throughout the 1920s the number of women
holding jobs outside the home continued to
grow. Most women had to take jobs considered
"women's" work, such as teaching and working
in offices as clerks and typists. At the same time,
increasing numbers of college-educated women

started professional careers, and more women
worked after marriage. But the vast majority of
married women remained within the home,
working as homemakers and mothers.

The flapper symbolized the new "liberated"
woman of the 1920s. Pictures of flappers—carefree young women with short, "bobbed" hair,
heavy makeup, and short skirts—appeared in
magazines. Many people saw the bold, boyish
look and shocking behavior of flappers as a sign
of changing morals. Though hardly typical of
American women, the flapper image reinforced
the idea that women now had more freedom. Pre-
war values had shifted, and many people were
beginning to challenge traditional ways.

✓ **Reading Check** **Describing** What did the
Nineteenth Amendment guarantee?

Entertainment

Changes in attitudes spread quickly
because of the growth of mass media—
forms of communication, such as newspapers and radio, that reach millions of people.
Laborsaving devices and fewer working
hours gave Americans more leisure time. In
those nonworking hours, they enjoyed tabloid-
style newspapers, large-circulation magazines,
phonograph records, the radio, and the movies.

The Movies and Radio

In the 1920s the motion picture industry in **Hollywood,** California, became one of the country's
leading businesses. For millions of Americans, the
movies offered entertainment and escape.

The first movies were black and white and
silent, with the actors' dialog printed on the
screen and a pianist playing music to accompany the action. In 1927 Hollywood introduced
movies with sound. The first "talkie," *The Jazz
Singer,* created a sensation.

The radio brought entertainment into people's homes in the 1920s. In 1920 the first commercial radio broadcast, which carried the
presidential election returns, was transmitted by
station KDKA in Pittsburgh. In the next three
years nearly 600 stations joined the airwaves.

The networks broadcast popular programs across the nation. The evening lineup of programs included something for everyone—news, concerts, sporting events, and comedies. Radio offered listeners a wide range of music—opera, classical, country and western, blues, and jazz. *Amos 'n' Andy* and the *Grand Ole Opry* were among the hit shows of the 1920s. Families sat down to listen to the radio together.

Businesses soon realized that the radio offered an enormous audience for messages about their products, so they began to help finance radio programs. Radio stations sold spot advertisements, or commercials, to companies.

Sports and Fads

Among the favorite radio broadcasts of the 1920s were athletic events. Baseball, football, and boxing soared in popularity. Americans flocked to sporting events, and more people participated in sports activities as well.

Sports stars became larger-than-life heroes. Baseball fans idolized **Babe Ruth,** the great outfielder, who hit 60 home runs in 1927—a record that would stand for 34 years. Football star Red Grange, who once scored four touchdowns in 12 minutes, became a national hero. Golfer Bobby Jones and Gertrude Ederle, the first woman to swim the English Channel, became household names.

In the 1920s Americans took up new activities with enthusiasm, turning them into fads. The Chinese board game *mah-jongg* (mah•ZHAHNG) and crossword puzzles were all the rage. Contests such as flagpole sitting and dance marathons—often lasting three or four days—made headlines. Americans also loved the Miss America Pageant, which was first held in 1921.

Reading Check **Comparing** What fads were popular in the 1920s? What are two comparable fads today?

The Jazz Age

During the 1920s people danced to the beat of a new kind of music called jazz. Jazz captured the spirit of the era so well that the 1920s is often referred to as the **Jazz Age.**

Jazz had its roots in the South in African American work songs and in African music. A blend of ragtime and blues, it uses dynamic rhythms and **improvisation**—new rhythms and melodies created during a performance. Among the best-known African American jazz musicians were trumpeter **Louis Armstrong,** pianist and composer **Duke Ellington,** and singer **Bessie Smith.** White musicians such as Paul Whiteman and Bix Biederbecke also played jazz and helped bring it to a wider audience.

Interest in jazz spread through radio and phonograph records. Jazz helped create a unique African American recording industry. Equally important, jazz gave America one of its most distinctive art forms.

Harlem Renaissance

The rhythm and themes of jazz inspired the poetry of **Langston Hughes,** an African American writer. In the 1920s, Hughes joined the growing number of African American writers and artists who gathered in **Harlem,** an African American section of New York City. Hughes described his arrival in Harlem:

❝I can never put on paper the thrill of the underground ride to Harlem. I went up the steps and out into the bright September sunlight. Harlem! I stood there, dropped my bags, took a deep breath and felt happy again.❞ *Langston Hughes*

Harlem witnessed a burst of creativity in the 1920s—a flowering of African American culture called the **Harlem Renaissance.** This movement instilled an interest in African culture and pride in being African American.

During the Harlem Renaissance, many writers wrote about the African American experience in novels, poems, and short stories. Along with Hughes were writers like James Weldon Johnson, Claude McKay, Countee Cullen, and Zora Neale Hurston.

Based in New Orleans, King Oliver's Creole Jazz Band was one of the best and most important bands in early jazz.

Bessie Smith   *Jazz record label*

A Lost Generation of Writers

At the same time that the Harlem Renaissance blossomed, other writers were questioning American ideals. Disappointed with American values and in search of inspiration, they settled in Paris. These writers were called expatriates—people who choose to live in another country. Writer **Gertrude Stein** called these rootless Americans "the lost generation."

Novelist **F. Scott Fitzgerald** and his wife, Zelda, joined the expatriates in Europe. In *Tender Is the Night,* Fitzgerald wrote of people who had been damaged emotionally by World War I. They were dedicated, he said,

❝to the fear of poverty and the worship of success.❞

Another famous American expatriate was novelist **Ernest Hemingway,** whose books *The Sun Also Rises* and *A Farewell to Arms* reflected the mood of Americans in postwar Europe.

While some artists fled the United States, others stayed home and wrote about life in America. Novelist **Sinclair Lewis** presented a critical view of American culture in such books as *Main Street* and *Babbitt.* Another influential American writer was **Sherwood Anderson.** In his most famous book, *Winesburg, Ohio,* Anderson explored small-town life in the Midwest.

☑ **Reading Check** **Describing** What type of music did Louis Armstrong play?

Prohibition

During the 1920s the number of people living in cities swelled, and a modern industrial society came of age. Outside of the cities, many Americans identified this new, urban society with crime, corruption, and immoral behavior. They believed that the America they knew and valued—a nation based on family, church, and tradition—was under attack. Disagreement grew between those who defended traditional beliefs and those who welcomed the new.

The clash of cultures during the 1920s affected many aspects of American life, particularly the use of alcoholic beverages. The temperance movement, the campaign against alcohol use, had begun in the 1800s. The movement was rooted both in religious objections to drinking alcohol and in the belief that society would benefit if alcohol were unavailable.

The movement finally achieved its goal in 1919 with the ratification of the **Eighteenth Amendment** to the Constitution. This amendment established Prohibition—a total ban on the manufacture, sale, and transportation of liquor throughout the United States. Congress passed the **Volstead Act** to provide the means of enforcing the ban. In rural areas in the South and the Midwest, where the temperance movement was strong, Prohibition generally succeeded. In the cities, however, Prohibition had little support. The nation divided into two camps: the "drys"—those who supported Prohibition—and the "wets"—those who opposed it.

Consequences of the Ban

A continuing demand for alcohol led to widespread lawbreaking. Some people began making wine or "bathtub gin" in their homes. Illegal bars and clubs, known as speakeasies, sprang up in cities. Hidden from view, these clubs could be entered only by saying a secret password.

With only about 1,500 agents, the federal government could do little to enforce the Prohibition laws. By the early 1920s, many states in the East stopped trying to enforce the laws.

Prohibition contributed to the rise of organized crime. Recognizing that millions of dollars could be made from **bootlegging**—making and selling illegal alcohol—members of organized crime moved in quickly and took control. They used their profits to gain influence in businesses, labor unions, and governments.

Crime boss Al "Scarface" Capone controlled organized crime and local politics in Chicago. Defending his involvement in illegal alcohol, Capone said,

> 66 I make my money by supplying a popular demand. If I break the law, my customers are as guilty as I am. 99

Al Capone

Eventually, Capone was arrested and sent to prison.

Over time many Americans realized that the "noble experiment," as Prohibition was called, had failed. Prohibition was repealed in 1933 with the **Twenty-first Amendment.** 📖 *(See pages 249 and 250 for the text of the Eighteenth and Twenty-first Amendments.)*

✓ **Reading Check** **Analyzing** Why was Prohibition difficult to enforce?

Nativism

The anxieties many native-born Americans felt about the rapid changes in society contributed to an upsurge of nativism—the belief that native-born Americans are superior to foreigners. With this renewed nativism came a revival of the **Ku Klux Klan.**

As you read in Chapter 17, the first Klan had been founded in the 1860s in the South to control newly freed African Americans through the use of threats and violence. The second Klan, organized in 1915, still preyed on African Americans, but it had other targets as well—Catholics, Jews, immigrants, and other groups believed to represent "un-American" values.

In the 1920s the new Klan spread from the South to other areas of the country, gaining considerable power in such states as Indiana and Oregon and in many large cities. For the most part, the Klan used pressure and scare tactics to get its way, but sometimes Klan members whipped or lynched people or burned property.

The Klan began to decline in the late 1920s, however, largely as a result of scandals and power struggles involving Klan leaders. Membership shrank, and politicians who had been supported by the Klan were voted out of office.

The concerns of the Red Scare days had not completely disappeared. Some Americans feared foreign radicals would overthrow the government. Others believed foreigners would take away their jobs. This anti-immigrant prejudice was directed mainly at southern and eastern Europeans and Asians.

People In History

Will Rogers 1879–1935

Part Native American, Will Rogers grew up in the West roping cattle and riding on the range. He landed jobs with Wild West shows and soon perfected his riding and trick-roping act, which, along with his personality and sense of humor, made him a star.

By 1920 Will Rogers was starring on both stage and screen. A daily newspaper column he started in 1926 spread his humorous views on life and politics. Claiming "I don't make jokes—I just watch the government and report the facts," he poked fun in a light-hearted way and was never hostile. One of his favorite sayings was "I never met a man I didn't like."

By the late 1920s, audiences were listening to his commentary on the radio. To Americans, Rogers had become a national treasure. They mourned when Rogers died in a plane crash near Point Barrow, Alaska, in August 1935.

In 1921 Congress responded to nativist fears by passing the **Emergency Quota Act.** This law established a quota system, an arrangement placing a limit on the number of immigrants from each country. According to the act, only 3 percent of the total number of people in any national group already living in the United States would be admitted during a single year. Because there had been fewer immigrants from southern and eastern Europe than from northern and western Europe at that time, the law favored northern and western European immigrants.

Congress revised the immigration law in 1924. The **National Origins Act** reduced the annual country quota from 3 to 2 percent and based it on the census of 1890—when even fewer people from southern or eastern Europe lived in America. The law excluded Japanese immigrants completely. An earlier law, passed in 1890, had already excluded the Chinese.

These quota laws did not apply to countries in the Western Hemisphere. As a result, immigration of Canadians and Mexicans increased. By 1930 more than one million Mexicans had come to live in the United States.

Reading Check **Describing** What is a quota system?

The Scopes Trial

Another cultural clash in the 1920s involved the role of religion in society. This conflict gained national attention in 1925 in one of the most famous trials of the era.

In 1925 the state of Tennessee passed a law making it illegal to teach evolution—the scientific theory that humans evolved over vast periods of time. The law was supported by Christian fundamentalists, who accepted the biblical story of creation. The fundamentalists saw evolution as a challenge to their values and their religious beliefs.

A young high school teacher named John Scopes deliberately broke the law against teaching evolution so that a trial could test its legality. Scopes acted with the support of the American Civil Liberties Union (ACLU). During the sweltering summer of 1925, the nation followed day-to-day developments in the **Scopes trial** with great interest. More than a hundred journalists from around the country descended on Dayton, Tennessee, to report on the trial.

Two famous lawyers took opposing sides in the trial. **William Jennings Bryan,** Democratic candidate for president in 1896, 1900, and 1908 and a strong opponent of evolution, led the prosecution. **Clarence Darrow,** who had defended many radicals and labor union members, spoke for Scopes.

Although Scopes was convicted of breaking the law and fined $100, the fundamentalists lost the larger battle. Darrow's defense made it appear that Bryan wanted to impose his religious beliefs on the entire nation. The Tennessee Supreme Court overturned Scopes's conviction, and other states decided not to prosecute similar cases.

The Scopes case may have dealt a blow to fundamentalism, but the movement continued to thrive. Rural people, especially in the South and Midwest, remained faithful to their religious beliefs. When large numbers of farmers migrated to cities during the 1920s, they brought fundamentalism with them.

✓ **Reading Check** **Explaining** What law did Scopes challenge?

The Election of 1928

In 1927 President Coolidge shocked everyone by announcing that he would not run for a second full term. **Herbert Hoover** declared his candidacy for the Republican nomination.

During World War I, Hoover had won respect as the head of a committee providing food relief for Europe. He showed such a gift in the role that "to Hooverize" came to mean "to economize, to save and share." Later, Hoover served Presidents Harding and Coolidge as secretary of commerce.

Hoover worked tirelessly to promote cooperation between government and business. A symbol of the forward-looking middle class, he easily won the Republican nomination.

The Democrats chose a far different kind of candidate—**Alfred E. Smith,** governor of New York. The son of immigrants and a man of the city, Smith opposed Prohibition and championed the poor and the working class. As the first Roman Catholic nominee for president, Smith was the target of anti-Catholic feeling. Hoover won the election by a landslide due to both the Republican prosperity of the 1920s and the prejudice against Smith. The contest reflected many of the tensions in American society—rural versus urban life, nativism versus foreign influences, "wets" versus "drys," Protestants versus Catholics, traditional values versus modern values.

✓ **Reading Check** **Identifying** Who was elected president in 1928?

SECTION 4 ASSESSMENT

Checking for Understanding

1. **Key Terms** Use each of these terms in a sentence that will help explain its meaning: flapper, mass media, expatriate, Prohibition, nativism, quota system, evolution.

2. **Reviewing Facts** What was the Harlem Renaissance? Name two writers associated with it.

Reviewing Themes

3. **Continuity and Change** How did the Scopes trial reflect the desire of many Americans to return to traditional values?

Critical Thinking

4. **Making Generalizations** Why do you think Gertrude Stein referred to many American writers as "the lost generation"?

5. **Drawing Conclusions** Re-create the diagram below and describe how each person contributed to his or her field.

	Contribution
Sherwood Anderson	
Countee Cullen	
Louis Armstrong	

Analyzing Visuals

6. **Picturing History** Study the photos on page 716. What does the mood of the country seem to be at this time? Write a short paragraph in which you explain your analysis.

Interdisciplinary Activity

Reading Find and read a poem by a writer who interests you. Find illustrations and photographs that help to communicate the meaning of the poem. Display the poem and illustrations on poster board.

Chapter Summary

The Jazz Age

Time of Turmoil

- Fear of communism grows.
- Labor strikes occur.
- Racial tensions grow.
- Voters elect leaders who promise isolation.
- Harding's administration is marred by scandal.
- Coolidge continues Harding's pro-business economic policies.

A Booming Economy

- Demand grows for products.
- Installment buying boosts consumer spending.
- The auto industry brings benefits and changes.

The Roaring Twenties

- Women gain the right to vote through the Nineteenth Amendment.
- Mass media grows.
- Entertainment industry grows.
- Harlem Renaissance instills interest in African culture.

Clashing Cultures

- The Eighteenth Amendment establishes Prohibition. The Twenty-first Amendment repeals Prohibition.
- Nativism helps revive the Ku Klux Klan.
- Congress passes quota laws to limit immigration.
- The Scopes trial symbolizes the tensions of the 1920s.

Reviewing Key Terms

On a sheet of paper, use the following vocabulary words to write two paragraphs about the decade of the 1920s.

1. isolationism
2. gross national product
3. installment buying
4. Prohibition
5. quota system

Reviewing Key Facts

6. What is capitalism?
7. How did Calvin Coolidge respond to the 1919 Boston police strike?
8. Who were the presidential candidates in 1920?
9. What did the Five-Power Treaty limit?
10. What is installment buying?
11. What did Charles Lindbergh accomplish?
12. Name three important jazz musicians.

Critical Thinking

13. **Determining Cause and Effect** How was the Red Scare used to turn the public against unions?
14. **Reviewing Themes: Global Connections** How did President Harding feel about the League of Nations?
15. **Analyzing Information** What new forms of entertainment were available to the American people in the 1920s as a result of new technology?
16. **Economic Factors** Re-create the diagram below and describe what you think are the advantages and disadvantages of scientific management.

Scientific management	
Advantages	Disadvantages

Citizenship Cooperative Activity

17. **The Political Process** With a partner, find out how political parties in your state nominate candidates for office. Then interview neighbors who are active in a political party. If any of them have participated in the nominating process, ask them about their experiences. Prepare a brochure on the nominating process to distribute in your neighborhood.

Geography and History Activity

Study the graph below; then answer the questions that follow.

Self-Check Quiz
Visit taj.glencoe.com and click on **Chapter 24—Self-Check Quizzes** to prepare for the chapter test.

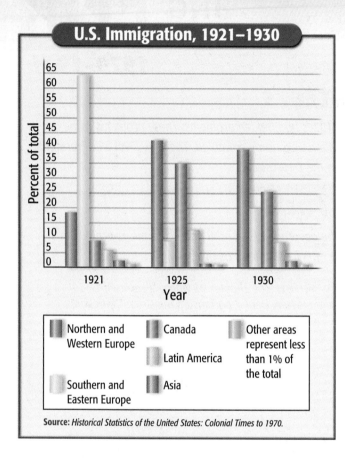

U.S. Immigration, 1921–1930

Percent of total

Year
1921   1925   1930

Northern and Western Europe

Canada

Latin America

Asia

Southern and Eastern Europe

Other areas represent less than 1% of the total

Source: *Historical Statistics of the United States: Colonial Times to 1970.*

18. What information is presented on the graph?

19. What percentage of emigrants came from Asia in 1925?

20. During which year shown was emigration from Canada the highest?

21. From what region was emigration the highest in 1921?

22. Use information presented in the graph to confirm or disprove this generalization: The percentage of emigrants from Canada remained constant throughout the decade.

Practicing Skills

23. **Making Generalizations** Over a period of weeks, read the editorials in your local newspaper. Then write a list of generalizations about the newspaper's position on issues such as politics or crime.

Economics Activity

24. Working with a partner, contact your local chamber of commerce to learn about some of the major businesses or industries in your area. Next conduct a business survey in your neighborhood. Find out where people work, what type of work they do, and how long they have worked. Encourage the people you survey to learn more about local businesses.

 ## Alternative Assessment

25. **Portfolio Project** Research the lives of people who were teenagers during the 1920s. Your local history museum or back issues of newspapers may be helpful. Try to learn about some of the following topics: education, styles of clothing, forms of recreation, and music. Look for pictures that record styles of clothing, hairdos, and social events of the period. Report your findings orally to the class. Then file your written summary in your portfolio.

 The Princeton Review

Standardized Test Practice

Directions: Choose the *best* answer to the following question.

In 1920, women won an important victory when the Nineteenth Amendment was ratified. What did this amendment accomplish?

F It required colleges to accept women.

G It guaranteed equal wages for equal work.

H It banned discrimination in the workplace.

J It granted women the right to vote.

Test-Taking Tip

Eliminate answers that don't make sense. For example, choice **F** is unlikely because the Nineteenth Amendment did not require colleges to accept women. Use the process of elimination to find the right answer.

CHAPTER 25

The Depression and FDR

1929–1941

Why It Matters

The prosperous times of the 1920s had hidden problems. These problems came out in the open in 1929 when the nation's economy crumbled. The New Deal was President Roosevelt's way of dealing with the Depression.

The Impact Today

The New Deal actively involved the government in social and economic concerns and created the Social Security system, which still affects us all.

 The American Journey *Video* *The chapter 25 video, "Fear Itself," examines the impact of FDR and his New Deal programs on the Great Depression.*

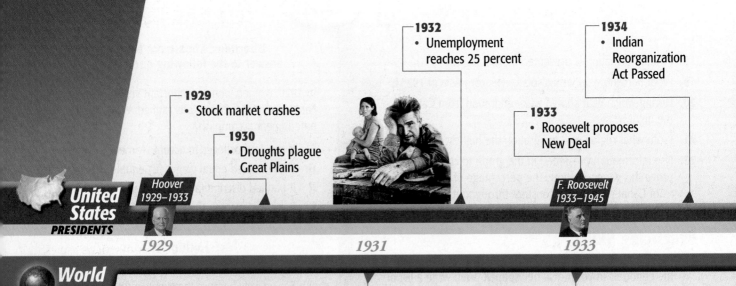

1932
• Unemployment reaches 25 percent

1934
• Indian Reorganization Act Passed

1929
• Stock market crashes

1930
• Droughts plague Great Plains

1933
• Roosevelt proposes New Deal

United States PRESIDENTS

Hoover 1929–1933

F. Roosevelt 1933–1945

1929   1931   1933

World

1931
• Japan invades Manchuria

1933
• Hitler comes to power in Germany

Work for the Unemployed Programs like the Works Progress Administration provided jobs during the Great Depression.

Cause-Effect Study Foldable Make this foldable to help you organize what you learn about the Great Depression and the New Deal.

Step 1 Fold a sheet of paper into thirds from top to bottom.

> This forms three rows.

Step 2 Open the paper and refold it into thirds from side to side.

> Fold it into thirds.

> This forms three columns.

Step 3 Unfold the paper and draw lines along the folds.

Step 4 Label your table foldable as shown.

EVENT	CAUSES	EFFECTS
Great Depression		
New Deal		

Reading and Writing As you read the chapter, use your foldable to record the causes and effects of the Great Depression and the New Deal.

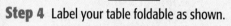

1935
• Social Security Act Passed

1939
• *Gone With the Wind* premieres

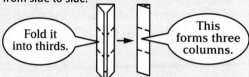

HISTORY Online

Chapter Overview
Visit taj.glencoe.com and click on **Chapter 25— Chapter Overviews** to preview chapter information.

1935   *1937*   *1939*

1935
• Italy invades Ethiopia

1936
• Spanish Civil War begins
• German Jews lose right to vote

1939
• Hitler invades Poland; World War II begins

The Great Depression

Main Idea

The Great Depression was a world-wide business and economic slump that lasted through the 1930s.

Key Terms

stock exchange, on margin, default, relief, public works

Reading Strategy

Organizing Information As you read the section, re-create the diagram below and explain how the Great Depression affected each of these groups.

Effects of the Great Depression		
industrial workers	farmers	home-owners

Read to Learn

• what caused the stock market crash.
• how the Great Depression plunged many Americans into poverty.
• how Hoover reacted to the Great Depression.

Section Theme

Economic Factors Many factors contributed to the economic crisis known as the Great Depression.

Preview of Events

◆1928   ◆1930   ◆1932

1928
Herbert Hoover is elected president

1929
Stock market crashes

1930s
The Great Depression strikes

1932
Bonus Army marches on Washington, D.C.

Stock market crash headline

AN American Story

The bubble of American prosperity burst when the New York stock market collapsed in October 1929. Thousands of investors lost all their savings. Wall Street—the nation's financial center—was in a state of shock. Many Americans suddenly found themselves out of work. In 1932 the popular actor and humorist Will Rogers remarked: "We'll hold the distinction of being the only nation in the history of the world that ever went to the poorhouse in an automobile."

The Stock Market

In the booming economy of the 1920s, confident business and government leaders said the nation had entered a new era of prosperity for all. The chairman of General Motors advised people to invest money in the stock market every month—and many followed his advice. "Grocers, motormen, plumbers, seam-stresses, and . . . waiters were in the market," reported writer Frederick Lewis Allen. The "market had become a national mania."

Suddenly, in October 1929, everything changed. Almost overnight the value of stocks plunged. Millionaires lost fortunes, and thousands of less wealthy investors lost their savings. The United States was about to enter its worst domestic crisis since the Civil War.

The Boom

A **stock exchange** is an organized system for buying and selling shares, or blocks of investments, in corporations. In the late 1920s, the value of stocks on the New York Stock Exchange climbed to dizzying heights, reaching record levels in September 1929.

Because many investors lacked the money to continue purchasing stock, they bought on margin. This means they paid only a fraction of the stock price and borrowed the rest from their brokers. Brokers, in turn, borrowed their money from banks. As long as the value of stocks continued to rise, the buyer could sell later, pay back what had been borrowed, and make a profit. If that value fell, though, investors and brokers would not have enough cash to pay off the loans.

The Crash

Fearing that the boom market would end, some investors began selling their stocks in late September. These sales made stock prices fall. Brokers began to demand repayment of loans, forcing investors who had bought on margin to sell their stock.

Prices declined steadily until October 21, but most financial experts thought the market was experiencing nothing more than a "period of readjustment." Then, for three straight days, stock prices plunged as investors sold millions of shares each day. Panicked traders sold almost 13 million shares on October 24, a day that became known as **"Black Thursday."**

Following a few days of calm, the decline and confusion continued on Monday. On Tuesday, October 29, the crisis worsened. By the end of the day, more than 16 million shares had changed hands and stock prices had plummeted. Journalist Jonathan Norton Leonard described the scene:

❝The selling pressure was . . . coming from everywhere. The wires to other cities were jammed with frantic orders to sell. So were the cables, radio, and telephones to Europe and the rest of the world. Buyers were few, sometimes wholly absent.❞

The New York Stock Exchange closed for a few days to prevent more panic selling. Shock spread across the country.

✓ **Reading Check** **Explaining** What is buying stock "on margin"?

The Great Depression

During the next two years, the United States slid into a severe economic crisis called the **Great Depression.** The nation's total economic output dropped 43 percent in three years, from $104 billion in 1929 to $58 billion in 1932.

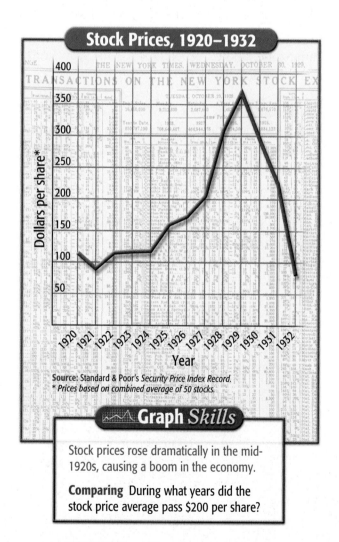

Stock Prices, 1920–1932

Source: Standard & Poor's *Security Price Index Record.*
* *Prices based on combined average of 50 stocks.*

Graph *Skills*

Stock prices rose dramatically in the mid-1920s, causing a boom in the economy.

Comparing During what years did the stock price average pass $200 per share?

While the stock market crash shook people's confidence in the economy, it did not cause the Depression. Other factors, working together, sent the economy into a long tailspin.

An Unbalanced Economy

The problems that led to the Great Depression began to give out warning signals in the early 1920s. Farm income shrank throughout the decade. Industries also declined. In the months before the stock market crash, the automobile and construction industries suffered from lagging orders. As a result, employers cut wages and laid off workers. With their incomes slashed, many Americans could no longer afford the consumer goods that the nation's industries had been churning out.

Another factor that fueled the Depression was the growing gap in wealth between rich people and most Americans. The prosperity of the 1920s did not help all Americans equally. In 1929 less than 1 percent of the population owned nearly one-third of the country's wealth. At the same time, about 75 percent of American families lived in poverty or on the very edge of it.

Credit Crisis

Borrowed money fueled much of the economy in the 1920s. Farmers bought land, equipment, and supplies on credit. Consumers used credit to buy cars. Investors borrowed to buy stocks. Many small banks suffered when farmers defaulted, or failed to meet loan payments. Large banks, which had bought stocks as an investment, suffered huge losses in the stock market crash. These losses forced thousands of banks across the nation to close between 1930 and 1933; millions of depositors lost their money.

International Depression

Weaknesses in the American economy also sapped the strength of foreign economies. European countries needed to borrow money from American banks and to sell goods to American consumers in order to repay their World War I debts to the United States. During the late 1920s, bank funds for loans dried up. International trade slowed down because, without American loans, other nations had less money to spend.

Joblessness and Poverty

As the Depression tightened its grip on the United States, millions lost their jobs. In 1932, 25 percent of American workers were out of work. The unemployment rate remained near 20 percent throughout the decade. Industrial cities were hardest hit. Workers who managed to keep their jobs worked only part-time or for reduced wages.

The newly unemployed felt devastated. New Yorker Sidney Lens, who lost his job, wrote about developing

❝ a feeling of worthlessness—and loneliness; I began to think of myself as a freak and misfit. ❞

Long lines of hungry people snaked through the streets of the nation's cities. They waited for hours to receive a slice of bread, a cup of coffee, or a bowl of soup from soup kitchens run by local governments or charities.

$100. WILL BUY THIS CAR. MUST HAVE CASH. LOST ALL ON THE STOCK MARKET

Picturing **History**

Forced to pay off debts for stocks that were suddenly worthless, Walter Thornton, shown here in October 1929, advertises his car for sale. **What was "Black Thursday"?**

MORE ABOUT...

Brother Can You Spare a Dime?

"Brother Can You Spare a Dime?" was a popular song in the 1930s during the Great Depression. In those days, prices were so low that if you were lucky enough to have a dime, you could actually buy something with it.

WORK-IS-WHAT-I WANT-AND-NOT-CHARITY WHO-WILL-HELP-ME-GET-A-JOB-7 YEARS-IN-DETROIT. NO MONEY SENT-AWAY. FURNISH-BEST-OF-REFERENCES PHONE RANDOLPH 8331 Room #59.

Prices During 1932–1934

Sirloin steak (per pound)	$0.29
Chicken (per pound)	.22
Bread (20-ounce loaf)	.05
Potatoes (per pound)	.02
Bananas (per pound)	.07
Milk (per quart)	.10
Cheese (per pound)	.29
Tomatoes (16-ounce can)	.09
Oranges (per dozen)	.27
Cornflakes (8 ounces)	.08

The Great Depression saw "Hoovervilles," such as this one in New York City, and unemployed workers standing on street corners pleading for jobs.

Listed here are Depression-era prices for selected foods. Read the list to see how far that "dime" from your "brother" would go.

Unemployed people tried to earn a few cents by shining shoes or selling apples on street corners. Those who had lost their homes built shelters out of old boxes and other debris, sometimes grouped together in pitiful "shantytowns." Some referred bitterly to the shantytowns as **Hoovervilles** because of President Hoover's failure to act. Across the country Americans wondered why the president did nothing to end the suffering. 📖 *(See page 974 of the Primary Sources Library for one account of life during the Depression.)*

✓ **Reading Check** **Describing** What percentage of American workers were out of work in 1932?

Hoover and the Crisis

President Hoover thought the economic crisis was only temporary and that prosperity was "just around the corner." He also believed that the "depression cannot be cured by legislative action or executive pronouncement." Instead,

Hoover called on business leaders not to cut wages or production of goods and on charities to do their best for the needy. Voluntary action by private citizens and local governments, Hoover said, would pull the nation through tough times.

Charities, churches, and volunteers worked heroically to provide relief—aid for the needy. So did state and local governments. Some cities withheld part of city workers' wages—already reduced—to fund soup kitchens. But the number who needed help was simply overwhelming.

Government Action

Eventually Hoover recognized that the federal government had to take steps to combat the Depression. In 1931 he authorized additional federal spending on public works—projects such as highways, parks, and libraries—to create new jobs. State and local governments ran out of money, however, and the combined spending by all three levels of government declined.

Bonus Army set up its camp near the Capitol.

Hoover tried a different measure in January 1932, when he asked Congress to create the **Reconstruction Finance Corporation** (RFC). The RFC lent money to businesses. It also provided funds for state and local programs providing relief. However, the RFC's directors were reluctant to make risky loans, and much of its budget remained unspent.

The Bonus Army

The march on Washington by the **Bonus Army** turned many Americans, who were already blaming Hoover for the Depression, firmly against the president. Congress had agreed to give each veteran of World War I a $1,000 bonus in 1945. Jobless veterans wanted the bonuses right away. In the summer of 1932, they formed the Bonus Army and marched to **Washington, D.C.,** to demand their money. At its peak the Bonus Army included about 20,000 veterans. Congress and the president turned the veterans down. Most of the veterans left, but about 2,000, joined by their families, vowed to remain until the bonuses were paid. When the police tried to disband the veterans' camp, conflict broke out and two people were killed.

Hoover responded by calling in the army. With tanks, machine guns, and cavalry, troops led by Army chief of staff General **Douglas MacArthur** and his aide **Dwight D. Eisenhower** entered the protesters' camp. Veterans and their families fled in terror as the troops burned their camp.

Hoover announced that "a challenge to the authority of the United States government has been met." Many Americans were horrified that the government had attacked its own citizens, particularly war veterans. Hoover seemed cold, distant, and out of touch with ordinary people. Many people thought the time had come for a change in government.

Reading Check **Explaining** What did the Reconstruction Finance Corporation provide?

SECTION 1 ASSESSMENT

Checking for Understanding

1. **Key Terms** Write a conversation between two friends at the time of the Great Depression. Include these terms in your writing: stock exchange, on margin, default, relief, public works.
2. **Reviewing Facts** What did the Bonus Army want? Where did it set up camp?

Reviewing Themes

3. **Economic Factors** How did buying stocks on margin contribute to the stock market crash?

Critical Thinking

4. **Drawing Conclusions** Do you think President Hoover followed the proper course in his handling of the Great Depression?
5. **Determining Cause and Effect** Re-create the diagram below and identify four major factors that led to the Great Depression.

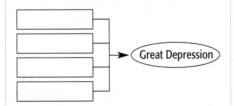

Analyzing Visuals

6. **Graph Skills** Study the graph on page 725. What period of time is shown? When did the average price of stocks reach its peak? During what years did the average drop below $100 per share?

Interdisciplinary Activity

Economics Using the food prices on page 727, make a grocery list of what you could buy on a budget of $3.00 a week. Make another list of which of the same items you could buy today if you only had $3.00 a week.

Roosevelt's New Deal

Guide to Reading

Main Idea

President Franklin Roosevelt promised to take action to get America out of the Great Depression.

Key Terms

Hundred Days, New Deal, work relief, subsidy

Reading Strategy

Classifying Information As you read the section, re-create the diagram below and identify each of the listed items.

	What is it?
The New Deal	
TVA	
CCC	
FDIC	

Read to Learn

- how Roosevelt tried to restore the confidence of the American people.
- what programs were created in FDR's first 100 days.

Section Theme

Government and Democracy New Deal legislation affected banking, the stock market, industry, agriculture, and welfare.

Preview of Events

1932 ——— 1933 ——— 1934

1932
Franklin Roosevelt is elected president

1933
Programs during the Hundred Days improve the economy

1934
Securities and Exchange Commission is created

Roosevelt inaugural button, 1933

AN American Story

Washington, D.C., was dark and dreary on March 4, 1933. President Franklin D. Roosevelt stood bareheaded in the chilly wind, tightly gripping the sides of the reading stand in front of him. His face was stern as he began his Inaugural Address. "This nation asks for action and action now!" he cried.

As Roosevelt spoke, his voice had an electric effect on the masses of people before him. The crowd shouted back its approval. To millions of despairing Americans, Roosevelt's voice was the symbol of hope. It seemed that the gloom was starting to lift.

Franklin D. Roosevelt

With the nation's economy crumbling, the Democrats believed they had a good chance of winning the presidency. Meeting in Chicago in June 1932, the Democrats chose Governor **Franklin D. Roosevelt** of New York as their candidate. Roosevelt—or FDR, as he was called—seemed to bring a fresh approach to politics.

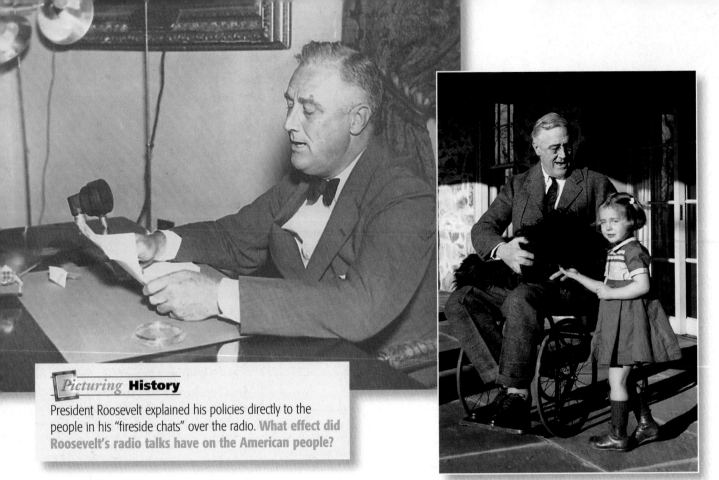

President Roosevelt explained his policies directly to the people in his "fireside chats" over the radio. **What effect did Roosevelt's radio talks have on the American people?**

Franklin Roosevelt, who was paralyzed by polio as a young man, is shown with Ruth Bie, the daughter of the caretaker at FDR's estate.

When Roosevelt learned that he had been nominated, he flew to Chicago to deliver the first acceptance speech ever made at a convention. He told the Democrats—and the nation—"I pledge you, I pledge myself, to a new deal for the American people."

As the Republicans and Democrats held their conventions in 1932, the Depression grew worse. The Republicans met in Chicago and nominated President Hoover for reelection. With the country's economy in trouble, Hoover's chances for winning reelection looked poor.

Early Years of Promise

Franklin D. Roosevelt, a distant cousin of former president Theodore Roosevelt, came from a wealthy family. Ambitious and charming, FDR decided on a career in politics. In 1905 he married Theodore Roosevelt's niece, **Eleanor Roosevelt,** and she became a tireless partner in his public life.

FDR's political career began with his election to the New York state senate in 1910. In 1913 he became assistant secretary of the navy, and in 1920 the Democrats chose him as their candidate

for vice president. The Democrats lost the election to Warren G. Harding, but Franklin Roosevelt's political future seemed bright.

Then in 1921 polio struck Roosevelt, paralyzing both his legs. Yet FDR's will remained strong. "Once I spent two years lying in bed trying to move my big toe," he said later. "After that, anything else seems easy."

Return to Politics

After a few years, FDR decided to return to politics. He never publicly mentioned his paralyzed legs, and he asked journalists not to photograph his leg braces or wheelchair. Elected governor of New York in 1928 and reelected in 1930, Roosevelt earned a national reputation as a reformer. He drew on the advice of a group of progressive lawyers, economists, and social workers—known as the **Brain Trust**—to develop relief programs for the state. When he decided to run for president, he counted on the Brain Trust to help him guide the nation to recovery.

During the 1932 campaign, Roosevelt declared that "the country needs and . . . demands bold, persistent experimentation." He also spoke of trying to help "the forgotten man at the bottom of the economic pyramid."

Reading Check **Identifying** Who were the Republican and Democratic candidates for president in 1932?

FDR Takes Charge

The American people were charmed by Roosevelt's confidence and his promise of action. On November 8, they went to the polls and elected Roosevelt in a landslide. He captured all but six states and received 472 of the 531 electoral votes. Democrats won important victories in Congress, also. People clearly wanted a change.

In the months before Roosevelt took office, the economy worsened. Protests in some cities erupted into violence. Meanwhile the banking system was collapsing. As more people rushed to withdraw their deposits, more and more banks went out of business. People became desperately afraid.

At his inauguration on March 4, 1933, Roosevelt told the nation that "the only thing we have to fear is fear itself—nameless, unreasoning, unjustified terror." He reassured people and pointed out that the "greatest primary task is to put people to work." He also promised immediate action on the banking crisis.

Restoring Confidence in Banks

Two days after the inauguration, Roosevelt ordered all banks closed for four days. He also called Congress to a special session, at which he presented the administration's plan for handling the banking problem. About seven hours later, Congress had passed and Roosevelt had signed the **Emergency Banking Relief Act.** The act proposed a wide range of presidential powers over banking and set up a system by which banks would open again or be reorganized. By mid-March half of the nation's banks had reopened.

Flood victims stand in line waiting for food and clothing. They are a sharp contrast to the happy family on the billboard.

At the end of his first week in office, FDR assured Americans in a radio broadcast "that it is safer to keep your money in a reopened bank than under the mattress." The next day deposits far exceeded withdrawals. The banking crisis had ended.

The president's radio talk was the first of many. He called these informal talks **fireside chats** because he sat next to a fireplace in the White House as he spoke. These fireside chats helped FDR gain the public's confidence.

The Hundred Days

After solving the banking crisis, President Roosevelt quickly tackled other areas of national concern. He sent Congress a stack of proposals for new programs to deal with the nation's economic problems. In all Roosevelt sent 15 proposals to Congress, and Congress approved every one of them.

Lasting about three months, the special session of Congress that Roosevelt called to launch his programs came to be called the Hundred Days. It was an amazingly productive time. Optimism swept through the capital. Journalist Thomas Stokes recalled, "The gloom, the tenseness, the fear of the closing months of the Hoover administration had vanished."

✓ Reading Check **Identifying** What law set up a plan to reorganize the nation's banks?

The New Deal

First New Deal Program	Initials	Begun	Purpose
Civilian Conservation Corps	CCC	1933	Provided jobs for young men to plant trees and build bridges
Tennessee Valley Authority	TVA	1933	Built dams to provide cheap electric power to seven Southern states; set up schools and health centers
Federal Emergency Relief Administration	FERA	1933	Gave relief to unemployed and needy
Agricultural Adjustment Administration	AAA	1933	Paid farmers not to grow certain crops
National Recovery Administration	NRA	1933	Helped set standards for production, prices, and wages
Public Works Administration	PWA	1933	Built ports, schools, and aircraft carriers
Federal Deposit Insurance Corporation	FDIC	1933	Insured savings accounts in banks approved by the government
Second New Deal Program			
Rural Electrification Administration	REA	1935	Loaned money to extend electricity to rural areas
Works Progress Administration	WPA	1935	Employed men and women to build hospitals, schools, parks, and airports; employed artists, writers, and musicians
Social Security Act	SSA	1935	Set up a system of pensions for the elderly, unemployed, and people with disabilities
Farm Security Administration	FSA	1937	Lent money to sharecroppers; set up camps for migrant workers
Fair Labor Standards Act	FLSA	1938	Established minimum wages and maximum hours for all businesses engaged in interstate commerce

〰️ Chart Skills

Under the Roosevelt New Deal during the 1930s, the federal government assumed responsibility for the welfare of many citizens.

Analyzing Information Why did setting up the FDIC help all Americans?

The New Deal Takes Shape

The new laws that Congress passed during the Hundred Days—and in the months and years that followed—came to be called the New Deal. New Deal laws and regulations affected banking, the stock market, industry, agriculture, public works, relief for the poor, and conservation of resources. These laws changed the face of America dramatically.

Frances Perkins, Roosevelt's secretary of labor, later recalled those early, exciting days of the New Deal:

>❝In March 1933, the New Deal was not a plan. . . . It was a happy phrase [FDR] had coined during the campaign. . . . It made people feel better, and in that terrible period of depression they needed to feel better.❞

💲Economics
Jobs and Relief

Roosevelt gave high priority to creating jobs. He planned to help the unemployed with work relief programs, giving needy people government jobs. During his first month in office, FDR asked Congress to create the **Civilian Conservation Corps** (CCC). Over the next 10 years, the CCC employed about 3 million young men to work on projects that benefited the public, planting trees to reforest areas, building levees for flood control, and improving national parks.

Roosevelt made aid to the poor and suffering another priority. FDR established the **Federal Emergency Relief Administration** (FERA) to give money to the states for use in helping people in need. Roosevelt appointed **Harry Hopkins,** a New York social worker, to lead the FERA. Hopkins became one of FDR's closest advisers and got involved in several other New Deal programs.

Roosevelt did not forget agriculture. On May 12, Congress passed the **Agricultural Adjustment Act** (AAA). The act had two goals: to raise farm prices quickly and to control production so that farm prices would stay up over the long term.

In the AAA's first year, though, the supply of food outstripped demand. The AAA could raise prices only by paying farmers to destroy crops, milk, and livestock. To many it seemed shocking to throw food away when millions of people went hungry. The New Dealers claimed the action was necessary to bring prices up.

To control production and farm prices, the AAA paid farmers to leave some of their land uncultivated. If market prices of key farm products such as wheat and cotton fell below a certain level, the AAA would pay farmers subsidies—grants of money—to make up the difference. In the first three years of the New Deal, farmers' incomes rose by about 50 percent. The Supreme Court ruled that the AAA was unconstitutional in *United States* v. *Butler* (1936) for invading the reserved powers of the states.

Rebuilding a Region

One of the boldest programs launched during the Hundred Days was the **Tennessee Valley Authority** (TVA). The TVA aimed to control flooding, promote conservation and development, and bring electricity to rural areas along the **Tennessee River.** By building new dams and improving others, the TVA ended the region's disastrous floods. And with hydroelectric power generating affordable electricity, thousands of farms and homes in some Southern states were wired for electricity for the first time.

Some critics charged that funds for the TVA should be used to support programs nationwide. Power companies also attacked the program as unfair and communistic. When the spring rains came in 1937, however, the system worked—the dams prevented the Tennessee River from flooding. In the end, most observers agreed that the TVA was an example of successful social and economic planning.

Driller, Fort Loudon Dam, Tennessee

Helping Business and Labor

On the last day of the Hundred Days, Congress passed the **National Industrial Recovery Act** (NIRA), which Roosevelt called "the most important and far-reaching legislation" ever passed in the United States. The NIRA aimed to boost the economy by helping business regulate itself.

The NIRA created the **National Recovery Administration** (NRA), which encouraged businesses to set a minimum wage and abolish child labor. In addition the NRA tried to set up codes governing pricing and other practices for every industry. **Hugh Johnson,** a former general named to head the NRA, launched a campaign to promote the agency. Before long the agency's blue eagle symbol and slogan—"We Do Our Part"—appeared everywhere.

The Blue Eagle, symbol of the NRA

Another program that the NIRA launched was the **Public Works Administration** (PWA). Its goal was to stimulate the economy through the building of huge public works projects that needed large numbers of workers. The agency employed people to work on the construction of roads, shipyards, hospitals, city halls, and schools. Many PWA projects—such as New York City's Lincoln Tunnel and Kentucky's Fort Knox—still stand. The PWA spent its funds slowly, though, and did not have much immediate impact on unemployment.

To avoid future banking crises, Roosevelt called for reform of the nation's financial system. Congress established the **Federal Deposit Insurance Corporation** (FDIC) to insure bank deposits. The government guaranteed that money placed in a bank insured by the FDIC would not be lost if the bank failed.

Congress also passed a law regulating the sale of stocks and bonds and created the **Securities and Exchange Commission** (SEC). This 1934 law gave the SEC the power to punish dishonest stockbrokers and speculators.

Assessing the Early New Deal

The New Deal did not cure the nation's ills. The Depression dragged on, bringing continued hardship. Farmers continued to lose their land. Unemployment remained at high levels. Many people still struggled to survive and to make ends meet.

Yet the darkest days had passed. The panic of 1932 and 1933 had receded, and the flurry of activity from the nation's capital had restored some measure of confidence.

Reading Check **Describing** What were the goals of the Agricultural Adjustment Act?

SECTION 2 ASSESSMENT

Checking for Understanding

1. **Key Terms** Write sentences about the New Deal; use these vocabulary terms: Hundred Days, work relief, subsidy.
2. **Reviewing Facts** For what region did the Tennessee Valley Authority provide electricity?

Reviewing Themes

3. **Government and Democracy** Describe the actions that Roosevelt took to restore confidence in banks and in the stock exchange.

Critical Thinking

4. **Comparing** Compare Hoover's and Roosevelt's programs to combat the Depression.
5. **Organizing Information** Re-create the diagram below and list three New Deal programs that Roosevelt established to create jobs or aid society as a whole.

Analyzing Visuals

6. **Chart Skills** Examine the table on page 732. Which programs were set up primarily to help farmers and rural areas? What was the purpose of the TVA?

Interdisciplinary Activity

Government Create a table that lists the positive and negative aspects of the New Deal farm program. Summarize in a brief paragraph what conclusions you can draw from your table.

SECTION 3 Life During the Depression

Guide to Reading

Main Idea
The Depression was a difficult time for Americans because many faced unemployment and the loss of land and other property.

Key Terms
Dust Bowl, migrant worker

Reading Strategy
Classifying Information As you read the section, re-create the diagram below and describe how different groups of people coped with difficult times.

Effects of the Great Depression		
Hispanic Americans	Great Plains farmers	African Americans

Read to Learn
- how the Depression affected minority groups.
- what radical political movements gained influence.

Section Theme
Economic Factors The Depression made life difficult for all Americans, and many migrated to other regions hoping for a better life.

Preview of Events

◆1930   ◆1935   ◆1940

1932
Hattie Caraway is elected first woman senator

1934
Indian Reorganization Act is passed

1939
Gone With the Wind film is released

AN American Story

"They hung around street corners and in groups. . . . They felt despised, they were ashamed of themselves. They cringed, they comforted one another. They avoided home." With these words, a social worker described unemployed Pennsylvania coal miners. Their pain was echoed across America by countless men, women, and children whose hopes were being crushed by the Depression.

Soup kitchen

Hard Times in America

Not every worker lost a job during the Depression. Not every family needed aid. Most Americans, however, had to make do with less: less income, less food, and less security.

Some families survived the Depression by pulling together. Parents and children shared homes with grandparents or other relatives to save money. Although the birthrate had decreased, school enrollment actually increased; because fewer young people could find work, they remained in school.

The strain shattered other families, however. Nearly two million men—and a much smaller number of women—abandoned their homes. They took to the road, drifting to warm places such as Florida and California.

Women Go to Work

Many people thought that women should not hold jobs as long as men were unemployed. Despite such prejudices, desperation drove a large number of women into the workforce. Many families survived on a woman's income—even though American women earned less than men.

Women also worked harder at home to make ends meet. Instead of buying clothes or groceries, they sewed their own clothing, baked their own bread, and canned their own vegetables. Some women started home businesses such as laundries or boardinghouses.

The New Deal era opened doors for women in public life. President Roosevelt appointed the first woman ever to serve in the cabinet, **Frances Perkins.** He also named more than 100 other women to federal posts. One—Ellen Sullivan Woodward—started a program to give jobs to women. In 1932 **Hattie Caraway** of Arkansas became the first woman to be elected to the United States Senate.

The best-known woman in American public life was **Eleanor Roosevelt,** who often acted as her husband's "eyes and ears." She made many fact-finding trips for the president because polio had limited his mobility. Mrs. Roosevelt campaigned vigorously for women and minorities and other humanitarian concerns. She wrote a daily newspaper column and used her boundless energy to meet people all over the country.

✓ **Reading Check** **Identifying** Who was the first woman to serve in a president's cabinet? How many other women were appointed to federal posts at this time?

The Dust Bowl

To make matters worse, the southern Great Plains suffered an environmental disaster during the 1930s. Hardest hit were western Kansas and Oklahoma, northern Texas, and eastern Colorado and New Mexico—the region dubbed the **Dust Bowl.**

People In History

Charles Drew 1904–1950

African American Charles Drew was born and raised in the segregated city of Washington, D.C., and refused to let racial prejudice stop him. His early interests were in education, particularly in medicine, but he was also an outstanding athlete. He starred at Dunbar High School in football, baseball, basketball, and track and field.

He graduated from Amherst College in Massachusetts and earned his medical degree at Canada's McGill University. In the 1930s Drew conducted pioneering research on blood plasma, and he created the model for blood and plasma storage that is used by the Red Cross today. When the United States entered World War II, Drew was in charge of the military's blood plasma program.

Drew's research changed transfusion methods so that stored plasma could be given to soldiers wounded on the battlefield—a medical advance that saved many lives. Drew later resigned to protest the military's decision to maintain racially segregated blood banks.

⭐Geography

What Caused the Dust Bowl?

Using new technology such as tractors and disc plows, farmers had cleared millions of acres of sod for wheat farming. They did not realize that the roots of the grass had held the soil in place. When a severe drought struck in 1931, crops died and the soil dried out. Strong prairie winds simply blew the soil away.

Each storm stripped away more soil. One storm in 1934 carried about 300 million tons of soil, depositing some of it on ships 300 miles out in the Atlantic Ocean. The drought—and the storms—continued for years.

People called the storms "black blizzards." A Texas boy wrote:

> ❝These storms were like rolling black smoke. We had to keep the lights on all day. We went to school with headlights on, and with dust masks on.❞

Thousands of Dust Bowl farmers went bankrupt and had to give up their farms. About 400,000 farmers migrated to California and became migrant workers, moving from place to place to harvest fruits and vegetables. So many came from Oklahoma that people called them "Okies." One observer described their arrival:

> ❝They came in decrepit [broken-down], square-shouldered [cars] . . . that looked like relics of some antique culture . . . piled high with mattresses and cooking utensils and children, with suitcases, jugs and sacks strapped to the running boards.❞

✓ **Reading Check** **Explaining** Where did many families move to escape the Dust Bowl?

The Plight of Minorities

The Depression fell especially hard on the minority groups who were already on the lower rungs of the American economic ladder. These groups included African Americans, Native Americans, and Hispanic Americans.

Dorothea Lange photographed a homeless Oklahoma family during Dust Bowl days.

African Americans

In the South more than half of the African American population had no jobs. African Americans who lived and worked in Southern cities found their jobs taken by white people who had lost theirs. The collapse of farm prices crushed African American farmers.

Seeking more opportunity, about 400,000 African American men, women, and children migrated to Northern cities during the decade of the 1930s. These migrants did not fare much better there, however. The jobless rate for African Americans remained high.

African Americans did make some political gains during the Depression. President Roosevelt appointed a number of African Americans to federal posts. He had a group of advisers, known as the Black Cabinet, that included Robert Weaver, a college professor, and **Ralph Bunche,** who worked for the State Department. **Mary McLeod Bethune,** who established Bethune-Cookman College in Florida, also served as an adviser.

African Americans continued to fight against prejudice. In 1939 opera singer Marian Anderson was denied permission to sing in Constitution Hall because she was black. Mrs. Roosevelt helped arrange for Anderson to give a historic concert at the Lincoln Memorial.

What *Life* Was Like...

Teen Entertainment

For a teenager in the 1930s, a dime would buy a round trip fare on a streetcar, or two apples from a corner vendor, or a malt at the drugstore fountain, or an afternoon at the movies.

Thrills and Chills
Young people flocked to the movies to see cartoons and monsters.

Escape
Radio programs, comics like *Little Orphan Annie* (right), and new novelty games provided an escape from the harsh reality of the Great Depression.

Native Americans

The 1930s did bring some benefits to Native Americans. The new head of the Bureau of Indian Affairs, **John Collier,** introduced a set of reforms known as the Indian New Deal.

Collier halted the sale of reservation land, got jobs for 77,000 Native Americans in the Civilian Conservation Corps, and obtained Public Works Administration funds to build new reservation schools. Most important, he pushed Congress to pass the **Indian Reorganization Act** of 1934. This law restored traditional tribal government and provided money for land purchases to enlarge some reservations.

Hispanic Americans

At the beginning of the 1930s, about two million people of Hispanic descent lived in the United States, mostly in California and the Southwest. Many had emigrated from Mexico. They worked as farmers, migrant workers, and laborers. As the Great Depression deepened, resentment against Mexican Americans grew. Many lost their jobs. Politicians and labor unions demanded that Mexican Americans be forced to leave the United States.

The government encouraged Mexican immigrants to return to Mexico. Authorities gave them one-way train tickets to Mexico or simply rounded them up and shipped them south across the border. More than 500,000 Mexican Americans left the United States during the early years of the Depression, often involuntarily.

Reading Check **Explaining** What was the purpose of the Indian Reorganization Act?

Radical Political Movements

Hard times helped **radical** political groups gain ground in the United States during the 1930s. Radical groups advocate extreme and immediate change. Socialists and Communists viewed the Depression not as a temporary economic problem but as the death of a failed system. They proposed sweeping changes.

Communism attracted workers, minority-rights activists, and intellectuals with promises to end economic and racial injustice. Although both socialism and communism had significant influence, neither became a major political force in the United States.

Another political development that caught the attention of many Americans was the rise of **fascists** in Germany and Italy. Fascism is a political philosophy that holds the individual second to the nation and advocates government by dictatorship. In 1936 the **Spanish Civil War** began. Germany and Italy supported fascists who were trying to take over the Spanish government. Although the United States remained neutral, more than 3,000 Americans went to Spain to fight the fascists.

Reading Check **Explaining** What is fascism?

Entertainment and the Arts

The Depression produced two separate trends in entertainment and the arts. One was escapism—light or romantic entertainment that helped people forget about their problems. The other was social criticism—portraits of the injustice and suffering of Depression America.

Radio became enormously popular during the 1930s. Daytime dramas sponsored by laundry detergents earned the nickname "soap operas." Adventure programs such as *Dick Tracy, The Lone Ranger,* and *Superman* had millions of listeners, as did variety shows featuring comedians George Burns, Gracie Allen, and Jack Benny.

At the Movies

Every week about 85 million people went to movie theaters, usually to escape their cares and worries. Some movies did explore serious topics. For example, *The Grapes of Wrath* (1940) was a screen version of John Steinbeck's powerful novel about farm families fleeing the Dust Bowl. The 1939 film of Margaret Mitchell's novel, *Gone With the Wind*, set in the Civil War era, also portrayed people coping with hard times.

Images of the Times

Many writers and painters portrayed the grim realities of Depression life. Richard Wright's novel *Native Son* told the story of an African American man growing up in Chicago. Writer James Agee and photographer Walker Evans depicted poor Southern farm families in *Let Us Now Praise Famous Men*.

Photographer Margaret Bourke-White also recorded the plight of American farmers, and Dorothea Lange took gripping photographs of migrant workers. Painters such as Grant Wood and Thomas Hart Benton showed ordinary people confronting the hardships of Depression life.

Reading Check **Analyzing** Would you consider *Gone With the Wind* social criticism or escapism? Explain.

SECTION 3 ASSESSMENT

Checking for Understanding

1. **Key Terms** Define Dust Bowl and migrant worker.
2. **Reviewing Facts** Describe three of the benefits that Native Americans received from the Indian New Deal including the Indian Reorganization Act.

Reviewing Themes

3. **Economic Factors** Why did many African Americans migrate from the South to the North during the 1930s?

Critical Thinking

4. **Determining Cause and Effect** Why did radical political movements gain popularity during the 1930s?
5. **Classifying Information** Re-create the diagram below and list the accomplishments of three individuals discussed in Section 3.

Individual	Accomplishments
1.	
2.	
3.	

Analyzing Visuals

6. **Picturing History** Look at the photograph by Dorothea Lange on page 737. Write a paragraph in which you describe why the family is leaving its home and where they are going.

Interdisciplinary Activity

Descriptive Writing Think of a modern story idea that would be considered social criticism. Using the outline of the story, write a short scene in which the characters point out a flaw in their society.

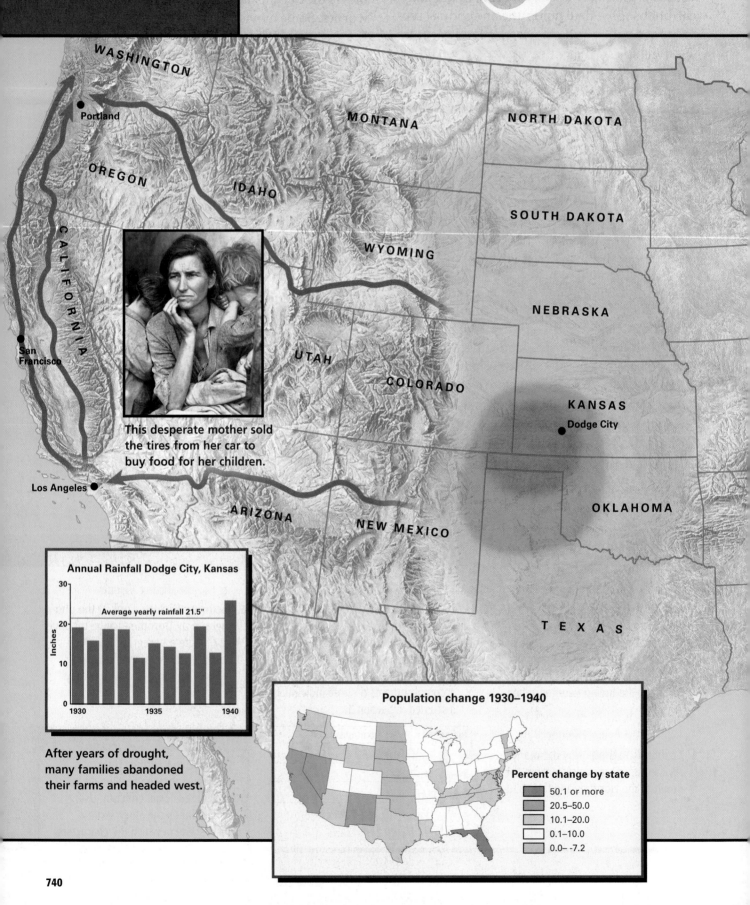

GEOGRAPHY & HISTORY

WASHINGTON

Portland

OREGON

IDAHO

MONTANA

NORTH DAKOTA

SOUTH DAKOTA

WYOMING

C A L I F O R N I A

San Francisco

UTAH

COLORADO

NEBRASKA

KANSAS

Dodge City

This desperate mother sold the tires from her car to buy food for her children.

Los Angeles

ARIZONA

NEW MEXICO

OKLAHOMA

T E X A S

Annual Rainfall Dodge City, Kansas

Average yearly rainfall 21.5"

Inches

30

20

10

0

1930   1935   1940

After years of drought, many families abandoned their farms and headed west.

Population change 1930–1940

Percent change by state

50.1 or more
20.5–50.0
10.1–20.0
0.1–10.0
0.0– -7.2

DUST BOWL

DURING THE 1930s, dust storms ravaged the Great Plains. This area was labeled the "Dust Bowl." Dust storms, dubbed "dusters" or "black blizzards" swept across the region darkening the sky and burying fences, fields, and even houses and barns.

LIVING ON THE PLAINS

Settlers had flocked to the plains and plowed up the grasses to plant wheat and other crops. Repeated deep plowing destroyed the protective root layer of the tough grasses and sod that held moisture and anchored the soil.

DARK CLOUDS

In the early 1930s a severe drought struck the region and the wind began to blow the fine-grained soil away. The drought lasted for years and caused many dust storms. Sometimes the storms lasted for weeks. High winds blew topsoil all the way to the Atlantic Ocean. Desperate farmers watched their crops shrivel and blow away.

HEADING WEST

Many families lost their jobs and their farms. They finally crammed their belongings into their old jalopies and headed west. During the 1930s half a million migrants traveled west searching for jobs. The migrants, many of them living out of their cars, would travel from farm to farm hoping to find work picking fruit, vegetables, or cotton.

RELIEF

New Deal programs finally brought relief to victims of the Dust Bowl. In addition to helping migrants, the federal government taught farmers in the Dust Bowl new conservation measures to preserve their land. Rains eventually fell, but true prosperity did not return to America until factories geared up production for World War II.

Dust storm in Hugoton, Kansas

Dust Bowl

← Migration route

Damage

Severe damage

Most severe damage

0   200 miles

0   200 kilometers

These "Dust Bowl refugees" were stranded on the highway when their truck broke down in New Mexico.

LEARNING *from* GEOGRAPHY

1. Which states suffered the most severe damage?

2. What states grew by more than 20 percent in population during 1930s? Why do you think these states experienced the greatest growth?

SECTION 4 Effects of the New Deal

Guide to Reading

Main Idea

As the Great Depression continued and the administration became the target of increasing criticism, Roosevelt launched the Second New Deal.

Key Terms

pension, Second New Deal, Social Security Act, unemployment insurance

Reading Strategy

Classifying Information As you read the section, re-create the diagram below and describe the aims of the programs and laws listed.

Program	Aims
Works Progress Administration	
Social Security Act	
Fair Labor Standards Act	

Read to Learn

- why people criticized Roosevelt and the New Deal.
- how the Second New Deal created new economic and social roles for government.

Section Theme

Government and Democracy Roosevelt continued to launch new programs to improve the economy.

Preview of Events

♦1934	♦1935	♦1936	♦1937

1935
FDR launches the Second New Deal

1936
FDR wins reelection

1937
Sit-down strike occurs in Flint, Michigan

Anti-New Deal button

AN American Story

Support for Franklin D. Roosevelt's efforts to end the Great Depression was far from unanimous. Many wealthy and conservative people attacked the president's "radical" policies. A political cartoon of the 1930s showed a boy writing the word *ROOSEVELT* on the sidewalk in front of his rich family's house. His sister calls out, "Mother, Wilfred wrote a bad word!"

New Deal Opponents

In the early days of his presidency, FDR counted on big business to support his efforts to revive the economy. The National Recovery Administration, for example, invited participation from the business community. In general, however, the business world opposed the New Deal.

Business leaders accused Roosevelt of spending too much government money and of trying to destroy free enterprise. In 1934 some of these conservative critics formed the Liberty League to "defend and uphold the Constitution." The League wanted government to let business alone and play a less active role in the economy. Although the Liberty League did not win widespread support, its existence convinced FDR that big business was against him.

Demanding More Reform

At the same time, Roosevelt drew fire from liberal critics. They wanted a more active government. Three men gained wide popularity with schemes to help the average American.

One of Roosevelt's critics was Father **Charles Coughlin,** a Detroit priest who reached millions of listeners through his weekly radio program. Coughlin, once a Roosevelt supporter, attacked FDR for not dealing firmly enough with big business, calling him "Franklin Double-Crossing Roosevelt." Coughlin used his radio show to attack bankers, Jews, Communists, and labor unions, as well as the New Deal. In time Coughlin lost support because of his extreme views.

Francis Townsend, a California doctor, rose to fame with his plan for a monthly pension, or payment, for older people. Older workers who quit their jobs, making them available to younger people, would receive a pension. Townsend's plan received little support from Congress. It did, however, force many Americans to think about the plight of the elderly poor and the needs of retired people.

Of greatest concern to Roosevelt, however, was Senator **Huey Long** of Louisiana. When he was governor of Louisiana, Long had won wide support with public works projects and attacks on big businesses.

In 1932 Long supported FDR, but within a year, the two men had split. One of Long's major complaints against the president was that he had not taken steps to redistribute wealth in the United States. By 1934 Long had developed his own plan for doing so. His "Share Our Wealth Plan" called for taxing the rich heavily, then using that money to give every American a home and $2,500 a year. As his appeal spread, Long became a threat to Roosevelt. Polls indicated that in 1936 he might receive as many as four million votes on a third-party ticket. But in 1935 he was assassinated.

✓ **Reading Check** **Describing** What group was Townsend's pension plan designed to help?

Economics
The Second New Deal

By the mid-1930s the economy had improved slightly, but the Depression was far from over. FDR took bolder steps.

FDR's critics: Huey Long (left) and Father Coughlin (right)

To bring in more government funds, Roosevelt pushed Congress to pass the **Revenue Act** of 1935. The act raised taxes on wealthy people and corporations. Critics accused him of "soaking the rich" to pay for his programs, but many Americans cheered.

In 1935 President Roosevelt launched a new set of programs and reforms, often called the Second New Deal. The laws passed at this time changed American life even more than the Hundred Days had done.

Creating Jobs

Millions of people—20 percent of the workforce—were still unemployed in 1935. In April Congress created the **Works Progress Administration** (WPA) to give people jobs and help the country. Led by Harry Hopkins, the WPA kept about two million people employed between 1935 and 1941. WPA workers built or repaired about 800 airports, 125,000 public buildings, 75,000 bridges, and 650,000 miles of roads.

The WPA also found work for unemployed writers, artists, and musicians. WPA painters decorated the new public buildings with murals. Writers and photographers documented life throughout America. The writers produced *Life in America,* 150 volumes that recorded folktales and songs, African American narratives, and Native American traditions.

Help for Those in Need

Before the Second New Deal, America was the only advanced industrial nation without a national government program to help the needy. In August 1935 Congress passed the Social Security Act.

The Social Security Act created a tax on workers and employers. That money provided monthly pensions for retired people. Another tax, on employers alone, funded unemployment insurance payments to people who lost their jobs. In addition, Social Security helped people with disabilities, the elderly poor, and children of parents who could not support them.

With the Social Security Act, the federal government took responsibility for the welfare of all citizens. It launched the American welfare system.

Reading Check Explaining How did the government raise money for Social Security?

The Labor Movement

Labor unions grew stronger as workers battled the Depression. In 1937 workers at the General Motors plant in **Flint, Michigan,** used a new technique—the sit-down strike. Strikers continuously occupied the plant and refused to work until management agreed to negotiate with them about their demands. For 44 days families

Picturing **History**

The glass sign was hand-painted by a member of the United Mine Workers Union. **How did workers benefit from the New Deal?**

ALL I SAID WAS "GIMME SIX MORE JUSTICES!"

and friends of the Flint strikers brought them food. Finally, the strikers won the right to organize their union.

The most influential labor leader during the 1930s was **John L. Lewis,** head of the United Mine Workers. To increase labor's power, Lewis strived to unite workers in every industry in a single union. Most unions in the American Federation of Labor (AFL) represented only skilled workers. Lewis called for industrial unions to include unskilled workers—the largest group in the labor force.

In 1935 Lewis formed a new union called the **Congress of Industrial Organizations** (CIO), which helped create industrial unions. By 1938 the CIO had four million members, including large numbers of women and African Americans.

Unions found support in the New Deal. The 1935 **National Labor Relations Act**—also called the **Wagner Act** after its sponsor, Senator Robert Wagner of New York—guaranteed workers the right to form unions to bargain collectively with employers. The act also created the National Labor Relations Board to enforce its provisions. In 1938 Congress passed the **Fair Labor Standards Act** (FLSA), which banned child labor and set a minimum wage of 40 cents an hour. The FLSA and the Wagner Act form the basis of American labor rights today.

Reading Check **Comparing** How did the CIO differ from the AFL?

The Supreme Court

Those who opposed the New Deal challenged many of its laws in the courts, claiming that they were unconstitutional. Several important cases reached the Supreme Court.

In May 1935, the Supreme Court ruled that the National Industrial Recovery Act was unconstitutional. In the opinion of the Court, Congress had exceeded its lawful power to regulate interstate commerce. In January 1936, the Supreme Court struck down the Agricultural Adjustment Act. Cases were also pending against the Wagner Act, the Social Security Act, and the Tennessee Valley Authority. It seemed as though the Supreme Court might destroy the New Deal.

A Second Term

The presidential campaign of 1936 was based on a single issue: Did the American people support FDR and the New Deal?

To run against Roosevelt, the Republicans nominated **Alfred M. Landon,** governor of Kansas. Landon attracted dissatisfied Democrats as well as Republicans. FDR campaigned as the champion of the average American. He denounced big business and the rich, who "are unanimous in their hate for me—and I welcome their hatred."

On Election Day FDR received 61 percent of the popular vote, the biggest landslide in an American presidential election to that time. Roosevelt's support came from progressives and liberals, the poor and unemployed, urban workers, and African Americans. These groups would form the core of the Democratic Party for decades to come.

Roosevelt's "Court-Packing" Plan

Soon after his reelection, FDR took action to prevent the Supreme Court from undoing the New Deal. He asked Congress to increase the number of justices on the Court from 9 to 15, saying that the 9 justices were overworked and needed additional help. FDR would appoint the 6 new justices—selecting, of course, justices who would uphold the New Deal.

The proposal aroused bitter opposition. Critics accused the president of trying to "pack" the Court and ruin the system of checks and balances set up in the Constitution. The issue died when the Court ruled in favor of the Wagner Act and the Social Security Act. The New Deal was no longer in serious danger from the Court. The unpopularity of the court-packing plan, however, cost Roosevelt a great deal of support and triggered a split in the Democratic Party.

The Roosevelt Recession

By the summer of 1937, the national income had nearly returned to its 1929 level. Believing that the Depression was finally over, Roosevelt tried to reduce the government's debt by cutting spending on relief and job programs.

The economy faltered immediately. Farm prices dropped. Four million people lost their jobs. Times nearly as hard as 1932–1933 returned. The new economic downturn, known to some as the **Roosevelt Recession,** lasted into 1938. Roosevelt helped to reverse it with a flood of government spending on public works.

The End of the New Deal

The court-packing fight and the Roosevelt Recession cost FDR support in Congress. The economy had not fully recovered, in spite of the wide-ranging New Deal programs. As the 1930s drew to a close, however, world events caused Americans to turn their attention from domestic to foreign affairs. Dangerous forces were on the rise in Asia and Europe.

Reading Check **Explaining** Why was Roosevelt's plan to change the Supreme Court criticized?

SECTION 4 ASSESSMENT

Checking for Understanding

1. **Key Terms** Write sentences about the Second New Deal; use these vocabulary terms: pension, Social Security Act, unemployment insurance.

2. **Reviewing Facts** Summarize the economic plan of Huey Long.

Reviewing Themes

3. **Government and Democracy** What was the aim of Social Security and exactly whom did it help?

Critical Thinking

4. **Making Generalizations** Why did many business leaders oppose Roosevelt's New Deal?

5. **Determining Cause and Effect** Why did Roosevelt propose to change the number of justices on the Supreme Court? Re-create the diagram below and list one cause and two effects of FDR's proposal.

Analyzing Visuals

6. **Political Cartoons** Review the cartoon "Packing the Court" on page 745. Does the cartoon show support for or opposition to the plan? How can you tell?

Interdisciplinary Activity

Government Research the effect of the New Deal in your community. Find out if the federal government in the 1930s supported any local projects in conservation, construction, or the arts.

Social Studies SKILLBUILDER

Analyzing News Media

Why Learn This Skill?

Every citizen needs to be aware of current issues and events to make good decisions when exercising citizenship rights.

Learning the Skill

To get an accurate profile of current events, you must learn to think critically about the news. The steps below will help you think critically.

- First, think about the source of the news story. Reports that reveal sources are more reliable than those that do not. If you know the sources, you can evaluate them. Can all facts be verified?
- Many news stories also interpret events. Such analyses may reflect a reporter's biases. Look for biases as you read or listen to news stories.
- Ask yourself whether the news is even-handed and thorough. Is it reported on the scene or secondhand? Does it represent both sides of an issue? The more sources cited for a fact, the more reliable it usually is.

Practicing the Skill

On this page is an excerpt from the New York Times *newspaper of February 6, 1937. Read the excerpt; then answer the following questions.*

① What point is the article trying to make?

② Is the article reporting something on the scene or secondhand?

③ Does the article reflect bias or strong opinion about the news item?

④ Is only one side of the issue presented? Explain.

AIM TO PACK COURT, DECLARES HOOVER

President Roosevelt's message to Congress asking for authority to appoint new Federal judges whenever existing ones were over 70 years old was characterized last night by Herbert Hoover, his predecessor in the White House, as a proposal for "packing" the Supreme Court to get through New Deal measures. . . .

"The Supreme Court has proved many of the New Deal proposals as unconstitutional. Instead of the ample alternatives of the Constitution by which these proposals could be submitted to the people through constitutional amendment, it is now proposed to make changes by 'packing' the Supreme Court. It has the implication of subordination of the court to the personal power of the Executive."

Applying the Skill

Analyzing News Media Think of an issue in your community on which public opinion is divided. Read newspaper features and editorials about the issue and listen to television reports. Can you identify biases? Which reports more fairly represent the issue and the solutions? Which reports are the most reliable?

 Glencoe's **Skillbuilder Interactive Workbook CD-ROM, Level 1,** provides instruction and practice in key social studies skills.

Chapter Summary

The Depression and FDR

Causes

- Income gap between rich and poor grows
- High tariffs and war debts
- Overuse of credit to make purchases
- Industry and agriculture supply exceeds demand
- Sales lag
- International market falters
- Stock market crash; financial panic

The Great Depression

Effects

- Millions lose jobs, poverty is widespread
- Businesses and banks close
- Depression spreads to other countries

- Roosevelt wins presidency
- New Deal legislation enacted
- Despite periods of economic upturn, the Depression remains

Reviewing Key Terms

On a sheet of paper, use at least six of the following terms to write a paragraph on the Great Depression or the New Deal.

1. default, relief, public works, Hundred Days, New Deal, Dust Bowl, migrant worker, pension, Social Security Act, subsidy, unemployment insurance

Reviewing Key Facts

2. What did the Bonus Army want the government to do?
3. What was the New Deal?
4. How did the CCC benefit the unemployed as well as the nation?
5. In what region was the Dust Bowl centered?
6. Summarize the advances made by African Americans and women during the Great Depression.
7. What was the purpose of the Social Security Act?
8. Describe two laws passed during the Second New Deal that helped workers and unions.

Critical Thinking

9. **Economic Factors** How did the trend of buying on credit in the 1920s affect banks during the Depression?
10. **Determining Cause and Effect** How did new technology help cause the Dust Bowl disaster?
11. **Reviewing Themes: Government and Democracy** Re-create the diagram below and list two ways the federal government changed during Roosevelt's administration.

Changing role of government

Practicing Skills

12. **Analyzing News Media** Find two articles, one in a current newspaper and the other in a newsmagazine, on a topic involving the economy. Compare the articles. Did either of the articles show any biases? List any unsupported claims.

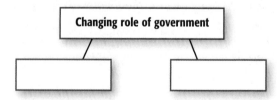

Geography and History Activity

Study the map below and answer these questions.

Self-Check Quiz
Visit **taj.glencoe.com** and click on **Chapter 25—
Self-Check Quizzes** to prepare for the chapter test.

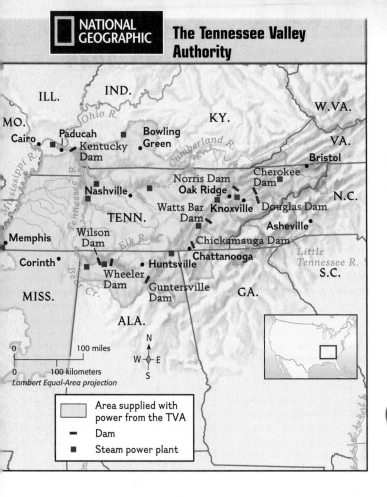

NATIONAL GEOGRAPHIC

The Tennessee Valley Authority

Legend:
- ☐ Area supplied with power from the TVA
- — Dam
- ■ Steam power plant

100 miles
100 kilometers
Lambert Equal-Area projection

13. Place What physical feature made Tennessee particularly suited for the Tennessee Valley Authority project?

14. Region Which states were supplied with power from the TVA?

15. Location On the map, what dams are located along the Tennessee River?

Economic Activity

16. Use the electronic card catalog at your school or community library to find information about the current Social Security Administration and its activities. Prepare a list of benefits and services that this organization provides to Americans today.

Citizenship Cooperative Activity

17. Research Work with members of your group to prepare a photo essay to document the hardships of the Depression. Photocopy some of the photos and display them in an interesting way on a sheet of cardboard. Write captions for each photo, provide photo credits, and write a title for your essay. Then, with the rest of the class, create a walk-through gallery to display all the photo essays.

Alternative Assessment

18. Portfolio Writing Activity Both Eleanor and Franklin Roosevelt received many letters from the public during the Depression asking for jobs, money, food, and clothing. Write a letter from either of the Roosevelts responding to a plea for help. Explain in your letter what you can or cannot do for this person. Use what you have learned about the Roosevelts' personalities to make your letters realistic.

Standardized Test Practice

Directions: Choose the *best* answer to the following question.

All of the following programs were created by Roosevelt in the First New Deal EXCEPT the

A Agricultural Adjustment Act (AAA).

B Civilian Conservation Corps (CCC).

C Fair Labor Standards Act (FLSA).

D Tennessee Valley Authority (TVA).

Test-Taking Tip.

Be careful when you see the word EXCEPT in a question. Read carefully all the answer choices and choose the one that *doesn't* fit with the question. Many times there are specific words in the question that tell you something specific. Here, the question asks about the First New Deal, not the Second New Deal.

CHAPTER 26

World War II

1939–1945

Why It Matters

World War II, the most destructive war in history, resulted in the deaths of more than 40 million people. More than half of the deaths were civilians, including about six million Jews and many others that were killed in the Holocaust. At the end of the war, the United States emerged as the strongest nation in the world and the possessor of a powerful weapon—the atomic bomb.

The Impact Today

World War II marked the beginning of the nation's role as a superpower. The war also transformed the American economy into an enormously productive and enduringly prosperous economy.

The American Journey *Video* *The chapter 26 video, "War on the Home Front," discusses what life was like in America during World War II.*

1942
- Japanese Americans sent to internment camps
- U.S. joins Allies in World War II

1940
- Selective Training and Service Act passed

1941
- U.S. enters the war
- Lend-Lease Act passed

F. Roosevelt
1933–1945

United States
PRESIDENTS

1940 *1941* *1942*

World

1939
- Germany seizes Czechoslovakia

1940
- German troops occupy Paris
- Germany bombs Britain

1941
- Germany attacks the Soviet Union

Mission Over Normandy by **William S. Phillips** During World War II, the Army Air Corps fought enemy aircraft, bombed targets, and transported soldiers.

FOLDABLES™
Study Organizer

Sequencing Events Study Foldable Make this foldable to describe and sequence the events of World War II.

Step 1 Collect 3 sheets of paper and place them about 1 inch apart.

> Keep the edges straight.

Step 2 Fold up the bottom edges of the paper to form 6 tabs.

> This makes all tabs the same size.

Step 3 When all the tabs are the same size, fold the paper to hold the tabs in place and staple the sheets together. Turn the paper and label each tab as shown.

World War II
Road to War
War Begins
On the Home Front
War in Europe and Africa
War in the Pacific

> Staple together along the fold.

Reading and Writing As you read the chapter, identify, sequence, and briefly describe the key events that belong under each heading on your foldable. Write information under each tab.

1945
• U.S. drops atomic bombs on Hiroshima and Nagasaki

1943   *1944*   *1945*

1944
• D-Day: Allies land in Normandy

1945
• Concentration camps found where Nazis killed millions
• World War II ends

HISTORY
Online

Chapter Overview
Visit taj.glencoe.com and click on **Chapter 26— Chapter Overviews** to preview chapter information.

Guide to Reading

Main Idea
As dictators threatened world peace, the United States tried to follow a policy of neutrality.

Key Terms
dictator, fascism, anti-Semitism, totalitarian, appeasement

Reading Strategy
Organizing Information As you read Section 1, re-create the diagram below and list three dictators and the countries they ruled in the 1920s and 1930s.

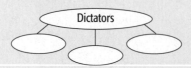

Dictators

Read to Learn
- why dictators came to power around the world.
- what actions led to the outbreak of World War II.

Section Theme
Global Connections Europe tried to avoid war by a policy of appeasement.

Preview of Events

♦*1930*   ♦*1935*   ♦*1940*

1931
Japan invades Manchuria

1933
Hitler becomes chancellor of Germany

1935
Italian forces invade Ethiopia

1939
Germany seizes Czechoslovakia

AN
American Story

Many people underestimated Adolf Hitler's influence, but not American journalist William Shirer. He described a rally for Hitler at Nuremberg in September 1934: "Like a Roman emperor Hitler rode into this medieval town. . . . The streets, hardly wider than alleys, are a sea of brown and black uniforms. . . . [W]hen Hitler finally appeared on the balcony for a moment . . . [people] looked up at him as if he were a Messiah, their faces transformed into something positively inhuman." The passion of the Nazis shocked Shirer, and soon it would shock the rest of the world.

Hitler at rally

The Rise of Dictators

In the late 1920s, Adolf Hitler achieved wide popularity in Germany. In his book *Mein Kampf* (My Struggle), Hitler set forth his political views.

❝He who wants to live must fight, and he who does not want to fight in this world, where eternal struggle is the law of life, has no right to exist.❞

When Hitler became the leader of Germany, he put his strong words into action. Hitler was among other ruthless leaders to rise to power in the 1920s and 1930s by taking advantage of people's anger and suffering. Some Europeans resented the terms of the Treaty of Versailles, signed in 1919, which ended World War I. When a worldwide economic depression hit in the 1930s, frustration and fear added to this anger.

Hitler and other leaders promised a better life. They described a glorious future to people humiliated by losing a war. Once they gained political power, these men became dictators—leaders who control their nations by force.

Italy

Benito Mussolini rose to power by appealing to the resentment of many Italians who felt they had not won enough in the Versailles treaty. Mussolini made fascism—extreme nationalism and racism—popular in Italy. By 1922 his **Fascist Party** had gained enough strength to force the king of Italy to declare Mussolini the head of the government. Within a few years, Mussolini had banned all political parties except his Fascist Party.

Known as *Il Duce* (the leader), Mussolini quickly put an end to democratic rule in Italy. Civil liberties and the free press ceased to exist. Boys and girls of all ages were enrolled in military organizations that taught them loyalty to the new government. Mussolini built up Italy's military and vowed to recapture the glory of the ancient Romans.

In 1935 Mussolini sent Italian forces to invade the African nation of **Ethiopia,** which it annexed—took over as its own territory. Ethiopian emperor Haile Selassie appealed to the League of Nations for help: "God and history will remember your judgment. It is us today. It will be you tomorrow." The League responded by banning trade in weapons and certain other materials with Italy, but it lacked the power to enforce the ban. Italy withdrew from the League and continued its aggressive policies, attacking and annexing its neighbor Albania in 1939.

Analyzing *Political Cartoons*

This American cartoon of Mussolini portrays him with a short body, small hands, a huge belly, and fear in his eyes. Mussolini's arm is raised in a familiar fascist salute. **What is the artist saying about Mussolini and fascism?**

Germany

The Great Depression had hit Germany extremely hard. Millions of people had lost their jobs, and its economy teetered on the edge of collapse. Germans rallied around Adolf Hitler, a shrewd politician and a spellbinding speaker. Hitler gained popularity by exploiting people's concern about unchecked inflation and severe unemployment. Hitler also played upon bitterness over the Versailles treaty. The treaty had forced Germany to give up some of its territory and to make heavy payments to the victors.

In 1921 Hitler became chairman of the National Socialist German Workers' Party, or the **Nazi Party.** Openly racist, Hitler and the Nazis portrayed the German people as superior to all others. They directed much of their anger against Jews, whom Hitler blamed for Germany's problems. His extreme anti-Semitism—hatred of the Jews—would later lead to unspeakable horrors.

Soon after he became chancellor, or chief minister, of Germany in 1933, Hitler ended all democracy and established totalitarian rule. In a

TWO VIEWPOINTS

Should We Intervene or Remain Neutral?

As Adolf Hitler's German army conquered parts of Europe, Americans debated their involvement. Should the United States stand back while the aggression continued and avoid the horrors of a war that was not its war? Or, should it help allies like Great Britain put an end to the destructive ambitions of Nazi Germany?

Petition Sent From the Fight for Freedom National Offices, 1940

We are not neutral. As freedom-loving citizens of the United States, we recognize that our liberty, that democracy everywhere will be ended unless the menace [threat] of Hitler is smashed. We, therefore, petition the Congress of the United States TO REPEAL OUR SUICIDAL, HYPOCRITICAL AND DANGEROUS NEUTRALITY ACT, to remove the prohibition against arming our merchant ships, and dissolve the ban which prevents vessels flying the American flag from sailing the seven seas. American policy has traditionally been that of freedom of the seas. Our Congress must reassert and uphold that right. Our Congress has pledged our resources to those nations fighting Axis aggression, and must reinforce that pledge by guaranteeing that our goods arrive at their destination in the hands of our allies.

Robert M. Hutchins, President of the University of Chicago, January 23, 1941

How can the United States better serve suffering humanity everywhere: by going into this war, or by staying out? I hold that the United States can better serve suffering humanity everywhere by staying out.…

If we go to war, we cast away our opportunity and cancel our gains. For a generation, perhaps for a hundred years, we shall not be able to struggle back to where we were. In fact, the changes that total war will bring may mean that we shall never be able to struggle back. Education will cease. Its place will be taken by vocational and military training. The effort to establish a democratic community will stop. We shall think no more of justice, the moral order, and the supremacy of human rights. We shall have hope no longer.

Learning From History

1. What did the members of Fight for Freedom want the U.S. Congress to do?
2. According to Robert Hutchins, what would happen to Americans if the United States entered World War II?
3. How strongly do each of these sides seem to feel about its opinions?

totalitarian state, a single party and its leader suppress all opposition and control all aspects of people's lives.

Hitler claimed that Germany had a right to expand its territory. Germany's neighbors watched uneasily as he rebuilt Germany's military strength in defiance of the Versailles treaty. To gain support in his expansion plans, Hitler formed an alliance with Italy in 1936.

Japan

During the Depression many Japanese grew frustrated with their government's failure to solve economic problems. As a result, military leaders rose to power in the early 1930s. These leaders thought they would solve Japan's problems by expanding Japanese power in Asia.

In September 1931, Japan launched an attack on the province of **Manchuria** in northeastern China. The League of Nations condemned the attack, but it took no action.

Left unchallenged, Japan set up a government in Manchuria. In 1937 Japan invaded northern China, moving southward until it occupied most of the country. Three years later Japan signed a pact of alliance, known as the "Axis," with Germany and Italy.

Soviet Union

In the late 1920s, **Joseph Stalin** rose to power as the Communist leader of the Soviet Union. Stalin demanded complete obedience from the people he ruled and got it through the use of force. Stalin executed his rivals, ordered the deaths of thousands suspected of supporting his rivals, and sent millions of Russians to labor camps. He also reorganized the nation's economy, forcing millions of people onto government-owned farms.

American Neutrality

While dramatic changes were taking place in the world, most Americans wanted to avoid involvement. To keep the nation out of future wars, Congress passed a series of **Neutrality Acts** between 1935 and 1937, which banned the sale of weapons to nations at war. The laws also allowed trade only to nations that could pay cash for goods and transport the goods in their own ships. Many American loans to European countries from World War I remained unpaid, and Congress wanted to prevent more debts.

✓ **Reading Check** **Explaining** What is fascism?

Germany on the March

Hitler began moving forward with his plans for expansion. In March 1936, he ordered troops into the **Rhineland.** The Treaty of Versailles had declared the Rhineland, a German territory west of the Rhine River, a neutral zone.

Hitler's next victim was **Austria.** Hitler insisted that Germany should be unified with Austria, a German-speaking nation. In March 1938, he sent troops into Austria and annexed it.

Hitler turned next to the **Sudetenland,** an area of Czechoslovakia where many German-speaking people lived. Falsely claiming that these people were being persecuted, Hitler announced Germany's right to annex the Sudetenland.

Czechoslovakia was prepared to fight to keep the Sudetenland. Britain and France, fearing a full-fledged war in the region, sought a peaceful solution to the crisis. In September 1938, European leaders met in Munich, Germany.

Britain and France thought that they could avoid war by accepting Germany's demands—a policy later known as appeasement. At the **Munich Conference,** the leaders agreed to turn the Sudetenland over to Germany. Hitler, in turn, promised not to expand Germany's territory further. The British prime minister, **Neville Chamberlain,** returned home to cheering crowds, declaring that the agreement had preserved "peace for our time."

Hopes for peace were shattered the following spring. In March 1939, Hitler's army seized the rest of Czechoslovakia. Now even Chamberlain realized that Hitler could not be trusted.

Meanwhile, Hitler was making plans to invade **Poland.** He worried, however, that such an attack would anger Stalin because Poland bordered the Soviet Union. Though bitter enemies, Hitler and Stalin signed a treaty called the **Soviet-German Non-Aggression Pact** in August 1939. The pact freed Hitler to use force against Poland without fear of Soviet intervention. The Nazi-Soviet pact shocked the leaders of Europe.

✓ **Reading Check** **Explaining** Did the policy of appeasement work? Explain.

SECTION 1 ASSESSMENT

Checking for Understanding

1. **Key Terms** Use each of these terms in a sentence that will help explain its meaning: dictator, fascism, anti-Semitism, totalitarian, appeasement.
2. **Reviewing Facts** What actions did Stalin use to gain obedience from the Russian people?

Reviewing Themes

3. **Global Connections** What was the aim of the policy of appeasement? Did it work?

Critical Thinking

4. **Comparing** What goals did the leaders of the nations of Germany, Italy, and Japan share in the 1930s?
5. **Sequencing Information** Re-create the time line below and list the major events in Hitler's rise to power in Germany.

1921	1933	1936	1938	1939
☐	☐	☐	☐	☐

Analyzing Visuals

6. **Analyzing Political Cartoons** Examine the cartoon on page 753. What do you think Mussolini's shadow represents? What word or phrase would you use to describe Mussolini's appearance?

Interdisciplinary Activity

Expository Writing Write newspaper headlines about three important events covered in Section 1.

What were people's lives like in the past?

What—and whom—were people talking about? What did they eat? What did they do for fun? These two pages will give you some clues to everyday life in the U.S. as you step back in time with TIME Notebook.

Star Quality

Apparently no one has told SHIRLEY TEMPLE *that this is 1934 and there is a Depression going on. Believe it or not, this six-year-old will earn $400,000 this year. What makes the young movie star such a success? Here is what the group who presented Temple with a special Academy Award said:*

"SHIRLEY TEMPLE BROUGHT MORE happiness to millions of children and grown-ups than any child of her years in the history of the world...."

Shirley Temple

ARCHIVE PHOTOS

Movies

Snow What and the Seven Who? Just in time for the holidays! On December 21, 1937, Disney movie studio has released *Snow White and the Seven Dwarfs*, the first animated full-length feature film. Snow White is joined by Happy, Sleepy, Dopey, Grumpy, Sneezy, Bashful, and Doc.

Snow White

© THE WALT DISNEY COMPANY/PHOTOFEST

Headlines from the Time

MISSING — Lindbergh Baby Search Still On Nearly two months have passed since famed flyer Charles Lindbergh and his wife Anne's baby boy was kidnapped in March 1932. A ladder leading up to the baby's window, muddy footprints, and a ransom note demanding $50,000 are the three clues that have been studied by over 5,000 FBI agents. About 100,000 police and volunteers have combed the horror-stricken country, searching for the baby.

Charles Lindbergh

TIME INC. PICTURE COLLECTION

" While I still have got breath in my lungs, I will tell you what a dandy car you make. I [have driven] Fords exclusively when I could get away with one. **"**

CLYDE BARROW,
(half the team of bank robbers Bonnie and Clyde) in a 1934 letter to Henry Ford

" I pledge you, I pledge myself, to a new deal for the American people. Let all us here assembled constitute ourselves prophets of a new order of competence and courage **"**

FRANKLIN D. ROOSEVELT,
accepting the Democratic presidential nomination in 1932

BROWN BROTHERS

" When these winds hit us, we and our misery were suddenly covered with dust.... If the wind blew one way, here came the dark dust from Oklahoma. Another way and it was the gray dust from Kansas. Still another way, the brown dust from Colorado and New Mexico. **"**

TEXAS FARMER,
in 1934, describing the worst agricultural disaster in U.S. history, the Dust Bowl. Dust has covered an area of 150 million square miles and has displaced more than 750,000 people

BETTMANN/CORBIS

AMERICAN SCENE
Depression Figures

Americans are truly suffering during this Great Depression. It is a time of enormous financial problems for millions of people—not just in the United States, but around the world. Banks are failing, people are losing their life savings, and businesses are closing their doors. The graphs on this page give an idea of this difficult time.

DEPRESSION INCOMES

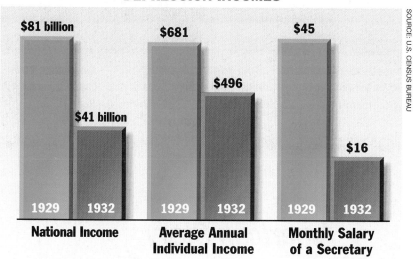

SOURCE: U.S. CENSUS BUREAU

National Income	Average Annual Individual Income	Monthly Salary of a Secretary
$81 billion (1929)	$681 (1929)	$45 (1929)
$41 billion (1932)	$496 (1932)	$16 (1932)

UNEMPLOYMENT IN THE U.S.

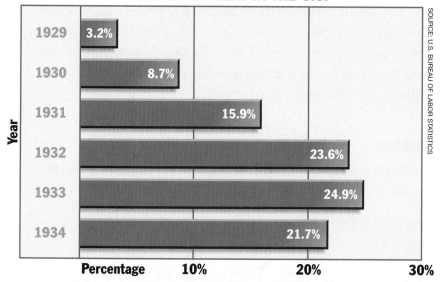

SOURCE: U.S. BUREAU OF LABOR STATISTICS

Year	Percentage
1929	3.2%
1930	8.7%
1931	15.9%
1932	23.6%
1933	24.9%
1934	21.7%

Percentage: 10% 20% 30%

Number One *Gone With the Wind* wins the Pulitzer Prize for 1937. Millions of readers set aside their worries as they experienced the epic drama, defeat, and triumphs of Mitchell's cast of characters.

- - - - - - - - - - - - - - - - -

Two is a charm for President Roosevelt, sworn in for the second time on January 20, 1937. FDR turned down a ride in a closed limousine—even though it was raining. He pointed toward the thousands of wet people who lined the streets of Washington, D.C., hoping to catch a glimpse of him, and said, "I'll ride in the open limo. If they can take it, I can!"

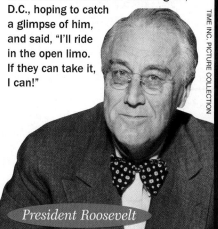

TIME INC. PICTURE COLLECTION

President Roosevelt

Three hundred miles per hour — on September 3, 1935, the Bluebird Special made history. This sleek car is the first land vehicle to top 300 mph (500 km).

- - - - - - - - - - - - - - - - -

Four gold medals. Adolf Hitler, Germany's Fascist leader, invited the world to Berlin for the 1936 Olympic Games. Hitler had hoped to prove the supposed "inferiority" of non-Aryan races. No one told that to U.S. superstar Jesse Owens, an African American athlete who won four gold medals in track and field events.

- - - - - - - - - - - - - - - - -

SECTION 2 War Begins

Guide to Reading

Main Idea

Many nations were drawn into the conflict, largely because of political alliances and economic relationships.

Key Terms

blitzkrieg, lend-lease, disarmament

Reading Strategy

Classifying Information As you read Section 2, re-create the diagram shown below and explain the importance of each event.

	Importance
The Battle of Britain	
Signing the Atlantic Charter	
Attack on Pearl Harbor	

Read to Learn

- which European nations fell to Germany in 1939 and 1940.
- how the United States responded to the war in Europe.

Section Theme

Global Connections The war expanded rapidly as nations became more involved and were drawn into the conflict.

Preview of Events

♦1939	♦1940	♦1941	♦1942
September 1939 Germany invades Poland	**August 1940** Britain is bombed by Germany	**June 1941** Hitler attacks the Soviet Union	**December 1941** Japan bombs Pearl Harbor

Newsboy the day after Pearl Harbor

AN American Story

Sixteen-year-old John Garcia, like others who witnessed the attack on Pearl Harbor, never forgot it: "My grandmother . . . informed me that the Japanese were bombing Pearl Harbor. I said, 'They're just practicing.' She said, no, it was real and the announcer is requesting that all Pearl Harbor workers report to work. . . . I was asked . . . to go into the water and get sailors out that had been blown off the ships. Some were unconscious, some were dead. So I spent the rest of the day swimming inside the harbor, along with some other Hawaiians. . . . We worked all day at that."

War in Europe

In a speech in 1937, President Franklin Roosevelt expressed the feeling of many Americans toward the growing "epidemic of world lawlessness":

❝We are determined to keep out of war, yet we cannot insure ourselves against the disastrous effects of war and the dangers of involvement.❞

On September 1, 1939, Hitler sent his armies into **Poland.** Two days later Great Britain and France declared war on Germany. World War II had begun.

The German attack on Poland was swift and fierce. German planes bombed and machine-gunned targets, German tanks blasted holes in Polish defenses, and thousands of soldiers poured into Poland. The Germans called the offensive a blitzkrieg, or "lightning war." Then Soviet troops moved into and occupied eastern Poland, acting on the Soviet agreement with Germany to divide Poland.

Great Britain and France could do little to help Poland because its defeat came so quickly. In late September 1939, the conquered country was split in half by Hitler and Stalin. Stalin also forced the **Baltic** republics of Latvia, Lithuania, and Estonia to accept Soviet military bases. When he tried to do the same with **Finland,** war broke out between the two nations. The Finns held out heroically until March 1940, when the Soviets forced them to surrender.

The War Expands

All through the winter of 1939–1940 the western front was quiet. British and French forces settled in at the **Maginot Line,** a string of steel-and-concrete bunkers along the German border from Belgium to Switzerland. In the spring the fighting began again. In April Hitler attacked **Denmark** and **Norway** to the north, and the following month he turned west to invade the **Netherlands** and **Belgium.** The Netherlands and Belgium immediately asked for help from Great Britain and France—the **Allies.** After terrible bombing raids in the Netherlands, the Dutch surrendered. The Belgians fought courageously, but they too were overwhelmed.

With the collapse of Belgium, Allied troops retreated to the port of **Dunkirk** in the northwest corner of France on the **English Channel.** They were now trapped between the advancing Germans and the French coast. In a daring move, more than 800 British ships—warships, ferries, and fishing boats—joined an operation to rescue the troops. Crossing the Channel again and again, the boats evacuated more than 300,000 French and British troops to safety.

In June the Germans crossed the Somme River and continued their sweep into France. Italy joined the war on the side of Germany

History *Through Art*

The Withdrawal from Dunkirk, June 1940 by Charles R.A. Cundall Boats crossed the English Channel to bring Allied troops from France back to safety in England. **Why did Allied forces retreat?**

Linking Past & Present

Aerial Warfare

Germany introduced jet planes late in World War II. The German jets could fly almost 550 miles per hour. By the 1960s American and Soviet jets roared through the skies at 1,000 miles per hour. Today United States military aircraft includes the F-117 stealth fighter. A winglike shape and flat surfaces that absorb radar energy make it difficult for enemy radar to detect it. **How do World War II planes differ from modern stealth bombers?**

Stealth bomber

Flying Grumman Wildcat fighter, 1942

and attacked France from the southeast. Germany and Italy—and later Japan—formed the **Axis Powers.** On June 14, 1940, German troops marched victoriously into Paris. The French surrendered a week later, stunned by the German blitzkrieg.

The Battle of Britain

All that stood between Hitler's domination of Western Europe was Great Britain. In August 1940, the Germans bombed British shipyards, industries, and cities, destroying entire neighborhoods of London and killing many civilians.

Hitler's goal was to break British morale before invading Britain. The British people endured, however, in part because of the inspiration of Prime Minister **Winston Churchill.** When Hitler called for Britain to surrender, Churchill responded defiantly:

> ❝We shall defend our island, whatever the cost may be. We shall fight on the beaches, we shall fight on the landing grounds, we shall fight in the fields and in the streets, we shall fight in the hills; we shall never surrender.❞

Although the **Battle of Britain** continued until October, the Germans never gained control of the skies over Britain. The British Royal Air Force (RAF) mounted a heroic defense and inflicted heavy losses on the German air force. Finally, Hitler ended the air attacks.

Germany Turns East

Frustrated by his failure in Britain, Hitler decided to realize one of his oldest dreams—to destroy the Soviet Union. Ignoring the pact he had made with Stalin, Hitler launched an attack on the Soviet Union in June 1941. Within months German armies had moved into Soviet territory. The Soviet Union joined the Allies in their fight against the Axis Powers.

✓ **Reading Check** **Examining** Why did Hitler bring the invasion of Britain to an end?

America and the War

The United States watched the war in Europe with growing concern. Although most Americans sympathized with the Allies, they were determined to avoid war. Isolationists banded together to form the **America First Committee.** Its members thought the United States should keep out of Europe's business. Among those who led this group were aviation hero Charles Lindbergh and automaker Henry Ford.

While vowing to remain neutral, Roosevelt took steps to prepare for war. In 1938, at his request, Congress voted to strengthen the navy. In 1939 the president asked Congress to pass a new Neutrality Act that allowed the United States to sell weapons to other countries on a "cash and carry" basis. In 1940 FDR signed the Selective Training and Service Act, the first peacetime draft in United States history. The law applied to American men between the ages of 21 and 35.

The 1940 Election

With the world in crisis, President Roosevelt decided to run for a third term, breaking the tradition set by George Washington. The Republicans chose as their candidate a former Democrat—business leader Wendell L. Willkie of Indiana. Willkie approved almost all of Roosevelt's New Deal reforms and generally agreed with his foreign policy. Public sentiment to stay out of the war was so strong that Roosevelt promised the American people, "Your boys are not going to be sent into any foreign wars." Roosevelt won an easy victory.

U.S. Involvement Grows

With the election won, Roosevelt moved to support the Allies openly. At Roosevelt's urging, Congress approved the Lend-Lease Act in March 1941. The Lend-Lease Act allowed America to sell, lend, or lease arms or other war supplies to any nation considered "vital to the defense of the United States." Britain, which was running out of cash, was the first to use lend-lease. Isolationists opposed the Lend-Lease Act, arguing that it would increase American involvement in the war.

German submarines in the Atlantic Ocean had been sinking British ships, including those carrying supplies from the United States. In mid-1941, American ships began escorting convoys of British merchant ships. After the Germans began firing on American destroyers, Roosevelt issued a "shoot-on-sight" order to American naval vessels that found German and Italian ships in certain areas.

The Atlantic Charter

In August 1941, President Roosevelt and British prime minister Churchill met and drew up the **Atlantic Charter.** While Roosevelt made no military commitments, he joined Churchill in setting goals for a world after "the final destruction of the Nazi tyranny." The two nations pledged that the people of every nation would be free to choose their own form of government and live free of "fear and want." They urged disarmament—giving up military weapons—and the creation of a "permanent system of general security."

Reading Check **Explaining** What did the Lend-Lease Act allow the United States to do?

The bombing of London caused much ruin. The Royal Air Force (inset) forced Hitler to abandon his invasion plans.

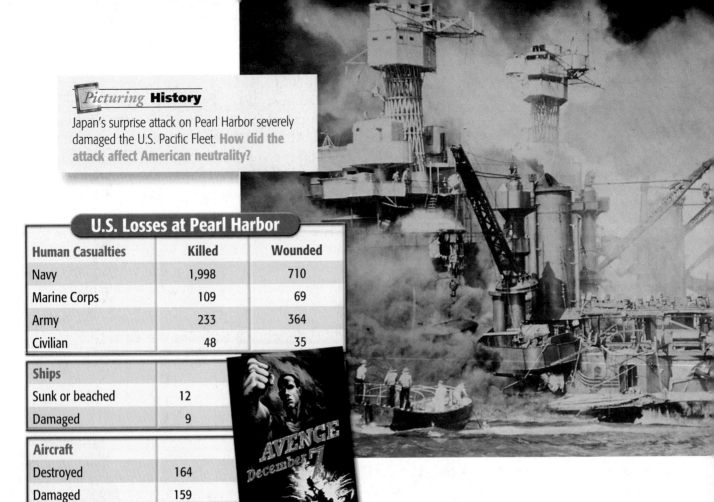

Picturing **History**

Japan's surprise attack on Pearl Harbor severely damaged the U.S. Pacific Fleet. **How did the attack affect American neutrality?**

U.S. Losses at Pearl Harbor		
Human Casualties	**Killed**	**Wounded**
Navy	1,998	710
Marine Corps	109	69
Army	233	364
Civilian	48	35
Ships		
Sunk or beached	12	
Damaged	9	
Aircraft		
Destroyed	164	
Damaged	159	

Source: USS *Arizona* Memorial.

The Japanese Threat

While Hitler and Mussolini were waging war in Europe, the Japanese were making military conquests in the Far East. After seizing much of China in the 1930s, the Japanese continued their expansion. After the fall of France in 1940, they seized the French colony of **Indochina** in Southeast Asia. Japan also planned to take the Dutch East Indies, British Malaya, and the American territory of the Philippines, primarily to acquire badly needed rubber and oil.

The United States Responds

The United States responded to Japan's aggression by applying economic pressure. Roosevelt froze all Japanese assets in American banks, preventing the Japanese from obtaining funds they had in the United States. He also stopped the sale of oil, gasoline, and other natural resources that Japan lacked. The action outraged the Japanese.

In October 1941, the Japanese prime minister, Fumimaro Konoye, resigned. Konoye had been willing to negotiate with the United States because he did not believe Japan could defeat America in a war. The new prime minister, General **Hideki Tōjō,** did not share Konoye's views. Still, on November 20, negotiations were opened in Washington between the United States and Japan. At the same time, confident of Japan's military might, the Tōjō government began planning an attack on the United States.

Attack on Pearl Harbor

At 7:55 A.M. on Sunday, December 7, 1941, Japanese warplanes attacked the American military base at **Pearl Harbor,** Hawaii. The American installations at Pearl Harbor could not have been more vulnerable to attack. Ships were anchored in a neat row and airplanes were grouped together on the airfield, easy targets for a Japanese air attack. The Americans at Pearl Harbor were taken completely by surprise. According to Rear Admiral William R. Furlong,

"In the Navy housing areas around Pearl Harbor, people couldn't imagine what was wrecking Sunday morning. Captain Reynolds Hayden, enjoying breakfast at his home on Hospital Point, thought it was construction blasting. . . . Lieutenant C. E. Boudreau, drying down after a shower, thought an oil tank had blown up near his quarters . . . until a Japanese plane almost grazed the bathroom window. Chief Petty Officer Albert Molter, puttering around his Ford Island flat, thought a drill was going on until his wife Esther called, 'Al, there's a battleship tipping over.'"

The attack devastated the American fleet, destroying many battleships, cruisers, and other vessels. Hundreds of planes were destroyed or damaged. More than 2,300 soldiers, sailors, and civilians were killed.

Fortunately, at the time of the attack, the navy's three aircraft carriers were at sea. Their escape from destruction provided the only good news that day.

Grace Tully, one of the president's secretaries, received an urgent call to report to the White House. She later recalled:

AVENGE PEARL HARBOR

OUR BULLETS WILL DO IT

"Most of the news on the . . . attack was then coming to the White House by telephone from Admiral Stark, Chief of Naval Operations, at the Navy Department . . . each report more terrible than the last, and I could hear the shocked unbelief in Admiral Stark's voice."

Pearl Harbor was the worst defeat in United States military history. Yet Pearl Harbor also united Americans. All debate about involvement in the war ended. On the day after Pearl Harbor, President Roosevelt asked Congress for a declaration of war, calling December 7 "a date which will live in infamy." Congress quickly approved the president's request to declare war on Japan.

On December 11, Germany and Italy, Japan's allies, declared war on the United States. Congress then declared war on them as well. The United States had joined the Allied nations—including Great Britain, France, China, and the Soviet Union—against the Axis Powers—Germany, Italy, and Japan—in World War II.

✓ Reading Check Explaining Why did the United States enter World War II?

SECTION 2 ASSESSMENT

Checking for Understanding

1. **Key Terms** Define the following key terms: blitzkrieg, lend-lease, disarmament.
2. **Reviewing Facts** What nations formed the Axis Powers?

Reviewing Themes

3. **Global Connections** What diplomatic actions did the United States take to prevent Japan from taking over nations in Asia?

Critical Thinking

4. **Predicting Consequences** Do you think the United States would have eventually joined the war even if Japanese forces had not attacked Pearl Harbor? Explain.
5. **Sequencing Information** Re-create the time line below and identify the important events.

Sept. 1, 1939	Mar. 1940	Jun. 14, 1940	Dec. 7, 1941
☐	☐	☐	☐

Analyzing Visuals

6. **Analyzing Art** Look at the painting on page 759. What event does the painting show? Why do you think the artist decided to portray this event in such a large view?

Interdisciplinary Activity

Descriptive Writing Write and record a 15-second radio news bulletin announcing the Japanese bombing of Pearl Harbor.

SECTION 3 On the Home Front

Guide to Reading

Main Idea
Demand for war goods created new industries and new jobs.

Key Terms
mobilization, ration, internment camp

Reading Strategy
Organizing Information As you read the section, re-create the diagram below and identify three ways Americans on the home front helped the war effort.

Helping the war effort

Read to Learn
• what steps the United States took to prepare for fighting the war.
• how the war affected Americans.

Section Theme
Economic Factors The United States had to switch rapidly from a peacetime economy to a wartime economy—providing arms and other supplies for thousands of troops.

Preview of Events

♦1941   ♦1942   ♦1943

1941
FDR establishes Fair Employment Practices Commission

1942
Revenue Act raises taxes to finance the war; Office of War Information promotes patriotism

1943
Navajo soldiers develop unbreakable radio code

AN
American Story

Audie Murphy

He wanted to join the Marines, but at 5 feet five inches tall he was too short. The Navy also turned him down. Reluctantly, Audie Murphy, the orphaned son of Texas sharecroppers, enlisted in the Army. By the end of the war, Murphy was the most decorated combat soldier of World War II. When victory was declared in Europe in May 1945, Murphy had still not reached his twenty-first birthday. Today, through the Audie Murphy Club, the Army honors noncommissioned officers who best represent Audie Murphy's motto, "You lead from the front."

America Prepares

The Japanese attack on Pearl Harbor united the American people as nothing else could. With astonishing speed the nation's economy and its people prepared to fight the war. Even before Pearl Harbor, the United States had begun raising an army under the Selective Service acts of 1940 and 1941. More than 15 million Americans joined the armed forces during the war, both as draftees and as volunteers.

For the first time, large numbers of women served in the military. About 250,000 women served in the **WACs** (Women's Army Corps), the **WAVES** (Women Appointed for Volunteer Emergency Service in the Navy), and women's units in the marines, Coast Guard, and army air corps. These women did not fight in combat—most performed clerical tasks or worked as nurses—but they played important roles in the war effort.

Equipping the troops and providing arms and other war materials required changes in the nation's economy. To speed up mobilization—military and civilian preparations for war—the American government created a number of new government agencies.

The **War Production Board** supervised the conversion of industries to war production. Under its guidance, automakers shifted from building cars to producing trucks and tanks. The **Office of Price Administration** set limits on consumer prices and rents to prevent inflation. The **National War Labor Board** helped resolve labor disputes that might slow down war production.

Financing the War

From 1941 to the end of World War II, the United States spent more than $320 billion on the war effort—10 times the amount spent in World War I. Much of this money was raised through taxes. The **Revenue Act of 1942** raised corporate taxes and required nearly all Americans to pay income taxes. Congress approved a system for withholding taxes from workers' paychecks—a practice still in effect.

The government also borrowed money to finance the war. As in World War I, the government sold war bonds. Movie stars and other celebrities urged people to buy bonds to support the war.

✔️ Reading Check **Explaining**
What was the purpose of the Revenue Act of 1942, and what did it do?

Wartime America

During the war, industry soared. Factories produced more than 70,000 ships, almost 100,000 tanks and airplanes, and millions of guns. Production speed increased as well. Some cargo ships were built in a matter of weeks.

Those who remained at home had to provide food and shelter for all those in uniform. Civilians also provided training, equipment, transportation, and medical care.

Wartime production helped restore prosperity to the nation after the long years of the Depression. Incomes rose and prices remained fairly stable.

Making Sacrifices

With the war effort came many sacrifices. For millions of American families, the war meant separation from loved ones serving overseas. Those at home lived in dread of receiving a telegram announcing that a family member had been killed, wounded, or captured.

With industries making war materials, Americans faced shortages of many consumer goods. After 1942, for example, automakers

About 2,000 women were accepted into the Women's Air Force Service Pilots.

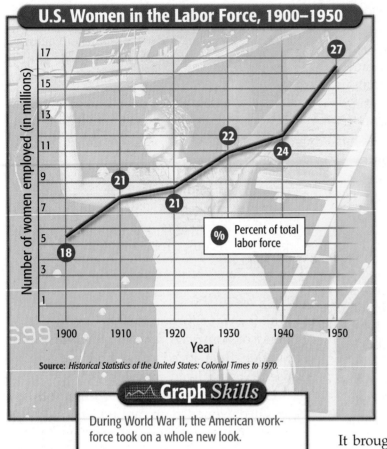

U.S. Women in the Labor Force, 1900–1950

Number of women employed (in millions)

17
15
13
11
9
7
5
3
1

18
21
21
22
24
27

% Percent of total labor force

1900   1910   1920   1930   1940   1950

Year

Source: *Historical Statistics of the United States: Colonial Times to 1970.*

Graph *Skills*

During World War II, the American workforce took on a whole new look.

Analyzing Information In 1940 what percent of the labor force was made up of women?

Many people joined in **civil defense**—protective measures in case of attack. For example, volunteer spotters scanned the skies for enemy aircraft that might try to approach America. Coastal cities enforced blackouts at night so that lights could not serve as beacons for enemy pilots.

The **Office of War Information,** established by the government, promoted patriotism and helped keep Americans united behind the war effort. It also broadcast messages all over the world. *(See page 975 for another way Americans were asked to contribute to the war effort.)*

Reading Check **Explaining** Why were many consumer goods in short supply?

Women and Minorities

The war had a tremendous impact on the lives of women and minorities. It brought opportunity for new jobs and a new role in society. Yet for some, unfair treatment left lasting scars.

As millions of men joined the armed forces, more women than ever before entered the labor force. In factories women worked as welders and riveters and in other jobs previously held by men. An advertising campaign featuring a character called **Rosie the Riveter** encouraged women to take factory jobs. For many women it was their first opportunity to work outside the home.

Although women had new job opportunities, they usually earned less than men. Moreover, when the war ended and the troops returned home, most women would lose their jobs. Still, the war opened new fields to women and changed public opinion about women's right to work.

African Americans During the War

About one million African American men and women served in the armed forces during the war. At first most were given low-level assignments and kept in segregated units. Gradually, military leaders assigned them to integrated

stopped making new cars and turned instead to making tanks, planes, and trucks. Women could not buy stockings—silk imports from war-torn Asia had halted, and nylon was needed to make parachutes.

In addition many resources and goods needed for the war effort were rationed—consumers could buy only limited numbers of them. Americans used government-issued books of ration coupons to purchase certain items, such as shoes, gasoline, tires, sugar, and meat. When people ran out of coupons, they did without the rationed items.

Helping the War Effort

People found other ways to help the war effort. Many planted "victory gardens" to grow vegetables, which were in short supply. Children collected scrap metal for use in industry.

Penicillin

Penicillin was first used on a large scale during World War II. Alexander Fleming's discovery of penicillin in 1928 happened accidentally in the course of research on influenza. The first widespread use of the medicine took place in 1943 to treat Allied troops in the North Africa campaign. Today penicillin is used in treating a wide range of diseases.

units. In 1942 the army began training whites and African Americans together in officer candidate school. Finally, African Americans were allowed to take combat assignments. The 332nd Fighter Group, known as the **Tuskegee Airmen,** shot down more than 200 enemy planes. **Benjamin Davis, Jr.,** who trained at the Tuskegee flying school, became the first African American general in the United States Air Force. His father, Benjamin Davis, Sr., had been the first African American general in the army.

In civilian life African Americans sought change. In the summer of 1941, labor leader **A. Philip Randolph** demanded that the government ban discrimination against African Americans in defense industries. He planned a large demonstration in Washington in support of his demands. President Roosevelt persuaded Randolph to call off the march by establishing the Fair Employment Practices Commission to combat discrimination in industries that held government contracts. The president announced that

66... there shall be no discrimination in the employment of workers in defense industries or government because of race, creed, color, or national origin.99

The war accelerated the population shift that had begun during World War I. Large numbers of African Americans moved from the rural South to industrialized cities in the North and the West in search of work. In some cities, racial tensions erupted in violence. The

violence sometimes resulted in death. The riots inspired the African American poet **Langston Hughes** to write:

66Yet you say we're fightin' for democracy.
Then why don't democracy
Include me?99

Native Americans

Many Native Americans left reservations to work in defense industries. Thousands of Native Americans served in the armed forces. **Ira Hayes** became a hero in the battle for Iwo Jima in the Pacific. A special group of Navajo formed the "code talkers." Many of the American radio communications about troop movements and battle plans were being intercepted by the Japanese. The "code talkers" used a special code based on the Navajo language to send messages—a code that the Japanese never broke.

Hispanic Americans

More than 250,000 Hispanic Americans served in the armed forces. The Medal of Honor, the nation's highest military medal, was awarded to 12 Mexican Americans. **Mercedes Cubría** of Cuba became the first Hispanic woman officer in the Women's Army Corps. **Horacio Rivero** of Puerto Rico became the first Hispanic four-star admiral since David Farragut to serve in the United States Navy.

Prompted by the wartime need for labor, United States labor agents recruited thousands of farm and railroad workers from Mexico. This program, called the **bracero** program, stimulated emigration from Mexico during the war years.

Tuskegee Airmen in Italy

The United States Marines recruited Navajo soldiers to develop a military code that the Japanese could not break.

Like African Americans, Mexican Americans suffered from discrimination, and their presence created tensions in some cities. In 1943, for example, a four-day riot started in **Los Angeles** when white sailors attacked Mexican American teens.

Japanese Americans

After the Japanese bombed Pearl Harbor, Japanese Americans were feared and hated by many other Americans. About two-thirds of Japanese Americans were **Nisei**—American citizens who had been born in the United States. But this fact made little difference to some who questioned the loyalty of Japanese Americans.

Military and political leaders worried about the loyalty of Japanese Americans if Japanese forces invaded the United States. The president directed the army to relocate more than 100,000 West Coast Japanese Americans to detention centers. Located mostly in desert areas, these internment camps were crowded and uncomfortable. Conditions were harsh.

With only days to prepare for the move, most Japanese Americans left valuable possessions behind. Many abandoned their homes and businesses or sold them at a loss. Most had to stay in internment camps for the next three years.

Peter Ota and his family were sent to a camp in Colorado. His father had come to California in 1904 and built up a successful fruit and vegetable business. After the war Ota remembered how his father had suffered.

❝After all those years, having worked his whole life to build a dream—having it all taken away. . . . He died a broken man.❞

In 1944, in *Korematsu* v. *United States,* the Supreme Court upheld the order providing for the relocation of Japanese Americans. In 1988 Americans acknowledged the injustice of relocation. Congress issued a formal apology and agreed to give each survivor $20,000, a token of the nation's regret. 📖 *(See page 998 for a summary of the* Korematsu *case.)*

✓ Reading Check Identifying Who were the Nisei?

SECTION 3 ASSESSMENT

Checking for Understanding

1. **Key Terms** Define the following key terms: mobilization, ration, internment camp.
2. **Reviewing Facts** List two ways the United States financed the war effort.

Reviewing Themes

3. **Economic Factors** How did wartime industrial production help the American economy recover from the Depression?

Critical Thinking

4. **Drawing Conclusions** Why did many Americans move to industrialized cities during the war?
5. **Organizing Information** Re-create the diagram below and explain how each of these actions helped the war effort.

Helping the war effort		
Civil defense	Bracero program	Rationing

Analyzing Visuals

6. **Graph Skills** Examine the graph on page 766. When did the number of women employed pass 10 million?

Interdisciplinary Activity

Writing Suppose you are a woman working in a defense factory during the war. This is the first job you have had outside of your home. Write a journal entry describing your first day on the job.

America's LITERATURE

Yoshiko Uchida (1921–1992)

Yoshiko Uchida grew up in California in the 1930s. As a Japanese American, she sometimes felt very different from the people around her. She wanted to be a "typical" American and often resented the Japanese ways of her family. Eventually Uchida learned to value the "invisible thread" that linked her to her heritage.

READ TO DISCOVER

During the war, the American government relocated to camps those Japanese people living in the West. How did Yoshiko and her sister, Kay, spend their time in the internment camp?

READER'S DICTIONARY

Tanforan: horse racing park used as a camp for Japanese Americans
mess hall: military-style dining area
canteen: a general store at a military camp
contraband: forbidden items
diversion: entertainment

The Invisible Thread

Gradually we became accustomed to life in **Tanforan**, especially to standing in long lines for everything. We lined up to get into the **mess hall** or to use a laundry tub or to buy something at the **canteen** (finding only shoelaces when we got in) or to get into the occasional movies that were shown.

We got used to rushing back to our stall after dinner for the 6:00 P.M. head count (we were still in bed for the morning count), and to the sudden unexpected campwide searches for **contraband** by the FBI when we were confined to our stalls for several hours.

For **diversion** we could also go to talent shows, recorded concerts, discussion groups, Saturday night dances, softball games, art classes, and hobby shows. . . .

Representatives from the university, the YMCA and YWCA, and various church groups also came to give us their support and help. They were working on arrangements to get students out of camp and back into schools as soon as possible.

One day our neighbor Mrs. Harpainter came to see us, bringing all sorts of snacks along with flowers from her garden for Mama. Her boys, however, were not allowed inside because they were under sixteen.

When Kay and I heard they were waiting outside the gate, we hurried to the fence to talk to them.

"Teddy! Bobby!"

We ran to greet them, squeezing our fingers through the chain links to touch their hands.

But an armed guard quickly shouted, "Hey, you two! Get away from the fence!"

FBI agent searches family's belongings

ANALYZING LITERATURE

1. **Recall and Interpret** Why did representatives from churches and other groups visit the camp?
2. **Evaluate and Connect** How do you think you would have felt in Uchida's place in the internment camp?

Interdisciplinary Activity

Art Draw plans for a community memorial suitable for remembering Japanese Americans treated unfairly during World War II.

SECTION 4 War in Europe and Africa

Guide to Reading

Main Idea
To win the war, the Allies had to regain control of North Africa and most of Europe.

Key Terms
D-Day, genocide, Holocaust

Reading Strategy
Sequencing Information As you read the section, re-create the time line below and identify important events during the war.

Nov. 1942	May 1943	Jun. 1944

Read to Learn
- what important battles took place in North Africa, Italy, and the Soviet Union between 1942 and 1944.
- what factors contributed to the Allied victory in Europe.

Section Theme
Global Connections The horrors of war continued as the Allies attempted to defeat the Axis Powers.

Preview of Events

♦1942 — ♦1944 — ♦1946

January 1942
U.S. joins Allies

June 1944
Allied ships land at Normandy

December 1944
Battle of the Bulge takes 75,000 lives

May 1945
Germany surrenders

AN American Story

Ernie Pyle

Ernie Pyle, a war correspondent, described the life of the World War II American soldier: "In the magazines war seemed romantic and exciting, full of heroics and vitality. . . . I saw instead men suffering and wishing they were somewhere else. . . . All of them desperately hungry for somebody to talk to besides themselves . . . cold and fairly dirty, just toiling from day to day in a world full of insecurity, discomfort, homesickness and a dulled sense of danger."

North African Campaign

On January 1, 1942—three weeks after Pearl Harbor—the United States joined Britain, the Soviet Union, and 23 other Allied nations in vowing to defeat the Axis Powers. Although the Japanese were conquering vast areas in the Pacific, the Allied leaders decided to concentrate first on defeating Hitler before dealing with Japan. The situation in Europe was desperate. German forces occupied almost all of Europe and much of North Africa. If the Germans defeated the Soviets, Germany might prove unstoppable.

Stalin and many American military leaders wanted the Allies to launch a major attack on continental Europe across the English Channel. Such an attack would force the Germans to defend the heart of their own empire. Churchill, however, argued that such an assault would be too difficult because of the German military presence in the area. FDR concluded that Churchill was right. The Allies made plans to attack North Africa instead. The Axis forces there were under the command of German general **Erwin Rommel,** known as the "Desert Fox" because of his success in desert warfare.

In November 1942, the British turned Rommel back at El Alamein. The victory prevented the Germans from capturing the Suez Canal, linking the Mediterranean and the Red Sea.

Landing in Algeria and Morocco on November 8, American, British, and Canadian troops under American general **Dwight D. Eisenhower**

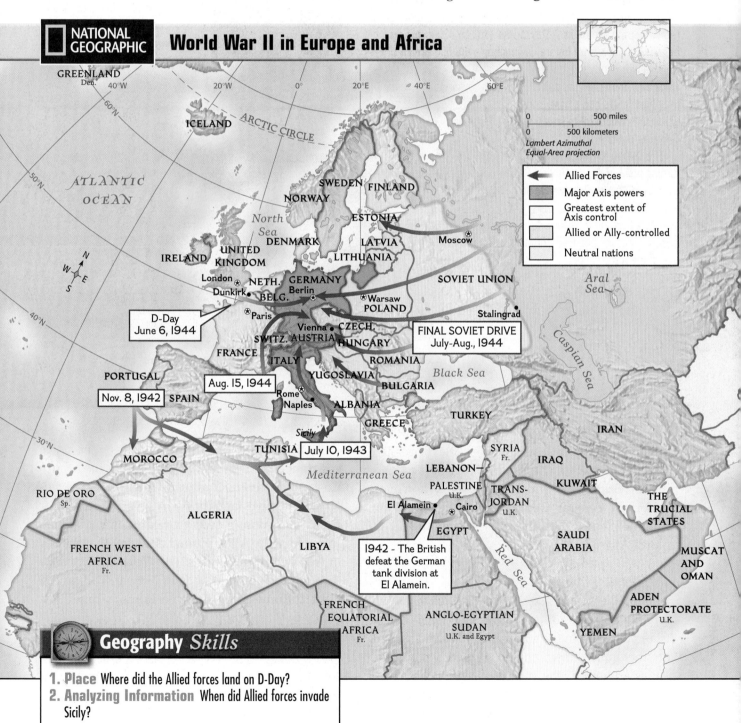

World War II in Europe and Africa

NATIONAL GEOGRAPHIC

Allied Forces
Major Axis powers
Greatest extent of Axis control
Allied or Ally-controlled
Neutral nations

500 miles
500 kilometers
Lambert Azimuthal Equal-Area projection

D-Day June 6, 1944

FINAL SOVIET DRIVE July-Aug., 1944

Aug. 15, 1944

Nov. 8, 1942

July 10, 1943

1942 - The British defeat the German tank division at El Alamein.

Geography *Skills*

1. Place Where did the Allied forces land on D-Day?
2. Analyzing Information When did Allied forces invade Sicily?

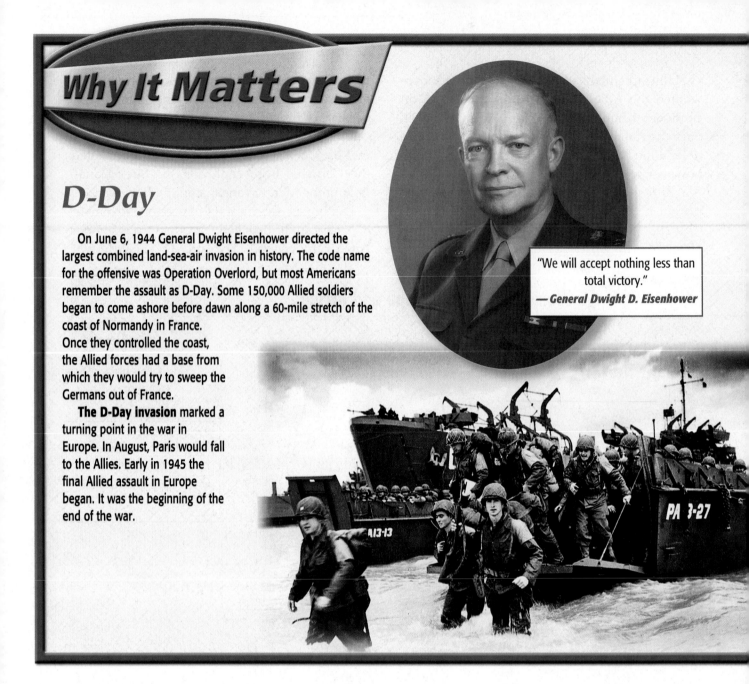

Why It Matters

D-Day

On June 6, 1944 General Dwight Eisenhower directed the largest combined land-sea-air invasion in history. The code name for the offensive was Operation Overlord, but most Americans remember the assault as D-Day. Some 150,000 Allied soldiers began to come ashore before dawn along a 60-mile stretch of the coast of Normandy in France. Once they controlled the coast, the Allied forces had a base from which they would try to sweep the Germans out of France.

The D-Day invasion marked a turning point in the war in Europe. In August, Paris would fall to the Allies. Early in 1945 the final Allied assault in Europe began. It was the beginning of the end of the war.

"We will accept nothing less than total victory."
— *General Dwight D. Eisenhower*

advanced eastward swiftly. The inexperienced Americans met defeat in Tunisia. With the backing of British air and naval power, however, American general **George Patton** closed in on Rommel. The Allies drove the Germans out of North Africa in May 1943.

The Invasion of Italy

The Allies used bases in North Africa to launch an invasion of southern Europe. They took the island of **Sicily** in the summer of 1943 and landed on the Italian mainland in September. As the Allies advanced, the Italians overthrew dictator Benito Mussolini and surrendered. However, German forces in Italy continued to fight.

In the winter of 1943, the Allies met fierce resistance at the monastery town of **Monte Cassino** in central Italy, and their advance faltered. The next January the Allies landed farther north at **Anzio,** a seaport near Rome. German forces kept the Allies pinned down on the beaches at Anzio for four months. The Allies finally broke through the German lines in May and advanced toward **Rome.** They liberated Rome in June 1944.

Air War Over Germany

While fighting raged in North Africa and Italy, the Allies launched an air war against Germany. In the summer of 1942, British and American air forces began a massive bombing campaign

D-Day Invasion

NATIONAL GEOGRAPHIC

Legend:
- Axis territory
- Allied territory
- British troops
- Canadian troops
- U.S. troops
- Airborne and glider landing zones force
- Major German fortifications

UNITED KINGDOM

London · 0°
Dover ·
Calais ·
Strait of Dover
Shoreham ·
Portsmouth
Southampton ·
Dieppe ·
JUNO
SWORD
GOLD
OMAHA
Portland ·
Seine River
Le Havre ·
Paris ⊛
Dartmouth ·
UTAH
50°N
Cherbourg ·
St.-Lô ·
Caen ·
Normandy
FRANCE
English Channel
3°W

Scale varies in this perspective

The invasion army was split into five forces. The two American forces, code-named Utah and Omaha, would strike in the west. British and Canadian forces, named Gold, Juno, and Sword, would land farther east.

Numbers

Allied Forces
- 150,000 troops (11 divisions)
- 1,500 tanks
- 5,300 ships and landing craft
- 12,000 airplanes
- 20,000 airborne troops

Casualties

By the end of the day, 2,500 Allied soldiers were killed.

D-Day planners had forecast 10,000 dead.

---

against Germany. Each day hundreds of American bombers pounded German factories and cities. Each night British bombers battered the same targets. The bombing caused massive destruction and killed thousands of German civilians. In July 1943 a week-long series of bombing raids on the port of Hamburg created a whirling tower of fire that engulfed the city. More than 30,000 people died in the raids. Yet the attacks failed to crack Germany's determination to win the war.

Reading Check **Explaining** Why did the Allies decide to attack North Africa rather than launch an attack on continental Europe?

The Tide Turns in Europe

Meanwhile, the Soviets and the Germans were locked in ferocious combat. For months the Soviet Union bore the main force of Germany's European war effort.

The Eastern Front

After invading the Soviet Union in June 1941, German troops had moved quickly into the nation's interior. By September the Germans surrounded **Leningrad** and began a **siege,** or military blockade, that lasted nearly 900 days. The German attack continued, but Leningrad did not fall. As food ran out, the people of the city ate horses, cats, and dogs—even bread made from wallpaper paste. Thousands died. The Germans could not take the city, however, and in early 1944 the siege was broken.

German forces also attacked other Soviet cities. In 1941 the Germans tried to capture the Soviet capital of **Moscow.** Heavy losses and bad weather slowed their advance, but the Germans reached Moscow's outskirts by December. When all seemed lost, the Soviets staged a counterattack and forced a German retreat.

In the spring of 1942, Germany launched another offensive. A major target was the city of **Stalingrad,** key to oil-rich lands to the south. To take the city, the Germans had to fight street by street and house by house. No sooner had the Germans won Stalingrad than Soviet forces surrounded the city, cutting off the German supply lines. Cold and starving, the German troops fought on until February 1943, when the tattered remains of their army finally surrendered.

After Stalingrad, a major Soviet offensive drove the Germans back hundreds of miles. The Germans mounted a counteroffensive in the summer of 1943, but their defeat at Stalingrad marked a major turning point in the war.

Invasion of France

As the Soviets pushed toward Germany from the east, the Allies were planning a massive invasion of France from the west. General Eisenhower, the commander of Allied forces in Europe, directed this invasion, known as **Operation Overlord.** Eisenhower later wrote of the tense days of preparation:

> ❝All southern England was one vast military camp, crowded with soldiers awaiting final word to go.❞

Eisenhower planned to land his troops on the French coast of **Normandy** on June 5, but rough seas forced him to delay the landing. Finally, on June 6, 1944—**D-Day**—the Allied ships landed on the coast of Normandy.

After wading ashore the troops faced land mines and fierce fire from the Germans. Many Allied troops were hit as they stormed across the beaches to establish a foothold on high ground. Within a few weeks, the Allies had landed a million troops in France.

From Normandy the Allies pushed across France. On August 25 French and American soldiers marched through joyful crowds and liberated Paris.

People In History

George S. Patton 1885–1945

Unpredictable and flamboyant, George S. Patton was one of the most remarkable U.S. Army commanders and also the leading authority on tank warfare. Patton was a clever planner, which helped make him one of the war's greatest combat commanders.

Patton distinguished himself in various World War II campaigns, including the invasion of North Africa and the capture of Sicily. The controversy that arose after Patton struck a soldier almost cost him his career. Eventually Patton was reassigned to lead the Third Army. After the invasion of Normandy in the summer of 1944, Patton's army swept across

Europe. In December, the Third Army helped win the Battle of the Bulge. By the end of the war, the Third Army liberated more than 80,000 square miles of territory and took thousands of prisoners. Patton died in December 1945 from injuries suffered in an automobile accident.

(Left) Polish Jews taken prisoner, 1943; (above) liberated prisoners at concentration camp at Ebensee, Austria in May 1945

Victory in Europe

Germany fought for survival on two fronts. In the east the Soviets pushed the Germans out of eastern Europe. In the west the British and Americans approached the German border.

The Allied advance across France moved so rapidly that some people thought the war would be over by the end of the year. In late 1944, however, the drive came to a halt at the Rhine River, stalled by German defenses and cold weather.

In mid-December the Germans mounted a last, desperate offensive. On December 16, 1944, they launched a surprise attack along a 50-mile front in Belgium. In the **Battle of the Bulge,** the Germans at first drove troops and artillery deep into a bulge in the Allied lines. After several weeks, however, the Allies pushed the Germans back. The battle, which resulted in more than 100,000 casualties, marked the end of serious German resistance.

The final phase of the war in Europe now began. By mid-April 1945, the Soviets had surrounded **Berlin,** the German capital. Hitler, who had spent the final months of the war in an underground bunker there, realized that the situation was hopeless and committed suicide on April 30. Germany signed an unconditional surrender on May 7, ending the war in Europe. The Allies declared May 8 **V-E Day** for "Victory in Europe."

Death of a President

President Roosevelt did not share in the Allied victory celebration. In February 1945, he had traveled to Yalta in the Soviet Union to meet with Churchill and Stalin. After returning home Roosevelt had gone to Warm Springs, Georgia, for a vacation. He died there suddenly on April 12, 1945.

Americans were saddened by the death of the man who had led them for 12 difficult years. When Vice President **Harry S Truman** heard the news, he asked Eleanor Roosevelt if there was anything he could do for her. She replied, "Is there anything *we* can do for *you?* You are the one in trouble now."

Reading Check **Explaining** Why was the Battle of the Bulge an important victory for the Allies?

The Holocaust

As the Allies liberated areas that had been under German control, they found horrifying evidence of Nazi brutality. Hitler had warned in 1939 that another war would result in "the destruction of the Jews in Europe." Nazi leaders developed what they called "the final solution of the Jewish question." Their "solution" was genocide—wiping out an entire group of people.

Ever since Hitler had gained power in 1933, the Nazis had persecuted Jews. This persecution became more deadly as German power spread through Europe. Once the war began, Nazis rounded up thousands of Jews, shooting them and throwing them into mass graves. One man who witnessed a massacre of Russian Jews wrote of the act:

❝I watched a family of about eight persons. . . . [A soldier] instructed them to go behind the earth mound. . . . They went down into the pit, lined themselves up against the previous victims and were shot.❞

Nazi troops crammed thousands more into railroad cars like cattle, depositing them in **concentration camps**—prison camps for civilians. Guards took the prisoners' belongings, shaved their heads, and tattooed camp numbers on their arms. Forced to live in horrible conditions, the prisoners often had only a crust of bread or watery soup to eat. Thousands became sick and died.

In the early 1940s, the Nazis embarked on their "final solution" to destroy the Jews. They built death camps where they killed thousands of people a day in gas chambers, then burned their bodies in ovens. At the largest camp—**Auschwitz** in Poland—the Nazis killed between 1 and 2 million people. As many as 6 million Jews died in what has become known as the Holocaust. Millions of others, including Soviet prisoners of war, Poles, Gypsies, and people with handicaps—were also ruthlessly killed.

As Allied forces moved through Germany and Poland after V-E Day, they saw firsthand the unspeakable horrors of the camps. R.W. Thompson, a British reporter, wrote about one such camp:

❝Across the sandy clearing is the incinerator, but it ran out of [fuel]. A rough record by the chief burner of bodies records 17,000 burned last month. They say each body was roughly clubbed as it went in.❞

People around the world were stunned by this terrible result of Nazi tyranny.

In Remembrance

The United States Holocaust Memorial Museum is located near the National Mall in Washington, D.C. This memorial provides a national mark of respect for all victims of Nazi persecution. In 2001 Congress passed legislation to approve construction of the National World War II Memorial on a site on the National Mall. This is the first national memorial dedicated to all who served during the war.

✓ Reading Check **Identifying** What groups of people were victims of the Holocaust?

SECTION 4 ASSESSMENT

Checking for Understanding

1. **Key Terms** Define D-Day, genocide, **and** Holocaust.
2. **Reviewing Facts** In what region did the Allies launch an invasion after they drove the German forces out of North Africa?

Reviewing Themes

3. **Global Connections** When the United States joined the Allies, why did the Allies concentrate first on defeating Hitler?

Critical Thinking

4. **Drawing Conclusions** Why do you think Hitler felt threatened by Jews and other minorities?
5. **Organizing Information** Re-create the diagram below and describe the significance of these events.

Significance	
D-Day	V-E Day

Analyzing Visuals

6. **Geography Skills** Examine the map on page 771. When did the Allied forces launch an attack on German forces in North Africa?

Interdisciplinary Activity

Geography Draw a map of the former Soviet Union and use symbols to show the outcome of the battles between German and Soviet forces.

War in the Pacific

Guide to Reading

Main Idea
Japan's surrender ends World War II.

Key Terms
island hopping, kamikaze

Reading Strategy
Classifying Information As you read the section, re-create the diagram below and explain the importance of each subject.

	Importance
Island hopping	
Manhattan Project	
V-J Day	

Read to Learn
- how the United States planned to gain control of the Pacific region.
- what role the atomic bomb played in ending the war.

Section Theme
Global Connections When Japanese leaders would not surrender, President Truman ordered the use of the atomic bomb.

Preview of Events

♦1942　　　　　　　　　♦1944　　　　　　　　　♦1946

April 1942
Allies surrender Bataan

March 1945
Americans seize Iwo Jima

August 1945
Atomic bomb is dropped on Hiroshima

September 1945
Japan surrenders; World War II ends

AN American Story

Bob Krell, a soldier in World War II, felt a need to describe his life in the war: "At night before a big airborne operation you crawl deeper in your sack, but you can't get away from the noise. Over the roar of engines, somebody is shouting a bunch of names. . . . [W]e will climb into our parachutes as dawn breaks. We will trudge out to the planes and climb in, not saying much of anything about anything. . . ." Bob Krell was killed in action 12 hours after he wrote these words.

The war brought sadness to separated families

The Pacific Front

On December 7, 1941, the same day the Japanese attacked Pearl Harbor, Japanese bombers struck American airfields in the **Philippines** and on the islands of **Wake** and **Guam**—key American bases in the Pacific. In the following days, the Japanese intensified their campaign in the Pacific. They invaded Thailand and Malaya and captured Guam, Wake Island, and the British colony of Hong Kong.

Japanese troops had landed in the Philippines in mid-December and quickly taken the capital of Manila. The defending forces—Filipino and American troops commanded by American general **Douglas MacArthur**—were forced to retreat to the rugged **Bataan** Peninsula west of Manila and the small island fortress of **Corregidor.**

The Philippines Fall

After months of fierce fighting, the exhausted Allied troops defending Bataan surrendered on April 9, 1942. The forces on Corregidor held out for another month. The Japanese forced their Bataan prisoners—many sick and near starvation—to march to a prison camp more than 60 miles away. Only much later did the public learn

World War II in the Pacific

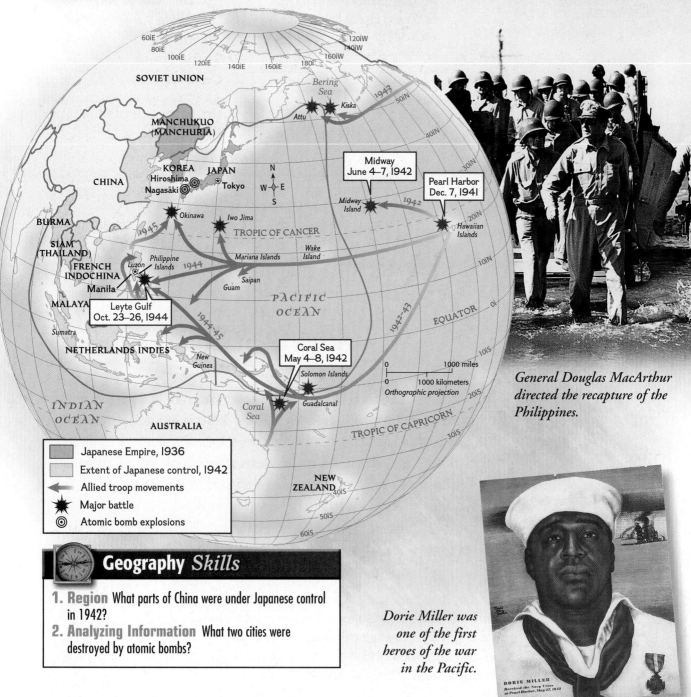

General Douglas MacArthur directed the recapture of the Philippines.

Dorie Miller was one of the first heroes of the war in the Pacific.

Geography *Skills*

1. **Region** What parts of China were under Japanese control in 1942?
2. **Analyzing Information** What two cities were destroyed by atomic bombs?

what these prisoners endured. About 76,000 prisoners started out, but only about 54,000 of those on the **Bataan Death March** reached the camp. As one survivor recalled:

> ❝Anybody that could walk, they forced 'em into line. . . . If you fell out to the side, you were either shot by the guards or you were bayoneted [stabbed] and left there.❞

Two months before the surrender, General MacArthur had left for Australia to take command of Allied forces in the Pacific. MacArthur promised the Filipinos, "I shall return."

Island Hopping

With Japan's string of quick victories, American morale was low. Then, in April, 16 American bombers, launched from an aircraft carrier in the Pacific, bombed **Tokyo.** This daring raid led by James Doolittle had little military importance, but it lifted Americans' spirits.

In May, American and Japanese fleets clashed in the Coral Sea northeast of Australia. American ships were heavily damaged, but the Japanese suffered crippling losses. The **Battle of the Coral Sea** was a strategic victory because it halted the Japanese advance on Australia.

An even greater victory followed in June 1942. In the **Battle of Midway,** northwest of Hawaii, the navy destroyed four Japanese aircraft carriers and hundreds of airplanes. This was the first major Japanese defeat.

The United States was now ready to go on the offensive against Japan. The commanders—General MacArthur and Admiral **Chester Nimitz**—adopted a strategy known as island hopping. This called for attacking and capturing certain key islands. The United States then used these islands as bases for leapfrogging to others, moving ever closer to the Philippines—and to Japan.

Between August 1942 and February 1943, American forces engaged in one of the most vicious campaigns of the war for the control of **Guadalcanal,** one of the Solomon Islands. Although the Japanese put up fierce resistance, the Americans finally secured the island.

In June 1944, American forces captured Guam and other islands nearby. Guam provided a base for launching bombing strikes on Japan. In October, American ships destroyed most of the Japanese fleet at the **Battle of Leyte Gulf** in the Philippines, the biggest naval battle in history—in all, 282 ships took part. MacArthur had fulfilled his promise to return to the Philippines.

HISTORY Online

Student Web Activity
Visit taj.glencoe.com and click on **Chapter 26— Student Web Activities** for an activity on World War II.

The Advance on Japan

American forces now closed in on Japan itself. In March 1945, they seized the island of **Iwo Jima** and in June the island of **Okinawa.** The Japanese fought fiercely to defend these islands so near to Japan. Thousands of Americans died in the battles, and many thousands more were wounded.

With most of Japan's air force and navy destroyed, American bombers pounded Tokyo and other Japanese cities. The raids killed thousands of civilians and crippled Japan's economy. In desperation, the Japanese unleashed a corps of suicide pilots known as kamikazes. They crashed planes loaded with explosives into American ships. Kamikaze pilots sank several destroyers during the battle for Okinawa.

☑ **Reading Check** **Explaining** What is significant about the Battle of Midway?

The Atomic Bomb

Although the Japanese faced certain defeat, they continued to fight. Their refusal to surrender led the United States to use a powerful new weapon: the atomic bomb.

In 1939 the German-born physicist **Albert Einstein** had written to President Roosevelt warning him that the Nazis might try to use the energy of the atom to build "extremely powerful bombs." Wanting to develop such weapons first, Roosevelt created a top-secret operation, the **Manhattan Project.** After years of work, scientists tested the atomic bomb in the New Mexico

Raising the U.S. flag at Iwo Jima

The War Ends

After the bombings, the Japanese government agreed to surrender. August 15, 1945, was proclaimed **V-J Day,** for "Victory over Japan." All around America, people expressed happiness and relief. Japan signed the formal surrender on September 2 aboard the battleship the U.S.S. *Missouri.* World War II had finally ended.

In the years immediately after the war, Allied authorities put the top Nazi and Japanese leaders on trial. They were accused of war crimes and crimes against humanity. The Allies held the trials in Nuremberg, Germany, and in Tokyo.

The Cost of the War

World War II was the most destructive conflict in history. More than 40 million people died during the war; more than half of these were civilians killed by bombing, starvation, disease, torture, and murder. American casualties—about 322,000 dead and 800,000 injured—were high, but light compared with those of other nations. The Soviet Union suffered more than 20 million deaths. Those who survived faced the huge task of trying to rebuild their lives and their countries. Nationalist movements grew, particularly in colonial nations that had suffered invasions by the warring powers. Many colonies began to seek independence in the postwar years.

desert on July 16, 1945. Truman now had to decide whether to use the bomb against Japan.

The Allies issued the **Potsdam Declaration,** warning that if Japan did not surrender, it faced "prompt and utter destruction." The Japanese leaders did not surrender, and Truman ordered the use of the bomb.

On August 6, 1945, an American B-29 bomber, the *Enola Gay,* dropped an atomic bomb on the Japanese city of **Hiroshima.** Three days later, a second bomb was dropped on the city of **Nagasaki.** The atomic bombs caused immense destruction. The first bomb leveled Hiroshima and killed about 70,000 people; the Nagasaki bomb killed about 40,000. Thousands more were injured, and many died later from radiation.

✓ **Reading Check** **Identifying** On what Japanese cities were atomic bombs dropped?

✓ **Reading Check** **Describing** Who was brought to trial at the Nuremberg trials?

SECTION 5 ASSESSMENT

Checking for Understanding

1. **Key Terms** Use each of these terms in a sentence that will help explain its meaning: island hopping, kamikaze.
2. **Reviewing Facts** Explain the significance of the Battle of Leyte Gulf.

Reviewing Themes

3. **Global Connections** Why did kamikaze missions pose such a deadly threat to Allied forces?

Critical Thinking

4. **Identifying Central Issues** If you had been president, would you have ordered the attacks on Hiroshima and Nagasaki? Why or why not?
5. **Sequencing Information** Re-create the time line below and list important events in the Pacific in 1945.

Mar. 1945	July 1945	Aug. 1945	Sept. 1945
☐	☐	☐	☐

Analyzing Visuals

6. **Geography Skills** Examine the map of World War II in the Pacific on page 778. What naval battle took place in May 1942? In June 1942?

Interdisciplinary Activity

Math Make a bar graph that compares the number of people killed during the war in the major Axis and Allied countries.

Writing a Paragraph

Why Learn This Skill?

Paragraphs are the building blocks of an essay or other composition. Each paragraph is a unit—a group of sentences about a single topic or idea.

Learning the Skill

Most well-written paragraphs share four characteristics.

- First, a paragraph expresses one main idea or is about one subject. A topic sentence states that main idea. The topic sentence may be located at the beginning, the middle, or the end of a paragraph.
- Second, the rest of the sentences in a paragraph support the main idea. The main idea may be developed by facts, examples, or reasons.
- Third, the sentences are arranged in a logical order.
- Fourth, transitional words link sentences within the paragraph. These words can also link one paragraph with the next. Examples include *next, then, finally, also, because, however,* and *as a result.*

Practicing the Skill

Use the following sentences to build a paragraph containing a topic sentence and other sentences that give supporting details. Put the sentences in a logical order and add transitional words if you need to. Underline your topic sentence.

1 Three days later an American plane dropped another bomb on Nagasaki.

2 The bomb killed about 70,000 people.

3 This second bomb killed nearly 40,000 people instantly and many more later.

Hiroshima after the atomic bomb

4 On August 6, 1945, the United States dropped an atomic bomb on Hiroshima, Japan.

5 About 100,000 others died later from the effects of radiation.

6 When the bomb exploded, a sheet of flame spread over the city.

Applying the Skill

Writing a Paragraph Choose a topic from the World War II era and write a paragraph about it. Then rewrite the paragraph with its sentences out of order. Exchange papers with a classmate. Can he or she find the topic sentence? Does it work logically?

 Glencoe's **Skillbuilder Interactive Workbook CD-ROM, Level 1,** provides instruction and practice in key social studies skills.

Chapter Summary
World War II

1931
- Japan invades Manchuria

1933
- Hitler becomes chancellor of Germany

1935
- Italian forces invade Ethiopia

1939
- Germany seizes Czechoslovakia
- Germany invades Poland

1940
- Germany bombs Britain

1941
- Hitler attacks the Soviet Union
- FDR establishes Fair Employment Practices Commission
- Japan bombs Pearl Harbor

1942
- Revenue Act raises taxes to finance the war
- Office of War Information promotes patriotism
- U.S. joins Allies
- Allies surrender Bataan

1943
- Navajo soldiers develop unbreakable radio code

1944
- Allied ships land at Normandy
- Battle of the Bulge

1945
- Germany surrenders
- Americans seize Iwo Jima
- Atomic bomb is dropped on Hiroshima
- Japan surrenders
- World War II ends

Reviewing Key Terms

Examine the pairs of words below. Then write a sentence explaining what the words in each pair have in common.

1. fascism, dictator
2. genocide, Holocaust
3. island hopping, blitzkrieg

Reviewing Key Facts

4. How did Britain and France try to prevent war with Germany?
5. When did Japan attack Pearl Harbor?
6. What did the government do to ensure that industries produced enough war materials?
7. What was Operation Overlord?
8. Who succeeded Franklin Roosevelt as president?
9. What actions by the Japanese convinced the United States to use the atomic bomb?

Critical Thinking

10. **Drawing Conclusions** Explain the importance to Hitler of Germany's 1939 non-agression treaty with the Soviet Union. Why do you suppose the Soviet Union signed it?
11. **Reviewing Themes: Economic Factors** Why did the government require rationing during the war?
12. **Drawing Conclusions** Why did the Allies focus first on the war in Europe rather than on the war in the Pacific?
13. **Comparing** Re-create the diagram below and compare the roles that the United States played in world affairs during the 1930s and 1940s.

	Role in world affairs
The U.S. in the 1930s	
The U.S. in the 1940s	

 Technology Activity

14. **Using the Internet** Search the Internet for a World War II site that includes memoirs or excerpts from veterans and/or civilians. Copy or print a part of the memoirs that you find interesting. Post the excerpts on the classroom bulletin board under the heading "Voices of World War II."

Geography and History Activity

The map below shows the attack on Pearl Harbor. Study the map and answer the questions that follow.

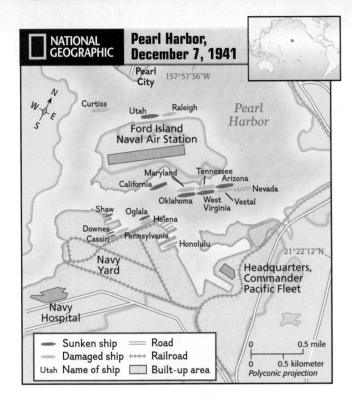

NATIONAL GEOGRAPHIC
Pearl Harbor, December 7, 1941

Pearl City   157°57'36"W

Curtiss
Utah   Raleigh
Pearl Harbor

Ford Island Naval Air Station

Maryland   Tennessee
California   Arizona
                              Nevada
Oklahoma   West   Vestal
                  Virginia

Shaw   Oglala
              Helena
Downes
Cassin   Pennsylvania
              Honolulu   21°22'12"N

Navy Yard

Headquarters, Commander Pacific Fleet

Navy Hospital

— Sunken ship   === Road
--- Damaged ship   +++ Railroad
Utah Name of ship   ▭ Built-up area

0   0.5 mile
0   0.5 kilometer
Polyconic projection

15. Location What ships are located along the eastern side of Ford Island?

16. Location What ships were nearest the *Nevada*?

17. Location What happened to the *Raleigh* during the attack?

Practicing Skills

Writing a Paragraph *Write a short paragraph for each of the topic sentences that follow. Each paragraph must have at least three sentences supporting the topic and arranged in a logical way. Use transitional words or phrases to connect your ideas smoothly.*

18. The leaders of Italy, Germany, and Japan attempted to restore their nations to their former greatness through the use of the military.

19. Minority groups played vital roles in World War II, both in the armed forces and at home.

HISTORY Online

Self-Check Quiz
Visit taj.glencoe.com and click on **Chapter 26— Self-Check Quizzes** to prepare for the chapter test.

Cooperative Citizenship Activity

20. Foreign Policy Goals With a partner, check current newspapers and newsmagazines for articles about United States relations with foreign nations. Clip the articles and build a table categorizing these relations under these headings: *Maintaining national security, Promoting world peace, Protecting free trade, Supporting democratic governments, and Promoting humane treatment of people.*

Economics Activity

21. How might rationing have changed the way families lived? Write a one-page paper in which you describe three ways rationing affected individuals and families during World War II.

 Alternative Assessment

22. Portfolio Writing Activity Choose a person discussed in this chapter. Research the life of this individual. Be sure to take notes about his or her life and accomplishments before, during, and after World War II. Write a one-page biography based on your findings.

The Princeton Review
Standardized Test Practice

Directions: Choose the *best* answer to the following question.

Which of the following was a turning point in Europe during World War II?

A The Treaty of Paris

B The election of Roosevelt

C The bombing of Pearl Harbor

D The German defeat at Stalingrad

Test-Taking Tip

Eliminate answers that you know are wrong. For example, choice **A,** the Treaty of Paris, was not made in World War II.

UNIT
10 Turning Points

1945–1975

Why It Matters

As you study Unit 10, *you will learn about the changes that came after World War II. Out of the war came a new sense of global responsibility as the United States made every effort to protect Western democracy. Many Americans pressed for social reform and equal rights. In addition, the use of new technology changed the way Americans lived and worked.*

Primary Sources Library

See pages 976–977 for primary source readings to accompany Unit 10.
Use the American history
Primary Source Document Library
CD-ROM *to find additional primary sources about the Cold War, the civil rights movement, and the Vietnam era.*

American soldier in
Vietnam, 1966

The Problem We All Live With
by Norman Rockwell

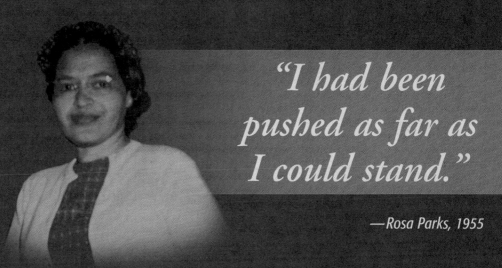

"I had been pushed as far as I could stand."

—Rosa Parks, 1955

The Cold War Era

1945–1954

Why It Matters

After the end of World War II, the United States and the Soviet Union entered into a bitter rivalry. Each side tried to gain allies and prove that its system—democracy and free enterprise or communism—was better.

The Impact Today

The rivalry between the United States and the Soviet Union shaped much of the modern world. The collapse of the Soviet Union in 1991 marked the end of the Cold War era.

The American Journey *Video* *The chapter 27 video, "The Wall and the Berlin Airlift," details the Berlin blockade and the effects of the Berlin airlift.*

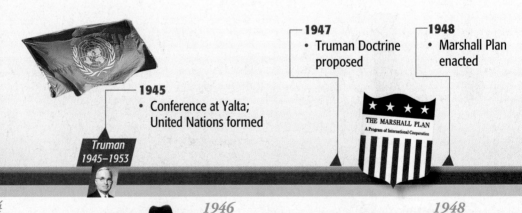

1945
• Conference at Yalta; United Nations formed

1947
• Truman Doctrine proposed

1948
• Marshall Plan enacted

THE MARSHALL PLAN
A Program of International Cooperation

United States
PRESIDENTS

Truman
1945–1953

1944   *1946*   *1948*

World

1946
• Churchill's "Iron Curtain" speech marks beginning of Cold War

1948
• Soviets blockade West Berlin
• State of Israel formed

Conflict in Korea United Nations troops fight in the streets of Seoul, South Korea, September 1950.

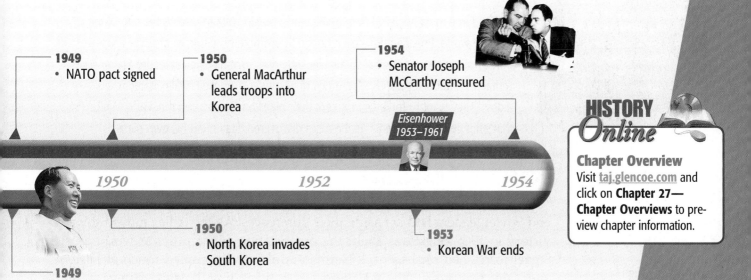

1949
• NATO pact signed

1950
• General MacArthur leads troops into Korea

1954
• Senator Joseph McCarthy censured

Eisenhower 1953–1961

1950   1952   1954

1950
• North Korea invades South Korea

1953
• Korean War ends

1949
• Communist victory in China under Mao Zedong

HISTORY Online

Chapter Overview Visit taj.glencoe.com and click on **Chapter 27— Chapter Overviews** to preview chapter information.

Cold War Origins

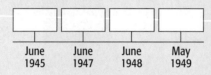

Guide to Reading

Main Idea
The United States struggled to prevent the spread of communism.

Key Terms
iron curtain, containment, airlift, cold war

Reading Strategy
Sequencing Information As you read the section, re-create the time line below and list important events in the Cold War.

June 1945	June 1947	June 1948	May 1949

Read to Learn
• how the United States attempted to stop the spread of communism.
• how foreign policy changed as a result of the Cold War.

Section Theme
Global Connections Soviet expansion led to a cold war between the forces of democracy and communism.

Preview of Events

♦ 1945   ♦ 1947   ♦ 1949

February 1945
Conference at Yalta is held

April 1945
Harry S Truman succeeds FDR

May 1948
Jewish leaders proclaim new state of Israel

June 1948
Soviets blockade West Berlin

October 1949
Mao Zedong forms Communist China

AN American Story

The Big Three at Yalta

The three most powerful men in the world met in Yalta to discuss the fate of the postwar world. President Roosevelt hoped to promote his vision of postwar cooperation. Prime Minister Churchill spoke elegantly and forcefully. Soviet leader Stalin remained stubbornly opposed to much of what was proposed. Stalin stated to his aides, "They want to force us to accept their plans on Europe and the world. Well, that's not going to happen." As the Allies discovered, Stalin had his own plans.

Wartime Diplomacy

While fighting a common enemy during World War II, Western democracies and Soviet leaders had set aside their differences. As the Allies moved toward victory in 1945, questions about the organization of the postwar world arose. Soviet forces had pushed back German armies and occupied much of Eastern and Central Europe. Should these areas—including Poland, Hungary, and Czechoslovakia—remain in Soviet hands?

In February 1945, the "Big Three" Allied leaders—**Franklin D. Roosevelt, Winston Churchill,** and **Joseph Stalin**—met at Yalta, a Soviet port on the Black Sea. They came to discuss issues affecting the postwar world. Out of this meeting came the Yalta agreement, in which the Soviet Union agreed to enter the war against Japan. In return, the Soviets received some territories in Asia.

Reaching an agreement on postwar arrangements proved more difficult. Roosevelt and Churchill feared the Soviet domination of Eastern Europe and the spread of communism. Stalin, on the other hand, wanted to keep a large area of land between the Soviet Union and its potential enemies in the West. Germany presented a special problem. The Allies finally agreed to divide Germany into four zones until elections could be held to determine its future. The Soviet Union, the United States, Britain, and France would each control a zone.

Stalin agreed to allow free elections in occupied Eastern Europe and to cooperate in planning for the new international organization proposed by the United States and Britain. Roosevelt and Churchill felt encouraged about a peaceful postwar world. Their hopes went unfulfilled.

NATIONAL GEOGRAPHIC

Europe After World War II

Communist control
Divided nation
NATO member
Neutral nation
⊙ Jointly-occupied city

Geography *Skills*

1. Place What nations of Europe remained neutral?
2. Region Were most of the nations of Eastern Europe NATO members or under Communist control?

The United Nations

President Roosevelt died suddenly on April 12, 1945. Vice President **Harry S Truman** succeeded him. Facing the enormous responsibilities of the presidency, Truman told reporters, "When they told me yesterday [of Roosevelt's death], I felt like the moon, the stars, and all the planets had fallen on me."

One of Truman's first decisions as president was to go ahead with the meeting to form the new international organization discussed at Yalta. On June 26, in San Francisco, California, 50 nations—including the Soviet Union—signed the charter creating the **United Nations** (UN). The members hoped the UN could settle disputes between nations and prevent future wars.

✓ **Reading Check** **Describing** How did the Allies agree to divide Germany?

⭐Geography

Soviet Expansion in Europe

The uneasy wartime alliance between the Western nations and the Soviet Union did not last. Stalin did not keep his promise to hold free elections in Eastern Europe. Instead the Soviets set up Communist governments in these countries, and Soviet forces remained in the region.

Developments in Eastern Europe led to a growing distrust between the Soviet Union and Western nations. Europe split into two camps—the Soviet-controlled Communist governments of the East and the capitalist democracies.

The Iron Curtain

Winston Churchill believed that the division between East and West was permanent. In 1946 he declared in a speech in Fulton, Missouri, that an *"iron curtain"* had descended on Europe. Churchill meant that the Soviets had cut off Eastern Europe from the West. Behind this iron curtain, he said, lay the countries of Eastern Europe "in what I must call the Soviet sphere, and all are subject to a very high . . . measure of control from Moscow."

Churchill warned that the Soviets would eventually look beyond Eastern Europe and try to gain control of other parts of the world. This idea alarmed Americans, who had feared the spread of communism ever since the Russian Revolution in 1917.

Civil war raged in **Greece,** as Communist rebels armed by the Soviet Union attempted to overthrow the Greek king and his pro-Western government. At the same time, the Soviets put enormous pressure on **Turkey** to give them naval bases on the straits leading to the Mediterranean Sea.

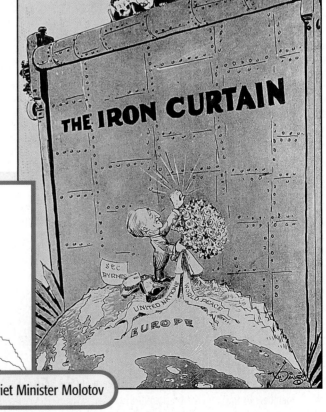

Analyzing *Political Cartoons*

The iron curtain represented a barrier to the free exchange of ideas between countries under Soviet control and the rest of the world. The iron curtain often appeared in cartoons about the Cold War. **What does the cartoon say about the attitude of Secretary of State Byrnes toward the Soviet leaders?**

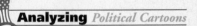

A Secretary of State Byrnes   **B** Joseph Stalin   **C** Soviet Minister Molotov

Containing the Soviets

Seeking ways to counter Soviet expansion, President Truman drew from the ideas of **George F. Kennan,** an American diplomat and an expert on Soviet history and culture. Kennan argued that the United States and the Soviet Union could not cooperate and that the United States must take forceful steps to stop Soviet expansion. His ideas led to the policy of containment. The United States would try to "contain" Soviet expansion through limited military means and nonmilitary means in areas of the world that were of strategic importance to the United States. Kennan defined these areas narrowly—mostly Western Europe and Japan. But other U.S. officials gradually expanded their view of what was of strategic importance to the country and its future.

The Truman Doctrine

The policy of containment soon went into effect. Speaking to Congress in March 1947, the president proposed a policy that became known as the **Truman Doctrine,** a commitment to help nations threatened by communism and Soviet expansion.

> 66 I believe that it must be the policy of the United States to support free peoples who are resisting attempted subjugation [conquest] by armed minorities or by outside pressures. 99

Congress voted to give military and economic assistance to Greece and Turkey to hold back the Soviet threat.

The Marshall Plan

At the end of World War II, much of Europe lay in ruins. Bombing had destroyed countless houses, factories, bridges, and roads. Many people lacked homes and jobs, and they often did not have enough food. Their war-ravaged societies provided fertile ground for communism, with its promises of housing and employment for all.

George Marshall, the U.S. secretary of state, saw Western Europe as strategically important to the United States. He believed that the best way to keep the countries of Western Europe free of communism would be to help restore their economies. In June 1947, Marshall proposed a plan to provide massive economic aid to Europe. At first his plan met some resistance in Congress. After Soviet-supported Communists took over the government of **Czechoslovakia** in February 1948, however, this resistance disappeared.

Congress approved the Marshall Plan, a program of economic aid for Europe that became a vital part of the policy of containment. Between 1948 and 1951, the Marshall Plan contributed nearly $13 billion to the rebuilding of the countries of Western Europe. As Marshall had predicted, no Western government in the region fell to a communist revolution.

Reading Check **Explaining** How was the Marshall Plan supposed to check communist expansion?

Crisis in Berlin

The Allied leaders at Yalta had divided Germany into four occupation zones. The Soviet Union controlled the eastern part of the country, while the United States, Britain, and France divided the western part. The German capital of **Berlin,** located deep within Soviet-controlled East Germany, was also divided among the four nations.

President Truman believed that a reunited Germany was essential to the future of Europe. Stalin, on the other hand, feared that a reunited Germany would once again pose a threat to the Soviet Union. He sought to maintain Soviet influence in a divided Germany. Tensions over the German issue led to a serious crisis in 1948.

The Berlin Blockade

On June 7, 1948, the United States, Britain, and France announced that they were uniting their zones to form a new West German republic. Each nation's section of Berlin would be included in this republic as well, even though the city lay within Soviet-held East Germany.

The **Berlin blockade** was Stalin's answer to the West's plans for West Germany. On June 24, 1948, Soviet troops rushed into position around the edge of West Berlin. Almost overnight they created a blockade, stopping traffic on all highway,

Berlin Airlift

In June 1948, the Soviet Union halted all traffic by land or water into or out of Western-controlled Berlin. Allied Powers began supplying the city's 2.5 million residents with the necessities of life—by air. Night and day for more than 10 months, British and United States cargo planes carried food, medicine, clothing, raw materials, and even coal to Berlin. World opinion turned against the Soviet Union and its tactics of starving innocent people to achieve its goals. Berlin became a symbol of America's fight against communism.

The effort—some 278,000 flights delivering 2 million tons of supplies—melted the hatred between former American and German enemies. In May 1949, the Soviet Union finally lifted its blockade.

railroad, and water routes through East Germany to West Berlin. As a result, West Berlin and its two million citizens were cut off from vital supplies. The Soviets hoped this blockade would drive the West out of Berlin.

The Berlin Airlift

President Truman refused to give in to the Soviets. "We stay in Berlin, period," he declared, but he did not want to risk war by using military force to end the blockade. Instead he organized a massive airlift to save the city. American and British cargo planes began flying food, fuel, and other supplies into West Berlin.

The **Berlin airlift** continued day and night for more than 10 months, delivering tons of supplies to West Berlin. Realizing that the Western powers intended to stay in the city, Stalin ended the Berlin blockade in May 1949. Despite the success of the airlift, Berlin and Germany remained divided. In October 1949, the division of Germany into two

nations—the **Federal Republic of Germany,** or West Germany, and the **German Democratic Republic,** or East Germany—became official.

✓ **Reading Check** **Analyzing** How did the Soviet Union respond to plans to form a new West German republic?

Two Armed Camps

The crisis in Berlin confirmed that the United States and the Soviet Union were locked in a cold war—a war in which the two enemies did not actually fight each other. Instead each nation began building up its military forces and arms to intimidate the other. European nations began to take sides in this mounting cold war.

The United States and the countries of Western Europe agreed that the best way to contain the Soviets was through mutual defense. In

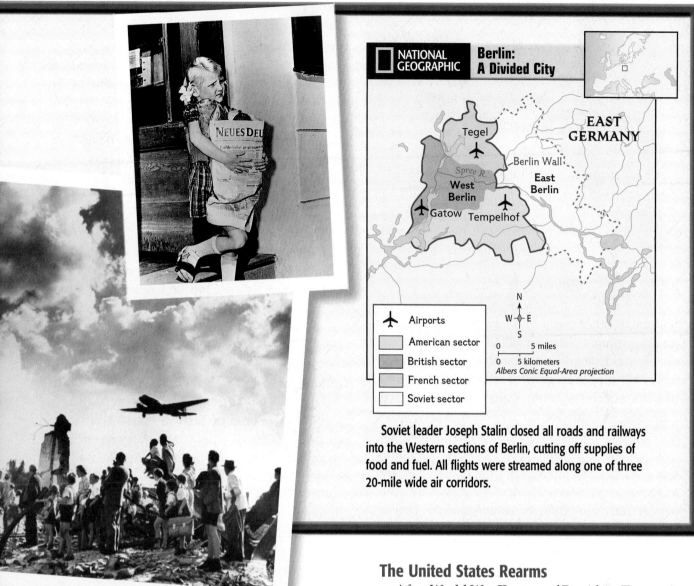

**Berlin:
A Divided City**

EAST
GERMANY

Tegel

Berlin Wall

Spree R.

East
Berlin

West
Berlin

Gatow   Tempelhof

N
W ◆ E
S

0   5 miles
0   5 kilometers
Albers Conic Equal-Area projection

✈ Airports

American sector

British sector

French sector

Soviet sector

Soviet leader Joseph Stalin closed all roads and railways
into the Western sections of Berlin, cutting off supplies of
food and fuel. All flights were streamed along one of three
20-mile wide air corridors.

April 1949, the United States, Canada, and 10 Western European nations signed a pact establishing the **North Atlantic Treaty Organization** (NATO). The agreement stated that "an armed attack against one or more of [the member nations] shall be considered an attack against all." To defend against a possible Soviet invasion of Western Europe, the NATO countries created a large military force.

In response to NATO, the Soviet Union created an alliance of its own with the Communist governments of Eastern Europe. The alliance, established in 1955 by mutual defense treaties known as the **Warsaw Pact,** had a military force that the Soviet Union controlled. The formation of NATO and the Warsaw Pact divided Europe into two armed camps.

The United States Rearms

After World War II, some of President Truman's foreign policy advisers in the **National Security Council** (NSC) argued that America could not rely on other nations to contain the Soviets and resist the spread of communism. Unlike George Kennan and the supporters of the containment policy, the NSC advisers believed the United States needed to take a more active stand against communism everywhere—not just in strategic locations.

In 1950 the NSC released a report, known as **NSC-68,** which said that the United States must actively

❝foster the seeds of destruction within the Soviet Union❞

and fight communist movements wherever they arose. The United States committed itself to combating communist expansion everywhere in the world.

Germany

Germany is reunified On October 3, 1990, the two parts of Germany finally reunited, and Berlin—rejoined as one city—again became the nation's official capital. The German government's move to Berlin from the West German capital of Bonn is scheduled to be completed in the year 2003.

Independence Movements

As the Cold War grew more bitter in Europe, nations in other parts of the world were undergoing dramatic changes. Many states broke free of colonial rule and established independence.

The Philippines gained independence from the United States in 1946. For years afterward Filipinos struggled with terrible poverty, government corruption, and civil war. In the late 1940s, Asian countries such as India, Pakistan, and Burma broke away from the British Empire to form new nations. During the 1950s and the early 1960s, more than 25 African nations gained independence from European colonial powers. The path to independence in Africa was often bloody. Once free, the new nations faced the enormous task of building modern societies.

In the Middle East, Jews and Arabs both claimed the region of **Palestine,** an area the British had controlled. In 1947 the United Nations proposed dividing Palestine into independent Jewish and Arab states with Jerusalem as an international city. The Jews accepted the plan, but the Arab states did not. After declaring its independence, the new Jewish state of **Israel** was attacked by Arab armies in the first of six major wars between the Arabs and Israel.

Communism in China

Perhaps the most threatening change of the postwar period occurred in **China,** the largest country in Asia. In 1949 a long civil war ended with the victory of Chinese Communist forces led by **Mao Zedong** (MAU ZUH•DUNG) over the armies commanded by **Chiang Kai-shek** (JEE•AHNG KY•SHEHK), the head of the Chinese government. Mao Zedong formed a new Communist state, the People's Republic of China, while Chiang Kai-shek retreated with his forces to the island of **Taiwan** off the southeastern coast of China. The United States recognized the government in Taiwan as the legitimate government of all China.

With Communists in control of mainland China, the Soviet Union had a powerful ally in Asia. It appeared to many people that the entire continent of Asia was in danger of converting to communism.

☑ **Reading Check** **Identifying** What new nation was formed in the Middle East in the 1940s?

SECTION 1 ASSESSMENT

Checking for Understanding

1. **Key Terms** Write a paragraph in which you use each of the following terms correctly: iron curtain, containment, airlift, cold war.

2. **Reviewing Facts** Did the Berlin blockade force the Western powers to leave the city? Explain.

Reviewing Themes

3. **Global Connections** What was the purpose of the Truman Doctrine?

Critical Thinking

4. **Analyzing Information** Explain why the United States's actions during the Berlin blockade were considered part of a "cold war."

5. **Determining Cause and Effect** Re-create the diagram below and explain how the Marshall Plan helped to contain the spread of communism.

| Marshall Plan | ⇨ | |

Analyzing Visuals

6. **Geography Skills** Examine the map of Europe on page 789. Was Spain a neutral nation? Was Turkey a NATO member?

Interdisciplinary Activity

Geography Compare a map of Africa after World War II to a map of Africa today. Photocopy or draw a modern map and indicate five countries that have changed their names or boundaries.

Critical Thinking SKILLBUILDER

Making Inferences

Why Learn This Skill?

Have you heard someone say, "You can't judge him on face value"? It means that people, things you see, or things you read might not be as they appear to be. There might be a double or hidden meaning to what you see or hear.

Learning the Skill

Inferences are ideas that are not directly stated. **Making Inferences** involves reading between the lines to interpret what you are seeing. You call upon some previous knowledge or just use common sense.

Practicing the Skill

First published at the beginning of the Cold War, *Animal Farm* by George Orwell tells the story of a farm taken over by its overworked, mistreated animals. The fable exposes the negative effects that totalitarian government can have on society. Read this passage from George Orwell's novel *Animal Farm.* Then answer the questions that follow.

> Squealer tries to persuade the animals that Napoleon is a good leader, saying, "Do not imagine, comrades, that leadership is a pleasure! On the contrary, it is a deep and heavy responsibility. No one believes more firmly than Comrade Napoleon that all animals are equal. He would be only too happy to let you make your decisions for yourselves. But sometimes you might make the wrong decisions, comrades, and then where should we be? Suppose you had decided to follow Snowball . . . ?"
>
> "He fought bravely at the Battle of the Cowshed," said somebody.
>
> "Bravery is not enough," said Squealer. "Loyalty and obedience are more important . . ."

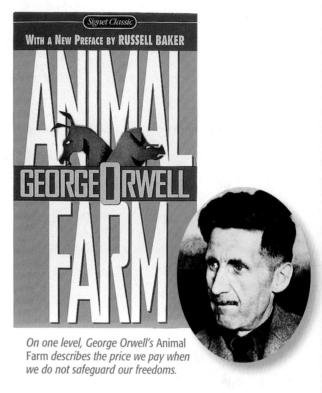

On one level, George Orwell's Animal Farm *describes the price we pay when we do not safeguard our freedoms.*

① Does Squealer represent the leaders or the common animals?

② Why does he say that leadership is a "deep and heavy responsibility?"

③ Squealer says that all animals are equal. Does he really believe this? Explain.

Applying the Skill

Making Inferences Choose a poem, or a quote found in a newspaper, that you think has more than one meaning. Share your selection with a classmate to see if they infer a hidden meaning.

 Glencoe's **Skillbuilder Interactive Workbook CD-ROM, Level 1,** provides instruction and practice in key social studies skills.

Postwar Politics

Guide to Reading

Main Idea
The Truman administration pushed for economic and social reform.

Key Terms
inflation, closed shop

Reading Strategy
Organizing Information As you read the section, re-create the diagram below and identify three measures that were part of Truman's Fair Deal.

The Fair Deal

Read to Learn
- what economic problems Americans faced after World War II.
- what actions President Truman and Congress proposed to deal with the nation's problems.

Section Theme
Economic Factors Americans tried to adjust to a peacetime economy after World War II.

Preview of Events

♦1944   ♦1946   ♦1948

1944
Congress approves the GI Bill of Rights

1946
Miners and railroad workers strike

1947
Taft-Hartley Act limits unions

1948
Truman wins the presidency

Harry S Truman

★ *AN* ★
American Story

When soldiers returned home after World War II, they came back to a nation facing the difficult task of changing from wartime to peacetime. Would the economy collapse again and another depression sweep the country? President Truman was optimistic: "We are having our little troubles now. Just a blow-up after a little let-down from war." Public concern, however, forced the nation's political leaders into a heated debate over the best way to deal with America's economic problems.

⑤ Economics

The Postwar Economy

After World War II, the nation and its economy had to adjust to peacetime life. Industries had to shift from producing war materials to making **consumer goods.** Defense workers had to be retrained to work in consumer industries, and returning soldiers needed jobs.

During the war, government price controls had kept the cost of consumer goods such as food and clothing quite stable. When the government removed these controls, prices began to surge. This rise in prices, or inflation, also resulted from a huge increase in consumer demand and spending. During the war years,

Americans had saved their money because many consumer goods were unavailable or rationed. Now they were eager to spend this money on new consumer products and services.

Workers Seek Higher Wages

As a result of inflation, consumer prices rose at a much faster rate than wages. During the war, workers had accepted government controls on wages and agreed not to strike. Now they would no longer be put off. When employers refused to raise wages, labor unions called for strikes. In 1945 and 1946, millions of steelworkers, railroad workers, and others walked off their jobs, demanding higher wages and better conditions.

Labor unrest and strikes disrupted the nation's economy. When miners went on strike in 1946, many Americans feared that dwindling coal supplies would cause the economy to grind to a halt. At about the same time, a strike by railroad workers caused a total shutdown of the nation's railroads, which were vital to the economy.

Truman Takes Action

Alarmed by the labor unrest, President Truman pressured the striking miners and railroad workers to go back to their jobs. In May 1946, he threatened to draft them into the army if they did not return to work. The president insisted he had the right to take such steps to keep vital industries operating.

President Truman finally forced striking miners back on the job by having the government take over the mines. At the same time, however, he persuaded the mine owners to grant many of the workers' demands. Truman also pressured railroad workers to return to work.

✓ Reading Check Describing What happened to the price of consumer goods when demand grew after the war?

Truman Faces the Republicans

In September 1945, President Truman, a Democrat, presented Congress with a plan of domestic reforms aimed at solving some of the nation's economic problems. Truman later called this program the **Fair Deal.**

Truman proposed to raise the minimum wage, expand Social Security benefits, increase federal spending to create jobs, build new public housing, and create a system of national health insurance. However, because of opposition by a coalition of Republicans and Southern Democrats, these measures failed to pass in Congress.

Republicans Control Congress

Many Americans blamed Truman and the Democratic Party for the nation's economic problems. In the congressional elections of 1946, the slogan "Had Enough?" helped Republicans win control of both houses of Congress.

The new Republican Congress moved quickly to create its own plans for the nation. Having rejected Truman's program for reform, the Republicans now set up proposals to enact a program that would limit government spending, control labor unions, reduce government regulation of the economy, and reverse policies adopted in the 1930s under FDR's New Deal.

For many Republicans in Congress, the most important problem facing the nation was labor unrest and the growing power of labor unions. Conservative Republicans favored big business

Analyzing *Political Cartoons*

President Truman and Congress were often at odds over the Fair Deal. **What is the cartoonist saying about Truman's power?**

KINDA PINCHES ACROSS THE TOES — GIMME A SIZE LARGER.

VAST PRESIDENTIAL AUTHORITY

CONGRESS

and wanted to limit the power of unions. In the spring of 1947, Congress introduced the **Taft-Hartley bill.** This bill limited the actions workers could take against their employers. It outlawed the closed shop, a workplace that hires only union members. It also allowed the government to temporarily stop any strike that endangered public health or safety. This provision aimed to prevent any future strikes like those of the miners and the railroad workers the year before. Union members and their leaders sharply criticized the Taft-Hartley Act, calling it a "slave labor bill." Although President Truman opposed recent strikes, he also knew that the Democrats needed the support of labor. Truman vetoed the act, but the Republican-controlled Congress overrode his veto.

Government Reorganization

One issue on which Truman and Congress agreed was the need to improve the administration of the federal government, which had greatly expanded since the New Deal. In 1947 Truman appointed a commission headed by former President Herbert Hoover to study ways of improving the efficiency of government. Out of the Hoover Commission's work came plans to create new government departments and agencies.

In 1947 Congress passed the **National Security Act.** It unified the army, navy, marines, and air force under the Department of Defense. A secretary of defense headed the new department. The act also set up a permanent Joint Chiefs of Staff, made up of the heads of each of the armed forces to coordinate military policy. A National Security Council, operating out of the White House, would advise the president on foreign and military matters.

The National Security Act also set up another institution, the **Central Intelligence Agency (CIA).** The CIA aids American foreign policy by collecting information about what is going on in other countries, evaluating it, and passing it

Trading Weapons for Textbooks

Welcome to Indiana University

The GI Bill

In 1944 Congress passed the Servicemen's Readjustment Act, better known as the GI Bill of Rights. GI stands for government issue. This law provided billions of dollars in loans to help returning GI's—soldiers, sailors, and marines—attend college, receive special training, set up businesses, or buy homes. It also provided unemployment and health benefits for the GI's as they looked for jobs.

By making it possible for millions of GI's to go to college, the GI Bill changed U.S. higher education forever. University education was now open to people from every income level.

on to the president and other foreign-policy decision makers. The CIA uses its own secret agents, paid informers, and friendly governments to collect such information.

Many Americans feared that the CIA would be used to spy on American citizens. Truman, however, promised that the new agency would operate only in foreign lands and would not bring "police state methods" into American society. The CIA was so successful that in 1949 Congress gave that agency the right to receive, exchange, and spend money without giving account to Congress.

The Election of 1948

As the 1948 presidential election approached, Truman appeared to be the underdog. Continuing economic problems made the president unpopular with many Americans, and his lack of success in winning passage of domestic reforms made Truman's administration look weak and ineffective.

Divisions within the Democratic Party also increased the chances of an easy Republican victory. At the party's national convention, a group of Southern Democrats walked out to protest Truman's support for civil rights legislation. The Southern Democrats formed the States' Rights Democratic Party, or Dixiecrats, and nominated Governor **Strom Thurmond** of South Carolina for president. At the same time, some liberal members of the Democratic Party left to form the Progressive Party, with **Henry Wallace** as their nominee for president. Wallace opposed Truman's foreign policy and called for closer ties between the United States and the Soviet Union.

Dewey Leads Polls

With the Democrats badly divided, it looked as though Governor **Thomas Dewey** of New York, the Republican nominee, would surely win the election. Opinion polls showed Dewey with a huge lead. One pollster remarked: "Mr. Dewey is still so clearly ahead that we might just as well get ready to listen to his inaugural."

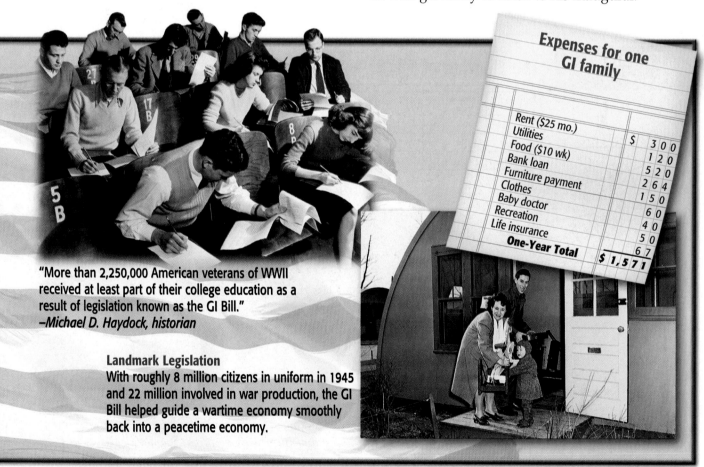

"More than 2,250,000 American veterans of WWII received at least part of their college education as a result of legislation known as the GI Bill."
–Michael D. Haydock, historian

Expenses for one GI family

Rent ($25 mo.)	$	3 0 0
Utilities		1 2 0
Food ($10 wk)		5 2 0
Bank loan		2 6 4
Furniture payment		1 5 0
Clothes		6 0
Baby doctor		4 0
Recreation		5 0
Life insurance		6 7
One-Year Total	$	**1,5 7 1**

Landmark Legislation
With roughly 8 million citizens in uniform in 1945 and 22 million involved in war production, the GI Bill helped guide a wartime economy smoothly back into a peacetime economy.

Truman campaigned aggressively. Traveling more than 30,000 miles (48,000 km) by train on a "whistle-stop" tour of the country, he gave some 250 speeches along the way. In town after town, he sharply attacked what he called "that do-nothing, good-for-nothing, worst Congress" for rejecting his Fair Deal legislation.

Truman Stages an Upset

On Election Day experts still expected Dewey to win. Expectations for a Republican victory were so great that on the evening of the election—before many votes were counted—the *Chicago Daily Tribune* newspaper issued a special edition announcing "Dewey Defeats Truman."

The nation was in for a great surprise. When all the ballots were counted, Truman had edged out Dewey by more than two million votes in a narrow upset victory. Democrats also regained control of both the House of Representatives and the Senate in the election.

Reading Check **Analyzing** Why was the outcome of the 1948 presidential election a surprise?

A Fair Deal for Americans

Truman took the election results as a sign that Americans wanted reform. He quickly reintroduced the **Fair Deal** legislation he had presented to Congress in 1945. Some of these reform measures passed, but his plan lacked broad support, and Congress defeated most of the measures. Congress did pass laws to raise the minimum wage, expand Social Security benefits for senior citizens, and provide funds for housing for low-income families.

◖Citizenship
A Stand on Civil Rights

In a message to Congress in 1948, President Truman declared:

❝We shall not, however, finally achieve the ideals for which this nation was founded so long as any American suffers discrimination as a result of his race, or religion, or color, or the land of origin of his forefathers.❞

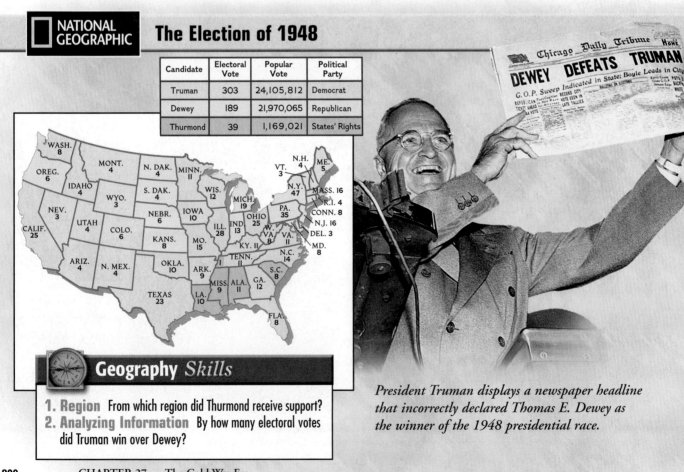

NATIONAL GEOGRAPHIC **The Election of 1948**

Candidate	Electoral Vote	Popular Vote	Political Party
Truman	303	24,105,812	Democrat
Dewey	189	21,970,065	Republican
Thurmond	39	1,169,021	States' Rights

Geography *Skills*

1. **Region** From which region did Thurmond receive support?
2. **Analyzing Information** By how many electoral votes did Truman win over Dewey?

President Truman displays a newspaper headline that incorrectly declared Thomas E. Dewey as the winner of the 1948 presidential race.

Picturing **History**

African Americans welcome Truman to Harlem during his 1948 presidential campaign. **How was Truman successful in advancing civil rights?**

1948 civil rights button

and ordered the armed forces to **desegregate**—to end the separation of races. The president also instructed the Justice Department to actively enforce existing civil rights laws. When Truman proposed his domestic agenda to Congress in 1949, he proclaimed that "every segment of our population and every individual has a right to expect from our government a fair deal." Truman asked for the clearance of slums, government-backed medical insurance, higher minimum wages, and more federal money for public schools. Although much of the president's Fair Deal vision went unfulfilled, he made an important start toward improving the lives of millions of Americans.

Although Truman championed ending such discrimination, he was unable to persuade Congress to pass legislation that would protect the voting rights of African Americans, abolish the poll tax, and make lynching a federal crime. Still, President Truman did take serious steps to advance the civil rights of African Americans. He ordered federal departments and agencies to end job discrimination against African Americans

---

SECTION 2 ASSESSMENT

Checking for Understanding

1. **Key Terms** Use the terms inflation and closed shop in sentences that will help explain their meaning.
2. **Reviewing Facts** What actions did President Truman take in order to advance the civil rights of African Americans?

Reviewing Themes

3. **Economic Factors** What factors caused inflation of prices after World War II?

Critical Thinking

4. **Determining Cause and Effect** How did the Taft-Hartley Act affect business and unions?
5. **Organizing Information** Complete a diagram like the one shown by describing the adjustments made in the United States to convert from a wartime to a peacetime economy.

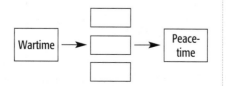

Analyzing Visuals

6. **Geography Skills** Examine the election map on page 800. Was the total number of votes cast for Dewey and Thurmond greater than Truman's total?

Interdisciplinary Activity

Economics At a library, view copies of newspapers published five years ago. Compare the prices of three items advertised at that time to the same items today. Calculate the percent of increase (or decrease) in price for each of the products.

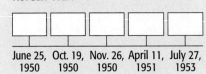

SECTION 3 The Korean War

Guide to Reading

Main Idea
Americans under the United Nations flag fought to stop a Communist takeover of the Korean peninsula.

Key Terms
stalemate, demilitarized zone

Reading Strategy
Sequencing Information As you read the section, re-create the time line below and list key events in the Korean War.

June 25, 1950   Oct. 19, 1950   Nov. 26, 1950   April 11, 1951   July 27, 1953

Read to Learn
• what events led to the Korean War.
• how America's war aims changed during the war.

Section Theme
Global Connections The United States fought in Korea to stop Communist expansion.

Preview of Events

◆1950   ◆1952   ◆1954

June 1950
North Korea invades South Korea

April 1951
Truman fires General MacArthur

July 1953
Cease-fire agreement is signed

Korean service medal

AN American Story

The bitter wind stung the raw faces of 12 U.S. Marine officers. They had just fought for five bloody days to lead their troops out of a Chinese trap in the icy wastes of northeast Korea. Now they listened to the words of their commander: "We are going to come out of this as Marines, not as stragglers. We're going to bring out our wounded and our equipment. We're coming out . . . as Marines or not at all." Two more days of fighting followed, as the tired but determined Marines held off fierce enemy attacks. With the arrival of air cover on the third day, the Marines were able to push back the Chinese and make their escape.

Conflict in Korea

Before June 1950, few Americans knew much about **Korea,** a small east Asian country located on the Korean Peninsula west of Japan. In 1945 Korea was a colony of Japan. At the end of World War II, Japan was stripped of its territorial possessions. The United States and the Soviet Union both sent troops into Korea and agreed to occupy it temporarily. They divided the peninsula in half along the **38th parallel** of latitude, with the Soviets controlling North Korea and the Americans controlling South Korea.

The Soviet Union and the United States could not agree on how to unify Korea. When these two nations removed their forces in 1949, Korea remained divided. Tensions between the two Koreas were high.

On June 24, 1950, President Truman flew to his home in Independence, Missouri, for a brief vacation. While sitting on his porch on a hot summer night, the president received a telephone call from Secretary of State Dean Acheson. "Mr. President," Acheson said in a grim tone, "I have very serious news. The North Koreans have invaded South Korea." Truman knew this meant only one thing: the United States soon would be involved in military action in Asia.

The Invasion of South Korea

After the American troops pulled out of South Korea, North Korea decided to unify the country by force. On June 25, 1950, the armies of North Korea crossed the 38th parallel into South Korea. Poorly armed, the South Koreans were no match for the North. Within days the Communist forces had gained control over much of South Korea, including **Seoul**, the capital city.

President Truman reacted quickly to the Korean invasion, which he believed was supported by the Soviet Union. Without asking Congress to actually declare war, Truman ordered the use of limited American air and sea forces in Korea. He called this "police action" necessary to carry out America's policy of containment. Truman said:

> 66Korea is the Greece of the Far East. If we are tough enough now, if we stand up to them like we did in Greece three years ago, they won't take any next steps.99

United Nations Responds

At the same time, President Truman asked the UN to send forces to defend the South Koreans. The United Nations condemned the invasion of South Korea and agreed to send a special force to the region under the United States's direction. President Truman quickly appointed General **Douglas MacArthur,** a hero of World War II, to command the UN forces.

On June 30, just days after the North Korean invasion, General MacArthur led American troops into Korea to stop the Communist advance. By the end of 1950, other nations were supplying troops or other assistance to the American-led war effort. Even so, Americans made up the majority of troops throughout the Korean War.

The United Nations had a clear but difficult goal—push the North Koreans back across the 38th parallel. When China intervened in the conflict, this goal changed, causing Truman and MacArthur to clash over military strategy.

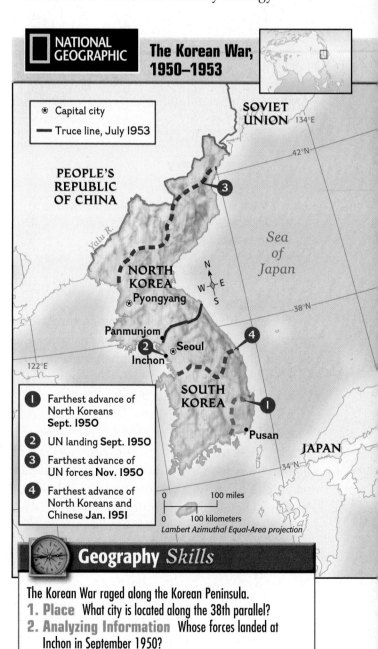

NATIONAL GEOGRAPHIC

The Korean War, 1950–1953

* Capital city
— Truce line, July 1953

PEOPLE'S REPUBLIC OF CHINA

SOVIET UNION

Sea of Japan

NORTH KOREA
⊛ Pyongyang

Panmunjom

Inchon
⊛ Seoul

SOUTH KOREA

Pusan

JAPAN

1. Farthest advance of North Koreans **Sept. 1950**
2. UN landing **Sept. 1950**
3. Farthest advance of UN forces **Nov. 1950**
4. Farthest advance of North Koreans and Chinese **Jan. 1951**

0   100 miles
0   100 kilometers
Lambert Azimuthal Equal-Area projection

Geography Skills

The Korean War raged along the Korean Peninsula.
1. **Place** What city is located along the 38th parallel?
2. **Analyzing Information** Whose forces landed at Inchon in September 1950?

Picturing **History**

American troops move forward to the battlefield, while South Korean women and children flee from the Communists. **What was the state of the Korean conflict by January 1951?**

Early Phases of the War

By September 1950, North Korean forces had pushed all the way to the southern tip of the Korean Peninsula. Only a small area in the southeast around the port city of **Pusan** was still held by the South Korean army.

After joining the South Koreans, General MacArthur designed a bold counterattack against North Korea. In September, United Nations forces made a daring landing midway on the Korean Peninsula near the port of **Inchon**. They took that strategic city and moved on to recapture Seoul.

Meanwhile American and UN troops began pushing north from Pusan. By October 1 the North Koreans, caught between UN forces advancing from both Seoul and Pusan, were forced to retreat north across the 38th parallel. South Korea now came under the control of the United Nations forces.

Taking the Offensive

Encouraged by this success, General MacArthur urged President Truman to order an invasion of North Korea. He assured Truman that neither **China** nor the Soviet Union would enter the war to help North Korea, and he promised to have troops "home by Christmas." Truman sought and received approval from the United Nations to cross the 38th parallel, invade the North, and create "a unified, independent and democratic Korea"—a new goal for the war.

After receiving these new orders, MacArthur moved his forces northward. The UN forces captured **Pyongyang,** the North Korean capital, on October 19, and then moved north toward the **Yalu River,** part of North Korea's border with China. Total victory seemed just days away.

As the UN forces advanced, the United States received a warning from the Chinese. If the invasion of North Korea continued, China would send in its army to support the North Koreans. Believing the Chinese warning was a bluff, President Truman allowed MacArthur to continue moving north.

The Chinese were not bluffing, however. By late October, thousands of Chinese troops began massing along the border, and some crossed the Yalu River southward into North Korea. On November 26, huge numbers of Chinese troops launched an attack on United Nations forces. Badly outnumbered, the UN forces retreated south back across the 38th parallel. Within weeks, the Communists had recaptured Seoul.

✔ Reading Check **Describing** What line separated North from South Korea?

American Leadership Divided

By January 1951, United Nations forces managed to stop their retreat. Launching a counteroffensive, they retook Seoul and pushed the Communists back across the 38th parallel. The war now became a stalemate, a situation in which neither side was able to gain much ground or achieve a decisive victory. The stalemate lasted for almost two years, with much bitter fighting along the 38th parallel.

Truman and MacArthur Disagree

As the stalemate dragged on, President Truman began to consider negotiating an end to the fighting. General MacArthur, however, argued that the UN forces should now attack China, either by invading the country or by bombing Chinese troops stationed in North Korea. Truman opposed MacArthur's plan, fearing that such actions would lead to a larger war with China or escalate into another world war.

In a letter to a member of Congress, MacArthur complained that he was being kept from doing his job. "We must win," he wrote. "There is no substitute for victory."

On April 11, 1951, President Truman relieved General MacArthur of his command in Korea. "I could do nothing else and still be president of the United States," Truman concluded. He wrote:

> ❝If I allowed him to defy the civil authorities in this manner, I myself would be violating my oath to uphold and defend the Constitution.❞

MacArthur's firing created a storm of protest in the United States. The general was extremely popular, and polls showed that a majority of Americans supported him against the president. Moreover, MacArthur did not go quietly. After receiving a hero's welcome on his return to the United States, he delivered a farewell speech to Congress. "Old soldiers never die," he said, "they just fade away."

Ending the Conflict

The two sides in the Korean War began negotiations in July 1951. The talks lasted for two years before a cease-fire agreement was signed on July 27, 1953, during the presidency of Dwight Eisenhower. This agreement ending the war created a demilitarized zone—a region where military forces could not enter—between North and South Korea. The zone extended roughly a mile and a half on either side of the 38th parallel.

The Korean War ended with neither side achieving victory and almost no change in territory. Losses had been great. More than 54,000 Americans died in the war, and another 103,000 were wounded. Nearly two million Koreans and Chinese lost their lives, and large portions of North and South Korea were devastated.

America's involvement in the Korean War sent a clear message to the Soviet Union: The United States was committed to fighting Communist expansion with money, arms, and even lives. At the same time, the inability of the United States to win a clear victory contributed to uncertainty at home about the nation's foreign policy.

HISTORY Online

Student Web Activity
Visit taj.glencoe.com and click on **Chapter 27— Student Web Activities** for an activity on the Korean War.

✓ Reading Check **Comparing** How did Truman's view on the Korean War differ from General MacArthur's view?

SECTION 3 ASSESSMENT

Checking for Understanding

1. **Key Terms** Define the following terms: stalemate, demilitarized zone.
2. **Reviewing Facts** How did the Korean War begin?

Reviewing Themes

3. **Global Connections** How did American goals change during the course of the Korean War?

Critical Thinking

4. **Identifying Central Issues** Do you think Truman should have allowed MacArthur to attack China? Why or why not?
5. **Organizing Information** Re-create the diagram below and provide two reasons for the Korean War ending in a stalemate.

Analyzing Visuals

6. **Geography Skills** Examine the map on page 803. When did UN forces make their farthest advance?

Interdisciplinary Activity

Persuasive Writing Write a one-page editorial in which you argue whether a U.S. military leader should or should not be able to override a president's decision.

Guide to Reading

Main Idea

Life in Cold War America was marked by a search for security.

Key Terms

subversion, blacklist, perjury, allege, censure

Reading Strategy

Classifying Information As you read the section, re-create the diagram below and explain why these individuals are important.

	Historical significance
Alger Hiss	
Ethel Rosenberg	
Joseph McCarthy	

Read to Learn

- what effect Cold War fears had on domestic politics.
- how McCarthyism affected the nation.

Section Theme

Government and Democracy Americans of the postwar era took steps to combat the spread of communism within the United States.

Preview of Events

♦1945 ♦1950 ♦1955

1947
House Un-American Activities Committee holds hearings

1950
Congress passes the McCarran Act

1953
The Rosenbergs are executed as spies

1954
McCarthy is censured

AN American Story

John Howard Lawson of the "Hollywood Ten"

In 1947, a congressional committee held public hearings on the alleged communist influence in the Hollywood film industry. Many witnesses called before the committee were asked the same questions: "Are you now or have you ever been a member of the Communist Party?" Two witnesses denied having communist ties, but 10 others refused to give a straight "yes" or "no" answer. In dramatic moments worthy of the movies, these "Hollywood Ten" challenged the committee's right to ask about their political beliefs. One of the accused yelled, "This is the beginning of an American concentration camp!"

Cold War Fears

The Cold War intensified Americans' fears of communist subversion, or sabotage. Stories of stolen government documents and spy rings gripped the country in the late 1940s. Then in 1949 Americans learned that the Soviet Union had built its own atomic bomb.

Many Americans worried that Communist spies and sympathizers—people friendly to Communists, or "Reds" as they were known—had penetrated all levels of American society and were attempting to weaken the government.

This **Red Scare** dominated the nation's politics for years and led to a massive hunt to uncover Communists. In this climate of fear, few Americans were safe from accusations of disloyalty—not even the president.

Republican critics began accusing President Truman of being too easy on Communists. In 1947 Truman responded by ordering an investigation into the loyalty of all federal employees. Millions of government workers had to undergo security checks, and thousands were investigated by the FBI. Although the investigations found little evidence of espionage, many federal employees lost their jobs.

Loyalty Oaths and Investigations

Many state and local governments, colleges, and businesses began similar campaigns to uncover communist subversion. Some organizations required individuals to sign oaths swearing their loyalty to the United States. Those who refused risked losing their jobs.

In 1950 Congress passed the **McCarran Act,** which required all Communist organizations to register with the government and to provide lists of members. President Truman vetoed the act. "In a free country, we punish men for crimes they commit," he said, "but never for the opinions they hold." Congress overrode his veto.

In 1947 a congressional committee, the **House Un-American Activities Committee** (HUAC), began investigating communist subversion in the nation. In widely publicized hearings, the committee questioned people about their knowledge of Communists or Communist sympathizers. Individuals came under suspicion because of the beliefs of their friends or coworkers—guilt by association. The committee's activities fueled an anti-Communist hysteria in the nation.

HUAC launched a sensational investigation of the Hollywood film industry, rumored to be full of Communists. A number of those who were summoned refused to testify, and several screenwriters and directors—the "Hollywood Ten"—went to jail for refusing to answer questions about their political beliefs or those of their colleagues. Reacting to public and government pressure, film companies created blacklists—lists of individuals whose loyalty was suspicious—that barred people from working in Hollywood's film industry.

American Spies Revealed

In 1948 **Whittaker Chambers,** a magazine editor, volunteered to testify before HUAC. After admitting that he had spied for the Soviet Union in the 1930s, Chambers accused **Alger Hiss,** a former State Department official, of giving him secret government documents in 1937 and 1938 to pass on to the Soviets.

Chambers produced secret State Department papers he claimed were written by Hiss and microfilm of other secret documents. Chambers swore that he had received the microfilm (which was hidden in a pumpkin) from Hiss. Investigators could not prosecute Hiss for spying because too much time had passed since the events had occurred. However, he was found guilty of perjury, or lying, and sent to prison.

Causes and Effects of the Cold War

Causes

- The Soviet Union expands into Eastern Europe.
- Communism extends into Western Europe, the Middle East, and Asia.
- Western governments fear Soviet aggression.

Effects

- The United States aids anti-Communist forces.
- Western powers form NATO.
- The Korean War erupts.
- A U.S.–Soviet arms race develops.

Graphic Organizer → Skills

The Cold War pitted the Soviet Union and its allies against the United States and its allies.

Analyzing Information What organization did the Western powers form?

People In History

Margaret Chase Smith 1897–1995

Margaret Chase Smith of Maine was the first woman to be elected to both houses of Congress.

First elected to the House in 1940, Smith made many contributions during her four terms. During World War II, she worked to improve the position of women in the military. She played a major role in the passage of a new law, the Women's Armed Services Integration Act (1948), that allowed women to serve as permanent, regular members of the nation's military forces.

Smith also served four terms in the Senate. Never afraid to speak out on the issues, she was one of the first to condemn the tactics used by Senator Joseph McCarthy in his crusade against communism.

In 1964 Smith was one of the presidential nominees at the Republican National Convention, making her the first woman to have her name placed in nomination by a major political party.

The most dramatic spy case to come before HUAC involved the atomic bomb. **Julius** and **Ethel Rosenberg,** a New York couple who were members of the Communist Party, were accused of plotting to pass secret information about the atomic bomb to the Soviet Union. Brought to trial in 1951, the Rosenbergs were convicted and sentenced to death. The judge in the case declared their crime "worse than murder."

Groups around the world protested the sentence as a gross injustice, but higher courts upheld the death sentence decision. Executed in 1953, the Rosenbergs maintained their innocence to the end and claimed that they were persecuted because of their political beliefs.

☑ **Reading Check** **Explaining** What did the McCarran Act require?

McCarthyism

From 1950 to 1954, the hunt for Communists in America was dominated by Senator **Joseph McCarthy** of Wisconsin. During those years, McCarthy publicly attacked many people alleged—declared without proof—to be Com-munists. His unfounded accusations destroyed the careers of many innocent Americans and heightened the atmosphere of anti-Communist hysteria in the country. A new word was coined, McCarthyism, which came to mean the use of unproved accusations against political opponents.

Joseph McCarthy rose to national attention almost overnight. In a speech in Wheeling, West Virginia, in February 1950, he announced that America had been betrayed by the "traitorous actions" of certain individuals. Raising a sheet of paper, he claimed to have in his hand a list of 205 State Department employees who were members of the Communist Party. Millions of Americans believed McCarthy's charges.

During the next four years, McCarthy continued to accuse government officials and others of being Communists. His congressional subcommittee attacked and bullied the people it called to testify. Many federal employees resigned or were dismissed as a result of McCarthy's investigations.

Even the most powerful government officials hesitated to oppose him. McCarthy often targeted Democrats. He and his Republican colleagues in

Congress saw anticommunism as an important issue to use against the Democratic Party. Some Republican candidates for Congress, including **Richard Nixon,** successfully smeared their opponents with charges of being soft on communism. Such tactics worked because so many Americans feared the threat of communism.

McCarthy's Downfall

In 1954 McCarthy launched an investigation of the United States Army. He made alarming claims that Communists had infiltrated the military. In a series of televised hearings watched by millions of Americans, McCarthy hurled wild accusations at highly respected army officials.

The televised Army-McCarthy Hearings proved the turning point in the McCarthy investigations. For weeks Americans witnessed McCarthy's sneering and cruel attacks. Toward the end of the hearings, **Joseph Welch,** an attorney for the army, said to McCarthy:

❝Until this moment, Senator, I think I never really gauged your cruelty or your recklessness. . . . Have you left no sense of decency?❞

Many Americans now came to view McCarthy as a cruel bully who had little basis for his accusations. Congress also turned against McCarthy. In December 1954, the Senate voted to censure, or formally criticize, him for "conduct unbecoming a senator." Censure and the

Analyzing *Political Cartoons*

This 1950 cartoon shows McCarthy spreading charges of disloyalty. **Why does the cartoonist portray McCarthy as the Statue of Liberty?**

loss of public support ended McCarthy's influence. Yet during the years when fears of communism had raged in the country, McCarthyism had damaged the lives of many innocent people.

Reading Check **Describing** What claims did McCarthy make against the United States Army?

SECTION 4 ASSESSMENT

Checking for Understanding

1. **Key Terms** Define the following terms: subversion, blacklist, perjury, allege, censure.
2. **Reviewing Facts** Describe the aim of loyalty oaths.

Reviewing Themes

3. **Government and Democracy** What negative effects did McCarthy's anti-Communist actions have on American society?

Critical Thinking

4. **Drawing Conclusions** How do you think television affected the outcome of the Army-McCarthy hearings?
5. **Organizing Information** Re-create the diagram below and give two examples of the government's response to growing fears of communism.

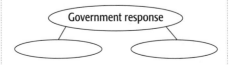

Government response

Analyzing Visuals

6. **Graphic Organizer Skills** Examine the cause-and-effect chart on page 807. Into what areas did the Soviet Union expand? What was one effect of the Cold War?

Interdisciplinary Activity

Art Draw a political cartoon that describes the effect you think Joseph McCarthy had on the American people. Make sure you include a caption with your cartoon.

Chapter Summary

The Cold War Era

Soviet Union

United States

Soviets occupy much of Eastern and Central Europe

THE MARSHALL PLAN
A Program of International Cooperation

Truman Doctrine proposed; Congress approves Marshall Plan

U.S., Britain, and France unite to form West German Republic

Berlin blockade

Berlin airlift

NATO Pact

With UN, U.S. fights in Korean War

Warsaw Pact

U.S. builds largest military force

Reviewing Key Terms

On graph paper, create a word search puzzle using the following terms. Crisscross the terms vertically and horizontally, then fill in the remaining squares with extra letters. Use the terms' definitions as clues to find the words in the puzzle. Share your puzzle with a classmate.

1. iron curtain
2. containment
3. airlift
4. cold war
5. inflation
6. closed shop
7. perjury
8. allege

Reviewing Key Facts

9. Who coined the phrase "iron curtain"? What did it represent?
10. What did the Marshall Plan provide?
11. What is a "cold war"?
12. Why did many labor unions strike after the war?
13. What did the GI Bill provide?
14. Who did the major parties nominate for the presidency in 1948? Who won the election?
15. What was the outcome of the conflict in Korea?
16. What was the purpose of the House Un-American Activities Committee?

Critical Thinking

17. **Analyzing Themes: Global Connections** What was the strategy behind the Marshall Plan?
18. **Analyzing Information** How did Truman exercise his power as commander in chief of the United States military during the Korean War?
19. **Drawing Conclusions** In addition to fighting communism, what other motivation do you think Senator McCarthy had for his actions?
20. **Determining Cause and Effect** Re-create the diagram below and identify two ways the United States used its position as the strongest and wealthiest nation in the world to shape economic recovery in Europe.

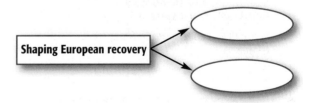

Shaping European recovery

Practicing Skills

Making Inferences *Examine the photograph that appears on pages 784 and 785. Then, answer the questions that follow.*

21. Describe the details in the painting.

22. What feelings does the face of the young girl express?

23. What do you know about the movement to integrate schools during the 1950s?

24. Putting all this together, what do you infer as the reason for the girl's expression?

25. Find a newspaper or magazine photograph and write at least three inferences based on the photo.

Geography and History Activity

Study the map on page 793. Then answer the questions that follow.

26. **Region** Among what four countries was Germany divided?

27. **Place** What country or countries occupied East Berlin?

28. **Place** What country or countries occupied West Berlin?

29. **Location** What is unusual about the location of the airports in Berlin? Explain your reasoning.

Citizenship Cooperative Activity

30. **Military Service** The GI Bill provided many benefits to soldiers returning from World War II. Through these benefits Americans who thought they could never go to college or own their own homes could now achieve these goals. Organize into four groups to explore the incentives offered today for people who join the United States Army, Navy, Marines, and Coast Guard. Use the list of questions that follow to guide your group's research.

- Is attending college or another institution of extended learning still an option?
- What kinds of economic incentives are offered to recruits?
- What advantages are awarded to those joining the armed services today that were not available at the end of World War II?

Use your information to design a recruitment plan to attract people to a particular branch of the service. Include all forms of media in your plan such as billboards, newspaper ads, radio, and television.

Self-Check Quiz
Visit taj.glencoe.com and click on **Chapter 27— Self-Check Quizzes** to prepare for the chapter test.

Technology Activity

31. **Using the Internet** Search the Internet for information about how the United Nations is organized. Design a flowchart or graphic organizer that shows the names of each of the main bodies of the UN and how they are related to each other.

Alternative Assessment

32. **Portfolio Writing Activity** The United States government was anxious to avoid military conflict after World War II. Review the chapter and make a list of examples of how the United States government used negotiation and other nonviolent means to resolve international problems without resorting to war.

The Princeton Review

Standardized Test Practice

Directions: Choose the *best* answer to the following question.

The United States started the Marshall Plan as a way to prevent an economic collapse in Europe that would open the door to communism. Which of the following was another purpose of the Marshall Plan?

A To shift the balance of power away from Asian nations

B To encourage European Allied efforts in World War II

C To build a strong Europe on which American economic security could depend

D To prevent the Soviet Union from becoming a major military power

Test-Taking Tip

This question requires you to remember a fact about the Marshall Plan. Remember that the plan was an economic program—that is it provided money to help rebuild European economies. Which answer fits best with this information?

CHAPTER 28

America in the 1950s

1953–1960

Why It Matters

The election of Dwight Eisenhower to the presidency ushered in one of the most prosperous periods in American history. Economic growth resulted in increased employment and higher wages throughout the 1950s.

The Impact Today

The prosperity of the 1950s raised questions that remain important in American society today. Can a period of economic growth bring benefits to all Americans—or are some groups likely to be excluded? Can the nation's economic growth be guided by cultural and social values—or does growth occur at the expense of those values? Americans still debate these issues today.

 The American Journey *Video* The chapter 28 video, "The Fifties Dream," explores popular culture and ideals during the 1950s.

1953
• Results of polio vaccine tests published

1956
• Federal Highway Act passed

1950s
• Baby boom increases U.S. population by over 20 percent

1955
• Eisenhower meets with Khrushchev at Geneva summit

United States
PRESIDENTS

Eisenhower
1953–1961

1952   1954   1956

World

1950s
• Abstract expressionism grows in popularity

1953
• Watson, Crick, and Franklin discover DNA structure

1955
• Warsaw pact signed

1956
• Egypt takes control of Suez Canal
• Uprising in Hungary is defeated by Soviet troops

Red Spy Hunt by **Thomas Maitland Cleland** The 1950s transformed our culture and shaped the way we live today.

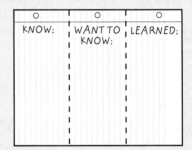
1957
- Kerouac's *On the Road* published

1958
- The United States launches *Explorer*

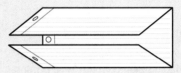

1959
- Alaska and Hawaii become states

1958   *1960*

1957
- Soviet Union launches *Sputnik*

1959
- Mary and Louis Leakey uncover hominid fossils

HISTORY *Online*

Chapter Overview
Visit taj.glencoe.com and click on **Chapter 28— Chapter Overviews** to preview chapter information.

Eisenhower in the White House

Guide to Reading

Main Idea
President Eisenhower promoted policies to compete with the Soviet Union for military and space leadership.

Key Terms
moderate, surplus, arms race, domino theory, summit, peaceful coexistence

Reading Strategy
Organizing Information As you read the section, re-create the diagram below and list examples of actions the United States took to solve problems in world affairs.

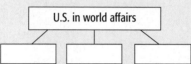

U.S. in world affairs

Read to Learn
• what beliefs and policies characterized the Eisenhower presidency.
• what foreign policy challenges the Eisenhower administration faced.

Section Theme
Science and Technology The United States worked to develop space technology and compete with the Soviets in space.

Preview of Events

♦ *1950*   ♦ *1955*   ♦ *1960*

1952
Eisenhower elected president

1953
Oveta Culp Hobby heads HEW

1957
The Soviets launch *Sputnik*

1959
Alaska and Hawaii enter the Union

Republican ad, 1952

AN American Story

"He merely has to smile at you, and you trust him at once." These words were used to describe Dwight D. Eisenhower, Republican presidential candidate in 1952. Eisenhower had an appeal that went far beyond his party label. His performance in World War II had made him an unquestioned hero in the eyes of almost every American. Above all, his personality and political style made many people feel safe, comfortable, and confident.

Republican Revival

By 1952 Harry S Truman faced widespread dissatisfaction with his presidency. Many Americans were frustrated over the stalemated war in Korea and worried about reports of communist subversion in government. To the Democrats' relief, Truman decided not to run for reelection. The Democrats nominated the respected governor of Illinois, **Adlai E. Stevenson,** for president and Senator John J. Sparkman of Alabama as his running mate.

To head their presidential ticket, the Republicans chose General **Dwight D. Eisenhower,** the popular World War II hero. For vice president, the Republicans selected **Richard M. Nixon,** a young senator from California who had won fame as a tough opponent of communism.

The Campaign

Born in Texas and raised in rural Kansas, Dwight D. Eisenhower graduated from the United States Military Academy at West Point. He rose steadily through the army to become supreme commander of the Allied forces in Europe during World War II. People called him Ike—and they trusted him. His warmth and sincerity attracted many voters.

Eisenhower's steadiness made Americans feel secure. He won wide support with his pledge to bring the Korean War to an "early and honorable end." "If that job requires a personal trip to Korea," he declared, "I shall make that trip."

The Republicans faced a brief crisis during the presidential campaign when the story broke that Richard Nixon had accepted political gifts from supporters. Nixon went on television to defend himself in what came to be known as the "Checkers" speech. He proclaimed that he had done nothing wrong and had kept only one gift—his family dog, Checkers. The speech won broad support for Nixon, persuading Eisenhower to keep him on the ticket.

Landslide Republican Victory

In November 1952, Americans elected Eisenhower to the presidency in a landslide victory—the first Republican to win the White House since 1928. Far more people voted in 1952 than in any previous presidential election. Eisenhower collected over six million popular votes more than Stevenson and carried the electoral college 442 to 89. The Republicans also won control of Congress. The election seemed to usher in a new era in national politics.

Reading Check **Identifying** Who was the candidate for vice president on Eisenhower's ticket?

Domestic Policy

Although Eisenhower had little political experience, he proved to be an effective politician. During his two terms in office, Eisenhower followed a moderate, or middle-of-the-road, approach to domestic policy. He described himself as "conservative when it comes to money and liberal when it comes to human beings."

Eisenhower helped steer the country on a steady course. He avoided ambitious new government programs, but resisted the pressure to abolish popular older ones, and sometimes he even expanded them. As he once told reporters:

❝I feel pretty good when I'm attacked from both sides. It makes me more certain I'm on the right track.❞

President Eisenhower wanted to make the federal government "smaller rather than bigger." He supported economic policies aimed at limiting government spending and encouraging private enterprise. With the support of Republicans and conservative Democrats in Congress, the president removed the wage and price controls that the Truman administration had established during the Korean War. He also managed to transfer some authority in financial matters to the states and to make some cuts in government spending. When he left office in 1961, the federal budget had a surplus, or excess, of $300 million.

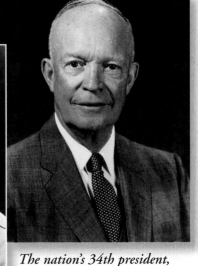

The nation's 34th president, Dwight Eisenhower, served in the military for more than 30 years.

The Nation Expands

The greatest domestic program of the Eisenhower presidency involved building a network of interstate highways. In June 1956 Congress passed the **Federal Highway Act.** The law funded the construction of more than 40,000 miles (64,000 km) of highways that tied the nation together. The highway program—the largest public works program in the nation's history—also spurred growth in many areas of the nation's economy, including the automobile and oil industries, while improving military mobility in case of an attack.

The nation itself also grew during Eisenhower's presidency. In 1959 **Alaska** and **Hawaii** entered the Union, bringing the number of states to 50. Alaska and Hawaii became the only states not bordering on the other states.

Social Programs

Eisenhower believed that government should protect the basic welfare of Americans. He refused to tamper with Social Security and other New Deal social programs. During his presidency, Eisenhower agreed to extend Social Security benefits to 10 million more people and to provide unemployment insurance to 4 million more. He also approved greater funding for public housing and, in 1955, agreed to an increase in the minimum wage from 75 cents an hour to $1.00.

The creation of the **Department of Health, Education, and Welfare** (HEW) in 1953 confirmed the government's role in helping Americans meet their basic social needs. Eisenhower named **Oveta Culp Hobby** as the first secretary of the new department. Hobby, only the second

America's Flags

Stars and Stripes Today Statehood for Alaska and Hawaii brought the number of stars to 50 (its current number) in the flag of 1960.

woman in American history to hold a cabinet post, had organized the Women's Army Corps (WACs) in World War II.

Eisenhower's moderation and leadership won the approval of a majority of Americans. In the 1956 presidential election, he ran against Democrat Adlai Stevenson again. This time Eisenhower won by an even bigger margin, receiving more than 57 percent of the popular vote.

Reading Check **Describing** How did the highway program affect the economy?

Eisenhower and the Cold War

On October 4, 1957, millions of Americans heard the startling news: the Soviets had sent into space the world's first artificial satellite, called *Sputnik*. Within a month, the Soviets successfully launched a second satellite. Americans were both horrified and in awe. They feared that the nation was lagging behind the Soviets. They also feared that the Soviets could launch atomic weapons from space.

Worry turned to embarrassment in December 1957, when the United States tried to launch its own space satellite—*Vanguard*. Hundreds of reporters and spectators watched the rocket rise a few feet off the launching pad—and then explode. The foreign press made fun of the launch, calling it "Flopnik" and "Stayputnik." America's status declined.

United States–Soviet Rivalry

During the 1950s the United States–Soviet rivalry kept the Cold War at the center of American foreign policy. The Eisenhower administration continued to oppose the spread of communism. At the same time, the president looked for ways to keep American–Soviet tensions from erupting into open conflict.

Secretary of State **John Foster Dulles** became Eisenhower's most important foreign policy adviser. Dulles condemned the containment policy of the Truman administration. Eisenhower and Dulles proposed a new, bolder policy. If the Soviet Union attacked any nation, the United States would launch a **massive retaliation**—an instant attack using nuclear weapons. Vice President Nixon explained:

66Rather than let the Communists nibble us to death all over the world in little wars, we will rely in the future on massive mobile retaliatory [attacking] powers.99

Dulles believed that the United States had to use threats to push the Soviets to the brink of war before they would agree to anything. Critics called this tough stance "brinkmanship."

By relying more on nuclear weapons, the Eisenhower administration could reduce the size of the army and the arsenal of **conventional,** or non-nuclear, weapons. These reductions would allow Eisenhower to cut the military budget. As Secretary of Defense Charles Wilson explained, nuclear weapons gave the United States "more bang for the buck."

The Arms Race

Despite Eisenhower's intentions, defense spending increased again. The policy of massive retaliation—and Soviet efforts to counter it—produced a nuclear arms race. Both nations built more and more weapons.

The superpowers built immensely destructive hydrogen bombs—nuclear weapons that were much more powerful than atomic bombs. They developed a variety of guided missiles capable of delivering nuclear warheads. The **intermediate-range ballistic missile** (IRBM) could reach targets up to 1,500 miles (2,414 km) away. The **intercontinental ballistic missile** (ICBM) had a range of many thousands of miles. Soon both sides had massive nuclear arsenals capable of destroying the other side many times over.

As the arms race continued, Americans began preparing for a nuclear attack. The **Civil Defense Administration** educated the public with pamphlets and radio and television messages. Some families built air-raid shelters in their basements or backyards. Schools held air-raid drills. One student described his school's drill: "Students lie on the floor and stick their heads under the lockers." He recalled that he believed this would make him safe during a nuclear attack. 📖 *(See page 976 for an article LIFE magazine published on what to do during a nuclear attack.)*

The Space Race

The launch of *Sputnik* shifted the space race into high gear. Nearly 12 years later, a spacecraft from *Apollo 11* landed on a level plain in the Sea of Tranquility on the moon. The long-lived dream of landing on the moon had come true.

At the end of the Cold War, the United States and Russia agreed to build a space station and cooperate on other projects in space. A rivalry that began in fear has become a partnership.

Astronaut on the moon

Competing in Space

The Soviet launch of *Sputnik* and the *Vanguard* failure led America to develop its own space program. Federal money poured into the **National Aeronautics and Space Administration (NASA),** the new government agency in charge of the space program. When the United States succeeded in launching the *Explorer* satellite in January 1958, the Associated Press reported:

66The missile took off in a beautiful launching. It rose slowly at first in a huge splash of flame with a roar that could be heard for miles. . . .99

The **space race** had begun, and the United States soon began pulling ahead. **Project Mercury** was the nation's first program to put an astronaut in space. Along with its commitment to space exploration and scientific research, the government also encouraged science education by providing more funds for the teaching of science and technology in the nation's schools.

✓**Reading Check** **Explaining** What is massive retaliation?

Foreign Policy Challenges

With the stakes in the nuclear arms race so high, the United States and the Soviet Union had to act carefully. A minor crisis, badly managed, could lead to all-out war.

Crisis in the Middle East

Trouble arose first in the Middle East. Arab states had attacked Israel soon after its founding in 1948, and tensions there had remained high ever since. Because the United States backed Israel, while the Soviet Union maintained ties with the Arab states, a Middle East conflict threatened to involve the superpowers as well as their allies.

Fighting did break out in the Middle East in 1956, when Egyptian president **Gamal Abdel Nasser** nationalized, or brought under government control, the **Suez Canal** from British control. Great Britain and France feared that Nasser might close the canal and cut off oil shipments to Europe. In October, the two European powers attacked Egypt. Great Britain and France hoped to overthrow Nasser and seize the canal. Israel, angered by repeated Arab attacks along its borders, agreed to help by invading Egypt.

The United States sponsored a United Nations resolution calling for an immediate truce. The Soviets threatened rocket attacks on British and French cities. In the face of this pressure, the three nations pulled out of Egypt.

Uprising in Hungary

Another crisis erupted in Europe. In October 1956, students and workers demonstrated in **Budapest,** the capital of **Hungary,** for changes in the government. Strikes and riots soon spread. A new government came to power and demanded withdrawal of Soviet troops. In early November, Soviet tanks and troops poured into Hungary and crushed the revolt. Hungarian rebels appealed to the United States for help. President Eisenhower condemned the Soviet crackdown but did not intervene.

War in Southeast Asia

Yet another trouble spot appeared in Southeast Asia, in France's former colony of **Vietnam.** In the early 1950s, the United States gave France billions of dollars in military aid to help it fight the **Vietminh,** nationalist rebels led by Communist leader **Ho Chi Minh.**

In spite of American aid, the French soon faced defeat. In March 1954, Vietminh forces trapped 13,000 French troops at the French base of **Dien Bien Phu.** The French pleaded with the United States to send forces, but Eisenhower refused. The Korean War was still fresh in his memory. "I can conceive of no greater tragedy," he said, "than for the United States to become engaged in all-out war in Indochina."

Analyzing *Political Cartoons*

Many cartoons used a bear to stand for the Soviet Union and an eagle to represent the United States. **What do you think the cartoonist was saying by showing the subjects on the edge of a cliff?**

The Language of the Cold War

These terms were first used during the Cold War era.

Fallout shelter Underground building designed to hold up against fallout from a nuclear attack

Hot line Direct phone line between U.S. and Soviet leaders established after the Cuban missile crisis

Hydrogen bomb Nuclear weapon hundreds of times more powerful than the atomic bombs dropped on Hiroshima and Nagasaki; first tested in 1952

Iron Curtain Term used to describe the separation between communist and democratic nations in Europe

Massive retaliation Policy that promised U.S. attacks in answer to Soviet expansion

Missile Gap Claim that the U.S. had fallen behind the Soviets in producing nuclear missiles

Space Race Rivalry for supremacy in outer space

Sputnik First artificial earth satellite, launched by USSR in 1957 (pictured above)

U-2 Spy plane with ability to take pictures from as high as 80,000 feet (24,400 m)

Intercontinental ballistic missile

Without American troops, the French were forced to surrender in May. Soon after, French and Vietminh representatives in **Geneva, Switzerland,** negotiated a cease-fire agreement. The agreement, known as the **Geneva Accords,** temporarily divided Vietnam. The Vietminh controlled the north, while other Vietnamese—more friendly to the French—held the south. The accords also arranged for the withdrawal of all French troops and called for free elections in a reunited Vietnam in 1956.

Eisenhower believed that if one nation in Asia fell to the Communists, others would also fall, one after the other. He described the danger in what came to be called the domino theory:

> 66You have a row of dominoes set up. You knock over the first one, and what will happen to the last one is that it will go over very quickly.99

To keep South Vietnam from becoming the first domino, the United States aided its anti-Communist government. In another step to defend against Communist aggression, the United States helped to create the **Southeast Asia Treaty Organization** (SEATO) in 1954. The United States, Great Britain, France, New Zealand, Australia, the Philippines, Pakistan, and Thailand made up the alliance. The nations pledged joint action against any aggressor.

Troubles in Latin America

The Eisenhower administration also faced communist challenges in Latin America. In 1954 the **Central Intelligence Agency** (CIA) helped overthrow the government of **Guatemala,** which some American leaders feared was leaning toward communism. Latin Americans resented the intervention in Guatemala.

Anti-American feeling became a part of the growing revolutionary movement in **Cuba.** Following the overthrow of dictator Fulgencio Batista (buh•TEES•tuh), rebel leader **Fidel Castro** formed a new government in January 1959. The United States supported Castro at first and welcomed his promise of democratic reforms. But Castro angered Americans when he seized foreign-owned property. His government became a dictatorship and formed close ties with the Soviet Union. During the last days of his presidency in 1961, Eisenhower cut diplomatic ties with Cuba. Relations between the two nations have remained strained ever since.

Cold War "Thaws"

After Soviet dictator Joseph Stalin died in 1953, **Nikita Khrushchev** (krush•CHAWF) emerged as the dominant leader. By the mid-1950s, both American and Soviet leaders were interested in easing Cold War tensions.

In July 1955, Eisenhower, NATO leaders, and Soviet officials met at a summit conference in Geneva, Switzerland. A summit is a meeting of heads of government. The leaders discussed disarmament and German reunification. The friendly atmosphere, promptly called the "Spirit of Geneva," renewed hopes for peace.

After the Geneva summit, a policy of peaceful coexistence began to emerge. This meant that the two superpowers would compete with one another but would avoid war. Khrushchev proposed to Eisenhower that the two leaders visit each other's country and attend another summit in **Paris** in 1960. Eisenhower agreed.

Khrushchev's 10-day trip to the United States in 1959 captured world headlines. As the leaders made plans for their next meeting in Paris, Eisenhower hoped to reach agreements on arms control and nuclear test bans.

The U-2 Incident

Hopes of peace fell to earth with an American plane. For years American pilots had flown high-altitude spy planes—**U-2s**—over Soviet territory to photograph Soviet nuclear sites and military bases.

When the Soviets shot down a U-2 plane on May 1, 1960, and captured its pilot, Francis Gary Powers, Khrushchev denounced the United States for invading Soviet airspace. Although the Paris summit began as scheduled on May 16, the mood had changed. The summit broke up the next day. The brief "thaw" in the Cold War had ended.

Eisenhower's Warning

In his January 1961 Farewell Address to the nation, President Eisenhower issued a warning about the influence of the military. The military budget had grown dramatically, he said, and military leaders had allied with business to seek bigger and more expensive weapons. Eisenhower feared that this alliance—a **"military-industrial complex"**—heated the arms race and could "endanger our liberties or democratic processes." In a twist of history, this former army general warned the nation of the close involvement of government and industry in preparing for war.

✓ **Reading Check** **Describing** How did relations between the superpowers change after the Geneva summit?

SECTION 1 ASSESSMENT

Checking for Understanding

1. **Key Terms** Use the following terms to write an article about life during the Cold War: arms race, domino theory, peaceful coexistence.

2. **Reviewing Facts** What two states were added to the Union during Eisenhower's presidency?

Reviewing Themes

3. **Science and Technology** How did the Soviet launch of *Sputnik* affect science and technology in the United States?

Critical Thinking

4. **Identifying Central Issues** Why was President Eisenhower willing to send massive aid to Vietnam?

5. **Comparing** Re-create the diagram below and describe how Eisenhower's view on foreign policy differed from Truman's view.

Foreign policy	
Eisenhower	Truman

Analyzing Visuals

6. **Analyzing Political Cartoons** Study the cartoon on page 818. Who do the figures in the cartoon represent? What idea do you think the cartoonist is presenting?

Interdisciplinary Activity

Science Make a two-level time line with the heading "United States" and "Soviet Union." Track the achievements of these two countries in space from 1957 to 1967.

1950s Prosperity

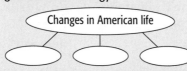

Guide to Reading

Main Idea
Economic growth changed the social and cultural life of Americans.

Key Terms
productivity, standard of living, affluence, baby boom

Reading Strategy
Organizing Information As you read Section 2, re-create the diagram below and describe three changes that occurred in American life as a result of the strong economy or the growth of technology.

Changes in American life

Read to Learn
- what factors helped the economy grow during the 1950s.
- how the era's prosperity affected American society and culture.

Section Theme
Continuity and Change The economic growth of the 1950s brought great changes to the nation.

Preview of Events

♦1945   ♦1950   ♦1955   ♦1960

1947
William Levitt starts first suburban development

1955
Polio vaccine given to school children

1956
Elvis Presley gains national popularity

New homes in the suburbs

AN
American Story

During the prosperous 1950s, many Americans left the cities to settle in the suburbs, hoping for a better life for themselves and their children. "Suburbia"—with its great distances between home, school, shopping areas, and downtown—gradually became not only a place but also a lifestyle. One suburban resident observed: "Before we came here, we used to live pretty much to ourselves. . . . Now we stop around and visit people or they visit us. I really think [suburban living] has broadened us."

A Booming Economy

After World War II, many experts predicted America's economy would level off or decline as production of war goods decreased. Instead, after a few years of adjustment, the economy began to grow rapidly and steadily. Between 1945 and 1960, the total value of goods and services produced in the United States increased about 250 percent.

Some of this amazing growth resulted from the burst of military spending during the Korean War. Government spending on housing, schools, welfare, highways, and veteran benefits also spurred the rapid economic expansion. Technological advances contributed to economic growth as well. Business, industry, and agriculture adopted new technology and new production methods, resulting in greater productivity—the ability to produce more goods with the same amount of labor. The demand for new technology led to greater investment in research and in the education and training of scientists, engineers, and technicians.

The **computer** was one of the 1950s' technological advances. Unlike today's small personal computers, early computers were immense, weighing tons and filling whole rooms. Although first used only by the military and the government, computers soon appeared in large corporations. By 1955 International Business Machines (IBM) was the leader in the field, with orders for 129 of its big computers.

Higher Incomes

The economic boom of the 1950s raised the standard of living—a measure of people's overall wealth and quality of life—of millions of Americans. Between 1945 and 1960, **personal income**—the average income, earned or unearned, of every individual in the nation—increased from $1,223 to $2,219. By the end of the 1950s, Americans had the highest standard of living in the world.

Prosperity and steady economic growth also led to new optimism. Economists began to think it was possible to maintain prosperity and

growth permanently. Americans felt confident that the government could, when necessary, take steps to avoid serious **recessions,** or downturns in the economy.

Reading Check **Comparing** How did the computers of the 1950s differ from modern computers?

A Changing Nation

Economic growth and prosperity brought many changes to America. These included a growth in population, increased affluence, or wealth, suburban expansion, and a greater demand for consumer goods.

The Baby Boom

Like the economy, the family enjoyed great growth during the postwar years. During the 1950s the nation's population rose from 150 million to 179 million, an increase of nearly 20 percent. People called the nation's soaring birthrate a baby boom.

Several factors encouraged the baby boom. Husbands and wives who had postponed having children during the Depression and World War II started having families. With higher incomes, couples felt they could afford to have more children. In addition, better health

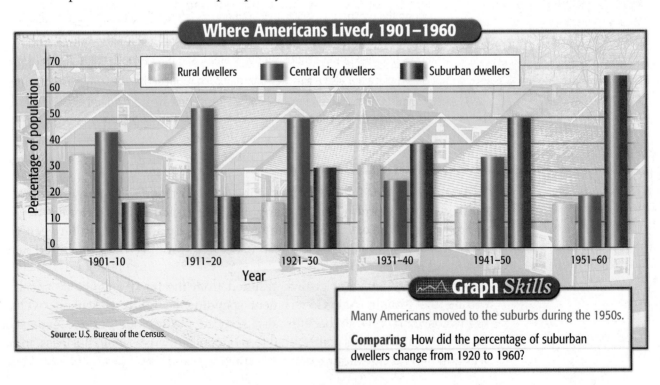

Where Americans Lived, 1901–1960

Legend: Rural dwellers | Central city dwellers | Suburban dwellers

Y-axis: Percentage of population (0–70)
X-axis: Year — 1901–10, 1911–20, 1921–30, 1931–40, 1941–50, 1951–60

Source: U.S. Bureau of the Census.

Graph Skills

Many Americans moved to the suburbs during the 1950s.

Comparing How did the percentage of suburban dwellers change from 1920 to 1960?

People In History

Jonas Salk 1914–1995

By the early 1950s, medical science had made great strides in combating childhood diseases. Antibiotics and vaccines helped control diseases such as diphtheria, influenza, and typhoid fever. A vaccine for polio, however, continued to escape the medical profession. Polio became the era's most dreaded disease because the disease left many of its victims paralyzed for life.

After many years of research, scientist Dr. Jonas Salk developed the first safe and effective vaccine against polio. After it was tested, the Salk vaccine was administered to schoolchildren beginning in 1955. The threat of polio has been almost completely eliminated. Salk was hailed as a hero not only for developing the vaccine, but also for refusing to patent the vaccine. The medical pioneer's last years were spent searching for a vaccine against AIDS.

---

care, improved nutrition, and medical breakthroughs against disease helped reduce the infant death rate.

The baby boom had a powerful impact on society. Many women left the workforce to stay home and raise their children. The demand for baby products and services grew, stimulating the economy. School enrollment soared as the "baby boomers" reached school age, putting a great strain on the educational system.

Expanding Suburbs

During the 1950s, 75 percent of new home construction took place in the **suburbs.** The new suburbs were usually located on the fringes of major cities.

William Levitt introduced mass-produced housing based on experience he had gained building houses for the navy. He started his first suburban development, called **Levittown,** on Long Island, New York, in 1947. Levittown included more than 17,000 identical houses, built from materials precut and preassembled at a factory and then erected quickly on designated lots. Other builders adopted Levitt's methods or used their own techniques for rapid construction, creating a massive house-building boom.

Suburban housing developments appealed to many Americans. In addition to affordable homes, they offered privacy, isolation from urban problems, space for cars, and a sense of belonging to a community formed by people similar in age, social background, and race.

Though affordable, the suburbs did not offer opportunities for home ownership to everyone. Many American cities had growing populations of middle-class minorities, particularly African American and Hispanic American, who longed to escape the noise and the crime of the cities. However, the developers of the nation's postwar suburbs often refused to sell homes to minorities.

A Nation on Wheels

The car made suburban escape possible. People needed cars to get to work, to go shopping, and to run errands. For suburban families, cars were not a luxury but a necessity.

The construction of thousands of miles of new highways in the 1950s encouraged the spread of suburbs. Suburban America became a "car culture" in which life centered on the automobile. Southern California came to symbolize suburban life and this car culture. In California, the drive-in capital of the nation, a person could go to the movies, eat fast food, do banking, and even attend religious services without leaving the car. One suburban California woman spoke for many other Americans when she explained her need for a car:

> 66I live in Garden Grove, work in Irvine, shop in Santa Ana . . . my husband works in Long Beach, and I used to be the president of the League of Women Voters in Fullerton.99

Air Travel

Americans were also finding it easier to travel by air. The jet engine was perfected in the 1950s, and the first jet-powered commercial aircraft began operation. By the early 1950s, the airliner

was on the way to replacing the railroad train and the ocean liner as the preferred transportation for long-distance travel.

A Consumer Society

Americans of the 1950s went on a buying spree. Affluence, the growing variety and quantity of products available, and expanded advertising all played a role in the increased demand for consumer goods. Buying goods became easier, too. Many Americans used credit cards, charge accounts, and easy-payment plans to purchase goods.

Consumers eagerly sought the latest products—dishwashers, washing machines, television sets, stereos, and clothes made from synthetic fabrics. The growing market for bigger and better cars prompted automakers to outdo

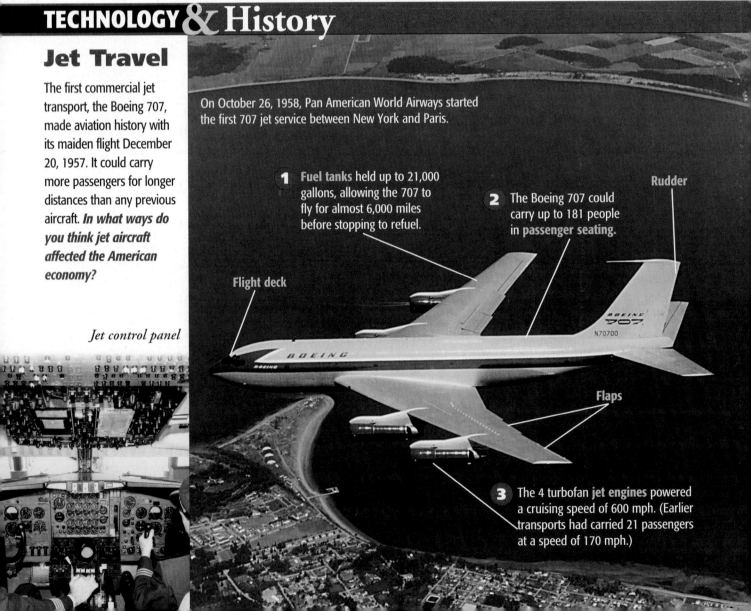

TECHNOLOGY & History

Jet Travel

The first commercial jet transport, the Boeing 707, made aviation history with its maiden flight December 20, 1957. It could carry more passengers for longer distances than any previous aircraft. *In what ways do you think jet aircraft affected the American economy?*

Jet control panel

On October 26, 1958, Pan American World Airways started the first 707 jet service between New York and Paris.

1 Fuel tanks held up to 21,000 gallons, allowing the 707 to fly for almost 6,000 miles before stopping to refuel.

2 The Boeing 707 could carry up to 181 people in passenger seating.

Rudder

Flight deck

Flaps

3 The 4 turbofan jet engines powered a cruising speed of 600 mph. (Earlier transports had carried 21 passengers at a speed of 170 mph.)

Architect Frank Lloyd Wright, who died in 1959, left behind a rich legacy of beautiful homes and buildings. The house "Fallingwater" in rural Pennsylvania appears to come out from the rocks above the waterfall. Wright's 70-year career influenced many architects.

one another by manufacturing bigger, faster, and flashier cars. They came out with new models every year, adding stylish features such as chrome-plated bumpers and soaring tail fins.

The advertising and marketing of products on television, on radio, and in magazines created consumer fads and crazes that swept the nation. In the late 1950s, Americans bought millions of hula hoops—large plastic rings they twirled around their waists. Other popular fads included crew cuts for boys, poodle skirts for girls, and a new snack—pizza.

An American Culture

By 1949 over 900,000 American households had television sets. These large wooden cabinets had small screens that displayed grainy black-and-white images. During the 1950s an average of 6.5 million sets were produced annually. By the end of the decade, most American families had television.

Television profoundly changed American life. It became the main form of entertainment for many people as well as an important source of news and information. Religious leaders helped spread religious commitment with the aid of modern communications. They had their own radio and television programs, best-selling books, and newspaper columns. **Billy Graham,** a popular Protestant minister and preacher, attracted thousands of people throughout the nation and in other parts of the world. **Fulton J. Sheen,** a Roman Catholic bishop, became a television personality through his weekly program. Protestant minister **Norman Vincent Peale** attracted many thousands of followers with his message of

"positive thinking." Another popular religious leader, Jewish rabbi **Joshua Loth Liebman** expressed tolerance for religious differences:

> 66Tolerance is the positive and cordial effort to understand another's beliefs, practices, and habits without necessarily sharing or accepting them.99

Billboards and television commercials proclaimed: "Bring the whole family to church" and "The family that prays together stays together." Messages like these clearly indicated that postwar society was focused on the family.

Millions of Americans watched the same programs. Families gathered to watch quiz shows such as *The $64,000 Question.* Children tuned in to programs such as *The Mickey Mouse Club* and *Howdy Doody.* Teens kept up with the latest hit songs on *American Bandstand.* Families followed weekly episodes of *I Love Lucy, Leave It to Beaver,* and *Father Knows Best.* The images shown in

One of the most popular cars of 1957, the Chevrolet Bel Air sold for about $2,500.

many programs—of happy middle-class families in neat middle-class homes—helped shape Americans' expectations for their own lives.

Finally, television had an important effect on the consumer culture. Television advertising helped create a vast national market for new products and fashions. Some shows—such as the *Philco Television Playhouse*—adopted the names of their sponsors, which brought the sponsors prestige.

A new form of music—rock 'n' roll—achieved great popularity in the 1950s. Many teens rejected the mellow popular music favored by their parents. They preferred the heavily accented beats and simple lyrics of rock 'n' roll.

Rock 'n' roll grew from the rhythm and blues music that African American musicians had created years before. It often had some elements of country music. In rock 'n' roll, the tempo was quicker, and electrically amplified instruments—mostly guitars—were used.

One of the first rock hits, reaching number one in 1955, was Bill Haley and the Comets' *Rock Around the Clock.* Adapting the style of African American performers such as Chuck Berry and Little Richard, **Elvis Presley** burst on the national scene in 1956. Presley quickly became known as the king of rock 'n' roll and was an idol to millions of young Americans. Many young men copied his ducktail haircut and swaggering mannerisms.

For teenagers, the shared experience of listening to the music helped forge a common identity and bond. The differing attitudes of the older and younger generations toward music, as well as other forms of popular culture, later came to be known as the **generation gap.**

Reading Check **Analyzing** Why did suburban life appeal to many Americans?

SECTION 2 ASSESSMENT

Checking for Understanding

1. **Key Terms** Use each of these terms in a sentence that will help explain its meaning: productivity, standard of living, affluence, baby boom.
2. **Reviewing Facts** How did Americans' per capita income change during the 1950s?

Reviewing Themes

3. **Continuity and Change** Describe the link between television and consumer spending in the 1950s.

Critical Thinking

4. **Compare and Contrast** Think about the ways television and the automobile changed the way Americans lived during the 1950s. How would your life be different without them?
5. **Analyzing Information** Re-create the diagram below and identify factors that stimulated economic growth in the 1950s.

Economic growth

Analyzing Visuals

6. **Graph Skills** Examine the graph on page 822. How did the percentage of rural dwellers change from 1920 to 1960?

Interdisciplinary Activity

Music Paste photographs or drawings on poster board of the musicians that you think represent the best of modern music. Write captions that include your explanation of why music is an important part of American culture.

Analyzing Information

Why Learn This Skill

Have you ever heard someone say, "Don't believe everything you read"? To be an informed citizen, you have to analyze information carefully as you read to make sure you understand the meaning and the intent of the writer.

Learning the Skill

❶ Identify the subject or topic of the information.

❷ How is the information organized? What are the main points?

❸ Think about how reliable the source of the information is.

❹ Summarize the information in your own words. Does the information agree with or contradict something you already know?

Practicing the Skill

In this chapter you read about new trends in music and the influence of Elvis Presley. The information that follows is from a biography of Presley. Analyze the paragraph and answer the questions that follow.

Elvis Presley may be the single most important figure in American twentieth-century popular music. Not necessarily the best, *and certainly not the most consistent. But no one could argue that he was not the musician most responsible for popularizing rock and roll. His 1950s recordings established the basic language of rock and roll; his explosive stage presence set standards for the music's visual image; his vocals were incredibly powerful and versatile.*

❶ Was the information easy to understand? Explain.

❷ Consider the source of the information. Does that make it seem more valid or less valid? Why?

Elvis Presley in a 1956 performance

❸ Summarize the paragraph in a sentence of your own.

❹ Do you think the writer admired or did not admire Presley? Why?

Applying the Skill

Analyzing Information Choose an article from a newsmagazine. Read it and analyze the information. Answer questions one, two, and three, as they apply to the article.

 Glencoe's **Skillbuilder Interactive Workbook CD-ROM, Level 1,** provides instruction and practice in key social studies skills.

Problems in a Time of Plenty

Guide to Reading

Main Idea
Many Americans did not share in the prosperity of the 1950s.

Key Terms
ghetto, automation, materialism

Reading Strategy
Classifying Information As you read the section, re-create the diagram below and describe the economic problems these groups faced.

	Economic problems
Small farmers	
Migrant farmworkers	
Factory workers	

Read to Learn
- which groups did not share in the prosperity of the 1950s.
- why some people criticized American values of the period.

Section Theme
Continuity and Change The prosperity that many Americans enjoyed in the 1950s was not shared by the rural and urban poor.

Preview of Events

♦1950	♦1955	♦1960
1950s More than 20 percent of Americans live in poverty	**1950s** "Beat" writers influence nonconformists	**1950s** Women and African Americans question their roles in society

Children in Washington, D.C.

AN American Story

Picture postcards of Washington, D.C. in the 1950s showed the Capitol and other government buildings. Hidden behind the tall buildings was a very different United States, however. It was a nation of crumbling streets and rat-infested tenements, hungry and, sometimes, homeless people. The "invisible poor" lived in a nation not of affluence and plenty, but of desperate need.

Poverty

In the 1950s more than 20 percent of Americans lived in poverty. Millions more struggled to survive on incomes only slightly above the poverty level. Such poverty marred the landscape of the affluent society.

Many farmers did not share in the prosperity of the 1950s. Huge crop surpluses during those years caused the prices of farm products—and thus farm income—to decline dramatically. Large business enterprises bought vast areas of available farmland. They used large sums of money to transform agriculture into a thriving business. New machines and chemicals helped produce an abundance of food for American and foreign consumers. While some farmers benefited from these changes, others suffered. Because small farms could not compete with large farms, many small-farm families sold their land and migrated to urban areas. Thousands of small farmers who remained in agriculture struggled to stay out of poverty.

Farmworkers suffered as well. In the South, African American sharecroppers and tenant farmers had always struggled to survive. Their problems increased when mechanized cotton pickers replaced workers. The popularity of synthetic fibers reduced the demand for cotton. Southern farmworkers lost their jobs, cotton production fell, and thousands of farmers lost their land.

Migrant farmworkers in the West and the Southwest—mostly Mexican Americans and Asian Americans—also suffered. They toiled long hours for very low wages and lived in substandard housing.

Rural poverty did not always come from agricultural problems. In **Appalachia,** a region stretching along the Appalachian Mountains through several states, the decline of the coal industry plunged thousands of rural mountain people into desperate poverty.

Urban Poverty

As increasing numbers of middle-class Americans moved to the suburbs in the 1950s, they left the poor behind. The inner cities became islands of poverty. To these islands people still came looking for work. Continuing their migration from rural areas of the South, more than three million African Americans moved to cities in the North and the Midwest between 1940 and 1960. Many poor Hispanics—Puerto Ricans in the East and Mexicans in the Southwest and the West—also moved to American cities.

The migration of poor African Americans and Hispanics to Northern cities hastened the departure of whites to the suburbs. This "white flight"

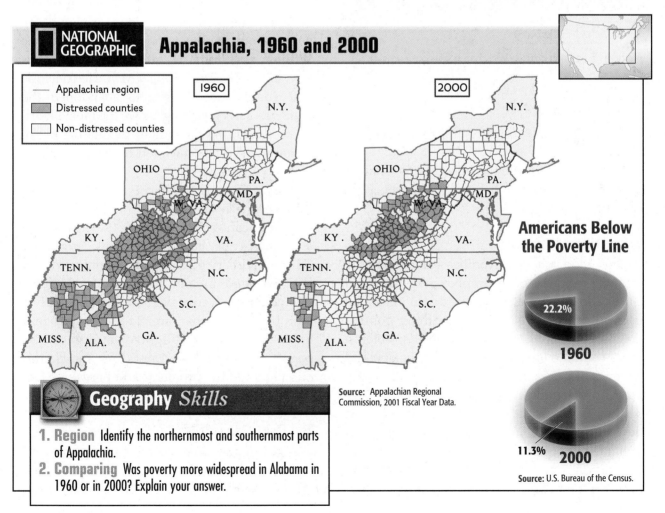

NATIONAL GEOGRAPHIC

Appalachia, 1960 and 2000

— Appalachian region
▨ Distressed counties
☐ Non-distressed counties

1960

2000

Source: Appalachian Regional Commission, 2001 Fiscal Year Data.

Americans Below the Poverty Line

22.2% — 1960

11.3% — 2000

Source: U.S. Bureau of the Census.

Geography Skills

1. **Region** Identify the northernmost and southernmost parts of Appalachia.
2. **Comparing** Was poverty more widespread in Alabama in 1960 or in 2000? Explain your answer.

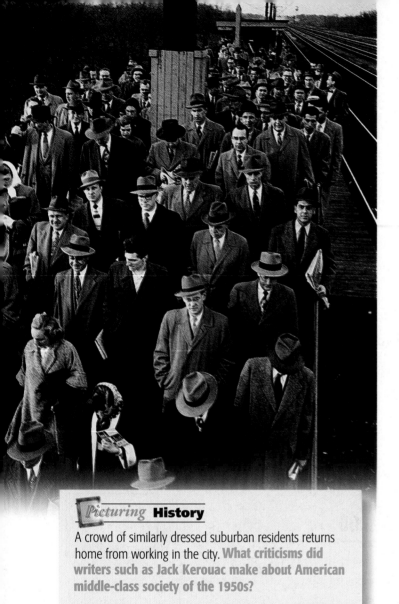

Picturing History

A crowd of similarly dressed suburban residents returns home from working in the city. **What criticisms did writers such as Jack Kerouac make about American middle-class society of the 1950s?**

turned some areas of cities into ghettos—neighborhoods that were inhabited mainly by poor minority groups.

Urban Unemployment

Few good job opportunities existed for the growing numbers of urban poor. As whites fled cities, factories and businesses also relocated into suburban areas. With a declining population, cities faced growing financial problems. Taxes could no longer keep up with the demand for such services as public transportation and police protection. Moreover, automation—producing goods using mechanical and electronic devices—reduced jobs in the industries that remained. It became more and more difficult for the urban poor to rise from poverty and improve their lives.

The urban poor struggled not only with poverty but also with racial discrimination in employment, housing, and education. Crime and violence often grew out of inner-city poverty, especially among young people who saw no hope for escape from life in the ghetto.

Reading Check **Explaining** What effect did automation have on factory jobs?

Voices of Dissent

Changes in American society in the 1950s caused some people to question the values that were emerging. Some critics charged that the sameness of suburban and corporate life had a cost—the loss of individuality. Others condemned American materialism—a focus on accumulating money and possessions rather than an interest in spiritual matters.

Social Critics

During the 1950s, leading social critics examined the complexity of modern society. Many wrote about its effects on individual behavior. **William H. Whyte, Jr.,** studied American business life in *The Organization Man*. He concluded that young executives who abandoned their own views to "get along" were the most likely to succeed. He drew a somber picture of "organization men" who "have left home spiritually as well as physically."

In his book *The Affluent Society*, economist **John Kenneth Galbraith** wrote of the prosperous American society of the 1950s. However, not all Americans shared in this prosperity. Galbraith described a suburban family, comfortably installed in an "air-conditioned, power-steered and power-braked automobile," driving "through cities that are badly paved, made hideous by litter, blighted buildings, billboards." Prosperous Americans, he claimed, often ignored the problems and hardships faced by other Americans.

The Beat Generation

A group of writers called the Beats had even sharper criticism of American society. The term "Beat," said novelist **Jack Kerouac,** meant "weariness with all forms of the modern industrial state." Kerouac, poet **Allen Ginsberg,** and other Beats rebelled against American culture.

Kerouac's novel *On the Road,* the most influential book of the Beats, described the wild adventures of friends who drove aimlessly around the country. Its main character was

> **❝**mad to live, mad to talk, mad to be saved, desirous of everything at the same time.**❞**

The novel made Kerouac an instant celebrity.

Millions of young Americans read the works of Beat writers. Some adopted Beat attitudes of rebellion and isolation from society.

Questioning Roles

With society changing, women and African Americans began questioning their roles. In the 1950s both groups strived to gain greater freedom and equality.

"The suburban housewife was the dream image of the young American woman," wrote **Betty Friedan,** herself a suburban wife and mother. "She was healthy, beautiful, educated, [and] concerned only about her husband, her children, and her home." Television, advertising, and magazines reinforced this image of women as perfect wives and mothers and presented the idea of suburban life as the path to a full and happy life.

As Friedan discovered, however, many suburban housewives were dissatisfied with this role and longed to express their individuality. Her book, *The Feminine Mystique,* described the frustration and unhappiness of these women.

African Americans also questioned their place in society in the 1950s. After years of struggling for their rights, African Americans became increasingly impatient for change and less willing to accept their status as second-class citizens. They launched a new campaign for full civil rights.

Three events in the 1950s proved especially important for African Americans. First, the Court decision in *Brown* v. *Board of Education of Topeka* (1954) declared racial segregation in public schools to be unconstitutional. Second, African Americans staged a successful boycott of segregated buses in Montgomery, Alabama. Third, President Eisenhower sent troops to Little Rock, Arkansas, to enforce a court order to integrate a high school. These three events, which you will learn more about in Chapter 29, paved the way for the successes of the civil rights movement in the 1960s.

✓ **Reading Check** **Describing** What criticisms were made about suburban and corporate life?

SECTION 3 ASSESSMENT

Checking for Understanding

1. **Key Terms** Write a short paragraph in which you use the following terms: ghetto, automation, materialism.
2. **Reviewing Facts** Problems in what industry led to unemployment and economic woes in Appalachia?

Reviewing Themes

3. **Continuity and Change** How were American inner cities changing during the 1950s?

Critical Thinking

4. **Drawing Conclusions** Why do you think some women were dissatisfied with their roles during the 1950s?
5. **Determining Cause and Effect** Re-create the diagram below and explain how automation affected each of the following groups.

Effects of Automation		
Factory owner	Small farmer	Industrial worker

Analyzing Visuals

6. **Picturing History** Examine the photographs in this section. Write a caption for each of the photographs in which you describe what the subjects are doing.

Interdisciplinary Activity

Descriptive Writing Write a poem at least 12 lines long that might have been written by a social critic of the 1950s.

What were people's lives like in the past?

What—and whom—were people talking about? What did they eat? What did they do for fun? These two pages will give you some clues to everyday life in the U.S. as you step back in time with TIME Notebook.

CULVER PICTURES

Profile

On July 20, 1969, **NEIL ARMSTRONG** *became the first human to walk on the moon. There he spoke the famous words "That's one small step for a man, one giant leap for mankind." Later, Armstrong reflected on his voyage and the "spaceship" we call Earth.*

"FROM OUR POSITION HERE ON THE EARTH, IT IS DIFFICULT to observe where the Earth is, and where it's going, or what its future course might be. Hopefully by getting a little farther away, both in the real sense and the figurative sense, we'll be able to make some people step back and reconsider their mission in the universe, to think of themselves as a group of people who constitute the crew of a spaceship going through the universe. If you're going to run a spaceship you've got to be pretty cautious about how you use your resources, how you use your crew, and how you treat your spacecraft."

—from the book First on the Moon

BETTMANN/CORBIS

Neil Armstrong

❝Riddle: What's college? That's where girls who are above cooking and sewing go to meet a man they spend their lives cooking and sewing for.❞

Ad for Gimbel's Department Store campus clothes in 1952

GEORGE SILK

❝I was looking… to the left, and I heard these terrible noises…. So I turned to the right, and all I remember is seeing my husband, he had this sort of quizzical look on his face, and his hand was up.❞

FIRST LADY JACQUELINE KENNEDY, *on the day her husband, President John F. Kennedy, was assassinated in 1963*

❝I have a dream that my four little children will one day live in a nation where they will not be judged by the color of their skin but by the content of their character.❞

REV. MARTIN LUTHER KING, JR. *August 28, 1963*

WHAT'S IN & WHAT'S OUT

ADAM SCULL/GLOBE PHOTOS

Kermit

TV GUIDE
Weekly magazine has circulation of about 6.5 million by 1959.

KERMIT
It's easy being green – when you're a hot Muppet on the hit show *Sesame Street* that first aired in 1969.

MINI SKIRTS
Skirts in 1964 reach new heights.

COLLIER'S
The respected magazine loses readership, publishing its final edition on Jan. 4, 1957.

TV'S BEAVER
After 234 episodes, *Leave It to Beaver* goes off the air in 1963.

POODLE SKIRTS
1950s girls wear these long skirts with a puffy crinoline underneath.

Leave It to Beaver

GLOBE PHOTOS

American Scene 1950-1960

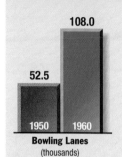
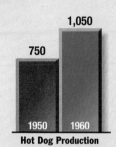
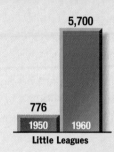
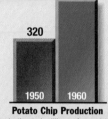

	1950	1960
Bowling Lanes (thousands)	52.5	108.0
Little Leagues	776	5,700
Hot Dog Production (estimated millions of pounds)	750	1,050
Potato Chip Production (estimated millions of pounds)	320	532
Encyclopedia Sales (millions of dollars)	72	300

Be Prepared

"Know the Bomb's True Dangers. Know the Steps You Can Take to Escape Them!—You Can Survive."
Government pamphlet, 1950

ARE YOU DIGGING YOUR OWN bomb shelter? Better go shopping. Below is a list of items included with the $3,000 Mark I Kidde Kokoon, designed to accommodate a family of five for a three- to five-day underground stay.

- 3-way portable radio
- air blower
- radiation detector
- protective apparel suit
- face respirator
- radiation charts (4)
- hand shovel combination (for digging out after the blast)
- gasoline-driven generator
- gasoline (10 gallons)
- chemical toilet
- toilet chemicals (2 gallons)
- bunks (5)
- mattresses and blankets (5)
- air pump (for blowing up mattresses)
- incandescent bulbs (2) 40 watts

- fuses (2) 5 amperes
- clock—non-electric
- first aid kit
- waterless hand cleaner
- sterno stove
- canned water (10 gallons)
- canned food (meat, powdered milk, cereal, sugar, etc.)
- paper products

Bomb Shelter

BETTMANN/CORBIS

POPPERFOTO/ARCHIVE PHOTO

WORD AND MUSIC
Translation, Please!

Match the jazz or bebop word to its meaning.

1 crazy   **a.** become enthusiastic

2 dig   **b.** wonderful, great

3 flip   **c.** understand, appreciate

4 hip   **d.** aware

answers: 1. b; 2. c; 3. a; 4. d

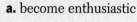

833

Chapter Summary
America in the Fifties

Eisenhower's Domestic Policy

- Attempts to limit government spending
- Federal Highway Act
- Extends social programs

The Cold War

- American leaders adopt policy of massive retaliation
- NASA is created
- Crisis in the Middle East
- Uprising in Hungary
- War in Southeast Asia
- Troubles in Latin America
- Geneva Summit encourages peaceful coexistence
- U-2 incident rekindles Cold War

Prosperity

- Productivity increased
- Per capita income and the standard of living increased
- The baby boom increases population
- Suburban housing developments boom
- Car culture grows
- Consumerism grows
- Television viewing increases

Problems and Issues

- Growing competition hurts small farmers
- Decline in coal industry increases poverty in rural areas
- Inner cities decay as businesses and residents relocate
- Social critics question conformity
- Women question their roles in society
- African Americans challenge segregation

Reviewing Key Terms

Examine the groups of words below. Then write a sentence explaining what each group has in common.

1. automation, productivity
2. affluence, standard of living
3. domino theory, arms race
4. summit, peaceful coexistence

Reviewing Key Facts

5. What states entered the Union in 1959?
6. Name three foreign policy challenges the Eisenhower administration faced.
7. What was the goal of Project Mercury?
8. How did the Geneva summit help to ease Cold War tensions?
9. Who formed a new government in Cuba in 1959?
10. Identify technological advances of the 1950s.
11. What are downturns in the economy called?
12. What medical breakthrough did Dr. Jonas Salk make?
13. Identify three religious leaders who influenced Americans in the 1950s.
14. How did the mass movement to the suburbs affect inner cities?

Critical Thinking

15. **Analyzing Information** What general economic policies did the Eisenhower administration support?
16. **Determining Cause and Effect** Why would the development of nuclear weapons have allowed Eisenhower to cut the military budget?
17. **Analyzing Themes: Continuity and Change** Why was there such a great demand for automobiles in the 1950s?
18. **Determining Cause and Effect** Re-create the diagram below and explain how these two factors created problems for farmers and farm workers.

Farm problems	
Crop surpluses	Synthetic fiber industry

Practicing Skills

Analyzing Information Reread the "People in History" feature on page 823 and answer the questions that follow.

19. Who is the subject of the feature?

20. How did polio affect its victims?

21. What effect did the use of the polio vaccine have?

 Geography and History Activity

Study the maps on page 829; then answer the questions that follow.

22. **Region** How many states are included in the Appalachia region?

23. **Location** In which states did poverty strike the hardest in 1960?

24. **Comparing Maps** Was poverty in the Appalachian region more widespread in 1960 or in 2000? How can you tell?

Citizenship Cooperative Activity

25. **Analyzing Social Issues** Throughout history social critics have tried to draw attention to the injustices of society. Working in groups of three, research to find three poems written by modern poets that deal with current social problems. Social problems might include, for example, poverty, prejudice, and the prevalence of violence. Mount each of your poems on an 8½" x 11" sheet of paper and use photographs or drawings to illustrate each. Your group might also want to include short descriptions or captions to identify your photographs or drawings. Combine your poems with those of other groups to create a poetry collection titled "A Decade of Dissent."

Economics Activity

26. **Math Practice** The Bureau of Labor Statistics issued these statistics on workers between the ages of 16 and 24 who were employed in July 1998. Use the statistics to create a bar graph showing the numbers of young people working in the different economic sectors.

About 7 in 8 employed youth worked in private business this summer. The largest employers were retail trade (7.4 million) and services (5.8 million). There were also large numbers of youth employed in manufacturing (2.2 million) and construction (1.2 million). Government employed a total of 1.5 million young people in July. Nearly 3 in 5 of the young people with government jobs worked in local government.

 HISTORY Online

Self-Check Quiz
Visit taj.glencoe.com and click on **Chapter 28— Self-Check Quizzes** to prepare for the chapter test.

 Technology Activity

27. **Using the Internet** In the 1950s it would have been hard to imagine the role computers would play in our lives today. One by-product of the computer revolution is the hundreds of new computer-related words we have added to our language. Words such as *surfing* and *megabyte* describe computers and how we use them. Do an internet search and compile a list of words that probably did not exist before computers were invented in the 1950s. Share your findings with the class.

Alternative Assessment

28. **Portfolio Writing Activity** Talk to a friend or relative who is a baby boomer. How is life different for people of your generation? What do you think will be the effect on society when baby boomers retire? Write a report that focuses on these questions. Place it in your portfolio.

 Standardized Test Practice

Directions: Choose the *best* answer for this multiple choice question.

The Cold War between the United States and the former Soviet Union was a rivalry between what two forms of government?

A communism and socialism

B communism and dictatorship

C communism and democracy

D democracy and monarchy

Test-Taking Tip
To answer this question, you need to remember various systems of government are defined. Did either the United States or the former Soviet Union live under a monarchy—rule by a king or queen? Since they did not, you know that answer **D** is incorrect.

The Civil Rights Era

1954–1973

Why It Matters

In the 1950s, a tide of protest began to rise in America against deeply rooted attitudes of racism and discrimination. The campaign for equality grew and gained momentum in the 1960s. Although the civil rights movement could not overcome all the obstacles, it achieved some great and long-lasting successes.

The Impact Today

Inspired by the movements of the 1950s and 1960s, many Americans work to secure full rights for all citizens.

The American Journey *Video* *The chapter 29 video, "Beyond Prejudice,"* *examines what it was like to be a young adult during the civil rights movement.*

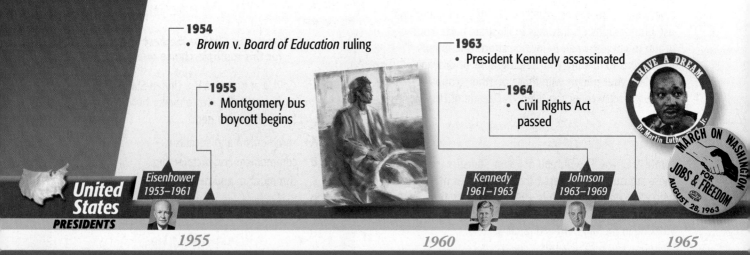

1954
• *Brown* v. *Board of Education* ruling

1955
• Montgomery bus boycott begins

1963
• President Kennedy assassinated

1964
• Civil Rights Act passed

United States
PRESIDENTS

Eisenhower
1953–1961

Kennedy
1961–1963

Johnson
1963–1969

1955   1960   1965

World

1954
• French forced out of Vietnam

1959
• Fidel Castro seizes power in Cuba

1962
• Algeria gains independence from France

1964
• Nelson Mandela receives life sentence in South Africa

March on Washington On August 28, 1963, more than 200,000 people gathered to urge support for civil rights legislation.

Study Organizer

Identifying Main Ideas Study Foldable
Make and use this foldable to identify the major issues about the Civil Rights era and to classify information under those topics.

Step 1 Collect 3 sheets of paper and place them about 1 inch apart.

Keep the edges straight.

Step 2 Fold up the bottom edges of the paper to form 6 tabs.

This makes all tabs the same size.

Step 3 When all the tabs are the same size, fold the paper to hold the tabs in place and staple the sheets together. Turn the paper and label each tab as shown.

The Civil Rights Era
Women's Rights
Hispanic Americans
Native Americans
Americans with Disabilities
African Americans

Staple together along the fold.

Reading and Writing As you read the chapter, write (under each appropriate tab) what you learn about the struggle for civil rights by different groups of Americans.

1968
- Dr. Martin Luther King, Jr., assassinated
- Indian Civil Rights Act passed

1970
- Grape workers gain increased pay and better conditions

1971
- Floppy disk introduced

Nixon
1969–1974

1970   *1975*

1967
- First heart transplant performed in South Africa

1972
- Britain imposes direct rule on Northern Ireland
- Terrorists kill Israeli Olympic athletes

HISTORY Online

Chapter Overview
Visit taj.glencoe.com and click on **Chapter 29— Chapter Overviews** to preview chapter information.

SECTION 1 The Civil Rights Movement

Guide to Reading

Main Idea

Despite obstacles, African Americans pressed for equal rights.

Key Terms

segregation, integrate, boycott, civil disobedience

Reading Strategy

Classifying Information As you read the section, re-create the diagram below and describe the roles these people played in the civil rights movement.

	Roles
Linda Brown	
Rosa Parks	
Martin Luther King, Jr.	

Read to Learn

• how a Supreme Court decision helped African Americans in their struggle for equal rights.
• why Dr. Martin Luther King, Jr., emerged as a leader.

Section Theme

Civic Rights and Responsibilities African Americans organized in an effort to secure equal rights.

Preview of Events

♦1954	♦1955	♦1956	♦1957

1954
Supreme Court strikes down segregation in education

1955
Rosa Parks is arrested; Montgomery bus boycott begins

1957
Dr. Martin Luther King, Jr., heads SCLC; Federal troops help integrate a Little Rock high school

AN
American Story

Jackie Robinson baseball card

Jackie Robinson could do everything on a baseball field—hit singles, slam home runs, and speed from base to base. Robinson was the first African American to play major league baseball. When his team, the Brooklyn Dodgers, reached the World Series in 1947, Robinson recalled, "I experienced a completely new emotion when the National Anthem was played. This time, I thought, it is being played for me, as much as for anyone else."

Equality in Education

African Americans had suffered from racism and discrimination in the United States since colonial times. As the nation entered the second half of the twentieth century, many African Americans believed that the time had come for them to enjoy an equal place in American life. They fought for equal opportunities in jobs, housing, and education. They also fought against segregation—the separation of people of different races.

The *Brown* Decision

The **NAACP** (National Association for the Advancement of Colored People) had worked on behalf of African Americans since its founding in 1909. In the 1950s, NAACP lawyers searched for cases they could use to challenge the laws allowing the segregation of public education.

The Supreme Court had upheld segregation laws in the past. In 1896 in *Plessy v. Ferguson,* it had ruled that "separate but equal" public facilities were legal. **Thurgood Marshall,** the chief lawyer for the NAACP, decided to challenge the idea of "separate but equal." The NAACP began to decide which among the nation's segregated school districts to bring before the Court. Seven-year-old African American Linda Brown was not permitted to attend an all-white elementary school just blocks from her house. The Brown family sued the school system but lost. Marshall and the NAACP appealed the case all the way to the Supreme Court.

The case of **Brown v. Board of Education of Topeka, Kansas,** combined with several similar cases, reached the Supreme Court in December 1952. Marshall argued that segregated schools were not and could not be equal to white schools. For that reason segregated schools violated the Fourteenth Amendment.

On May 17, 1954, the Court unanimously ruled in *Brown* v. *Board of Education of Topeka, Kansas,* that it was unconstitutional to separate schoolchildren by race. The *Brown* decision reversed the Court's decision in *Plessy* v. *Ferguson.* *(See page 997 for a summary of the* Brown *decision.)*

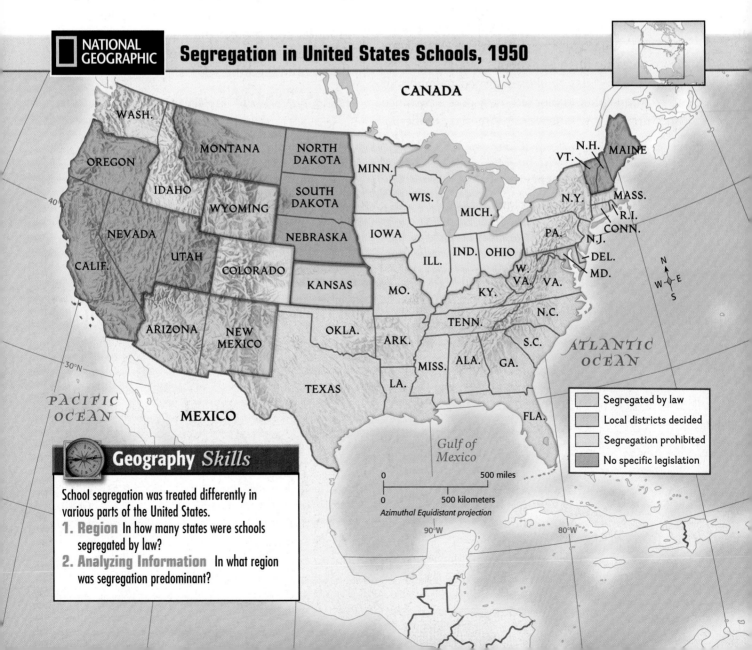

NATIONAL GEOGRAPHIC

Segregation in United States Schools, 1950

CANADA

WASH. · OREGON · MONTANA · NORTH DAKOTA · MINN. · IDAHO · WYOMING · SOUTH DAKOTA · WIS. · MICH. · N.H. · VT. · MAINE · N.Y. · MASS. · R.I. · CONN. · NEVADA · UTAH · NEBRASKA · IOWA · ILL. · IND. · OHIO · PA. · N.J. · DEL. · CALIF. · COLORADO · KANSAS · MO. · W. VA. · VA. · MD. · ARIZONA · NEW MEXICO · OKLA. · ARK. · TENN. · N.C. · S.C. · MISS. · ALA. · GA. · LA. · TEXAS · FLA.

PACIFIC OCEAN · MEXICO · ATLANTIC OCEAN · Gulf of Mexico

Legend:
- Segregated by law
- Local districts decided
- Segregation prohibited
- No specific legislation

0 — 500 miles
0 — 500 kilometers
Azimuthal Equidistant projection

90°W · 80°W · 40° · 30°N

Geography *Skills*

School segregation was treated differently in various parts of the United States.
1. **Region** In how many states were schools segregated by law?
2. **Analyzing Information** In what region was segregation predominant?

Integrating the Schools

The Court's decision in *Brown* v. *Board of Education* called on school authorities to make plans for integrating—bringing races together—in public schools. The Court also ordered that integration was to be carried out "with all deliberate speed"—as fast as reasonably possible.

Some school systems integrated quickly. However, in parts of the South, local leaders vowed to keep African American children out of white schools. A clash between the federal government and these states seemed unavoidable.

Confrontation in Little Rock

In 1957 a federal judge ordered Central High School in **Little Rock, Arkansas,** an all-white school, to admit African American students. Arkansas governor **Orval Faubus** opposed integration. In September he called out the state's National Guard to prevent African Americans from entering the high school.

On the first day of classes, armed members of the National Guard blocked the school's entrance and turned away nine African American students.

One of them, 15-year-old **Elizabeth Eckford,** recalled that when she tried to squeeze past a member of the guard,

> 66 He raised his bayonet, and then the other guards moved in and raised their bayonets. 99

For the first time since the Civil War, a Southern state had defied the authority of the federal government. Although Eisenhower had some doubts about the *Brown* decision, he believed it was his duty to enforce the law. The president warned Faubus that, if the governor did not admit the students, the federal government would act.

When a federal judge ruled that the governor had violated federal law, Faubus removed the National Guard. Eisenhower sent hundreds of soldiers to Little Rock to patrol the school grounds and protect the students. Shielded by the federal troops, the nine African American students entered the school.

Reading Check **Explaining** What did the Supreme Court rule in *Brown* v. *Board of Education*?

Picturing **History**

Elizabeth Eckford (center) braves the insults of white citizens to enter Central High School in Little Rock, Arkansas. **How did President Eisenhower respond to the crisis in Little Rock?**

People In History

Dr. Martin Luther King, Jr. 1929–1968

After the Montgomery bus boycott, Dr. Martin Luther King, Jr., emerged as the leader of the African American protest movement. What drove him into this demanding role in history?

The son of a Baptist minister, King attended Morehouse College, and when he was 18 years old decided on a career in the ministry. By the time he first arrived in Montgomery in September 1954 as pastor of the Dexter Avenue Baptist Church, he had also met and married Coretta Scott.

From the beginning of the Montgomery bus boycott, King encouraged his followers to use nonviolent resistance. This meant that those who carried out the demonstrations should not fight with authorities. In spite of his stand on nonviolence, King often became the target of violence.

In April 1968, King was in Memphis, Tennessee, to support a strike of sanitation workers. There, the minister was shot while standing on a motel balcony.

Gains on Other Fronts

While school integration continued, African Americans made other advances in securing their rights. More and more took part in a movement dedicated to securing fair and equal treatment.

The Montgomery Bus Boycott

On the evening of December 1, 1955, **Rosa Parks** boarded a bus in downtown **Montgomery, Alabama.** Parks, a seamstress, was secretary of the local chapter of the NAACP. She found an empty seat in the section reserved for whites.

When white passengers entered the bus, the driver told Parks, an African American, to move to the rear of the bus. Parks refused. At the next bus stop, she was taken off the bus by police, arrested for breaking the law, and fined $10. The episode could have ended there—but it did not.

Rosa Parks's arrest led African Americans in Montgomery to organize a boycott—a refusal to use—the city's buses. The boycott organizers hoped to hurt the city financially and force it to alter its policies. They had strength in numbers—almost 75 percent of the bus company's riders were African American.

At a boycott meeting, a young Baptist minister came forward to speak. Not widely known at the time, **Dr. Martin Luther King, Jr.,** made an impact on the crowd. He declared:

> 66We're here because, first and foremost, we are American citizens, and we are determined to acquire our citizenship to the fullness of its meaning. We are tired—tired of being segregated and humiliated, tired of being kicked about by the brutal feet of oppression.99

The boycott upset many people's daily lives, but the African Americans of Montgomery pulled together to make it work. Students hitchhiked to school; workers walked or rode bikes to their jobs. King helped organize car pools to shuttle people from place to place.

The bus boycott lasted for more than a year. City officials arrested King and other leaders at different times, but African Americans held firm. The local bus company lost thousands of dollars in fares, and downtown businesses lost customers. Finally, the Supreme Court settled the matter by ruling that the Montgomery bus segregation law was unconstitutional. In December 1956, the boycott ended.

Causes and Effects of the Move Toward Equality

Causes

- 1955, Rosa Parks is arrested
- 1955, Montgomery bus boycott begins
- 1957, Conflict at Little Rock
- 1957, SCLC is organized
- 1960, Students stage sit-ins
- 1963, March on Washington, D.C.

Effects

- 1962, James Meredith enrolls at University of Mississippi
- 1967, Thurgood Marshall appointed to Supreme Court
- 1968, Shirley Chisholm elected to House of Representatives
- 1972, Barbara Jordan elected to Congress

Graphic Organizer ➤ Skills

African Americans faced many obstacles in their struggle for equal rights.

Analyzing Information What protest followed the arrest of Rosa Parks?

Nonviolent Protest

With the victory in Montgomery, King became a leader of the civil rights movement. He followed the tactics of **A. Philip Randolph,** the nation's most prominent African American labor leader. King was also strongly influenced by **Mohandas Gandhi,** who had used nonviolent protest to help India gain independence from Great Britain. In keeping with his beliefs, Gandhi used protest methods based on civil disobedience, or the refusal to obey laws that are considered unjust.

In January 1957, King and 60 other ministers started a new organization called the **Southern Christian Leadership Conference** (SCLC). SCLC leaders emphasized nonviolent protest. They showed civil rights workers how to protect themselves from violent attacks. The SCLC also discussed how to identify targets for protests and how to organize people for support. In taking these steps, the SCLC prepared African Americans for the struggle for equal rights.

✓ **Reading Check** **Describing** How did the Montgomery bus boycott begin?

SECTION 1 ASSESSMENT

Checking for Understanding

1. **Key Terms** Use these terms in sentences that explain important events in the civil rights movement: segregation, integrate, boycott, civil disobedience.
2. **Reviewing Facts** Name the Supreme Court decision that banned segregation in education.

Reviewing Themes

3. **Civic Rights and Responsibilities** How did the Montgomery bus boycott end?

Critical Thinking

4. **Drawing Conclusions** Why do you think Dr. Martin Luther King, Jr., believed nonviolent protest was the most effective course to gain civil rights?
5. **Sequencing Information** Re-create the time line below and list important events in the civil rights movement in the 1950s.

May 1954	Dec. 1955	Jan. 1957	Sept. 1957
☐	☐	☐	☐

Analyzing Visuals

6. Examine the map on page 839. In what states did local school districts decide whether schools were integrated or not? In what states in the far northwest was segregation prohibited?

Examine the map on page 839.

Interdisciplinary Activity

Descriptive Writing Write song lyrics to be sung at a civil rights march. Base your lyrics on the story of Rosa Parks and her courage the night of her arrest.

America's LITERATURE

Maya Angelou (1928–   )

Maya Angelou, born in 1928, has written poetry, fiction, and plays. Born Marguerite Johnson, Angelou and her brother, Bailey, were raised by their grandmother, Annie Henderson, the owner of a general store in Stamps, Arkansas.

READ TO DISCOVER

In the following excerpt from Angelou's autobiography, she is about 10 years old. Bright but painfully self-conscious, she has become withdrawn and refuses to speak to anyone. As you read, notice the influence that Mrs. Flowers has on Marguerite.

READER'S DICTIONARY

familiar: close friend or associate

Her World by Philip Evergood

I Know Why the Caged Bird Sings

Mrs. Bertha Flowers was the aristocrat of Black Stamps. She had the grace of control to appear warm in the coldest weather, and on the Arkansas summer days it seemed she had a private breeze which swirled around, cooling her. . . .

She was one of the few gentlewomen I have ever known, and has remained throughout my life the measure of what a human being can be.

Momma had a strange relationship with her. Most often when she passed on the road in front of the Store, she spoke to Momma in that soft yet carrying voice, "Good day, Mrs. Henderson." Momma responded with "How you, Sister Flowers?"

Mrs. Flowers didn't belong to our church, nor was she Momma's **familiar.** Why on earth did she insist on calling her Sister Flowers? Shame made me want to hide my face. Mrs. Flowers deserved better than to be called Sister. Then, Momma left out the verb. Why not ask, "How *are* you, *Mrs.* Flowers?" With the unbalanced passion of the young, I hated her for showing her ignorance to Mrs. Flowers. It didn't occur to me for many years that they were as alike as sisters, separated only by formal education. . . .

Occasionally, though, Mrs. Flowers would drift off the road and down to the Store and Momma would say to me, "Sister, you go on and play." As I left I would hear the beginning of an intimate conversation. Momma persistently using the wrong verb, or none at all. . . .

I heard the soft-voiced Mrs. Flowers and the textured voice of my grandmother merging and melting. They were interrupted from time to time by giggles that must have come from Mrs. Flowers. . . .

She acted just as refined as whitefolks in the movies and books and she was more beautiful, for none of them could have come near that warm color without looking gray by comparison.

From *I Know Why the Caged Bird Sings*, by Maya Angelou. Copyright © 1969 by Maya Angelou. Reprinted by permission of Random House, Inc.

ANALYZING LITERATURE

1. **Recall and Interpret** Describe the relationship between Momma and Mrs. Flowers.
2. **Evaluate and Connect** Do you think you would like Mrs. Flowers? Explain.

Interdisciplinary Activity

Informative Writing Write a one-page sketch describing an encounter you had with a person who influenced your life in a positive way.

SECTION 2 Kennedy and Johnson

Guide to Reading

Main Idea
John Kennedy's New Frontier and Lyndon Johnson's Great Society were government programs to fight poverty, help cities and schools, and promote civil rights.

Key Terms
poverty line, Medicare, Medicaid

Reading Strategy
Organizing Information As you read the section, re-create the diagram below and list four programs that were part of the War on Poverty.

Read to Learn
• what the goals were for Kennedy's New Frontier.
• what new programs were created as part of the Great Society.

Section Theme
Government and Democracy Presidents Kennedy and Johnson proposed increased spending on social programs.

Preview of Events

♦1960	♦1962	♦1964	♦1966
Jan. 1961 John F. Kennedy takes office as president	**Nov. 1963** Kennedy is assassinated	**Jan. 1964** President Johnson announces war on poverty	**July 1964** Civil Rights Act of 1964 is passed

1960 presidential campaign items

AN American Story

They stood together on the inaugural platform: 43-year-old John F. Kennedy—tanned, vigorous, and coatless despite the subfreezing weather—and 70-year-old Dwight D. Eisenhower, wearing a muffler, looking like a tired general. The appearances of the two men, a generation apart in age, symbolized the change of leadership. Kennedy's speech promised so much: "Let every nation know . . . that we shall pay any price, bear any burden, meet any hardship, support any friend, oppose any foe to assure the survival and the success of liberty. . . ."

Election of 1960

By 1960, the crusade for civil rights had become a national movement. Against this background, the nation prepared for a presidential election. The Republican candidate, Vice President **Richard M. Nixon,** pledged to continue the policies of President Eisenhower. The Democratic candidate, **John F. Kennedy,** promised new programs to "get the country moving again."

For much of the campaign, polls showed Nixon in the lead. One reason for this was the fact that Kennedy was Roman Catholic. No Catholic had ever been president, and many Americans feared that if Kennedy won he might show more loyalty to his church than to his country. Kennedy answered by stressing his belief in the separation of church and state.

John F. Kennedy

Kennedy came from one of the country's wealthiest and most powerful families. His father, Joseph P. Kennedy, was a successful business leader and the American ambassador to Britain at the start of World War II.

John Kennedy joined the United States Navy during World War II and was assigned to active duty in the Pacific. When the Japanese sank the PT (patrol torpedo) boat he commanded, Kennedy saved the life of a crew member by swimming to shore with the injured man on his back. The rescue effort led to navy and marine medals for Kennedy but also aggravated an old back injury he had. The story of the rescue was later described in Robert Donovan's book *PT 109.*

Kennedy's political career began in 1946 when he won a seat in Congress from Massachusetts. Six years later, he was elected to the United States Senate. The young senator wrote a book, *Profiles in Courage,* which described difficult political decisions made by past United States senators. The book became a best-seller and received a Pulitzer Prize. After easily winning reelection to the Senate in 1958, Kennedy campaigned for the presidency in 1960.

A New President

The turning point in the 1960 election came when the candidates took part in the first televised presidential debates. Kennedy appeared handsome and youthful. Nixon, who was recovering from an illness, looked tired and sick. Kennedy spoke with confidence about the future. Many viewers thought that Kennedy made a better impression.

In November, nearly 70 million voters turned out to choose between Nixon and Kennedy. For the first time, the people of Alaska and Hawaii took part in a presidential election. The results were extremely close. In the popular vote, Kennedy won 49.7 percent, while Nixon received 49.5 percent. In the electoral vote, Kennedy gained a greater margin over Nixon—303 to 219 votes.

Reading Check **Identifying** Who were the presidential candidates in 1960?

The New Frontier

On January 20, 1961, snow covered Washington, D.C., and icy winds whipped through the city. Still, thousands of people streamed to the Capitol to see John Fitzgerald Kennedy become the thirty-fifth president of the United States. *(See page 995 for part of President Kennedy's Inaugural Address.)*

Richard Nixon and John Kennedy took part in the first televised presidential debates in 1960.

In 1960 for the first time, radio and television played a major factor in a presidential campaign. This advertisement for television sets focuses on the televised presidential debates.

He offered the nation youth, energy, and hope. In his Inaugural Address, Kennedy spoke of a new era:

> 66Let the word go forth from this time and place . . . that the torch has been passed to a new generation of Americans.99

The young president promised to face the nation's challenges with determination. In closing, Kennedy roused the American people to action:

> 66And so, my fellow Americans: ask not what your country can do for you—ask what you can do for your country.99

Domestic Policies

Kennedy drew up plans for the **New Frontier,** a group of proposals involving social programs. One bill he sent to Congress called for more federal funds for education. Another bill aimed to help poor people get jobs. Reluctant to commit to Kennedy's expensive programs, Congress failed to pass most of these bills.

Another area of concern for Kennedy was civil rights. The president wished to help African Americans in their fight for equal rights. At the same time he worried that moving too quickly would anger Southern Democrats in Congress, whose support he needed to enact legislation.

Lyndon Johnson takes the oath of office aboard Air Force One after the assassination of President Kennedy.

In 1963 Kennedy decided to ask Congress to pass a bill guaranteeing civil rights. The House approved the measure, but it stalled in the Senate. Meanwhile, the president left for a campaign trip to Dallas, Texas.

Kennedy Assassinated

On November 22, 1963, Kennedy arrived in Dallas with his wife, Jacqueline. As the president and the First Lady rode through the streets in an open car, several shots rang out. Kennedy slumped against his wife. The car sped to a hospital, but the president was dead. Shortly afterward, Vice President **Lyndon B. Johnson** took the oath of office as president.

The assassination stunned the nation. Television networks broadcast the news almost without interruption for the next few days. Millions of Americans numbly watched the funeral.

In the midst of the grief came another shock. The day of Kennedy's shooting, Dallas police had arrested **Lee Harvey Oswald** and charged him with killing the president. Two days later, as police moved Oswald from one jail to another, Jack Ruby jumped through the circle of police officers and journalists and shot and killed Oswald.

Rumors that a group of enemies had plotted the assassination swirled around the country. Soon afterward, President Johnson appointed **Earl Warren,** chief justice of the United States, to head a commission to investigate the Kennedy shooting. After months of study, the **Warren Commission** issued its report. Oswald had acted on his own, it said. The report did not satisfy everyone, however. Many people believed the assassination was a conspiracy, or secret plot.

Reading Check **Describing** What happened on November 22, 1963?

The "Great Society"

Soon after becoming president, Lyndon B. Johnson outlined a set of programs even more ambitious than Kennedy's New Frontier. He called his proposals the **"Great Society."** In a speech he explained his vision of America:

> "In a land of great wealth, families must not live in hopeless poverty. In a land rich in harvest, children must not go hungry. . . . In a great land of learning and scholars, young people must be taught to read and write."

Johnson had acquired great skill as a legislator during his 22 years in Congress. He used this skill to persuade Congress to launch programs that would make the Great Society real.

The War on Poverty

In January 1964, President Johnson declared "an unconditional war on poverty in America." The first part of his plan for a Great Society consisted of programs to help Americans who lived below the poverty line—the minimum income needed to survive. A program called **Head Start** provided preschool education for the children of poor families. **Upward Bound** helped poor students attend college. The **Job Corps** offered training to young people who wanted to work. **Volunteers in Service to America** (VISTA) was a kind of domestic peace corps of citizens working in poor neighborhoods.

Among the most important laws passed under Johnson were those establishing Medicare and Medicaid. Medicare helped pay for medical care for senior citizens. Medicaid helped poor people pay their hospital bills.

Helping Cities and Schools

Other parts of the Great Society targeted the nation's crumbling cities. In 1966 President Johnson established the **Department of Housing and Urban Development** (HUD), which helped fund public housing projects. Another program, Model Cities, provided money to help rebuild cities. Schools received a boost from the Elementary and Secondary Education Act of 1965, which greatly increased spending for education.

Civil Rights

Although raised in the South, Lyndon Johnson was not a segregationist. He believed that the nation must protect the rights of all American citizens. When Johnson took office, he vowed to turn the civil rights bill Kennedy had proposed into law. In early 1964 he warned Congress that: "We are going to pass a civil rights bill if it takes all summer."

With growing support across the nation for the goals of the civil rights movement, Congress passed the **Civil Rights Act of 1964** in July. The act prohibited discrimination against African Americans in employment, voting, and public accommodations. It banned discrimination not only by race and color, but also by sex, religion, or national origin.

✓ **Reading Check** **Comparing** What did Medicare and Medicaid do?

SECTION 2 ASSESSMENT

Checking for Understanding

1. **Key Terms** Use each of the following words in sentences about the Great Society: poverty line, Medicare, Medicaid.
2. **Reviewing Facts** What was the purpose of the Job Corps?

Reviewing Themes

3. **Government and Democracy** Describe Johnson's policies toward civil rights.

Critical Thinking

4. **Drawing Conclusions** Should televised debates influence how Americans choose their president? Explain your reasoning.
5. **Organizing Information** Re-create the diagram below and identify three proposals that Kennedy asked Congress to act on.

Kennedy proposals

Analyzing Visuals

6. **Analyzing Artifacts** Examine the campaign items on page 844. What are the ideas that each is trying to present to voters? Compare these items to current campaign buttons and posters you have seen.

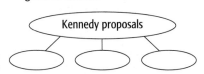

Interdisciplinary Activity

Citizenship Choose one of President Kennedy's or President Johnson's programs and create a poster supporting or opposing it.

The Struggle Continues

Guide to Reading

Main Idea

New leaders emerged as growing numbers of African Americans became dissatisfied with the slow progress of civil rights.

Key Terms

sit-in, interstate

Reading Strategy

Classifying Information As you read the section, re-create the diagram below and describe the roles these people played in the civil rights movement.

	Roles
James Meredith	
Malcolm X	
Stokely Carmichael	

Read to Learn

• what actions African Americans took in the early 1960s to secure their rights.
• how tensions erupted in violence in many American cities.

Section Theme

Continuity and Change New African leaders, such as Malcolm X, called for changes in strategies and goals.

Preview of Events

♦1960   ♦1965   ♦1970

—1961   —1962   —1963   —1968
Freedom Riders move   James Meredith enrolls   More than 200,000 people   Dr. Martin Luther King, Jr.,
through the South   at University of Mississippi   march in Washington, D.C.   is assassinated

AN American Story

Supporting the sit-ins

On February 1, 1960, four African American students walked into a store in Greensboro, North Carolina. After buying a few items, they sat down at a "whites-only" lunch counter. When a waitress questioned what they were doing, one of the students replied, "We believe since we buy books and papers in the other part of the store, we should get served in this part." They were refused service, and the four sat at the counter until the store closed. By the end of the week, hundreds of students had joined the protest. Angry whites jeered at the students and dumped food on them. The protesters refused to leave or strike back.

The Movement Grows

A new wave of civil rights activity swept across the nation in the 1960s. Early activity targeted segregation in the South. Segregation existed in the North as well. In Northern cities and suburbs, African Americans and whites often lived in different neighborhoods; as a result, their children often attended different schools.

Soon African Americans expanded their goal to fighting discrimination and racism in the North as well as in the South.

High school and college students staged sit-ins in nearly 80 cities. A sit-in is the act of protesting by sitting down. Sit-ins were staged throughout the nation against stores that practiced segregation. Store managers wanted to end the disturbances and the loss of business. Gradually many stores agreed to desegregate.

The sit-ins helped launch a new civil rights group, the **Student Nonviolent Coordinating Committee** (SNCC). Civil rights activist **Ella Baker** was a guiding spirit behind SNCC and one of its organizers. Earlier, Baker had played important roles in both the NAACP and the SCLC. SNCC was a key player in the civil rights movement for several years.

Freedom Rides

The Supreme Court had ruled in 1960 against segregated bus facilities. Another civil rights group, the **Congress of Racial Equality** (CORE), decided to see whether the ruling was being enforced. On May 4, 1961, a group of African American and white CORE members left Washington, D.C., on two buses bound for New Orleans. They called themselves **Freedom Riders.**

The bus trip went smoothly until it reached Alabama, where angry whites stoned and beat the Freedom Riders.

Television and newspapers broadcast reports of the beatings. **Robert Kennedy,** the United States attorney general, asked CORE to stop the Freedom Rides for a "cooling-off period." CORE leader **James Farmer** responded: "We have been cooling off for 350 years. If we cool off any more, we will be in a deep freeze."

Violence and Arrests

The Freedom Riders pressed on, only to meet more violence in Birmingham and Montgomery, Alabama. There were no mobs waiting for the Freedom Riders in Jackson, Mississippi. However, police, state troopers, and Mississippi National Guard units were everywhere. As the Riders stepped off the bus and tried to enter the whites-only waiting room at the bus station, they were arrested for trespassing and jailed.

Despite the violence and the jail sentences, more Freedom Riders kept coming all summer. In the fall the Interstate Commerce Commission took steps to enforce the Supreme Court ruling, issuing new regulations that banned segregation on interstate buses—those that crossed state lines—and in bus stations.

Picturing **History**

Police in Birmingham, Alabama, used high-pressure water hoses against civil rights marchers. Sit-ins were another form of protest. **What was the purpose of the Freedom Rides?**

Integrating Universities

African Americans continued to apply pressure to secure their civil rights. They spurred President Kennedy to take a more active role in the civil rights struggle.

In 1962 a federal court ordered the University of Mississippi to enroll its first African American student, **James Meredith.** However, Mississippi governor **Ross Barnett,** with the aid of state police, prevented Meredith from registering. When President Kennedy sent federal marshals to escort Meredith to the campus, riots erupted. A mob stormed the administration building armed with guns and rocks. The marshals fought back with tear gas and nightsticks. Meredith succeeded in registering but two people were killed. Federal troops were stationed at the university to protect him until he graduated in 1963.

Another confrontation between state and federal power took place in June 1963—this time in Alabama. Governor **George Wallace** vowed he would "stand in the schoolhouse door" to block the integration of the University of Alabama in Tuscaloosa. President Kennedy, acting on the advice of his brother, sent the Alabama National Guard to ensure the entry of African Americans to the university. As a result, Wallace backed down.

Birmingham

In the spring of 1963, Dr. Martin Luther King, Jr., and the SCLC targeted **Birmingham, Alabama,** for a desegregation protest. Police arrested hundreds of demonstrators, including King, but the demonstrations continued. During King's two weeks in jail, he wrote the eloquent "Letter from Birmingham Jail," in which he wrote:

> ❝For years now I have heard the word 'Wait!' It rings in the ear of every Negro with piercing familiarity. This 'Wait' has almost always meant 'Never.' We must come to see . . . that 'justice too long delayed is justice denied.'❞

What If...

Jackie Robinson Failed to Make the Major Leagues?

Can you imagine major league baseball without such superstars as Sammy Sosa or Ken Griffey, Jr.? Yet these great players may never have had the chance if not for Jackie Robinson. When Robinson first played for the Brooklyn Dodgers on April 15th, 1947, he became the first African American in the twentieth century to play major league baseball. His outstanding play and courage in the face of adversity led to the signing of many more African American players.

Yet what if Robinson had failed? Some sports historians believe that many more years might haved passed before another chance opened for an African American player. Robinson's wife, Rachel, notes, "Jack knew that by breaking the color barrier, he was not only paving the way for minorities in professional sports, but was also providing opportunities in all facets of life. . . ."

Houston Federal Judge David Hittner echoes those sentiments:

❝I think the start of the heavy civil rights movement came with the breaking of the color barrier in major league baseball. It was one of the great indications of the impetus of the civil rights movement in the United States. To me, it really was the start. It showed a lot of folks that, here was the concept of equality. It nailed many nails in the coffin, particularly in terms of the perception of inferiority. Jackie Robinson was a pioneer. He had to stand there and take it, just so others could maybe someday get to where he was.❞

With Robinson's success came integration in other sports. By the mid-1950s African American athletes had established themselves as a powerful force in almost all professional sports.

National television carried vivid pictures of police setting snarling police dogs on unarmed demonstrators and washing small children across streets with the powerful impact of fire hoses. President Kennedy sent 3,000 troops to restore peace. On June 11, 1963, in Jackson, Mississippi, **Medgar Evers,** state field secretary for the NAACP, was murdered. The murder and the events in Alabama forced President Kennedy to make a decision. Appearing on national television, Kennedy spoke of the "moral issue" facing the nation:

> ❝The heart of the question is whether all Americans are to be afforded equal rights and equal opportunities, whether we are going to treat our fellow Americans as we want to be treated. If an American, because his skin is dark, cannot . . . enjoy the full and free life which all of us want, then who among us would be content to have the color of his skin changed and stand in his place?❞

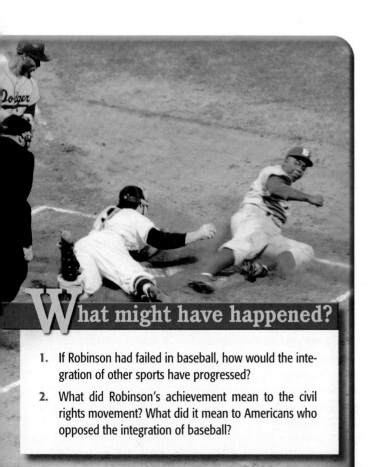

What might have happened?

1. If Robinson had failed in baseball, how would the integration of other sports have progressed?

2. What did Robinson's achievement mean to the civil rights movement? What did it mean to Americans who opposed the integration of baseball?

Days later, the president introduced new legislation giving all Americans the right to be served in public places and barring discrimination in employment.

March on Washington

To rally support for the civil rights bill, Dr. Martin Luther King, Jr., and the SCLC organized a massive march in Washington, D.C., on August 28, 1963. More than 200,000 people, of all colors and from all over the country, arrived to take part. Emily Rock, a 15-year-old African American, described how she felt at the march:

> ❝There was this sense of hope for the future—the belief that this march was the big step in the right direction. It could be heard in the voices of the people singing and seen in the way they walked. It poured out into smiles.❞

About 6,000 police officers stood nearby, but they had nothing to do but direct traffic. There was no trouble. Proceeding with great dignity and joy, the marchers carried signs urging Congress to act. They sang songs, including one that was becoming the anthem of the civil rights movement: "We Shall Overcome." 📖 *(See page 977 of the Primary Sources Library for the words to this song.)*

Late in the afternoon, Dr. Martin Luther King, Jr., spoke to the crowd in ringing words of his desire to see America transformed:

> ❝I have a dream that one day this nation will rise up and live out the true meaning of its creed: 'We hold these truths to be self-evident; that all men are created equal.' . . . When we let freedom ring, . . . we will be able to speed up that day when all of God's children . . . [will] join hands and sing in the words of the old . . . spiritual, 'Free at last! Free at last! Thank God Almighty, we are free at last!'❞

📖 *(See page 996 for more of this famous speech.)*

Freedom Summer

Congress did not pass Kennedy's civil rights bill until after his death. President **Lyndon B. Johnson,** who succeeded Kennedy, finally

this there can be no argument," he said. "Every American citizen must have an equal right to vote." In August Johnson signed the **Voting Rights Act of 1965** into law. The act gave the federal government the power to force local officials to allow African Americans to register to vote.

The act led to dramatic changes in political life in the South. In 1966 about 100 African Americans held elective office in the South. By 1972 that number had increased 10 times.

✓ Reading Check **Analyzing** Why were sit-ins an effective strategy against segregation?

Other Voices

By the mid-1960s, the civil rights movement had won numerous victories. Yet a growing number of African Americans grew tired of the slow pace of change and bitter over white attacks.

Malcolm X, a leader in the Nation of Islam (or Black Muslims), emerged as an important new voice for some African Americans. Malcolm X criticized the civil rights goal of integration, declaring that the best way for African Americans to achieve justice was to separate themselves from whites.

Malcolm X gained increasing support. By 1965, however, he had begun to change his ideas. Instead of racial separation, he called for "a society in which there could exist honest white-black brotherhood." Soon afterwards, he was killed by an assassin from a rival group among the Black Muslims. His fiery words and passionate ideas, contained in his autobiography and other writings, continued to influence the civil rights movement after his death.

Black Power

Other African American leaders embraced more radical approaches. **Stokely Carmichael,** who became the leader of SNCC, advanced the idea of **Black Power.** This was a philosophy of racial pride that said African Americans should create their own culture and political institutions. Carmichael and other radicals called at times for revolution, a complete transformation

persuaded Congress to pass the bill. The Civil Rights Act of 1964 outlawed discrimination in hiring and ended segregation in stores, restaurants, theaters, and hotels. Yet, in many states, African Americans still could not vote. Poll taxes and other discriminatory laws prevented them from exercising this right.

During the summer of 1964, thousands of civil rights workers spread throughout the South to help African Americans register to vote. They called the campaign **Freedom Summer,** but the workers faced strong, sometimes violent, opposition.

The Right to Vote

The next year SNCC organized a major demonstration in **Selma, Alabama,** to protest the continued denial of African Americans' right to vote. Police attacks on the marchers again dramatized the cause.

President Johnson stepped in. On March 15, 1965, in a televised speech, the president urged passage of a voting rights bill. "About

of society. Although rejected by such groups as the NAACP, the idea of Black Power had a great impact on the civil rights movement.

Violence Erupts

In Oakland, California, a group of young radicals formed the **Black Panther Party.** The Panthers symbolized a growing tension between African Americans and urban police. Large numbers of African Americans in urban areas felt frustrated about poverty and unemployment. The Panthers demanded reforms and armed themselves in opposition to the police. Several armed clashes with the police occurred.

The first major urban riots since the 1940s took place in the summer of 1965 in the **Watts** section of **Los Angeles.** In a week of rioting, 34 people died and much of Watts burned to the ground. National Guard troops were called in to end the uprising. The Watts riot was the first of a series of racial disorders that hit cities in the summers of 1965, 1966, and 1967.

Between the years of 1965 and 1967 rioting broke out in more than 40 Northern cities, including San Francisco, Chicago, and Cleveland. In July 1967, five days of protests, looting, and burning of buildings in Newark, New Jersey, ended with the deaths of 26 people and more than $10 million in damage. The next week, a massive uprising in Detroit shut the city down for several days.

President Johnson named a commission to study the causes of the riots and to suggest steps to improve conditions. The report of this group, the Kerner Commission, warned that "our nation is moving toward two societies, one black, one white—separate and unequal."

The wave of urban riots devastated many African American neighborhoods. The riots ended—but not before one last burst of rage.

King Is Assassinated

On April 4, 1968, racial tension in the United States took another tragic turn. On that night in Memphis, Tennessee, an assassin shot and killed Dr. Martin Luther King, Jr. King's assassination set off angry rioting in more than 100 cities. Fires burned in the nation's capital, just blocks from the Capitol and the White House.

Thousands of people attended King's funeral in Atlanta. Millions more watched on television. All mourned the death of an American hero who, the night before his death, had said God "has allowed me to go up to the mountain, and I've seen the promised land. I may not get there with you. But I want you to know tonight, that we, as a people, will get to the promised land!"

Reading Check **Explaining** Why did some African American leaders criticize the goal of integration?

SECTION 3 ASSESSMENT

Checking for Understanding

1. **Key Terms** Using complete sentences, define the following terms: sit-in, interstate.

2. **Reviewing Facts** What idea did Stokely Carmichael advance?

Reviewing Themes

3. **Continuity and Change** How did the beliefs and strategies of groups such as the Black Panthers differ from the beliefs and strategies of Dr. Martin Luther King, Jr.?

Critical Thinking

4. **Predicting Consequences** What do you think would have happened in the civil rights movement had King not been assassinated?

5. **Analyzing Information** Re-create the diagram below and describe three events of racial unrest that spread to major cities during the summers of 1965–1967.

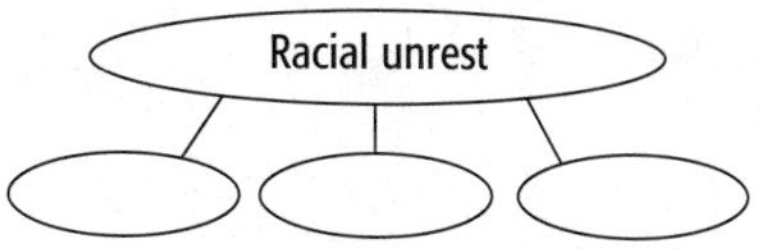

Racial unrest

Analyzing Visuals

6. **Picturing History** Examine the photographs on page 849. Write a caption that describes what is happening in the pictures. If you were a reporter interviewing these people, what would you ask them?

Interdisciplinary Activity

Expository Writing Choose a civil rights figure from the section. Research this person and write a personal profile. Include copies of photographs, speeches, and so on, as appropriate.

FREEDOM RIDERS

SEGREGATED WAITING ROOMS, restaurants, restrooms, and buses still existed in the South in 1961, despite Supreme Court orders to integrate facilities serving passengers traveling from state to state.

ON THE ROAD

On May 4th, 1961, 13 neatly dressed African-American and white Freedom Riders boarded buses in Washington, D.C. Determined to challenge segregation, these men and women knew they might encounter violence or be arrested as they headed toward New Orleans. The Riders were turned away from a bus station in Danville, Virginia, and police stopped a scuffle in Rock Hill, South Carolina. Despite these incidents, the trip through Virginia, the Carolinas, and Georgia went fairly smoothly.

TROUBLE DEVELOPS

In Alabama, however, trouble started. White mobs ambushed the Riders in Anniston and Birmingham, torching one of the buses. When many of the battered Freedom Riders decided to abandon the buses in Birmingham and fly to New Orleans, new groups took up the cause in Nashville, Tennessee, and other cities. They eventually made it to Jackson, Mississippi, where they were arrested.

ENFORCING THE LAW

Freedom Riders continued these non-violent protests until they got what they wanted. In September 1961 Attorney General Robert Kennedy persuaded the Interstate Commerce Commission to enforce the Supreme Court's ruling prohibiting racial discrimination on buses and in transportation facilities.

LEARNING *from* GEOGRAPHY

1. Why do you think the Freedom Riders decided to protest in this region of the United States?

2. Where did Freedom Riders encounter the greatest difficulties? Were they successful in reaching their goal?

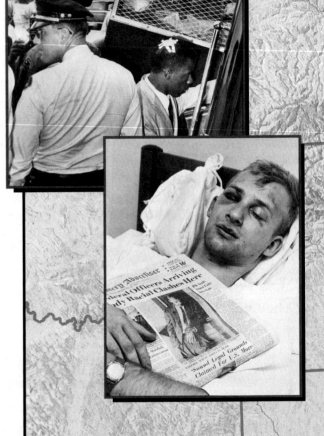

Police arrest Freedom Rider John Lewis (top) in Jackson, Mississippi. Jim Zwerg (below) lies in a hospital bed after beatings by people in favor of segregation at a Montgomery, Alabama, bus terminal.

LOUISIANA

Freedom Riders

⬅ First bus route

⬅ Second bus route

⬅ - - Air route

0   50 miles

0   50 kilometers

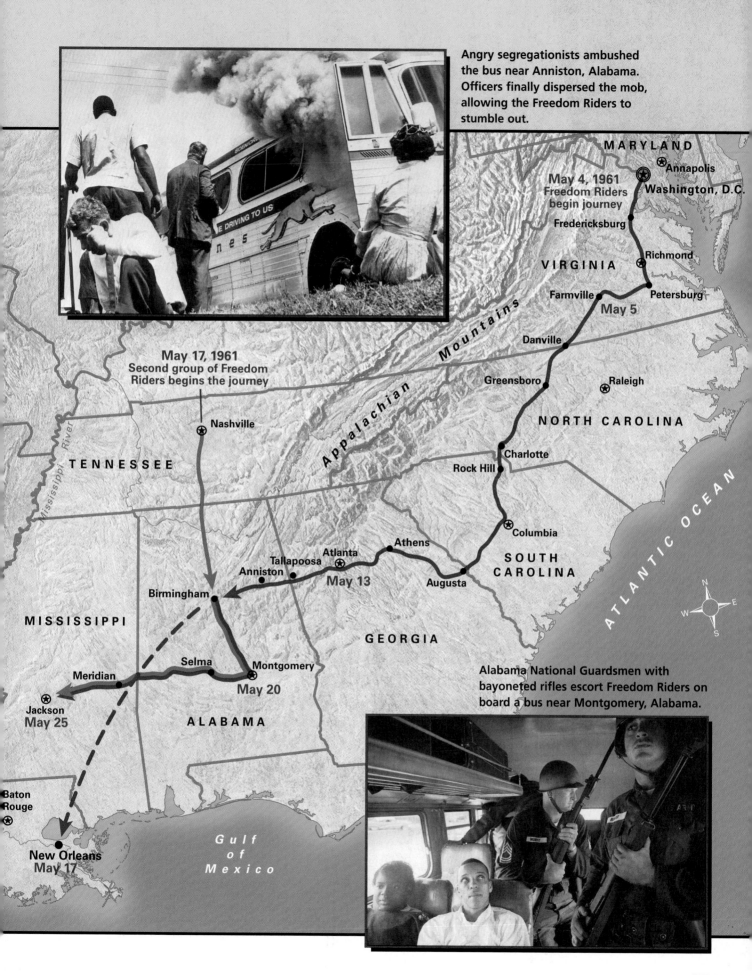

Angry segregationists ambushed the bus near Anniston, Alabama. Officers finally dispersed the mob, allowing the Freedom Riders to stumble out.

MARYLAND
Annapolis
Washington, D.C.

May 4, 1961
Freedom Riders begin journey

Fredericksburg

Richmond

VIRGINIA

Farmville   Petersburg

May 5

Danville

Greensboro   Raleigh

NORTH CAROLINA

Appalachian Mountains

May 17, 1961
Second group of Freedom Riders begins the journey

Nashville

TENNESSEE

Charlotte

Rock Hill

Columbia

SOUTH CAROLINA

Athens

Atlanta

Tallapoosa

Anniston   May 13   Augusta

Birmingham

GEORGIA

MISSISSIPPI

Selma

Montgomery

Meridian   May 20

Jackson
May 25

ALABAMA

Baton Rouge

New Orleans
May 17

Gulf of Mexico

ATLANTIC OCEAN

Mississippi River

N
W E
S

Alabama National Guardsmen with bayoneted rifles escort Freedom Riders on board a bus near Montgomery, Alabama.

855

SECTION 4 Other Groups Seek Rights

Guide to Reading

Main Idea

In the 1960s and 1970s, growing numbers of women, Hispanic Americans, Native Americans, and disabled Americans entered the struggle for equal rights.

Key Terms

feminist, Hispanic

Reading Strategy

Organizing Information As you read the section, re-create the diagram below and describe the role each person played in the 1960s and 1970s.

	Roles
Phyllis Schlafly	
César Chávez	
Herman Badillo	

Read to Learn

- what steps women and minorities took to improve their lives.
- what new leaders emerged.

Section Theme

Continuity and Change During the 1960s and 1970s, women and minorities used political action to shatter stereotypes and improve their lives.

Preview of Events

♦1960	♦1965	♦1970	♦1975
1963 Congress passes Equal Pay Act; *The Feminine Mystique* is published	**1966** National Organization for Women is created	**1973** American Indian Movement protests at Wounded Knee, South Dakota	

AN American Story

Jesse de la Cruz

Mexican American farmworker Jesse de la Cruz had labored for decades in the grape and cotton fields of the Southwest. In 1972 she began working for the United Farm Workers Union. Cruz made speaking tours, trying to bring women into the union. "Women can no longer be taken for granted—that we're just going to stay home and do the cooking and cleaning," she told her listeners. "It's way past the time when our husbands could say, 'You stay home! You have to take care of the children! You have to do as I say!'"

Women's Rights

The effects of the civil rights movement reached well beyond the African American community. Women, Hispanics, Native Americans, and people with disabilities all found inspiration in the struggles of African Americans. In 1961 President John F. Kennedy created the Commission on the Status of Women. It reported that women—an ever-growing part of the workforce—received lower pay than men, even for performing the same jobs. In 1963 Kennedy convinced Congress to pass the **Equal Pay Act,** which prohibited employers from paying women less than men for the same work.

Uniting for Action

In 1966 feminists—activists for women's rights—created the **National Organization for Women** (NOW). NOW fought for equal rights for women in all aspects of life—in jobs, education, and marriage.

Among its early successes, NOW helped end separate classified employment ads for men and women, and airline rules that required female flight attendants to retire at age 32. In the 1960s and 1970s, NOW and similar groups worked to increase the number of women entering the professions. Banks, realtors, and department stores were forced to grant loans, mortgages, and credit that they long had denied to female applicants.

In the early 1970s, NOW launched a campaign for an **Equal Rights Amendment** (ERA) to the Constitution. The amendment stated that "equality of rights under the law shall not be denied or abridged by the United States or by any state on account of sex." **Phyllis Schlafly** and other opponents of the ERA warned that the amendment would upset the traditional roles of society and lead to the breakdown of the family. Some people argued that the amendment was unnecessary because the Constitution already provided women with adequate protection. In the end, not enough states ratified the amendment to make it law.

Women Gain Opportunities

Despite the defeat of the Equal Rights Amendment, women progressed in a number of areas in the 1970s. In 1972 the federal government outlawed discrimination against women in educational programs receiving federal funds. This law, along with the efforts of many businesses, helped women begin to make advances in the world of work.

HISTORY *Online*

Student Web Activity
Visit taj.glencoe.com and click on **Chapter 29— Student Web Activities** for an activity on the women's rights movement.

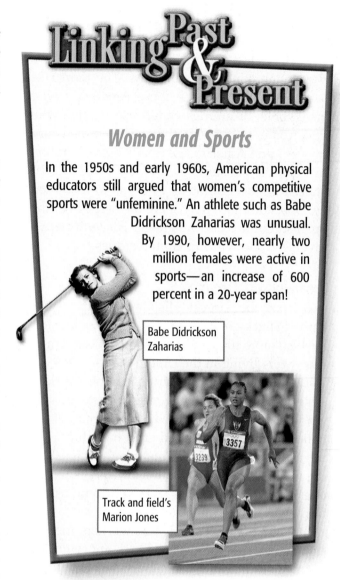

Linking Past & Present

Women and Sports

In the 1950s and early 1960s, American physical educators still argued that women's competitive sports were "unfeminine." An athlete such as Babe Didrickson Zaharias was unusual. By 1990, however, nearly two million females were active in sports—an increase of 600 percent in a 20-year span!

Babe Didrickson Zaharias

Track and field's Marion Jones

Women gained more job opportunities, and more women rose to higher-level jobs in their companies. *(See page 977 for one woman's struggle to gain equal pay in the work place.)*

Most of the nation's all-male colleges and universities began admitting women. More women than ever entered medical school and law school to become doctors and lawyers.

Women also made progress in the political arena. Many women gained local and state offices. Several women won seats in the Senate and the House of Representatives and appointments to the president's cabinet. In 1981 President Ronald Reagan appointed **Sandra Day O'Connor** as the first female justice of the Supreme Court.

Reading Check **Summarizing** What happened to the Equal Rights Amendment?

Hispanic Americans

In the 1960s the rapidly growing Hispanic population sought equal rights. The term *Hispanic American* refers to those Americans who have come, or are descended from others who have come, to the United States from the countries of Latin America and Spain. From 3 million in 1960, the Hispanic population in the United States rose to 9 million by 1970 and to 15 million by 1980. Although they share the heritage of the Spanish culture and language, Hispanics are a diverse group with different histories.

Farmworkers Organize

By far, the largest Hispanic group in the United States comes from the country of Mexico. By 1980 more than eight million Mexican Americans were living in the United States.

The fight for rights started among Mexican American migrant farmworkers. These people, who planted and harvested a large share of the nation's food supply, faced great hardships. The migrant farmers did backbreaking work, laboring from dawn until dusk for low wages. When one job ended, they had to travel from farm to farm in search of the next job.

In the early 1960s, migrant workers formed unions to fight for better wages and working conditions. Their leader, **César Chávez,** organized thousands of farmworkers into the United Farm Workers (UFW).

The union went on strike and organized nationwide boycotts. Consumers across the country supported the UFW by refusing to buy grapes, lettuce, and other farm produce under boycott. The success of the boycotts enabled the UFW to win higher wages and shorter work hours for many farmworkers.

The union boycott was followed by emerging political power among Hispanic Americans. In the years that followed, Hispanic Americans would join together in an organization called **La Raza Unida** to fight discrimination and to elect Hispanics to government posts. **The League of United Latin American Citizens** (LULAC) won lawsuits in federal court to guarantee Hispanic Americans the right to serve on juries and the right to send their children to unsegregated schools.

Puerto Ricans

Puerto Ricans, another major group of Hispanics, come from the island of Puerto Rico, a commonwealth of the United States. They are American citizens who have made major contributions to the United States.

In 1970 the first representative to Congress of Puerto Rican origin, **Herman Badillo,** was elected from New York City. After four terms, Badillo served as the city's deputy mayor. Baseball all-time great **Roberto Clemente** performed heroically both on and off the baseball diamond. In 1972 Clemente died in a plane crash while delivering relief supplies to earthquake victims in Nicaragua.

Because Puerto Rico is not a wealthy island, many Puerto Ricans have migrated to American cities in search of jobs. By 1970 they made up 10 percent of the population of New York City. As with African Americans, though, they often faced discrimination in their job search, leading to no work or work for low pay. Many of the children and grandchildren of the Puerto Ricans who arrived in New York in the 1960s migrated to neighboring states, but many Puerto Ricans remained in New York City.

Cubans Arrive

After the Cuban Revolution of 1959, dictator Fidel Castro established a Communist government and seized the property of many Cubans. More than 200,000 people opposed to Castro fled to the United States in the 1960s. Thousands more came in the 1980s.

These immigrants settled all over the United States. The largest number of Cubans settled in south Florida, where they have established a thriving community.

César Chávez

In 1975 Hispanic people and other groups won a victory with the extension of voting rights. The new law required that registration and voting be carried out in other languages as well as in English. This was designed to help those citizens who might not read or speak English. Election materials, for example, are available in Spanish and English in many states.

✓ **Reading Check** **Explaining** Why did many Cubans flee their homeland in the 1960s?

Native Americans

The years after World War II were a time of transition for Native Americans. Starting in the early 1950s, the federal government urged Native Americans to leave the reservations to work in cities. Federal policy also tried to weaken the power of tribal government.

This policy did not improve the lives of Native Americans. Many could not find jobs in the cities. Those still crowded on reservations enjoyed few jobs or other opportunities. More than one-third of Native Americans lived below the poverty line. Unemployment was widespread—as high as 50 percent in some areas. A 1966 study revealed that Native Americans suffered so much from malnutrition and disease that their life expectancy was only 46 years.

Efforts to Organize

In the 1960s Native Americans organized to combat these problems. They wanted political power and they demanded independence from the United States government. Native Americans also increasingly emphasized their own history, language, and culture in their schools. The **National Congress of American Indians** (NCAI) sought more control over Native American affairs.

In 1961 more than 400 members of 67 Native American nations gathered in Chicago. In a Declaration of Indian Purpose, these delegates

Wounded Knee button

Picturing **History**
In the 1973 AIM takeover of Wounded Knee, Native American leaders Russell Means (left) and Dennis Banks (right) protested broken treaties and civil rights violations. **Why was Wounded Knee chosen as the place for the AIM protest?**

stated that Native Americans have the "right to choose our own way of life," and maintained that "a treaty, in the minds of our people, is an eternal word."

The federal government recognized the Native Americans' issues. Congress passed the **Indian Civil Rights Act of 1968,** which formally protected the constitutional rights of all Native Americans. At the same time, the new law recognized the right of Native American nations to make laws on their reservations.

A Supreme Court decision in the 1970s reaffirmed the independence of tribal governments. Other court decisions confirmed Native Americans' rights to land granted in treaties.

American Indian Movement

Believing the process of change too slow, some younger Native Americans began taking stronger actions. In 1968 a group established the **American Indian Movement** (AIM), which worked for equal rights and improvement of living conditions.

AIM was founded by Clyde Bellecourt, Dennis Banks, and others. Later, Russell Means became a leader. AIM carried out several protests. In

November 1969, for example, AIM was one of the Native American groups that took over Alcatraz Island, a former prison in San Francisco Bay. AIM wanted the island to serve as a cultural center. The incident ended in June 1971 when the groups surrendered to U.S. marshals.

In the fall of 1972, AIM members occupied the Bureau of Indian Affairs in Washington, D.C. They demanded the lands and rights guaranteed under treaties with the United States. They surrendered the building after the government agreed to review their complaints.

In February 1973, AIM occupied the small town of **Wounded Knee, South Dakota,** the site of the 1890 massacre of Sioux by federal troops. In the early 1970s, Wounded Knee was part of a large Sioux reservation. The people there suffered from terrible poverty and ill health.

AIM leaders vowed to stay until the government met demands for change and investigated the treatment of Native Americans. The siege ended on May 8, but it focused national attention on the terrible conditions under which Native Americans lived.

Americans With Disabilities

People with physical disabilities also sought equal treatment in the 1960s and the 1970s. Congress responded by passing a number of laws.

One law concerned the removal of barriers that prevented some people from gaining access to public facilities. Another required employers to offer more opportunities for disabled people in the workplace. Yet another asserted the right of children with disabilities to equal educational opportunities. As a result of these actions, people with disabilities enjoy more job opportunities, better access to public facilities, and a greater role in society.

Reading Check **Identifying** What act protects the rights of all Native Americans?

SECTION 4 ASSESSMENT

Checking for Understanding

1. **Key Terms** Use each of these terms in a sentence that will help explain its meaning: feminist, Hispanic.
2. **Reviewing Facts** Who was the first female justice to serve on the Supreme Court?

Reviewing Themes

3. **Continuity and Change** What was the purpose of the American Indian Movement? What rights did Native Americans gain in the 1960s?

Critical Thinking

4. **Analyzing Information** Identify two organizations that Native Americans developed to help them take more control of their own lives.
5. **Drawing Conclusions** Re-create the diagram below and list two reasons why you think people with disabilities felt the need to work for equal treatment in the 1960s and 1970s.

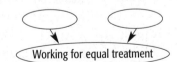

Working for equal treatment

Analyzing Visuals

6. **Political Cartoons** Bring to class a copy of a political cartoon from a recent newspaper or magazine. Try to find a cartoon in which the topic is the rights of people. Explain the cartoonist's viewpoint and the tools used to make the point.

Interdisciplinary Activity

Citizenship Create a poster that might have been used in a march to support or oppose the ERA.

SKILLBUILDER

Drawing Conclusions

Why Learn This Skill?

Drawing conclusions allows you to understand ideas that are not stated directly.

Learning the Skill

Follow these steps in learning to draw conclusions:
- Review the facts that are stated directly.
- Use your knowledge and insight to develop some conclusions about these facts.
- Look for information to check the accuracy of your conclusions.

Practicing the Skill

The excerpt on this page was written by Dr. Martin Luther King, Jr., after he was arrested in Birmingham, Alabama, for peaceably demonstrating against segregation. King began writing this letter in response to a newspaper ad in which a group of white ministers called for an end to the demonstrations. King's words attempt to explain to the white ministers his use of civil disobedience.

Dr. Martin Luther King, Jr.

After reading the excerpt, answer the questions, which require you to draw conclusions.

> ❝We know through painful experience that freedom is never voluntarily given by the oppressor; it must be demanded by the oppressed. . . . For years now I have heard the word 'Wait!' It rings in the ear of every Negro with piercing familiarity. This 'Wait' has almost always meant 'Never.' We must come to see, with one of our distinguished jurists, that 'justice too long delayed is justice denied.'❞

—*Dr. Martin Luther King, Jr.*
"Letter from Birmingham Jail," 1963

1. How does King say that freedom is earned?

2. What were the African Americans "waiting" for?

3. What happens to justice if it is delayed?

4. What conclusions can you draw from King's overall tone in his letter?

5. What evidence could help prove your conclusions?

Applying the Skill

Drawing Conclusions Read a newspaper or newsmagazine article about a criminal court case. Use the facts in the article to draw a conclusion about the innocence or guilt of the accused.

Glencoe's **Skillbuilder Interactive Workbook CD-ROM, Level 1,** provides instruction and practice in key social studies skills.

Chapter Summary

The Civil Rights Era

African Americans challenge segregation

- *Brown v. Board of Education of Topeka, Kansas*
- Montgomery bus boycott
- Freedom Riders
- March on Washington
- Civil Rights Act of 1964
- Voting Rights Act of 1965

Hispanic Americans organize

- César Chávez organizes United Farm Workers
- La Raza Unida and LULAC fight discrimination
- Voting rights extended

Native Americans demand rights

- Indian Civil Rights Act of 1968
- NCAI and AIM call attention to problems

Women fight for equal rights

- Equal Pay Act
- National Organization for Women
- ERA brings attention to women's rights

Reviewing Key Terms

Use these key terms to create a newspaper article in which you describe important events during the civil rights era.

1. poverty line
2. integrate
3. segregation
4. boycott
5. sit-in

Reviewing Key Facts

6. What Supreme Court case abolished segregation in schools?
7. Whose arrest sparked the Montgomery bus boycott?
8. What is civil disobedience?
9. What was the main goal of President Kennedy's New Frontier program?
10. What conclusion did the Warren Commission reach?
11. What did the Civil Rights Act of 1964 prohibit?
12. What is significant about James Meredith?
13. Why was the March on Washington organized?
14. What was the goal of Black Power?
15. What did Herman Badillo accomplish?

Critical Thinking

16. **Making Generalizations** Why do you think the civil rights movement gained momentum during this era?
17. **Analyzing Themes: Civic Rights and Responsibilities** According to Thurgood Marshall, what constitutional amendment was violated by allowing school segregation? Explain why Marshall argued that segregated schools were unconstitutional.
18. **Compare and Contrast** How did the idea of Black Power differ from Martin Luther King's goals for the civil rights movement?
19. **Determining Cause and Effect** Re-create the diagram below and describe two impacts that the African American civil rights movement had on other minorities.

Practicing Skills

Drawing Conclusions *Read the passage below and answer the questions that follow. Remember to review the information and add your own knowledge before drawing any conclusions.*

Malcolm X, a strong African American leader, bitterly and regretfully recalled his youthful efforts at straightening his hair in order to look more like a white person:

> 66 This was my first big step toward self-degradation: when I endured all of that pain, literally burning my flesh to have it look like a white man's hair. I had joined that multitude of Negro men and women in America who are brainwashed into believing that the black people are 'inferior'—and white people 'superior.' 99

> —Malcolm X, *Autobiography of Malcolm X,* 1965

20. What reason does Malcolm X give for straightening his hair?

21. As an adult, how did Malcolm X view his youthful actions?

22. What conclusion can you draw about the views of many African American people toward white people at that time?

23. What statement from the passage supports your conclusion?

 ## Geography and History Activity

Study the map on page 839. Then answer the questions that follow.

24. **Location** What law regarding segregation did Colorado have in place?

25. **Region** Explain why you agree or disagree with this statement: Many states in the West had no specific legislation concerning segregation in schools.

Citizenship Cooperative Activity

26. **Researching** With members of your group research to find out how many people of different ethnic backgrounds live in your county. Make a graph to illustrate your findings. Then choose one of the minority ethnic groups to research. Prepare a written report with illustrations to provide more information about this particular ethnic group in your county. You may want to find out if members of this ethnic group have settled in one particular area of the county, if they have formed special clubs or organizations, or if they observe any special holidays.

 ## Technology Activity

27. The United Farm Workers are still active today. Search the Internet for information about this organization and create a brochure that explains its goals.

 ## Alternative Assessment

28. **Creating a Time Line** Review the chapter for dates important to minority groups. Create a time line that traces the progress of African Americans, Hispanics, Native Americans, and women in their struggle for equal rights during the 1950s and 1960s.

 ### Standardized Test Practice

Directions: Choose the *best* answer to the following question.

In *Brown* v. *Board of Education of Topeka, Kansas,* the Supreme Court ruled that Topeka's school district had engaged in which unconstitutional practice?

A Prohibited school prayer

B Bussed students to schools far away from their homes

C Had set up different schools for white and African American students

D Refused to offer required courses

Test-Taking Tip

The important word in this question is *unconstitutional.* Transporting students great distances seems inconvenient, but it is not specifically banned by the Constitution. Therefore, you can eliminate answer **B.**

The Vietnam Era

1960–1975

Why It Matters

The United States became involved in Vietnam because it believed that if all of Vietnam fell under a Communist government, communism would spread throughout Southeast Asia and beyond. The Vietnam War was the longest war in the nation's history.

The Impact Today

More than 58,000 U.S. troops died in Vietnam. The war damaged people's confidence in their government. Americans grew more willing to challenge the president on military and foreign policy issues after Vietnam. The war also became a yardstick to gauge whether to involve American troops in later crises.

The American Journey *Video* *The chapter 30 video, "The First TV War," explores how televised images brought the Vietnam War into American households and influenced public opinion about the war.*

1962
- Cuban missile crisis

1965
- U.S. involvement in Vietnam grows

United States
PRESIDENTS

Eisenhower
1953–1961

Kennedy
1961–1963

Johnson
1963–1969

1960

1963

1966

World

1959
- Civil war begins in Vietnam

1961
- Berlin Wall erected

1966
- Cultural Revolution in China

Helping a Comrade Members of the First Marine Division carry a wounded marine to safety during battle in South Vietnam.

FOLDABLES™
Study Organizer

Sequencing Events Study Foldable Sequence the actions of the United States's presidents during the Vietnam War by making and using this foldable.

Step 1 Fold one sheet of paper in half from side to side.

Step 2 Turn the paper and fold it into thirds.

Step 3 Unfold and label the foldable as shown.

J.F.K.   L.B.J.   Nixon

Step 4 Cut the top layer only along both fold lines.

J.F.K.   L.B.J.   Nixon

This will make three tabs.

Reading and Writing As you read the chapter, record facts about the actions and policies of the presidents in office during the Vietnam era. Be sure to also record the dates of these important events.

1968
- Robert Kennedy assassinated

1969
- Armstrong walks on moon

1973
- Paris peace accords end U.S. involvement in Vietnam

Nixon 1969–1974

1970
- Kent State shootings

Ford 1974–1977

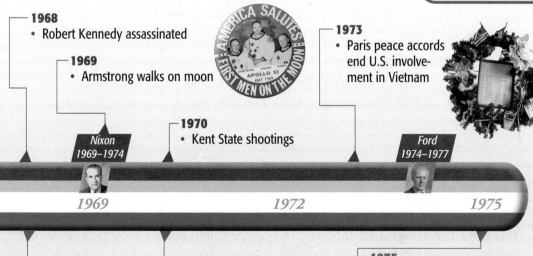

1969   1972   1975

1968
- North Vietnam launches Tet offensive

1970
- Civil War begins in Cambodia

1975
- Vietnam War ends after fall of Saigon

HISTORY Online

Chapter Overview
Visit taj.glencoe.com and click on **Chapter 30— Chapter Overviews** to preview chapter information.

Kennedy's Foreign Policy

Guide to Reading

Main Idea
In the early 1960s, the nation faced Soviet threats relating to Cuba and to Berlin.

Key Terms
guerrilla warfare, flexible response, executive order, exile, blockade, hot line

Reading Strategy
Organizing Information As you read Section 1, re-create the diagram below and describe the actions the Kennedy administration took in response to these crises.

Response to Crises	
Berlin Wall	Cuban missile crisis

Read to Learn
• how the Kennedy administration handled challenges to foreign affairs.
• what happened during the Cuban missile crisis.

Section Theme
Geography and History The Kennedy administration faced crises in Cuba and Berlin.

Preview of Events

♦1960	♦1965	♦1970

1961	1962	1963	1969
Bay of Pigs invasion fails	Cuban missile crisis occurs	Telephone hot line links U.S., Soviet leaders	Neil Armstrong walks on the moon

Kennedy inaugural ribbon

AN American Story

"In the long history of the world, only a few generations have been granted the role of defending freedom in its hour of maximum danger. I do not shrink from this responsibility—I welcome it." So spoke John F. Kennedy in his Inaugural Address. Although Kennedy talked of approaching this responsibility with "energy" and "devotion," events unfolding around the world—in Cuba, Eastern Europe, and Vietnam—would challenge his determination. The new president and nation soon faced a series of crises.

New Directions

President Kennedy continued the anti–Communist foreign policy begun under Presidents Truman and Eisenhower. In pursuing that policy, though, Kennedy tried some new approaches.

During the presidential campaign, Kennedy led Americans to believe that the nation had fewer nuclear missiles than the Soviet Union. As president, Kennedy increased spending on nuclear arms. At the same time, he tried to convince Nikita Khrushchev, the Soviet leader, to agree to a ban on nuclear testing.

Strength Through Flexibility

Kennedy also worked to improve America's ability to respond to threats abroad. In certain areas of the world, Communist groups fought to take control of their nation's government. Many of these groups received aid from the Soviet Union. They employed guerrilla warfare, or fighting by small bands using tactics such as sudden ambushes.

The United States needed a new approach for fighting guerrilla wars. Kennedy introduced a plan called flexible response, which relied on special military units trained to fight guerrilla wars. One of these units was the Special Forces, known as the **Green Berets.** The Special Forces provided the president with troops ready to fight guerrilla warfare anywhere around the world.

Strength Through Aid

President Kennedy understood that the poverty in Latin America, Asia, and Africa made the Communist promises of economic equality seem attractive. He decided to provide aid to countries in those areas to counteract the appeal of communism. On March 1, 1961, the president signed an executive order creating the **Peace Corps.** An executive order is a rule issued by the chief executive.

Americans who volunteered for the Peace Corps worked in other countries as teachers, health workers, and advisers in farming, industry, and government. By 1963 some 5,000 volunteers were working in more than 40 countries.

To promote Latin America's growth, Kennedy proposed a 10-year development plan called the **Alliance for Progress.** In his Inaugural Address, Kennedy promised Latin American leaders that the United States would "assist free men and free governments in casting off the chains of poverty." He hoped as well to prevent the rise of Communist states in the region.

Reading Check **Explaining** Why did President Kennedy form the Peace Corps?

Cold War Confrontations

In 1961, just a few months after taking office, President Kennedy faced a foreign policy crisis in Cuba. That same year, the United States and the Soviet Union clashed in Europe.

As you read in Chapter 28, **Fidel Castro** had seized power in Cuba in 1959. When Castro formed an alliance with the Soviet Union, Americans felt threatened because Cuba lies only 90 miles (144 km) south of Florida. Late in Eisenhower's presidency, officials in the Central

History *Through Art*

The Peace Corps in Ethiopia, 1966 by Norman Rockwell Volunteers worked in many developing countries in Africa. **Which Kennedy program dealt with Latin America's economy?**

Intelligence Agency (CIA) forged a plan to overthrow Castro. The CIA recruited refugees who had fled Castro's Cuba and settled in the United States. The plan called for these exiles, or persons forced from their homes, to land in Cuba, spark an uprising, and overthrow Castro. Although Kennedy had doubts about the plan, he accepted the advice of military advisers and the CIA and allowed it to go forward.

On April 17, 1961, about 1,500 CIA-trained Cuban exiles landed at the **Bay of Pigs** in southern Cuba. Many blunders occurred, and at a crucial moment, Kennedy refused to provide American air support. Within days Cuban forces crushed the invasion and captured the survivors.

The Bay of Pigs embarrassed Kennedy, who took the blame for the failure. The disaster had three consequences. First, Kennedy never again completely trusted military and intelligence advice. Second, other nations in Latin America lost trust in Kennedy. Third, Soviet premier Khrushchev concluded that Kennedy was not a strong leader and could be bullied.

The Berlin Wall

Though 16 years had passed since the end of World War II, the wartime Allies had still not settled the status of Germany. West Germany gained complete independence in 1949, but the Soviet Union continued to control East Germany.

The location of **Berlin**—fully within Soviet-controlled East Germany—posed special problems. American, British, and French troops still remained in the western part of the city, and they sometimes had difficulty getting into West Berlin and maintaining control there. Meanwhile a steady flow of people fled to West Berlin from Communist East Berlin, hoping to escape economic hardship and find freedom.

At a June 1961 summit conference in Vienna, Austria, Premier Khrushchev told President Kennedy that the West must move out of Berlin, and he insisted on an agreement by the end of the year. Kennedy rejected Khrushchev's demand. To emphasize the West's right to stay in West Berlin, the United States later sent more troops to protect the city.

People In History

Alan Shepard 1923–1998

Alan Shepard became a national hero on May 5, 1961, when he became the first American in space. His flight aboard the tiny *Freedom 7* spaceship lasted 15 minutes and reached an altitude of about 120 miles. Although the flight was brief, it was a key step forward for the United States in its space race with the Soviet Union.

After graduating from the United States Naval Academy in 1944, Shepard served during World War II. After the war, he attended the Naval Test Pilot School. In 1959 Shepard was named one of NASA's original seven astronauts.

Ten years after his flight aboard *Freedom 7*, Shepard commanded the *Apollo 14* moon mission, during which he spent a record 33.5 hours on the surface of the moon.

In 1974 Shepard retired from both NASA and the Navy and entered private business. He served as the president of the Mercury Seven Foundation, which provides college science scholarships for deserving students.

Later that summer, a large number of East Germans fled to the West. On August 13, the East German government, with Soviet backing, closed the border between East and West Berlin and built a wall of concrete blocks and barbed wire along it. The Soviets posted armed guards along the wall to stop more East Germans from fleeing to the West. The **Berlin Wall** cut communications between the two parts of the city.

The Western Allies continued to support the independence of West Berlin. They could do little, however, to stop the building of the wall, which came to symbolize Communist repression.

✓**Reading Check** **Explaining** Why did the Soviet Union build the Berlin Wall?

The Cuban Missile Crisis

The most dangerous Cold War dispute between the Americans and Soviets came in 1962. Once again the dispute involved Cuba.

In mid-October 1962, an American spy plane flying over Cuba made a disturbing discovery. Photographs revealed that the Soviets were building launching sites for nuclear missiles. These missiles could easily reach the United States in a matter of minutes.

For the next week, President Kennedy met secretly with advisers to determine how to deal with the **Cuban missile crisis.** They explored several options, including invading Cuba and bombing the missile sites. New spy photographs showed the bases nearing completion faster than expected. A decision had to be made.

On October 22, President Kennedy, speaking on national television, revealed the "secret, swift, and extraordinary buildup" of missiles in Cuba. Kennedy ordered the navy to blockade, or close off, Cuba until the Soviets removed the missiles. He threatened to destroy any Soviet ship that tried to break through the blockade. The president also declared:

❝It shall be the policy of this nation to regard any nuclear missile launched from Cuba against any nation in the Western Hemisphere as an attack by the Soviet Union on the United States.❞

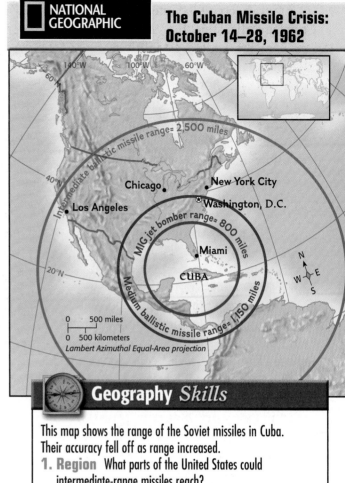

NATIONAL GEOGRAPHIC

The Cuban Missile Crisis: October 14–28, 1962

Geography *Skills*

This map shows the range of the Soviet missiles in Cuba. Their accuracy fell off as range increased.
1. **Region** What parts of the United States could intermediate-range missiles reach?
2. **Analyzing Information** What strategy did the United States use to respond to the Soviet threat in Cuba?

The United States would respond, he warned, with a nuclear attack against the Soviet Union.

As the two superpowers neared the brink of nuclear war, people all over the world waited nervously. However, Khrushchev was not ready to back down, and Soviet ships—some carrying missiles—continued to approach Cuba.

Two days after Kennedy's announcement, a breakthrough occurred. Some Soviet ships nearing the blockade turned back.

However, some Soviet ships still headed toward Cuba, and work on the missile bases continued. The president's advisers worked on plans for an air attack on the missile sites—just in case.

After five agonizing days, when the world appeared on the brink of nuclear war, the Soviet ships turned back from the blockade. Soviet leaders also decided to withdraw their missiles from Cuba.

Having come so close to nuclear disaster, the superpowers worked to establish a better relationship. In the summer of 1963, Kennedy and Khrushchev created a direct telephone link, called the hot line, between Moscow and Washington to allow the leaders to communicate instantly in times of crisis.

That same summer, the two nations signed a treaty banning nuclear tests aboveground and underwater.

Rivalry in Space

The United States competed with the Soviet Union in another area during the Kennedy administration—outer space. The space race began when the Soviet Union launched *Sputnik,* the world's first successful satellite, in 1957. In April 1961, Soviet cosmonaut **Yuri Gagarin** (guh•GAHR•uhn) became the first person to orbit the earth. One month later, **Alan Shepard, Jr.,** became the first American to make a spaceflight.

Shortly after Shepard's flight, Kennedy challenged the nation to a great undertaking. In a speech to Congress, he said:

❝I believe that this nation should commit itself to achieving the goal, before this decade is out, of landing a man on the moon and returning him safely to the earth.❞

The president asked Congress for more money for **NASA** (the National Aeronautics and Space Administration), which ran the space program. NASA expanded its launching facility in Florida and built a control center in Houston, Texas.

Astronaut **John Glenn** thrilled the country in February 1962 when he orbited the earth in a spacecraft, the first American to do so. An even greater triumph for the space program came on July 20, 1969, with the **Apollo project.** Awestruck television viewers around the world watched the spacecraft *Eagle* land on the surface of the moon. Hours later, with millions still watching, astronaut **Neil Armstrong** took the first human step on the moon and announced: "That's one small step for a man, one giant leap for mankind." By the end of the Apollo project in 1972, 10 more Americans had landed on the moon.

✓ **Reading Check** **Explaining** Why did President Kennedy order a blockade of the island of Cuba?

SECTION 1 ASSESSMENT

Checking for Understanding

1. **Key Terms** Write a sentence in which you correctly use each of the following terms: guerrilla warfare, flexible response, executive order, exile, blockade, hot line. Below each sentence write the definition of the term used.

2. **Reviewing Facts** Who was the first American to orbit the earth in a spacecraft?

Reviewing Themes

3. **Geography and History** Why did West Berlin's location make it difficult for the allies to defend it?

Critical Thinking

4. **Making Inferences** Why do you think Khrushchev sent missiles to Cuba?

5. **Analyzing Information** Re-create the diagram below and identify strategies that the Kennedy administration considered to stop the buildup of missiles in Cuba.

```
         Cuban missile crisis
        /                    \
   (        )            (        )
```

Analyzing Visuals

6. **Geography Skills** Examine the map of the Cuban missile crisis on page 869. According to the map, was Washington, D.C., within the range of a medium ballistic missile? Could a medium-range missile reach Los Angeles?

Interdisciplinary Activity

Persuasive Writing Write a speech that President Kennedy might have written to defend his actions during the Cuban missile crisis.

War in Vietnam

Main Idea

U.S. military involvement in Vietnam increased steadily throughout the 1960s.

Key Terms

Vietcong, coup, escalate, search-and-destroy mission

Reading Strategy

Organizing Information Re-create the diagram below and fill in the main events that occurred after the Gulf of Tonkin Resolution.

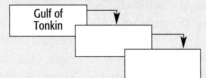

Gulf of Tonkin

Read to Learn

- how Vietnam became a divided country.
- why America increased its involvement in the Vietnam War.

Section Theme

Global Connections Unable to end the Vietnam War quickly, the United States found itself increasingly drawn into the conflict.

Preview of Events

♦1950   ♦1960   ♦1970

1954
Geneva Accords divide Vietnam

1959
Civil war in Vietnam begins

1964
Gulf of Tonkin Resolution passed

1968
More than 500,000 U.S. troops are in Vietnam

Soldier's boots, Vietnam War

★★★★★★★ AN American Story

In March 1967 David Parks, an African American soldier serving in Vietnam, described an enemy attack on his camp: "I was asleep when the first shell exploded. The earth shook and I rolled to the ground as someone hollered, 'Incoming!' . . . I shook like jelly as the shrapnel burst all around our bunker. . . . All we could do was open up with our 50-caliber and small arms. . . . I'm not sure the native people are with us. They smile at us in the daytime and their sons shoot at us at night. It's hard to spot the real enemy."

The U.S. and Vietnam

In the early 1960s, the United States became involved in a fight against communism in Southeast Asia. The war in **Vietnam** did not unfold as Americans had hoped, however. General Maxwell Taylor, who served as American ambassador to Vietnam, reflected on the war in Vietnam years after it had ended:

❝First, we didn't know ourselves. We thought we were going into another Korean war, but this was a different country. Secondly, we didn't know our South Vietnamese allies. We never understood them, and that was another surprise. And we knew even less about North Vietnam.❞

CHAPTER 30   The Vietnam Era   **871**

Origins of the War

The roots of the Vietnam conflict can be traced back to World War II, when Japanese forces captured the French colony of Indochina in Southeast Asia. Vietnamese forces led by Communist **Ho Chi Minh** (hoh chee MIHN) fought against the Japanese.

When Japan surrendered at the end of World War II, Ho Chi Minh declared Vietnam's independence. The French, however, were unwilling to give up their empire. Their Indochina colony—the present-day nations of Cambodia, Laos, and Vietnam—was among the richest of France's colonies, supplying such valuable resources as rice, rubber, and tin. Ho Chi Minh and his forces fought the French in a long, bloody war, finally defeating the French in 1954 at Dien Bien Phu.

The Geneva Accords

That same year, diplomats from the United States, France, Great Britain, the Soviet Union, China, and Vietnam met in Geneva, Switzerland, to work out a peace agreement. According to the **Geneva Accords,** Vietnam would be divided temporarily. Ho Chi Minh's Communist nationalists would control the North.

Hanoi served as its capital. Non-Communist forces—supported by the United States—would control the South, with **Saigon** as the capital. Vietnam would be unified in 1956 after national elections.

Neither the United States nor South Vietnam had signed the agreement, but they did not oppose its provisions. At the same time, an American representative warned that the United States reserved the right to step in if Communist North Vietnam moved aggressively against the South.

In 1955 **Ngo Dinh Diem** (NOH DIHN deh •EHM), the French-educated Vietnamese leader, gained control of the government of South Vietnam. The following year, Diem, with American support, refused to hold the elections. Diem's brutal policies and his refusal to hold elections angered many Vietnamese.

Communist supporters of Ho Chi Minh remained in the South after Vietnam was divided. In the late 1950s, Diem launched a campaign to destroy the power of the Communists. In response, the Communists organized themselves as the **National Liberation Front** (NLF)—better known to Americans as the Vietcong. In 1959 the Vietcong, on orders from Ho Chi Minh, began a war against the Diem regime.

Ho Chi Minh

Picturing History

Buddhist monks often led protests against unpopular South Vietnamese governments and their leaders. **Why did Vietnam's Buddhists protest against the Diem government?**

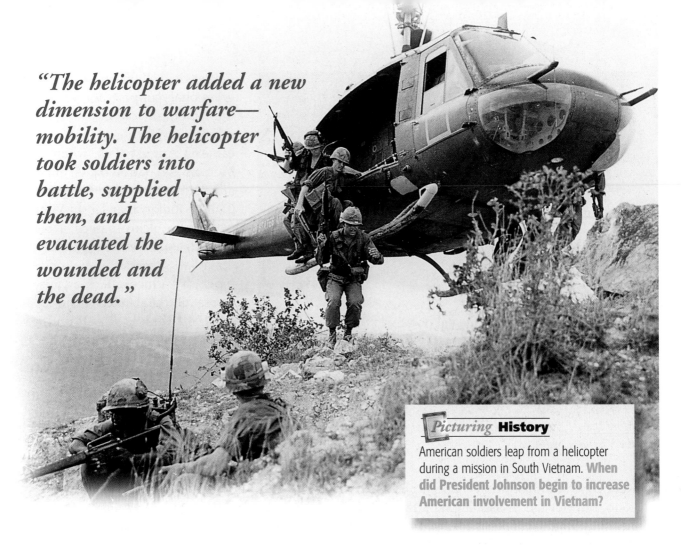

"The helicopter added a new dimension to warfare— mobility. The helicopter took soldiers into battle, supplied them, and evacuated the wounded and the dead."

A Growing American Role

The United States had replaced the French as the dominant foreign power in the South in 1955. If Communists took South Vietnam, President Eisenhower once said, the other countries of Southeast Asia would fall to communism like a row of dominoes—one right after the other. This **domino theory** helped shape American policy in Vietnam for the next 20 years.

To support South Vietnam, the Eisenhower administration sent the country billions of dollars in aid. It also dispatched a few hundred soldiers, who acted as advisers to the South Vietnamese government and army.

Like Eisenhower, President Kennedy saw Vietnam as part of the global struggle in the fight against communism. Kennedy sent more Special Forces troops—the Green Berets—to train and advise South Vietnamese troops. Kennedy also pressured Diem to make political and economic reforms to eliminate the conditions that had allowed communism to take root in the first place. But Diem refused to comply.

Instead of paying for new schools, health clinics, or land reform, American funds often ended up in the pockets of corrupt South Vietnamese officials. At the same time, North Vietnam sent aid and troops to the South to help the Vietcong in a guerrilla war against Diem that began in 1959.

The Diem government lost support throughout the country. His government took rights away from **Buddhists**—the majority of the people in South Vietnam—and favored Catholics, like himself. Buddhists responded with protests, some of which ended in bloodshed when government troops fired into the crowds.

In early 1963 Buddhist monks showed their opposition to Diem's rule by setting themselves on fire on busy streets. Horrifying photographs of monks engulfed in flames appeared in newspapers and on television screens around the world. The Kennedy administration found it difficult to continue to support Diem.

On November 1, 1963, a group of South Vietnamese army officers staged a coup—overthrew the government—and assassinated Diem. The

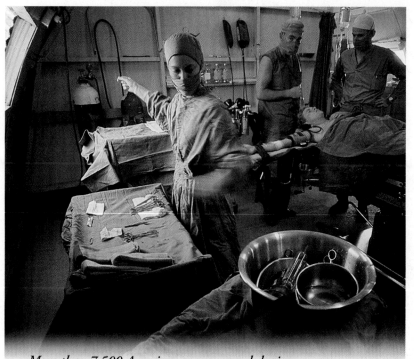

More than 7,500 American nurses served during the Vietnam conflict.

Kennedy administration had supported the coup, but not the assassination. After President Kennedy was assassinated later that same month, the question of what to do in Vietnam fell on the shoulders of President **Lyndon B. Johnson.**

✔ **Reading Check** **Analyzing** How did the domino theory affect the decision regarding the conflict in Vietnam?

The Conflict Deepens

At the time of Kennedy's death, the United States had nearly 16,000 American troops in Vietnam as advisers. President Johnson sent Secretary of Defense **Robert McNamara** to Vietnam on a fact-finding mission.

McNamara told the president that South Vietnam could not resist the Vietcong rebels without more help from the United States. In a May 1964 conversation, taped but not made public until 1997, Johnson himself expressed doubts about American commitment. "I don't think it's worth fighting for," he said, "but I don't think we can get out." Nevertheless, as Vietcong attacks continued, the United States moved toward deeper involvement.

President Johnson wanted congressional support for expanding the American role in Vietnam. The opportunity to get that support came in August 1964, when North Vietnamese patrol boats allegedly attacked American destroyers in the Gulf of Tonkin near North Vietnam. Congress quickly passed a resolution that allowed the president to "take all necessary measures to repel any armed attack against the forces of the United States." The **Gulf of Tonkin Resolution** gave Johnson broad authority to use American forces in Vietnam.

In 1965 Johnson began to escalate—gradually increase—United States involvement in Vietnam. The buildup included both ground troops and an air campaign.

United States Marines landed near **Da Nang,** South Vietnam, on March 8, 1965. During the next three years, the number of American troops in Vietnam increased sharply. About 180,000 soldiers were in Vietnam by the end of 1965, almost 400,000 by the end of 1966, and more than 500,000 by 1968.

The United States also unleashed an intense bombing campaign called Operation Rolling Thunder. Some planes attacked the **Ho Chi Minh Trail,** a network of roads, paths, and bridges that wound from North Vietnam through Cambodia and Laos into South Vietnam. North Vietnamese troops used this route to bring equipment south. Other planes targeted bridges, docks, factories, and military bases in the North.

The bombing increased in intensity from 1965 through 1968. By then American planes had dropped more bombs on North Vietnam than they had dropped on Germany, Italy, and Japan during World War II.

Fighting the War

The American troops found fighting a ground war in Vietnam difficult. Dense jungles, muddy trails, and swampy rice paddies hampered troop movement. The South Vietnamese army did not always fight effectively. As the Vietcong guerrillas blended with the population, American soldiers found it hard to tell friends and enemies apart.

The American forces began to conduct search-and-destroy missions. The goal was to seek out Vietcong or North Vietnamese units and destroy them. The Americans hoped to eventually defeat the Communists or force them to negotiate.

Ground troops coordinated their moves with air support. Patrols on the ground radioed their location, and helicopter gunships roared to the scene to blast the enemy with cannon and machine-gun fire.

Planes bombed areas of South Vietnam in an effort to drive guerrillas from their jungle cover. Both sides used planes to drop **napalm,** an explosive that burned intensely, to destroy jungle growth. North Vietnamese and Vietcong forces also used napalm in flamethrowers, devices that expel fuel or a burning stream of liquids. To improve visibility, chemical herbicides were sprayed in Vietnam to clear out forests and tall grasses. One herbicide, **Agent Orange,** is believed to have contaminated many Americans and Vietnamese, causing serious health problems.

Frustration Grows

The bombing of the Ho Chi Minh Trail and the North did not stop the constant flow of troops and equipment south. Neither did it break the morale of the North Vietnamese. As one of their leaders later said,

> 66The Americans thought that the more bombs they dropped, the quicker we would fall to our knees and surrender. But the bombs heightened, rather than dampened, our spirit.99

Picturing **History**

A wounded American soldier reaches for a fallen comrade. **How many American troops were in Vietnam by late 1967?**

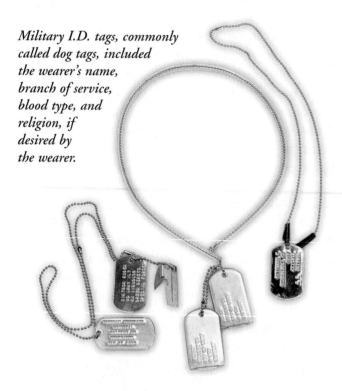

Military I.D. tags, commonly called dog tags, included the wearer's name, branch of service, blood type, and religion, if desired by the wearer.

The search-and-destroy missions killed thousands of North Vietnamese and Vietcong troops—but the troops always seemed to be replaced. What Ho Chi Minh had said to the French became true again:

> ❝You can kill ten of my men for every one I kill of yours. But even at those odds, you will lose and I will win.❞

American troops advanced into rice paddies, jungles, and small villages and killed scores of Vietcong. Yet the next day, the same area had to be attacked again.

American soldiers grew frustrated. Philip Caputo, a young marine lieutenant, recalled the changing attitude:

> ❝When we marched into the rice paddies on that damp March afternoon, we carried, along with our packs and rifles, the implicit convictions that the Vietcong could be quickly beaten. We kept the packs and rifles; the convictions, we lost.❞

Debate in the White House

Officials in the Johnson administration saw the mounting Communist losses and believed at first that the United States could succeed. As the war dragged on, however, some government officials saw a gloomier situation. Secretary of Defense McNamara began to argue that the ground war and the air attacks had failed and that the war could not be won. Outside the nation's capital, opposition to the war grew. Soon it swelled to anger.

✓ **Reading Check** **Identifying** What is Agent Orange? What are its effects?

SECTION 2 ASSESSMENT

Checking for Understanding

1. **Key Terms** Use the following terms in sentences or short paragraphs: Vietcong, coup, escalate. Relate them by using two or more of the terms in each sentence or paragraph.
2. **Reviewing Facts** How many American troops were in Vietnam by the end of 1965?

Reviewing Themes

3. **Global Connections** How did President Johnson gain congressional approval to use American forces in Vietnam?

Critical Thinking

4. **Making Inferences** Explain how Americans' view of communism influenced policy to support South Vietnam.
5. **Organizing Information** Re-create the diagram below and explain the purpose of the military strategies.

Strategy	Purpose
Search-and-destroy missions	
Operation Rolling Thunder	

Analyzing Visuals

6. **Picturing History** Examine the photograph on page 875. Write a caption expressing what you think the soldier is saying to his fallen comrade.

Interdisciplinary Activity

Research and Sequencing Use books, magazines, and newspapers to learn about the plight of American POWs (prisoners of war) and MIAs (soldiers missing in action) in Vietnam. Make a time line to show what the government and private citizens have done on their behalf.

SECTION 3 The Vietnam Years at Home

Guide to Reading

Main Idea

Many Americans opposed the nation's involvement in Vietnam. Many others believed that U.S. leaders were not doing enough to win the war.

Key Terms

counterculture, deferment, dove, hawk, credibility gap, silent majority

Reading Strategy

Organizing Information As you read the section, re-create the diagram below and state how you think people known as doves and hawks differed on these issues.

	The Draft	Escalation
Doves		
Hawks		

Read to Learn

- what factors contributed to the rise of the protest movement.
- how Americans at home responded to the war in Vietnam.

Section Theme

Continuity and Change As the war continued, disagreement over the nation's role in Vietnam grew.

Preview of Events

```
    ♦1967                              ♦1968                                    ♦1969
```

October 1967
War protesters march on Pentagon

April 1968
Dr. Martin Luther King, Jr., is assassinated

June 1968
Robert F. Kennedy is assassinated

November 1968
Richard Nixon wins presidency

AN American Story

Demonstration at the Pentagon

As the Vietnam War dragged on, Americans became divided over the U.S. presence in that country. Even reporters showed their biases when they covered the antiwar demonstrations at the Pentagon in 1967. On one hand, older reporters, who stood behind the police, wrote about radicals storming the Pentagon. On the other side of the police barricade, younger reporters wrote about the brutality of the U.S. Marshals. Each side of the generation gap firmly believed that its version of the story was correct.

The Youth Protest

While fighting raged in Vietnam, the American people disagreed sharply over the war. Prowar and antiwar groups attacked each other with mounting anger. Antiwar demonstrators called President Johnson and his supporters "killers." Supporters of the war referred to the protesters as "traitors." The war seemed to split America—and much of the division resulted from what people called the **generation gap.**

As United States involvement in the war increased, so did opposition to it. Some Americans felt that the conflict in Vietnam was a civil war and should not involve the United States. Others were concerned that the cost of America's commitment to Vietnam was hurting domestic programs. All condemned the devastation of the countryside and lives lost during the course of the war.

Many who opposed the war were part of the counterculture, a movement that rejected traditional American values. Some common symbols of the counterculture—torn blue jeans and long hair for males—aroused opposition from parents. Popular music played a role in communicating the ideas of the counterculture.

Other parts of the counterculture represented a more serious challenge to traditional middle-class values. Some young people refused to follow customary social roles of study, work, and family. They aimed to reject aspects of American society—the competition for material goods and personal success.

Opposition to the Draft

Student protests targeted the selective service system—the **draft** that supplied soldiers for the war. The law required all men to register for the draft when they reached age 18. Opposition to the draft had two sources.

Those strongly opposed to American involvement in Vietnam believed that by forcing an end to the draft they could halt the supply of soldiers needed to fight there. Others called the draft unfair. Draft boards had the power to give

Texas business executive H. Ross Perot attempted to deliver food, medicine, mail, and clothing to U.S. prisoners of war in Vietnam.

people deferments that excused them from the draft for various reasons. Full-time students attending college—mostly from the middle class—received such deferments. As a result an increasing percentage of soldiers came from poor or working-class families. Many who opposed the draft argued that deferments discriminated against the poor.

Some protesters became **conscientious objectors,** claiming that their moral or religious beliefs prevented them from fighting in the war. Other protesters showed their opposition by burning their draft cards—their military registration forms. Congress responded with a law making the burning of draft cards a crime.

Doves and Hawks

Students and other opponents of the Vietnam War came to be called doves. Supporters of the war became known as hawks.

Across the nation more and more Americans came to view the war unfavorably. Some thought the United States should not be fighting in Vietnam. Others opposed the way the government conducted the war. Both hawks and doves criticized President Johnson for his handling of the war in Vietnam, and his approval rating declined dramatically.

The War Loses Support

As opposition to the war mounted, the opponents staged larger demonstrations. In October 1967, more than 50,000 people marched to the **Pentagon**—headquarters of the Defense Department—to protest the war.

Attacks by opponents of the war grew sharper and more bitter. The Secret Service, charged with guarding President Johnson, feared for his safety and urged him not to speak in public. He began to appear only before crowds known to be sympathetic.

The president had often urged people to come together to discuss issues calmly. "Let us reason together," he had said. By 1968 Americans showed less willingness to talk reasonably, and violent events often overtook discussion.

Reading Check **Explaining** What are draft deferments? Who received them?

Reacting against the antiwar demonstrations, many Americans countered with demonstrations in support of American troops.

1968—Year of Crisis

The year 1968 opened with a shock for the American people. On January 23, North Korean boats seized the **USS** *Pueblo,* a navy spy ship cruising in international waters off the coast of Korea. The news that a foreign country had captured an American ship and its crew shocked the nation.

The next week brought another staggering blow as North Vietnam launched a major series of attacks in South Vietnam. As Americans soon learned, 1968 would be a long, dramatic, and very difficult year.

The Tet Offensive

On January 31, 1968, the North Vietnamese and Vietcong launched a series of attacks throughout South Vietnam. The attacks, which began on the Vietnamese new year—Tet— became known as the **Tet offensive.** Tet marked a turning point in the Vietnam War.

The Tet offensive targeted American military bases and South Vietnam's major cities. Vietcong troops raided the United States embassy in **Saigon,** the capital. The Vietcong also struck in **Hue,** the ancient capital of Vietnam, and fought for almost a month.

All across South Vietnam, Americans and South Vietnamese troops fought bravely to retake the cities. They finally drove the Vietcong back and inflicted thousands of casualties. The enormous losses that the Vietcong suffered

forced North Vietnam to take over a larger share of the fighting. In military terms, the Americans and the South Vietnamese won the battle.

Impact Back Home

In the United States, however, the Tet offensive turned many more Americans against the war—and against President Johnson. The sight of Vietcong guerrillas killing Americans in the embassy shocked television viewers. The many days needed to defeat the assault on Hue undermined the army's statements about the United States winning the war.

Major newspapers and magazines openly criticized the Johnson administration's conduct of the war. The *Wall Street Journal* wrote, "The American people should be getting ready to accept . . . the prospect that the whole Vietnam effort may be doomed."

Most Americans seemed to agree. Fewer people believed that the army was making progress in the war. More people believed that the army was losing ground. The Johnson administration developed a credibility gap—fewer people trusted its statements about the war.

As opposition to the war grew, President Johnson faced challenges in his own party. In late 1967, Democratic senator **Eugene McCarthy** of Minnesota had announced that he would run for the party's nomination for the presidency as a protest against the war. Not well known, McCarthy seemed to have little chance of winning. In the March 12 primary in New Hampshire, however,

TWO VIEWPOINTS

Should We Be Fighting the Vietnam War?

As the war in Vietnam dragged on, political support for it began to evaporate. While government politicians coaxed Americans to support goals of liberty and democracy, antiwar protesters counted the corpses sent home and argued that the war was useless.

President Johnson addresses the nation, March 31, 1968

Tonight I renew the offer I made in August—to stop the bombardment of North Vietnam. We ask that talks begin promptly, that they be serious talks on the substance of peace. . . .

There is division in the American house now. There is divisiveness among us all tonight. And holding the trust that is mine, as President of all the people, I cannot disregard the peril to the progress of the American people and the hope and the prospect of peace for all peoples. . . .

Accordingly, I shall not seek, and I will not accept, the nomination of my party for another term as your President.

But let men everywhere know, however, that a strong, a confident, and a vigilant America stands ready tonight to seek an honorable peace—and stands ready tonight to defend an honored cause—whatever the price, whatever the burden, whatever the sacrifices that duty may require. . . .

Walter Cronkite, news broadcaster, after the Tet offensive, February 27, 1968

We have too often been disappointed by the optimism of the American leaders, both in Vietnam and Washington, to have faith any longer in the silver linings they find in the darkest clouds. . . . To say that we are closer to victory today is to believe, in the face of evidence, the optimists who have been wrong in the past. To suggest we are on the edge of defeat is to yield to unreasonable pessimism. To say that we are mired in stalemate seems the only realistic, yet unsatisfactory conclusion. . . .

[I]t is increasingly clear to this reporter that the only rational way out then will be to negotiate, not as victors, but as an honorable people who lived up to their pledge to defend democracy, and did the best they could.

Walter Cronkite

Learning From History

1. What does Johnson mean by "division in the American house"?
2. Why might Americans like Walter Cronkite be frustrated with the war?
3. Do the president's words seem realistic? How might Cronkite respond to the president's address?

McCarthy surprised everyone by taking 42 percent of the popular vote. Although Johnson won the primary, McCarthy's strong showing indicated widespread opposition to the war.

Later, another antiwar candidate entered the race. **Robert F. Kennedy,** attorney general during his brother's presidency and now a senator from New York, announced that he, too, would seek the Democratic nomination.

The President Responds

Events in Vietnam and the growing antiwar movement disturbed President Johnson. Following the Tet offensive, the American commander in Vietnam, General **William Westmoreland,** had requested still more troops. Instead of agreeing, the president ordered a reevaluation of the war. He also reevaluated his own campaign for reelection in 1968.

On March 31, 1968, after consulting advisers, President Johnson appeared on television to announce a "new step toward peace"—he would halt the bombing of North Vietnam's cities. He asked North Vietnam for a comparable action so that peace negotiations could begin.

The president concluded his speech with a startling announcement. He said, "I shall not seek, and I will not accept, the nomination of my party for another term as your president."

✓ **Reading Check** **Identifying** What candidates from President Johnson's own party challenged him?

Violence Erupts

A few days after Johnson's withdrawal from the presidential race, tragedy struck the nation. A sniper in Memphis, Tennessee, shot and killed

Dr. Martin Luther King, Jr., the leading activist in the civil rights movement.

The King assassination triggered a rash of riots across the country. Army troops were called on to control unruly crowds in various cities. Already saddened by King's death, Americans worried about the renewed urban violence.

While the nation agonized over unrest at home and war abroad, the presidential race picked up speed. Vice President **Hubert H. Humphrey** joined Eugene McCarthy and Robert Kennedy in seeking the Democratic nomination. Kennedy edged out McCarthy in a number of primary elections, but McCarthy rebounded and scored a primary victory in Oregon. Humphrey, meanwhile, avoided the primaries. He gathered support among Democratic Party leaders, who in some states chose the delegates.

In early June 1968, Kennedy and McCarthy faced each other in the primary election in California, the state with the most delegates. That night, after Kennedy won, an assassin shot and killed him—and the nation reeled with the shock of yet another assassination.

The Democratic Convention

By the time the Democrats held their convention in **Chicago,** Humphrey appeared to have enough votes to win the nomination. As a long-time supporter of civil rights and labor causes, Humphrey had considerable backing in his party. As a supporter of Johnson's Vietnam policy, however, Humphrey was linked to the prowar faction of the party.

Antiwar Democrats felt angry and excluded from the convention. Tension filled the air. When trouble broke out, though, it did not occur as much in the convention hall as in the city's streets.

Frustrated by the almost certain victory of Humphrey, thousands of antiwar activists flocked to Chicago to protest. Chicago's mayor, **Richard J. Daley,** feared violence from the demonstrators and had the police out in force. The police made some arrests the first two nights, but no major problems developed.

On the third day, the antiwar protesters planned to march to the convention site to protest Humphrey's nomination. Police blocked the marchers at the hall. When the marchers headed in another direction, the police stopped them again. The protesters began to pelt the police with sticks and bottles. The police threw tear gas and charged in, wielding nightsticks. They pursued those who fled, beating some and arresting many.

Humphrey won the Democratic nomination, but the violence outside and the anger within the hall—all shown on television—had damaged his candidacy. The Democrats appeared unable to control their own convention. Humphrey admitted, "Chicago was a catastrophe."

✓ **Reading Check** **Identifying** What two popular leaders were assassinated in 1968?

Election of 1968

A majority of Americans disapproved of the police action in Chicago, but at the same time, strongly opposed the actions of the protesters. The years of protest and dissent had taken their toll and a backlash had set in. Most Americans fervently wished for a return to "law and order."

The Wallace Candidacy

One presidential candidate who used the "law and order" theme was Governor **George C. Wallace** of Alabama. Running as a third-party candidate, Wallace promised to crack down on "long-hair . . . draft card-burning youth." In addition, he criticized efforts to integrate schools by busing students and ridiculed "pointy-headed" bureaucrats in Washington for telling people how to run their lives.

Wallace's tough stand on law and order and his appeal to racial fears attracted many voters. Some political reporters predicted Wallace could win as much as 20 percent of the vote.

The "Silent Majority"

The Republican presidential nominee, former vice president **Richard M. Nixon,** also tried to tap into voters' growing conservative sentiment. Nixon pledged to represent the "quiet voice" of the "great majority of Americans, the non-shouters, the nondemonstrators." He called these people the "silent majority." Declaring that the "first civil right of every American is to be free from domestic violence," Nixon promised a return to law and order.

Nixon remained vague on his views of Vietnam. He promised that he would achieve "peace with honor," but he would not provide details of his plan.

During the election campaign, Nixon sought to win some of the traditionally Democratic Southern states with the law-and-order issue. This "Southern strategy" paid off. Although Wallace did take five Southern states and 46 electoral votes, Nixon won seven Southern states and their 78 electoral votes.

Nixon Wins

The popular vote was close. Nixon edged out Humphrey by about 500,000 votes—a difference of less than 1 percent. In the electoral vote, however, Nixon won a solid majority—301 votes to Humphrey's 191.

Nixon entered the presidency with the votes of only 43.4 percent of the people. Nixon and Wallace together, however, had won almost 57 percent of the vote. It seemed that a substantial majority of Americans wanted the government to restore order.

Reading Check **Identifying** What presidential candidate provided a strong third-party challenge in 1968?

SECTION 3 ASSESSMENT

Checking for Understanding

1. **Key Terms** Define counterculture, deferment, dove, hawk, credibility gap, silent majority.
2. **Reviewing Facts** What did conscientious objectors declare?

Analyzing Themes

3. **Continuity and Change** What was the result of the 1968 presidential election?

Critical Thinking

4. **Making Inferences** How do you think the credibility gap affected Johnson's ability to be an effective president?
5. **Determining Cause and Effect** Re-create the diagram below and explain why support for war in Vietnam eroded.

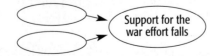

Support for the war effort falls

Analyzing Visuals

6. **Picturing History** Look at the photographs on page 879. Write a paragraph to describe what is happening.

Interdisciplinary Activity

Research Interview friends and relatives who lived during the Vietnam War era to see how people in your community reacted to the conflict. Present an oral report of your findings.

Building a Database

Why Learn This Skill?

Have you ever collected baseball cards or cataloged the CDs in your collection? Have you ever kept a list of the names and addresses of your friends and relatives? If you have collected information and kept some sort of list or file, then you have created a database.

Learning the Skill

An electronic database is a collection of facts that are stored in files on the computer. The information is organized in fields.

A database can be organized and reorganized in any way that is useful to you. By using a database management system (DBMS)—special software developed for record keeping—you can easily add, delete, change, or update information. You give commands to the computer telling it what to do with the information, and it follows your commands. When you want to retrieve information, the computer searches through the files, finds the information, and displays it on the screen.

Nixon greets well-wishers at a campaign rally.

Practicing the Skill

Richard M. Nixon is one of the presidents discussed in this chapter. Follow these steps to build a database of the political and cultural events that took place during his presidency.

1 Determine what facts you want to include in your database.

2 Follow instructions in the DBMS you are using to set up fields. Then enter each item of data into its assigned field.

3 Determine how you want to organize the facts in the database—chronologically by the date of the event, or alphabetically by the name of the event.

4 Follow the instructions in your computer program to place the information in order of importance.

5 Check that the information in your database is all correct. If necessary, add, delete, or change information or fields.

Applying the Skill

Building a Database Bring current newspapers to class. Using the steps just described, build a database of political figures mentioned in the newspapers. Explain to a partner why the database is organized the way it is and how it might be used in this class.

SECTION 4 Nixon and Vietnam

Guide to Reading

Main Idea
President Nixon put a plan in place to train and equip South Vietnamese soldiers to take the place of American troops.

Key Terms
Vietnamization, martial law, MIAs

Reading Strategy
Organizing Information As you read the section, re-create the diagram below and identify three strategies Nixon used to end the war.

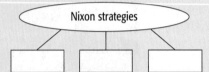
Nixon strategies

Read to Learn
• what steps Nixon took to end the war in Vietnam.
• what the costs of the Vietnam War were.

Section Theme
Continuity and Change President Nixon changed the strategy of the conflict that included intense bombing and Vietnamization.

Preview of Events

♦1968   ♦1970   ♦1972   ♦1974

June 1969
Nixon begins to withdraw troops from Vietnam

April 1970
Nixon sends troops to Cambodia

May 1970
Six students killed at Kent State and Jackson State

January 1973
Paris peace accords end U.S. involvement in Vietnam

Nixon inaugural button

AN American Story

President Nixon's inauguration in January 1969 took place on a cold, gloomy day. Hundreds of demonstrators chanting antiwar slogans and holding anti-Nixon posters stood along Pennsylvania Avenue in Washington, D.C. At one point Nixon's limousine was pelted with sticks, stones, and bottles. Offended by this behavior, World War II veterans shouted at the demonstrators, labeling the protesters "communists" and "traitors." This marked the first time an inaugural parade was disrupted in the 180 years of the presidency.

A New Strategy

In his Inaugural Address in January 1969, **Richard M. Nixon** appealed to the American people for calm:

❝We cannot learn from one another until we stop shouting at one another—until we speak quietly enough so that our words can be heard as well as our voices.❞

Nixon had campaigned on a pledge of "peace with honor" in Vietnam. He wanted to pull American forces out of Vietnam, but he did not want American withdrawal to be seen as a sign of defeat. Nixon's strategy of peace with honor had three parts—reform of the selective service system, giving South Vietnam more responsibility in fighting the war, and expanding the bombing campaign.

Under President Nixon the selective service system changed. College students could no longer obtain draft deferments, only 19-year-olds could be called for service in Vietnam, and draftees would be chosen by lottery on the basis of their birthday. Protests against the draft faded with these reforms because the government began calling up fewer young men and because President Nixon promised to eliminate the selective service in the future.

President Nixon started withdrawing American troops from Vietnam in June 1969. He did not, however, want to abandon South Vietnam to the Communists. By the end of the year, Nixon had developed his plan of Vietnamization and announced it to the American people. Vietnamization called for the army of South Vietnam to take a more active role in fighting the war— and for Americans to become less involved. While stepping up the training of South Vietnamese soldiers, American ground troops would gradually withdraw from the country.

When Nixon took office in January 1969, more than 540,000 American troops were in Vietnam. By the end of 1970, the number had fallen to 334,000 and by 1971 to about 60,000.

In the third part of his Vietnam policy, Nixon expanded the bombing campaign. Hoping to relieve pressure on troops in South Vietnam, the president ordered the bombing of enemy supply routes and hideouts in neighboring Cambodia and Laos. Although the Nixon administration sought publicity for changes to the draft and the

American soldiers on patrol

withdrawal of troops, it kept the bombing of Cambodia secret.

Reading Check **Explaining** Why did the U.S. expand its bombing campaign?

Renewed Opposition at Home

A new round of antiwar demonstrations began in late 1969, reflecting the growing sentiment for ending the war. In October more than 300,000 people took part in an antiwar protest in Washington, D.C.

The government also tried to end the war through peace talks with North Vietnam. **Henry Kissinger,** the president's national security adviser, represented the United States in the Paris talks. The United States had launched the bombing campaign to persuade the North Vietnamese to agree to settlement terms, but the North Vietnamese adopted a wait-and-see attitude. They believed that the strength of the antiwar movement in the United States would force the Americans to withdraw.

The new antiwar protests and North Vietnam's unyielding attitude alarmed President Nixon. In his speech on Vietnamization in November, he appealed to the "silent majority" of Americans for support for his policy. "North Vietnam cannot defeat or humiliate the United States," he said. "Only Americans can do that."

Expanding the War

Further conflict gripped Southeast Asia when Cambodia plunged into a civil war between Communist and non-Communist forces. Nixon decided in April 1970 to send American troops to destroy Communist bases in Cambodia.

The attack aroused outrage in Congress and elsewhere. By sending American troops to Cambodia, critics charged, Nixon invaded a neutral country and overstepped his constitutional authority as president.

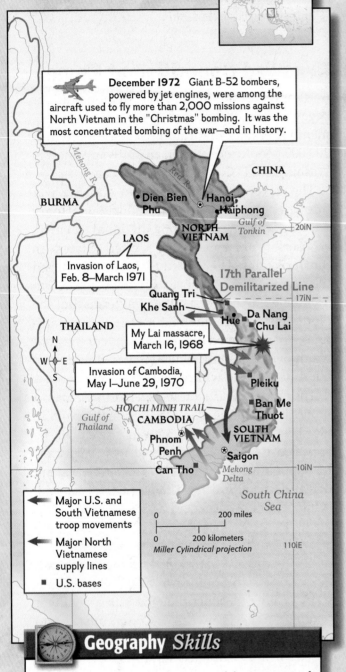

December 1972 Giant B-52 bombers, powered by jet engines, were among the aircraft used to fly more than 2,000 missions against North Vietnam in the "Christmas" bombing. It was the most concentrated bombing of the war—and in history.

Invasion of Laos, Feb. 8–March 1971

My Lai massacre, March 16, 1968

Invasion of Cambodia, May 1–June 29, 1970

⬅ Major U.S. and South Vietnamese troop movements

⬅ Major North Vietnamese supply lines

■ U.S. bases

CHINA
BURMA
• Dien Bien Phu
Hanoi ✪
• Haiphong
Gulf of Tonkin
NORTH VIETNAM
LAOS
17th Parallel Demilitarized Line
Quang Tri
Khe Sanh
Hue •
■ Da Nang
■ Chu Lai
THAILAND
Pleiku ■
HO CHI MINH TRAIL
■ Ban Me Thuot
Gulf of Thailand
CAMBODIA
SOUTH VIETNAM
Phnom Penh ✪
✪ Saigon
Can Tho ■
Mekong Delta
South China Sea

0   200 miles
0   200 kilometers
Miller Cylindrical projection

Geography *Skills*

Throughout the war United States troops and the government of South Vietnam controlled the major cities.

1. **Location** Along what line of latitude did the demilitarized zone run?
2. **Analyzing Information** Through which countries did the Ho Chi Minh Trail run?

United States Troops in Vietnam, 1965—1973

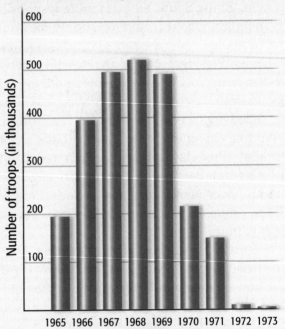

Number of troops (in thousands)

Year

Source: *Statistical Abstract of the United States.*

Opposition to the War

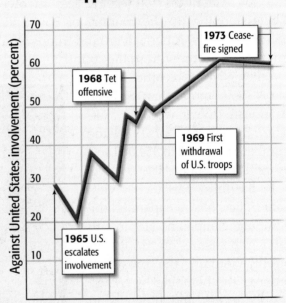

Against United States involvement (percent)

1973 Cease-fire signed

1968 Tet offensive

1969 First withdrawal of U.S. troops

1965 U.S. escalates involvement

Year

Source: *The Gallup Poll: Public Opinion.*

Picturing **History**

A stunned woman kneels beside the body of a student killed at Kent State. **What event sparked the student unrest at Kent State?**

PROTEST!

Kent State

The Cambodian invasion provoked a storm of antiwar protests on campuses across the nation. Most proceeded peacefully. However, two protests ended in tragedy.

At a protest at Kent State University in **Kent, Ohio,** students burned a military building on campus. Ohio's governor declared martial law—emergency military rule—on the campus and ordered 3,000 National Guard troops to Kent.

On May 4 armed troops arrived on campus. Eighteen-year-old Leone Keegan, a freshman, remembered going to class that morning:

> ❝I saw all these young men in uniforms standing on the street corners with their rifles, and I was thinking, What is this?❞

At noon students gathered for a protest rally on the campus lawn. The National Guard members—young, inexperienced, and nervous—told the protesting students to leave. "Evacuate the area. You have no right to assemble," they shouted through bullhorns. The students shouted back, "We don't want your war." Some students threw stones.

The troops shot tear gas toward the students; many students ran. One National Guard unit chased some students between two buildings.

Then—for reasons that are unclear—the troops opened fire. ". . . [T]hey're killing us," screamed one student in disbelief. Four students were dead and at least nine more were wounded.

Jackson State

Violence flared again on May 15 at the nearly all-African American college of **Jackson State** in Mississippi. Following a night of campus violence, two students were shot and killed. Witnesses charged that the police had recklessly blasted the residence hall with shotguns. The police claimed they were protecting themselves from sniper fire.

A wave of student strikes followed the tragedies at Kent State and Jackson State. Hundreds of colleges and universities suspended classes or closed down completely.

The president took a hard line. The Kent State shootings, he said, "should remind us once again that when dissent turns to violence it invites tragedy." A commission that investigated events at Kent State found that the shootings were unjustified. A majority of Americans, however, seemed to agree with the president.

✓ **Reading Check** **Identifying** Who represented the United States in the Paris talks?

"Peace Is at Hand"

Meanwhile, the Nixon administration continued to negotiate with representatives of the North Vietnamese government. These talks stalled, however.

In March 1972, the North Vietnamese launched another major offensive in the South. Because the United States had few troops left in Vietnam, Nixon resumed bombing. Nixon ordered American planes to bomb targets near **Hanoi,** the capital of North Vietnam. He also ordered the navy to plant mines in North Vietnamese harbors.

The president stopped insisting that North Vietnam remove all its troops from South Vietnam before a full American withdrawal. Nixon sent Henry Kissinger to negotiate. In the fall of 1972—just before the presidential election in the United States—they reached a tentative agreement. "Peace is at hand," Kissinger announced.

His statement came too soon. The agreement collapsed because the South Vietnamese president objected to allowing North Vietnamese forces to remain in South Vietnam.

Paris Peace Accords

After his reelection, Nixon unleashed American airpower against North Vietnam. In December 1972, the heaviest bombardment of the war fell on North Vietnam's cities, provoking outrage in the United States and abroad.

Nixon stood firm, and North Vietnam returned to the peace talks. The Americans pressured the South Vietnamese to accept the peace terms. On January 27, 1973, the negotiators signed the peace agreement.

The United States agreed to pull its remaining troops out of the country. The North Vietnamese agreed to return all American prisoners of war. While the Paris peace accords ended American involvement in Vietnam, they did not end the conflict.

The War Ends

The North Vietnamese never abandoned their goal of unifying Vietnam under their control. In early 1975 they launched a final major offensive. The weakened South Vietnamese army collapsed suddenly on all fronts. Within a few weeks, North Vietnamese tanks reached the outskirts of Saigon.

As North Vietnamese forces closed in on Saigon, the last Americans scrambled to escape the country, some by helicopter from the roof of the American embassy. Thousands of Vietnamese citizens who had supported or worked for the Americans also fled to the United States. Many more could not escape. In the early hours of April 30, 1975, Saigon fell to the Communists. Soon after, South Vietnam surrendered. The long war was over.

✓ Reading Check **Analyzing** What was the result of the Paris peace agreements?

Legacy of the War

The Vietnam War took a staggering toll of life and suffering. More than one million Vietnamese—civilians as well as soldiers on one side or the other—died between 1965 and the end of the conflict. Vietnam lay in ruins with many villages destroyed.

More than 58,000 Americans were dead; 300,000 were wounded, many of them permanently disabled. The United States had poured more than $150 billion into the war.

About 2.7 million Americans had served in Vietnam. Unlike the veterans of World War II, they found no hero's welcome when they returned home. Many Americans simply wanted to forget the war. They paid little attention to those who had fought and sacrificed in Vietnam.

The relatives of the American soldiers who had been classified as missing in action, or as MIAs, continued to demand that the government press the Vietnamese for information. The Vietnamese did allow a number of American groups to search the countryside. As the years passed, however, the likelihood of finding anyone alive faded.

HISTORY Online

Student Web Activity
Visit taj.glencoe.com and click on **Chapter 30— Student Web Activities** for an activity on the Vietnam War.

A Step Toward Healing

The construction of the **Vietnam Veterans Memorial** in Washington, D.C., provided a step toward healing the country's wounds. Designed by **Maya Ying Lin,** the striking memorial is a polished black granite wall in the shape of a private's stripes. It bears the names of all the Americans who died or were missing in action in the conflict.

When they visit the wall, families, friends, and comrades in war seek out the names of those who fought in Vietnam and did not return. Since the memorial was dedicated in 1982, visitors have left thousands of keepsakes and remembrances there. The flowers, letters, poems, and pictures left at the wall pay a proud and moving tribute to the Americans who died in the service of their country.

✓ Reading Check **Identifying** What are MIAs?

SECTION 4 ASSESSMENT

Checking for Understanding

1. **Key Terms** Define Vietnamization, martial law, MIAs.
2. **Reviewing Facts** Why did Nixon's actions in Cambodia anger many people?

Analyzing Themes

3. **Global Connections** Explain the process of Vietnamization. Who proposed this plan?

Critical Thinking

4. **Drawing Conclusions** Do you think Nixon succeeded in attaining "peace with honor?" Explain.
5. **Sequencing Information** Re-create the time line below and identify key dates and events in the Vietnam War during the Nixon presidency.

```
                  ┌──────┐   ┌──────┐
                  └──────┘   └──────┘
June 1969                            April 1975
┌──────┐        ┌──────┐   ┌──────┐
└──────┘        └──────┘   └──────┘
```

Analyzing Visuals

6. **Geography Skills** Examine the map of the Vietnam War on page 886. Where was the demilitarized zone located?

Interdisciplinary Activity

Expository Writing Imagine you are a reporter during the Vietnam era. Research and write a news story on one aspect of the war that you find especially interesting or important.

Chapter Summary

The Vietnam Era

1954
- Geneva Accords divide Vietnam

1957
- Soviet Union launches *Sputnik*

1959
- Civil War begins in Vietnam

1961
- Bay of Pigs invasion fails
- Berlin Wall erected

1962
- Cuban Missile crisis occurs

1963
- John F. Kennedy is assassinated
- Lyndon B. Johnson sworn in as president

1964
- Gulf of Tonkin Resolution passed

1967
- More than 500,000 U.S. troops in Vietnam
- War protesters march on Pentagon

1968
- North Korea captures USS *Pueblo*
- North Vietnamese launch Tet offensive
- Dr. Martin Luther King, Jr., is assassinated
- Robert Kennedy is assassinated
- Violence erupts at Democratic convention in Chicago
- Richard Nixon wins presidency

1969
- Neil Armstrong walks on the moon
- Nixon begins to withdraw troops from Vietnam

1970
- Nixon sends troops to Cambodia
- Six students killed at Kent State and Jackson State

1973
- Paris peace accords end U.S. involvement in Vietnam

Reviewing Key Terms

On a sheet of paper, use all of the following terms to write sentences relating to the information in the chapter.

1. flexible response
2. hot line
3. Vietcong
4. domino theory
5. escalate
6. deferment
7. Vietnamization
8. MIAs

Reviewing Key Facts

9. Why did the Soviets build the Berlin Wall?
10. Why did President Kennedy blockade Cuba?
11. In what way did the Gulf of Tonkin Resolution extend President Johnson's power?
12. What is Agent Orange?
13. What was the Tet offensive?

Critical Thinking

14. **Comparing** Why do you think most Americans supported the war effort during World War II, but many did not support the Vietnam War?

15. **Drawing Conclusions** President Johnson made the decision not to run for reelection in 1968. Determine whether you believe that President Johnson's decision was a good one or a bad one for the country. On a diagram like the one shown, write at least three reasons to support your decision.

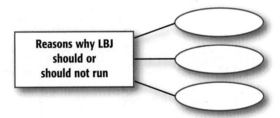

Reasons why LBJ should or should not run

Practicing Skills

16. **Using a Database** Prepare a database of the major battles of the Vietnam War involving United States troops. At your local library, research to find information about the sites of the battles, who the commanding officer was, how many American soldiers were killed or wounded at the sites, and how many North Vietnamese were killed or wounded. Share your database with the rest of your class.

Geography and History Activity

Study the two maps on this page; then answer the questions that follow.

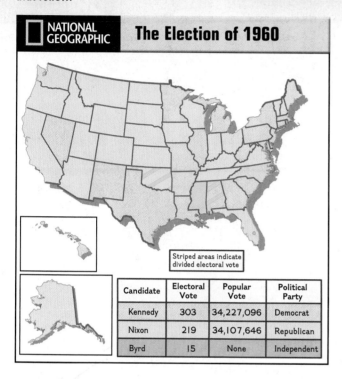

NATIONAL GEOGRAPHIC — The Election of 1960

Striped areas indicate divided electoral vote

Candidate	Electoral Vote	Popular Vote	Political Party
Kennedy	303	34,227,096	Democrat
Nixon	219	34,107,646	Republican
Byrd	15	None	Independent

NATIONAL GEOGRAPHIC — The Election of 1968

Striped area indicates divided electoral vote

Candidate	Electoral Vote	Popular Vote	Political Party
Nixon	301	31,785,480	Republican
Humphrey	191	31,275,166	Democrat
Wallace	46	9,906,473	Independent

17. **Region** In what regions of the country did Kennedy receive the strongest support in the 1960 election? In which regions was support for Kennedy weakest?

18. **Region** What regions supported Nixon in 1960? In 1968?

19. **Region** Explain why you agree or disagree with the following: The Northeast was Nixon's strongest region in 1968.

Citizenship Cooperative Activity

20. **Individual Involvement** With two other students, research to find what opportunities exist in your community for individual involvement on issues. For example, does your community have a recycling program? Find out what you might do to assist in these efforts. Report your findings to the class.

Alternative Assessment

21. **Portfolio Writing Activity** United States involvement in Vietnam officially ended in 1973. What effects of the war are still part of American life? Write a paragraph discussing what these effects are.

Standardized Test Practice

Directions: Choose the *best* answer to the following question.

What happened in Vietnam after the last American troops left?

A The process of Vietnamization began.

B South Vietnam surrendered to North Vietnam.

C The two sides met at Paris.

D President Johnson decided not to seek a second term.

Test-Taking Tip

Be aware of the order of events asked about in a question. This question asks about events in Vietnam after the United States pulled out. Choice **A** is an event that occurred before the pull out.

11 Modern America

1968–Present

Why It Matters

Incredible change marked the last part of the twentieth century. The Cold War came to an end. Faith in government was shaken by presidential scandal. As the United States entered a new century, new challenges emerged. The American people responded to terrorism by looking for new ways to preserve and protect their ideals in a changing world. The following resources offer more information about this period in American history.

Decorative flag, computer art

Primary Sources Library

See pages 978–979 for primary source readings to accompany Unit 11.
Use the American history
Primary Source Document Library
CD-ROM *to find additional primary sources about Modern America.*

The International Space Station

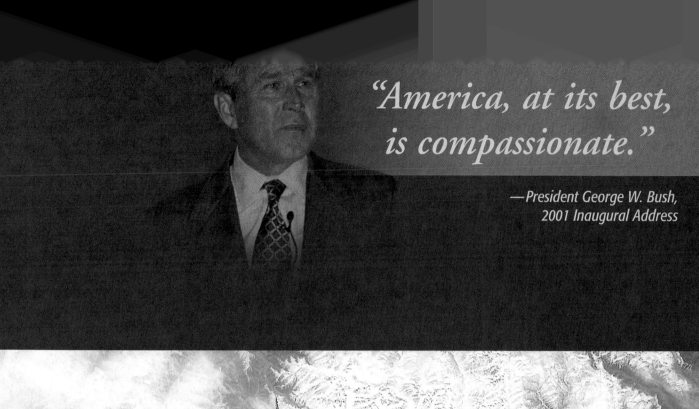

"*America, at its best, is compassionate.*"

—*President George W. Bush,*
2001 Inaugural Address

CHAPTER 31

Search for Stability

1968–1981

Why It Matters

During the 1960s and 1970s, the American people's view of the nation and the government changed. Some believed that the United States had lost its position as the economic and political leader of the free world. Yet the American system of constitutional government worked and survived.

The Impact Today

Today many Americans continue to express doubts about the political system. Mistrust of politicians, especially "Washington insiders," has reduced voter turnout in elections. It has also spurred the creation of political movements outside the two major parties.

 The American Journey Video *The chapter 31 video, "Watergate," details the events in the Watergate controversy.*

1972
- Nixon visits Beijing
- SALT I signed

1973
- Watergate hearings

1974
- Nixon resigns presidency

 **United States PRESIDENTS**

| Nixon 1969–1974 | Ford 1974–1977 |

1966   *1970*   *1974*

 World

1967
- Six-Day Arab-Israeli War

Temporarily...
10 GALLONS PER CUSTOMER
We appreciate your business & cooperation.

1973
- OPEC imposes embargo of oil to U.S.

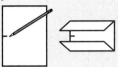

FOLDABLES™
Study Organizer

Evaluating Information Study Foldable
Make and use this foldable to organize information about America's search for stability at the end of the twentieth century.

Step 1 Mark the midpoint of a side edge of one sheet of paper. Then fold the outside edges in to touch the midpoint.

Step 2 Fold in half from side to side.

Step 3 Open and cut along the inside fold lines to form four tabs. Label your foldable as shown.

What led to better relations with China?

What happened in Iran in 1979?

Why did President Nixon resign?

Who won the election of 1980?

Cut along the fold lines on both sides.

Reading and Writing As you read the chapter, search for the answers to these four questions. Write answers under each of the tabs.

Celebrating the Bicentennial Fireworks light up the Statue of Liberty during celebration of the nation's 200th birthday on July 4, 1976.

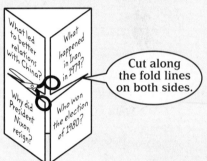

1977
- Panama Canal treaties signed

1979
- Iranians take 52 U.S. hostages
- Accident at Three Mile Island

1980
- U.S. boycotts Moscow Olympics

1981
- Iranians release U.S. hostages

Carter 1977–1981

Reagan 1981–1989

1978

1982

1975
- 36 nations agree to Helsinki Accords

1978
- First test-tube baby born in London

1979
- Soviet troops invade Afghanistan

1981
- Scientists identify AIDS

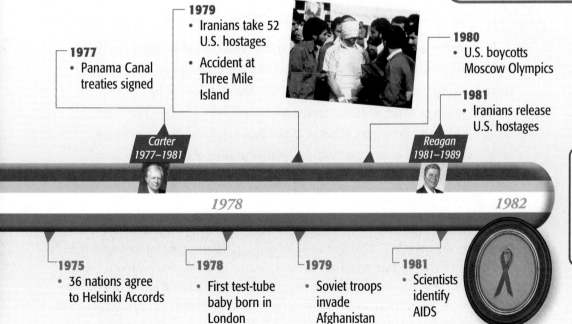

HISTORY
Online

Chapter Overview
Visit taj.glencoe.com and click on **Chapter 31— Chapter Overviews** to preview chapter information.

Nixon's Foreign Policy

Main Idea

President Nixon tried to ease cold war tensions but pursued active policies in the Middle East and Latin America.

Key Terms

détente, balance of power, embargo, shuttle diplomacy

Reading Strategy

Classifying Information As you read the section, re-create the diagram below and describe the goals of these strategies and policies.

```
        Goals
   ┌──────┼──────────┐
Détente:  Balance   Shuttle
          of power: diplomacy:
```

Read To Learn

- how Richard Nixon changed U.S. political relations with the Soviet Union and China.
- what actions the U.S. took regarding the Middle East and Latin America.

Section Theme

Global Connections Richard Nixon pursued a very active foreign policy.

Preview of Events

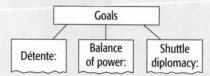

♦1970   ♦1972   ♦1974

April 1971
American table-tennis team visits China

February 1972
President Nixon visits Beijing

May 1972
Leaders sign the first Strategic Arms Limitation Treaty

October 1973
Arab countries impose oil embargo on the U.S.

1972 election button

AN American Story

To improve relations with the Communist world, President Richard Nixon made a historic visit to China in February 1972. Nixon later described how he felt upon his arrival in Beijing, the Chinese capital: ". . . 'The Star Spangled Banner' had never sounded so stirring to me as on that windswept runway in the heart of Communist China. . . . As we left the airport, [Chinese leader Zhou Enlai] said, 'Your handshake came over the vastest ocean in the world—twenty-five years of no communication.' "

Easing the Cold War

In his Inaugural Address on January 20, 1969, President Richard M. Nixon told the American people, "The greatest honor . . . is the title of peacemaker." Many Americans wondered whether Nixon fit the role of peacemaker. During his years in Congress, he had gained a reputation as a fierce enemy of communism. Few people imagined that Nixon, the anti-Communist crusader, would introduce policies to improve America's relations with the Communist world.

Behind the Iron Curtain

President Nixon intended to leave his mark on foreign policy. He hoped to build a more stable, peaceful world by reaching out to the Soviet Union and the People's Republic of China. In the summer of 1969, Nixon visited several countries, including Romania—the first time an American president had gone behind the iron curtain. Nixon wanted to find areas of common interest and cooperation with these Cold War opponents.

Détente

To help him in this task, Nixon appointed **Henry Kissinger,** a Harvard University professor, as his national security adviser. Kissinger and Nixon shared a belief in *realpolitik*—policies based on national interests rather than political ideology. They believed that peace among nations would come through negotiation rather than through threats or force. President Nixon formulated a foreign policy plan of détente—attempts at relaxing, or easing, international tensions. As détente replaced confrontation, the United States and Communist states could begin working together to resolve issues that divided them.

Nixon realized that détente would work only if a balance of power existed. A balance of power is a distribution of power among nations to prevent any one nation from becoming too powerful. "It will be a safer world and a better world," he declared,

66if we have a strong, healthy United States, Europe, Soviet Union, China, Japan—each balancing the other, not playing one against the other.99

Picturing **History**

Henry Kissinger (below) helped President Nixon handle foreign policy matters. Premier Zhou Enlai and President Nixon (right) inspect troops during Nixon's 1972 visit to China. **When did the United States and China establish full diplomatic relations?**

China

Since the Communist takeover of China in 1949, the United States had refused to recognize the **People's Republic of China,** the most populated nation on the earth. Instead the United States recognized the anti-Communist Chinese government under **Chiang Kai-shek** in exile on the island of Taiwan.

By the time Nixon became president, however, each side had good reasons for wanting to improve relations. China distrusted and feared the Soviet Union. The United States hoped that recognition of China would help end the war in Vietnam and drive a deeper wedge between the two Communist powers.

The winds of change began to blow in the fall of 1970 when Nixon told reporters that he wanted to go to China. Noting this change in tone, the Chinese responded by inviting an American table-tennis team to visit the country in April 1971. A week later the United States announced the opening of trade with China.

"Ping-Pong diplomacy" was accompanied by secret talks between American and Chinese officials about forging closer ties between the two nations. After Kissinger made a secret trip to China in July 1971, President Nixon announced that he would visit **Beijing,** the Chinese capital, "to seek the normalization of relations."

In February 1972 Nixon arrived in China for a week-long visit. Nixon and China's premier **Zhou Enlai** agreed to allow greater scientific and cultural exchange and to resume trade. Although formal diplomatic relations were not established until 1979, Nixon's trip marked the first formal contact with China in more than 25 years.

The Soviet Union

Nixon followed his history-making trip to China with a visit to **Moscow,** the Soviet capital, in May 1972. The Soviets eagerly welcomed the thaw in Cold War politics. They wanted to prevent a Chinese-American alliance and to slow the costly arms race. They also hoped to gain access to United States technology and to buy badly needed American grain. Soviet leader **Leonid Brezhnev** remarked,

66There must be room in this world for two great nations with different systems to live together and work together.99

While in Moscow, President Nixon signed the Strategic Arms Limitation Treaty, or **SALT I.** This landmark treaty, the result of talks begun in 1969, restricted the number of certain types of nuclear missiles in American and Soviet arsenals. Although SALT I did not end the arms race, it greatly reduced tensions between the United States and the Soviet Union.

The United States and the Soviet Union also agreed to work together in trade and science. Nixon—and the world—hoped that a new era of cooperation would bring greater stability to world affairs.

Reading Check **Identifying** What is détente?

High Lob

Analyzing *Political Cartoons*

"Ping-Pong diplomacy" improved relations between the United States and the People's Republic of China. **What nations do the players represent?**

Many Palestinians lived in exile, scattered throughout the Middle East, North Africa, and Europe. **What was the cause of the Yom Kippur War?**

The Middle East

President Nixon's foreign policy aimed to maintain world stability without being drawn into regional disputes. The president wanted to avoid any involvement that might lead to another situation like Vietnam. Nixon stated that the United States would help in "the defense and development of allies and friends" but not take "basic responsibility" for the future of those nations. A crisis soon arose in the Middle East that tested this policy.

Arab-Israeli Tensions

Since the founding of the Jewish state of Israel in 1948, the United States had supported Israel in its struggles against its Arab neighbors. Tensions between Israel and the Arab states had erupted in war in 1948, 1956, and 1967. The Six-Day War of 1967 left Israel in control of east Jerusalem, the **West Bank,** the **Golan Heights** of Syria, and the **Gaza Strip** and **Sinai Peninsula** of Egypt. The 1967 war also increased the number of Arab refugees. Thousands of Palestinians now lived in Israeli-held territory, and thou-

sands more lived in neighboring Arab states. The Palestinians' demand for their own homeland became another source of instability.

Yom Kippur War

War erupted again on October 6, 1973. Egypt and Syria attacked Israel in an attempt to regain territory lost in the Six-Day War. Because the attack occurred on Yom Kippur, a major Jewish holiday, the conflict became known as the **Yom Kippur War.**

The United States pressured Israel to accept a cease-fire. A cease-fire came, but not before the Israelis had regained most of the territory lost in the initial Arab advance. Israel also had taken additional territory from Syria and Egypt.

Angry at the United States for supporting Israel, Arab oil-producing states imposed an embargo—a ban on shipments—of oil to the United States and to other nations not seen as "friendly." The embargo caused an oil shortage in the United States. Long lines of cars formed at gas pumps and Americans became angry as gas prices skyrocketed.

Shuttle Diplomacy

President Nixon sent Kissinger, now secretary of state, to the region to gain the trust of Arab leaders and to negotiate some type of agreement between Israel and its Arab neighbors. During the next two years, Kissinger engaged in shuttle diplomacy—traveling back and forth between the capitals of Israel, Egypt, and Syria trying to resolve the oil crisis and forge a lasting peace.

Early in 1974, **Golda Meir,** the prime minister of Israel, and **Anwar el-Sadat,** the president of Egypt, reached agreements that separated Israeli and Arab forces in the Sinai Peninsula and Golan Heights. Then in March 1974, Kissinger persuaded the Arab nations to end the oil embargo. Kissinger also improved relations with Egypt, the largest and most powerful Arab state, by promising large amounts of foreign aid.

Israeli leader Golda Meir

Reading Check **Summarizing** What happened in the U.S. as a result of the oil embargo?

Latin America

The Nixon administration sought to protect its interests in Latin America and to prevent the spread of communism. In 1970 the South American country of **Chile** elected **Salvador Allende** president. Allende was a follower of **Karl Marx,** the founder of communism. When the new Chilean government took over American businesses in Chile, the United States protested. Nixon and his foreign-policy advisers feared an increase in Soviet influence in Chile and the spread of communism in Latin America.

With the backing of the CIA (Central Intelligence Agency), a small group of Chilean military leaders under General **Augusto Pinochet** overthrew the government and killed Allende. The United States immediately recognized the new military dictatorship and restored foreign aid to Chile.

The situation in Chile reflected another aspect of Nixon's foreign policy. Although willing to pursue détente with China and the Soviet Union, the president was still determined to contain the spread of communism—and Soviet influence—in the world.

Reading Check **Explaining** Why did the United States oppose Salvador Allende?

SECTION 1 ASSESSMENT

Checking for Understanding

1. **Key Terms** Use each of these terms in a sentence that will help explain its meaning: détente, balance of power, embargo, shuttle diplomacy.
2. **Reviewing Facts** How did Henry Kissinger contribute to Nixon's presidency?

Reviewing Themes

3. **Global Connections** What was Nixon's main foreign policy goal?

Critical Thinking

4. **Drawing Conclusions** Why did Nixon think that improving relations with China would make the Soviet Union more cooperative?
5. **Organizing Information** Re-create the diagram below and identify each leader.

Zhou Enlai ⟶ ◯

Anwar el-Sadat ⟶ ◯

Golda Meir ⟶ ◯

Analyzing Visuals

6. **Sequencing Events** Study the time line that appears on pages 894–895. When did OPEC impose the oil embargo? Who was the nation's president when the Panama Canal treaties were signed?

Interdisciplinary Activity

Current Events Find a newspaper article that discusses the Israeli-Arab relationship today and compare it to the relationship that existed in the 1960s and 1970s.

Nixon and Watergate

Guide to Reading

Main Idea
Nixon tried to deal with the nation's economic problems, but was forced to resign due to the Watergate scandal.

Key Terms
revenue sharing, affirmative action, stagflation, deficit, impeachment, amnesty, underemployment

Reading Strategy
Organizing Information As you read the section, list three challenges that Nixon faced during his presidency.

Challenges

Read To Learn
• how Nixon struggled with domestic problems.
• how the Watergate scandal affected politics.

Section Theme
Continuity and Change Economic problems and political scandal marked the 1970s and troubled both Richard Nixon and Gerald Ford.

Preview of Events

♦1972   ♦1973   ♦1974   ♦1975

June 1972
Break-in at Watergate occurs

1973
OPEC oil embargo reduces U.S. supplies

August 1974
Nixon resigns the presidency

December 1974
CIA's secret files revealed

1968 Republican campaign button

AN American Story

President Nixon had grave concerns about the state of American society. "We live in a deeply troubled and profoundly unsettled time. Drugs, crime, campus revolts, racial discord, draft resistance—on every hand we find old standards violated, old values discarded." Nixon believed that a "silent majority" of middle-class Americans shared his concerns about increasing crime and social disorder. In an ironic twist of events, however, the Nixon administration itself would get caught up in a web of illegal activities.

Nixon's Domestic Program

In his 1968 presidential campaign, Nixon had pledged to bring "law and order" back to American society. He also vowed to reduce government's role in people's lives.

Nixon's drive to restore law and order involved "cracking down on crime" and imposing stiffer penalties on lawbreakers. To strengthen the power of the police Nixon used federal funds to help state and city police forces.

The Courts

Nixon thought the federal courts should be tougher on criminals. "As a judicial conservative," he said, "I believe some Court decisions have gone too far in weakening the peace forces against the criminal forces in our society." During his presidency, four vacancies arose on the Supreme Court. Nixon hoped that the justices he appointed—**Warren Burger** as chief justice, and **Harry Blackmun, Lewis Powell,** and **William Rehnquist**—would shift the Court to a more conservative position. The decisions of the new justices did not fully meet the president's conservative goals, however.

New Federalism

Nixon wanted to reduce federal involvement in people's lives and to cut federal spending. He pledged to "reverse the flow of power and resources from the states and communities to Washington and start power and resources flowing back . . . to the people." To accomplish this goal, he introduced a program called the **New Federalism.**

One part of the New Federalism called for giving the states some of the revenue earned from federal taxes for use at the state and local levels. This revenue sharing became law in 1972.

Nixon also sought to end or scale back many Great Society programs begun under President Johnson. He promised to "quit pouring billions of dollars into programs that have failed." He abolished the Office of Economic Opportunity, the agency that had led Johnson's War on Poverty.

On civil rights issues, Nixon took a conservative position aimed at appealing to white voters. For example, Nixon opposed **busing.** Busing was used to promote racial integration by transporting students from mostly white or African American neighborhoods to racially mixed schools.

At the same time, however, his administration worked to carry out federal court orders to integrate schools. The Nixon administration also promoted affirmative action, or preference to minorities in jobs where they had previously been excluded. A practical politician, President Nixon did accept new government programs that had popular support. He approved the creation of two new agencies—the **Occupational Safety and Health Administration (OSHA)** to ensure workers' safety and the **Environmental Protection Agency (EPA)** to protect the environment.

Economics

Economic Problems

While attempting to change the direction of government, President Nixon had to deal with serious economic problems. Industry and manufacturing were declining because of foreign competition. Businesses and consumers struggled with **inflation**—a general rise in the prices of goods and services—fueled by international competition for raw materials and the increasing cost of oil. The United States also faced slow economic growth and high unemployment.

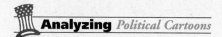

Analyzing *Political Cartoons*

This cartoon reflects how the value of the American dollar declined during the early 1970s. **What does the image of George Washington suggest about the mood of the country?**

Seeking Economic Stability

President Nixon tried a number of approaches to reduce inflation. He began by cutting federal spending. At the same time, he called for a **tight money policy.** Interest rates were raised so that people would borrow less and spend less. With less money in circulation, prices dropped. However, as demand slowed, business began to cut back and output fell. These steps slowed economic growth and brought on stagflation—a combination of rising prices and a sluggish economy.

Nixon then switched tactics. He temporarily froze wages and prices and issued guidelines for any future increases. This put a brake on inflation, but the economy remained in a recession.

Later, Nixon tried a third approach—increasing federal spending to stimulate the economy. Although this policy helped revive the economy for a short time, it also created a budget deficit in which government spending was greater than government revenue. None of Nixon's policies managed to restore the economy to its previous strength, and economic problems continued to trouble his administration.

✓ **Reading Check** **Analyzing** What was stagflation?

Nixon's Second Term

Looking ahead in 1971 to the presidential campaign of 1972, Nixon had doubts about his chances for reelection. The war in Vietnam had not yet ended, and the easing of tensions with China had not yet occurred. Businesses and consumers had to struggle with the effects of inflation. The president and his supporters wanted to ensure his reelection.

A Campaign Against Enemies

To help plan his campaign strategy, Nixon relied on a small group of loyal aides. The aides closest to the president were **John Ehrlichman,** his chief domestic adviser, and **H.R. Haldeman,** his chief of staff.

In their drive to win reelection, the president and his closest advisers, it was later revealed, stretched, and sometimes crossed, the bound-aries of the law. In 1971, for example, Nixon asked his aides for an "enemies list" of people considered unfriendly to the administration. He then ordered the FBI and the Internal Revenue Service (IRS) to investigate some of these people. Nixon justified such actions as necessary to maintain national security, arguing that those who challenged government policies posed a serious danger to the nation.

Nixon's campaign committee collected millions of dollars. It used some of this money to create a secret group—nicknamed "the plumbers"—to stop leaks of information that might hurt the administration. Some campaign money also went to pay for operations against Nixon's Democratic foes, but that party had many problems of its own.

Landslide Victory

The Democratic Party was split. Candidates competing for the nomination included: former vice president **Hubert Humphrey,** Senators **Edmund Muskie** of Maine and **George McGovern** of South Dakota, and former governor of Alabama **George Wallace.** Muskie and Humphrey could not gain enough support. Wallace's campaign was cut short in May 1972 by a would-be assassin's bullet that left him paralyzed.

McGovern, the most liberal of the four candidates, won the nomination. Many democrats and labor union leaders were cool towards McGovern's candidacy.

The Democrats' lack of unity as well as an upsurge in the economy and the prospect of peace in Vietnam

Nixon button and McGovern tie

led to a landslide victory for Nixon. He won 60.7 percent of the popular vote. The Republican victory in the electoral college was even more lopsided—520 to 17.

The Energy Crisis

During Nixon's second term as president, severe economic problems confronted the nation. One of the most critical problems was the cost of fuel, especially imported oil.

The U.S. economy depended heavily on oil. Much of this oil came from the Middle East. Arab oil-producing countries belonged to **OPEC**, the Organization of Petroleum Exporting Countries. In 1973 these countries placed an embargo on all oil shipments to the United States. At the same time, they raised their prices.

The sharp price increases and the five-month embargo damaged the nation's economy. Many companies had to lay off workers, while others raised their prices. Angry consumers complained about the high prices and the long lines at gas stations.

The president imposed emergency measures to conserve oil. Nixon also urged Americans to conserve energy voluntarily. Congress reduced speed limits on highways because a vehicle burns less fuel at lower speeds.

To deal with the long-range problem of dependence on imported oil, Nixon urged development of domestic oil, especially in **Alaska,** which possessed vast, untapped oil reserves.

Reading Check **Evaluating** Why were gasoline prices increasing during this period?

The Watergate Crisis

During Nixon's second term, what seemed like a small scandal turned into a presidential crisis. The scandal began with the president's reelection campaign. In June 1972, his reelection committee had wanted information about the Democrats' campaign plans. Members of the Nixon campaign ordered "the plumbers" to break into the headquarters of the Democratic National Committee to install telephone listening devices—bugs. This break-in set events in motion that would rock the presidency and the nation.

A Third-Rate Burglary

Sometime after midnight on June 17, 1972, Frank Wills, a security guard at the **Watergate** office-apartment complex in Washington, D.C., noticed tape covering the locks on doors leading to an underground parking garage. "I took the tape off," he later recalled, "but I didn't think anything of it." About an hour later, he found that someone had retaped the locks. Wills decided to call the police.

Frank Wills's discovery led to the arrest of five men who had broken into Democratic Committee headquarters in the Watergate complex. The arrests of "plumbers" Gordon Liddy and E. Howard Hunt followed soon afterward. Investigations revealed that Liddy and Hunt were connected to the Nixon campaign and were paid from White House funds.

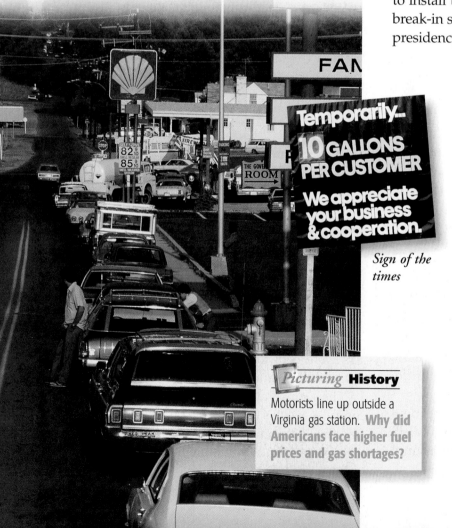

Sign of the times

Picturing **History**

Motorists line up outside a Virginia gas station. **Why did Americans face higher fuel prices and gas shortages?**

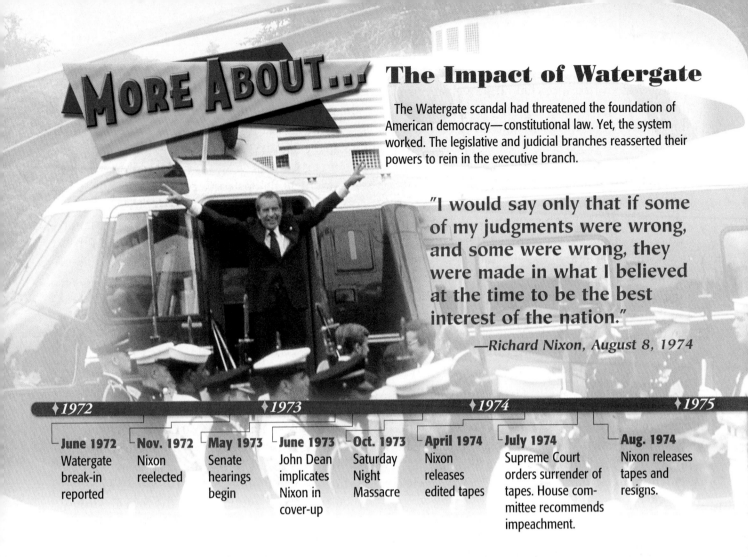

MORE ABOUT... The Impact of Watergate

The Watergate scandal had threatened the foundation of American democracy—constitutional law. Yet, the system worked. The legislative and judicial branches reasserted their powers to rein in the executive branch.

> "I would say only that if some of my judgments were wrong, and some were wrong, they were made in what I believed at the time to be the best interest of the nation."
>
> —*Richard Nixon, August 8, 1974*

♦ 1972   ♦ 1973   ♦ 1974   ♦ 1975

June 1972 Watergate break-in reported

Nov. 1972 Nixon reelected

May 1973 Senate hearings begin

June 1973 John Dean implicates Nixon in cover-up

Oct. 1973 Saturday Night Massacre

April 1974 Nixon releases edited tapes

July 1974 Supreme Court orders surrender of tapes. House committee recommends impeachment.

Aug. 1974 Nixon releases tapes and resigns.

The White House denied any involvement. Nixon's press secretary, Ronald Ziegler, dismissed the break-in as a "third-rate burglary." The president declared that "no one in the White House staff, no one in the administration . . . was involved in this bizarre incident."

Investigation

Meanwhile, two newspaper reporters for the *Washington Post,* **Bob Woodward** and **Carl Bernstein,** began publishing a series of articles that linked the burglary to the Nixon campaign. As the election approached, however, fewer than half of the American people had even heard of the Watergate break-in.

John Sirica, the federal district court judge presiding over the trial of the Watergate burglars, resolved to uncover the truth. Eventually, one of the burglars, James McCord, admitted that White House aides had lied about their involvement and had pressured the burglars "to plead guilty and remain silent."

A Scandal Unravels

Early in 1973 the Senate voted to hold hearings on Watergate. As pressures mounted, Nixon shook up the White House staff. He fired the White House counsel, **John Dean,** and forced aides H.R. Haldeman and John Ehrlichman to resign. He also declared that he would take responsibility for the mistakes of others because "there can be no whitewash at the White House." Nixon also agreed to Senate demands to appoint a special prosecutor—someone independent of the Justice Department—to investigate Watergate. **Archibald Cox** took the job.

The Senate Watergate hearings began in May 1973. Chaired by Senator **Sam Ervin** of North Carolina, the hearings slowly revealed the inner workings of the Nixon White House. The most damaging testimony came from John Dean. Dean testified that there had been a cover-up and that Nixon himself directed it, but he produced no evidence to confirm his account.

Then in July investigators learned that a secret taping system had recorded all conversations in the president's office. Ervin and Cox demanded the tapes. President Nixon refused and claimed **executive privilege,** insisting that release of the tapes would endanger national security.

When Cox requested a court order to get the tapes in October, Nixon ordered his attorney general, Elliot Richardson, to fire Cox. Richardson refused—and then resigned. Deputy Attorney General William Ruckelshaus also refused to carry out the order and resigned. Finally, Nixon found a Justice Department official willing to fire Cox. This **Saturday Night Massacre,** as the resignations and firing became known, resulted in a storm of public protest.

In the middle of this turmoil, another scandal struck the administration. The Justice Department charged Vice President **Spiro Agnew** with taking bribes while governor of Maryland. On October 10, 1973, he resigned. Nixon appointed Representative **Gerald R. Ford** of Michigan, the Republican leader of the House, to succeed Agnew. Congress quickly confirmed the nomination.

The Crisis Deepens

Public outrage over the Saturday Night Massacre forced Nixon to appoint a new special prosecutor, **Leon Jaworski.** Meanwhile, the House of Representatives began considering impeachment—the constitutional provision to remove a president from office. If the House charged Nixon with committing "high crimes and misdemeanors," he would then be tried in the Senate. If a two-thirds majority of senators found him guilty, he would no longer be president.

In April 1974, Nixon decided to release printed copies of some of the tapes. These transcripts, heavily edited and missing significant portions, led to new protests. Nixon refused court orders to hand over the unedited tapes. Appeals reached the Supreme Court, which ruled on July 24 that the president had to surrender the tapes.

At the end of July, after weeks of closed hearings, the House Judiciary Committee adopted three articles of impeachment, charging the president with obstruction of justice, abuse of power, and contempt of Congress. Nixon released the tapes on August 5. A conversation on one tape revealed that the president had ordered a cover-up of the Watergate break-in just a few days after it happened. The conversation provided the crucial piece of evidence that linked Nixon to Watergate.

Nixon Resigns

Public reaction and the prospect of an impeachment trial forced Nixon to resign. On the evening of August 8, 1974, he went on national television to announce his decision.

The next morning a tearful Richard Nixon said good-bye to his staff and then left the White House by helicopter. He was succeeded by Gerald Ford, who became the first U.S. president never elected to the office of president or vice president.

The Watergate crisis revealed that the system of checks and balances could work to remove a president that abused his power and violated the Constitution. Congress passed laws to correct some of the abuses. However, the scandal damaged the public's faith in their political institutions and leaders.

Time magazine,
August 19, 1974

✔ **Reading Check** **Identifying**
Who succeeded President Nixon?

A Time for Healing

After Nixon's helicopter left the White House, Gerald Ford was sworn in as president. Ford assured Americans, "Our long national nightmare is over." To fill the office of vice president, Ford selected Nelson Rockefeller, a highly respected

The changing of presidents on August 9, 1974, is symbolized in this replacement of former president Nixon's official portrait by one of the new president, Gerald Ford. **What position did Ford hold before becoming president?**

Republican and former governor of New York. Relieved to put the Watergate crisis behind them, most Americans welcomed the new president and a fresh start for the nation.

One of Ford's first acts, however, destroyed much of this confidence. On September 8, 1974, only a month after taking office, Ford granted Richard Nixon a **pardon** for any crimes he may have committed as president.

This meant that the former president could not be prosecuted for his part in the cover-up. Ford hoped that the pardon would help heal the wounds of Watergate. Instead, the pardon stirred controversy. Many Americans questioned why Nixon should escape punishment when others involved in the Watergate scandal went to jail. Some even accused Ford of striking a bargain with Nixon in advance—the promise of a pardon in exchange for Nixon's resignation. Although

Ford defended his action, the new president never fully regained the trust and popularity he had enjoyed in his first weeks in office.

Spying on American Citizens

In December 1974, Americans were startled to learn that the CIA had spied and kept secret files on some American citizens. A few months later, they discovered that the FBI also had secret files. President Ford appointed special commissions to investigate CIA and FBI misconduct. He and Congress began working on new laws to regulate the activities of the two agencies.

Vietnam Amnesty

Yet another controversy arose when President Ford offered amnesty, or protection from prosecution, to men who had illegally avoided military service during the Vietnam War. Ford promised that these people would not be punished if they pledged loyalty to the United States and performed some type of national service. While many people approved of amnesty, others thought it was too lenient. Supporters of the Vietnam War argued that draft dodgers and deserters should be punished.

Ford and Foreign Affairs

With little experience in foreign affairs, Ford relied on Henry Kissinger, his secretary of state, and continued the policies of the Nixon administration. Ford extended the policy of détente with the Soviet Union. In late 1974, he met with Soviet leader **Leonid Brezhnev** to discuss arms control. The two leaders reached a preliminary agreement on limiting nuclear weapons.

In July 1975, Ford traveled to Helsinki, Finland, where he signed the **Helsinki Accords** with the Soviet Union and various Western nations. The countries pledged to respect the human rights and civil liberties of their citizens.

The Ford administration also worked to improve relations with China. When Chinese Communist chairman **Mao Zedong** died in 1976, a more moderate government came to power. The new Chinese leaders wanted to expand economic and political ties to the United States, and the two nations moved a little closer.

A Troubled Economy

The economic problems that the Nixon administration faced continued to plague President Ford. Inflation remained high and unemployment rose.

By the 1970s Europe and Japan challenged America's world economic supremacy. Inexpensive and efficient Japanese cars flooded the American market. European products also provided strong competition to American-made goods.

This foreign competition led to factory closings in the United States and massive layoffs of workers. America began to suffer from underemployment; that is, people worked in jobs for which they were overqualified or that did not fully use their skills. Underemployment resulted, in part, from the loss of jobs to foreign competition.

The actions of OPEC continued to influence the American economy, also. Although the oil shortage caused by the embargo of 1973–1974 had eased, OPEC kept oil prices high, and the high prices contributed to inflation. The American economy seemed to be crumbling and Ford struggled for a solution.

Ford's Response

To fight inflation Ford launched a campaign called Whip Inflation Now (WIN), a voluntary program of wage and price controls. He called on Americans to save their money rather than spend it and to plant their own gardens to counter rising food prices. Although the effort led to a small drop in inflation, the economy declined and the nation headed into recession.

HISTORY Online
Student Web Activity
Visit taj.glencoe.com and click on **Chapter 31— Student Web Activities** for an activity on the Watergate crisis.

Spending Cuts

Another approach Ford urged for controlling inflation was to cut government spending. However, the Democratic-controlled Congress wanted to maintain or increase spending for social programs. Ford vetoed several congressional spending bills in an attempt to control spending, but his actions did not curb inflation.

To stimulate the economy and encourage economic growth, Ford persuaded Congress to pass a tax cut. Although the cut did bring some improvement in the economy, it led to larger budget deficits as government revenue declined and spending remained the same or increased. Despite his efforts, President Ford was unable to solve the nation's economic problems.

✔ **Reading Check** **Evaluating** How did Europe and Japan challenge the U.S. economy?

SECTION 2 ASSESSMENT

Checking for Understanding

1. **Key Terms** Use each of these terms in a sentence that will help explain its meaning: revenue sharing, affirmative action, stagflation, deficit, impeachment, amnesty, underemployment

2. **Reviewing Facts** List two actions that Nixon took to restore law and order.

Reviewing Themes

3. **Continuity and Change** Explain how Gerald Ford came to be president.

Critical Thinking

4. **Synthesizing Information** Explain how the government's checks and balances system worked when Nixon abused his power as president.

5. **Organizing Information** Re-create the diagram below and list reasons each person might have problems being reelected.

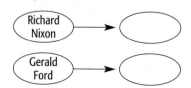

Analyzing Visuals

6. **Political Cartoons** Study the cartoon on page 902. Explain why George Washington is barely visible on the dollar bill. If you were a cartoonist, explain another way to express this idea.

Interdisciplinary Activity

Art Create a bumper sticker that supports or opposes Ford's pardon of President Nixon in the Watergate scandal.

Predicting Consequences

Why Learn This Skill?

Did you ever wish you could see into the future? Predicting future events is very difficult. You can, however, develop skills that will help you identify the logical consequences of decisions or actions.

Learning the Skill

Follow these steps to help you accurately predict consequences.

- Review what you already know about a situation by listing facts, events, and people's responses. The list will help you recall events and how they affected people.
- Analyze patterns. Try to determine what the patterns show. Are some consequences more likely to occur than others?
- Use your knowledge and observations of similar situations. In other words, ask yourself, "What were the consequences of a similar decision or action that occurred in the past?"
- Map out all possible consequences or outcomes.
- Analyze each of the potential consequences by asking, "How likely is it that this will occur?"
- Make a prediction.

Practicing the Skill

Candidates for public office often make campaign promises based on how they think voters will respond. Use the information in the chart below to help you predict what type of candidate would be elected president in 1980. Answer the questions.

1 Review the facts and events listed on the chart. What patterns do you notice? What do the facts tell you about the 1970s?

2 Recall similar situations in which voters faced hard times. What kind of president do you think Americans would want?

Applying the Skill

Predicting Consequences Read newspapers for articles about an event that affects your community. Make an educated prediction about what will happen. Explain your reasoning.

 Glencoe's **Skillbuilder Interactive Workbook CD-ROM, Level 1,** provides instruction and practice in key social studies skills.

Events of the 1970s ➤	Results and Reactions
OPEC oil embargo causes a shortage of fuel.	Americans feel helpless and angry.
President Ford vetoes programs in health, housing, and education to reduce government spending.	Many people lose jobs, and the nation suffers the worst recession in 40 years.
Ford pardons Nixon.	Americans feel frustrated.
To conserve energy, Americans buy smaller, imported cars.	American workers suffer unemployment as several automobile plants close.
Americans learn CIA and FBI have secret files on citizens.	Americans become angry at government's abuse of power.

The Carter Presidency

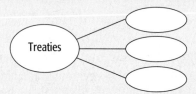

Guide to Reading

Main Idea
Jimmy Carter approached economic and foreign policy issues differently than Nixon or Ford, but was still unable to win reelection.

Key Terms
trade deficit, human rights, apartheid, fundamentalist

Reading Strategy
Classifying Information As you read the section, re-create the diagram below and list three treaties that the Carter administration negotiated.

Treaties

Read To Learn
• how President Carter emphasized human rights in foreign policy.
• what actions Carter took to improve the economy.

Section Theme
Global Connections Despite some failures, Carter saw success in treaties dealing with the Middle East and arms reductions.

Preview of Events

◆*1976* ◆*1977* ◆*1978* ◆*1979*

1976
Jimmy Carter wins the presidency

1977
Panama Canal treaties signed

1978
Camp David Accords lead toward Arab-Israeli peace

1979
Iranians take 52 Americans hostage

English-Spanish campaign poster

AN
American Story

Jimmy Carter brought a simple lifestyle to the White House. For example, to save money President Carter once planned to visit his hometown of Plains, Georgia, by car instead of by helicopter. He soon discovered that it was much less expensive to go by helicopter. Carter later stated about going by car: "A good portion of the Georgia State Patrol had been marshaled to block every country crossroads for more than 60 miles! It was obvious that I was not simply one of the people anymore."

The Election of 1976

As the 1976 elections approached, President Ford hoped to win the election outright. But Ford's prospects did not look particularly good. Although he had helped to restore confidence in government, Watergate was still fresh in the minds of the American people. In early 1976, **Jimmy Carter** ran as a Democratic candidate in the presidential primary election in New Hampshire. Few voters knew who Carter was. Then Carter began winning key primary elections.

Stressing his integrity, religious faith, and his standing as an outsider, Carter gathered enough delegates to win the Democratic nomination. Senator **Walter Mondale** of Minnesota ran as vice president.

Meanwhile President Ford had struggled to gain the Republican nomination. He faced a strong challenge from the former governor of California, **Ronald Reagan,** who was favored by party conservatives. Ford chose Senator **Bob Dole** of Kansas as his running mate.

During the campaign, Ford tried to stress his achievements as president. Carter promised to clean up the government and ran as much against the memory of Nixon and government corruption as against Ford. Carter won in a very close election, gaining 50.1 percent of the popular vote to Ford's 48 percent. To a great extent, Carter owed his margin of victory to support from African American Southern voters.

✓ **Reading Check** **Explaining** How did Carter represent himself in the 1976 presidential campaign?

An Informal Presidency

Carter, an "outsider" with no experience in national politics, did not fit the image of a typical politician. A former governor of Georgia, Carter liked to say he was just a peanut farmer from a small town called Plains who wanted to serve his country.

From the beginning, Carter set a down-to-earth tone. At his inauguration he wore an ordinary business suit rather than formal clothing. After the ceremony, Carter and his family walked up Pennsylvania Avenue from the Capitol to the White House instead of riding in

the traditional limousine. These gestures symbolized Carter's desire to create a more informal presidency. Carter wanted to be seen as an average American.

Struggling With the Economy

When Carter took office, the nation still suffered from high inflation and unemployment. Carter tried to jolt the economy out of recession by increasing federal spending and cutting taxes. Both measures were meant to stimulate economic growth. Unemployment came down, but inflation took off. Carter then reversed course and proposed spending cuts and a delayed tax cut.

Carter's reversals on economic policies made him seem weak and uncertain. As an outsider, the president had trouble gaining support for his programs in Congress. Although Carter needed the backing of congressional Democrats, his administration made little effort to work with them.

Energy Crisis

Carter made energy policy a priority. The high costs of energy added to inflation. In addition, as American money flowed overseas to purchase oil, the nation faced a growing trade deficit—the value of foreign imports exceeded the value of American exports.

In April 1977, Carter presented the **National Energy Plan,** aimed at resolving the energy crisis. To stress the need to reduce energy use, for example, the president turned down the thermostat in the White House.

Carter's plan included the creation of a Department of Energy to coordinate energy policy, research funds to explore alternative sources of energy, and tax policies to encourage domestic oil production and energy conservation. Congress enacted a weakened version of the plan in 1978.

Nuclear Power

In the late 1970s, Americans became more concerned about the threats of nuclear power. In March 1979 a major accident occurred at the **Three Mile Island** nuclear power plant near Harrisburg, Pennsylvania.

An anti-nuclear protest movement soon spread. President Carter, however, was unwilling to halt the nuclear energy program, which provided more than 10 percent of the nation's energy needs. At the same time, supporters of nuclear power argued that, with proper safeguards, nuclear power provided no danger to the environment.

✓ **Reading Check** **Identifying** What economic problems did Carter face when he took office?

Foreign Affairs

Carter based his foreign policy on human rights—a concern that governments around the world grant greater freedom and opportunity without the threat of persecution or violence. He proposed that any nation that violated human rights should not receive aid and support from the United States.

Carter withdrew economic and military aid from such countries as Argentina, Uruguay, and Ethiopia because of human rights violations. He condemned South Africa for its policy of apartheid, racial separation and economic and political discrimination against non-whites.

Carter's human rights diplomacy sometimes caused problems in the United States. In 1980 Cuban dictator Fidel Castro allowed thousands of Cubans, including criminals and political prisoners, to leave Cuba.

Beginning in April, Cuban refugees began leaving from **Mariel Harbor;** most were en route to Florida. The United States, however, had trouble absorbing such large numbers of people. Some of the emigrants were detained in refugee

People In History

Wilma Mankiller 1945–

During the 1960s, Wilma Mankiller lived in California and was active in the women's rights movement and the Native American rights movement. In the 1970s, she took this activism back to her roots in northeast Oklahoma and applied it to the government of her tribe, the Cherokee Nation.

In 1985, Wilma Mankiller became the Cherokee chief, the first woman to ever serve as a chief of a major Native American group. She often faced opposition, but was reelected and held the top position for almost ten years. As chief, she was responsible for 140,000 people and a 75 million-dollar budget.

During her time as the leader of the Cherokee, Mankiller focused on lowering unemployment, increasing educational opportunities, and improving community health care. She also created the Institute for Cherokee Literacy to preserve Cherokee traditions and culture.

camps. In June, President Carter ordered other Cubans be moved to federal prisons to await removal hearings. Then, in September, Castro sealed off the boatlift. About 125,000 Cuban refugees had entered the United States.

Carter had learned that a foreign policy based on a single issue, human rights, had many limitations. Even so, the president continued to speak out on the issue.

The Panama Canal

Carter also acted to end Latin American bitterness over the Panama Canal. Over the years, U.S. ownership of the canal and its control of the Canal Zone had caused friction between the United States and **Panama.** Carter signed two treaties with Panama in 1977. The treaties turned the U.S.-controlled Panama Canal over to Panama by the year 2000 but guaranteed that the canal would remain a neutral waterway open to all shipping. Some Republicans in the Senate tried to block ratification of the treaties, charging that Carter was giving away U.S. property. The Senate approved the treaties in 1978.

The Middle East

President Carter sought to bring peace to the Middle East. When peace talks between Israel and Egypt stalled in 1978, Carter invited Israeli prime minister **Menachem Begin** and Egyptian president **Anwar el-Sadat** to Camp David, Maryland, for a summit meeting.

For two weeks, the three leaders discussed issues dividing Israel and Egypt. In September 1978 they announced an agreement. Known as the **Camp David Accords,** the agreement led to an Egyptian-Israeli peace treaty signed at the White House in March 1979. The treaty marked the first time that Israel and an Arab nation had reached a peace agreement.

The Soviet Union

Carter criticized Soviet human-rights violations, but at the same time, he continued negotiations on arms control. In June 1979, the president signed a second Strategic Arms Limitation Treaty, or **SALT II.** Critics in the Senate charged that the treaty gave the Soviets an advantage, and the Senate delayed ratification.

Picturing **History**
President Carter meets with Egyptian president Anwar el-Sadat (left) and Israeli prime minister Menachem Begin (right). **Why were the Camp David Accords important?**

Any hope of the Senate approving SALT II disappeared in December 1979, when Soviet troops invaded **Afghanistan,** a country in southwestern Asia bordering the Soviet Union. Carter ordered sanctions against the Soviet Union. The United States and other nations refused to take part in the Olympic Games in Moscow. In addition, the United States imposed a grain embargo on the Soviet Union.

Crisis in Iran

In the 1970s, **Iran** was one of the strongest U.S. allies in the Persian Gulf region, an area vital to Western oil needs. Shah Mohammed Reza Pahlavi, the ruler of Iran, used U.S. aid to build up a powerful military force. Many Iranians, however, complained about corruption in the government. Others objected to Western influence in the country, which they felt weakened traditional Muslim values.

In January 1979, Islamic fundamentalists—people who believe in strict obedience to religious laws—forced the shah to flee Iran. The new ruler, Muslim leader **Ayatollah Khomeini,** was hostile to the United States because of its support of the shah.

Iranians present a blindfolded and handcuffed American hostage.

In November 1979, Iranian students, with the support of fundamentalists in the government, stormed the American embassy in **Tehran,** the capital of Iran, and held 52 Americans hostage. The United States was outraged. Attempts to negotiate the release of the hostages failed, and a daring desert rescue attempt ended in tragedy with the death of 8 American soldiers. The hostage crisis dragged on and became a major issue in the presidential election of 1980.

✓ **Reading Check** **Summarizing** Why did the United States boycott the 1980 Olympic Games?

The Election of 1980

The Iranian crisis damaged the president politically. By the time the election campaign began, Carter's popularity among the public had declined dramatically.

The Republicans nominated **Ronald Reagan** for president in 1980. In marked contrast to Carter, Reagan radiated charm and confidence. His conservative message of lower taxes, reduced spending, stronger defense, and a restoration of American pride attracted Americans weary of government and economic problems. When Reagan asked, "Are you better off now than you were four years ago?" most Americans answered, "No!"

Reagan swept to victory, with an electoral vote margin of 489 to 49. Republicans also gained control of the Senate for the first time since 1954. The election resulted in a bitter defeat for Jimmy Carter, who only 4 years earlier had promised a new era in American politics.

A final disappointment for Carter came in January 1981. During the last weeks of his presidency, he worked to obtain the release of the hostages. The Iranians finally did release them— after Ronald Reagan took the oath of office.

✓ **Reading Check** **Evaluating** How was Reagan perceived differently than Carter?

SECTION 3 ASSESSMENT

Checking for Understanding

1. **Key Terms** Use the following terms in a paragraph to help explain their meaning: trade deficit, human rights, apartheid, fundamentalist.
2. **Reviewing Facts** How did Jimmy Carter's manner differ from many other presidents'?

Reviewing Themes

3. **Global Connections** What issue guided Carter's foreign policy? How did the president attempt to implement this policy?

Critical Thinking

4. **Drawing Conclusions** Which of Carter's actions do you think did the greatest damage to his chances for reelection?
5. **Organizing Information** Re-create the diagram below and identify three problems facing the Carter administration and the actions taken in response.

Problems	Actions

Analyzing Visuals

6. **Picturing History** Study the picture at the top of this page. What effect do you think this image on television had on the American people? How do you think this picture and similar images affected Carter's campaign for a second term?

Interdisciplinary Activity

Geography Draw a world map and label the different countries that Carter dealt with during his presidency.

America's LITERATURE

Ernesto Galarza (1905–1984)

Like many immigrants who come to the United States, Ernesto Galarza arrived facing the challenge of adjusting to his adopted country. This excerpt from his autobiography, *Barrio Boy,* tells the story of how Galarza and his mother, Doña Henriqueta traveled from Mexico to California to meet his uncles, Gustavo and José. His story describes experiences common to those arriving in the United States then and now.

READ TO DISCOVER

Unable to speak English and unfamiliar with the customs in the United States, 6-year-old Galarza and his mother embarked on a new life. Their trip was a journey into another world for young Ernesto. As you read, think about what it would be like to move to a new country.

READER'S DICTIONARY

barrio: Spanish word for "neighborhood"

Tucson: a city in southeastern Arizona

Sacramento: the capital of California

Barrio Boy

In the sunny morning of the next day we walked back to the station. Our train was still there, the flats and boxcars and coaches deserted, Mexican and American soldiers walking back and forth. "Look, the American flag," my mother said. It was flying over a building near us. Down the street, beyond the depot, there was a Mexican flag on a staff. "We are in the United States. Mexico is over there." . . .

. . . In **Tucson** we found our way to the address Gustavo had sent. It was a small hotel where the clerk spoke Spanish. He took us down a long, dark hall to a room, where I immediately began to explore the remarkable inventions of the Americans.

. . . Regularly we went to the hotel to ask for mail from Gustavo. Almost always there was a letter with money, but it was many weeks before we received the most important one of all, the one that had the pass and the instructions for the trip. We were to take the train to **Sacramento,** go to the Hotel Español and stay there until Gustavo and José came for us.

. . . And from what I saw in the coach on that long ride, the Americans were indeed different. They ate the repulsive sandwiches with relish. They put their feet, shoes and all, on

the seats in front of them. When the men laughed it seemed more like a roar, and if they were close by it scared me. Doña Henriqueta frowned and admonished me. "Be careful I never hear you braying like that." Many of them kept their hats on as if they didn't know that the inside of a coach was like the inside of a house, and wearing your hat in either a sure sign of being *mal educado* [ill-mannered].

From *Barrio Boy* by Ernesto Galarza. © 1971 by the University of Notre Dame Press. Used by permission of the publisher.

ANALYZING LITERATURE

1. **Recall and Interpret** What observations do Ernesto and his mother make about Americans?
2. **Evaluate and Connect** What parts of Ernesto's story are probably shared by all people coming to a new place?

Interdisciplinary Activity

Descriptive Writing Imagine that you are Ernesto writing a postcard to a friend in Mexico. Describe your impressions of America and of the people you've seen.

915

What were people's lives like in the past?

What might our lives be like in the future? These two pages will give you some clues to everyday life in the U.S. as you step back—and look ahead—with TIME Notebook.

Profile

After getting HIV from a blood-clotting drug when he was just 13, **RYAN WHITE** *was asked to speak before a Presidential Commission on AIDS in 1988:*

"I CAME FACE TO FACE WITH DEATH AT thirteen years old. I was diagnosed with AIDS: a killer. Doctors told me I'm not contagious. Given six months to live and being the fighter that I am, I set high goals for myself. It was my decision to live a normal life, go to school, be with my friends, and enjoy day-to-day activities. It was not going to be easy.

The school I was going to said they had no guidelines for a person with AIDS.... We began a series of court battles for nine months, while I was attending classes by telephone. Eventually, I won the right to attend school, but the prejudice was still there."

Ryan White

HUBBARD-LIAISON

Future Medicine

"TAKE 200 TINY ROBOTS and call me in the morning." Don't laugh. Your doctor may be saying that to you sometime during the next few decades.

Nanotechnologists are researchers and makers of microscopic robots. In the future, these germ-sized robots—called nanomachines—will cruise through your body, making sure everything's running in order. They'll report back to a mainframe that's also in your body to report on your condition. Then the tiny robots will scrape away blockages in the arteries, clean up dangerous cancer cells, and blast away blood clots.

Doctors predict that living to be 100 or older won't be any big deal—possibly in this generation. And you may have the nanorobots to thank for it!

FUTURE SHOCK

Population Growth in the United States

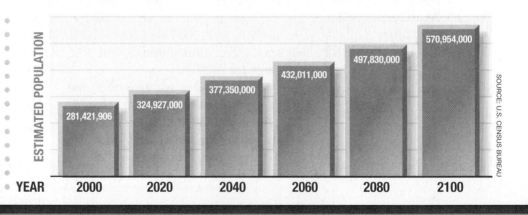

YEAR	2000	2020	2040	2060	2080	2100
ESTIMATED POPULATION	281,421,906	324,927,000	377,350,000	432,011,000	497,830,000	570,954,000

SOURCE: U.S. CENSUS BUREAU

MILESTONES

EVENTS AND PEOPLE OF THE TIME

HARMONIZED. MICHAEL JACKSON with 45 rock stars as they sing the tune Jackson co-wrote with Lionel Ritchie called "We Are the World." On April 5, 1985, about 5,000 radio stations around the world played the song at the same time—all in an effort to raise money for starving people in Africa. After just one year, "We Are the World" made over $44 million.

RELEASED. Fifty-two American **HOSTAGES** after 444 days in captivity in Iran. Held by terrorists who were angry over America's favorable treatment of Iran's former ruler, the group was snatched from the U.S. Embassy in Iran. The fact that the U.S. couldn't negotiate their release was a factor in **PRESIDENT JIMMY CARTER'S** 1980 election loss.

SPILLED. Over 11,000,000 gallons of crude oil in the clean waters of Prince William Sound, Alaska, in March 1989. A huge tanker struck a coral reef, dumping hundreds of thousands of barrels of crude oil into the water, devastating commercial fishing and wiping out precious Alaskan wildlife.

Oil-covered sea bird found in Prince William Sound, Alaska.

AL GRILLO/ALASKA STOCK

President Carter

BETTMANN/CORBIS

NUMBERS

U.S. AT THE TIME

11,600 The number of air traffic controllers who went on strike in 1981, grounding the nation's commercial airlines

70¢ The amount earned by a woman for every dollar earned by a man in 1987

E.T.

PHOTOFEST

$229,000,000 Ticket sales from the movie, *E.T., the Extra-Terrestrial*, released in 1982—one of the highest-grossing films ever

50% The percent of all African American children living in poverty in 1989

1,200,000 Los Angeles children in 1986 who observed a moment of silence in honor of astronaut and teacher Christa McAuliffe who was killed when the space shuttle *Challenger* exploded

Christa McAuliffe

TIME INC. PICTURE COLLECTION

FUTURE SHOCK

What You Do Today Affects Tomorrow's World

In May 2001, there were about 284 million people in the United States. India's population was about 1.03 billion. But Americans use 25 percent of the world's resources and cause 25 to 30 percent of the world's waste. Compared to the typical person in India, the average U.S. citizen uses:

50 times more steel

56 times more energy

170 times more synthetic rubber

170 times more newsprint

250 times more motor fuel

300 times more plastic

Chapter Summary
Search for Stability

Nixon's Foreign Policy

- Nixon opens relations with China and the Soviet Union
- U.S. backs an overthrow of Communist Chilean government

Nixon and Watergate

- Nixon introduces New Federalism
- Economy suffers under inflation
- White House involvement with Watergate break-in revealed
- Vice President Agnew resigns
- Nixon appoints Gerald Ford as new vice president
- Nixon resigns presidency

Ford and Carter

- Ford grants pardon to Nixon
- Ford continues détente with Soviet Union
- Inflation rises
- Carter makes energy policy a priority
- Carter bases foreign policy on human rights
- Carter works to bring peace in Middle East

- Islamic fundamentalists take 53 Americans hostage in Iran
- Carter loses 1980 election to Ronald Reagan

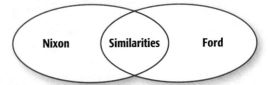

Reviewing Key Terms

On graph paper, create a word search puzzle using the following terms. Crisscross the terms vertically and horizontally, then fill in the remaining squares with extra letters. Use the terms' definitions as clues to find the words in the puzzle. Share your puzzle with a classmate.

1. détente
2. embargo
3. shuttle diplomacy
4. stagflation
5. deficit
6. impeachment
7. amnesty
8. human rights

Reviewing Key Facts

9. Which two nations were the focus of Nixon's attempt to ease Cold War tensions?
10. What was shuttle diplomacy?
11. Explain why President Nixon was forced to resign.
12. What did Congress do in the aftermath of Watergate?
13. Why did the United States lose its place as a world economic leader in the 1970s?
14. What did President Carter do to resolve the energy crisis?
15. How did Carter bring temporary peace to the Middle East?

Critical Thinking

16. **Analyzing Themes: Global Connections** What was Nixon's main reason for establishing friendly relations with the Soviet Union?
17. **Analyzing Information** What did Nixon do to create a New Federalism?
18. **Analyzing Themes: Global Connections** What did Carter think the United States should do to any nation that violated human rights?
19. **Drawing Conclusions** How did Carter's support of the shah of Iran ignore the interest of Islamic fundamentalists in that country?
20. **Analyzing Themes: Continuity and Change** Re-create the diagram below and describe how the foreign policies of Ford and Nixon were alike.

Nixon — Similarities — Ford

HISTORY Online

Self-Check Quiz
Visit taj.glencoe.com and click on **Chapter 31—Self-Check Quizzes** to prepare for the chapter test.

Geography and History Activity

In 1973 Saudi Arabia imposed an embargo, or a restriction of trade, on oil shipped to Israel's allies including the United States. At the same time, other OPEC countries raised their prices. Although the embargo was lifted in 1974, its economic effects continued through the end of the decade. Study the chart below; then answer the questions that follow.

Year	Consumption (Billions of gallons)	Cost per Gallon		
		Reg.	Prem.	No lead
1973	110.5	$ .40	.45	NA
1974	106.3	.53	.57	.55
1975	109.0	.57	.61	.60
1976	115.7	.59	.64	.61
1977	119.6	.62	.67	.66
1978	125.1	.63	.69	.67
1979	122.1	.86	.92	.90
1980	115.0	1.19	1.28	1.25

Gasoline Consumption and Prices

Source: *Statistical Abstract of the United States*

21. In what year did gasoline consumption first exceed 120 billion gallons?

22. How much more did a gallon of regular gasoline cost in 1980 than in 1973?

23. Based on billions of gallons of gas consumed, in which year shown on the chart was the environment most polluted with automobile fumes?

Practicing Skills Activity

24. **Predicting Consequences** Review the skill on predicting consequences on page 909. Then read the following statements and predict three consequences for each. Rank the three consequences in order of most likely to occur to least likely to occur.

   - If a person in a public office, including the president, commits a crime, he or she should not be pardoned.
   - Engineers develop an effective, efficient electric-powered automobile.
   - The school year is lengthened by 30 days.

Citizenship Cooperative Activity

25. **Serving on a Jury** Find people from your school or city who have served on a jury. Ask them to recall their impressions of the experience. With a partner, think about what happens if you have received a jury notice in the mail. Write a description of what you would do next and what you would expect to happen. Then note what you plan to tell the judge about your understanding of a juror's responsibilities. Share your writing with the class.

Alternative Assessment

26. **Expository Writing** Review the chapter and make a list of the successes and failures of Presidents Nixon, Ford, and Carter. Based on your list, which of the three would you vote for in a presidential election today? Explain your choice.

Standardized Test Practice

The Princeton Review

Directions: Choose the *best* answer to the following question.

Which of the following was a key feature of the Carter administration?

A   foreign policy based on human rights

B   emphasis on formality

C   clear economic policies

D   close cooperation with Congress

Test-Taking Tip:
Eliminate answers that you know are wrong. For example, Carter was different from his predecessors because he was personally casual. Therefore answer **B** must be wrong.

CHAPTER 32

New Challenges

1981–Present

Why It Matters

The 1980s and 1990s ushered in a period of great change. With the collapse of communism in Europe, relations between East and West changed dramatically. Former foes sought closer ties. At home, new advances in technology, medicine, and industry helped the nation move forward.

The Impact Today

The technological innovation during this period accounts for today's communications revolution and globalized economy.

 The American Journey Video *The chapter 32 video, "America Responds to Terrorism," focuses on how Americans united after the events of September 11, 2001.*

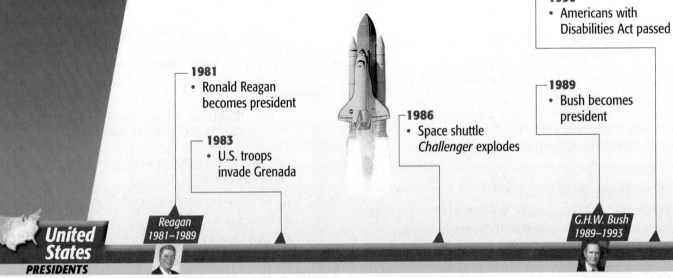

1990
• Americans with Disabilities Act passed

1981
• Ronald Reagan becomes president

1983
• U.S. troops invade Grenada

1986
• Space shuttle *Challenger* explodes

1989
• Bush becomes president

Reagan 1981–1989

G.H.W. Bush 1989–1993

United States
PRESIDENTS

1980

1985

1990

World

1980
• Solidarity trade union formed in Poland

1989
• Students protest in Tiananmen Square
• Fall of communism in Eastern Europe

1990
• Nelson Mandela released from South African prison

A New President George W. Bush was inaugurated the nation's forty-third president on January 20, 2001.

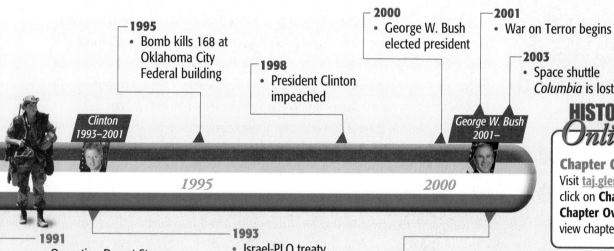

1995
• Bomb kills 168 at Oklahoma City Federal building

1998
• President Clinton impeached

2000
• George W. Bush elected president

2001
• War on Terror begins

2003
• Space shuttle *Columbia* is lost

Clinton 1993–2001

George W. Bush 2001–

1995

2000

1991
• Operation Desert Storm
• Breakup of Soviet Union; Apartheid ends in South Africa

1993
• Israel-PLO treaty signed

2001
• Former Yugoslav president Slobodan Milosevic arrested

HISTORY Online

Chapter Overview
Visit taj.glencoe.com and click on **Chapter 32— Chapter Overviews** to preview chapter information.

The Reagan Presidency

Main Idea
Ronald Reagan took a conservative approach to both domestic and foreign policy.

Key Terms
deregulation, federal debt, glasnost, perestroika

Reading Strategy
Classifying Information As you read the section, re-create the diagram below and provide three conservative actions taken by Ronald Reagan.

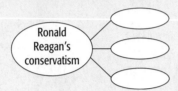

Ronald Reagan's conservatism

Read To Learn
- how Ronald Reagan implemented supply-side economics.
- how Ronald Reagan was active in foreign policy.
- how the Soviet Union changed.

Section Theme
Economic Factors Ronald Reagan was conservative at home and built up the military to counter the Soviet Union.

Preview of Events

◆1980   ◆1985   ◆1990

1981
Sandra Day O'Connor appointed to Supreme Court

1985
Mikhail Gorbachev becomes leader of Soviet Union

1987
Reagan and Gorbachev sign INF Treaty

AN American Story

President Reagan views a giant get-well card

On March 30, 1981, President Reagan gave a speech at the Washington Hilton. After the speech, the president left the hotel through a side entrance and passed through a line of press photographers and TV cameras. As he walked to his car, gunshots rang out. The president had been shot in the chest. Also injured were two security officers and the president's press secretary, James Brady. The assassin, John Hinckley, Jr., was quickly subdued. Despite the attempt on his life, the president never lost his sense of humor. In the operating room, he told the surgeons, "Please tell me you're Republicans."

The Reagan Revolution

Ronald Reagan's election to the presidency in 1980 marked a significant conservative shift in America. The conservative movement grew across the country, particularly in the South and Southwest, a region known as the **Sunbelt.** When the Sunbelt's population increased during the 1970s, the conservative movement gained political power.

Many Americans wanted a return to what President Ronald Reagan, a former actor with Illinois small-town roots, called "traditional American values"—an emphasis on family life, hard work, respect for law, and patriotism. They shared the conservative view that the federal government made too many rules, collected too much in taxes, and spent too much money on social programs.

Air Traffic Controllers' Strike

A few months after Ronald Reagan became president, the nation's air traffic controllers went on strike. They refused to go back to work despite the president's orders to do so. President Reagan acted at once, firing the controllers and ordering military staff to oversee air traffic while new controllers were trained to do the work.

President Carter had been criticized for his lack of leadership and indecision. With this action, Ronald Reagan showed that he would stand firm and use his position as president to carry out the policies in which he believed.

Deregulation

As part of his promise to reduce government and "get the government off the backs of the American people," President Reagan pursued a policy of deregulation. This meant cutting the rules and regulations government agencies placed on businesses. Under President Reagan, for example, the Department of Transportation wrote new rules for automobile exhaust systems and safety measures that were easier for car manufacturers to meet.

The Supreme Court

Reagan also put a conservative stamp on the Supreme Court by naming justices to the Court who shared his views. He appointed **Sandra Day O'Connor** in 1981, the first woman ever appointed to the Court. Reagan later appointed **Antonin Scalia** and **Anthony Kennedy.**

Reaganomics

Deregulation and his court appointments showed President Reagan's commitment to a conservative view of government. It was his

Picturing **History**

Sandra Day O'Connor appears with Supreme Court Chief Justice Warren Burger on the steps of the Supreme Court building. **Why was O'Connor's appointment significant?**

economic policies, however, that formed the core of the "Reagan Revolution." Reagan believed that lower taxes would allow individuals and corporations to invest in new businesses. Because a tax cut would mean less income, Reagan also called for less government spending. Supporters called Reagan's economic policy **supply-side economics** because it proposed to stimulate the economy by increasing the supply of goods and services. The president's critics ridiculed the policy as "Reaganomics."

In 1981 Congress lowered taxes and slashed nearly $40 billion from federal programs such as school lunches, student aid, welfare, low-income housing, and food stamps. Critics charged that these cuts hurt both the working poor and unemployed people. Supporters argued that Reaganomics would boost the economy, helping everybody in the long run.

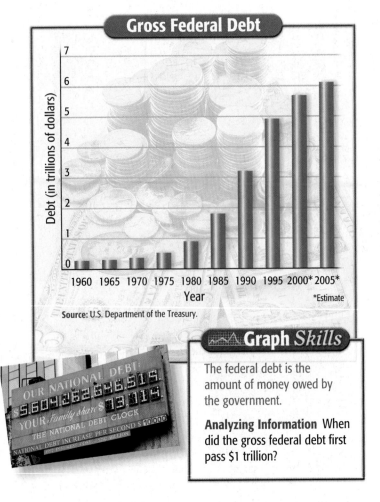

Gross Federal Debt

Debt (in trillions of dollars)

Year

*Estimate

Source: U.S. Department of the Treasury.

OUR NATIONAL DEBT:
$5,604,626,646,515.
YOUR *Family share* $73,014
THE NATIONAL DEBT CLOCK
NATIONAL DEBT INCREASE PER SECOND $10,000

Graph Skills

The federal debt is the amount of money owed by the government.

Analyzing Information When did the gross federal debt first pass $1 trillion?

While Reagan cut domestic programs, he pushed for sharp increases in military spending. The president declared that the Soviet threat made it necessary to build up the military.

Government Debt

With higher defense spending and lower taxes, the government spent more money than it collected in revenue. It had to borrow money to make up the difference. This borrowing increased the federal debt—the amount of money owed by the government. Between 1970 and 1980, the federal debt had grown from $381 to $909 billion. By 1990 the debt had jumped to $3.2 trillion.

$ Economics
Recession and Recovery

President Reagan's new economic policies seemed to falter when a serious recession began early in his first term. However, the economy recovered a year later and began to boom.

In 1983 the economy began a long, steady rise. Businesses expanded, and the high jobless rate of 1982 declined. Investors showed confidence in the economy with a boom in stock trading.

The federal debt continued to grow as well. In 1985 Congress tried to halt growth of the debt by passing the **Gramm-Rudman-Hollings Act.** The act set a series of targets for eliminating the federal budget deficit by 1991. If Congress and the president could not agree on *voluntary* spending cuts, the law called for *automatic* spending cuts to balance the budget. The provision for automatic cuts did not apply to all areas of the budget, however, so it had limited success.

Reading Check **Explaining** What is the amount of money the government owes called?

Reagan's Foreign Policy

Ronald Reagan pledged in his campaign to wage a tough fight against communism. To carry out his policy, President Reagan launched a massive buildup of the military. He expanded the American arsenal of tanks, ships, aircraft, and nuclear missiles. He defended these actions by quoting George Washington's advice: "To be prepared for war is one of the most effective means of preserving peace."

Reagan also proposed an antimissile defense system, the **Strategic Defense Initiative** (SDI). Nicknamed "Star Wars," the SDI would provide a defensive shield against enemy missiles. However, scientists were unable to develop the technology for the SDI.

Latin America

Besides building up the nation's military strength, Reagan also committed American forces and aid to the fight against communism, especially in nearby Latin America.

Late in the Carter presidency, Communist rebels in **Nicaragua**—called **Sandinistas**—had overthrown the government. After becoming president, Reagan sent aid to the **contras,** a group battling the Sandinistas. The fighting in Nicaragua continued for many years and became a source of disagreement between President Reagan and Congress.

In October 1983, President Reagan took direct military action in the Caribbean. Rebels on the tiny Caribbean island of Grenada staged an uprising. Concerned about the fate of 800 American medical students on the island, Reagan dispatched troops to rescue the Americans and establish a prodemocracy government. Reagan's action won widespread approval at home.

The Middle East

President Reagan was less successful with peace efforts in the Middle East. In 1982, he sent a force of marines to help keep the peace in the war-torn nation of Lebanon. The Americans soon were caught in a web of violence. A car bomb blast killed more than 60 people at the U.S. embassy in Beirut in April 1983. Then in October, 241 Americans and 58 French died in attacks on U.S. and French military headquarters. Rather than become more deeply involved in the struggle, the president withdrew all U.S. forces from Lebanon.

✓ Reading Check **Summarizing** What is SDI?

Reagan's Second Term

By 1984 the American economy was booming. In his State of the Union Address, President Reagan declared:

❝America is back—standing tall, looking [toward the future] with courage, confidence and hope.❞

President Reagan and Vice President **George Bush** continued using this optimistic theme in their campaign for reelection. The Democrats chose **Walter Mondale,** vice president under Jimmy Carter, and **Geraldine Ferraro,** a member of Congress from New York. Ferraro became the first woman to run for vice president on a major political party ticket.

Reagan won the electoral votes of 49 out of 50 states. It was one of the most lopsided presidential elections in American history. Spurred on by high employment, a strong economy, and low interest rates, Reagan enjoyed high popularity ratings early in his second term.

Fact · Fiction Folklore

Presidents and Labor Unions

President Reagan was once president of a labor union. The former broadcaster, Hollywood screen actor, and governor of California was president of the Screen Actors' Guild. He is the only president to have also been the chief official of a union.

The Iran-Contra Scandal

Despite his popularity, a scandal cast a shadow over part of President Reagan's second term. Terrorists, with ties to the Iranian government, held U.S. citizens hostage in Lebanon. Hoping to secure the release of the hostages, Reagan officials made a deal with Iran.

Marine lieutenant colonel **Oliver North** and Navy vice admiral John Poindexter, both assigned to the White House National Security Council, arranged for the sale of weapons to Iran in return for help in freeing American hostages. North and Poindexter decided to funnel money from this secret arms sale to help the Nicaraguan contras.

News of these deals—which came to be known as the **Iran-Contra scandal**—created an uproar. Critics charged that these deals violated federal laws barring officials from aiding the contras. They also said that the deals violated the Constitution by interfering with Congress's role in making foreign policy. Congress held hearings to determine whether the president took part in breaking the law. But there was never any proof of the president's involvement.

A Changing Soviet Policy

A remarkable shift in Soviet-American relations began to take shape at the beginning of Reagan's second term as president. Changes in Soviet leadership helped trigger the change. In 1985 Communist Party leaders of the Soviet Union chose a new general secretary, or leader—**Mikhail Gorbachev.** To the surprise of people all around the world, Gorbachev was committed to reforming the Soviet government. He called for a policy of glasnost—opening Soviet society to new ideas.

Picturing **History**

President Reagan and Soviet leader Gorbachev shake hands at their June 1988 summit meeting in Moscow. **What major step did both leaders take earlier toward ending the threat of nuclear war?**

Gorbachev also tried to change the way his country was governed. Moving away from the government's near-total control of the economy, he allowed more democracy and local economic planning. This new policy, perestroika, encouraged the Soviets to seek even greater changes.

With the Soviet economy in trouble, Gorbachev knew that the Soviet Union could not afford to build nuclear weapons. At several meetings he tried to convince President Reagan that he wanted to end the nuclear arms race. These early meetings accomplished little.

In 1987, however, President Reagan and Premier Gorbachev signed an agreement, the **Intermediate-Range Nuclear Forces (INF) Treaty.** The treaty aimed to reduce the number of nuclear missiles in each superpower's arsenal. Reagan explained the agreement by quoting what he said was a Russian proverb: "Trust, but verify." While both nations still held vast nuclear arsenals, they had taken a major step toward reducing the threat of nuclear war.

✓ **Reading Check** **Explaining** What were glasnost and perestroika?

SECTION 1 ASSESSMENT

Checking for Understanding

1. **Key Terms** Use each of these terms in a complete sentence that will help explain its meaning: deregulation, federal debt, glasnost, perestroika
2. **Reviewing Facts** List two of President Reagan's actions that proved he was committed to creating a more conservative government.

Reviewing Themes

3. **Economic Factors** Why did President Reagan believe that lowering taxes would aid the economy?

Critical Thinking

4. **Drawing Conclusions** Do you think Reagan administration officials were justified in violating congressional laws in the Iran-Contra incident? Explain.
5. **Organizing Information** Re-create the diagram below and explain why each of these people was in the news.

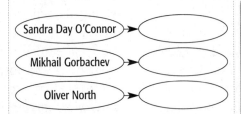

Sandra Day O'Connor →

Mikhail Gorbachev →

Oliver North →

Analyzing Visuals

6. **Graph Skills** Review the graph of the Gross Federal Debt shown on page 924. What years are shown? What was the first year the debt was almost twice the amount it was five years before?

Interdisciplinary Activity

Research Find the literal meaning of the terms *contras* (Spanish) and *perestroika* (Russian). Then find an English word or phrase that has the same meaning. Use the two terms in a complete sentence.

Technology SKILLBUILDER

Using an Electronic Spreadsheet

Why Learn This Skill?

People use electronic spreadsheets to manage numbers quickly and easily. You can use a spreadsheet any time a problem involves numbers that you can arrange in rows and columns.

Learning the Skill

A spreadsheet is an electronic worksheet. All spreadsheets follow a basic design of rows and columns. Each column (vertical) is assigned a letter or a number. Each row (horizontal) is assigned a number. Each point where a column and row intersect is called a *cell*. The cell's position on the spreadsheet is labeled according to its corresponding column and row—Column A, Row 1 (A1); Column B, Row 2 (B2), etc.

Spreadsheets use *standard formulas* to calculate the numbers. You create a simple mathematical equation that uses these standard formulas and the computer does the calculations for you.

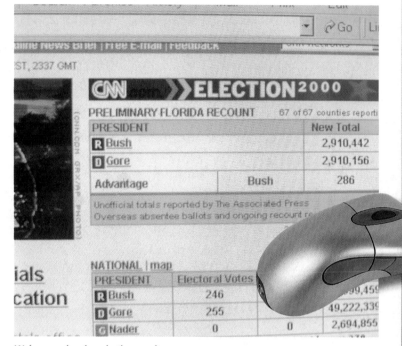

Web page showing election results

Practicing the Skill

Suppose you want to know how many votes the Republican, Democratic, and Independent candidates received across six states in the 2000 presidential election. Use these steps to create a spreadsheet that will provide this information:

1 In cells B1, C1, and D1 respectively, type a candidate's name or political party. In cell E1, type the term *total*.

2 In cells A2–A7, type the name of a state. In cell A8, type the word *total*.

3 In row 2, enter the number of votes each candidate received in the state named in cell A2. Repeat this process in rows 3–7.

4 Create a formula to calculate the votes. The formula for the equation tells what cells (B2 + C2 + D2) to add together.

5 Copy the formula down in the cells for the other five states.

6 Use the process in steps 4 and 5 to create and copy a formula to calculate the total number of votes each candidate received.

Applying the Skill

Using a Spreadsheet Use a spreadsheet to enter your test scores and your homework grades. At the end of the grading period, the spreadsheet will calculate your average grade.

The Bush Presidency

Guide to Reading

Main Idea
George Bush had an active foreign policy and presided over the fall of the Soviet Union and the end of the Cold War.

Key Terms
coup, bankruptcy

Reading Strategy
Organizing Information As you read the section, re-create the time line below and provide three key events leading to the fall of communism.

1980	1989	1990

Read To Learn
- how the Soviet Union collapsed.
- how George Bush used the military overseas.
- how George Bush had difficulty domestically.

Section Theme
Global Connections Great political changes marked the global situation during George Bush's presidency.

Preview of Events

♦1988   ♦1990   ♦1992

1988
George Bush is elected president

June 1989
Chinese students protest in Tiananmen Square

November 1989
The Berlin Wall is torn down

January 1991
Allies launch Operation Desert Storm

December 1991
The Soviet Union is dismantled

AN
American Story

On September 2, 1944, a young pilot took part in a bombing mission against Japanese bases. World War II was raging. His plane—launched from an aircraft carrier—suffered a direct hit from a Japanese anti-aircraft gun. The pilot and his two crew members bailed out into the Pacific Ocean. A U.S. submarine rescued the pilot from a life raft, but the other two men were never found. For his heroism, the pilot—George Bush—was awarded the Distinguished Flying Cross. More than 40 years later, Bush would become the forty-first president of the United States.

Navy pilot George Bush during World War II

A New World Order

As Ronald Reagan's second term drew to a close, the election campaign for his successor heated up. Vice President **George H.W. Bush** swept through the 1988 primaries to win the Republican presidential nomination. Bush chose Indiana senator **Dan Quayle** as his running mate. Many Democrats vied for their party's nomination, but the field quickly narrowed to two candidates—civil rights leader **Jesse Jackson** and Massachusetts governor **Michael Dukakis.** Dukakis, who ran the most effective primary campaign, won the nomination and chose Senator **Lloyd Bentsen** of Texas as his running mate.

On Election Day, Bush carried 40 states, giving him 426 electoral votes to 112 for Dukakis. However, Bush's victory did not extend to Congress. The Democrats retained control of the House and the Senate.

A Changing Soviet Union

With much experience in foreign affairs, newly elected president George Bush was called upon to steer the United States through a time of sweeping change facing the world. Many important changes dealt with the Soviet Union.

In December 1988, Soviet leader Mikhail Gorbachev stood before the United Nations to describe the "new world order" to come. Gorbachev stressed that people throughout the world wanted "independence, democracy, and social justice."

Gorbachev wanted to end the arms race so he could focus on reforms within the Soviet Union. He sought to continue the progress on arms control begun with President Reagan. In 1990 Gorbachev and President Bush agreed with European leaders to destroy tanks and other conventional weapons positioned throughout Europe. In 1991, with the **Strategic Arms Reduction Treaty** (START), they achieved a breakthrough. For the first time, two nuclear powers agreed to destroy existing nuclear weapons.

Unrest in the Soviet Union

Most Soviet citizens, however, were more concerned about their own problems than about arms control. For years they had endured shortages of food and basic items such as shoes and soap because of government mismanagement

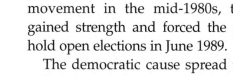

Lech Walesa

and heavy defense spending. Gorbachev's policies aimed to solve the economic problems, but changes came slowly. The shortages continued, and people grew impatient with the conditions.

With Gorbachev's policy of glasnost, Soviet citizens began to express their dissatisfaction openly. Thousands of people marched through Moscow in February 1990, demanding an end to Communist rule. Unrest and calls for democracy had also spread throughout the Soviet Union. Many of the republics that made up the Soviet Union demanded independence.

A Rising Tide of Freedom

While events were unfolding in the Soviet Union, the people of Eastern Europe also grew restless. Many people sensing change occurring in the Soviet Union under Gorbachev's leadership felt freer to demand change in their countries as well.

The first democratic moves outside of the Soviet Union occurred in **Poland,** where shipyard workers had won the right to form an independent labor union—called **Solidarity**—in August 1980. **Lech Walesa,** the leader of Solidarity, emerged as a symbol of resistance to Communist rule. He led the Poles in calling for reforms. Although the government cracked down on the democratic movement in the mid-1980s, the movement gained strength and forced the government to hold open elections in June 1989.

The democratic cause spread to neighboring countries. Across Eastern Europe demonstrators filled the streets of major cities. As a result of a relaxation of Soviet control and public pressure, long-sealed national borders were opened and Communist governments toppled. In the last three months of 1989, the iron curtain that had separated Eastern and Western Europe for more than 40 years began to crumble. Throughout 1989 Gorbachev not only refused to intervene, but he encouraged reform.

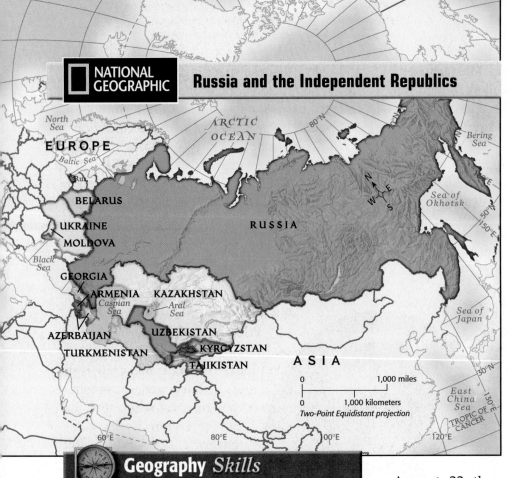

Geography *Skills*

By the early 1990s, all the republics had declared independence from the Soviet Union.

1. Location What republics border Belarus?

2. Location Which of the republics have the best access to shipping lanes in the Black Sea?

The Wall Comes Tumbling Down

Freedom also came to East Germany—the focus of so much cold war tension. With protests raging and thousands of citizens fleeing to West Germany, the Communist government opened the Berlin Wall on November 9, 1989.

Germans brought hammers and chisels to chop away at the Berlin Wall, long the symbol of the barrier to the West. In 1990 East Germany voted to reunite with West Germany.

Collapse of the Soviet Union

As Europe was changing, Gorbachev faced mounting opposition from political rivals within the Soviet Union. Some reformers demanded that he move more quickly. Hard-line Communists in the military and secret police resisted his changes and feared the collapse of the Soviet empire.

In August 1991, the hard-liners struck back. A group of Communist officials and army generals staged a coup, an overthrow of the government. They held Gorbachev captive and ordered soldiers to seize the parliament building.

As the world waited anxiously, about 50,000 Russians surrounded the parliament building to protect it from the soldiers. **Boris Yeltsin,** president of the Russian Republic and a reformer, stood on top of a tank and declared, "Democracy will win!" President Bush telephoned Yeltsin to express America's support. On August 22 the coup collapsed. Freed, Gorbachev returned to Moscow.

The defeat of the coup turned the tide of democracy into a tidal wave. Soon all 15 republics had declared their independence from the Soviet Union. Yeltsin outlawed the Communist Party in Russia. On December 25, 1991, Gorbachev announced the end of the Soviet Union and the Soviet flag that flew over the Kremlin was lowered for the last time.

The End of the Cold War

President Bush responded quickly to the new situation. In the spring of 1992, Bush and other world leaders pledged $24 billion in assistance to the former Soviet republics. President Bush declared:

    ❝❝For over 40 years, the United States led the West in the struggle against communism and the threat it posed to our most precious values. That confrontation is over.❞❞

✓ **Reading Check** **Cause and Effect** How did the fall of communism in Eastern Europe affect Germany?

A New Foreign Policy

With the end of the Cold War came both renewed hope and new challenges to maintaining world peace. While trying to redefine the goals of American foreign policy, President Bush had to deal with crises in Central America, China, the Middle East, and the Balkans.

Panama

President Bush had declared that a "war on drugs" was one of the major goals of his administration. This war played a role in Bush's policy in Central America.

Under the rule of General **Manuel Noriega,** political repression and corruption had become widespread in Panama. In 1988 Noriega was charged with drug trafficking by an American court. Previously, he had refused to yield power to the newly elected president of Panama, Guillermo Endara. In December 1989, Bush ordered U.S. troops to the Central American nation to overthrow Noriega. When the troops gained control of the country, Noriega surrendered. Endara became Panama's new president, and the U.S. troops left Panama. In 1992 Noriega was tried and convicted in the United States.

China

George Bush had served as the first U.S. **envoy**—diplomatic representative—to China, when the two countries reopened relations in 1974. He took a special interest in China, claiming, "I know the Chinese." During the 1980s, China's Communist government began to reform the economy, but it refused to make political reforms. In May 1989, students and workers in China held demonstrations calling for more democracy. As the protests spread, the country seemed on the verge of revolution.

The Chinese government sent troops to crush the uprising. On June 4, 1989, soldiers and tanks killed several hundred protesters gathered in **Tiananmen Square** in the center of Beijing. World leaders condemned the slaughter. Although President Bush disapproved of the Chinese leaders' use of force, he carefully avoided words or actions that might lead the Chinese to break off relations with the United States. He did not believe that international pressure or trade sanctions would result in a change in Chinese policies. Although Bush's policy met opposition, it permitted U.S. trade with China to continue to grow.

The Persian Gulf War

The Bush administration—and the world—faced a serious challenge to stability in 1990. On August 2 Iraq's dictator, **Saddam Hussein** (hoo•SAYN), sent his army into **Kuwait,** a small neighboring country rich in oil. Kuwait was quickly overwhelmed. The fear grew that Iraq would also invade Saudi Arabia.

Vowing to "draw a line in the sand," President Bush persuaded other nations to join what he called **Operation Desert Shield.** Hundreds of thousands of troops moved to Saudi Arabia to prevent an invasion of that country. The coalition forces were under the command of U. S. general **Norman Schwarzkopf.** Hussein was ordered to withdraw his troops from Kuwait—but the Iraqi troops did not leave and tension mounted. The United Nations set a deadline. Iraq must withdraw by January 15, 1991, or the allies would use force to remove them. Congress voted to support military action if Iraq did not withdraw.

Operation Desert Storm

Iraq refused to budge, and on January 16 the allies launched **Operation Desert Storm.** Laser-guided missiles and thousands of tons of bombs

Students demanding democratic reform gathered in Tiananmen Square.

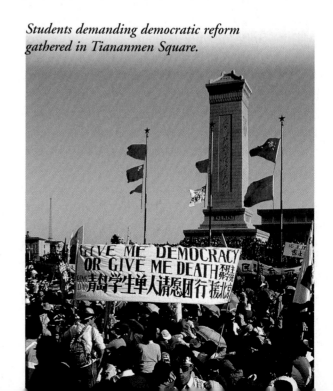

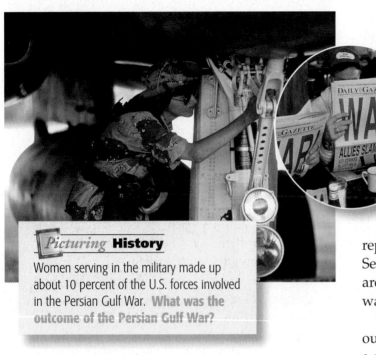

Women serving in the military made up about 10 percent of the U.S. forces involved in the Persian Gulf War. **What was the outcome of the Persian Gulf War?**

fell on Iraq, destroying its air defenses and other military targets and damaging many civilian sites. President Bush explained the attack:

❝The world could wait no longer. . . . While the world waited, Saddam Hussein met every overture of peace with open contempt.❞

After almost six weeks of round-the-clock bombardment, Hussein's forces still refused to leave Kuwait. In late February the allies opened the second phase of Desert Storm—a ground war in which they attacked Iraqi troops from the side and rear. At the same time, planes bombarded Iraqi positions.

Thousands of Iraqi soldiers died. Thousands more surrendered. Just 100 hours after the ground war began, President Bush suspended military action. "Kuwait is liberated," he announced. "America and the world have kept their word." Iraq accepted the allied cease-fire terms, and Saddam Hussein's troops finally left Kuwait.

Americans celebrated the sudden victory. They hailed the leaders of Desert Storm, Norman Schwarzkopf and General **Colin Powell,** chairman of the Joint Chiefs of Staff, and held parades for the troops. President Bush's approval rating in opinion polls soared above 90 percent. After the war, the United States helped rebuild Kuwait. It took nine months to extinguish the hundreds of oil well fires set by fleeing Iraqi troops.

War in the Balkans

Another challenge to world peace arose in Yugoslavia. Yugoslavia had been composed of several republics. After the collapse of Yugoslavia's government, the republics of **Slovenia, Croatia,** and **Bosnia-Herzegovina** declared independence in 1991. The population of Croatia and Bosnia included many Serbs—people from the Yugoslav republic of Serbia. These Serbs, backed by the Serbian republic, fought to hold on to certain areas of Croatia and Bosnia. In the terrible civil war that followed, thousands died.

Reports of atrocities committed by the Serbs outraged world leaders. In 1992 the UN passed a resolution that placed a boycott on trade with Serbia until the fighting stopped.

✓**Reading Check** **Evaluating** How long did Operation Desert Storm last?

Domestic Issues

Early in his presidency, Bush faced a banking crisis. During the 1980s, the Reagan administration had cut regulations in many industries. New laws eased restrictions on savings and loan associations (S&Ls)—financial institutions that specialized in making loans to buy homes.

The new laws allowed managers of S&Ls to become more aggressive in offering attractive returns to savers—and in making far more risky loans. When many borrowers could not repay their loans and real estate values declined, S&Ls began to lose millions of dollars. Many failed completely and closed their doors. Individual deposits in S&Ls were insured by the government, which now had to pay out billions of dollars to the customers of the failed institutions. To prevent the crisis from spreading, the government bailed out other struggling S&Ls. This policy eventually cost taxpayers almost $500 billion.

Economic Downturn

The heavy borrowing of the 1980s loomed as another source of trouble for the economy. As the federal debt continued to reach new highs, business and personal debt grew as well. In 1990, when the economy slowed to a recession, many people and businesses could not meet loan payments. Some had to declare bankruptcy, selling off everything they owned to pay debts. Across the country businesses closed. Cuts in military spending, made possible by the end of the Cold War, led to additional job losses.

Many people called for the government to step in to stimulate the economy. President Bush refused to increase federal spending. He did agree to extend unemployment benefits for people who had lost their jobs, but he opposed further government involvement. The nation had to wait out the recession.

Accomplishments

While the president and Congress disagreed on many issues, they cooperated on some legislation. In 1990, for example, the president signed a law updating the Clean Air Act. The next year he signed a law combating job discrimination.

Bush and Congress agreed on a major civil rights law as well. The Americans with Disabilities Act of 1990 outlawed job discrimination against people with disabilities. It also required institutions to provide disabled people with easier access to workplaces, communications, transportation, and housing.

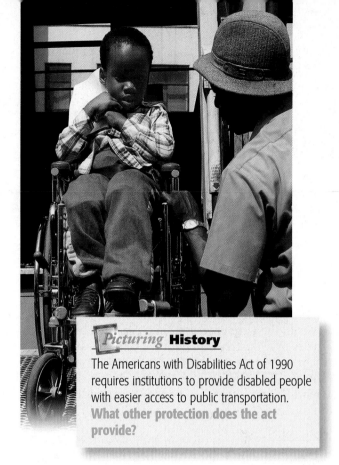

Picturing **History**

The Americans with Disabilities Act of 1990 requires institutions to provide disabled people with easier access to public transportation. **What other protection does the act provide?**

Another important part of the president's domestic agenda was the war on illegal drugs. In 1989 President Bush created the Office of National Drug Control Policy. This department coordinates the activities of more than 50 federal agencies involved in the war on drugs.

✓ Reading Check **Identifying** What is an S&L?

SECTION 2 ASSESSMENT

Checking for Understanding

1. **Key Terms** Use each of these terms in a complete sentence that will help explain its meaning: coup, bankruptcy

2. **Reviewing Facts** Explain why the people of Eastern Europe abandoned communism.

Reviewing Themes

3. **Global Connections** Compare President Bush's handling of the Tiananmen Square incident in China to his handling of Iraq's invasion of Kuwait.

Critical Thinking

4. **Determining Cause and Effect** What economic issues reduced Bush's popularity?

5. **Organizing Information** Re-create the diagram below and list what each person did to cause Bush to respond with military power.

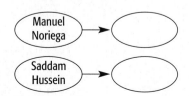

Analyzing Visuals

6. **Geography Skills** Examine the map on page 930. Which of the independent states is larger—Georgia or Uzbekistan? What bodies of water does Russia border?

GLOBAL CANDY

THE CHOCOLATE CANDY that you buy at your local store is produced by a vast network of people and businesses all around the world.

The raw ingredients for chocolate are grown all over the world, then are processed into candy in high-tech factories in industrialized nations. Cacao beans, chocolate's primary raw material, are gathered from trees in countries along the Equator. Approximately 40 percent of the world's cacao comes from the West African nation of Côte d'Ivoire.

Sugar to sweeten chocolate is processed from sugarcane and sugar beets. Major exporters of sugar are found in nearly every continent.

Almond trees grow in Morocco, Iran, in southern Europe, and on the west coast of the United States.

Cacao beans are processed into cocoa butter and mixed with other ingredients in factories located mainly in Western Europe and North America. The exact process and the proportions of ingredients are usually closely guarded secrets.

Chocolate is an international product. Before World War II most products were made in a single country. As transportation and communication networks have improved, more and more multinational companies have come to rely on natural resources and manufacturing facilities in many countries. Now roughly one third of all products produced involve several nations. What we decide to buy today affects people and businesses all around the world.

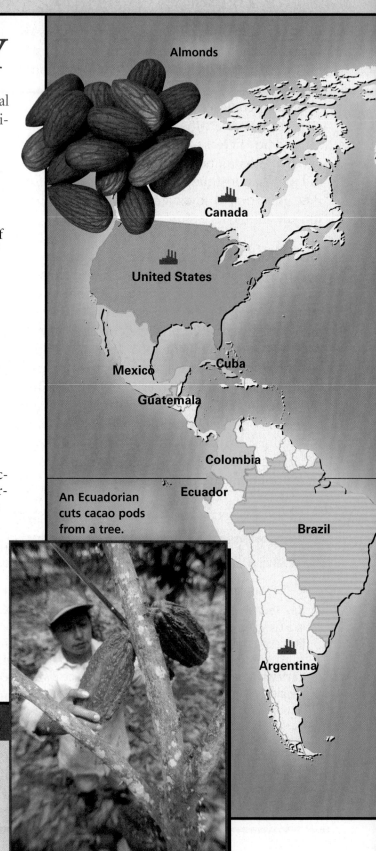

An Ecuadorian cuts cacao pods from a tree.

LEARNING from GEOGRAPHY

1. **Why would a nation need to import resources rather than use its own?**

2. **What patterns do you see in the locations of the countries that grow cacao? Almonds?**

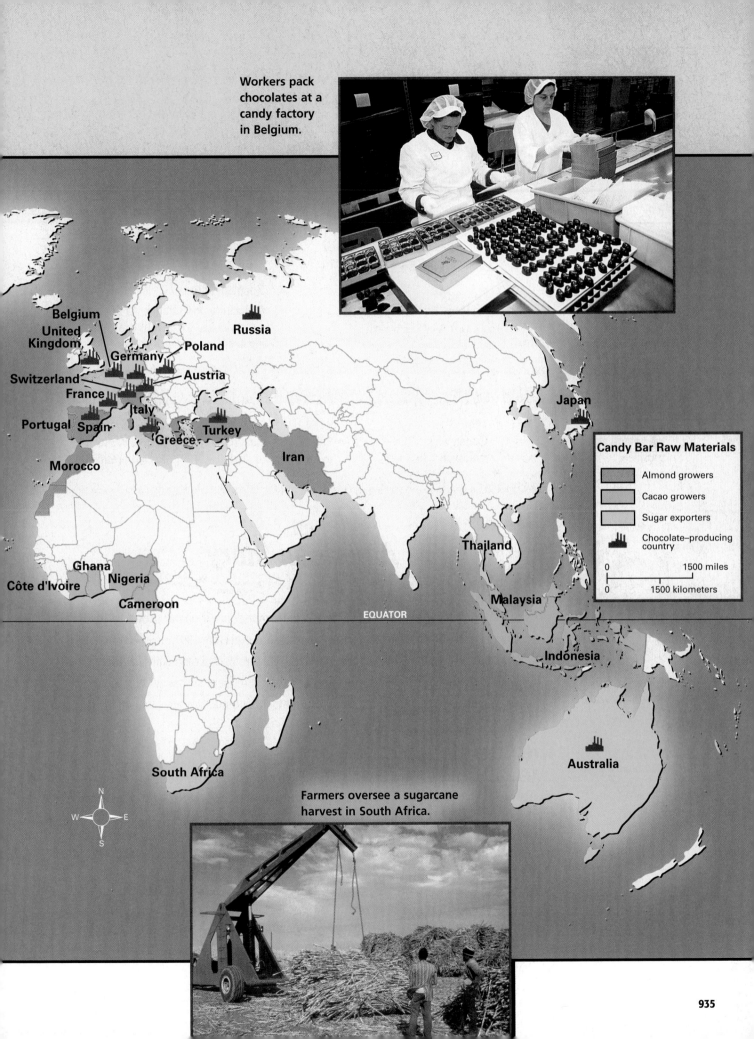

Workers pack chocolates at a candy factory in Belgium.

Belgium
United Kingdom
Switzerland
France
Portugal
Spain
Morocco

Germany
Italy
Greece

Russia
Poland
Austria
Turkey
Iran

Japan

Ghana
Côte d'Ivoire
Nigeria
Cameroon

Thailand
Malaysia

EQUATOR

Indonesia

South Africa

Australia

Candy Bar Raw Materials

	Almond growers
	Cacao growers
	Sugar exporters
🏭	Chocolate–producing country

0	1500 miles
0	1500 kilometers

Farmers oversee a sugarcane harvest in South Africa.

A New Century

Guide to Reading

Main Idea
During the Clinton and Bush administrations, the nation faced new challenges at home and abroad.

Key Terms
grassroots, budget deficit, line-item veto, gross domestic product, impeach, incumbent, Internet, ozone, global warming, terrorism

Reading Strategy
Classifying Information As you read the section, re-create the diagram below and describe three domestic programs of the 1990s.

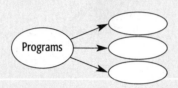

Read to Learn
• why President Clinton was impeached by Congress.
• why the election of 2000 triggered controversy.

Section Theme
Continuity and Change As the nation looked to the future, a changing world created new challenges.

Preview of Events

1992 — 1996 — 2000

1992
Bill Clinton elected president

1996
Clinton wins reelection

1998
Impeachment trial results in Clinton's acquittal

2000
George W. Bush elected president

Clinton inaugural button

AN American Story

A president appears on MTV. Politicians perform rock music on talk shows. What would George Washington have thought about such events? In 1991, polls showed that voters were turned off by politics. So the 1992 presidential candidates found new ways to reach the public—especially young people. President Bush and challenger Bill Clinton appeared on TV and radio talk shows. Both candidates appeared on MTV.

The Clinton Administration

After the Gulf War victory, President Bush's popularity soared. A troubled economy, however, hurt Bush's reelection chances for 1992 and encouraged challengers to enter the race. The Democrats nominated Arkansas governor **Bill Clinton** to run against President Bush. Clinton chose Tennessee senator **Al Gore** as his running mate. The Clinton campaign focused on the economy and the high unemployment rate.

Unhappy with "politics as usual," many Americans did not want to vote for either Bush or Clinton. A grassroots movement—people organizing at the local level around the nation—put Texas businessman **H. Ross Perot** on the ballot as a third-party candidate. Perot stressed the need to end the government's **deficit spending,** or spending more money than it takes in.

Americans elected Clinton, the first president born after World War II. Clinton received 43 percent of the popular vote, Bush 38 percent, and Perot 19 percent. Clinton received less than a majority of the votes because of Perot's strong showing, the highest percentage of popular votes for any third-party candidate since Theodore Roosevelt in 1912.

Domestic Program

One of the new president's goals was reducing the budget deficit—the amount by which spending exceeds revenue. Clinton proposed cutting government spending, raising taxes for middle- and upper-income Americans, and providing tax credits to the poorest. Most Republicans in Congress opposed this plan, but it narrowly passed.

Clinton faced even stronger opposition to his plan for health-care reform. His goal was to control rising health-care costs and provide adequate health insurance for every American. The president named the First Lady, **Hillary Rodham Clinton,** to head the task force.

Congress rejected the Clinton plan, calling it too expensive and too reliant on government control. Later, Congress did pass a number of measures that provided more health-care protection for workers who changed jobs, the elderly, children, and other groups not covered.

During his first term, President Clinton won some legislative battles. Despite strong opposition, the president succeeded in passing the Brady Bill of 1993. The law imposed a waiting period and background checks for handgun purchases. The 1994 crime bill banned 19 kinds of assault weapons and provided for 100,000 new police officers.

Another Clinton proposal that became law was the Family and Medical Leave Act of 1993. It permitted workers to take time off from their jobs for special family situations.

Contract with America

Before the 1994 congressional elections, a group of Republicans crafted a new plan of action. Led by Representative Newt Gingrich of Georgia, congressional Republicans declared a **Contract with America** to

> ❝return to the basic values that had built the country: work and family and the recognition of a higher moral authority.❞

In the contract, Republicans promised to reduce the federal government, balance the budget, lower taxes, and reform how Congress operates. They also pledged to pass laws to reduce crime, reform welfare, and strengthen the family.

The result was a strong Republican victory in the 1994 elections. For the first time in 40 years, the Republicans controlled both houses of Congress. In their first hundred days in office, the Republicans passed many parts of the Contract with America.

Congress passed a line-item veto bill. Intended as a way to reduce wasteful spending, the line-item veto allowed the president to cancel any individual items within a spending bill. The Supreme Court later overturned the law. It ruled that such an increase in the president's power could be granted only through a constitutional amendment.

Other parts of the Contract with America were also rejected. Some proposals stalled in the Senate, and President Clinton vetoed several Republican bills on welfare reform and the budget. Clinton argued that budget cuts would hurt elderly people on Medicare, damage the environment, and damage education.

Health Care for America's Families

Picturing **History**

Health-care reform was an important program for both the president and Congress. **Why did Congress reject the Clinton plan?**

Analyzing *Political Cartoons*

Cartoonists often use the elephant to represent the Republican Party and the donkey to represent the Democratic Party. **What statement is the cartoonist making about Congress and the president?**

Budget Problems and Compromise

Disagreement between the president and congressional Republicans continued. A major dispute blocked passage of the 1996 budget, causing the federal government to run out of money. The government shut down nonessential services twice for a total of 27 days. Congress and the president recognized that compromise was needed.

Both the Republicans in Congress and President Clinton proposed plans for a balanced budget. The president also pushed for an increase in the minimum wage and sponsored a welfare reform bill that set a work requirement for people receiving benefits and put a five-year time limit on benefits.

Clinton Wins a Second Term

The Republicans hoped to recapture the White House in 1996. However, passage of the Brady Act and the Crime Act weakened Republican arguments that Clinton was soft on crime. Most important, the economy was healthy and unemployment was at a 30-year low. President Clinton easily won reelection, beating the Republican candidate, former Senate majority leader **Robert Dole.**

The American economy continued to grow. One measure of this growth is the gross domestic product (GDP), which is the value of all the goods and services produced in a nation in a year. In 1996 and 1997, the GDP grew by about 4 percent a year—one of the highest rates of growth since the post-World War II boom.

The economy's growth increased the amount of tax money the government received. At the same time, the president and Congress cut back the size of the federal budget. The federal budget is prepared for a **fiscal year**—a 12-month planning period. The 1998 fiscal year ended with a federal **budget surplus**—the amount of money remaining after all expenditures—of about $80 billion, the first surplus in three decades.

Under Investigation

In 1994 legal questions arose relating to real estate investments Clinton had made while governor of Arkansas. Attorney General **Janet Reno** appointed an independent counsel to investigate the president. **Kenneth Starr,** a former federal judge, led the investigation. As other scandals were exposed, Starr widened the scope of the investigation.

In early 1998 a new scandal emerged involving a personal relationship between the president and a White House intern. Evidence suggested that the president may have committed **perjury,** or lied under oath, about the relationship. In September, Starr sent a report to Congress claiming that President Clinton had committed perjury and obstructed justice in an effort to conceal the personal relationship.

The House of Representatives voted to hold hearings to decide whether to impeach the president, in response to Starr's report. To impeach is to make a formal accusation of wrongdoing against a public official. The House scheduled the hearings for November, following the 1998 congressional elections.

With Clinton in trouble, the Republicans expected to make major gains in the 1998 elections. Instead, the Democrats gained 5 seats in the House, although they still trailed the Republicans 223 to 211. The Senate remained unchanged, with 55 Republicans and 45 Democrats. Incumbents—the current officeholders—did extremely well in the 1998 elections.

Impeachment

Although there was general agreement that the president had lied, Congress was divided over whether his actions justified impeachment. Clinton's supporters argued that his offenses did not qualify as "high crimes and misdemeanors," as stated in the Constitution. Clinton's accusers insisted that the "rule of law" is a fundamental principle of American society, and that the president should be held accountable if his actions were illegal.

On December 19, 1998, the House of Representatives passed two articles of impeachment, one for perjury and one for obstruction of justice. With this action, Bill Clinton became only the second president ever to be impeached. The case moved to the Senate for trial. A two-thirds majority Senate vote is needed to convict and remove a president from office.

On February 12, 1999, the senators cast their votes. The result was 45 guilty to 55 not guilty on the perjury article, and 50 guilty to 50 not guilty on the obstruction of justice article. Acquitted of both charges, Bill Clinton had survived the challenge to his presidency.

✔ Reading Check Describing What role did Kenneth Starr play?

Foreign Policy

Even as the nation struggled with domestic issues, international matters presented new challenges.

TWO VIEWPOINTS

Should We Convict the President?

In 1998 a political storm brewed in the nation's capital over the future of President Bill Clinton. The House of Representatives accused President Clinton of lying under oath and obstructing justice, and voted to impeach him. Now it was up to the Senate to convict and remove him from office. Passionate voices cried out for and against conviction.

Statement of Senator Paul Sarbanes (D-Md.), 1999

The gravity of what is at stake—the democratic choice of the American people—and the solemnity of the proceedings dictate that a decision to remove the President from office should follow only from the most serious of circumstances. . . .

The Articles of Impeachment that have been exhibited to the Senate fall far short of what the Founding Fathers had in mind when they placed in the hands of Congress the power to impeach and remove a President from office. They fall far short of what the American people demand to be shown and proven before their democratic choice is reversed. . . .

Statement of Senator Pete Domenici (R-N.M.), 1999

The President had a choice to make during this entire, lamentable episode. At a number of critical junctures, he had a choice either to tell the truth or to lie, first in the civil rights case, before the grand jury and on national television. Each time he chose to lie. He made that fateful choice. . . .

The President has committed high crimes and misdemeanors, in violation of his oath of office. He lied under oath. He obstructed justice. His behavior was unworthy of the Presidency of the United States.

President Clinton

Analyzing Primary Sources

1. What reasons does Senator Sarbanes give for his vote to not remove President Clinton from office?
2. Why does Senator Domenici believe that the president should be removed from office?
3. Would you have voted to remove President Clinton from office? Why or why not?

Important decisions faced American policy-makers on defining the nation's role in the post-Cold War world.

In 1993 Clinton persuaded Congress to ratify the **North American Free Trade Agreement,** or NAFTA. Under NAFTA the United States, Canada, and Mexico agreed to eliminate trade barriers among the three nations. NAFTA opponents feared a loss of U.S. jobs. Farmers also feared NAFTA, saying that low-priced Mexican produce would undercut American goods. Supporters argued that the treaty would lower prices for American consumers and expand markets.

Middle East Peace Accords

In September 1993 President Clinton invited Israeli prime minister Yitzhak Rabin and Yassir Arafat, head of the Palestine Liberation Organization (PLO), to the White House for the signing of a historic agreement between the two leaders. Israel recognized the PLO as the representative of the Palestinian people, and the PLO recognized Israel's right to exist. The agreement created a plan for limited Palestinian self-government over certain areas in Israel.

Opposition to the plan emerged on both sides and the violence continued. In 1995 an Israeli extremist assassinated Prime Minister Rabin. In 2001 Ariel Sharon, the new Israeli prime minister, pledged to put Israel's security above the peace process. The region remained as far from peace as ever.

Peacekeeping in the Balkans

As you read earlier, civil war had erupted in the former Yugoslavia. Bitter fighting followed, especially in Bosnia, where Serbs engaged in **ethnic cleansing**—forcibly removing or killing members—of the Muslim population. NATO air strikes on their positions brought Serbs to the bargaining table. The Clinton administration then led peace talks, which produced the Dayton Accords in December 1995.

In 1998 Serbian leader **Slobodan Milosevic** attempted to drive the Muslims out of the Kosovo region. The United States and NATO launched air strikes against Serbia, until Serb troops withdrew from Kosovo and its Muslim population could return.

✔ **Reading Check** **Summarizing**
What did critics say NAFTA would cause?

Picturing **History**

The Senate has tried two presidents on impeachment charges: Andrew Johnson and Bill Clinton. Johnson was acquitted by only one vote in 1868. **What was the verdict in Clinton's trial?**

Andrew Johnson and ticket of admission to impeachment trial

A New President for a New Century

President Clinton's two terms in office left the country divided. Many Americans were pleased with the economy, but were disappointed with the president's personal behavior. As the 2000 election approached, the major parties looked for candidates who appealed to a broad cross section of voters.

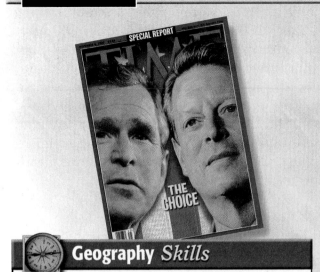

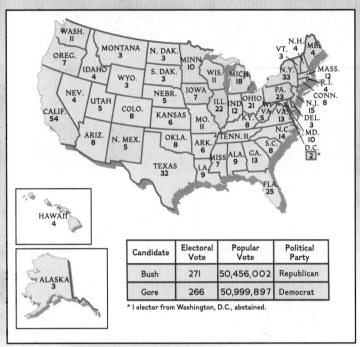

Candidate	Electoral Vote	Popular Vote	Political Party
Bush	271	50,456,002	Republican
Gore	266	50,999,897	Democrat

* I elector from Washington, D.C., abstained.

Geography *Skills*

The 2000 election marked the first election in 112 years where the candidate who won the popular vote did not win the electoral vote.

1. **Location** What states have more than 20 electoral votes?
2. **Location** What candidate won the electoral votes in each of these states?

The Election of 2000

The Democrats nominated Vice President Al Gore for president, hoping that the popularity of Clinton's policies would convince Americans to vote for Gore. The large Republican field eventually came down to two men: Governor **George W. Bush** of Texas and Senator **John McCain** of Arizona. Ultimately, the Republicans chose Bush, the son of former President Bush, as their nominee.

Gore made history by naming Senator **Joseph Lieberman** as his running mate. This marked the first time in U.S. history that a Jewish American ran on a national ticket. George W. Bush chose **Richard Cheney** as his running mate. Cheney served as chief of staff to President Gerald Ford and defense secretary to former President George Bush in 1989.

A major issue of the campaign of 2000 was what to do with the budget surplus. Gore and Bush agreed that Social Security and Medicare needed reform, but disagreed on the details. Both also supported tax cuts and plans to help seniors pay for prescription drugs. Consumer

activist **Ralph Nader** also entered the race. Noting that "too much power in the hands of the few has further weakened our democracy," Nader ran as the nominee of the Green Party.

The 2000 election was extraordinarily close between Bush and Gore. Although Bush had a slim lead in Florida, the results were so close an automatic recount was required by law. Without Florida's 25 electoral votes, neither Bush nor Gore had the 270 electoral votes needed to win.

Gore also asked for manual recounts in several counties, and a battle began over whether and how to conduct them. Lawsuits were filed in state and federal courts. The issue ultimately reached the United States Supreme Court. On December 12, five weeks after the election, the Court issued its decision after a five-to-four vote. In *Bush* v. *Gore,* the Court ruled that a hand recount of selected votes in Florida ordered by the Florida Supreme Court violated the equal protection clause of the Constitution. It further held that there was not enough time to conduct a recount that would pass constitutional standards.

President Bush meets with the cabinet.

In a televised speech the following day, Gore conceded. On January 20, 2001, Bush became the 43rd president of the United States.

The Bush Administration

Protests followed the election. Some groups claimed the Florida counts were unfair. Others criticized the decision of the Supreme Court. In his Inaugural Address, President Bush repeated his campaign message of "inclusion, not division," saying America should be united.

The need for unity and cooperation was important in Congress as well. After the election the Senate was evenly split—50 Republicans and 50 Democrats. This meant that the Republicans held control because Vice President Richard Cheney, as president of the Senate, could cast the deciding vote when there was a tie.

Then Vermont senator James Jeffords left the Republican Party in May 2001 and became an independent. This led to a historic switch in power, transferring control to the Democrats in mid-session.

Cabinet and Advisers

Nominating the members of the cabinet was one of the new president's first responsibilities. President Bush named popular retired General of the Army **Colin Powell** as secretary of state. The Senate quickly approved Powell and most of Bush's other nominees. However, Bush's choice for secretary of labor, Linda Chavez, was forced to withdraw when questions arose over her housing an illegal immigrant. Replacing Chavez was

Elaine Chao, the first Asian American woman to serve in a president's cabinet. Chao had previously served as director of the Peace Corps.

Other women played leading roles in the new administration. **Condoleezza Rice,** the first woman in history to hold the job of national security adviser, was instrumental in shaping foreign policy. First Lady **Laura Bush** promoted education. She organized a series of book festivals to raise money for libraries. She also called attention to the need for recruiting more teachers and improving reading skills.

Tax Cut

During the campaign, Bush promised a tax cut, and he quickly presented his proposal to Congress. The proposal caused much debate. Republicans argued that it was the peoples' money and that they deserved it back. They also claimed that the tax cut would help the slowing economy. Opponents argued that the money could be used more responsibly elsewhere, such as for Social Security or for paying off the national debt.

In June 2001 President Bush signed into law the largest reduction in federal taxes since 1981. Joined by a bipartisan group from the House and Senate, the President signed a 10-year, $1.3 trillion tax-cut bill into law.

International Affairs

The Bush administration proposed a National Missile Defense system, designed to protect the United States from any incoming missiles by shooting them down before they reach American airspace. Supporters viewed the system as a means of protection against an unstable leader who might use nuclear weapons. Critics countered that the system would renew an international arms race.

As President Bush's top military adviser, Colin Powell laid out a blueprint for intervention in international conflict. The **Powell Doctrine** calls for using American troops only when a vital national interest is at stake and there is a clear and realistic goal.

Reading Check **Describing** What is Elaine Chao's role in the Bush administration?

Looking to the Future

As Americans entered a new century, they faced many uncertainties—and opportunities. New technologies and a changing society had begun to transform America in new ways.

The Global Economy

President Bush said one of his major aims was to stimulate global economic growth. He called for a world trading system that is dramatically more open and more free:

> 66We know that nations that open their economies to the benefits of trade are more successful in climbing out of poverty. . . . We also know that free trade encourages the habits of liberty that sustain freedom. . . . 99

Since 1995 the World Trade Organization (WTO) has administered trade practices between many nations. The WTO has more than 140 members and many other countries have applied for membership.

Growth of technology industries boosted economic growth. Telecommunications grew rapidly as Americans watched television by cable or satellite, spoke on cellular phones, and exchanged messages by fax. Personal computers were being used in homes, schools, and businesses in greater numbers than ever before. Through the Internet, a worldwide linking of computer networks, American students could communicate with students in countries halfway around the world.

A Changing Society

As America entered the twenty-first century, its population had begun to change significantly. Because Americans were living longer than in the past, elderly people formed an increasing portion of the population. The Census Bureau reported that more than 12 percent of the population was over 65 years of age in the year 2000. As the baby boom generation ages, this population will grow even larger. This will require greater government payments for Social Security and Medicare.

People In History

Colin Powell 1937-

During the Persian Gulf War, the highest-ranking military officer serving was Colin Powell, the chairman of the Joint Chiefs of Staff. He was the youngest person and the first African American to hold that position. A four-star general, Powell had a very distinguished military career for thirty-five years, serving twice in Vietnam and working for four presidents.

Born to Jamaican immigrants, Powell was raised in Harlem and the South Bronx of New York City. He attended public school and the City College of New York, where he studied geology and began military training.

After the Gulf War, Powell wrote an autobiography and established a charitable organization, America's Promise—the Alliance for Youth, that helps children.

In 2001, Powell went to work for his fifth president, George W. Bush, as the first African American secretary of state.

Immigration also changed the composition of American society. By 2000 more than 10 percent of the population was foreign-born. Latin America and Asia provided the greatest number of immigrants. Asian Americans made up about 4 percent of the population; Hispanic Americans more than 12 percent. If trends continue, Hispanic Americans will soon become the largest minority in the United States.

Environmental Challenges

For years, scientists noted that the earth's atmosphere was losing ozone. This layer of gas protects life on Earth from cancer-causing rays of the sun. In 1987, the United States and 23 other nations agreed to stop making chemicals that might be weakening the ozone layer.

Scientists continued to debate the effects of global warming. They warned that the steady increase in average world temperatures could bring about major changes in weather patterns, the environment, and crop production.

Threats to Peace and Security

Preserving peace remains the most pressing global issue. In the late 1900s and early 2000s, acts of terror multiplied. New dangers lurked with the development of new kinds of warfare, including chemical weapons and biological weapons, which deliberately spread disease among humans.

Terrorism—the use of violence by groups against civilians to achieve a political goal—threatened the security of the nation. On April 19, 1995, a massive bomb exploded at the Murrah Federal Building in downtown Oklahoma City, leaving 168 dead. The tragedy focused national attention on the violent anti-government feelings of private American militia groups. In January 1998, Theodore Kaczynski pleaded guilty to a string of mail bombings, dating from 1978 to 1995, which killed 3 and injured 29 others. Kaczynski hoped to inspire a rebellion against modern industrial society. These are examples of domestic terrorism. People engage in **domestic terrorism** when they attack people in their own country.

In addition to concern about domestic terrorism, the United States also faced **international terrorism.** As the world's most powerful nation, the United States frequently served as a target for terrorists—either acting independently or with the support of a hostile government. The attack on the World Trade Center and the Pentagon on September 11, 2001, was an example of international terrorism.

HISTORY Online

Student Web Activity
Visit taj.glencoe.com and click on **Chapter 32—Student Web Activities** for an activity on today's technology.

SECTION 3 ASSESSMENT

Checking for Understanding

1. **Key Terms** Use each of these terms in a complete sentence that will help explain its meaning: budget deficit, gross domestic product, impeach, incumbent.
2. **Reviewing Facts** Summarize the events of Clinton's impeachment.

Reviewing Themes

3. **Continuity and Change** How did the 1994 election affect the balance of parties in Congress?

Critical Thinking

4. **Predicting Consequences** How might an aging population affect the nation's workforce?
5. **Determining Cause and Effect** Use a diagram like the one below to list the effects of recent technological advances on your life.

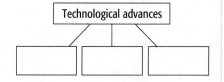

Analyzing Visuals

6. **Geography Skills** Examine the election map on page 941. What was the difference in the electoral vote count?

Interdisciplinary Activity

Citizenship During the next week, pay attention to the news to find what actions the president has taken on different issues. Write down your findings. Next to each entry, indicate your stand on the issue and whether or not you agree with the president's actions.

SECTION 4 The War on Terrorism

Guide to Reading

Main Idea
After suffering the worst terrorist attack in its history, the United States launched an effort to fight international terrorism.

Key Terms
counter-terrorism

Reading Strategy
Organizing Information As you read about America's war on terrorism, complete a diagram like the one below to explain how Americans responded to the events of September 11, 2001.

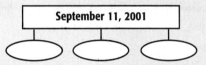

September 11, 2001

Read to Learn
• how Americans responded to terrorism.
• what actions the government took to fight terrorism.

Section Theme
Global Connections The United States called for a worldwide coalition to fight against terrorism.

Preview of Events

◆1975	◆1985	◆1995	◆2005
1979 Soviet Union invades Afghanistan	**1988** Al-Qaeda is organized	**1998** Bombs explode at U.S. embassies in Kenya and Tanzania	**2001** Attack on the Pentagon and World Trade Center

AN American Story

The first airliner hit the World Trade Center's north tower in New York City at about 8:45 in the morning. Eighteen minutes later, a second plane hit the south tower. Those who died on the airplanes were the first victims. Fire and falling wreckage from the twin towers of the World Trade Center killed thousands more, and hundreds of rescuers—fire fighters, police officers, and volunteers—themselves became victims. "The smoke was so bad, I was suffocating. When the buildings toppled, it was like a volcano," one survivor noted. "We have a lot of heroes," said one firefighter, "and we lost a lot of good people."

Rescue workers carry out an injured man at the World Trade Center.

The crash of two passenger airplanes into the World Trade Center was not an accident. Early on the morning of September 11, 2001, terrorist hijackers had seized control of the planes, then deliberately flew them into the buildings. Terrorists took control of a third plane and crashed into the Pentagon, the headquarters of the nation's Department of Defense. Hijackers also seized a fourth airplane, but passengers heroically attacked the hijackers, causing that plane to crash in Pennsylvania. In all, thousands of people died.

Terrorist attacks destroyed the World Trade Center (left), one of the nation's economic centers. Three New York City firefighters (right) raise the American flag amid the rubble.

Many New York City rescue workers who went to help also lost their lives when the towers collapsed. Hundreds of firefighters, police officers, and volunteers gave their lives in the line of duty trying to save others. Among those who died were Fire Department chaplain Mychal Judge and first deputy commissioner William Feehan, a 42-year veteran of the fire department. The largest number of New York City firefighters to have died in a single disaster before the terrorist attack was 12.

The Terrorist Threat

The attacks on the World Trade Center and the Pentagon were acts of terrorism. Terrorism is the use of violence by groups against civilians to achieve a political goal.

Who Was Responsible?

Intelligence sources and FBI investigators quickly identified **Osama bin Laden** as the prime suspect. Like most people in the Middle East, bin Laden is a **Muslim**—someone who believes in and practices the religion of Islam. Although the vast majority of the 1 billion Muslims worldwide believe Islam rejects terrorism, militant **fundamentalists** like bin Laden do not. They believe that any action is justified to drive American influence out of the Arab world.

Bin Laden believed that Western ideas had harmed Muslim society. His experience in Afghanistan convinced him that superpowers could be beaten.

War in Afghanistan

In 1979 the Soviet Union had invaded the nation of **Afghanistan,** in Southwest Asia, to support that nation's pro-communist government.

Muslims from across the Middle East went to Afghanistan to fight against the Soviets. Among them was bin Laden, who came from one of Saudi Arabia's wealthiest families. In 1988, he founded an organization called **al-Qaeda** (al KY•duh), or "the Base." Al-Qaeda recruited Muslims to fight against the Soviets and bought arms for the Afghanistan soldiers. After Soviet forces withdrew from Afghanistan, bin Laden became a hero to many fundamentalists.

Terrorist Acts

Operating first from Sudan and then from Afghanistan—then under the control of Muslim fundamentalists known as the **Taliban**—bin Laden led al-Qaeda on a mission to drive Americans and other non-Muslims out of the Middle East. In 1998 terrorist truck bombs exploded at the American embassies in the African countries of **Kenya** and **Tanzania.** The bombs killed more than 200 people, including 12 Americans, and injured over 4,500.

In late 1999, terrorists linked to al-Qaeda were arrested trying to smuggle explosives into the United States in an attempt to bomb targets in Seattle, Washington. In October 2000, terrorists backed by al-Qaeda crashed a boat loaded with explosives into the **USS Cole,** an American warship, while it was refueling in Yemen.

✓ **Reading Check** **Describing** How did Osama bin Laden become so influential in Afghanistan?

A New War Begins

Then on September 11, 2001, terrorists struck on an even greater scale. The shock was felt across the nation, and thousands of people sought a way to help.

The Spirit of America

From coast to coast, thousands attended prayer services and vigils. Across the nation, Americans lined up to donate blood. Others raised money and collected food, blankets, and other supplies for the victims and rescue workers. Firefighters and medical workers from many cities headed to New York to help.

Using a combination of imagination and hard work, young people throughout the nation volunteered to help. Students in Western Springs, a village near Chicago, Illinois, encouraged their entire community to take part in a toys, books, and games garage sale to raise money. Students at a school in Cedar Rapids, Iowa, started a project called Working for America. The students worked by doing chores for family and neighbors

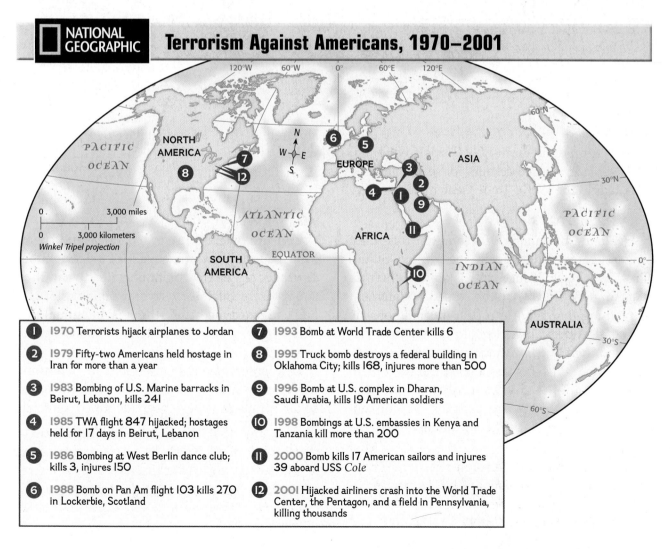

NATIONAL GEOGRAPHIC
Terrorism Against Americans, 1970–2001

1. 1970 Terrorists hijack airplanes to Jordan

2. 1979 Fifty-two Americans held hostage in Iran for more than a year

3. 1983 Bombing of U.S. Marine barracks in Beirut, Lebanon, kills 241

4. 1985 TWA flight 847 hijacked; hostages held for 17 days in Beirut, Lebanon

5. 1986 Bombing at West Berlin dance club; kills 3, injures 150

6. 1988 Bomb on Pan Am flight 103 kills 270 in Lockerbie, Scotland

7. 1993 Bomb at World Trade Center kills 6

8. 1995 Truck bomb destroys a federal building in Oklahoma City; kills 168, injures more than 500

9. 1996 Bomb at U.S. complex in Dharan, Saudi Arabia, kills 19 American soldiers

10. 1998 Bombings at U.S. embassies in Kenya and Tanzania kill more than 200

11. 2000 Bomb kills 17 American sailors and injures 39 aboard USS Cole

12. 2001 Hijacked airliners crash into the World Trade Center, the Pentagon, and a field in Pennsylvania, killing thousands

AMERICA'S HEROES

New York City Fire Department chaplain Mychal Judge, shown here in prayer, was killed while administering last rites to a firefighter.

New York City firefighter Tony James salutes during a funeral service.

Jessica Malone, who comes from a large family of firefighters, went to New York City to help.

and donated money they earned to the Red Cross. The South Bronx Job Corps Center put together canine care packages for search and rescue dogs at the World Trade Center site.

Fair Treatment

Realizing that many people might turn their anger against Muslims in the United States, President Bush visited the Islamic Center in Washington, D.C. There he issued a statement explaining that Islam is a peaceful religion. He urged all Americans to uphold the nation's values and treat Muslim Americans fairly.

President Bush created a special fund to help the children of Afghanistan. Many of the children in Afghanistan are orphans and do not have enough to eat. The president asked the children of the United States to send $1—or whatever they could—to America's Fund for Afghan Children.

New Threats

Concern over the use of biological and chemical weapons grew in the wake of the September 11 tragedy. Letters containing deadly anthrax spores were mailed to several political leaders and the news media. **Anthrax** is an animal disease that has existed for tens of thousands of years.

Law enforcement investigated to determine the identity and the motives of the attackers, but so far, no suspects have been identified. Officials do not think al-Qaeda sent the anthrax.

"In the face of all this evil, we remain strong and united, one nation under God." —President George W. Bush

Protecting America

President Bush and his advisers began planning a response to the terrorist attacks. The president placed the armed forces on high alert. Fighter aircraft began patrolling the skies over major cities. Security at airports was increased, and the FBI began a massive investigation. The president created a new cabinet-level post, **Homeland Security,** to coordinate counter-terrorism efforts. Counter-terrorism involves military or political activities intended to combat terrorism. He named Pennsylvania governor Tom Ridge as head of the department. 📖 *(See pages 978–979 of the Appendix for President Bush's address to Congress after the attacks.)*

The Office of Homeland Security had trouble coordinating counter-terrorism efforts. In June 2002, President Bush asked Congress to combine all of the agencies responsible for the public's safety into a new department to be called the Department of Homeland Security. The new department would control the Coast Guard, the Border Patrol, the Immigration and Naturalization Service, the Customs Service, the Federal Emergency Management Agency, and many other agencies.

In late October 2001, Congress passed and the president signed into law new measures to combat terrorism. The **USA Patriot Act of 2001** gave federal prosecutors and FBI agents new powers to investigate those who plot or carry out acts of terrorism. The law expanded the power of federal agents to tap telephones and track Internet usage in the hunt for terrorists. It also permits agents to conduct secret searches of a suspect's home or office without giving prior notice to the owner of the property.

Attorney General **John Aschroft** promised that government agents would waste no time putting the new tools to use in the hunt for terrorists. Although both houses of Congress passed the bill overwhelmingly, some critics expressed concern that measures could be used not only against suspected terrorists, but people and organizations engaged in lawful activity. To make sure civil liberties were not compromised by the new law, many of its powers will expire in late 2005, unless extended by Congress.

Building a Coalition

The death and devastation caused by the terrorism affected not only Americans, but also people around the world. World leaders responded with statements of sympathy and outrage. NATO members promised to support the United States as did other nations including Pakistan, India, Turkey, and Israel. Some Muslim nations, including Saudi Arabia and Egypt, offered more limited support because they feared widespread protests from their people.

Secretary of State Colin Powell began building an international coalition to support the United States. Secretary of Defense Donald Rumsfeld began to position troops, aircraft, and warships in the Middle East. The president promised that

66We will direct every resource at our command—every means of diplomacy, every tool of intelligence, every instrument of law enforcement, every financial influence, and every necessary weapon of war—to the disruption and defeat of the global terror network.99

On the Trail of Terrorism

The war against terrorism first concentrated on Afghanistan where bin Laden was reported to be in hiding. The Taliban controlled most of Afghanistan and imposed their religious views on the Afghan people. Taliban leaders had come under criticism for discriminating against women and being intolerant of other religions. Since 1996, when the Taliban captured the Afghan capital, **Kabul,** the main opposition force, the **Northern Alliance,** had battled the Taliban but had made little headway.

President Bush demanded that the Taliban in Afghanistan turn over bin Laden and his supporters. After the Taliban refused, on October 7 the U.S. military attacked Taliban and al-Qaeda forces. Cargo jets also dropped food, medicine, and supplies to the Afghan people.

The air strikes by U.S. warplanes allowed the Northern Alliance to quickly take control of the country. After the Taliban fell from power, the United States and its allies worked with Afghan leaders to create an interim—or temporary—

Americans gathered at parks, churches, and fire stations across the nation to express not only their grief but their patriotism.

government to run the country. Nations around the world pledged a total of more than four billion dollars to help Afghanistan.

Meanwhile, the war against al-Qaeda continued. American troops began searching the mountains of Afghanistan for al-Qaeda terrorists. Others were sent to the Philippines, Yemen, and the country of Georgia to train local soldiers to fight terrorists.

Although the war in Afghanistan was going well, terrorist attacks in South Asia and the Middle East created new problems. In December 2001, terrorists from Kashmir—a region in northern India—attacked India's parliament. India has fought many wars with Pakistan over Kashmir. India's leaders believed the terrorists had been trained by Pakistan. They blamed Pakistan for the attack on the parliament, and began mobilizing India's army.

By June 2002, the two nations were ready to go to war. The situation was very dangerous because both sides had nuclear weapons. President Bush sent Colin Powell and Donald Rumsfeld to the region to try to prevent war from breaking out.

Pakistan promised to crack down on terrorists in its territory, but tensions remained high.

South Asia was not the only region where terrorism created problems. In the Middle East, Palestinian terrorists sent suicide bombers into Israel. These bombers concealed explosives under their clothing. They detonated the bombs in Israeli restaurants, shops, and buses, killing dozens of other people. After several suicide bombings took place in Israel, the Israeli army invaded several Palestinian cities where they believed the terrorist groups were based.

In response to the violence in the Middle East, President Bush outlined a plan for ending the Israeli-Palestinian conflict. He announced his support for the creation of a Palestinian state living in peace beside Israel. He asked Israel to stop raiding Palestinian cities. At the same time, he demanded Palestinian leaders stop terrorist attacks and reform their government to make it more democratic and less corrupt.

Continuing the War on Terrorism

President Bush made it clear that while the war on terrorism would start by targeting al-Qaeda, it would not end there. "It will not end," the president announced, "until every terrorist group of global reach has been found, stopped, and defeated." He also warned that the United States would regard "any nation that continues to harbor or support terrorism" as an enemy.

The war against terrorism, President Bush warned Americans, would not end quickly, but it was a war the people of the United States were now called to fight:

66 Great harm has been done to us. We have suffered great loss. And in our grief and anger we have found our mission and our moment.... We will not tire, we will not falter, and we will not fail. 99

Confrontation with Iraq

President Bush and his advisers were worried that terrorist groups might acquire **weapons of mass destruction.** These weapons can kill tens of thousands of people all at once. Nuclear, chemical, and biological weapons are examples of weapons of mass destruction.

While continuing the fight against terrorist groups, the Bush administration turned its attention to a familiar foe: Saddam Hussein, the leader of Iraq. After the Gulf War ended in 1991, UN weapons inspectors found evidence that Iraq had developed biological weapons and had nearly succeeded in building a nuclear bomb. UN Security Council resolutions called for Iraq to disarm its chemical, biological, and nuclear weapons programs. Iraq repeatedly violated these resolutions.

On September 12, 2002, President Bush asked the UN to pass a new resolution against Iraq. If Saddam Hussein wanted peace, he had to give up Iraq's weapons of mass destruction, readmit the UN weapons inspectors he had expelled in 1998, stop supporting terrorism, and stop oppressing his people. In mid-October, Congress voted to authorize the use of force against Iraq. On November 8, the UN Security Council unanimously approved a resolution imposing tough new arms inspections on Iraq. The resolution pledged Iraq would face "serious consequences" if it did not cooperate. The United States then began preparing for war. In February 2003, Secretary of State Colin Powell gave the UN evidence that Iraq was still hiding its weapons. On March 20, U.S. aircraft attacked Baghdad. The war with Iraq had begun.

✔ Reading Check **Describing** What steps did President Bush take in response to the terrorist attacks?

SECTION 4 ASSESSMENT

Checking for Understanding
1. **Key Terms** Define: counter-terrorism.
2. **Reviewing Facts** What happened to the USS *Cole* when it was refueling in Yemen?

Reviewing Themes
3. **Global Connections** Do you think the dangers of terrorism require global cooperation? Explain and support your point of view with reasons.

Critical Thinking
4. **Drawing Conclusions** Why do you think President Bush specifically chose to visit the Islamic Center in Washington, D.C.?
5. **Organizing Information** Use a diagram like the one below to identify what you think are the three major effects of terrorism on Americans.

Effects of terrorism

Analyzing Visuals
6. **Geography Skills** Examine the map on terrorism on page 947. How many Americans were taken hostage in Iran? What events on the map took place in the 1990s?

Interdisciplinary Activity
Expository Writing How will world events affect your future? Write an essay entitled "The World's Future and My Own" identifying important issues and explaining how events could affect your life.

Chapter Summary
New Challenges

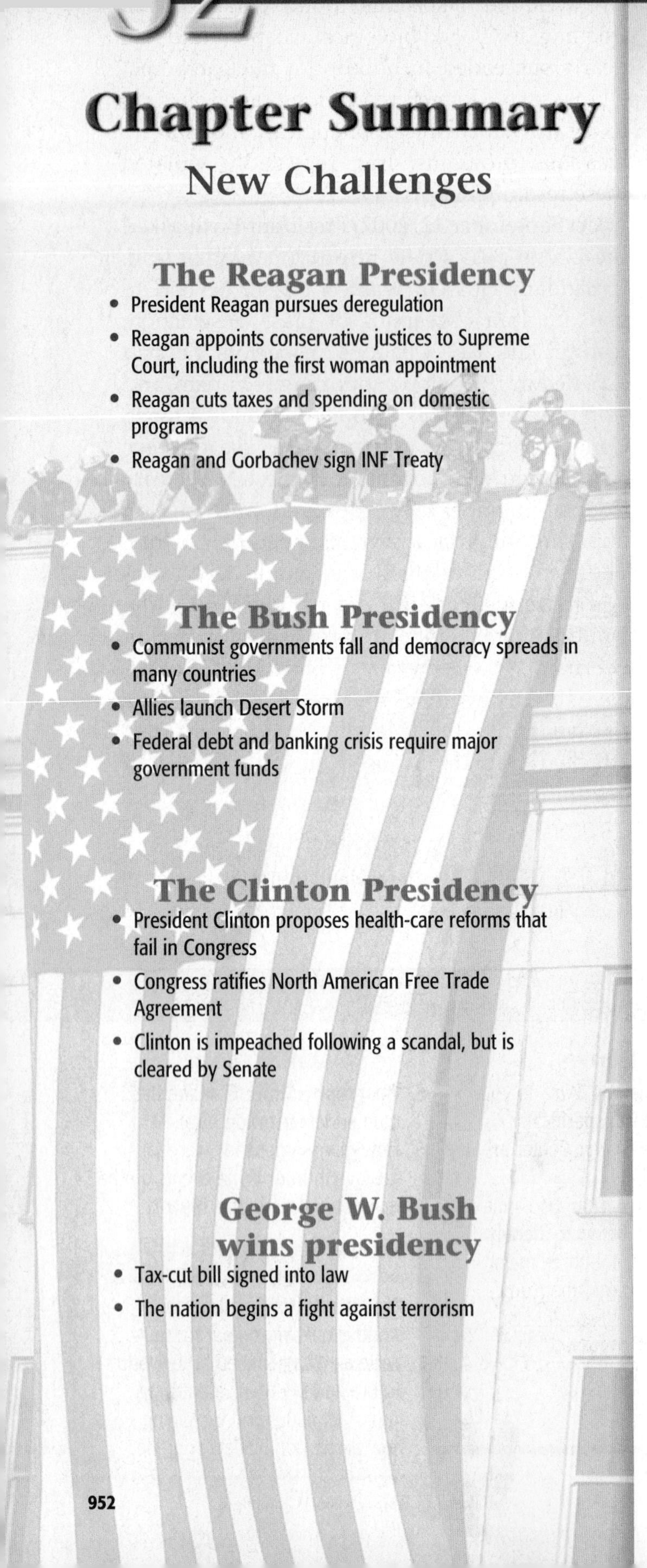

The Reagan Presidency
- President Reagan pursues deregulation
- Reagan appoints conservative justices to Supreme Court, including the first woman appointment
- Reagan cuts taxes and spending on domestic programs
- Reagan and Gorbachev sign INF Treaty

The Bush Presidency
- Communist governments fall and democracy spreads in many countries
- Allies launch Desert Storm
- Federal debt and banking crisis require major government funds

The Clinton Presidency
- President Clinton proposes health-care reforms that fail in Congress
- Congress ratifies North American Free Trade Agreement
- Clinton is impeached following a scandal, but is cleared by Senate

George W. Bush wins presidency
- Tax-cut bill signed into law
- The nation begins a fight against terrorism

Reviewing Key Terms
On a sheet of paper, define the following terms:

1. deregulation
2. federal debt
3. perestroika
4. coup
5. incumbent
6. global warming
7. ozone
8. line-item veto

Reviewing Key Facts

9. What was Reagan's economic policy?
10. How did Mikhail Gorbachev try to reform the Soviet government?
11. How did Poland lead the way in toppling communism in Eastern Europe?
12. What triggered the Persian Gulf War?
13. Why was health care an important issue in the 1990s?
14. What was the significance of the Middle East Peace Accords?
15. What was the outcome of President Clinton's impeachment trial?
16. Who won the presidential election in 2000? Why was the election unusual?

Critical Thinking

17. **Economic Factors** What was the goal of President Reagan's policy of deregulation?
18. **Global Connections** What event marked the end of the Cold War?
19. **Groups and Institutions** Why did the federal government run out of money in the mid-1990s?
20. **Groups and Institutions** What message do you think voters were sending by electing a majority of Republicans to both houses of Congress in 1994?
21. **Evaluating** Re-create the diagram below and rank the four presidents that you studied in this chapter from best to worst. Then explain why you ranked them as you did.

President	Your reasons
1	
2	
3	
4	

Geography and History Activity

Study the map and answer the questions that follow.

Self-Check Quiz
Visit taj.glencoe.com and click on **Chapter 32—Self-Check Quizzes** to prepare for the chapter test.

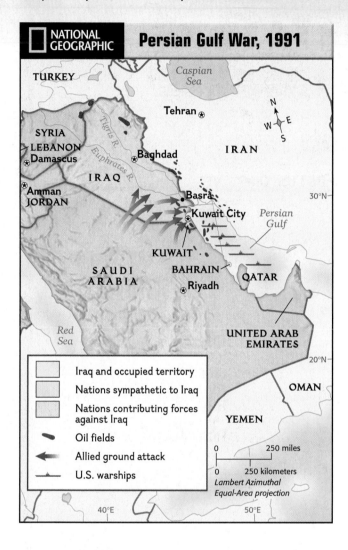

NATIONAL GEOGRAPHIC **Persian Gulf War, 1991**

TURKEY

Caspian Sea

Tehran ⊕

SYRIA
LEBANON
Damascus ⊕ Baghdad ⊕   IRAN

Tigris R.
Euphrates R.

IRAQ

Amman ⊕
JORDAN

Basra ⊕
Kuwait City ⊕   Persian Gulf   30°N

KUWAIT

SAUDI ARABIA   BAHRAIN ⊕
Riyadh ⊕   QATAR

Red Sea

UNITED ARAB EMIRATES

20°N

	Iraq and occupied territory
	Nations sympathetic to Iraq
	Nations contributing forces against Iraq

OMAN

⬟ Oil fields
← Allied ground attack
⊢ U.S. warships

YEMEN

0   250 miles
0   250 kilometers
Lambert Azimuthal Equal-Area projection

40°E   50°E

22. Region What country borders Iraq to the northeast?

23. Movement The blue lines indicate invasion forces. From what country was the invasion launched?

24. Location In what body of water were warships present?

Practicing Skills

25. Using an Electronic Spreadsheet Use a spreadsheet to enter the daily high, average, and low temperatures for your community for four weeks. At the end of this period, calculate your average local temperature. Then use the spreadsheet to make line graphs showing the monthly high temperatures, average temperatures, and low temperatures for your community.

Technology Activity

26. Using the Internet Use a search engine to search the Internet for information about Afghanistan. Write a short description of the change in power in that country during the past 20 years.

Citizenship Cooperative Activity

27. Your Community and the World Ask family members and neighbors about ways in which your community is connected to other parts of the world. Prepare a short fact sheet on the international connections of your community and the world. Discuss your view with the other groups.

Alternative Assessment

28. Portfolio Writing Activity Review the chapter for information about how the three presidents in office from 1980 to 2000 viewed the role of the federal government. Record the information in your journal. Use your notes to summarize each president's view in a single sentence.

The Princeton Review **Standardized Test Practice**

Directions: Choose the *best* answer to the following question.

The government had to shut down nonessential services twice in 1996 in response to what situation?

F power outages
G disputes over the budget
H bipartisan agreement
J the "Contract with America"

Test-Taking Tip

Eliminate answers that don't make sense. For example, why would the government shut down because of "bipartisan agreement"? Answer **H** must be wrong.

Appendix

Contents

What Is an Appendix and How Do I Use One?

An appendix is the additional material you often find at the end of books. The following information will help you learn how to use the appendix in **The American Journey.**

Primary Sources Library

The **Primary Sources Library** provides additional first-person accounts of historical events. Primary sources are often narratives by a person who actually experienced what is being described.

Presidents of the United States

The **presidents** have served as our nation's leaders. In this resource you will find information of interest on each of the nation's presidents, including their term in office, political affiliation, and their occupations before they became president.

Documents of American History

This is a collection of some of the most important writings in American history. Each **document** begins with an introduction describing the author and placing the selection within its historical context.

Supreme Court Case Summaries

The **Supreme Court Case Summaries** provide readable discussions of important Supreme Court cases. The summaries are listed in alphabetical order and include a summary of the facts of the case and its impact.

Gazetteer

A **gazetteer** (GA•zuh•TIHR) is a geographical dictionary. It lists some of the largest countries, cities, and several important geographic features. Each entry also includes a page number telling where this place can be found in your textbook.

Glossary

A **glossary** is a list of important or difficult terms found in a textbook. Since words sometimes have other meanings, you may wish to consult a dictionary to find other uses for the term. The glossary gives a definition of each term as it is used in the book. The glossary also includes page numbers telling you where in the textbook the term is used.

Spanish Glossary

A **Spanish glossary** contains everything that an English glossary does, but it is written in Spanish. A Spanish glossary is especially important to bilingual students, or those Spanish-speaking students who are learning the English language.

Index

An **index** is an alphabetical listing that includes the subjects of the book and the page numbers where those subjects can be found. The index in this book also lets you know that certain pages contain maps, graphs, photos, or paintings about the subject.

Acknowledgements and Photo Credits

This section lists photo credits and/or literary credits for the book. You can look at this section to find out where the publisher obtained the permission to use a photograph or to use excerpts from other books.

Test Yourself

Find the answers to these questions by using the Appendix on the following pages.

1. **What does ironclad mean?**
2. **Who was the sixth president of the United States?**
3. **On what page can I find out about Anne Hutchinson?**
4. **Where exactly is Roanoke located?**
5. **What was the Supreme Court's decision in *Marbury v. Madison?***

Primary Sources Library

Working With Primary Sources

Suppose that you have been asked to write a report on changes in your community over the past 25 years. Where would you get the information you need to begin writing? You would draw upon two types of information—primary sources and secondary sources.

Definitions

Primary sources are often first-person accounts by someone who actually saw or lived through what is being described. In other words, if you see a fire or live through a great storm and then write about your experiences, you are creating a primary source. Diaries, journals, photographs, and eyewitness reports are examples of primary sources. **Secondary sources** are secondhand accounts. For instance, if your friend experiences the fire or storm and tells you about it, or if you read about the fire or storm in the newspaper, and then you write about it, you are creating a secondary source. Textbooks, biographies, and histories are secondary sources.

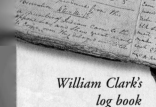

William Clark's log book

Checking Your Sources

When you read primary or secondary sources, you should analyze them to figure out if they are dependable or reliable. Historians usually prefer primary sources to secondary sources, but both can be reliable or unreliable, depending on the following factors.

Time Span

With primary sources, it is important to consider how long after the event occurred the primary source was written. Chances are the longer the time span between the event and the account, the less reliable the account is. As time passes, people often forget details and fill in gaps with events that never took place. Although we like to think we remember things exactly as they happened, the fact is we often remember them as we wanted them to occur.

Reliability

Another factor to consider when evaluating a primary source is the writer's background and reliability. First, try to determine how this person knows about what he or she is writing. How much does he or she know? Is the writer being truthful? Is the account convincing?

Opinions

When evaluating a primary source, you should also decide whether the account has been influenced by emotion, opinion, or exaggeration. Writers can have reasons to distort the truth to suit their personal purposes. Ask yourself: Why did the person write the account? Do any key words or expressions reveal the author's emotions or opinions? You may wish to compare the account with one written by another witness to the event. If the two accounts differ, ask yourself why they differ and which is more accurate.

Interpreting Primary Sources

To help you analyze a primary source, use the following steps:

- **Examine the origins of the document.**
  You need to determine if it is a primary source.

- **Find the main ideas.**
  Read the document and summarize the main ideas in your own words. These ideas may be fairly easy to identify in newspapers and journals, for example, but are much more difficult to find in poetry.

- **Reread the document.**
  Difficult ideas are not always easily understood on the first reading.

- **Use a variety of resources.**
  Form the habit of using the dictionary, the encyclopedia, and maps. These resources are tools to help you discover new ideas and knowledge and check the validity of sources.

George Washington's compass

Classifying Primary Sources

Primary sources fall into different categories:

Printed publications include books such as autobiographies. Printed publications also include newspapers and magazines.

Songs and poems include works that express the personal thoughts and feelings, or political or religious beliefs, of the writer, often using rhyming and rhythmic language.

Visual materials include a wide range of forms: original paintings, drawings, sculptures, photographs, film, and maps.

Oral history collects spoken memories and personal observations through recorded interviews. By contrast, oral tradition involves stories that people have passed along by word of mouth from generation to generation.

Personal records are accounts of events kept by an individual who is a participant in, or witness to, these events. Personal records include diaries, journals, and letters.

Artifacts

Artifacts are objects such as tools or ornaments. Artifacts present information about a particular culture or a stage of technological development.

Different Worlds Meet

Until the arrival of Christopher Columbus, the lifestyle and culture of Native Americans had endured for centuries. They told stories, sang songs, and recited tales that recounted their past and their close relationship with the natural world. These stories and songs survived through oral tradition. This means that each generation passed down its stories and songs to its young people by word of mouth. As you read, think about how oral history, folklore, and tradition connect us to the past.

Reader's Dictionary

Lakota: a member of the Sioux people of central and eastern North America

prophecy: a prediction about the future

Black Hills: mountains in the western Dakotas and northeast Wyoming

elder: a person who is honored for his or her age and experience

Pinta: one of the three ships under Columbus's command during his first trip to the Americas

White Buffalo Calf Woman Brings the First Pipe

Joseph Chasing Horse of the Lakota people tells the story of the White Buffalo Calf Woman.

We **Lakota** people have a **prophecy** about the white buffalo calf. How that prophecy originated was that we have a sacred bundle, a sacred pipe, that was brought to us about 2,000 years ago by what we know as the White Buffalo Calf Woman.

The story goes that she appeared to two warriors at that time. These two warriors were out hunting buffalo . . . in the sacred **Black Hills** of South Dakota, and they saw a big body coming toward them. And they saw that it was a white buffalo calf. As it came closer to them, it turned into a beautiful young Indian girl.

[At] that time one of the warriors [had bad thoughts] and so the young girl told him to step forward. And when he did step forward, a black cloud came over his body, and when the black cloud disappeared, the warrior who had bad thoughts was left with no flesh or blood on his bones. The other warrior kneeled and began to pray.

And when he prayed, the white buffalo calf, who was now an Indian girl told him to go back to his people and warn them that in four days she was going to bring a sacred bundle.

So the warrior did as he was told. He went back to his people, and he gathered all the **elders,** and all the

Kiowa animal hide calendar

leaders, and all the people in a circle and told them what she had instructed him to do. And sure enough, just as she said she would, on the fourth day, she came.

They say a cloud came down from the sky, and off of the cloud stepped the white buffalo calf. As it rolled onto the earth, the calf stood up and became this beautiful young woman who was carrying the sacred bundle in her hand.

As she entered into the circle of the nation, she sang a sacred song and took the sacred bundle to the people who were there to take [it from] her.

. . . And she instructed our people that as long as we performed these ceremonies we would always remain caretakers and guardians of sacred land. She told us that as long as we took care of it and respected it that our people would never die and would always live.

The sacred bundle is known as the White Buffalo Calf Pipe because it was brought by the White Buffalo Calf Woman. . . .

When White Buffalo Calf Woman promised to return again, she made some prophecies at that time. One of those prophecies was that the birth of a white buffalo calf would be a sign that it would be near the time when she would return again to purify the world. What she meant by that was that she would bring back [spiritual] harmony. . . .

Astrolabe

Columbus Crosses the Atlantic

Christopher Columbus reached the new world on October 12, 1492. At sea for over two months, his sailors worried that they would not find land before their food and water ran out. Columbus's entries in his logs show the mood of his crew, and their impressions of the natives.

October 11:

The crew of the **Pinta** spotted some . . . reeds and some other plants; they also saw what looked like a small board or plank. A stick was recovered that looks man-made, perhaps carved with an iron tool . . . but even these few [things] made the crew breathe easier; in fact the men have even become cheerful.

October 12:

The islanders came to the ships' boats, swimming and bringing us parrots and balls of cotton thread . . . which they exchanged for . . . glass beads and hawk bells . . . they took and gave of what they had very willingly, but it seemed to me that they were poor in every way. They bore no weapons, nor were they acquainted with them, because when I showed them swords they seized them by the edge and so cut themselves from ignorance.

Analyzing Primary Sources

1. What did the Indian girl tell the Lakota warriors?
2. What prophecy did the White Buffalo Calf Woman make to the people?
3. What does the use of the animal hide tell you about the people who made the calendar?
4. Why were the members of Columbus's crew cheerful when they spied the objects at sea?

Colonial Settlement

Early America was a nation of people unafraid to experiment. Because colonists often had to learn new ways of obtaining food and shelter in a primitive country, they grew to appreciate ingenuity. Because of the need to cooperate—for companionship, and even for survival—they overlooked the differences in cultures that separated them in the old country. As you read these primary source selections, think about how the necessity to adapt affected the way the colonists approached everyday situations.

Reader's Dictionary

enlightened: informed

haughty: proud, vain

indigence: poverty

habitation: home

phial: small bottle

blunder: mistake

tolerable: satisfactory

What is an American?

 **Printed Publications**

J. Hector St. John Crevecoeur of France traveled widely in the American colonies and farmed in New York. His Letters from an American Farmer *was published in 1782.*

I wish I could be acquainted with the feelings and thoughts which must . . . present themselves to the mind of an **enlightened** Englishman, when he first lands on the continent. . . . If he travels through our rural districts he views not the hostile castle, and the **haughty** mansion, contrasted with the clay-built hut and miserable cabin, where cattle and men help to keep each other warm, and dwell in meanness, smoke, and **indigence.** A pleasing uniformity of decent competence appears throughout our **habitations.** The meanest of our log-houses is dry and comfortable. . . . What then is the American, this new man? He is either a European, or the descendant of a European, hence that strange mixture of blood, which you will find in no other country. I could point out to you a family whose grandfather was an Englishman, whose wife was Dutch, and whose son married a French woman, and whose present four sons have now four wives of different nations. . . . There is room for everybody in America; has he particular talent, or industry? He exerts it in order to produce a livelihood, and it succeeds. . . .

Butter churn

Ben Franklin

Personal Records

We often think of Benjamin Franklin as a successful diplomat and inventor. In 1750, Franklin wrote to a friend about an experiment that did not go as well as he had planned.

I have lately made an experiment in electricity, that I desire never to repeat. Two nights ago, being about to kill a turkey by the shock from two large glass jars, containing as much electrical fire as forty common **phials,** I . . . took the whole [charge] through my own arms and body, by receiving the fire from the united top wires with one hand, while the other held a chain connected with the outsides of both jars. The company present (whose talking to me, and to one another, I supposed occasioned my inattention to what I was about) say, that the flash was very great, and the crack as loud as a pistol; yet, my senses being instantly gone, I neither saw the one nor heard the other. . . . Nothing remains now of this shock, but a soreness in my breast-bone, which feels as if it had been bruised. I did not fall, but suppose I should have been knocked down, if I had received the stroke in my head. The whole was over in less than a minute.

You may communicate this to Mr. Bowdoin, as a caution to him, but do not make it more public, for I am ashamed to have been guilty of so notorious a **blunder;**. . . . I am yours . . .

B. Franklin

P.S. The jars hold six gallons each.

Penn's Colony

Personal Records

In a letter written in 1683, William Penn describes the growth of his colony.

Our capital town is advanced to about 150 very **tolerable** houses for wooden ones; they are chiefly on both the navigable rivers that bound the ends or sides of the town. The farmers have got their winter corn in the ground. I suppose we may be 500 farmers strong. I settle them in villages, dividing 5,000 acres among ten, fifteen, or twenty families, as their ability is to plant it. . . .

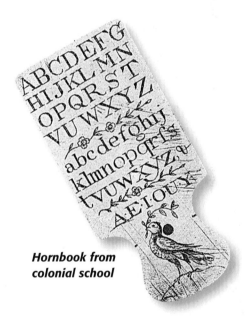

Hornbook from colonial school

Analyzing Primary Sources

1. How does de Crevecoeur describe the typical home in the colonies in the late 1700s?
2. What do you think Franklin was trying to learn with his experiment?
3. During what season of the year did Penn write this letter? How can you tell?

Creating a Nation

In settling North America, the colonists developed a sense that they were taking part in the birth of a new society, where people had the opportunity to better themselves. As you read these primary source selections, think about the reasons the colonists began to find fault with Great Britain. What words would you use to describe the American "spirit" that made them determined to fight for independence?

Reader's Dictionary

sovereign: king or leader

destitute: lacking

procure: gain or obtain

gall: to become sore by rubbing

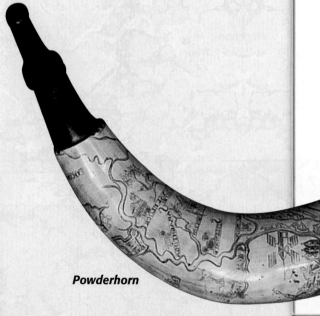

Powderhorn

Common Sense

Printed Publications

In Common Sense, written in January 1776, patriot Thomas Paine called upon the colonists to break away from Great Britain.

Every thing that is right begs for separation from [Great] Britain. The Americans who have been killed seem to say, 'TIS TIME TO PART. England and America are located a great distance apart. That is itself strong and natural proof that God never expected one to rule over the other.

The Bold Americans

Songs & Poems

Broadside ballads—emotionally-charged story poems printed on a single sheet of paper—were distributed widely and helped fuel colonists' passion for freedom.

Come all you bold young Bostonians, come
    listen unto me:
I will sing you a song concerning liberty.
Concerning liberty, my boys, the truth I will
    unfold,
Of the bold Americans, who scorn to be
    controlled.
We'll honor George, our **sovereign,** on any
    reasonable terms,
But if he don't grant us liberty, we'll all lay down
    our arms.
        But if he will grant us liberty, so plainly
            shall you see,
        We are the boys that fear no noise!
           Success to liberty!

Surviving at Valley Forge

Below are excerpts from the personal records of two different people who served at Valley Forge. The first selection is by Albigence Waldo, a surgeon who tended the sick and injured.

I am sick—discontented . . . Poor food—hard lodging—cold weather—fatigue—nasty cloathes—nasty cookery. . . . I can't endure it—Why are we sent here to starve and freeze? . . .

In this selection, soldier Joseph Plumb Martin, age 16 at the time, remembers the hardships on the way to Valley Forge.

The army was not only starved but naked. The greatest part were not only shirtless and barefoot, but **destitute** of all other clothing, especially blankets. I **procured** a small piece of rawhide and made myself a pair of moccasins, which

Military drum of the American Revolution

kept my feet (while they lasted) from the frozen ground, although, as I well remember, the hard edges so **galled** my ankles, while on a march, that it was with much difficulty and pain that I could wear them afterwards; but the only alternative I had was to endure this inconvenience or to go barefoot, as hundreds of my companions had to, till they might be tracked by their bloods upon the rough frozen ground.

Immigrant Life in America

A German immigrant wrote this account of his experiences.

But during the voyage there is on board these ships terrible misery, stench, fumes, horror, vomiting, many kinds of sea-sickness, fever . . . all of which comes from old and sharply salted food and meat, also from very bad and foul water, so that many die miserably. . . .

Many parents must sell and trade away their children like so many head of cattle. . . . [I]t often happens that such parents and children, after leaving the ship, do not see each other again for many years, perhaps no more in all their lives.

Analyzing Primary Sources

1. What is the main point that Thomas Paine makes in the excerpt from *Common Sense*?
2. What do the bold Americans scorn?
3. What might have kept the soldiers from leaving Valley Forge, under such horrible conditions?

The New Republic

The Constitution established a completely new framework of government that was meant to be flexible and lasting. Along with the excitement of starting a new nation came challenges and growing pains. Many people, both American-born and foreign-born, wondered: Can this new kind of government last? As you read these primary source selections, think about how well the government served the people as the nation grew.

Reader's Dictionary

gallery: outdoor balcony

proclamation: announcement

agitated: upset and nervous

ungainly: awkward, clumsy

plainest manner: in a simple way

discord: disagreement, conflict

rapture: joy

marsh: soft, wet land

corduroy-road: a road made of logs laid side by side

Washington's First Inaugural

Personal Records

Pennsylvania Senator William Maclay was one of the many witnesses to the nation's first presidential inauguration.

The President was conducted out of the middle window into the **gallery** [overlooking Wall Street], and the oath was administered by the Chancellor [the highest judicial officer in the state of New York]. Notice that the business done was communicated to the crowd by **proclamation** . . . who gave three cheers, and repeated it on the President's bowing to them.

As the company returned into the Senate chamber, the President took the chair and the Senators and Representatives their seats. He rose, and all arose also, and [he] addressed them. This great man was **agitated** and embarrassed more than ever he was by the leveled cannon or pointed musket. He trembled, and several times could scarce make out to read, though it must be supposed he had often read it before. . . . When he came to the words *all the world*, he made a flourish with his right hand, which left rather an **ungainly** impression. I sincerely, for my part, wished all set ceremony in the hands of the dancing-masters, and that this first of men had read off his address in the **plainest manner,** without ever taking his eyes from the paper, for I felt hurt that he was not first in everything.

Copy of letter written by President Washington

Song of Liberty

The following song is one of the hundreds of anonymous patriotic songs written, printed, and distributed in little song books during the early 1800s.

The fruits of our country, our flocks and
    our fleeces,
What treasures immense, in our mountains
    that lie,
While **discord** is tearing Old Europe to
    pieces,
Shall amply the wants of the people
    supply;
New roads and canals, on their bosoms
    conveying,
Refinement and wealth through our forests
    shall roam,
And millions of freemen, with **rapture**
    surveying,
Shall shout out "O Liberty! this is thy home!"

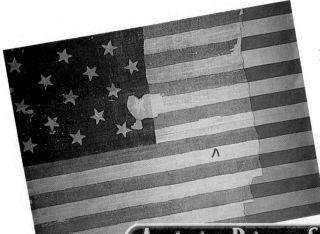

Flag flown at Fort McHenry during War of 1812

On the Road

Printed Publications

David Stevenson described a journey by stage-coach along a typical route of the time.

Sometimes our way lay for miles through extensive **marshes,** which we crossed by **corduroy-roads.** . . . At others the coach stuck fast in mud, from which it could be [moved] only by the combined efforts of the coachman and passengers; at one place we traveled . . . through a forest flooded with water, which stood to a height of several feet. . . . The distance of the route from Pittsburgh to Erie is 128 miles, which was accomplished in forty-six hours . . . although the [stagecoach] by which I traveled carried the mail, and stopped only for breakfast, dinner and tea, but there was considerable delay by the coach being once upset and several times "mired."

A woman named Elizabeth Smith Geer wrote about winter travel in her diary:

My children gave out with cold and fatigue and could not travel, and the boys had to unhitch the oxen and bring them and carry the children on to camp. It was so cold and numb I could not tell by feeling that I had any feet at all. . . . I have not told you half we suffered.

Analyzing Primary Sources

1. What was it about Washington's public speaking manner that Maclay criticized?
2. In the song, what does the phrase "treasures immense" mean?
3. How did roads of the early 1800s differ from roads that we travel on today?

The Growing Nation

In the early 1800s, the United States had a firmly established democracy, but the freedoms it guaranteed did not extend to everyone. Native Americans were forced from their lands, while African Americans were enslaved—torn from their homelands and often separated from their families. As you read these primary source selections, think about how long these conditions existed before ideas of reform began to take hold.

Reader's Dictionary

detachment: group or body of people

inclemency: harsh conditions

auction block: site where enslaved people were bought and sold

piteous: sad, distressed

vociferously: loudly

battery: a grouping of weapons

rent: opened or parted

Trail of Tears

Printed Publications

Although recognized as a separate nation by several U.S. treaties, the Cherokee people were forced to leave their lands because white people wanted it for farming. Thousands died before they reached Indian Territory, the present-day state of Oklahoma. This forced journey came to be called the Trail of Tears. A newspaper published this account.

On Tuesday evening we fell in with a **detachment** of the poor Cherokee Indians . . . about eleven hundred Indians—sixty wagons—six hundred horses, and perhaps forty pairs of oxen. We found them in the forest camped for the night by the road side . . . under a severe fall of rain accompanied by heavy wind. With their canvas for a shield from the **inclemency** of the weather, and the cold wet ground for a resting place, after the fatigue of the day, they spent the night . . . many of the aged Indians were suffering extremely from the fatigue of the journey, and the ill health consequent upon it . . . several were then quite ill, and one aged man we were informed was then in the last struggles of death.

Map of Georgia in 1826 showing Cherokee land (left) and seal of Cherokee Nation (right)

Delicia Patterson

Oral Histories

Delicia Patterson provided this look at life under slavery. She was 92 years old when she was interviewed.

I was born in Boonville, Missouri, January 2, 1845. Mother had five children but raised only two of us. I was owned by Charles Mitchell until I was fifteen years old. They were fairly nice to all of their slaves. . . .

When I was fifteen years old, I was brought to the courthouse, put up on the **auction block** to be sold. Old Judge Miller from my county was there. I knew him well because he was one of the wealthiest slave owners in the county, and the meanest one. He was so cruel all the slaves and many owners hated him because of it. He saw me on the block for sale, and he knew I was a good worker. So, when he bid for me, I spoke right out on the auction block and told him:

"Old Judge Miller, don't you bid for me, 'cause if you do, I would not live on your plantation. I will take a knife and cut my own throat from ear to ear before I would be owned by you. . . ."

So he stepped back and let someone else bid for me. . . . So I was sold to a Southern Englishman named Thomas Steele for fifteen hundred dollars. . . .

Religious Camp Meeting

Personal Records

The desire for self-improvement was closely connected to a renewed interest in religion. By the 1830s, the Second Great Awakening, the second great period of religious revival in the United States, was in full swing. The camp meeting was especially important to isolated frontier families. One preacher, James Finley, described a revival meeting:

The noise was like the roar of Niagara. . . . Some of the people were singing, others praying, some crying for mercy in the most **piteous** accents, while others were shouting most **vociferously.** . . . At one time I saw at least five hundred swept down in a moment, as if a **battery** of a thousand guns had been opened upon them, and then immediately followed shrieks and shouts that **rent** the very heavens.

Anti-slavery banner

Analyzing Primary Sources

1. Do you think the writer of the newspaper article feels sympathy toward the Cherokee?
2. Why did Delicia, the formerly enslaved woman, not want to serve on Judge Miller's plantation?
3. What scene is James Finley describing?

Civil War and Reconstruction

The American Civil War, or the War Between the States, was a major turning point for the American people. When the fighting ended, 600,000 Americans had lost their lives, slavery had been abolished, and most of the South lay in ruin. Leaders argued over how to reunite the shattered nation. And even though slavery had been abolished, African Americans quickly discovered that freedom did not mean equality. As you read these selections, think about the changes that took place during this era.

Reader's Dictionary

exterminating: destructive

bondage: slavery

suffrage: the right to vote

musket: soldier's rifle

Swing Low, Sweet Chariot

Songs & Poems

Spirituals—songs of salvation—provided the enslaved African Americans who wrote and sang them with not only a measure of comfort in bleak times but with a means for communicating secretly among themselves.

Swing low, sweet chariot,
Coming for to carry me home,
Swing low, sweet chariot,
Coming for to carry me home.

I looked over Jordan and what
    did I see
Coming for to carry me home,
A band of angels coming after me.
Coming for to carry me home.

If you get there before I do,
Coming for to carry me home,
Tell all my friends I'm coming too,
Coming for to carry me home.

I'm sometimes up and sometimes down,
Coming for to carry me home,
But still my soul feels heavenly bound,
Coming for to carry me home.

The Fisk Jubilee Singers

On the Plight of African Americans

Personal Records

In 1867 Frederick Douglass appealed eloquently to Congress on behalf of African Americans.

. . . Yet the Negroes have marvelously survived all the **exterminating** forces of slavery, and have emerged at the end of 250 years of **bondage,** not [sad and hateful], but cheerful, hopeful, and forgiving. They now stand before Congress and the country, not complaining of the past, but simply asking for a better future.

. . . It is true that a strong plea for equal **suffrage** might be addressed to the national sense of honor. Something, too, might be said of national gratitude. A nation might well hesitate before the temptation to betray its allies. There is something . . . mean, to say nothing of the cruelty, in placing the loyal Negroes of the South under the political power of their rebel masters. . . . We asked the Negroes to [support] our cause, to be our friends, to fight for us and against their masters; and now, after they have done all that we asked them to do . . . it is proposed in some quarters to turn them over to the political control of the common enemy of the government and of the Negro. . . .

What, then, is the work before Congress? . . . In a word, it must [allow African Americans to vote], and by means of the loyal Negroes and the loyal white men of the South build up a national party there, and in time bridge the [gap] between North and South, so that our country may have a common liberty and a common civilization. . . .

The Fire of Battle

Personal Records

Union soldier George Sargent served in the area west of Washington, D.C., throughout the Shenandoah Valley. He wrote his impressions of how soldiers react in battle.

Can you imagine a fellow's feelings about that time, to have to face thousands of **muskets** with a prospect of having a bullet put through you? If you can, all right; I can't describe it. I've heard some say that they were not scared going into a fight, but I think it's all nonsense. I don't believe there was ever a man who went into battle but was scared, more or less. Some will turn pale as a sheet, look wild and ferocious, some will be so excited that they don't know what they are about while others will be as cool and collected as on other occasions.

Analyzing Primary Sources

1. What does "Swing Low, Sweet Chariot" show about the condition and faith of the people who sang it?
2. What did Frederick Douglass urge Congress to do?
3. What does George Sargent say happens to all soldiers in battle?

Reshaping the Nation

In the period from the end of the Civil War to 1900, America grew at a remarkable rate. The settlement of the West was filled with tragedy for Native Americans, adventure for the settlers, and hardship for just about everyone. The trend toward large-scale industrial operations led to the Age of Big Business. Immigrants from Europe flocked to America, arriving with the hope of a better life. However, the growth of factories and new ways of working caused problems between workers and owners.

Reader's Dictionary

reservation: land set aside for Native Americans

abide: follow

kosher: approved by Jewish law

Sioux ghost dance shirt

Indian School

Ah-nen-la-de-ni of the Mohawk people describes his first experience in school.

After the almost complete freedom of **reservation** life the cramped quarters and the dull routine of the school were maddening to all us strangers. There were endless rules for us to study and **abide** by, and hardest of all was the rule against speaking to each other in our own language. We must speak English or remain silent, and those who knew no English were forced to be dumb or else break the rules in secret. This last we did quite frequently, and were punished, when detected, by being made to stand in the "public hall" for a long time or to march about the yard while the other boys were at play.

The Sweat Shop

Oral Histories

In factories, people had to work at an inhumane pace. Following is the account of a young woman employed in New York City's garment industry.

At seven o'clock we all sit down to our machines and the boss brings to each one the pile of work that he or she is to finish during the day. . . . This pile is put down beside the machine and as soon as a skirt is done it is laid on the other side of the machine. . . . The machines go like mad all day, because the faster you work, the more money you get. Sometimes in my haste I get my finger caught and the needle goes right through it. . . . We all have accidents like that. . . . Sometimes a finger has to come off. . . . All the time we are working the boss walks about examining the finished garments and making us do them over again if they are not just right. So we have to be careful as well as swift. . . .

Young coal miners in Kingston, Pennsylvania

An Emigrant's Story

Printed Publications

In her book The Promised Land, *Mary Antin tells of leaving her native country, Poland, to come to America when she was 13 years old.*

What did they not ask, the eager, foolish, friendly people? They wanted to handle the ticket, and mother must read them what is written on it. How much did it cost? Was it all paid for? Were we going to have a foreign passport or did we intend to steal across the border? Were we not going to have new dresses to travel in? Was it sure that we could get **kosher** food on the ship?

[After we boarded the train] when the warning bell rang out, it was drowned in—fragments of blessings, farewells—"Don't forget!"—"Take care of—" "Keep your tickets—" "Moshele—newspapers!—" "Garlick is best!" "Happy journey!" "God help you!" "Good-bye!" "Remember—"

Analyzing Primary Sources

1. How does the boy at the Indian school compare life there with the life on the reservation?
2. Why did the workers in the sweat shop work quickly?
3. What words does Mary Antin use to describe the people of her town who asked the many questions?

Reform, Expansion, and War

As city populations grew, living and working conditions became worse. The Progressive movement worked to protect workers and the poor, while much attention was turned overseas. During the late 1800s and early 1900s, the United States used the Monroe Doctrine to oppose European involvement in Latin America. By enforcing it in a war with Spain, the United States became a colonial power. World War I was a global conflict with unprecedented casualties. This war meant the fall of the old-world empires, and an end to a quieter way of life. As you read these primary source selections, think about how the focus of average citizens changed from the Civil War to World War I.

Reader's Dictionary

bewildered: confused

damages: money

ruefully: regretfully

starboard: the right side of the ship

periscope: a viewing device for submarines to see above the ocean surface

stern: the rear of the ship

score: twenty

Hull House

 **Printed Publications**

Social workers established settlement houses in the slums of the large cities. One of the more famous was Hull House, founded in Chicago by Jane Addams. This excerpt explains how settlement houses helped poor and disadvantaged people living in the city.

We early found ourselves spending many hours in efforts to secure support for deserted women, insurance for **bewildered** widows, **damages** for injured operators, furniture from the clutches of the installment store. The Settlement is valuable as an information and interpretation bureau. It constantly acts between the various institutions of the city and the people for whose benefit these were erected. The hospitals, county agencies, and State asylums are often but vague rumors to the people who need them most. Another function of the Settlement to its neighborhood resembles that of the big brother whose mere presence on the playground protects the little one from bullies.

Propaganda poster

Aboard the *Lusitania*

Despite the threat of German submarine attacks, Theodate Pope, an American, boarded the Lusitania to sail home from Europe. On May 7, 1915, a torpedo sank the British ship. After being rescued, Pope wrote this letter.

Friday morning we came slowly through fog, blowing our fog horn. It cleared off about an hour before we went below for lunch. A young Englishman at our table had been served with his ice cream, and was waiting for the steward to bring him a spoon to eat it with. He looked **ruefully** at it and said he would hate to have a torpedo get him before he ate it. We all laughed, and then commented on how slowly we were running. We thought the engines had stopped.

Mr. Friend [another passenger] and I went up on deck B on the **starboard** side and leaned over the railing, looking at the sea, which was a marvellous blue and very dazzling in the sunlight. I said, "How could the officers ever see a **periscope** there?" The torpedo was on its way to us at that moment, for we went a short distance farther toward the **stern,** . . . when the ship was struck on the starboard side. The water and timbers flew past the deck. Mr. Friend struck his fist in his hand and said, "By Jove! they've got us." The ship steadied herself a few seconds and then listed [tilted] heavily to starboard, throwing us against the wall of a small corridor. . . .

. . . [The] deck suddenly looked very strange, crowded with people, and I remember that two women were crying in a pitifully weak way. An officer was shouting orders to stop lowering the boats, and we were told to go down to deck B. We first looked over the rail and watched a boat filled with men and women being lowered. The stern was lowered too quickly and half the boatload were spilled backwards into the water. We looked at each other, sickened by the sight. . . .

The United States and Cuba

Sympathy for Cubans under Spanish rule grew as newspapers competed with each other in reporting stories of Spanish atrocities. An editorial in Joseph Pulitzer's New York World is a case in point:

How long are the Spaniards to drench Cuba with the blood and tears of her people?

. . . How long shall old men and women and children be murdered by the **score,** the innocent victims of Spanish rage against the patriot armies they cannot conquer?

. . . How long shall the United States sit idle and indifferent . . . ?

Analyzing Primary Sources

1. According to Jane Addams, what is the role of the settlement house?
2. The *Lusitania* passengers were aware that Germany had threatened to attack British ships. From Theodate Pope's account, do you think they took the threat seriously?
3. What action do you think the newspaper editorial wants the United States to take? Explain.

Turbulent Decades

After World War I, Americans enjoyed a decade of relative prosperity. The Great Depression ended that. The terrible economic slump shook the lives of the rich and made life even harder for those who were already poor. In the 1940s, international events became the center of attention, and fighting in World War II became the nation's top priority. As you read these selections, think about the various ways Americans demonstrated personal courage, in the good times and in the bad.

Reader's Dictionary

soup line: outdoor kitchen set up to distribute free food to needy people

contemptuous: scornful

A fruit seller

Standing in the Soup Line

Peggy Terry came from the hills of Kentucky, but her family spent the hard years of the Depression in Oklahoma City. She describes how the family managed to eat during the tough times.

I first noticed the difference when we'd come home from school in the evening. My mother'd send us to the **soup line**. . . . If you happened to be one of the first ones in line, you didn't get anything but water that was on top. So we'd ask the guy that was ladling out the soup into the buckets—everybody had to bring their own bucket to get the soup—he'd dip the greasy, watery stuff off the top. So we'd ask him to please dip down to get some meat and potatoes from the bottom of the kettle. . . .

Then we'd go across the street. One place had bread, large loaves of bread. Down the road just a little piece was a big shed, and they gave milk. My sister and me would take two buckets each. And that's what we lived off for the longest time.

I can remember one time, the only thing in the house to eat was mustard. My sister and I put so much mustard on biscuits that we got sick. And we can't stand mustard till today. . . .

When they had food to give to people, you'd get a notice and you'd go down. So Daddy went down that day and he took my sister and me. They were giving away potatoes and things like that. But they had a truck of oranges parked in the alley. Somebody asked them who the oranges were for, and they wouldn't tell 'em. So they said, well, we're gonna take those oranges. And they did. My dad was one of the ones that got up on the truck. They called the police, and the police chased us all away. But we got the oranges.

It's different today. People are made to feel ashamed now if they don't have anything. Back then, I'm not sure how the rich felt. I think the rich were as **contemptuous** of the poor then as they are now. But among the people that I knew, we all had an understanding that it wasn't our fault. It was something that had happened to the machinery. . . .

I remember it was fun. It was fun going to the soup line. 'Cause we all went down the road, and we laughed and we played. The only thing we felt is that we were hungry and we were going to get food. Nobody made us feel ashamed. There just wasn't any of that.

On the Home Front

The U.S. government appealed to civilians to support the war effort in many ways. This bulletin was posted in meat markets.

1] THE NEED IS URGENT—War in the Pacific has greatly reduced our supply of vegetable fats from the Far East. It is necessary to find substitutes for them. Fat makes glycerine. And glycerine makes explosives for us and our Allies—explosives to down Axis planes, stop their tanks, and sink their ships. We need millions of pounds of glycerine and you housewives can help supply it.

Wartime conservation poster

2] DON'T throw away a single drop of used cooking fat, bacon fat, meat drippings, fry fats—every kind you use. After you've got all the cooking good from them, pour them through a kitchen strainer into a clean, wide-mouthed can. Keep it in a cool dark place. . . .

3] TAKE THEM to your meat dealer when you've saved a pound or more. He is cooperating patriotically. He will pay you for your waste fats and get them started on their way to war industries. . . .

Analyzing Primary Sources

1. What does Peggy Terry mean when she says that the hard times were due to "something that had happened to the machinery"?
2. For what purpose did the government ask people to save their cooking fats and meat drippings?

Turning Points

During the Cold War era, the world lingered on the edge of nuclear disaster as the superpowers—the United States and the Soviet Union— both tried to extend their influence around the world. At home, families tried to prepare for a nuclear attack as best they could. At the same time, African Americans began to demand better treatment from their govern- ment. The nation found a voice in protest. Protest against injustice toward African Americans marked the late 1950s. In the 1960s, the youth of America protested involvement in the Vietnam War. Women demanded equal pay for equal work. As you read these selections, think about how the government reacted to the passions of the American citizens. Did their actions make a difference?

Reader's Dictionary

fallout: particles of radioactive material that drift through the atmosphere after a nuclear explosion

Conelrad: (from "<u>Con</u>trol of <u>El</u>ectromagnetic <u>Rad</u>iation") a radio broadcasting system that would replace normal broadcasts in an emergency

Fallout Fears

 **Printed Publications**

By 1961 fears of nuclear war were so great that the government urged people to be prepared for a nuclear attack. LIFE *magazine reminded Americans what to do during such an attack.*

The standard Civil Defense signal for an alert is a steady 3- to 5-minute blast of a siren or whistle. The warning to take cover is a 3-minute period of short blasts or a wailing siren. If an attack should come, however, the first warning you may get could be the flash itself. Your first move should be to close your eyes and bury your head in your arms or clothing to block out the light. The flash may last for several seconds, so keep covered until it begins to dim.

The shockwave will come next. Take cover so you will not be knocked down. If you are in a car, roll down windows to avoid flying glass and lie on the floor. Try to count the seconds between the flash and shockwave. This will help you estimate how far away the bomb has hit and how long you have to find better cover before the **fallout** can reach you. . . .

Wherever you are, try to reach a radio— preferably a battery radio since the electricity may be out—and tune it to 640 or 1240 on your dial, which are the **Conelrad** frequencies for emergency instructions. If you have a shelter, go to it immediately. . . .

If you have no shelter and there is an hour or so left before the fallout is due to reach your area, you can block up the windows of your basement with one foot of earth, and take shelter there under tables on which you have piled books and magazines for extra shielding. You should also get together a supply of food and water and take it to the basement with you. . . .

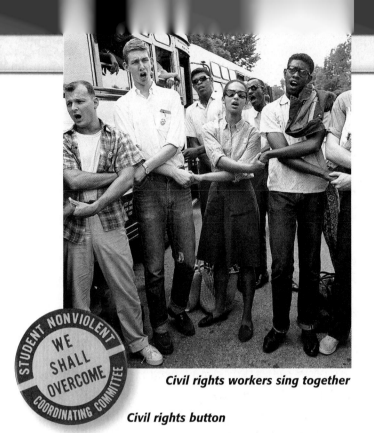

Civil rights workers sing together

Civil rights button

We'll walk hand in hand someday
Oh deep in my heart, I do believe
We shall overcome someday

We shall live in peace, we shall live in peace
We shall live in peace someday
Oh deep in my heart, I do believe
That we shall overcome someday

We Shall Overcome

Songs & Poems

As civil rights supporters marched in protest, they often raised their voices in unison to drown out their fears and bolster their hopes. Many considered this song the civil rights anthem.

We shall overcome, we shall overcome
We shall overcome someday
Oh deep in my heart, I do believe
That we shall overcome someday

We'll walk hand in hand, we'll walk hand
   in hand

Working Women

During the 1960s and 1970s, women began demanding equal pay for equal work. Women such as Joanne Gus, a warehouse worker, filed lawsuits to get back pay from their employers. In this excerpt, Gus describes the difficulties she and her coworkers faced after receiving a disappointing $500 offer to settle their lawsuit.

. . . I was ready to cry. You can't realize all the aggravation and amount of work that had been done so far. The really sad part about it was that most of the women were willing to settle. They were afraid to take it any further. Well, I can be very stubborn, especially if I know I'm right about an issue. So I refused the offer for them all. Well, the next few days were really [awful] at work. Still, I knew I was worth more.

The case made it to federal court. A settlement of $548,000 in back pay for 246 women was reached.

Analyzing Primary Sources

1. According to the *LIFE* magazine article, in what order would someone probably experience the effects of a nuclear attack some distance away?
2. What things did workers in the civil rights movement want to "overcome" as is implied in the song?
3. How did Joanne Gus's attitude differ from those of her coworkers?

Modern America

World events since the 1970s have moved with breathtaking speed. The Soviet Union collapsed, ending the Cold War. New advances in technology helped the world move forward. Millions of immigrants came to the United States, following the promise of freedom and economic opportunity. At the same time, terrorism threatened the American way of life. As you examine these selections, think of the challenges and opportunities facing the United States today.

Reader's Dictionary

extremism: the holding of unreasonable views

humanitarian: committed to improving the lives of other people

pluralism: society with different ethnic and religious groups

tolerance: acceptance of and fairness toward people who hold different views

Proud to Be an American

"God Bless the USA," by singer Lee Greenwood, topped the country music charts in the 1980s. It was adopted as a theme song for President Reagan's 1984 reelection campaign.

I'm proud to be an American
where at least I know I'm free,
And I won't forget the men who died
who gave that right to me,
And I gladly stand up next to you
and defend her still today,
'Cause there ain't no doubt I love this land
God Bless the U.S.A.

Address to Congress

On September 20, 2001, President George W. Bush addressed Congress, nine days after New York City and Washington, D.C., were shaken by suicide aircraft attacks.

On September the eleventh, enemies of freedom committed an act of war against our country. Americans have known wars—but for the past 136 years, they have been wars on foreign soil, except for one Sunday in 1941 [the attack on Pearl Harbor]. Americans have known the casualties of war—but not at the center of a great city on a peaceful morning. Americans have known surprise attacks—but never before on thousands of civilians. All of this was brought upon us in a single day—and night fell on a different world, a world where freedom itself is under attack. . . .

The terrorists [who carried out the attack] practice a fringe form of Islamic **extremism** that has been rejected by Muslim scholars and the vast majority of Muslim clerics— a fringe movement that perverts the peaceful teachings of Islam. . . .

This group [al-Qaeda] and its leader, a person named Osama bin Laden, are linked to many other organizations in different countries. . . . The leadership of al-Qaeda has great influence in Afghanistan and supports the Taliban regime in controlling most of that country. . . .

The United States respects the people of Afghanistan—after all, we are currently its largest source of **humanitarian** aid—but we condemn the Taliban regime.

[The terrorists] hate what we see right here in this chamber—a democratically elected government. Their leaders are self-appointed. They hate our freedoms—our freedom of religion, our freedom of speech, our freedom to vote and assemble and disagree with each other. . . .

This is not, however, just America's fight. And what is at stake is not just America's freedom. This is the world's fight. This is civilization's fight. This is the fight of all who believe in progress and **pluralism, tolerance,** and freedom. . . .

The civilized world is rallying to America's side. They understand that if this terror goes unpunished, their own cities, their own citizens may be next. Terror, unanswered, can not

President Bush thanks rescue workers

only bring down buildings, it can threaten the stability of legitimate governments. And we will not allow it. . . .

I ask you to uphold the values of America, and remember why so many have come here. We are in a fight for our principles, and our first responsibility is to live by them. No one should be singled out for unfair treatment or unkind words because of their ethnic background or religious faith. . . .

Great harm has been done to us. We have suffered great loss. And in our grief and anger we have found our mission and our moment. Freedom and fear are at war. The advance of human freedom—the great achievement of our time, and the great hope of every time— now depends on us. Our Nation—this generation—will lift a dark threat of violence from our people and our future. We will rally the world to this cause, by our efforts and by our courage. We will not tire, we will not falter, and we will not fail.

Analyzing Primary Sources

1. What themes does Lee Greenwood express in his song?
2. To what other tragic event does President Bush compare the events of September 11, 2001?
3. Why does the president believe other nations should help in the fight against terrorism?

Presidents of the United States

In this resource you will find portraits of the individuals who served as presidents of the United States, along with their occupations, political party affiliations, and other interesting facts.

**The Republican Party during this period developed into today's Democratic Party. Today's Republican Party originated in 1854.*

1 George Washington

Presidential term: 1789–1797
Lived: 1732–1799
Born in: Virginia
Elected from: Virginia
Occupations: Soldier, Planter
Party: None
Vice President: John Adams

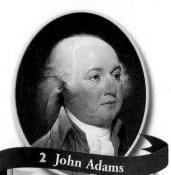

2 John Adams

Presidential term: 1797–1801
Lived: 1735–1826
Born in: Massachusetts
Elected from: Massachusetts
Occupations: Teacher, Lawyer
Party: Federalist
Vice President: Thomas Jefferson

3 Thomas Jefferson

Presidential term: 1801–1809
Lived: 1743–1826
Born in: Virginia
Elected from: Virginia
Occupations: Planter, Lawyer
Party: Republican**
Vice Presidents: Aaron Burr, George Clinton

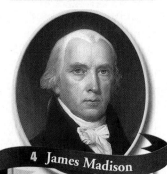

4 James Madison

Presidential term: 1809–1817
Lived: 1751–1836
Born in: Virginia
Elected from: Virginia
Occupation: Planter
Party: Republican**
Vice Presidents: George Clinton, Elbridge Gerry

5 James Monroe

Presidential term: 1817–1825
Lived: 1758–1831
Born in: Virginia
Elected from: Virginia
Occupation: Lawyer
Party: Republican**
Vice President: Daniel D. Tompkins

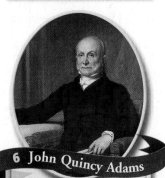

6 John Quincy Adams

Presidential term: 1825–1829
Lived: 1767–1848
Born in: Massachusetts
Elected from: Massachusetts
Occupation: Lawyer
Party: Republican**
Vice President: John C. Calhoun

7 Andrew Jackson

Presidential term: 1829–1837
Lived: 1767–1845
Born in: South Carolina
Elected from: Tennessee
Occupations: Lawyer, Soldier
Party: Democratic
Vice Presidents: John C. Calhoun, Martin Van Buren

8 Martin Van Buren

Presidential term: 1837–1841
Lived: 1782–1862
Born in: New York
Elected from: New York
Occupation: Lawyer
Party: Democratic
Vice President: Richard M. Johnson

9 William H. Harrison

Presidential term: 1841
Lived: 1773–1841
Born in: Virginia
Elected from: Ohio
Occupations: Soldier, Planter
Party: Whig
Vice President: John Tyler

10 John Tyler

Presidential term: 1841–1845
Lived: 1790–1862
Born in: Virginia
Elected as V.P. from: Virginia
Succeeded Harrison
Occupation: Lawyer
Party: Whig
Vice President: None

11 James K. Polk

Presidential term: 1845–1849
Lived: 1795–1849
Born in: North Carolina
Elected from: Tennessee
Occupation: Lawyer
Party: Democratic
Vice President: George M. Dallas

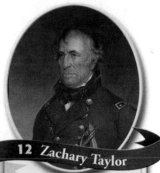

12 Zachary Taylor

Presidential term: 1849–1850
Lived: 1784–1850
Born in: Virginia
Elected from: Louisiana
Occupation: Soldier
Party: Whig
Vice President: Millard Fillmore

13 Millard Fillmore

Presidential term: 1850–1853
Lived: 1800–1874
Born in: New York
Elected as V.P. from: New York
Succeeded Taylor
Occupation: Lawyer
Party: Whig
Vice President: None

14 Franklin Pierce

Presidential term: 1853–1857
Lived: 1804–1869
Born in: New Hampshire
Elected from: New Hampshire
Occupation: Lawyer
Party: Democratic
Vice President: William R. King

15 James Buchanan

Presidential term: 1857–1861
Lived: 1791–1868
Born in: Pennsylvania
Elected from: Pennsylvania
Occupation: Lawyer
Party: Democratic
Vice President: John C. Breckinridge

16 Abraham Lincoln

Presidential term: 1861–1865
Lived: 1809–1865
Born in: Kentucky
Elected from: Illinois
Occupation: Lawyer
Party: Republican
Vice Presidents: Hannibal Hamlin, Andrew Johnson

17 Andrew Johnson

Presidential term: 1865–1869
Lived: 1808–1875
Born in: North Carolina
Elected as V.P. from: Tennessee
Succeeded Lincoln
Occupation: Tailor
Party: Republican
Vice President: None

18 Ulysses S. Grant

Presidential term: 1869–1877
Lived: 1822–1885
Born in: Ohio
Elected from: Illinois
Occupations: Farmer, Soldier
Party: Republican
Vice Presidents: Schuyler Colfax,
Henry Wilson

19 Rutherford B. Hayes

Presidential term: 1877–1881
Lived: 1822–1893
Born in: Ohio
Elected from: Ohio
Occupation: Lawyer
Party: Republican
Vice President: William A.
Wheeler

20 James A. Garfield

Presidential term: 1881
Lived: 1831–1881
Born in: Ohio
Elected from: Ohio
Occupations: Laborer, Professor
Party: Republican
Vice President: Chester A.
Arthur

21 Chester A. Arthur

Presidential term: 1881–1885
Lived: 1830–1886
Born in: Vermont
Elected as V.P. from: New York
Succeeded Garfield
Occupations: Teacher, Lawyer
Party: Republican
Vice President: None

22 Grover Cleveland

Presidential term: 1885–1889
Lived: 1837–1908
Born in: New Jersey
Elected from: New York
Occupation: Lawyer
Party: Democratic
Vice President: Thomas A.
Hendricks

23 Benjamin Harrison

Presidential term: 1889–1893
Lived: 1833–1901
Born in: Ohio
Elected from: Indiana
Occupation: Lawyer
Party: Republican
Vice President: Levi P. Morton

24 Grover Cleveland

Presidential term: 1893–1897
Lived: 1837–1908
Born in: New Jersey
Elected from: New York
Occupation: Lawyer
Party: Democratic
Vice President: Adlai E.
Stevenson

25 William McKinley

Presidential term: 1897–1901
Lived: 1843–1901
Born in: Ohio
Elected from: Ohio
Occupations: Teacher, Lawyer
Party: Republican
Vice Presidents: Garret Hobart,
Theodore Roosevelt

26 Theodore Roosevelt

Presidential term: 1901–1909
Lived: 1858–1919
Born in: New York
Elected as V.P. from: New York
Succeeded McKinley
Occupations: Historian, Rancher
Party: Republican
Vice President: Charles W.
    Fairbanks

27 William H. Taft

Presidential term: 1909–1913
Lived: 1857–1930
Born in: Ohio
Elected from: Ohio
Occupation: Lawyer
Party: Republican
Vice President: James S.
    Sherman

28 Woodrow Wilson

Presidential term: 1913–1921
Lived: 1856–1924
Born in: Virginia
Elected from: New Jersey
Occupation: College Professor
Party: Democratic
Vice President: Thomas R.
    Marshall

29 Warren G. Harding

Presidential term: 1921–1923
Lived: 1865–1923
Born in: Ohio
Elected from: Ohio
Occupations: Newspaper Editor,
    Publisher
Party: Republican
Vice President: Calvin Coolidge

30 Calvin Coolidge

Presidential term: 1923–1929
Lived: 1872–1933
Born in: Vermont
Elected as V.P. from:
    Massachusetts
Succeeded Harding
Occupation: Lawyer
Party: Republican
Vice President: Charles G. Dawes

31 Herbert C. Hoover

Presidential term: 1929–1933
Lived: 1874–1964
Born in: Iowa
Elected from: California
Occupation: Engineer
Party: Republican
Vice President: Charles Curtis

32 Franklin D. Roosevelt

Presidential term: 1933–1945
Lived: 1882–1945
Born in: New York
Elected from: New York
Occupation: Lawyer
Party: Democratic
Vice Presidents: John N. Garner,
    Henry A. Wallace, Harry S
    Truman

33 Harry S Truman

Presidential term: 1945–1953
Lived: 1884–1972
Born in: Missouri
Elected as V.P. from: Missouri
Succeeded Roosevelt
Occupations: Clerk, Farmer
Party: Democratic
Vice President: Alben W.
    Barkley

34 Dwight D. Eisenhower

Presidential term: 1953–1961
Lived: 1890–1969
Born in: Texas
Elected from: New York
Occupation: Soldier
Party: Republican
Vice President: Richard M.
    Nixon

35 John F. Kennedy

Presidential term: 1961–1963
Lived: 1917–1963
Born in: Massachusetts
Elected from: Massachusetts
Occupations: Author, Reporter
Party: Democratic
Vice President: Lyndon B. Johnson

36 Lyndon B. Johnson

Presidential term: 1963–1969
Lived: 1908–1973
Born in: Texas
Elected as V.P. from: Texas
Succeeded Kennedy
Occupation: Teacher
Party: Democratic
Vice President: Hubert H. Humphrey

37 Richard M. Nixon

Presidential term: 1969–1974
Lived: 1913–1994
Born in: California
Elected from: New York
Occupation: Lawyer
Party: Republican
Vice Presidents: Spiro T. Agnew, Gerald R. Ford

38 Gerald R. Ford

Presidential term: 1974–1977
Lived: 1913–
Born in: Nebraska
Appointed as V.P. upon Agnew's resignation; succeeded Nixon
Occupation: Lawyer
Party: Republican
Vice President: Nelson A. Rockefeller

39 James E. Carter, Jr.

Presidential term: 1977–1981
Lived: 1924–
Born in: Georgia
Elected from: Georgia
Occupations: Business, Farmer
Party: Democratic
Vice President: Walter F. Mondale

40 Ronald W. Reagan

Presidential term: 1981–1989
Lived: 1911–
Born in: Illinois
Elected from: California
Occupations: Actor, Lecturer
Party: Republican
Vice President: George H.W. Bush

41 George H.W. Bush

Presidential term: 1989–1993
Lived: 1924–
Born in: Massachusetts
Elected from: Texas
Occupation: Business
Party: Republican
Vice President: J. Danforth Quayle

42 William J. Clinton

Presidential term: 1993–2001
Lived: 1946–
Born in: Arkansas
Elected from: Arkansas
Occupation: Lawyer
Party: Democratic
Vice President: Albert Gore, Jr.

43 George W. Bush

Presidential term: 2001–
Lived: 1946–
Born in: Connecticut
Elected from: Texas
Occupation: Business
Party: Republican
Vice President: Richard B. Cheney

The Magna Carta

The Magna Carta, signed by King John in 1215, marked a decisive step forward in the development of constitutional government in England. Later, it became a model for colonists who carried the Magna Carta's guarantees of legal and political rights to America.

1. . . . [T]hat the English Church shall be free, and shall have its rights entire, and its liberties unimpaired. . . . we have also granted for us and our heirs forever, all the liberties written out below, to have and to keep for them and their heirs, of us and our heirs:

39. No free man shall be seized or imprisoned, or stripped of his rights or possessions, or outlawed or exiled, or deprived of his standing in any other way, nor will we proceed with force against him, or send others to do so, except by the lawful judgment of his equals, or by the law of the land.

40. To no one will we sell, to no one deny or delay right or justice.

41. All merchants may enter or leave England unharmed and without fear, and may stay or travel within it, by land or water, for purposes of trade, free from all illegal exactions, in accordance with ancient and lawful customs. This, however, does not apply in time of war to merchants from a country that is at war with us. . . .

42. In future it shall be lawful for any man to leave and return to our kingdom unharmed and without fear, by land or water, preserving his allegiance to us, except in time of war, for some short period, for the common benefit of the realm. . . .

60. All these customs and liberties that we have granted shall be observed in our kingdom in so far as concerns our own relations with our subjects. Let all men of our kingdom, whether clergy or laymen, observe them similarly in their relations with their own men. . . .

63. . . . Both we and the barons have sworn that all this shall be observed in good faith and without deceit. Witness the abovementioned people and many others. Given by our hand in the meadow that is called Runnymede, between Windsor and Staines, on the fifteenth day of June in the seventeenth year of our reign.

Illuminated manuscript, Middle Ages

The Mayflower Compact

On November 21, 1620, 41 colonists aboard the Mayflower drafted this agreement. The Mayflower Compact was the first plan of self-government ever put in force in the English colonies.

In the Name of God, Amen. We, whose names are underwritten, the Loyal Subjects of our dread Sovereign Lord King James, by the Grace of God, of Great Britain, France, and Ireland, King, Defender of the Faith, etc. Having undertaken for the Glory of God, and Advancement of the Christian Faith, and the Honour of our King and Country, a Voyage to plant the first Colony in the northern Parts of Virginia; Do by these Presents, solemnly and mutually, in the Presence of God and one another, covenant and combine ourselves together into a civil Body Politick, for our better Ordering and Preservation, and Furtherance of the Ends aforesaid: And by Virtue hereof do enact, constitute, and frame, such just and equal Laws, Ordinances, Acts, Constitutions, and Officers, from time to time, as shall be thought most meet and convenient for the general Good of the Colony; unto which we promise all due Submission and Obedience. In Witness whereof we have hereunto subscribed our names at Cape-Cod the eleventh of November, in the Reign of our Sovereign Lord King James, of England, France, and Ireland, the eighteenth, and of Scotland, the fifty-fourth, Anno Domini, 1620.

The Federalist, No. 10

James Madison wrote several articles supporting ratification of the Constitution for a New York newspaper. In the excerpt below, Madison argues for the idea of a federal republic.

By a faction, I understand a number of citizens . . . who are united and actuated by some common impulse . . . adverse to the rights of other citizens. . . . The inference to which we are brought is that the causes of faction cannot be removed and that relief is only to be sought in the means of controlling its *effects.* . . .

James Madison

A republic, by which I mean a government in which the scheme of representation takes place . . . promises the cure for which we are seeking. . . .

The two great points of difference between a democracy and a republic are: first, the delegation of the government, in the latter, to a small number of citizens elected by the rest; secondly, the greater number of citizens, and greater sphere of country, over which the latter may be extended.

The effect of the first difference is . . . to refine and enlarge the public views, by passing them through the medium of a chosen body of citizens, whose wisdom may best discern the true interest of their country, and whose patriotism and love of justice will be least likely to sacrifice it to temporary or partial considerations. . . .

Washington's Farewell Address

At the end of his second term as president, George Washington spoke of the dangers facing the young nation. He warned against the dangers of political parties and sectionalism, and he advised the nation against permanent alliances with other nations.

. . . Citizens by birth or choice of a common country, that country has a right to concentrate your affections. The name of American, which belongs to you in your national capacity, must always exalt the just pride of patriotism more than any appellation derived from local discriminations. With slight shades of difference, you have the same religion, manners, habits, and political principles. You have in a common cause fought and triumphed together. . . .

In contemplating the causes which may disturb our union it occurs as matter of serious concern that any ground should have been furnished for characterizing parties by *geographical* discriminations. . . .

George Washington

No alliances, however strict, between the parts can be an adequate substitute. They must inevitably experience the infractions and interruptions which all alliances in all times have experienced. . . .

The great rule of conduct for us in regard to foreign nations is, in extending our commercial relations to have with them as little *political* connection as possible. . . .

. . . I anticipate with pleasing expectation that retreat in which I promise myself to realize . . . the sweet enjoyment of partaking in the midst of my fellow citizens the benign influence of good laws under a free government—the ever-favorite object of my heart, and the happy reward, as I trust, of our mutual cares, labors, and dangers.

The Star-Spangled Banner

During the British bombardment of Fort McHenry during the War of 1812, a young Baltimore lawyer named Francis Scott Key was inspired to write the words to "The Star-Spangled Banner." Although it became popular immediately, it was not until 1931 that Congress officially declared "The Star-Spangled Banner" as our national anthem.

O! say can you see by the dawn's early light,
What so proudly we hailed at the twilight's last gleaming,

Whose broad stripes and bright stars through the perilous fight,
O'er the ramparts we watch'd, were so gallantly streaming?
And the Rockets' red glare, the Bombs bursting in air,
Gave proof through the night that our Flag was still there;
O! say does that star-spangled Banner yet wave,
O'er the Land of the free, and the home of the brave!

The Monroe Doctrine

In an 1823 address to Congress, President James Monroe proclaimed the Monroe Doctrine. Designed to end European influence in the Western Hemisphere, it became a cornerstone of United States foreign policy.

. . . With the existing colonies or dependencies of any European power we have not interfered and shall not interfere. But with the Governments who have declared their independence and maintained it, and whose independence we have, on great consideration and on just principles, acknowledged, we could not view any interposition for the purpose of oppressing them, or controlling in any other manner their destiny, by any European power in any other light than as the manifestation of any unfriendly disposition toward the United States. . . .

Our policy in regard to Europe, which was adopted at an early stage of the wars which have so long agitated that quarter of the globe, nevertheless remains the same, which is, not to interfere in the internal concerns of any of its powers; to consider the government *de facto* as the legitimate government for us; to cultivate friendly relations with it, and to preserve those relations by a frank, firm, and manly policy, meeting in all instances the just claims of every power, submitting to injuries from none. . . .

James Monroe

Memorial of the Cherokee Nation

Beaded shoulder bag, Cherokee people

The Indian Removal Act of 1830 called for the relocation of Native Americans to territory west of the Mississippi River. Cherokee leaders protested the policy.

We are aware that some persons suppose it will be for our advantage to remove beyond the Mississippi. We think otherwise. Our people universally think otherwise. . . .

We wish to remain on the land of our fathers. We have a perfect and original right to remain without interruption or molestation. The treaties with us, and laws of the United States made in pursuance of treaties, guaranty our residence and our privileges, and secure us against intruders. Our only request is, that these treaties may be fulfilled, and these laws executed. . . .

. . . We have been called a poor, ignorant, and degraded people. We certainly are not rich; nor have we ever boasted of our knowledge, or our moral or intellectual elevation. But there is not a man within our limits so ignorant as not to know that he has a right to live on the land of his fathers, in the possession of his immemorial privileges, and that this right has been acknowledged by the United States; nor is there a man so degraded as not to feel a keen sense of injury, on being deprived of his right and driven into exile. . . .

The Seneca Falls Declaration

One of the first documents to express the desire for equal rights for women is the Declaration of Sentiments and Resolutions, issued in 1848 at the Seneca Falls Convention in Seneca Falls, New York. Led by Lucretia Mott and Elizabeth Cady Stanton, the delegates adopted a set of resolutions that called for woman suffrage and opportunities for women in employment and education. Excerpts from the Declaration follow.

When, in the course of human events, it becomes necessary for one portion of the family of man to assume among the people of the earth a position different from that which they have hitherto occupied, but one to which the laws of nature and of nature's God entitle them, a decent respect to the opinions of mankind requires that they should declare the causes that impel them to such a course.

We hold these truths to be self-evident: that all men and women are created equal; that they are endowed by their Creator with certain inalienable rights; that among these are life, liberty, and the pursuit of happiness; that to secure these rights governments are instituted, deriving their just powers from the consent of the governed. Whenever any form of government becomes destructive of these ends, it is the right of those who suffer from it to refuse allegiance to it, and to insist upon the institution of a new government, laying its foundation on such principles, and organizing its powers in such form as to them shall seem most likely to effect their safety and happiness. Prudence, indeed, will dictate that governments long established should not be changed for light and transient causes; . . . But when a long train of abuses and usurpations, pursuing invariably the same object, evinces a design to reduce them under absolute despotism, it is their duty to throw off such government, and to provide new guards for their future security. . . .

The history of mankind is a history of repeated injuries and usurpations on the part of man toward woman, having in direct object the establishment of an absolute tyranny over her. To prove this, let facts be submitted to a candid world. . . .

Now, in view of the entire disfranchisement of one-half the people of this country, their social and religious degradation—in view of the unjust laws above mentioned, and because women do feel themselves aggrieved, oppressed, and fraudulently deprived of their most sacred rights, we insist that they have immediate admission to all the rights and privileges which belong to them as citizens of these United States. . . .

Elizabeth Cady Stanton

The Emancipation Proclamation

On January 1, 1863, President Abraham Lincoln issued the Emancipation Proclamation, which freed all enslaved people in states under Confederate control. The Proclamation was a step toward the Thirteenth Amendment (1865), which ended slavery in all of the United States.

. . . That on the 1st day of January, in the year of our Lord 1863, all persons held as slaves within any state or designated part of a state, the people whereof shall then be in rebellion against the United States, shall be then, thenceforward, and forever free; and the Executive Government of the United States, including the military and naval authority thereof, will recognize and maintain the freedom of such persons, and will do no act or acts to repress such persons, or any of them, in any efforts they may make for their actual freedom.

That the Executive will, on the 1st day of January aforesaid, by proclamation, designate the states and parts of states, if any, in which the people thereof, respectively, shall then be in rebellion against the United States; and the fact that any state, or the people thereof, shall on that day be in good faith represented in the Congress of the United States, by members chosen thereto at elections wherein a majority of the qualified voters of such states shall have participated, shall, in the absence of strong countervailing testimony, be deemed conclusive evidence that such state, and the people thereof, are not then in rebellion against the United States. . . .

And, by virtue of the power and for the purpose aforesaid, I do order and declare that all persons held as slaves within said designated states and parts of states are, and henceforward shall be, free; and that the Executive Government of the United States, including the military and naval authorities thereof, will recognize and maintain the freedom of said persons.

And I hereby enjoin upon the people so declared to be free to abstain from all violence, unless in necessary self-defense; and I recommend to them that, all cases when allowed, they labor faithfully for reasonable wages.

And I further declare and make known that such persons, of suitable condition, will be received into the armed service of the United States. . . .

And upon this act, sincerely believed to be an act of justice, warranted by the Constitution upon military necessity, I invoke the considerate judgement of man-kind and the gracious favor of Almighty God. . . .

Abraham Lincoln

Members of the 4th Infantry

The Gettysburg Address

On November 19, 1863, President Abraham Lincoln gave a short speech at the dedication of a national cemetery on the battlefield of Gettysburg. His simple yet eloquent words expressed his hopes for a nation divided by civil war.

Four score and seven years ago our fathers brought forth on this continent a new nation, conceived in liberty, and dedicated to the proposition that all men are created equal.

Now we are engaged in a great civil war, testing whether that nation, or any nation so conceived and so dedicated, can long endure. We are met on a great battlefield of that war. We have come to dedicate a portion of that field as a final resting place for those who here gave their lives that that nation might live. It is altogether fitting and proper that we should do this.

But, in a larger sense, we can not dedicate—we can not consecrate—we can not hallow—this ground. The brave men, living and dead, who struggled here, have consecrated it far above our poor power to add or detract. The world will little note nor long remember what we say here, but it can never forget what they did here. It is for us, the living, rather, to be dedicated here to the unfinished work which they who fought here have thus far so nobly advanced. It is rather for us to be here dedicated to the great task remaining before us—that from these honored dead we take increased devotion to that cause for which they gave the last full measure of devotion; that we here highly resolve that these dead shall not have died in vain; that this nation, under God, shall have a new birth of freedom; and that government of the people, by the people, for the people, shall not perish from the earth.

Soldier's kit, Civil War

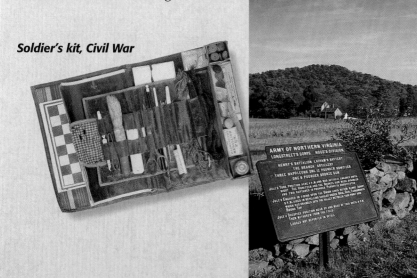

Gettysburg Memorial

I Will Fight No More

Shield made of buffalo hide

In 1877 the Nez Perce fought the government's attempt to move them to a smaller reservation. After a remarkable attempt to escape to Canada, Chief Joseph realized that resistance was hopeless and advised his people to surrender.

Tell General Howard I know his heart. What he told me before I have in my heart. I am tired of fighting. . . . The old men are all dead. It is the young men who say yes or no. He who led the young men is dead. It is cold and we have no blankets. The little children are freezing to death. My people, some of them have run away to the hills, and have no blankets, no food; no one knows where they are—perhaps freezing to death. I want to have time to look for my children and see how many of them I can find. Maybe I shall find them among the dead. Hear me, my chiefs. I am tired; my heart is sick and sad. From where the sun now stands I will fight no more forever.

The Pledge of Allegiance

In 1892 the nation celebrated the 400th anniversary of Columbus's landing in America. In connection with this celebration, Francis Bellamy, a magazine editor, wrote and published the Pledge of Allegiance. The words "under God" were added by Congress in 1954 at the urging of President Dwight D. Eisenhower.

I pledge allegiance to the Flag of the United States of America and to the Republic for which it stands, one Nation under God, indivisible, with liberty and justice for all.

Students in a New York City school recite the Pledge of Allegiance

The American's Creed

William Tyler Page of Friendship Heights, Maryland, wrote The American's Creed. This statement of political faith summarizes the true meaning of freedom available to all Americans. The U.S. House of Representatives adopted the creed on behalf of the American people on April 3, 1918.

I believe in the United States of America as a Government of the people, by the people, for the people; whose just powers are derived from the consent of the governed; a democracy in a republic; a sovereign Nation of many sovereign States; a perfect union, one and inseparable; established upon those principles of freedom, equality, justice, and humanity for which American patriots sacrificed their lives and fortunes.

I therefore believe it is my duty to my Country to love it; to support its Constitution; to obey its laws; to respect its flag, and to defend it against all enemies.

The Fourteen Points

On January 8, 1918, President Woodrow Wilson went before Congress to offer a statement of aims called the Fourteen Points. Wilson's plan called for freedom of the seas in peace and war, an end to secret alliances, and equal trading rights for all countries. The excerpt that follows is taken from the President's message.

. . . We entered this war because violations of right had occurred which touched us to the quick and made the life of our own people impossible unless they were corrected and the world secured once for all against their recurrence. What we demand in this war, therefore, is nothing peculiar to ourselves. It is that the world be made fit and safe to live in; and particularly that it be made safe for every peace-loving nation which, like our own, wishes to live its own life, determine its own institutions, be assured of justice and fair dealing by the other peoples of the world as against force and selfish aggression. All the peoples of the world are in effect partners in this interest, and for our own part we see very clearly that unless justice be done to others it will not be done to us. The program of the world's peace, therefore, is our program; and that program, the only possible program, as we see it, is this:

I. Open covenants of peace, openly arrived at, after which there shall be no private international understandings of any kind but diplomacy shall proceed always frankly and in the public view.

II. Absolute freedom of navigation upon the seas, outside territorial waters, alike in peace and in war, except as the seas may be closed in whole or in part by international action for the enforcement of international covenants.

XIV. A general association of nations must be formed under specific covenants for the purpose of affording mutual guarantees of political independence and territorial integrity to great and small states alike. . . .

Brown v. Board of Education

On May 17, 1954, the Supreme Court ruled in **Brown** *v.* **Board of Education of Topeka, Kansas,** *that racial segregation in public schools was unconstitutional. This decision provided the legal basis for court challenges to segregation in every aspect of American life.*

. . . The plaintiffs contend that segregated public schools are not "equal" and cannot be made "equal" and that hence they are deprived of the equal protection of the laws. Because of the obvious importance of the question presented, the Court took jurisdiction. . . .

Our decision, therefore, cannot turn on merely a comparison of these tangible factors in the Negro and white schools involved in each of the cases. We must look instead to the effect of segregation itself on public education.

In approaching this problem, we cannot turn the clock back to 1868 when the Amendment was adopted, or even to 1896 when *Plessy* v. *Ferguson* was written. We must consider public education in the light of its full development and its present place in American life throughout the Nation. Only in this way can it be determined if segregation in public schools deprives these plaintiffs of the equal protection of the laws.

Today, education is perhaps the most important function of state and local governments. Compulsory school attendance laws and the great expenditures for education both demonstrate our recognition of the importance of education to our democratic society. . . . In these days, it is doubtful that any child may reasonably be expected to succeed in life if he is denied the opportunity of an education. Such an opportunity, where the state has undertaken to provide it, is a right which must be made available to all on equal terms.

We come then to the question presented: Does segregation of children in public schools solely on the basis of race, even though the physical facilities and other "tangible" factors may be equal, deprive the children of the minority group of equal educational opportunities? We believe that it does.

. . . We conclude that in the field of public education the doctrine of "separate but equal" has no place. Separate educational facilities are inherently unequal. Therefore, we hold that the plaintiffs and others similarly situated for whom the actions have been brought are, by reason of the segregation complained of, deprived of the equal protection of the laws guaranteed by the Fourteenth Amendment. . . .

Troops escort students to newly integrated school

John F. Kennedy's Inaugural Address

President Kennedy's Inaugural Address on January 20, 1961, set the tone for his administration. In his address Kennedy stirred the nation by calling for "a grand and global alliance" to fight tyranny, poverty, disease, and war.

We observe today not a victory of party but a celebration of freedom—symbolizing an end as well as a beginning—signifying renewal as well as change. For I have sworn before you and Almighty God the same solemn oath our forebears prescribed nearly a century and three-quarters ago.

The world is very different now. For man holds in his mortal hands the power to abolish all forms of human poverty and all forms of human life. And yet the same revolutionary beliefs for which our forebears fought are still at issue around the globe—the belief that the rights of man come not from the generosity of the state but from the hand of God.

We dare not forget today that we are the heirs of that first revolution. Let the word go forth from this time and place, to friend and foe alike, that the torch has been passed to a new generation of Americans—born in this century, tempered by war, disciplined by a hard and bitter peace, proud of our ancient heritage—and unwilling to witness or permit the slow undoing of those human rights to which this nation has always been committed, and to which we are committed today at home and around the world.

Let every nation know, whether it wishes us well or ill, that we shall pay any price, bear any burden, meet any hardship, support any friend, oppose any foe to assure the survival and the success of liberty.

This much we pledge—and more.

To those old allies whose cultural and spiritual origins we share, we pledge the loyalty of faithful friends. United, there is little we cannot do in a host of cooperative ventures. Divided, there is little we can do. . . .

Let us never negotiate out of fear. But let us never fear to negotiate.

Let both sides explore what problems unite us instead of belaboring those problems which divide us. . . .

Let both sides seek to invoke the wonders of science instead of its terrors. Together let us explore the stars, conquer the deserts, eradicate disease, tap the ocean depths, and encourage the arts and commerce. . . .

And so, my fellow Americans: ask not what your country can do for you—ask what you can do for your country.

My fellow citizens of the world: ask not what America will do for you, but what together we can do for the freedom of man. . . .

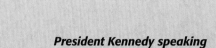

President Kennedy speaking at his inauguration

I Have a Dream

On August 28, 1963, while Congress debated wide-ranging civil rights legislation, Dr. Martin Luther King, Jr., led more than 200,000 people in a march on Washington, D.C. On the steps of the Lincoln Memorial he gave a stirring speech in which he eloquently spoke of his dreams for African Americans and for the United States. Excerpts of the speech follow.

. . . There are those who are asking the devotees of civil rights, "When will you be satisfied?"

We can never be satisfied as long as the Negro is the victim of the unspeakable horrors of police brutality. . . .

We cannot be satisfied as long as the Negro's basic mobility is from a smaller ghetto to a larger one.

We can never be satisfied as long as a Negro in Mississippi cannot vote and a Negro in New York believes he has nothing for which to vote. . . .

I say to you today, my friends, that in spite of the difficulties and frustrations of the moment I still have a dream. It is a dream deeply rooted in the American dream. I have a dream that one day this nation will rise up and live out the true meaning of its creed: "We hold these truths to be self-evident, that all men are created equal."

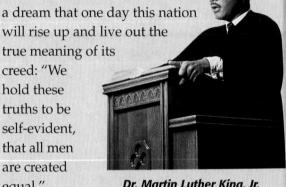

Dr. Martin Luther King, Jr.

I have a dream that one day on the red hills of Georgia the sons of former slaves and the sons of former slaveowners will be able to sit down together at the table of brotherhood.

I have a dream that one day even the state of Mississippi, a desert state sweltering with the heat of injustice and oppression, will be transformed into an oasis of freedom and justice.

I have a dream that my four little children will one day live in a nation where they will not be judged by the color of their skin but by the content of their character. . . .

. . . When we let freedom ring, when we let it ring from every village and every hamlet, from every state and every city, we will be able to speed up that day when all of God's children, black men and white men, Jews and Gentiles, Protestants and Catholics, will be able to join hands and sing in the words of the old Negro spiritual: "Free at last! Free at last! Thank God Almighty, we are free at last!"

The March on Washington

Supreme Court Case Summaries

The following summaries give details about important Supreme Court cases.

Brown v. Board of Education (1954)

In *Brown* v. *Board of Education of Topeka, Kansas*, the Supreme Court overruled *Plessy* v. *Ferguson* (1896) [see p. 999] making the separate-but-equal doctrine in public schools unconstitutional. The Supreme Court rejected the idea that truly equal but separate schools for African American and white students would be constitutional. The Court explained that the Fourteenth Amendment's requirement that all persons be guaranteed equal protection of the law is not met simply by ensuring that African American and white schools "have been equalized…with respect to buildings, curricula, qualifications and salaries, and other tangible factors."

The Court then ruled that racial segregation in public schools violates the Equal Protection Clause of the Constitution because it is inherently unequal. In other words, nothing can make racially segregated public schools equal under the Constitution because the very fact of separation marks the separated race as inferior. In practical terms, the Court's decision in this case has been extended beyond public education to virtually all public accommodations and activities.

Dred Scott v. Sandford (1857)

Dred Scott was taken by slaveholder, John Sandford, to the free state of Illinois and to the Wisconsin Territory, which had also banned slavery. Later they returned to Missouri, a slave state. Several years later, Scott sued for his freedom under the Missouri legal principle of "once free, always free." In other words, under Missouri law enslaved people were entitled to freedom if they had lived in a free state at any time. Missouri courts ruled against Scott, but he appealed the case all the way to the United States Supreme Court.

Dred Scott

The Supreme Court decided this case before the Fourteenth Amendment was added to the Constitution. (The Fourteenth Amendment provides that anyone born or naturalized in the United States is a citizen of the nation and of his or her state of residence.) The court held that enslaved African Americans were property, not citizens, and thus had no rights under the Constitution. The decision also declared that it was unconstitutional to prohibit slavery in the territories. Many people in the North were outraged by the decision, which moved the nation closer to civil war.

Furman v. Georgia (1972)

This decision put a halt to the application of the death penalty under state laws then in effect. For the first time, the Supreme Court ruled that the death penalty amounted to cruel and unusual punishment, which is outlawed in the Constitution. The Court explained that existing death penalty laws did not give juries enough guidance in deciding whether or not to impose the death penalty. As a result, the death penalty in many cases was imposed arbitrarily, that is, without a reasonable basis in the facts and circumstances of the offender or the crime.

The Furman decision halted all executions in the 39 states that had death penalty laws at that time. Since the decision, 38 states have rewritten death penalty laws to meet the requirements established in the Furman case.

Gibbons v. Ogden (1824)

Thomas Gibbons had a federal license to operate a steamboat along the coast, but he did not have a license from the state of New York to travel on New York waters. He wanted to run a steamboat line between Manhattan and New Jersey that would compete with Aaron Ogden's company. Ogden had a New York license. Gibbons sued for the freedom to use his federal license to compete against Ogden on New York waters.

Gibbons won the case. The Supreme Court made it clear that the authority of Congress to regulate interstate commerce (among states) includes the authority to regulate intrastate commerce (within a single state) that bears on, or relates to, interstate commerce.

Before this decision, it was thought that the Constitution would permit a state to close its borders to interstate commercial activity—which, in effect, would stop such activity in its tracks. This case says that a state can regulate purely internal commercial activity, but only Congress can regulate commercial activity that has both intrastate and interstate dimensions.

Gideon v. Wainwright (1963)

After being accused of robbery, Clarence Gideon defended himself in a Florida court because the judge in the case refused to appoint a free lawyer. The jury found Gideon guilty. Eventually, Gideon appealed his conviction to the United States Supreme Court, claiming that by failing to appoint a lawyer the lower court had violated his rights under the Sixth and Fourteenth Amendments.

The Supreme Court agreed with Gideon. In *Gideon v. Wainwright* the Supreme Court held for the first time that poor defendants in criminal cases have the right to a state-paid attorney under the Sixth Amendment. The rule announced in this case has been refined to apply whenever the defendant, if convicted, can be sentenced to more than six months in jail or prison.

Korematsu v. United States (1944)

After the Japanese bombing of Pearl Harbor in 1941, thousands of Japanese Americans on the West Coast were forced to abandon their homes and businesses, and they were moved to internment camps in

In 1983 Fred Korematsu (center) won a reversal of his conviction.

California, Idaho, Utah, Arizona, Wyoming, Colorado, and Arkansas. The prison-like camps offered poor food and cramped quarters.

The Supreme Court's decision in *Korematsu v. United States* upheld the authority of the federal government to move Japanese Americans, many of whom were citizens, from designated military areas that included almost the entire West Coast. The government defended the so-called exclusion orders as a necessary response to Japan's attack on Pearl Harbor. Only after his reelection in 1944 did President Franklin Roosevelt rescind the evacuation orders, and by the end of 1945 the camps were closed.

Marbury v. Madison (1803)

During his last days in office, President John Adams commissioned William Marbury and several other men as judges. This action by Federalist president Adams angered the incoming Democratic-Republican president Thomas Jefferson. Jefferson then ordered James Madison, his secretary of state, not to deliver the commissions, thus blocking the appointments. William Marbury sued, asking the Supreme Court to order Madison to deliver the commission that would make him a judge.

The Court ruled against Marbury, but more importantly, the decision in this case established one of the most significant principles of American constitutional law. The Supreme Court held that it is the Court itself that has the final say on what the Constitution means. This is known as judicial review. It is also the Supreme Court that has the final say in whether or not an act of government—legislative or executive at the federal, state, or local level—violates the Constitution.

McCulloch v. Maryland (1819)

Following the War of 1812, the United States experienced years of high inflation and general economic turmoil. In an attempt to stabilize the economy, the United States Congress chartered a Second Bank of the United States in 1816. Maryland and several other states, however, opposed the competition that the new national bank created and passed laws taxing its branches. In 1818, James McCulloch, head of the Baltimore branch of the Second Bank of the United States, refused to pay the tax to the state of Maryland. The case worked its way through the Maryland state courts all the way to the United States Supreme Court.

The Supreme Court declared the Maryland tax unconstitutional and void. More importantly, the decision established the foundation for expanded Congressional authority. The Court held that the necessary and proper clause of the Constitution allows Congress to do more than the Constitution expressly authorizes it to do. The decision allows Congress to enact nearly any law that will help it achieve any of its duties as set forth in the Constitution. For example, Congress has the express authority to regulate interstate commerce. The necessary and proper clause permits Congress to do so in ways not actually specified in the Constitution.

Miranda v. Arizona (1966)

In 1963, police in Arizona arrested Ernesto Miranda for kidnapping. The court found Miranda guilty on the basis of a signed confession. The police admitted that neither before nor during the questioning had Miranda been advised of his right to consult with an attorney before answering any questions or of his right to have an attorney present during the interrogation. Miranda appealed his conviction, claiming that police had violated his right against self-incrimination under the Fifth Amendment by not informing him of his legal rights during questioning.

Miranda won the case. The Supreme Court held that a person in police custody cannot be questioned unless told that he or she has: 1) the right to remain silent, 2) the right to an attorney (at government expense if the accused is unable to pay), and 3) that anything the person says after stating that he or she understands these rights can be used as evidence of guilt at trial. These rights have come to be called the

In 1963, the arrest of Ernesto Miranda (left) led to a landmark decision.

Miranda warning. They are intended to ensure that an accused person in custody will not unknowingly give up the Fifth Amendment's protection against self-incrimination.

New York Times Company v. United States (1971)

In June 1971, the *New York Times* published its first installment of the "Pentagon Papers," a classified document about government actions in the Vietnam War era. The secret document had been leaked to the *Times* by antiwar activist Daniel Ellsberg, who had previously worked in national security for the government. President Richard Nixon went to court to block further publication of the Pentagon Papers. The *New York Times* appealed to the Supreme Court to allow it to continue publishing without government interference.

The Supreme Court's ruling in this case upheld earlier decisions that established the doctrine of prior restraint. This doctrine protects the press (broadly defined to include newspapers, television and radio, filmmakers and distributors, etc.) from government attempts to block publication. Except in extraordinary circumstances, the press must be allowed to publish.

Plessy v. Ferguson (1896)

In the late 1800s railroad companies in Louisiana were required by state law to provide "separate-but-equal" cars for white and African American passengers. In 1890 a group of citizens in New Orleans selected Homer Plessy to challenge that law. In 1892, Plessy boarded a whites-only car and refused to move. He was arrested. Plessy appealed to the Supreme Court, arguing that the Louisiana separate-but-equal law violated his right to equal protection under the Fourteenth Amendment.

Homer Plessy lost the case. The Plessy decision upheld the separate-but-equal doctrine used by Southern states to perpetuate segregation following the Civil War. The court ruled that the Fourteenth Amendment's equal protection clause required only equal public facilities for the two races, not equal access to the same facilities. This decision was overruled in 1954 by *Brown* v. *Board of Education of Topeka, Kansas,* (discussed previously).

Roe v. Wade (1973)

Roe v. *Wade* challenged restrictive abortion laws in both Texas and Georgia. The suit was brought in the name of Jane Roe, an alias used to protect the privacy of the plaintiff.

In this decision, the Supreme Court ruled that females have a constitutional right under various provisions of the Constitution—most notably, the due process clause—to decide whether or not to terminate a pregnancy. The Supreme Court's decision in this case was the most significant in a long line of decisions over a period of 50 years that recognized a constitutional right of privacy, even though the word *privacy* is not found in the Constitution.

Tinker v. Des Moines School District (1969)

During the Vietnam War, some students in Des Moines, Iowa, wore black armbands to school to protest American involvement in the conflict. Two days earlier, school officials had adopted a policy banning the wearing of armbands to school. When the students arrived at school wearing armbands, they were suspended and sent home. The students argued that school officials violated their First Amendment right to free speech.

The Supreme Court sided with the students. In a now-famous statement the court said that "it can hardly be argued that either students or teachers shed their constitutional rights of freedom of speech or expression at the schoolhouse gate." The Supreme Court went on to rule that a public school could not suspend students who wore black armbands to school to symbolize their opposition to the Vietnam War. In so holding, the Court likened the students' conduct to pure speech and decided it on that basis.

United States v. Nixon (1974)

In the early 1970s, President Nixon was named an unindicted co-conspirator in the criminal investigation that arose in the aftermath of a break-in at the offices of the Democratic Party in Washington, D.C. A federal judge had ordered President Nixon to turn over tapes of conversations he had with his advisers about the break-in. Nixon resisted the order, claiming that the conversations were entitled to absolute confidentiality by Article II of the Constitution.

The decision in this case made it clear that the president is not above the law. The Supreme Court held that only those presidential conversations and communications that relate to performing the duties of the office of president are confidential and protected from a judicial order of disclosure. The Court ordered Nixon to give up the tapes, which revealed evidence linking the president to the conspiracy to obstruct justice. He resigned from office shortly thereafter.

Worcester v. Georgia (1832)

State officials in Georgia wanted to remove the Cherokees from land that had been guaranteed to them in earlier treaties. Samuel Worcester was a Congregational missionary who worked with the Cherokee people. He was arrested for failure to have a license that the state required to live in Cherokee country and for refusing to obey an order from the Georgia militia to leave Cherokee lands. Worcester then sued the state of Georgia. He claimed that Georgia had no legal authority on Cherokee land because the United States government recognized the Cherokee in Georgia as a separate nation.

The Supreme Court agreed with Worcester by a vote of 5 to 1. Chief Justice John Marshall wrote the majority opinion which said that Native American nations were a distinct people with the right to have independent political communities and that only the federal government had authority over matters that involved the Cherokee.

President Andrew Jackson supported Georgia's efforts to remove the Cherokee to Indian Territory and refused to enforce the court's ruling. After the ruling Jackson remarked, "John Marshall has made his decision. Now let him enforce it."

The gazetteer is a geographical dictionary that lists political divisions, natural features, and other places and locations. Following each entry is a description, its latitude and longitude, and a page reference that indicates where each entry may be found in this text.

A

Abilene city in Kansas (39°N/97°W) 535

Afghanistan country in southwestern Asia (33°N/63°E) RA11, 949

Africa continent of the Eastern Hemisphere south of the Mediterranean Sea and adjoining Asia on its northeastern border (10°N/22°E) RA13, 41

Alabama state in the southeastern United States; 22nd state to enter the Union (33°N/87°W) RA3, 319

Alamo Texas mission captured by Mexican forces in 1836 (29°N/98°W) 365

Alaska state in the United States, located in northwestern North America (64°N/150°W) RA4, 640

Albany capital of New York State located in the Hudson Valley; site where Albany Congress proposed first formal plan to unite the 13 colonies (42°N/74°W) 119

Allegheny River river in western Pennsylvania uniting with the Monongahela River at Pittsburgh to form the Ohio River (41°N/79°W) 123

Andes mountain system extending along western coast of South America (13°S/75°W) 27

Antietam Civil War battle site in western Maryland (40°N/77°W) 492

Appalachian Mountains chief mountain system in eastern North America extending from Quebec and New Brunswick to central Alabama (37°N/82°W) RA5, 105

Appomattox Court House site in central Virginia where Confederate forces surrendered, ending the Civil War (37°N/78°W) 491

Arizona state in the southwestern United States; 48th state to enter the Union (34°N/113°W) RA2, 28

Arkansas state in the south central U.S.; acquired as part of Louisiana Purchase (35°N/94°W) RA3, 397

Asia continent of the Eastern Hemisphere forming a single landmass with Europe (50°N/100°E) RA13, 17

Atlanta capital of Georgia located in the northwest central part of the state (34°N/84°W) RA5, 406

Atlantic Ocean ocean separating North and South America from Europe and Africa (5°S/25°W) RA12, 16

Australia continent and country southeast of Asia (25°S/125°E) RA13

Austria-Hungary former monarchy in central Europe (47°N/12°E) 668

B

Baltimore city on the Chesapeake Bay in central Maryland (39°N/77°W) 87

Barbary Coast north coast of Africa between Morocco and Tunisia (35°N/3°E) 289

Bay of Pigs site of 1961 invasion of Cuba by U.S.-trained Cuban exiles (22°N/79°W) 868

Beijing capital of China located in the northeastern part of the country (40°N/116°E) 647

Belgium country in northwest Europe (51°N/3°E) RA13, 668

Bering Strait waterway between North America and Asia where a land bridge once existed (65°N/170°W) 17

Beringia land bridge that linked Asia and North America during the last Ice Age (65°N/170°W) 17

Berlin city in east central Germany; former capital divided into sectors after World War II (53°N/13°E) 775

Birmingham city in north central Alabama; scene of several civil rights protests (33°N/86°W) 570

Black Hills mountains in southwestern South Dakota; site of conflict between the Sioux and white settlers during 1870s (44°N/104°W) 545

Boston capital of Massachusetts located in the eastern part of the state; founded by English Puritans in 1630 (42°N/71°W) 78

Brazil country in eastern South America (9°S/53°W) RA12, 55

Breed's Hill site near Boston where the Battle of Bunker Hill took place (42°N/71°W) 145

Buffalo industrial city and rail center in New York State (43°N/79°W) 318

Bull Run site of two Civil War battles in northern Virginia; also called Manassas (39°N/77°W) 466

C

Cahokia largest settlement of the Mound Builders, built in Illinois after A.D. 900 (39°N/90°W) 30

California state in the western United States; attracted thousands of miners during gold rush of 1849 (38°N/121°W) RA2, 371

Cambodia country in Southeastern Asia bordering Gulf of Siam; official name Democratic Kampuchea (12°N/105°E) RA13, 874

Canada country in northern North America (50°N/100°W) RA9, 17

Cape of Good Hope southern tip of Africa (34°S/18°E) 44

Caribbean Sea tropical sea in the Western Hemisphere (15°N/75°W) RA8

Central America area of North America between Mexico and South America (11°N/86°W) RA8, 17

Chancellorsville Virginia site of 1863 Confederate victory (38°N/78°W) 486

Charleston city in South Carolina on the Atlantic coast; original name Charles Town (33°N/80°W) 89

Chesapeake Bay inlet of the Atlantic Ocean in Virginia and Maryland (38°N/76°W) 71

Chicago largest city in Illinois; located in northeastern part of the state along Lake Michigan (42°N/88°W) 318

Chile South American country (35°S/72°W) RA12, 900

China country in eastern Asia; mainland (People's Republic of China) under Communist control since 1949 (37°N/93°E) RA13, 639

Chisholm Trail pioneer cattle trail from Texas to Kansas (34°N/98°W) 535

Cincinnati city in southern Ohio on the Ohio River; grew as a result of increasing steamship traffic during the mid-1800s (39°N/84°W) 265

Cleveland city in northern Ohio on Lake Erie (41°N/82°W) 423

Colombia country in South America (4°N/73°W) RA12, 26

Colorado state in the western United States (39°N/107°W) RA3, 29

Colorado River river that flows from the Colorado Rockies to the Gulf of California (36°N/113°W) RA4, 284

Columbia River river flowing through southwest Canada and northwestern United States into the Pacific Ocean (46°N/120°W) RA4, 357

Concord village northwest of Boston, Massachusetts; site of early battle of the American Revolution (42°N/71°W) 143

Connecticut state in the northeastern United States; one of the original 13 states (42°N/73°W) RA3, 79

Cuba country in the West Indies, North America (22°N/79°W) RA8, 47

Czechoslovakia former country in central Europe; now two countries, the

Czech Republic and Slovakia (49°N/ 16°E) RA13, 791

Dallas a leading city in Texas (33°N/ 97°W) 846

Delaware state in the northeastern United States; one of the original 13 states (39°N/75°W) RA3, 83

Detroit city in southeastern Michigan; site of significant battles during the French and Indian War and the War of 1812; center of automobile industry (42°N/83°W) 125

Dien Bien Phu site in northwestern Vietnam where French troops were defeated by Vietminh troops in 1954 (21°N/102°E) 872

Dodge City Kansas cattle town during the 19th century (37°N/100°W) 535

Dominican Republic country in the West Indies on the eastern part of Hispaniola Island (19°N/71°W) RA8, 47

Dust Bowl area of the Great Plains where the drought of the 1930s turned the soil to wind-borne dust (37°N/98°W) 756

East Germany country in central Europe; reunified with West Germany in 1990 (52°N/12°E) 792

Egypt country in northeastern Africa (27°N/27°E) RA10, 771

England division of the United Kingdom of Great Britain and Northern Ireland (52°N/2°W) 40

Erie Canal the waterway connecting the Hudson River with Lake Erie through New York State (43°N/ 76°W) 318

Ethiopia country in eastern Africa, north of Somalia and Kenya (8°N/ 38°E) RA13, 753

Europe continent of the northern part of the Eastern Hemisphere between Asia and the Atlantic Ocean (50°N/ 15°E) RA13, 38

Florida state in the southeastern United States (30°N/85°W) RA3, 53

Fort McHenry fort in Baltimore harbor; inspired poem that later became "The Star-Spangled Banner" (39°N/ 76°W) 299

Fort Necessity Pennsylvania fort built by George Washington's troops in 1754 (40°N/80°W) 118

Fort Sumter Union fort during the Civil War located on island near Charleston, South Carolina; site of first military engagement of Civil War (33°N/80°W) 453

Fort Ticonderoga British fort on Lake Champlain (44°N/73°W) 144

France country in western Europe (50°N/1°E) RA13, 40

Fredericksburg city and Civil War battle site in northeast Virginia (38°N/ 77°W) 486

Freeport city in northern Illinois; site of 1858 Lincoln-Douglas campaign debate (42°N/89°W) 448

Gadsden Purchase portion of present-day Arizona and New Mexico; area purchased from Mexico in 1853 (32°N/111°W) RA7, 374

Galveston city on the Gulf of Mexico coast in Texas; created nation's first commission form of city government (29°N/95°W) 611

Gaza Strip narrow coastal strip along the Mediterranean (31°N/34°E) RA10, 899

Georgia state in the southeastern United States (33°N/84°W) RA3, 90

Germany country in central Europe; divided after World War II into East Germany and West Germany; unified in 1990 (50°N/10°E) RA13, 667

Gettysburg city and Civil War battle site in south central Pennsylvania; site where Lincoln delivered the Gettysburg Address (40°N/77°W) 486

Great Britain commonwealth comprising England, Scotland, and Wales (56°N/2°W) 667

Great Lakes chain of five lakes, Superior, Erie, Michigan, Ontario, and Huron, in central North America (45°N/87°W) RA5, 61

Great Plains flat grassland in the central United States (45°N/104°W) RA4, 390

Great Salt Lake lake in northern Utah with no outlet and strongly saline waters (41°N/113°W) RA3, 378

Greece country in southeastern Europe (39°N/21°E) RA13, 790

Greensboro northern North Carolina city; scene of sit-ins to protest segregation (36°N/80°W) 848

Grenada country in the Caribbean (12°N/61°W) 925

Guadalcanal island in the Solomons east of Australia (10°S/159°E) 779

Guam U.S. possession in the western Pacific Ocean (14°N/143°E) 653

Guatemala country in Central America, south of Mexico (16°N/92°W) RA8, 23

Gulf of Mexico gulf on the southeast coast of North America (25°N/94°W) RA5, 92

Gulf of Tonkin gulf in South China Sea east of northern Vietnam (20°N/ 108°E) 874

Haiti country on Hispaniola Island in the West Indies (19°N/72°W) RA8, 47

Hanoi capital of Vietnam (21°N/106°E) 872

Harlem northern section of Manhattan in New York City; cultural center of African Americans in the early and mid-1900s (41°N/74°W) 700

Harpers Ferry town in northern West Virginia on the Potomac River (39°N/78°W) 448

Hartford capital of Connecticut located along the Connecticut River (42°N/ 73°W) 79

Hawaii state in the United States located in the Pacific Ocean (20°N/ 157°W) RA5, 644

Hiroshima city in southern Japan; site of first military use of atomic bomb, August 6, 1945 (34°N/132°E) 780

Hispaniola island in the West Indies in North America (17°N/73°W) RA8, 47

Horseshoe Bend Alabama site where Creek-U.S. battled in 1814 (33°N/ 86°W) 298

Hudson Bay large bay in northern Canada (60°N/86°W) RA8, 61

Hudson River river flowing through New York State (53°N/ 74°W) 316

Hungary country in central Europe (47°N/20°E) RA13, 690

Idaho state in the northwestern U.S.; ranks among top states in silver production (44°N/115°W) RA2, 530

Illinois state in the north central United States; one of the states formed in the Northwest Territory (40°N/91°W) RA3, 195

Indian Territory land reserved by the United States government for Native Americans, now the state of Oklahoma (36°N/98°W) 342

Indiana state in the north central United States; one of the states formed in the Northwest Territory (40°N/ 87°W) RA3, 195

Indochina region in Southeast Asia (17°N/105°E) 762

Iowa state in the north central U.S. acquired as part of the Louisiana Purchase (42°N/94°W) RA3

Iran country in southwestern Asia (31°N/53°E) RA11, 913

Iraq country in southwestern Asia (32°N/42°E) RA11, 931

Ireland island west of England, occupied by the Republic of Ireland and by Northern Ireland (54°N/8°W) RA12, 771

Israel country of the Middle East in southwestern Asia along the Mediterranean Sea (33°N/34°E) RA10, 794

Italy country in southern Europe along the Mediterranean (44°N/11°E) RA13, 39

Jackson Mississippi capital (32°N/90°W) 406

Jamestown first permanent English settlement in North America; located in southeastern Virginia (37°N/77°W) 72

Japan island country in eastern Asia (36°N/133°E) RA13, 639

Kansas state in the central United States; fighting over slavery issue in 1850s gave territory the name "Bleeding Kansas" (38°N/99°W) RA3, 442

Kentucky state in the south central United States; border state that sided with the Union during the Civil War (37°N/87°W) RA3, 282

Korea peninsula in eastern Asia between China, Russia, and the Sea of Japan, on which are located the countries North Korea and South Korea (38°N/127°E) RA13, 802

Kuwait country of the Middle East in southwestern Asia between Iraq and Saudi Arabia (29°N/49°E) RA11, 931

Lake Erie one of the five Great Lakes between Canada and the U.S. (42°N/81°W) RA5, 298

Lake Huron one of the five Great Lakes between Canada and the U.S. (45°N/83°W) RA5, 298

Lake Michigan one of the five Great Lakes between Canada and the U.S. (43°N/87°W) RA5, 298

Lake Ontario the smallest of the five Great Lakes (43°N/79°W) RA5, 298

Lake Superior the largest of the five Great Lakes (48°N/89°W) RA5, 298

Laos southeast Asian country, south of China and west of Vietnam (20°N/102°E) RA13, 874

Latin America Central and South America; settled by Spain and Portugal (14°N/90°W) RA12, 327

Lexington Revolutionary War battle site in eastern Massachusetts; site of first clash between colonists and British, April 19, 1775 (42°N/71°W) 143

Leyte island of the east central Philippines, north of Mindanao (10°N/125°E) 779

Little Rock capital of Arkansas located in the center of the state; site of 1957 conflict over public school integration (35°N/92°W) 423

London capital of United Kingdom located in the southeastern part of England (51°N/0°) 73

Los Angeles city along Pacific coast in southern California; industrial, financial, and trade center of western United States (34°N/118°W) 531

Louisiana state in the south central United States (31°N/93°W) RA3, 298

Louisiana Territory region of west central United States between the Mississippi River and the Rocky Mountains purchased from France in 1803 (40°N/95°W) RA7, 124

Lowell city in Massachusetts (43°N/83°W) 308

Maine state in the northeastern United States; 23rd state to enter the Union (45°N/70°W) RA3, 324

Mali country in Western Africa (16°N/0°) RA12, 41

Manchuria region of northeast China; invaded by Japan in 1931 (48°N/125°E) 754

Manila capital and largest city of the Philippines located on southwest Luzon Island and Manila Bay (14°N/121°E) RA13, 651

Maryland state in the eastern United States; one of the original 13 states (39°N/76°W) RA3, 87

Massachusetts state in the northeastern United States; one of the original 13 states (42°N/72°W) RA3, 79

Massachusetts Bay Colony Pilgrim settlements along the Charles River (42°N/71°W) 78

Mediterranean Sea sea between Europe and Africa (36°N/13°E) RA13, 39

Memphis Tennessee city on the Mississippi River near the Mississippi border (35°N/90°W) 403

Mexican Cession territory gained by the United States after war with Mexico in 1848 (37°N/111°W) 374

Mexico country in North America south of the United States (24°N/104°W) RA8, 19

Mexico City capital and most populous city of Mexico (19°N/99°W) 24

Michigan state in the north central United States; one of the states formed in the Northwest Territory (45°N/85°W) RA3, 195

Midway Islands U.S. possession in the central Pacific Ocean (28°N/179°W) 778

Milwaukee city in eastern Wisconsin (43°N/88°W) 605

Minnesota state in the north central United States; fur trade, good soil, and lumber attracted early settlers (46°N/96°W) RA3

Mississippi state in the southeastern United States; became English territory after French and Indian War (32°N/90°W) RA3, 319

Mississippi River river flowing through the United States from Minnesota to the Gulf of Mexico; explored by French in 1600s (29°N/89°W) RA5, 30

Missouri state in the south central U.S.; petition for statehood resulted in sectional conflict and the Missouri Compromise (41°N/93°W) RA3, 324

Missouri River river flowing through the United States from the Rocky Mountains to the Mississippi River near St. Louis (39°N/90°W) RA5, 284

Montana state in the northwestern United States; cattle industry grew during 1850s (47°N/112°W) RA3, 530

Montgomery capital of Alabama located in the central part of the state; site of 1955 bus boycott to protest segregation (32°N/86°W) 406

Montreal city along the St. Lawrence River in southern Quebec, Canada (45°N/73°W) 60

Moscow capital of former Soviet Union and capital of Russia (56°N/37°E) 774

Nagasaki Japanese city; site of the second atom-bombing in 1945, ending World War II (32°N/130°E) 780

Nashville capital of Tennessee located in the north central part of the state (36°N/87°W) 423

Natchez city in western Mississippi along the Mississippi River (32°N/91°W) 316

National Road road from Baltimore, Maryland, to Vandalia, Illinois (40°N/81°W) 315

Nebraska state in the central United States (42°N/101°W) RA3, 442

Netherlands country in northwestern Europe (53°N/4°E) RA13, 77

Nevada state in the western United States (39°N/117°W) RA2, 510

New Amsterdam town founded on Manhattan Island by Dutch settlers in 1625; renamed New York by British settlers (41°N/74°W) 62

New England region in northeastern United States (42°N/72°W) RA5, 77

New France French land claims stretching from Quebec to Louisiana (39°N/85°W) 92

New Hampshire state in the northeastern United States; one of the original 13 states (44°N/72°W) RA3, 80

New Jersey state in the northeastern United States; one of the original 13 states (40°N/75°W) RA3, 84

New Mexico state in the southwestern United States; ceded to the United States by Mexico in 1848 (34°N/107°W) RA3, 369

New Netherland Dutch Hudson River colony (42°N/72°W) 83

New Orleans city in Louisiana in the Mississippi Delta (30°N/90°W) 92

New Spain part of Spain's empire in the Western Hemisphere (35°N/110°W) RA7, 92

New York state in the northeastern United States; one of the original 13 states (43°N/78°W) RA3, 83

New York City city in southeastern New York State at the mouth of the Hudson River; first capital of nation (41°N/74°W) 84

Newfoundland province in eastern Canada (48°N/56°W) RA8, 46

Nicaragua country in Central America (13°N/86°W) RA8, 707

Normandy region along French coast and site of D-Day invasion, June 6, 1944 (48°N/2°W) 772

North America continent in the northern part of the Western Hemisphere between the Atlantic and Pacific oceans (45°N/100°W) RA12, 16

North Carolina state in the southeastern United States; one of the original 13 states (36°N/81°W) RA3, 89

North Dakota state in the north central U.S.; Congress created Dakota Territory in 1861 (47°N/102°W) RA3, 530

North Korea Asian country on the northern Korean Peninsula (40°N/127°E) RA13, 802

North Vietnam communist nation in Southeast Asia; unified with South Vietnam in 1976 to form Vietnam (21°N/106°E) RA13, 872

Northwest Territory territory north of the Ohio River and east of the Mississippi River (47°N/87°W) RA6, 196

O

Ohio state in the north central United States; first state in the Northwest Territory (40°N/83°W) RA3, 195

Ohio River river flowing from Allegheny and Monongahela rivers in western Pennsylvania into the Mississippi River (37°N/85°W) RA5, 116

Oklahoma state in the south central United States; Five Civilized Tribes moved to territory in the period 1830–1842 (36°N/98°W) RA3, 539

Oregon state in the northwestern United States; adopted woman suffrage in 1912 (44°N/124°W) RA2, 356

Oregon Trail pioneer trail from Independence, Missouri, to the Oregon Territory (42°N/110°W) 358

P

Pacific Ocean world's largest ocean, located between Asia and the Americas (0°/175°W) RA12–13, 48

Palestine historical region in southwest Asia between the Mediterranean Sea and the Jordan River; area sometimes called the Holy Land (32°N/35°E) 794

Panama country in the southern part of Central America, occupying the Isthmus of Panama (8°N/81°W) RA8, 656

Panama Canal canal built across the Isthmus of Panama through Panama to connect the Caribbean Sea and the Pacific Ocean (9°N/80°W) 657

Pearl Harbor naval base at Honolulu, Hawaii; site of 1941 Japanese attack, leading to United States entry into World War II (21°N/158°W) 645

Pennsylvania state in the northeastern United States (41°N/78°W) RA3, 84

Persian Gulf gulf in southwestern Asia between Iran and the Arabian Peninsula (28°N/50°E) RA11, 931

Peru country in South America, south of Ecuador and Colombia (10°S/75°W) RA12, 327

Philadelphia city in eastern Pennsylvania on the Delaware River; Declaration of Independence and the Constitution both adopted in city's Independence Hall (40°N/75°W) 85

Philippines island country in southeast Asia (14°N/125°E) RA13, 651

Pikes Peak mountain in Rocky Mountains in central Colorado (38°N/105°W) 285

Pittsburgh city in western Pennsylvania; one of the great steelmaking centers of the world (40°N/80°W) 118

Plymouth town in eastern Massachusetts, first successful English colony in New England (42°N/71°W) 77

Poland country on the Baltic Sea in Eastern Europe (52°N/18°E) RA13, 755

Portugal country in southwestern Europe (38°N/8°W) RA12, 44

Potomac River river flowing from West Virginia into Chesapeake Bay (38°N/77°W) 87

Providence capital of Rhode Island; site of first English settlement in Rhode Island (42°N/71°W) RA3

Puerto Rico United States commonwealth in the West Indies (18°N/67°W) RA8

Pullman a company town south of Chicago; site of 1897 railroad strike (42°N/87°W) 575

Q

Quebec city in Canada, capital of Quebec Province, on the St. Lawrence River; first settlement in New France (47°N/71°W) 62

R

Rhode Island state in the northeastern United States; one of the original 13 states (41°N/72°W) RA3, 80

Richmond capital of Virginia located in the central part of the state; capital of the Confederacy during the Civil War (37°N/77°W) 388

Rio Grande river between the United States and Mexico in North America; forms the boundary between Texas and Mexico (26°N/97°W) RA4, 372

Roanoke island off the coast of present-day North Carolina that was site of early British colonizing efforts (35°N/76°W) 71

Rocky Mountains mountain range in western United States and Canada in North America (50°N/114°W) RA14, 32

Russia name of republic; former empire of eastern Europe and northern Asia coinciding with Soviet Union (60°N/64°E) RA13, 640

S

Sacramento capital of California located in the north central part of the state (38°N/121°W) 371

Saigon present-day Ho Chi Minh City; former capital of South Vietnam (11°N/106°E) 879

Salt Lake City capital of Utah located in the northern part of the state; founded by Mormons in 1847 (41°N/112°W) 361

San Antonio city in south central Texas (29°N/98°W) 365

San Diego city in southern California (33°N/117°W) 93

San Francisco city in northern California on the Pacific coast (38°N/122°W) 376

Santa Fe capital of New Mexico located in the north central part of the state (36°N/106°W) 92

Santa Fe Trail cattle trail from Independence, Missouri, to Santa Fe, New Mexico (36°N/106°W) 369

Saratoga Revolutionary War battle site in the Hudson Valley of eastern New York State (43°N/74°W) 168

Savannah city in far eastern Georgia (32°N/81°W) 90

Seattle Washington city bordered by Puget Sound and Lake Washington (47°N/122°W) RA2

Selma Alabama city; site of a 1965 voter-registration drive (32°N/87°W) 852

Seneca Falls town in New York State; site of women's rights convention in 1848 (43°N/77°W) 426

Shiloh site of 1862 Union victory in Tennessee (35°N/88°W) 469

Sicily Italian island in the Mediterranean (37°N/13°E) 772

Sierra Nevada mountain range in eastern California (39°N/120°W) RA4, 32

Sinai Peninsula peninsula in the Middle East separating Egypt from Israel (29°N/34°E) 899

South America continent in the southern part of the Western Hemisphere lying between the Atlantic and Pacific oceans (15°S/60°W) RA12, 16

South Carolina state in the southeastern United States; one of the original 13 states (34°N/81°W) RA3, 89

South Dakota state in the north central United States; acquired through the Louisiana Purchase (44°N/102°W) RA3, 530

South Korea country in Asia on the Korean Peninsula (36°N/128°E) RA13, 802

South Vietnam country in Southeast Asia united in 1976 with North Vietnam to form Vietnam (11°N/107°E) RA13, 873

Soviet Union former country in northern Europe and Asia (60°N/64°E) 754

Spain country in southwestern Europe (40°N/4°W) RA12, 46

St. Augustine city in northeastern Florida on the Atlantic coast; oldest permanent existing European settlement in North America, founded in 1565 (30°N/81°W) 53

St. Lawrence River river flowing from Lake Ontario, between Canada and the United States, through parts of Canada to the Atlantic Ocean (48°N/69°W) 92

Stalingrad city in the former Soviet Union on the Volga River; present name Volgograd (49°N/42°E) 774

Sudetenland region in northwest Czechoslovakia; taken by Hitler's forces in 1938 (50°N/18°E) 755

Suez Canal canal built between the Mediterranean Sea and the Red Sea through northeastern Egypt (31°N/32°E) 771

Switzerland European country in the Alps (47°N/8°E) RA13

Taiwan island country off the southeast coast of China; seat of the Chinese Nationalist government (24°N/122°E) RA13, 794

Tehran capital of Iran (36°N/52°E) RA11, 914

Tennessee state in the south central United States; first state readmitted to the Union after the Civil War (36°N/88°W) RA3, 319

Tenochtitlán Aztec capital at the site of present-day Mexico City (19°N/99°W) 24

Texas state in the south central United States; Mexican colony that became a republic before joining the United States (31°N/101°W) RA3, 363

Tokyo capital of Japan located on the eastern coast of Honshu Island (36°N/140°E) 779

Toronto city in Canada on Lake Ontario; capital of the province of Ontario (44°N/79°W) RA12

Trenton capital of New Jersey located on the Delaware River in the central part of the state; site of Revolutionary War battle in December 1776 (40°N/75°W) 167

Union of Soviet Socialist Republics See Soviet Union.

United Kingdom country in northwestern Europe made up of England, Scotland, Wales, and Northern Ireland (56°N/2°W) RA12, 771

United States country in central North America; fourth largest country in the world in both area and population (38°N/110°W) RA2–3, RA12

Utah state in the western United States; settled by Mormons in 1840s (39°N/113°W) RA2, 378

Valley Forge Revolutionary War winter camp northwest of Philadelphia (40°N/75°W) 173

Venezuela South American country on the Caribbean Sea (8°N/65°W)RA12, 658

Vermont state in the northeastern United States; 14th state to enter the Union (44°N/73°W) RA3, 144

Vicksburg city and Civil War battle site in western Mississippi on the Mississippi River (42°N/85°W) 486

Vietnam country in southeastern Asia (16°N/108°E) RA13, 871

Virginia state in the eastern United States; colony of first permanent English settlement in the Americas (37°N/80°W) RA3, 72

Wake Island island in the central Pacific Ocean; annexed by United States in 1898 (19°N/167°E) 777

Washington state in the northwestern United States; territory reached by Lewis and Clark in 1805 (47°N/121°W) RA2, 530

Washington, D.C. capital of the United States located on the Potomac River at its confluence with the Anacostia River, between Maryland and Virginia coinciding with the District of Columbia (39°N/77°W) RA3, 261

West Indies islands in the Caribbean Sea, between North America and South America (19°N/79°W) RA8, 47

West Virginia state in the east central United States (39°N/81°W) RA3, 462

Willamette Valley valley of the Willamette River in western Oregon (45°N/123°W) 359

Wisconsin state in the north central United States; passed first state unemployment compensation act, 1932 (44°N/91°W) RA3, 195

Wounded Knee site of massacre of Native Americans by soldiers in southern South Dakota in 1890 and of American Indian Movement protest in 1973 (43°N/102°W) 547

Wyoming state in the western United States; territory provided women the right to vote, 1869 (43°N/108°W) RA3, 530

Yalu River river in eastern Asia, between China and North Korea (41°N/126°E) 804

Yorktown town in southeastern Virginia and site of final battle of Revolutionary War (37°N/76°W) 184

Yugoslavia country in southeast Europe, on the Adriatic Sea (44°N/20°E) RA13, 690

Gazetteer

A

abolitionist a person who strongly favors doing away with slavery (p. 418)

abstain to not take part in some activity, such as voting (p. 439)

adobe a sun-dried mud brick used to build the homes of some Native Americans (p. 32)

affirmative action an active effort to improve educational and employment opportunities for minority groups and women (p. 902)

affluence the state of having much wealth (p. 822)

airlift a system of transporting food and supplies by aircraft into an area otherwise impossible to reach (p. 792)

alien an immigrant living in a country in which he or she is not a citizen (p. 271)

allege state as a fact but without proof (p. 808)

alliance a close association of nations or other groups, formed to advance common interests or causes (p.122)

alliance system defense agreements among nations (p. 667)

ambush a surprise attack (p. 187)

amendment an addition to a formal document such as the Constitution (pp. 213, 221)

American System policies devised by Henry Clay to stimulate the growth of industry (p. 324)

amnesty the granting of pardon to a large number of persons; protection from prosecution for an illegal act (pp. 501, 907)

anarchist person who believes that there should be no government (p. 701)

anarchy disorder and lawlessness (p. 658)

annex to add a territory to one's own territory (p. 367)

annexation bringing an area under the control of a larger country (p. 645)

Antifederalists individuals who opposed ratification of the Constitution (p. 212)

anti-Semitism hostility toward or discrimination against Jews (p. 753)

apartheid racial separation and economic and political discrimination against nonwhites, a policy formerly practiced in the Republic of South Africa (p. 912)

appeasement accepting demands in order to avoid conflict (p. 755)

apprentice assistant who is assigned to learn the trade of a skilled craftsman (p. 112)

appropriate to set something aside for a particular purpose, especially funds (p. 223)

arbitration settling a dispute by agreeing to accept the decision of an impartial outsider (p. 621)

archaeology the study of ancient peoples (p. 17)

armistice a temporary peace agreement to end fighting (pp. 652, 680)

arms race the competition between the United States and the Soviet Union to build more and more weapons in an effort to surpass the other's military strength (p. 817)

arsenal a storage place for weapons and ammunition (p. 448)

article a part of a document, such as the Constitution, that deals with a single subject (p. 209)

artifact an item left behind by early people that represents their culture (p. 17)

assembly line a production system with machines and workers arranged so that each person performs an assigned task again and again as the item passes before him or her (p. 565)

assimilate to absorb a group into the culture of a larger population (p. 585)

astrolabe an instrument used by sailors to observe positions of stars (p. 40)

autocracy government in which one person has unlimited power (p. 675)

automation a system or process that uses mechanical or electronic devices that replace human workers (p. 830)

B

baby boom a marked increase in the birthrate, especially in the United States immediately following World War II (p. 822)

backcountry a region of hills and forests west of the Tidewater (p. 105)

balance of power the distribution of power among nations so that no single nation can dominate or interfere with another (pp. 667, 897)

bankruptcy the condition of being unable to pay one's debts; one's property is managed or sold to pay those to whom one owes money (p. 933)

barrio a Spanish-speaking neighborhood in a city, especially in the southwest U.S. (p. 633)

bicameral consisting of two houses, or chambers, especially in a legislature (p. 193)

black codes laws passed in the South just after the Civil War aimed at controlling freedmen and enabling plantation owners to exploit African American workers (p. 505)

blacklist list of persons who are disapproved of and are punished, such as by being refused jobs (p. 807)

blitzkrieg name given to the sudden, violent offensive attacks the Germans used during World War II; "lightning war" (p. 759)

blockade cut off an area by means of troops or warships to stop supplies or people from coming in or going out; to close off a country's ports (pp. 179, 463, 869)

blockade runner ship that sails into and out of a blockaded area (p. 468)

bond a note issued by the government, which promises to pay off a loan with interest (p. 261)

boomtown a community experiencing a sudden growth in business or population (p. 376)

border ruffians Missourians who traveled in armed groups to vote in Kansas's election during the mid-1850s (p. 443)

border states the states between the North and the South that were divided over whether to stay in the Union or join the Confederacy (p. 461)

bounty money given as a reward, such as to encourage enlistment in the army (p. 482)

boycott to refuse to buy items from a particular country (p. 134); to refuse to use in order to show disapproval or force acceptance of one's terms (p. 841)

brand a symbol burned into an animal's hide to show ownership (p. 534)

budget deficit the amount by which government spending exceeds revenue (p. 937)

bureaucracy system in which nonelected officials carry out laws and policies (p. 337)

burgesses elected representatives to an assembly (p. 73)

cabinet a group of advisers to the president (p. 259)

Californios Mexicans who lived in California (p. 373)

canal an artificial waterway (p. 318)

capital money for investment (pp. 308, 399)

capitalism an economic system based on private property and free enterprise (pp. 308, 701)

caravel small, fast ship with a broad bow (p. 40)

carbon dating a scientific method used to determine the age of an artifact (p. 19)

carpetbaggers name given to Northern whites who moved South after the Civil War and supported the Republicans (p. 510)

cash crop farm crop raised to be sold for money (pp. 103, 518)

casualty a military person killed, wounded, or captured (p. 469)

caucus a meeting held by a political party to choose their party's candidate for president or decide policy (pp. 269, 337)

cede to give up by treaty (p. 374)

censure to express formal disapproval of some action (p. 809)

census official count of a population (p. 314)

charter a document that gives the holder the right to organize settlements in an area (p. 71)

charter colony colony established by a group of settlers who had been given a formal document allowing them to settle (p. 110)

checks and balances the system in which each branch of government has a check on the other two branches so that no one branch becomes too powerful (p. 210)

circumnavigate to sail around the world (p. 49)

citizen a person who owes loyalty to and is entitled to the protection of a state or nation (p. 229)

civil disobedience refusal to obey laws that are considered unjust as a nonviolent way to press for changes (p. 842)

civil service the body of nonelected government workers (p. 612)

civil war conflict between opposing groups of citizens of the same country (p. 444)

civilization a highly developed culture, usually with organized religions and laws (p. 22)

classical relating to ancient Greece and Rome (p. 39)

clipper ship a fast sailing ship with slender lines, tall masts, and large square sails (p. 387)

closed shop a workplace in which the employer by agreement hires only union members (p. 798)

coeducation the teaching of male and female students together (p. 427)

cold war a struggle over political differences between nations carried on by methods short of war (p. 792)

collective bargaining discussion between an employer and union representatives of workers over wages, hours, and working conditions (p. 574)

Columbian Exchange exchange of goods, ideas, and people between Europe and the Americas (p. 60)

commission a group of persons directed to perform some duty (p. 516)

committee of correspondence an organization that spread political ideas through the colonies (p. 137)

compromise agreement between two or more sides in which each side gives up some of what it wants (p. 204)

concurrent powers powers shared by the states and the federal government (p. 219)

Conestoga wagon sturdy vehicle topped with white canvas and used by pioneers to move west (p. 283)

conquistador Spanish explorer in the Americas in the 1500s (p. 51)

conservation the protection and preservation of natural resources (p. 622)

consolidation the practice of combining separate companies into one (p. 557)

constituents people that members of Congress represent (p. 223)

constitution a formal plan of government (pp. 89, 193)

containment the policy or process of preventing the expansion of a hostile power (p. 791)

convoy a group that travels with something, such as a ship, to protect it (p. 678)

cooperative store where farmers bought products from each other; an enterprise owned and operated by those who use its services (p. 549)

corporation a business in which investors own shares (p. 568)

corruption dishonest or illegal actions (p. 510)

cotton gin a machine that removed seeds from cotton fiber (pp. 308, 398)

counterculture a social movement whose values go against those of established society (p. 878)

counter-terrorism military or political activities intended to combat terrorism (p. 949)

coup a sudden overthrow of a government by a small group (pp. 873, 930)

coureur de bois French trapper living among Native Americans (p. 62)

court-martial to try by a military court (p. 326)

credibility gap lack of belief; a term used to describe the lack of trust in the Johnson administration's statements about the Vietnam War (p. 879)

credit a form of loan; ability to buy goods based on future payment (p. 403)

culture a way of life of a group of people who share similar beliefs and customs (p. 19)

customs duties taxes on foreign imported goods (p. 280)

D

D-Day the day on which the Allied forces invaded France during World War II; June 6, 1944 (pp. 772, 774)

debtor person or country that owes money (p. 90)

decree an order given by one in authority (p. 364)

default to fail to meet an obligation, especially a financial one (p. 726)

deferment an excuse, issued by the draft board, that lets a person be excused from military service for various reasons (p. 878)

deficit the shortage that occurs when spending is greater than income (p. 903)

demilitarize to remove armed forces from an area (p. 326)

demilitarized zone a region where no military forces or weapons are permitted (p. 805)

deport to send out of a country aliens who are considered dangerous (p. 701)

depreciate to fall in value (p. 197)

depression a period of low economic activity and widespread unemployment (pp. 199, 350)

deregulation the act of cutting the restrictions and regulations that government places on business (p. 923)

desert to leave without permission (p. 173)

détente a policy which attempts to relax or ease tensions between nations (p. 897)

dictator a leader who rules with total authority, often in a cruel or brutal manner (p. 753)

disarmament removal of weapons (pp. 326, 761)

discrimination unfair treatment of a group; unequal treatment because of a person's race, religion, ethnic background, or place of birth (pp. 392, 628)

dissent disagreement with or opposition to an opinion (pp. 76, 685)

diversity variety or difference (p. 104)

dividend a stockholder's share of a company's profits, usually as a cash payment (p. 568)

dollar diplomacy a policy of joining the business interests of a country with its diplomatic interests abroad (p. 659)

domestic tranquility maintaining peace within the nation (p. 217)

domino theory the belief that if one nation in Asia fell to the Communists, neighboring countries would follow (pp. 819, 873)

dove a person who opposes war or warlike policies, such as one who opposed the Vietnam War (p. 878)

draft the selection of persons for military service (p. 481)

drought a long period of time with little rainfall (p. 29)

dry farming a way of farming dry land in which seeds are planted deep in ground where there is some moisture (p. 539)

due process of law idea that the government must follow procedures established by law and guaranteed by the Constitution (p. 228)

Dust Bowl the name given to the area of the southern Great Plains severely damaged by droughts and dust storms during the 1930s (p. 736)

E

effigy rag figure representing an unpopular individual (p. 134)

Electoral College a special group of voters selected by their state's voters to vote for the president and vice president (p. 210)

emancipate to free from slavery (p. 475)

embargo an order prohibiting trade with another country (pp. 290, 899)

emigrant a person who leaves a country or region to live elsewhere (p. 358)

emigrate to leave one's homeland to live elsewhere (p. 583)

empresario a person who arranged for the settlement of land in Texas during the 1800s (p. 363)

encomienda system of rewarding conquistadors with tracts of land and the right to tax and demand labor from Native Americans who lived on the land (p. 55)

Enlightenment movement during the 1700s that spread the idea that knowledge, reason, and science could improve society (p. 208)

entente an understanding between nations (p. 667)

entrenched occupying a strong defensive position (p. 486)

enumerated powers powers belonging only to the federal government (p. 219)

escalate to increase or expand (p. 874)

espionage spying (p. 686)

ethnic group a minority that speaks a different language or follows different customs than the majority of people in a country (pp. 583, 667)

evolution the scientific theory that humans and other living things have evolved over time (p. 718)

executive branch the branch of government, headed by the president, that carries out the nation's laws and policies (p. 210)

executive order a rule issued by a chief executive that has the force of law (p. 867)

exile a person forced to leave his or her country (p. 868)

expansionism a policy that calls for expanding a nation's boundaries (p. 639)

expatriate a person who gives up his or her home country and chooses to live in another country (p. 716)

export to sell goods abroad (p. 109)

factory system system bringing manufacturing steps together in one place to increase efficiency (p. 309)

famine an extreme shortage of food (p. 393)

fascism a political system, headed by a dictator, that calls for extreme nationalism and racism and no tolerance of opposition (p. 753)

favorite son candidate that receives the backing of his home state rather than of the national party (p. 335)

federal debt the amount of money owed by the government (p. 924)

federalism the sharing of power between federal and state governments (pp. 208, 219)

Federalists supporters of the Constitution (p. 211)

federation a type of government that links different groups together (p. 33)

feminist a person who advocates or is active in promoting women's rights (p. 857)

fixed costs regular expenses such as housing or maintaining equipment that remain about the same year after year (p. 403)

flapper a young woman of the 1920s who defied conventions in her behavior and dress (p. 714)

flexible response a plan that used special military units to fight guerrilla wars (p. 867)

forty-niners people who went to California during the gold rush of 1849 (p. 375)

Fourteen Points the peace plan to end World War I and restructure the countries of Europe, proposed by Woodrow Wilson (p. 689)

free enterprise the freedom of private businesses to operate competitively for profit with minimal government regulation (p. 308)

free silver the unlimited production of silver coins (p. 550)

freedman a person freed from slavery (p. 502)

frigate warship (p. 297)

front a region where warfare is taking place (p. 679)

fugitive runaway or trying to run away (p. 438)

fundamentalist a person who believes in the literal meaning of religious texts and strict obedience to religious laws (p. 913)

genocide the deliberate destruction of a racial, political, or cultural group (p. 775)

ghetto a part of a city in which a minority group lives because of social or economic pressure (p. 830)

ghost town former mining town that became deserted (p. 530)

Gilded Age the name associated with America in the late 1800s, referring to the extravagant wealth of a few and the terrible poverty that lay underneath (p. 592)

glasnost a Soviet policy allowing more open discussion of political and social issues, as well as more widespread news and information (p. 925)

global warming a steady increase in average world temperatures (p. 944)

grandfather clause a clause that allowed individuals who did not pass the literacy test to vote if their fathers or grandfathers had voted before Reconstruction began; an exception to a law based on preexisting circumstances (p. 519)

grassroots society at the local and popular level away from political or cultural centers (p. 936)

greenback a piece of U.S. paper money first issued by the North during the Civil War (p. 483)

gross domestic product the value of all the goods and services produced in a nation during a one-year period (p. 938)

gross national product the total value of all goods and services produced by a nation's residents during a year, regardless of where production takes place (p. 709)

guerrilla tactics referring to surprise attacks or raids rather than organized warfare (p. 344)

guerrilla warfare a hit-and-run technique used in fighting a war; fighting by small bands of warriors using tactics such as sudden ambushes (pp. 180, 867)

habeas corpus a legal order for an inquiry to determine whether a person has been lawfully imprisoned (p. 481)

hawk a person who advocates war or warlike policies, such as a supporter of the Vietnam War (p. 878)

hieroglyphics an ancient form of writing using symbols and pictures to represent words, sounds, and concepts (p. 24)

Hispanic a person from or descended from people who came from the countries of Latin America or Spain (p. 858)

Holocaust the name given to the mass slaughter of Jews and other groups by the Nazis during World War II (p. 776)

homestead to acquire a piece of U.S. public land by living on and cultivating it (p. 537)

horizontal integration the combining of competing firms into one corporation (p. 569)

hot line a direct telephone line for emergency use (p. 870)

human rights rights regarded as belonging to all persons, such as freedom from unlawful imprisonment, torture, and execution (p. 912)

Hundred Days a special session of Congress that dealt with problems of the Depression (p. 732)

Ice Age a period of extremely cold temperatures when part of the planet's surface was covered with massive ice sheets (p. 17)

impeach to formally charge a public official with misconduct in office (pp. 223, 507, 938)

impeachment charging a public official with misconduct in office; if proven guilty before a designated court, the official is removed from office (p. 906)

imperialism the actions used by one nation to exercise political or economic control over smaller or weaker nations (p. 640)

implied powers powers not specifically mentioned in the Constitution (pp. 221, 268)

import to buy goods from foreign markets (p. 109)

impressment forcing people into service, as in the navy (pp. 265, 290)

incumbent someone who currently holds an office or position (p. 939)

indentured servant laborer who agreed to work without pay for a certain period of time in exchange for passage to America (p. 87)

Industrial Revolution the change from an agrarian society to one based on industry which began in Great Britain and spread to the United States around 1800 (p. 307)

inflation a continuous rise in the price of goods and services (pp. 175, 483, 796)

initiative the right of citizens to place a measure or issue before the voters or the legislature for approval (p. 614)

injunction a court order to stop an action, such as a strike (p. 575)

installment buying a system of paying for goods in which customers promise to pay small, regular amounts over a period of time (p. 711)

integrate to end separation of different races and bring into equal membership in society (pp. 512, 840)

interchangeable parts uniform pieces that can be made in large quantities to replace other identical pieces (p. 309)

internal improvements federal projects, such as canals and roads, to develop the nation's transportation system (p. 322)

Internet a worldwide linking of computer networks (p. 943)

internment camps the detention centers where Japanese Americans were moved to and confined during World War II (p. 768)

interstate across state lines; connecting or existing between two or more states (p. 849)

iron curtain the political and military barrier that isolated Soviet-controlled countries of Eastern Europe after World War II (p. 790)

ironclad armored naval vessel (p. 468)

Iroquois Confederacy a powerful group of Native Americans in the eastern part of the United States made up of five nations: the Mohawk, Seneca, Cayuga, Onondaga, and Oneida (p. 117)

island hopping a strategy used during World War II that called for attacking and capturing certain key islands and using these islands as bases to leapfrog to others (p. 779)

isolationism a national policy of avoiding involvement in world affairs (pp. 639, 707)

isthmus a narrow strip of land connecting two larger land areas (p. 657)

joint occupation the possession and settling of an area shared by two or more countries (p. 357)

joint-stock company a company in which investors buy stock in the company in return for a share of its future profits (p. 71)

judicial branch the branch of government, including the federal court system, that interprets the nation's laws (p. 210)

judicial review the right of the Supreme Court to determine if a law violates the Constitution (pp. 222, 281)

kamikaze during World War II, a Japanese suicide pilot whose mission was to crash into his target (p. 779)

laissez-faire policy that government should interfere as little as possible in the nation's economy (pp. 279, 350, 621)

land-grant college originally, an agricultural college established as a result of the 1862 Morrill Act that gave states large amounts of federal land that could be sold to raise money for education (p. 598)

landslide an overwhelming victory (p. 336)

League of Nations an association of nations to preserve peace and resolve international disputes proposed in Wilson's Fourteen Points (p. 689)

lease to hand over property in return for rent (p. 705)

legislative branch the branch of government that makes the nation's laws (p. 209)

lend-lease the act passed during World War II allowing the United States to sell, lend, or lease arms or other war supplies to any nation considered "vital to the defense of the United States" (p. 761)

line of demarcation an imaginary line running down the middle of the Atlantic Ocean from the North Pole to the South Pole dividing the Americas between Spain and Portugal (p. 47)

line-item veto the power that allows the president to cancel individual spending items in a budget or bill (p. 937)

literacy the ability to read and write (p. 113)

literacy test a method used to prevent African Americans from voting by requiring prospective voters to read and write at a specified level (p. 519)

lock in a canal, an enclosure with gates at each end used in raising or lowering boats as they pass from level to level (p. 318)

lode a mass or strip of ore sandwiched between layers of rock (p. 529)

log cabin campaign name given to William Henry Harrison's campaign for the presidency in 1840, from the Whigs' use of a log cabin as their symbol (p. 351)

Loyalists American colonists who remained loyal to Britain and opposed the war for independence (p. 145)

lynching putting to death a person by the illegal action of a mob (p. 520)

maize an early form of corn grown by Native Americans (p. 19)

majority more than half (p. 335)

Manifest Destiny the idea popular in the United States during the 1800s that the country must expand its boundaries to the Pacific (p. 360)

manumission the freeing of some enslaved persons (p. 201)

martial law the law applied by military forces in occupied territory or in an emergency (p. 887)

martyr a person who sacrifices his or her life for a principle or cause (p. 448)

mass media types of communication that reach large numbers of people, such as newspapers, radio, and television (p. 714)

mass production the production of large quantities of goods using machinery and often an assembly line (p. 566)

materialism attaching too much importance to physical possessions and comforts (p. 830)

Mayflower Compact a formal document, written in 1620, that provided law and order to the Plymouth colony (p. 77)

Medicaid a social program that gives the states money to help those who cannot afford to pay for their hospital bills (p. 847)

Medicare a social program that helps pay for medical care for the elderly (p. 847)

mercantilism the theory that a state's or nation's power depended on its wealth (pp. 59, 109)

mercenary paid soldier who serves in the army of a foreign country (p. 164)

merger the combining of two or more businesses into one (p. 571)

MIAs soldiers classified as missing in action (p. 889)

migrant worker a person who moves from place to place to find work harvesting fruits and vegetables (p. 737)

migration a movement of a large number of people into a new homeland (p. 17)

militarism a buildup of military strength within a country (p. 667)

militia a group of civilians trained to fight in emergencies (pp. 118, 142)

minutemen companies of civilian soldiers who boasted that they were ready to fight on a minute's notice (p. 142)

mission religious settlement (pp. 54, 92)

mobilization gathering resources and preparing for war (pp. 683, 765)

moderate opposed to major social change or extreme political ideas (p. 815)

monopoly total control of a type of industry by one person or one company (p. 570)

Morse code a system for transmitting messages that uses a series of dots and dashes to represent the letters of the alphabet, numbers, and punctuation (p. 389)

mosque a Muslim house of worship (p. 42)

mountain man a frontiersman living in the wilderness, as in the Rocky Mountains (p. 357)

muckraker a journalist who uncovers abuses and corruption in a society (p. 613)

mudslinging attempt to ruin an opponent's reputation with insults (p. 336)

national debt the amount of money a national government owes to other governments or its people (p. 260)

National Grange the first farmers' organization in the United States (p. 549)

Glossary

nationalism loyalty to a nation and promotion of its interests above all others (pp. 293, 667)

nativism the belief that those born in a country are superior to immigrants (p. 717)

nativist a person who favors those born in his country and is opposed to immigrants (p. 395)

naturalization to grant full citizenship to a foreigner (p. 229)

neutral taking no side in a conflict (p. 163)

neutral rights the right to sail the seas and not take sides in a war (p. 290)

neutrality a position of not taking sides in a conflict (p. 265)

New Deal the name given to the new laws aimed at relieving the Depression, which were passed by Congress during the Hundred Days and the months that followed (p. 733)

nomadic moving from place to place with no permanent home (p. 543)

nomads people who move from place to place, usually in search of food or grazing land (p. 17)

nominating convention system in which delegates from the states selected the party's presidential candidate (p. 337)

nonimportation the act of not importing or using certain goods (p. 134)

normal school a two-year school for training high school graduates as teachers (p. 413)

Northwest Passage water route to Asia through North America sought by European explorers (p. 60)

nullify to cancel or make ineffective (pp. 271, 338)

O

offensive position of attacking or the attack itself (p. 463)

on margin to buy stock by paying only a fraction of the stock price and borrowing the rest (p. 725)

Open Door policy a policy that allowed each foreign nation in China to trade freely in the other nations' spheres of influence (p. 647)

open range land not fenced or divided into lots (p. 534)

ordinance a law or regulation (p. 196)

ore a mineral mined for the valuable substance it contains, such as silver (p. 529)

override to overturn or defeat, as a bill proposed in Congress (p. 505)

overseer person who supervises a large operation or its workers (pp. 106, 403)

ozone the layer of gas composed of a form of oxygen that protects the earth and its people from cancer-causing sun rays (p. 944)

P

pacifist person opposed to the use of war or violence to settle disputes (pp. 85, 686)

partisan favoring one side of an issue (p. 268)

patent a document that gives an inventor the sole legal right to an invention for a period of time (p. 308)

Patriots American colonists who were determined to fight the British until American independence was won (p. 145)

patronage another name for the spoils system, in which government jobs or favors are given out to political allies and friends (p. 612)

patroon landowner in the Dutch colonies who ruled like a king over large areas of land (p. 83)

peaceful coexistence agreement between opposing countries that they will compete with one another but will avoid war (p. 820)

pension a sum paid regularly to a person, usually after retirement (p. 743)

perestroika a policy of government and economic reform in the Soviet Union in the mid-1980s (p. 926)

perjury lying when one has sworn an oath to tell the truth (p. 807)

persecute to treat someone harshly because of that person's beliefs or practices (p. 76)

petition a formal request (pp. 148, 196)

philanthropy charitable acts or gifts of money to benefit the community (p. 570)

pilgrimage a journey to a holy place (p. 42)

Pilgrims Separatists who journeyed to the colonies during the 1600s for a religious purpose (p. 77)

plantation a large estate run by an owner or manager and farmed by laborers who lived there (p. 55)

plurality largest single share (p. 335)

political machine an organization linked to a political party that often controlled local government (p. 610)

poll tax a tax of a fixed amount per person that had to be paid before the person could vote (p. 519)

pool a group sharing in some activity, for example, among railroad barons who made secret agreements and set rates among themselves (p. 559)

popular sovereignty political theory that government is subject to the will of the people (p. 218); before the Civil War, the idea that people living in a territory had the right to decide by voting if slavery would be allowed there (p. 442)

Populist Party U.S. political party formed in 1892 representing mainly farmers, favoring free coinage of silver and government control of railroads and other monopolies (p. 550)

poverty line a level of personal or family income below which one is classified as poor according to government standards (p. 847)

preamble the introduction to a formal document, especially the Constitution (pp. 151, 217)

precedent a tradition (p. 259)

prejudice an unfair opinion not based on facts (p. 392)

Glossary

presidio Spanish fort in the Americas built to protect mission settlements (p. 54)

primary an election in which voters choose their party's candidate (p. 614)

privateer armed private ship (pp. 179, 297)

productivity how much work each worker does (pp. 710, 822)

prohibition the forbidding by law of the making or selling of alcoholic beverages (p. 619)

Prohibition the nationwide ban on the manufacture, sale, and transportation of liquor in the United States that went into effect when the Eighteenth Amendment was ratified in 1919 (p. 717)

propaganda ideas or information designed and spread to influence opinion (pp. 137, 672)

proportional to be the same as or corresponding to (p. 203)

proprietary colony colony run by individuals or groups to whom land was granted (pp. 83, 111)

protectorate a country that is technically independent, but is actually under the control of another country (p. 653)

public works projects such as highways, parks, and libraries built with public funds for public use (p. 727)

pueblo home or community of homes built by Native Americans (pp. 29, 54)

Puritans Protestants who, during the 1600s, wanted to reform the Anglican Church (p. 77)

─────── Q ───────

quota system an arrangement placing a limit on the number of immigrants from each country (p. 718)

─────── R ───────

radical extreme (p. 501)

ragtime a type of music with a strong rhythm and a lively melody with accented notes, which was popular in early 1900s (p. 601)

ranchero Mexican ranch owner (p. 371)

rancho huge properties for raising livestock set up by Mexican settlers in California (p. 371)

ratify to give official approval to (pp. 185, 211, 476)

ration to give out scarce items on a limited basis (p. 766)

realism an approach to literature, art, and theater that shows things as they really are (p. 600)

rebate discount or return of part of a payment (p. 559)

Rebel Confederate soldier, so called because of opposition to the established government (p. 464)

recall the right that enables voters to remove unsatisfactory elected officials from office (p. 614)

recession a downward turn in business activity (p. 709)

reconciliation settling by agreement or coming together again (p. 514)

Reconstruction the reorganization and rebuilding of the former Confederate states after the Civil War (p. 501)

recruit to enlist soldiers in the army (p. 165)

referendum the practice of letting voters accept or reject measures proposed by the legislature (p. 614)

regionalism in art or literature, the practice of focusing on a particular region of the country (p. 600)

relief aid for the needy; welfare (p. 727)

relocate to force a person or group of people to move (p. 342)

Renaissance a period of intellectual and artistic creativity, c. 1300–1600 (p. 39)

rendezvous a meeting (p. 357)

reparations payment by the losing country in a war to the winner for the damages caused by the war (p. 690)

repeal to cancel an act or law (p. 134)

republic a government in which citizens rule through elected representatives (p. 193)

republicanism favoring a republic, or representative democracy, as the best form of government (p. 218)

reservation an area of public lands set aside for Native Americans (p. 543)

reserved powers powers retained by the states (p. 219)

resolution a formal expression of opinion (p. 134)

revenue incoming money (p. 133)

revenue sharing money raised from federal taxes and given to the states for use at the state and local levels (p. 902)

revival a series of meetings conducted by a preacher to arouse religious emotions (p. 413)

royal colony colony run by a governor and a council appointed by the king or queen (p. 111)

─────── S ───────

sabotage secret action by enemy agents or sympathizers to damage a nation's war effort (p. 686)

scalawags name given by former Confederates to Southern whites who supported Republican Reconstruction of the South (p. 510)

search-and-destroy mission a strategy used in Vietnam in which American forces sought Vietcong and North Vietnamese units to destroy them (p. 875)

secede to leave or withdraw (pp. 285, 338, 438)

secession withdrawal from the Union (p. 451)

Second New Deal a new set of programs and reforms launched by Franklin D. Roosevelt in 1935 (p. 744)

sectionalism loyalty to a region (pp. 322, 437)

sedition activities aimed at weakening established government (p. 271)

segregation the separation or isolation of a race, class, or group (pp. 519, 838)

Glossary

Separatists Protestants who, during the 1600s, wanted to leave the Anglican Church in order to found their own churches (p. 77)

settlement house institution located in a poor neighborhood that provided numerous community services such as medical care, child care, libraries, and classes in English (p. 593)

sharecropping system of farming in which a farmer works land for an owner who provides equipment and seeds and receives a share of the crop (p. 512)

shareholder a person who invests in a corporation by buying stock and is a partial owner (p. 568)

shuttle diplomacy negotiations between nations carried on by a person who travels back and forth between them (p. 900)

silent majority the phrase used by Nixon to describe the majority of Americans, those who did not protest or demonstrate (p. 882)

sit-in the act of occupying seats or sitting down on the floor of an establishment as a form of organized protest (p. 849)

slave code the laws passed in the Southern states that controlled and restricted enslaved people (p. 405)

slum poor, crowded, and run-down urban neighborhoods (p. 591)

smuggling trading illegally with other nations (p. 109)

Social Security Act a law requiring workers and employers to pay a tax; the money provides a monthly pension for retired people (p. 744)

socialist person who believes industries should be publicly owned and run by the government rather than by private individuals (p. 686)

sodbuster a name given to the Plains farmer (p. 539)

speculator person who risks money in order to make a large profit (pp. 125, 261)

sphere of influence section of a country where one foreign nation enjoys special rights and powers (p. 647)

spiritual an African American religious folk song (p. 405)

spoils system practice of handing out government jobs to supporters; replacing government employees with the winning candidate's supporters (p. 337)

square deal Theodore Roosevelt's promise of fair and equal treatment for all (p. 621)

stagflation a combination of rising prices and a sluggish economy with relatively high unemployment (p. 903)

stalemate a situation during a conflict when action stops because both sides are equally powerful and neither will give in (p. 804)

standard gauge the uniform width of 4 feet, 8.5 inches for railroad tracks, adopted during the 1880s (p. 558)

standard of living a measure of people's overall wealth and quality of life; a minimum of necessities and luxuries that a group is accustomed to (p. 822)

states' rights rights and powers independent of the federal government that are reserved for the states by the Constitution; the belief that states' rights supersede federal rights and law (pp. 271, 451)

steerage cramped quarters on a ship's lower decks for passengers paying the lowest fares (p. 584)

stock shares of ownership a company sells in its business which often carry voting power (p. 568)

stock exchange a place where shares in corporations are bought and sold through an organized system (p. 725)

strait a narrow passageway connecting two larger bodies of water (p. 49)

strike a stopping of work by workers to force an employer to meet demands (p. 392)

strikebreaker person hired to replace a striking worker in order to break up a strike (p. 575)

subsidy grant of money from the government to a person or a company for an action intended to benefit the public (pp. 530, 733)

subsistence farming farming in which only enough food to feed one's family is produced (p. 101)

suburbs residential areas that sprang up close to or surrounding cities as a result of improvements in transportation (p. 592)

subversion an attempt to overthrow a government by persons working secretly from within (p. 806)

suffrage the right to vote (pp. 336, 426)

suffragist a man or woman who fought for a woman's right to vote (p. 616)

summit a meeting of heads of government (p. 820)

surplus excess; amount left over after necessary expenses are paid (p. 815)

sweatshop a shop or factory where workers work long hours at low wages under unhealthy conditions (pp. 573, 585)

tariff a tax on imports or exports (pp. 262, 338)

technology the application of scientific discoveries to practical use (pp. 40, 308)

Tejano a Mexican who claims Texas as his home (p. 363)

telegraph a device or system that uses electric signals to transmit messages by a code over wires (p. 389)

temperance the use of little or no alcoholic drink (p. 413)

tenant farmer farmer who works land owned by another and pays rent either in cash or crops (pp. 92, 402)

tenement a building in which several families rent rooms or apartments, often with little sanitation or safety (p. 591)

terrace a raised piece of land with the top leveled off to promote farming (p. 26)

terrorism the use of violence by groups against civilians to achieve a political goal (p. 944)

theocracy a form of government in which the society is ruled by religious leaders (p. 23)

Tidewater a region of flat, low-lying plains along the seacoast (p. 105)

toleration the acceptance of different beliefs (p. 79)

total war war on all aspects of the enemy's life (p. 490)

totalitarian a political system in which the government suppresses all opposition and controls most aspects of people's lives (p. 754)

trade deficit the situation when the value of a country's foreign imports exceeds the value of its exports (p. 911)

trade union organization of workers with the same trade or skill (pp. 392, 573)

transcendentalist any of a group of New England writers who stressed the relationship between human beings and nature, spiritual things over material things, and the importance of the individual conscience (p. 415)

transcontinental extending across a continent (p. 531)

triangular trade a trade route that exchanged goods between the West Indies, the American colonies, and West Africa (p. 102)

tribute money paid for protection (pp. 52, 289)

trust a combination of firms or corporations formed by a legal agreement, especially to reduce competition (pp. 569, 612)

trustbuster someone who breaks up a trust into smaller companies (p. 621)

turnpike a road that one must pay to use; the money is used to pay for the road (p. 315)

unalienable right a right that cannot be surrendered (p. 154)

unconstitutional not agreeing or consistent with the Constitution (p. 262)

underemployment the condition when people work at jobs for which they are overqualified or that do not utilize their skills (p. 908)

Underground Railroad a system that helped enslaved African Americans follow a network of escape routes out of the South to freedom in the North (p. 422)

unemployment insurance payments by the government for a limited period of time to people who have lost their jobs (p. 744)

utopia community based on a vision of a perfect society sought by reformers (p. 412)

vaquero Hispanic ranch hand (p. 536)

vaudeville stage entertainment made up of various acts, such as dancing, singing, comedy, and magic shows (p.602)

vertical integration the combining of companies that supply equipment and services needed for a particular industry (p. 570)

veto to reject a bill and prevent it from becoming a law (p. 349)

Vietcong the guerrilla soldiers of the Communist faction in Vietnam, also known as the National Liberation Front (p. 872)

Vietnamization Nixon's policy that called for South Vietnam to take a more active role in fighting the war and for Americans to become less involved (p. 885)

vigilantes people who take the law into their own hands (pp. 377, 529)

War Hawks Republicans during Madison's presidency who pressed for war with Britain (p. 293)

work relief programs that gave needy people government jobs (p. 733)

writ of assistance legal document that enabled officers to search homes and warehouses for goods that might be smuggled (p. 133)

Yankee Union soldier (p. 464)

yellow journalism writing which exaggerates sensational, dramatic, and gruesome events to attract readers, named for stories that were popular during the late 1800s (p. 600); a type of sensational, biased, and often false reporting (p. 650)

yeoman Southern owner of a small farm who did not have enslaved people (p. 402)

Glossary

Spanish Glossary

A

abolitionist/abolicionista una persona que favorece firmemente suprimir la esclavitud (p. 418)

abstain/abstenerse no tomar parte de una actividad, como de votar (p. 439)

adobe/adobe un ladrillo de lodo, seco al sol, usado para construir las casas de los Nativos Americanos (p. 32)

affirmative action/acción afirmativa un esfuerzo activo para mejorar las oportunidades de educación y empleo para grupos de minorías y de la mujer (p. 902)

affluence/afluencia la condición de tener mucha riqueza (p. 822)

airlift/puente aéreo un sistema de transportar comida y abastos por vehículos aéreos hasta un área que no se puede alcanzar de otras maneras (p. 792)

alien/extranjero una persona inmigrante que vive en un país en el cual no es ciudadano (p. 271)

alleged/alegado dicho como un hecho pero sin pruebas (p. 808)

alliance/alianza una asociación íntima entre naciones u otros grupos formada para avanzar intereses o causas que llevan en común (p. 122)

alliance system/sistema de alianza acuerdos de defensa entre naciones (p. 667)

ambush/emboscada un ataque por sorpresa (p. 187)

amendment/enmienda una adición a un documento formal tal como la Constitución (pp. 213, 221)

American System/Sistema Americano políticas ideadas por Henry Clay para estimular el crecimiento de la industria (p. 324)

amnesty/amnistía el otorgar perdón a un número grande de personas; la protección del proceso a causa de una acción ilegal (pp. 501, 907)

anarchist/anarquista una persona que cree que no debe de haber ningún gobierno (p. 701)

anarchy/anarquía desorden y sin ley (p. 658)

annex/anexar añadir un territorio a su propio territorio (p. 367)

annexation/anexión traer un área bajo el control de un país más grande (p. 645)

Antifederalists/antifederalistas personas que estaban en contra de que se ratificara la Constitución (p. 212)

anti-Semitism/antisemitismo hostilidad hacia o discriminación en contra de los judíos (p. 753)

apartheid/apartheid la separación racial y discriminación económica y política en contra de la gente no blanca, una política anteriormente practicada en la República de África del Sur (p. 912)

appeasement/apaciguamiento aceptar demandas para evitar conflictos (p. 755)

apprentice/aprendiz asistente asignado para aprender el oficio de un artesano experto (p. 112)

appropriate/destinar apartar para un propósito en particular, dicho especialmente de fondos (p. 223)

arbitration/arbitraje arreglo de una disputa por medio de un acuerdo para aceptar la decisión de una persona imparcial (p. 621)

archaeology/arqueología el estudio de pueblos antiguos (p. 17)

armistice/armisticio un acuerdo temporal de paz para suprimir combates (pp. 652, 680)

arms race/carrera de armas la competición entre los Estados Unidos y la Unión Soviética para construir más y más armas, cada uno con el propósito de sobrepasar el poder militar del otro (p. 817)

arsenal/arsenal un lugar para el almacenaje de armas y municiones (p. 448)

article/artículo una parte de un documento tal como la Constitución que trata de un solo tema (p. 209)

artifact/artefacto un artículo dejado por pueblos antiguos que representa su cultura (p. 17)

assembly line/línea de montaje un sistema de producción arreglado con máquinas y trabajadores para que cada persona haga vez tras vez su trabajo designado mientras el artículo pasa por en frente de él (p. 565)

assimilate/asimilar introducir a un grupo dentro de la cultura de una población más grande (p. 585)

astrolabe/astrolabio un instrumento usado por los marineros para observar las posiciones de las estrellas (p. 40)

autocracy/autocracia gobierno en el cual una persona lleva el poder sin límite (p. 675)

automation/automatización un sistema o proceso que usa aparatos mecánicos o electrónicos para reemplazar a los trabajadores humanos (p. 830)

B

baby boom/auge de nacimientos un aumento marcado de la proporción de nacimientos, como el de los Estados Unidos inmediatamente después de terminar la Segunda Guerra Mundial (p. 822)

backcountry/monte una región de colinas y bosques al oeste de la orilla del mar (p. 105)

balance of power/balance de poder la distribución de poder entre naciones para que ninguna nación en particular pueda dominar o interferir con otra (pp. 667, 897)

bankruptcy/bancarrota la condición de no poder pagar sus deudas; la propiedad de uno es manejada o vendida para pagar a las personas a las cuales uno debe dinero (p. 933)

barrio/barrio una vecindad hispanoparlante de una ciudad, especialmente en el sudoeste de EE.UU. (p. 633)

bicameral/bicameral que consiste de dos cámaras, especialmente dicho en una legislatura (p. 193)

black codes/códigos negros leyes establecidas en el Sur al terminar la Guerra Civil para controlar a los libertos y permitir a los dueños de plantaciones la explotación de los trabajadores afroamericanos (p. 505)

blacklist/lista negra una lista de personas que son desaprobadas y castigadas, tal como rehusar a darles trabajo (p. 807)

blitzkrieg/*blitzkrieg* nombre dado a los ataques ofensivos súbitos y violentos usados por los alemanes durante la Segunda Guerra Mundial; "guerra relámpago" (p. 759)

blockade/bloqueo el cerrar un área por medio de tropas o de buques de guerra para prohibir el entrar y el salir de abastos y de personas; cerrar los puertos de un país (pp. 179, 463, 869)

blockade runner/forzador de bloqueo un buque que navega adentro y afuera de un área bloqueada (p. 468)

bond/bono una obligación hecha por el gobierno la cual promete pagar un préstamo con interés (p. 261)

boomtown/pueblo en bonanza una comunidad experimentando un auge repentino de comercio o población (p. 376)

border ruffians/rufianes fronterizos hombres de Missouri que viajaban en grupos armados a votar en la elección de Kansas a mediados de los años 1850 (p. 443)

border states/estados fronterizos los estados entre el Norte y el Sur que fueron divididos sobre el problema de quedarse en la Unión o de unirse a la Confederación (p. 461)

bounty/gratificación dinero dado como recompensa, como para animar el alistamiento en el ejército (p. 482)

boycott/boicotear rehusar comprar artículos de un país en particular (p. 134); rehusar usar (p. 841)

brand/marca a fuego un símbolo quemado en la piel de un animal para mostrar título de propiedad (p. 534)

budget deficit/déficit del presupuesto la cantidad por la cual los gastos exceden las rentas, especialmente referente al gobierno (p. 937)

bureaucracy/burocracia sistema en el cual oficiales no elegidos administran las leyes y políticas (p. 337)

burgesses/burgueses representantes elegidos para una asamblea (p. 73)

— **C** —

cabinet/gabinete un grupo de consejeros al presidente (p. 259)

Californios/californios mexicanos que vivían en California (p. 373)

canal/canal vía artificial de agua (p. 318)

capital/capital dinero para inversión (pp. 308, 399)

capitalism/capitalismo un sistema económico basado en la propiedad particular y la empresa libre (pp. 308, 701)

caravel/carabela un buque pequeño y veloz con una proa ancha (p. 40)

carbon dating/datar con carbón un método científico usado para determinar la edad de un artefacto (p. 19)

carpetbaggers/*carpetbaggers* nombre dado a los blancos norteños que se trasladaban al Sur después de la guerra y apoyaban a los republicanos (p. 510)

cash crop/cultivo comercial cosecha cultivada para vender por dinero (pp. 103, 518)

casualty/baja un miliciano muerto, herido, o capturado (p. 469)

caucus/junta electoral una reunión llevada a cabo por un partido político para escoger el candidato a la presidencia de su partido o para decidir políticas (pp. 269, 337)

cede/ceder abandonar por tratado (p. 374)

censure/censurar expresar desaprobación formal de alguna acción (p. 809)

census/censo registro oficial de una población (p. 314)

charter/carta de privilegio un documento que otorga los derechos de organizar establecimientos en una área (p. 71)

charter colony/colonia a carta colonia establecida por un grupo de colonizadores a quienes se les había dado un documento formal permitiéndoles colonizar (p. 110)

checks and balances/inspecciones y balances el sistema en el cual cada rama de gobierno refrena las otras dos ramas para que ninguna rama vuelva a ser demasiado poderosa (p. 210)

circumnavigate/circunnavegar navegar alrededor del mundo (p. 49)

citizen/ciudadano una persona que debe ser leal y tiene derecho a la protección de un estado o nación (p. 229)

civil disobedience/desobediencia civil el rehusar obedecer las leyes que uno considera injustas como una manera pacífica para insistir en cambios (p. 842)

civil service/servicio civil el cuerpo de trabajadores gubernamentales no elegidos (p. 612)

civil war/guerra civil conflicto entre grupos opuestos de ciudadanos del mismo país (p. 444)

civilization/civilización una cultura sumamente desarrollada, generalmente con religiones y leyes organizadas (p. 22)

classical/clásico relacionado a Grecia y Roma antigua (p. 39)

clipper ship/buque clíper un buque veloz con líneas delgadas, mástiles altos, y grandes velas cuadradas (p. 387)

closed shop/taller cerrado un lugar de trabajo en el cual, por acuerdo, el empresario contrata sólo a los miembros del sindicato (p. 798)

coeducation/coeducación la enseñanza conjunta de estudiantes hombres y mujeres (p. 427)

cold war/guerra fría una lucha sobre diferencias políticas entre naciones llevada a cabo por métodos fuera de guerra (p. 792)

collective bargaining/negociaciones colectivas discusión entre el empresario y los representantes sindicales de los trabajadores sobre salario, horas, y condiciones del taller (p. 574)

Columbian Exchange/Cambio Colombiano el cambio de productos, ideas, y personas entre Europa y las Américas (p. 60)

commission/comisión un grupo de personas dirigidas a hacer algún deber (p. 516)

Spanish Glossary

committee of correspondence/comité de correspondencia una organización que usaba reuniones, cartas, y panfletos para propagar ideas políticas para las colonias (p. 137)

compromise/compromiso un acuerdo entre dos o más partidos en el cual cada partido abandona algo de lo que quiere (p. 204)

concurrent powers/poderes concurrentes poderes compartidos por los estados y el gobierno federal (p. 219)

Conestoga wagon/conestoga vehículo firme cubierto de lona blanca usado por los pioneros para moverse hacia el oeste (p. 283)

conquistador/conquistador explorador español en las Américas en los años 1500 (p. 51)

conservation/conservación la protección y preservación de recursos naturales (p. 622)

consolidation/consolidación la práctica de juntar compañías particulares en una (p. 557)

constituents/constituyentes personas representadas por miembros del Congreso (p. 223)

constitution/constitución un plan formal de gobierno (pp. 89, 193)

containment/contención la política o proceso de prohibir la expansión de un poder hostil (p. 791)

convoy/convoy un grupo que viaja con algo, tal como un buque, para protegerlo (p. 678)

cooperative/cooperativa una tienda donde los granjeros compraban productos uno al otro; una empresa poseída y operada por los que usan sus servicios (p. 549)

corporation/sociedad anónima un grupo autorizado por ley a montar una actividad pero con los derechos y deberes de una persona particular (p. 568)

corruption/corrupción acciones deshonestas o ilegales (p. 510)

cotton gin/despepitadora de algodón una máquina que sacaba las semillas de las fibras de algodón (pp. 308, 398)

counterculture/contracultura un movimiento social cuyos valores están en contra de los de la sociedad establecida (p. 878)

counter-terrorism/*contraterrorismo* actividades militares o políticos con el fin de combatir el terrorismo (p. 949)

coup/golpe derrocamiento súbito de un gobierno por un grupo pequeño (pp. 873, 930)

coureur de bois/*coureur de bois* cazador de pieles francés viviendo entre los Nativos Americanos (p. 62)

court-martial/consejo de guerra someter a juicio por un tribunal militar (p. 326)

credibility gap/resquicio de credibilidad falta de creencia; un término usado para describir la falta de confianza en los anuncios de la administración de Johnson referente a la Guerra en Viet Nam (p. 879)

credit/crédito una forma de préstamo; la capacidad de comprar productos basada en pagos futuros (p. 403)

culture/cultura la manera de vivir de un grupo de personas que tienen en común sus creencias y costumbres (p. 19)

customs duties/derechos de aduana impuestos sobre productos importados del extranjero (p. 280)

D

D-Day/D-Day el día en el cual las fueras Aliadas invadieron Francia durante la Segunda Guerra Mundial; el 6 de junio de 1944 (pp. 772, 774)

debtor/deudor persona o país que debe dinero (p. 90)

decree/decreto una orden o decisión dada por alguién de autoridad (p. 364)

default/incumplimiento de pago fallar en hacer una obligación, especialmente una financiera (p. 726)

deferment/aplazamiento un perdón, aprobado por la junta de reclutamiento, que permite que sea perdonada una persona del servicio militar por varias razones (p. 878)

deficit/déficit escasez que ocurre cuando los gastos son más que los ingresos (p. 903)

demilitarize/desmilitarizar quitar fuerzas armadas de un área (p. 326)

demilitarized zone/zona desmilitarizada una región donde no se permite ninguna fuerza militar ni armas (p. 805)

deport/deportar mandar afuera de un país a los extranjeros que se consideran peligrosos (p. 701)

depreciate/depreciar caer en valor (p. 197)

depression/depresión un período de poca actividad económica y de desempleo extenso (pp. 199, 350)

deregulation/deregulación el acto de quitar las limitaciones y reglamentos que el gobierno había puesto en el comercio (p. 923)

desert/desertar salir sin permiso (p. 173)

détente/*détente* una política que intenta relajar o aliviar tensiones entre naciones (p. 897)

dictator/dictador un líder que manda con plena autoridad, a menudo de una manera cruel o brutal (p. 753)

disarmament/desarme el quitar armas (pp. 326, 761)

discrimination/discriminación trato injusto de un grupo; trato parcial a causa de la raza, la religión, los antecedentes étnicos, o lugar de nacimiento de alguién (pp. 392, 628)

dissent/disensión desacuerdo con u oposición a una opinión (pp. 76, 685)

diversity/diversidad variedad o diferencia (p. 104)

dividend/dividendo cheque que se paga a los accionistas, por lo general trimestralmente, representa una porción de las ganancias de la corporación (p. 568)

dollar diplomacy/diplomacia del dólar una política de unir los intereses comerciales de un país con sus intereses diplomáticos al extranjero (p. 659)

domestic tranquility/tranquilidad doméstica mantener la paz dentro de la nación (p. 217)

domino theory/teoría dominó la creencia de que si una nación de Asia hubiera caído a los comunistas los países vecinos la habrían seguido (pp. 819, 873)

dove/paloma una persona que se opone a la guerra y las políticas de guerra, tal como una persona que se oponía a la Guerra en Viet Nam (p. 878)

draft/reclutamiento la selección de personas a servicio militar requerido (p. 481)

drought/sequía un largo período con poca lluvia (p. 29)

dry farming/agricultura seca una manera de cultivar tierra seca en la cual las semillas se plantan al fondo de la tierra donde hay un poco de humedad (p. 539)

due process of law/proceso justo de ley idea de que el gobierno debe de seguir los procesos establecidos por ley y garantizados por la Constitución (p. 228)

Dust Bowl/Cuenca de Polvo el nombre dado al área del sur de las Grandes Llanuras extensivamente dañada por las sequías y las tempestades del polvo durante los años 1930 (p. 736)

E

effigy/efigie una figura rellenada de trapos que representa una persona impopular (p. 134)

Electoral College/Colegio Electoral un grupo especial de votantes escogidos por los votantes de sus estados para elegir al presidente y al vicepresidente (p. 210)

emancipate/emancipar liberar de la esclavitud (p. 475)

embargo/embargo una orden que prohibe el comercio con otro país (pp. 290, 899)

emigrant/emigrante una persona que sale de un país o una región para vivir en otras partes (p. 358)

emigrate/emigrar dejar su patria para vivir en otras partes (p. 583)

empresario/empresario una persona que arregló la colonización de tierra en Texas durante los años 1800 (p. 363)

encomienda/encomienda sistema de recompensar a los conquistadores con extensiones de tierra y el derecho de recaudar impuestos y exigir mano de obra a los Nativos Americanos que vivían en la tierra (p. 55)

Enlightenment/Siglo de las Luces movimiento durante los años 1700 que propagaba la idea de que el conocimiento, la razón, y la ciencia podrían mejorar la sociedad (p. 208)

entente/convenio un acuerdo entre naciones (p. 667)

entrenched/atrincherado que ocupa una fuerte posición defensiva (p. 486)

enumerated powers/poderes enumerados poderes que pertenecen solamente al gobierno federal (p. 219)

escalate/intensificar aumentar o extender (p. 874)

espionage/espionaje espiar (p. 686)

ethnic group/grupo étnico una minoría que habla un idioma diferente o que sigue costumbres diferentes que la mayoría de la gente de un país (pp. 583, 667)

evolution/evolución la teoría científica de que los seres humanos y otros seres vivos se han desarrollado tras largos períodos de tiempo (p. 718)

executive branch/rama ejecutiva la rama de gobierno, dirigida por el presidente, que administra las leyes y la política de una nación (p. 210)

executive order/orden ejecutiva una regla emitida por un jefe ejecutivo que lleva la fuerza de ley (p. 867)

exile/exilio una persona forzada a abandonar su patria (p. 868)

expansionism/expansionismo una política que demanda el extender las fronteras de una nación (p. 639)

expatriate/expatriado una persona que abandona su patria y decide vivir en otro país (p. 716)

export/exportar vender bienes en el extranjero (p. 109)

F

factory system/sistema de fábrica sistema que junta en un solo lugar las categorías de fabricación para aumentar la eficiencia (p. 309)

famine/hambre una escasez extrema de comida (p. 393)

fascism/fascismo un sistema político, dirigido por un dictador, que demanda nacionalismo y racismo extremo, y ninguna tolerancia de oposición (p. 753)

favorite son/hijo favorito candidato que recibe el apoyo de su estado natal en lugar del partido nacional (p. 335)

federal debt/deuda federal la cantidad de dinero debido por el gobierno (p. 924)

federalism/federalismo el compartir el poder entre el gobierno federal y los gobiernos estatales (pp. 208, 219)

Federalists/federalistas apoyadores de la Constitución (p. 211)

federation/federación una forma de gobierno que une grupos diferentes (p. 33)

feminist/feminista una persona que aboga por o está activa en promulgar los derechos de la mujer (p. 857)

fixed costs/costos fijos gastos regulares tal como de vivienda o mantenimiento de equipo que se quedan casi iguales año tras año (p. 403)

flapper/*flapper* una jovencita de los años 1920 que retaba las costumbres de comportamiento e indumentaria (p. 714)

flexible response/respuesta flexible un plan que usaba unidades militares especiales para montar guerras al estilo guerrilla (p. 867)

forty-niners/*forty-niners* personas que fueron a California durante la fiebre del oro en 1849 (p. 375)

Fourteen Points/Catorce Puntos el plan de paz para suprimir la Primera Guerra Mundial y reestructurar los países de Europa, propuesto por Woodrow Wilson (p. 689)

free enterprise/libre comercio la libertad de empresas privadas para operarse competetivamente para ganancias con la mínima regulación gubernamental (p. 308)

free silver/plata libre la producción sin límite de monedas de plata (p. 550)

freedman/liberto una persona liberada de la esclavitud (p. 502)

frigate/fragata buque de guerra (p. 297)

front/frente una región donde la guerra activa se lleva a cabo (p. 679)

fugitive/fugitivo evadido que trata de huir (p. 438)

fundamentalist/fundamentalista una persona que cree en el sentido literal de escrituras religiosas y la obediencia estricta a leyes religiosas (p. 913)

G

genocide/genocidio el eradicar un grupo racial, político, o cultural (p. 775)

Spanish Glossary

ghetto/*ghetto* una parte de una ciudad en la cual vive un grupo de minoría a causa de presión económica o social (p. 830)

ghost town/pueblo de espectros pueblo anterior de mineros que se dejó (p. 530)

Gilded Age/la Época Dorada el nombre asociado con América al final de los años 1800, referente a la gran riqueza de los tiempos y la terrible pobreza que estaba debajo (p. 592)

glasnost/*glasnost* una política soviética que permitía discusión más abierta de cuestiones políticas y sociales, y la promulgación más amplia de noticias e información (p. 925)

global warming/calentamiento mundial un aumento contínuo del promedio de temperaturas mundiales (p. 944)

grandfather clause/cláusula de abuelo una cláusula que permitía votar a las personas que no aprobaron el examen de alfabetismo si sus padres o sus abuelos habían votado antes de que empezó la Reconstrucción; una excepción a una ley basada en circunstancias preexistentes (p. 519)

grassroots/la gente común la sociedad al nivel local y popular afuera de los centros políticos y culturales (p. 936)

greenback/billete de dorso verde un billete de la moneda de EE.UU. expedido primeramente por el Norte durante la Guerra Civil (p. 483)

gross domestic product/producto interno bruto valor de todos los productos dentro de las fronteras nacionales de un país en un año (p. 938)

gross national product/producto nacional bruto valor total de todos los productos producidos en un año con la mano de obra y la propiedad suplidas por los residentes de un país, sin importar donde toma lugar la producción (p. 709)

guerrilla tactics/tácticas de guerrilla referente a ataques sorpresas o incursiones en lugar de la guerra organizada (p. 344)

guerrilla warfare/contienda a guerrilleros una técnica de tirar y darse a la huída usada en combates de guerra (pp. 180, 867)

habeas corpus/hábeas corpus una orden legal para una encuesta para determinar si una persona ha sido encarcelada legalmente (p. 481)

hawk/halcón una persona que aboga por la guerra y las políticas de guerra, tal como un apoyador de la Guerra en Viet Nam (p. 878)

hieroglyphics/jeroglíficos una forma antigua de escribir usando símbolos y dibujos para representar palabras, sonidos, y conceptos (p. 24)

Hispanic/hispano una persona o descendiente de la gente que vinieron de los países de Latinoamérica o de España (p. 858)

Holocaust/Holocausto el nombre dado a la matanza extensa de judíos y otros grupos por los nazis durante la Segunda Guerra Mundial (p. 776)

homestead/*homestead* adquirir una pieza de tierra pública de EE.UU. por medio de vivir en ella y cultivarla (p. 537)

horizontal integration/integración horizontal la asociación de firmas competitivas en una sociedad anónima (p. 569)

hot line/línea de emergencia una línea telefónica directa para uso en caso de emergencia (p. 870)

human rights/derechos humanos derechos, tal como la libertad de encarcelamiento ilegal, tortura, y ejecución, considerados como pertenecientes a todas las peronas (p. 912)

Hundred Days/Cien Días una sesión especial del Congreso llamada por Franklin D. Roosevelt para tratar los problemas de la Depresión (p. 732)

Ice Age/Época Glacial un período de temperaturas extremadamente frías cuando parte de la superficie del planeta estaba cubierta de extensiones masivas de hielo (p. 17)

impeach/acusar acusación formal a un oficial público de mala conducta en la oficina (pp. 223, 507, 938)

impeachment/acusación el acusar a un oficial público de mala conducta en la oficina; si se le prueba culpable ante una corte designada, se le despide de la oficina (p. 906)

imperialism/imperialismo las acciones usadas por una nación para ejercer control político o económico sobre naciones más pequeñas y débiles (p. 640)

implied powers/poderes implícitos poderes no mencionados específicamente en la Constitución (pp. 221, 268)

import/importar comprar bienes de mercados extranjeros (p. 109)

impressment/requisición captura de marineros para forzarlos a servir en una marina extranjera (pp. 265, 290)

incumbent/titular alguién que actualmente tiene un oficio o posición (p. 939)

indentured servant/sirviente contratado trabajador que consiente trabajar sin pago durante un cierto período de tiempo a cambio del pasaje a América (p. 87)

Industrial Revolution/Revolución Industrial el cambio de una sociedad agraria en una basada en la industria que empezó en la Gran Bretaña y se promulgó a los Estados Unidos alrededor del año 1800 (p. 307)

inflation/inflación aumento contínuo del precio de productos y servicios (pp. 175, 483, 796)

initiative/iniciativa el derecho de los ciudadanos de poner una medida o tema ante los votantes o la legislatura para aprobación (p. 614)

injunction/amonestación una orden judicial para terminar una acción, tal como una huelga (p. 575)

installment buying/compra a plazos un sistema de comprar productos en el cual los clientes prometen hacer pagos pequeños y regulares a través de un período de tiempo (p. 711)

integrate/integrar suprimir la segregación de las razas diferentes e introducir a membrecía igual y común en la sociedad (pp. 512, 840)

interchangeable parts/partes intercambiables piezas uniformes que pueden ser hechas en grandes cantidades para reemplazar otras piezas idénticas (p. 309)

internal improvements/mejoramientos internos proyectos federales, tal como canales y carreteras, para desarrollar el sistema de transportación de una nación (p. 322)

Internet/Internet enlaze a través de todo el mundo de redes de computadoras (p. 943)

internment camps/campos de internamiento los centros de detención adonde los americanos japoneses fueron trasladados y allí encerrados durante la Segunda Guerra Mundial (p. 768)

interstate/interestatal a través de fronteras estatales; que conecta o existe entre dos o más estados (p. 849)

iron curtain/cortina de hierro la barrera política y militar para los países de Europa Oriental controlados por los soviéticos que los aislaba después de la Segunda Guerra Mundial (p. 790)

ironclad/acorazado buque armado (p. 468)

Iroquois Confederacy/Confederación Iroquesa un grupo poderoso de Nativos Americanos de la región oriental de los Estados Unidos compuesto de cinco naciones: los pueblos mohawk, séneca, cayuga, onondaga y oneida (p. 117)

island hopping/saltar islas una estrategia usada durante la Segunda Guerra Mundial que demandó el atacar y capturar ciertas islas importantes para usarlas como bases para saltar por encima de otras (p. 779)

isolationism/aislacionismo una política nacional de evitar el involucramiento en asuntos mundiales (pp. 639, 707)

isthmus/istmo una faja estrecha de tierra que conecta dos áreas de tierra más grandes (p. 657)

joint occupation/ocupación en común la posesión y colonización de un área como esfuerzo compartido por dos o más países (p. 357)

joint-stock company/compañía por acciones una compañía en la cual los inversionistas compran acciones de la compañía a cambio de una porción de las ganancias en el futuro (p. 71)

judicial branch/rama judicial la rama de gobierno, incluyendo el sistema de tribunales federales, que interpreta las leyes de una nación (p. 210)

judicial review/repaso judicial el derecho del Tribunal Supremo para determinar si una ley viola la Constitución (pp. 222, 281)

kamikaze/kamikase durante la Segunda Guerra Mundial, un piloto suicida japonés cuya misión era chocar con el blanco (p. 779)

laissez-faire/*laissez-faire* la creencia de que el gobierno no debe de involucrarse en los asuntos comerciales y económicos del país (pp. 279, 350, 621)

land-grant college/colegio de tierras donadas originalmente, un colegio agrícola establecido como resultado del Decreto Morrill de 1862 que dio a los estados, grandes cantidades de tierras federales que podrían ser vendidas para recaudar dinero para la educación (p. 598)

landslide/victoria arrolladora una victoria abrumadora (p. 336)

League of Nations/Liga de Naciones una asociación de naciones para mantener la paz y resolver disputas internacionales propuesta en los Catorce Puntos de Wilson (p. 689)

lease/arrendar entregar propiedad en cambio de renta (p. 705)

legislative branch/rama legislativa la rama de gobierno que redacta las leyes de una nación (p. 209)

lend-lease/prestar-arrendar el decreto aprobado durante la Segunda Guerra Mundial que permitía a los Estados Unidos que vendiera, prestara, o arrendara armas u otros abastos de guerra a cualquier nación considerada "vital para la defensa de los Estados Unidos" (p. 761)

line of demarcation/línea de demarcación una línea imaginaria a lo largo del medio del Océano Atlántico desde el Polo Norte hasta el Polo Sur para dividir las Américas entre España y Portugal (p. 47)

line-item veto/veto de partida el poder que permite al presidente que cancele partidas particulares de gastos de un presupuesto o proyecto de ley (p. 937)

literacy/alfabetismo la capacidad de leer y escribir (p. 113)

literacy test/examen de alfabetismo un método usado para prohibir a los afroamericanos a votar por requerir a presuntos votantes que pudieran leer y escribir a niveles especificados (p. 519)

lock/esclusa en un canal un recinto con puertas en cada extremo y usado para levantar y bajar los buques mientras pasan de un nivel al otro (p. 318)

lode/filón una faja o venero de mena intercalada entre estratos de piedra (p. 529)

log cabin campaign/campaña de cabaña rústica el nombre dado a la campaña para la presidencia de William Henry Harrison en 1840, debido al uso de una cabaña rústica de troncos como su símbolo por los whigs (p. 351)

Loyalists/lealistas colonizadores americanos que quedaron leales a la Bretaña y se opusieron a la guerra para la independencia (p. 145)

lynching/linchamiento matar a una persona a través de la acción ilegal de una muchedumbre airada (p. 520)

maize/maíz una forma antigua de elote cultivado por los Nativos Americanos (p. 19)

majority/mayoría más de la mitad (p. 335)

Spanish Glossary

Manifest Destiny/Destino Manifiesto la idea popular en los Estados Unidos durante los años 1800 de que el país debería de extender sus fronteras hasta el Pacífico (p. 360)

manumission/manumisión el liberar a unas personas esclavizadas (p. 201)

martial law/ley marcial ley administrada por las autoridades civiles en una situación de emergencia (p. 887)

martyr/mártir una persona que sacrifica su vida por un principio o una causa (p. 448)

mass media/difusoras de información formas de comunicación que alcanzan a grandes números de personas, tal como periódicos, radio, y televisión (p. 714)

mass production/fabricación en serie la producción de grandes cantidades de productos usando máquinas y muchas veces una línea de montaje (p. 566)

materialism/materialismo atribuir demasiada importancia a las posesiones y comodidades físicas (p. 830)

Mayflower Compact/Convenio del Mayflower un documento formal escrito en 1620 que proporcionó leyes para el mantenimiento del orden público en la colonia de Plymouth (p. 77)

Medicaid/*Medicaid* un programa social que da dinero a los estados para ayudar a las personas que no pueden pagar la factura del hospital (p. 847)

Medicare/*Medicare* un programa social que ayuda en pagar el esmero médico para los ancianos (p. 847)

mercantilism/mercantilismo idea de que el poder de una nación dependía de ampliar su comercio y aumentar sus reservas de oro (p. 59, 109)

mercenary/mercenario soldado remunerado para servir en el ejército de un país extranjero (p. 164)

merger/fusión de empresas la asociación de dos o más negocios en uno (p. 571)

MIAs/*MIAs* soldados clasificados como extraviados en la guerra, inglés *missing in action* (p. 889)

migrant worker/obrero migrante una persona que se mueve de un lugar a otro para buscar trabajo en la cosecha de frutas y vegetales (p. 737)

migration/migración el movimiento de un gran número de personas hacia una nueva patria (p. 17)

militarism/militarismo un desarrollo de poder militar dentro de un país (p. 667)

militia/milicia un grupo de civiles entrenados para luchar durante emergencias (pp. 118, 142)

minutemen/*minutemen* compañías de soldados civiles que se jactaban de que podrían estar listos para tomar armas en sólo un minuto (p. 142)

mission/misión una comunidad religiosa (pp. 54, 92)

mobilization/mobilización juntar recursos y preparar para la guerra (pp. 683, 765)

moderate/moderado opuesto a gran cambio social o ideas políticas extremas (p. 815)

monopoly/monopolio control total de una industria por una persona o una compañía (p. 570)

Morse code/código Morse un sistema para transmitir mensajes que usa una serie de puntos y rayas para representar las letras del abecedario, los números, y la puntuación (p. 389)

mosque/mezquita una casa de alabanza musulmana (p. 42)

mountain man/hombre montañés colonizador que vivía en el monte, como en las Montañas Rocosas (p. 357)

muckraker/expositor de corrupción periodista que descubre abusos y corrupción en una sociedad (p. 613)

mudslinging/detractar intentar arruinar la reputación de un adversario con insultos (p. 336)

national debt/deuda nacional la cantidad de dinero que un gobierno debe a otros gobiernos o a su pueblo (p. 260)

National Grange/Granja Nacional la primera organización de granjeros de los Estados Unidos (p. 549)

nationalism/nacionalismo lealtad a una nación y promoción de sus intereses sobre todos los demás (pp. 293, 667)

nativism/nativismo la creencia de que aquellos que nacieron en un país son mejores que los inmigrantes (p. 717)

nativist/nativista una persona que favorece a los nacidos en su patria y se opone a los inmigrantes (p. 395)

naturalization/naturalización el otorgar la plena ciudadanía a un extranjero (p. 229)

neutral/neutral que no toma partido a ninguna persona ni a ningún país en un conflicto (p. 163)

neutral rights/derechos neutrales el derecho para navegar en el mar sin tomar partido en una guerra (p. 290)

neutrality/neutralidad una posición de no tomar partido en un conflicto (p. 265)

New Deal/Nuevo Trato el nombre dado a las leyes nuevas con la meta de aliviar la Depresión que fueron estatuidas por el Congreso durante los Cien Días y los meses siguientes (p. 733)

nomadic/nómada que se mueve de un lugar a otro sin hogar permanente (p. 543)

nomads/nómadas personas que se mueven de lugar a lugar, generalmente en busca de comida o de tierras para pastar (p. 17)

nominating convention/convención nominadora sistema en el cual los diputados estatales escogieron al candidato para la presidencia de su partido (p. 337)

nonimportation/no importación la acción de evitar la importación o uso de ciertos productos (p. 134)

normal school/escuela normal una escuela con programa de dos años para entrenar a los graduados de preparatoria para ser maestros (p. 413)

Northwest Passage/Paso Noroeste ruta acuática para Asia por América del Norte buscada por exploradores europeos (p. 60)

nullify/anular cancelar o hacer sin efecto (pp. 271, 338)

offensive/ofensiva la posición de atacar o el mismo ataque (p. 463)

on margin/al margen comprar acciones por pagar sólo una fracción del precio del valor y el resto del préstamo recibido a un corredor (p. 725)

Open Door policy/política de Puerta Abierta una política que permitía a cada nación extranjera en China que comerciara libremente en las esferas de influencia de las otras naciones (p. 647)

open range/terreno abierto tierra sin cercas ni dividida en solares (p. 534)

ordinance/ordenanza una ley o regulación (p. 196)

ore/mena un mineral minado por la sustancia valorable que contiene, tal como plata (p. 529)

override/vencer rechazar o derrotar, como un proyecto de ley propuesto en el Congreso (p. 505)

overseer/capataz persona que supervisa una operación grande o a sus trabajadores (pp. 106, 403)

ozone/ozono el estrato de gas compuesto de una forma de oxígeno que protege la tierra y a su gente de los rayos del sol que causan el cáncer (p. 944)

pacifist/pacifista persona opuesta al uso de guerra o violencia para arreglar disputas (pp. 85, 686)

partisan/partidario a favor de una parte de un asunto (p. 268)

patent/patente un documento que da al inventor el derecho exclusivo legal de una invención durante un período de tiempo (p. 308)

Patriots/patriotas colonizadores americanos que estaban determinados para luchar en contra de los británicos hasta que se ganara la independencia americana (p. 145)

patronage/patronazgo otro nombre del sistema de recompensa política en el cual puestos y favores gubernamentales se dan a aliados políticos y a amigos (p. 612)

patroon/_patroon_ terrateniente de las colonias holandesas que gobernaba áreas grandes de tierra como un rey (p. 83)

peaceful coexistence/coexistencia pacífica acuerdo entre países opuestos de que competirán uno con el otro pero evitarán la guerra (p. 820)

pension/pensión una cantidad pagada a una persona, generalmente después de la jubilación (p. 743)

perestroika/_perestroika_ una política de gobierno y economía empezada por Gorbachev en la Unión Soviética a mediados de los años 1980 (p. 926)

perjury/perjurio el mentir después de haber jurado decir la verdad (p. 807)

persecute/perseguir tratar cruelmente a alguién a causa de sus creencias o prácticas (p. 76)

petition/petición una solicitud formal (pp. 148, 196)

philanthropy/filantropía acciones caritativas o donaciones de dinero para beneficiar a la comunidad (p. 570)

pilgrimage/peregrinación un viaje a un sitio sagrado (p. 42)

Pilgrims/peregrinos separatistas que viajaron a las colonias durante los años 1600 por un propósito religioso (p. 77)

plantation/plantación una finca grande manejada por el dueño o un gerente y cultivada por trabajadores que vivían allí (p. 55)

plurality/pluralidad el mayor número de individuos (p. 335)

political machine/máquina política una organización aliada con un partido político que muchas veces controlaba el gobierno local (p. 610)

poll tax/impuesto de capitación un impuesto de una cantidad fija por cada persona que tenía que ser pagada antes de que pudiera votar la persona (p. 519)

pool/consorcio un grupo compartiendo de una actividad, por ejemplo, entre barones ferrocarrileros que hacían acuerdos secretos y fijaban tipos entre ellos mismos (p. 559)

popular sovereignty/soberanía popular la teoría política de que el gobierno está sujeto a la voluntad del pueblo (p. 218); antes de la Guerra Civil, la idea de que la gente que vivía en un territorio tenía el derecho de decidir por votar si allí sería permitida la esclavitud (p. 442)

Populist Party/Partido Populista partido político de los EE.UU. formado en 1892 que representaba principalmente a los granjeros, que favorecía la acuñación libre de plata y el control gubernamental de ferrocarriles y otros monopolios (p. 550)

poverty line/línea de pobreza el nivel de ingresos personales o familiares clasificado de pobre según la norma del gobierno (p. 847)

preamble/preámbulo la introducción de un documento formal, especialmente la Constitución (pp. 151, 217)

precedent/precedente una tradición (p. 259)

prejudice/prejuicio una opinión injusta no basada en los hechos (p. 392)

presidio/presidio un fuerte español en las Américas construido para proteger las colonias misioneras (p. 54)

primary/elección preliminar una elección en la cual los votantes escogen al candidato de su partido (p. 614)

privateer/buque corsario buque armado privado (pp. 179, 297)

productivity/productividad la cantidad de trabajo que hace cada trabajador (pp. 710, 822)

prohibition/prohibición leyes que prohiben el hacer o vender de bebidas alcohólicas (p. 619)

Prohibition/Prohibición entredicho contra la fabricación, transportación, y venta de bebidas alcohólicas por todo los Estados Unidos (p. 717)

propaganda/propaganda ideas o información diseñadas para influenciar la opinión (pp. 137, 672)

proportional/proporcional que son iguales o que corresponden (p. 203)

proprietary colony/colonia propietaria colonia dirigida por personas o grupos a quienes se les había otorgado la tierra (pp. 83, 111)

protectorate/protectorado un país que es técnicamente independiente, pero que en realidad está bajo el control de otro país (p. 653)

public works/proyectos públicos proyectos tal como carreteras, parques, y bibliotecas construidos con fondos públicos para el uso del público (p. 727)

pueblo/pueblo una casa o una comunidad de casas construidas por Nativos Americanos (pp. 29, 54)

Puritans/puritanos protestantes que, durante los años 1600, querían reformar la iglesia anglicana (p. 77)

Q

quota system/sistema de cuotas un arreglo que pone un límite en el número de inmigrantes de cada país (p. 718)

R

radical/radical extremo (p. 501)

ragtime/*ragtime* una clase de música con un ritmo fuerte y una melodía animada con notas acentuadas que era popular al principio del siglo (p. 601)

ranchero/ranchero dueño de rancho mexicano (p. 371)

rancho/rancho propiedades grandísimas para producir ganado establecidas por colonizadores mexicanos en California (p. 371)

ratify/ratificar dar aprobación oficial para (pp. 185, 211, 476)

ration/racionar distribuir los artículos escasos sobre una base limitada (p. 766)

realism/realismo una perspectiva de literatura, arte, y teatro que representa las cosas tal como son (p. 600)

rebate/rebaja descuento o devolución de una porción de un pago (p. 559)

Rebel/rebelde soldado confederado, así nombrado a causa de su oposición al gobierno establecido (p. 464)

recall/elección de revocación el derecho que permite a los votantes que despidan de la oficina a los oficiales elegidos que son inadecuados (p. 614)

recession/recesión un deslizamiento en actividades comerciales (p. 709)

reconciliation/reconciliación arreglar por acuerdo o por reunirse de nuevo (p. 514)

Reconstruction/Reconstrucción la reorganización y la reconstrucción de los anteriores estados confederados después de la Guerra Civil (p. 501)

recruit/reclutar enlistar a soldados para el ejército (p. 165)

referendum/referéndum la práctica de permitir a los votantes que acepten o rechacen medidas propuestas por la legislatura (p. 614)

regionalism/regionalismo en arte o literatura, la práctica de enfocar en una región en particular del país (p. 600)

relief/ayuda social ayuda para los pobres; asistencia pública (p. 727)

relocate/reubicar forzar a una persona o a un grupo de personas a trasladarse (p. 342)

Renaissance/Renacimiento un período de creatividad intelectual y artística, alrededor de los años 1300–1600 (p. 39)

rendezvous/*rendezvous* una reunión (p. 357)

reparations/reparaciones pago por el país que pierde una guerra al país que gana por los daños causados por la guerra (p. 690)

repeal/revocar cancelar un decreto o ley (p. 134)

republic/república un gobierno en el cual ciudadanos gobiernan por medio de representantes elegidos (p. 193)

republicanism/republicanismo que favorece una república, o sea una democracia representativa, como la mejor forma de gobierno (p. 218)

reservation/reservación un área de tierra pública apartada para los Nativos Americanos (p. 543)

reserved powers/poderes reservados poderes retenidos por los estados (p. 219)

resolution/resolución una expresión formal de opinión (p. 134)

revenue/ingresos entrada de dinero (p. 133)

revenue sharing/ingreso compartido dinero recaudado de impuestos federales y dado a los estados para uso a los niveles estatales y locales (p. 902)

revival/renacimiento religioso una serie de reuniones dirigidas por un predicador para animar emociones religiosas (p. 413)

royal colony/colonia real colonia administrada por un gobernador y un consejo nombrados por el rey o reina (p. 111)

S

sabotage/sabotaje acción secreta por agentes del enemigo o los que compadecen para dañar el esfuerzo de guerra de una nación (p. 686)

scalawags/*scalawags* nombre dado por los confederados anteriores a los blancos sureños que apoyaban la Reconstrucción republicana del Sur (p. 510)

search-and-destroy mission/misión de buscar y destruir una estrategia usada en Viet Nam en la cual las fuerzas americanas buscarían las unidades norvietnameses y vietconenses para destruirlas (p. 875)

secede/separarse abandonar o retirar (pp. 285, 338, 438)

secession/secesión retiro de la Unión (p. 451)

Second New Deal/Segundo Nuevo Trato un nuevo juego de programas y reformas lanzados por Franklin D. Roosevelt en 1935 (p. 744)

sectionalism/regionalismo lealtad a una región (pp. 322, 437)

sedition/sedición actividades con el propósito de debilitar un gobierno establecido (p. 271)

segregation/segregación la separación o aislamiento de una raza, una clase, o un grupo (pp. 519, 838)

Separatists/separatistas protestantes que, durante los años 1600, querían dejar la iglesia anglicana para fundar sus propias iglesias (p. 77)

settlement house/casa de beneficencia institución colocada en una vecindad pobre que proveía numerosos servicios a la comunidad tal como cuidado médico, cuidado de niños, bibliotecas, y clases de inglés (p. 593)

sharecropping/aparcería sistema de agricultura en el cual un granjero labra la tierra para un dueño que provee equipo y semillas y recibe una porción de la cosecha (p. 512)

shareholder/accionista una persona que invierte en una sociedad anónima por comprar acciones y que es un dueño parcial (p. 568)

shuttle diplomacy/diplomacia de lanzadera negociaciones entre naciones llevada a cabo por una persona que viaja entre ellas yendo y viniendo (p. 900)

silent majority/mayoría callada la frase usada por Nixon para describir la mayoría de los americanos, los que no protestaban ni demostraban (p. 882)

sit-in/plantón el acto de ocupar asientos o de sentarse en el suelo de un establecimiento como una forma de protesta organizada (p. 849)

slave code/código de esclavos las leyes aprobadas en los estados sureños que controlaban y restringían a la gente esclavizada (p. 405)

slum/barrio bajo vecindad pobre, superpoblada, y de de vecindades ruinosas (p. 591)

smuggling/contrabandear cambiar ilegalmente con otras naciones (p. 109)

Social Security Act/Decreto de Seguro Social una ley que exige a los empleados y a los empresarios que paguen un impuesto; el dinero provee una pensión mensual para personas jubiladas (p. 744)

socialist/socialista una persona que cree que las industrias deben de ser poseídas por el público y manejadas por el gobierno en lugar de personas particulares (p. 686)

sodbuster/rompedor de césped nombre dado al granjero de las Llanuras (p. 539)

speculator/especulador persona que arriesga dinero para hacer una ganancia grande (pp. 125, 261)

sphere of influence/esfera de influencia sección de un país donde una nación extranjera tiene derechos y poderes especiales (p. 647)

spiritual/espiritual una canción popular religiosa afroamericana (p. 405)

spoils system/sistema de despojos la práctica de dar puestos gubernamentales a los partidarios; reemplazar a los empleados del gobierno con los partidarios del candidato victorioso (p. 337)

square deal/trato justo la promesa de Theodore Roosevelt para el trato justo e igual para todos (p. 621)

stagflation/stagflación una combinación del alza de precios y una economía estancada con una tasa alta de desempleo (p. 903)

stalemate/estancamiento una situación durante un conflicto cuando la acción se para debido a que ambos partidos son igualmente poderosos y ningún de los dos lo abandonará (p. 804)

standard gauge/medida normal la anchura uniforme de 4 pies, 8.5 pulgadas de las vías ferroviarias, adoptada durante los años 1880 (p. 558)

standard of living/norma de vivir una medida de calidad comprensiva de vida y riqueza de la gente; el mínimo de las necesidades y lujos a los cuales un grupo está acostumbrado (p. 822)

states' rights/derechos estatales derechos y poderes independientes del gobierno federal que son reservados a los estados por la Constitución (pp. 271, 451)

steerage/entrepuente los cuarteles apretados de las cubiertas bajas de un barco para los pasajeros que pagan los pasajes más bajos (p. 584)

stock/acciones valores de propiedad de comercio que vende una compañía que llevan muchas veces el poder de votar (p. 568)

stock exchange/mercado de acciones un lugar donde acciones de sociedades anónimas se venden y se compran a través de un sistema organizado (p. 725)

strait/estrecho un paso angosto que conecta dos extensiones más grandes de agua (p. 49)

strike/huelga un paro de trabajo por los trabajadores para forzar al empresario a satisfacer demandas (p. 392)

strikebreaker/esquirol una persona contratada para reemplazar a un huelguista para suprimir una huelga (p. 575)

subsidy/subsidio donación de dinero del gobierno a una persona o una compañía para una acción con el propósito de beneficiar al público (pp. 530, 733)

subsistence farming/agricultura para subsistencia labranza que produce solamente la comida que se necesita para dar de comer a la familia del trabajador (p. 101)

suburbs/suburbios áreas residenciales que brotaron cerca de o alrededor de ciudades como resultado de mejoramientos de transportación (p. 592)

subversion/subversión un esfuerzo para derrocar un gobierno montado por personas trabajando secretamente desde adentro (p. 806)

suffrage/sufragio el derecho al voto (pp. 336, 426)

suffragist/sufragista un hombre o mujer que luchaba para el derecho al voto de la mujer (p. 616)

summit/conferencia cumbre una reunión de altos jefes de gobierno (p. 820)

surplus/superávit exceso; la cantidad que sobra después de pagar los gastos necesarios (p. 815)

sweatshop/fábrica-opresora un taller o fábrica donde se explota a los trabajadores, trabajándolos muchas horas por poco pago y en condiciones malsanas (pp. 573, 585)

tariff/tarifa impuesto sobre productos importados o exportados (pp. 262, 338)

technology/tecnología el uso de conocimientos científicos para propósitos prácticos (pp. 40, 308)

Tejano/tejano un mexicano que reclama Texas como su patria (p. 363)

telegraph/telégrafo un aparato o sistema que usa señales eléctricas para transmitir mensajes a códigos a través de alambres (p. 389)

Spanish Glossary

temperance/templanza el uso de poca o de ninguna bebida alcohólica (p. 413)

tenant farmer/granjero arrendatario un granjero que labra la tierra de otro dueño y paga renta ya sea con la cosecha o al contado (pp. 92, 402)

tenement/casa de vecindad un edificio en el cual varias familias alquilan cuartos o apartamentos, a menudo con pocas medidas sanitarias o seguridad (p. 591)

terrace/terraza una parcela de tierra elevada y allanada para fomentar la agricultura (p. 26)

terrorism/*terrorismo* el uso de la violencia contra ciudadanos para lograr un gol político (p. 944)

theocracy/teocracia una forma de gobierno en la cual la sociedad está gobernada por líderes religiosos (p. 23)

Tidewater/Orilla del Mar una región de llanuras planas y bajas alrededor de la costa del mar (p. 105)

toleration/tolerancia el aceptar creencias diferentes (p. 79)

total war/guerra total la guerra en todo aspecto de la vida del enemigo (p. 490)

totalitarian/totalitario un sistema político en el cual el gobierno suprime toda oposición y controla muchos aspectos de la vida de la gente (p. 754)

trade deficit/déficit de cambio la situación cuando el valor de las importaciones de un país excede el valor de las exportaciones (p. 911)

trade union/gremio una organización de artesanos con el mismo oficio o destreza (pp. 392, 573)

transcendentalist/transcendentalista uno de un grupo de escritores de Nueva Inglaterra que acentuaban la relación entre los seres humanos y la naturaleza, asuntos espirituales sobre asuntos materiales, y la importancia de la conciencia particular (p. 415)

transcontinental/*transcontinental* que se extiende a través del continente (p. 531)

triangular trade/trato triangular una ruta de comercio para cambiar productos entre las Antillas, las colonias americanas, y África del Oeste (p. 102)

tribute/tributo dinero pagado para protección (pp. 52, 289)

trust/cártel una combinación de firmas o sociedades anónimas formada por un acuerdo legal, especialmente para reducir la competición (pp. 569, 612)

trustbuster/rompedor de cárteles alguién que divide un cártel en compañías más pequeñas (p. 621)

turnpike/autopista una carretera que uno debe de pagar para usar; el dinero se usa para pagar el costo de la carretera (p. 315)

unalienable right/derecho inalienable un derecho al que no se puede renunciar (p. 154)

unconstitutional/anticonstitucional no de acuerdo ni consistente con la Constitución (p. 262)

underemployment/empleo insuficiente la condición cuando la gente trabaja en puestos para los cuales están sobrecalificados o que no utilizan sus destrezas (p. 908)

Underground Railroad/Ferrocarril Subterráneo un sistema que ayudó a los afroamericanos esclavizados a seguir una red de rutas de escape afuera del Sur hacia la libertad del Norte (p. 422)

unemployment insurance/seguro de desempleo pagos por el gobierno durante un cierto período limitado de tiempo a las personas que han perdido sus trabajos (p. 744)

utopia/utopía una comunidad basada en una visión de la sociedad perfecta buscada por los reformistas (p. 412)

vaquero/vaquero trabajador ranchero hispánico (p. 536)

vaudeville/teatro de variedades entretenimiento compuesto de varios actos, tal como baile, canción, comedia, y espectáculos de mágica (p. 602)

vertical integration/integración vertical la asociación de compañías que abastecen con equipo y servicios necesarios para una industria particular (p. 570)

veto/vetar rechazar un proyecto de ley y prevenir que vuelva a ser una ley (p. 349)

Vietcong/*Vietcong* los soldados guerrillistas de la facción comunista en Viet Nam, también conocidos por el Frente Nacional para Liberación (p. 872)

Vietnamization/vietnamización la política de Nixon que demandó que Viet Nam del Sur tomara un papel más activo en luchar la guerra y que los americanos se involucraran menos (p. 885)

vigilantes/vigilantes gente que toman la ley en sus propias manos (pp. 377, 529)

War Hawks/halcones de guerra republicanos durante la presidencia de Madison que insistían en la guerra con la Bretaña (p. 293)

work relief/ayuda de trabajo programas que dieron trabajos gubernamentales a los pobres (p. 733)

writ of assistance/escrito de asistencia documento legal que permitía a los oficiales que exploraran las casas y bodegas en busca de productos que tal vez pudieran ser de contrabandeado (p. 133)

XYZ

Yankee/yanqui soldado de la Unión (p. 464)

yellow journalism/periodismo amarillista escritura que exageraba acontecimientos sensacionales, dramáticos, y repulsivos para atraer a los lectores, citando historias que fueron populares durante los fines de los años 1800 (p. 600); una clase de reportaje sensacional, prejuzgado, y a menudo falso (p. 650)

yeoman/terrateniente menor dueño sureño de una granja pequeña que no tenía esclavos (p. 402)

Italicized page numbers refer to illustrations. The following abbreviations are used in the index:
m = map, c = chart, p = photograph or picture, g = graph, crt = cartoon, ptg = painting, q = quote

Index

Index

Index

Index

Index

Index

Acknowledgements and Photo Credits

Acknowledgements

50   From *Morning Girl* by Michael Dorris. Text © 1992 by Michael Dorris. Reprinted with permission from Hyperion Books for Children.

107   From *The Kidnapped Prince* by Olaudah Equiano. Adapted by Ann Cameron. Copyright © 1995 by Ann Cameron. Reprinted by permission of Alfred A. Knopf, Inc.

140   Excerpt from *Johnny Tremain* by Esther Forbes. Copyright © 1943 by Esther Forbes Hoskins, © renewed 1971 by Linwood M. Erskine, Jr., Executor of the Estate of Esther Forbes Hoskins. Reprinted by permission of Houghton Mifflin Co. All rights reserved.

295   From *Night Flying Woman: An Ojibway Narrative* by Ignatia Broker. Copyright © 1983 by the Minnesota Historical Society. Reprinted by permission.

769   Reprinted with the permission of Simon & Schuster Books for Young readers, an imprint of Simon & Schuster Children's Publishing Division from *The Invisible Thread* by Yoshiko Uchida. Copyright © 1991 by Yoshiko Uchida.

841, 996   Reprinted by arrangement with the Heirs to the Estate of Martin Luther King, Jr., c/o Writers House, Inc. as agent for the proprietor. Copyright © 1963 by Martin Luther King, Jr., copyright renewed 1991 by Coretta Scott King.

843   From *I Know Why the Caged Bird Sings*, by Maya Angelou. Copyright © 1969 by Maya Angelou. Reprinted with permission of Random House, Inc.

915   From *Barrio Boy* by Ernesto Galarza. Copyright © 1971 by the University of Notre Dame Press. Used by permission of the publisher.

978   "God Bless the USA," words and music by Lee Greenwood. Copyright © 1984 Songs of Universal Inc. and Universal-Songs of Polygram International Inc. (BMI) International Copyright Secured. All Rights Reserved.

Glencoe would like to acknowledge the artists and agencies who participated in illustrating this program: Morgan Cain & Associates; Ortelius Design, Inc.; QA Digital

Photo Credits

CORBIS, (br)Henry Diltz/CORBIS; 321 James Monroe Museum & Memorial Library; 324 (t)Boot Hill Museum/Henry Groskinsky, (b)Peter Menzel; 325 (l)Library of Congress, (r)Collection of the Boston Public Library, Print Division; 326 Schalkwijk/Art Resource, NY; 328 (t)Smithsonian Institution, (tc)The Metropolitan Museum of Art, Rogers Fund, 1942. (42.95.11), (l)Craig McDougal, (r)Anthony Richardson, (b)New York Historical Society, (bc)James Monroe Museum & Memorial Library; 330 Collection of David J. & Janice L. Frent; 330–331 Collection of Mrs. J. Maxwell Moran; 331 Brown Brothers; 332 (l)National Museum of American Art, Washington, DC/Art Resource, NY, (r)Collection of David J. & Janice L. Frent; 333 (c)Archives & Manuscripts Division of the Oklahoma Historical Society, (b)Indiana Historical Society, Boatmen's National Bank of St. Louis; 334 Collection of David J. & Janice L. Frent; 335 New York Historical Society; 337 Library Company of Philadelphia; 338 North Wind Picture Archive; 340 The Philbrook Center; 340–341 Kevin C. Chadwick/National Geographic Society; 341 Stock Montage; 343 SuperStock; 344 National Museum of American Art, Smithsonian Institution. Gift of Mrs. Joseph Harrison, JR/Art Resource, NY; 348 Bettman-CORBIS; 349 New York Historical Society; 350 (l)National Portrait Gallery, Smithsonian Institution/Art Resource, NY, (r)Smithsonian Institution; 352 (tr)Collection of David J. & Linda L. Frent, (tl)SuperStock, (background)New York Historical Society; 354 (l)Stock Montage, (r)Collection of David J. & Janet L. Frent; 355 (t)The Manoogian Foundation, on loan to the National Gallery of Art, Washington. Photo by Lyle Peterzell, (bl)Archives Division, Texas State Library, (r)Collection of David J. & Janice L. Frent; 356 Nikki Pahl; 357 Hutton Archive/Getty Images; 359 (b)Henry Groskinsky, (t)Mongerson-Wunderlich Gallery, Chicago; 362 Archives Division, Texas State Library; 363 Institute of Texas Culture; 364–365 Friends of the Governor's Mansion, Austin; 366 Archives Division, Texas State Library; 369 Panhandle Plains Historical Museum; 370 Thomas Gilcrease Institute of American Art, Tulsa OK; 371 file photo; 373 California State Library; 375 courtesy The Oakland Museum; 376 (l)Levi Strauss & Company, (r)Doug Martin; 377 SuperStock; 378 Bettman-CORBIS; 379 (l)Bettman-CORBIS, (r)Wenham Museum; 380 courtesy Denver Public Library Western History Department; 382 American Museum, Bath, England/Bridgeman Collection/SuperStock, Inc.; 383 Timothy Fuller; 384 (tr)Smithsonian Institution, (others)file photo; 385 (t)SuperStock, (bl)North Wind Picture Archive, (br)National Portrait Gallery, Smithsonian Institution; 386 Smithsonian Institution/Charles Phillips; 387 Peabody Essex Museum, Salem, MA/Mark Sexton; 389 (l)The Chessie System, B70 Railroad Museum Archives (Photo by Robert Sherbow/UNIPHOTO), (r)CORBIS; 391 Jack Naylor; 392 Museum of Fine Arts, Boston, M. & M. Karolik Collection; 394 (l)The Bayard Harbor of New York c.1953–1855 Samuel B. Waugh (1814–1885) Watercolor on canvas, 99/5 x 198/4 Gift of Mrs. Robert L. Littlejohn, Museum of the City of New York, 33.169 (detail), (r)Bostonian Society/Mark Sexton; 397 Grant Heilman Photography; 399 (l)Bettman-CORBIS, (r)Smithsonian Institution; 401 Courtesy of Deere & Company, Moline, Ill. USA; 402 (l)The J. Paul Getty Museum, (r)Bettman-CORBIS; 404 (background)Photo Researchers, (t)New York Historical Society, (cr)Adam Woolfitt/CORBIS, (bl)courtesy of Charleston Museum, (br)Valentine Museum; 406 Stock Montage; 408 (tr)Smithsonian Institution/Charles Phillips, (c)file photo, (b)T.W. Wood Art Gallery, Montpelier, VT; 410 (t)The American Antiquarian Society, (b)Bettman-CORBIS, (br)FPG; 411 (t)St. Louis Art Museum, St. Louis, Missouri, USA/SuperStock, (bl)Chicago Historical Society, (br)Oberlin College Archives, Oberlin, Ohio; 412 National Portrait Gallery, Smithsonian Institution, Washington DC; 414 (t)City Art Museum of St. Louis/SuperStock, (bc)Brown Brothers, (bl)Museum of American Textile History, (br)FPG; 418 Peabody Essex Museum/Mark Sexton; 419 Library of Congress; 420 Collection of William Gladstone; 422 Library of Congress; 425 Mount Holyoke College Art Museum, South Hadley, Massachusetts; 426 (l)Chicago Historical Society, (r)Meserve Collection; 427 (tl)Maria Mitchell Association, (tr)National Archives of Canada, (br)Nebraska State Historical Society, (bc)Hulton Archive, (bl)CORBIS; 430 (t)New York Historical Society, (c)Peabody Essex Museum/Mark Sexton, (b)Library of Congress; 432 Mark Burnett; 432–433 Painting by Don Troiani/photo courtesy of Historical Art Prints, Ltd.; 433 PhotoDisc; 435 (t)CORBIS, (l)Missouri State Historical Society, (r)Photo Network; 436 Frank & Marie-Therese Wood Print Collection, Alexandria, VA; 437 Collection of David J. & Janice L. Frent; 438 New York Historical Society; 440 CORBIS; 441 Library of Congress; 442 Schlesinger Library, Radcliffe College; 444 H. Armstrong Roberts; 445 North Wind Picture Archive; 446 (l)Al Fenn/Timepix, (r)Missouri State Historical Society; 447 courtesy Illinois State Historical Library; 449 Chicago Historical Society; 450 (t)courtesy Chicago Historical Society, (b)The Library of Congress; 456 (t)North Wind Picture Archive, (tc)Missouri State Historical Society, (bc)courtesy Chicago Historical Society, (b)Bettman-CORBIS; 458 (l)Museum of the Confederacy, (c)Museum of the Confederacy, (r)Museum of the Confederacy; 459 (t)Painting by John Troiani/courtesy Historical Art Prints, Ltd., (bl) National Archives, (bc)©1986 Time-Life Books Inc. from the series "Civil War"/Edward Owen, (r)Illinois State Historical Library; 460 PhotoDisc; 461 Seventh Regiment Fund, New York City; 462–463 PhotoDisc; 464 National Archives; 465 (r)file photo, (l)Bettman-CORBIS; 466 Manassas National Battlefield Park/Larry Sherer; 467 National Archives; 468 PhotoDisc; 471 Medford Historical Society Collection/CORBIS; 473 McLellan Lincoln Collection, The John Hay Library, Brown University/John Miller; 474, 475 PhotoDisc; 476 file photo; 478 Collection of Larry Williford; 479 (l)Museum of the Confederacy, (r)PhotoDisc; 480 FPG; 481 Library of Congress; 482 (l)Brown Brothers, (r)CORBIS; 484 MAK I; 485 Picture Research Consultants; 486 Michigan Capitol Committee, photography by Peter Glendinning; 490 (l)Matt Meadows, (r)Picture Research Consultants; 491 (l)Brown Brothers, (r)CORBIS; 494 (t)McLellan Lincoln Collection, The John Hay Library, Brown University/John Miller, (ct)CORBIS, (bc)Painting by Don Troiani/courtesy Historical Arts Prints, Ltd., (b)National Archives; 496 file photo; 497 Aaron Haupt; 498 North Wind Picture Archive; 499 (t)CORBIS, (b)Museum of American Political Life; 500 National Museum of American History/ Smithsonian Institution; 501 Gettysburg National Military Park; 502 (l)©1986 Time-Life Books Inc. from the series "Civil War"/Edward Owen, (r)Illinois State Historical Library; 504 Chicago Historical Society; 505 Tennessee Botanical Gardens & Museum of Art, Nashville; 509 CORBIS; 511 Chester County Historical Society, West Chester, PA; 512 National Museum of American History, Smithsonian Institution/Rudolf Eickmeyer; 513 North Wind Picture Archive; 516 file photo; 516–517 CORBIS; 517 Bettman-CORBIS; 520 Museum of American Political Life, University of Hartford; 521 National Portrait Gallery, Smithsonian Institution/Art Resource, NY; 522 (t)file photo, (c)Collection of David J. & Janice L. Frent, (b)Corcoran Gallery of Art; 524 National Park Service Collection; 524–525 Peter Harholdt/CORBIS; 525 Brown Brothers; 526 (tl)Library of Congress, (tr)Archive Photos, (b)Stock Montage; 526–527 (b)White House Historical Association; 527 (b)Collection of David J. & Janice L. Frent; 527–528 From the original painting by Mort Kunstler, The Race, Mort Kunstler, Inc., 528 courtesy The Oakland Museum; 530 Colorado Historical Society; 531 (l)Brown Brothers, (r)L. Berger/SuperStock; 534 Bob Mullenix; 535 Thomas Gilcrease Institute of American Art; 536 Photograph from the book: The Life and Adventures of Nat Love, Better Known in the Cattle Country as "Deadwood Dick" – BY HIMSELF – A True History of Slavery Days, Life on the Great Cattle Ranges and on the Plains of the "Wild and Wooly" West, Based on Facts, and Personal Experiences of the Author/Rare Book and Manuscripts, Special Collections Library, Duke University, Durham, North Carolina; 537 (l)Nebraska State Historical Society, Lincoln, Tulsa, OK, (r)Montana Historical Society, Helena; 538 Kansas Collection/University of Kansas Libraries; 542 The Museum of the American Indian, Hye Foundation, NY; 543 (r)Smithsonian Institution, National Museum of American Art, Washington, DC/Art Resource, NY; 545 Denver Public Library, Western History Collection; 546 Smithsonian Institution, National Museum of American Art, Washington, DC/Art Resource, NY; 546 Stock Montage; 548 New York Historical Society; 550 AP/Wide World Photos; 552 (t)the Oakland Museum, (bl)The Beinecke Rare Book & Manuscript Library, Yale University, (br)The Museum of the American Indian, Hye Foundation, NY; 554 (t)courtesy Rockefeller Archive Center, (c)Stanford University Museum of Art, (b)Michael Freeman; 555 (t)Fine Arts Museum of San Francisco, Gift of Mr. and Mrs. John D. Rockefeller 3rd 1979.7.4, (b)National Air and Space Museum; 556 Picture Research Consultants; 561 W.H. Clark/H. Armstrong Roberts; 562 NASA; 562–563 Brown Brothers; 563 National Air and Space Museum; 564 Stock Montage; 565 (tl)Smithsonian Institution, (tc)Picture Research Consultants, (tr)Lewis Latimer Collection, Queens Borough Public Library/Long Island Division, NY, (bl)Picture Research Consultants, (br)courtesy George Eastman House; 566 courtesy Ford Motor Company; 567 courtesy Rockefeller Archive Center; 568 CORBIS; 569 Library of Congress; 570 National Portrait Gallery/Smithsonian Institution/Art Resource, NY; 572, 573 Library of Congress; 576 (t)Library of Congress, (c)National Portrait Gallery/Smithsonian Institution/Art Resource, NY, (b)Westmoreland Museum of Art, Greensburg, PA, (background)Hulton Archive; 578 Michael Freeman; 579 (t,c)Aaron Haupt, (br)Timothy Fuller; 580 (b)Hulton Deutsch/CORBIS, (t)courtesy California History Room, California State Library, Sacramento; 581 (t)Orchard Films, (b)White House Historical Association, Bettman-CORBIS; 582 Karen Yamauchi for Chermayeff & Geismar Inc./Metaform; 583 Library of Congress; 585 Jacob A. Riis Collection, Museum of the City of New York; 586 (t)Rykoff Collection/CORBIS, (b) CORBIS; 588–589 Library Company of Philadelphia; 590 Smithsonian Institution; 592 Archive Photo; 593 University of Illinois at Chicago. The University Library, Jane Addams Memorial Collection; 594 Brown Brothers; 596 Rudi von Briel; 597 Collection of Sue & Lars Hotham/Rob Huntley/Lightstream; 598 Library of Congress; 599 (br)Bettman-CORBIS, (others)Library of Congress; 600 Smithsonian Institution; 601 Winslow Homer American, 1836–1910. Girls with Lobster, 1873. Watercolor and gouache over graphite, 24.2 x 32.9 cm. © The Cleveland Museum of Art, 2002. Purchase from the J.H. Wade Foundation, 1943.60; 603 (l)National Portrait Gallery, Smithsonian Institution/Art Resource, NY, (r)from the collection of Paul Urbahn at Steamboats.com; 604 (t)Bettman-CORBIS, (c, chart)Library of Congress, (b)Smithsonian Institution, (background)Edwin Levick/Hulton/Archive; 606 National Archives; 606–607 Ansel Adams Publishing Rights Trust/CORBIS; 607 CORBIS; 608 (t)Collection of David J. & Janice L. Frent, (b)CORBIS; 609 (t)National Gallery of Art, Washington. Chester Dale Collection, (b)White House Historical Association, (l)By permission of the Houghton Library, Harvard University, (br)The Schomberg Center for Research in Black Culture, New York Public Library; 610 Doug Martin; 611 Library of Congress; 613 The Ida M. Tarbell Collection, Pelletier Library, Alleghany College; 615 Museum of the City of New York; 616 CORBIS; 618 Schlesinger Library, Radcliffe College; 619 (l)CORBIS, (r)Picture Research Consultants; 620, 621 Collection of David J. & Janice L. Frent; 622 David J. & Janice Frent Collection/CORBIS; 623 (t)David J. & Janice L. Frent Collection/CORBIS, (c)Collection of David J. & Janice L. Frent, (cr)file photo, (bl)The Museum of American Political Life, University of Hartford, (br)Library of Congress; 625 Theodore Roosevelt Collection/Harvard College Library/by permission of the Houghton Library/Harvard University; 626 Daniel J. Cox/naturalexposures.com; 627 Robin Brandt; 628 CORBIS; 629 Brown Brothers; 630 (l)Bettman-CORBIS; 630 (r)Private Collection; 631 Culver Pictures; 632 The Schomberg Center for Research in Black Culture, New York Public Library; 633 Oscar B. Willis/The Schomburg Center for Research in Black Culture, New York Public Library; 634 (tl)By permission of the Houghton Library, Harvard University, (tr)Doug Martin, (c)Collection of David J. & Janice L. Frent, (b)file photo; 635 Steve Kelley/Copley News Service; 636 Franklin D. Roosevelt Library; 636–637 (t)Woodfin Camp & Associates, (b)White House Historical Association; 637 (l)United States Military Museum, West Point, (r)Picture Research Consultants; 638 Picture Research Consultants; 639 courtesy US Naval Academy Museum; 640 (l)Historic Seward House/James M. Via, (r)Hulton-Deutsch/CORBIS; 644 National Postal Museum; 645 Bishop Museum; 647 Library of Congress; 649 United States Military Museum, West Point; 650 (l)CORBIS, (c)Library of Congress, (r)Bettman-CORBIS; 652 Brown Brothers; 653 Library of Congress; 655 Aaron Haupt; 656 Picture Research Consultants; 657 (l)Leonard de Selva/CORBIS, (r)Private Collection/courtesy R.H. Love Galleries, Chicago; 658 National Archives; 659 Library of Congress; 660 Courtesy of the Webb County Heritage Foundation; 661 CORBIS; 662 (t)National Postal Museum, (c)Frederic Remington Art Museum, Ogdensburg, NY; (b)Picture Research Consultants; 664 (tl)Bettman-CORBIS,